HERMETICA

The Ancient Greek and Latin Writings Which Contain Religious or Philosophic Teachings Ascribed to Hermes Trismegistus

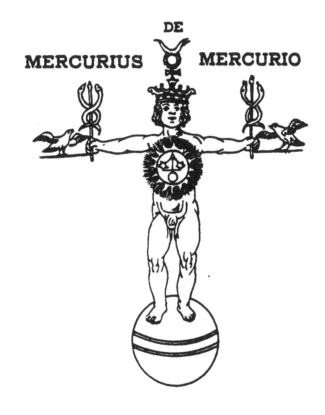

(Volume 4)

TESTIMONIA WITH INTRODUCTION, ADDENDA AND INDICES BY A.S. FURGUSON

Walter Scott

ISBN 1-56459-484-X

KESSINGER PUBLISHING'S
RARE MYSTICAL REPRINTS

THOUSANDS OF SCARCE BOOKS
ON THESE AND OTHER SUBJECTS:

Freemasonry * Akashic * Alchemy * Alternative Health * Ancient Civilizations * Anthroposophy * Astrology * Astronomy * Aura * Bible Study * Cabalah * Cartomancy * Chakras * Clairvoyance * Comparative Religions * Divination * Druids * Eastern Thought * Egyptology * Esoterism * Essenes * Etheric * ESP * Gnosticism * Great White Brotherhood * Hermetics * Kabalah * Karma * Knights Templar * Kundalini * Magic * Meditation * Mediumship * Mesmerism * Metaphysics * Mithraism * Mystery Schools * Mysticism * Mythology * Numerology * Occultism * Palmistry * Pantheism * Parapsychology * Philosophy * Prosperity * Psychokinesis * Psychology * Pyramids * Qabalah * Reincarnation * Rosicrucian * Sacred Geometry * Secret Rituals * Secret Societies * Spiritism * Symbolism * Tarot * Telepathy * Theosophy * Transcendentalism * Upanishads * Vedanta * Wisdom * Yoga * *Plus Much More!*

DOWNLOAD A FREE CATALOG AT:
www.kessinger.net

OR EMAIL US AT:
books@kessinger.net

HERMETICA

THE ANCIENT GREEK AND LATIN WRITINGS WHICH CONTAIN RELIGIOUS OR PHILOSOPHIC TEACHINGS ASCRIBED TO

HERMES TRISMEGISTUS

PUBLISHERS' NOTE

WHEN Walter Scott died suddenly in February 1925, he left manuscript materials for a considerable part of the fourth volume he projected; but the task of gathering up the threads and completing his unfinished work was one of unusual difficulty. The publishers were fortunate enough to enlist the aid of Professor A. S. Ferguson of the University of Aberdeen, who supervised the third volume in its final stages. To his patience and his regard for Scott's disinterested scholarship, the appearance of this final volume is due.

April 1936.

CONTENTS

viii CONTENTS

INTRODUCTION

I

THIS volume is printed from Mr. Scott's manuscript as far as
p. 352; there is reason to believe that the text and interpretation
give his final view. Some small excisions have been made, and
I have added a few notes, which are indicated by square brackets.
The only change that requires mention is the substitution of Clarke's
text of Ammianus Marcellinus for that used by Mr. Scott. I did not
feel justified in intervening further.

For the material printed after p. 352 I am responsible. There is
evidence that Mr. Scott intended to add Appendixes; they were not
written, and I have ventured to replace them by Addenda. Another
edition on a large scale will hardly appear in this generation; and it
may be convenient to have the additional matter gathered under one
cover. It is necessary to remember that the war made access to
foreign periodicals difficult during the years when Mr. Scott's commentary was taking shape; there are no signs, for example, that he
ever saw Bousset's remarkable article in the *Göttingische gelehrte
Anzeigen* for 1914. So far as space allowed, I have tried to give an
account of recent work. The debt I owe to the works of Bousset
and Reitzenstein requires special acknowledgement; I have felt bound
to quote their opinions even when I could not follow the whole way.

Material also accumulated in my own hands, and I have used
some of it. It is but respectful to explain why these notes frequently
diverge from Mr. Scott's interpretation. I agree with him that the
documents are largely in the Platonic-Stoic tradition, and have added
evidence in support of that view. I am unable to follow his theory
of the textual history of the documents. If that were all, it would
not have fallen within my province to express an opinion. But in
using my material I repeatedly found myself driven to the conclusion
that the order given in the manuscripts is a valuable clue to the
meaning. Without this working assumption, I could make no head-
way. Contradictions did not especially trouble Hermetists. They
worked upon a school tradition, which they were not concerned to
trim into consistency or to state in logical order; they often reveal
most of themselves when they are least intelligible. The problem of
interpretation is not so much to distinguish and state a Hermetic

doctrine [1] as to trace, passage by passage, what strand of tradition the writer was following ; and the context is a clue. So far as space will allow, I shall try to discern how a Hermetist writer worked, and shall select portions of the *Asclepius* and the *Kore Kosmu* for that purpose.

'It is to be hoped,' wrote Mr. Scott, 'that the process of recovering the thoughts of the Hermetic writers, to which I have tried to contribute, will be taken up and carried farther by others.' My intimate acquaintance with Mr. Scott's work has left me with a feeling of respect for the patience and candour with which he approached a complicated problem. The Introduction and Addenda will, I trust, be taken as an attempt to revalue some of the evidence, without controversial intent.

II

THE *ASCLEPIUS*

A. The *Asclepius* is a compilation. One document, the Apocalypse (cc. 24–27 d), contains indications that may be used to date it. Upon the hypothesis that the invasion (or rather, the settlement) of Egypt by Indians and Scythians ('vicina barbaria', 340. 25) [2] was an historical event, the most reasonable answer is that given by Mr. Scott: it could plausibly be supposed that they formed part of the Palmyrene army that invaded Egypt under Zabdas. Since Lactantius knew the *Asclepius* as a whole, the assumption that the Apocalypse narrates historical facts means (a) that the prophecy was written, and then embodied in the *Asclepius*, between A.D. 268 and the first decade of the fourth century ; (b) that certain sentences, prophesying penalties and even capital punishment for the pious, were inserted later, after the edicts of Constantine (A.D. 353, 356).

The Indian and the Scythian appear to date this document. But they have a pedigree in literary tradition ; for the poet Horace they were the 'neighbouring barbarism' that threatened *Roman* peace. [3] Let us ask another question : at what time could it be believed, upon credible authority, that the disasters foretold by the Apocalypse would befall Egypt ? Egypt need not have been invaded, much less

[1] An attempt to state the characteristic Hermetic teaching will be found in Bousset's article, mentioned above.

[2] References to the texts in vol. i, and to the notes upon them in the Addenda, are given by page and line. References to Mr. Scott's notes in vols. ii and iii are given by volume and page. ' *T.*' signifies the *Testimonia* printed at the foot of the page in vol. i.

[3] See p. 416 below.

settled, by outlandish men ; penalties need not have been imposed by Roman law, and against the religion of Egypt. It is enough if calamity was foretold, and was feared by Egyptians.

There is no element in this prophecy that has not its parallel in the *Oracula Sibyllina*, which bore the authority of the Sibyls. The Alexandrian author of Book V makes the Indians and the Scythians the scourge of Egyptian idolatry, to be overwhelmed in their turn by a cosmic outbreak. This invasion is no more historical than the war among the stars. When the fifth book describes Isis as forgotten and the Serapeum of Alexandria in ruins,[1] though it fell under Theodosius in A.D. 391, the oracle expresses the desires of an Alexandrian Jew through the Sibyl's mouth ; and the conflict of the stars, with which the book ends, is a Stoic theme adapted to apocalyptic use,[2] as our Apocalypse ends with the *senectus* and the *regenitura mundi*.[3] The theme of this conflict was itself probably adapted by the Jewish author from a pagan Alexandrian poem.[4]

These Jewish writings bear witness to the temper of Egyptian Jews at the end of the first and the beginning of the second centuries of our era. The great Jewish outbreaks under Trajan (*c.* A.D. 115) were the open manifestations of that temper. In that crisis the oracles of the Sibyls could lead Egyptians to fear not only the downfall of their religion, but the end of the Empire and of the age.

The Sibyls and 'Hystaspes'[5] foretold the disappearance of the Roman Empire and the Roman name ; this wider context explains how Scythians and Indians come to be called 'neighbours'.[6] For the thesis was that Asia would again prevail, and the Roman name was destined to be blotted out.[7] Egypt would be the first in the Empire to suffer for her superstitions and would be bathed in blood.[8] As Egypt suffered plagues when the people of God was oppressed in Egypt alone, so the whole world (over which the Jews

---

[1] *Orac. Sibyll.* v. 484 *sqq.* ; see vol. i, p. 61, n. 1.

[2] Seneca, *Consolatio ad Marciam*, 26. 4. Compare the *Book of Enoch*, 18. 13-16. 21. 3-6.

[3] 344. 11, 346. 5 ; see vol. iii. 177.

[4] Roscher, *Mythol. Lex.* iii. 2190. In v. 514 ὁ θεός is not the Jewish God, and Οὐρανὸς αὐτός (v. 528) is openly pagan.

[5] Hystaspes' book may rank with the works of 'Ostanes'. The prophecy ascribed to him was known before A.D. 150. See p. 25, n. 4 below and E. von Dobschütz, *Das Kerugma Petri*, p. 124.

[6] The Jewish equivalents would be Gog and Magog (*Orac. Sibyll.* iii. 512-19, *Rev.* 20. 8-9), and again the Parthians and Medes (*Enoch*, 66. 5).

[7] *Op. cit.* 7. 15. 11. Compare the catchword Ῥώμη ῥύμη (*Orac. Sibyll.* iii. 364, viii. 165).

[8] Lactantius, *div. inst.* 7. 15. 10 (p. 24. 27 below).

are now scattered) would be stricken now, 'ut iustus et cultor dei populus liberetur'.[1]

As later writers observe, the last great outburst of Jewish nationalism was preceded or accompanied by signs and portents: the Pantheon was struck by lightning and many cities were overwhelmed by earthquakes.[2] Orosius draws a parallel with the plagues of Egypt: 'hic itidem tertia sub Traiano plaga Iudaeos excitauit, qui . . . toto orbe saeuierunt, absque magnis multarum urbium ruinis, quas crebri terrae motus isdem temporibus subruerunt.'[3] Egypt and Libya suffered from the Jews with special severity: 'incredibili deinde motu sub uno tempore Iudaei quasi rabie efferati per diuersas terrarum partes exarserunt. nam et per totam Libyam aduersus incolas atrocissima bella gesserunt: quae adeo tunc interfectis cultoribus desolata est, ut, nisi postea Hadrianus imperator collectas illuc aliunde colonias deduxisset, uacua penitus terra abraso habitatore mansisset. Aegyptum uero totam et Cyrenen et Thebaidam cruentis seditionibus turbauerunt. in Alexandria autem commisso proelio uicti et adtriti sunt.'[4] Dio's account of Jewish ferocity may well report the fears of contemporary Alexandrians;[5] and one of Hadrian's first acts was to rebuild the ruined city of Alexandria.[6] In our Apocalypse we may still trace the warning to Rome behind the forebodings about Egypt; and the cosmic disaster is common to both Egyptian and Jewish prophecies. The Palmyrene war did not, so far as we know, affect the religion of Egypt. On the other hand, the records attest the fierce religious animosity that inspired the Jewish outbreaks.

In such apocalypses the 'just' or 'cultores dei' are persecuted;[7] it is a commonplace that law breaks down in this dissolution of all order, cosmic and human.[8] While the Jews triumphed, such fears

---

[1] Lactantius, *div. inst.* 7. 15. 5. Compare the language of Orosius below.

[2] Orosius, 7. 12. 6.   [3] *Op. cit.* 7. 27. 6.

[4] *Op cit.* 7. 12. 6. As the Jews of Jerusalem were slain or expelled, so Egypt would lose her inhabitants (340. 14, 26).

[5] Dio, 68. 32. 1.   [6] Eusebius, *Chronicon, ann.* 2133.

[7] 'De cultoribus etiam dei duae partes interibunt et tertia quae fuerit probata remanebit' (*div. inst.* 7. 16. 14). Compare 340. 20–342. 2. 'Tunc eruere templum dei conabitur et iustum populum persequetur' (*op. cit.* 7. 17. 6). It seems doubtful whether the 'mentis religio' (342. 27) is the 'religion of Mind' whose adherents are to be persecuted. In 340. 9 'pia mente' means εὐσεβεῖ ψυχῇ, as often in the *Asclepius* (336, 27, 25; cf. 200. 6); we should probably translate τῆς ψυχῆς εὐσέβεια. The εὐσεβεῖς are constantly mentioned as victims in the *Oracula*, and the application is simply changed.

[8] 'Nova iura . . . lex noua' (342. 28); 'noua consilia . . . uolutabit, ut . . . leges commutet et suas sanciat' (*div. inst.* 7. 16. 4): 'idem iustos homines obuoluet libris prophetarum atque ita cremabit . . . non lex aut ordo aut militiae disciplina seruabitur' (*ibid.* 7. 17. 8–9). When 'Hystaspes' states that the 'pii

were natural ; and it is possible that Egyptians took over Jewish—not to say pagan—material about the oppression of the 'pious'; the Christian Lactantius did so later under the menace of a great persecution. It must be remembered that traces of heathen martyrologies survive, imitating the Jewish and the Christian.[1] There need be no allusion to Imperial legislation against a pagan cult, and a later date is not required.

Prophecy of this kind ends with the assurance of final triumph (through God's intervention) after suffering, the *regenitura mundi* after its senescence. The Jewish formula in the *Oracula* combined the Stoic theory of a world rejuvenated with the national ideal of a city where God should reign over the just. The *deorum secessio* in our text is but the first stage. If our hypothesis is correct, it would not be surprising to find traces of a pagan analogue to the Jewish ideal ; and they are to be found, outside the limits ordinarily assigned to the Apocalypse. The passage in question is c. 27 d, which has the appearance of being an isolated fragment. In the reign of impiety the gods depart from the land, and evil angels remain (340. 25, 344. 3); we might well expect a return of the gods to complete the cycle.[2]

In our text order and religion are said to be restored by the Will of God, which is identical with Good (344. 15). The writer gives a typical account of this Will, which is Good (346. 8),[3] and of the Cosmos, its image, 'boni bonus'. This opens an account of the hierarchy of dispensers of goods. Outside the Cosmos is the *ultramundanus deus* ; within are two great deities, *Iuppiter ⟨vitae?⟩ dispensator*[4] and *Iuppiter Plutonius nutritor animantium*. This may be an insertion in the original Apocalypse ; but it is a classification distinct in character from the list of ousiarchs (324), the intelligible deities who are contrasted with the sensible (star-gods). As will be seen, this hierarchy ends with local (not cosmic) deities, who are the chief concern of the Apocalypse, and in virtue of whose beneficent presence Egypt is the temple of the whole globe.

---

ac fideles' held up their hands to Jupiter (pp. 25–6 below), and that Jupiter had pity on them, we see the pagan and the Jewish tradition mingling.

Historically, after the Jewish revolts, no Jew might land on Cyprus or enter Jerusalem upon pain of death (Dio, 68. 32. 3 ; Eusebius, *Hist. evang.* 4. 6. 3). See in general Juster, *Les Juifs dans l'Empire romain*, ii. 171.

[1] A. Bauer, *Heidnische Märtyrerakten* (*Archiv für Papyrusforschung*, vol. 1, pp. 29–47).

[2] In 346. 6 read 'peracto temporis cursu' ; see *Suppl. lect.*, p. 572 below.

[3] In l. 9 perhaps : 'Dei enim natura consilium est [voluntatis], bonitas summa (βούλησις. τὸ ἀκρότατον ἀγαθὸν ὄν). *Ascl.* Consilium, O Trismegiste ? Cf. 344. 15.

[4] Ζεὺς ⟨ζωὴν⟩ χορηγῶν ; compare 324. 5, 348. 20, 26 ; also note on 330. 21.

After the two Jupiters the future tense is abruptly resumed, 'aliorum vero vires et effectus per omnia quae sunt *distribuentur*. ⌜*Distribuentur*⌝ vero qui terrae dominantur, et *conlocabuntur* in civitate in summo initio Aegypti, quae a parte solis occidentis *condetur*, ad quam terra marique *festinabit* omne mortale genus' (346. 31).

Who are these 'alii', and what are their activities (ἐνέργειαι)? They are the subordinate dispensers of goods, the gods of the land or μερικοὶ θεοί, with their specialized functions,[1] under the great deities just named. They departed when evil triumphed (344. 3), and will return when God ('restitutor deus') restores the earth to righteousness. In this setting the phrase 'qui terrae dominantur' (346. 33) must mean the old gods of Egypt, the *dii terreni*.

The text has been confused by a dittography, owing to homoeoteleuton. The first verb should read 'distribu*u*ntur'; the clause completes the classification of beneficent deities by explaining that the μερικοὶ θεοί have specialized activities.[2] It leads up to the second sentence, which prophesies their restoration (*resti*t*uentur*) and the establishment of their worship in a new city. This explains the return to the future tense. In this context the writer can hardly mean that Alexandria will be a great emporium. The new city is the city of man's desire; and the old gods of Egypt, now gathered in the Libyan mountain, will draw the whole human race as worshippers.[3]

This prophecy is illustrated by the mingling of pagan, Jewish, and Christian elements by Lactantius under the stress of persecution:[4] the just will triumph; the *princeps daemonum* will fall, and will be in ward 'mille annis caelestis imperii, quo iustitia in orbe regnabit . . .

---

[1] So in 362. 9 caelestes dii catholicorum dominantur)(terreni incolunt *singula*; 'hi nostri vero, singillatim quaedam curantes (362. 4: τὰ καθ' ἕκαστα ἐπισκοποῦντες). See p. 429 below. In the myth of the *Politicus* (272 E), which may have contributed something indirectly to this apocalypse, the minor gods " ἀφίεσαν αὖ τὰ μέρη τοῦ κόσμου τῆς αὑτῶν ἐπιμελείας " when God relinquished the helm; but there is no mention of *nocentes angeli*.

[2] The scribal error is easily made—distribuuntur. restituentur＞distribuentur. distribuentur—and the change of tenses shows that the text passes from theology to prophecy. Translate : τῶν δ' ἄλλων αἱ τε δυνάμεις καὶ αἱ ἐνέργειαι κατὰ πάντα μεμερισμέναι εἰσίν.

[3] Lact., *op. cit.* 7. 24. 15 : 'homines . . . regnabunt cum deo, pariter reges gentium uenient a finibus terrae cum donis et muneribus, etc.' Cf. *epitome*, 67. 3, *Isaiah*, 60. 3, 11, *Revelation*, 21. 24-6. It may be recalled that Hadrian, returning from Britain by Gaul, was 'Alexandrina seditione turbatus, quae nata est ob Apidem, qui, cum repertus esset post multos annos, turbas inter populos creauit, apud quem deberet locari, omnibus studiose certantibus ' (Spartianus, *Vita Hadriani*, 12). Apis was again discovered in 362, after long search.

[4] *Div. inst.* 7. 24. 6. Compare the *epitome*, 68. 1 : ' Cum eadem Trismegistus, eadem Hystaspes, eadem Sibyllae cecinerint, dubitari non potest, etc.'

post cuius aduentum congregabuntur iusti ex omni terra peractoque
iudicio ciuitas sancta constituetur in medio terrae, in qua ipse conditor
deus cum iustis dominantibus commoretur. quam ciuitatem Sibylla
designat cum dicit :

καὶ πόλιν, ἣν ἐπόθησε θεός, ταύτην ἐποίησεν
λαμπροτέραν ἄστρων ἠδ' ἡλίου ἠδε σελήνης.

(*Orac. Sibyll.* v. 420.)

Here an Alexandrian Jew speaks through the mouth of the Sibyl,
and foretells a golden age of justice and peace. The *Asclepius*
describes God's dealings with evil and the return of the *dii terreni* to
a new city of Egypt—a pagan 'new Jerusalem'—to which the whole
world will make pilgrimage. Egypt will again be 'mundi totius
templum'.[1] An editorial join marks the end of the prophecy.

It has been argued that the prophecy fits the conditions of the last
great uprising of the Jews, which was heralded by ominous natural
disasters and wrought immense havoc in Egypt and Libya. The
literary evidence shows that prophecies, circulated in Egypt under
names of power, foretold the end of Rome, with a special visitation
for Egypt and the religion of Egypt, and the end of the age. Such
prophecies depicted the sufferings of the 'just and pious', their appeal
to God (or Jupiter) for succour (Hystaspes),[2] their restoration in a
city of God after a cosmic purification. The hypothesis is that pagan
Egyptians took what such writers as the 'Sibyls' and (possibly)
'Hystaspes' said about the just and pious to themselves, and sought
a recompense for present tribulations in the final triumph of their
gods. Their sufferings and the prophecies (not penal law) are the
historical facts behind the Apocalypse. This hypothesis has enabled
us to restore a portion of the prophecy that is otherwise unintelligible. There seems to be no reason why an Alexandrian should not
have written this apocalypse under Trajan or Hadrian. As no great
danger threatened the Egyptian religion after this time and before
Lactantius, there is no sufficient reason for assigning it to a later date.

This apocalyptic document, which may reasonably be assigned to
the first quarter of the second century, provides a philosophical

---

[1] The Apocalypse is introduced apropos of the description of Egypt as the
temple of the whole terrestrial globe (340. 7) ; though hardly composed for this
position in our treatise, it is not entirely inappropriate, because it gives an account of
the flight and re-establishment of the deities whom it is man's privilege to make—a
theme begun in c. 23 and not resumed till c. 37. See analysis (pp. xxx, xxxi), B. 9, 14.

[2] Compare the appeals to God in the primitive barbarism, discussed in section
III below (p. xxxvi, n. 7).

background for the Egyptian and Jewish elements. The Cosmos, the instrument of God's Will and the image of God, made for man's delight and love, belongs to the Posidonius-*Timaeus* tradition;[1] the senescence and rejuvenation is Stoic,[2] bound up with the Platonic conception of the great year; the chain of dispensers of good also belongs to the theory of the Cosmos as a 'multiformis adunata congestio', where the *ultramundanus deus* is linked with the departmental deities, who execute God's providence for man. But when the good deities withdraw before the *nocentes angeli*, another strain appears—a dualism between the good and the evil forces in the Cosmos; it is significant that the doctrine has a Jewish setting. We must link this with the account of the *summus daemon* (366. 11) and of the just man whose protection from daemons is piety (370. 4). As we shall see, these passages do not necessarily belong to a document composed by a single author. But it can be said, with some probability, that the characteristic Hermetic dualism appears in a document the occasion for which was the great Jewish revolt. This is consistent with the hypothesis that the writings of Cornelius Labeo show knowledge of this Hermetic doctrine, and that his date has the reign of Hadrian as a *terminus ante quem*,[3] although the two arguments are independent of one another. We are therefore not obliged to assign a later date to passages containing this doctrine.

Such passages, however, do not necessarily belong to the same document. Since c. 37 (358. 12), after an editorial join, again takes up the theme of man, the maker of gods, from c. 23 b (338. 6), we can say with some confidence that the sections on departmental and local deities form a group. But they are separated by two other documents, both of which are abruptly introduced.

After an editorial join ('et haec usque eo narrata sunt', 364. 25), the first of these is introduced by the words 'de inmortali aut de mortali'.[4] The clue to this section lies in Macrobius.[5] He reports

---

[1] 342. 13 : 'Hoc totum bonum (τοῦτο τὸ πᾶν, ἀγαθὸν ὄν) . . . machina voluntatis dei summo (*Bradwardine*) suo operi (*G*) absque invidia suffragantis'. *Timaeus*, 29 e.

[2] Ultimately from the myth of the *Politicus*.

[3] Benno Boehm advanced the hypothesis about Labeo's date, and Bousset used it to elucidate the early history of Hermetism. See pp. 474-7 below. For the other side see W. Kroll, *Die Zeit des Cornelius Labeo*, *Rheinisches Museum*, N.F. 71 (1916), pp. 308-57.

[4] See below in the analysis of the *Asclepius*, B 11 (below, p. xxx).

[5] *Commentarius*, 1. 11. His source was probably Porphyry (*de reditu animae*) and ultimately Numenius ; see F. Cumont, *Rev. des Études grecques*, 32, pp. 113-20.

that certain followers of Pythagoras and Plato believe in two deaths, the death of the animal when the soul leaves the body, and the death of the soul when it is embodied and separated from the simple and undivided fount of nature.[1] As my notes show, the Hermetist presupposes a theory that the bodily organism dissolves after the fixed *logos* of determined numbers that constitutes the *harmonia* of soul and body comes to an end (*mors fatalis* or *naturalis*); to cut short the time of purgation in the body by force renders the soul unfit for its heavenly abode. Macrobius uses this theory to distinguish between the consequences of natural and of violent death, especially suicide.[2] It is not obvious that the Hermetist had before him the same distinction. The text, as we have it, launches into a general account of the punishment meted out for sin, especially for sin concealed in life, and only at the end (368. 8) mentions the penalties incurred by those who have their life cut short by the law. This divergence occurs at a point where *mors necessaria* (366. 6) is taken by the writer to mean the eternal punishment of the soul by the *summus daemon*, not the εἱμαρμένος θάνατος of the body by natural causes. Thus the contrast between natural and violent death (368. 9–10) has been almost submerged; the writer's interest lies in the second death of the wicked and the security of the just (368. 10, 370. 4 *sqq.*).[3]

What unprotected man must fear is the power of evil daemons and of fate (370, *T.*, vol. iv, p. 231). This again introduces the fundamental Hermetic dualism between the evil forces of the Cosmos and the good. The demonology of c. 33 b (transferred to 368. 11) is not germane to this context. The daemons and heroes of c. 33 (318. 22), who inhabit the lower and the upper air, have their proper place under the theme *de inani* (316. 31). The argument is that there is no void; or rather, the argument from the absence of a physical void is used to justify the theme of an intelligible world full of living beings: apparent emptiness is filled with invisibles, daemons or heroes. Upon this theory there are *medietates* among living beings as well as among the

---

[1] See on νοῦς ὑλικός below. In these chapters Macrobius also gives an account of the descent and ascent of the soul through the spheres, a doctrine characteristic of Hermetism.

[2] *Comment.* I. 13. 5–20. Compare *naturae anima debita* and *vitam violenter amittunt* (368. 8–9).

[3] In 358. 28 the 'mundanus homo' of Asclepius is said to lie in earth; reliquus enim, vel potius totus, si est homo totus in sensu vitae ⌜melior⌝, remeavit in caelum'. Bradwardine (see below) reads *melioris*, and this is supported by Macrobius' 'spe uitae uerioris' (*Comm.* I. 13. 18). The doctrine of the two deaths then applies: 'quid aliud intellegendum est quam mori animam, cum ad corporis inferna demergitur, uiuere autem, cum ad supera post corpus euadit' (*ibid.* I. 10. 17).

elements. It is an optimistic demonology, based upon unity and continuity of life throughout the Cosmos, and contrasted with the Hermetic dualism found in the section *de inmortali*.[1] Though apparently a fragment as it stands, it follows naturally upon the section on Aion, the dispenser of life.

This tract *de inmortali* may serve as an example of the deformation of an intelligible doctrine by the Hermetist, and of the distinction between the Posidonian optimism that pervades many of the documents and the astral fatalism that stands in contrast to it.

The mention of the sun at the end of this section (370. 16) is used as a transition to the second god (348. 8), Aeternitas (Aion) who is identified with the sun. The sun is not an alien interpolation; he helps to determine what Aeternitas is. For Chalcidius says of the World-Soul that it is stretched from the centre of the mundane body and enwraps it; it nourishes the Cosmos 'uitali uigore' within and without.[2] He then reports the opinion of 'some' that this centre is not the earth, but the Sun: 'a regione uitalium, id est a sole animae uigorem infusum esse mundano corpori potius intellegendum pronuntiant. siquidem terra inmobilis, sol uero semper in motu ... ideoque solem cordis obtinere rationem et uitalia mundi totius in hoc igne posita esse dicunt'. Theon of Smyrna[3] uses identical language, and the common source is probably Adrastus.[4] This is exegesis of the *Timaeus*. The background of the argument is that the Cosmos is 'vitae aeternitatisque plenissimus' from the source of life. The theme is treated by Macrobius: 'constat, inquam, nihil intra uiuum mundum perire, sed eorum, quae interire uidentur, solam mutari speciem'.[5]

---

[1] It should be observed that the accounts of the source of life (cc. 29 c–32), of the living beings whose continuity fills the invisible void (cc. 33–4; pp. 316. 31, 322. 14, 326. 12), of the connexion of Ἀιδης with *inferi* and its context (c. 17 b; p. 316. 12), of the changes of *species* (cc. 35–6; p. 328. 16)—all fit into one theory of the continuity of life. See notes in Addenda *ad loca*. The change of *species* may be illustrated by the quotation from Macrobius in the next paragraph.

[2] cc. 99–100 (*Tim.* 34 b); cf. 208. 25, 436. 18 *seq.*

[3] P. 187. 15.

[4] Switalski, *Des Chalcidius Kommentar zu Plato's Timaeus*, p. 70. Probably Posidonius is the ultimate source; the sun as 'cor caeli' is commonplace (e.g. Theon, 138. 16, Chalcidius c. 100), and is part of the comparison of microcosmos and macrocosmos; see K. Reinhardt, *Kosmos und Sympathie*, pp. 335 *sq.* The conception of the sun as enwrapping is found in 268. 25. In 266. 8 the sun is the ὄγκος of νοητὴ οὐσία.

[5] *Comment.* 2. 12. 13. This again arises from the microcosm-macrocosm argument; Macrobius is directly inspired by Plotinus, *Enn.* 2. 1. For the Cosmos as a πλήρωμα τῆς ζωῆς compare 232. 12 *sqq.* Compare also 318. 2 with Macrobius, *Sat.* 1. 8. 8: 'cumque semina rerum omnium post caelum gignendarum de caelo

In the printed text (vol. i, pp. 362-4) two sections on Aeternitas, obviously related, are placed together. It will be convenient to take the latter of these first (c. 40 b). This passage occurs in the MSS. after the account of god-making, explained in the Addenda.[1] Why is it that a discussion of εἱμαρμένη and Aeternitas is attached to an explanation of the nature of terrestrial gods? It is said that their activities are not by *chance* (*fortuitos* = τύχη, 362. 1); their sphere is specialized, whereas that of the celestial gods is universal: οἱ δ' ἡμέτεροι (θεοί) τὰ καθ' ἕκαστα ἐπισκοποῦντες—τὰ μὲν χρησμοῖς τε καὶ μαντείᾳ[2] προσημαίνοντες, τῶν δὲ προνοοῦντες καὶ τούτοις ὡσαύτως βοηθοῦντες—τοὺς ἀνθρώπους φίλῳ τινὶ συνδέσμῳ[3] φυλάττουσι.

ΑΣΚΛ. τίνα οὖν τοῦ λόγου μοῖραν[4] ἡ εἱμαρμένη διοικεῖ, ὦ Τρισμέγιστε, εἰ (si F) οἱ μὲν οὐράνιοι θεοὶ τῶν καθολικῶν ἄρχουσιν, οἱ δ' ἐπίγειοι τῶν καθ' ἕκαστα προΐστανται; (362. 3).

In this document, which is extremely confused, the main theme is the divine law (νόμος or λόγος), which is said to have 'parts'. The particular acts which the terrestrial gods oversee are distinguished alike from the καθολικά and from τύχη, about which a mere fragment remains (364. 23). This fragment is followed by the words 'Dictum est vobis de singulis' (372. 1), which are, I suggest, the formal *explicit* of a section περὶ τῶν καθ' ἕκαστα.

The origin of this theory is a piece of *Timaeus* exegesis;[5] it is based upon that passage where God showed to the souls 'the nature of the whole'[6] and revealed the εἱμαρμένοι νόμοι[7] (*Tim.* 41). The

---

fluerent (288. 18), et elementa uniuersa, quae mundo plenitudinem facerent ex illis seminibus fundarentur, ubi mundus omnibus suis partibus membrisque perfectus est, etc.' The origin is *Tim.* 41 c.

[1] See p. 426 below.

[2] This is commonplace in such discussions of Pronoia and εἱμαρμένη; see Chalcidius, cc. 157, 168 *seqq.*, Nemesius, *de nat. hominis*, 748 A, 791 A (Migne).

[3] See on 290. 22, p. 396 below.

[4] It will be seen that there are three 'parts' of the law. Upon the theory to be stated they are presided over by Atropos, Clotho, and Lachesis, who receives the heavenly ἐνέργειαι from her sisters. Cf., Ps.-Plutarch, *de fato*, 574 C: εἰ γε καὶ ἡ κατ' οὐσίαν εἱμαρμένη ὀρθῶς ἡμῖν εἰς τὰς τρεῖς μοίρας διανενέμηται. For the three sisters see Chalcidius, c. 144, *de fato* 568 E-F. Since our text is mutilated or muddled, it should be remembered that the sisters appear in the βίων αἵρεσις of *Republic* X, and that the theory about acts in our power is intended to relieve God from the responsibility for evil; cf. 442. 27 ἐν ἀρχῇ ἑλομένη βίον τὸν καθ' εἱμαρμένην.

[5] See A. Gercke, *Rheinisches Museum* (1886, pp. 266-91) for the theory. The sources are Pseudo-Plutarch, *de fato*, Chalcidius, Apuleius, Nemesius, and Albinus, *Eisagoge*. Switalski (*op. cit.*) adds Alexander Aphrodisiensis, *de fato*.

[6] The phrase is used in 436. 18 and (Φ. πάντων) in 438. 4. When the Hermetist writes of the κίνησις κινοῦσα τὸ πᾶν (436. 17), he is platonizing; he means the 'motus se movens' which imparts circular motion to the heavens and life to the individuals in the Cosmos (see Macrobius, *Comm.* 2. 16. 22-3).

[7] Translated 'uniuersa fatorum series' by Chalcidius, c. 143.

nature of the whole is identified with the World-Soul; it is called
εἰμαρμένη κατ᾽ οὐσίαν,[1] and is divided into three parts. The laws[2]
are the laws imparted to the highest and passed down through the
Cosmos. This is εἰμαρμένη κατ᾽ ἐνέργειαν, and answers to the 'fatalis
series' of the Stoics. The *substance* (οὐσία) is apprehended by the
mind; its *activity* (ἐνέργεια) is recognized by what it does.[3] The
purpose of this theory is to evade the consequences of the Stoic
theory of Pronoia: if, said Nemesius, it were an unbroken series of
causes, it would bring on its effects (τέλη) according to its own
motion and necessity, not according to utility; so the nature of the
immutable law must be considered if room is to be left for freedom.[4]

It will be convenient to take the account of Nemesius as a basis.[5]
'Plato' makes Providence govern both τὰ καθόλου and τὰ καθ᾽ ἕκαστα,
and divides the λόγος of Providence into three. The Providence[6]
of the first God cares for the forms, the Cosmos as a whole, the
heavens and the stars, kinds, being, quantity and quality, and the
forms subordinate to them.[7] The celestial gods look after the genesis
of animals, and plants, and all that becomes and passes away.[8] 'τῆς
δὲ διεξαγωγῆς καὶ τοῦ τέλους τῶν πρακτῶν καὶ τῆς τάξεως
τῶν κατὰ βίον, τῶν τε φυσικῶν καὶ τῶν ὑλικῶν τε καὶ ὀργανικῶν καλουμένων ἀγαθῶν, καὶ τῶν τούτοις ἀντικειμένων, τὴν τρίτην εἶναι πρόνοιαν Πλάτων ἀποφαίνεται. Προΐστασθαι δὲ ταύτης τινὰς τεταγμένους
δαίμονας περὶ τὴν γῆν, φύλακας τῶν ἀνθρωπίνων πράξεων.' This
answers to the division found in Apuleius:[9] Providentia summi
exsuperantissimique deorum; caelicolae susceptam provinciam secundae providentiae retinent; daemones ... ministri dei ... custodes hominum et interpretes.[10] Thus God governs all δυνάμει; his

[1] *De fato*, 568 D, Chalcidius, c. 143, Nemesius 753 B.
[2] The sources quote not only the νόμος ἀκόλουθος τῇ τοῦ παντὸς φύσει of the *Timaeus*, but the θεσμὸς Ἀδραστείας of the *Phaedrus* (248 c), and the Λαχέσεως λόγος of the *Republic* (617 D).
[3] The substance is Providentia, the power 'ex Providentia'. [4] 752 B.
[5] 793 A. His account is probably derived from Porphyry.
[6] The word comes from *Tim.* 30 C 2. [7] *Tim.* 41 D, Chalc. c. 147.
[8] Cf. *de fato*, 573 F: ἡ δὲ τῶν νέων θεῶν (*Tim.* 42 D) τάξις καὶ δημιουργία τὴν δευ-τέραν πρόνοιαν δηλοῖ. Compare 362. 3 and 336. 14.
[9] *De Platone*, I. 12; cf. Ps.-Plut. *de fato*, c. 9.
[10] The phrase of Ps.-Plutarch is: τῶν ἀνθρωπίνων πράξεων φύλακές τε καὶ ἐπίσκο-ποι. It can now be seen that the 'dii (qui) pio affectu (cf. 362. 6) humana omnia respiciunt atque custodiunt' (336. 26) are not the star-gods of l. 9, but the third providence. In short, c. 22 gives the same doctrine, even to the *voluntas dei* (336. 22); cf. Chalcidius, c. 135, 'diligentiam uero hominibus inpertiens propter dei uoluntatem, qui custodes dedit'. It may also be noted that the account in *de fato* marches from the general theory based upon the *Timaeus* to theurgy, while the *Asclepius* follows the reverse order (cc. 37–40). A further link is perhaps given by the account of the invisibility of Ἅιδης (316. 12; see p. 406 below). This theme

Will or Mind is the first or highest Providence, and a trace of this is preserved in the phrase, 'haec ergo tria . . . vel maxime dei *nutu* sunt effecta' (364. 5). This conception of the Will of God has its ultimate source in the *Timaeus*.[1] The second providence is, as Nemesius writes, Fate and Necessity; its mark is τάξις. For the third providence is reserved the sphere of human acts. Since the text, as it stands, omits to explain the reason for this refinement. it need only be noticed that the daemons are, upon the theory, pressed into service to vindicate human freedom and to acquit God of responsibility for evil. 'Causa penes optantem, deus extra culpam. . . . uel cum ait animis Lachesis nullam earum sortito sub dicionem daemonibus esse uenturam, sed ipsas sponte lecturas sibi daemonem, quem quaeque putauerit deligendum.' Similarly Ps.-Plutarch brings in the Socratic daemon.[2] The Hermetist is following school tradition, but hardly comprehending it.

It was said above that εἱμαρμένη κατ' οὐσίαν was identified with the World-Soul, and that it was tripartite—the regions are those of the fixed stars, the planets, and the sublunary sphere,[3] presided over by Atropos, Clotho, and Lachesis. If the World-Soul is in a sense the law-giver, in another it is the law—'ut si quis periti legum latoris animam legem uocet' (Chalc., c. 177).[4] In our text (362. 11) the writer begins with a 'εἱρμός' definition of Fate,[5] identifying it with necessity; this is so far consistent with orthodox Stoicism. Then he

is connected by Chalcidius (c. 134) with a general discussion of the invisibility of daemons; as we have seen, in the *Asclepius* the argument occurs apart, in a discussion *de inani* (cc.33-4).

[1] 29 E (cf. *de fato* 573 C): ἀγαθὸς ἦν . . . βουληθεὶς γὰρ ὁ θεὸς ἀγαθὰ μὲν πάντα, φαῦλον δὲ μηδὲν εἶναι κατὰ δύναμιν . . . εἰς τάξιν ἦγεν ἐκ τῆς ἀταξίας; cf. *Tim.* 42 E and Nemesius 796 A. It may be suspected that 'vel maxime' (364. 5) is a blundered rendering of κατὰ δύναμιν. Compare 'quantum rationabiliter potuisset' in c. 16 (314. 19), and 'voluntati' (l. 27); in that passage there is not an absolute dualism, but on the contrary the question is why there is evil if the Cosmos is 'quasi membrum (dei)' (314. 18). The answer is that God, as far as possible, safeguarded man with ἐπιστήμη and that the Cosmos is an *organon* subordinate to his Will (or Providence). This is the answer in 366. 1 *sq.*, a passage undoubtedly inspired by the *Timaeus* tradition. The connexion of βούλησις and τάξις may be seen, e.g. in 234. 14.

[2] Chalc., c. 154, *de fato*, 574 B (= *Theages*, 129 E).

[3] Ps.-Plutarch, *de fato*, c. 2.

[4] The law: 'dei iussum, cui parent dii secundi, ratio est, opinor, continens ordinationem perpetuam, quae fatum uocatur' (Chalc., c. 146, on *Tim.* 42 E); cf. Apuleius, *de Platone*, 1. 12. The laws, when taught, 'fatum est idque diuina lex est mundi animae insinuata, salubre omnium rerum regimen' (Ch. c. 147). We can now understand the phrase in 336. 13, 'propter unitatem rationis' (διὰ τὸ ἓν εἶναι τὸν λόγον); one law embraces both the τάξις of the stars and the ἐπιστήμη of men. *De fato* (573 E-74 A) quotes *Laws* 875 C in the same connexion: ἐπιστήμης γὰρ οὔτε νόμος οὔτε τάξις οὐδεμία κρείττων.

[5] εἰ δὲ εἱμαρμένη εἱρμός τις οὖσα αἰτιῶν ἀπαράβατος . . . (Nemesius, 752 B).

adds four alternative identifications,[1] the first of which is 'effectrix rerum'. This could be plausibly identified with *natura creatrix*; but the Greek of Lydus and the preceding sentence suggest that this εἱμαρτὴ ἐνέργεια (as Lydus calls it) is no other than εἱμαρμένη κατ᾽ ἐνέργειαν. The *summus deus* who is the second alternative is not the Stoic deity, but that God whose Mind or Will the second god is;[2] the latter is the third alternative, and is the Providentia described as the 'lator legis utriusque uitae' by Chalcidius. The last alternative is 'omnium caelestium terrenarumque rerum firmata divinis legibus disciplina'. This I take to be the system of the whole, with its law given—εἱμαρμένη κατ᾽ οὐσίαν; in Chalcidius' list it is the World-Soul, 'secunda mens, quasi custos legis aeternae'. It is not a coincidence that Chalcidius gives these four: *summus deus, prouidentia, fatum, secunda mens* or *anima mundi tripertita*.[3] For the triple division of εἱμαρμένη, *necessitas*, and *ordo* follows at once in our text, and we can explain why the first two are respectively connected with ἀρχαί and τέλη. The law of nature is given καθόλου, and embraces τὰ καθ᾽ ἕκαστα δυνάμει.[4] It prescribes against treachery, and punishes if there is treachery; but it does not make the traitor. 'Lex omnia conplexa causas praecedentes ex meritis nostris habet ut *initia* quaedam; quae porro necessitatibus constricta proueniunt (sc. τέλη), iuxta praecessionem necessitatemque eius *consequenter* (ἑπομένως) *eueniunt*'.[5] Since our text omits the application, it is unnecessary to enter upon the details of this naïve theory here. The discussion is specifically relevant to human action, although the Hermetist omits to apply the argument.

It must now be shown how Aeternitas fits this context. In its nature the *fatalis series* is infinite and in infinite time; but the law or λόγος or fate that enwraps everything cannot be other than determinate, since it is divine.[6] The answer is given in terms of the

---

[1] For the form of the sentence see Macrobius, *Comm.* 1. 6. 20: 'aut enim deus summus est aut mens ex eo nata . . . aut mundi anima . . . aut caelestia sunt . . . aut terrena natura est' (quinarius numerus).

[2] Chalcidius, c. 176. His lists are given in cc. 176-7, 188.

[3] cc. 176-7.

[4] *De fato*, c. 4, Nemesius 756 A, Chalcidius, c. 150. Ἀρχαί are ἐξ ὑποθέσεως, τέλη are καθ᾽ ὑπόθεσιν; and the 'individuum glutinum' (862. 16) of Fate and Necessity may be expressed in the formula, 'si hoc erit, sequetur illud' (Chalc. c. 152). The division is: 'quod in nobis positum est, et ipsum fatum, et quod secundum fati legem pro meritis inminet' (Chalcidius, c. 151).

[5] Chalcidius, c. 150. The three sisters find no place in our text; but the description of the three powers in c. 40 a, acting without anger or favour, perhaps indicates that the original account referred to individuals.

[6] Chalcidius, c. 148.

perfectus annus of the *Timaeus* (39 d); this law is made manifest in the return of the heavens to the same. '*ἐν γὰρ τούτῳ τῷ λόγῳ ὡρισμένῳ τ' ὄντι καὶ θεωρουμένῳ πάνθ' ὅσα τε κατ' οὐρανὸν ἅ τ' ἐπὶ τὴν γῆν ἐξ ἀνάγκης ἄνωθεν συνίσταται, πάλιν μὲν εἰς ταὐτὸ καταστήσεται, πάλιν δ' ἐξ ἀρχῆς ὅλα κατὰ ταὐτὰ ὡσαύτως ἀποδοθήσεται, μόνη γοῦν ἡ κατ' οὐρανὸν σχέσις αὐτὴ πρὸς ἑαυτὴν κατὰ πάντα τεταγμένη πρός τε τὴν γῆν καὶ πρὸς τὰ ἐπίγεια πάντα διὰ μακρῶν περιόδων πάλιν ἐπανήξει ποτέ· αἵ τε μετ' αὐτὴν ἐφεξῆς καὶ ἐχόμεναι ἀλλήλαις ἐχομένως παρέσονται, ἑκάστη τὰ αὑτῆς ἐξ ἀνάγκης φέρουσαι. . . . ὡς γὰρ ἡ τοῦ κύκλου κίνησις ὅ τε ταύτην παραμετρῶν χρόνος κύκλος τίς ἐστιν, οὕτω καὶ τῶν κατὰ κύκλον γιγνομένων ὁ λόγος κύκλος ἂν νομισθείη.*'[1] This remarkable parallel with c. 40 b shows beyond question what the 'volubilis ratio' is. The ingenuity of the commentators linked this theory with the soul in the *Phaedrus* who walks with God, and will be secure 'ad alterius circuitus tempus';[2] and if he always does this, he will always be secure. Thus Socrates, by following the law, will be always secure 'iuxta fatum'.[3]

[1] *De fato*, c. 3; Chalcidius, c. 148. See also the quotations from Lydus and Basil, p. 430 below. Lydus shows the influence of the number theory prominent in Philo and Macrobius. There are frequent traces in the *Hermetica*; see, e.g. 248. 1, and 154. 28, where the μονάς is the World-Soul stated in Pythagorean terms (see Macrobius, *Comm.* 1. 6. 75, and 2. 1. 16 *sq.*).

[2] The use of this phrase links up the perfect year with the Stoic doctrine of the eternal return. See *Phaedrus* 248 c, Chalc., c. 152, *de fato* 568 c. A curious further identification of the Christian ἀνάστασις with the eternal return will be found on p. 260, n. 4 below; it is a development of this doctrine. See Nemesius 761 A, Tatian, *Oratio*, 3. 13–14.

[3] With the doctrine of Providences here implied we must connect ἡ ἄνω πρόνοια (514. 24), ἡ καθόλου πρόνοια (516. 5), and ἡ ἄλλη πρόνοια (512. 1) which has a province between the summit of heaven and the moon.

It is also probable that those parts of *Ascl.* I which describe man, the microcosm, as having a double function are derived from *Timaeus* exegesis. C. 11 a (p. 306) evidently contrasts the earthly functions of man with his heavenly nature. The chapter begins with *cupiditas*, and should continue (as my notes argue) with the service man does on earth. Though this appears in our text, the Hermetist gives it a twist whereby man is made to despise his mortal part ('despiciat atque contemnat'). Now Chalcidius, upon the theory, suggests that divination, oracles, and astrology are in the realm of conjecture, about things pertaining to the service of the body; and he bases this upon the distinction between God's work of creating souls and the work of the νέοι θεοί in the *Timaeus*. The passions, *ira et cupiditas*, are useful instruments for life; and they are necessary 'ut .... curaret, intueretur etiam caelestia, cum uero *ad terrena despiceret, despectus* aeque ne esset otiosus, sed ex eadem inclinatione cura rerum terrestrium nasceretur' (c. 187). Upon this theory there are two sets of virtues, 'una in comprehensione diuinarum rerum, quae sapientia est, altera in dispositione rerum mortalium, quae prudentia nominatur' (c. 180; cf. c. 137). The Hermetist, in cc. 9–12, bases this contrast upon man's double nature as a microcosm; this is an exposition of his earthly duties (see e.g. 300. 20 *seq.*). But in 306. 17 he suddenly lays stress upon contempt for man's mortal part. The body, consisting of four elements and symmetrically disposed, is contrasted with the four parts of the soul (306. 21; see analysis below, B. 3).

The sum of the whole matter is : 'quae uero reguntur hac lege, ratione ordine ac sine ui reguntur. nihil enim ratione et ordine carens non uiolentum' (Chalc., c. 177). This law is the theme of

But these parts (*animus, sensus, memoria, providentia*) are surely θυμός, αἴσθησις, μνήμη, φρόνησις, which use the body according to reason. They should be contrasted, not identified, with the four 'higher' elements of man—*anima et sensus, spiritus ac ratio* (ψυχή, νοῦς, πνεῦμα, λόγος) in 304. 21. The background is thus a doctrine based upon the psychology of the *Timaeus*—the 'cut' between the principle (42 E) and the mortal (69 C),* like the *anima mundi* with its two circles. (The counterpart of this theory for the World-Soul is given crudely in 194. 9 *sqq*.) When he expounds *philosophia moralis*, and gives priority to *theoria*, the writer imperfectly distinguishes the two senses of *prudentia*, theoretical and practical (Chalc., c. 264). In making the same contrast, Macrobius reports the more austere view in terms that are parallel to our document :

'prudentiae esse mundum istum et omnia, quae in mundo insunt, diuinorum contemplatione despicere omnemque animae cogitationem in sola diuina dirigere.' *Comment*. 1. 8. 4.

'homo hactenus esse debuit, ut contemplatione diuinitatis partem, quae sibi iuncta mortalis est mundi inferioris necessitate seruandi, despiciat atque contemnat.' *Ascl*. 306. 14.

Those who reason in this way, says Macrobius, deny that rulers can be happy ; he himself prefers the more liberal doctrine of Plato and Plotinus. But whatever colour the Hermetist may have added to this document, its doctrine is that given by Macrobius. Those who put off their 'mundana custodia' have their heavenly reward. The 'parentes' (308. 4) are men like Asclepius, the inventor of medicine, and Hermes (358. 26 *seq*.), or benefactors like Isis and Osiris, who return to heaven when their work is done (494. 10). The aretalogy of Isis and Osiris (see note on 492. 1, p. 465 below) should be connected with the account of kingly souls in the following *Excerpt* (494. 24 *seq*.). We are here upon the traces of a general theory about those who

sui memores alios fecere merendo (*Aen*. 6. 664).

This belief has two pillars : that, having descended from heaven, they are animated 'maiestate promissae beatitudinis et caelestis habitaculi' (*Comment*. 1. 8. 2), and that the 'rectores quondam urbium recepti in caelum curam regendorum hominum non relinquunt' (*ibid*. 1. 9. 9 ; cf. 358. 31, 514. 20, 520. 2). I shall return to this point in section III (p. xxxviii).

In the second place, the writer mentions the choir of the Muses (302. 14), and the true music which is the order of all things conjoined ('coniunctarum† omnium rerum ordinem scire', 310. 14)—i.e. 'concentum quendam melo divino dulcissimum': or 'ordo rerum singularium *in unum* omnium artifici ratione conlata(rum)' (τεχνικῷ λόγῳ συνηρμοσμένων), means the music of the spheres, as the parallel of Macrobius shows (*Comment*. 2. 3). He refers to the Platonic Sirens, to Apollo Μουσηγέτης (the Sun, *mens mundi*), and says, 'inesse enim mundanae animae causas musicae' (2. 3. 11). This is exegesis of the *Timaeus* (cf. Proclus, *in Tim*. ii. 208. 9 Diehl). Macrobius rests upon the *theologi* (Orphics, Chaldaean oracles) and the Etruscans (antiquarians of the stamp of Varro and Labeo), who called the Muses 'mundi cantum' (*ibid*. § 4). We are enabled to conjecture that the Hermetist and Macrobius draw upon a common tradition from two signs used by the latter to justify the theory of celestial music. In the first place the *theologi* introduced music into religious services 'canere caelum . . . conprobantes' (2. 3. 4–5) ; this recalls the account of the religious use of music in 302. 16–20, and is 'Chaldaic' (see on 248. 18, p. 389 below). Again music accompanies the burial of the dead, who return 'ad originem dulcedinis musicae' (§ 6) ; this should be compared with the account

---

* Cf. *Tim*. 42 A. For the 'cut', see p. xxviii, n. 1, below.

† Codd. *cunctarum omnium* ; Bradwardine (see below) has *iunctarum*. Both readings may be explained from 9*iunctarum* (συνηρμοσμένων).

cc. 39-40. But the Hermetist has omitted the reason for the theory : to show (Fate notwithstanding) that our acts are in our power.[1] That the original document set forth the theory can hardly be doubted. The introductory matter distinguishes the sphere of the celestial gods from τὰ καθ' ἕκαστα, for which the local gods care (362. 2-6). Asclepius' question, in the catechetical manner, asks explicitly about the *rationis pars* occupied by Fate, and about the *catholica* and *singula* (τὰ καθ' ἕκαστα) governed by the celestial and the terrestrial gods respectively (326. 8-10). The questions are asked, but not all answered ; yet the final words—'dictum est vobis de singulis' (372. 1)— imply that they have somewhere been answered. These words follow upon an unfinished sentence on Chance or Fortune (364. 23-4). Now the theory as set forth by its exponents treats systematically of *proui-dentia, fatum in substantia positum et in munere inuentum, quid in hominis potestate sit, quid quod iuxta fati decretum prouenit*—and then of *fortuna* and *casus* (Chalc., c. 158).[2] Our text clearly contained

of the return of Isis and Osiris to heaven in the *Kore Kosmu* (494. 12). The back-ground is a theory of the nature and fate of the soul, and of the music that is the world order. A further sign is the allusion to the transmigration of wicked souls into the bodies of beasts (308. 12). When Arnobius attacks the followers of Mercury, Pythagoras, and Plato, there is some reason to suppose that Cornelius Labeo may be his opponent.* It is common to this unnamed opponent and to Servius that souls descend from heaven, that they are purged (cf. *Ascl.*, c. 28), that they reascend or enter the bodies of beasts.† This doctrine recurs in the *Kore Kosmu* (478. 20), where the writer is obviously influenced by the *Timaeus*: we are dealing with a doctrine of the soul in the tradition of Platonic exegesis.

Lastly, a traditional division of Philosophy underlies this section : *moralis* ('dili-genter cum mundo viventibus', 308. 10), *rationalis* (*de deo et anima*), and *natura-lis*. But dialectic is omitted, and mathematics expressly excluded (310. 5). If we turn to Macrobius' triple division (*Comment.* 2. 17. 15), *philosophia naturalis* has the same limitation : it is physics, and physics means the study of the celestial harmony and of the earth. A comparison of *Asclepius*, c. 13 with the text of Macrobius and with Chalcidius, c. 264, *seq.*, shows that the three depend upon a common doctrine. The centre of physics is 'suspicere caelum' (302. 20); that is pure philosophy and is contrasted with the other divine service, 'gubernare terrena' or 'terrenus cultus' (304. 1).

This doctrine belongs to the tradition of Platonic interpretation, probably mediated through Posidonius. The number theory so prominent in Macrobius and Chalcidius (Adrastus), is contemned by the Hermetist (310. 5) ; but traces of it may be found not only in the *concentus*, but also in the conception of a deity who is bisexual (332. 11). Whatever Oriental elements are merged in this concep-tion, the μονάς of the *Timaeus*, which is even and odd, male and female, and generates all numbers, is an element in it (Macrobius, *Comment.* 2. 2. 17). As I have shown (note on 364. 25, p. 431 below), a number theory is also implied in 366. 2.

[1] In 362. 20 the phrase 'rerum perficiendarum' should probably be translated τῶν πρακτῶν ; compare Nemesius as quoted above on the third providence (p. xx).

[2] So in *de fato*, c. 6 : ἑξῆς ῥητέον, ὡς τό γ' ἐφ' ἡμῖν καὶ ἡ τύχη, τό τε δυνατὸν καὶ

---

* See my note on iv. 7. 8, p. 474 below.

† Arnobius, *adv. nationes*, ii. 14, 30, 33, 16 ; Servius, *ad Aen.* 6. 741, 719.

more about the latter.[1] We may therefore consider two hypotheses: that the Hermetist's further explanation of things in our power has fallen out after an account of *eventus vel fors*, though it should come earlier, or that he has again completely muddled the theory as he muddled the account of violent death. In any case he has muddled the theory, and something has fallen out of the text.

For our purpose it is not necessary to consider whether Gercke was right in arguing that this is an early Neo-Platonic doctrine, or whether it is of Posidonian origin, as later writers have maintained. In either case the *terminus a quo* need not be later than the first part of the second century of our era; that is the date given by Gercke. We have already assigned the same date to the Apocalypse on other grounds.

Since the *Timaeus*—or rather *Timaeus* commentary—sheds light on the theory of Aeternitas, we can now briefly attempt to explain the distinction between the 'sensus aeternitatis' and the 'sensus mundi' in c. 32 b. Aeternitas (Aion) is 'plenissimus omnium sensibilium et totius disciplinae (τάξεως), consistens ... cum deo', and the 'sensus mundi receptaculum est sensibilium omnium specierum et disciplinarum' (354. 12–15). The manner in which Aion contains all sensibles may be understood from the description of the Orphic Phanes: "πάντα δὲ τὰ συγγενῆ περιέχον" ὅτι τῶν αἰσθητῶν ἐστι περιληπτικὸν ἁπάντων (Proclus, *in Tim.* 1. 435. 6 Diehl).

When Proclus interprets the World-Soul—after the *theologi*!—he says that νοῦς is the ἀμέριστος οὐσία of Dionysus, τὸ δὲ γόνιμον αὐτοῦ τὴν μεριστὴν αὐτὴν περὶ τὸ σῶμα ζωὴν φυσικὴν οὖσαν καὶ σπερμάτων οἰστικήν, ἣν δὲ καὶ τὴν Ἄρτεμίν φησι τὴν πάσης προεστῶσαν τῆς ἐν τῇ φύσει γεννήσεως καὶ μαιευομένην τοὺς φυσικοὺς λόγους ἄνωθεν διατείνειν ἄχρι τῶν ὑποχθονίων . . ., τὸ δὲ λοιπὸν τοῦ θεοῦ σῶμα πᾶν τὴν ψυχικὴν σύστασιν, εἰς ἑπτὰ καὶ τοῦτο διηρημένον·

ἑπτὰ δὲ πάντα μέλη κούρου διεμοιρήσαντο,

φησίν ὁ θεόλογος περὶ τῶν Τιτάνων, καθάπερ καὶ ὁ Τίμαιος εἰς ἑπτὰ διαιρεῖ μοίρας αὐτήν.[2] In short, the dismemberment of Dionysus by the Titans

τὸ ἐνδεχόμενον, καὶ τὰ τούτων συγγενῆ, ταχθέντα ἐν τοῖς προηγουμένοις, αὐτά τε σώζοιτ᾽ ἄν, καὶ τὴν εἱμαρμένην σώζοι. In terms of the theory τύχη is αἰτία κατὰ συμβεβηκὸς τῶν ἕνεκά του ἐν τοῖς κατὰ προαίρεσιν; i.e., it is τοῦ ἐφ᾽ ἡμῖν within the sphere of προαίρεσις (c. 7).

[1] The sphere of the local gods was expressly distinguished from that of τύχη in 362. 1.

[2] *In Tim.* 2. 146. 3. The Soul, he says, enwraps the *All*, but is also stretched through it. So Plato properly called indivisible substance the substance immediately above soul, or briefly mind shared by soul. See 208. 18 *sqq.*

represents the soul stretched through the Cosmos, and Plato followed the Orphics. The material for illustrating this interpretation will be found in Kern, *Orphica*, 207 *sqq.*; it will suffice to quote two passages: 'Quod figmentum discipuli Orphei interpretati leguntur, nihil aliud Bacchum quam animam mundi asserentes; quae ut ferunt philosophi quamvis quasi membratim per mundi corpora dividatur, semper tamen se redintegrare videtur, corporibus emergens et se formans, dum semper una eademque perseverans nullam simplicitatis suae patitur sectionem' (*Mythogr. Vat.* iii. 12. 5). In Macrobius' account of the descent of the soul (*Comment.* 1. 12. 12) it is said: 'Ipsum autem Liberum patrem Orphici νοῦν ὑλικὸν suspicantur intellegi, qui ab illo indiuiduo natus in singulos ipse diuiditur, ideo in illorum sacris traditur Titanio furore in membra discerptus et frustis sepultis rursus unus et integer emersisse, quia νοῦς, quem diximus mentem uocari, ex indiuiduo praebendo se diuidendum et rursus ex diuiso ad indiuiduum reuertendo et mundi inplet officia et naturae suae arcana non deserit'.[1]

The purpose of this section is first to explain the nature of Aion, who is (with God) an intelligible ἀρχή (352. 21), and then to show how man's mind is capable of apprehending what they are. This is part of the discussion of intelligibles (see Analysis below). It has, however, a different function from the account of the divine law, fate, and eternity that follows the division of spheres among the gods in cc. 39–40, though both doctrines have their ultimate source in the *Timaeus.*

B. *Analysis.* It has been seen that the compiler was a botcher, and that consistency of doctrine need not be sought in the *Asclepius.* We have to do with a school tradition, which gave the 'right' answer to important questions.[2] It may be convenient to give a rough list of contents, without pressing any theory of structure. The evidence of editorial joins, of abrupt transitions, of solemn formulas such as introduce the extant *libelli*, may indicate that extracts from different documents or discontinuous extracts from the same documents were used in compiling the *Asclepius.* The joins, as they appear to be, are frequently accompanied by some conventional phrases about the importance of the λόγος to be revealed; and it may be observed that characteristic Hermetic material about νοῦς or about piety is often loosely attached to extracts in the Platonic-Stoic tradition.

---

[1] Cf. 190. 20. This passage, too, supposes that evil men pass into the bodies of beasts.
[2] On school tradition see A. D. Nock, *Sallustius*, pp. xxxvii–xxxix.

1. The theme of the first section is *de coniunctione deorum* (296. 19). It may be suspected that the exposition begins with the words 'de caelo cuncta in terram et in aquam et in aera' (288. 18; 38. 1 Thomas); the previous sentence is editorial. The first of the characteristic λόγος passages appears in 290. 6–10, after a triple εἰς formula. It emphasizes the main theme—the *continuatio* of living beings in their different grades throughout the Cosmos. The *medietas* of man in the series gives rise to a diatribe passage about his marvellous nature (294. 11–296. 3). The writer then treats briefly of life below the human level (296. 4). A clause about νοῦς is clumsily tacked on (l. 12), so clumsily that it bears the appearance of an editorial addition to ordinary Posidonian material—it precedes an obvious editorial section, which promises to deal with νοῦς along with πνεῦμα. It is possible that c. 7 as a whole is transitional matter.

The *divinus Cupido* who speaks through Hermes (288. 6) may be a character from an older document, the φιλόσοφος Ἔρως of the Orphics πρὸς τὴν νοητὴν σοφίαν ἀνάγων (Proclus, *in Tim.* 1. 169. 14 Diehl).

2. *Incipit:* Dominus et omnium conformator, quem recte dicimus deum (298. 14; 43. 2 Th.). Introduced by a prayer to impart the *ratio* (λόγος) *de tota summitate* faithfully. *Theme:* man's double relation to God and the Cosmos, with his double function as earthly governor and as practising *divinitatis dilectus*. Each part is introduced by the formula *audi itaque* (298. 14, 302. 9). The *voluntas dei* is here introduced, and the section appears to be based upon *Timaeus* commentary.

3. *Incipit:* Aeternitatis dominus deus primus est, secundus est mundus, homo est tertius (304. 6; 45. 15 Th.). This is formally introduced as an εἰλικρινὴς καὶ ἀληθὴς λόγος. It is possible to hold that this simply continues the previous theme; I suspect, however, that the editor has patched together two extracts dealing with the same subject, and has called each a λόγος. The peculiarity of this section is that man's double nature is illustrated by a garbled account of a double set of elements, and a psychology in which four higher parts answer to four lower parts.[1] The section ends with diatribe material on

---

[1] The theory of symmetry is found in Philo and the Clementine *Recognitiones* (8. 29): see p. xxiii n. 3 and Addenda, p. 402 below. The principle governing the 'cut' between upper and lower may be illustrated from Proclus, *in Tim.* 1. 206. 7: προϋφέστηκέ πως ἐν τοῖς οὐρανίοις ἡ ἐναντίωσις ἢ κατὰ τὰς διττὰς περιφορὰς τῶν σωμάτων ... ἢ κατὰ τοὺς διττοὺς κύκλους τῶν ψυχῶν ... ἢ κατ' ἄλλην ὑποιανοῦν τοιαύτην τομήν.

true as opposed to false philosophy. Again *Timaeus* material. The λόγος is formally closed and a new section announced in 310. 24-5.

4. *Incipit:* Fuit deus et ὕλη . . . et mundo comitabatur spiritus (310. 26 ; 49. 17 Th.).[1] *Title: de spiritu et de his similibus.* This was anticipated in 296. 27, and introduces the invisible ἀρχαί. A garbled account of ἀγέννητα that are γεννητικά is followed by the traditional denial that God is responsible for evil, and by an account of the safeguard provided against it—the promised section on νοῦς ? The function of *spiritus* is stated in the closing words (314. 25). Again there is a formal *explicit* (l. 28).

5. *Incipit:* Mente sola intellegibilis summus qui dicitur deus (314. 29 ; 51. 13 Th.). This treats of the conception of the invisible and intelligible, and is illustrated by an etymologizing explanation of Ἄιδης, the invisible. It is perhaps best to take this section as an account of invisible ἀρχαί in the Cosmos ('principalia et antiquiora et quasi capita . . . omnium', 316. 25). The main theme is still *spiritus*, and a passage on νοῦς is again roughly tacked on (320. 14).

6. *Incipit:* Sunt ergo omnium specierum principes dii (322. 21 ; 53. 25 Th.).[2] The formula of introduction about the *sublimis ratio* (c. 19 a) is elaborate. We should read the transition in 320. 24 (53. 10 Th.) thus : 'ego vero nec eorum dico omnium (*scilicet* deorum) sed magnorum ⟨anti⟩qu⟨i⟩orumque et principalium'; this will answer to the description quoted above in 5. The verbal parallel suggests that the writer is now dealing with intelligible *deities*, after intelligible ἀρχαί. The general thesis (to be resumed later) is that the intelligible world is distinct from the sensible. The governors of life and order, the ousiarchs, are the intelligible deities. The list breaks off with the *secundus* ⟨deus ?⟩, probably Aion, whose creative instrument is *aer* or πνεῦμα. At present it is enough to note the break.

The mutilated passage which follows (326. 1 ; 54. 18 Th.) describes the continuity of life that in all its variety is one ; individuals, though one, are made 'alia' (ἀλλοῖα) by the Will of God.[3] The differentiating process is not explained till 13 below.[4]

---

[1] Compare the *incipit* of *Libellus* III : ἦν γὰρ σκότος . . . καὶ ὕδωρ καὶ πνεῦμα λεπτὸν νοερόν (146. 1). The preceding phrases in *lib.* III are a summary ; see note *ad loc.*

[2] Εἰσὶ μὲν οὖν ἁπάσων ἰδεῶν ἀρχαὶ θεοί τινες.

[3] In 326. 9 distantia)(adunata = διαιρούμενα)(ἡνωμένα ; cf. *Suppl. Lect.* on 288. 25.

[4] It is perhaps worth noting that this fragment supplies the proper commentary to c. 5, which deals with the *continuatio*, and that its last lines may explain the curious fragment on making (292. 21-5), where *species* (l. 24) may translate ἀγάλματα (τῶν θεῶν). Cf. 338. 16.

7. *Incipit*: Deus etenim vel pater vel dominus omnium (330. 22; 55. 11 Th.). A pedantically expressed invocation leads to the description of a creative bisexual God and to diatribe material on procreation. As the transitional question shows—'haec iterum ratio quae est?' (330. 21; 55. 10 Th.)—this continues the λόγος of creation.

8. A short transition on piety leads to man's special gift—νοῦς. *Introductory formula*: audi itaque. *Incipit*: Deus pater et dominus cum post deos homines efficeret (336. 3; 58. 9 Th.). *Theme*: an argument about the double nature of man in which νοῦς is made his differentiating characteristic. The order presupposed here is stargods, daemons (l. 26) and men, under the *voluntas dei*. This order is also presupposed by the doctrine of the three providences in 15.

9. *Incipit*: Dominus et pater vel . . . deus (338. 5; 59. 12 Th.) The theme of this fragmentary λόγος is man's *potestas visque*: as God made the star-gods, so man is *fictor deorum*. These are the gods with whom he has *cognatio et consortium* (l. 3). The relation of 8 and 9 resembles that between 2 and 3; it is convenient to treat them separately, and the transition may indicate that they are separate—ἐπειδὴ ὁ λόγος . . . παραδέδοται (? l. 3).

10. Section 9 is broken into by *The Apocalypse* (340. 4: 60. 20 Th.), which must once have been a separate document. (Analysis given above, p. x.)

11. After an abrupt transition, this section appears to begin with a title *de inmortali aut de mortali*[1] (364. 25; 65. 18 Th.), As explained above, this is a garbled account of two kinds of death, and has Neo-Pythagorean elements (p. xvi).

12. *Incipit*: Secundum etenim deum hunc crede (348. 8; 67. 26 Th.). The thread of connexion is the mention of the Sun at the close of the last section. The ἀρχαί are *deus* and *Aion*, which is the source of life, itself eternal. There are obvious affinities with 6 above, though it would be rash to contend that this supplies the missing account of the *secundus* ⟨deus⟩ in 324. 18. At the close the writer discusses how an intelligible ἀρχή can be apprehended by men. It is arguable that the section ends at *Vides ergo* and the brief prayer in 356. 13, and that the following paragraph is editorial matter.

---

[1] Stobaeus gives only περὶ τοῦ θανάτου. Our text may be confused, concealing a contrast between *mors inmortalis* (ἀίδιος) and *mors fatalis* (εἱμαρμένος). Compare 'inmortali sententia' (καταδίκη) in 366. 18.

13. This section begins abruptly: De inani vero . . . sic sentio (316. 31; 72. 12 Th.). It continues, as I suggest, the arguments of 5 and 6. These chapters on the void and space, like the chapter on Ἄιδης, are physical examples introduced to explain the conception of invisible beings or ἀρχαί. This is the argument found in Apuleius and Chalcidius, that the Cosmos is filled with a continuous chain of invisible beings, the daemons. The general thesis is: 'omnia enim mundi membra sunt plenissima, ut ipse mundus sit plenus atque perfectus' (318. 2; 72. 15 Th.). The physical analogies lead up to the formula of application: '*His ergo sic se habentibus* . . . scitote intellegibilem mundum . . . esse incorporalem' (322. 14; 74. 10 Th.). This catches up the theme of 5 and 6. What is the relation of the two worlds? The intelligible enwraps the sensible like a garment, and all the variety of the sensible world is from it and in it and through it. If we observe the reference to the corporeals and in-corporeals from which the forms (αἰσθηταὶ ἰδέαι) are constituted,[1] together with the clear allusion to the function of Omniformis (the ousiarch),[2] it would appear that this is the necessary supplement to the mutilated doctrine of ousiarchs. For here we have an astrological argument, accounting for the continuous production of individuals in all their variety; and the last words of 6 were 'cuius nutu effici-untur alia' (ἀλλοῖα). The *sublimis ratio* (322. 8, 330. 21) is at last explained. C. 36, on change of form (*species*) in the Cosmos, is another physical illustration.

It will further be observed that the mutilated passage in 6, describing the continuity between sensibles and invisibles (326. 1) pieces out the reference to the daemons in the illustration from the void (318) and helps to explain the nature of the argument.

14. The transition to this section begins 'iterum ad hominem rationemque eius redeamus' (358. 12; 76. 15 Th.). This formally resumes the interrupted account of man as *fictor deorum* in 9 above. The *explicit* is 'sic deorum fictor est homo' (360. 25).

15. The fragment on εἱμαρμένη (362. 8; 78. 19 Th.) gives no proper answer to the question about Fate, the celestial and terrestrial gods, *catholica* and *singula* (362. 9; 78. 20 Th.). Probably the editor linked this section to the discussion of terrestrial deities by the phrase, 'et ne putassis *fortuitos* (τύχῃ) effectus esse terrenorum

---

[1] Read 'haec duo, ex quibus constant formae, corpora (et) incorporalia' with Kroll (328. 25; cf. 316. 16).

[2] (Omniformis) qui diversis speciebus diversas formas facit (324. 11); so εἱμαρ-μένη πάντα ἀλλοιοῖ (324, *Testim.*).

deorum' (362. 1 ; 78. 12 Th.), after the *explicit* of the previous section. The analysis has been given on p. xix. *Explicit*: 'dictum est vobis de singulis' (372. 1 ; 80. 7 Th.).

16. *The Prayer* (374. 1 ; 80. 24 Th.). This is plainly borrowed material, like the aretalogy ending the *Kore Kosmu*.

However the facts are interpreted, the first part of the dialogue can be analysed into a number of sections, opening with solemn language, introduced as λόγοι, and sometimes ending with a formal *explicit*. The later portion has no *incipits*, makes abrupt transitions, refers back to themes previously treated, and has some formal *explicits*. Some doctrines are badly garbled, and unessential or illustrative matter is so treated as to seem the main subject of a section. If a Hermetist threw the contents of a commonplace-book into continuous narrative, with some dialogue insertions, the effect would not be much more incoherent.

The first thesis, *de coniunctione deorum*, is announced in the prologue—'alterum alterius consentaneum esse'; the chain of living beings is continuous and connected throughout the Cosmos. This is a main theme—or the main theme—of the treatise: unity in variety. The *sublimis ratio*, it will be recalled, is that the Will works through the chain of life and creates the infinite diversity of living beings. The account of the ousiarchs should lead directly to the account of diversity of individuals (6); but c. 20 diverts the argument to another aspect of the *ratio*, the bisexuality of God and diatribe matter on procreation. It is only in 12 and 13 that the writer winds up the theme, with an account of Aion (an ἀρχή), the source of life in a Cosmos that is all life. In the chain man's *medietas* gives him special importance, and the writer devotes 2 and 3 to his position in the Cosmos. At a later stage (8 and 9) the writer returns to man as the possessor of νοῦς, and god-maker in virtue of his position ; this is not carried through till 14. Another group of themes may perhaps be classified as follows. Among the entities in the Cosmos some are invisible, and the concept needs explanation. Sections 4 and 5 deal with invisibles that may be called cosmic ; section 6 begins the theme of invisible and intelligible beings, but it is not carried through till 12 and 13, where the writer treats first of Aion the source of life, and then of the intelligible world enwrapping the sensible and imposing upon it the variety of forms. The sections interposed form a series of excursions. With section 7 the theme passes from creation to procreation, and so to the good man, to piety, νοῦς, and god-making (9), to the special pieties of Egypt, and to the fate of man after death. Again, one special theme in this group is broken off and only resumed after the intelligibles have been disposed of: the return to god-making in 14 certainly resumes 9, and god-making again carries the writer on to the miserably mishandled section on *singula*.

The form of the treatise is consistent with the hypothesis of a writer who extracts and abridges λόγοι without much intelligence, dropping the thread to pursue a topic suggested by the context, and resuming arbitrarily. On the whole, the signs of editorial joins tell against the supposition that the writer was simply inconsequent; and the inclusion of arguments without beginning, end, or obvious application taken by themselves—although their background elsewhere shows how they apply—indicates that the writer helped himself from more fully developed arguments. It is difficult to conceive that a series of mischances to the text could have produced the kind of disorder present in this document.

III

KORE KOSMU

The *Kore Kosmu*, a narrative in dialogue form, illustrates a different method of compiling and adapting material.[1] If Bousset's theory is right, the Platonizing tale of the embodiment of souls is superimposed upon an older tale of the fall of πνεύματα from their heavenly seats. The very disorder or inconsistency of the narrative is therefore a valuable clue, not to be smoothed away. As the text stands, there is one main theme that holds the fabric together. It is the theme of Ignorance, Search, and Discovery.[2] From the grandiose opening, where the splendours above are contrasted with the fears and ignorance and seekings of the 'things below', through the Hellenistic conceit of Nature embracing Work[3] with laughter[4] and bearing Discovery, and the burlesque of the souls gingerly investigating the Father's soul-brew as if they were alchemists,[5] to Momus' diatribe about the dangers of curiosity and the final aretalogy in praise of

---

[1] For details throughout, see notes in the Addenda, pp. 448 *sqq.* below.

[2] Ἀγνωσία, Ζήτησις, Εὕρεσις.

[3] 'Verum idem, qui Labor ab eadem uocabatur ... *caelum* cum domina impiger permeauit' (Martianus Capella, 2. 143).

[4] Read γελάσασα (the laughter of procreation) for λαλήσασα (462. 26).

[5] In 468. 27 read τὸ τοῦ πατρὸς [πρὸς = πατρός] ἐκύκων (codd. προσεκύνουν) κρᾶμα καὶ ... ἐπεζήτουν. The language in the context is alchemical.

those who gave the gifts of knowledge and civilization to men, this theme is woven into the narrative.

The theme is knowledge, forbidden knowledge and disorder, revealed knowledge and the *cultus vitae*. Let us see how the episodes, blending different traditions, bear upon this issue. It will be convenient to select the last part of the narrative.[1]

As it stands, it is disjointed. Momus appears abruptly, and is named by an afterthought; the primitive barbarism is confusedly sketched; the Elements make their complaint and disappear; Isis and Osiris are praised in an aretalogy that bears traces of a Hermes document, though Isis has up to this point been the narrator. The knowledge imparted by Isis and Osiris brings piety[2] and justice; but the souls evidently sought forbidden knowledge (468. 25), and the speech of Momus is directed against the dangers of knowledge—περιεργία[3] breeds ἀταξία.

The mighty spirit that springs from the earth, only later identified with the critic Momus, is a figure from the East. In form his speech is diatribe, and the material such as might be used to praise the achievements of man or to castigate his presumption, as Philo did. The text, as it stands, is not uniformly in the language of prophecy. It falls into the present tense[4] to describe man's conquest of land and sea; and the spirit speaks as if all that remained for man was to scale the heavens—ἀταξία again. When Heeren emended present into future tenses, he may have removed the last traces of an accusation; for the words are such as might have come from the mouth of a Jewish 'accuser', standing before the maker of mankind (482. 4). But the accuser is merged in the person of the Greek (or Jewish-Greek) critic of the creator Hermes-Prometheus when he asks for desire and fear[5] and disease to curb man's presumption.

As the notes in the Addenda show, this brings the tale of Hermes, the maker of man, into the cycle of Prometheus, the maker of man; and Momus is a figure common to both versions. The *Kore Kosmu*, as we have it, is a patchwork of fragments. It seems possible, however, to indicate the background that lends to them a certain unity.

---

[1] I leave the sections on creation entirely out of this analysis.

[2] The opening sentence should perhaps read: οὗτοι ⟨τοῦ⟩ ὁσίου (codd. βίου) τὸν βίον ἐπλήρωσαν (492. 3).

[3] Περιεργία, which alarms Momus, is personified in Martianus Capella, 2. 146.

[4] 482. 17, 19. 23; cf. 15. The counterpart of Momus' diatribe is the last part of God's speech in 480. 3–19, which also exhibits uncertainty about tenses, and is connected with the theory of the origin of the arts.

[5] The text might be *Timaeus*. 42 A 3–B 1. with Hesiod. *O.D.* 00–10:.

The presumption of the souls led God to decree that they should be subject to Eros and Ananke (476. 33). Momus still fears the presumption that will scale the heavens like the race of Iapetus.[1] Hermes curbs the exercise of their intelligence by endowing them with feeble bodies and with desire. The fragment on the primitive κατάστασις again appears to describe the rivalry of embodied souls with the gods (486. 12). Beyond question the common element is presumption, springing from knowledge men should not possess.

If we turn to the lost *Hermetica* of which Zosimus preserves traces, Isis tells her son that she was spied by an angel from above, who desired her, and she refused to yield unless he revealed to her the working of gold and silver. He did not possess those powers ; and the first of the angels, Amnael, came to her. She did not yield to him until he told the mysteries she sought. This tale shows that the Hermetic myth had become fused with the tale of the fallen angels in the *Book of Enoch*.[2] They imparted forbidden knowledge to women, and to men. Bousset has pointed out that the *Kore Kosmu* has some resemblance to the fall of the children of heaven in *Enoch*, and that the complaint of the four Elements is parallel to the complaint of the four Archangels.[3] Now in *Enoch* the fallen angels taught[4] the making of weapons and the working of metals,[5] ornaments, costly stones [6] and colouring tinctures,[7] enchantments,[8] root-digging,[9] astrology,[10] the constellations, etc. Momus enumerates such

---

[1] 482. 27 ; cf. Horace, *Od.* 1. 3. 27. and note on 482. 4.

[2] In *Enoch*, cc. 6 and 9. the influence of the *Genesis* myth of the sons of God and the daughters of men is evident ; but in cc. 18. 13 and 21. 3 the seven planets who transgressed the commandments and did not come forth at the appointed time are punished. This recalls the command of God to the souls to keep their station and to turn the ' cylinder ', the axis of the Cosmos ; the passage from Photius quoted on p. 509 of vol. iii gives this meaning, and I now see that περιστροβῶσι (466. 13) is active. The planets, of course, had subordinate daemons or spirits attached to them (268. 30). This is therefore an astrological myth showing how spirits fell under the power of εἱμαρμένη.

[3] *Enoch*, 6. 2, 9. 1. Passages from Christian tradition will be found collected in H. J. Lawlor, *Early Citations from the Book of Enoch* (*Journal of Philology*, 1897, pp. 164–225), and R. H. Charles, *The Book of Enoch*, 1912, pp. lxxxi–xcv.

[4] 8. 1–3.

[5] Zosimus. pp. 45–6 below ; Pseudo-Clement, *Homiliae*, 8. 14, has the whole list of arts.

[6] Possibly λίθων φύσεις (482. 14) ; this may refer especially to the magic power of precious stones ; compare *Homil.*, 8. 14 (σὺν τούτοις δὲ τοῖς μαγευθεῖσιν λίθοις) and 360. 19.

[7] ποιότητα χυλῶν (482. 14).   [8] 494. 7.   [9] 482. 13 ; cf. 480. 6.

[10] 482. 22 'reading τὰ μετέωρα) ; 494. 1 : cf. Tertullian, *de cultu feminarum*, 1. 2, 'metallorum opera nudaverunt (illi angeli) et herbarum ingenia traduxerunt et incantationum vires provulgaverunt et omnem *curiositatem* (περιεργίαν !) usque ad stellarum interpretationem designaverunt'. Tatian, *Oratio* 8 : διάγραμμα γὰρ

arts in a group by themselves; they were traditionally enumerated in the various forms the legend assumed. We find the legend closely associated with Hermetic doctrine. Syncellus repeats the story of the 'Watchers' in *Enoch*, the arts they revealed, and their descendants the giants, together with a Hermetic extract about the origin of alchemy.[1] Lactantius also treats of the fallen angels in connexion with Hermetic doctrine.[2] Forbidden knowledge was reputed to come from the fallen angels;[3] and the theory of Fate was bound up with it, as the argument of Zosimus and others shows.

It was supposed that the evil daemons who beset men were the spirits of these fallen angels, or of their offspring, the giants.[4] They used men as their instruments,[5] and satisfied their craving for blood with flesh, and finally with human flesh. They caused mutual slaughter. One element in the theory of this primitive κατάστασις is Orphic.[6] But it must be observed that the Clementine *Homilies* give a close parallel to the theme of pollution caused by the giant brood.[7] The *Kore Kosmu* still gives some evidence, corroborated

αὐτοῖς ἀστροθεσίας ἀναδείξαντες ... τὴν εἱμαρμένην εἰσηγήσαντο, ⟨βασιλείαν⟩ λίαν ἄδικον. The introduction of Fate into the myth, in connexion with astrology, is noteworthy.

[1] P. 150, n. 1 below. The *Watchers* (ἐγρήγοροι) are first mentioned in *Daniel*, 4. 10, 14, 20, and the word is used in *Enoch*, 1. 5, and elsewhere. Their original function was to watch over men (see p. 13. 17 below). Compare the ἔφοροι (local deities) in Zosimus (p. 137 below), and perhaps the Zophasemin (οὐρανοῦ κατό-πται) of Sanchuniathon in vol. ii. 114.

[2] P. 13. 14 below.

[3] ('Αζαήλ) ἐδήλωσεν τὰ μυστήρια τοῦ αἰῶνος, τὰ ἐν τῷ οὐρανῷ ἃ ἐπιτηδεύουσι (*Enoch*, 9. 6). Cf. Julius Africanus (Syncellus i, p. 35 Dindorf).

[4] Chalcidius identifies the evil daemons with the fallen angels (c. 135); the *Homilies* give this status to the souls of the giants (8. 18; see below). See Lactantius, p. 13. 22 below; the point is that the souls of the giants are earth-bound, fit neither for heaven nor for hell (*Enoch*, 15. 11–16. 1).

[5] *Homil.* 9. 10; cf. 270. 26, δι' ὀργάνων τῶν ἡμετέρων σωμάτων; Tatian, *Oratio* 8 (of the fallen angels), ὑπόθεσις δὲ αὐτοῖς (τοῖς δαίμοσι) τῆς ἀποστασίας οἱ ἄνθρωποι γίνονται. See also p. 5. 8 below and note on 486. 10.

[6] See note on 490. 23.

[7] Compare (with Bousset) the following (*Homil.* 8. 17) with the complaint of the Elements: ἐπὶ δὲ τῇ πολλῇ τῶν αἱμάτων ῥύσει ὁ καθαρὸς ἀὴρ ἀκαθάρτῳ ἀναθυμιάσει μιανθεὶς καὶ νοσήσας τοὺς ἀναπνέοντας αὐτὸν νοσώδεις ἀπειργάζετο, ὡς τοὺς ἀνθρώπους λοιπὸν ἀώρους ἀποθνήσκειν (cf. 488. 14: αὐτὸς θολοῦμαι .... καὶ ἀπὸ τῶν νεκρῶν σωμάτων ἀναθυμιάσεως νοσώδης τέ εἰμι καὶ ὑγιεινὸς οὐκέτι). ἡ δὲ γῆ ἐκ τούτων σφόδρα μιανθεῖσα .... For the motive of complaint compare the following: 'Cave igitur quantum potes effundere sanguinem hominum, quia doctor egregius Hermogines (*sc.* Hermes) scripsit, dicens: Quando creatura interficit creaturam sibi similem, ut homo hominem, *virtutes celorum clamabunt* ad divinam magestatem dicentes Domino: Domine, servus Tuus vult esse Tibi similis. Quia si injuste interficitur, respondet Creator excelsus: Perimite eum qui interficit quia ipse interficietur: Mihi vindictam et Ego retribuam', etc. (*Secretum Secretorum, Opera hactenus inedita Rogeri Baconi*, fasc. v, p. 55, ed. R. Steele).

from other Hermetic sources, that knowledge was held to be of daemonic origin.

In the *Asclepius* it is said that the Egyptians once were in ignorance, and then learned to make gods (358. 17). The theme here is essentially the same. Though our sources are confused, Euhemerizing, Judaizing, Christianizing, the outlines of the theory can be discerned. In *Oracula Sibyllina* (3. 97-154) is embodied a heathen oracle, which narrates how men built a tower after the flood to reach heaven; God (the gods) sent winds and overthrew them.[1] This is followed by the Euhemerizing account of the advent of Kronos, Titan, and Iapetus as kings, and of their wars. The Titans were ἄγριοι ἄνδρες (137). The purpose of this tale is to explain the origin of war (154), and (as we know from Lactantius)[2] of kingship and godship. The assault on the heavens answers to Momus's fear that men will arm against heaven and reach out their souls to the stars (στοιχεῖα, 482. 28); this is what the souls are said to attempt. The Euhemerist version naturally gives no trace of the use of men as instruments by the spirits. In the Pseudo-Clementine writings[3] Ham (the first magician) did not receive and did not pass on his father's religion to his descendants; again, the desire for kingship led them to wars and deceits. His son Mesraim (Zoroaster)[4] was the father of the Egyptians, Babylonians, and Persians. In the clear air of Egypt—so the explanation runs—the courses and the energies of the stars were first observed.[5] Mesraim-Zoroaster drew down lightning from the stars and was finally consumed by lightning through the jealousy of daemons. The folly of men represented

[1] For details, See J. Geffcken, *Die Babylonische Sibylle* (*Nachr. K. Gesell-schaft, Göttingen,* 1900, pp. 88-102; *Texte u. Untersuchungen,* N.F. 8. The order of events is inverted in the text; for the Babylonian tale of the tower is made to precede the Berosian account of Kronos. It should be noted that Josephus preserves the pagan θεοί, replaced by the Jewish God in our *Oracula* (*Antiq.* I. 4, 3). Alexander Polyhistor, using the Sibylline account, puts Titan and *Prometheus* (not Iapetus) after the Flood, and then the tower-building (Eusebius, Cyril, *adv. Iul.* I. 9). The relevant texts will be found in Syncellus, i. 80-2 Dind., and in Geffcken's notes to the *Oracula.*

[2] *Div. inst.* 2. 13. 7.

[3] *Recogn.* 4. 27; *Homil.* 9. 3. I have not troubled to distinguish between the two accounts. See also Joannes Malalas, *Chron.* 84-85 Migne.

[4] The version of the wars after the Flood in Moses of Khoren pits Zerovanus (Zoroaster) against Titan and 'Japetosthe' (Müller, *Fragm. Hist. Graec.* ii. 502). In these tales the giants, Titans, and Typhonians played the same part. For Hermes and the flood see Syncellus (vol. iii, p. 491).

[5] Lact. 2. 13. 10. The object of Lactantius was to establish that the *cultus dei* was original, and was followed (after the period of ἀγνωσία) by god-making; this is Euhemerism adapted to his special purpose.

him as being carried to heaven in a chariot of lightning, and they honoured him with statues, temples, and altars.[1] The rationalizing forms of the story are intended to account for the origin of astronomy and magic, for the origin of wars, and for the deification of kings and benefactors.[2]

It is arguable that a number of episodes in the *Kore Kosmu* are intelligible in the light of a common background, that knowledge is a dangerous power derived from evil sources; this is consistent with Bousset's hypothesis of the πνεύματα. We still have traces of the assault upon the heavens by fallen souls and of the strife among men caused by the 'souls' (cf. *Book of Jubilees*, 10. 1). They are but traces. For the main theme in the document has shifted to a different theory of the origin of knowledge—the divine gift of the *cultus vitae* after primitive barbarism. The instruments of God, Osiris and Isis, teach mankind order, peace, justice, the rites of religion, astrology, philosophy, magic, and medicine; and Hermes is their instructor.

The theory has Greek elements, in so far as the ἄγριος πολιτεία, through need,[3] is replaced by civilization. In the aretalogy Isis is not the world-goddess of the Cymean inscription, but a benefactor who returns to her heavenly seat, with the accompaniment of music. Reference has been made above to the theory that rulers come down from above and are animated by the hope of return after they have put off their mundane guardianship.[4] If we now consider the account

---

[1] *Homil.* 9. 4–6 identifies Nebrod (Nimrod, *Gen.* 10. 9) with Zoroaster. The account of the origin of fire-worship in Egypt (§ 6) etymologizes: Phtha means fire, and the god Phtha is identical with Hephaestus or Osiris. He was their first king; altars were set up, and so forth. For Hermes and Zoroaster see Zosimus, p. 105 below.

[2] The origin of knowledge and the arts was attributed to the fallen daemons by Lactantius, *op. cit.* 2. 16. Cf. Commodianus, *Instructiones*, 1. 3:

> Ab ipsis in terra artis prolatae fuere,
> Et tingere lanas docuerunt et quaeque geruntur,
> Mortales et illi mortuos simulacro ponebant.

The last line brings in the art of god-making. See the account of statues in the *Asclepius* (cc. 23–4, 37–8).

[3] Χρεία. Compare χρη[ματι]ζοντι τῷ κόσμῳ (486. 37), τῷ[ν] πάντων δεομένῳ κόσμῳ (492. 1). See references in note on 486. 10. Primitive irreligion and barbarism are one: ἄθεος ἀπανθρώπων (sic legendum) ἐπ' ἐμὲ χορὸς ἔπεστι (488. 31). It may be that the curious phrase τοῖς λειπομένοις ἀνθρώποις ὀργάνοις χρώμεναι (486. 15) represents an account of men deserted by God; cf. 422. 14, (ψυχὴ) ὑπολειφθεῖσα ὑπὸ τοῦ θεοῦ; and 486. 32, μέχρι πότε ... ἄθεον καταλεῖψαι τὸν θνητῶν βίον προ[σ]αίρεσιν ἔχεις;

[4] Cf. 494. 10, where ἀπητούμεθα λοιπόν may conceal οἶκον, the *habitaculum* or *propria sedes* of returning souls (Macrobius, *Comment.* 1. 8. 2). See p. xxiii, n. 3 above for the return, and the music.

of kingly souls in *Excerpt* XXVI, which is part of the Isis group, the Posidonian background of this Egyptian passage will be clear.

It runs as follows : πολλαὶ γάρ εἰσι βασιλεῖαι· αἱ μὲν γάρ εἰσι ψυχῶν, αἱ δὲ σωμάτων, αἱ δὲ τέχνης, αἱ δὲ ἐπιστήμης, αἱ δὲ ⌈αὐτῶν⌉[1] . . . ἀπογεγονότων ἤδη ψυχῶν μὲν Ὄσιρις, ὁ πατήρ σου· σωμάτων δὲ ὁ ἑκάστου ἔθνους ἡγεμών· βουλῆς δὲ ὁ πατὴρ πάντων καὶ καθηγητὴς ὁ Τρισμέγιστος Ἑρμῆς· ἰατρικῆς δὲ ὁ Ἀσκληπιὸς ὁ Ἡφαίστου· ἰσχύος δὲ καὶ ῥώμης πάλιν Ὄσιρις . . . φιλοσοφίας δὲ Ἀρνεβεσχῆνις, ποιητικῆς πάλιν ὁ Ἀσκληπιὸς ⟨ὁ⟩ Ἰμούθης (520. 3). The choice of names suggests that Egyptian figures (too few for the purpose) are imposed upon a Greek list of benefactors.

It will be remembered that Virgil places *fortes, sacerdotes, vates,* and *philosophi* in his group in Elysium : [2]

> hic manus ob patriam pugnando volnera passi ;
> quique sacerdotes casti, dum vita manebat ;
> quique pii vates, et Phoebo digna locuti ;
> inventas aut qui vitam excoluere per artes ;
> quique sui memores aliquos fecere merendo.
>
> (*Aen.* 6. 660.)

Manilius puts Hermes, the 'kingly soul'[3] who revealed the heavens to man, at the head of a similar list :

> et natura dedit uires seque ipsa reclusit
> *regalis animos* primum dignata mouere
> proxima tangentis rerum fastigia caelo,
> qui domuere feras gentes oriente sub ipso,
> qua mundus redit et nigras super euolat urbes.
> tum qui templa sacris coluerunt omne per aeuum
> delectique sacerdotes in publica uota
> officio uinxere deum ; quibus ipsa potentis
> numinis accendit castam praesentia mentem,
> inque deum deus ipse tulit patuitque ministris.   (1. 40.)

This doctrine may be traced in the second *logos* of God (480. 3), where the more righteous souls are to become kings, founders of

---

[1] *Fortasse ἐπιτηδευμάτων.*

[2] See Norden's edition of *Aeneid* VI, pp. 33–6. The *philosophi* are the *cultores vitae*; see the passages from Macrobius discussed on p. xxiii, n. 3 above, and Lactantius, *de ira*, 11. 7: 'ii omnes qui coluntur ut dii, homines fuerunt et idem primi et maximi reges, sed eos aut ob uirtutem qua profuerunt hominum generi diuinis honoribus adfectos esse post mortem aut ob beneficia et inuenta quibus humanam uitam excoluerunt inmortalem memoriam consecutos quis ignorat?' The idea of gifted souls descending from heaven was perhaps influenced by commentary on the *Phaedrus* myth (248 D).

[3] Cf. 494. 23 *sqq.*, 514. 20. See Ps.-Ecphantus, Stobaeus, *Anthol.* 4. 7. 64.

cities, and lawgivers, seers and prophets, astronomers and philosophers, priests exact in their rites—καὶ ὅποσαι ἐστὲ καλῶν κἀγαθῶν ἄξιαι.[1]

The theory is that the benefactors of the race are souls divinely sent to assume mundane duties. Let us now look at specific instances, from a rationalizing list:[2]

Lactantius, *div. inst.*	Isidorus, *etymologiae*, 8. 11. 3.
artes quoque inuentoribus suis inmortalitatem peperisse dicuntur, ut Asclepio medicina, Volcano fabrica. (1. 18. 21.)	nam quorundam et inventiones artium cultu peperisse dicuntur, ut Aesculapio medicina, Vulcano fabrica. ab actibus autem vocantur, ut Mercurius, quod mercibus praeest ; Liber a libertate. fuerunt etiam et quidam viri fortes aut urbium conditores, quibus mortuis homines, qui eos dilexerunt, simulacra finxerunt.
ipsi reges . . . magnum sui desiderium mortui reliquerunt, itaque homines eorum simulacra finxerunt. (1. 15. 4.)	

The character of our Egyptian list is now evident. The class of *fortes* is represented by the king of might and strength, Osiris;[3] poetry and philosophy are conjoined because they were joined in Greek tradition, and names are attached to them ; Asclepius is naturally the king of healing, as Hephaestus of crafts in the Greek tradition. If the clause about Hermes is not corrupt, it is a tumid way of saying that he is the interpreter of God's Will.[4] It was the task of certain

---

[1] This answers closely to the Virgilian line about *philosophi* (6. 664) quoted above. The bestiary passage that follows has a curious interest. These ensouled animals are benefactors. Now the Clementine Homilies (8. 12) tell how the lower angels besought God to permit them to visit the earth, that by becoming men themselves they might turn men to God. Since their divine nature allowed them to become all things, some turned into precious stones and gold, and others became animals, creeping things, fish, and birds, and whatever they wished. These are the 'Watchers' (see *Book of Jubilees*, 4. 15). We may compare the remains of the Hermetic Ἀρχαϊκὴ βίβλος, a treatise associated with the 'Kuranis' and the 'Koiranides' (1st century A.D.). It probably dealt with the origins and φύσεις of animals; compare the story of the cock on p. 151 below and note on p. 487. (Malalas gives a Euhemerist version in *Chron.* p. 89 Migne.) Cf. φύσις in 480. 11 *sqq.* See further M. Wellmann, *Philologus, Suppl.-Band* XXVII, Heft 2.

[2] See A. Schmekel, *Isidorus von Sevilla*, p. 200, where the quotation from Isidore is compared with the second passage in Lactantius.

[3] Athenagoras gives the same theory of the god-king as Lactantius : τί θαυμαστὸν τοὺς μὲν ἐπὶ ἀρχῇ καὶ τυραννίδι ὑπὸ τῶν κατ' αὐτοὺς κληθῆναι θεούς . . . τοὺς δ' ἐπ' ἰσχύϊ, ὡς Ἡρακλέα καὶ Περσέα, τοὺς δ' ἐπὶ τέχνῃ, ὡς Ἀσκληπιόν. He quotes (*Libellus*, c. 30) the Euhemerizing account of Kronos in *Orac. Sibyll.* 3 given above, p. xxxvii. See p. 2 below, where perhaps read συνάπτων τὸ ἀνθρώπειον αὐτοῖς γένος in l. 8 (ΑΝΙΟΝ : ΑΙΔΙΟΝ).

[4] The change in emphasis from God's Mind to his Will or Providence may be seen in Chalcidius' rendering of the *Timaeus* : 'hac igitur dei ratione *consilioque* huius modi genituram temporis *uolentis creari* sol et luna et aliae quinque stellae... factae sunt' (38 c). It is the development of the theme "βουληθείς . . . κατὰ δύναμιν". Varro's etymology of Sibyllae is θεοβούλη, 'quia divinam voluntatem hominibus interpretari solebant' (Lactant. *div. inst.* 1. 6. 7 ; Isidorus, 8. 8. 1)

'gods' or divinely inspired souls like Hermes (458. 17), who had 'sympathy' with the stars, to seek and to interpret. As the aretalogy at the end of the *Kore Kosmu* shows, Hermes taught the hidden ordinances of God to Isis and Osiris.[1] The role of the prophet in relation to the king he instructs is well known in this type of reve-lation literature;[2] and this Hermes may perhaps be taken as the head of the class *vates* in the traditional list.

From this tangle some main threads may be picked out. The aretalogy of Isis and Osiris is an addition the nature of which can be recognized from the inscriptions at Andros and elsewhere. They serve here as the indigenous *cultores vitae humanae*, as other god-kings might have served in another context.[3] The complement to this passage is the description of men and women who continue to benefit man after their return to the sky (*Asclepius*, c. 37); upon the theory civilization owes its origin to divine souls sent down to rule, in due course to return to the stars. We have found it, in a rationalist form, in Lactantius and others to explain the *cultus deorum*. The general theory covers the fragment of the speech of God about the mission of benefactors, and the account of kingly souls in *Excerpts* XXIV and XXVI.

In the *Asclepius* (c. 37) the discovery of god-making ended primi-tive ignorance, as here. Though we have but a fragment, it describes more than original ἀγνωσία. As Bousset suggests, the presumption of the souls in heaven, their revolt against the star-gods after they were embodied, their use of men as instruments, Hermes' teaching about daemons (492. 27) all belong to one tradition; but we must add the diatribe of Momus against knowledge, notwithstanding its form. The diatribe is not 'world-weary pessimism' (Reitzenstein); it is part of a theory resting upon a myth. The myth can be under-stood in the light of such pagan tales as the Sibylline account of Babel; the souls in their rebellion had daemonic knowledge and ambitions, and they caused faction among men.[4] In our setting the theory is an astrological account of Fate. God gave over the souls to Ἔρως and Ἀνάγκη; Hermes so compounded the material of men

That is the relation in which Hermes stands to God. Perhaps read ὁ πατήρ (*sc.* Ὄσιρις), καὶ πάντων καθηγητὴς ὁ Τρ. Ἑ.; see *Suppl. Lectionum*, p. 574 below.

[1] 492. 12, 27, 494. 1.

[2] See F. Boll, *Aus der Offenbarung Johannis, Anhang II, Könige als Offen-barungsträger.* Compare (with Boll) *Libellus* XVII, and 262. 12. For the general conception see note on 132. 4 (p. 359 below).

[3] See Macrobius, *Comment,* 1. 9. 7, with its use of Hesiod and Virgil.

[4] See *Book of Jubilees*, 10. 1–12.

that they should not be strong as well as intelligent (474. 7) ; Momus begged for the πάθη to offset intelligence ; Hermes promised the engine of Fate. There are obvious discrepancies here in the borrowed material ; we may discern *Timaeus* matter in it, and it is of particular interest to observe the parallel with Stoic teleological debates in which Prometheus figured. He actually appears in a fragment of dialogue preserved by Zosimus, which perhaps ran something like this :

Prometheus—'What is the greatest happiness ?'

Epimetheus— 'A pretty woman and plenty of money.'

Prometheus—' Do not take a gift from Zeus Olympios (Fate), but send it back' (iv. 105 below).

Here we come upon the traces of allegorizing Hesiodic commentary, as often in these discussions of origins ; and we may see the ultimate source of Momus' demand for the plagues of love and fever and deceitful hopes (*O.D.*, 90–105). It would be tempting to pursue the connexion of Hermes, Prometheus, and Zoroaster with the theme of the origin of civilization, the first man, Fate and the superiority of the philosopher to Fate ; but it would lead us too far. Enough has been said to show that the *Kore Kosmu* is a document of great complexity. The compiler doubtless did not always comprehend the full bearing of his material. That material is drawn from myth, allegory, and theory upon man, fate, and daemons, knowledge forbidden and lawful, and the *cultus vitae*.

IV

THE FRAGMENTS

The Fragments are of varying value as evidence. Iamblichus (*Abammonis responsum*)[1] and Zosimus contribute to our knowledge of the astral fatalism that is one aspect of Hermetism ; the Christian Fathers stand on a different plane. They quote to confute, or to confirm their faith by pagan testimony. Lactantius gives little that is not contained in the extant documents or may not be interpreted as a reminiscence of them. With Didymus [2] we enter dubious territory. Fragments 23 and 24 appear in a chain of heathen oracles that are

---

[1] The ascription to Iamblichus is vindicated by C. Rasche, *De Iamblicho libri qui inscribitur de mysteriis auctore* (1911).

[2] I take the opportunity to emend a passage at the end of the extract from Didymus (iv. 176. 10) : man should, he says, regard his time on earth as a sojourn at an inn, παρασκευαζόμενος [ἰν'] εὐφρύνης (codd. εὖ φρονῇ) ἐφ' ἑκάστης πρὸς τὴν ἐκ τούτου ἔξοδον.

supposed to bear upon the doctrine of the Trinity; they are themselves oracles. Fragment 24 is said to come from the three discourses to Asclepius. It has traces of iambic rhythm, and fragment 23 is clearly an oracle in hexameters. They cannot be derived from the Hermetic writings; they form part of a chain of heathen testimonies to Christian doctrine.

Cyril's treatment is even more instructive. He assumes that they belong to the same Hermetic document, though they are metrical and in different metres; and he specifies their source as the 'third book' addressed to Asclepius (iv. 207. 7). It can hardly be doubted that he improved upon the vague reference given by Didymus or his source; conceivably the whole construction rests upon a dittography ($\lambda \acute{o} \gamma \omega \nu$ $\gamma \omega \nu > \gamma'$).[1] There is no decisive evidence that Cyril knew at first hand a body of Hermetic writings. A genuine (though expanded) quotation from the *Asclepius* (iv. 220. 1), is cited under the same title[2] as a cosmogony unconnected with the *Asclepius* (iv. 213. 3), and the letter to Asclepius in *Corpus* XIV is not differentiated from the other *Asclepius* documents (iv. 217. 3). He does not distinguish between the documents, and where he distinguishes he is wrong. The much-quoted extract about God's ineffability (*Stobaei Exc.* I) follows upon its proper source (*Timaeus* 28 c); Cyril runs it into fragment 25 with no indication that the two are unconnected; fragment 26 follows after a perfunctory break, and again there is no indication that it contains two independent fragments (iv. 197. 17). This order is consistent with the hypothesis that he had access to a *catena* of quotations. In iv. 211. 1 he gives a garbled title, 'Hermes to his *nous*' instead of 'Nous to Hermes'. Fragment 34 is almost certainly a loose reference to speeches in the *Kore Kosmu*, which is not mentioned. We may therefore suspect the precision of the title $\acute{e} \nu$ $\tau \hat{\omega}$ $\pi \rho \grave{o} s$ $\tau \grave{o} \nu$ $T \grave{a} \tau$ $\delta \iota \epsilon \xi o \delta \iota \kappa \hat{\omega}$ $\lambda \acute{o} \gamma \omega$ $\pi \rho \acute{\omega} \tau \omega$ (iv. 215. 1);[3] it has no greater claim to authority than the title of the preceding extract, $\acute{e} \nu$ $\tau \hat{\omega}$ $\pi \rho \grave{o} s$ $\grave{A} \sigma \kappa \lambda \eta \pi \iota \acute{o} \nu$. The common note of the Cyril quotations is the nature of the creative Logos. It is probable that Didymus and Cyril drew upon a collection of sayings from Greek writers, perhaps formed during the Arian controversy.[4]

[1] Cf. iv. 227. 3, 487. It is perhaps pressing an explanation too far to suggest that the title 'the first diexodic logos to Tat' (*Frr*. 30, 33) has a similar origin: the $\sigma \upsilon \mu \phi \omega \nu \acute{\iota} a$ in iv. 225. 17 reads, $\tau o \hat{\upsilon}$ $a \grave{\upsilon} \tau o \hat{\upsilon}$ $\pi \rho \grave{o} s$ $\tau \grave{a}$ $(T \acute{a} \tau)$ $\delta \iota \epsilon \xi o \delta \iota \kappa \grave{a}$ $\pi \rho \acute{\omega} \tau o \upsilon$ $\lambda \acute{o} \gamma o \upsilon$.

[2] $\acute{e} \nu$ $\tau \hat{\omega}$ $\pi \rho \grave{o} s$ $\grave{A} \sigma \kappa \lambda \eta \pi \iota \acute{o} \nu$.

[3] We need look no further than *Asclepius*, c. 1, for the title itself.

[4] The $\sigma \upsilon \mu \phi \omega \nu \acute{\iota} a$ given in iv. 225 should be compared. It purports to be from Cyril and I am unable to contest this; but it gives extracts not in Cyril. The

Little need be said here about the Arabic *Testimonia*; but it is perhaps possible to reduce the names of the Sabian prophets to some order and to connect them with the Hermetism of our documents. Pseudo-Justin (vol. iv. 7. 1) gives Akmon and Hermes as the two earliest philosophers. One manuscript reads Ἄμμωνος, and Casaubon preferred the easier reading. Now Hesychius reads (*s. v.* ἄκμων) Κρόνος, Οὐρανός; and (*s. v.* Ἀκμωνίδης) ὁ Χάρων (?) καὶ ὁ Οὐρανός· Ἄκμωνος γὰρ παῖς. *Etymologicum Magnum* has Ἄκμων . . . Ὠκεάνου δὲ υἱὸν τὸν οὐρανόν.[1] Since Ouranos and Kronos were regarded by the Hermetists as prophets and teachers before Hermes,[2] we need not hesitate to retain the reading Ἄκμωνος. It is unnecessary to determine whether Akmon should be identified with one or the other, for reasons to be seen. There was a Sabian tradition that the Ka'bah was an ancient temple of Saturn, founded by Seth (i.e. Agathodaemon or Oráni). More to the point is the identification of Kronos, Agathodaemon, and Aion with one another in religious tradition.[3]

The Arabic sources present great textual confusion, which is partly due to uncertainty about Greek names. Agathodaemon and Hermes are major prophets, and with them are linked others (Greek or Indian or Iranian), whose names have been mutilated. Aráni (*v. l.* Oráni)

extract, with full title, ascribed to Hermes in l. 20 is a garbled oracle in hexameters; and another garbled set of hexameters on the following page (l. 16) may be found among the oracles in Buresch's *Klaros*.

[1] For Akmon see Mövers, *Phönic.* i. 98, Chwolsohn, *Die Ssabier*, ii. 673, Pauly-Wissowa, *Real-Encycl. s.v. Akmon*. These authorities omit our passage, since Casaubon had removed the word. We should also restore it in the superscription to *Exc.* XIII, where Wachsmuth and Scott read Ἑρμοῦ ἐκ τῶν πρὸς Ἄμμωνα. This excerpt is one of a series of short extracts in Stobaeus (I. 4. 5-7 c, vol. 1, p. 72 W.), the lemmata of which are in disorder. The order of extracts is Sophocles, Euripides, Thales, Hermes, Pythagoras (5-7 c). After the second F reads in the text Θάλητος. Σοφοκλῆ. Θυέστη. Εὐριπίδ. Διδύμῳ. Ἑρμου ἐκ τῶν Πλάτωνος, with ἄκμωννα Πυθαγόρου in the margin. At the same point in the text P reads θάλητος . . . ἑρμοῦ ἐκ τοῦ πλάτωνος. ἄκμωνα πυθαγόρου. It was supposed by Wachsmuth that ἐκ τῶν πρὸς had been corrupted into τῶν Πλάτωνος; but this leaves ἄκμωνα unaccounted for, and it is evident that ἄκμωννα πυθαγόρου purports to give the authors of two successive extracts. We must take Πλάτωνος as an attempt to substitute a known name, and recognize that the copyist was in a difficulty because there were more names than extracts. Read Ἑρμοῦ ἐκ τῶν Ἄκμωνος. This is another of those Agathodaemon utterances of which examples are found in *Corpus* XII. i. 8-9 and *Frr.* 29, 31. The statement that ἀνάγκη is the κρίσις βεβαία καὶ ἀμετάτρεπτος δύναμις προνοίας (*lex in munere et in actu*) should be taken with the definition of πρόνοια in *Exc.* XII as the αὐτοτελὴς λόγος τοῦ ἐπουρανίου θεοῦ (the self-complete or perfect law; connect αὐτοτελής with προηγούμενος). Whether any of the other Ammon excerpts dealing with fate are really Akmon excerpts cannot be said.

[2] 190. 2, *Fr.* 5. In Manetho's list of the first Egyptian dynasty Agathodaemon and Kronos follow Helios and precede Osiris and Isis.

[3] Reitzenstein, *Das iranische Erlösungsmysterium* p. 191. 2 etc.

stands before the two prophets in Al-Kindí (iv. 249. 4), and in Al-Maqdísí (iv. 251). Masudi names the first and second Oráni (*v. l.* Oráfí) together with Hermes and Agathodaemon, and identifies the first pair with the second (iv. 255, C. p. 624). Further, El-Basthání says that Seth, who founded the Ka'bah, was called Agathodaemon by the Sabians and Oráfí (*v. l.* Oráni) by the Greeks.[1] Since the name is said to be Greek, and since there is nothing to commend the conjectures Orpheus and Ouranios, the evidence of the extant *Hermetica* should be brought to bear upon the persistent forms Aráni and Oráni. This astral religion preserved the name of Ouranos, and identified both Hermes and Agathodaemon with him by the simple device of doubling him. Since Al-Qifthí makes the same identification for Ludin (*v. l.* Lurin) the first and the second,[2] it can hardly be doubted that the Arabic article has still further deformed this name.

In the list of the sons of Hermes (iv. 256) if Şá is the ancestor of the Sabians, Qoft is presumably the eponymous ancestor of the Kopts or ancient Egyptians. Athríb is more difficult; the clue perhaps lies in the statement of Dimeshqí[3] that, according to the Kopts, the pyramids were the graves of king Súreid, of his brother Hergíb (Hermes), and of Hergíb's son Afrúbín (Afríbún : Al-Sojúthí). These are names of peoples ; but the most probable explanation of Ashmun is that he is Agathodaemon.[4]

Lastly, why is Solon among the prophets of Sabianism (iv. 262) ? This is probably a trace of the persistent influence of the *Timaeus*. The Sabians honoured him as that ancestor of Plato who learned from Egypt the tale of Atlantis (*Tim.* 20 D–E) ; and his name travelled to Harran along with the text that man is a plant of heaven.[5]

I have added some *Testimonia* of no great importance. Since Bousset has used Arnobius to exhibit the nature of the astral fatalism that is a significant aspect of Hermetism, and to argue for its early date, the Addenda give further extracts from his treatise. Mr. Scott included no *Testimonia* from scholastic or medieval sources, and I have not attempted to fill up the gap. I have used one hardly genuine passage from the *Secretum Secretorum* above to illustrate the

[1] Chwolsohn, ii. 635. El-Basthání flourished in the fifteenth century.
[2] *Op. cit.* i. 243, 793.
[3] *Cosmography* (Chwolsohn, ii. 409). Al-Sojúthí also gives the same account (*ibid.* ii. 617).
[4] See Manetho (Syncellus, i, p. 72), quoted in vol. iii. 491 ; punctuate ὑπὸ τοῦ Ἀγαθοδαίμονος, υἱοῦ τοῦ δευτέρου Ἑρμοῦ.
[5] See vol. iii. 36, n. 1.

complaint of the Elements; others may be found in Mr. Robert Steele's edition of Roger Bacon.

One problem may, however, be mentioned. The work of Bernardus Silvestris entitled *de mundi universitate*[1] is known to be influenced by Chalcidius and Macrobius. It has not been recognized to be largely a cento, with a good deal of the *Asclepius* patched in. The doctrine is as nearly pagan and fatalist as a clerk's work may safely be. The Ousiarchs of the *Asclepius* make, so far as I know, their only other appearance in literature here, disguised as Oyarses, *genii caelestes*—Pantomorphos, Saturn, Jupiter, the Sun, Pluto.[2] Combined with some extracts from the *Asclepius* are other passages, colourably Hermetic in character. If we compare Bernardus with the *de causa dei*[3] of Thomas Bradwardine, Warden of Merton and Archbishop of Canterbury under Edward III, the *Asclepius* (under the title *Hermetis de verbo aeterno*) is abundantly quoted by Bradwardine; and he also uses occasionally a work which he calls *Hermetis de mundo et caelo*, the source (in his view) of the *de mundo*. As an example will show, his quotations from this document prove that Bernardus also used it:

Bernardus.	*Bradwardine.*
In qua vitae viventis imagines, notiones aeternae, mundus intelligibilis, rerum cognitio praefinita . . . Illic in genere, in specie, in individuali singularitate conscripta, quicquid hyle, quicquid mundus, quicquid parturiunt elementa. Illic exarata supremi digito dispunctoris textus temporis, fatalis series, dispositio saeculorum (13. 157).	Qui et De Mundo et caelo 1 . . . sic ait; Cuncta regit et componit; illic iunguntur in specie in individuali singularitate conscripta, quicquid *hyle*, quicquid mundus, quicquid mundi machina, quicquid tempus, quicquid in temporalibus parturiunt elementa: illic textus operis fatalis series, saeculorum dispositio, temporalium omnium meta summi digito dispositoris exarata, illic nodus perpetuitatis (711 c).

It is sufficient here to add that Bradwardine attributes a form of a famous saying to the same document: 'sicut ad centrum circulus, sic ad aeternitatem consistit mundus temporarius' (845 c). I have been unable to trace the tract *de mundo et caelo*.

[1] *Ed.* C. S. Barach and J. Wrobel (Innsbruck, 1876). The date is about 1150. I hope to deal with the subject elsewhere.

[2] *Op. cit.* pp. 38. 92, 41. 46, 42. 76, 44. 131. 50. 118.

[3] Edited by Sir Henry Savile, 1618. My friend Dr. Richard McKeon introduced me to Bernardus and Bradwardine.

V

The Indexes of Greek and Latin words offer a fairly full guide to the religious and philosophical terminology, with some indication of the range of the Hermetic vocabulary. It seemed on the whole more convenient to cite words by their traditional place, where the printed text allows, though the choice was not made without difficulty. Some words from the *apparatus criticus* are included. I have also entered certain emendations not noted by Mr. Scott, though always with due warning. Zielinski's καταπονῆσαι (*codd.* κατανοῆσαι 120. 21) and ἐκφθορά (*codd.* ἐκφορά 130. 5) deserve record. The examples collected in the vocabulary sometimes suggest or support an emendation. In 172. 17 the parallels almost impose τὸ ἓν καὶ μόνον (ἐγκεί-μενον) ἀγαθόν. I venture to restore two Platonic personifications in ἡ Φύσις πάντων, φύουσα... σπείρουσα... γενεσιουργοῦσα (γένεσις ἔχουσα 438. 6), and ἀκολουθήσει Δίκη νέμουσα (διὰ γένους) μισθο⟨ὺ⟩ς ἐπα-ξίο⟨υ⟩s (490. 23). If I mention two suggestions for *Libellus* III— εἰς κατοπτίαν οὐρανοῦ καὶ ἱερᾶς πορείας οὐρανίων θεῶν (146. 29),[1] and ἀμοιβὰς κυκλουμένας (μοίρας ὀχλουμένης) γνῶναι ἀγαθῶν καὶ φαύλων (148. 2)—it is to take the opportunity of noting that this tumid piece as a whole is less Biblical than it would appear to be. The gods who create living things (146. 19) are the star gods of the *Timaeus*,[2] and the character of § 3 b is astrological—men are intended to observe the heavens. The cycle of life described in the confused text of § 4 has perhaps its nearest parallel in the περὶ πολιτείας attri-buted to Hippodamus the Pythagorean; the conceptions of ἀνάγκη, φύσις, of ἀρχή, τέλος and ἀνανέωσις appear in both.[3]

---

[1] A scribe perhaps wrote:

δρομήματος θεῶν ἐγκυκλίων

εἰς κατοπτίαν οὐρανοῦ καὶ

ἱερᾶς πορίας δρομήματος οὐρανίων θεῶν

καὶ ἔργων καὶ θείων φύσεως

Having copied δρομήματος a second time, he inserted the correction in the margin: it became corrupted to the meaningless τερασπορίας, and slipped back into the text before εἰς.

[2] Cf. 468. 6.

[3] *Stobaei Anthologium*, 4. 34. 71 (vol. 5, p. 846 Hense): πάντα μὲν ὦν τὰ θνατὰ δι' ἀνάγκαν φύσιος ἐν μεταβολαῖς καλινδεῖται... γενόμενα γὰρ ἀέξεται τὰ πράγματα καὶ ἀεξηθέντα ἀκμάζει καὶ ἀκμάσαντα γηράσκει καὶ τέλος ὕστατα φθείρεται· τὰ μὲν ὑπὸ φύσιος γινόμενα δι' αὐτᾶς τᾶς φύσιος ἐς τὸ ἄδηλον αὖτις τερματιζόμενα, καὶ πάλιν ἐκ τῶ ἀδήλω ἐς τὸ ὁρατὸν ἐπισυνερχόμενα ἀμοιβᾷ γενέσιος καὶ ἀνταποδόσει φθορᾶς κύκλον αὐταύτας ἀναποδιζοίσας... οἶκοί τε καὶ πόλεις ὑπὸ μεγάλων εὐτυχημάτων ἀερθεῖσαι καὶ †βίον βαθυπλούτων ἅμα τοῖς μακαριζομένοις ἀγαθοῖς ἐς τὸν ὄλεθρον ἔβα-σαν, κ.τ.λ.

Some of the more important words have been classified according to sense, and I have tried to make up for the necessary limitations imposed upon my notes. If στοιχεῖον can mean a 'support', and a body as the support of the soul,[1] then we are justified in retaining the description of the sky as πρῶτον στοιχεῖον (432. 10); the stars are στοιχεῖα (482. 28) because they are ensouled; and a regenerated man may regard his body as a πλαστὸν στοιχεῖον (240. 18). This explains the triple division of *Caelum*, *terra*, and *elementa* in 330. 7; the last are not the elements, but stars. The fiery sun and the moon change like earth and sky—all signs that μεταβολή is the rule of life. It is therefore unnecessary to suppose that the 'stationes et cursus' (330. 14) of fruits on the earth's surface are instances of the mobility of the fourth element, water. They are ⟨βλα⟩στήσεις καὶ φοραί of the products of earth—*fructuum nativitas, augmenta et maturitas* (346. 22). Since the *Asclepius* is a translation, and not a good translation, the senses ascribed to such words as *mens* or *mundus* are open to doubt. I have not hesitated to depart from the rendering given in the translation or notes in this edition where there seemed to be reason. A word like *totum* is used to translate τὸ πᾶν, and *animus* may render θυμός; but in too many cases, I fear, the exact shade of meaning remains to be determined.

Professor A. D. Nock has most generously given me a list of the more important readings in the Corpus MSS.—A, C, and M. They are printed after the Addenda.

Thomas Bradwardine extracted numerous passages from the *Asclepius* in his work *de. causa Dei*, under the title *Hermetis de verbo aeterno*. Some specimen readings are subjoined; where his text coincides with one or more MSS. the fact is noted.

286. 12 utroque (GPLF)   304. 9 cum homine ipso gubernatorem composuit, ipso gubernatore compositi: *om.* cum homine ipso PL: *om.* ipso gubernatorem composuit *cett.*   308. 20 immortalitatem   310. 14 iunctarum omnium   19 vera scientia puraque philosophia   29 quando (GLF)   326. 6 gubernatorum superiorum et inferiorum   332. 9 *om.* esse   334. 2 percipito *om.* omni   342. 17 summo suo operi (suo operi G)   344. 7 innavigabitur   16 corruptelas omnium errorum   346. 6 per coactum cursum (GL)   352. 3 stabilitas fixa fiat lege ista   5 stabilitas enim L (stabilistas enim G)   358. 30 melioris   362. 17 quarum (GF)

---

[1] Cf. ὄχημα, σκῆνος. The senses of στοιχεῖον (στείχω) run parallel to those of βάσις (βαίνω); see O. Lagercrantz, *Elementum* (*Skr. Kungl. Humanistika Veten-skaps Samfundet*, Upsala, Bd. XI). Probably στήριγμα applies to the body in the sense of a support or ground of evil in 172. 11.

18 cogit ad effectum (*man.* 2B *et ed. Rom.*) . . . illis   366. 6 est et
15 ignis (GPL)   368. 4 saevioribus (GPLF).

These readings agree most frequently with G, and never with BM against the other manuscripts. Bradwardine's text anticipates Hildebrand's *percipito* in 334. 2. Some other readings appear to restore sense where the MSS. are defective : e.g., *iunctarum omnium rerum ordinem scire* (τὴν συνηρμοσμένων πάντων τάξιν γνῶναι) for *cunctarum* (*giunctarum ?*) *omnium* (310. 14); *summo suo operi absque invidia suffragantis* (342. 17) ; *si est homo totus in sensu vitae melioris* for *melior* (358. 30).

I regret that the issue of this volume has been delayed, in part by pressing calls, and in part because the work had to be carried further than I had anticipated ; it would have been easier if I could have made a fresh start. My thanks are due to the late Professor F. Ll. Griffith, to Professor Margoliouth, and to Professor H. J. Rose for the help they kindly gave me on various points. I have already acknowledged the generosity of Professor A. D. Nock ; he has also been good enough to allow me to use some of his notes from the *Journal of Egyptian Archaeology*, quoted under the initials A. D. N. Mr. John Macdonald, Reader in Celtic in this University, has been a resource on questions of scholarship. Mr. E. H. Blakeney most kindly read through the proofs of the Indexes. I have again to thank Mr. S. Dixon, reader to the University Press, for the unfailing and valuable help he has given throughout.

A. S. FERGUSON.

KING'S COLLEGE
   OLD ABERDEEN

TESTIMONIA

ATHENAGORAS

Libellus pro Christianis[1] 28: Ἡρόδοτος μὲν οὖν καὶ Ἀλέξανδρος ὁ τοῦ Φιλίππου ἐν τῇ πρὸς τὴν μητέρα ἐπιστολῇ . . . φασὶ παρ' ἐκείνων ἀνθρώπους αὐτοὺς γενέσθαι μαθεῖν.[2] . . . ⸢εἰ τοίνυν Ἡρόδοτος ἔλεγεν περὶ τῶν θεῶν ὡς περὶ ἀνθρώπων ἱστορεῖν Αἰγυπτίους, καίτοι λέγοντι τῷ Ἡροδότῳ·[3] " τὰ μέν νυν θεῖα τῶν ἀφηγημάτων, οἷα ἤκουον, οὐκ εἰμὶ 5 πρόθυμος διηγεῖσθαι ἔξω ἢ τὰ ὀνόματα αὐτέων μοῦνα"[4] ἐλάχιστα μὴ[5] πιστεύειν ὡς μυθοποιῷ ἔδει· ἐπεὶ δὲ Ἀλέξανδρος καὶ Ἑρμῆς ὁ Τρισμέγιστος ἐπικαλούμενος συνάπτων τὸ ἀίδιον[6] αὐτοῖς γένος⸥[7] καὶ ἄλλοι μυρίοι, ἵνα μὴ καθ' ἕκαστον καταλέγοιμι, οὐδὲ λόγος ἔτι καταλείπεται βασιλεῖς ὄντας αὐτούς· μὴ νενομίσθαι θεούς.[8] καὶ ὅτι μὲν ἄνθρωποι, δηλοῦσι μὲν καὶ 10 Αἰγυπτίων οἱ λογιώτατοι, . . . δηλοῖ δὲ καὶ Ἀπολλόδωρος ἐν τῷ Περὶ θεῶν.

[1] Edited by Schwartz, *Texte und Untersuchungen* IV. 2, 1891. Athenagoras probably wrote this in A.D. 177; the date certainly falls within A.D. 177–180 (Harnack, *Chronol.* I, pp. 318 and 710).

[2] I. e. Herodotus and Alexander say that they learnt from the Egyptians that the persons worshipped as gods in Egypt were men.

[3] Schwartz brackets τῷ Ἡροδότῳ.

[4] Hdt. 2. 3.

[5] Schwartz brackets μὴ.

[6] ἀίδιον MS.: ἴδιον coni. Schwartz.

[7] This passage (εἰ τοίνυν . . . αὐτοῖς γένος) is unintelligible, and manifestly corrupt. What Athenagoras probably meant might be expressed by writing εἰ τοίνυν ⟨μόνος⟩ Ἡρόδοτος ἔλεγεν περὶ τῶν θεῶν ὡς περὶ ἀνθρώπων ἱστορεῖν Αἰγυπτίους, [καίτοι λέγοντι . . . αὐτέων μοῦνα] ἐλάχιστα ⟨ἂν τούτῳ⟩ [μὴ] πιστεύειν ὡς μυθοποιῷ ἔδει· ἐπεὶ δὲ ⟨ταὐτὸ λέγει⟩ Ἀλέξανδρος, καὶ Ἑρμῆς ὁ Τρισμέγιστος ἐπικαλούμενος, συνάπτων τὸ [ἀ]ίδιον αὐτοῖς γένος, κ.τ.λ. The statement about Hermes implies that Athenagoras knew of some writing ascribed to Hermes in which Egyptian gods were spoken of as men; and if ἴδιον is the right reading, this statement implies also that Athenagoras knew of a document in which Hermes said that he was himself descended from persons who were commonly regarded as gods. The Hermetic passage of which he was thinking must have resembled *Corp.* X. 5 (cf. Lactant. *Div. inst.* I. 11. 61) and *Ascl. Lat.* III. 37.

[8] Perhaps ⟨⟨μὴ⟩⟩ βασιλεῖς ὄντας αὐτοὺς [[μὴ]] νενομίσθαι θεούς.

TERTULLIAN

Adv. Valentinianos[1] 15 : Age nunc discant Pythagorici, agno-
scant Stoici, Plato ipse, unde materia, quam innatam volunt, et
originem et substantiam traxerit in omnem hanc struem mundi ; quod
nec Mercurius ille Trismegistus, magister omnium physicorum,[2]
5 recogitavit.[3]

De anima[4] 2 : Plane non negabimus aliquando philosophos iuxta
nostra sensisse. ... Visa est quidem sibi (*sc.* philosophia) et ex
sacris, quas putant, litteris hausisse, quia plerosque[5] auctores etiam
deos existimavit antiquitas, nedum divos, ut Mercurium Aegyptium,
10 cui praecipue Plato adsuevit,[6] ut Silenum Phrygem, cui a pastoribus
perducto ingentes aures suas Midas tradidit, ut Hermotimum,[7]
cui Clazomenii mortuo templum contulerunt, ut Orpheum, ut
Musaeum, ut Pherecydem Pythagorae magistrum.[8]

---

[1] Edited by Kroymann (*Corp. script. eccl. Lat.* vol. xxxxvii), 1906. The date
of Tertull. *Adv. Valentin.* is about A. D. 207-208.

[2] Hermes was ' the teacher of all the *physici*' (or ' of all *physica*'). Tertullian
apparently believed that all the theories of Greek philosophers concerning the
universe were derived from the teaching of an Egyptian named Hermes Trismegistus. He doubtless thought that Pythagoras and Plato had studied in Egypt,
and had there learnt the doctrines of that ancient philosopher.

[3] Hermes ' did not reflect about' the origin of matter. Tertullian can hardly
have supposed that all the thoughts of Hermes, or even the contents of all the
writings of Hermes, were completely known to him ; and without complete knowledge of them it would be impossible to make sure that Hermes had not reflected
on a certain subject. But perhaps Tertullian means merely that Hermes, like the
Platonists, taught that matter was *innata* ($\dot{\alpha}\gamma\acute{\epsilon}\nu\nu\eta\tau\sigma s$), and that it was to be
inferred thence that he had not adequately considered the question of its origin.
Even this however would seem to imply some definite knowledge of the contents
of philosophic writings ascribed to Hermes. Did Tertullian know of some
Hermetic document (such as *Ascl. Lat.* II. 14 b-16 a, for instance,) in which it was
said that $\H{\upsilon}\lambda\eta$ is $\dot{\alpha}\gamma\acute{\epsilon}\nu\nu\eta\tau\sigma s$? Or did he, knowing only that Platonists said this,
assume that, since they said it, their teacher Hermes must have said the same?

[4] Edited by Reifferscheid and Wissowa (*Corp. script. eccl. Lat.* vol. xx), 1890.
The date of Tertull. *De an.* is probably A. D. 208-213 (Harnack).

[5] *Plerosque* means ' many ', but not necessarily ' the greater number'.

[6] This most likely means that Plato learnt more of his philosophy from Hermes
than from any other teacher; though it would be possible to take the words as
meaning that Plato followed the teaching of Hermes more closely than any other
Greek philosopher did.

[7] Hermotimus of Clazomenae probably lived in the sixth century B. C. He seems
to have been a seer of the same type as Epimenides and Aristeas; see Rohde,
Psyche, pp. 385-391. Hermotimus was said to have originated the doctrine of
$\nu\sigma\hat{\upsilon} s$ which was taught by Anaxagoras (Arist. *Metaph.* A. 3, 984 b 19).

[8] Hermes is here placed first in a list of writers of whom Tertullian says that in

De anima 28: Quis ille nunc vetus sermo apud memoriam Platonis de animarum reciproco discursu, quod hinc abeuntes eant illuc, et rursus huc veniant et vivant, et dehinc e vita abeant, rursus ex mortuis effici vivos? Pythagoricus, ut volunt quidam; divinum Albinus[1] existimat, Mercurii forsitan Aegyptii.[2] Sed nullus sermo 5 divinus nisi dei unius, quo prophetae, quo apostoli, quo ipse Christus intonuit.

De anima 33: Etiam cum iudicii nomine vindicatur hoc dogma, quod animae humanae pro vita et meritis genera animalium sortiantur, . . .; et hic dicam: si demutantur, non ipsae dis- 10 pungentur quae merebuntur,[3] et evacuabitur ratio iudicii, si meritorum deerit sensus. Deerit autem sensus meritorum, si status verterit animarum; vertit autem status animarum, si non eaedem

ancient times they were believed to be not merely *divi* (i. e. men deified after their deaths? or men inspired by the gods?), but *dei*, and their writings were thought to be 'sacred'; and it is implied that the doctrines of the Greek philosophers were derived, in part at least, from those writings.

We have some fragments of the *Theologia* of Pherecydes; and there may have been writings ascribed to Hermotimus, though I have not found any mention of them except in this passage. There were numerous writings ascribed to Orpheus and his pupil Musaeus; and it is possible that in Tertullian's time there may have been in existence writings ascribed to Silenus. Servius reports a story told by Theopompus, according to which Silenus answered questions put to him by king Midas *de rebus naturalibus et antiquis*; and Virgil, *Ecl.* 6, makes Silenus sing (but not write) a poem beginning with a *cosmogonia*. Had Virgil read a poem, such as he there describes, that was attributed to Silenus? Or was some one induced by Virgil's eclogue to write such a poem? Or is Tertullian's mention of *writings* ascribed to Silenus a blunder?

[1] The man meant is, no doubt, the Albinus (sometimes mistakenly called Alcinous) who taught Platonic philosophy in the latter part of the second century A. D. Some of his writings are extant.

[2] This appears to mean that Albinus thought that the doctrine of *metensomatosis*, or transmigration of souls, was 'divine',—that is to say, that the man by whom it was first taught received it from the gods by inspiration,—and that this inspired teacher was perhaps Hermes Trismegistus. It does not necessarily follow from this that Albinus knew of any writings ascribed to Hermes in which the doctrine of *metensomatosis* was taught. He knew that Pythagoras, who taught that doctrine to the Greeks, was said to have been a pupil of Egyptian teachers; and if he also knew that Hermes Trismegistus was reputed to have been the earliest and greatest of Egyptian teachers, and to have been a man divinely inspired, that would be enough to make him think that the doctrine was *divinum, Mercurii forsitan Aegyptii*. This passage therefore affords no proof that our *Hermetica*, or Hermetic writings of similar character, were known to Albinus.

[3] *Dispungentur* apparently means 'will have their accounts settled', i. e. will receive reward or suffer punishment. Tertullian argues that, if a soul which has inhabited a human body afterwards inhabits the body of a beast, it is no longer the same soul, but has been changed into another, and therefore the good or evil that befalls it in its second body cannot be regarded as reward or punishment for what it has done in its first body. The pig-soul will not say to itself 'I am now being punished for the sins which I committed when I was a man'; for it will have no memory of the human life which preceded, and will not feel itself to be the same soul that lived that life.

perseveraverint [aeque si perseveraverint]¹ in iudicium. Quod et Mercurius Aegyptius novit, dicens animam digressam a corpore non refundi in animam universi,² sed manere determinatam, uti rationem, inquit, patri reddat eorum quae in 5 corpore gesserit.³

CYPRIANUS

*Quod idola dii non sint*⁴ 6: Spiritus sunt insinceri et vagi, qui posteaquam terrenis vitiis inmersi sunt et a vigore caelesti terreno contagio recesserunt, non desinunt perditi perdere, et depravati errorem pravitatis infundere. Hos et poetae daemonas norunt, et 10 Socrates instrui se et regi ad arbitrium daemonii praedicabat, et magis⁵ inde est ad perniciosa vel ludicra potentatus : quorum tamen praecipuus Ostanes⁶ et formam veri dei negat conspici posse, et

---

¹ aeque si perseveraverint *delevit Wissowa.*

² in animam universi *om. A.*

³ *Frag.* 1. This is a quotation from a lost *Hermeticum.* In many of the extant *Hermetica* the separate existence of the individual soul after death is assumed ; but in none of them is its reabsorption into the world-soul explicitly denied. We know from *Corp.* X. 7 (οὐκ ἤκουσας ἐν τοῖς γενικοῖς, ὅτι ἀπὸ μιᾶς ψυχῆς τῆς τοῦ παντὸς πᾶσαι αἱ ψυχαὶ εἰσιν αὗται 《ὥσπερ ἀπονενεμημέναι》 ;) that the *anima mundi* was spoken of in one of the Γενικοὶ λόγοι πρὸς Τάτ ; and it is possible that the passage quoted by Tertullian occurred in that same Γενικὸς λόγος. [Stob. *Exc.* XXV. 3 denies that the individual soul is diffused μετὰ τοῦ ἄλλου ἀπείρου πνεύματος, and asserts that each soul goes to its proper place. But this is hardly what Tertullian says.]

⁴ Cyprianus, ed. Hartel (*Corp. script. eccl. Lat.* vol. iii), 1868-1871. If the *Quod idola dii non sint* was written by Cyprian, its date must be about A. D. 250. But Harnack (*Chronol.* II, pp. 336 ff.) gives strong reasons for doubting whether the writer of this treatise was Cyprian ; and if not, it may be a good deal later.

⁵ Dat. plur. of *magus.*

⁶ Ostanes was 'chief among magicians'. Pliny *Nat. Hist.* 30. 8-11 : 'Primus, quod exstet, ut equidem invenio, commentatus est de ea (*sc.* de magica) Osthanes, Xerxen regem Persarum bello quod is Graeciae intulit comitatus, ac velut semina artis portentosae sparsit obiter infecto quacumque commeaverat mundo. . . . Hic maxime Osthanes ad rabiem, non aviditatem modo scientiae eius Graecorum populos egit. . . . Non levem et Alexandri Magni temporibus auctoritatem addidit professioni (magices) secundus Osthanes comitatu eius exornatus.' Pliny knew a book about magic which he believed to have been written by Osthanes, and refers to it several times (*N. H.* 28. 6, 69, 256, 261 ; 30. 14). Alchemists, from the third century A. D. onward, referred to Ostanes as an authority on their art. (See Berthelot, *Alchimistes grecs*, I, pp. 151, 165, &c.)

Herodotus (3. 68 ff.) says that the leader of the seven conspirators by whom the Magian Pseudo-Smerdis was killed, and Darius made king in his place, was Otanes son of Pharnaspes. (In the Behistun inscription, this man is called Utána son of Thukhra.) Herodotus also says (7. 61) that the Persian contingent in the

angelos veros sedi eius dicit adsistere. In quo et Plato pari ratione consentit, et unum deum servans ceteros angelos vel daemonas dicit. Hermes quoque Trismegistus unum Deum loquitur, eumque inconprehensibilem adque inaestimabilem confitetur.[1] 7. Hi ergo spiritus sub statuis adque imaginibus consecratis delitescunt. 5

PSEUDO-JUSTINUS

Cohortatio ad gentiles [2] 36 E–37 B: Εἰ τοίνυν, ὦ ἄνδρες Ἕλληνες, μὴ προτιμοτέραν ἡγεῖσθε τῆς ὑμῶν αὐτῶν σωτηρίας τὴν περὶ τῶν μὴ ὄντων θεῶν ψευδῆ φαντασίαν, πείσθητε, ὥσπερ ἔφην, τῇ ἀρχαιοτάτῃ καὶ σφόδρα παλαιᾷ Σιβύλλῃ, ἧς τὰς βίβλους ἐν πάσῃ τῇ οἰκουμένῃ σώζεσθαι συμβαίνει, περὶ μὲν τῶν λεγομένων θεῶν, ὡς μὴ ὄντων, ἀπό τινος δυνατῆς 10 ἐπιπνοίας διὰ χρησμῶν ὑμᾶς διδασκούσῃ, περὶ δὲ τῆς τοῦ σωτῆρος ἡμῶν Ἰησοῦ Χριστοῦ μελλούσης ἔσεσθαι παρουσίας καὶ περὶ πάντων τῶν ὑπ' αὐτοῦ γίνεσθαι μελλόντων σαφῶς καὶ φανερῶς προαναφωνούσῃ· ἔσται γὰρ ὑμῖν ἀναγκαῖον προγύμνασμα ἡ τούτων γνῶσις τῆς τῶν ἱερῶν ἀνδρῶν προφητείας. εἰ δέ τις οἴοιτο παρὰ τῶν [[πρεσβυτάτων παρ' 15 αὐτοῖς ὀνομασθέντων]] [3] φιλοσόφων τὸν περὶ θεοῦ μεμαθηκέναι λόγον,

army of Xerxes was commanded by 'Otanes, the father of Xerxes' wife Amestris (cf. Plin. *l. c.*: 'Xerxen ... bello quod is Graeciae intulit comitatus'). This can hardly have been the same person as Otanes the conspirator, who would have been about eighty years old at the time of the expedition of Xerxes; but readers of Herodotus, if not Herodotus himself, might easily identify the two men. It seems probable then that the imaginary 'Ostanes the magician' was evolved partly out of the historical Otanes (Utána) who was a comrade of Darius and an opponent of the Magus, and partly out of the man of the same name who held command under Xerxes. (Another Persian named Otanes, son of Sisamnes, is mentioned in Hdt. 5. 25.)

[1] The Hermetic passage referred to is probably Herm. *ap.* Stob. *Exc.* I θεὸν νοῆσαι μὲν χαλεπόν, κ.τ.λ. Cf. *Frag.* 2.

Chs. 1–9 of the *Quod idola* are an abridgement of the *Octavius* of Minucius Felix; and the passage here printed ('Spiritus sunt ... consecratis delitescunt') agrees closely with Min. Fel. 26. 7–27. 1 in all except the sentence about Hermes, who is not mentioned by Min. Fel. This sentence ('Hermes quoque...confitetur'), since it contains nothing about daemons, has no bearing on the main subject of the paragraph; and it interrupts the sequence of thought. It may therefore be suspected that it was written as a marginal note on *Plato ... unum deum servans*, and has been inserted in the text by error.

[2] Otto, *Justini opera*, tom. ii ('*Opera Justini addubitata*'), 1879. The date of the *Cohort. ad gent.* is certainly later than A. D. 221, and is probably between A. D. 260 and 302 (Harnack, *Chronol.* II, pp. 151–158).

[3] The words πρεσβυτάτων παρ' αὐτοῖς ὀνομασθέντων are evidently out of place here. The writer's meaning must have been 'If any one should think that he has learnt the (true) doctrine about God from the Pagan philosophers, let him note what ⌜Akmon⌝ and Hermes say (viz. that the truth about God cannot be told by

⌐Ἄκμωνός⌐¹ τε καὶ Ἑρμοῦ ἀκουέτω, ⟨τῶν⟩ ⟨⟨πρεσβυτάτων παρ' αὐτοῖς [ὀ]νομισθέντων,⟩⟩ ⌐Ἄκμωνος⌐ μὲν ἐν τοῖς περὶ αὐτοῦ ² λόγοις πάγκρυφον τὸν θεὸν ὀνομάζοντος, Ἑρμοῦ δὲ σαφῶς καὶ φανερῶς λέγοντος· "θεὸν νοῆσαι μέν ἐστι χαλεπόν, φράσαι δὲ ἀδύνατον ᾧ καὶ νοῆσαι δυνατόν.³" πανταχόθεν τοίνυν εἰδέναι προσήκει, ὅτι οὐδαμῶς ἑτέρως περὶ θεοῦ ἢ τῆς ὀρθῆς θεοσεβείας μανθάνειν οἷόν τε, ἢ παρὰ τῶν προφητῶν μόνων, τῶν διὰ τῆς θείας ἐπιπνοίας διδασκόντων ὑμᾶς.⁴

ARNOBIUS

*Adv. nat.*⁵ 2. 13 : Interea tamen o isti, qui admiramini, qui stupetis doctorum et philosophiae scita, ita non iniustissimum ducitis
10 inequitare, inludere tamquam stulta nobis et bruta dicentibus, cum vel ea vel talia reperiamini et vos dicere quae nobis dici pronuntiarique ridetis ? Nec mihi cum his sermo est qui per varia sectarum deverticula dissipati has atque illas partes opinionum diversitate fecerunt : vos,

a philosopher)'. On the other hand, something like τῶν πρεσβυτάτων (*sc.* φιλοσόφων) is wanted as a qualification of ⌐Ἄκμωνός⌐ τε καὶ Ἑρμοῦ ; I have therefore inserted τῶν πρεσβυτάτων παρ' αὐτοῖς (i.e. among the Pagans) ὀνομασθέντων after ἀκουέτω, and altered ὀνομασθέντων (which, in this position, is closely followed by ὀνομάζοντος,) into νομισθέντων.

¹ '"Ἄμμωνος C hic et paulo post, ἄκμωνος (*bis*) F et omn. edd., ἄκμονος (*bis*) DG, ἄκμωνος et dein ἄκμονος B. Legendum esse "Ἄμμωνος iam Casaubonus monuit' Otto.
⌐Akmon⌐ and Hermes are here spoken of as two ancient philosophers whose teachings are preserved in written documents ; and it is apparently implied that ⌐Akmon⌐ was the earlier of the two. But nothing is known of any teacher named Akmon ; and the reading "Ἄμμωνος, which is adopted by Otto, does not suit the context. Ammon was known to the Greeks as a god and as a king of Egypt, but not as a philosopher ; and in the extant *Hermetica*, king Ammon receives instruction from Hermes and from Asclepius, but is nowhere represented as a teacher. It seems to me most likely that the true reading is Ἀγ⟨αθοῦ δαί⟩μονος. We know from *Corp*. XII. i and from other evidence that there were Hermetic *libelli* in which the part of teacher was assigned to Agathos Daimon, and that of pupil to Hermes ; and a man who had read some of those *libelli* might very well say that the two earliest philosophers whose names were known and whose teachings were recorded were Agathos Daimon and Hermes. The Hermetists regarded Agathos Daimon as a god, and Hermes as a man ; but a Christian writer would naturally assume that both were men. If Ἀγαθοῦ δαίμονος is the right reading, it may be inferred that the author of the *Cohortatio* knew of a *Hermeticum* in which Agathos Daimon was made to tell his pupil Hermes that God is πάγκρυφος, i. e. wholly hidden from men's sight.
² αὐτοῦ] ἑαυτοῦ CF. αὐτοῦ apparently means τοῦ θεοῦ.
³ Herm. *ap*. Stob. *Exc*. I.
⁴ ὑμᾶς BF : ἡμᾶς CDEG.
⁵ Edited by Reifferscheid (*Corp. script. eccl. Lat.* vol. iv), 1875. Arnobius wrote his *Adv. nat.* in A. D. 304-310 (Harnack, *Chronol.* II, p. 415).

vos appello, qui Mercurium, qui Platonem Pythagoramque sectamini, vosque ceteros, qui estis unius mentis et per easdem vias placitorum inceditis unitate.[1]

[1] It is evident from what follows that the men here addressed are Platonists. Arnobius goes on to say that these men jeer at the Christians, and speak contemptuously of certain Christian beliefs. C. 13: 'Audetis ridere nos, quod patrem rerum ac dominum veneramur ... Audetis ridere nos, quod animarum nostrarum provideamus saluti?' C. 14: 'Audetis ridere nos, cum gehennas dicimus et inextinguibiles quosdam ignes ...?' C. 32: 'Quid est quod a vobis tamquam bruti et stolidi iudicemur, si propter hos metus (i. e. fear lest our souls should perish) liberatori dedidimus ... nos deo?' C. 34: 'quaenam iniustitia tanta est, ut fatui vobis credulitate in ista videamur?' C. 35: 'si animae, inquiunt, mortales (sunt) ..., immortales quemadmodum fieri ... possunt?' C. 47: 'si parens et genitor animarum, inquitis, deus non est, quo auctore progenitae (sunt animae)?' C. 51: 'risui vobis est nostra responsio, quod cum regias suboles esse animas abnegemus, non referamus contra, ex quibus sint causis atque originibus procreatae.' The point on which Arnobius lays most stress in these chapters (II. 13–62) is that his Platonist opponents maintain that the human soul has issued immediately from the supreme God, and is, of its own nature, divine and immortal, whereas he holds that the soul is mortal if left to itself, and can become immortal only by God's grace.

It may be inferred that Arnobius had before him a book written by a Platonist (or possibly two or more books written by Platonists) in which Christianity was attacked and ridiculed. The best-known book of that character was the work of Porphyry against the Christians, which was written not long before A. D. 300, and must have been much read at the time at which Arnobius wrote. Lactantius (*Div. inst.* 5. 2) speaks of two men (Hierocles and another) who wrote against the Christians soon after A. D. 302; and there were doubtless other writings of the same kind, of which we know nothing. To which of these writings Arnobius is replying, it seems impossible to ascertain.

The words *qui Mercurium ... sectamini* cannot mean the writers of our *Hermetica*; for in most of these the Christians are ignored; in none of them are Christian doctrines expressly spoken of and ridiculed; and in the one or two passages in which Christians are referred to (see *Ascl. Lat.* III. 24 b–26 a and *Corp.* IX. 4 b), they are not mentioned by name. 'Followers of Mercurius' must therefore be taken to mean Platonists who said, or of whom it was said, that their doctrines were derived from the teaching of Hermes Trismegistus. And as that might be said by any one who believed that Plato was a disciple of Egyptian teachers, and that the wise men of Egypt had been taught their wisdom by Hermes, these words cannot be held to prove that Greek documents in which the teaching of Hermes was supposed to be recorded were known either to Arnobius himself or to the Platonists of whom he speaks; though we know from other evidence that such documents were in existence in his time.

But the language of this sentence ('vos, vos appello ... inceditis unitate') is far from clear. Platonists might be called 'followers of Plato and Pythagoras' (it was commonly thought that both Pythagoras and Plato had studied in Egypt, and that Plato had learnt from Pythagoras as well as from Egyptian priests); but we should have expected the three names to be written either in the order *Mercurium, Pythagoram, Platonem*, or in the order *Platonem, Pythagoram, Mercurium*. And what can be meant by *vosque ceteros*? Arnobius apparently divides the men of whom he speaks into two distinct groups, and at the same time says that the men of the second group hold the same opinions as the men of the first group. But if their opinions are the same, in what respect do the two groups differ? It may be suspected that there is some corruption in the text. Possibly Arnobius said that the followers of Pythagoras held the same opinions as the followers of Plato. If that is what he meant, one might conjecture that he had in his hands two books against the Christians, one written by a man who called himself a Platonist, and the other by a man who called himself a Pythagorean, and that he found that they agreed in doctrine. The so-called Pythagoreans of his time were in fact Platonists.

LACTANTIUS

Div. inst.[1] 1. 6. 1–5 : Nunc ad divina testimonia transeamus. 1
Sed prius unum proferam quod est simile divino, et ob nimiam
vetustatem, et quod is quem nominabo ex hominibus in deos
relatus est. Apud Ciceronem[2] C. Cotta . . . disputans contra 2
5 Stoicos . . . quinque fuisse Mercurios ait, et . . . quintum fuisse eum
a quo sit Argus occisus, ob eamque causam in Aegyptum profugisse,
atque Aegyptiis leges ac litteras tradidisse. Hunc Aegyptii Thoyth 3
appellant, . . . Idem oppidum condidit quod etiam nunc Graece
vocatur Mercurii civitas[3], et Pheneatae[4] colunt eum religiose.
10 Qui tametsi homo fuit, antiquissimus tamen, et instructissimus omni
genere doctrinae, adeo ut ei multarum rerum et artium scientia
Trismegisto cognomen inponeret. Hic scripsit[5] libros, et quidem 4
multos, ad cognitionem divinarum rerum pertinentes, in quibus
maiestatem summi ac singularis dei asserit, isdemque nominibus
15 appellat quibus nos dominum et patrem.[6] Ac ne quis nomen eius
requireret, ἀνώνυμον esse dixit, eo quod nominis proprietate non
egeat, ob ipsam scilicet unitatem. Ipsius haec verba sunt : ὁ δὲ θεὸς
εἷς. ὁ δὲ εἷς ὀνόματος οὐ προσδέεται· ⌜ἔστι γὰρ ὁ ὢν ἀνώνυμος⌝.[7]

---

[1] Edited by Brandt and Laubmann (*Corp. script. eccl. Lat.* vol. xix), 1890.
[2] Cic. *De nat. deor.* 3. 22. 56.   [3] I. e. Hermopolis in Egypt.
[4] The people of Pheneus in Arcadia. There was a well-known cult of Hermes in
that Arcadian town (Paus. 8. 14. 4 ff.); and Lactantius follows Cicero *l. c.* in identifying the Egyptian Thoth-Hermes with the Greek Hermes worshipped at Pheneus.
[5] Lactantius assumes that the *libelli* in which Hermes is represented as speaking
to a pupil were written by Hermes himself. (Cf. *ad filium scribentis* in *Epit.* 4. 5.)
Did he suppose that the dialogues actually took place, and that Hermes afterwards
wrote down what he and his pupil had said? Or did he think that Hermes, like
Plato, composed fictitious dialogues in order to convey by means of them the
truths which he wished to teach, but, unlike Plato, made himself the chief speaker
in these fictitious dialogues?
[6] I. e. κύριον and πατέρα. God is frequently called κύριος and πατήρ in extant
Hermetica. See *Ascl. Lat.* III. 20 a : 'Deus etenim vel pater vel dominus
omnium' &c. *Ib.* 22 b, 23 b, 26 a, 29 b.
[7] *Frag. 3.* Compare *Epit.* below. The Greek here given might be made to agree
with the Latin rendering in *Epit.* by writing ὁ δὲ θεὸς εἷς. ὁ δὲ εἷς ⟨⟨ὢν ἀνώνυμος⟩⟩·
ὀνόματος ⟨⟨γὰρ⟩⟩ οὐ προσδέεται, ⟨ἐπεὶ μόνος⟩ ἐστι [[γὰρ]] [ὁ] [[ὢν ἀνώνυμος]]. A similar
thought is expressed in different words in *Ascl. Lat.* III. 20 a (as emended) : 'hunc
vero innominem vel potius omninominem esse, siquidem is sit unus omnia'; and
in *Corp.* V. 10 a : αὐτὸς ὀνόματα ἔχει ἅπαντα . . . αὐτὸς ὄνομα οὐκ ἔχει. Cf. Philo
Vita Mos. I. 14. 75 : λέγε, φησίν, αὐτοῖς ὅτι ἐγώ εἰμι ὁ ὤν (*Exod.* 3. 14), ἵνα, μαθόντες
διαφορὰν ὄντος τε καὶ μὴ ὄντος, προσαναδιδαχθῶσιν ὡς οὐδὲν ὄνομα τὸ παράπαν ἐπ'
ἐμοῦ κυριολογεῖται, ᾧ μόνῳ πρόσεστι τὸ εἶναι. Ps.-Justinus *Cohort. ad gent.* 19 B–C :
οὐδὲν γὰρ ὄνομα ἐπὶ θεοῦ κυριολογεῖσθαι δυνατόν. τὰ γὰρ ὀνόματα εἰς δήλωσιν καὶ
διάγνωσιν τῶν ὑποκειμένων κεῖται πραγμάτων, πολλῶν καὶ διαφόρων ὄντων· θεῷ δὲ
οὔτε ὁ τιθεὶς ὄνομα προϋπῆρχεν, οὔτε αὐτὸς ἑαυτὸν ὀνομάζειν ᾠήθη δεῖν, εἷς καὶ μόνος
ὑπάρχων.

5 Deo igitur nomen ⟨non⟩ est, quia solus est, nec opus est proprio
vocabulo, nisi cum discrimen exigit multitudo, ut unam quamque
personam sua nota et appellatione designes. Deo autem, quia
semper[1] unus est, proprium nomen ⌈est deus⌉.[2]

4 *Epitome* 4. 4 *sq.* : Hermes, qui ob virtutem multarumque artium 5
scientiam Trismegistus meruit nominari, qui et doctrina et vetustate
philosophos antecessit, quique aput Aegyptios ut deus colitur,
maiestatem dei singularis infinitis adserens laudibus, dominum
et patrem nuncupat, eumque esse sine nomine, quod proprio
vocabulo non indigeat, quia solus sit; nec habere ullos 10
5 parentes, quia ex se et per se ipse sit.[3] Huius ad filium
scribentis exordium tale est: 'Deum quidem intellegere difficile
est, eloqui vero inpossibile, etiam cui intellegere possibile
est: perfectum enim ab inperfecto, invisibile a visibili non
potest conprehendi.'[4]   15

Div. inst. 1. 7. 2 : Quid quod Mercurius ille Termaximus, cuius
supra feci mentionem, non modo ἀμήτορα, ut Apollo,[5] sed
ἀπάτορα quoque appellat deum, quod origo illi non sit
aliunde?[6] Nec enim potest ab ullo esse generatus qui ipse
universa generavit.   20

Div. inst. 1. 11. 61 : Apparet ergo non ex caelo esse natum (*sc.*
Saturnum), quod fieri non potest, sed ex eo homine cui nomen
Urano fuit. Quod esse verum Trismegistus auctor est, qui cum
diceret admodum paucos extitisse in quibus esset perfecta
doctrina, in his Uranum Saturnum[7] Mercurium[8] nominavit 25
cognatos suos.

2 *Epit.* 14. 2–4 : Saturnus caelo et terra traditur natus. Hoc utique
incredibile est; sed cur ita traditur, ratio certa est : quam qui ignorat,

---

[1] semper *secludendum*?   [2] *Fortasse* est nullum.
[3] *Eumque esse . . . solus sit* corresponds to ὁ δὲ θεὸς . . . ἀνώνυμος in *Div. inst.*
1. 6. 4 : *nec habere . . . ipse sit* corresponds to *non modo* ἀμήτορα . . . *sit aliunde* in
Div. inst. 1. 7. 2. Lactantius here (in *Epit.*) puts together two Hermetic passages
which he gives separately in *Div. inst.*, and which he may have found in different
Hermetic *libelli*; and he appends to them a third ('Deum quidem intellegere' &c.)
which is not given in *Div. inst.* *Frag.* 3, 4.
[4] Herm. *ap.* Stob. *Exc.* I. That Hermetic passage is not given in *Div. inst.*;
but an allusion to it occurs in *De ira* II. 11.
[5] In an oracle ascribed to Apollo, which Lactantius has quoted just before this,
it is said that God is ἀμήτωρ. *Frag.* 4.
[6] See *Div. inst.* 4. 13. 2 below.
[7] See *Corp.* X. 5; *Frag.* 5.
[8] See *Ascl. Lat.* III. 37, where an earlier Hermes, grandfather of Hermes Trismegistus the teacher, is spoken of.

tamquam fabulam respuit. Saturni patrem Uranum fuisse vocita-
tum[1] et Hermes auctor est et Sacra Historia[2] docet. Trismegistus 3
paucos admodum fuisse cum diceret perfectae doctrinae
viros, in iis cognatos suos enumeravit Uranum Saturnum
5 Mercurium. Euhemerus eundem Uranum primum in terra 4
regnasse commemorat.

  Div. inst. 2. 8. 48 : Nam divina providentia effectum esse mundum, ut taceam de Trismegisto, qui hoc praedicat,[3] taceam de carminibus Sibyllarum, quae idem nuntiant, taceam de prophetis, qui
10 opus mundi et opificium dei uno spiritu et pari voce testantur, etiam
inter philosophos paene universos convenit ; id enim Pythagorei[4]
Stoici Peripatetici,[5] quae sunt principales omnium disciplinae.

  Div. inst. 2. 8. 68 : Opera ipsius (*sc.* dei) videntur oculis ; quomodo
autem illa fecerit, ne mente quidem videtur, quia, ut Hermes ait,
15 mortale inmortali, temporale perpetuo, corruptibile in-
corrupto propinquare non potest,[6] id est propius accedere et
intellegentia subsequi. Et ideo terrenum adhuc animal rerum
caelestium perspectionem non capit, quia corpore quasi custodia
saeptum tenetur,[7] quominus soluto ac libero sensu cernat omnia.

20 *Div. inst.* 2. 10. 3–15 : Tum fecit sibi ipse (*sc.* deus) simulacrum 3
sensibile atque intellegens, id est ad imaginis suae formam, qua nihil
potest esse perfectius : hominem figuravit ex limo terrae. . . . De hac 5
hominis fictione poetae quoque, quamvis corrupte, tamen non aliter
tradiderunt : namque hominem de luto a Prometheo factum esse
25 dixerunt. Res eos non fefellit, sed nomen artificis. . . . Non dico 12
(poetas) esse mentitos, sed primum omnium Promethea simulacrum
hominis formasse de molli ac pingui luto, ab eoque primo natam esse

---

  [1] The thing which Lactantius is trying to prove is that Saturn was a man, and
son of a man named Uranus.
  [2] I. e. Ennius' translation of the Ἱερὰ ἀναγραφή of Euemerus.
  [3] *Hermetica* passim ; e. g. *Ascl. Lat.* I. 8 &c. ; *Frag.* 6.
  [4] The term *Pythagorei* may be taken to include the Platonists.
  [5] It would have been difficult to find a *Peripateticus* who taught *divina providentia effectum esse mundum.* The Aristotelian view was that the world is without
beginning. Cf. Lact. *Div. inst.* 2. 10. 17 : ' Aristoteles autem labore se ac molestia
liberavit, dicens semper fuisse mundum : itaque et humanum genus et cetera quae
in eo sunt initium non habere, sed fuisse semper ac semper fore.' But the Aristotelian teaching about φύσις resembled the Stoic teaching about *divina providentia*
(πρόνοια) in giving prominence to teleology.
  [6] See Herm. *ap.* Stob. *Exc.* I ; *Frag.* 7.
  [7] The body is *mortale, temporale,* and *corruptibile* ; therefore the mind, as long
as it is imprisoned in the body, cannot *rerum caelestium perspectionem capere.* The
thought expressed in this last sentence occurs repeatedly in extant *Hermetica.* It
is derived from Plato ; but Lactantius may perhaps have got it from a *Hermeticum.*

13 artem statuas et simulacra fingendi. . . . Sic . . . illut, quod a deo
   factum ferebatur, homini, qui opus divinum imitatus est, coepit
14 adscribi.   Ceterum fictio veri ac vivi hominis e limo dei est.   Quod
   Hermes quoque tradit, qui non tantum hominem ad imaginem
   dei factum esse dixit a deo,[1] sed etiam illut explanare temptavit, 5
   quam subtili ratione singula quaeque in corpore hominis
   membra formaverit, cum eorum nihil sit quod non tan-
   tundem ad usus necessitatem quantum ad pulchritudinem
15 valeat.[2]   Id vero etiam Stoici, cum de providentia disserunt, facere
   conantur, et secutus eos Tullius pluribus quidem locis,[3] sed tamen 10
   materiam tam copiosam et uberem strictim contingit.   Quam ego
   nunc idcirco praetereo, quia nuper proprium de ea re librum [4] ad
   Demetrianum auditorem meum scripsi.

4   *Div. inst.* 2. 12. 4–14: Empedocles . . . quattuor elementa constituit,
   ignem aerem aquam terram, fortasse Trismegistum secutus, qui nostra 15
   corpora ex his quattuor elementis constituta esse dixit a deo:
5 habere namque in se aliquid ignis, aliquid aeris, aliquid
   aquae, aliquid terrae, et neque ignem esse neque aerem
   neque aquam neque terram.[5]   Quae quidem falsa non sunt: nam
   terrae ratio in carne est, umoris in sanguine, aeris in spiritu, ignis in 20
6 calore vitali.   Sed neque sanguis a corpore secerni potest sicut umor a
   terra, neque calor vitalis a spiritu sicut ignis ab aere : adeo rerum
   omnium duo sola reperiuntur elementa, quorum omnis ratio in nostri
7 corporis fictione conclusa est.   Ex rebus ergo diversis ac repugnanti-
   bus homo factus est, sicut ipse mundus, ex luce ac tenebris, ex vita et 25
   morte :[6] quae duo inter se pugnare in homine praecepit, ut si anima

---

[1] This may be Lactantius' interpretation of the words μάθε τίς ὁ δημιουργῶν τὴν
καλὴν ταύτην καὶ θείαν [τοῦ ἀνθρώπου] εἰκόνα in *Corp.* V. 6. Compare *Ascl. Lat.*
I. 7 b : '(hominis) una pars simplex, quae, ut Graeci aiunt, οὐσιώδης, quam vocamus
divinae similitudinis formam.' *Ascl. Lat.* I. 10 : '(dei) sunt imagines duae mundus
et homo.' *Corp.* I. 12 : περικαλλὴς γὰρ (ἦν) (*sc.* the Archanthropos), τὴν τοῦ
πατρὸς εἰκόνα ἔχων. See *Div. inst.* 7. 4. 3.   *Frag.* 8.
     [2] The passage to which Lactantius here refers is probably *Corp.* V. 6. It is true
that in that passage little is said about the adaptation of man's bodily organs *ad
usus necessitatem* ; but their adaptation *ad pulchritudinem* is spoken of, and the
human body is compared to a statue.
     [3] In *De opif. dei* I. 12, Lactantius refers to three such passages in Cicero, viz.
De rep. lib. 4, *De legg.* lib. 1 (§§ 26, 27), and *De nat. deor.* lib. 2 (§§ 133–153).
The passage in *De rep.* is lost, and that in *De legg.* contains little ; but in *De nat.
deor.* 2. 133–153 (probably from Posidonius) the adaptation of the bodily organs
ad usus necessitatem is spoken of at some length.
     [4] Viz. *De opif. dei.*
     [5] Herm. *ap.* Stob. *Exc.* II A. 2.
     [6] Cf. *Corp.* I, in which φῶς and ζωή are similarly contrasted with darkness and
death.

superaverit, quae oritur ex deo, sit inmortalis et in perpetua luce verse-
tur, si autem corpus vicerit animam dicionique subiecerit, sit in tenebris
sempiternis et in morte.[1] . . . In hac igitur societate caeli atque 10
terrae, quorum effigies expressa est in homine, superiorem partem
5 tenent ea quae sunt dei, anima scilicet, quae dominium corporis
habet, inferiorem autem ea quae sunt diaboli, corpus utique, quod
quia terrenum est, animae debet esse subiectum sicut terra caelo : est 11
enim quasi vasculum, quo tamquam domicilio temporali spiritus hic
caelestis utatur. Utriusque officia sunt, ut hoc, quod est ex caelo et
10 deo, imperet, illut vero, quod ex terra et diabolo, serviat. . . .
Quodsi anima ignis est, ut ostendimus, in caelum debet eniti sicut 14
ignis, ne exstinguatur, hoc est ad inmortalitatem, quae in caelo
est.

Div. inst. 2. 14. 1–15. 8 :[2] Cum ergo numerus hominum coepisset 14.
15 increscere, providens deus ne fraudibus suis diabolus, cui ab initio
dederat terrae potestatem, vel corrumperet homines vel disperderet,
. . . misit angelos ad tutelam cultumque generis humani. . . . Itaque 2
illos cum hominibus commorantes dominator ille terrae fallacissimus
consuetudine ipsa paulatim ad vitia pellexit, et mulierum congressibus
20 inquinavit. Tum in caelum ob peccata quibus se inmerserant non 3
recepti ceciderunt in terram. Sic eos diabolus ex angelis dei suos
fecit satellites ac ministros. Qui autem sunt ex his procreati, quia 4
neque angeli neque homines fuerunt, sed mediam quandam naturam
gerentes, ⌈non sunt ad inferos recepti sicut in caelum parentes
25 eorum⌉.[3] Ita duo genera daemonum facta sunt, unum caeleste, 5
alterum terrenum.[4] Hi sunt immundi spiritus, malorum quae geruntur

---

[1] This description of a fight between the two parts or elements of which man is
composed resembles in some respects *Exc.* II B. 6–8 (as emended): ἑνὸς γὰρ
γίγνεται πρὸς δύο ἡ στάσις, τοῦ μὲν ἄνω σπεύδοντος, τῶν δὲ καθελκόντων κάτω· καὶ
ἔρις καὶ μάχη πολλὴ πρὸς ἄλληλα τούτων γίγνεται, κ.τ.λ. If we assume that, in the
volume of *Hermetica* which Lactantius had before him, *Exc.* II B followed immediately on *Exc.* II A, he must have read that passage very soon after the sentence
in *Exc.* II A which he quotes in § 5. But if what he says in §§ 7–14 was suggested
to him by *Exc.* II B. 6–8, it would seem that he misunderstood that document, and
took τὸ ἕν to mean the soul (which, in agreement with his Stoic authorities, he held
to consist of *spiritus caelestis* or *ignis*), and τὰ δύο to mean the two gross elements,
earth and water, of which the body is composed ; whereas the Hermetist meant by
τὸ ἕν the λογιστικόν or νοῦς, and by τὰ δύο the θυμοειδές and the ἐπιθυμητικόν.

[2] A large part of the contents of this passage is derived from Minucius Felix
26. 7–27. 7. But in writing it, Lactantius probably had in mind also *Ascl. Lat.*
III. 37–38 b, in which the worship of *dei terreni* is advocated by a Pagan.

[3] There is something wrong here. We have just been told that *parentes eorum*
were not *in caelum recepti* ; and the statement that the sons ‘were not admitted
into hell’ is irrelevant. Something like *daemones appellati sunt sicut parentes
eorum* would suit the context.

[4] The *daemones caelestes* are demons of heavenly origin, i. e. fallen angels ; the

6 auctores, quorum idem diabolus est princeps. Unde illum Trismegi-
9 stus daemoniarchen[1] vocat. ... Philosophi quoque de his (sc.
daemonibus) disserunt : nam Plato etiam naturas eorum in Symposio[2]
exprimere conatus est, et Socrates esse circa se adsiduum daemona
11 loquebatur. ... Hi, ut dico, spiritus contaminati ac perditi per 5
omnem terram vagantur, et in solacium perditionis suae perdendis
12 hominibus operantur. Itaque omnia insidiis fraudibus dolis errori-
13 bus conplent. ... (Homines) daemonas venerantur quasi terrestres
deos, et quasi depulsores malorum quae ipsi faciunt et inrogant.
14 Qui quoniam spiritus sunt tenues et inconprehensibiles, insinuant 10
se corporibus hominum, et occulte in visceribus operati valetu-
dinem vitiant, morbos citant, somniis animos terrent, mentes
furoribus quatiunt, ut homines his malis cogant ad eorum auxilia
decurrere.[3]

15. 1   Quarum omnium fallaciarum ratio expertibus veritatis obscura est : 15
prodesse enim putant eos, cum nocere desinunt, qui nihil possunt
2 aliut quam nocere. Dicat fortasse aliquis colendos ergo esse, ne
noceant, siquidem possint nocere. Nocent illi quidem, sed iis a quibus
timentur, quos manus dei potens et excelsa non protegit, qui profani
3 sunt a sacramento veritatis. Iustos autem, id est cultores dei, metuunt, 20
cuius nomine adiurati de corporibus excedunt : quorum verbis tamquam
flagris verberati non modo daemonas esse se confitentur, sed etiam
5 nomina sua edunt, illa quae in templis adorantur. ... Tantum habet
cognitio dei ac iustitia potestatis. Cui ergo nocere possunt nisi iis
6 quos habent in sua potestate ? Denique adfirmat Hermes eos qui 25
cognoverint deum non tantum ab incursibus daemonum tutos esse,
verum etiam ne fato quidem teneri. μία inquit φυλακὴ εὐσέβεια.
εὐσεβοῦς γὰρ ἀνθρώπου οὔτε δαίμων κακὸς οὔτε εἱμαρμένη
κρατεῖ. θεὸς γὰρ ῥύεται τὸν εὐσεβῆ ἐκ παντὸς κακοῦ. τὸ γὰρ

---

daemones terreni are demons born on earth, sons of fallen angels and mortal women. Compare the distinction between *dei caelestes* and *dei terreni* in *Ascl. Lat.* III. 38 b. Lactantius here assumes the *dei* worshipped by the Pagans to be *daemones*, i.e. *immundi spiritus*; though he elsewhere says that they are the souls of dead men.

[1] The passage referred to is probably *Ascl. Lat.* III. 28 *init.*, where it is said that after death the soul *transiet in summi daemonis potestatem*. It is most likely that *summi daemonis* is the translator's rendering of δαιμονιάρχου. The *summus daemon* there spoken of is the judge of the dead, and has little resemblance to the *diabolus* of the Christians; but that would not prevent Lactantius from taking the term to mean 'the Devil'. He uses *daemoniarches* as a synonym for *diabolus* in *Epit.* 24. 1. *Frag.* 9.

[2] Pl. *Sympos.* 202 E.

[3] Compare what Porphyry, *De abst.* 2. 38–43, says about evil daemons and men's worship of them.

ἓν καὶ μόνον ἐν ἀνθρώποις ἐστὶν ἀγαθὸν εὐσέβεια.[1] Quid sit
autem εὐσέβεια, ostendit alio loco his verbis: ἡ γὰρ εὐσέβεια γνῶσίς
ἐστιν τοῦ θεοῦ.[2] Asclepius quoque auditor eius eandem sententiam[3] 7
latius explicavit in illo sermone [perfecto] quem scripsit ad regem.[4]

5 Uterque[5] vero daemonas esse adfirmat inimicos et vexatores 8
hominum, quos ideo Trismegistus ἀγγέλους πονηρούς[6] appellat;
adeo non ignoravit ex caelestibus depravatos terrenos esse coepisse.

Div. inst. 4. 6. 1–13. 5: Deus igitur machinator constitutorque 6. 1
rerum, . . . antequam praeclarum hoc opus mundi adoriretur,
10 sanctum et incorruptibilem spiritum genuit, quem filium nuncuparet.
Et quamvis alios postea innumerabiles creavisset, quos angelos 2
dicimus, hunc tamen solum primogenitum divini nominis appellatione
dignatus est, patria scilicet virtute ac maiestate pollentem. Esse 3
autem summi dei filium, qui sit potestate maxima praeditus, non
15 tantum congruentes in unum voces prophetarum, sed etiam Trismegisti
praedicatio et Sibyllarum vaticinia demonstrant. Hermes, in eo libro 4
qui Λόγος τέλειος inscribitur, his usus est verbis:[7] ὁ κύριος καὶ τῶν
πάντων ποιητής, ὃν θεὸν καλεῖν νενομίκαμεν, ἐπεὶ τὸν δεύτερον
ἐποίησε θεὸν ὁρατὸν καὶ αἰσθητόν — αἰσθητὸν δέ φημι οὐ
20 διὰ τὸ αἰσθάνεσθαι αὐτόν, περὶ γὰρ τούτου, πότερον αὐτὸς
αἰσθάνεται ⟨ἢ μή, εἰσαῦθις ῥηθήσεται⟩,[8] ἀλλὰ ὅτι εἰς αἴσθησιν
⌜ὑποπέμπει⌝[9] καὶ εἰς ὅρασιν—ἐπεὶ οὖν τοῦτον ἐποίησε πρῶτον
καὶ μόνον καὶ ἕνα, καλὸς δὲ αὐτῷ ἐφάνη καὶ πληρέστατος

---

[1] This is almost certainly the Greek original of *Ascl. Lat.* III. 29 b *init.* The
same passage (down to παντὸς κακοῦ) is quoted, with some additions, by Cyril,
Migne vol. 76, col. 701 A (*Testim.*).

[2] This is either an inaccurate quotation from *Corp.* IX. 4 a, where our MSS.
give εὐσέβεια δέ ἐστι θεοῦ γνῶσις, or a quotation from a lost *Hermeticum.* Lactantius quotes these words to justify his substitution of *eos qui cognoverint deum* for
pios in his summary of the preceding quotation, μία φυλακὴ εὐσέβεια κ.τ.λ. *Frag.* 10.

[3] Viz. ‘ eos qui cognoverint deum non tantum ab incursibus daemonum tutos
esse, verum etiam ne fato quidem teneri.’

[4] The passage referred to is *Corp.* XVI. 15 *fin.* and 16 : τὸ δὲ λογικὸν μέρος τῆς
ψυχῆς ἀδέσποτον τῶν δαιμόνων ἔστηκεν. . . . ταύτην δὲ τὴν διοίκησιν Ἑρμῆς εἱμαρμένην ἐκάλεσεν. *Corp.* XVI is rightly described as *sermo quem Asclepius scripsit
ad regem* (sc. *Ammonem*). But the word *perfecto* must have been added by mistake.
Sermo perfectus (Λόγος τέλειος) is the name by which the Greek original of *Ascl.
Lat.* was known to Lactantius and others.

[5] I. e. Hermes (in *Ascl. Lat.* III and elsewhere) and Asclepius (in *Corp.* XVI).

[6] *Ascl. Lat.* III. 25 : ‘ nocentes angeli ’.

[7] *Ascl. Lat.* I. 8. This passage is also quoted by Pseudo-Anthimus (*Testim.*).

[8] ⟨ἢ μή, εἰσαῦθις ῥηθήσεται⟩ *Wachsmuth and Brandt* : ⟨ἢ μή, ὕστερον ῥηθήσεται⟩
Struve. Ascl. Lat. I. 8 : ‘ de hoc enim, an ipse sentiat an non, alio dicemus
tempore.’

[9] Lactantius probably read and wrote ὑποπέμπει (cf. *sed quod in sensum mittat*
in *Epit.*) ; but the Hermetic author must have written ὑποπίπτει. If a copyist
wrote -πείπτει, this might easily be altered into -πέμπει.

πάντων τῶν ἀγαθῶν, ἠγάσθη τε καὶ πάνυ ἐφίλησεν ὡς ἴδιον
9 τόκον.[1] Sibylla...[2] ... Idcirco illum Trismegistus δημιουργὸν
τοῦ θεοῦ[3] et Sibylla σύμβουλον[4] appellat, quod tanta sapientia et
virtute sit instructus a deo patre, ut consilio eius et manibus uteretur
in fabricatione mundi.

5

1   Fortasse quaerat aliquis hoc loco, quis sit iste tam potens, tam deo
carus, et quod nomen habeat, cuius prima nativitas non modo
antecesserit mundum, verum etiam prudentia disposuerit, virtute
2 construxerit.   Primum scire nos convenit nomen eius ne angelis quidem notum esse qui morantur in caelo, sed ipsi soli ac deo patri, nec 10
ante id publicabitur, ut est sanctis litteris traditum, quam dispositio
3 dei fuerit impleta; deinde nec enuntiari posse hominis ore, sicut
Hermes docet, haec dicens: αἴτιον[5] δὲ τούτου[6] ⌜τοῦ αἰτίου⌝[7] ἡ τοῦ
ΘΕΑΓΕΝΕΤΟΥΑΓΑΘΟ[8] βούλησις, οὗ τὸ ὄνομα οὐ δύναται
ἀνθρωπίνῳ στόματι λαληθῆναι.[9]   Et paulo post ad filium: ἔστιν 15

---

[1] The 'second god' spoken of in this passage is the Kosmos. But Lactantius
supposed the Hermetist to have meant by 'the second god', not the Kosmos itself,
but a 'Son of God' by whom the Kosmos was made.
[2] Here follow three quotations from the *Oracula Sibyllina*.
[3] *Ascl. Lat.* III. 26 a, as quoted by Lactantius *Div. inst.* 7. 18. 4: ὁ κύριος καὶ
πατὴρ καὶ θεὸς καὶ ⌜τοῦ πρώτου καὶ ἑνὸς θεοῦ⌝ δημιουργός. Lactantius had before
him a corrupt reading of that passage, and misunderstood its meaning. In the
Hermetic document, as originally written, it must have been the supreme God that
was called δημιουργός; but Lactantius thought that ὁ τοῦ πρώτου καὶ ἑνὸς θεοῦ
δημιουργός meant 'he who was employed by the supreme God to make the world',
i. e. not God himself, but a Son of God.
[4] *Orac. Sibyll.* 8. 264 (written by a Christian, and based on *Gen.* I. 26): αὐτὸν
γὰρ πράτιστα λαβὼν σύμβουλον ἀπ' ἀρχῆς | εἶπεν ὁ παντοκράτωρ· Ποιήσωμεν, τέκνον,
ἄμφω | εἰκόνος ἡμετέρης ἀπομαξάμενοι βροτὰ φῦλα.
The application of the terms δημιουργός and σύμβουλος to the Son of God is
again referred to by Lactantius in *Div. inst.* 4. 11. 7: 'illum filium suum primogenitum, illum opificem rerum et consiliatorem suum delabi iussit e caelo.'
[5] αἴτιον *B*: αἴτιος *RH Sedulius*: αἴγιος *S*.   [6] τούτου *om. B*.
[7] ΤΟΥΑΙΤΙΟΥ *B*: ΤΟΥ ΑΙΝΟΥ *R*: ΕΑΙΟΥ *H*: ΤΟΥΑΙΑΙΟΓ *S*: ΤΟΥΔΙ-
ΚΙΟΥ (?) *P*: ΤΟΥΤΟΥ ΑΙΤΙΟΥ *V*: ΑΥΤΙΟΥ *Sedulius*.   Perhaps τοῦ αἰτίου
ought to be bracketed.
[8] ΘΕΑΓΕΝΕΤΟΥΑΓΑΘΟ *B*: ΑΤΑΘΟΥ *R*: ΘΕΤΟΥΑΤΑ ΤΟΥ ΒΟΥ *H*:
ΘΕΑΓΕΤΟΥ ΑΓΑΕΟΥ *S*: ΘΕΑΓΕΤΟΥΑΓΑΟΘΥ *P*: ΘΕΑΓΕΤΟΥΑΓΑΘΟΥ *V*:
ΘΕΑΓΕΤΥ ΛΓΑΘΟΥ *Sedulius*, following Stadtmüller, prints in his text
αἴτιος δὲ τούτου τοῦ αἰτίου ἡ τοῦ θεοῦ ἅτε τοῦ ἀγαθοῦ βούλησις, and compares *Corp.*
XIV. 9 : πᾶν δὲ τὸ γέννητον ὑπὸ τοῦ θεοῦ γέγονεν, ὅπερ ἐστὶν ὑπὸ τοῦ ἀγαθοῦ καὶ
τοῦ τὰ πάντα δυναμένου ποιεῖν. But ἅτε τοῦ ἀγαθοῦ is surely impossible.
Lactantius must have read in this clause something which made him think that
the Son of God was spoken of. Possibly the reading of his copy may have been
ἡ τοῦ θεογενήτου ἀγαθοβούλησις (which differs little from the reading of *B*, the
earliest MS.), and he may have supposed that ὁ θεογένητος meant the Son of God.
But we may be sure that the Hermetist, when he spoke of One 'whose name cannot
be uttered by human lips', was speaking, not of a Son of God, but of the supreme
God himself. ΘΕΑΓΕΝΕΤΟΥΑΓΑΘΟ must therefore be a corruption of some term
or phrase denoting God; and it may be conjectured that the original reading was
αἴτιον δὲ τούτου ἡ τοῦ ἀγενήτου βούλησις, that ἀγαθοῦ was written as a variant for
ἀγενήτου, and that θε(οῦ) was inserted as a gloss.   [9] *Frag.* 11.

γάρ τις, ὦ τέκνον, ἀπόρρητος λόγος ⌜σοφίας ὅσιος ὁσίου⌝[1] περὶ[2]
τοῦ μόνου κυρίου πάντων καὶ προεννοουμένου[3] θεοῦ[4] ὃν εἰπεῖν
ὑπὲρ ἄνθρωπόν ἐστιν.[5] Sed quamvis nomen eius, quod ei a 4
principio pater summus inposuit, nullus alius praeter ipsum sciat,
5 habet tamen et inter angelos aliut vocabulum et inter homines aliut.
Iesus quippe inter homines nominatur. . . .

Nunc vero de prima eius nativitate dicamus. In primis enim 8. 1
testificamur illum bis esse natum, primum in spiritu, postea in carne.
. . . Qui cum esset a principio filius dei, regeneratus est denuo 2
10 secundum carnem. . . . Qui audit dei filium dici, non debet tantum 3
nefas mente concipere, ut existimet ex conubio ac permixtione feminae
alicuius deum procreasse, quod non facit nisi animal corporale morti-
que subiectum. Deus autem cum solus adhuc esset, cui permiscere 4
se potuit?[6] ⌜Aut⌝ cum esset tantae potestatis, ut quidquid vellet
15 efficeret, utique ad creandum societate alterius non indigebat : nisi forte
existimabimus deum, sicut Orpheus[7] putavit, et marem esse et feminam,
quod aliter generare non quiverit, nisi haberet vim sexus utriusque,[8]
quasi aut ipse secum coierit aut sine coitu non potuerit procreare. Sed 5

[1] OCIOCOCIOY *B* : OCIOCIC *R* : OCIOOCCIOIK *H* : OYIOCOCIOIC
SP : OCIOC *V Sedulius* ; ὅσιός τε *coni. Brandt.* Perhaps σοφίας ὁσίου ⟨μ⟩εστός.

[2] ΠΕΡΙ *RV Sedulius* : ΤΙΕΡΙ *S* : ΤΕΡΙ *P* : *om. BH.*

[3] Brandt conjectures (πάντα) προεννοουμένου, which he takes to mean *omnia
praescientis*. But προεννοουμένου could not mean *praescientis*; and if the insertion
of πάντα is accepted, it would be better to write πάντα προνοουμένου (*omnia provi-
dentis*). That, however, is hardly satisfactory.

[4] τὸν προεννοούμενον θεόν occurs in *Abammonis resp.* 10. 3, and in Ps.-Anthimus
§ 15 (*Testim.*) ; cf. τὸν προεγνωσμένον θεόν in Cyril 553 B. In each of these places
a term denoting the supreme God is required ; but what is meant by the word
προεννοούμενος ?

[5] Below, in 4. 9. 3, Lactantius expresses what he takes to be the meaning of this
Hermetic passage by writing 'esse ineffabilem quendam sanctumque sermonem,
cuius enarratio modum hominis excedat'. There is nothing there to correspond to
σοφίας, and nothing to correspond to περὶ τοῦ . . . θεοῦ. Probably the Greek text
which he had before him, and transcribed in 4. 7. 3, was already corrupt, and he
disregarded the words which he could not make sense of. He assumed that λόγος
meant the Son of God ; and he made ὅν refer to λόγος. If ὅν had been immediately preceded by θεοῦ in his copy, he could hardly have failed to see that ὅν
meant God, and not the λόγος ; it therefore seems most likely that θεοῦ was neither
written by the Hermetist nor read by Lactantius, but has been added later.
Perhaps καὶ προεννοουμένου θεοῦ ought to be bracketed. *Frag. 12.*
The Hermetist's words cannot be restored with certainty ; but there can be little
doubt that his meaning was ' There is a secret teaching . . . concerning Him who
alone is Lord of all . . ., whom it is beyond man's power to describe'.

[6] Cf. *Corp.* VI. 1 b (as emended) : οὔτε σύζυγόν ἐστιν αὐτοῦ, [ ] οὗ ἐρασθήσεται.
Corp. XI. ii. 14 a (with reference to God's generative activity) : οὐδὲ γὰρ ἄλλο ἔχει
συνεργόν.

[7] Abel, *Orphica*, fr. 62 : θῆλυς καὶ γενέτωρ κρατερὸς θεὸς Ἠρικεπαῖος. *Ib.* fr. 46,
l. 4 and fr. 123, l. 3 : Ζεὺς ἄρσην γένετο, Ζεὺς ἄμβροτος ἔπλετο νύμφη.

[8] Cf. *Ascl. Lat.* III. 20 b (as emended) : ' solus omni utriusque sexus fecunditate
plenissimus, . . . parit semper quicquid voluerit procreare.' Cf. vol. iii, p. 135.

et Hermes in eadem fuit opinione,[1] cum dicit eum αὐτοπάτορα et αὐτομήτορα.[2] Quod si ita esset, ut a prophetis pater dicitur, sic

6 etiam mater diceretur. Quomodo igitur procreavit? Primum nec sciri a quoquam possunt nec enarrari opera divina; sed tamen sanctae litterae docent, in quibus cautum est illum dei filium dei esse 5 sermonem, itemque ceteros angelos dei spiritus esse : nam sermo est

7 spiritus cum voce aliquid significante prolatus. Sed tamen, quoniam spiritus et sermo diversis partibus proferuntur, siquidem spiritus naribus, ore sermo procedit,[3] magna inter hunc dei filium ceterosque angelos differentia est : illi enim ex deo taciti spiritus exierunt, quia 10 non ad doctrinam dei tradendam, sed ad ministerium creabantur;

8 ille vero, cum sit et ipse spiritus, tamen cum voce ac sono ex dei ore processit, sicut verbum, ea scilicet ratione, quia voce eius ad populum fuerat usurus, id est, quod ille magister futurus esset doctrinae dei et caelestis arcani ad homines perferendi. Ipsum primo locutus est, ut 15 per eum ad nos loqueretur, et ille vocem dei ac voluntatem nobis

9 revelaret. Merito igitur sermo ac verbum dei dicitur, quia deus procedentem de ore suo vocalem spiritum, quem non utero sed mente conceperat, inexcogitabili quadam maiestatis suae virtute ac potentia in effigiem, quae proprio sensu et sapientia vigeat, conprehendit; et 20

10 alios item spiritus suos in angelos figuravit.[4] Nostri spiritus dissolubiles sunt, quia mortales sumus, dei autem spiritus et vivunt et manent et sentiunt, quia ipse immortalis est et sensus ac vitae dator.

11 Nostrae voces licet aurae misceantur atque vanescant, tamen plerumque permanent litteris conprehensae : quanto magis dei vocem 25 credendum est et manere in aeternum et sensu ac virtute comitari,

12 quam de deo patre tamquam rivus de fonte traduxerit! Quodsi quis miratur ex deo deum prolatione vocis ac spiritus potuisse generari, si sacras voces prophetarum cognoverit, desinet profecto mirari. . . . 30

9. 1   Sed melius Graeci λόγον dicunt quam nos verbum sive sermonem :

---

[1] I. e. the opinion that God is ἀρσενόθηλυς.

[2] To say that God is αὐτοπάτωρ and αὐτομήτωρ is equivalent to saying that God is both ἀρσενόθηλυς and αὐτογέννητος.

[3] Lactantius has learnt from *Ev. Joh.* I. 1 that the Son is God's λόγος, and from *Ps.* 104. 4 (*Heb.* 1. 7) that the angels are God's πνεύματα; and taking the words λόγος (speech) and πνεῦμα (breath) in their literal and primary sense, he infers that the Son issued from God's mouth (*ex dei ore processit* below), and the angels issued from God's nose. (The latter statement is clearly implied, though not directly asserted.)

[4] I. e. God made the ' vocal breath ' which he emitted into a living person who is called the Son of God, and also fashioned the voiceless ' breaths ' which he emitted into living persons, who are called angels.

λόγος enim et sermonem significat et rationem, quia ille est et vox
et sapientia dei.   Hunc sermonem divinum ne philosophi quidem **2**
ignoraverunt, siquidem Zenon rerum naturae dispositorem atque
opificem universitatis λόγον praedicat, quem et fatum et necessitatem
5 rerum et deum et animum Iovis nuncupat, ea scilicet consuetudine,
qua solent Iovem pro deo accipere.   Sed nihil obstant verba, cum **3**
sententia congruat veritati.   Est enim spiritus dei quem ille animum
Iovis nominavit.   Nam Trismegistus, qui veritatem paene universam
nescio quo modo investigavit, virtutem maiestatemque verbi saepe **1**
10 descripsit, sicut declarat superius illut exemplum, quo fatetur e s s e
i n e f f a b i l e m q u e n d a m s a n c t u m q u e s e r m o n e m, c u i u s e n a r-
r a t i o m o d u m h o m i n i s e x c e d a t.[2]

Dixi de nativitate prima breviter, ut potui.   Nunc de secunda.... **4**

Summus igitur deus ac parens omnium, cum religionem suam **13. 1**
15 transferre voluisset, doctorem iustitiae misit e caelo, ut novis cultoribus
novam legem in eo vel per eum daret, non sicut antea fecerat per
hominem, sed tamen nasci eum voluit tamquam hominem, ut per
omnia summo patri similis existeret.   Ipse enim pater deus, origo et **2**
principium rerum, quoniam parentibus caret, ἀπάτωρ atque ἀμήτωρ
20 a Trismegisto verissime nominatur, quod ex nullo sit procreatus.[3]
Idcirco etiam filium bis nasci oportuit, ut et ipse fieret ἀπάτωρ atque
ἀμήτωρ.   In prima enim nativitate spiritali ἀμήτωρ fuit, quia sine **3**
officio matris a solo deo patre generatus est ; in secunda vero carnali **4**
ἀπάτωρ fuit, quoniam sine patris officio virginali utero procreatus est,
25 ut mediam inter deum hominemque substantiam gerens nostram
hanc fragilem inbecillamque naturam quasi manu ad inmortalitatem
posset educere.   Factus est et dei filius per spiritum et hominis per **5**
carnem, id est et deus et homo.

Epit. 37. 1–9 : Deus in principio, antequam mundum insti- **1**
30 tueret, de aeternitatis suae fonte deque divino ac perenni spiritu
suo filium sibi ipse progenuit incorruptum ⌐fidelem⌐ virtuti ac
maiestati patriae respondentem.[4]   Hic est virtus, hic ratio, hic sermo **2**

---

[1] A hypostatized λόγος of God is spoken of in *Corp.* I, which may or may not
have been known to Lactantius, and in some Hermetic passages quoted by Cyril.   •
But in some at least of the Hermetic passages of which Lactantius was thinking
when he wrote *saepe,*—e. g. in *Corp.* XII. ii. 23 b (*Div. inst.* 6. 25. 10),—he misunderstood the Greek, and took the word λόγος in a sense not intended by the
Hermetic writer. *Frag.* 12.

[2] *Div. inst.* 4. 7. 3 (p. 17. 1 above).

[3] See *Div. inst.* 1. 7. 2 (p. 10 above).

[4] incorruptum fidelem, virtuti ... patriae respondentem *Brandt.*   But what is
the point of *fidelem* ?   Read rather *incorruptum, fideliter virtuti ... patriae respondentem.*

dei, hic sapientia. Hoc opifice,[1] ut Hermes ait, et consiliatore, ut Sibylla, [et] praeclaram et mirabilem huius mundi fabricam machinatus

3 est. Denique ex omnibus angelis, quos idem deus de suis spiritibus figuravit, solus in consortium summae potestatis adscitus est, solus deus nuncupatus. Omnia enim per ipsum, et sine ipso nihil· 5

4 Denique Plato[2] de primo ac secundo deo non plane ut philosophus sed ut vates locutus est, fortasse in hoc Trismegistum secutus, cuius

5 verba[3] de Graecis conversa subieci: Dominus et factor universorum quem deum vocare[4] existimavimus, secundum fecit deum visibilem et sensibilem. Sensibilem autem dico non 10 quod ipse sensum accipiat, sed quod in sensum mittat et visum. Cum ergo hunc fecisset primum et solum et unum, optimus ei apparuit et plenissimus omnium bonorum.[5]

8 Sibylla quoque . . . Huius nomen nulli est notum nisi ipsi et patri, sicut docet Iohannes in Revelatione.[6] Hermes ait non posse 15

9 nomen eius mortali ore proferri.[7] Ab hominibus tamen duobus vocabulis nuncupatur, Iesus, quod est salvator, et Christus, quod est rex.

[1] δημιουργόν Div. inst. 4. 6. 9 (p. 16. 2 above).
[2] Of what passage in Plato was Lactantius thinking, when he said that 'Plato spoke of a first and a second God'? Brandt refers to the two passages which Eusebius (Pr. ev. 11. 16) quotes with the object of showing that Plato recognized both a Maker of the world and a supreme God above the Maker; viz. Pl. Epinomis 986 C (κόσμον, ὃν ἔταξε λόγος ὁ πάντων θειότατος) and Epist. 6. 323 D (τὸν τῶν πάντων θεὸν ἡγεμόνα . . . τοῦ τε ἡγεμόνος καὶ αἰτίου πατέρα κύριον). To these might be added the often quoted passage Id. Epist. 2. 312 E : περὶ τὸν πάντων βασιλέα πάντ' ἐστί, καὶ ἐκείνου ἕνεκα πάντα, καὶ ἐκεῖνο αἴτιον ἁπάντων τῶν καλῶν· δεύτερον δὲ πέρι τὰ δεύτερα, καὶ τρίτον πέρι τὰ τρίτα. (As formerly printed, περὶ τὰ δεύτερα and περὶ τὰ τρίτα. But δεύτερον πέρι and τρίτον πέρι are required to make sense: see Burnet's text and Mayor on Clem. Alex. Strom. 7. 2. 9.) But it seems more likely that Lactantius was thinking of such passages as Timaeus 28 C, and especially of the end, 92 C, εἰκὼν τοῦ νοητοῦ (al. ποιητοῦ) θεὸς αἰσθητός . . . γέγονεν, . . . μονογενὴς ὤν. Those were the words of Plato which the Hermetist had in mind when he wrote ὁ . . . τῶν πάντων ποιητὴς . . . ἐπεὶ τὸν δεύτερον ἐποίησε θεὸν ὁρατὸν καὶ αἰσθητόν, and Lactantius saw the resemblance, but believing the Hermetic document to be the earlier, thought that Plato was 'perhaps following Trismegistus'. The θεὸς αἰσθητός of whom Plato and the Hermetist spoke was the Kosmos; but Lactantius supposed that they meant by that term the person whom he called 'the Son of God'.
[3] Div. inst. 4. 6. 4 (p. 15. 17 above).
[4] vocare Davis (= καλεῖν) : vocari MS.
[5] In this translation, Lactantius (if the MS. of the Epitome gives rightly what he wrote) has broken up the complex Greek sentence into three separate sentences, and has omitted the clauses περὶ γὰρ τούτου, πότερον αὐτὸς αἰσθάνεται (ἢ μή, εἰσαῦθις ῥηθήσεται) and ἠγάσθη τε καὶ πάνυ ἐφίλησεν ὡς ἴδιον τόκον. It is possible that in his copy of the Λόγος τέλειος the words ἢ μή, εἰσαῦθις ῥηθήσεται were already missing, and the preceding words (περὶ γὰρ . . . αἰσθάνεται) were consequently unintelligible to him.
[6] Apoc. Joh. 19. 12.
[7] Div. inst. 4. 7. 3 (p. 16. 14 above).

Div. inst. 4. 27. 18–20 : Nam si quis studet altius inquirere, **18**
congreget eos quibus peritia est ciere ab inferis animas.   Evocent
Iovem Neptunum Volcanum Mercurium Apollinem patremque
omnium Saturnum : respondebunt ab inferis omnes, et interrogati
5 loquentur et de se ac deo fatebuntur.   Post haec evocent Christum : **19**
non aderit, non adparebit, quia non amplius quam biduo aput inferos
fuit.   Quid hac probatione certius proferri potest ?   Ego vero non **20**
dubito quin ad veritatem Trismegistus hac aliqua ratione[1] pervenerit,
qui de deo patre omnia, de filio locutus est multa[2] quae divinis
10 continentur arcanis.[3]

Div. inst. 5. 14. 9–12 : Iustitia quamvis omnes simul virtutes **9**
amplectatur, tamen duae sunt omnium principales quae ab ea
divelli separarique non possunt, pietas et aequitas. . . .   Pietas **11**
vero et aequitas quasi venae sunt eius[4], his enim duobus fontibus
15 constat tota iustitia : sed caput eius et origo in illo primo est, in
secundo vis omnis ac ratio.   Pietas autem nihil aliud est quam
dei notio, sicut Trismegistus verissime definivit, ut alio loco diximus.[5]
Si ergo pietas est cognoscere deum, cuius cognitionis haec summa **12**
est ut colas, ignorat utique iustitiam qui religionem dei non tenet.

20 *Div. inst.* 6. 25. 1–12 : Nunc de sacrificio ipso pauca dicamus. **1**
. . . Duo sunt quae offerri debeant, donum et sacrificium ; donum **5**
in perpetuum, sacrificium ad tempus.   Verum apud istos, qui nullo **6**
modo rationem divinitatis intellegunt, donum est quidquid auro
argentoque fabricatur, item quidquid purpura et serico texitur,
25 sacrificiumque victima et quaecumque in ara cremantur.   Sed **7**
utroque non utitur deus, quia et ipse incorruptus est et illud totum
corruptibile.   Itaque deo utrumque incorporale offerendum est, ⌈quo
utitur.   Donum est⌉[6] integritas animi, sacrificium laus et hymnus.

---

[1] Lactantius said (*Div. inst.* 4. 9. 3, p. 19. 8 above) that he did not know how
Hermes had acquired his knowledge of the truth ('veritatem paene universam nescio
quo modo investigavit').   Here however he seems to have given an answer to that
question.   The meaning of this passage seems to be that Hermes evoked the souls of
the dead men whom the Pagans thought to be gods, and learnt the truth by ques-
tioning them.   Possibly Lactantius knew of Hermetic dialogues in which Hermes
was represented as receiving instruction from a divine visitant (e. g. from the
Agathos Daimon), and assumed this teacher to be the soul of a dead man evoked
by necromantic rites.

[2] See note on *Div. inst.* 4. 9. 3.

[3] The *divina arcana* are the Christian Scriptures.

[4] *I. e.* iustitiae.

[5] *Div. inst.* 2. 15. 6 (p. 15. 2 above).

[6] *Quo utitur* is unintelligible ; and *donum* ought to be accompanied by some
qualifying phrase, such as *quod deo offerri debet.*   (Brandt proposes *utatur* in place
of *utitur* ; but the difficulty would not be got rid of by that alteration.)

10 . . . Hoc autem duplex sacrificii genus[1] quam sit verissimum, Trismegistus Hermes idoneus testis est, qui nobiscum, id est cum prophetis quos sequimur, tam re quam verbis congruit. De iustitia sic locutus est: 'Hoc verbum, o fili, adora et cole: cultus 11 autem dei unus est malum non esse.'[2] Idem[3] in illo sermone 5 perfecto, cum exaudisset Asclepium quaerentem a filio suo[4] utrum placeret patri eius[5] proferri tus et alios odores ad sacrificium dei, exclamavit: 'Bene, bene ominare, o Asclepi: est enim maxima inpietas tale quid de uno illo ac singulari bono in animum inducere. Haec et his similia huic non con- 10 veniunt: omnium enim quaecumque sunt plenus est, et omnium minime indigens. Nos vero gratias agentes adoremus: huius enim sacrificium sola benedictio est'.[6] 12 Et recte: verbo enim sacrificari oportet deo, siquidem deus verbum est, ut ipse confessus est. Summus igitur colendi dei ritus est ex ore 15 iusti hominis ad deum directa laudatio.

Div. inst. 7. 4. 3 : (Stoici) ignorant unum hominem a deo esse formatum, putantque homines in omnibus terris et agris tamquam fungos esse generatos.[7] At Hermes non ignoravit hominem et a deo[8] et ad dei similitudinem fictum.[9]

20

[1] The things which are here called 'two kinds of *sacrificium*' are *integritas animi* (= *iustitia*) and *laus et hymnus*. We are told in § 7 that *integritas animi* is a *donum*, and *laus et hymnus* a *sacrificium*; but the word *sacrificium* is here used in a wider sense, and includes *donum* as well as what was previously called *sacrificium*. The meaning might have been made clearer by writing *duplex oblationis* (or *cultus*) *genus* instead of *duplex sacrificii genus*.
  In the first of the two passages which Lactantius proceeds to quote, Hermes speaks *de iustitia* (i. e. *de dono quod deo debetur*); in the second, Hermes speaks *de laude et hymno* (i. e. *de sacrificio quod deo debetur*).
[2] *Corp.* XII. ii. 23 b. Lactantius had before him the same corrupt reading that is given by our MSS. of the *Corpus*, viz. τοῦτον τὸν λόγον, ὦ τέκνον, προσκύνει καὶ θρήσκευε, κ.τ.λ.; and he supposed that τοῦτον τὸν λόγον meant the Son of God. But if the word λόγον occurred at all in the Hermetic passage as originally written, it probably meant 'discourse' or 'teaching'. See note on *Div. inst.* 4. 9. 3. Lactantius takes *malum non esse* (μὴ εἶναι κακόν) to be equivalent to *iustum esse*, and accordingly says that Hermes is here speaking *de iustitia*.
[3] idem *coni. Heumann* : item *MSS., Brandt*.   [4] I. e. asking Tat.
[5] *patri eius* means Tat's father, i. e. Hermes. Hermes heard Asclepius asking Tat whether Hermes would like incense to be burnt.
[6] This is a translation of the Greek original of *Ascl. Lat.* III. 41 a.
[7] Cf. Cic. *De legg.* 1. 8. 24: 'disputari solet . . . perpetuis cursibus conversioni-busque caelestibus exstitisse quandam maturitatem serendi generis humani, quod sparsum in terras atque satum divino auctum sit animorum munere.' Origen *c. Cels.* 1. 37. 355: καὶ κατ' αὐτοὺς δὲ τοὺς Ἕλληνας οὐ πάντες ἄνθρωποι ἐξ ἀνδρὸς καὶ γυναικὸς ἐγένοντο· εἰ γὰρ γεννητός ἐστιν ὁ κόσμος, ὡς καὶ πολλοῖς Ἑλλήνων ἤρεσεν, ἀνάγκη τοὺς πρώτους μὴ ἐκ συνουσίας γεγονέναι, ἀλλ' ἀπὸ γῆς, σπερματικῶν λόγων συστάντων ἐν τῇ γῇ.
[8] The making of man by God is spoken of, for instance, in *Ascl. Lat.* I. 8.
[9] See notes on *Div. inst.* 2. 10. 14 (p. 12 above).

Div. inst. 7. 9. 11: An aliquis cum ceterarum animantium naturam consideraverit, quas pronis corporibus abiectas in terramque prostratas summi dei providentia effecit, ut ex hoc intellegi possit nihil eas rationis habere cum caelo, potest non intellegere solum ex
5 omnibus caeleste ac divinum animal esse hominem? Cuius corpus ab humo excitatum, vultus sublimis, status rectus originem suam quaerit, et quasi contempta humilitate terrae ad altum nititur, quia sentit summum bonum in summo sibi esse quaerendum, memorque condicionis suae, qua deus illum fecit eximium, ad artificem suum
10 spectat. Quam spectationem Trismegistus ΘΕΟΠΙΔΑ[1] rectissime nominavit: quae in mutis animalibus nulla est.

Div. inst. 7. 13. 1–4: Declaravi, ut opinor, animam non esse 1 solubilem: superest citare testes, quorum auctoritate argumenta firmentur. Neque nunc prophetas in testimonium vocabo, . . . sed 2
15 eos potius, quibus istos qui respuunt veritatem credere sit necesse. Hermes, naturam hominis describens, ut doceret quemadmodum esset 3 a deo factus, haec intulit: ⌈καὶ τὸ αὐτὸ²⌉ ἐξ ἑκατέρων φύσεων, τῆς τε ἀθανάτου καὶ τῆς θνητῆς, μίαν ἐποίει φύσιν τὴν τοῦ ἀνθρώπου, τὸν αὐτὸν πῇ μὲν ἀθάνατον, πῇ δὲ θνητὸν ποιήσας,³
20 καὶ τοῦτον φέρων ἐν μέσῳ τῆς θείας καὶ ἀθανάτου φύσεως καὶ τῆς θνητῆς καὶ μεταβλητῆς ἵδρυσεν, ἵνα πάντα μὲν ὁρῶν πάντα θαυμάζῃ.⁴ Sed hunc fortasse aliquis in numero philosopho- 4 rum⁵ conputet, quamvis in deos relatus Mercurii nomine ab Aegyptiis

---

1 ΟΠΙδΑ *in ras.* (*in marg.* d͞i inspectionem) *B* : ΘΕΟΠΙda *R* : ΘΕⲰΠΙΔΑ *HS* : ΘΗⲰΠΙΔΑ *P*. θεοππίαν (conjectured by.Fritzsche, and accepted by Brandt) gives the sense required. The word θεοππία does not occur in the extant *Hermetica*; but θεοπτικὴ δύναμις occurs in Herm. *ap.* Stob. *Exc.* II A. 6 (i. e. in a *libellus* which was certainly known to Lactantius) and *Exc.* VII. 3. In both these documents the passage which contains that term is probably an interpolation; but the words may have been inserted in one or both of them before the time of Lactantius. *Frag.* 14.

2 αὐτὸ *om. B.*

3 ἐξ ἑκατέρων . . . θνητὸν ποιήσας. Cf. *Ascl. Lat.* I. 8 (as emended): 'Itaque hominem conformat ex animi et corporis, id est, ex aeterna atque mortali natura, ⟨⟨ex utraque natura in unum confundens miscensque quantum satis esse⟨t⟩ ⟩⟩.' *Ib.* c. 10 *fin.*: 'humanitas, ex parté divina, ex alia parte effecta mortalis est.' *Ascl. Lat.* III. 22 b: 'Denique et ⌈bonum⌉ hominem et qui posset inmortalis esse ex utraque natura conposuit, divina atque mortali.' *Frag.* 15.

4 If μέν is sound, this clause must have been followed, in the Hermetic document, by a clause introduced by δέ. But what can have been the word that stood in antithesis to πάντα? And why is πάντα repeated? We should rather have expected ἵνα τὰ μὲν . . ., τὰ δὲ . . . . The corresponding passage in *Ascl. Lat.* I. 8 is 'ut . . . utraeque origini suae satisfacere possit, et mirari atque ⟨ad⟩orare caelestia et [in]colere atque gubernare terrena'.

5 I. e. it may be thought that Hermes was merely a human philosopher, and not a god.

honoretur, nec plus ei auctoritatis tribuat quam Platoni aut Pythagorae. Maius igitur testimonium[1] requiramus.

14. 9 *Div. inst.* 7. 14. 9–18. 5: Per saecula sex, id est annorum sex milia, manere in hoc statu mundum necesse est.[2] . . . Et rursus . . . necesse est ut in fine sexti millesimi anni malitia omnis aboleatur e terra, et regnet per annos mille iustitia, sitque tranquillitas et requies a laboribus quos mundus iam diu perfert. . . . Quomodo autem consummatio futura sit, et qualis exitus humanis rebus inpendeat, si quis divinas litteras fuerit scrutatus, inveniet. Sed et saecularium prophetarum congruentes cum caelestibus voces finem rerum et occasum post breve tempus adnuntiant, describentes quasi fatigati et dilabentis mundi ultimam senectutem.[3] Quae vero a prophetis et vatibus futura esse dicantur priusquam superveniat extrema illa conclusio, collecta ex omnibus et coacervata subnectam.[4] . . .

15. 7 Propinquante igitur huius saeculi termino, humanarum rerum statum commutari necesse est, et in deterius nequitia invalescente prolabi. . . .

8 Ita enim iustitia rarescet, ita inpietas et avaritia et cupiditas et libido crebrescet, ut si qui forte tum fuerint boni, praedae sint sceleratis ac divexentur undique ab iniustis, soli autem mali opulenti sint, boni vero in omnibus contumeliis atque in egestate iactentur. Confundetur omne ius, et leges interibunt. Nihil quisquam tunc habebit nisi aut quaesitum aut defensum manu, audacia et vis omnia possidebunt. Non fides in hominibus, non pax, non humanitas, non pudor, non veritas erit, atque ita neque securitas neque regimen neque requies a malis ulla.

10 Omnis enim terra tumultuabitur, frement ubique bella, omnes gentes in armis erunt et se invicem obpugnabunt, civitates inter se finitimae proeliabuntur. Et prima omnium Aegyptus stultarum superstitionum luet poenas, et sanguine velut flumine operietur:[5] tum peragrabit

---

[1] I. e. the testimony of one whom the Pagans believed to be a god. Lactantius here goes on to quote an oracle of Apollo.

[2] This means that the *consummatio* will come to pass as soon as 6,000 years shall have elapsed since the creation of the world. Lactantius thought that this period would be completed 'not more than 200 years' after the time at which he wrote, i. e. at a date not later than A.D. 511 (*Div. inst.* 7. 25. 5).

[3] *Ascl. Lat.* III. 26 a *init.* Cf. Lact. *Epit.* 66. 6: 'et hanc esse mundi senectutem ac defectionem Trismegistus elocutus est.'

[4] Lactantius constructs his eschatology by combining together, and working up into a more or less consistent whole, predictions which he has found chiefly, if not solely, in (1) the Jewish and Christian Scriptures, (2) the *Oracula Sibyllina*, (3) an apocalypse ascribed to Hystaspes, and (4) the Prophecy of Hermes in the Λόγος τέλειος (*Ascl. Lat.* II. 24 b–26 a). Cf. *Epit.* 68. 1: 'cum haec omnia vera et certa sint, prophetarum omnium consona adnuntiatione praedicta, cum eadem Trismegistus, eadem Hystaspes, eadem Sibyllae cecinerint,' &c.

[5] This special mention of Egypt was probably suggested by *Ascl. Lat.* III. 24 b *sq.* The words *sanguine velut flumine operietur* correspond to *torrenti*

gladius orbem, metens omnia, et tamquam messem cuncta pro-
sternens. . . .

Tum vero detestabile atque abominandum tempus existet, quo 16. 5
nulli hominum sit vita iucunda.¹ Eruentur funditus civitates atque
5 interibunt, non modo ferro atque igni, verum etiam terrae motibus
adsiduis et eluvie aquarum et morbis frequentibus et fame crebra.
Aer enim vitiabitur et corruptus ac pestilens fiet, modo inportunis 6
imbribus modo inutili siccitate, nunc frigoribus nunc aestibus nimiis.
Nec terra homini dabit fructum : non seges quicquam, non arbor, non
10 vitis feret, sed cum in flore spem maximam dederint, in fruge
decipient. Fontes quoque cum fluminibus arescent, ut ne potus 7
quidem suppetat, et aquae in sanguinem aut amaritudinem mutabun-
tur. Propter haec deficient et in terra quadrupedes et in aere volucres 8
et in mari pisces. Prodigia quoque in caelo mirabilia mentes homi-
15 num maximo terrore confundent.² . . .

Illi vero³ ubi se clausos undique atque obsessos viderint, exclama- 17. 11
bunt ad deum voce magna, et auxilium caeleste inplorabunt ; et
exaudiet eos deus, et mittet regem magnum de caelo, qui eos eripiat
ac liberet, omnesque inpios ferro ignique disperdat. Haec ita futura 18. 1
20 esse, cum prophetae omnes ex dei spiritu, tum etiam vates ex instinctu
daemonum cecinerunt. Hystaspes enim, quem superius nominavi,⁴ 2

---

sanguine plenus adusque ripas erumpes (addressed to the Nile) in that passage.
But in the *Oracula Sibyllina* also there are numerous predictions of woe to Egypt.

¹ Cf. *Ascl. Lat.* III. 25 : 'tunc taedio hominum non admirandus videbitur
mundus. . . . mors vita utilior iudicabitur.'

² §§ 5–8 ('terrae motibus . . . aer enim vitiabitur . . . nec terra homini dabit
fructum . . . prodigia quoque in caelo'). Cf. *Ascl. Lat.* III. 25 *fin.* : 'Tunc nec
terra constabit, . . . nec siderum cursus constabit in caelo ; . . . fructus terrae con-
rumpentur, nec fecunda tellus erit, et aer ipse maesto torpore languescet.'

³ Sc. *iusti et sectatores veritatis*, persecuted and threatened with destruction by
Antichrist.

⁴ *Div. inst.* 7. 15. 19 : 'Hystaspes quoque, qui fuit Medorum rex antiquissimus,
a quo amnis nomen accepit qui nunc Hydaspes dicitur, admirabile somnium sub
interpretatione vaticinantis pueri ad memoriam posteris tradidit : sublaturi ex orbe
imperium nomenque Romanum multo ante praefatus est quam illa Troiana gens
conderetur.' Cf. Justin *Apol.* 1. 20. 1 : καὶ Σίβυλλα δὲ καὶ Ὑστάσπης γενήσεσθαι
τῶν φθαρτῶν ἀνάλωσιν διὰ πυρὸς ἔφασαν. *Ib.* 44. 12 : κατ' ἐνέργειαν δὲ τῶν φαύλων
δαιμόνων θάνατος ὡρίσθη (by the Roman government) κατὰ τῶν τὰς Ὑστάσπου ἢ
Σιβύλλης ἢ τῶν προφητῶν βίβλους ἀναγιγνωσκόντων, ὅπως διὰ τοῦ φόβου ἀποστρέψωσιν
ἐντυγχάνοντας τοὺς ἀνθρώπους τῶν καλῶν γνῶσιν λαβεῖν. Clem. Alex. *Strom.*
6. 5. 43 : λάβετε καὶ τὰς Ἑλληνικὰς βίβλους, ἐπίγνωτε Σίβυλλαν, ὡς δηλοῖ ἕνα θεὸν
καὶ τὰ μέλλοντα ἔσεσθαι· καὶ τὸν Ὑστάσπην λαβόντες ἀνάγνωτε, καὶ εὑρήσετε πολλῷ
τηλαυγέστερον καὶ σαφέστερον γεγραμμένον τὸν υἱὸν τοῦ θεοῦ, καὶ καθὼς παράταξιν
ποιήσουσι τῷ Χριστῷ πολλοὶ βασιλεῖς μισοῦντες αὐτὸν καὶ τοὺς φοροῦντας τὸ ὄνομα
αὐτοῦ καὶ τοὺς πιστοὺς αὐτοῦ, καὶ τὴν ὑπομονὴν καὶ τὴν παρουσίαν αὐτοῦ. In the
Excerpta e Theosophia (Buresch, *Klaros*, p. 95) we are told that in the *Theosophia*
(a work written in A. D. 474–491) were quoted χρήσεις Ὑστάσπου τινὸς βασιλέως
Περσῶν ἢ Χαλδαίων, εὐλαβεστάτου, φησί, γεγονότος, καὶ διὰ τοῦτο θείων μυστηρίων

descripta iniquitate saeculi huius extremi, pios ac fideles a nocentibus segregatos ait cum fletu et gemitu extenturos esse ad caelum manus et inploraturos fidem Iovis: Iovem respecturum ad terram et auditurum voces hominum, atque inpios extincturum. Quae omnia vera sunt praeter unum, quod Iovem dixit illa facturum quae deus faciet. 5

3 Sed et illut non sine daemonum fraude subtractum, missuiri a patre tunc filium dei, qui deletis omnibus malis pios liberet. Quod Hermes tamen non dissimulavit: in eo enim libro qui λόγος τέλειος inscribitur, post enumerationem malorum de quibus diximus subiecit haec:[1]

4 ἐπὰν δὴ ταῦτα γένηται, ὦ Ἀσκληπιέ, τότε ὁ κύριος καὶ πατὴρ 10 ⌜καὶ θεὸς καὶ τοῦ πρώτου καὶ ἑνὸς θεοῦ δημιουργός⌝,[2] ἐπι-

ἀποκάλυψιν δεξαμένου περὶ τῆς τοῦ σωτῆρος ἐνανθρωπήσεως. Lydus *De mens.* 14. 9 mentions χρήσεις Ὑστάσπου τινὸς βασιλέως Περσῶν ἢ Χαλδαίων.

Justin's mention of 'the books of Hystaspes' shows that this apocalypse was known to Christians before A. D. 150. Scherer (*Gesch. des iudischen Volkes*, 1909, vol. iii, p. 594, thinks that it was probably written by a Jew. But it seems more likely that it was a Zoroastrian document, written originally in the Persian language, and translated into Greek by a Pagan. The Hystaspes to whom it was attributed must have been Vishtâspa, the king of eastern or western Iran in whose reign and under whose protection Zarathushtra lived and preached (Moulton, *Early Religious Poetry of Persia*, p. 50 ff.). The name Jupiter (Ζεύς), by which, as Lactantius tells us, the supreme God was called in it, would not have been thus used either by a Christian or by a Jew; but Ζεύς might very well be written by a Pagan Greek as a translation of Ahuramazda. If the prophecy spoke of a final and decisive conflict between good and evil, and of the coming of a saviour, and said that the enemies of God and of God's faithful servants would be destroyed by fire, it was in those respects in agreement with genuine Zoroastrian tradition. Lactantius tells us that Hystaspes said nothing about the coming of the Son of God; on the other hand, in Clem. *Strom.* 6. 5. 43 and the *Theosophia* (Buresch), we are told that Hystaspes predicted the παρουσία Χριστοῦ and the ἐνανθρώπησις τοῦ σωτῆρος. This contradiction might be accounted for by assuming that the Zoroastrian apocalypse spoke of the coming of a saviour, and that some Christians identified the saviour spoken of with Christ, but others did not. Lactantius says also that Hystaspes predicted the destruction of the Roman empire; but this statement may have resulted from Christian interpretation of a prophecy in which the enemies of God and his people were spoken of in general terms, and there is no need to suppose that Rome was mentioned by name. Possibly the document was of Persian origin, but was more or less altered by Jewish or Christian interpolations before it came into the hands of Lactantius.   [1] *Ascl. Lat.* III. 26 a.

[2] καὶ θεὸς καὶ τοῦ πρώτου καὶ ἑνὸς θεοῦ δημιουργός *Lactant.*: deus primipotens et unius gubernator dei *Ascl. Lat.*

Lactantius and the translator of *Ascl. Lat.* had before them different readings of the Greek phrase, both of which were corrupt. In place of τοῦ πρώτου καὶ ἑνὸς θεοῦ (unius dei *Ascl. Lat.*), some term denoting the Kosmos is needed. The Hermetist may have written either τοῦ πρωτογενοῦς θεοῦ (Davis), or τοῦ πρώτου καὶ ἑνὸς (αἰσθητοῦ) θεοῦ. For the latter, cf. the Greek original of *Ascl. Lat.* I. 8, given in *Div. inst.* 4. 6. 4: ἐπεὶ τὸν δεύτερον ἐποίησε θεὸν ὁρατὸν καὶ αἰσθητόν, ... ἐπεὶ οὖν τοῦτον ἐποίησε πρῶτον καὶ μόνον καὶ ἕνα...

Lactantius took the words τοῦ πρώτου καὶ ἑνὸς θεοῦ δημιουργός to signify the Son of God (see *Div. inst.* 4. 6. 9), and thereby contrived to interpret the passage as meaning 'missuiri a patre tunc filium dei, qui deletis omnibus malis pios liberet'. He assumed that it was the Son of God that was spoken of as doing, either alone or in conjunction with His Father, all that is here described. But how he disposed of the words ὁ κύριος καὶ πατήρ, it is difficult to guess.

βλέψας τοῖς γενομένοις, καὶ τὴν ἑαυτοῦ βούλησιν, τοῦτ'
ἔστιν τὸ ἀγαθόν, ἀντερείσας τῇ ἀταξίᾳ, καὶ ἀνακαλεσάμενος
τὴν πλάνην,[1] καὶ τὴν κακίαν ⌜ἐκκαθάρας⌝ πῇ μὲν ὕδατι
πολλῷ κατακλύσας,[2] πῇ δὲ πυρὶ ὀξυτάτῳ διακαύσας, ἐνίοτε
5 δὲ πολέμοις καὶ λοιμοῖς ἐκπαίσας,[3] ἤγαγεν[4] ἐπὶ τὸ ἀρχαῖον
καὶ ἀποκατέστησεν τὸν ἑαυτοῦ κόσμον. Sibyllae quoque non 5
aliter fore ostendunt quam ut dei filius a summo patre mittatur, qui
et iustos liberet de manibus inpiorum, et iniustos cum tyrannis
saevientibus deleat.

10 *De ira* 11. 11 *sq.*: Unus est igitur princeps et origo rerum 11
deus, sicut Plato in Timaeo et sensit et docuit: cuius maiestatem
tantam esse declarat, ut nec mente conprehendi nec lingua exprimi
possit.[5] Idem testatur Hermes,[6] quem Cicero[7] ait in numero deorum 12
apud Aegyptios haberi, eum scilicet qui ob virtutem multarumque
15 artium scientiam Termaximus nominatus est, et erat non modo
Platone, verum etiam Pythagora septemque illis sapientibus longe
antiquior.

---

[1] καὶ ἀνακαλεσάμενος τὴν πλάνην *Lactant.* : errorem revocans *Ascl. Lat.* The
long string of participles is awkward ; and it may be suspected that the Hermetist
wrote ἀνεκαλέσατο τὴν πλάνην.

[2] καὶ τὴν κακίαν ⌜ἐκκαθάρας⌝ πῇ μὲν ὕδατι πολλῷ κατακλύσας *Lactant.* : maligni-
tatem omnem vel inluvione diluens *Ascl. Lat.* ἐκκαθάρας was probably read by
Lactantius, but cannot have been written by the Hermetist; it may have been
substituted by error for πᾶσαν, the reading implied by *Ascl. Lat.*

[3] ἐκπαίσας *Brandt* (malitia ... percussa *interpretat. Lat. in B*) : ΕΚΙΤΕΣΑΣ *B* :
ecpesas *H* : ΕΚΠΑΣΑΣ *S* : ΗΚΠΣΑΣ *P* : ΕΚΠΗΣΑΣ *Sedulius* : ἐκπιέσας
Bernays. *Ascl. Lat.* gives *finiens*, from which it may be inferred that the translator read either ἐκπαύσας or ἐκτελέσας.

[4] Perhaps ⟨ἀν⟩ήγαγεν.

[5] Pl. *Tim.* 28 C.

[6] Stob. *Exc.* I. In writing *nec mente conprehendi possit*, Lactantius misrepre-
sents both Plato and the Hermetist; for both alike imply that *deum mente comprehendere*, though difficult, is not impossible.

[7] *De nat. deor.* 3. 22. 56.

ABAMMONIS AD PORPHYRIUM
RESPONSUM

('*Iamblichi de mysteriis liber*')

Ἀβάμμωνος διδασκάλου πρὸς τὴν Πορφυρίου πρὸς Ἀνεβὼ ἐπιστολὴν ἀπόκρισις, καὶ τῶν ἐν αὐτῇ ἀπορημάτων λύσεις.

I. 1 a θεὸς ὁ τῶν λόγων ἡγεμὼν Ἑρμῆς πάλαι δέδοκται ⌜καλῶς⌝ ἅπασι τοῖς ἱερεῦσιν εἶναι κοινός, ⌜ὁ δὲ⌝ τῆς περὶ θεῶν ἀληθινῆς ἐπιστήμης προεστηκὼς 5 εἷς ἐστιν ὁ αὐτὸς ἐν ὅλοις· ᾧ δὴ καὶ οἱ ἡμέτεροι πρόγονοι τὰ αὐτῶν τῆς σοφίας εὑρήματα ἀνετίθεσαν, Ἑρμοῦ πάντα τὰ οἰκεῖα συγγράμματα ἐπονομάζοντες. ⌜εἰ δὲ⌝ τοῦδε τοῦ θεοῦ καὶ ἡμεῖς τὸ ἐπιβάλλον καὶ δυνατὸν ἑαυτοῖς μέρος μετάσχοιμεν.

b σύ τε καλῶς ποιεῖς ⌜ἅτινα εἰς γνῶσιν⌝ τοῖς ἱερεῦσιν ⌜ὡς φιλοῦσι⌝ 10 περὶ θεολογίας προτείνων ἐρωτήματα, ἐγώ τε, εἰκότως τὴν πρὸς Ἀνεβὼ τὸν ἐμὸν μαθητὴν πεμφθεῖσαν ἐπιστολὴν ἐμαυτῷ γεγράφθαι νομίσας, ἀποκρινοῦμαί σοι αὐτὰ τἀληθῆ ὑπὲρ ὧν πυνθάνῃ. οὐδὲ γὰρ ἂν εἴη πρέπον Πυθαγόραν μὲν καὶ Πλάτωνα καὶ Δημόκριτον καὶ Εὔδοξον καὶ πολλοὺς ἄλλους τῶν παλαιῶν Ἑλλήνων τετυχηκέναι διδαχῆς 15 τῆς προσηκούσης ὑπὸ τῶν καθ' ἑαυτοὺς γινομένων ἱερογραμματ⟨έ⟩ων, σὲ

---

1 Editiones: T. Gale, Oxon. 1678; G. Parthey, Berolini 1857. De codicibus vide infra. Adhibui textum Galei et lectiones codicum D, M, Aᵖ, Bᵖ, Cᵖ. Accedunt codicis F lectiones nonnullae a Galeo nuntiatae.   2 Ἀβάμμωνος Gale: Ἀβάμωνος DMAᵖCᵖ | Ante Ἀβάμωνος add. Ἰαμβλίχου τοῦ μεγάλου εἰς τὴν ἐπιστολὴν τοῦ Πορφυρίου D   3 λύσεις Gale: λύσις MBᵖ | 'Addit quidam MS. περὶ τῶν Αἰγυπτίων μυστηρίων. Hinc Ficinus ... de Mysteriis Aegyptiorum. Plerique Codd. haec non addunt' Gale   4 θεὸς Gale, M: πρὸς D | λόγων Gale: ὅλων M | ὁ Ἑρμῆς Gale: Ἑρμῆς (om. ὁ) DMAᵖCᵖ   5 κοινῶς Bᵖ | Fortasse πάλαι δέδοκται κ(αὶ) ἄλ(λ)ως ἅπασι(ν) [τοῖς ἱερεῦσιν] εἶναι κοινός, καὶ τῆς περὶ θεῶν   6 ὅλοις Gale, M: λόγοις Aᵖ | πρόγονοι (corr. πρόγονοι) M   7 ἀνετίθεσαν M | τὰ om. M   8 εἰ δὲ M: εἰ καὶ cett.: fortasse εἴθε 8-9 καὶ δυνατὸν secludendum?   9 μετάσχοιμεν Gale, M: μετέχομεν AᵖBᵖ: μετεχόμενον (corr. μετέχομεν) Cᵖ   10 ἅτινα εἰς γνῶσιν Gale, F (recentior manus): ἀγνῶς ἀγνῶσι DM: ἀγνῶς ἀγνῶσι Bᵖ | ὡς φιλοῦσι Gale, M: om. D   11 προτείνων ἐρωτήματα Gale, M: προτείνων πρός τε τὰ ἐρωτήματα BᵖF: inter προτείνων et ἐρωτήματα lacunam indicant AᵖCᵖ: fortasse καλῶς ποιεῖς [[ ]] τοῖς ἱερεῦσιν ὡς ⟨⟨ἀγνῶς⟩⟩ φιλ(οσοφ)οῦσι (vel ὡς ⟨⟨γνῶσιν⟩⟩ ἔχουσι) περὶ θεολογίας προτείνων ἐρωτήματα | τὴν πρὸς Gale: πρὸς τὴν M   12 πεμφθεῖσαν ἐπιστολὴν Gale: ἐπιστολὴν πεμφθεῖσαν M: τιμῶν ἐπιστολὴν F: τιμῶν ... ἐπιστολὴν (i.e. post τιμῶν lacunam indicant) AᵖCᵖ | ἐμαυτῷ om. Aᵖ   13 νομίσας Gale, M: ὁμολογῶν FAᵖCᵖ   13-14 γὰρ ἂν εἴη FBᵖCᵖ: γὰρ εἴη Gale: γὰρ εἶεν DM   14 μὲν DM: om. Gale | Δημόκριτον καὶ AᵖCᵖ: Δημόκριτόν τε καὶ Gale, M   14-15 καὶ Δημόκριτον καὶ Εὔδοξον secludendum?   16 ἱερογραμματέων Gale: ἱερογραμμάτων DMAᵖCᵖ

δ' ἐφ' ἡμῶν ὄντα, καὶ τὴν αὐτὴν ἐκείνοις ἔχοντα γνώμην, διαμαρτεῖν τῆς ὑπὸ τῶν νῦν ζώντων καὶ καλουμένων κοινῶν διδασκάλων ὑφηγήσεως.

ἐγὼ μὲν οὖν οὕτως ἐπὶ τὸν λόγον τὸν παρόντα πρόσειμι· σὺ δ', εἰ μὲν **c** βούλει, τὸν αὐτὸν ἡγοῦ σοι πάλιν ἀντιγράφειν ὧπερ ἐπεστείλας· εἰ δὲ καὶ
5 φαίνοιτό σοι δεῖν, ἐμὲ θὲς εἶναι [[σοι]] τὸν ἐν γράμμασί ⟨⟨σοι⟩⟩ διαλεγόμενον ἢ τινα ἄλλον προφήτην Αἰγυπτίων· οὐδὲ⟨ν⟩ γὰρ τοῦτο διενήνοχεν· ἢ ἔτι βέλτιον, οἶμαι, τὸν μὲν λέγοντα ἄφες, εἴτε χείρων εἴτε ἀμείνων εἴη, τὰ δὲ λεγόμενα σκόπει, εἴτε ἀληθῆ εἴτε ψευδῆ λέγεται, προθύμως ἀνεγείρας τὴν διάνοιαν.

10 ἐν ἀρχῇ δὴ διελώμεθα τὰ γένη, πόσα τέ ἐστι καὶ ὁποῖα, τῶν νυνὶ **d** προκειμένων προβλημάτων, ἀπὸ τίνων τε εἴληπται ⌈θείων θεολογιῶν⌉ τὰ ἀπορήματα διέλθωμεν, καὶ κατὰ ποίας τινὰς ἐπιστήμας ἐπιζητεῖται ⟨. . .⟩ τὴν πρόθεσιν αὐτῶν ποιησώμεθα.

τὰ μὲν οὖν ἐπιποθεῖ διάκρισίν τινα τῶν κακῶς συγκεχυμένων· τὰ δ' **e**
15 ⌈ἐστὶ περὶ⌉ τὴν αἰτίαν δι' ἢν ἕκαστά ἐστί τε οὑτωσὶ καὶ νοεῖται· τὰ δ' ἐπ' ἄμφω τὴν γνώμην ἕλκει [κατ' ἐναντίωσίν τινα προβαλλόμενα]· ἔνια δὲ καὶ τὴν ὅλην ἀπαιτεῖ παρ' ἡμῶν μυσταγωγίαν.

τοιαῦτα δὲ ὄντα πολλαχόθεν εἴληπται, καὶ ἀπὸ διαφερουσῶν ἐπιστημῶν. **f** τὰ μὲν γὰρ ἀφ' ὧν οἱ Χαλδαίων σοφοὶ παραδεδώκασι τὰς ἐπιστάσεις
20 προσάγει· τὰ δ' ἀφ' ὧν Αἰγυπτίων οἱ προφῆται διδάσκουσι ποιεῖται τὰς ἀντιλήψεις· ἔνια δὲ καὶ τῆς τῶν φιλοσόφων θεωρίας ἐχόμενα τὰς ἐρωτήσεις ἑπομένως αὐτοῖς ποιεῖται· ἤδη δέ τινα καὶ ἀπ' ἄλλων οὐκ ἀξίων λόγου δοξασμάτων ἐφέλκεταί τινα ἀπρεπῆ διαμφισβήτησιν· τὰ δ' ἀπὸ τῶν κοινῶν ὑπολήψεων [παρ' ἀνθρώποις] ὥρμηται.

---

1 Post σὲ δὲ lacunam indicant A^pC^p. Fortasse σὲ δέ, ⟨ὦ Πορφύριε⟩ | ἐκείνοις ἔχοντα γνώμην DMA^pC^p : γνώμην ἐκείνοις ἔχοντα Gale | τῆς Gale, M : τῶν A^pC^p 3 οὖν om. M 4 βούλει Gale, M : προσδέῃ A^pC^p | ὥσπερ D 5 σοι Gale, M : om. A^pC^p : σοι del. B | Ante δεῖν spatium 9 litt. vacuum habet M : ibidem lacunam indicant A^pB^pC^p : fortasse σοι ⟨μᾶλλον⟩ δεῖν | σοι huc transposui 6 ἢ τινα ἄλλον Gale, M : οἷον τινα (sed post τινα lacunam indicat) C^p : οἷον τινα A^p : fortasse [ἐμὲ] τὸν ἐν γράμμασί σοι διαλεγόμενον θὲς εἶναι ὁντινοῦν ἄλλον | οὐδὲν scripsi : οὐδὲ codd. 7 ἢ ἔτι Gale : ἤ τι M | βέλτιον οἶμαι Gale, M : οἶμαι βέλτιον F : om. DB^p sed lacunam indicant | Post οἶμαι vacuum habet spatium unius versus M : ibidem lacunam indicant A^pC^p 8 σκόπει Gale : περισκόπει DM | εἴτε ψευδῆ Gale, M : εἴτε καὶ ψευδῆ A^p 10 διελώμεθα B^p | πόσῳ B^p 11 τε om. M | θεολογιῶν Gale : λογίων M : om. DB^p sed lacunam indicant. Post θεολογιῶν lacunam indicat A^p 12 ἀπορρήματα M | ἐπιζητεῖται Gale : ἐπιζητεῖ τε B^p : ἐπιζητῆσαι M 13 Lacunam signavi. Fortasse ⟨ἡ λύσις· καὶ οὕτω δὴ⟩ 14 συγκεχυμένων C^p 15 ἕκαστά om. DMB^p | τε DM : τι Gale | οὑτωσὶ M : οὑτωσὶ B^p : οὕτω δὲ D : οὕτω δὴ Gale 16 προβαλλόμενα D : προβαλλόμεθα MB^p : προβαλλώμεθα Gale | κατ'. . . προβαλλόμενα seclusi 17 ἀπετεῖ D 19 παραδεδώκασι M 20 Αἰγυπτίων om. F | οἱ om. M 22 ποιεῖται codd. : fortasse προτείνει | ἀξίῳ M 23 διαμφισβήτησιν M 24 ἀνθρώποις Gale, M : ἀνθρώπων B^p | παρ' ἀνθρώποις seclusi : fortasse τῶν ⟨⟨πᾶσ(ιν) ἀνθρώποις⟩⟩ κοινῶν ὑπολήψεων

g αὐτά τε οὖν καθ᾽ ἑαυτὰ ἕκαστα ποικίλως διάκειται, καὶ πρὸς ἄλληλα πολυειδῶς συνήρμοσται· ὅθεν δὴ [διὰ] πάντα ταῦτα λόγου τινός ἐστιν ἐπιδεῆ τοῦ κατευθυνο⟨ῦ⟩ντος αὐτὰ προσηκόντως.

2 a ἡμεῖς οὖν τὰ μὲν Ἀσσυρίων πάτρια δόγματα ⟨. . .⟩ παραδώσομέν σοι μετ᾽ ἀληθείας τὴν γνώμην, τὰ δὲ ἡμέτερά σοι σαφῶς ἀποκαλύψομεν, 5
τὰ μὲν ἀπὸ τῶν ἀρχαίων ⌜ἀπείρων⌝ γραμμάτων ⌜ἀναλογιζόμενοι τῇ γνώσει⌝, τὰ δ᾽ ἀφ᾽ ὧν ὕστερον ⟨. . .⟩ εἰς πεπερασμένον βιβλίων ⟨πλῆθος⟩ συνήγαγον [οἱ παλαιοὶ] τὴν ὅλην περὶ τῶν θείων εἴδησιν. φιλόσοφον δ᾽ εἴ τι προβάλλεις ἐρώτημα, διακρινοῦμέν σοι καὶ τοῦτο κατὰ τὰς Ἑρμοῦ παλαιὰς στήλας, ἃς Πλάτων ἤδη πρόσθεν καὶ Πυθαγόρας δια- 10
ναγνόντες φιλοσοφίαν συνεστήσαντο. τὰ δ᾽ ⌜ἀλλόφυλα⌝ ζητήματα ἢ ἀντιλογικὰ καὶ δυσεριστίαν τινὰ ἐμφαίνοντα πρᾴως καὶ ἐμμελῶς παρα- μυθούμενοι, [ἢ] τὴν ἀτοπίαν αὐτῶν ἀποδείξομεν· καὶ ὅσα προχωρεῖ κατὰ τὰς κοινὰς ἐννοίας, γνωρίμως πάνυ καὶ σαφῶς πειρασόμεθα διαλέγεσθαι.

b καὶ τὰ μὲν ἔργων θείων πείρας δεόμενα πρὸς ἀκριβῆ κατανόησιν 15
⟨ἀ⟩δύνατον [μόνον] διὰ λόγων ⟨ἐξηγεῖσθαι⟩· τὰ δὲ νοερᾶς θεωρίας ⟨ἐχόμενα⟩ ⌜πλήρη τε καθαιρεῖσθαι⌝ ⟨. . .⟩, σημεῖα δ᾽ αὐτῶν ἀξιόλογα δυνατὸν φράζειν, ἀφ᾽ ὧν δύνασαι καὶ σὺ καὶ οἱ σοὶ ὅμοιοι τῷ νῷ ⌜παράγεσθαι περὶ⌝ τὴν οὐσίαν τῶν ὄντων. ὅσα δὲ τυγχάνει διὰ λόγων ὄντα γνωστά, τούτων οὐδὲν ἀπολείψομεν εἰς τὴν τελείαν ἀπόδειξιν. 20

c τὸ δ᾽ οἰκεῖον ἐπὶ πᾶσιν ἀποδώσομέν σοι προσηκόντως, καὶ τὰ μὲν θεολογικὰ θεολογικῶς, ⟨τὰ⟩ ⟨⟨δὲ⟩⟩ θεουργικὰ [[δὲ]] θεουργικῶς ἀποκρινού-

1 ποικοίλως M   2 διὰ seclusi | πάντα ταῦτα Gale, M : ταῦτα πάντα Bᴾ   3 κατευθυνοῦντος scripsi : κατευθύνοντος codd.   4 Ἀσσυρίων Gale : ἀσυρίων DMAᴾBᴾCᴾ | πρῶτα F ut videtur | Lacunam signavi | παραδό- σωμέν Bᴾ   5 μετ᾽ ἀκριβείας καὶ post σοι addit F ut videtur | τὰ δ᾽ ἡμέτερά Gale, M : τῷ δ᾽ ἡμέτερον Bᴾ. | ἀποκαλύψωμεν M   7 ἐφ᾽ Aᴾ | Lacunam signavi | Fortasse τὰ μὲν ⟨⟨τῆς γνώσεως⟩⟩ ἀπὸ τῶν ἀρχαίων [[ ]] γραμμάτων, ⟨⟨ἀπείρων⟩⟩ ⟨ὄντων⟩, ἀναλογιζόμενοι [[ ]], τὰ δ᾽ ἀφ᾽ ὧν ὕστερον ⟨συγγράψαντες νεώτεροί τινες⟩ | εἰς πεπερασμένον βιβλίων πλῆθος scripsi : ἐν πεπερασμένῳ βιβλίῳ F : εἰς πεπερασμένον βιβλίον (βιβλίων Cᴾ) cett.   8 οἱ παλαιοὶ seclusi | περὶ Gale, M : παρὰ AᴾCᴾ : παρὰ (corr. περὶ) D | φιλόσοφοι Cᴾ   9 εἴ τοι D | προβάλλεις Gale, M : παραβάλλεις (corr. προβάλλεις) D : προβάλλῃς Aᴾ   10 ἤδη πρόσθεν Gale, M : om. DBᴾ sed lacunam indicant   10-11 διαναγνόντες FAᴾCᴾ : διαγνόντες Gale, M   11 διεστήσαντο FCᴾ | τὰ δ᾽ ἀλλόφυλα Gale : om. DBᴾ sed lacunam indicant : om. M. Fortasse τὰ δ᾽ ἀλλόκοτα   11-12 ἢ ἀντι- λογικὰ secludendum?   13 ἢ seclusi | καὶ om. AᴾCᴾ | προχωρεῖ Gale : προχωροῦσι DMBᴾ   14 καὶ σαφῶς Gale, M : om. F et spatio vacuo relicto AᴾCᴾ   15 ἀκριβῆ om. F : puncta habet Aᴾ | Post κατανόησιν spatium 18 litt. vacuum habet M : ibidem lacunam indicat D   16 ἀδύνατον διὰ λόγων μόνων ἐξηγεῖσθαι coni. Gale in notis : δυνατὸν μόνον διὰ λόγων Gale in textu : μόνον διὰ λόγων δυνατόν DM | ἐχόμενα addidi   17 τε καθαιρεῖσθαι Gale : τε καθαίρεσθαι Cᴾ : om. D : om. Bᴾ sed lacunam indicat | καθαιρεῖσθαι om. M vacuo relicto spatio 9 litt. | Lacunam signavi | αὐτῶν scripsi : αὐτῆς codd. | δυνατὸν scripsi : δύναται codd.   18 δύνασαι Gale, M : δύνασθαι Aᴾ : fortasse δυνήσῃ | σὺ M : σοὶ cett. | παράγεσθαι DMAᴾCᴾ : περιάγεσθαι Gale   19 περὶ om. AᴾCᴾ sed lacunam indicant   20 τούτων οὐδὲν Gale : τούτου οὐδὲν AᴾCᴾ : om. MBᴾ : om. D lacuna relicta | ἀπολλείψωμεν M | τελέαν Aᴾ   22 θεολογικῶς, τὰ δὲ θεουργικὰ θεουργικῶς om. MBᴾ : θεουργικὰ δὲ θεουργικῶς Gale : θεουργικῶς δὲ τὰ θεουργικὰ DAᴾCᴾ : τὰ δὲ θεουργικὰ θεουργικῶς scripsi | ἀποκρινούμεθα Gale : ἀποκρινόμεθα DM

μεθα, φιλοσόφως δὲ τὰ φιλόσοφα μετὰ σοῦ συνεξετάσομεν· καὶ τούτων
ὅσα μὲν εἰς τὰ πρῶτα αἴτια διήκει, ⌜κατὰ τὰς πρώτας ἀρχὰς⌝ συνακολουθοῦντες εἰς φῶς προάξομεν, ὅσα δὲ περὶ ἠθῶν ἢ περὶ τελῶν εἴρηται, κατὰ τὸν
ἠθικὸν τύπον διαιτήσομεν δεόντως, καὶ τἄλλα ὡσαύτως κατὰ τὸν οἰκεῖον
5 τρόπον ἐν τάξει διαθησόμεθα. ἤδη δὲ ἀψώμεθα τῶν σῶν ἐρωτήσεων.

φῂς τοίνυν πρῶτον κ.τ.λ.   **3**

τούτων δὲ ἀποστάς, ὡς φῄς, βούλει σοι δηλωθῆναι τί τὸ πρῶτον αἴτιον **8. 1 a**
ἡγοῦνται εἶναι Αἰγύπτιοι, πότερον νοῦν ἢ ὑπὲρ νοῦν, καὶ μόνον ἢ μετ' ἄλλου
ἢ ἄλλων, καὶ πότερον ἀσώματον ἢ σωματικόν, καὶ εἰ τῷ δημιουργῷ τὸ αὐτό
10 ἢ πρὸ τοῦ δημιουργοῦ, καὶ εἰ ἐξ ἑνὸς τὰ πάντα ἢ ἐκ πολλῶν, καὶ εἰ ὕλην
ἴσασιν ⌜ἢ σώματα ποιὰ πρῶτα⌝, καὶ ἀγέννητον ὕλην ἢ γεννητήν.

ἐγὼ δή σοι πρῶτον ἐρῶ τὴν αἰτίαν δι' ἣν ἔν τε ⟨τοῖς⟩ γράμμασι τῶν **b**
ἀρχαίων ἱερογραμματέων πολλαὶ καὶ ποικίλαι δόξαι περὶ τούτων φέρονται,
καὶ παρὰ τοῖς ἔτι ζῶσι ⌜τῶν σοφῶν τὰ μεγάλα⌝ οὐχ ἁπλῶς ὁ λόγος
15 παραδίδοται. λέγω δὴ οὖν ὡς, πολλῶν οὐσιῶν ὑπαρχουσῶν, καὶ τούτων
διαφερουσῶν παμπληθές, πολλαὶ παρεδόθησαν αὐτῶν καὶ ἀρχαί, διαφόρους
ἔχουσαι τάξεις, ἄλλαι παρ' ἄλλοις τῶν παλαιῶν ἱερέων. τὰς μὲν οὖν ὅλας
Ἑρμῆς ἐν ταῖς δισμυρίαις βίβλοις, ἃς Σέλευκος ἀπεγράψατο, ἢ ⌜ταῖς⌝
τρισμυρίαις τε καὶ ἑξακισχιλίαις καὶ πεντακοσίαις καὶ εἴκοσι πέντε, ὡς
20 Μανεθὼς ἱστορεῖ τελέως ἀνέδειξε· τὰς δ' ἐπὶ τῶν κατὰ μέρος οὐσιῶν
ἄλλοι ἄλλας διαλ όντες τῶν παλαιῶν πολλαχοῦ ⌜διερμηνεύουσι⌝. δεῖ
δὲ τἀληθὲς περὶ πασῶν ⌜ἀνευρεθῆναι⌝, συντόμως τε αὐτό σοι κατὰ τὸ
δυνατὸν διερμηνεῦσαι.

καὶ πρῶτον μέν, ὃ πρῶτον ἠρώτησας, περὶ τούτου ἄκουε. πρὸ τῶν ὄντως **2 a**
25 ὄντων καὶ τῶν ὅλων ἀρχῶν ἐστι θεὸς εἷς, πρότερος καὶ τοῦ πρώτου θεοῦ καὶ
βασιλέως, ἀκίνητος ἐν ⟨τῇ⟩ μονότητι τῆς ἑαυτοῦ ἑνότητος μένων· οὔτε
γὰρ νοητὸν αὐτῷ ἐπιπλέκεται οὔτε ἄλλο τι. παράδειγμα δὲ ἵδρυται τοῦ αὐτοπάτορος ⟨⟨καὶ⟩⟩ αὐτογόνου [[καὶ]] [μονοπάτορος] θεοῦ,[1] τοῦ ὄντως ἀγαθοῦ.
μεῖζον γάρ τι ⟨ὁ εἷς⟩, καὶ πρῶτον, καὶ πηγὴ τῶν πάντων, καὶ πυθμὴν

<hr />

1 συνεξετάσομεν· καὶ τούτων Gale: ἐξετάσομεν· καὶ τούτων M : συνε(om. ξετάσομεν
καὶ τούτων sed lacunam indicant) AᴾCᴾ   2 ὅσα μὲν Cᴾ : μὲν ὅσα Gale, MAᴾ
2-3 συνακολουθοῦντες Gale : συνεξακολουθοῦντες DM   4. τύπον Gale, FM :
τρόπον Bᴾ   7 ἀποστάς Gale, M: om. D   8 νοῦν (post πότερον) Gale:
οὖν MAᴾ   9 τὸ αὐτὸ scripsi : τὰ αὐτὰ codd.   11 σώματα ποιὰ DAᴾ : σωμα-
τοποιὰ Gale, M   12 πρότερον M | τοῖς addidi   14 παρὰ Gale : περὶ
DMAᴾBᴾCᴾ | τῶν σοφῶν τὰ μεγάλα secludendum !   16 διαφόρους Gale:
διαφόρως DMCᴾ   18 ἃς scripsi : ὡς codd. | ταῖς seclusi   20 Μανεθῶς F :
Μενεθὼς AᴾCᴾ | τὰ (corr. τὰς) M   21 διαλαβόντες coni. Gale in notis :
διαβάλλοντες codd.   22 δὴ Aᴾ   25 πρότερος Aᴾ : πρώτιος DMBᴾCᴾ :
πρῶτος Gale   25-26 Fortasse τοῦ πρωτ(ογόν)ου θεοῦ καὶ ⟨θεῶν⟩ βασιλέως
26 τῇ addidi   27 ἵδρυται ⟨οὗτος⟩?   27-28 αὐτοπάτορος καὶ αὐτογόνου θεοῦ
scripsi : αὐτοπάτορος αὐτογόνου καὶ μονοπάτορος θεοῦ codd.   28 ὄντως Gale :
ὄντος MCᴾ   29 ὁ εἷς addidi | Fort. πηγὴ [ ] καὶ πυθμὴν ⟨πάντων⟩ τῶν
νοουμένων

τῶν νοουμένων, πρὸ τῶν ἰδεῶν ὤν[των]· ⟨⟨αὐτὸς γὰρ τὸ προόντως ⟨ἀγαθ⟩όν
ἐστι, καὶ τῶν νοητῶν ἀρχή· διὸ καὶ νοητάρχης προσαγορεύεται.⟩⟩

b ἀπὸ δὲ τοῦ ἑνὸς τούτου ὁ [αὐτάρκης] ⟨⟨αὐτοπάτωρ⟩⟩ θεὸς ἑαυτὸν ἐξέλαμψε·
διὸ καὶ [[αὐτοπάτωρ]] [καὶ] αὐτάρχης ⟨ὀνομάζεται⟩. ἀρχὴ γὰρ οὗτος ⟨ἀρχῶν⟩,
καὶ θεὸς θεῶν, μονὰς ἐκ τοῦ ἑνός, προούσιος, καὶ ἀρχὴ τῆς οὐσίας· ἀπ' 5
αὐτοῦ γὰρ ἡ οὐσιότης καὶ ἡ οὐσία· διὸ καὶ οὐσιοπάτωρ καλεῖται. [[αὐτὸς
γὰρ τὸ προόντως ὄν ἐστι, τῶν νοητῶν ἀρχή· διὸ καὶ νοητάρχης προσαγορεύεται.]]

c αὗται μὲν οὖν εἰσιν ἀρχαὶ πρεσβύταται πάντων· ἃς Ἑρμῆς πρὸ τῶν
αἰθερίων καὶ ἐμπυρίων θεῶν προτάττει καὶ τῶν ἐπουρανίων, ἑκατὸν μὲν 10
περὶ τῆς ἱστορίας τῶν ἐμπυρίων, καὶ ἰσάριθμα τούτοις περὶ τῶν αἰθερίων
συγγράμματα παραδούς, χίλια δὲ περὶ τῶν ἐπουρανίων.

3 a κατ' ἄλλην δὲ τάξιν ⟨. . .⟩ προ[σ]τάττει θεὸν τὸν Κμήφ, [τῶν ἐπουρανίων θεῶν ἡγούμενον], ὅν φησι νοῦν εἶναι αὐτὸν ἑαυτὸν νοοῦντα καὶ τὰς
νοήσεις εἰς ἑαυτὸν ἐπιστρέφοντα· ⟨⟨ἐν ᾧ δὴ τὸ πρῶτόν ἐστι νοοῦν καὶ τὸ 15
b πρῶτον νοητόν.⟩⟩ τούτου δὲ τὸ ἓν ἀμερές, καὶ ὅ φησι πρῶτον μάγευμα,
προτάττει, ὃν καὶ Εἰχτὼν ἐπονομάζει [[ἐν ᾧ δὴ τὸ πρῶτόν ἐστι νοοῦν
c καὶ τὸ πρῶτον νοητόν]], ὃ δὴ καὶ διὰ σιγῆς μόνης θεραπεύεται. ἐπὶ
δὲ τούτοις ⟨τῆς⟩ τῶν ἐμφανῶν δημιουργίας ἄλλοι προεστήκασιν ἡγεμόνες. ὁ γὰρ δημιουργικὸς νοῦς, ⟨ὁ⟩ καὶ [τῆς] ἀληθείας προστάτης καὶ σοφίας, 20
ἐρχόμενος μὲν ἐπὶ γένεσιν, καὶ τὴν ἀφανῆ τῶν κεκρυμμένων λόγων
δύναμιν εἰς φῶς ἄγων, Ἀμοῦν κατὰ τὴν τῶν Αἰγυπτίων γλῶσσαν λέγεται,
συντελῶν δὲ ἀψευδῶς ἕκαστα καὶ τεχνικῶς μετ' ἀληθείας, Φθά,—Ἕλληνες
δὲ εἰς Ἥφαιστον μεταλαμβάνουσι τὸν Φθά, τῷ τεχνικῷ μόνῳ προσβάλλον-
τες,—ἀγαθῶν δὲ ποιητικὸς ὤν, Ὄσιρις κέκληται· καὶ ἄλλας δι' ἄλλας 25
δυνάμεις τε καὶ ἐνεργείας ἐπωνυμίας ἔχει.

---

1 πρὸ τῶν scripsi : πρώτων codd. | ἰδεῶν DMAᴾCᴾ : εἰδεῶν Bᴾ : εἰδῶν Gale
| ὤν scripsi : ὄντων codd. | αὐτὸς γὰρ (an οὗτος γὰρ ?) . . . προσαγορεύεται huc
a § 2 b fin. transposui | τὸ DMAᴾ : τε FCᴾ | προόντως FMAᴾCᴾ : παρόντως D
| ἀγαθόν scripsi : ὄν DMAᴾCᴾ : om. F   2 ἐστι· καὶ τῶν M : ἐστι τῶν D   3 δὲ
Gale : δὴ DMAᴾ | αὐτάρκης (perperam scriptum pro αὐτάρχης) seclusi :
αὐτοπάτωρ huc transposui   4 καὶ seclusi | αὐτάρχης Dᴾ (αὐτάρκης Parthey) :
ὀνομάζεται addidi | ἀρχῶν addidi   5 Fort. τοῦ ἑνός. προούσιος ⟨οὗτος⟩
6-7 διὸ καὶ οὐσιοπάτωρ . . . νοητῶν ἀρχή om. Gale   10 ἑκατῶν Aᴾ   11 ἐθε-
ρίων M   13 Lacunam signavi : fortasse πρὸ τοῦ δημιουργικοῦ νοῦ | προ-
τάττει coni. Gale in notis : προστάττει codd. | Κμήφ scripsi : ἡμήφ codd.
13-14 τῶν . . . ἡγούμενον seclusi   14 φησὶν M | αὐτὸν om. M   15 ἐν ᾧ . . .
νοητόν huc transposui | ἐν ᾧ codd. : fort. ὅς | νοῦν M   16 ἐν om. M
| καὶ ὅ codd. : fort. ὁ καὶ | μάγευμα codd. : μαίευμα coni. Gale in notis :
fortasse μάγμα | καὶ . . . μάγευμα secludendum ?   17 ὃν codd. : fortasse ὁ
| εἰχτὼν vel εἰχταν DMCᴾ : Εἰχτὼν Gale   19 τῆς addidi | δημιουργίαν
Bᴾ | ἄλλη M   20 ὁ καὶ scripsi : καὶ τῆς codd. | σοφίας Gale : σοφία
DMCᴾ   21 ἀρχόμενος D   22 Ἀμοῦν D : ἀμοῦν AᴾCᴾ : Ἀμῶν Gale :
ἀμῶν M   23 δὴ M | Φθά Gale : φασὶν Φθὰ Aᴾ : φασὶν (om. Φθά) DMBᴾCᴾ
24 μόνῳ M : μόνον Gale   25 ἀγαθὸν D | ποιητικῶς M : ποιητικοὶ Cᴾ
| κέκτηται M

ἔστι δὴ οὖν καὶ ἄλλη τις ἡγεμονία παρ' αὐτοῖς τῶν περὶ γένεσιν ⌐ὅλων⌐ d
στοιχείων καὶ τῶν ἐν αὐτοῖς δυνάμεων, τεττάρων μὲν ἀρρενικῶν τεττάρων δὲ
θηλυκῶν, ἥντινα ἀπονέμουσιν ἡλίῳ· καὶ ἄλλη τῆς φύσεως ὅλης τῆς περὶ
γένεσιν ἀρχή, ἥντινα σελήνῃ διδόασι.

5 κατὰ μέρη τε διαλαμβάνοντες τὸν οὐρανὸν εἰς δύο μοίρας, ἢ τέτταρας, ἢ e
δώδεκα, ἢ ἓξ καὶ τριάκοντα, ἢ διπλασίας τούτων, ἢ ἄλλως ὁπωσοῦν αὐτὸν
διαιροῦντες, ἡγεμόν[ι]ας καὶ τούτων προτάττουσι πλείονας ἢ ἐλάττονας,
⌐πᾶσι δὲ αὐτὸν⌐ ὑπερέχοντα αὐτῶν ἕνα προτιθέασι.

καὶ οὕτως ἄνωθεν ἄχρι τῶν τελευταίων ἡ περὶ τῶν ἀρχῶν Αἰγυπτίοις f
10 πραγματεία ἀφ' ἑνὸς ἄρχεται, καὶ πρόεισιν εἰς πλῆθος, τῶν πολλῶν αὖθις
ὑφ' ἑνὸς διακυβερνωμένων, καὶ πανταχοῦ τῆς ἀορίστου φύσεως ἐπικρατουμένης ὑπό τινος ὡρισμένου μέτρου καὶ τῆς ἀνωτάτω ἑνιαίας πάντων
αἰτίας.

ὕλην δὲ παρήγαγεν ὁ θεός, ἀπὸ τῆς οὐσιότητος ⌐ὑποσχισθείσης⌐ ὑλό- g
15 τητος, ἣν παραλαβὼν ὁ δημιουργός, ζωτικὴν οὖσαν, τὰς ⟨μὲν⟩ [ἁπλᾶς
καὶ] ἀπαθεῖς σφαίρας ἀπ' αὐτῆς ἐδημιούργησε, τὸ δὲ ἔσχατον αὐτῆς εἰς
τὰ γεννητὰ καὶ φθαρτὰ σώματα διεκόσμησε.

διευκρινηθέντων δὴ οὖν τούτων οὕτως, καὶ τῶν ἐν τοῖς συγγράμμασιν οἷς 4 a
λέγεις περιτετυχηκέναι σαφής ἐστιν ἡ διάλυσις. τὰ μὲν γὰρ φερόμενα ὡς
20 Ἑρμοῦ Ἑρμαϊκὰς περιέχει δόξας, εἰ καὶ τῇ τῶν φιλοσόφων γλώττῃ
πολλάκις χρῆται· μεταγέγραπται γὰρ ἀπὸ τῆς Αἰγυπτίας γλώττης ὑπ'
ἀνδρῶν φιλοσοφίας οὐκ ἀπείρως ἐχόντων.

Χαιρήμων δέ, καὶ εἴ τινες ἄλλοι τῶν περὶ τὸν κόσμον ἅπτονται [πρώτων] b
αἰτίων, τὰς τελευταίας ἀρχὰς ἐξηγοῦνται· ὅσοι τε τοὺς πλανήτας, καὶ τὸν
25 ζῳδιακόν, τούς τε δεκανοὺς καὶ ὡροσκόπους, καὶ τοὺς λεγομένους κραταιοὺς
[καὶ] ἡγεμόνας παραδιδόασι, τὰς μεριστὰς τῶν ἀρχῶν διανομὰς ἀναφαίνουσι.

τά τε ἐν τοῖς σαλμεσχινιακοῖς μέρος τι βραχύτατον περιέχει τῶν Ἑρμαϊκῶν c
διατάξεων· καὶ τὰ περὶ ἀστέρων [ἢ] φάσεων καὶ κρύψεων καὶ σελήνης αὐξή-
σεων καὶ μειώσεων ἐν τοῖς ἐσχάτοις ⌐εἶχε⌐ τῆς παρ' Αἰγυπτίοις αἰτιολογίας.

1 ὅλων Gale, M : ὅλως Bᵖ : secludendum ? 2 ἀρρενικῶν DMAᵖCᵖ : ἀρσε-
νικῶν Gale 4 ἀρχὴ D : ἀρχῆς Gale, M 5 κατὰ Gale, M : καὶ τὰ Cᵖ :
καὶ τὰ μὲν κατὰ F 6 αὐτὸν scripsi : αὐτὰς codd. 6–7 ἢ ἄλλως ... καὶ
τούτων om. M : haec eadem omittit Gale in textu, sed in notis scribit ' Adde ex
aliis, ἢ ἄλλως ὁπωσοῦν αὐτὰς διαιροῦντες, ἡγεμονίας καὶ τούτων προτάττουσι'
7 ἡγεμόνας scripsi : ἡγεμονίας codd. 8 πᾶσι Gale, M : πάλιν Aᵖ 11 διακυ-
βερνομένων DAᵖ | τῆς D (et M ?) : τοῦ Gale 12 ὁρισμένου M | ἐνίαις D
14 παρήγαγον Cᵖ | Fortasse ὁ ⟨πρῶτος⟩ θεός | ὑποσχισθείσης Gale : ἀποσχι-
σθείσης M 15 μὲν addidi 15–16 ἁπλᾶς καὶ seclusi 16 Fortasse ἀπ⟨ὸ
τοῦ καθαρωτέρου⟩ αὐτῆς 17 ἄφθαρτα M 23 Χαιρήμων Gale : Χαιρημὴν D :
χαιρήμην M : χαιρὴ μὴν Cᵖ | εἴτινες Gale : οἴτινες DMAᵖCᵖ | τὸν om. M
πρώτων seclusi 24 Post αἰτίαν addit εἰ Aᵖ 26 καὶ seclusi (cf. Porphyr. ap.
Euseb. Praep. Ev. 3. 4. 1) | παραδιδόασι DM : παραδίδωσι Gale 27 σαλμε-
σχινιακοῖς DMBᵖCᵖ : σαλαμινιακοῖς Aᵖ : ἀλμενιχιακοῖς Porphyr. ap. Euseb. 28 ἢ
seclusi | Fortasse φάνσεων vel φαύσεων 28–29 καὶ ter scripsi : ἢ ter codd.
29 εἶχε codd. : fortasse κεῖται | τῆς ... αἰτιολογίας scripsi : τὴν ... αἰτιολογίαν codd.

d φυσικά τε οὐ λέγουσιν εἶναι πάντα Αἰγύπτιοι, ἀλλὰ καὶ τὴν τῆς ψυχῆς
ζωὴν καὶ τὴν νοερὰν ἀπὸ τῆς φύσεως διακρίνουσιν, οὐκ ἐπὶ τοῦ παντὸς
μόνον, ἀλλὰ καὶ ἐφ' ἡμῶν· νοῦν τε καὶ λόγον προστησάμενοι καθ' ἑαυτοὺς
ὄντας, οὕτως δημιουργεῖσθαί φασι τὰ γιγνόμενα. προπάτορά τε ⟨πρὸ τοῦ⟩
τῶν ἐν γενέσει δημιουργοῦ προτάττουσι, καὶ τὴν πρὸ τοῦ οὐρανοῦ καὶ τὴν 5
ἐν τῷ οὐρανῷ ζωτικὴν δύναμιν ⟨δια⟩γιγνώσκουσι· καθαρόν τε νοῦν ὑπὲρ
τὸν κόσμον προτιθέασι, καὶ ἕνα ἀμέριστον ἐν ὅλῳ τῷ κόσμῳ, καὶ διῃρημένον
ἐπὶ πάσας τὰς σφαίρας ἕτερον.

e καὶ ταῦτα οὐδὲ λόγῳ ψιλῷ θεωροῦσιν, ἀλλὰ καὶ διὰ τῆς ἱερατικῆς
θεουργίας ἀναβαίνειν ἐπὶ τὰ ὑψηλότερα καὶ καθολικώτερα καὶ τῆς 10
εἱμαρμένης ὑπερκείμενα παραγγέλλουσι πρὸς τὸν θεὸν καὶ δημιουργόν,
μήτε ὕλην προσποιουμένους μήτε ἄλλο τι προσπαραλαμβάνοντας ἢ μόνον
καιροῦ παρατήρησιν.

5 a ὑφηγήσατο δὲ καὶ ταύτην τὴν ὁδὸν Ἑρμῆς, ⟨. . .⟩ ἡρμήνευσε δὲ Βίτυς
προφήτης [Ἄμμωνι βασιλεῖ], ἐν ἀδύτοις εὑρὼν ἀναγεγραμμένην ἐν ἱερογλυ- 15
φικοῖς γράμμασι κατὰ Σάϊν τὴν ἐν Αἰγύπτῳ. [τό τε τοῦ θεοῦ ὄνομα παρέδωκε
τὸ διῆκον δι' ὅλου τοῦ κόσμου]. εἰσὶ δὲ καὶ ἄλλαι πολλαὶ περὶ αὐτῶν
συντάξεις.

b ὥστε οὐκ ὀρθῶς μοι δοκεῖς πάντα ἐπὶ φυσικὰ ἀνάγειν αἴτια τὰ παρ'
Αἰγυπτίοις. εἰσὶ γὰρ ἀρχαὶ παρ' αὐτοῖς πλείονες καὶ περὶ πλειόνων οὐσιῶν, 20
ὑπερκόσμιοί τε δυνάμεις, ἃς καὶ διὰ τῆς ἱερατικῆς ἁγιστείας ἐθεράπευσαν.

c ἐμοὶ μὲν οὖν κοινὰς ταῦτα δοκεῖ παρέχεσθαι ἀφορμὰς εἰς τὴν διάλυσιν
καὶ τῶν μετὰ ταῦτα ἐπιζητουμένων ὅλων. ἀλλ' ἐπεὶ δεῖ μηδὲν ἀνεξέταστον
αὐτῶν παραλιπεῖν, προσιστώμεθα καὶ τούτοις τοῖς προβλήμασι, περικρούσωμέν τε αὐτὰ πανταχόθεν, ἵν' εἰδῶμεν εἴ πη σαθρόν τι διαδοξάζει. 25

6 a λέγεις τοίνυν ὡς Αἰγυπτίων οἱ πλείους καὶ τὸ ἐφ' ἡμῖν ἐκ τῆς τῶν
ἀστέρων ἀνῆψαν κινήσεως. τὸ δὲ πῶς ἔχει, δεῖ διὰ πλειόνων ἀπὸ τῶν
Ἑρμαϊκῶν σοι ⌜νοημάτων⌝ διερμηνεῦσαι. δύο γὰρ ἔχει ψυχάς, ὡς ταὐτά
φησι τὰ γράμματα, ὁ ἄνθρωπος· καὶ ἡ μέν ἐστιν ἀπὸ τοῦ πρώτου νοητοῦ,

2-3 Fortasse οὐκ ἐφ' ἡμῶν μόνον, ἀλλὰ καὶ ἐπὶ τοῦ παντός   4 πρὸ τοῦ addidi
5 δημιουργοῦ scripsi : δημιουργὸν codd.   6 διαγιγνώσκουσι scripsi : γιγνώσκουσι
vel γινώσκουσι codd.   9 οὐδὲ λόγῳ ψιλῷ Aᵖ : οὐδόλως ψιλῷ M : οὐδ' ὅλως
ψιλῷ F : ⟨οὐδ' ὅλως?⟩ ψιλῷ BᵖCᵖ : οὐδ' ὅλως ψιλῷ λόγῳ Gale | διὰ Gale : ἐπὶ
DMAᵖCᵖ   10 ὑψιλότερα D   11 παραγγέλουσι Aᵖ   12-13 ἢ μόνον
καιροῦ παρατήρησιν secludendum?   14 Lacunam signavi | Βίτυς Gale :
βίτις M   15 Ἄμμωνι (Ἄμμονι Aᵖ) βασιλεῖ seclusi   16 Σάϊν Gale : σῶϊν
Cᵖ : σαῖν (σῶιν man. post.) M   16-17 τό τε . . . κόσμου seclusi   17 περὶ
αὐτῶν Gale, M : περὶ τῶν αὐτῶν AᵖCᵖ : fortasse περὶ τούτων   19 αἴτια τὰ παρ'
Gale : αἴτια παρ' M   20 εἰσὶ γὰρ Gale, M : εἰσί τε γὰρ AᵖCᵖ   22 κοινὰς
codd. : fortasse ἱκανὰς   23 ἐπιζητουμένων Gale : ἐπεξητημένων DAᵖCᵖ : ἐπιζητη-
μένων MBᵖ | ἐπεὶ δεῖ Gale : ἐπεὶ δεῖ M : ἐπειδὴ D ·   24 παραλειπεῖν M
| προσιστώμεθα DMAᵖCᵖ : προστιθώμεθα Gale | καὶ secludendum?   25 εἴ
πη scripsi : ὅπη Gale : ὅπη M | διαδοξάζει Gale : διασώζει M   27 ἀστέρων
Gale : ἀέρων M : ἀέρων (corr. ἀστέρων) Cᵖ | ἀνῆψαι M   28 σοι om. M
| νοημάτων Gale, M : fortasse ὑπομνημάτων vel ἀπομνημονευμάτων

μετέχουσα καὶ τῆς τοῦ δημιουργοῦ δυνάμεως, ἡ δὲ ἐνδιδομένη ἐκ τῆς τῶν
οὐρανίων περιφορᾶς, εἰς ἣν ἐπεισέρπει ἡ θεοπτικὴ ψυχή.

τούτων δὴ οὕτως ἐχόντων, ἡ μὲν ἀπὸ τῶν κόσμων εἰς ἡμᾶς καθήκουσα b
ψυχὴ ταῖς περιόδοις συνακολουθεῖ τῶν κόσμων· ἡ δὲ ἀπὸ τοῦ νοητοῦ, νοητῶς
5 παροῦσα, τῆς γενεσιουργοῦ κυκλήσεως ὑπερέχει, καὶ κατ' αὐτὴν ἥ τε λύσις
γίνεται τῆς εἱμαρμένης καὶ ἡ πρὸς τοὺς νοητοὺς θεοὺς ἄνοδος, θεουργία τε,
ὅση πρὸς τὸ ἀγέννητον ἀνάγε[τα]ι, κατὰ τὴν τοιαύτην ζωὴν ἀποτελεῖται.

《⌜ἀλλ' οὐδὲ πᾶν δέχεται ἐν τῇ φύσει τῆς εἱμαρμένης⌝. ἀλλ' ἔστι 7《《c》》
καὶ ἑτέρα τῆς ψυχῆς ἀρχή, κρείττων πάσης φύσεως καὶ γενέσεως, καθ' ἣν
10 καὶ θεοῖς ἑνοῦσθαι δυνάμεθα καὶ τῆς κοσμικῆς τάξεως ὑπερέχειν, ἀιδίου τε
ζωῆς καὶ τῶν ὑπερουρανίων θεῶν τῆς ἐνεργείας μετέχειν. κατὰ δὴ ταύτην
οἷοί τέ ἐσμεν καὶ ἑαυτοὺς λύειν· ὅταν γὰρ δὴ τὰ βελτίονα τῶν ἐν ἡμῖν
ἐνεργῇ, καὶ πρὸς τὰ κρείττονα ἀνάγηται [αὐτῆς] ἡ ψυχή, τότε χωρίζεται
παντάπασι τῶν κατεχόντων αὐτὴν εἰς τὴν γένεσιν, καὶ ἀφίσταται τῶν
15 χειρόνων, ζωήν τε ἑτέραν ἀνθ' ἑτέρας ἀλλάττεται, καὶ δίδωσιν ἑαυτὴν εἰς
ἄλλην διακόσμησιν, τὴν προτέραν ἀφεῖσα παντελῶς.》》

οὐκέτι δὴ οὖν, ὃ σὺ ἀπορεῖς, δεσμοῖς ἀλύτοις ἀνάγκης, ἣν εἱμαρμένην a
καλοῦμεν, ἐνδέδεται πάντα· ἔχει γὰρ ἀρχὴν οἰκείαν ἡ ψυχὴ τῆς εἰς τὸ
νοητὸν περιαγωγῆς, καὶ τῆς ἀποστάσεως μὲν ἀπὸ τῶν γιγνομένων, ἐπὶ δὲ
20 τὸ ὂν καὶ τὸ θεῖον συναφῆς.

οὐδ' αὖ τοῖς θεοῖς τὴν εἱμαρμένην ἀνήψαμεν οὓς ὡς λυτῆρας τῆς b
εἱμαρμένης ἔν τε ἱεροῖς καὶ ξοάνοις θεραπεύομεν· ἀλλ' οἱ μὲν θεοὶ λύουσι
τὴν εἱμαρμένην, αἱ δ' ἀπ' αὐτῶν ἔσχαται φύσεις καθήκουσαι, καὶ
συμπλεκόμεναι τῇ γενέσει τοῦ κόσμου καὶ τῷ σώματι, τὴν εἱμαρμένην
25 ἐπιτελοῦσιν. εἰκότως ἄρα τοῖς θεοῖς ἁγιστείαν πᾶσαν προσάγομεν, ὅπως
ἂν ⌜μόνοι διὰ πειθοῦς νοερᾶς⌝ τῆς ἀνάγκης ἄρχοντες τὰ ἀπὸ τῆς εἱμαρμένης
ἀποκείμενα κακὰ ἀπολύωσιν.

[[ἀλλ' οὐδὲ πᾶν δέχεται ... ἀφεῖσα παντελῶς.]]   [[c]]

τί οὖν; οἷόν τέ ἐστι διὰ τῶν πολευόντων θεῶν λύειν ἑαυτόν; ⟨. . .⟩ καὶ 8 a
30 τοὺς αὐτοὺς ἡγεῖσθαι μοιρηγέτας καὶ δεσμοῖς ἀλύτοις τὸν βίον δεσμεύοντας;
κωλύει μὲν ἴσως οὐδὲν καὶ τοῦτο, εἰ τῶν θεῶν πολλὰς περιεχόντων οὐσίας καὶ
δυνάμεις [ἐν ἑαυτοῖς], ἐνυπάρχουσιν ἐν αὐτοῖς [ἄλλαι τε] ἀμήχανοι ὅσαι

---

2 εἰς ἣν . . . ψυχή secludendum ?   3 δὴ Gale : δὲ MAᵖ   4 κόσμων codd. :
fortasse ἄστρων   5 κυκλήσεως AᵖCᵖ : κινήσεως Gale : κλήσεως DM : κυκλώ-
σεως F   7 ἀνάγει scripsi : ἀνάγεται codd. | τοιαύτην codd. : fortasse ταύτης
8 § 7 c (ἀλλ' οὐδὲ . . . ἀφεῖσα παντελῶς) huc transposui | πᾶν δέχεται DMCᵖ :
πᾶν δέδεται Aᵖ : πάντα ἔχεται Gale : fortasse [ἀλλ'] οὐ δὴ πάντα δέδεται [ἐν
τῇ φύσει] τῇ εἱμαρμένῃ   9 γενέσεως Aᵖ : γνώσεως DMCᵖ : γεννήσεως Gale
10 ἀιδίων M   13 αὐτῆς seclusi   14 τὴν om. M   17 ἀνάγκην M   19 ἐπὶ δὲ
Gale : ἐπειδὲ M   21 οὐδ' αὖ τοῖς DM : οὐδ' αὐτοῖς Gale : fortasse οὐδ(ὲ τοῖς) αὐτοῖς
vel οὐδ' αὐτοῖς ⟨τοῖς⟩   24 συμπεκόμεναι M   29 Lacunam signavi   30 τὸν
βίον scripsi : τοὺς βίους codd.   32 ἐν ἑαυτοῖς seclusi | ἄλλαι τε seclusi

διαφοραὶ καὶ ἐναντιώσεις. οὐ μὴν ἀλλὰ καὶ τοῦτο ἔνεστι λέγειν, ὡς ἐν
ἑκάστῳ τῶν θεῶν, καὶ τῶν ἐμφανῶν, εἰσί τινες [οὐσίας] νοηταὶ ἀρχαί, δι'
ὧν γίνεται ἡ ἀπὸ τῆς γενέσεως [τῶν κόσμων] ταῖς ψυχαῖς ἀπαλλαγή.
εἰ δ' ἄρα τις καὶ δύο γένη περικοσμίων τε καὶ ὑπερκοσμίων θεῶν ἀπολείποι,
διὰ τῶν ὑπερκοσμίων ἔσται ταῖς ψυχαῖς ἀπόλυσις.   5

b   ταῦτα μὲν οὖν ἐν τοῖς περὶ θεῶν ἀκριβέστερον λέγεται, τίνες τέ εἰσιν
ἀναγωγοὶ καὶ κατὰ ποίας αὐτῶν δυνάμεις, πῶς τε τὴν εἱμαρμένην λύουσι,
καὶ διὰ τίνων ἱερατικῶν ἀνόδων, τάξις τε ὁποία τῆς κοσμικῆς ἐστι φύσεως,
καὶ ὅπως ἡ νοερὰ ταύτης ἐπικρατεῖ ⌜τελειοτάτη⌝ ἐνέργεια.

c   ὥστε οὐδ' ὅπερ ἐκ τῶν Ὁμηρικῶν σὺ παρέθηκας, τὸ στρεπτοὺς εἶναι τοὺς   10
θεούς, ὅσιόν ἐστι φθέγγεσθαι. νόμοις γὰρ ἀχράντοις [καὶ νοεροῖς]
ὥρισται πάλαι τὰ ἔργα τῆς ἱερᾶς ἁγιστείας· τάξει τε μείζονι καὶ δυνάμει
λύεται τὰ καταδεέστερα, εἰς βελτίονά τε μεθισταμένων ἡμῶν λῆξιν
ἀπόστασις γίνεται τῶν καταδεεστέρων· καὶ οὐ παρὰ τὸν ἐξ ἀρχῆς τι
θεσμὸν ἐπιτελεῖται ⌜ἐν τῷ τοιῷδε⌝, ἵνα μεταστραφῶσιν οἱ θεοὶ κατὰ τὴν   15
ὕστερον γιγνομένην ἱερουργίαν, ἀλλ' ἀπὸ τῆς πρώτης καθόδου ἐπὶ τούτῳ
κατέπεμψεν ὁ θεὸς τὰς ψυχάς, ἵνα πάλιν εἰς αὐτὸν ἐπανέλθωσιν. οὔτε οὖν
μεταβολή τις γίνεται διὰ τῆς τοιαύτης ἀναγωγῆς, οὔτε μάχονται αἱ κάθοδοι
τῶν ψυχῶν καὶ αἱ ἄνοδοι. ὥσπερ γὰρ ἐν τῷ παντὶ τῇ νοερᾷ οὐσίᾳ ἡ
γένεσις καὶ τὸ πᾶν τόδε συνήρτηται, οὕτω καὶ ἐν τῇ τῶν ψυχῶν διακοσμήσει   20
τῇ περὶ γένεσιν αὐτῶν ⌜ἐπιμελείᾳ⌝ συμφωνεῖ καὶ ἡ ἀπὸ γενέσεως λύσις.

I a   λείπεται δὴ τελευταῖος ὁ περὶ εὐδαιμονίας λόγος, περὶ οὗ σὺ ποικίλως
ἐπεζήτησας, τὰ μὲν πρῶτα ἐπιστάσεις ὑποτείνων, ἔπειτα ἀπορῶν, καὶ μετὰ
ταῦτα διαπυνθανόμενος. θέντες οὖν ἕκαστα τῶν σῶν ᾗπερ αὐτὰ προήγαγες,
ἀποκρινούμεθά σοι πρὸς αὐτὰ συμμέτρως.   25

b   ἐπέστησας γὰρ μήποτε ἄλλη τις λανθάνῃ οὖσα ἡ πρὸς εὐδαιμονίαν
ὁδός. καὶ τίς ἂν γένοιτο ἑτέρα, ἀφισταμένη τῶν θεῶν, εὔλογος πρὸς
αὐτὴν ἄνοδος; εἰ γὰρ ἐν τοῖς θεοῖς ἡ οὐσία τῶν ἀγαθῶν ὅλων καὶ τελειότης
περιέχεται, καὶ ἡ πρώτη δύναμις αὐτῶν καὶ ἀρχή, παρὰ μόνοις ἡμῖν, καὶ
τοῖς ὁμοίως ἐχομένοις τῶν κρειττόνων γνησίως τε τῆς πρὸς αὐτοὺς ἑνώσεως   30
ἀντιλαμβανομένοις, ἡ τῶν ἀγαθῶν ὅλων ἀρχὴ καὶ τελευτὴ σπουδαίως
ἐπιτηδεύεται. ἐνταῦθα δὴ οὖν καὶ ἡ τῆς ἀληθείας πάρεστι θέα καὶ ἡ τῆς

1 ἐν om. Cᴾ   2 οὐσίας seclusi   3 ἡ D: om. Gale et M | τῶν κόσμων
seclusi | ἀπαλλαγή Gale, M: ἡ ἀπόλυσις AᴾCᴾ   4 ἡ δ' M   7 πᾶς Bᴾ:
πῶς cett.   8 ἀνόων Aᴾ   9 τελειοτάτη secludendum? An legendum καὶ
ὅπως ἡ νοερὰ ⟨τάξις vel οὐσία⟩ ταύτης ἐπικρατεῖ τελειοτέρᾳ ἐνεργείᾳ!   11 αἰσχράν-
τοις D | καὶ νοεροῖς seclusi   12–14 τάξει τε μείζονι ... τῶν καταδεεστέρων
secludendum!   14 τὸν] τῶν M   15 οἱ θεοὶ om. M   15–16 τὴν ὕστερον M,
Gale: τὴν εἰς ὕστερον AᴾCᴾ   16 ἀλλ' ἀπὸ Gale: ἀλλὰ πῇ (!) M   19 Post
ψυχῶν scriptum et deletum habet ἐν τῷ παντὶ νοερὰ οὐσία M | γὰρ ἐν scripsi:
γὰρ καὶ ἐν Gale: ἐν (om. γὰρ καὶ) M | τῇ νοερᾷ Gale: τῇ νοερὰ M: νοερῷ τῇ Aᴾ
21 Fortasse τῇ περὶ γένεσιν αὐτῶν (sc. τῶν ψυχῶν ἐπιπλοκῇ)   26 ἡ secludendum!
27 ἀφισταμένοις!

νοερᾶς ἐπιστήμης ⟨. . .⟩. καὶ μετὰ τῆς τῶν θεῶν γνώσεως ἡ πρὸς
ἑαυτοὺς ἐπιστροφὴ καὶ ἡ γνῶσις ἑαυτῶν συνέπεται.

μάτην οὖν διαπορεῖς ⟨. . .⟩ ὡς οὐ δεῖ πρὸς δόξας ἀνθρωπίνας βλέπειν. **2a**
τίς γὰρ σχολὴ τῷ πρὸς τοῖς θεοῖς τὴν διάνοιαν ἔχοντι κάτω βλέπειν εἰς
5 ἀνθρώπων ἐπαίνους;

ἀλλ' οὐδὲ τὸ ἐπὶ τούτῳ πρὸς ἔπος ἐπαπορεῖς, ὡς ἡ ψυχὴ ἐκ τοῦ τυχόντος **b**
ἀναπλάττει μεγάλα. τίς γὰρ δὴ ἐν τοῖς ὄντως οὖσι πλασμάτων ἀρχὴ
συνίσταται; οὐχ ἡ μὲν φανταστικὴ δύναμις ἐν ἡμῖν ἐστιν εἰδωλοποιός,
φαντασία δ' οὐδεμία ἐγείρεται τῆς νοερᾶς ζωῆς τελείως ἐνεργούσης; οὐ
10 [παρὰ] τοῖς θεοῖς συνυπάρχει ἡ ἀλήθεια, κατ' οὐσίαν, ἀλλ' οὐχὶ κατὰ
συμφωνίαν, ἐνιδρυμένη τοῖς νοητοῖς; εἰκῆ τοίνυν τὰ τοιαῦτα καὶ παρὰ σοὶ
καὶ παρ' ἄλλοις τισὶ θρυλεῖται.

ἀλλ' οὐδὲ ὅσα ὡς ἀγύρτας καὶ ἀλαζόνας διασύρουσί τινες τοὺς τῶν θεῶν **c**
θεραπευτάς, οἷς καὶ σὺ παραπλήσια εἴρηκας, οὐδὲν οὐδὲ ταῦτα ἅπτεται τῆς
15 ἀληθινῆς θεολογίας τε καὶ θεουργίας. εἰ δέ πού τινες παραφύονται
τοιοῦτοι παρὰ τὰς τῶν ἀγαθῶν ἐπιστήμας, ὥσπερ καὶ παρὰ τὰς ἄλλας
τέχνας αἱ κακοτεχνίαι παραβλαστάνουσιν, ἐναντιώτεραι δήπου αὗται πρὸς
αὐτὰς ὑπάρχουσι μᾶλλον ἢ πρὸς ἄλλο ὁτιοῦν· τῷ γὰρ ἀγαθῷ τὸ κακὸν
διαμάχεται μᾶλλον ἢ τῷ μὴ ἀγαθῷ.

20 βούλομαι δὴ τὸ μετὰ τοῦτο καὶ τὰ ἄλλα ἐπιδραμεῖν, ὅσα διαβάλλων **3**
τὴν θείαν πρόγνωσιν, ἄλλας τινὰς μεθόδους αὐτῇ παραβάλλεις περὶ τὴν
τοῦ μέλλοντος προμήνυσιν διατριβούσας. ἐμοὶ γὰρ οὔτε εἴ τις ἐκ φύσεως
ἐπιτηδειότης εἰς σημασίαν τοῦ ἐσομένου παραγίνεται, ὥσπερ ἡ τοῖς
ζώοις τῶν σεισμῶν ἢ τῶν ἀνέμων ἢ τῶν χειμώνων συμπίπτει πρόγνωσις,
25 τίμιος εἶναι δοκεῖ· κατ' αἰσθήσεως γὰρ ὀξύτητα ἢ κατὰ συμπάθειαν **ἢ**
κατ' ἄλλην τινὰ φυσικῶν δυνάμεων συγκίνησιν ἡ τοιαύτη ἔμφυτος συνέπεται
μαντεία, οὐδὲν ἔχουσα σεμνὸν καὶ ὑπερφυές· οὔτε εἴ τις κατὰ λογισμὸν
ἀνθρώπινον ἢ τεχνικὴν παρατήρησιν ἀπὸ σημείων τεκμηριοῦται ἐκεῖνα ὧν
ἐστι τὰ σημεῖα δηλωτικά, ὡς ἀπὸ συστολῆς ἢ φρίκης τὸν μέλλοντα πυρετὸν
30 προγινώσκουσιν οἱ ἰατροί, οὐδὲν οὐδὲ οὗτός μοι δοκεῖ τίμιον ἔχειν καὶ
ἀγαθόν. ἀνθρωπίνως τε γὰρ ἐπιβάλλει καὶ συλλογίζεται τῇ ἡμετέρᾳ
διανοίᾳ, περί τε τῶν ἐν τῇ φύσει, τοῖς γιγνομέ<ν>οις ὁμολογουμένως, οὐ
πόρρω τῆς σωματοειδοῦς τάξεως ποιεῖται τὴν διάγνωσιν. ὥστε οὐδ' εἰ
φυσική τις ἔνεστιν ἐν ἡμῖν ἐπιβολὴ τοῦ μέλλοντος, ὥσπερ καὶ ἐν τοῖς
35 ἄλλοις ἅπασιν ἡ δύναμις ἥδε ἐναργῶς ἐνεργοῦσα διαφαίνεται, οὐδὲν οὐδὲ
αὕτη μακαριστὸν τῷ ὄντι κέκτηται· τί γὰρ ἂν εἴη γνήσιον καὶ τέλειον καὶ
ἀΐδιον ἀγαθὸν τῶν ὑπὸ τῆς φύσεως τῆς ἐν γενέσει εἰς ἡμᾶς ἐμφυομένων;

1 ἐπιστήμης] τελειότης Aᵖ: fortasse ἐπιστήμη τελειότης   10 παρά seclusi
15–16 τε καὶ θεουργίας . . . ὥσπερ] τε καὶ φιλοσοφίας, ἀλλ' ὥσπερ Aᵖ ceteris omissis:
τε, ὥσπερ Cᵖ ceteris omissis   20 τὸ secludendum!   23 Ante εἰς add.
τῷ Aᵖ | ἢ secludendum!

4 a   μόνη τοίνυν ἡ θεία μαντικὴ συναπτομένη τοῖς θεοῖς ὡς ἀληθῶς ἡμῖν τῆς
θείας ζωῆς μεταδίδωσι, τῆς τε προγνώσεως καὶ τῶν θείων νοήσεων μετέχουσα,
καὶ ἡμᾶς θείους ὡς ἀληθῶς ἀπεργάζεται, ἡ δὲ αὐτὴ καὶ τὸ ἀγαθὸν ἡμῖν
γνησίως παρέχει, διότι πεπλήρωται τῶν ἀγαθῶν ὅλων ἡ μακαριωτάτη τῶν
θεῶν νόησις.   5

b   οὐ τοίνυν προορῶσι μέν, ὡς σὺ τοπάζεις, οἱ ταύτην ἔχοντες τὴν μαντικήν,
οὐ μὴν εἰσιν εὐδαίμονες· ἀγαθοειδὴς γάρ ἐστι πᾶσα ἡ θεία πρόγνωσις.
οὐδὲ προορῶσι μὲν τὰ μέλλοντα, χρῆσθαι δὲ αὐτοῖς καλῶς οὐκ ἐπίστανται·
ἀλλ' αὐτὸ τὸ καλὸν καὶ τὴν τάξιν τὴν ἀληθῆ καὶ πρέπουσαν μετὰ τῆς
προγνώσεως παραδέχονται.   10

c   πάρεστι δ' αὐτῇ καὶ τὸ ὠφέλιμον· οἱ γὰρ θεοὶ καὶ δύναμιν τοῦ φυλάξασθαι
τὰ ἐπιόντα ἀπὸ τῆς φύσεως δεινὰ παραδιδόασι. καὶ ὅταν μὲν ἀσκεῖν δέῃ
τὴν ἀρετήν, καὶ συμβάλληται πρὸς τοῦτο ἡ τοῦ μέλλοντος ἀδηλία,
ἀποκρύπτουσι τὰ ἐσόμενα, ἕνεκα τοῦ τὴν ψυχὴν βελτίονα ἀπεργά-
ζεσθαι· ὅταν δὲ πρὸς τοῦτο μηδὲν διαφέρῃ, λυσιτελῇ δὲ ταῖς ψυχαῖς τὸ 15
προγινώσκειν, ἕνεκα τοῦ σώζειν αὐτὰς καὶ ἀνάγειν τὴν ἐν ταῖς μαντείαις
πρόγνωσιν ἐν μέσαις αὐτῶν ταῖς οὐσίαις ἐντιθέασιν.

5 a   ἀλλὰ τί ταῦτα ἀπομηκύνω, διὰ πολλῶν ἐν τοῖς ἔμπροσθεν τὸ τῆς θείας
μαντικῆς πρὸς τὴν ἀνθρωπίνην ἐπιδείξας ὑπερέχον; βέλτιον οὖν, ὅπερ
ἀπαιτεῖς παρ' ἡμῶν, τὴν εἰς εὐδαιμονίαν ὁδὸν ἐπιδεῖξαί σοι, καὶ ἐν τίνι 20
κεῖται ἡ αὐτῆς οὐσία· ἀπὸ γὰρ τούτου τό τε ἀληθὲς εὑρίσκεται, καὶ ἅμα τὰς
ἀπορίας πάσας ἔνεστι διαλύειν ῥᾳδίως.

b   λέγω τοίνυν ὡς ὁ ⌜θεατὸς νοούμενος⌝ ἄνθρωπος, ἡνωμένος τὸ πρόσθεν ⌜τῇ
θέᾳ τῶν θεῶν⌝, ἐπεισῆλθεν ἑτέρᾳ ψυχῇ τῇ περὶ τὸ ἀνθρώπινον μορφῆς εἶδος
συνηρμοσμένῃ, καὶ διὰ τοῦτο ἐν τῷ τῆς ἀνάγκης καὶ εἱμαρμένης ἐγένετο 25
δεσμῷ. σκοπεῖν δὴ δεῖ τίς αὐτοῦ γίνεται λύσις καὶ ἀπαλλαγὴ τῶν δεσμῶν.

c   ἔστι τοίνυν ⌜οὐκ ἄλλη τις ἢ⌝ τῶν θεῶν γνῶσις· ἰδέα γάρ ἐστιν
εὐδαιμονίας τὸ ἐπίστασθαι τὸ ἀγαθόν, ὥσπερ τῶν κακῶν ἰδέα συμβαίνει ἡ
λήθη τῶν ἀγαθῶν καὶ ἀπάτη [περὶ τὸ κακόν]. ἡ μὲν οὖν ⟨. . .⟩ τῷ
θείῳ σύνεστιν, ἡ δὲ χείρων μοῖρα ἀχώριστός ἐστι τοῦ θνητοῦ· καὶ ἡ μὲν 30
τὰς τῶν νοητῶν οὐσίας [ἱερατικαῖς ὁδοῖς] ἀναμετρεῖ, ἡ δέ, παρακρουσθεῖσα
τῶν ἀρχῶν, προΐησιν ἑαυτὴν ἐπὶ τὴν ⌜καταμέτρησιν⌝ τῆς τοῦ σώματος ἰδέας·
καὶ ἡ μὲν γνῶσίς ἐστι τοῦ πατρός, ἡ δὲ παραγωγὴ ἀπ' αὐτοῦ καὶ λήθη τοῦ
⌜προουσίου αὐταρχοῦντος πατρὸς⌝ θεοῦ· καὶ ἡ μὲν σώζει τὴν ἀληθινὴν

15 λυσιτελῇ scripsi : λυσιτελεῖ codd.   23 θεατὸς Aᴾ: θεωτὸς Gale (θεητὸς
in notis): θεοπτικὸς ? θεατικὸς ⟨τῶν θείων⟩ ? | τὸ scripsi : τῷ codd.   24 θεία Dᴾ
27 οὐκ om. Cᴾ: fortasse ἔστι τοίνυν [οὐκ] ἄλλη ⟨μέν⟩ τις ἢ   29 περὶ
τὸ κακόν seclusi   ⌜Lacunam significavi: supplendum τῶν θεῶν γνῶσις ?
31 ἱερατικαῖς ὁδοῖς seclusi: fortasse ἡ μὲν ⟨τὴν πρὸς⟩ τὰς τῶν νοητῶν οὐσίας [ ]
ὁδὸν ἀναμετρεῖ   34 αὐταρχοῦντος Cᴾ: αὐταρκοῦντος cett. | πατρὸς] πρὸς
Dᴾ | Fortasse ἡ μὲν γνῶσίς ἐστι τοῦ ⟨⟨αὐταρχοῦντος⟩⟩ πατρός, ἡ δὲ . . . λήθη τοῦ
προουσίου [[ ]] [ ] θεοῦ

ζωήν, ἐπὶ τὸν πατέρα αὐτῆς ἀνάγουσα, ἡ δὲ κατάγει τὸν ⌈γενάρχουντα⌉ ἄνθρωπον ἄχρι τοῦ μηδέποτε μένοντος ἀλλ᾽ ἀεὶ ῥέοντος.

αὕτη μὲν οὖν νοείσθω σοι πρώτη τῆς εὐδαιμονίας ὁδός, νοερὰν ἔχουσα τῆς θείας ἑνώσεως ἀποπλήρωσιν τῶν ψυχῶν.

5 ἡ δ᾽ ἱερατικὴ καὶ θεουργικὴ τῆς εὐδαιμονίας δόσις καλεῖται μὲν " θύρα d πρὸς θεὸν τὸν δημιουργὸν τῶν ὅλων ", ἢ " τόπος " ἢ " αὐλὴ τοῦ ἀγαθοῦ "· δύναμιν δ᾽ ἔχει πρῶτον μὲν ἁγνείαν τῆς ψυχῆς, πολὺ τελειοτέραν τῆς τοῦ σώματος ἁγνείας· ἔπειτα κατάρτυσιν τῆς διανοίας εἰς μετουσίαν καὶ θέαν τοῦ ἀγαθοῦ καὶ τῶν ἐναντίων πάντων ἀπαλλαγήν· μετὰ δὲ ταῦτα, πρὸς 10 τοὺς τῶν ἀγαθῶν δοτῆρας θεοὺς ἕνωσιν.

ἐπειδὰν δὲ κατ᾽ ἰδίαν ταῖς μοίραις τοῦ παντὸς συνάψῃ καὶ ταῖς διηκούσαις 6 a δι᾽ αὐτῶν ὅλαις θείαις δυνάμεσι, τότε τῷ ὅλῳ δημιουργῷ τὴν ψυχὴν προσάγει καὶ παρακατατίθεται, καὶ ἐκτὸς πάσης ὕλης αὐτὴν ποιεῖ, μόνῳ τῷ ἀιδίῳ λόγῳ συνηνωμένην.

15 ⌈οἷον δ᾽⌉ λέγω· τῇ αὐτογόνῳ ⟨δυνάμει⟩, καὶ τῇ αὐτοκινήτῳ, καὶ τῇ b ἀνεχούσῃ πάντα, καὶ τῇ νοερᾷ, καὶ τῇ διακοσμητικῇ τῶν ὅλων, καὶ τῇ πρὸς ἀλήθειαν τὴν νοητὴν ἀναγωγ⟨ικ⟩ῇ, καὶ τῇ αὐτοτελεῖ, καὶ τῇ ποιητικῇ, καὶ ταῖς ἄλλαις δημιουργικαῖς δυνάμεσι τοῦ θεοῦ κατ᾽ ἰδίαν συνάπτει, ὡς ἐν ταῖς ἐνεργείαις αὐτῶν καὶ ταῖς νοήσεσι [καὶ ταῖς δημιουργικαῖς] τελέως 20 ⟨ἐν⟩ίστασθαι τὴν θεουργικὴν ψυχήν· καὶ τότε δὴ ἐν ὅλῳ τῷ δημιουργικῷ θεῷ τὴν ψυχὴν ἐντίθησι. καὶ τοῦτο τέλος ἐστὶ τῆς παρ᾽ Αἰγυπτίοις ἱερατικῆς ἀναγωγῆς.

⌈αὐτὸ δὲ⌉ τἀγαθὸν τὸ μὲν θεῖον ἡγοῦνται τὸν προεννοούμενον θεόν, τὸ δὲ 7 a ἀνθρώπινον τὴν πρὸς αὐτὸν ἕνωσιν· ὅπερ Βίτυς ἐκ τῶν Ἑρμαϊκῶν βίβλων 25 μεθηρμήνευσεν.

οὐκ ἄρα παρεῖται τοῦτο τὸ μέρος τοῖς Αἰγυπτίοις, ὃ σὺ ὑπονοεῖς, ἀλλὰ b θεοπρόπως παρεδόθη. οὐδὲ περὶ σμικρῶν οἱ θεουργοὶ τὸν θεῖον νοῦν ἐνοχλοῦσιν, ἀλλὰ περὶ τῶν εἰς ψυχῆς κάθαρσιν καὶ ἀπόλυσιν καὶ σωτηρίαν ἀνηκόντων. οὐδὲ χαλεπὰ μὲν διαμελετῶσιν οὗτοι, ἄχρηστα δὲ 30 τοῖς ἀνθρώποις, ἀλλὰ τοὐναντίον τὰ τῇ ψυχῇ πάντων ὠφελιμώτατα. οὐδ᾽ ὑπὸ πλάνου τινὸς φενακίζονται δαίμονος οἱ ἐν πᾶσι τὴν ἀπατηλὴν καὶ δαιμονίαν φύσιν ἐπικρατήσαντες, ἐπὶ δὲ τὴν νοητὴν καὶ θείαν ἀναχθέντες.

τοσαῦτά σοι καθ᾽ ἡμετέραν δύναμιν ἀπεκρινάμεθα περὶ ὧν ἠπόρησας περὶ 8 a τῆς θείας μαντικῆς τε καὶ θεουργίας.

εὔχομαι δὴ οὖν τὸ λοιπὸν τοῖς θεοῖς ἐπὶ τῷ τέλει τῶν λόγων, τῶν ἀληθῶν b

1 ⟨τὴν ψυχὴν⟩ ἀνάγουσα? 3 πρώτη] πρὸ BP : ⟨ἡ⟩ πρώτη? 4 ⟨τὴν⟩ τῆς? 7 πρῶτον scripsi : πρώτην codd. 15 δυνάμει addidi 17 τῇ ⟨ἀγαθῶν⟩ ποιητικῇ? 19 ταῖς post καὶ secludendum? | καὶ ταῖς δημιουργικαῖς seclusi 20 ἐνίστασθαι scripsi : ἵστασθαι codd. 27 θεοπρόπως scripsi : θεοπρεπῶς codd.

νοημάτων ἐμοί τε καὶ σοὶ παρέχειν τὴν φυλακὴν ἀμετάπτωτον, εἴς τε τὸν
ἀίδιον αἰῶνα ⌜δι' αἰωνίων⌝ ἀλήθειαν ἐντιθέναι, καὶ τελειοτέρων νοήσεων περὶ
θεῶν χορηγεῖν μετουσίαν, ἐν αἷς δὴ τὸ μακαριστὸν τέλος τῶν ἀγαθῶν
ἡμῖν πρόκειται, καὶ ⌜αὐτὸ⌝ τὸ κῦρος τῆς ὁμονοητικῆς φιλίας τῆς πρὸς
ἀλλήλους.

                                                    5

         3 ἐν οἷς (sc. τοῖς θεοῖς)?

NOTES ON
ABAMMONIS AD PORPHYRIUM RESPONSUM
('*Iamblichi de mysteriis liber*')[1]

THE book commonly but incorrectly called '*Iamblichi de mysteriis
(Aegyptiorum) liber*' was written in reply to a letter addressed by
Porphyry to an Egyptian priest named Anebo. Porphyry's letter is
not extant; but extracts from it have been preserved by Eusebius
and others, and an epitome of some parts of it is given by Augustine
(*De civ. dei* 10. 11); and from these data, combined with those
supplied by the *De myst.* itself, it is possible to recover the substance
and meaning of the letter as a whole, though not to reconstruct the
actual text of it.[2] Porphyry asked for information about the theology
of the Egyptian priests, and the significance of their religious usages;
and his questions implied that there was much in their rituals and
theurgic practices that he found it difficult to reconcile with his
own beliefs. In Augustine's words, '(Porphyrius) consulenti similis
et quaerenti et prodit artes sacrilegas (Aegyptiorum) et evertit'.[3]

The Reply is ostensibly written by an Egyptian priest of high
standing, named Abammon; and its title, as given by the MSS., is
Ἀβάμ(μ)ωνος διδασκάλου πρὸς τὴν Πορφυρίου πρὸς Ἀνεβὼ ἐπιστολὴν
ἀπόκρισις, καὶ τῶν ἐν αὐτῇ ἀπορημάτων λύσεις (al. λύσις). But in some

---

[1] Greek text, Latin translation, and notes: T. Gale, Oxford 1678. Greek text.
and Latin translation: G. Parthey, Berlin 1857. German translation and notes:
Th. Hopfner, Leipzig 1922.

[2] Gale printed in his edition of the *De myst.* a reconstructed text of Porphyry's
letter, and this is reprinted by Parthey. But it is only in those sections of Gale's
text of the letter which he has transcribed from Eusebius and other Christian
writers that we have the very words which Porphyry wrote; the rest of it is made
up by putting together passages extracted from the Reply, in which things said by
Porphyry are probably given in a more or less altered and abbreviated form.

[3] Cf. Aug. *De civ. dei* 10. 26: 'Nescio quo modo, quantum mihi videtur, amicis
suis theurgis erubescebat Porphyrius.'

MSS. this title is preceded by a note [1] in which we are told that Proclus, in his commentary on Plotinus, said that the author of the book was Iamblichus.   This anonymous note is the only evidence for the authorship of Iamblichus; for there can be little doubt that the insertion of his name before the title Ἀβάμωνος κ.τ.λ. in some of the MSS. was suggested by the note, and rests on no other authority.

If we judge from internal evidence, it seems very unlikely that the book was written by Iamblichus.   It is true that the writer's religious and philosophic tenets agree in the main [2] with what we know of the teaching of Iamblichus; but there were many men of the time who held similar tenets; and it is difficult to imagine any motive that could have induced the Syrian Neoplatonist to masquerade as an Egyptian priest, and write a reply to Porphyry in that assumed character.   The evidence of the anonymous note is hardly sufficient to outweigh the improbability; and it may be suspected that either Proclus was mistaken, or the writer of the note misunderstood what Proclus said.   Moreover, the note itself hints a doubt; if the statement of Proclus had been positive and indisputable, there would have been no need to support it, as the writer of the note does, by referring to the evidence of style and contents.   Possibly the view that Iamblichus was the author was put forward by Proclus merely as a conjecture of his own; and if so, we are not bound to accept it. Or again, Proclus may have been speaking, not of our ' *De mysteriis* ', but of another writing.   Porphyry's letter was widely known, and must have been a stumbling-block to those who were disposed to agree with Iamblichus in his high estimate of the value and efficacy

---

[1] ἰστέον ὅτι ὁ φιλόσοφος Πρόκλος, ὑπομνηματίζων τὰς τοῦ μεγάλου Πλωτίνου ἐννεάδας, λέγει ὅτι ὁ ἀντιγράφων εἰς τὴν προκειμένην τοῦ Πορφυρίου ἐπιστολὴν ὁ θεσπέσιός ἐστιν Ἰάμβλιχος, καὶ διὰ τὸ τῆς ὑποθέσεως οἰκεῖον καὶ ἀκόλουθον ὑποκρίνεται πρόσωπον Αἰγυπτίου τινὸς Ἀβάμωνος. ἀλλὰ καὶ τὸ τῆς λέξεως κομματικὸν καὶ ἀφοριστικὸν καὶ τὸ τῶν ἐννοιῶν πραγματικὸν καὶ γλαφυρὸν καὶ ἔνθουν μαρτυρεῖ τὸν Πρόκλον καλῶς καὶ κρίναντα καὶ ἱστορήσαντα. This note is printed by Gale, under the heading ' Anonymi Testimonium praefixum Codd. MSS. Iamblichi '. Leemans says that it is present in cod. B, and I have seen it in cod. M; which of the other MSS. have it, I do not know.   In M, the note is preceded by the title τοῦ αὐτοῦ Ἰαμβλίχου εἰς τὴν ἐπιστολὴν Πορφυρίου, and is followed by the title Ἀβάμωνος διδασκάλου κ.τ.λ.; in D, the note is omitted, but the title Ἀβάμωνος διδασκάλου κ.τ.λ. is preceded by the words Ἰαμβλίχου τοῦ μεγάλου εἰς τὴν ἐπιστολὴν τοῦ Πορφυρίου.

[2] Not however in all respects; see notes on 8. 1, 2 a, b, and 4 d. The writer is, like Iamblichus, a Neoplatonist (i. e. a Platonist who accepts such modifications of Platonic doctrine as were introduced, or first made widely known, by Plotinus); and, like Iamblichus, he attaches much importance to *theurgia*. But the *Responsum* shows, as far as I have observed, none of those special characteristics by which the teaching of Iamblichus was distinguished from that of other Neoplatonists after Plotinus.

of *theurgia*; Iamblichus would therefore have good reason to deal with the ἀπορίαι put forward in it; and it is possible that he wrote a reply to it in his own person, that Proclus spoke of that reply, and that the writer of the note, having before him the 'Reply of Abammon', and knowing of no other, wrongly supposed this to be the writing to which Proclus referred.

If we disregard the note, there seems to be no sufficient reason for rejecting the view that the book is what it professes to be, and that its author was an Egyptian priest, who had acquired Greek culture and studied Greek philosophy, and sought to reconcile and combine the religious traditions of his country with the Neoplatonic teaching that was current in his time.[1] If Abammon is not a real person, he is well invented, and his character is consistently maintained. He speaks with the authority of a high-placed ecclesiastic, and addresses the foreign inquirer *de haut en bas*, in a tone of courteous and dignified condescension which is well suited to his position, but differs widely from that which we should have expected Iamblichus to adopt towards his teacher Porphyry.

It is best then to discard the spurious title *Iamblichi de mysteriis liber*, and to use in place of it the title *Abammonis ad Porphyrium responsum*, which leaves the question of authorship open.

The date of the book cannot be precisely determined. Porphyry was in his sixty-eighth year in A. D. 301, and must have died within a few years after that date (Zeller III. ii, p. 694). He may have written his letter to Anebo at any time before his death; and Abammon's Reply, though it may have been written after some interval, can hardly be many years later than Porphyry's letter. We may therefore date it roughly at 'about A. D. 300.'[2]

[1] Similarly, the earlier Egyptian priest Chaeremon, in the first century A.D., when Stoicism was dominant, accepted the teaching of the Stoics, and interpreted the religious traditions of the Egyptians in accordance with Stoic doctrine. It should be remembered that Plotinus and his teacher Ammonius Saccas were Egyptians; there is therefore no reason to be surprised at a learned Egyptian being proficient in Neoplatonic philosophy.

[2] G. Wolff, *Porphyrii de philosophia ex oraculis haurienda librorum reliquiae*, Berlin 1856, p. 27, says he thinks that Porphyry was *still in his youth* when he wrote to Anebo; for his letter shows that 'de philosophica deorum interpretatione nondum sibi persuaserat, sed incertus fluctuabat'. And if he was already a pupil of the Egyptian Plotinus, why (asks Wolff) did he not consult *him*, rather than an Egyptian priest?

For these reasons Wolff thinks that Porphyry wrote this letter towards the end of his stay at Athens, shortly before he migrated to Rome and became a pupil of Plotinus, and that the date of the letter must therefore be about A. D. 260.

If Wolff's conclusion is to be accepted, it would seem to follow that the *Responsum* must have been written soon after A. D. 260, and can hardly be later

There is no trustworthy printed text of Abammon's Reply. The *editio princeps* is Gale's edition, 1678. Gale was a good scholar, and his notes show extensive knowledge of Neoplatonic literature; but he gives no systematic *apparatus criticus*. The MSS. known to him were

B = codex Leidensis Vossianus, *c.* A.D. 1600, handed over to Gale by Isaac Voss;

F = codex Basiliensis Feschianus, saec. XVI, collated for Gale by Sebastian Fesch; and certain 'Codices Regii' of the Royal Library at Paris,[1] collated for Gale by Ed. Bernard and J. Mabillon.

Gale's printed text is based on B, but must not be assumed to be an exact reproduction of that manuscript, In his notes, Gale gives some variant readings of F and the 'Regii', as well as conjectural emendations of his own.

The only later edition known to me is that of G. Parthey, 1857. Parthey made use of a collation of B by G. H. Moser, and took over from Gale those variants of F and the 'Regii' which were given in Gale's notes; and he used in addition the following MSS :—

A = codex Florentinus Laurentianus, saec. XV, collated for Parthey by F. de Furia;

C = codex Vindobonensis, saec. XV (?), collated by Schubart;

D = codex Gothanus, saec. XV, collated by Parthey himself.

In Gale's and Parthey's editions, the *De myst.* is divided into ten Parts. Of these, Part 1, §§ 1 and 2, Part 8, and Part 10 are here given. In my revision of Parts 1 and 8, I have made use of Gale's statements as to F,[2] and Parthey's statements as to B, A, and C.

---

than 270. But on the other hand, its author shows knowledge of doctrines which were first made widely current, if not originated, by Plotinus (e. g. that of τὸ ἐπέκεινα νοῦ); and as Plotinus died in A.D. 270, and the *Enneads* were not published until after his death, this fact points rather to a date more nearly approaching A.D. 300. If we assume a later date than Wolff's for Porphyry's letter, the answer to Wolff's question 'why did he not consult Plotinus?' might be 'because Plotinus was dead'. And the appearance of 'fluctuation' or uncertainty of opinion which presents itself in the questions asked by Porphyry may be merely a sort of Socratic εἰρωνεία. Augustine's description of Porphyry's attitude, 'consulenti similis et quaerenti artes (Aegyptiorum) evertit', seems to me to be nearer the truth than Wolff's.

[1] According to Omont, *Inventaire des MSS. grecs de la Bibl. Nat.*, 1886–1898, there are now in the Bibliothèque Nationale at Paris four MSS. of the *De myst.*, viz. no. 1978, saec. XV; no. 1979, written in A.D. 1620; no. 1980, written by Vergetius (A.D. 1535–1568); and Suppl. gr. 292, saec. XVII. Gale's 'Regii' are probably the first three of these. Gale sometimes speaks of the 'Regii' collectively, and sometimes refers to one or another of them as 'Regius'; but in the latter case, he does not say which of them he means.

[2] I have thought it best to ignore Gale's mentions of the 'Regii', because it is uncertain which MS. or MSS. he is speaking of when he refers to them.

But what I have seen of Parthey's work on the *Corpus Hermeticum* has given me reason to doubt whether his reports of the readings of MSS. are to be relied on ; and in order to indicate this doubt, I have marked as B^p, A^p, and C^p the readings of B, A, and C which I have taken over from him. With regard to D, I have ignored Parthey, and have used a collation of this manuscript by Jacobs, which is entered in a copy of Gale's edition in the Bodleian Library.[1] And I have added the readings of an Oxford MS. collated by me (Bodleianus 20598, Miscell. Gr. 198, saec. XVI), which I call M.[2] Thus the only readings which I can give with perfect confidence are those of D, which are reported by Jacobs, and those of M, which I have seen. M is closely related to D, but is not copied from it.[3]

In Part 10, I have used Parthey's edition alone.

PAGE 28, ll. 4–5. θεὸς ὁ τῶν λόγων ἡγεμὼν Ἑρμῆς πάλαι δέδοκται ⌜καλῶς⌝ ἅπασι τοῖς ἱερεῦσιν εἶναι κοινός. The Hermes here spoken of is not the man and teacher, but the god. It seems that the writer, identifying the Egyptian god Thoth-Hermes with the Greek god Hermes, alludes to the Greek saying κοινὸς Ἑρμῆς, which commonly meant 'I claim a share in your good luck', but employs that familiar phrase in a different sense. But there is something wrong in the text. If we write καὶ ἄλλως or κἄλλως in place of the meaningless καλῶς, and cut out τοῖς ἱερεῦσιν (which may have come from τοῖς ἱερεῦσιν in 1 b *init.*), the meaning will be 'The saying "Hermes is common to all" holds good in theology as well as in other things'; that is, all men who have any knowledge of the gods have got it by the working in them of one and the same god Hermes, the god of reason or true thought. Cf. Proclus *In Pl. Alcib. I.* 104 A : τὰ μὲν γὰρ πάθη μερισμοῦ καὶ διαστάσεώς ἐστιν αἴτια ταῖς ψυχαῖς· ... ὁ δὲ λόγος κοινός ἐστι πᾶσι καὶ ἡ τοῦ λόγου προβολή, καὶ διὰ τοῦτο " κοινὸς ὁ Ἑρμῆς ", ἵνα δὴ καὶ ἠθικῶς αὐτοῦ ποιησώμεθα τὴν ἐξήγησιν. Proclus *Circa Providentiam* (Cousin) prooem. : 'Donec enim placentia dicimus nobis ipsis, nostra utique et haec dicere et scribere videbimur, aliterque et communem Mercurium ducem habentes (i. e. ἄλλως τε καὶ κοινὸν τὸν

---

[1] In those of my foot-notes in which Gale's reading is given and D is not mentioned, it is to be understood that Jacobs has not noted any difference between D and Gale's text.

[2] This MS. was acquired by the Bodleian Library in 1824. It is one of the Meerman MSS., nearly all of which came from the Jesuit College of Clermont at Paris. In the margin of M are numerous variants, added by two different hands. In my foot-notes, M means the reading of the first hand.

[3] A revised edition of *Abammonis responsum* as a whole is much to be desired; and with a view to this, a more thorough investigation of the MSS. is wanted.

'Ἑρμῆν ἡγεμόνα ἔχοντες), qui indocibiles praeacceptiones (i. e. προλήψεις) communium conceptuum omni animae imponere dicitur.'

6-8. οἱ ἡμέτεροι πρόγονοι . . . Ἑρμοῦ πάντα τὰ οἰκεῖα συγγράμματα ἐπονομάζοντες. The sacred books of the Egyptians were called 'the books of Thoth'. The writer is aware that these books were written by Egyptian priests; but he holds that they are none the less 'books of Thoth', inasmuch as the priests who wrote them were inspired by Thoth-Hermes, who is ὁ τῶν λόγων ἡγεμών. He is here speaking of ancient Egyptian writings, and not of the Greek *Hermetica*.

8-9. ⌜εἰ δὲ⌝ (εἴθε?) τοῦδε τοῦ θεοῦ καὶ ἡμεῖς . . . μετάσχοιμεν. Abammon prays that, in what he is now about to write, he too may be inspired by that same god. Cf. 3. 18 : οὐδὲ λόγον περὶ θεῶν ἄνευ θεῶν λαλεῖν δυνατόν.

10-11. σύ τε καλῶς ποιεῖς ⌜ἅτινα εἰς γνῶσιν (al. ἀγνῶς ἀγνῶσι)⌝ τοῖς ἱερεῦσιν ⌜ὡς φιλοῦσι⌝ περὶ θεολογίας προτείνων ἐρωτήματα. ὡς φιλοῦσι cannot be right. It would be possible to write ὡς φίλοις; but the corruption is probably more extensive. The general meaning must have been 'I am glad you have applied to the Egyptian priests, and thereby acknowledged that they know the truth about the gods, and can give true answers to your questions'.[1]

11-12. τὴν πρὸς Ἀνεβὼ τὸν ἐμὸν μαθητὴν πεμφθεῖσαν ἐπιστολὴν ἐμαυτῷ γεγράφθαι. Abammon describes himself below as one of 'those who are called κοινοὶ διδάσκαλοι'; and he is called διδάσκαλος in the title. He is apparently president of a college of ἱερογραμματεῖς, and perhaps the supreme head of the system of priestly teaching in Egypt. Anebo, to whom Porphyry wrote, was one of his pupils. Abammon considers Porphyry's letter to be virtually addressed to the whole body of Egyptian priests, and therefore to himself as representative and spokesman of that body; he consequently takes upon himself the task of answering it.

14. Πυθαγόραν μὲν καὶ Πλάτωνα κ.τ.λ. Abammon pays Porphyry a compliment by putting him on a par with Pythagoras and Plato, but at the same time takes for granted his own superiority. It is the Egyptian priesthood that is in possession of the absolute truth (αὐτὰ τὰ ἀληθῆ); and the relation of Greek philosophers to Egyptian

---

[1] Cf. 1. 8, where Abammon refutes the hypothesis that the gods are locally confined to the heavens, and cannot be present here on earth. On that assumption, he says, οὐδὲ ἡμεῖς οὖν οἱ ἱερεῖς (i. e. we Egyptian priests) οὐδὲν παρὰ τῶν θεῶν μεμαθήκαμεν (by means of theurgic operations) . . . οὐδὲ σὺ ὀρθῶς ἡμᾶς ἐρωτᾷς εἰδότας τι περιττότερον, ἐπείπερ μηδὲν τῶν ἄλλων ἀνθρώπων διαφέρομεν (which is absurd). His argument in that passage implies that gods, when invoked with certain rites, appear to Egyptian priests, and reveal things to them.

priests must necessarily be, as it has always been, that of pupils to
teachers. Cf. Herm. *ap.* Stob. *Exc.* XXIV. 11–16.

29. 1. τὴν αὐτὴν ἐκείνοις ἔχοντα γνώμην. ἐκείνοις means 'Pythagoras,
Plato, Democritus, Eudoxus, and many other ancient Greeks' who
received instruction from Egyptian priests. It might very well be
said that Porphyry agreed in opinion with Pythagoras and Plato;
but it would be strange to say that he held the same opinions as
Democritus; and there would not be much point in speaking thus of
Eudoxus, who was known as an astronomer and mathematician rather
than as a theologian. It is possible that the names of Democritus
and Eudoxus have been added by a later hand; but if we retain
those names, we must understand τὴν αὐτὴν ἐκείνοις ἔχοντα γνώμην to
mean 'having the same purpose or aim that they had', i.e. seeking,
as they did, to learn from the Egyptian priests.

4–7. εἰ δὲ καὶ φαίνοιτό σοι ⟨μᾶλλον?⟩ δεῖν, ἐμὲ θὲς εἶναι [[σοι]] τὸν ἐν
γράμμασι ⟨⟨σοι⟩⟩ διαλεγόμενον, ἢ (al. οἷόν) τινα ἄλλον προφήτην Αἰγυ-
πτίων· οὐδὲ⟨ν⟩ γὰρ τοῦτο διενήνοχεν. προφήτης sometimes meant an
Egyptian priest of a certain special rank or order; but it here seems
to mean an Egyptian priest of any kind, including the ἱερογραμματεῖς.

Abammon's meaning is 'you must take this Reply as expressing
the view of the Egyptian priesthood as a whole. Who it is that acts
as their spokesman,—whether Anebo, or I, or any other of them,—is
a matter of indifference.' He might have claimed to speak with
superior authority as their chief, or one of their chiefs; but he
magnanimously refrains from insisting on that personal claim.

ἐμὲ θὲς εἶναι . . . ἢ τινα ἄλλον can hardly be right. A better sense
might be got by writing τὸν ἐν γράμμασί σοι διαλεγόμενον θὲς εἶναι
ὁντινοῦν ἄλλον προφήτην Αἰγυπτίων.

10–11. διελώμεθα τὰ γένη . . . τῶν . . . προβλημάτων. This is done in
1 e, where four different γένη are mentioned.

11–12. ἀπὸ τίνων τε εἴληπται ⌜θείων θεολογιῶν⌝ τὰ ἀπορήματα διέλθωμεν. This is done in 1 f, where we are told that Porphyry's questions
or objections are based on (1) the doctrines of the wise men of
Chaldaea, (2) those of the Egyptian priests, (3) those of the (Greek)
philosophers, (4) certain 'contemptible opinions', and (5) the
common notions of mankind. We might strike out θείων and retain
θεολογιῶν (or θεολόγων), which would be applicable to (1), (2), and
perhaps (3), though not to (4) and (5).

12–13. καὶ κατὰ ποίας τινὰς ἐπιστήμας ἐπιζητεῖται ⟨. . .⟩. Cf. καὶ ἀπὸ διαφερουσῶν ἐπιστημῶν (εἴληπται) in 1 f. The ἐπιστῆμαι of which the writer is thinking are probably θεολογία, θεουργία, and φιλοσοφία; see 2 c.

14–15. τὰ δ᾽ ⌜ἐστὶ περὶ⌝ τὴν αἰτίαν δι᾽ ἣν ἕκαστά ἐστί τε οὑτωσὶ καὶ νοεῖται. What is wanted is something parallel to ἐπιποθεῖ διάκρισίν τινα and τὴν ὅλην ἀπαιτεῖ μυσταγωγίαν. Abammon is describing the different kinds of *answers* that Porphyry's ἀπορήματα require; and we should get nearer to his meaning if we wrote τὰ δ᾽ ἐξήγησιν (sc. ἐπιποθεῖ) τῆς αἰτίας δι᾽ ἣν κ.τ.λ.

The αἰτία δι᾽ ἣν ἕκαστά ἐστί τε οὑτωσὶ καὶ νοεῖται perhaps means 'the reason why the Egyptian priests do so-and-so and think so-and-so'. But if so, the sense would be more clearly expressed by writing πράττεταί τε in place of ἐστί τε.

16. [κατ᾽ ἐναντίωσίν τινα προβαλλόμενα]. These words are clearly out of place here; they may have occurred somewhere else in the chapter, but I have failed to find any suitable place for them. Cf. τὰ ... ἀντιλογικὰ καὶ δυσεριστίαν τινὰ ἐμφαίνοντα in 2 a.

19–20. τὰ μὲν γὰρ ἀφ᾽ ὧν οἱ Χαλδαίων σοφοὶ παραδεδώκασι τὰς ἐπιστάσεις προσάγει, κ.τ.λ. This division of the sources or grounds of Porphyry's ἀπορήματα into five classes is repeated in 2 a, where τὰ Ἀσσυρίων πάτρια δόγματα = ἃ οἱ Χαλδαίων σοφοὶ παραδεδώκασι:—τὰ ἡμέτερα = ἃ Αἰγυπτίων οἱ προφῆται διδάσκουσι:—φιλόσοφον εἴ τι προβάλλεις ἐρώτημα = τῆς τῶν φιλοσόφων θεωρίας ἐχόμενα:—τὰ δ᾽ ⌜ἀλλόφυλα⌝ ζητήματα ἢ ἀντιλογικὰ καὶ δυσεριστίαν τινὰ ἐμφαίνοντα = τινα καὶ ἀπ᾽ ἄλλων οὐκ ἀξίων λόγου δοξασμάτων ἐφέλκεταί τινα ἀπρεπῆ διαμφισβήτησιν:—and ὅσα προχωρεῖ κατὰ τὰς κοινὰς ἐννοίας = τὰ δ᾽ ἀπὸ τῶν κοινῶν ὑπολήψεων ὥρμηται.

For ἐπιστάσεις, which seems here to be nearly equivalent to ἐνστάσεις, 'objections', cf. 10. 1 : τὰ μὲν πρῶτα ἐπιστάσεις ὑποτείνων, ἔπειτα ἀπορῶν, ... ἐπέστησας γὰρ κ.τ.λ.

What is meant by 'the doctrines handed down by the Chaldaean sages'? These words may perhaps be taken as referring to the 'Chaldaean Oracles', a theosophic poem or collection of poems which was known to Porphyry (Aug. *De civ. dei* 10. 32 : see Kroll *De oraculis Chaldaicis*, p. 6), and was regarded as an inspired scripture by the Neoplatonists from Iamblichus onward. Those 'Oracles' might, for instance, have been quoted as an authority on the question discussed by Abammon in 8. 1, 'whether the supreme God is νοῦς or ὑπὲρ νοῦν'; and on the question mentioned in 8. 1 a, 'whether ὕλη is ἀγέννητος or γεννητή', which is answered in 8. 3 g (ὕλην παρήγαγεν ὁ θεός).[1] But there is no evidence that Porphyry mentioned the 'Chaldaean Oracles' in his letter to Anebo; and it is possible that the 'Chaldaean' or 'Assyrian' doctrines here spoken of are those of astrology, which was known to be of Babylonian origin, and is discussed in 9. 2–4. Abammon there says to Porphyry περὶ γενεθλιαλογίας ποιεῖς τὸν λόγον, εἴτε ὑφέστηκεν εἴτε μή.

21–22. τὰς ἐρωτήσεις . . . ποιεῖται. As this follows close on ποιεῖται τὰς ἀντιλήψεις, it is probable that ποιεῖται has been wrongly substituted for some other verb, e.g. προτείνει.

23–24. τὰ δ' ἀπὸ τῶν κοινῶν ὑπολήψεων [παρ' ἀνθρώποις] ὥρμηται. παρ' ἀνθρώποις must be struck out. We might insert πᾶσιν ἀνθρώποις before κοινῶν; but its insertion would make no difference in the sense.

κοιναὶ ὑπολήψεις (= κοιναὶ ἔννοιαι in 2 a) is a term of Stoic origin. 'These primary conceptions, or κοιναὶ ἔννοιαι,[2] are . . . those conceptions which, by the nature of thought, can be equally deduced by all men from experience' (Zeller, Stoics, Eng. tr. 1880, p. 81).

30. 4–5. τὰ μὲν Ἀσσυρίων πάτρια δόγματα ⟨. . .⟩ παραδώσομέν σοι μετ' ἀληθείας τὴν γνώμην. The meaning was probably '(In dealing with) the Assyrian doctrines, I will frankly and sincerely tell you what I think about them'.

6–8. τὰ μὲν ἀπὸ τῶν ἀρχαίων ⌈ἀπείρων⌉ γραμμάτων ⌈ἀναλογιζόμενοι τῇ γνώσει⌉, τὰ δ' ἀφ' ὧν ὕστερον ⟨. . .⟩ εἰς πεπερασμένον βιβλίων ⟨πλῆθος⟩ συνήγαγον [οἱ παλαιοὶ] τὴν ὅλην περὶ τῶν θείων εἴδησιν. The general sense of this corrupt passage appears to be 'The sources from which I shall draw when I speak of Egyptian religion are (1) the ancient writings (i.e. the "books of Thoth", written in ancient times by Egyptian priests), and (2) books in which recent writers have condensed or summarized the contents of the ancient writings'.[3] The

---

[1] Wolff, Porphyr. de philos. ex oraculis haur., speaks of 'ea quae Aeneas Gazaeus sophista Theophrasti p. 51 Boiss. praebet : οὐ γὰρ ἀγένητος οὐδὲ ἄναρχος ἡ ὕλη. τοῦτό σε καὶ Χαλδαῖοι διδάσκουσι καὶ ὁ Πορφύριος. ἐπιγράφει δὲ (Περὶ?) Καθόδου τὸ βιβλίον, ἐν ᾧ εἰς μέσον προάγει τῶν Χαλδαίων τὰ λόγια, ἐν οἷς γεγονέναι τὴν ὕλην ἰσχυρίζεται, i. e. quorum testimonio confirmat materiam esse natam'.

In 3. 3, Abammon reports, and apparently accepts as true, a doctrine which he says he 'once heard Chaldaean προφῆται teaching'. In that doctrine, 'gods' who are good, and make men good, are contrasted with 'daemons' who are bad, and make men bad; and the relation between the 'good gods' and the 'bad daemons' is compared to that between light and darkness. It looks as if the 'Chaldaean prophets' there spoken of were Zoroastrians, or had at any rate been influenced by Zoroastrianism. (Is it possible that they were Manichaean missionaries?) See also 6. 7 fin., where it appears to be said that 'Chaldaeans' worship gods alone, not daemons (holding 'daemons' to be bad?).

[2] The Stoics used the terms κοιναὶ ἔννοιαι, φυσικαὶ ἔννοιαι, and προλήψεις as equivalents.

[3] As a matter of fact, Abammon doubtless draws much more from sources of this second class than from the 'ancient writings' themselves.

combination of the two epithets ἀρχαίων ἀπείρων is impossible; and so is the phrase πεπερασμένον βιβλίον, 'a limited book', which would imply by contrast the conception of an unlimited or infinite book. But the writer may have spoken of a limited *number* of recent books (πεπερασμένον βιβλίων ⟨πλῆθος⟩), in contrast to the vast mass of the ancient writings (cf. '36,525 books of Hermes' in 8. 1 b). The subject of συνήγαγον has been lost; in place of [οἱ παλαιοὶ] we should have expected something like νεώτεροί τινες. Among the recent books in which the ancient doctrines were reproduced in an abridged form, the author presumably included the writings of Manetho and Seleucus (see 8. 1 b), and those of Chaeremon (see 8. 4 b); but he may have meant this description to apply to the Greek *Hermetica* also (see 8. 4 a, 8. 5 a, and 10. 7).

9–11. τὰς Ἑρμοῦ παλαιὰς στήλας, ἃς Πλάτων ἤδη πρόσθεν καὶ Πυθαγόρας διαναγνόντες φιλοσοφίαν συνεστήσαντο. The writer accepts the current view that the Greek philosophers got their doctrines from Egyptian sources; he therefore intends, in dealing with questions of philosophy, to refer to those Egyptian sources, rather than to the writings of the Greek philosophers.

15–16. τὰ μὲν ἔργων θείων πείρας δεόμενα πρὸς ἀκριβῆ κατανόησιν ⟨ἀ⟩δύνατον [μόνον] διὰ λόγων ⟨⟨μόνων?⟩⟩ ⟨ἐξηγεῖσθαι⟩. ἔργα θεῖα = θεουργία. It is impossible to explain by mere words the meaning and effect of *theurgia*, i. e. of ritual or sacramental actions. In order to understand such things fully, a man must have experienced their working in his own person.

16–19. τὰ δὲ νοερᾶς θεωρίας ⟨ἐχόμενα?⟩ ⌜πλήρη τε καθαιρεῖσθαι⌝ ⟨...⟩, σημεῖα δ' αὐτῶν (αὐτῆς MSS.) ἀξιόλογα δυνατὸν (δύναται MSS.) φράζειν, ἀφ' ὧν δύνασαι (δυνήσῃ?) κ.τ.λ. The clause which begins with τὰ δὲ νοερᾶς θεωρίας must have ended with some phrase similar in meaning to ἀδύνατον διὰ λόγων ἐξηγεῖσθαι; something of that sort is needed to stand in contrast to the following clause σημεῖα δὲ . . . δυνατὸν φράζειν. 'With regard to νοητά', says Abammon, 'words are inadequate; each man must behold τὰ ὄντως ὄντα for himself with his own mental eyes. But it is possible to give suggestions which will help you and others to attain to the contemplation of them; and this I will do.' Cf. *Corp. Herm.* 9. 10, and Plotinus 6. 9. 4.

δύνασαι (or δυνήσῃ), following closely on δυνατόν, is awkward; it may perhaps have been substituted by error for some other verb.

19. ὅσα δὲ τυγχάνει διὰ λόγων ὄντα γνωστά. These things are contrasted with the two kinds of things which, as we have just been told,

are not (or at least not completely) διὰ λόγων γνωστά, viz. τὰ ἔργων θείων πείρας δεόμενα and τὰ νοερᾶς θεωρίας ⟨ἐχόμενα⟩.

31. 2. ὅσα μὲν εἰς τὰ πρῶτα αἴτια διήκει. This refers especially to 8. 1 ff., where Abammon answers Porphyry's question τί τὸ πρῶτον αἴτιον ἡγοῦνται εἶναι Αἰγύπτιοι.

3. ὅσα δὲ περὶ ἠθῶν ἢ περὶ τελῶν εἴρηται. τέλη here means the 'ends' or 'aims' of human action, the word τέλος being used in the same sense as when Epicureanism was summed up in the phrase ἡδονὴ τέλος. This seems to refer chiefly to 10. 1–7, where ὁ περὶ εὐδαιμονίας λόγος is discussed. Abammon there says that τὸ ἀνθρώπινον ἀγαθόν (i. e. the τέλος in the ethical sense) is 'union with God' (ἡ πρὸς τὸν θεὸν ἕνωσις).

7–8. τί τὸ πρῶτον αἴτιον ἡγοῦνται εἶναι Αἰγύπτιοι, πότερον νοῦν ἢ ὑπὲρ νοῦν. Aristotelians would have said that the First Cause is νοῦς; the later Platonists said that the First Cause (the ἕν or ἀγαθόν of Plotinus) is ἐπέκεινα νοῦ. See notes on Corp. Herm. II. 12 b–16.

8–9. μόνον ἢ μετ' ἄλλου ἢ ἄλλων. Some Platonists recognized ὕλη as an independent αἴτιον beside God; see Ascl. Lat. II. There were men who spoke of φύσις as a πρῶτον αἴτιον distinct from God (see Corp. Herm. III); Porphyry may have been thinking of them, and perhaps also of some who spoke similarly of τύχη, ἀνάγκη, or εἱμαρμένη.

9. πότερον ἀσώματον ἢ σωματικόν. This is equivalent to asking ' Are the Egyptians Platonists or Stoics? '

9–10. εἰ τῷ δημιουργῷ τὸ αὐτό (τὰ αὐτὰ MSS.) ἢ πρὸ τοῦ δημιουργοῦ. The Platonists in general, from Numenius onward, distinguished the Demiurgus from the supreme God, and held the latter to be πρὸ τοῦ δημιουργοῦ.

10. εἰ ἐξ ἑνὸς τὰ πάντα ἢ ἐκ πολλῶν. The Atomists held ἐκ πολλῶν εἶναι τὰ πάντα. Cf. Dionysius, bishop of Alexandria (A. D. 247–265), ap. Euseb. Pr. ev. 14. 23. 1 : πότερον ἕν ἐστι συναφὲς τὸ πᾶν, ὡς ἡμῖν τε (sc. the Christians) καὶ τοῖς σοφωτάτοις Ἑλλήνων Πλάτωνι καὶ Πυθαγόρᾳ καὶ τοῖς ἀπὸ τῆς στοᾶς καὶ Ἡρακλείτῳ φαίνεται, ἢ δύο, ὡς ἴσως τις ὑπέλαβεν,[1] ἢ καὶ πολλὰ καὶ ἄπειρα, ὡς τισιν ἄλλοις (sc. Democritus and Epicurus) ἔδοξεν ;

10–11. εἰ ὕλην ἴσασιν ⌜ἢ σώματα ποιὰ (al. σωματοποιὰ) πρῶτα⌝. τὰ

---

[1] Who is the man who ἴσως ὑπέλαβε δύο ? Perhaps Aristotle, who distinguished the ' fifth substance ' of which the heavens consist from the elements of which the lower world is composed. Or is Dionysius thinking of those Platonists (such as the writer of Ascl. Lat. II) who said that there are two ἀγέννητα, viz. God and ὕλη ? Or of Zoroastrian dualism ?

πρῶτα σώματα would mean the cosmic elements; but it is difficult to see why the elements should be mentioned here. Perhaps ἢ σώματα ποιὰ (or ποῖα?) πρῶτα ought to be bracketed; it may have come from a marginal note. Another remedy would be to strike out ἢ σώματα and πρῶτα, and read εἰ ὕλην ἴσασιν ἄποιον.

12–13. ἔν τε ⟨τοῖς⟩ γράμμασι τῶν ἀρχαίων ἱερογραμματέων πολλαὶ καὶ ποικίλαι δόξαι περὶ τούτων φέρονται. The 'writings of the ancient ἱερογραμματεῖς' are 'the books of Thoth', i.e. the sacred writings which were in the keeping of the Egyptian priests, and of which we have specimens in the Pyramid-texts, the 'Book of the Dead', and other documents of similar character. We may be sure that those writings contained no answers to the questions asked by Porphyry (πότερον νοῦς ἢ ὑπὲρ νοῦν τὸ πρῶτον αἴτιον; &c.), because the conceptions on which those questions are based were unknown to the early Egyptians, and the terms in which the questions are stated would have been unintelligible to them.[1] But some Egyptian priests of the Roman period imagined that they found in the ancient writings doctrines which they had really learnt from the Greek philosophers, just as Philo imagined that he found the doctrines of Platonism in the Books of Moses. According to the methods of interpretation which were commonly employed in those times, an inspired text meant whatever the reader chose that it should mean. A large part of the contents of the ancient Egyptian documents consisted of formulae the original meaning of which had long been lost. It is probable that many of the priests of Roman Egypt were unable, or very imperfectly able, even to decipher the ancient scripts and read the words; and those who did read them, and tried to make sense of them, could do so only by inventing arbitrary interpretations in accordance with their own beliefs and ways of thinking, whatever these might be. Thus Chaeremon thought that the teaching of the old documents agreed with that of the Stoics; Abammon (or the writer of 'Abammon's Reply') thought that it agreed with that of the Neoplatonists. As there is no reason to suppose that the early Egyptians had attained to the conception of ἀσώματα (a conception which hardly existed among the Greeks before the time of Plato), it

---

[1] Eusebius (Pr. ev. 3. 9. 12, p. 103 b), criticizing Porphyry's statement that the 'Zeus' described in an Orphic poem is ὁ δημιουργικὸς νοῦς, says πῶς δ' ἂν αὐτὸν τοῦτον ἐθεολόγει, ὃν μηδὲ τὴν ἀρχὴν ἔγνω ὁ τῶν ἐπῶν ποιητής, εἴτε ὁ Θρᾷξ εἴη Ὀρφεὺς εἴτε τις ἄλλος; εἰ δὴ παρ' Αἰγυπτίων ἢ καὶ παρὰ τῶν πρώτων Ἑλλήνων ἥκοντα ἦν εἰς αὐτὸν τὰ τῆς θεολογίας, οἱ δέ γε ἀπεδείχθησαν οὐδὲν νοητὸν ἐπιστάμενοι οὐδ' ἐν ἀφανεῖ καὶ ἀσωμάτῳ οὐσίᾳ περιεχόμενον. On the assumption that the Orphic poem was written at an early date, that is a sound argument.

is to be presumed that, in respect of such questions as πότερον ἀσώματον ἢ σωματικὸν τὸ πρῶτον αἴτιον ἡγοῦνται εἶναι Αἰγύπτιοι, Chaeremon came nearer to the true answer than Abammon; but neither the one nor the other can have known much about the meaning of the ancient writings, or the beliefs of those who wrote them. The author of 'Abammon's Reply' did indeed know enough about the matter to be aware that the ancient documents differed among themselves, and presented various and apparently inconsistent doctrines (8. 1 b); but he got over this difficulty by assuming that each of the documents contained only a detached portion of a complex system of theology, which he supposed to have been known as a whole to the ancient ἱερογραμματεῖς by whom the books were written.

14–15. παρὰ τοῖς ἔτι ζῶσι ⌜τῶν σοφῶν τὰ μεγάλα⌝ οὐχ ἁπλῶς ὁ λόγος παραδίδοται. ὁ λόγος means the theology taught in the ancient writings. There were men in Abammon's time who thought they knew what that theology was, and tried to restate it in their own words; but they differed in their accounts of it.

15–17. πολλῶν οὐσιῶν ὑπαρχουσῶν, . . . πολλαὶ παρεδόθησαν αὐτῶν καὶ ἀρχαί, διαφόρους ἔχουσαι τάξεις. Cf. 8. 5 b: εἰσὶ γὰρ ἀρχαὶ παρ' αὐτοῖς πλείονες καὶ περὶ πλειόνων οὐσιῶν. There are different grades or orders of things (e.g. that of τὰ νοητά and that of τὰ αἰσθητά, with sub-divisions of the one and the other); and each of these different orders of things is brought into being or maintained in being by a separate group of gods. These groups of gods together constitute one all-comprehensive hierarchy, culminating in τὸ ἐπέκεινα νοῦ, which is the supreme ἀρχή or First Cause of all. But each of the several writers has spoken of one such group alone, and said nothing about the rest. Each of the documents therefore, says Abammon, contains a part of the truth, but a part only; and in order to get the whole truth, we must combine these separate parts into one coherent system.

In what he says about the different τάξεις of gods, the writer shows that he had gone some way at least in the direction of that extraordinarily complicated system of theology which was formulated by Iamblichus, and was further elaborated by succeeding Neoplatonists down to Proclus.[1] But in Abammon's scheme, τὸ ἐπέκεινα νοῦ καὶ νοητῶν is represented by the θεὸς εἷς alone; whereas Iamblichus added a παντάπασιν ἀπόρρητον above or beyond the ἁπλῶς ἕν, and thus

[1] That system was analogous in principle to the divine genealogies of Valentinus and other Christian Gnostics of the second century, but was much more elaborately developed. As to Iamblichus' 'classification of the higher beings', see Zeller III. ii, 1903, pp. 744–755.

divided τὸ ἐπέκεινα into two distinct entities (or rather 'pre-entities').[1] Moreover, in 'Abammon's Reply' there is no trace of that distinction between θεοὶ νοητοί and θεοὶ νοεροί which is prominent in the system of Iamblichus, nor of the series of 'triads' into which Iamblichus divided each of these two orders of gods.

17–20. τὰς μὲν οὖν ὅλας (sc. ἀρχὰς) Ἑρμῆς ἐν ταῖς δισμυρίαις βίβλοις, ᾶς (ὡς MSS.) Σέλευκος ἀπεγράψατο, ἢ [ταῖς] τρισμυρίαις τε καὶ ἑξακισχιλίαις καὶ πεντακοσίαις καὶ εἴκοσι πέντε, ὡς Μανεθὼς ἱστορεῖ, τελέως ἀνέδειξε. The writer has told us in 1. 1 a what he meant by 'books of Hermes'. He believed these books to have been written by ancient ἱερογραμματεῖς inspired by the god Thoth-Hermes. It is evident that he cannot have read, or known, at first hand, more than a very small proportion of the enormous number of books of which he speaks;[2] he had not even counted them himself, and could only refer to the varying reports as to their number which were given by earlier writers. Seleucus had 'registered' (ἀπεγράψατο) or catalogued the books, and gave the number as 20,000; Manetho gave it as 36,525 (i.e. 25 for each day of the four-year period of 1461 days, or in other words, 100 for each day of the year of 365¼ days).

Suidas says that Seleucus of Alexandria wrote περὶ θεῶν βιβλία ρ'; and he is doubtless the man who is called Σέλευκος ὁ θεολόγος by Porphyry, De abst. 2. 55. Manetho is the Egyptian priest who lived in the reign of the first Ptolemy, and wrote in Greek a book on the religion of the Egyptians (τῶν φυσικῶν ἐπιτομή, Diog. Laert. Prooem. 10).

---

[1] Damascius De princ. c. 43: πότερον δύο εἰσὶν αἱ πρῶται ἀρχαὶ πρὸ τῆς νοητῆς πρώτης τριάδος, . . . καθάπερ ἠξίωσεν ὁ μέγας Ἰάμβλιχος. Ib. c. 45: ἆρα οὖν οὕτω θετέον δύο τὰς ἐπέκεινα τῶν νοητῶν τριάδων ἀρχάς, καὶ ὅλως εἰπεῖν τῶν νοητῶν ἀπάντων, ὡς ἠξίωσεν ὁ Ἰάμβλιχος, ὅσον ἐμέ γε εἰδέναι μόνος ἀξιώσας τῶν πρὸ ἡμῶν ἀπάντων. Ib. c. 51: Iamblichus spoke of τὸ ἁπλῶς ἕν as distinct from ἡ παντάπασιν ἀπόρρητος ἀρχή.

Zeller indeed (III. ii, p. 746 n. 2) interprets De myst. 8. 2 a, b as asserting that same doctrine of the 'doubled One' (or more exactly, 'the One' and 'that which is beyond the One'); that is, he thinks both the 'first God' and the 'second God' here spoken of by Abammon to be ἐπέκεινα νοῦ καὶ νοητῶν, and takes them to correspond respectively to the παντάπασιν ἀπόρρητον and the ἁπλῶς ἕν of Iamblichus. But he is surely mistaken in this. Abammon, after speaking of his first and second Gods, passes on immediately to the gods of the material universe (θεοὶ αἰθέριοι, ἐμπύριοι, and ἐπουράνιοι, 2 c); so that if both his first God and his second God were ἐπέκεινα νοῦ, there would be no God in his scheme to stand for νοῦς. It must therefore be his first God alone that is ἐπέκεινα νοῦ; and his second God must be νοῦς. In this respect Abammon agrees with Plotinus, and differs from Iamblichus.

[2] Clem. Alex. Strom. 6. 4. 35–37 gives a list of the 'books of Hermes' (i.e. Egyptian writings, not Greek Hermetica) which the several orders of Egyptian priests were required to study. His total amounts to 42 only; but these 42 books,

21-23. δεῖ δὲ τἀληθὲς περὶ πασῶν (sc. τῶν ἀρχῶν) ⌐ἀνευρεθῆναι⌐, συντόμως τε αὐτό σοι κατὰ τὸ δυνατὸν διερμηνεῦσαι. In place of ἀνευρεθῆναι,
an active verb is wanted. If διερμηνεῦσαι is right, διερμηνεύουσι at the
end of the preceding sentence is probably wrong.

24-26. πρὸ τῶν ὄντως ὄντων καὶ τῶν ὅλων ἀρχῶν ἐστι θεὸς εἷς, πρότερος
(al. πρώτιος) καὶ τοῦ ⌐πρώτου θεοῦ καὶ βασιλέως⌐. τὰ ὄντως ὄντα = τὰ
νοητά. The θεὸς εἷς here spoken of corresponds to τὸ ἕν of Plotinus,
which is ἐπέκεινα νοῦ καὶ οὐσίας (i.e. νοῦ καὶ τῶν νοητῶν). The God
denoted by the words τοῦ ⌐πρώτου θεοῦ καὶ βασιλέως⌐ must be that
second God of whom it is said below that he ἀπὸ τοῦ ἑνὸς τούτου ἑαυτὸν
ἐξέλαμψε, and who corresponds to the νοῦς of Plotinus. But a God
who issued from another God could not be called ὁ πρῶτος θεός.
The sense required might be got by reading τοῦ πρωτ⟨ογόν⟩ου θεοῦ καὶ
⟨θεῶν⟩ βασιλέως. The variant πρώτιος for πρότερος is difficult to
account for; is it a corruption of προαίτιος?

According to the old Heliopolitan myth, Tum, the eldest of the
personal gods, and progenitor of all the rest,[1] issued from a primal
ocean, which was called Nu. In Abammon's time, Egyptian priests
who had studied Greek philosophy may have read this myth in the
old writings, and taken Nu and Tum to signify respectively the 'first
God' and the 'second God' of the Neoplatonists. The phrase
ἑαυτὸν ἐξέλαμψε, used below to describe the process by which the
second God issued from the first God, would be exactly appropriate
in speaking of the rising of Tum the Sun-god out of the waters of Nu.

27-28. παράδειγμα δὲ ἵδρυται τοῦ αὐτοπάτορος ⟨⟨καὶ⟩⟩ αὐτογόνου [[καὶ]]
[μονοπάτορος] θεοῦ, τοῦ ὄντως ἀγαθοῦ. μονοπάτορος is most likely a
variant for αὐτοπάτορος. The second God is αὐτοπάτωρ and αὐτόγονος,
'his own father and his own son'; that is to say, he is αὐτογέννητος.
(See note on Ascl. Lat. II. 14 b.) The first God (ὁ εἷς) is ἀκίνητος;
no activity can be ascribed to him; and the writer consequently says
that the second God was not engendered by the first God, but ἐκ τοῦ
ἑνὸς ἑαυτὸν ἐξέλαμψε. Compare Plotinus 5. 1. 6: δεῖ οὖν, ἀκινήτου
ὄντος (τοῦ ἑνός, neut.), εἴ τι δεύτερον μετ' αὐτό, οὐ προσνεύσαντος οὐδὲ
βουληθέντος οὐδὲ ὅλως κινηθέντος (τοῦ ἑνός) ὑποστῆναι αὐτό (sc. τὸ
δεύτερον). πῶς οὖν; ... (δεῖ νοῆσαι) περίλαμψιν ἐξ αὐτοῦ μέν, ἐξ αὐτοῦ
δὲ μένοντος, οἷον (ἐξ) ἡλίου τὸ περὶ αὐτὸν λαμπρὸν φῶς περιθέον, ἐξ αὐτοῦ
ἀεὶ γεννώμενον μένοντος. Ib. 5. 3. 12: οὐ γὰρ οἷον προυθυμήθη (τὸ ἕν)

---

[1] In the 'Book of the Dead', Tum is called 'Creator of heaven, maker of
beings, procreator of all that is, who gave birth to the gods, self-created, lord of
life' (Wiedemann, *Religion of the ancient Egyptians*, Eng. tr. p. 31).

νοῦν γενέσθαι, εἶτα ἐγένετο νοῦς· ... ἀλλὰ δῆλον ὅτι, εἴ τι ὑπέστη μετ'
αὐτό, μένοντος ἐκείνου ἐν τῷ αὐτοῦ ἤθει ὑπέστη· δεῖ οὖν, ἵνα τι ἄλλο
ὑποστῇ, ἡσυχίαν ἄγειν ἐφ' ἑαυτοῦ πανταχοῦ ἐκεῖνο. ... ἢ κατὰ λόγον
θησόμεθα τὴν [μὲν] ἀπ' αὐτοῦ οἷον ῥυεῖσαν ἐνέργειαν ὡς ἀπὸ ἡλίου ⟨φῶς⟩.
φῶς τι οὖν θησόμεθα καὶ πᾶσαν τὴν νοητὴν φύσιν, αὐτὸν δέ, ἐπ' ἄκρῳ τῷ
νοητῷ ἑστηκότα, βασιλεύειν ἐπ' αὐτοῦ, ... ἐπιλάμπειν δέ, ἀεὶ μένον ἐπὶ
τοῦ νοητοῦ. *Ib.* 5. 3. 15: how can anything issue from the One?
ἔστιν εἰπεῖν, οἷον ἐκ φωτὸς τὴν ἐξ αὐτοῦ περίλαμψιν.[1] *Ib.* 6. 8. 18 (with
reference to the relation between νοῦς and τὸ ἕν): ὥσπερ φωτὸς ἐπὶ
πολὺ σκεδασθέντος ἐξ ἑνός τινος ἐν αὐτῷ ὄντος διαφανοῦς, εἴδωλον μὲν τὸ
σκεδασθέν, τὸ δ' ἀφ' οὗ τὸ ἀληθές.[2] Porphyr. (?) *ap.* Cyril. *c. Jul.* 545 B
(*Testim.*): προῆλθε δὲ (νοῦς) προαιώνιος, ἀπ' αἰτίου τοῦ θεοῦ (i.e. from
the first God) ὡρμημένος, αὐτογέννητος ὢν καὶ αὐτοπάτωρ· οὐ γὰρ
ἐκείνου κινουμένου πρὸς γένεσιν τὴν τούτου ἡ πρόοδος γέγονεν, ἀλλὰ τούτου
παρελθόντος αὐτογόνως ἐκ θεοῦ.

The first God is παράδειγμα of the second God; in other words,
the second God is εἰκών (or, as Plotinus says, εἴδωλον) of the first.

τοῦ ὄντως ἀγαθοῦ is probably masculine. The second God differs
from the first in being actively creative, and as such is called ὁ ὄντως
ἀγαθός. (Cf. Pl. *Tim.* 29 E, where the Demiurgus is called ἀγαθός.)
The phrase ὁ ὄντως ἀγαθός, applied to the second God, is contrasted
with τὸ προόντως ⟨ἀγαθ⟩όν, which (if my correction is right) is applied
to the first God (ὁ πρὸ τῶν ὄντως ὄντων), in agreement with Plotinus,
who uses τὸ ἀγαθόν as a synonym for τὸ ἕν. Cf. Numenius *ap.* Euseb.
Pr. ev. 11. 22. 3 (p. 544 a): εἰ δ' ἔστι μὲν νοητὸν ἡ οὐσία καὶ ἡ ἰδέα, ταύτης
δ' ὡμολογήθη πρεσβύτερον καὶ αἴτιον εἶναι ὁ ⌜νοῦς⌝,[3] αὐτὸς οὗτος μόνος
εὕρηται ὢν τὸ ἀγαθόν. καὶ γὰρ [εἰ] ὁ μὲν δημιουργὸς θεός (i.e. the second
God) ἐστι γενέσεως ἀρχή, τὸ ⟨δὲ⟩ ἀγαθὸν οὐσίας ἐστιν[4] ἀρχή. ἀνάλογον
δὲ τούτῳ μὲν (sc. τῷ ἀγαθῷ, neut. = τῷ πρώτῳ θεῷ) ὁ δημιουργὸς θεός, ὢν
αὐτοῦ μιμητής,[5] τῇ δ' οὐσίᾳ ἡ γένεσις, εἰκὼν αὐτῆς οὖσα[6] καὶ μίμημα. εἰ
⌜γὰρ⌝[7] ὁ δημιουργὸς τῆς γενέσεως (i.e. the second God) ἐστιν ἀγαθός, ἦ που
ἔσται [καὶ] ὁ τῆς οὐσίας δημιουργὸς (i.e. the first God) αὐτοάγαθον. .... ὁ
μὲν πρῶτος θεὸς αὐτοάγαθον, ὁ δὲ τούτου μιμητὴς δημιουργὸς ἀγαθός.

---

[1] There is something wrong here. The sense required is rather οἷον ἐξ ἡλίου τὴν
τοῦ φωτὸς αὐτοῦ περίλαμψιν.

[2] 'The light diffused (i. e. νοῦς) is an image; the source from which it comes
(i. e. τὸ ἕν) is the reality.'

[3] In place of ὁ νοῦς, some term denoting the first God ὁ (πρῶτος) νοῦς would
serve the purpose; for the first and second Gods of Numenius are ὁ πρῶτος νοῦς and
δεύτερος νοῦς.

[4] ἐστὶν Vigerus; εἶναι MSS.

[5] Cf. Abammon's phrase παράδειγμα ἵδρυται κ.τ.λ.

[6] οὖσα Vigerus: ἐστὶ MSS.   [7] εἰ γὰρ Vigerus: εἴπερ MSS.

32. 1. πρὸ τῶν ἰδεῶν ὤν (πρώτων ἰδεῶν ὄντων MSS.). αἱ ἰδέαι, the eternal archetypes of τὰ αἰσθητά, are νοητά; and the first God is prior to νοῦς and νοητά.

1–2. ⟨⟨αὐτὸς (οὗτος?) γὰρ τὸ προόντως ⟨ἀγαθ⟩όν ἐστι, καὶ τῶν νοητῶν ἀρχή· διὸ καὶ νοητάρχης προσαγορεύεται.⟩⟩ These words, as they stand in the MSS., are applied to the second God. But they are evidently applicable to the first God only, and not to the second. I have therefore transposed them, and placed them at the end of the passage in which the first God is spoken of.

Abammon says that the first God is called νοητάρχης, because he is ἀρχή (source or cause) of τὰ νοητά; that the second God is called αὐτάρχης (i. e. αὐτὸς ἑαυτοῦ ἀρχὴ ὤν, 'cause of himself'), because he ἑαυτὸν ἐξέλαμψε, 'produced himself by shining forth' from the first God; and that the second God is also called οὐσιοπάτωρ, because he is ἀρχὴ τῆς οὐσίας, 'cause of corporeal substance'. The words νοητάρχης, αὐτάρχης,[1] and οὐσιοπάτωρ do not, as far as I know, occur anywhere else in Greek literature. They are presumably translations of Egyptian words used in ritual formulae as titles or epithets of certain gods. If so, Abammon (or rather, the recent writer from whom Abammon is here drawing) gave to the Egyptian word which he translated by νοητάρχης a sense which cannot have been meant in the old writings; for the early Egyptians knew nothing of νοητά in the Platonic sense.

As to οὐσιοπάτωρ (= ἀρχὴ τῆς οὐσίας), cf. οὐσιάρχης in *Ascl. Lat.* III. 19 b, and see notes *ad loc.* The word οὐσία, since it is contrasted with νοητά, must be taken as meaning αἰσθητά; that is, it is here used in the sense 'corporeal substance', in which it was commonly employed by the Stoics, and not as an equivalent for τὰ ὄντως ὄντα = τὰ νοητά, the sense more usually given to it by Platonists (e. g. by Numenius *ap.* Euseb. *Pr. ev.* 11. 22. 3, quoted above). Abammon's second God (νοῦς) is Demiurgus of the αἰσθητὸς κόσμος; and that is what is meant by calling him ἀρχὴ τῆς οὐσίας. In *Resp.* I. 5, on the other hand, Abammon uses οὐσία in its Platonic sense; he there says ἔστι δὴ οὖν τἀγαθὸν τό τε ἐπέκεινα τῆς οὐσίας καὶ τὸ κατ᾽ οὐσίαν ὕπαρχον·[2] ἐκείνην λέγω τὴν οὐσίαν τὴν πρεσβυτάτην καὶ τιμιωτάτην

---

[1] The word αὐταρχή is used by Simplicius, in the sense 'principle of principles' (Liddell and Scott). If my conjecture, ἀρχὴ γὰρ οὗτος (ἀρχῶν), is right, Abammon implies that his word αὐτάρχης might be taken in the sense 'principle of principles' or 'cause of causes', *as well as* in the sense 'cause of himself'.

[2] τἀγαθὸν τὸ ἐπέκεινα τῆς οὐσίας is the ἀγαθόν = ἕν of Plotinus, and is identical with the θεὸς εἷς of 8. 2 a, who is called τὸ προόντως ⟨ἀγαθ⟩όν.—τἀγαθὸν τὸ κατ᾽ οὐσίαν ὕπαρχον corresponds to the second God of 8. 2 a, who is called ὁ ὄντως ἀγαθός.

καὶ καθ' αὑτὴν οὖσαν, ἀσώματον, θεῶν ἰδίωμα ἐξαίρετον, κ.τ.λ. But in that passage, the words ἐκείνην λέγω τὴν οὐσίαν τὴν πρεσβυτάτην show that the writer admitted the use of οὐσία in another sense also. In his use of οὐσία in 8. 2 b (προούσιος καὶ ἀρχὴ τῆς οὐσίας κ.τ.λ.) he may perhaps be following the Stoic Chaeremon.

4–5. ἀρχὴ γὰρ οὗτος ⟨ἀρχῶν⟩ καὶ θεὸς θεῶν. This second God is ἀρχή of the whole hierarchy of subordinate gods, each of whom again is an ἀρχή within his special sphere of action. The first God, out of whom the second God issued, is πρὸ τῶν ὅλων ἀρχῶν (8. 2 a), and might be called πρόαρχος more fitly than ἀρχή; though in 2 c the first and second Gods together are called ἀρχαὶ πρεσβύταται πάντων.

5. μονὰς ἐκ τοῦ ἑνός. The second God (who is νοῦς) is called μονάς. Cf. Aetius 1. 3. 8 (Diels *Doxogr.* p. 281): ' Pythagoras ' τὴν μονάδα καὶ τὴν ἀόριστον δυάδα ἐν ταῖς ἀρχαῖς· σπεύδει δὲ αὐτῷ τῶν ἀρχῶν ἡ μὲν (sc. ἡ μονὰς) ἐπὶ τὸ ποιητικὸν αἴτιον καὶ ⌈εἰδικόν⌉,[1] ὅπερ ἐστὶ νοῦς ὁ θεός (al. νοῦς καὶ θεός). *Ib.* p. 282 : νοῦς μὲν οὖν ἡ μονάς ἐστιν· ὁ γὰρ νοῦς κατὰ μονάδα θεωρεῖ.[2] οἷον πολλῶν ὄντων ἀνθρώπων οἱ μὲν ἐπὶ μέρους εἰσὶν ⌈ἀναίσθητοι⌉ ἀπερίληπτοι καὶ ἄπειροι,[3] ἀλλ' αὐτὸ τοῦτο ἄνθρωπον ἕνα μόνον νοοῦμεν, ᾧ οὐδεὶς ⟨τῶν ἐπὶ μέρους?⟩ ἔτυχεν ὅμοιος· καὶ ἵππον ἕνα νοοῦμεν, οἱ δὲ ἐπὶ μέρους εἰσὶν ἄπειροι. τὰ γὰρ εἴδη ταῦτα πάντα καὶ γένη κατὰ μονάδας εἰσί. . . . διὰ τοῦτο οὖν νοῦς ἡ μονάς, ᾧ ταῦτα νοοῦμεν. Theo Smyrn. (Diels *Vorsokr.*[2] I, p. 235) says that Archytas and Philolaus (Pythagoreans) ἀδιαφόρως τὸ ἓν καὶ μονάδα καλοῦσι, καὶ τὴν μονάδα ἕν. But Abammon, being a Neoplatonist, distinguishes them, and applies the term μονάς to νοῦς, and the term ἕν or θεὸς εἷς to τὸ ἐπέκεινα νοῦ.

9–10. ἃς Ἑρμῆς πρὸ τῶν αἰθερίων καὶ ἐμπυρίων θεῶν προτάττει καὶ τῶν ἐπουρανίων. In 8. 2 a, b, c the writer is giving an abstract of a theological system which he found in some Graeco-Egyptian source, and which was there ascribed to 'Hermes',—i. e. said to be taught in the Egyptian 'books of Thoth'. The system may be tabulated thus :—

Supracosmic gods :
{ First God (ὑπὲρ νοῦν), called νοητάρχης.
{ Second God (νοῦς), called αὐτάρχης and οὐσιοπάτωρ.

Cosmic gods :
{ θεοὶ ἐπουράνιοι.
{ θεοὶ ἐμπύριοι.
{ θεοὶ αἰθέριοι.

[1] εἰδικὸν Plnt. : ἴδιον Stob. : ἀίδιον coni. Heeren.
[2] I. e. apprehends the one universal, not the many particulars.
[3] Read οἱ μὲν ἐπὶ μέρους, [[ ]] [ἀν]αίσθητοί ⟨ὄντες⟩ ἀπερίληπτοί ⟨⟨εἰσι⟩⟩ καὶ ἄπειροι, or something to that effect.

Porphyry divided the cosmic gods into the same three classes. Aug. *De civ. dei* 10. 27 (addressed to Porphyry): 'Tu autem hoc didicisti non a Platone, sed a Chaldaeis magistris tuis,[1] ut in *aetherias* vel *empyreas* mundi sublimitates et firmamenta *caelestia* extolleres vitia humana, ut possent di vestri theurgis pronuntiare divina.' A partly similar division is spoken of by Proclus, *ap.* Simplic. *in phys.* 613. 4: τοῦτο γὰρ εἶναι τὸ φῶς[2] τὸ ὑπὲρ τὸ ἐμπύριον, μονάδα ὂν πρὸ τριάδος τῆς τοῦ ἐμπυρίου καὶ αἰθερίου καὶ ὑλαίου. Proclus *in Tim.* 156 E: τί οὖν; φαίη τις ἂν τῶν ἐκ τῆς ἱερορίου θεοσοφίας ὡρμημένων καὶ τὰ πάντα διαιρουμένων εἰς ἐμπύριον, αἰθέριον, ὑλαῖον, καὶ μόνον τὸ ἐμφανὲς ὑλαῖον καλούντων. Lydus *De mens.* 19. 2: τρεῖς δὲ σωμάτων διαφοραί· τὰ μὲν γάρ ἐστιν ὑλικά, τὰ δὲ ἀέρια (α(ἰθ)έρια?), τὰ δὲ ἐμπύρια, ὡς ὁ Χαλδαῖος παραδίδωσιν.[3]

Proclus evidently placed τὸ αἰθέριον below τὸ ἐμπύριον (as in Pseudo-Pl. *Epinomis* αἰθήρ is placed below πῦρ), and Abammon must have done likewise; that is, his series (αἰθερίων, ἐμπυρίων, ἐπουρανίων) must be understood as running upward from below. Perhaps the domain of the ἐπουράνιοι θεοί is the outermost sphere of heaven; that of the ἐμπύριοι θεοί, the sphere of the fixed stars; and that of the αἰθέριοι θεοί, the region of the planet-spheres. If so, the system in that respect agrees with the list of departments assigned to the several οὐσιάρχαι in *Ascl. Lat.* 19 b.

10–12. ἑκατὸν μὲν περὶ τῆς ἱστορίας τῶν ἐμπυρίων . . . συγγράμματα παραδούς, κ.τ.λ. It seems almost certain that the writer got these numbers from that catalogue (ἀπογραφή), of the 'books of Hermes' by Seleucus which is spoken of in 8. 1 b; and consequently, that the source of 8. 2 a, b, c as a whole was the work of Seleucus περὶ θεῶν. If that is so, it would follow from the close resemblance of the system summarized in 2 a, b, c to that of Plotinus, that the date at which Seleucus wrote can hardly have been earlier than the death of Plotinus in A. D. 270.

13. κατ' ἄλλην δὲ τάξιν ⟨. . .⟩ προ[σ]ράττει (*sc.* Ἑρμῆς) θεὸν τὸν Κμήφ (ἠμήφ MSS.). In 8. 3 a, b, c Abammon gives a scheme which is un-

---

[1] This apparently means the 'Chaldaean Oracles'.

[2] This φῶς corresponds to Abammon's θεοὶ ἐπουράνιοι. There is nothing in Abammon's list to correspond to the ὑλαῖον of Proclus, which apparently means the sublunar region.

[3] Kroll, *De orac. Chald.* p. 31, thinks that the division spoken of by Proclus was based on an obscure passage in the 'Chaldaean Oracles', in which it was said that out of Hecate, the source of 'soul' or life, πολλὴ ἄδην βλύζει ψυχῆς λιβὰς ἀρχεγενέθλου, | ἄρδην ἐμψυχοῦσα φάος, πῦρ, αἰθέρα, κόσμους. (φάος in that passage may perhaps be taken to correspond to τὸ ἐπουράνιον, πῦρ to τὸ ἐμπύριον, αἰθέρα to τὸ αἰθέριον, and κόσμους to τὸ ὑλαῖον.)

connected with that of 8. 2 a, b, c, and must have come from a different source. It is a second and independent attempt to state in terms of Greek philosophy the teaching of the 'Books of Thoth'. Its constructor identified each of the chief Egyptian gods with one of the component parts of his philosophic system.

For Κμήφ (Καμῆφις in Herm. *ap*. Stob. XXIII. 32) the Greeks sometimes wrote the form Κνήφ. See Addenda. Cf. Porphyr. *ap*. Euseb. *Pr. ev.* 3. 11. 45 : τὸν δημιουργόν, ὃν Κνὴφ οἱ Αἰγύπτιοι προσαγορεύουσιν. . . . τὸν δὲ θεὸν τοῦτον ἐκ τοῦ στόματος προίεσθαί φασιν ᾠόν, ἐξ οὗ γεννᾶσθαι θεὸν ὃν αὐτοὶ προσαγορεύουσι Φθᾶ, οἱ δὲ Ἕλληνες Ἥφαιστον· ἑρμηνεύειν δὲ τὸ ᾠὸν τὸν κόσμον. Plutarch, *Is. et Os.* 21, after speaking of the grave of Osiris, says οὐ μόνον δὲ τούτου (*sc.* Ὀσίριδος) οἱ ἱερεῖς λέγουσιν, ἀλλὰ καὶ τῶν ἄλλων θεῶν, ὅσοι μὴ ἀγέννητοι μηδ᾽ ἄφθαρτοι, τὰ μὲν σώματα παρ᾽ αὐτοῖς κεῖσθαι καμόντα καὶ θεραπεύεσθαι, τὰς δὲ ψυχὰς ἐν οὐρανῷ λάμπειν ἄστρα, . . . εἰς δὲ τὰς ταφὰς¹ τῶν τιμωμένων ζῴων τοὺς μὲν ἄλλους συντεταγμένα τελεῖν, μόνους δὲ μὴ διδόναι τοὺς Θηβαΐδα κατοικοῦντας, ὡς θνητὸν θεὸν οὐδένα νομίζοντας, ἀλλ᾽ ὃν καλοῦσιν αὐτοὶ Κνήφ, ἀγέννητον ὄντα καὶ ἀθάνατον. According to Plutarch's informants then, Osiris, Isis, and Horus had lived and died on earth as human beings, but Kneph had never thus lived and died ; he had been an immortal god from the first, and had never been incarnated.

14–15. ὃν φησι νοῦν εἶναι αὐτὸν ἑαυτὸν νοοῦντα καὶ τὰς νοήσεις εἰς ἑαυτὸν ἐπιστρέφοντα. νοῦς ἑαυτὸν νοῶν is the supreme God of the Aristotelians, and the second God of Plotinus.

This νοῦς must necessarily be supracosmic ; but the ἐπουράνιοι θεοί (if the term is used in the same sense as in 2 c) are cosmic. Consequently, if we retain the words τῶν ἐπουρανίων θεῶν ἡγούμενον, we must understand them to mean, not that this god is himself one of the ἐπουράνιοι θεοί and is first among them, but that he, a supracosmic god, has under his immediate guidance or command the ἐπουράνιοι θεοί, who, as the cosmic gods of highest rank, stand next below him. But to this there are two objections. In the first place, it is difficult to understand how one whose thoughts are directed wholly and solely on himself can act as ἡγεμών to others ; and in the second place, such a statement would be inconsistent with the following sentences, in which we are told that next below νοῦς ἑαυτὸν νοῶν stands, not an order of gods called ἐπουράνιοι, but another νοῦς (viz. ὁ δημιουργικός), who, in respect of his several δυνάμεις, is identified with the Egyptian gods Amun, Ptah, Osiris, &c. It is therefore necessary to bracket

---

¹ ταφάς Salmasius : γραφάς codd.

τῶν ἐπουρανίων θεῶν ἡγούμενον as an interpolation. Something like πρὸ τοῦ δημιουργικοῦ νοῦ has probably been lost before προτάττει.

15–16. ⟨⟨ἐν ᾧ (perhaps ὅς) δὴ τὸ πρῶτόν ἐστι νοοῦν καὶ τὸ πρῶτον νοητόν.⟩⟩ In the MSS., these words are made to refer to the ἓν ἀμερές. But they must have been intended to refer to νοῦς ἑαυτὸν νοῶν; and I have transposed them accordingly.[1] The words imply that this νοῦς is πρῶτος, and consequently that there is a δεύτερος νοῦς also.

τὸ νοοῦν is indistinguishable from νοῦς; the meaning would therefore be clearer if ὅς were written in place of ἐν ᾧ. In saying that this νοῦς contains in itself (or is) τὸ νοητόν as well as τὸ νοοῦν, the writer is in agreement with Plotinus, who identifies τὸ νοητόν (= τὸ ὄντως ὄν) with νοῦς.[2] That identification is indeed implied in Aristotle's statement that ὁ νοῦς ἑαυτὸν νοεῖ; for τὸ νοητόν means that which νοῦς νοεῖ.

16–17. τούτου δὲ τὸ ἓν ἀμερές, καὶ ὅ (ὃ καί?) φησι πρῶτον μάγευμα προτάττει. The ἓν ἀμερές is the ἕν of Plotinus, which is ἐπέκεινα νοῦ. It is called ἀμερές in contrast to νοῦς, which, according to Plotinus, is μεριστόν, both in the sense that it has two sides or aspects (τὸ νοοῦν and τὸ νοούμενον, subject and object), and in the sense that the νοητά with which it is identified, or to which it is correlative, are πολλά.

If the reading of the MSS. is right, we are told that the term πρῶτον μάγευμα was used 'by Hermes' (i.e. in one or more of the Egyptian 'Books of Thoth') to denote the One. μάγευμα elsewhere means 'a piece of magic art', a charm or spell, from μαγεύειν and μάγος. In that sense the word is impossible here. Gale conjectured μαίευμα; but this would mean 'a thing brought forth by a midwife's aid', and would not be applicable to the One, which is ἀγέννητον, and is prior to all else. μάγευμα might however (by analogy with μαγεύς, μαγεῖον, and ἐκμαγεῖον) be connected with μάσσειν, to knead, and taken as equivalent to μάγμα, 'a thing kneaded'; and it is possible that the author wrote either μάγμα, or μάγευμα in the sense of μάγμα, and meant by it 'a plastic mass' (of moist clay or the like). A

[1] There is another reason also for transposing them. In the MSS., a clause beginning with ἐν ᾧ δή is immediately followed by a clause beginning with ὃ δή; which is hardly admissible.

[2] Plot. 5. 1. 4: ἕκαστον δὲ αὐτῶν (sc. τῶν νοητῶν) νοῦς καὶ ὄν ἐστι, καὶ τὸ σύμπαν πᾶς νοῦς καὶ πᾶν ὄν. . . . ἅμα [μὲν] γὰρ ἐκεῖνα καὶ συνυπάρχει καὶ οὐκ ἀπολείπει ἄλληλα, ἀλλὰ δύο ὄντα ⌜τοῦτο τὸ ἕν⌝ ὁμοῦ νοῦς καὶ ὄν, καὶ νοοῦν καὶ νοούμενον, ὁ μὲν νοῦς κατὰ τὸ νοεῖν, τὸ δὲ ὂν κατὰ τὸ νοούμενον.—(δύο ὄντα τοῦτο τὸ ἕν is unintelligible; but the meaning must have been something like δύο ὄντα ἕν ἐστιν). Cf. Porphyr. ap. Cyril c. Jul. 552 B (Testim.): νοῦν . . ., ἐν ᾧ δὴ τὰ ὄντως ὄντα καὶ ἡ πᾶσα οὐσία τῶν ὄντων.

primal mud or slime out of which the world was evolved occurs in some cosmologies (e.g. in that of Sanchuniathon). An Egyptian might have used some such term to denote the mud out of which grew the lotus from which the Sun-god issued; and a Neoplatonist might see in it a symbol or figure of the One, in which all things are implicitly contained, but in which they are as yet undifferentiated and, as it were, 'kneaded together'.

But it is possible that καὶ ὅ φησι πρῶτον μάγευμα has been wrongly inserted. In the MSS., there are here four relative clauses in succession; and after removing both this one and ἐν ᾧ δὴ . . . νοούμενον, we should still have two remaining, which is as much as can easily be tolerated.

17. ὃν καὶ Εἰχτὼν ἐπονομάζει. Εἰχτών is probably an Egyptian god-name. Cf. Griffith and Thompson, *Demotic Magical Pap.*, col. vi, l. 20 (in an invocation addressed to the lamp in a *lychnomanteia*): 'You (must) say again "Esex, Poe, Ef-khe-ton", otherwise said, "Khet-on".' (Note *ad loc.*: 'The pronunciation of both groups was probably almost identical, ḥetôn.') In *Pistis Sophia*, c. 126 (C. Schmidt, p. 207), the 'first archon', who 'has a crocodile-face, and whose tail is in his mouth', is named *Enchthonin*; which may perhaps be a corrupt form of the same name.

Is it possible that ῥηξίχθων, which occurs as a god-name in magic Papyri, is connected? Could it be ῥη-σι(or π-σι)-ιχθων, *Re son of Ichthon*, altered to make it sound like a Greek word?

18. ὃ δὴ καὶ διὰ σιγῆς μόνης θεραπεύεται. In the traditional text, these words appear to refer to τὸ πρῶτον νοοῦν καὶ τὸ πρῶτον νοητόν, i.e. to the first νοῦς. But that is impossible; for the first νοῦς is identified with Kmeph, who was a temple-god with an established cult, and must have been like all other temple-gods, worshipped with vocal adoration. It must be the One (τὸ ἓν ἀμερές, named Εἰχτών,) that 'is worshipped only by silent contemplation'; and we get that clearly said, when the intervening words ἐν ᾧ δὴ . . . νοητόν have been removed.

As to 'silent worship' of the supreme God, cf. Porphyr. *De abst.* 2. 34: διὸ οὐδὲ λόγος τούτῳ (*sc.* θεῷ τῷ ἐπὶ πᾶσιν) ὁ κατὰ φωνὴν οἰκεῖος, οὐδ' ὁ ἔνδον, ὅταν πάθει ψυχῆς ᾖ μεμολυσμένος, διὰ δὲ σιγῆς καθαρᾶς καὶ τῶν περὶ αὐτοῦ καθαρῶν ἐννοιῶν θρησκεύομεν αὐτόν. . . . τοῖς δὲ αὐτοῦ ἐκγόνοις, νοητοῖς δὲ θεοῖς, ἤδη καὶ τὴν ἐκ τοῦ λόγου ὑμνῳδίαν προσθετέον.

20. ὁ γὰρ δημιουργικὸς νοῦς κ.τ.λ. In distinguishing a first νοῦς (ὁ ἑαυτὸν νοῶν) and a second νοῦς (ὁ δημιουργικός), the constructor of

this system agreed with Numenius (Euseb. *Pr. ev.* 11. 18. 22). In recognizing a ἕν above νοῦς, he agreed with Plotinus.

⟨ὁ⟩ καὶ [τῆς] ἀληθείας προστάτης καὶ σοφίας. The second νοῦς is 'president' or 'patron' of truth and wisdom. This appears to mean that, besides being Demiurgus of the universe, the second νοῦς has another function also, viz. that of revealing truth to men and inspiring them with wisdom. To say that he does this is equivalent to saying that he puts νοῦς into men; i.e. that the νοῦς of the individual man comes to him from a divine and universal νοῦς.

The function which in these words is assigned to the second νοῦς is the same, or nearly the same, as that which in 1. 1 was assigned to the god Thoth-Hermes.

20–22. (ὁ δημιουργικὸς νοῦς) ἐρχόμενος μὲν ἐπὶ γένεσιν, καὶ τὴν ἀφανῆ τῶν κεκρυμμένων λόγων δύναμιν εἰς φῶς ἄγων, Ἀμοῦν . . . λέγεται. The κεκρυμμένοι λόγοι correspond to the σπερματικοὶ λόγοι of the Stoics. A Platonist would take these λόγοι to be thoughts or designs of the Demiurgus. They are the conceptions of things which do not yet exist; and to them is attributed the force by which things are brought into existence. To 'bring their hidden force into light', i.e. to make it manifest, signifies to bring things into visible existence by means of the force inherent in the λόγοι.

The name Amun was thought by Egyptians to mean 'the Hidden One'; and the writer was thinking of this explanation of the name when he used the words ἀφανῆ and κεκρυμμένων. Cf. Plut. *Is. et Os.* 9: τῶν πολλῶν νομιζόντων ἴδιον παρ' Αἰγυπτίοις ὄνομα τοῦ Διὸς εἶναι τὸν Ἀμοῦν (ὃ παράγοντες ἡμεῖς Ἄμμωνα λέγομεν), Μανεθὼς μὲν ὁ Σεβεννίτης τὸ κεκρυμμένον οἴεται καὶ τὴν κρύψιν ὑπὸ ταύτης δηλοῦσθαι τῆς φωνῆς· Ἑκαταῖος δὲ ὁ Ἀβδηρίτης φησὶ τούτῳ καὶ πρὸς ἀλλήλους τῷ ῥήματι χρῆσθαι τοὺς Αἰγυπτίους, ὅταν τινὰ προσκαλῶνται· προσκλητικὴν γὰρ εἶναι τὴν φωνήν. διὸ τὸν πρῶτον θεόν, ὃν τῷ παντὶ τὸν αὐτὸν νομίζουσιν, ὡς ἀφανῆ καὶ κεκρυμμένον ὄντα, προσκαλούμενοι καὶ παρακαλοῦντες ἐμφανῆ γενέσθαι καὶ δῆλον αὐτοῖς, Ἀμοῦν λέγουσιν.

23. συντελῶν δὲ ἀψευδῶς ἕκαστα καὶ τεχνικῶς μετ' ἀληθείας (λέγεται) Φθά. As bringing things into existence, the demiurgic νοῦς is called Amun; as working on things already in existence, and 'finishing them off' (συντελῶν) or bringing them to perfection, he is called Ptah. In doing the latter, he works as a skilled craftsman (τεχνικῶς); and it is because of this aspect of his work, Abammon adds, that the Greeks identify Ptah with their craftsman-god Hephaistos.

[Professor F. L. Griffith informs me that Ptah is much associated with Mê'it, 'Truth', perhaps because good workmanship needs 'exactitude', though that is uncertain.][1]

25. ἀγαθῶν δὲ ποιητικὸς ὤν, Ὄσιρις κέκληται. Cf. Plut. *Is. et Os.* 42 : ὁ γὰρ Ὄσιρις ἀγαθοποιός· ... τὸ δ' ἕτερον ὄνομα τοῦ θεοῦ, ⌜τὸν Ὄμφιν⌝, εὐεργέτην ὁ Ἑρμαῖός φησι δηλοῦν ἑρμηνευόμενον. (τὸν Ὄμφιν must be a corruption of Ὀννωφ(ρ)ιν or some such Greek transliteration of Wen-nofre.) [But ἀγαθοποιός is not a correct translation of *Wen-nofre*, which has some such meaning as 'the good being' or 'the beautiful being'; so Professor Griffith tells me.]

The scheme given in 8. 3 a, b, c is this :—

(1) τὸ ἕν ; called Eichton (and πρῶτον μάγευμα).

(2) First νοῦς (ἑαυτὸν νοῶν) ; called Kmeph.

(3) Second νοῦς (δημιουργικός) ; called Amun, Ptah, Osiris, &c., in respect of his several δυνάμεις or modes of action.

33. 1–3. ἔστι δὴ οὖν καὶ ἄλλη τις ἡγεμονία παρ' αὐτοῖς . . ., ἥντινα ἀπονέμουσιν ἡλίῳ. παρ' αὐτοῖς means παρὰ τοῖς Αἰγυπτίοις. This is a system which seems to be unconnected with that of 8. 3 a, b, c, and to have been taken from another source.

τῶν περὶ γένεσιν ⌜ὅλων⌝ στοιχείων καὶ τῶν ἐν αὐτοῖς δυνάμεων, τεττάρων μὲν ἀρρενικῶν τεττάρων δὲ θηλυκῶν. Cf. Sen. *Nat. quaest.* 3. 12. 2 : 'Aegyptii quatuor elementa fecerunt, deinde ex singulis bina, maria et feminea.'

In Egyptian inscriptions, from the time of Amasis (*c.* 550 B.C.) onward, there is frequently mentioned an Ogdoad consisting of four male and four female deities, to whom collectively was assigned a part in the making of the world. (Brugsch *Rel. und Myth.* pp. 125–160). Their names are given (with some variations) as Nun and Nunet, Ḥeh and Ḥehet, Kek and Keket, Nenu and Nenut. The four males are depicted in the form of frog-headed men, and the four females in the form of snake-headed women. As this Ogdoad can be traced back to the middle of the sixth century B.C., and the doctrine of the four cosmic elements was not clearly formulated among the Greeks before the time of Empedocles (*c.* 450 B.C.), and was probably unknown in Egypt until introduced there by Greeks, these four pairs of deities

---

[1] Brugsch, *Rel. und Myth.* p. 85, says that in Egyptian inscriptions Ptah is frequently entitled 'father' or 'lord of the craftsmen' and 'of the crafts'. That corresponds to Abammon's statement that Ptah works τεχνικῶς. But Brugsch also says (*ib.* p. 111) that Ptah is sometimes called 'the lord of truth', 'the maker of truth', and 'he who establishes truth throughout the world'; and perhaps the addition of ἀψευδῶς and μετ' ἀληθείας has something to do with the aspect of Ptah's action that is implied in these latter phrases.

cannot have originally meant the four elements; but they came to be identified with the four elements in the Hellenistic period.

We are told that these four pairs of element-gods are presided over by the Sun-god; which implies that in this system the Sun-god is the maker of all things on earth, and constructs them out of the elements with the assistance of the Ogdoad.

3-4. καὶ ἄλλη τῆς φύσεως ὅλης τῆς περὶ γένεσιν ἀρχή, ἥντινα σελήνῃ διδόασι. This is another system again, in which it is the Moon, and not the Sun, that presides over all γένεσις in the sublunar world. That would not necessarily exclude the existence of supracosmic gods, and of οὐράνιοι θεοί (fixed stars, Sun and other planets) above the Moon; but it can hardly have been combined with the preceding doctrine of Sun and elements.

5-6. διαλαμβάνοντες τὸν οὐρανὸν εἰς δύο μοίρας, ἢ τέτταρας, ἢ δώδεκα, ἢ ἓξ καὶ τριάκοντα, ἢ διπλασίας τούτων. The twelve parts of heaven correspond to the twelve Signs of the Zodiac; and the 36 parts, to the 36 Decani among whom the Zodiac was portioned out. (On the Decani, see Herm. *ap*. Stob. *Exc*. VI.) Hence it is probable that the divisions of heaven into 2, 4, and 72 parts also were based on divisions of the Zodiac. The meaning seems to be that the zodiacal circle was marked off into segments of 180°, 90°, 30°, 10°, and 5°, and each of these segments, larger or smaller, together with that portion of the celestial sphere which ʻrises along with itʼ (παρανατέλλει), was placed under the command of a particular god (each of the ten-degree parts, for instance, being assigned to one of the Decani). As χρονοκράτορες, these gods would preside over spaces of time varying from half a year to five days.

Since ἤ, and not καί, is used, the writer apparently meant that heaven was differently divided in different documents known to him; i. e. that one of his authorities divided it into two parts, another into four, and so on. But if their several statements were combined together into one system (as he would consider that they ought to be), there would be a hierarchy of οὐράνιοι θεοί of different ranks, headed by the one god who presides over heaven as a whole, and extending to the seventy-two gods each of whom has charge of a space of five degrees.

All the gods of this system have to do with the sphere of the fixed stars, and nothing is here said about sun, moon, or other planets.

8. ⌜πᾶσι δὲ αὐτὸν⌝ ὑπερέχοντα αὐτῶν ἕνα προτιθέασι. The author must have written something like πάντων δὲ τούτων ὑπερέχοντα

ἕνα προτιθέασι. This 'one god' is the first and highest of the gods ; whether those who thus 'divided heaven into parts' spoke also of a supracosmic God above him or not, we are not told.

9–13. καὶ οὕτως ἄνωθεν . . . πάντων αἰτίας. This is a summary description of the theological system which the writer supposed to be contained in the 'books of Thoth', and in which he considered all the distinct systems spoken of in 8. 2 a–3 e to be comprehended. Cf. *Ascl. Lat.* III. 19 c, where the list of οὐσιάρχαι concludes with a sentence to the same effect as this.

11–13. πανταχοῦ τῆς ἀορίστου φύσεως ἐπικρατουμένης ὑπό τινος ὡρισμέ. νου μέτρου καὶ τῆς ἀνωτάτω ἑνιαίας πάντων αἰτίας. The lower is ἀόριστον as compared with the higher ; e. g. the sublunar world is ἀόριστον in comparison with the heavens, and the material universe as a whole is ἀόριστον in comparison with τὰ νοητά.

The ἑνιαία πάντων αἰτία is the θεὸς εἷς of 8. 2 a, the ἓν ἀμερές of 3 b.

14. ὕλην δὲ παρήγαγεν ὁ θεός· 'Matter was brought into being by God.' This, or something like it, was the doctrine of the Neoplatonists, from Plotinus [1] onward ; whereas the earlier Platonists regarded ὕλη as pre-existing side by side with God.

14–15. ἀπὸ τῆς οὐσιότητος ⌈ὑποσχισθείσης (*al.* ἀποσχισθείσης)⌉ ⟨τῆς ?⟩ ὑλότητος. Cf. Iamblichus *ap.* Proclum *in Tim.* 117 D (*Testim.*): Ἰάμβλιχος ἱστόρησεν ὅτι καὶ Ἑρμῆς ἐκ τῆς οὐσιότητος τὴν ὑλότητα παράγεσθαι βούλεται. If the meaning of Abammon's phrase is the same as that of the phrase ascribed to Hermes by Iamblichus, τῆς οὐσιότητος must be equivalent to τῶν νοητῶν (cf. Procl. *ib.*, Ὀρφεὺς . . . ἀπὸ τῆς πρωτίστης τῶν νοητῶν ὑποστάσεως παράγει τὴν ὕλην), and ὑποσχισθείσης must have been wrongly substituted for some participle equivalent to παραχθείσης.

Is *Abammonis resp.* 8. 3 g the passage to which Proclus refers?

---

[1] As to the origin of ὕλη, Plotinus speaks somewhat ambiguously; e. g. 4. 8. 6 : εἴτ' οὖν ἦν ἀεὶ ἡ τῆς ὕλης φύσις . . . εἴτ' ἐπηκολούθησεν ἐξ ἀνάγκης ἡ γένεσις αὐτῆς τοῖς πρὸ αὐτῆς αἰτίοις. (ὕλη is, according to Plotinus, τὸ μὴ ὄν ; and it is difficult to speak definitely of an origin of the non-existent.) His view on this question is thus stated by B. A. G. Fuller, *The problem of evil in Plotinus.* p. 306 : 'The passages we have been considering appear to teach a substantial derivation of Matter from the One. Matter is τὸ ἔσχατον in a chain of which the One is τὸ πρῶτον, and in which each link is derived from and dependent upon its antecedent. Just as the One overflows into Mind [say rather "as the One, by overflowing, gives rise to Mind", and so on] Mind into Soul, and Soul into the world, so the lower powers of Soul in their final exhaustion pass over into blind nothingness [i. e. into ὕλη], or in other words, beget or produce it. The last glimmer of light, we might say, by its extinction, gives rise to darkness.' Cf. Zeller III. ii, pp. 599–601.

If so, it would follow that Proclus believed 'Abammon's Reply' to have been written by Iamblichus.

Proclus says that Iamblichus ascribed the statement about ὑλότης and οὐσιότης to Hermes. Abammon does not explicitly ascribe it to Hermes; but he gives it to be understood that all the doctrines which he sets forth in Part 8 of his Reply, including this, were taught in the Egyptian 'Books of Hermes'. It would therefore be possible to say that the writer of 'Abammon's Reply' ἱστόρησεν ὅτι καὶ Ἑρμῆς κ.τ.λ. It cannot, however, be considered certain that Proclus is referring to 'Abammon's Reply'; for it may be that the statement about ὑλότης and οὐσιότης was taken by the author of 'Abammon's Reply' from a Greek *Hermeticum*; that Iamblichus, in one of his lost writings, quoted it from that same *Hermeticum*; and that Proclus refers to that lost writing of Iamblichus.

15. ἣν παραλαβὼν ὁ δημιουργός. ὕλη was brought into being by (the supreme) God, and was 'taken over' from him by the Demiurgus. This agrees with the doctrine of Proclus, who says (*Plat. theol.* 218) that ὕλη was not made by the Demiurgus, but was generated by the Powers above him, and that he found it already in existence: πρόεισιν οὖν καὶ ἡ ὕλη καὶ πᾶν τὸ ὑποκείμενον τῶν σωμάτων ἄνωθεν ἀπὸ τῶν πρωτίστων ἀρχῶν, αἳ δὴ διὰ περιουσίαν δυνάμεως ἀπογεννᾶν δύνανται καὶ τὸ ἔσχατον τῶν ὄντων. Cf. Procl. *In Tim.* 116 F–117 D (*Testim.*) and Procl. *Instit.* 72 (Zeller III. ii, p. 869). In this way a Neoplatonist could reconcile his opinion that ὕλην παρήγαγεν ὁ θεός with the teaching of the *Timaeus* concerning the Demiurgus and his dealings with the ὑποδοχή (which was called ὕλη by those who wrote after Plato).

ζωτικὴν οὖσαν. ὕλη had in it the potentiality of life, and was thereby suited to be used as the raw material out of which living bodies (both that of the Kosmos and those of all living things contained in it) were made. This statement is hardly consistent with the commonly accepted view that the primal ὕλη was ἄμορφος, ἀνείδεος, or ἄποιος, i.e. devoid of all qualities; but some Platonists (e.g. Plutarch, *Is. et Os.* 58) denied that ὕλη was wholly ἄποιος. See preliminary note on *Ascl. Lat.* II.

15–17. τὰς ⟨μὲν⟩ [ἁπλᾶς καὶ] ἀπαθεῖς σφαίρας ἀπ⟨ὸ τοῦ καθαρωτέρου?⟩ αὐτῆς ἐδημιούργησε, τὸ δὲ ἔσχατον αὐτῆς εἰς τὰ γεννητὰ καὶ φθαρτὰ σώματα διεκόσμησε. ἁπλᾶς is probably a variant for ἀπαθεῖς. The spheres of heaven, and the gods who dwell in them, are ἀπαθεῖς, i.e. exempt from perturbations; but there is no good reason for calling them 'simple'.

The phrase τὸ ἔσχατον αὐτῆς (which requires as its antithesis something like τὸ καθαρώτερον αὐτῆς) implies not only that the ὕλη spoken of was not ἄποιος, but also that one part of it differed in quality from another part. Out of the purer part of it the Demiurgus made the unchanging heavens; out of the coarse residuum he made the mortal organisms of the sublunar world. Cf. *Corp.* VIII. 3; and Methodius Περὶ τοῦ αὐτεξουσίου 2–4, quoted in preliminary note on *Ascl. Lat.* II.

19–20. τὰ μὲν γὰρ φερόμενα ὡς Ἑρμοῦ. These are the Greek *Hermetica*. They are included among the writings which Porphyry, in his letter to Anebo, said that he had read (οἷς λέγεις περιτετυχηκέναι); and he could not have read books written in the Egyptian language. This proves that some of our *Hermetica* (or at any rate Greek *Hermetica* of the same kind) were known to Porphyry.

Abammon says that they are translations or paraphrases of documents written in the Egyptian language. In that, he is mistaken. He rightly recognizes that their terminology is not Egyptian, but is that of Greek philosophy (τῇ τῶν φιλοσόφων γλώττῃ πολλάκις χρῆται); but he accounts for this by saying that the translators were experts in Greek philosophy, and expressed the substance of the ancient Egyptian doctrines (Ἑρμαϊκὰς δόξας) in terms which they had learnt in the Greek schools.

23. Χαιρήμων δέ. Chaeremon wrote about the middle of the first century A. D. He was an Egyptian priest (a ἱερογραμματεύς, Porphyr. *ap.* Euseb. *Pr. ev.* 5. 10. 5), and won high repute by his proficiency in Greek learning. He is said to have been chief librarian of the Alexandrian library; and he was one of the teachers appointed to give lessons to the boy Nero (Suidas *s. v.* Ἀλέξανδρος Αἰγαῖος). He was an adherent of Stoicism[1] (perhaps the syncretic Stoicism of Posidonius); and he wrote an Αἰγυπτιακὴ ἱστορία, in which he gave an account of Egyptian theology, interpreting it in accordance with Stoic doctrine.

The paragraph of Porphyry's letter which Abammon, from this point on to 8. 8 *fin.* is answering, is given as follows by Eusebius, *Pr. ev.* 3. 3 *fin.* (p. 92 a): ἄκουε δ᾽ οὖν ἃ καὶ ὁ Πορφύριος ἐν τῇ πρὸς Ἀνεβὼ τὸν Αἰγύπτιον ἐπιστολῇ περὶ τῶν αὐτῶν ἱστορεῖ· (4. 1)

---

[1] He is called Χαιρήμων ὁ Στωικός by Porphyry, *De abst.* 4. 6. *Ib.* 4. 8 *fin.*: (Χαιρήμονος,) ἀνδρὸς φιλαλήθους τε καὶ ἀκριβοῦς, ἔν τε τοῖς Στωικοῖς πραγματικώτατα φιλοσοφήσαντος.

"Χαιρήμων¹ μὲν γὰρ καὶ οἱ ἄλλοι οὐδ' ἄλλο τι² πρὸ τῶν ὁρωμένων κόσμων³ ⌈ἡγοῦνται, ἐν ἀρχῆς λόγῳ τιθέμενοι τοὺς Αἰγυπτίων⌉,⁴ οὐδ' ἄλλους θεοὺς πλὴν τῶν πλανητῶν λεγομένων,⁵ καὶ τῶν συμπληρούντων τὸν ζῳδιακόν,⁶ καὶ ὅσοι τούτοις παρανατέλλουσι ⟨. . .⟩ τάς τε εἰς τοὺς δεκανοὺς τομὰς καὶ τοὺς ὡροσκόπους,⁷ καὶ τοὺς λεγομένους κραταιοὺς ἡγεμόνας,⁸ ὧν καὶ τὰ ὀνόματα ἐν τοῖς ⌈ἀλμενιχιακοῖς⌉⁹ φέρεται, καὶ θεραπεῖαι

¹ Cf. Euseb. *Pr. ev.* 3. 9. 15 : καὶ ὁ Χαιρήμων δὲ μικρῷ ἔμπροσθεν ἐμαρτύρει οὐδ' ἄλλο τι πρὸ τοῦ ὁρωμένου κόσμου τοὺς Αἰγυπτίους ἡγεῖσθαι, οὐδ' ἄλλους θεοὺς πλὴν τῶν πλανητῶν καὶ τῶν λοιπῶν ἀστέρων, πάντα τε εἰς τὰ ὁρώμενα τοῦ κόσμου μέρη καὶ οὐδὲν εἰς ἀσωμάτους καὶ ζώσας οὐσίας ἑρμηνεύοντας. The first part of that sentence (καὶ ὁ Χαιρήμων . . . τῶν λοιπῶν ἀστέρων) is a repetition, with slight changes, of Χαιρήμων μὲν . . . τούτοις παρανατέλλουσι in 3 4. 1; the second part of it (πάντα τε . . . ἑρμηνεύοντας) is an almost exact repetition of καὶ ὅλως πάντα . . . ἑρμηνεύοντας in 3. 4. 2. Is the awkwardness of the grammatical construction (ἐμαρτύρει . . . ἡγεῖσθαι . . . πάντα τε . . . ἑρμηνεύοντας, a participle coupled to an infinitive) due to an error in the text? Or does it result from Eusebius' carelessness in putting together phrases copied from two different parts of the earlier passage?

² οὐδέ is difficult to account for. We should have expected οὐδὲν ἄλλο; but οὐδ' ἄλλο τι is repeated in 3. 9. 15.

³ τῶν ὁρωμένων κόσμων may perhaps be a conflation of two different readings, τοῦ ὁρωμένου κόσμου (3. 9. 15) and τῶν ὁρωμένων (neuter). But the plural κόσμων is used in *Abammon* 8. 6 b; it there appears to mean the stars or the spheres of heaven.

⁴ There can be little doubt that the unintelligible words ἡγοῦνται . . . Αἰγυπτίων ought to be so corrected as to make them yield the same sense as the corresponding words in 3. 9. 15. The question with which Porphyry is concerned is not what sort of gods Chaeremon and others like him believed in, but what sort of gods they said the (early) Egyptians believed in. I would propose to emend the passage thus : Χαιρήμων μὲν γὰρ καὶ οἱ ἄλλοι ⟨μαρτυροῦσιν⟩ οὐδ' ἄλλο τι πρὸ τῶν ὁρωμένων [κόσμων] ἡγεῖσθαι [[ἐν ἀρχῆς λόγῳ τιθέμενοι]] τοὺς Αἰγυπτίους, οὐδ' ἄλλους θεοὺς πλὴν τῶν . . . καὶ ὅσοι τούτοις παρανατέλλουσι(ν), ⟨⟨ἐν ἀρχῆς λόγῳ τιθεμένο⟨υς⟩⟩⟩ τάς τε εἰς τοὺς δεκανοὺς τομὰς κ.τ.λ. The accusative τὰς τομάς has no grammatical construction; something therefore must have been lost before it, and ἐν ἀρχῆς λόγῳ τιθεμένους makes good sense when shifted to this place.

⁵ λεγομένων secludendum? The Christian Eusebius, in his comment on the passage, speaks of 'the stars called ἀπλανεῖς and those which are named πλανῆται'; but that the Pagan philosopher Porphyry should speak of 'the so-called planets' is almost as strange as if he were to speak of 'the so-called sun'.

⁶ οἱ συμπληροῦντες τὸν ζῳδιακόν are the gods of the twelve Signs and the other divisions of the Zodiac mentioned in 8. 3 e. The stars of the Zodiac and the παρανατέλλοντες of the several Zodiac-divisions together make up the whole number of fixed stars; so that τῶν πλανητῶν . . . παρανατέλλουσι is equivalent to τῶν ἀστέρων τῶν τε ἀπλανῶν ὀνομαζομένων καὶ τῶν πλανητῶν καλουμένων in 3. 4. 3, and to τῶν πλανητῶν καὶ τῶν λοιπῶν ἀστέρων in 3. 9. 15.

⁷ For the meaning of ὡροσκόποι, see note on *quorum vocabulum est Horoscopi* in *Ascl. Lat.* III. 19 b (vol. iii, p. 119). It is possible that ὡροσκόποι, as here used, is merely another name for the Decani; but if so, there must be some slight error in the text, both here and in the corresponding words of Abammon's Reply (τούς τε δεκανοὺς καὶ ὡροσκόπους, 8. 4 b).

⁸ The κραταιοὶ ἡγεμόνες must be astral gods of similar nature to the Decani; but there is nothing to show what particular class of astral gods is meant by this term. Cf. *Pap. mag. Berl.* i. 207 : ὁ κτίσ[τ]ας δεκανοὺς ⟨καὶ?⟩ κραταιοὺς καὶ ἀρχαγγέλους. (In another version of the same invocation, *Pap. mag. Par.* i. 1203, ὁ κτίσας θεοὺς καὶ ἀρχαγγέλους καὶ δεκανούς; i. e. the word κραταιούς is there omitted.)

⁹ ἀλμενιχιακοῖς codd. Euseb.: in codd. Abammon, σαλμεσχινιακοῖς (which is

παθῶν,[1] καὶ ἀνατολαὶ καὶ δύσεις, καὶ μελλόντων σημειώσεις. (2) ἑώρα
γὰρ[2] ⟨αὐ⟩τοὺς[3] τὸν ἥλιον δημιουργὸν φαμένους, καὶ τὰ περὶ τὸν Ὄσιριν καὶ
τὴν Ἶσιν καὶ πάντας τοὺς ἱερατικοὺς μύθους ἢ εἰς τοὺς ἀστέρας καὶ τὰς τούτων
φάνσεις καὶ κρύψεις καὶ ἐπιτολὰς[4] αἰνιττομένους,[5] ἢ εἰς τὰς τῆς σελήνης
αὐξήσεις καὶ μειώσεις, ἢ εἰς τὴν τοῦ ἡλίου πορείαν, ἢ τό γε νυκτερινὸν
ἡμισφαίριον ἢ τὸ ἡμερινόν, ἢ τόν γε ποταμόν· καὶ ὅλως πάντα εἰς τὰ
φυσικὰ καὶ οὐδὲν εἰς ἀσωμάτους καὶ ζώσας οὐσίας[6] ἑρμηνεύοντας. ὧν οἱ

given by the astrologer Hephaestion also), with the variants σαλαμινιακοῖς, σαλ-
μενισχιακοῖς, ἀλμενικιανοῖς. In cod. Paris. gr. 2. 417, fol. 112 R (Kroll *Philol.* 57,
p. 125; Hopfner *Über die Geheimlehren* p. 262) it is said that the astrologer
Nechepso got something ἐκ τῶν σαλμεσχοινιακῶν; and as this spelling of the word
agrees almost exactly with the best reading of codd. Abammon, it is probable that
it is right, or nearly right, and that ἀλμενιχιακοῖς, the reading of codd. Euseb., is
wrong. The word is most likely either Egyptian or Chaldaean.

From what is here said, it appears that the things denoted by this word were
writings known and used in Egypt, which contained (1) the names of the Decani
and other astral gods, (2) the times of rising and setting of the stars or constellations to which those names belonged, (3) predictions of future events by inference
from the movements of the stars, or directions for thus predicting them, and (4)
instructions how to heal diseases by methods based on these data (e. g. by invoking
this or that astral god, or by the use of certain remedies at times indicated by the
movements of the stars). That is, they were what we might call astronomical
almanachs, with astrological and 'astromedical' notes appended.

Is it possible that our word *almanach* is derived from ἀλμενιχ-ιακά? According
to the *Oxford English Dictionary*, the word (*almanach*) first occurs in Roger
Bacon's writings (A.D. 1267), and 'the immediate source of it was apparently a
Spanish-Arabic *al-manākh*. An Arabic-Castilian vocabulary of 1505 has *manākh*,
almanaque, calendario. . . . But the word occurs nowhere else as Arabic, has no
etymon in the language, and its origin is uncertain'. The writer of the article
in the *O. E. D.* concludes that 'the difficulties of connecting (ἀλμενιχιακοῖς)
historically either with the Spanish-Arabic *manākh*, or with med.L. *almanach*
without Arabic intermediation, seem insurmountable'. To this it might be
answered that, if the word used by Porphyry and Abammon continued to be used
by astrologers in Egypt down to the time of the Arab conquest, it may have been
carried thence to Spain by the Arabs; and if they took the first syllable of it to be
their article *al*, that may perhaps have given rise to the otherwise inexplicable
word *manākh*. But on the other hand, there is reason to think that the true form
of the word used in Egypt was σαλμεσχινιακά or something like it, and that
ἀλμενιχιακοῖς is a corruption; and if so, the resemblance between the latter and
almanach must be merely accidental.

[1] καὶ θεραπεῖαι παθῶν seems to be wrongly placed; perhaps it ought to follow
μελλόντων σημειώσεις.

[2] Sc. ὁ Χαιρήμων.

[3] αὐτοὺς scripsi: τοὺς MSS.

[4] The κρύψις of a star is the disappearance of it which is caused by the sun's
approach to it; and its φάνσις is its reappearance when the distance of the sun from
it has increased. The ἐπιτολή of a star is its (visible) rising above the eastern
horizon, and more especially its first visible rising after κρύψις. But perhaps it
would be better either to bracket ἐπιτολάς or to write ἐπιτολὰς ⟨καὶ δύσεις⟩.

[5] αἰνιττομένους scripsi: ἐλιττομένους codd.

[6] Both νοητοὶ θεοί, and the souls and minds of αἰσθητοὶ θεοί (star-gods, the Nile,
&c.), might be called ἀσώματοι οὐσίαι. The word ζώσας seems to imply that τὰ
φυσικά (= τὰ σωματικά), with which these οὐσίαι are contrasted, are not 'living'.
The Egyptians, as reported by Chaeremon, regarded the stars as gods, and must
therefore have held them to be 'living'; but according to him, they did not

πλείους καὶ τὸ ἐφ' ἡμῖν ἐκ τῆς τῶν ἀστέρων ἀνῆψαν κινήσεως, οὐκ οἶδ' ὅπως δεσμοῖς ἀλίτοις ἀνάγκη(ς),[1] ἣν εἱμαρμένην λέγουσι, πάντα καταδήσαντες, καὶ πάντα τούτοις ἀνάψαντες τοῖς θεοῖς, ⌜οὕτω⌝ λυτῆρας τῆς εἱμαρμένης ⌜μόνους⌝ ἔν τε ἱεροῖς καὶ ξοάνοις καὶ τοῖς ἄλλοις θεραπεύουσι."[2] (3) ταῦτα μὲν οὖν (says Eusebius) ἀπὸ τῆς δηλωθείσης ἐπιστολῆς κείσθω, σαφῶς διαγορεύοντα ὅτι καὶ ἡ τῶν Αἰγυπτίων ἀπόρρητος θεολογία οὐδὲ[3] ἄλλοις πλὴν τῶν κατ' οὐρανὸν ἀστέρων τῶν τε ἀπλανῶν ὀνομαζομένων καὶ τῶν πλανητῶν καλουμένων ἐθεολόγει, δημιουργόν τε τῶν ὅλων εἰσῆγεν οὕτινα οὖν ἀσώματον, . . . μόνον δὲ τὸν ὁρώμενον ἥλιον, κ.τ.λ.

23–24. Χαιρήμων δέ, καὶ εἴ τινες ἄλλοι τῶν περὶ τὸν κόσμον ἅπτονται [πρώτων] αἰτίων, τὰς τελευταίας ἀρχὰς ἐξηγοῦνται. The cosmic gods of whom Chaeremon and others like him speak are the ' last ' (i.e. proximate) causes of things ; the supracosmic gods, who are the primary causes, are not mentioned by them. πρώτων is unintelligible, and inconsistent with τελευταίας.

24–26. ὅσοι τε τοὺς πλανήτας . . . παραδιδόασι. These words look as if they referred to persons other than Chaeremon and those associated with him. But in the corresponding passage of Porphyry's letter, it appears to be said (though the reading is doubtful) that ' Chaeremon and the others ' spoke of the planets and the other star-gods. Perhaps the two passages can be reconciled by taking ὅσοι . . . παραδιδόασι to mean those Egyptians whose statements were reported by Chaeremon.

27–28. τά τε ἐν τοῖς σαλμεσχινιακοῖς μέρος τι βραχύτατον περιέχει τῶν Ἑρμαϊκῶν διατάξεων. The Ἑρμαϊκαὶ διατάξεις are the systems which the writer believed to be contained in the Egyptian ' Books of Thoth ', and to be portions of a single system in which they were all comprehended. The data supplied by the 'almanachs' belonged to one small part only of that comprehensive system.

34. 1–8. φυσικά τε οὐ λέγουσιν εἶναι πάντα . . . σφαίρας ἕτερον. Chaeremon said that the Egyptians φυσικὰ λέγουσιν εἶναι πάντα, i.e. that they (like the Stoics) do not admit the existence of anything except the material universe and its contents, and know nothing of supracosmic gods. Abammon denies this, and, in opposition to Chaeremon, here

recognize minds or souls, whether divine or human, *as things distinct from bodies, or existing apart from bodies.* Cf. the denial of Chaeremon's view in Abammon's Reply, 8. 4 d : φυσικά τε οὐ λέγουσιν εἶναι πάντα Αἰγύπτιοι, ἀλλὰ καὶ τὴν τῆς ψυχῆς ζωὴν καὶ τὴν νοερὰν ἀπὸ τῆς φύσεως διακρίνουσιν.

[1] ἀνάγκης Gale (cf. *Abammon* 8. 7 a) : ἀνάγκην A : ἀνάγκῃ Dindorf.

[2] Perhaps : καταδήσαντες· καὶ πάντα τούτοις ἀνάψαντες τοῖς θεοῖς, (τοὺς) αὐτ(οὺς) ὡ(ς) λυτῆρας, τῆς εἱμαρμένης [μόνους] (ὄντας) . . . θεραπεύουσι.

[3] οὐδέ is strange ; cf. οὐδ' ἄλλο τι in Porphyry's letter.

gives a summary of the theology which he himself considers to be
that of 'the Egyptians', i. e. of the doctrine which he supposes to be
taught in the ancient Egyptian writings, and which he accepts as his
own creed.

1–2. καὶ τὴν τῆς ψυχῆς ζωὴν καὶ τὴν νοερὰν ἀπὸ τῆς φύσεως διακρίνουσιν.
ἡ φύσις here means the material universe. The Stoics held ψυχή and
νοῦς to be corporeal things; the Platonists held them to be incorporeal. The Egyptians, says Abammon, agree with the Platonists in
this.

2–3. οὐκ ἐπὶ τοῦ παντὸς μόνον, ἀλλὰ καὶ ἐφ' ἡμῶν. The subject under
discussion is not man, but the universe and the gods by whom it is
governed; and it is not the human νοῦς that Abammon goes on to
speak of, but the divine and universal νοῦς. A better sense would
therefore be got by writing οὐκ ἐφ' ἡμῶν μόνον, ἀλλὰ καὶ ἐπὶ τοῦ
παντός.

3–4. νοῦν τε καὶ λόγον προστησάμενοι καθ' ἑαυτοὺς ὄντας. καθ' ἑαυτούς
means apart from matter; the νοῦς and λόγος spoken of are incorporeal.

Is λόγος a synonym for νοῦς? Or does the writer mean that the
Egyptians recognize two incorporeal gods, one of whom is here called
νοῦς, and the other λόγος? In the latter case, the λόγος would seem
to be identical with the second νοῦς spoken of below.

4–5. προπάτορά τε ⟨πρὸ τοῦ⟩ τῶν ἐν γενέσει δημιουργοῦ (προπάτορά τε
τῶν ἐν γενέσει δημιουργὸν MSS.) προτάττουσι. As to the word προπάτωρ,
see note on Herm. ap. Stob. Exc. II A. 13.

According to the reading of the MSS., the προπάτωρ is τῶν ἐν
γενέσει δημιουργός. But the meaning must have been that the
Egyptians recognize a προπάτωρ distinct from and prior to the
δημιουργὸς τῶν ἐν γενέσει; and I have corrected the text accordingly.
The προπάτωρ is the same God that is described as νοῦς καθ' ἑαυτὸν
ὤν, and as καθαρὸς νοῦς ὑπὲρ τὸν κόσμον; the δημιουργὸς τῶν ἐν γενέσει
is the same that is described as νοῦς ἀμέριστος ἐν ὅλῳ τῷ κόσμῳ.

The doctrine ascribed to 'the Egyptians' in this paragraph, and
apparently accepted by the writer, is not that of Iamblichus, nor is
it that of Plotinus; but it resembles that of Numenius.[1] There is
a first νοῦς, entirely detached from the Kosmos, and a second νοῦς,
who has made the Kosmos and governs it; but there is no mention

[1] Cf. Numenius ap. Euseb. Pr. ev. 11. 18. 6: καὶ γὰρ οὔτε (οὔ τι Gifford)
δημιουργεῖν ἐστι χρεὼν τὸν πρῶτον (sc. θεόν), καὶ τοῦ δημιουργοῦντος δὲ θεοῦ χρὴ
εἶναι νομίζεσθαι πατέρα τὸν πρῶτον θεόν. Numenius called these two Gods the
first νοῦς and the second νοῦς.

here of anything that is ὑπὲρ νοῦν or ἐπέκεινα νοῦ. In ignoring the ἕν which is ἐπέκεινα νοῦ, the system formulated in this passage (4 d) differs both from that of 8. 2 a, b, c and from that of 3 a, b, c; in distinguishing a first νοῦς and a second νοῦς, it agrees with that of 3 a, b, c.

7–8. καὶ ἕνα ἀμέριστον ἐν ὅλῳ τῷ κόσμῳ, καὶ διῃρημένον ἐπὶ πάσας τὰς σφαίρας ἕτερον. Besides the second νοῦς, which is present everywhere in the universe made and governed by it, but is 'undivided', there is also a third νοῦς, which is divided, and a portion of which is assigned to each of the several spheres. The second νοῦς and the third νοῦς together apparently correspond to the demiurgic νοῦς of 3 c, who is called by various names (Amun, Ptah, Osiris, &c.) in respect of his several δυνάμεις.

9–11. ἀλλὰ καὶ διὰ τῆς ἱερατικῆς θεουργίας ἀναβαίνειν... παραγγέλλουσι πρὸς τὸν θεὸν καὶ δημιουργόν. Abammon here says that 'the Egyptians' (i. e. Egyptian Books of Thoth and the priests who base their teaching on those books) tell men to make use of certain 'theurgic' or sacramental rites, and say that those who do so are, by means of those rites, raised to the world of νοῦς and νοητά, placed above the reach of εἱμαρμένη, and brought into conjunction with the Demiurgus. The theurgic rites here spoken of are evidently the same system of initiations that is described in 10. 5 d–6 b, q. v.

12–13. ἢ μόνον καιροῦ παρατήρησιν. If we retain these words, the meaning would seem to be that those who seek to be united with the Demiurgus by means of theurgic rites must perform each of the rites, or be admitted to each of the successive initiations, at a certain prescribed time. But there is no apparent reason for saying this. Perhaps ἢ ... παρατήρησιν may have been added by a later hand.

14. ὑφηγήσατο δὲ καὶ ταύτην τὴν ὁδὸν Ἑρμῆς. 'This way' must be taken to mean the method of *theurgia* spoken of in the preceding sentence. Not only a system of theology, says Abammon, but also instructions how to attain to union with the Demiurgus by means of sacramental rites, were given by 'Hermes', i. e. in writings ascribed to Thoth.

14–15. ⟨...⟩ ἡρμήνευσε δὲ Βίτυς προφήτης [Ἄμμωνι βασιλεῖ], ἐν ἀδύτοις εὑρὼν ἀναγεγραμμένην. In these words the writer is speaking of one particular document, apparently a treatise on the theurgic rites. (He adds below that 'there are also many other treatises' on the same subject.) If we accept the reading of the MSS., we must understand ἡρμήνευσε (ταύτην τὴν ὁδόν), ... εὑρὼν (ταύτην τὴν ὁδὸν) ἀναγεγραμμένην. But it is strange to call a document inscribed on a temple-wall 'this *way*'; and it seems most likely that some words, in which the particular treatise referred to was explicitly mentioned, have been lost before ἡρμήνευσε.

Abammon says that this document was inscribed, in hieroglyphic writing, in a temple at Saïs, and that Bitys 'discovered' the inscription and 'translated' it into Greek. (Cf. 10. 7 a : ὅπερ Βίτυς ἐκ τῶν Ἑρμαϊκῶν βίβλων μεθηρμήνευσεν.) A προφήτης means an Egyptian priest of a certain grade ; and 'Bitys the *prophetes*' must have been an Egyptian priest of recent date. It seems that he wrote in Greek a book on *theurgia*, and sought to give it authority by pretending that it was a translation of an ancient inscription, which he said he had found at Saïs.[1] The writer of Abammon's Reply accepted without doubt or question the statements of Bitys about the inscription, and consequently thought that the system of theurgic rites which was set forth in this recent book rested on ancient and indisputable authority.[2]

If Bitys wrote in Greek, and was believed to be the recent discoverer and translator of an ancient document, he cannot have been supposed to have been a contemporary of the prehistoric King Ammon ; the words Ἄμμωνι βασιλεῖ must therefore be struck out.[3]

[1] In doing this, he followed a common practice. Cf. *Pap. mag. Par.* i. 885 : δεῦρό μοι . . ., ἐπεί σοι λέγω τὰ ⟨ὀνόματα ?⟩ ἃ ἔγραψεν ἐν Ἡλιουπόλει ὁ τρισμέγιστος Ἑρμῆς ἐν ἱερογλυφικοῖς γράμμασι. For other instances, see note on *Herm. ap.* Stob. *Exc.* XXIII. 7.

[2] In saying this, I am assuming good faith on the part of the writer. But it is not impossible that Abammon (supposing him to have been a real person, and the author of the *De myst.*,) knew more about the origin of the document 'found' by Bitys than he thought fit to tell, and that he had connived at the pious fraud, or even co-operated in it.

One might compare the finding of 'the Book of the Law' (i.e. the Book of Deuteronomy) in the temple at Jerusalem in the reign of Josiah (2 Kings 22. 3 ff.). In that case also, important innovations in religious usage were authorized by a sacred book 'found' at the time when it was wanted for that purpose.

[3] Reitzenstein, *Poimandres*, p. 107, rightly strikes out Ἄμμωνι βασιλεῖ after Βίτυς προφήτης ; but he inserts those words after Ἑρμῆς. That is, he writes the passage thus : ὑφηγήσατο δὲ καὶ ταύτην τὴν ὁδὸν Ἑρμῆς ⟨⟨Ἄμμωνι βασιλεῖ⟩⟩, ἡρμήνευσε δὲ Βίτυς προφήτης [[ ]], ἐν ἀδύτοις εὑρὼν κ.τ.λ. This would imply that the book which Bitys wrote, and which he said he had translated from a hieroglyphic inscription, took the form of a discourse or epistle addressed by Hermes to King Ammon. That is not impossible ; but we have no reason to think that it was so.

Reitzenstein, *ib.* p. 108, identifies this Βίτυς with a Βίτος mentioned by the alchemist Zosimus (see *Testim.*), and with a Πίτυς spoken of as a magician in *Pap. mag. Par.* i (Wessely 1888, pp. 95, 92, 98 : Πίτυος ἀγωγή — βασιλεῖ Ὀστάνῃ Πίτυς χαίρειν — ἀγωγὴ Πίτυος βασιλέως — Πίτυος Θεσσαλοῦ), and thinks he may also be identical with a 'Bithus of Dyrrhachium' mentioned (as an authority on magical remedies) by Pliny, *N. H.* 28. 82. But there is no ground for these conjectures. The passage in Zosimus is corrupt and unintelligible ; if Bitys was an Egyptian *prophetes*, he cannot have been either a king or a Thessalian ; and Dyrrhachium was neither in Egypt nor in Thessaly.

Perhaps the person who inserted them was thinking of the Greek *Hermetica* which bore the superscription Ἑρμοῦ πρὸς Ἄμμωνα, and supposed them to be the writings to which Abammon referred. But the document spoken of must have differed in character for the *Hermes to Ammon* libelli of which specimens have been preserved by Stobaeus; for these are not treatises on *theurgia*, and, like the rest of our religious and philosophical *Hermetica*, show little interest in ritual.

16–17. [τό τε τοῦ θεοῦ ὄνομα παρέδωκε τὸ διῆκον δι᾽ ὅλου τοῦ κόσμου.] Who is the subject of παρέδωκε? Bitys, or Hermes? Whether the one or the other is meant, there is no intelligible connexion between this clause and those which precede it. A statement about something which pervades the universe has nothing to do with the topic of *theurgia*, with which the writer is dealing in this paragraph. It therefore seems most likely that τό τε . . . τοῦ κόσμου has been inserted here by error.

The Stoics spoke of a divine πνεῦμα which διήκει δι᾽ ὅλου τοῦ κόσμου;[1] and it is possible that ὄνομα is a misreading for πνεῦμα. But there are instances of ὄνομα in a similar connexion. *Pap. mag. Par.* i. 1209: ἐπικαλοῦμαί σου τὸ ἑκατονταγράμματον ὄνομα, τὸ διῆκον ἀπὸ τοῦ στερεώματος μέχρι τοῦ βάθους τῆς γῆς. (In another recension of the same invocation, *Pap. mag. Berl.* i. 217: ἐπικαλοῦμαί σου τὸ κρυ(π)τὸν ⌈υποδιηκον⌉ (*lege* ὄνομα, τὸ διῆκον) ἀπὸ τοῦ στερεώματος ἐπὶ τὴν γῆν.) In passages such as this, the god's *name* is identified with the god's *power* or *energy*.

It would be possible to read τό τε τοῦ θεοῦ ὄνομα παρέδωκε το(ῦ) διῆκον⟨τος⟩ δι᾽ ὅλου τοῦ κόσμου. This god might be one of the νόες that are spoken of in 8. 4 d (ἕνα ⟨νοῦν⟩ ἀμέριστον ἐν ὅλῳ τῷ κόσμῳ, καὶ διῃρημένον ἐπὶ πάσας τὰς σφαίρας ἕτερον); and we might suppose the writer of the words τό τε . . . τοῦ κόσμου to have meant that Bitys or Hermes, in the document spoken of, told the name of that god (said, perhaps, that his name was Kmēph? Cf. 8. 3 a). But whatever the person who wrote these words may have meant, it seems best to bracket them.

21. ὑπερκόσμιοί τε δυνάμεις, ἃς καὶ διὰ τῆς ἱερατικῆς ἁγιστείας ἐθεράπευσαν. ἡ ἱερατικὴ ἁγιστεία = ἡ ἱερατικὴ θεουργία (8. 4 e). The Demiurgus and his δυνάμεις, with whom the worshipper is united by

---

[1] Cf. a magic invocation in *Pap. mag. Par.* i. 1117: χαῖρε, τὸ πνεῦμα τὸ διῆκον ἀπὸ οὐρανοῦ ἐπὶ γῆν, καὶ ἀπὸ γῆς τῆς ἐν μέσῳ κύτ(ε)ι τοῦ κόσμου ἄχρι τῶν περάτων τῆς ἀβύσσου (i. e. of space).

means of theurgic rites, are present in the material universe (cf. 8. 4 d) ; but they may at the same time be called ὑπερκόσμιοι (supracosmic), inasmuch as they are not identified with the material universe or any parts of it, but are regarded as incorporeal beings who govern it.

22. κοινὰς ταῦτα δοκεῖ παρέχεσθαι ἀφορμάς. What does κοινάς mean ? ἱκανάς would give a clearer sense.

22-23. εἰς τὴν διάλυσιν καὶ τῶν μετὰ ταῦτα ἐπιζητουμένων ὅλων. τὰ μετὰ ταῦτα ἐπιζητούμενα are, or include, the questions about εἱμαρμένη which are spoken of in the last sentence of the extract from Porphyry's letter given by Eusebius, *Pr. ev.* 3. 4. 2 (see p. 70). Abammon apparently means 'you ought to be able to solve those problems for yourself, by applying to them the truths which I have already told you ; but in order to guard against the possibility of error, I will go on to discuss them directly and explicitly'.

24-25. περικρούσωμέν τε αὐτὰ πανταχόθεν, ἵν' εἰδῶμεν εἴ πη (ὅπη MSS.) σαθρόν τι διαδοξάζει. Cf. Pl. *Phileb.* 55 C: γενναίως δέ, εἰ πή τι σαθρὸν ἔχει (ἠχεῖ coni. Wytt.),[1] πᾶν περικρούωμεν. Pl. *Theaet.* 179 D : προσιτέον οὖν ἐγγυτέρω, . . . καὶ σκεπτέον τὴν φερομένην ταύτην οὐσίαν διακρούοντα εἴτε ὑγιὲς εἴτε σαθρὸν φθέγγεται. The metaphor is taken from the testing of an earthen or metallic vessel by rapping it. [διαδοξάζει may be taken as middle ; cf. Liddell and Scott, 9th edition.]

As the text stands, αὐτά means ταῦτα τὰ προβλήματα. But it is not the problems, but the solutions of them, that need testing. It may therefore be suspected that some words have been lost before περικρούσωμεν.

28-29. δύο γὰρ ἔχει ψυχάς, ὡς ταῦτά φησι τὰ γράμματα, ὁ ἄνθρωπος. The 'Hermaic' writings here spoken of are apparently those called τὰ φερόμενα ὡς Ἑρμοῦ in 8. 4 a, i.e. the Greek *Hermetica*. In none of the extant *Hermetica* is it explicitly said that 'man has two souls'; but a doctrine which is the same in substance, though expressed in other words, occurs in many of them.[2] That doctrine is indeed the foundation of all Platonic psychology. The lower of the 'two souls' is the thing which is called the θνητὸν εἶδος ψυχῆς in the *Timaeus*, and τὸ ἄλογον τῆς ψυχῆς in Aristotle's *Ethics*, but is divided into two parts, τὸ θυμοειδές and τὸ ἐπιθυμητικόν, in Plato's *Republic*; the higher of the two souls is that which is called the νοῦς in the *Timaeus*, and τὸ

---

[1] Badham retains ἔχει, objecting to ἠχεῖ that 'if this had been the meaning, the future must have been used'. Ought we then to read ἠχήσει? But the objection, if valid, would apply equally to φθέγγεται in *Theaet.*

[2] See, for instance, Herm. *ap.* Stob. *Exc.* II B. 6 and 7.

λογιστικόν in the *Republic*. These two things must have been called δύο ψυχαί in one or more Hermetic *libelli* which were known to the writer of 'Abammon's Reply', but are now lost.

They were so called by Numenius among others.[1] Porphyr. *ap.* Stob. 1. 49. 25 a, vol. i, p. 350 W.: ἄλλοι δέ, ὧν καὶ Νουμήνιος, οὐ τρία μέρη ψυχῆς μιᾶς, ἢ δύο γε, τὸ λογικὸν καὶ ⟨τὸ⟩[2] ἄλογον, ἀλλὰ δύο ψυχὰς ἔχειν ἡμᾶς οἴονται, ὥσπερ καὶ ⌜ἄλλοι⌝,[3] τὴν μὲν λογικήν, τὴν δὲ ἄλογον· ὧν πάλιν οἱ μὲν ἄμφω ἀθανάτους, οἱ δὲ τὴν ⟨μὲν⟩[4] λογικὴν ἀθάνατον, τὴν δὲ ἄλογον οὐ ⌜κατὰ τὰς ἐνεργείας μόνον ἀφίστασθαι τῆς ποιᾶς κινήσεως⌝,[5] ἀλλὰ καὶ κατ' οὐσίαν διαλύεσθαι. τοῖς δὲ ἐδόκει δύο ψυχῶν εἰς ταὐτὸ συμπλακεισῶν ἀλλήλαις, ⌜διπλασίας⌝ εἶναι τὰς κινήσεις,[6] ὁμοιουμένων ἀλλήλαις ἐκ τοῦ ἀπολαύειν ἑκατέραν τῶν τῆς ἑτέρας παθημάτων κατὰ τὴν ἕνωσιν. Cf. Clem. Alex. *Strom.* 2. 20. 114 (quoted in note on Herm. *ap.* Stob. *Exc.* IV A. 7): δύο γὰρ δὴ ψυχὰς ὑποτίθεται καὶ οὗτος (*sc.* Isidorus son of Basilides) ἐν ἡμῖν, καθάπερ οἱ Πυθαγόρειοι. (Numenius was commonly called a Pythagorean; but in that period there was little difference of meaning between the terms 'Pythagorean' and 'Platonist'.) Origen *De princip.* 3. 4. 1: 'Haberi a quibusdam quaestio solet huiusmodi, utrumnam velut duae animae in nobis dicendae sint, una quaedam divinior et caelestis, et alia inferior.' Plotinus 6. 7. 5: (ἡ θειοτέρα ψυχὴ) ἐποχεῖται τῇ ἥτις προσχρῆται πρώτως σώματι. ἡ δὲ (θειοτέρα προσχρῆται σώματι) δευτέρως· ἤδη γὰρ

---

[1] The earliest instance of the statement that 'man has two souls' occurs in Xen. *Cyrop.* 6. 1. 41, where the Mede Araspas, speaking of the struggle between his sense of honour and his illicit love of the captive Pantheia entrusted to his charge, says to Cyrus: δύο ... σαφῶς ἔχω ψυχάς· νῦν τοῦτο πεφιλοσόφηκα μετὰ τοῦ ἀδίκου σοφιστοῦ τοῦ Ἔρωτος. οὐ γὰρ δὴ μία γε οὖσα ἅμα ἀγαθή τέ ἐστι καὶ κακή, οὐδ' ἅμα καλῶν τε καὶ αἰσχρῶν ἔργων ἐρᾷ, καὶ ταὐτὰ ἅμα βούλεταί τε καὶ οὐ βούλεται πράττειν· ἀλλὰ δῆλον ὅτι δύο ἐστὸν ψυχά, καὶ ὅταν μὲν ἡ ἀγαθὴ κρατῇ, τὰ καλὰ πράττεται, ὅταν δὲ ἡ πονηρά, τὰ αἰσχρὰ ἐπιχειρεῖται. (The argument by which Xenophon's Araspas demonstrates his *philosophema* that 'man has two souls' is of the same kind as that by which Plato's Socrates, in *Rep.* 4. 435 sqq., proves that there are three distinct εἴδη in the human soul.) But the Hermetic writers of whom Abammon speaks are not likely to have borrowed this doctrine directly from Xenophon's romance.

[2] τὸ addidi.

[3] ἄλλοι MSS.: ἄλλα coni. Wachsmuth, who says 'ἄλλα sunt aures, oculi, manus &c.' (i. e. man has two souls, as he has two eyes and two ears). Cf. Macarius, quoted below.

[4] μὲν addidi.

[5] Perhaps either οὐ τῆς κατ' ἐνέργειαν μόνον ἀφίστασθαι κινήσεως, or οὐ τῆς ἐνεργείας μόνον ἀφίστασθαι [τῆς ποιᾶς κινήσεως]. The meaning must be that at death the ἄλογος ψυχὴ not only ceases to act, but ceases to exist.

[6] Perhaps, ⟨τοῦ⟩τοις δὲ (i. e. to those who said that man has two souls) ἐδόκει ⟨τῶν⟩ δύο ψυχῶν εἰς ταὐτὸ συμπλακεισῶν ἀλλήλαις ἁπλᾶς [ιας] εἶναι τὰς κινήσεις. Those who said what is reported in this sentence must have been explaining how it is that a man, though he has two souls, yet acts as one person and not as two.

αἰσθητικοῦ ὄντος τοῦ γενομένου ἐπηκολούθησεν αὕτη (sc. ἡ θειοτέρα ψυχή), τρανοτέραν ζωὴν διδοῦσα. μᾶλλον δὲ οὐδ' ἐπηκολούθησεν, ἀλλὰ οἷον προσέθηκεν αὐτήν· οὐ γὰρ ἐξίσταται τοῦ νοητοῦ (ἡ θειοτέρα ψυχή), ἀλλὰ συναψαμένη οἷον ἐκκρεμαμένην ἔχει τὴν κάτω, συμμίξασα ἑαυτὴν ⌜λόγῳ πρὸς λόγον⌝.[1] Plot. 2. 1. 5 fin. : ἡμεῖς δέ, πλασθέντες ὑπὸ τῆς διδομένης παρὰ τῶν ἐν οὐρανῷ θεῶν ψυχῆς[2] καὶ αὐτοῦ τοῦ οὐρανοῦ, κατ' ἐκείνην καὶ σύνεσμεν τοῖς σώμασιν. ἡ γὰρ ἄλλη ψυχή, καθ' ἣν ἡμεῖς,[3] τοῦ εὖ εἶναι, οὐ τοῦ εἶναι αἰτία· ἤδη γοῦν τοῦ σώματος ἔρχεται γενομένου. See also Plot. 2. 3. 9; 4. 3. 27 init. τῆς μὲν (ψυχῆς) λεγομένης ὑφ' ἡμῶν θειοτέρας, καθ' ἣν ἡμεῖς, τῆς δὲ ἄλλης τῆς παρὰ τοῦ ὅλου; 4. 3. 31; 4. 4. 18; 4. 4. 29; 4. 4. 43; 6. 4. 14 fin. Porphyr. De abst. 1. 40 : οὐδὲ τῶν δύο ψυχὰς ἡμᾶς ἔχειν λεγόντων δύο προσοχὰς[4] ἡμῖν δεδωκότων· δύο γὰρ ἂν οὕτω ζῴων ⌜συνέρξεις⌝[5] ἐποίουν, ἃ ἐνεδέχετο, ἄλλου πρὸς ἄλλοις ὄντος, τὸ ἕτερον τοῦ ἑτέρου μὴ προσποιεῖσθαι τὰ ἔργα. Macarius Aegyptius, Hom.[6] 52. 5 : καὶ ὥς, [τὸ σῶμα] ἐὰν ᾖ παρὰ χεῖρα ἢ παρὰ πόδα ἢ παρ' ὀφθαλμόν, ἐπίμωμός ἐστιν ὁ ἄνθρωπος, οὕτω καὶ [ἡ ψυχὴ][7] χωρὶς τῆς ἐπουρανίου ψυχῆς ⟨τῆς ἐ⟩κ [αι][8] τοῦ θεϊκοῦ πνεύματος ἀτελὴς καὶ ἐπίμωμός ἐστιν, . . . δύο γὰρ χεῖρας καὶ δύο πόδας καὶ δύο ὦτα ⟨ἔχων⟩ τέλειος ⟨ὁ⟩[9] ἄνθρωπός ἐστιν. . . . οὕτω καὶ τὸν ἀληθῆ Χριστιανὸν εἶναι δεῖ· ὁ γὰρ Κύριος εὐδόκησεν αὐτὸν ἔχειν δύο ψυχάς, μίαν τὴν κτισθεῖσαν καὶ μίαν ἐπουράνιον ἐκ τοῦ θεϊκοῦ πνεύματος, καὶ οὕτω δύνανται εἶναι τέλειοι. Proclus De providentia et fato et eo quod in nobis, Cousin, col. 148 : 'aliam quidem esse animam separabilem a corpore et devenientem in hunc mortalem locum desuper alicunde a diis, aliam autem esse in corporibus consistentem et inseparabilem a subiectis ; et hanc quidem dependere a Fato, illam autem a Providentia secundum sui ipsius substantiam.' Proclus ib. col. 150 : 'omnes Platonis amatores duplicem divulgantes animam' ; i. e. 'all the Platonists say that the (human) soul is twofold'.

---

[1] Perhaps ὡς λόγος πρὸς λόγον? According to Plotinus, souls are λόγοι.

[2] This is the lower soul, which is implanted in the body at birth by the operation of the astral influences (cf. Abammon 8. 6 a ἐνδιδομένη ἐκ τῆς τῶν οὐρανίων περιφορᾶς). and manifests itself in bodily growth.

[3] This is the 'diviner' soul, which is the man's true self.

[4] 'Even those who say that we have two souls do not say that we have two attentions'; i. e. they do not say that one of the two souls can attend to one thing at the same time that the other soul is attending to another thing.

[5] Perhaps σύνερξιν; 'a shutting-up-together of two living beings'.

[6] This is one of seven Homilies ascribed to Macarius, which are preserved in a Bodleian MS., and have recently been published for the first time by Mr. G. L. Marriott, Macarii Anecdota, Harvard Theological Studies V, 1918.

[7] I have bracketed τὸ σῶμα and ἡ ψυχή.

[8] I have written τῆς ἐκ (cf. ἐκ τοῦ θεϊκοῦ πνεύματος below; the heavenly soul is 'that which is born of the Spirit', Ev. Joh. 3. 6): καὶ MSS.

[9] I have written χεῖρας and πόδας (χεῖρες and πόδες MS.), and added ἔχων and ὁ.

29-35. 1. ἡ μέν ἐστιν ἀπὸ τοῦ πρώτου νοητοῦ, μετέχουσα καὶ τῆς τοῦ δημιουργοῦ δυνάμεως. The higher of the two souls emanates from 'the first νοητόν' (or in other words, from the 'first νοῦς' of 8. 3 a, b, c and 4 d); and it partakes of the power of the Demiurgus, who is the 'second νοῦς'. Inasmuch as the second νοῦς likewise emanates from the first νοῦς, the higher soul of the individual man is, so to speak, a younger brother of the Demiurgus.[1] The meaning would be clearer if καὶ μετέχει were written in place of μετέχουσα καὶ.

The lower soul is called ἡ ἐνδιδομένη ἐκ τῆς τῶν οὐρανίων περιφορᾶς (= τῆς γενεσιουργοῦ κυκλήσεως), and ἡ ἀπὸ τῶν κόσμων ('from the stars' or 'from the spheres of heaven') εἰς ἡμᾶς καθήκουσα ψυχή. It is put into the body at birth[2] by the working of the stars, which are the instruments of εἱμαρμένη, and it is throughout life governed by astral influence (ταῖς περιόδοις συνακολουθεῖ τῶν κόσμων); the man in whom the lower soul has the command is therefore a slave of εἱμαρμένη, —or, as we might say, is subject to the laws of nature. But κατὰ τὴν ἐκ τοῦ νοητοῦ ψυχὴν ἡ λύσις γίνεται τῆς εἱμαρμένης; that is to say, the man in whom the higher soul is given full scope for its activity, and the lower soul is suppressed or subordinated, rises above the material world, which is subject to the working of the stars; his life is united with that of the νοητοὶ θεοί, and he is thus released from the domination of εἱμαρμένη. Cf. 10. 5 b, where the 'two souls' are again spoken of.

2. εἰς ἣν ἐπεισέρπει ἡ θεοπτικὴ ψυχή. εἰς ἣν ἐπεισέρπει corresponds to ἐπεισῆλθεν ἑτέρᾳ ψυχῇ in 10. 5 b. The writer's view seems to be that the lower soul is present in the body from the moment of birth, but the higher soul inserts itself into the lower soul (and so becomes incarnate) at a later stage,—perhaps at adolescence. The higher soul is the human νοῦς; and it is only adults (and indeed, according to one way of speaking, only a few among them) that have νοῦς.

For the word θεοπτικός, see note on τὴν θεοπτικὴν δύναμιν in Herm. ap. Stob. Exc. II A. 6. Cf. Criton Pythagoreus ap. Stob. 2. 8. 24, vol. ii, p. 158 W.: (ὁ θεὸς) ὄψιν αὐτῷ (sc. τῷ ἀνθρώπῳ) ἐνέφυσε τοιαύταν, τὸν προσαγορευόμενον νόον, ᾧ τὸν θεὸν ὄψεται. οὔτε γὰρ ...

---

[1] It agrees with this that Abammon says the aim of the Egyptian thurgia is to unite the human soul (not with τὸ ἕν, nor with the first νοῦς, but) with the Demiurgus.

[2] Whether the lower soul begins to exist at the moment of birth, or has been in existence before its embodiment, we are not explicitly told; but the words ἐνδιδομένη and καθήκουσα seem to imply its pre-existence. Probably those who said that it is immortal (Porphyr. ap. Stob. 1. 49. 25 a) would have asserted its pre-existence, and those who said that it is mortal would have denied this.

ἄνευ νόῳ (ἦν) ἰδεῖν τὸν θεὸν αὐτόν. The higher of the two souls is here called ἡ θεοπτικὴ ψυχή. But there is nothing in what precedes to account for its being so called ; and the sequence of thought would be clearer if εἰς ἦν . . . ψυχή were struck out.

At what point in this passage (8. 6 a, b) does Abammon's report of the teaching of the *Hermetica* end, and the statement of his own inferences from it begin ? The earlier part of the passage at least, from δύο γὰρ ἔχει ψυχάς down to ἐκ τῆς τῶν οὐρανίων περιφορᾶς, must have been taken (in substance if not verbally) from a Greek *Hermeticum*. On the other hand, it is not likely that anything like the last sentence of 6 b (θεουργία . . . ἀποτελεῖται) occurred in a *Hermeticum* ; for the writers of the extant *Hermetica* attached no importance to *theurgia*. As to the intervening passage (τούτων δὴ οὕτως ἐχόντων . . . ἡ πρὸς τοὺς νοητοὺς θεοὺς ἄνοδος, 6 b), there may be some doubt. Its contents agree with the doctrine of our *Hermetica* in general ; but as the words τούτων δὴ οὕτως ἐχόντων with which it begins (cf. τὸ δὲ πῶς ἔχει above) seem to show that it is an inference drawn by Abammon, and as it is closely linked (by τε) with the following sentence about *theurgia*, it is probably not to be taken as included in what Abammon tells us that 'the Hermetic writings say'. We may conclude then that the Hermetic passage ends at θεοπτικὴ ψυχή (or at οὐρανίων περιφορᾶς, if we bracket εἰς ἦν ἐπεισέρπει ἡ θεοπτικὴ ψυχή).

6–7. θεουργία τε, ὅση πρὸς τὸ ἀγέννητον ἀνάγει (ἀνάγεται MSS.), κατὰ τὴν τοιαύτην ζωὴν ἀποτελεῖται. ὅση . . . ἀνάγει implies that there are other kinds of θεουργία besides that of which the writer is speaking in this passage. The ordinary rites of temple-worship (offerings, hymn-singing, &c.) might be called θεουργία ; but the sort of θεουργία with which Abammon is here concerned is the series of sacramental initiations by which men are raised to τὸ ἀγέννητον (i. e. to the world of νοητά), and are thereby set free from εἱμαρμένη.

τὴν τοιαύτην ζωήν means the life of the higher soul. But that meaning would be more clearly expressed if τὴν ταύτης (sc. τῆς ψυχῆς) ζωήν were written. κατά is used as in κατ' αὐτὴν ἡ λύσις γίνεται above, and καθ' ἣν καὶ θεοῖς ἐνοῦσθαι δυνάμεθα and κατὰ δὴ ταύτην οἷοί τέ ἐσμεν καὶ ἑαυτοὺς λύειν in 7 ⟨⟨c⟩⟩.

8–16. ἀλλ' οὐδὲ πᾶν . . . ἀφεῖσα παντελῶς. There is some confusion in the text of 8. 7 a, b, c. In 7 b, Abammon is speaking on the question raised by the words καὶ πάντα τούτοις ἀνάψαντες τοῖς θεοῖς, ⌐οὕτω⌐ λυτῆρας τῆς εἱμαρμένης . . . θεραπεύουσι in Porphyry's letter ; i. e. on the question whether the gods through whom εἱμαρμένη works can without inconsistency be worshipped as releasing men from εἰμαρμένη. And he continues to deal with that same question in 8 a. But in the traditional text, the two parts of this discussion (7 b and 8 a) are separated by the interposition of 7 c, the contents of which have nothing to do with that question, but are closely related to the passage about the two souls (6 a, b). It appears therefore that 7 c ought to precede 7 b instead of following it.

But there is another difficulty. 7 c is merely an amplified statement of what is said in 7 a. Either 7 a alone, or 7 c alone, might very well stand next after 6 b; but if we place either of them in that position, the other seems superfluous.

This latter difficulty is however diminished if we put 7 c before 7 a, and take 7 a, the shorter of these two passages, to be a summing up of what has been more fully said in 7 c. I have therefore placed these sections in the order 6 a, b, 7 ⟨⟨c⟩⟩ a, b, 8 a. Thus rearranged, the text becomes intelligible. Abammon says in 6 a that he will discuss the question of τὸ ἐφ' ἡμῖν at some length (διὰ πλειόνων); and he does so in 6 a, b, 7 ⟨⟨c⟩⟩. He then, in 7 a, briefly recapitulates what he has just been saying in answer to Porphyry's statement about that matter, and having done so, passes on, in 7 b, to discuss the other topic spoken of in the same sentence of Porphyry's letter, viz. that of the λυτῆρες τῆς εἰμαρμένης. The discussion of this latter topic, begun in 7 b, is continued in 8 a.

The Platonic doctrine which is set forth in 7 ⟨⟨c⟩⟩ and 7 a is stated as follows by Iamblichus, *Ep. ad Macedonium* (Stob. 2. 8. 43, vol. ii, p. 173 W.): οὐσία ἐστιν ἄϋλος ἡ τῆς ψυχῆς καθ' ἑαυτήν, ἀσώματος, ἀγέννητος πάντη καὶ ἀνώλεθρος, παρ' ἑαυτῆς ἔχουσα τὸ εἶναι καὶ τὸ ζῆν, αὐτοκίνητος παντελῶς, καὶ ἀρχὴ τῆς φύσεως καὶ τῶν ὅλων κινήσεων. αὕτη δὴ οὖν, καθ' ὅσον ἐστὶ τοιαύτη, καὶ τὴν αὐτεξούσιον[1] καὶ τὴν ἀπόλυτον περιείληφεν ἐν ἑαυτῇ ζωήν. (καὶ)[2] καθ' ὅσον μὲν δίδωσιν ἑαυτὴν εἰς τὰ γιγνόμενα, καὶ ὑπὸ τὴν τοῦ παντὸς φορὰν ἑαυτὴν ὑποτάττει, κατὰ τοσοῦτον καὶ ὑπὸ τὴν εἰμαρμένην ἄγεται, καὶ δουλεύει ταῖς τῆς φύσεως ἀνάγκαις· καθ' ὅσον δὲ αὖ τὴν νοερὰν ἑαυτῆς καὶ τῷ ὄντι ἄφετον ἀπὸ πάντων καὶ αὐθαίρετον ἐνέργειαν ἐνεργεῖ κατὰ τοσοῦτον τὰ ἑαυτῆςἑκουσίως πράττει, καὶ τοῦ θείου καὶ ἀγαθοῦ καὶ νοητοῦ μετ' ἀληθείας ἐφάπτεται. *Ib*. 44: τὸν κατὰ νοῦν ἄρα βίον καὶ τὸν ἐχόμενον τῶν θεῶν διαζῆν μελετητέον· οὗτος γὰρ ἡμῖν μόνος ἀποδίδωσι τὴν ἀδέσποτον τῆς ψυχῆς ἐξουσίαν, ἀπολύει τε ἡμᾶς τῶν ἀνάγκης[3] δεσμῶν, καὶ ποιεῖ ζῆν οὐκ ἀνθρώπινόν τινα

---

[1] Perhaps τὸ αὐτεξούσιον.   [2] καὶ add. Meineke.
[3] ἀνάγκης Heeren : ἀναγκαίων MSS.

βίον, ἀλλὰ τὸν θεῖον¹ καὶ [τῇ βουλήσει τῶν]² θείων ἀγαθῶν ἀποπληρούμενον. Iamblichus ib. 45 : τούτων δὲ οὕτως ἐχόντων, καὶ ἡ τῶν ἀνθρώπων ἀρχὴ τοῦ πράττειν ἔχει μὲν συμφωνίαν πρὸς ἀμφοτέρας ταύτας τὰς
τοῦ παντὸς ἀρχάς (sc. εἱμαρμένην καὶ πρόνοιαν)· ἔστι δὲ καὶ ἀφειμένη[ν]
ἀπὸ τῆς φύσεως καὶ ἀπόλυτος ἀπὸ τῆς τοῦ παντὸς κινήσεως ἐν ἡμῖν τῶν]
πράξεων ἀρχή[ν].³ διὰ τοῦτο ⌜οὐκ ἔνεστιν ἐν τῇ τοῦ παντός⌝.⁴ διότι μὲν
γὰρ ⟨⟨οὐκ⟩⟩⁵ ἀπὸ τῆς φύσεως παράγεται, οὐδὲ ἀπὸ τῆς τοῦ παντὸς κινήσεως,
πρεσβυτέρα ⟨ἐστί⟩, καὶ [[οὐκ]] ⟨τῆς⟩ ἀπὸ τοῦ παντὸς ἐνδιδομέν⟨ς⟩ προτέ-
τακται·⁶ διότι γε μὴν ἀφ' ὅλων τῶν τοῦ κόσμου μερίδων καὶ ἀπὸ πάντων
⟨τῶν⟩⁷ στοιχείων μοίρας τινὰς κατενείματο⁸ καὶ ταύταις πάσαις χρῆται,
περιέχετ⟨αι⟩ ⟨⟨καὶ⟩⟩ αὐτὴ [[καὶ]]⁹ ἐν τῇ τῆς εἱμαρμένης διατάξει, συντελεῖ τε
εἰς αὐτήν, καὶ συμπληροῖ τὴν ἐν αὐτῇ κατασκευήν, καὶ χρῆται αὐτῇ
δεόντως, καὶ καθ' ὅσον μὲν λόγον καθαρὸν αὐθυπόστατον καὶ αὐτοκίνητον
ἀφ' ἑαυτοῦ τε ἐνεργοῦντα καὶ τέλειον ἡ ψυχὴ συνείληφεν ἐν ἑαυτῇ, κατὰ
τοσοῦτον ἀπόλυτός ἐστι πάντων τῶν ἔξωθεν· καθ' ὅσον γε μὴν καὶ ζωὰς
ἄλλας προβάλλει ῥεπούσας εἰς τὴν γένεσιν, καὶ ἐπικοινωνεῖ τῷ σώμα⟨τι⟩,¹⁰
κατὰ τοσοῦτον ἔχει συμπλοκὴν καὶ πρὸς τὴν τοῦ κόσμου διάταξιν.

8. ⌜ἀλλ' οὐδὲ πᾶν δέχεται ἐν τῇ φύσει τῆς εἱμαρμένης⌝. The meaning required might be got by writing either πάντα ἔχεται (Gale) τῆς
εἱμαρμένης, or πάντα δέδεται (πᾶν δέδεται Cᴾ) τῇ εἱμαρμένῃ. The
words ἐν τῇ φύσει cannot be right. If the sense intended were 'all
things in the material universe', we ought rather to read οὐ πάντα
τὰ ἐν τῇ φύσει δέδεται τῇ εἱμαρμένῃ. But the following context
shows that Abammon is not speaking of all things in the universe,
but of all things in *man*. That might perhaps be expressed by πάντα

¹ Perhaps οὐκ ἀνθρώπινον βίον, ἀλλὰ θεῖόν τινα.
² τῇ βουλήσει τῶν seclusi. καὶ τῇ βουλήσει τῶν θεῶν ἀγαθῶν ἀποπληρούμενον
Wachsmuth.
³ ἔστι δὲ καὶ ἀφειμένη . . . καὶ ἀπόλυτος . . . ἀρχή Wachsmuth : ἔχει δὲ καὶ
ἀφειμένην . . . καὶ ἀπόλυτον . . . ἀρχήν MSS. Cf. Abammon 8. 7 ⟨⟨c⟩⟩ : ἀλλ' ἔστι
καὶ ἑτέρα τῆς ψυχῆς ἀρχή κ.τ.λ.
⁴ τῇ τοῦ παντός may have come from τῆς τοῦ παντός above, and may have taken
the place of some other words which originally stood here.
⁵ οὐκ addidit Wachsmuth.
⁶ πρεσβυτέρα ἐστί, καὶ τῆς ἀπὸ τοῦ παντὸς ἐνδιδομένης (sc. ἀρχῆς) προτέτακται
scripsi : πρεσβυτέρα καὶ οὐκ ἀπὸ τοῦ παντὸς ἐνδιδομένη προτέτακται (προστέτακται F)
MSS. These two ἀρχαὶ τῶν πράξεων correspond to the 'two souls' spoken of in
Abammon 8. 6.
⁷ τῶν addidi.
⁸ κατενείματο seems to mean 'has taken possession of' or 'has taken under its
charge'. By entering a body, composed of material elements, and thereby taking
on itself the management of a portion of the material world, even the higher ἀρχή
(or ψυχή) has to some extent subjected itself to the influence of cosmic forces.
⁹ περιέχεται καὶ αὐτὴ scripsi : περιέχει ταύτῃ καὶ MSS. : περιέχεται αὐτὴ
Heeren.
¹⁰ τῷ σώματι Heeren : τὸ σῶμα MSS.

τὰ ἐν τῇ φύσει ⟨ἡμῶν⟩; but it seems more probable that ἐν τῇ φύσει has been inserted by error. (φύσει may have come from πάσης φύσεως below.)

If we assume that 7 ⟨⟨c⟩⟩ originally stood next after b, the connexion is not rightly expressed by ἀλλ' οὐδέ. Perhaps we ought to bracket ἀλλ' (which may be a misplaced doublet of ἀλλ' in the following line), and read οὐ δή.

8–9. ἀλλ' ἔστι καὶ ἑτέρα τῆς ψυχῆς ἀρχή, κρείττων πάσης φύσεως καὶ γενέσεως. φύσις καὶ γένεσις means the operation of the forces which work in the material world. The ἑτέρα τῆς ψυχῆς ἀρχή is the higher of the 'two souls' spoken of in 8. 6 a, b. The two things which were there called 'two souls' are here called two ἀρχαί belonging to or contained in the (single) soul. The word ἀρχή is used again in 7 a (ἔχει γὰρ ἀρχὴν οἰκείαν ἡ ψυχὴ τῆς εἰς τὸ νοητὸν περιαγωγῆς); and in both places it seems to mean 'origin of action' (ἀρχὴ κινήσεως or πράξεως). Each of the two parts of the soul is an ἀρχή, inasmuch as each of them originates action; but they differ, in that the action originated by the lower part is determined by φύσις καὶ γένεσις (i. e. by forces governed by εἱμαρμένη), but the action originated by the higher part is not thus determined.

21–22. οὐδ' αὖ τοῖς (οὐδ⟨ὲ τοῖς⟩ αὐτοῖς?) θεοῖς τὴν εἱμαρμένην ἀνήψαμεν οὓς ὡς λυτῆρας τῆς εἱμαρμένης ἔν τε ἱεροῖς καὶ ξοάνοις θεραπεύομεν. Cf. Porphyry's letter (Euseb. Pr. ev. 3. 4. 2): καὶ πάντα τούτοις ἀνάψαντες τοῖς θεοῖς, ⌜οὕτω⌝ λυτῆρας τῆς εἱμαρμένης ⌜μόνους⌝ ἔν τε ἱεροῖς καὶ ξοάνοις καὶ τοῖς ἄλλοις θεραπεύουσι. There seems to be some corruption in both passages. The sense wanted might be got by writing τοὺς αὐτοὺς ὡς λυτῆρας τῆς εἱμαρμένης ὄντας . . . θεραπεύουσι in Porphyry's letter, and οὐδὲ τοῖς αὐτοῖς θεοῖς in Abammon's Reply. Cf. καὶ τοὺς αὐτοὺς ἡγεῖσθαι κ.τ.λ. in 8. 8 a init. Porphyry's point is that the Egyptians are inconsistent in worshipping as 'liberators from εἱμαρμένη' the very same gods by whom, according to their doctrine, the bonds of εἱμαρμένη are imposed on men; and Abammon answers this by saying that, according to the true Egyptian doctrine, the gods who liberate men from εἱμαρμένη are not the same as the powers by whose working men are subjected to εἱμαρμένη (οἱ μὲν θεοὶ λύουσι τὴν εἱμαρμένην, αἱ δ' ἀπ' αὐτῶν ἔσχαται φύσεις καθήκουσαι . . . τὴν εἱμαρμένην ἐπιτελοῦσιν).

ἔν τε ἱεροῖς καὶ ξοάνοις is the reading given by the MSS. both in Porphyry's letter ap. Euseb. and in Abammon's Reply; but the τε is difficult to explain.

22–23. οἱ μὲν θεοὶ λύουσι τὴν εἱμαρμένην. The gods of whom

Abammon is here speaking are those worshipped in the Egyptian temples (ἐν ἱεροῖς καὶ ξοάνοις). According to 8. 3 c, those gods are aspects or manifestations of the demiurgic νοῦς.

The λύσις τῆς εἱμαρμένης of which Abammon speaks is chiefly that λύσις which consists in the transference of men from the world of αἰσθητά to the world of νοητά; but in this sentence he may perhaps be thinking also of such suspensions of natural law in the world of αἰσθητά as the temple-gods were believed to grant in answer to men's prayers, e. g. miraculous healings of sickness.

Abammon's view appears to be that the decrees of εἱμαρμένη are executed (or in other words, the laws of nature are put in operation) by certain ἔσχαται φύσεις (daemons?) derived from the gods and subordinate to them, but that the working of those laws is sometimes suspended in particular cases by the intervention of the gods themselves.

Compare a discussion of the same subject by Iamblichus, *Ep. ad Poemenium* (Stob. 1. 1. 35, vol. i, p. 43 W.): οἱ θεοὶ τὴν εἱμαρμένην συνέχοντες διὰ παντὸς ἐπανορθοῦνται· ἡ δ' ἐπανόρθωσις αὐτῶν ποτὲ μὲν ἐλάττωσιν κακῶν, ποτὲ δὲ παραμυθίαν, ἐνίοτε δὲ καὶ ἀναίρεσιν ἀπεργάζεται·[1] ἀφ' οὗ δὴ διακοσμεῖται ἡ εἱμαρμένη [τοῖς ἀγαθοῖς],[2] διακοσμουμένη δὲ ⟨. . .⟩[3] ⌜οὐκ ὑποφαίνεται πᾶσα[4] πρὸς⌝ τὴν ἄτακτον φύσιν τῆς γενέσεως. οὐκοῦν ἔτι μᾶλλον σῴζεται ἡ πεπρωμένη διὰ τῆς τοιαύτης ἐπανορθώσεως, ⟨⟨διότι οὐκ ἐᾶται ὑπορρεῖν εἰς τὴν ἄτακτον πλημμέλειαν·⟩⟩[5] καὶ τὸ παρατρέπον αὐτῆς μένει κατὰ τὴν ἄτρεπτον τῶν θεῶν ἀγαθότητα συνεχόμενον [[διότι οὐκ ἐᾶται ὑπορρεῖν εἰς τὴν ἄτακτον πλημμέλειαν]]. τούτων δὴ οὕτως ἐχόντων τό τε ἀγαθοειδὲς τῆς προνοίας τό τε αὐτεξούσιον τῆς ψυχῆς καὶ πάντα τὰ κάλλιστα διασῴζεται, τῇ βουλήσει[6] τῶν θεῶν συνυπάρχοντα. ·'The gods maintain destiny throughout, but at the same time correct it. Their correction of destiny sometimes diminishes evils, sometimes consoles us under them, and sometimes wholly removes them. Destiny is in this way reduced to order, and thereby ⟨the good which is lacking to it is supplied; for the goodness of destiny⟩ fails to manifest itself in all its fullness, by reason of the disorderly nature of the world of change with which it has to deal. By such correction then destiny is the more truly maintained, in that it is prevented from falling away into the aberrations of disorder; and in its swervings, it is kept in steadfast accord with the unswerving goodness

---

[1] ἀπεργάζεται Heeren : ἀπεργάζονται MSS.   [2] τοῖς ἀγαθοῖς seclusi.
[3] Lacunam signavi.   [4] πᾶσαν P.
[5] διότι . . . πλημμέλειαν huc transpos i.   [6] βουλῇ P.

of the gods. This being so, the goodness of Providence, the freedom of the human will, and all things of highest worth are upheld; all these things are coexistent with the will of the gods.'[1] In that passage Iamblichus apparently says that εἱμαρμένη is maintained by the same gods by whom it is corrected when it needs correction; and if that is his meaning, Abammon differs from him in that respect.

25–27. ὅπως ἄν ⌜μόνοι διὰ πειθοῦς νοερᾶς⌝ τῆς ἀνάγκης ἄρχοντες τὰ ἀπὸ τῆς εἱμαρμένης ἀποκείμενα κακὰ ἀπολύωσιν. The gods cannot be said to govern necessity 'by means of intelligent persuasion'. Perhaps μόνοι διὰ πειθοῦς νοερᾶς ought to be bracketed; it may be a misplaced fragment.

29–30. τί οὖν; οἷόν τέ ἐστι διὰ τῶν πολευόντων θεῶν λύειν ἑαυτόν; ⟨...⟩ καὶ τοὺς αὐτοὺς ἡγεῖσθαι μοιρηγέτας καὶ δεσμοῖς ἀλύτοις τὸν βίον (τοὺς βίους MSS.) δεσμεύοντας; The πολεύοντες θεοί (called οἱ ἐμφανεῖς θεοί below) are the star-gods. They are here regarded as a class of gods distinct from the temple-gods spoken of in 7 b. 'Is it possible', Abammon asks, 'to get release by the agency of the star-gods? ⟨How can a man think that possible,⟩ if at the same time he thinks that those same gods bind human life with bonds from which there is no release?' The star-gods were commonly held to be the agents through whom Heimarmene works; and assuming that belief to be true, it would seem useless to try to get release from the bonds of Heimarmene by worshipping the star-gods.

That is apparently the meaning of the passage. But in the text of the MSS., the meaning is not clearly expressed; the second clause (καὶ τοὺς αὐτοὺς ἡγεῖσθαι κ.τ.λ.) does not fit on rightly to the first. If we read the two clauses as parts of one sentence, the verb 'to think' (ἡγεῖσθαι) ought to occur either in both or in neither. It therefore

---

[1] The meaning of the passage ἀφ' οὗ δὴ διακοσμεῖται ... τῆς γενέσεως is doubtful; but the general sense of the extract is clear. εἱμαρμένη is the law of nature. By this law the processes of the Kosmos are 'ordered', i. e. directed to good ends. But owing to the inherent 'disorderliness' or intractability of ὕλη, the laws of nature, though ordained for the purpose of producing good, sometimes produce evil. When evils thus arise, the gods intervene, and 'correct' destiny: i. e. they suspend or modify the laws of nature, as far as may be needed to remedy the particular evil. E. g. a man falls sick by the operation of destiny or natural law. A god miraculously heals the sick man; that is a 'correction' of destiny. Iamblichus, however, maintains that by such corrections the law of destiny is not violated, but is rather upheld in a higher degree; for the purpose of destiny is to work good, and this purpose is more fully attained by occasional suspensions of natural laws than it would be by their invariable maintenance. The only law that is valid without exception is the will of the gods to do good. This is the law of destiny in the highest sense; and to this, in case of conflict, all other laws must yield.

seems probable that there is a lacuna before καὶ τοὺς αὐτοὺς ἡγεῖσθαι. The gap might be filled in some such way as this : ⟨πῶς εὔλογον τούτους ὡς λυτῆρας θεραπεύειν,⟩ καὶ τοὺς αὐτοὺς ἡγεῖσθαι... δεσμεύοντας;

The words δεσμοῖς ἀλύτοις τὸν βίον δεσμεύοντας are an explicit statement of what is implied in the term μοιρηγέτας.

31–36. 1. εἰ τῶν θεῶν πολλὰς περιεχόντων οὐσίας καὶ δυνάμεις [ἐν ἑαυτοῖς], ἐνυπάρχουσιν ἐν αὐτοῖς [ἄλλαι τε] ἀμήχανοι ὅσαι διαφοραὶ καὶ ἐναντιώσεις. ἐν ἑαυτοῖς is doubtless a doublet of ἐν αὐτοῖς.

Cf. 8. 1 b : πολλῶν οὐσιῶν ὑπαρχουσῶν, καὶ τούτων διαφερουσῶν παμπληθές, πολλαὶ παρεδόθησαν αὐτῶν καὶ ἀρχαί, διαφόρους ἔχουσαι τάξεις. What was there said of the gods in general seems to be here applied to the star-gods in particular. They are divided into different classes or orders (e. g. there is the τάξις of the zodiac-gods and that of the planet-gods) ; and it is conceivable that men may be bound in the bonds of εἱμαρμένη by the working of one class of star-gods, and released from those bonds by another class of star-gods.

That appears to be the only possible way to make sense of the words τῶν θεῶν . . . καὶ ἐναντιώσεις, if we read them in their present context. But the sequence of thought in this paragraph is not clear ; and it may be suspected that there is some dislocation of the text.

1–2. ἐν ἑκάστῳ τῶν θεῶν, καὶ τῶν ἐμφανῶν, εἰσί τινες [οὐσίαι] νοηταὶ ἀρχαί. We were told in 8. 7 c that there is a νοητὴ ἀρχὴ (πράξεως) in the human soul ; and if so, there must a fortiori be a νοητὴ ἀρχή in a star-god. The star-god then may discharge his function as an agent of εἱμαρμένη by the action of the lower and corporeal part of his complex being, but at the same time release men from εἱμαρμένη by the action of his νοητὴ ἀρχή, which is incorporeal.

4–5. εἰ δ' ἄρα τις καὶ δύο γένη περικοσμίων τε καὶ ὑπερκοσμίων θεῶν ἀπολείποι, διὰ τῶν ὑπερκοσμίων ἔσται ταῖς ψυχαῖς ἀπόλυσις. The star-gods are θεοὶ περικόσμιοι. The preceding part of the paragraph is an argumentum ad hominem, addressed to those who (like Chaeremon) recognized cosmic gods alone. Abammon maintains that even those who held that view might without inconsistency admit the possibility of λύσις. But Abammon himself believes in the existence of supra-cosmic gods as well as cosmic gods, and holds that the λύσις which men seek is to be got chiefly, if not solely, from the former. Perhaps he may have thought that λύσις in respect of αἰσθητά or σωματικά (e. g. healing of sickness) can sometimes be obtained by prayer to a star-god ; but he does not explicitly say so.

6. ταῦτα μὲν οὖν ἐν τοῖς περὶ θεῶν ἀκριβέστερον λέγεται. Abammon

refers Porphyry to a book which he calls τὰ περὶ θεῶν for fuller information about the things which he has been discussing.

Iamblichus is said to have written a book entitled περὶ θεῶν (Damasc. *De princip.* c. 61, p. 132 Ruelle) ; and Gale, assuming that to be the book here referred to, says that Iamblichus (whom he takes to be the author of 'Abammon's Reply') 'oblitus est Noster susceptae personae, seque huius responsionis auctorem manifesto declarat, dum ad hoc suum opus nos mittit'. But there is no reason to think that the book here spoken of is the περὶ θεῶν which Iamblichus wrote. There must have been in circulation dozens of works which bore that title. Abammon, if we suppose him to have been a real person, may have written one himself, and may mean 'see my περὶ θεῶν'. Or he may be referring to a well-known work περὶ θεῶν written by some one else,—possibly the περὶ θεῶν βιβλία ρ' of Seleucus.

10–11. ὅπερ ἐκ τῶν Ὁμηρικῶν σὺ παρέθηκας, τὸ στρεπτοὺς εἶναι τοὺς θεούς. Hom. *Il.* 9. 497 : στρεπτοὶ δέ τε καὶ θεοὶ αὐτοί. This passage is quoted in Pl. *Rep.* 364 D. Cf. Hierocles *ap.* Stob. 1. 3. 53, vol. i, p. 63 W.: ἔτι προσδιαληπτέον καὶ ταῦθ' ὑπὲρ τῶν θεῶν, ὡς εἰσὶν ἄτρεπτοι καὶ ἀραρότες τοῖς κρίμασιν, ὥστε τοῦ ἀπ' ἀρχῆς δόξαντος μηδέποτε ἐξίστασθαι.... καὶ τὰ τοιαῦτα ἔοικεν αὐτοσχεδίως καὶ ⌈μετ' οὐδενὸς⌉[1] λέγειν ἡ ποιητική· "καὶ ⟨μὲν τοὺς⟩ θυσίαισι ... παρατρωπῶσ' ἄνθρωποι | λισσόμενοι, ὅτε κέν τις ὑπερβαίη καὶ ἁμάρτῃ", καὶ τὸ " στρεπτοὶ δέ τε καὶ θεοὶ αὐτοί".

11–12. νόμοις γὰρ ἀχράντοις [καὶ νοεροῖς] ὥρισται πάλαι τὰ ἔργα τῆς ἱερᾶς ἁγιστείας. The release of the soul from the bonds of Heimarmene by means of *theurgia* is not a breach of divine ordinances, but a fulfilment of them ; for it has been ordained from the first, not only that souls should be bound by those bonds, but also that they should be released from them by certain means.

12–14. τάξει τε μείζονι καὶ δυνάμει λύεται τὰ καταδεέστερα, εἰς βελτίονά τε μεθισταμένων ἡμῶν λῆξιν ἀπόστασις γίνεται τῶν καταδεεστέρων. This passage has no direct bearing on the question whether the gods are στρεπτοί, which is dealt with in the preceding and following clauses ; and the connexion of thought would be clearer if τάξει τε μείζονι ... τῶν καταδεεστέρων were cut out. The words εἰς βελτίονα ... τῶν καταδεεστέρων are a repetition of what was said in the last lines of 7 ⟨⟨c⟩⟩.

17–18. οὔτε οὖν μεταβολή τις γίνεται διὰ τῆς τοιαύτης ἀναγωγῆς. μεταβολή τις means a change in God's purpose.

26–27. μήποτε ἄλλη τις λανθάνῃ οὖσα [ἢ ?] πρὸς εὐδαιμονίαν ὁδός.

---

[1] μετ' οὐδενὸς MSS.: κατ' οὐδενὸς Usener: μετ' οὐδενὸς λόγου Meineke.

ἄλλη apparently means other than the way of *theurgia*. The Egyptian priests say that happiness is to be got by means of sacramental rites ; but is there not perhaps some other way of attaining to it, of which they are not aware? The 'other way' of which Porphyry was thinking may have been philosophic contemplation. See note on 10. 5 c, pp. 91–92.

27–28. καὶ τίς ἂν γένοιτο ἑτέρα, ἀφισταμένη τῶν θεῶν, εὔλογος πρὸς αὐτὴν (*sc.* εὐδαιμονίαν) ἄνοδος ; The sense required by the context might be more clearly expressed by writing τίς ἂν γένοιτο [ἑτέρα] ἀφισταμένοις τῶν θεῶν εὔλογος πρὸς αὐτὴν ἄνοδος ; To reject *theurgia* is ἀφίστασθαι τῶν θεῶν, 'to withdraw oneself from the gods'; and how can men reasonably expect to attain to happiness if they do that ?

29. καὶ ἡ πρώτη δύναμις αὐτῶν καὶ ἀρχή. Does αὐτῶν mean τῶν θεῶν, or τῶν ἀγαθῶν ? If it means τῶν θεῶν, we might rather have expected καὶ τούτων (ἐστὶν) ἡ πρώτη δύναμις καὶ ἀρχή, 'to the gods belongs the supreme power and government '. But it seems better to take αὐτῶν as meaning τῶν ἀγαθῶν (cf. ἡ τῶν ἀγαθῶν ὅλων ἀρχὴ καὶ τελευτή below), and translate thus : 'if the being and perfection of all goods, and supreme power over all goods and origination of them, are contained in the gods (i.e. are to be found in the gods, and in them alone), then it is only among us (Egyptian priests), and those (others) who, like us, cling to the Powers above, and genuinely lay hold on union with the gods,—it is only among us and such as us, I say, that is employed in earnest that procedure which is the beginning and end of all goods.' Gods and goods are correlative and inseparable ; therefore, it is only those who attain to union with the gods (as the Egyptian priests do) that can get true goods, i. e. be happy.

29–31. παρὰ μόνοις ἡμῖν, καὶ τοῖς ὁμοίως . . . ἀντιλαμβανομένοις. Abammon could not (especially when writing to a foreigner) go so far as to say that happiness is unattainable for all mankind except a small number of Egyptian priests. It is with the Egyptian rites of initiation (those rites which are spoken of below, 10. 5 d–6 b) that he is personally concerned ; but he admits that there may be in other countries other forms of *theurgia* that are equally efficacious. And perhaps he might even admit that it was possible for men such as Plotinus and Porphyry to attain to εὐδαιμονία by philosophic contemplation, without making use of any theurgic or sacramental rites ; for they too might be described as ἐχόμενοι τῶν κρειττόνων and τῆς πρὸς αὐτοὺς ἑνώσεως ἀντιλαμβανόμενοι. See note on 5 c.

32–37. 1. ἐνταῦθα δὴ οὖν καὶ ἡ τῆς ἀληθείας πάρεστι θέα καὶ ἡ τῆς νοερᾶς ἐπιστήμης ⟨τελειότης or τελείωσις?⟩. ἐνταῦθα means in the theurgic rites or initiations. The initiated 'see reality'; that is equivalent to saying that they see the gods or God. (For ἀλήθεια, cf. τοῖς θεοῖς συνυπάρχει ἡ ἀλήθεια in 10. 2 b; and see Herm. ap. Stob. II A.) In 2. 3 ff., Abammon has described in detail visible apparitions (ἐπιφάνειαι) of gods and superhuman beings of various grades, apparitions which men obtain by means of appropriate rites; and he seems to assume that the sight of such apparitions makes men 'see God' in the higher sense in which the term θεοπτία was understood by Neoplatonic mystics. How or why it should do so, it is difficult to understand; but that, perhaps, is one of the things which, as he says in 1. 2 b, cannot be explained in words, and can be learnt only by religious experience.

ἐπιστήμης θέα ('to see knowledge') is impossible; some substantive therefore is needed after ἐπιστήμης; and τελειότης (A^p) may be right. ἡ τῆς νοερᾶς ἐπιστήμης τελειότης is equivalent to γνῶσις (τῶν θεῶν), and is accordingly referred to in the words μετὰ τῆς τῶν θεῶν γνώσεως which follow.

3. μάτην οὖν διαπορεῖς ⟨. . .⟩ ὡς οὐ δεῖ πρὸς δόξας ἀνθρωπίνας βλέπειν. There is nothing in the context to account for this mention of 'men's opinions about us' and 'men's praises of us'; a passage in which the ἀπορία to which Abammon is here replying was stated must therefore have been lost. We may suppose that Porphyry, in what he said about εὐδαιμονία, spoke of the approval of one's fellow men as one of the possible τέλη of human action; and to this Abammon answers 'He whose thoughts are fixed on the gods will not care what men say about him'.

6-7. ὡς ἡ ψυχὴ ἐκ τοῦ τυχόντος ἀναπλάττει μεγάλα. The rites of initiation culminate in a vision of 'great things' (i. e. of gods and things divine). Porphyry has suggested that the things which men see in such visions are not realities, but are merely phantasms produced by their own imagination. Abammon denies this. In the men who see these visions, it is not φαντασία, he says, but νοῦς, that is at work; and νοῦς does not produce phantasms, but apprehends τὰ ὄντως ὄντα.

9-10. οὐ [παρὰ] τοῖς θεοῖς συνυπάρχει ἡ ἀλήθεια; The initiated are united with the gods; and that must mean that they are brought into contact with reality; for 'reality coexists with the gods', and must be present where the gods are present.

10-11. κατ' οὐσίαν, ἀλλ' οὐχὶ κατὰ συμφωνίαν, ἐνιδρυμένη τοῖς νοητοῖς.

Reality is involved in the very being of τὰ νοητά; it is not a thing distinct from τὰ νοητά, and with which they are merely in harmony or agreement. That must, I think, be what the writer meant; but if so, he does not say it clearly. ἐνιδρυμένη is a suitable word to go with κατ᾽ οὐσίαν, but not with κατὰ συμφωνίαν; and he ought rather to have written something like κατ᾽ οὐσίαν ἐνιδρυμένη τοῖς νοητοῖς, ἀλλ᾽ οὐχὶ κατὰ συμφωνίαν συνακολουθοῦσα αὐτοῖς.

13–14. ὅσα ὡς ἀγύρτας καὶ ἀλαζόνας διασύρουσί τινες τοὺς τῶν θεῶν θεραπευτάς. Some people say that the priests by whom the theurgic rites are conducted are impostors, and that the effects of the theurgic operations (e. g. the apparitions or visions seen by the initiated) are produced by fraud or trickery; and Porphyry himself has said something of the sort (παραπλήσια τούτοις). In reply to this, Abammon admits that there are sorcerers who ape the true 'worshippers of the gods', and produce apparently similar effects by fraudulent devices (or possibly by getting aid from evil daemons); but he regards such persons as scoundrels, and indignantly denies that the Egyptian priests are to be classed with them.

20–22. διαβάλλων τὴν θείαν πρόγνωσιν κ.τ.λ. In §§ 3 and 4, Abammon discusses divination (μαντική). This is a digression, and seems, at first sight, to have nothing to do with the main topic of 10. 1–7, viz. εὐδαιμονία, to which he returns in § 5 a (ἀλλὰ τί ταῦτα ἀπομηκύνω κ.τ.λ.). But the connexion of the digression with the main topic is explained in § 4 b. Porphyry, we are there told, has said that men are not made εὐδαίμονες by the possession of μαντική (i. e. by being able to foresee future events); and it is·to this passage in Porphyry's letter that Abammon is replying in §§ 3 and 4. μαντική has already been discussed by Abammon in Part 3. It is closely connected with *theurgia*; and the ἀπορίαι put forward by Porphyry had to do with both. In 10. 8, the contents of the whole treatise are summed up in the words τοσαῦτά σοι . . . ἀπεκρινάμεθα περὶ ὧν ἠπόρησας περὶ τῆς θείας μαντικῆς τε καὶ θεουργίας.

21. ἄλλας τινὰς μεθόδους αὐτῇ (*sc.* τῇ θείᾳ προγνώσει) παραβάλλεις. ἡ θεία πρόγνωσις is foreknowledge obtained by men through direct action of the gods. Abammon says that this θεία μαντική does contribute to men's true happiness; but he distinguishes from it two other ways of getting foreknowledge, which are not 'divine' or supernatural, but merely 'human' or natural, and which he regards as of little value or importance. These are (1) *instinctive* anticipation of something that is about to take place (a sort of foreknowledge that

is of the same kind as the foreknowledge of weather-changes shown by some birds and beasts, and results from keenness of-sense-perception, or from the working of physical forces on our bodies); and (2) *scientific* inference from indications that are already present (as when a physician infers from his patient's pulse that fever is impending).

38. 1-2. μόνη τοίνυν ἡ θεία μαντικὴ συναπτομένη τοῖς θεοῖς ὡς ἀληθῶς ἡμῖν τῆς θείας ζωῆς μεταδίδωσι, τῆς τε προγνώσεως καὶ τῶν θείων νοήσεων μετέχουσα. The participles συναπτομένη and μετέχουσα are grammatically applied to ἡ μαντική; but it is the μάντις himself, and not his art, that 'is joined to the gods' and 'partakes of the thoughts which the gods think'. This is what the writer must have meant; and his meaning would have been more clearly expressed if he had written συνάπτουσα ἡμᾶς (or συναπτομένων ἡμῶν) τοῖς θεοῖς, and τῶν θείων νοήσεων μετεχόντων ἡμῶν.

The kind of μαντική of which Abammon is here thinking must be the prophesying of a man who is possessed or inspired by a god. (There were other kinds of μαντική which might also be called θεῖαι, e. g. *extispicium*; but what is here said would hardly be applicable to them.) Such a man was 'united with' his god, in nearly the same sense that those who were initiated by the rites spoken of in §§ 5 d– 6 b were united with the gods; and it is possible that a gift of power to prophesy was included among the benefits obtained by means of those initiations.

11. πάρεστι δ᾽ αὐτῇ καὶ τὸ ὠφέλιμον. τὸ ὠφέλιμον (*utile*) is contrasted with τὸ καλόν (*honestum*). In §§ 4 a, b, Abammon has been speaking of the prophet's union with his god; he who enjoys such union is thereby made εὐδαίμων. In 4 c, he goes on to speak of the prophet's foreknowledge of the future. The gods grant men foreknowledge of some future events, and withhold foreknowledge of others. They grant foreknowledge if and when it is 'better for the soul' to know the future, and withhold it if and when the soul is 'made better' by not knowing the future. That is, in both cases alike the gods do that which best promotes men's εὐδαιμονία.

18. ἐν τοῖς ἔμπροσθεν: i. e. in Part 3, which is a discussion of μαντική.

20-21. τὴν εἰς εὐδαιμονίαν ὁδὸν ἐπιδεῖξαί σοι, καὶ ἐν τίνι κεῖται ἡ αὐτῆς οὐσία. In these words Abammon sums up the contents of §§ 5 b–8, the passage with which the treatise concludes, and to which all that has preceded was intended to lead up. His conclusion is this :—

that happiness consists in union with God, and the way which leads
to it (or at any rate one of the ways, and the way which he himself
prefers,) is *theurgia*.

The Hermetists agreed with him in holding that happiness is
union with God, but would have denied that the way to it is
theurgia.

23–25. λέγω τοίνυν ὡς ὁ ⌜θεατὸς νοούμενος⌝ ἄνθρωπος . . . ἐπεισῆλθεν
ἑτέρᾳ ψυχῇ κ.τ.λ. As to the 'two souls', cf. 8. 6 a. It is evident from
the context that ὁ ⌜θεατὸς νοούμενος⌝ ἄνθρωπος means the higher of the
two souls. For θεατός one might conjecture either θεοπτικός (cf. ἡ
θεοπτικὴ ψυχή in 8. 6 a) or θεατικός (with τῶν θείων or something
equivalent either added or implied); and νοούμενος may possibly be
a corrupted doublet of ἡνωμένος.

23–24. ἡνωμένος τὸ πρόσθεν ⌜τῇ θέᾳ τῶν θεῶν⌝. A man cannot be
said to be 'made one with' a θέα. The simplest remedy would be to
write ἡνωμένος τοῖς θεοῖς. (θέᾳ may perhaps have come from ⌜θεατός⌝
in the line above.) The higher soul, before it came down and
'entered into' the lower soul, dwelt in the world above, in union with
the gods. On the other hand, if τῇ θέᾳ τῶν θεῶν is to be retained,
ἡνωμένος must be altered; it would be possible to write, for instance,
χρώμενος τὸ πρόσθεν τῇ θέᾳ τῶν θεῶν, which would mean that the
higher soul, before it came down, 'enjoyed the (beatific) vision of
the gods' in the world above.

26. σκοπεῖν δὴ δεῖ τίς αὐτοῦ (sc. τοῦ τῆς εἱμαρμένης δεσμοῦ) γίνεται
λύσις. Abammon, here and elsewhere, identifies εὐδαιμονία with
'release from the bonds of Heimarmene'. To find out how men can
get this release is equivalent to finding out how they can get happiness. Heimarmene has dominion over bodily things alone; and
'the bonds of Heimarmene' means the bonds of the body. The
soul that has detached its affections from the body and corporeal
things, and is united with the gods, lives in a world that is beyond
the reach of Heimarmene.

27. ἔστι τοίνυν (sc. λύσις καὶ ἀπαλλαγὴ τῶν δεσμῶν τῆς εἱμαρμένης) ⌜οὐκ
ἄλλη τις ἢ⌝ τῶν θεῶν γνῶσις. As the text stands, Abammon here says
that there is only one way to 'release' and happiness (cf. 10. 1 b, μήποτε
ἄλλη τις λανθάνῃ οὖσα ἡ πρὸς εὐδαιμονίαν ὁδός), and this one way is 'knowledge of the gods'. To make that statement agree with his general
attitude, it must be supplemented by a tacit assumption that knowledge of the gods is to be got by means of *theurgia*. But even with
that supplement, it can hardly be accepted, because it is contradicted

by what is said at the end of 10. 5 c: αὕτη μὲν οὖν νοείσθω σοι πρώτη τῆς εὐδαιμονίας ὁδός, . . . · ἡ δ' ἱερατικὴ καὶ θεουργικὴ κ.τ.λ. In this latter passage, we are told that there are two different ways to happiness; one of the two is 'knowledge of the gods', and the other is *theurgia*. The author cannot have thus contradicted himself; one of the two contradictory sentences must therefore be corrupt. The first statement can be made to agree with the second by a small change in the text; a much larger change would be needed in the second to make it agree with the first. It therefore seems best to alter the first sentence of 5 c; and I would propose to write there ἔστι τοίνυν [οὐκ (omitted in C)] ἄλλη ⟨μέν⟩ τις (sc. λύσις τῶν δεσμῶν) ἢ τῶν θεῶν γνῶσις. With that alteration, the meaning of 5 c *sq.* will be this: 'There are two ways to happiness. One of them is ἡ γνῶσις τῶν θεῶν,—which is also called, in 5 c *fin.*, ὁδὸς νοερὰν (in contrast to θεουργικὴν) ἔχουσα ⟨τὴν?⟩ τῆς θείας ἑνώσεως ἀποπλήρωσιν τῶν ψυχῶν, "a method by which the union of men's souls with the gods is accomplished *intellectually*"; (this is philosophic contemplation, the way chosen by Plotinus and Porphyry, and by the Hermetists;) the other way is *theurgia* (i.e. a course of sacramental initiations, which is the way preferred by Abammon himself, and described by him in 5 d–6 b).'

If this is the right interpretation of the passage, Abammon here admits that it is possible for philosophers such as Porphyry to attain to union with the gods (and thereby to εὐδαιμονία) by contemplation alone, without making use of sacramental rites; but he himself, though he has learnt and accepted the Neoplatonic philosophy, is more priest than philosopher; and it is in the theurgic rites practised in Egypt that he finds salvation for himself and his fellow priests.

27–29. ἰδέα γάρ ἐστιν εὐδαιμονίας τὸ ἐπίστασθαι τὸ ἀγαθόν, ὥσπερ τῶν κακῶν ἰδέα συμβαίνει ἡ λήθη τῶν ἀγαθῶν. Gods and good being correlative, it may be said indifferently either that happiness consists in knowledge of the gods, or that it consists in knowing the good; either statement implies the other.

The word ἰδέα must here be taken as a synonym for οὐσία, the logical 'essence' of a thing.

29. καὶ ἀπάτη [περὶ τὸ κακόν]. The ἀπάτη which goes with λήθη τῶν ἀγαθῶν can hardly be called 'delusion that has to do with evil'. περὶ τοῦ κακοῦ or τῶν κακῶν would be preferable; but it seems best to strike out these words. What is meant is rather ἀπάτη περὶ τῶν ἀγαθῶν, the delusion that makes men think things to be good which re not really good.

29-30. ἡ μὲν οὖν ⟨. . .⟩ τῷ θείῳ σύνεστιν, ἡ δὲ χείρων μοῖρα ἀχώριστός ἐστι τοῦ θνητοῦ. Some substantive is wanted here to stand in contrast to ἡ χείρων μοῖρα, and to be understood with ἡ μέν in each of the following clauses. As the text stands, we have to guess the missing term from the preceding context; it might be λύσις τῶν δεσμῶν, or τῶν θεῶν γνῶσις, or εὐδαιμονία. But the author can hardly have been so careless as to leave it unexpressed, and thereby make the meaning of the whole paragraph doubtful; and it is most likely that he wrote ἡ μὲν οὖν ⟨τῶν θεῶν γνῶσις⟩ τῷ θείῳ σύνεστιν. (The omission may have been caused by the similarity of τῶν θεῶν and τῷ θείῳ.) If so, ἡ χείρων μοῖρα, the opposite of the missing term, is ἀγνωσία τῶν θεῶν.

ἡ μὲν ⟨τῶν θεῶν γνῶσις⟩ τῷ θείῳ σύνεστι, κ.τ.λ. must be taken to mean οἱ μὲν τοὺς θεοὺς ἐγνωκότες τῷ θείῳ σύνεισι, οἱ δὲ τοὺς θεοὺς ἀγνοοῦντες ἀχώριστοί εἰσι τοῦ θνητοῦ. 'Those who know the gods enjoy communion with that which is divine'; (knowledge of God involves union with God;) 'but those who do not know the gods are inseparably joined with that which is mortal' (i. e. the body and things corporeal). And similarly, in the next clause, ἡ μὲν . . . ἀναμετρεῖ must be taken to mean οἱ μὲν τοὺς θεοὺς ἐγνωκότες . . . ἀναμετροῦσι. In the two other clauses which begin with ἡ μέν, an abstract term such as ἡ τῶν θεῶν γνῶσις is more appropriate.

30-31. ἡ μὲν τὰς τῶν νοητῶν οὐσίας [ἱερατικαῖς ὁδοῖς] ἀναμετρεῖ. In this paragraph, Abammon is speaking of a way to happiness which he calls 'the first' (of two different ways); and 'the *hieratic and theurgic* process by which happiness is conferred' is the other way which he distinguishes from it (5 d *init.*, if I understand that passage rightly). There ought therefore to be no mention of '*hieratic* ways' (i. e. priestly ways, or ways of ritual,) in 5 c; and for this reason it seems necessary to strike out ἱερατικαῖς.

τὰς τῶν νοητῶν οὐσίας perhaps means 'τὰ νοητά, which are τὰ ὄντως ὄντα'. But what can be meant by ἀναμετρεῖ in this connexion? A man might be said to *get knowledge of* τὰ νοητά, or to *see* them (with the mental eye), but hardly to *measure* them. The verb ἀναμετρεῖν may mean *to retrace* a road, that is, to travel along it a second time (whether in the same direction as before or in the reverse direction). It is possible that the word was here used in this sense, and that ὁδοῖς has been written by mistake for ὁδόν. One might conjecture ἡ μὲν ⟨τὴν πρὸς⟩ τὰς τῶν νοητῶν οὐσίας [ ] ὁδὸν ἀναμετρεῖ. The soul has come down from the νοητὸς κόσμος to be incarnated on earth; the soul which, in its life on earth, attains to knowledge of the gods 'retraces the road', that is, travels back to the νοητὸς κόσμος from which it came. When ὁδόν had been altered into ὁδοῖς, some one may have tried to give a meaning to ὁδοῖς by adding ἱερατικαῖς.

31–32. ἡ δέ (sc. τῶν θεῶν ἀγνωσία), παρακρουσθεῖσα τῶν ἀρχῶν, προίησιν ἑαυτὴν ἐπὶ τὴν ⌈καταμέτρησιν⌉ τῆς τοῦ σώματος ἰδέας. The man who does not know the gods is 'turned aside' or 'led astray' from the (or his) ἀρχαί, and consequently abandons himself to a merely corporeal life. That, or something like it, must be the general meaning; but it is difficult to make out the exact sense of the words.

What are the ἀρχαί? They might be the causes or sources of all things in the αἰσθητὸς κόσμος; and in this sense, the term might denote either the gods themselves, or τὰ νοητά. Or they might be the divine sources from which the human soul has issued.

καταμέτρησιν (the 'measuring out' of something that belongs to the body) cannot be right; the word must have been corrupted by the influence of ἀναμετρεῖ. The phrase τῆς τοῦ σώματος ἰδέας might possibly mean either 'the visible form or shape of the body' or 'the class of things to which the body belongs'. It may perhaps be equivalent to τῶν σωματικῶν; but as the word on which it depends is corrupt, there is nothing to tell us what the author meant by it.

33. ἡ μὲν (sc. τῶν θεῶν γνῶσις) γνῶσίς ἐστι τοῦ πατρός. The repetition of γνῶσις (if we assume that the term understood is ἡ τῶν θεῶν γνῶσις) is somewhat awkward; but the statement is not merely tautological. Knowledge of the several gods leads on to and culminates in knowledge of 'the Father', i. e. the Demiurgus, who is θεὸς θεῶν (8. 2 b), and is, for all practical purposes, the supreme God, since the One, who alone is 'prior to' the Demiurgus, is held by Abammon to be wholly inaccessible.

33–34. ἡ δὲ (sc. τῶν θεῶν ἀγνωσία) παραγωγὴ (ἐστίν) ἀπ' αὐτοῦ καὶ λήθη τοῦ ⌈προουσίου αὐταρχοῦντος πατρὸς⌉ θεοῦ. τοῦ . . . θεοῦ is again the Demiurgus, who is called προούσιος and αὐτάρχης in 8. 2 b. But the three terms προουσίου αὐταρχοῦντος πατρός could hardly be thus used together as epithets of θεοῦ; and the repetition of πατρός is objectionable. Perhaps the author may have written ἡ μὲν γνῶσίς ἐστι τοῦ αὐταρχοῦντος πατρός, ἡ δὲ . . . λήθη τοῦ προουσίου θεοῦ.

39. 1. ἐπὶ τὸν πατέρα αὐτῆς ἀνάγουσα. The Demiurgus is πατὴρ ζωῆς. He is the generator of physical life in the Kosmos and all living beings in it; and (inasmuch as he is νοῦς) he is also the generator of 'the *true* life', i. e. the higher life of the νοερὰ ψυχή.

1-2. ἡ δὲ (sc. τῶν θεῶν ἀγνωσία) κατάγει τὸν ⌜γεναρχοῦντα⌝ ἄνθρωπον ἄχρι τοῦ μηδέποτε μένοντος ἀλλ' ἀεὶ ῥέοντος. The meaning must be that, if a man does not know the gods, he is thereby brought down from the world of immutable reality (τὰ ὄντως ὄντα) to the world of change (τὰ γιγνόμενα καὶ ἀπολλύμενα). But what can be meant by γεναρχοῦντα? The word γενάρχης means the *founder* or *first ancestor of a family*. Adam might be called ὁ γεναρχῶν ἄνθρωπος, as being the first ancestor of the human race; and the term would be applicable to the Archanthropos of *Corp. Herm.* I, and the 'Primal Man' spoken of by some of the Christian Gnostics and by Mani. The Archanthropos of *Corp.* I is a mythical prototype of the οὐσιώδης ἄνθρωπος, the incorporeal human soul; and if ὁ γεναρχῶν ἄνθρωπος could be taken in that sense here, the sentence might be understood as meaning that *the incorporeal soul*, unless saved by knowledge of the gods, sinks down into the world of matter. But there is no trace elsewhere in *Abammonis resp.* of anything like the Anthropos-doctrine of *Corp.* I; and it is hardly possible that the author alluded to that doctrine in a single word alone, and left the allusion unexplained. It seems then that the text must be corrupt. Perhaps we ought to read something like κατάγει τὸν ἄνθρωπον ἀπὸ τοῦ γεναρχοῦντος, i. e. from the Demiurgus, who is called 'the Father' in the preceding clauses.

5. ἡ δ' ἱερατικὴ καὶ θεουργικὴ τῆς εὐδαιμονίας δόσις. This phrase stands in contrast to (ἡ) πρώτη τῆς εὐδαιμονίας ὁδός, and the meaning would have been clearer if εὐδαιμονίας ὁδός had been written in both clauses; but the author has chosen to writ δόσις (if the reading is right) instead of ὁδός in the second clause.

In this passage (10. 5 d–6 b) Abammon describes the particular kind of *theurgia* which he most highly values, and which he is most earnestly concerned in upholding. It consists of a certain course or series of initiations, or sacramental rites, by means of which some few Egyptian priests attain to 'union with the gods'. The Greek may be translated thus :

'The hieratic and theurgic process by which bliss is conferred is called "the door of access to the God who is Maker of the universe", or "the place" or "court of the good"; but the thing meant is this :— to begin with, purity of soul, a purity much nearer to perfection than mere bodily purity ; then, a course of mental preparation (i. e. religious training and instruction) that will make the aspirant fit to partake of the good and to contemplate the good, and will rid his mind of all that is opposed to this ; and after that, (the sacramental rite itself, by which) he is made one with the gods, who are the givers of all goods. And when the theurgic process has (by a series of such initiations) successively joined the man's soul with the several departments of the universe, and with all the divine Powers that permeate the several departments, then at last it brings the soul up to the Demiurgus in his wholeness, and deposits it with Him, and puts it outside of all matter ; and there the soul abides, made one with the eternal Logos, and with Him alone.

'What I mean is this : the theurgic process joins the soul with the *self-generating* Power of God, and with the *self-moved* Power, and' &c., 'and with the other demiurgic powers of God, one after another, so that the theurgic soul (i. e. the soul of the man who subjects himself to this theurgic process) is completely placed in (i. e. blended with or absorbed into) the activities and thoughts of the several Powers ; and then at last (by the final initiation) it implants the soul in (or makes it one with) the Demiurgus-God in his wholeness. This (union with the Demiurgus) is the consummation of the hieratic rites by which the soul is raised to the world above, as those rites are practised among the Egyptians.'

Abammon tells us then that the Egyptian priests aspired to union with a God whom he calls the Demiurgus (and whom he identifies with νοῦς, the second of the three divine *hypostases* of Plotinus), and that they could and did attain to union with this God by means of a long series of sacramental rites. (It is implied in what he says that this was the utmost limit of their aspiration, and that the One, the first *hypostasis* of the Plotinian triad, was inaccessible to them.)

5–8. καλεῖται μὲν " θύρα πρὸς θεὸν τὸν δημιουργὸν τῶν ὅλων", ἢ "τόπος" ἢ " αὐλὴ τοῦ ἀγαθοῦ " · δύναμιν δ' ἔχει κ.τ.λ. There can be little doubt that θύρα πρὸς θεὸν κ.τ.λ. and τόπος or αὐλὴ τοῦ ἀγαθοῦ are translations of Egyptian phrases used by the priests to describe their sacramental rites. They may have been titles of Egyptian ritual-books.

δύναμιν ἔχει is equivalent to δύναται, 'it means', in contrast to καλεῖται.

7–8. ἁγνείαν τῆς ψυχῆς, πολὺ τελειοτέραν τῆς τοῦ σώματος ἁγνείας. In mystery-cults of all kinds, including those of the Greeks, the *mystae* were required to observe, before and during the ceremonies, certain rules of ἁγνεία (e. g. to abstain from certain kinds of food, and from sexual intercourse). But such rules had to do merely with *bodily* purity ; and for the Egyptian rites of which Abammon is here speaking, that alone, he says, is not enough; the *soul* of the aspirant must be pure (i. e. free from evil passions).

13. ἐκτὸς πάσης ὕλης αὐτὴν (*sc.* τὴν ψυχὴν) ποιεῖ (ἡ θεουργία). The soul of the man who is united with the Demiurgus is wholly detached from the material world (or in other words, 'released from the bonds of Heimarmene', which has dominion over material things alone).

13–14. μόνῳ τῷ ἀιδίῳ λόγῳ συνηνωμένην. The word λόγος seems to be here used as a synonym for νοῦς; it is employed to denote the Demiurgus, who is νοῦς. Whence did the author get this use of the word? It is of Stoic origin; but it may perhaps have come to him from the Jewish (Philo's) conception of God's λόγος, transmitted through Pagan writings such as *Corp. Herm.* I and the Hermetic passages quoted by Cyril; and it is not quite impossible that some influence from the Christian λόγος-doctrine also may have reached him.

15. τῇ αὐτογόνῳ ⟨δυνάμει⟩ (*sc.* κατ' ἰδίαν συνάπτει τὴν ψυχὴν ἡ θεουργία), καὶ τῇ αὐτοκινήτῳ, κ.τ.λ. What are these 'Powers' of the Demiurgus? The gods by whom the various functions of divine government of the world are severally discharged are regarded by their worshippers as distinct persons; but they are at the same time 'Powers' or modes of activity (different aspects, as we might say,) of one God, in whom they are all included. (Compare the δυνάμεις spoken of in *Corp. Herm.* I, and by Philo.) It is evident that Abammon identifies each of the different Powers he mentions with one of the gods worshipped in Egyptian temples; and what he says amounts to this:—that the aspirant must, by a distinct and separate rite of initiation in each case, be united with each of a number of Egyptian temple-gods, one after another; and that, when this has been done, he must, by a final initiation, be united with the one God in whom all the other gods are contained together.

As the text stands, eight different Powers are explicitly mentioned, and we are told that there are others also. But seeing that any two consecutive items in the list would coalesce into one if the τῇ which separates them were struck out, and the article might easily be inserted in copying, it is uncertain how many the author specified; he may, for instance, have written τῇ αὐτογόνῳ καὶ [τῇ] αὐτοκινήτῳ to denote a single Power.

The names of the Egyptian gods meant are not here given; but there can be little doubt that each of these terms, vague as they may seem to us, was intended to indicate one particular temple-god, and would suffice to indicate him to those who were acquainted with

the formulae employed in his cult. Is it possible for us to discover
the god-names implied, or any of them? Some help in this may be
got from 8. 3 (pp. 32, 58 sqq.), where a sketch of a Neoplatonic
system of theology is given, with Egyptian god-names appended. It
can be inferred from that passage that the Demiurgus is Κμῆφ; and
it is to be presumed that the three other temple-gods there named,
viz. Amun, Ptah, and Osiris, occur here also, and very likely in
the same order. τῇ διακοσμητικῇ τῶν ὅλων καὶ [τῇ?] πρὸς ἀλήθειαν τὴν
νοητὴν ἀναγωγ⟨ικ⟩ῇ (δυνάμει) might possibly mean Ptah, who (as we are
told in 8. 3 c) συντελεῖ ἕκαστα τεχνικῶς μετ' ἀληθείας. (Or is ἡ πρὸς
ἀλήθειαν τὴν νοητὴν ἀναγωγική rather Thoth, who could hardly be
omitted? Or is ἡ νοερὰ δύναμις Thoth?) Is the first item in the
list (τῇ αὐτογόνῳ καὶ [τῇ?] αὐτοκινήτῳ [καὶ?] τῇ ἀνεχούσῃ πάντα) Amun?
And is the last Osiris? τῇ ποιητικῇ is too vague to indicate any
particular god; but one might conjecture τῇ ⟨ἀγαθῶν⟩ ποιητικῇ,
and compare Plut. Is. et Os. 42 (see p. 63 above).

There must have been, from early times, rites of consecration by
which a priest was devoted to the service of some one god in this
or that temple, and in some sense 'united with' that particular
god; and there must have been rites by which a man was raised
from a lower order of the priesthood to a higher. But is there any
evidence elsewhere of the existence in Egypt of a course of
initiations such as is here described, that is, a comprehensive system
in which the various consecration-rites connected with the cults of all
the chief gods of Egypt are fitted together as parts of one process,
and the aspirant is required to go through all these initiations in
succession? Perhaps not; but even if no other evidence for it can
be found, the testimony of Abammon (or of the author who speaks
under that assumed name, if Abammon is held to be a figment)
seems sufficient to establish the fact that about A.D. 300 such
a system was in being. To what extent it was actually put in
practice, we do not know. As each of the successive initiations
would have to be preceded by a time set apart for preparation
(κατάρτυσις τῆς διανοίας),[1] the whole course would probably extend
over a number of years, and might even occupy the greater part of
a lifetime. We can hardly suppose that more than a very few
completed it, and attained to 'union with the Demiurgus in his

---

[1] We may compare the description given by Apuleius of the preparation required
before initiation in the Isis-cult at Corinth, and before a subsequent initiation in
the cult of Osiris at Rome.

wholeness'; but a larger number may have begun it, and passed through some of the earlier stages of it.

If there was such a system at the time when *Abammonis resp.* was written, it is most likely that it had not been long in existence. It may have been an innovation, adopted by the Egyptian priesthood (or by a progressive party among them, a party that had been influenced by Greek philosophy,) in the hope of putting fresh life and vigour into their national Church, and enabling it to hold its own against the growing and threatening power of Christianity.

It may be suspected that Bitys, the Egyptian *prophetes* spoken of in 8. 5 a (p. 34), had a hand in the introduction of this new system, and promoted its acceptance by forging the Book of Thoth in which it was set forth, and which he said he had found at Saïs.

18–19. ὡς ἐν ταῖς ἐνεργείαις αὐτῶν (*sc.* of the several 'Powers' or gods) καὶ ταῖς νοήσεσι [καὶ ταῖς δημιουργικαῖς] τελέως ⟨ἐν⟩ίστασθαι τὴν θεουργικὴν ψυχήν. The words καὶ ταῖς δημιουργικαῖς are probably a misplaced repetition of καὶ ταῖς ἄλλαις δημιουργικαῖς above.

The effect of the initiation is that the man's soul 'is placed in', or comes to coincide with, the god's activities and thoughts; that is, the man does what the god does, and thinks what the god thinks. It is implied that this is what ἔνωσις πρὸς τὸν θεόν means. But the meaning would have been clearer if νοήσεις alone had been spoken of, and ἐνέργειαι omitted. 'What the god does' (as a 'demiurgic' Power) is to govern a department of the universe; and in what sense can it be said that the initiated man does that? Possibly what the writer meant may have been rather that the man's *will* is blended with his god's will; he willingly and gladly accepts, as if it were done by his own action, whatever the god does.

23. τἀγαθὸν τὸ μὲν θεῖον ἡγοῦνται (οἱ Αἰγύπτιοι) τὸν προεννοούμενον θεόν. 'The Egyptians think this' means that this is taught in the Books of Thoth, from which the Egyptian priests have learnt their wisdom.

The phrase ὁ προεννοούμενος θεός appears to denote the supreme God. Cf. Herm. *Fragm.* 12 (Lact. *Div. inst.* 4. 7. 3): τοῦ μόνου κυρίου πάντων καὶ προεννοουμένου θεοῦ. *Fr.* 36 (Ps.-Anthimus): εἰσόμεθα τὸν ⟨τε⟩ προεννοούμενον θεὸν ⟨καὶ τὸν δεύτερον⟩. *Fr.* 30 (Cyril c. *Jul.* 553 A, B): ὁ τοῦ δημιουργοῦ λόγος, . . . εἷς ὢν [ὁ] μετὰ τὸν προεγνωσμένον θεόν. But how is this use of προεννοούμενος to be explained? The word might mean either 'conceived before' (passive) or 'conceiving before' (middle); but if προεγνωσμένος in *Fr.* 30 is a synonym for it, it must be passive. ὁ προεννοούμενος θεός might then be translated 'the God who is preconceived'; but why the supreme God should be so called, I do not know.[1]

In any case, Abammon here identifies the supreme God with τὸ θεῖον ἀγαθόν (which seems to be equivalent to τὸ αὐτοαγαθόν or ἡ ἰδέα τοῦ ἀγαθοῦ). Cf. 8. 2 a (p. 32), where the θεὸς εἷς, the One, is called τὸ προόντως ἀγαθόν (if that conjecture is accepted).

23-24. τὸ δὲ ἀνθρώπινον (ἀγαθὸν ἡγοῦνται) τὴν πρὸς αὐτὸν (sc. τὸν προεννοούμενον θεὸν) ἕνωσιν. The good of man (the τέλος or *summum bonum* in the ethical sense, that is to say, man's εὐδαιμονία) is union with the supreme God.

It appears from what has preceded that the *summum bonum* for Egyptian priests was union with the Demiurgus, and that union with the One was unattainable for them. If then ὁ προεννοούμενος θεός means the supreme God, the writer must have used that term here to denote the Demiurgus, ignoring the One (who is indeed 'prior to' the Demiurgus, but is inaccessible), or disregarding for the moment the distinction between the first God and the second God.

24. ὅπερ Βίτυς ἐκ τῶν Ἑρμαϊκῶν βίβλων μεθηρμήνευσεν. ὅπερ certainly refers to the second of the two preceding clauses (i. e. the definition of τὸ ἀνθρώπινον ἀγαθόν); it is uncertain whether it does or not refer to the first clause also (i. e. the definition of τὸ θεῖον ἀγαθόν).

As to Bitys, see 8. 5 a (pp. 34, 72). He 'translated' the preceding statement 'from the Hermaic books'; that is, he wrote it in a Greek *Hermeticum* which he said he translated from an Egyptian Book of Thoth. It is possible that the book in which he wrote it was that same book which is spoken of in 8. 5 a, that is, the document which contained directions for the course of initiations described in 10. 5 d–6 b; a writing in which the Egyptian priests were told how to attain to union with the Demiurgus by means of theurgic rites might very well begin or end with the statement that the good of man is union with God. If that is not the writing here referred to, Bitys must have written one or more other Greek *Hermetica* also; but since he was interested in *theurgia*, it is most likely that whatever he may have written differed in character from our extant *Hermetica*.

26-27. οὐκ ἄρα παρεῖται τοῦτο τὸ μέρος τοῖς Αἰγυπτίοις, . . . ἀλλὰ

---

[1] Does the phrase mean 'The God of whom we have a πρόληψις', i. e. an innate or *a priori* notion?

The supreme God might perhaps be called ὁ πρὸ ἐννοίας ὤν, 'prior to ἔννοια', or προεννόητος in a similar sense, 'prior to all ἐννοητά'; but the participle προεννοούμενος could hardly be used with that meaning.

θεοπρόπως παρεδόθη. τοῦτο τὸ μέρος means τὸ ἀνθρώπινον ἀγαθόν or εὐδαιμονία. The Egyptian priests have not disregarded this, as Porphyry is inclined to think they have; and their teaching about it, and the rites by which they seek to obtain it, (are not mere human inventions or delusions, but) 'have been transmitted to them from the gods by inspiration'. The priests have learnt these things from the Books of Thoth (books which, if not literally written by Thoth with his own hand, were written by men of old who were inspired by the god Thoth); and the definition of man's good which Abammon has just quoted, and which he believes to have been translated from a Book of Thoth, is an instance of the θεοπροπίαι of which he speaks.

27. οὐδὲ περὶ σμικρῶν κ.τ.λ. Porphyry has suggested that the sacramental rites with which the Egyptian priests are occupied do not contribute to men's welfare, but are useless, and that perhaps the priests who put their trust in them are deceived by evil daemons, who pretend to be gods. Abammon replies: 'These theurgic rites are very far from being useless; for by means of them we obtain the truest and greatest goods, namely, purification and deliverance and salvation of the soul. And we who use these rites are not deceived by daemons; for we have attained to mastery over the daemons who deceive (τὴν ἀπατηλὴν καὶ δαιμονίαν φύσιν ἐπικρατήσαντες), and have risen to that higher world of thought in which the gods dwell (ἐπὶ τὴν νοητὴν καὶ θείαν φύσιν ἀναχθέντες).'

40. 1-2. εἴς τε τὸν ἀίδιον αἰῶνα ⌜δι' αἰωνίων⌝ ἀλήθειαν ἐντιθέναι. The sentence might be conjecturally emended in some such way as this: (εὔχομαι τοῖς θεοῖς) τῶν ἀληθῶν νοημάτων ἐμοί τε καὶ σοὶ παρέχειν τὴν φυλακὴν ἀμετάπτωτον εἰς [τε] τὸν ἀίδιον αἰῶνα, [⟨καὶ τελειοτέραν⟩ δι' αἰών[ι]ων (or διαιωνίως) ἀλήθειαν ἐντιθέναι] καὶ τελειοτέρων ⟨ἀεὶ⟩ νοήσεων [περὶ θεῶν?] χορηγεῖν μετουσίαν. There would then be two distinct petitions: (1) 'may both you and I keep our present beliefs unchanged for ever, so far as they are true'; and (2) 'may we go on for ever acquiring fuller and more perfect knowledge'. But the second petition is expressed in two different forms (ἀλήθειαν ἐντιθέναι being equivalent to νοήσεων χορηγεῖν μετουσίαν); it looks as if one of these two phrases had been written as an alternative for the other; and the sentence would read better if the first of them were cut out.

The words εἰς τὸν ἀίδιον αἰῶνα show that the writer is here thinking of an everlasting life after death. But little is said in *Abammonis resp.* about life after death. The 'union with the gods' of which Abammon repeatedly speaks is a state to which men may attain

during the present life ; and the notion that initiation is the means
of obtaining a happier lot *after death*, which was so prominent in
some of the Greek mystery-cults, seems to be almost entirely absent
in this treatise.   It may perhaps be tacitly implied, but it is hardly
ever explicitly spoken of.   Considering the great interest in the welfare
of the dead that was shown by the Egyptians in their funeral rites, it
is somewhat surprising that so little is said on this subject in a treatise
written (either really or ostensibly) by an Egyptian priest.

3. ἐν αἷς δὴ τὸ μακαριστὸν τέλος τῶν ἀγαθῶν ἡμῖν πρόκειται. ἐν αἷς
means ἐν τελειοτέραις νοήσεσι περὶ θεῶν. But perhaps we ought to
read ἐν οἷς, which would mean ἐν τοῖς θεοῖς. According to the view
maintained by Abammon, it is not in *thoughts about* the gods, but in
the gods themselves, and in that union with them which is to be got
(chiefly if not solely) by means of *theurgia*, that bliss is to be sought
and found.

4-5. καὶ ⌜αὐτὸ⌝ τὸ κῦρος τῆς ὁμονοητικῆς φιλίας τῆς πρὸς ἀλλήλους.
πρὸς ἀλλήλους means 'between you and me', rather than 'between
one man and another.' in general.   Abammon ends his Reply to
Porphyry with a courteous phrase implying a wish for agreement and
friendly feeling between them.   The fulfilment of that wish (τὸ κῦρος)
depends, like all else, on the gods (not on 'thoughts about' the
gods) ; and this is an additional reason for writing ἐν οἷς instead of
ἐν αἷς in the preceding clause.   In place of αὐτό, one might propose
ἅμ' αὐτῷ (*sc.* τῷ τέλει τῶν ἀγαθῶν), or something equivalent.

IAMBLICHUS

Proclus *in Tim.* 116 F–117 D (Diehl): περὶ δὲ τῆς ὕλης αὐτῆς ζητήσειεν ἄν τις, εἴτε ἀγένητός ἐστιν ἀπ' αἰτίας, ὥς φασιν οἱ περὶ Πλούταρχον[1] καὶ Ἀττικόν, εἴτε γενητή, καὶ ἐκ ποίας αἰτίας. Ἀριστοτέλης 117 A μὲν γὰρ ἀγένητον ἄλλως ἀπέδειξεν αὐτήν, ... · ὁ δὲ παρὼν λόγος ἀΐδιον μὲν αὐτὴν εἶναί φησιν, ἐπιζητεῖ δὲ εἰ ἀπ' αἰτίας ἐστὶν ἀγένητος, καὶ εἰ δύο ταύτας ἀρχὰς θετέον κατὰ Πλάτωνα τῶν ὅλων, ὕλην καὶ θεόν, μήτε τοῦ θεοῦ τὴν ὕλην παράγοντος μήτε τῆς ὕλης τὸν θεόν, ἵνα ἡ μὲν ἀΐδιος ᾖ πάντη καὶ ἄθεος, ὁ δὲ ἄϋλος πάντη καὶ ἁπλοῦς.

αὐτὸ μὲν οὖν τὸ πρᾶγμα τῶν σφόδρα ζητουμένων ἐστί, καὶ εἴρηται ἡμῖν ἐν ἄλλοις. νῦν δὲ ἀπόχρη πρὸς τούσδε τοὺς ἄνδρας ἐπιδεικνύναι τὴν τοῦ Πλάτωνος διάνοιαν ὁποία τίς ἐστιν. ὅτι μὲν γὰρ οὐχ ὁ δημιουργὸς πρώτως ὑφίστησι τὴν ὕλην, δῆλον ἐξ ὧν ἐρεῖ προελθών [Pl. *Tim.* 52 D]. ... δοκεῖ γοῦν διὰ τούτων τὴν μὲν ὕλην ὥσπερ ἀντιδιελεῖν τῷ δημιουργῷ ..., τὴν B δὲ γένεσιν ἀπὸ τοῦ δημιουργοῦ παράγειν καὶ τῆς ὕλης. μήποτε οὖν ἀπ' ἄλλης τάξεως, τῆς πρὸ τοῦ δημιουργοῦ τεταγμένης, ὑφίστησιν αὐτήν. ἐν γοῦν τῷ Φιλήβῳ [23 C] γράφει διαρρήδην· "τὸν θεὸν ἐλέγομέν που τὸ μὲν πέρας δεῖξαι τῶν ὄντων, τὸ δὲ ἄπειρον." ... δῆλον τοίνυν ὡς τὴν μὲν ὕλην ἀπειρίαν φήσομεν, τὸ δὲ εἶδος πέρας. εἰ οὖν ... ὁ θεὸς πᾶσαν ἀπειρίαν ὑφίστησι, καὶ τὴν ὕλην ὑφίστησιν, ἐσχάτην οὖσαν ἀπειρίαν. ...

τὰ δ' αὐτὰ ταῦτα καὶ Ὀρφεὺς παραδίδωσιν. ... ὥστε καὶ Ὀρφεὺς κατὰ C, D τοῦτον τὸν λόγον ἀπὸ τῆς πρωτίστης τῶν νοητῶν ὑποστάσεως παράγει τὴν ὕλην. ...

καὶ μὴν καὶ ἡ τῶν Αἰγυπτίων παράδοσις τὰ αὐτὰ περὶ αὐτῆς (*sc.* τῆς ὕλης) φησιν· ὅ γέ τοι θεῖος Ἰάμβλιχος ἱστόρησεν ὅτι καὶ Ἑρμῆς ἐκ τῆς οὐσιότητος τὴν ὑλότητα παράγεσθαι βούλεται.[2] καὶ δὴ καὶ εἰκὸς κἀκ τούτου τὸν Πλάτωνα τὴν τοιαύτην περὶ τῆς ὕλης δόξαν ἔχειν.

---

[1] Plutarch of Chaeronea, not Plutarchus the Neoplatonist of the fifth century.
[2] Cf. *Abammonis responsum* 8. 3 g (p. 33 above); *Fr.* 18.

ZOSIMUS PANOPOLITANUS

i. τοῦ αὐτοῦ Ζωσίμου περὶ ὀργάνων καὶ καμίνων.

1 [γνήσια ὑπομνήματα περὶ τοῦ Ω στοιχείου.] τὸ Ω στοιχεῖον, στρογγύλον ⟨ὂν⟩ [τὸ] ⟨καὶ⟩ διμερές, ⟨. . .⟩ τὸ ἀνῆκον τῇ ἑβδόμῃ Κρόνου ζώνῃ κατὰ τὴν ἔνσωμον φράσιν. κατὰ γὰρ τὴν ἀσώματον, ἄλλο τί ἐστιν ἀνερμήνευτον, ὃ μόνος Νικόθεος ⟨ὁ⟩ κεκρυμμένος οἶδεν· κατὰ δὲ τὴν ἔνσωμον, τὸ λεγόμενον 5 ὠκεανός, θεῶν, φησί, πάντων γένεσις καὶ σπορά, καθάπερ, φησίν, ⌈αἱ μοναρχικαὶ τῆς ἐνσώμου φράσεως⌉.

τὸ δὲ [λεγόμενον] μέγα καὶ θαυμαστὸν Ω στοιχεῖον περιέχει τὸν περὶ ὀργάνων [ὕδατος θείου] λόγον καὶ καμίνων ⌈πασῶν μηχανικῶν καὶ ἁπλῶν καὶ ἁπλῶς πασῶν⌉. 10

2 Ζώσιμος Θεοσεβείῃ ευηειαει. αἱ καιρικαὶ καταβαφαί, ὦ γύναι, εἰς χλευασμὸν ἐποίησαν τὴν περὶ καμίνων βίβλον· πολλοὶ γάρ, εὐμένειαν ἐσχηκότες παρὰ τοῦ ἰδίου δαιμονίου ⌈ἐπιτυγχάνειν τῶν καιρικῶν⌉, ἐχλεύασαν [καὶ] τὴν περὶ καμίνων καὶ ὀργάνων βίβλον ὡς οὐκ οὖσαν ἀληθῆ. καὶ οὐδεὶς λόγος αὐτοὺς ἀποδεικτικὸς ἔπεισεν ὅτι ⌈ἀλήθειά⌉ ἐστιν, εἰ μὴ αὐτὸς 15 ὁ ἴδιος αὐτῶν δαίμων κατὰ τοὺς χρόνους ⟨. . .⟩. τῆς ⟨γὰρ⟩ αὐτῶν εἱμαρμένης μεταβληθείσ⟨ης, καὶ⟩ παραλαβόντος αὐτοὺ⟨ς⟩ κακοποιοῦ δαί⟨μονος⟩, ⌈εἰπεῖν καὶ⌉ τῆς τέχνης· καὶ τῆς εὐδαιμονίας αὐτῶν πάσης κωλυθείσης, καὶ ⌈ἐφ᾽ ἑκάτερα τραπέντων τῶν αὐτῶν τύχῃ ῥημάτων⌉, μόλις ἐκ τῶν ἐναργῶν

3 τῆς εἱμαρμένης [αὐτῶν] ἀποδείξεων ὡμολόγησαν εἶναί τι καὶ ⌈μετ᾽ ἐκείνων 20 ὧν πρότερον ἐφρόνουν⌉. ἀλλ᾽ οἱ τοιοῦτοι οὐκ ἀποδεκτ[ε]οὶ οὔτε παρὰ θεῷ οὔτε φιλοσόφοις ἀνθρώποις. πάλιν γὰρ ⌈τῶν χρόνων σχηματισθέντων κατὰ τοὺς λεπτοὺς χρόνους καλῶς⌉, καὶ τοῦ δαιμονίου σωματικῶς αὐτοὺς εὐεργετοῦντος, πάλιν μεταβάλλονται ἐφ᾽ ἑτέραν ὁμολογίαν, τῶν πρότερον

1 Berthelot, *Alchimistes grecs*, 1888, Tom. II, p. 228 sqq.   Codices:—M, saec. XI; K, saec. XVI   2 γνήσια . . . στοιχείου seclusi   3 ὂν καὶ scripsi : τὸ codd. | Lacunam signavi | ἑβδόμῃ [Κρόνου]? An [ἑβδόμη] Κρόνου?   5 ὁ add. Reitzenstein   6 Hom. *Il*. 14. 201: Ὠκεανόν τε, θεῶν γένεσιν   8 λεγόμενον seclusi   9 ὕδατος θείου seclusi | Fortasse ⟨καὶ⟩ πασῶν μηχανῶν   11 ευηειαει M: εὐήει ἀεὶ K. Fortasse εὐη⟨μερ⟩εῖ⟨ν⟩ ἀεί | καιρικαὶ Ruelle : κερικαὶ MK   13 Fortasse ⟨ὥστε⟩ ἐπιτυγχάνειν ⟨διὰ⟩ τῶν καιρικῶν (*sc*. καταβαφῶν)   14 καὶ seclusi   15 Fortasse ὅτι ⟨οὐκ⟩ ἀληθής ἐστιν (*sc*. ἡ βίβλος).   An secludendum ὅτι ἀλήθειά ἐστιν?   16 Lacunam signavi: fortasse ⟨εὐμενὴς ὤν⟩ | γὰρ addidi   17 μεταβληθείσης καὶ scripsi : μεταβληθείς codd. | αὐτοὺς κικοποιοῦ δαίμονος scripsi : αὐτοῦ κακοποιοῦ δὲ codd.   18 Desideratur verbum 3 pers. pl., e. g. ἐξέπεσον   19 Fortasse ἐπὶ θάτερα τραπέντων, ἐὰν οὕτω τύχῃ, τῶν πραγμάτων   20 αὐτῶν seclusi   20-21 Fortasse ἐν ἐκείνοις ὧν πρότερον κατεφρόνουν   21 ἀποδεκτοὶ scripsi : ἀποδεκτέοι codd.   22-23 Fortasse πάλιν γὰρ τῶν πραγμάτων μετασχηματισθέντων . εἰς τὸ καλόν   24 μεταβάλλονται coni. Ruelle : μεταβάλλεται codd

ἐναργῶν πραγμάτων πάντων λελησμένοι, πάντοτε τῇ εἱμαρμένῃ ἀκολου-
θοῦντες καὶ εἰς ⸢τὰς λεγομένας⸣ καὶ εἰς τὰ ἐναντία, μηδὲν ἕτερον τῶν
σωματικῶν φανταζόμενοι, ἀλλὰ ⸢τὴν εἱμαρμένην⸣.

τοὺς τοιούτους δὲ ἀνθρώπους ὁ Ἑρμῆς ἐν τῷ περὶ φύσεων ἐκάλει ἄνοας, 4
5 τῆς εἱμαρμένης μόνον ὄντας πομπάς, μηδὲν τῶν ἀσωμάτων
φανταζομένους, μηδὲ αὐτὴν τὴν εἱμαρμένην τὴν αὐτοὺς ἄγουσαν
δικαίως ⟨ὑπολαμβάνοντας⟩ ἀλλὰ [τοὺς] δυσφημοῦντας αὐτῆς τὰ
σωματικὰ παιδευτήρια, καὶ τῶν εὐδαιμόνων αὐτῆς ἐκτὸς ⟨μηδὲν⟩
ἄλλο φανταζομένους.

10 ὁ δὲ Ἑρμῆς καὶ ὁ Ζωροάστρης τὸ φιλοσόφων γένος ἀνώτερον τῆς 5
εἱμαρμένης εἶπον, τῷ μήτε τῇ εὐδαιμονίᾳ αὐτῆς χαίρειν—
ἡδονῶν γὰρ κρατοῦσι—μήτε τοῖς κακοῖς αὐτῆς ⸢βάλλεσθαι⸣,
πάντοτε ἐν ἀϋλίᾳ ἄγοντας.

[μήτε τὰ καλὰ δῶρα παρ' αὐτῆς καταδεχόμενοι] [ἐπείπερ εἰς πέρας κακῶν
15 βλέπουσι].

διὰ τοῦτο καὶ ὁ Ἡσίοδος τὸν Προμηθέα εἰσάγει τῷ Ἐπιμηθεῖ παραγ- 6
γέλλοντα [τίνα οἴονται οἱ ἄνθρωποι πασῶν μείζονα εὐδαιμονίαν; γυναῖκα
εὔμορφον, φησί, σὺν πλούτῳ πολλῷ] [καὶ φησὶ] " μή⟨πο⟩τε δῶρον δέξασθαι
παρὰ Ζηνὸς Ὀλυμπίου, ἀλλ' ἀποπέμπειν ἐξοπίσω ", διδάσκων τὸν ἴδιον
20 ἀδελφὸν διὰ φιλοσοφίας ἀποπέμπειν τὰ τοῦ Διός, τουτέστι τῆς εἱμαρμένης
δῶρα.

Ζωροάστρης δέ, ⟨⟨αὐχῶν⟩⟩ ⟨ἐπὶ τῇ⟩ εἰδήσει τῶν ἄνω πάντων, καὶ μαγείᾳ 7
[[αὐχῶν]] [τῆς ἐνσώμου φράσεως] φάσκει ἀποστρέφεσθαι πάντα τῆς εἱμαρμένης τὰ κακά, καὶ μερικὰ καὶ καθολικά. ὁ μέντοι Ἑρμῆς ἐν τῷ περὶ [αν]
25 ἀϋλίας διαβάλλει [καὶ] τὴν μαγείαν, λέγων ὅτι οὐ δεῖ [τὸν πνευματικὸν
ἄνθρωπον] τὸν ἐπιγνόντα ἑαυτὸν [οὔτε] διὰ μαγείας κατορθοῦν
τι, ἐὰν καὶ κακὸν νομίζηται, μηδὲ βιάζεσθαι τὴν ἀνάγκην, ἀλλ'

1 πραγμάτων secludendum? 2 τὰ λεγόμενα coni. Ruelle. An τὰ ⟨ὑφ'
ἡμῶν⟩ λεγόμενα? 3 Fortasse ἀλλὰ ⟨δοῦλοι ὄντες⟩ τῆς εἱμαρμένης 5 μόνον
Reitz.: μόνους codd. 6 φανταζομένους codd.: fortasse ἐννοοῦντας | μηδὲ
Reitz.: μήτε codd. | τὴν Reitz.: τοὺς codd. 7 ὑπολαμβάνοντας
addidi | τοὺς seclusit Reitz. 8 μηδὲν add. Reitz. 10 Ζωροάστρης
Ruelle: Ζωροάστρις ΜΚ 10–11 Fortasse ⟨⟨τὸ ⟨⟨δὲ⟩⟩ φιλοσόφων γένος⟩⟩ ὁ [[δὲ]]
Ἑρμῆς [καὶ ὁ Ζωροάστρης] [[ ]] ἀνώτερον τῆς εἱμαρμένης εἶπεν 12 βλάπτεσθαι?
An ⟨εἰς λύπην κατα⟩βάλλεσθαι? 13 ἐν ἀϋλίᾳ scripsi: ἐναυλία Κ: ἐναυλίαν Μ
| ἄγοντας Reitz.: ἄγοντες codd. 14–15 μήτε . . . καταδεχόμενοι et ἐπείπερ . . .
βλέπουσι seclusi 17–18 τίνα . . . πολλῷ delevit Reitz. 18 καὶ φησὶ seclusi
| 'Lire μήποτε (?)' Ruelle: μήτε codd. 18–19 Hes. Op. et d. 86 21 Fortasse
δῶρα, ⟨⟨μηδὲ τὰ καλὰ [δῶρα] παρ' αὐτῆς καταδεχόμενον (l. 14)⟩⟩. 22 αὐχῶν
huc transposui: ἐπὶ τῇ addidi 23 τῆς ἐνσώμου φράσεως seclusi (vide § 1). An
αὐχῶν ἐπὶ τῇ εἰδήσει τῶν τε ἄνω πάντων καὶ τῆς ἐνσώμου φύσεως, μαγείᾳ φάσκει
κ.τ.λ.? 24–25 περὶ ἀϋλίας scripsi: περὶ ἀναυλίας codd. 25 καὶ seclusi
25–26 τὸν πνευματικὸν ἄνθρωπον seclusi 26 ἐπιγνῶντα codd. | οὔτε seclusi
27 κακὸν scripsi: καλὸν codd. | Fortasse οὐδὲ. Fortasse ἐὰν ⟨αὐτὴν⟩ (sc. τὴν ἀνάγκην)

ἐὰν ὡς ἔχει φύσεως [καὶ κρίσεως] πορεύεσθαι. ⌜δὲ διὰ μόνου
τοῦ⌝ ζητεῖν ἑαυτὸν καὶ θεὸν ἐπιγνόντα κρατεῖν ⟨ . . . ⟩ [τὴν
ἀκατονόμαστον τριάδα], καὶ ἐὰν τὴν εἱμαρμένην ὃ θέλει[ν]
ποιεῖν τῷ ἑαυτῆς πηλῷ, τουτέστι τῷ σώματι. καὶ οὕτως, φησί,
νοήσας καὶ πολιτευσάμενος, ⟨ . . . ⟩.   5

8   [[θεάσῃ τὸν θεοῦ υἱὸν πάντα γινόμενον τῶν ὁσίων ψυχῶν ἕνεκεν, ἵνα
αὐτὴν ἐκσπάσῃ ἐκ τοῦ χώρου τῆς εἱμαρμένης ἐπὶ τὸν ἀσώματον. ὅρα
αὐτὸν γινόμενον πάντα, θεόν, ἄγγελον, ἄνθρωπον παθητόν· πάντα γὰρ
δυνάμενος, πάντα ὅσα θέλει γίνεται, καὶ πατρὶ ὑπακούει, διὰ παντὸς
σώματος διήκων· φωτίζων τὸν ἑκάστης νοῦν, εἰς τὸν εὐδαίμονα χῶρον   10
ἀνώρμησεν, ὅπουπερ ἦν καὶ πρὸ τοῦτο σωματικὸν γενέσθαι, αὐτῷ ἀκολουθοῦντα καὶ ὑπ᾽ αὐτοῦ ὀρεγόμενον καὶ ὁδηγούμενον εἰς ἐκεῖνο τὸ φῶς.]]
[καὶ βλέψαι τὸν πίνακα ὃν ⌜καὶ βιτος γράψας⌝].

9   ⟨ . . . ⟩ καὶ ὁ τρίσμεγας Πλάτων, καὶ ὁ μυριόμεγας Ἑρμῆς, [ὅτι]
[Θώυθος ἑρμηνεύεται τῇ ἱερατικῇ [πρώτῃ] φωνῇ] [ὁ πρῶτος ἄνθρωπος] ⟨ὁ⟩   15
ἑρμηνεὺς πάντων τῶν ὄντων καὶ ⌜ὀνοματοποιὸς⌝ πάντων τῶν σωματικῶν.

10   ⟨ . . . ⟩ οἱ δὲ Χαλδαῖοι καὶ Πάρθοι καὶ Μῆδοι καὶ Ἑβραῖοι καλοῦσιν αὐτὸν
Ἀδάμ, ᾧ ἐστιν ἑρμηνεία γῆ παρθένος, καὶ γῆ αἱματώδης, καὶ γῆ πυρ(ρ)ά,
καὶ γῆ σαρκίνη. ταῦτα δὲ ἐν ταῖς βιβλιοθήκαις τῶν Πτολεμαίων ηὕρη[ν]ται,
⟨ . . . ⟩ ⌜ὃν⌝ ἀπέθε[ν]το εἰς ἕκαστον ἱερόν, μάλιστα ⟨δ᾽ εἰς⟩ τὸ ΣαραπεῖοΝ,   20
ὅτε παρεκάλεσεν Ἀσενὰν τὸν ἀρχ(ιερέα) Ἱεροσολύμων πέμψαι [τα] ἑρμη-
ν(έα), ὃς ἡρμήνευσε πᾶσαν τὴν Ἑβραΐδα Ἑλληνιστὶ καὶ Αἰγυπτιστί.

11   οὕτως οὖν καλεῖται ὁ πρῶτος ἄνθρωπος [ὁ παρ᾽ ἡμῖν Θωὺθ καὶ] παρ᾽
ἐκείνοις Ἀδάμ [τῇ τῶν ἀγγέλων φωνῇ αὐτὸν καλέσαντες]. οὐ μὴν [δὲ]
ἀλλὰ καὶ συμβολικῶς ⟨ . . . ⟩, διὰ τεσσάρων στοιχείων [ἐκ πάσης τῆς   25

1 καὶ κρίσεως seclusi   1–2 Fortasse δεῖ δὲ μόνον [τοῦ]   2 ἐπιγνῶντα codd.
| Lacunam signavi: fortasse ⟨τῶν παθῶν⟩ vel ⟨τοῦ ἀλόγου⟩   2–3 τὴν . . . τριάδα
seclusi   3 θέλει Ruelle: θέλειν MK   4 τῷ ἑαυτῆς πηλῷ K (Reitz.): τῷ
ἐὰν τῇ σπηλῷ M   5 Lacunam signavi   6–12 (θεάσῃ τὸν . . . τὸ φῶς) hinc
transposui: vide post § 15   13 καὶ βλέψαι . . . γράψας seclusi   14–15 ὅτι et
Θώυθος . . . φωνῇ seclusi   15 πρώτῃ seclusit Reitz. | ὁ πρῶτος ἄνθρωπος
seclusi | ὁ add. Reitz.   17 Lacunam signavi   18–19 Locum
Ἀδάμ . . . ηὕρηται ita repetit posterior alchemista Olympiodorus (Berthelot p.
89): ἐκ τοῦ Ἀδάμ· οὗτος γὰρ πάντων ἀνθρώπων πρῶτος ἐγένετο ἐκ τῶν τεσσάρων
στοιχείων· καλεῖται δὲ καὶ παρθένος γῆ, καὶ πυρ(ρ)ὰ γῆ, καὶ σαρκίνη γῆ, καὶ γῆ
αἱματώδης. ταῦτα δὲ εὑρήσεις ἐν ταῖς Πτολεμαίου βιβλιοθήκαις   18 πυρρά coni.
Ruelle: πυρα codd.   19 ηὕρηται scripsi: ηὕρηνται codd.   20 Lacunam
signavi | ἀπέθετο scripsi: ἀπέθεντο codd.   Fortasse ⟨ἐν τῷ βιβλίῳ⟩ ὃ[ν] (vel ἐν
τοῖς βιβλίοις ἃ) ἀπέθετο ⟨ὁ Φιλάδελφος⟩ | δ᾽ εἰς τὸ Σαραπεῖον scripsi: τῷ
Σαραπείῳ codd.   21 τὸν ἀρχιερέα Ἱεροσολύμων Reitz.: τῶν ἱερυσολύμων codd.
21–22 πέμψαι ἑρμηνέα scripsi: πέμψαντα Ἑρμῆν codd.   (An legendum πέμψαι
ἑρμην(έας) οἳ ἡρμήνευσαν?)   22 ἑρμήνευσε M: εἱρμήνευσε Ruelle (ex K?)
23 ὁ . . . καὶ seclusi   24 Ἀδάμ secludendum? | τῇ τῶν . . . καλέσαντες
seclusi | δὲ seclusi   25 Lacunam signavi. Fortasse⟨ἐκάλεσαν αὐτὸν Ἀδάμ⟩
25–p. 107. 1 ἐκ . . . σφαίρας seclusi

σφαίρας] αὐτὸν εἰπόντες, κατὰ τὸ σῶμα. [τὸ γὰρ ἄλφα αὐτοῦ στοιχεῖον
ἀνατολὴν δηλοῖ [τὸν ἀέρα], τὸ δὲ δέλτα αὐτοῦ στοιχεῖον δύσιν δηλοῖ [⟨γῆν⟩,
τὴν κάτω καταδύσασαν διὰ τὸ βάρος]· ⟨τὸ δὲ δεύτερον Α στοιχεῖον ἄρκτον
δηλοῖ·⟩ τὸ δὲ Μ στοιχεῖον μεσημβρίαν δηλοῖ] [τὸ μέσον τούτων τῶν σωμά-
5 των πεπαντικὸν πῦρ, τὸ εἰς τὴν μέσην [τετάρτην] ζώνην ⟨. . .⟩.] [οὕτως
οὖν] ὁ ⟨μὲν γὰρ⟩ σάρκινος ⟨ἄνθρωπος⟩ Ἀδὰμ [κατὰ τὴν φαινομένην περί-
πλασιν] [Θωὶθ] καλεῖται· ὁ δὲ ἔσω αὐτοῦ ἄνθρωπος, ὁ πνευματικός, καὶ
κύρ⟨ιον⟩ [[ομα]] ἔχει ὄν⟨⟨ομα⟩⟩ καὶ προσηγορικόν. τὸ μὲν οὖν κύριον
ἀγνοῶ[ν διὰ τὸ] τέως· μόνος γὰρ Νικόθεος, ὁ ἀνεύρετος ⟨γενόμενος⟩, τοῦτο
10 οἶδεν· τὸ δὲ προσηγορικὸν αὐτοῦ ὄνομα Φῶς καλεῖται, ἀφ' οὗ καὶ φῶτας
παρηκολούθησε λέγεσθαι τοὺς ἀνθρώπους. ⟨. . .⟩ ὅτε ἦν ⟨ὁ⟩ Φῶς ἐν τῷ 12
Παραδείσῳ, ⌐διαπνεόμενος ὑπὸ⌐ τῆς εἱμαρμένης, ἔπεισαν αὐτὸν ⟨οἱ . . .⟩,
ὡς ἄκακον ⟨ὄντα⟩ καὶ ⌐ἀνενέργητον⌐, ἐνδύσασθαι τὸν παρ' αὐτῶν Ἀδὰμ [τὸν
ἐκ τῆς εἱμαρμένης], τὸν ἐκ τῶν τεσσάρων στοιχείων· ὁ δὲ διὰ τὸ ἄκακον οὐκ
15 ἀπεστράφη· οἱ δὲ ἐκαυχῶντο ὡς δεδουλαγωγημένου αὐτοῦ.

⟨. . .⟩ τὸν ἔξω ἄνθρωπον δεσμὸν εἶπεν ὁ Ἡσίοδος ὃν ἔδησεν ὁ Ζεὺς τὸν 13
Προμηθέα. εἶτα μετὰ ⟨τοῦτον⟩ τὸν δεσμὸν ἄλλον αὐτῷ δεσμὸν ἐπιπέμπει
τὴν Πανδώρην, ἣν οἱ Ἐβραῖοι καλοῦσιν Εὖαν. ⟨. . .⟩ ⟨⟨διὰ τὴν παρακοὴν
τοῦ Ἐπιμηθέως, ἣν παρήκουσεν τοῦ Προμηθέως, ⟨τουτέστι⟩ τοῦ ἰδίου⟩⟩
20 ⟨νοός⟩. ὁ γὰρ Προμηθεὺς καὶ Ἐπιμηθεὺς εἷς ἄνθρωπός ἐστι κατὰ τὸν
ἀλληγορικὸν λόγον, [τουτέστι ψυχὴ καὶ σῶμα,] καὶ [ποτὲ] ⟨⟨νοός⟩⟩ μὲν
[ψυχῆς] ἔχει εἰκόνα ὁ Προμηθεύς, [ποτὲ δὲ] [[νοὸς]] [ποτὲ δὲ] σαρκὸς ⟨δὲ ὁ
Ἐπιμηθεύς⟩. [[διὰ τὴν παρακοὴν τοῦ Ἐπιμηθέως ἣν παρήκουσεν τοῦ
Προμηθέως τοῦ ἰδίου]] φησὶ γὰρ ὁ νοῦς ἡμῶν ⟨. . .⟩.
25 ⟨. . .⟩ ὁ δὲ υἱὸς τοῦ θεοῦ, πάντα δυνάμενος, καὶ πάντα γινόμενος ὅσα 14

1–5 τὸ γὰρ ἄλφα . . . τετάρτην ζώνην seclusi (τὸ γὰρ ἄλφα . . . Θωὶθ καλεῖται
delevit Reitz.)   2 τὸν ἀέρα seclusi   2–3 γῆν τὴν . . . βάρος
seclusi | γῆν τὴν scripsi : τὴν codd. : γῆν Reitz.   3–4 τὸ δὲ . . .
δηλοῖ addidi   4–5 τὸ μέσον . . . ζώνην seclusi   5 τετάρτην seclusi
| Lacunam signavi   Fortasse τὸ εἰς τὴν μέσην [   ] ζώνην ⟨⟨ἐκ πάσης τῆς
σφαίρας⟩⟩ ⟨συνηθροισμένον⟩   5–6 ὁ μὲν γὰρ σάρκινος ἄνθρωπος scripsi :
οὕτως οὖν ὁ σάρκινος codd.   6–7 κατὰ . . . περίπλασιν et Θωὶθ seclusi
7 αὐτοῦ secludendum?   8 κύριον ἔχει ὄνομα Reitz. : κυρομα εχειον
codd.   9 ἀγνοῶ scripsi (ἀγνοῶ διὰ τὸ Reitz.) : ἀγνοῶν διὰ τὸ τέως codd.
| γενόμενος addidi | τοῦτο scripsi : ταῦτα codd.   11 Lacunam
signavi : fortasse ⟨λέγει δὲ ὁ Νικόθεος ὡς⟩ | ὁ addidi   12 For-
tasse διατετμημένος ἀπὸ | ἔπεισαν ⟨οἱ ἄρχοντες⟩ αὐτὸν Reitz.   13 ὄντα
addidi | αὐτῶν Reitz. : αὐτοῦ codd.   13–14 τὸν ἐκ τῆς εἱμαρμένης seclusi
15 οἱ Reitz. : εἰ codd. | Fortasse ὡς δεδουλαγωγημένου αὐτοῦ ⟨ὑπὸ τῆς εἱμαρ-
μένης⟩   16 Lacunam signavi   17 τοῦτον add. Ruelle   18 Lacunam
signavi : διὰ τὴν . . . ἰδίου huc transposui   19 τουτέστι addidi   20 νοός
addidi   21 τουτέστι . . . σῶμα seclusi | ποτὲ seclusi : νοός huc transposui
22 ψυχῆς seclusi | Fortasse ⟨παρ⟩έχει | ποτὲ δὲ bis seclusi   22–23 δὲ
ὁ Ἐπιμηθεύς addidi   24 Lacunam signavi.   Fortasse ⟨τὰ ἀπὸ τῆς εἱμαρμένης
δεῖν ἀπωθεῖσθαι (?)⟩. ⟨⟨μηδὲ τὰ καλὰ δῶρα παρ' αὐτῆς καταδεχόμενος⟩⟩ (vide § 5 fin.)
25 Lacunam signavi | ὅσα scripsi : ὅτε codd.

θέλει, ὡς θέλει φαίνετ⟨αι⟩ ἑκάστῳ. ['Αδὰμ προσῆν] ['Ιησοῦς Χριστὸς]
[[ἀνήνεγκεν ὅπου καὶ τὸ πρότερον διῆγον φῶτες καλούμενοι]] ἐφάνη δὲ καὶ
τοῖς πάνυ ἀδυνάτοις ἀνθρώποις, ἄνθρωπος γεγονὼς παθητός, καὶ ῥαπιζόμενος
καὶ ⟨⟨κοπτόμενος καὶ φονευόμενος παρ' αὐτῶν⟩⟩ [λάθρα] [[τοὺς ἰδίους φῶτας
συλήσας]]· ⟨καὶ⟩ ἅτε μηδὲν παθών, τὸν δὲ θάνατον δείξας καταπατεῖσθαι, [καὶ 5
ἐῶσθαι], ⟨⟨τοὺς ἰδίους [φῶτας] συλήσας⟩⟩ ⟨⟨ἀνήνεγκεν ὅπου καὶ τὸ πρότερον
15   διῆγον φῶτες καλούμενοι⟩⟩.   καὶ ἕως ἄρτι καὶ τοῦ τέλους τοῦ κόσμου, [το]
τοῖς ⟨μὲ⟩ν λάθρα ⟨τοῖς δὲ⟩ καὶ φανερὰ συνὼν ⟨ὁδηγεῖ⟩ τοὺς ἑαυτοῦ, συμβουλεύων αὐτοῖς [λάθρα καὶ] διὰ τοῦ νοὸς αὐτῶν [κ]ἀπαλλαγὴν ἔχειν τοῦ [παρ']
αὐτῶν 'Αδάμ, [[κοπτομένου καὶ φονευομένου παρ' αὐτῶν]] ⌜τυφληγοροῦντος⌝ 10
καὶ διαζηλουμένα τῷ πνευματικῷ καὶ φωτεινῷ ἀνθρώπῳ. [τὸν ἑαυτῶν 'Αδὰμ
ἀποκτείνουσι.]

⟨⟨8⟩⟩   ⟨. . .⟩ ⟨⟨θεάσῃ τὸν θεοῦ υἱὸν πάντα γινόμενον τῶν ὁσίων ψυχῶν ἕνεκεν,
ἵνα αὐτὰς ἐκσπάσῃ ἐκ τοῦ χώρου τῆς εἱμαρμένης ἐπὶ τὸν ἀσώματον.   ὅρα
αὐτὸν γινόμενον πάντα, θεόν, ἄγγελον, ἄνθρωπον παθητόν· πάντα γὰρ 15
δυνάμενος, πάντα ὅσα θέλει γίνεται [καὶ πατρὶ ὑπακούει], διὰ παντὸς σώματος
διήκων.   ⟨. . .⟩ φωτίζων τὸν ἑκάστου νοῦν ⟨. . .   . . .⟩ εἰς τὸν εὐδαίμονα
χῶρον ἀνώρμησεν, ὅπουπερ ἦν καὶ πρὸ τοῦ[το] σωματικὸς γενέσθαι.
⟨. . .⟩ αὐτῷ ἀκολουθοῦντα καὶ ὑπ' αὐτοῦ ⌜ὀρεγόμενον⌝ καὶ ὁδηγούμενον εἰς
ἐκεῖνο τὸ φῶς.⟩⟩
20

16   ταῦτα δὲ γίνεται ἕως οὗ ἔλθῃ ὁ ἀντίμιμος δαίμων, διαζηλούμενος αὐτῷ,
καὶ θέλων ὡς τὸ πρῶτον πλανῆσαι, λέγων ἑαυτὸν υἱὸν θεοῦ, ἄμορφος ὢν
καὶ ψυχῇ καὶ σώματι.   οἱ δὲ φρονιμώτεροι γενόμενοι ἐκ τῆς καταλήψεως
τοῦ ὄντως υἱοῦ τοῦ θεοῦ [δι]δώ⟨σου⟩σιν αὐτῷ τὸν ἴδιον 'Αδὰμ εἰς φόνον, τὰ

1 φαίνεται scripsi : φαίνει codd.   1–2 'Αδὰμ προσῆν et 'Ιησοῦς Χριστὸς seclusi :
ἀνήνεγκεν . . . καλούμενοι hinc transposui   4 κοπτόμενος . . . αὐτῶν huc a
§ 15 transposui | κοπτόμενος καὶ φονευόμενος scripsi (an κοπτόμενος, καὶ
ἐφονεύθη ?) : κοπτομένου καὶ φονευομένου codd. | λάθρα seclusi   4–5 τοὺς . . .
συλήσας hinc transposui : καὶ addidi   5–6 καὶ ἐῶσθαι seclusi   6 φῶτας
seclusi   5–7 Fortasse ⟨καὶ ἐκ νεκρῶν ἠγέρθη,⟩ ἅτε μηδὲν παθών· τὸν δὲ θάνατον
δείξας καταπατεῖσθαι, ⟨⟨τοὺς ἰδίους συλήσας⟩⟩ ⟨⟨ἀνήνεγκεν κ.τ.λ.⟩⟩   7 καὶ
τοῦ τέλους τοῦ κόσμου secludendum ?   8 τοῖς μὲν λάθρα τοῖς δὲ καὶ φανερὰ
συνὼν scripsi : τόποις ἰλάθρα καὶ φανερὰ συλλῶν codd. | ὁδηγεῖ τοὺς scripsi :
τοῖς codd.   9 λάθρα καὶ seclusi | ἀπαλλαγὴν scripsi : καταλλαγὴν
codd. | παρ' seclusit Reitz.   10 κοπτομένου . . . αὐτῶν seclusit Reitz.
| Fortasse τυφλοδηγοῦντος   11–12 τὸν . . . ἀποκτείνουσι seclusit Reitz.   13 Lacu-
nam signavi.   Fortasse ⟨⟨καὶ βλέψας⟨α εἰς⟩ τὸν πίνακα ὃν [καὶ βιτος] ⟨ἔ⟩γραψα[ς]
(vel ὃν ὁ Νικόθεος ἔγραψε), § 8 fin.⟩⟩ θεάσῃ κ.τ.λ.   Κέβης τε ἔγραψε Ruelle   14 αὐτὰς
scripsi : αὐτὴν codd.   (An τῶν ὁσίων [ψυχῶν] ἕνεκεν, ἵνα αὐτοὺς ?) | τὸν
codd. : fortasse τὸ   16 καὶ πατρὶ ὑπακούει seclusi   17 Lacunam signavi
| ἑκάστου coni. Ruelle : ἑκάστης codd. | Lacunam signavi   18 τοῦ
σωματικὸς scripsi : τοῦτο σωματικὸν codd.   19 Lacunam signavi | ὀρεγό-
μενον codd. : fortasse ὀρθούμενον vel ἐγειρόμενον   [An αὐτοῦ ὀρεγόμενον καὶ ὑπ'
αὐτοῦ ὁδηγούμενον ? A. S. F.]   21 διαζηλούμενος Reitz. : δι' οὗ ζηλούμενος codd.
| αὐτῷ scripsi : αὐτοῖς codd.   22 πρῶτον scripsi : πρῴην codd. | Fortasse
πλανῆσαι ⟨τοὺς ἀνθρώπους⟩   23 φρονιμώτεροι γενόμενοι Ruelle : φρονιμώτερον
γενάμενοι ΜΚ   24 δώσουσιν scripsi : δίδωσιν ΜΚ

ἑαυτῶν φωτεινὰ πνεύματα σώζοντες ⟨εἰς τὸν⟩ ἴδιον χῶρον, ὅπουπερ καὶ
πρὸ ⟨τοῦ⟩ κόσμου ἦσαν.

πρὶν ἢ δὲ ταῦτα τολμῆσαι τὸν ἀντίμιμον [τὸν ζηλωτήν], πρῶτον ἀπο- 17
στέλλει αὐτοῦ πρόδρομον ἀπὸ τῆς Περσίδος, μυθοπλάνους λόγους λαλοῦντα,
5 καὶ περὶ τὴν εἱμαρμένην ἄγοντα τοὺς ἀνθρώπους· εἰσὶ δὲ τὰ στοιχεῖα τοῦ
ὀνόματος αὐτοῦ ἐννέα, [τῆς διφθόγγου σωζομένης,] κατὰ τὸν τῆς εἱμαρ
μένης ὅρον.

εἶτα μετὰ περίοδον πλέον ἢ ἔλαττον ἑπτὰ ⟨. . . ων⟩ καὶ αὐτὸς ⌜ἑαυτῷ
φύσει⌝ ἐλεύσεται.

10 καὶ ταῦτα μὲν οἱ Ἑβραῖοι [καὶ αἱ ἱεραὶ Ἑρμοῦ βίβλοι], περὶ τοῦ 18
φωτεινοῦ ἀνθρώπου, καὶ τοῦ ὁδηγοῦ αὐτοῦ υἱοῦ θεοῦ, καὶ τοῦ γηΐνου
Ἀδάμ, καὶ τοῦ ὁδηγοῦ αὐτοῦ ἀντιμίμου, τοῦ δυσφημίᾳ λέγοντος ἑαυτὸν
εἶναι υἱὸν θεοῦ [πλάνῃ]· οἱ δὲ Ἕλληνες καλοῦσι ⟨τὸ⟩ν γήϊ⟨ν⟩ον Ἀδὰμ
Ἐπιμηθέα, συμβουλευόμενον ὑπὸ τοῦ [[ἰδίου νοῦ]] ⟨⟨ἀδελφοῦ αὐτοῦ⟩⟩,
15 τουτέστι τοῦ [[ἀδελφοῦ αὐτοῦ]] ⟨⟨ἰδίου νοῦ⟩⟩, μὴ λαβεῖν τὰ δῶρα τοῦ Διός.
⌜ὅμως⌝ [καὶ σφαλεὶς καὶ μετανοήσας καὶ τὸν εὐδαίμονα χῶρον ζητήσας]
⟨. . .⟩ πάντα ἑρμηνεύει καὶ πάντα συμβουλεύει τοῖς ἔχουσιν ἀκοὰς νοεράς.
οἱ δὲ τὰς σωματικὰς ἔχοντες μόνον ἀκοὰς τῆς εἱμαρμένης εἰσὶ ⟨δοῦλοι⟩,
μηδὲν ἄλλο καταδεχόμενοι ἢ ὁμολογοῦντες.

20 ⟨. . .⟩ ὅσοι τὰς καιρικὰς ⟨. . .⟩, εὐτυχοῦντες, οὐδὲν ἕτερον ⌜λέγουσι⌝ τῆς 19
τέχνης, χλευάζοντες [ἢ] τὴν μεγάλην περὶ καμίνων βίβλον. καὶ οὐδὲ τὸν
ποιητὴν κατανοοῦσι λέγοντα "ἀλλ' οὔπως ἅμα ⟨πάντα⟩ θεοὶ δόσαν
ἀνθρώποισι" καὶ τὰ ἑξῆς· καὶ οὐδὲν ἐνθυμοῦνται, [οὐδὲ] βλέποντες ⟨εἰς⟩
τὰς τῶν ἀνθρώπων διαγωγάς, ὅτι καὶ εἰς μίαν τέχνην ἄνθρωποι διαφόρως
25 εὐτυχοῦσι, καὶ διαφόρως τὴν μίαν τέχνην ἐργάζονται, διὰ τὸ [ἤθη καὶ]
διάφορα ⟨ὄντα τὰ⟩ σχήματα τῶν ἀστέρων ⟨διάφορον καὶ τὴν⟩ μίαν τέχνην
ποιεῖν, καὶ τὸν μὲν ἄκρον ⟨εἶναι⟩ τεχνίτην, [τὸν δὲ μόνον τεχνίτην,] τὸν δὲ
ὑποβεβηκότα, τὸν δὲ [χείρονα] ἀπρόκοπον.

1 εἰς τὸν addidi (εἰς add. Reitz.) | ἴδιον codd. : fortasse εὐδαίμονα 2 τοῦ
addidi 3 τὸν ζηλωτήν seclusi 4 Fortasse μυθοπλάστους 6 Indicatur
Μανιχαῖος | τῆς . . . σωζομένης seclusi 8 περίοδον scripsi : περιόδου MK
| Lacunam signavi : fortasse ⟨ἐτῶν⟩ 8-9 καὶ αὐτός, φησίν, ἐλεύσεται? 10 μὲν
οἱ scripsi : μόνοι codd. | καὶ αἱ . . . βίβλοι seclusi 12 λέγοντος MK
13 πλάνῃ seclusi | καλοῦσι τὸν Reitz. : καλοῦσιν codd. | γήϊνον Reitz. :
γήϊον codd. 14-15 τοῦ ἀδελφοῦ αὐτοῦ, τουτέστι τοῦ ἰδίου νοῦ scripsi : τοῦ ἰδίου
νοῦ, τουτέστι τοῦ ἀδελφοῦ αὐτοῦ codd. 16 καὶ σφαλεὶς . . . ζητήσας seclusi
17 Lacunam indicavit Reitz. | Fortasse ὅμοια [ ] ⟨δὲ παραινοῦσι ⟨⟨καὶ αἱ ἱεραὶ
Ἑρμοῦ βίβλοι⟩⟩. ὁ γὰρ Ἑρμῆς τὰ περὶ τῆς εἱμαρμένης⟩ πάντα ἑρμηνεύει 18 δοῦλοι
addidi 19 καταδεχόμενοι ἢ secludendum? 20 Lacunam signavi
| Lacunam signavi. Fortasse ταῖς καιρικαῖς (sc. καταβαφαῖς) ⟨χρῶνται⟩ | λέ-
γουσι codd. : fortasse καταδέχονται 21 ἢ seclusi 22 πάντα addidi
23 βλέποντες εἰς scripsi : οὐδὲ βλέπουσι codd. 25-26 διὰ τὸ διάφορα ὄντα τὰ
scripsi : διὰ τὰ ἤθη καὶ διάφορα codd. 26 διάφορον καὶ τὴν addidi 27 ἄκρον
scripsi : ἄγαν codd. | εἶναι addidi | τὸν δὲ μόνον τεχνίτην seclusi
28 χείρονα seclusi | καὶ τὸν μὲν . . . ἀπρόκοπον secludendum?

20 οὕτως ἔστιν ⟨εὑρεῖν⟩ ἐπὶ πασῶν τῶν τεχνῶν [καὶ] διαφόροις ἐργαλείοις
καὶ ἀγωγαῖς τὴν αὐτὴν τέχνην ἐργαζομένους, καὶ διαφόρως ἔχοντας τὸ
[νοερὸν καὶ] ἐπιτευκτικόν. καὶ μάλιστα ὑπὲρ πάσας τὰς τέχνας ἐν τῇ
ἱερατικῇ ταῦτά ἐστι θεωρῆσαι. φέρε εἰπεῖν κατεαγότος ὀστέου, ἐὰν ⟨μὲν⟩
εὑρεθῇ ἱερεὺς ὀστ⟨ε⟩οδέ⟨της, οὗτος⟩ ⌜διὰ τῆς ἰδίας δεισιδαιμονίας ποιῶν⌝ 5
κολλᾷ τὸ ὀστοῦν, ὥστε καὶ τρισμὸν ἀκοῦσαι συνερχομένων εἰς ἄλληλα τῶν
ὀστέων· ἐὰν δὲ μὴ εὑρεθῇ ἱερεύς, [οὐ ⌜μὴ φοβηθῇ ἄνθρωπος ἀποθανεῖν,
ἀλλὰ] φέρονται ἰατροὶ ἔχοντες βίβλους ⌜κατὰ ζωγράφους γραμμικὰς
σκιαστὰς ἐχούσας γραμμὰς καὶ ὁσαιδηποτοῦν εἰσι γραμμαί⌝, καὶ ἀπὸ
βιβλίου περιδεσμεῖται ὁ ἄνθρωπος μηχανικῶς, καὶ ζῇ [χρόνον], τὴν ὑγείαν 10
πορισάμενος· καὶ οὐ δήπου ἀφίεται ⟨ὁ⟩ ἄνθρωπος ἀποθανεῖν διὰ τὸ μὴ εὑρη-
κέναι ἱερέα ὀστ⟨ε⟩οδέτην. οὗτοι δὲ ἀποτυχόντες τῷ λιμῷ τελευτῶσι, μὴ
καταξιοῦντες τὴν [ὀστοδητικὴν] τῶν καμίνων διαγραφὴν νοῆσαι καὶ ποιῆσαι,
ἵνα μακάριοι γενόμενοι νικήσωσι πενίαν, τὴν ἀνίατον νόσον.

21 καὶ ταῦτα μὲν ἐπὶ τοσοῦτον· ἐγὼ δὲ ἐπὶ τὸ προκείμενον ἐλεύσομαι, ὅ[ς] 15
ἐστι περὶ ὀργάνων. λαβὼν γάρ σου τὰς ἐπιστολὰς ἃς ἔγραψας, εὑρόν σε
παρακαλοῦσαν ὅπως καὶ τὴν τῶν ὀργάνων ἔκδοσίν σοι συγγράψω. ἐθαύμασα
δέ σε ὅτιπερ καὶ τὰ μὴ ὀφειλόμενα [συγγραφεῖς] ⟨ἀξιοῖς⟩ τυχεῖν παρ' ἐμοῦ.
ἢ οὐκ ἤκουσας τοῦ φιλοσόφου λέγοντος ὅτι ⟨. . .⟩; ταῦτα ἑκὼν παρεσιώ-
πησα, διὰ τὸ ἀφθόνως αὐτὰ ἐγκεῖσθαι καὶ ἐν ταῖς ἄλλαις [μου] γραφαῖς· σὺ 20
δὲ παρ' ἐμοῦ ταῦτα μαθεῖν ἠβουλήθης. ἀλλὰ μὴ οἴου ἀξιοπιστότερον ἐμὲ
τῶν ἀρχαίων ξυγγράψαι· γίνωσκε ὡς οὐκ ἂν δυναίμην. ἀλλ' ἵνα [[καὶ]]
πάντα ⟨⟨νοήσωμεν⟩⟩, ⟨⟨καὶ⟩⟩ τὰ παρ' ἐκείνων λαληθέντα [[νοήσωμεν]]
[τοίνυν] [τὰ παρ' ἐκείνων] σοι ὑποθήσω.

22 ἔχει δὲ οὕτως. βίκος ὑέλεος κ.τ.λ. 25

ii. τὸ πρῶτον βιβλίον τῆς τελευταίας ἀποχῆς Ζωσίμου ⌜Θηβαίου⌝
[ἔνθεν βεβαίωται ἀληθὴς ⟨. . .⟩ βίβλος].

§ 1. Ζώσιμος Θεοσεβείᾳ χαίρειν. ὅλον τὸ τῆς Αἰγύπτου βασίλειον, ὦ
γύναι, κ.τ.λ. . . .

1 εὑρεῖν add. Ruelle | καὶ seclusi   2 διαφόρως coni. Ruelle : διαφόρους codd.
3 νοερὸν καὶ seclusi   4 μὲν addidi   5 ὀστεοδέτης, οὗτος scripsi : ὃς
τόδε codd. | Fortasse διὰ τῆς ἰδίας ⟨τέχνης (vel λειτουργίας) τοὺς⟩ [δεισι]-
δαιμον[ί]ας ⟨εὐμενεῖς⟩ ποιῶν   7-8 οὐ μὴ . . . ἀλλὰ seclusi. Fortasse οὐ [μὴ
φοβηθῇ] ⟨δήπου ἀφίεται ὁ⟩ ἄνθρωπος ἀποθανεῖν (quod infra iteratur), ἀλλὰ   8 Fortasse καὶ διαγραφὰς [γραμ] ⟨ἀνατο⟩μικάς   10 χρόνον seclusi   11 ἀφίεται ὁ
scripsi : ἐφίεται codd.   12 ὀστεοδέτην scripsi : ὀστοδέτην codd.   13 ὀστο-
δητικὴν seclusi   15 ὃ coni. Ruelle : ὡς codd.   17 Fortasse ἔκθεσιν
18 ὀφειλόμενα scripsi : ὀφείλοντα codd. | συγγραφεῖς seclusi : ἀξιοῖς addidi
19 Lacunam signavi   20 μου seclusi. Fortasse ταῖς ἀρχαίαις γραφαῖς
23 νοήσωμεν et καὶ huc transposui. (Fortasse νοήσῃς)   24 τοίνυν et τὰ
παρ' ἐκείνων seclusi   26 Berthelot, Alchimistes grecs, Tom. II, p. 239 sqq.
(cod. A, saec. XV)   27 ἔνθεν . . . βίβλος seclusi | ⟨εἶναι ἤ⟩?   28-29 Olym-
piodorus alchymista, Berthelot, p. 90 (codd. MAKL): Ζώσιμος τοίνυν ἐν τῇ
τελευταίᾳ ἀποχῇ, πρὸς Θεοσέβειαν ποιούμενος τὸν λόγον, φησίν· Ὅλον τὸ τῆς

§ 7 *fin.* ὥστε ⟨τοῦτο⟩ καὶ σοὶ θέλουσιν ποιῆσαι, ὦ γύναι, διὰ τοῦ ψευδοπροφήτου αὐτῶν· κολακεύουσί σε τὰ κατὰ τόπον . . . ., πεινῶντα οὐ μόνον θυσίας, ἀλλὰ καὶ τὴν σὴν ψυχήν.   § 8. σὺ γοῦν μὴ περιέλκου, ὦ[ς] γύναι, ὡς καὶ ἐν τοῖς κατ᾽ ἐν⟨έργ⟩ειαν ἐξεῖπόν σοι· καὶ μὴ περι⟨ρ⟩ρέμβου
5 ζητοῦσα θεόν, ἀλλ᾽ οἴκαδε καθέζου, καὶ θεὸς ἥξει πρός σε, ὁ πανταχοῦ ὤν, καὶ οὐκ ἐν τόπῳ ἐλαχίστῳ ὡς τὰ δαιμόνια. καθεζομένη δὲ τῷ σώματι, καθέζου καὶ τοῖς πάθεσιν [ἐπιθυμίᾳ, ἡδονῇ, θυμῷ, λύπῃ, καὶ ταῖς ιβ΄ μοίραις τοῦ θανάτου]· καὶ οὕτως ⟨ἑ⟩αυτὴν διευθύνασα, προσκάλεσον πρὸς ἑαυτὴν τὸ θεῖον, καὶ οὕτως ἥξει [τ] ὁ πανταχοῦ ὢν καὶ οὐδαμοῦ. καὶ
10 [μὴ καλουμένη] πρόσφερε θυσίας τοῖς ⟨δαιμονίοις⟩ [μὴ τὰς προσφόρους] μὴ τὰς θρεπτικὰς αὐτῶν καὶ προσηνεῖς, ἀλλὰ τὰς ἀποτρεπτικὰς αὐτῶν καὶ ἀναιρετικάς, ἃς προσεφώνησε Μεμβρῆς τῷ Ἱεροσολύμων βασιλεῖ Σολομῶντι, αὐτὸς δὲ μάλιστα Σολομὼν ὅσας ἔγραψεν ἀπὸ τῆς ἑαυτοῦ σοφίας· καὶ οὕτως ἐνεργοῦσα, ἐπιτεύξῃ τῶν γνησίων καὶ φυσικῶν καιρικῶν.
15 ταῦτα δὲ [ἐ]ποίει ἕως [π] ἂν τελειωθῇς τὴν ψυχήν· ὅταν δὲ ἐπιγνῷς ἑαυτὴν τελειωθεῖσαν, τότε [καὶ τῶν φυσικῶν] τῆς ὕλης κατάπτυσον, καὶ καταδραμοῦσα ἐπὶ τὸν Ποιμ[εν]άνδρη⟨ν⟩, καὶ βαπτισθεῖσα τῷ κρατῆρι, ἀνάδραμε ἐπὶ τὸ γένος τὸ σόν.

Αἰγύπτου βασίλειον, ὦ γύναι, κ.τ.λ.   Cuius loci pars prior sine nomine scriptoris Olympiodori iteratur, Berthelot, p. 209 (codd. AELb)

1 τοῦτο addidi   2 Fortasse κολακεύουσι (vel κολακεύει) ⟨γάρ⟩ σε τὰ κατὰ τύπον ⟨δαιμόνια⟩   4 ὦ γύναι scripsi (ὦ γυνή coni. Ruelle): ὡς γυνή A | ἐνέργειαν coni. Ruelle: ἐνείαν A   4–16 μὴ περιρέμβου . . . τῶν φυσικῶν τῆς ὕλης κατάπτησον A. Locum ita citat Olympiodorus, Berthelot, p. 83 (codd. MAKL): Ζώσιμος τοίνυν, τὸ στέφος τῶν φιλοσόφων, ἡ ὠκεανόβρυτος (ὠκεανόρρυτος ?) γλῶσσα, ὁ νέος θεηγόρος, Μελίσσῳ τὸ πλεῖστον ἀκολουθήσας [κατὰ τὴν τέχνην], [[ὡς καὶ θεὸς εἷς]] μίαν τὴν τέχνην ἔλεγεν εἶναι, ⟨⟨ὡς καὶ θεὸς εἷς (ἐστι add. L)⟩⟩. καὶ ταῦτα ἐν μυρίοις τόποις πρὸς τὴν Θεοσέβειαν θεηγορεῖ καὶ ἀληθὴς ὁ λόγος. θέλων γὰρ αὐτὴν ἐλευθερῶσαι τῆς πολυπληθείας τῶν λόγων καὶ τῆς ὕλης ἁπάσης, ἐπὶ τὸν ἕνα θεὸν καταφεύγειν παραινεῖ, καί φησιν· " οἴκαδε καθέζου, ἐπιγνοῦσα ἕνα θεὸν καὶ μίαν τέχνην, καὶ μὴ ῥέμβου ζητοῦσα θεὸν ἕτερον· θεὸς γὰρ ἥξει πρός σε, ὁ πανταχοῦ ὤν, καὶ οὐκ ἐκ τόπῳ ἐλαχίστῳ ὡς τὸ δαιμόνιον. καθεζομένη δὲ τῷ σώματι, καθέζου καὶ τοῖς πάθεσιν· καὶ οὕτως σαυτὴν διευθύνασα, προσκαλέσῃ πρὸς ἑαυτὴν τὸ θεῖον, καὶ ὄντως (οὕτως A) ἥξει πρός σε ⌐τὸ θεῖον τὸ¬ (lege ὁ θεὸς ὁ) πανταχοῦ ὤν. ὅταν δὲ ἐπιγνῷς σαυτήν, τότε ἐπιγνώσῃ καὶ τὸν μόνον ὄντως (ὄντα add. L) θεόν· καὶ οὕτως ἐνεργοῦσα ἐπιτεύξῃ τῶν γνησίων καὶ φυσικῶν, καταπτύουσα τῆς ὕλης."   7–8 ἐπιθυμίᾳ . . . θανάτου seclusi (om. Olymp.)   8 μοίραις coni. Ruelle: μύραις A | ἑαυτὴν scripsi: αὐτὴν A | διευθύνουσα A (διευθύνασα Olymp.) | προσκάλεσον scripsi: προσκαλέσῃ A   9 ὁ coni. Ruelle: τὸ A   9–15 καὶ μὴ καλουμένη πρόσφερε . . . ἕως παντελειωθῇς τὴν ψυχήν A: om. Olymp.   10 μὴ καλουμένη seclusi. Fortasse [ἥξει δὲ καὶ] μὴ καλούμενος] | δαιμονίοις addidi (δαίμοσιν add. Reitz.) | μὴ τὰς προσφόρους seclusi   11 ἀποτρεπτικὰς coni. Ruelle: ἀποθρεπτικὰς A   14 καιρικῶν Ruelle: κυρικῶν A   15 ποίει Ruelle: ἐποίει A | ἕως ἂν τελειωθῇς coni. Ruelle: ἕως παντελειωθῇς A   15–16 ἐπιγνῷς ἑαυτὴν scripsi (ἐπιγνῷς αὐτὴν coni. Ruelle): ἐπιγνοῦσα αὐτὴν A   16 καὶ τῶν φυσικῶν seclusi | κατάπτυσον Reitz.: κατάπτησον A   17 Ποιμάνδρην scripsi: Ποιμένανδρα A

§ 9. ἐγὼ δὲ ἐπὶ τὸ προκείμενον ἐλεύσομαι, τῆς σῆς ἀτελειότητος ⟨...⟩. ἀλλ' ὀλίγον ἐπεκτεῖναι καὶ ἀνενέγκαι χρή με κ.τ.λ.

1 Lacunam signavi: fortasse ⟨λόγον ἔχων⟩ | χρή με scripsi: χρῆμα A   2 ὀλίγον scripsi: ὀλίγῳ A

NOTES ON ZOSIMUS

Zosimus, of Panopolis in Egypt, was an alchemist of high repute. He is the earliest writer on alchemy known to us that wrote books in his own name; though pseudonymous writings on that subject, attributed to Hermes and other ancient sages, were in existence before his time.[1] His date is uncertain; but he probably wrote not long after A. D. 300.[2] Of his voluminous writings, only detached portions and extracts have been preserved. Those parts of them which are extant in the original Greek have come down to us in a *Corpus* of excerpts from Greek writers on alchemy, which seems to have been compiled by Byzantine scholars in the eighth or ninth century, and is best represented by a Venetian manuscript (M) of the eleventh century. Numerous alchemistic manuscripts of later date (thirteenth to seventeenth centuries), containing collections based on the same *Corpus*, but varied by the omission of some excerpts and the addition of others, exist in the Bibliothèque Nationale of Paris and elsewhere.[3] These documents have been published by Berthelot, *Alchimistes grecs*, 1887–1888. In that publication, the work of editing

[1] See note on Zosimus i, § 21, l. 21; p. 136. An alchemist who probably wrote in the seventh or eighth century·gives a list of the chief authorities on alchemy as follows (Berthelot, *Origines de l'alchimie*, p. 127; cod. M): ' Exposition of the rules of gold-making, beginning with the names of those who were skilled in the art. Hermes Trismegistus was the first to write on the great mystery. He was followed by John, high priest of . . .* and of the sanctuaries which are there. Democritus, the celebrated philosopher of Abdera, spoke after them, as well as the excellent prophets who followed them. Men quote also the very wise Zosimus. These are the oecumenical and renowned philosophers. (After them,) the commentators [on the theories of Plato and Aristotle] Olympiodorus and Stephanus, having made investigations and discoveries, wrote great treatises on the art of making gold. Such are the very wise books, the authority of which will guide us.'

* In Berthelot's translation, this John is called ' l'archiprêtre de la Tuthie en Evagie'. But in a later and longer list of the same kind (Berthelot, *Alch. gr.* p. 25), he is called Ἰωάννης ἀρχιερεὺς (al. ἱερεὺς) τῆς ἐν ⌈εὐαγίᾳ⌉ (al. τῆς ἰνευασία and τῆς ἐνεβαγία) τῇ θείᾳ. ' Tuthie' therefore probably stands for a corruption of τῇ θείᾳ. Is the place Jerusalem (ἡ ἁγία καὶ θεία πόλις)? And is the man John Hyrcanus? If so, the writer has made a mistake in putting him before Democritus.

[2] ' Probably in the beginning of the fourth century', says Krumbacher, *Byz. litt.* p. 632.

[3] There is an alchemistic MS. of this character in Oxford (Bodl. *Canon Gr.* 95, saec. XV).

the Greek texts was done by Ruelle, who made use of M and some twelve other manuscripts.

A Syriac translation of some other portions of the writings of Zosimus is extant in a Cambridge manuscript of the fifteenth century. A French translation (by Duval) of the Syriac text has been published by Berthelot, *La chimie au moyen âge*, 1893.[1]

Among the titles of books written by Zosimus are Ἡ κατ᾽ ἐνέργειαν βίβλος, Περὶ ἀρετῆς, Πρᾶξις β' and Πρᾶξις γ',[2] Ἡ περὶ ἀφορμῶν σύνθεσις, Ἡ τελευταία ἀποχή, and Πρὸς Θεόδωρον. But his most extensive work seems to have been one which was addressed to a lady named Theosebeia, and consisted of numerous books, each of which was denoted by one of the letters of the alphabet.[3] Of this work, Book Ω is extant in Greek, and a large part of the first twelve books has been preserved in Syriac. The subjects of some of these books are given as follows in the Syriac translation :—'Second Book, concerning silver.' 'Sixth Book, on the working of copper; letter *vau* ' (i.e. ϛ). 'Seventh Book, which is called *sealed* and *seal* and *Houphestion*', on methods of softening silver and other bodies. 'Eighth Book, on the working of tin; letter *heth* ' (i.e. H). 'Ninth Book; letter *têt* ' (i.e. Θ), on the working of mercury. 'Tenth Book; letter concerning lead; it is the letter *yod*' (i.e. I). 'Eleventh Book; book on iron; letter *kaf*' (i.e. K). 'Twelfth Book; book on electrum.' And Book Ω is περὶ ὀργάνων καὶ καμίνων.

Among the Syriac texts there is also a treatise by Zosimus concerning earths and minerals. In that treatise the author finds occasion to speak of his travels; he says that he has been in Cyprus, Coelesyria, Troas, Thrace, Italy, Macedonia, Thasos, and Lemnos, and he describes diggings and metal-workings that he has seen in some of those places. It is called 'the Ninth Book', and is addressed

---

[1] Berthelot (*La chimie au moyen âge* I, p. 249) mentions also a Latin treatise on alchemy, entitled *Rosinus* (probably a corruption of Zosimus) *ad Euthiciam* (Theosebeiam ?). In this treatise are quoted Aros (Horus ?), Maria, Hermes and his work entitled *Key of the philosophers*, Bilonius (Apollonius of Tyana ?), Agadamon (Agathodaemon), Democritus and his *Chrysopoeia*. Of these authorities some at least were, and all may have been, quoted by Zosimus. But the treatise also contains references to Mahomet, and to writers who lived long after Mahomet; and Berthelot concludes that it cannot be earlier than the twelfth century, and was not written by Zosimus. It must, however, have been written by some one who had access, directly or indirectly, to Greek alchemistic writings of early date.

[2] In these two documents (and in the Περὶ ἀρετῆς also) the speaker narrates dreams in which alchemistic truths have been revealed to him.

[3] The books of which this work consisted are said to have been twenty-eight in number. If so, the Greek alphabet must have been for this purpose supplemented by four obsolete or foreign letters.

to Theosebeia. It may perhaps have been one of the twenty-eight books of the work described above; but if so, it is wrongly numbered.

Of the religion of Zosimus we know only what can be gathered from some of the digressions by which his technical writings on metallurgy are here and there interrupted. It appears from these passages that his religious creed was a blend of Pagan Platonism with Christian Gnosticism;[1] and among the sources from which he drew his Platonism were some of the philosophic *Hermetica*.[2] He doubtless assumed that those documents contained the philosophic and religious teaching of that same Hermes Trismegistus whom he believed to have been the author of the earliest writings on alchemy.

PAGE 104. ll. 8–9. τὸ . . . Ω στοιχεῖον περιέχει τὸν περὶ ὀργάνων [ ] λόγον κ.τ.λ. The extract here printed is the beginning of the book marked by the letter Ω (presumably the last book) in the comprehensive work on alchemy addressed by Zosimus to Theosebeia. In this book Zosimus dealt with the subject of alchemistic apparatus. A note on the symbolic meanings of the letter Ω is prefixed; and the fact that Nicotheus (of whom Zosimus speaks in § 11) is mentioned in it makes it probable that this preliminary note was written by Zosimus himself.

11. εὐηειαει. Groups of vowels frequently occur in magic invocations. Has such a vowel-group been intentionally substituted for the usual word of greeting? Or is this an accidental corruption of εὐη⟨μερ⟩εῖ⟨ν⟩ ἀεί or something of the sort?

---

[1] In Book XII (Syriac translation), Zosimus speaks of Aristotle as follows :— ' Though a philosopher for visible things, he has not well distinguished the existence of the invisible things, that is to say, that of the intelligences or spiritual substances. The angels who inspired him did not know them (*sc.* the invisible things), and consequently could not communicate to him that which they did not possess. He himself did not know that which he had not received from his masters (the meaning must be " He did not know these things, because he had not received them from his masters "); for there was no one who possessed the tradition of it. ⌐Neither was he the holy spirit⌐ (Zosimus probably said or meant that Aristotle had not in him, as some men have, a πνεῦμα which is an ἀπόσπασμα of the divine πνεῦμα), but he was ⟨merely⟩ a mortal man, a mortal intelligence in a mortal body. He was the most brilliant of the non-luminous beings, in contrast to the incorporeal beings. He possessed a power ⌐of appropriation or of resistance⌐ over the corporeal and non-luminous beings; (but these are (?)) other than the superior intelligences and the great celestial bodies. As he was ⟨merely⟩ mortal, he could not raise himself to the celestial sphere, and he did not know how to make himself worthy of it. That is why his science and his actions remained in the region inferior to that sphere.' That is, in substance, a Platonist's criticism of Aristotle; but the terms and phrases employed in it are Christian-Gnostic rather than Platonic.

[2] Plato, he says, is τρίσμεγας, but Hermes is μυριόμεγας (i, § 9).

αἱ καιρικαὶ καταβαφαί. βαφαί or καταβαφαί are 'tinctures applied to pieces of base metal for the purpose of changing them into gold (or so colouring them as to make them look like gold). The epithet καιρικαί has some unknown technical meaning; see notes on Zosimus ii, p. 136 ff.

12. τὴν περὶ καμίνων βίβλον Cf. τὴν μεγάλην περὶ καμίνων βίβλον in § 19. The 'book about furnaces' which is here spoken of cannot be that which Zosimus was engaged in writing. It must be one that was already in circulation; and it was probably a book written, not by Zosimus himself, but by an earlier alchemist.

The meaning appears to be that certain alchemists, having used with success the method of καιρικαὶ καταβαφαί, jeered at the book περὶ καμίνων, in which a different method was recommended. (Cf. ὅσοι τὰς καιρικὰς κ.τ.λ. in § 19.) These people have sometimes succeeded (in making gold); but their successes have been due to the favour of 'their own daemon'; and a man's daemon (or fortune) is not always favourable to him. The action of the daemons is determined by εἱμαρμένη; and εἱμαρμένη is sometimes adverse.

18. τῆς εὐδαιμονίας αὐτῶν κωλυθείσης. εὐδαιμονία is the condition of a man whose δαίμων is εὐμενής.

19–21. μόλις ... ὡμολόγησαν εἶναί τι καὶ ⌜μετ' ἐκείνων ὧν πρότερον ἐφρόνουν⌝. Perhaps εἶναί τι καὶ ἐν ἐκείνοις ὧν πρότερον κατεφρόνουν. When they fail to make gold by their own method, they are forced to admit that there is something to be said for a method which they have previously despised.

22–24. πάλιν γὰρ κ.τ.λ. They alternately accept and reject what Zosimus holds to be the true doctrine. They accept it when they are unsuccessful, but reject it when they are successful.

23–24. τοῦ δαιμονίου σωματικῶς αὐτοὺς εὐεργετοῦντος. Heimarmene and her agents the daemons act on bodily things alone.

105. 2–3. μηδὲν ἕτερον τῶν σωματικῶν φανταζόμενοι. They 'see nothing but bodily things'. What then are the incorporeal things which they ought to take into account and do not? If this phrase is to be taken in connexion with what precedes, it seems necessary to understand it as meaning that these men's conclusions are based solely on the 'bodily' (i. e. visible and tangible) results of their metallurgical operations, and therefore vary as those results vary; whereas the truth can be discovered only by theoretical reasoning (λόγος ἀποδεικτικός above). They say at one time 'I have made gold by my method, therefore my view was right', and at another time 'I have

failed to make gold by my method, therefore my view was wrong'; but they ignore the *a priori* arguments by which it can be demonstrated that one view is right and another wrong. They are mere empiricists.

4–109. 19. τοὺς τοιούτους δὲ κ.τ.λ. The statement that the opponents of Zosimus are 'slaves of Heimarmene' (*sc.* in respect of their opinions on a question of alchemy) gives occasion for a digression concerning subjection to and freedom from Heimarmene in a wider and more general sense. This digression extends from § 4 *init.* to § 18 *fin.*

4. ὁ Ἑρμῆς ἐν τῷ περὶ φύσεων κ.τ.λ. (*Fr.* 19). Zosimus knew and used treatises on alchemy which were supposed to have been written by Hermes Trismegistus, or to be written reports of his oral teaching. But the Hermetic document to which he refers in this section, and which (if the reading is right) he calls τὸ περὶ φύσεων, cannot have been a treatise on alchemy. It must have been a philosophic or religious *Hermeticum*; and if not *Corp.* IV, it must have been a lost *libellus* the contents of which closely resembled those of *Corp.* IV. Compare especially *Corp.* IV. 4 (οὗτοι οἱ . . . νοῦν μὴ προσειληφότες), and *ib.* 7 (καθάπερ αἱ πομπαὶ . . ., τὸν αὐτὸν τρόπον καὶ οὗτοι μόνον πομπεύουσιν ἐν τῷ κόσμῳ, παραγ[εν]όμενοι ὑπὸ τῶν σωματικῶν [ἡδονῶν]). Neither the word ἄνοες nor the word εἱμαρμένη occurs in *Corp.* IV; but the thought is the same, though somewhat differently expressed.

5–6. μηδὲν τῶν ἀσωμάτων φανταζομένους. Note the close proximity of μηδὲν . . . φανταζόμενοι above, and ⟨μηδὲν⟩ ἄλλο φανταζομένους below. The repetition of the phrase is awkward; perhaps φανταζομένους has here been wrongly substituted for some other participle, such as ἐννοοῦντας.

6–7. μηδὲ (μήτε MSS.) αὐτὴν τὴν εἱμαρμένην . . . δικαίως ⟨ὑπολαμβάνοντας⟩. They do not rightly understand the nature of the power by which they are led.

7–8. δυσφημοῦντας αὐτῆς τὰ σωματικὰ παιδευτήρια. They complain of the bodily chastisements inflicted on them by Heimarmene, e.g. poverty or physical pain. For the man who takes these apparent evils rightly, they are goods; they serve as a training, and teach him to despise the body.

8–9. τῶν εὐδαιμόνων αὐτῆς ⟨μηδὲν⟩ ἄλλο φανταζομένους. They have no conception of any other sort of happiness than that which Heimarmene confers, namely, bodily pleasure, or worldly prosperity.

10. ὁ δὲ Ἑρμῆς καὶ ὁ Ζωροάστρης κ.τ.λ. (*Fr.* 20). From what source did Zosimus get his information about the teaching of 'Zoroastres'? Porphyry, *Vita Plotini* 16, gives a list of books used as authorities by

the Gnostic sect against which Plotinus wrote ; and among those books are ἀποκαλύψεις Ζωροάστρου . . . καὶ Νικοθέου. Porphyry *ib.* says that he had himself examined this 'Apocalypse of Zoroastres', and had proved it to be a forgery of recent date, written by the founders of that Gnostic sect.[1] The teaching of the book must therefore have been in agreement with the Gnostic doctrines controverted by Plotinus, *Enn.* 2. 9. Now Zosimus (§ 1 and § 11) mentions Nicotheus as one to whom hidden things were known ; and it may be inferred from this that Zosimus derived the Gnostic doctrine which he sets forth in §§ 10-17 from a sect which recognized Nicotheus as a seer. Hence it is probable that the book of Zoroastres to which Zosimus refers is that same 'Apocalypse of Zoroastres' which was used, together with the 'Apocalypse of Nicotheus', by the Gnostic sect of which Porphyry speaks.

The seer Nicotheus is mentioned in the 'Unknown Gnostic Work' published by C. Schmidt, *Koptisch-Gnostische Schriften*, p. 342. We are there told that 'Nicotheus has spoken of him, and has seen him'. The sentence is obscure ; but 'him' probably means a divine person who is shortly afterwards called the μονογενής, and who may be identified with the 'Son of God' in the Gnostic doctrine reported by Zosimus.

The names of Hermes and Zoroastres are strangely coupled together in this section. It seems to be implied that these two teachers not only taught similar doctrines, but spoke in the same words ; but that can hardly have been meant. The language of § 5 is Hermetic rather than Christian-Gnostic ; (note especially the word αὐλία, and compare Ἑρμῆς ἐν τῷ περὶ αὐλίας in § 7 ;) and I am inclined to think that καὶ ὁ Ζωροάστρης has been wrongly inserted here, and that what Zosimus wrote was τὸ δὲ φιλοσόφων γένος (in contrast to the ἄνοες of § 4) ὁ Ἑρμῆς ἀνώτερον τῆς εἱμαρμένης εἶπεν. If so, Zoroastres was mentioned by Zosimus only in § 7 *init.*

13. πάντοτε ἐν αὐλίᾳ ἄγοντας (ἄγοντες MSS.). ἐν αὐλίᾳ is equivalent to ἐν τῷ ἀσωμάτῳ or ἐν τῷ νοητῷ. Cf. Porphyr. *De abst.* I. 41 : πρὸς τοῖς αὔλοις εἶναι.

14-15. [ἐπείπερ εἰς πέρας κακῶν βλέπουσι.] [§ 5 appears to be a piece of rhetoric, with three double clauses stating how philosophers are saved from εἱμαρμένη and why they are saved. The third pair seems to give a better balance and to lead directly to § 6. The phrase ἐπεὶ

---

[1] Porphyry was a good judge of such matters, and his decision on this point may be accepted.

... βλέπουσι perhaps means 'since they look to an end of evils', i. e. beyond the evils of εἱμαρμένη.

We should expect καταδέχεσθαι, as we should expect ἄγοντας ; but it is impossible to say whether Zosimus was copying and forgot the structure of his sentence. βάλλεσθαι seems to be an error for καταβάλλεσθαι, or perhaps for σφάλλεσθαι in the sense 'tripped up'.]

16. καὶ ὁ Ἡσίοδος. Hesiod's story of Pandora is interpreted by Zosimus as meaning that we ought to 'reject the gifts of Heimarmene'. The teaching of Hesiod, when thus explained, agrees with and confirms the teaching of Hermes concerning Heimarmene.

The story of Pandora is spoken of again in § 13 and in § 18.

17–18. [τίνα οἴονται οἱ ἄνθρωποι πασῶν μείζονα εὐδαιμονίαν; γυναῖκα εὔμορφον, φησί, σὺν πλούτῳ πολλῷ.] This note, wrongly inserted in the text, was written to explain the point of the Hesiodic story. Pandora, the gift sent by Zeus to Epimetheus, was a beautiful and wealthy woman, who was offered to him in marriage ; and most men think that marriage with such a woman is the highest happiness.

22–106. 5. Ζωροάστρης δέ, ⟨⟨αὐχῶν⟩⟩ ⟨ἐπὶ τῇ⟩ εἰδήσει τῶν ἄνω πάντων, καὶ μαγείᾳ [[ ]] [ ] φάσκει ἀποστρέφεσθαι πάντα τῆς εἱμαρμένης τὰ κακά .... ὁ μέντοι Ἑρμῆς κ.τ.λ. Zoroastres (in his Apocalypse) 'prides himself on his knowledge of heavenly or supracosmic things', but at the same time admits the utility of magic (which is not a heavenly or supracosmic thing) as a means of averting the evils with which we are threatened by Heimarmene ; and in that respect he differs from Hermes, who disapproves of magic.

In our extant (philosophic or religious) *Hermetica*, magic is ignored, but is nowhere explicitly condemned. The Hermetic passage referred to must have occurred in a lost *libellus* which was known to Zosimus by the title Ἑρμοῦ τὸ περὶ ἀϋλίας. *Fr.* 21.

23. [τῆς ἐνσώμου φράσεως]. This phrase seems to have come from § 1. But it may possibly be a corruption of τῆς ἐνσώμου φύσεως, 'corporeal things', in contrast to τῶν ἄνω.

25–26. [τὸν πνευματικὸν ἄνθρωπον] τὸν ἐπιγνόντα (ἐπιγνῶντα MSS.) ἑαυτόν. ὁ ἐπιγνοὺς ἑαυτὸν (καὶ τὸν θεόν) is the man who has attained to *gnosis*; cf. *Corp*. I. 19–21. The word πνευματικός was used in a similar sense by Christian Gnostics (cf. ὁ ἔσω αὐτοῦ ἄνθρωπος, ὁ πνευματικός, § 11 : τῷ πνευματικῷ καὶ φωτεινῷ ἀνθρώπῳ, § 15 : τὰ ἑαυτῶν φωτεινὰ πνεύματα, § 16), but is not thus employed in our *Hermetica*; I have therefore bracketed τὸν πνευματικὸν ἄνθρωπον, which I take to be a gloss on τὸν ἐπιγνόντα ἑαυτόν. [It is characteristic of Zosimus' style to set side by side without a connective two words or phrases each preceded by the article; cf. the example from § 11 quoted above. Compare perhaps also i. 1 τὸ Ω στοιχεῖον ⟨τὸ?⟩ στρογγύλον, τὸ διμερές, τὸ ἀνῆκον κ.τ.λ.; i. 12 τὸν ἐκ τῆς εἱμαρμένης, τὸν ἐκ τῶν τεσσάρων στοιχείων; i. 17 τὸν ἀντίμιμον, τὸν ζηλωτήν.]

27. μηδὲ (οὐδὲ?) βιάζεσθαι τὴν ἀνάγκην. ἀνάγκη means the working of Destiny or natural law. To use magic is to 'apply force to ἀνάγκη', i. e. to try to compel the powers by which the laws of nature are put in action to alter or suspend the operation of those laws.

106. 1. ἐὰν ⟨αὐτὴν?⟩ ὡς ἔχει φύσεως [καὶ κρίσεως] πορεύεσθαι. 'To let necessity go its way according to its nature.' This is equivalent to what is said below, ἐὰν τὴν εἱμαρμένην ὃ θέλει ποιεῖν τῷ ἑαυτῆς πηλῷ. If κρίσεως is retained, we must take ὡς ἔχει κρίσεως to mean 'as it (sc. necessity) may decide'; but it is better to bracket καὶ κρίσεως.

1-2. ⌜δὲ διὰ μόνου τοῦ⌝ ζητεῖν κ.τ.λ. If there is a stop after πορεύεσθαι, the verb on which ζητεῖν depended is lost. Sense may be made by writing δε⟨ῖ⟩ δὲ μόνον [τοῦ] ζητεῖν κ.τ.λ. [Berthelot punctuates after κρίσεως.]

2-3. [τὴν ἀκατονόμαστον τριάδα]. This phrase must be of Christian (orthodox or Gnostic) origin, and can hardly have occurred in a *Hermeticum*. It may have been inserted as an alternative for θεόν in ἑαυτὸν καὶ θεὸν ἐπιγνόντα.

6-12. [[θεάσῃ τὸν θεοῦ υἱὸν ... εἰς ἐκεῖνο τὸ φῶς.]] This section is evidently out of place. It has no connexion with what has been said in §§ 4-7 about the teaching of Hermes; and it is impossible to believe that the doctrine of the Son of God which is expounded in it was taught in a *Hermeticum*. On the other hand, the contents of § 8 are closely related to those of §§ 14 and 15; and if we place it next after § 15, the whole digression on εἱμαρμένη (§§ 4-18) falls into an intelligible order. Zosimus first sets forth a Pagan doctrine about εἱμαρμένη, which he found in the philosophic *Hermetica* (§§ 4-7), and then a Christian-Gnostic doctrine on the same subject (§§ 10-17), which he probably found in the Apocalypse of Nicotheus; and he shows that his Pagan and Christian-Gnostic authorities, while differing in their modes of expression, are fundamentally in agreement (§ 18).

In §§ 4-7, he speaks chiefly of Hermes; but he refers to Hesiod also (§ 6), as a Pagan Greek authority whose teaching is to the same effect as that of Hermes; and he incidentally mentions 'Zoroastres' (i. e. a Christian-Gnostic document) as differing from Hermes on a certain point (§ 7). In §§ 10-17, he refers to Hesiod again (§ 13), in order to bring the Greek poet's teaching into connexion with the Christian-Gnostic doctrine with which he is there dealing, just as he had previously brought it into connexion with that of Hermes.

13. [καὶ βλέψαι τὸν πίνακα κ.τ.λ.] See p. 129, ll. 13–20.

14. ⟨...⟩ καὶ ὁ τρίσμεγας Πλάτων, καὶ ὁ μυριόμεγας Ἑρμῆς. τρίσμεγας and μυριόμεγας are variations of τρισμέγιστος, the epithet commonly applied to Hermes the teacher.

14–15. [ὅτι] [Θώυθος ἑρμηνεύεται τῇ ἱερατικῇ [πρώτῃ] φωνῇ] [ὁ πρῶτος ἄνθρωπος]. These words cannot be connected with the preceding Πλάτων καὶ ... Ἑρμῆς. Plato certainly did not say that the first man was called Thoth in the Egyptian language ; and it is not likely that any such statement occurred in a *Hermeticum*. Θωύθ (dhwty, Coptic Θοοστ) was the name of the Egyptian god whom the Greeks called Ἑρμῆς. It might very well be assumed that this god, like other gods, had once been a man ; (indeed, the notion of a man and teacher named Hermes Trismegistus grew out of that assumption ;) but it is unlikely that any one supposed him to have been ' *the first* man ',—i. e. to be an Egyptian Adam, and as such (according to the doctrine of §§ 10–17) a symbol of ' the flesh ' as opposed to ' the spirit '. It therefore seems necessary to cut out both ὁ πρῶτος ἄνθρωπος here, and ὁ παρ' ἡμῖν Θωὶθ καί in § 11 *init*. It may be conjectured that [Θώυθος ἑρμηνεύεται τῇ ἱερατικῇ φωνῇ] is a marginal note on ὁ μυριόμεγας Ἑρμῆς, to the effect that ' Thoth is the Egyptian equivalent of the name Hermes'; and that [ὁ πρῶτος ἄνθρωπος] has been accidentally transferred to this place from the lost passage at the beginning of § 10. The insertion of ὁ παρ' ἡμῖν Θωύθ after ὁ πρῶτος ἄνθρωπος in § 11 *init.* may have resulted from a misunderstanding caused by the insertion of ὁ πρῶτος ἄνθρωπος in proximity to Θώυθος in § 9. The name Θωύθ occurs again further on in § 11, but is evidently out of place there.

[Plato names Thoth in *Phaedr.* 274 c (as inventor of γράμματα), and in *Phileb.* 18 b.]

14–16. ὁ μυριόμεγας Ἑρμῆς, [ ] ⟨ὁ⟩ ἑρμηνεὺς πάντων τῶν ὄντων καὶ ⌜ὀνοματοποιὸς⌝ πάντων τῶν σωματικῶν. It is probable that ὁ ἑρμηνεὺς κ.τ.λ. is a description of Hermes the teacher, and that the writer meant to suggest that the name Ἑρμῆς is etymologically connected with ἑρμηνεύς. [Cf. *Cratylus* 407 e.] This is an additional reason for cutting out the intervening words ὅτι Θώυθος . . . ὁ πρῶτος ἄνθρωπος.

Hermes the teacher might very properly be called ' the expounder of all things that are ' ; but why should he, or indeed any one, be called ' the *name-maker* of all bodily things ' ? In place of ὀνοματοποιός, we should rather have expected some word meaning 'despiser' or 'rejecter' (ἀποποιούμενος πάντα τὰ σωματικά?). [See Addenda.]

With the alterations which I have proposed, § 9 appears to be a remnant of a paragraph in which Zosimus summed up the teachings of Pagan philosophy (§§ 4–7) concerning εἱμαρμένη. 'The leading thinkers agree in telling us to reject the gifts of εἱμαρμένη, or in other words, to look on the so-called "goods" of the body with contempt; on this subject, the great Plato and the greater Hermes speak alike.'

17–18. ⟨. . .⟩ οἱ δὲ Χαλδαῖοι καὶ Πάρθοι καὶ Μῆδοι καὶ Ἑβραῖοι καλοῦσιν αὐτὸν (sc. τὸν πρῶτον ἄνθρωπον) Ἀδάμ. The exposition of Christian-Gnostic doctrine begins at this point; but the opening words of the passage have been lost. We must suppose a clause to have preceded in which it was said that some other nation called the first man by a different name. Compare the first paragraph of the Naassene document in Hippolytus *Ref. haer.* 5. 7, where there is a list of the names given to the first man or men by a number of different peoples, ending with Χαλδαῖοι δὲ τὸν Ἀδάμ. The Hebrews, being descended from Abraham, were, according to the narrative of *Genesis*, a branch of the Chaldaean race; and it may have been thence inferred that the name Adam was used by the Chaldaeans as well as by the Hebrews. But why Πάρθοι and Μῆδοι? Adam may have been spoken of in the Christian-Gnostic 'Apocalypse of Zoroastres'; and it was known that Zoroaster, by whom that book was supposed to have been written, was a Mede. But what reason Zosimus had for thinking that the *Parthians* called the first man Adam, I cannot guess.

18–19. Ἀδάμ, ᾧ ἐστιν ἑρμηνεία γῆ παρθένος, καὶ γῆ αἱματώδης, καὶ γῆ πυρ⟨ρ⟩ά, καὶ γῆ σαρκίνη. The name Adam is the Hebrew word *ādām*, 'man', which is (or sounds as if it were) derived from a root meaning 'red'. πυρρά, 'red', would suggest αἱματώδης,[1] and thence σαρκίνη; and this explanation of the name is in agreement with the Gnostic doctrine that follows, according to which Adam stands for the σάρξ or σῶμα. [Professor Margoliouth writes: 'The interpretation of *Adam* as γῆ παρθένος is clearly a combination of the derivation from the Hebrew *adamah* = γῆ (Philo ed. Mangey i. 62) and from the Greek ἀδμής = παρθένος. Hesychius gives ἀδάμα· παρθενικὴ γῆ. The sense is doubtless Josephus, *Ant.* I. i. 2 σημαίνει δὲ τοῦτο (Ἄδαμος) πυρρός, ἐπειδήπερ ἀπὸ τῆς πυρρᾶς γῆς ἐγεγόνει, τοιαύτη γάρ ἐστιν ἡ παρθένος γῆ.' Compare

---

[1] Possibly some may have thought that the name Adam was derived from the Hebrew word *dām*, 'blood'.

Olympiodorus (Berthelot, p. 89): οὗτος (Ἀδάμ) γὰρ πάντων ἀνθρώπων πρῶτος ἐγένετο ἐκ τῶν τεσσάρων στοιχείων. καλεῖται δὲ καὶ παρθένος γῆ, καὶ πυρ(ρ)ὰ γῆ, καὶ σαρκίνη γῆ, καὶ γῆ αἱματώδης.]

Cf. Euseb. *Pr. ev.* 11. 6. 10 *sq.*: παρ' Ἑβραίοις Ἀδὰμ ἡ γῆ καλεῖται, παρ' ὃ καὶ ὁ πρῶτος γηγενὴς ἐτύμως Ἀδὰμ ὑπὸ Μωσέως ἀνείρηται. ἔχοι δ' ἂν καὶ ἄλλην ἡ προσηγορία διάνοιαν, εἰς τὸ ἐρυθρὸν μεταλαμβανομένη, καὶ τὴν τοῦ σώματος παριστῶσα φύσιν. ἀλλὰ τὸν μὲν γεώδη καὶ γήινον καὶ γηγενῆ, ἢ τὸν σωματικὸν καὶ σάρκινον ἄνθρωπον, τῷ τοῦ Ἀδὰμ ἐπεσήμαντο προσρήματι· καλοῦσι δὲ καὶ ἄλλως παῖδες Ἑβραίων τὸν ἄνθρωπον, Ἐνὼς ἐπονομάζοντες, ὃν δή φασιν εἶναι τὸν ἐν ἡμῖν λογικόν, ἕτερον ὄντα τὴν φύσιν τοῦ γεώδους Ἀδάμ. Eusebius' distinction between Ἀδάμ and Ἐνώς corresponds to the distinction between Ἀδάμ and Φώς in the Gnostic source of Zosimus.

19–22. ταῦτα δὲ ἐν ταῖς βιβλιοθήκαις τῶν Πτολεμαίων ηὕρη[ν]ται ... Ἑλληνιστί καὶ Αἰγυπτιστί. Zosimus is here describing the source of the Jewish and Christian-Gnostic teaching about Adam. That source was, as a matter of fact, the Book of Genesis (as interpreted by Hellenistic Jews and Christians). His account of it is an inaccurate version of the Jewish legend about the origin of the Septuagint, which is told in the forged 'Epistle of Aristeas' (see Schürer, *Gesch. des jüd. Volkes*, III, pp. 424 ff. and 608 ff.). Ἀσενάς[1] has been substituted, by a slip of memory, for Eleasar, the name of the High Priest of Jerusalem in the Epistle of Aristeas. The seventy-two translators have been reduced to one (unless ὃς ἡρμήνευσε is a misreading for οἳ ἡρμήνευσαν); and the statement that the Hebrew books were translated into the Egyptian language as well as into Greek is a baseless addition.

This curiously circuitous description of the Book of Genesis shows that Zosimus had not himself read Genesis, and did not know much about it. His information about Adam, and about the Hebrew source of the Adam-doctrine also, was probably limited to what he got from such books as the Apocalypses of Nicotheus and Pseudo-Zoroastres, or from members of the Christian-Gnostic sect by which those books were used as authorities.

24–107. I. οὐ μὴν [δὲ] ἀλλὰ καὶ συμβολικῶς ⟨ἐκάλεσαν αὐτὸν Ἀδάμ (?)⟩, διὰ τεσσάρων στοιχείων [ ] αὐτὸν εἰπόντες, κατὰ τὸ σῶμα. Zosimus meant that the name Ἀδάμ, inasmuch as it consists of four letters (στοιχεῖα), is symbolical of the body, which is composed of the four material

---

[1] Asenath (Ἀσεννέθ in LXX) is the name of the Egyptian wife of Joseph, *Gen.* 41. 45.

elements (στοιχεῖα). Cf. τὸν . . . Ἀδάμ, τὸν ἐκ τῶν τεσσάρων στοιχείων, in § 12. But some one added a passage (τὸ γὰρ ἄλφα . . . μεσημβρίαν δηλοῖ) in which the significance of the name was explained in a different way: 'ΑΔΑΜ means the four quarters of the world; the first A stands for ἀνατολή (the East), the Δ for δύσις (the West), ⟨the second A for ἄρκτος (the North)⟩, and the M for μεσημβρία (the South).' (Cf. *Orac. Sib.* 3. 24: αὐτὸς δὴ θεός ἐσθ' ὁ πλάσας τετραγράμματον Ἀδάμ | τὸν πρῶτον πλασθέντα, ⌜καὶ οὔνομα πληρώσαντα⌝ | ἀντολίην τε δύσιν τε μεσημβρίην τε καὶ ἄρκτον. Slavonic Enoch, c. 30: 'And I gave him a name of four parts, of East, of West, of North, of South.') And some one else inserted into this added passage words in which an attempt was made to supplement the original statement of Zosimus, by showing how each of the letters might be taken to represent one of the elements: 'A stands for ἀήρ; Δ stands for δύσις, and therefore for γῆ, which, being heavy, κάτω δύεται; M stands for μέσον, and therefore for πῦρ, which is μέσον' (in what sense? Possibly in the sense that the sphere of the sun, which is the source or gathering-place of fire, occupies the middle position among the seven planetary spheres). This second interpolator says nothing about ὕδωρ; and his attempts to make Δ and M mean γῆ and πῦρ are absurd.[1]

107. 5–6. [οὕτως οὖν] ὁ ⟨μὲν γὰρ⟩ σάρκινος κ.τ.λ. οὕτως οὖν, wrongly repeated from the beginning of the section, has caused the omission of μὲν γάρ or some such connecting particles.

6–7. [κατὰ τὴν φαινομένην περίπλασιν]. This appears to be an alternative for κατὰ τὸ σῶμα above.

9–10. μόνος γὰρ Νικόθεος, ὁ ἀνεύρετος ⟨γενόμενος⟩, τοῦτο (ταῦτα MSS.) οἶδεν. τοῦτο means τὸ κύριον ὄνομα.

---

[1] [A reference to Olympiodorus (pp. 87 ff. Berthelot) should be appended to this note. The alchemists not only had many technical terms for one thing, but allegorized one thing in many different ways:—It is said (§ 30) that the Egyptians had the entrances and exits of their temples orientated to the cardinal points, assigning the East to the white substance and the West to the yellow. Thus the temple of Isis at Teremouthi had yellow mineral at its western door three cubits down. These things about the gold mines are inscribed upon the mountain of the East and the Libyan mountain, and have a hidden sense. (§ 31) The ἀρχή of the alchemical operation is λεύκωσις, as opposed to ξάνθωσις, and the white substance is assigned to the East (ἀνατολή), the ἀρχή of day. As for sunset, this is the yellowing, the end of the process. Hence the instruction, 'You will find a black vein . . .',—that is, sulphurous matter or our lead. This is extracted from the scoriae after the whitening, by means of decomposition under heat and by fixation. It was lead that the Egyptian prophets desired to obtain. (§ 32) But this is an allegory, not really about minerals, but about substances (οὐσίαι). Whence do we say that East was assigned to the male, West to the female? It is from Adam.—Here follows the passage quoted on p. 122, l. 1.]

ὁ ἀνεύρετος γενόμενος, 'the man who could not be found', is an allusion to some mysterious disappearance of the holy seer. Cf. § 1, where we are told that Νικόθεος ⟨ὁ⟩ κεκρυμμένος (= ὁ ἀνεύρετος γενόμενος) is the only man who knows a certain secret. It must have been said, either by Nicotheus himself in his Apocalypse or by others, that he had been snatched away to heaven. Compare Enoch, who οὐχ ηὑρίσκετο, διότι μετέθηκεν αὐτὸν ὁ θεός, *Gen.* 5. 24. Epiphanius, *Haer.* 40. 7, speaking of a sect called Archontici, says οὗτοι δὲ καὶ ἄλλους προφήτας φασὶν εἶναι, Μαρτιάδην τινὰ καὶ Μαρσιανόν, ἁρπαγέντας εἰς τοὺς οὐρανοὺς καὶ διὰ ἡμερῶν τριῶν καταβεβηκότας. This Μαρσιανός is doubtless identical with a prophet named Marsanes who is mentioned, in close connexion with Nicotheus, in C. Schmidt's 'Unknown Gnostic Work', p. 341, l. 36.

10. τὸ δὲ προσηγορικὸν αὐτοῦ ὄνομα Φὼς καλεῖται. The Gnostic writer whose teaching Zosimus reports took the word φώς (man) to be derived from φῶς (light), and assumed that φώς properly meant, not man in general, but ὁ φωτεινὸς ἄνθρωπος, the 'man of light', or spiritual man, as opposed to the corporeal man. In the mystical narrative of § 12, the man named Φώς is a prototype of all φωτεινοὶ ἄνθρωποι, in the same sense that Adam is a prototype of all σάρκινοι ἄνθρωποι. This Φώς corresponds in some respects to the Anthropos of *Corp.* I, who was made ἐκ ζωῆς καὶ φωτός.

We are told by Zosimus that 'Nicotheus alone knows the κύριον ὄνομα'. Nicotheus then must have said in his Apocalypse that the κύριον ὄνομα had been revealed to him, but that he was not permitted to divulge it. And if Nicotheus spoke of the κύριον ὄνομα, he must also have spoken of the προσηγορικὸν ὄνομα with which it is contrasted, and must have said what this name was. The statement that the προσηγορικὸν ὄνομα is Φώς must therefore have been taken from the Apocalypse of Nicotheus; and hence it follows that Zosimus, in the passages in which he uses or refers to the name Φώς (§ 12, ὅτε ἦν ὁ Φὼς ἐν τῷ Παραδείσῳ κ.τ.λ., and § 14, ὅπου ... διῆγον φῶτες καλούμενοι), is repeating what was said in that book. Moreover, as the contents of §§ 11–17 (with the exception of the digression on Hesiod in § 13, and perhaps the first part of § 17), hang together, and make up a consistent whole, it can hardly be doubted that they are all derived from one source, and consequently, from that same Apocalypse. And if so, we have in §§ 11–17 a summary of the teaching of the Christian-Gnostic seer Nicotheus.

11–12. ⟨...⟩ ὅτε ἦν ⟨ὁ⟩ Φὼς ἐν τῷ Παραδείσῳ κ.τ.λ. This story must have been introduced by some words which have been lost. In the missing passage, it was very likely said explicitly that the story was told by Nicotheus.

'Paradise' must here mean a celestial or supercelestial region (such as that in which the Anthropos of *Corp.* I resided before his fall and incarnation), and not the Garden of Eden upon earth.

12. ⌜διαπνεόμενος ὑπὸ⌝ τῆς εἱμαρμένης. Perhaps διατετμημένος ἀπό, 'cut off from'. It is through his incarnation that man becomes subject to Heimarmene. Before his incarnation, he lived in 'Paradise', i. e. in the incorporeal world; and as long as he remained there, he was beyond her reach. Heimarmene has power over corporeal things alone.

12–13. ἔπεισαν αὐτὸν ⟨οἱ . . .⟩ . . . ἐνδύσασθαι τὸν παρ' αὐτῶν (αὐτοῦ MSS.) Ἀδάμ. τὸν Ἀδάμ means the body. If the plural verbs ἔπεισαν and ἐκαυχῶντο are right, αὐτοῦ must be altered into αὐτῶν. Nicotheus must have said that the human body was made by a group of maleficent daemons or *archontes*.

13. ὡς ἄκακον ⟨ὄντα⟩. Having no knowledge or experience of evil, he did not suspect their malicious design, and was easily persuaded.

15. οἱ (εἱ MSS.) δὲ ἐκαυχῶντο, ὡς δεδουλαγωγημένου αὐτοῦ ⟨ὑπὸ τῆς εἱμαρμένης (?)⟩. The maleficent beings by whom the body was made were agents or ministers of Heimarmene, and their object was to bring man under her dominion.

16–17. ⟨. . .⟩ τὸν ἔξω ἄνθρωπον δεσμὸν εἶπεν ὁ Ἡσίοδος ὃν ἔδησεν ὁ Ζεὺς τὸν Προμηθέα. Hes. *Theog.* 521: δῆσε δ' (*sc.* Ζεὺς) ἀλυκτοπέδῃσι Προμηθέα ποικιλόβουλον | δεσμοῖς ἀργαλέοισι μέσον διὰ κίον' ἐλάσσας, | καὶ οἱ ἐπ' αἰετὸν ὦρσε κ.τ.λ. *Ib.* 614: οὐδὲ γὰρ . . . Προμηθεὺς | τοῖό γ' (*sc.* Διὸς) ὑπεξήλυξε βαρὺν χόλον, ἀλλ' ὑπ' ἀνάγκης | καὶ πολύιδριν ἐόντα, μέγας κατὰ δεσμὸς ἐρύκει. Zosimus interprets this δεσμός as meaning the imprisonment of the spiritual man in a material body, and thus makes it correspond to the imprisonment of Φώς in 'Adam' as described by Nicotheus. Perhaps the eagle by which the liver of Prometheus was devoured may have been taken to symbolize the bodily passions.

17–18. εἶτα . . . ἄλλον αὐτῷ δεσμὸν ἐπιπέμπει τὴν Πανδώρην. This refers to Hes. *Op.* 56–105. The story is told also in Hes. *Theog.* 510–514 and 570–589; but the woman, who is called Pandora in *Opera et Dies*, is nameless in the *Theogonia*.

The first δεσμός is the incarnation of the spiritual or incorporeal man; the second δεσμός is the further and more complete enslavement of man (already incarnate) which takes place when he 'accepts the gifts of Heimarmene', that is, when he allows himself to be dominated by desire for bodily pleasure or worldly prosperity. All men alike, during their life on earth, are necessarily bound by the the first δεσμός; but men can, if they will, escape from the second δεσμός, by 'rejecting the gifts of Heimarmene'.

18. τὴν Πανδώρην, ἣν οἱ Ἑβραῖοι καλοῦσιν Εὔαν. It may be inferred from this that Eve, as well as Adam, was spoken of in the Christian-Gnostic source from which Zosimus drew. Perhaps Nicotheus gave to the story of Eve an allegorical meaning similar to that which Zosimus gives to the story of Pandora.

18–20. ⟨. . .⟩ ⟨⟨διὰ τὴν παρακοὴν τοῦ Ἐπιμηθέως, ἣν παρήκουσεν τοῦ Προμηθέως, ⟨τουτέστι⟩ τοῦ ἰδίου⟩⟩ ⟨νοός⟩. The words ὁ γὰρ Προμηθεὺς καὶ Ἐπιμηθεὺς κ.τ.λ. must have been preceded by some mention of Epimetheus as well as of Prometheus; and if we place διὰ τὴν παρα- κοὴν τοῦ Ἐπιμηθέως κ.τ.λ. here, it supplies a connecting-link such as is required. We may suppose the sense to have been '⟨For men were brought into bondage⟩ in consequence of the neglect of Epi- metheus to heed the warning of Prometheus,—that is to say, the warning of his own νοῦς'.

20–23. ὁ γὰρ Προμηθεὺς . . . σαρκὸς ⟨δὲ ὁ Ἐπιμηθεύς⟩. Zosimus must have meant that Prometheus signifies the νοῦς, and Epimetheus the σάρξ; and I have rewritten this corrupt passage so as to make it express that meaning.

24. φησὶ γὰρ ὁ νοῦς ἡμῶν ⟨. . .⟩. ὁ νοῦς ἡμῶν (our νοῦς, as opposed to our σάρξ,) is the thing signified by Prometheus in the Hesiodic story of which Zosimus has just been speaking.[1] An object-clause de-

---

[1] Reitzenstein (*Poimandres* p. 105 and p. 215) says that ὁ νοῦς ἡμῶν means Poimandres. He prints the passage thus: φησὶ γὰρ ὁ Νοῦς ἡμῶν· "ὁ δὲ υἱὸς τοῦ ἀνθρώπου πάντα δυνάμενος καὶ πάντα γινόμενος ὅτι θέλει ὡς θέλει φαίνει ἑκάστῳ"; and he takes the words ὁ δὲ υἱὸς . . . φαίνει ἑκάστῳ to be a quotation from a Hermetic document which contained a collection of 'Sayings of Poimandres'. (He thinks that a phrase in *Corp.* XIII. 15 is another of these 'Sayings of Poimandres', and is quoted from the same Hermetic document.)

Now it is true that Zosimus, in one of his other writings (ii, § 8 below), mentions Poimandres; but that proves nothing more than that he had read *Corp.* I. I can see no ground whatever for supposing that he was thinking of Poimandres when he wrote the passage before us; and I can find no evidence, either here or else- where, that a collection of 'Sayings of Poimandres', such as Reitzenstein speaks of, ever existed. ὁ νοῦς ἡμῶν does not mean Poimandres; it means simply 'man's νοῦς'. It seems to me certain that ὁ δὲ υἱὸς τοῦ ἀνθρώπου κ.τ.λ. is not dependent on φησὶ γὰρ ὁ νοῦς ἡμῶν, but is separated from those words by a lacuna; and that the sentence ὁ δὲ υἱὸς . . . φαίνετ⟨αι⟩ ἑκάστῳ, together with all that follows down to the end of § 16, was taken by Zosimus, not from a *Hermeticum*, but from a Christian-Gnostic document. And it seems to me almost, if not quite, certain that this Christian-Gnostic document was the Apocalypse of Nicotheus.

pendent on φησί ('that we ought to reject the gifts of Heimarmene', or something to that effect) has been lost.

25–108. 20. ⟨. . .⟩ ὁ δὲ υἱὸς τοῦ θεοῦ κ.τ.λ. The exposition of Christian-Gnostic doctrine, which has been interrupted by the digression on Hesiod (§ 13), is here resumed. In § 12 we were told how man has become subject to Heimarmene; in §§ 14, 15, and ⟨⟨8⟩⟩ we are told how, by the aid of 'the Son of God', we may escape from our subjection to Heimarmene. But § 14 must have been preceded by a connecting passage, now lost, in which the topic of 'the Son of God' was introduced.

25–108. 1. πάντα γινόμενος ὅσα (ὅτε MSS.) θέλει. The correction ὅσα for ὅτε is confirmed by πάντα ὅσα θέλει γίνεται in § ⟨⟨8⟩⟩. Cf. the Naassene document in Hippol. *Ref. haer.* 5. 7 (Duncker and Schneidewin p. 142, l. 20): λέγουσιν οὖν¹ περὶ τῆς τοῦ πνεύματος² οὐσίας, ἥτις ἐστὶ πάντων τῶν γινομένων αἰτία, ὅτι τούτων ἐστὶν οὐδέν, γεννᾷ δὲ καὶ ποιεῖ πάντα τὰ γινόμενα, λέγοντες οὕτως, "γίνομαι ὃ θέλω, καὶ εἰμὶ ὃ εἰμί", διὰ [τοῦ]τὸ [φημὶ]³ ἀκίνητον εἶναι τὸ πάντα κινοῦν· μένει γὰρ ὅ ἐστι, ποιοῦν τὰ πάντα, καὶ οὐδὲν τῶν γινομένων γίνεται. In that passage, τὸ ἀκίνητον εἶναι τὸ πάντα κινοῦν is a reminiscence of Aristotle (*Metaph.* γ. 8, 1012 b 31); but the notion of a πνεῦμα which pervades the universe and is the cause of all life and movement in it, and which assumes all manner of forms and yet retains its identity, is of Stoic origin. (Compare, for instance, Orig. *c. Cels.* 6. 71 : τῶν Στωικῶν φασκόντων ὅτι ὁ θεὸς πνεῦμά ἐστι διὰ πάντων διεληλυθός, καὶ πάντ' ἐν ἑαυτῷ περιέχον.) Nicotheus seems to have adopted this notion, and applied it to his 'Son of God'.

108. 1–3. ὡς θέλει φαίνεται (φαίνει MSS.) ἑκάστῳ. ['Αδὰμ προσῆν] ['Ιησοῦς Χριστὸς] [ ]] ἐφάνη δὲ καὶ τοῖς πάνυ ἀδυνάτοις ἀνθρώποις, ἄνθρωπος γεγονὼς παθητός. The words which I have bracketed break the connexion between φαίνεται and ἐφάνη δέ. The Son of God manifests himself in various ways (e. g. he appears to seers such as Nicotheus in visions); but above all, he manifested himself to men in general, 'even to the very feeble', by his incarnation.

['Ιησοῦς Χριστός] is probably a marginal note on ὁ υἱὸς τοῦ θεοῦ. Nicotheus (or at any rate Zosimus in his report of the doctrine of Nicotheus) does not seem to have used the name Jesus Christ in speaking of the Son of God.

¹ Perhaps λέγουσι γοῦν. (There is a mention of τὸ πάντα κινοῦν in the preceding sentence.)
² πνεύματος cod. The editors alter πνεύματος into σπέρματος; but why?
³ διὰ τὸ scripsi : διὰ τοῦτο φημὶ cod.

3-4. ῥ πιζόμενος καὶ ⟨⟨κοπτόμενος καὶ φονευόμενος (κοπτομένου καὶ φονευομένου MSS.) παρ' αὐτῶν.⟩⟩ ῥαπιζόμενος is an allusion to an incident in the narrative of the Gospels; whence it may be inferred that Nicotheus accepted that narrative as a whole. If he mentioned the buffeting and scourging, he surely cannot have omitted to mention the crucifixion, in which the πάθη of the incarnate Son of God reached their culmination; and if he mentioned the crucifixion, Zosimus, for the same reason, is not likely to have omitted it in reporting what Nicotheus said. I have therefore inserted here the words κοπτόμενος καὶ φονευόμενος παρ' αὐτῶν, taken, with a slight alteration, from l. 10, where the phrase is certainly misplaced. But perhaps it might be better to put a stop after κοπτόμενος, and write καὶ ἐφονεύθη παρ' αὐτῶν; the crucifixion would then be given its due prominence.

It seems probable that there was also an explicit mention of the resurrection, which is indirectly referred to in τὸν δὲ θάνατον δείξας καταπατεῖσθαι; but if so, the words in which it was mentioned have been lost.

4-5. [λάθρα] [[τοὺς ἰδίους φῶτας συλήσας]]. In the MSS., λάθρα occurs three times within a few lines. I have retained it where it stands in contrast to φανερά, and bracketed it in the two other places.

The rescue, by the Son of God, of 'the men that are his own' ought to come after, and not before, the resurrection of the Son of God himself; I have therefore transposed the words τοὺς ἰδίους συλήσας, and placed them, together with ἀνήνεγκεν κ.τ.λ., after θάνατον δείξας καταπατεῖσθαι. By this alteration, we also get the advantage of bringing θάνατον κ.τ.λ. nearer to φονευόμενος.

5-6. καταπατεῖσθαι [καὶ ἐῶσθαι]. καὶ ἐῶσθαι has resulted from duplication of καὶ ἕως, § 15 init.

6-7. ⟨⟨ἀνήνεγκεν ὅπου καὶ τὸ πρότερον διῆγον φῶτες καλούμενοι⟩⟩. See § 11 fin. and 12. The word φώς, as there explained, means man as a spiritual or incorporeal being; and men were in that sense φῶτες when (like their mythical prototype, ὁ Φώς,) they lived in 'Paradise' before their incarnation upon earth. It appears that Nicotheus adopted the Platonic doctrine of the pre-existence of human souls, but expressed it in terms which differed from those used by the Platonists.

7. ἕως ἄρτι καὶ τοῦ τέλους τοῦ κόσμου. Perhaps καὶ τοῦ τέλους τοῦ κόσμου ought to be cut out; it is hardly consistent with ταῦτα δὲ γίνεται ἕως οὗ κ.τ.λ. in § 16 init.

8. τοῖς μὲν λάθρα ⟨τοῖς δὲ⟩ καὶ φανερὰ συνών (τόποις ἰλάθρα καὶ φανερὰ συλλῶν MSS.). The Son of God presents himself 'visibly' or 'openly' to a seer or prophet here and there; but he is present 'secretly' in the heart of every man who is worthy to receive him.

8–9. συμβουλεύων αὐτοῖς [λάθρα καὶ] διὰ τοῦ νοὸς αὐτῶν. It is man's νοῦς that guides him rightly; but it guides him rightly only when it is itself guided by the Son of God.

9–10. ἀπαλλαγὴν (καταλλαγὴν MSS.) ἔχειν τοῦ [παρ'] αὐτῶν Ἀδάμ. 'Adam' is the body, as in §§ 11 and 12; and 'their Adam' means that part of them which is corporeal. 'Rid yourselves of your Adam' is the Christian-Gnostic equivalent of the Hermetic warnings against 'loving the body' (Corp. XI. ii. 21 a, &c.).

Plotinus, 2. 9. 17, speaking of the Gnostics to whom he was opposed (and who, as we know from Porphyry, made use of the Apocalypse of Nicotheus), says καίτοι, εἰ καὶ μισεῖν αὐτοῖς ἐπῄει τὴν τοῦ σώματος φύσιν, διότι ἀκηκόασι Πλάτωνος πολλὰ μεμψαμένου τῷ σώματι οἷα ἐμπόδια παρέχει τῇ ψυχῇ, καὶ πᾶσαν τὴν σωματικὴν φύσιν εἰπεῖν χείρονα, ἐχρῆν κ.τ.λ.

10. ⌜τυφληγοροῦντος⌝. Perhaps τυφλοδηγοῦντος. Cf. Luke 6. 39: μήτι δύναται τυφλὸς τυφλὸν ὁδηγεῖν; The body is a blind guide.

11. διαζηλουμένου τῷ πνευματικῷ καὶ φωτεινῷ ἀνθρώπῳ. Cf. Paul, Gal. 5. 17: ἡ σὰρξ ἐπιθυμεῖ κατὰ τοῦ πνεύματος, τὸ δὲ πνεῦμα κατὰ τῆς σαρκός, ταῦτα γὰρ ἀλλήλοις ἀντίκειται.

11–12. [τὸν ἑαυτῶν Ἀδὰμ ἀποκτείνουσι.] Probably a fragment of a marginal note.

13–20. ⟨. . .⟩ θεάσῃ τὸν θεοῦ υἱὸν πάντα γινόμενον κ.τ.λ. In this section, things that have been said in §§ 14 and 15 are repeated in almost the same words. A connecting passage has been lost; if it had been preserved, we might perhaps have found in it some reason for this repetition.

θεάσῃ and ὅρα are difficult to understand. How, when, and where was Theosebeia to 'see' the Son of God becoming all things? A possible answer to that question might be got by transposing from the end of § 8 to the beginning of it the unintelligible words καὶ βλέψαι τὸν πίνακα ὃν ⌜καὶ βιτος γράψας⌝,[1] and writing here something

---

[1] [The MSS. τὸν πίνακα ὃν καὶ βιτος γράψας suggests that the text originally read Κέβητος, perhaps τ. Π. τὸν Κέβητος. With καὶ βιτος once established—and there is no difficulty in the interchange of ι and η—an attempt to rectify the grammar might give rise to the present reading. Ruelle's text reads ὃν Κέβητος γράψας, and his apparatus suggests Κέβης τε ἔγραψε. The point is the struggle between the higher and the lower man as illustrated in the Gospel (if the MS. order is right), the Tabula of Cebes, Plato, and Hermes.]

like ⟪καὶ βλέψασα εἰς τὸν πίνακα ὃν ἔγραψα (or ὃν ὁ Νικόθεος ἔγραψε?)⟫ θεάσῃ τὸν θεοῦ υἱὸν κ.τ.λ. We know that there were Gnostic books in which the teaching was illustrated by pictures or diagrams;[1] and it is possible to imagine a diagram depicting the descent of the Son of God from heaven into all parts of the world below, and the various forms in which he has manifested himself at different times and places. If we suppose that the book of Nicotheus contained a diagram of this kind, and that Zosimus drew a copy of it beside the text which he was writing,[2] he might very well say 'look at the drawing, and you will see the Son of Man becoming all things'.

15. γινόμενον πάντα, θεόν, ἄγγελον, ἄνθρωπον παθητόν. The Son of God must have been a god by origin and nature ; perhaps Nicotheus said that he became an angel at an intermediate stage on his way to incarnation as a man. It may have been assumed that the apparitions of the 'angel of God' in the Old Testament were apparitions of the Son of God in angel-form.

16. [καὶ πατρὶ ὑπακούει]. These words are out of place here, but may perhaps have occurred in the lost passage which preceded § ⟪8⟫.

17–18. ⟨...⟩ εἰς τὸν εὐδαίμονα χῶρον ἀνώρμησεν, ὅπουπερ ἦν καὶ πρὸ τοῦ σωματικὸς (πρὸ τοῦτο σωματικὸν MSS.) γένεσθαι. Cf. ἀνήνεγκεν ὅπου καὶ τὸ πρότερον διῆγον φῶτες καλούμενοι, in § 14, and ⟨εἰς τὸν⟩ ἴδιον χῶρον, ὅπουπερ καὶ πρὸ ⟨τοῦ⟩ κόσμου ἦσαν, in § 16 fin. If ἀνώρμησεν ('ascends') is right, the subject of the verb must be the man whose νοῦς has been illumined by the Son of God.

19–20. ⟨...⟩ αὐτῷ ἀκολουθοῦντα, καὶ ὑπ' αὐτοῦ ... ὁδηγούμενον εἰς ἐκεῖνο τὸ φῶς. It would seem that these words, in which (as in φωτίζων τὸν ἑκάστου νοῦν above) the guidance of men during their earthly life is spoken of, ought to precede rather than follow εἰς τὸν εὐδαίμονα χῶρον ... σωματικὸς γενέσθαι, which has to do with the ascent of men to heaven when their earthly life is ended. [Perhaps Zosimus wrote αὐτῷ ... αὐτοῦ ὀρεγόμενον καὶ ὑπ' αὐτοῦ ὁδηγούμενον. Once a scribe had written ὑπ' αὐτοῦ in error for αὐτοῦ, he might naturally omit the phrase before ὁδηγούμενον. Compare the repetition of πάντα above.]

21. ἕως οὗ ἔλθῃ ὁ ἀντίμιμος δαίμων. 'The daemon who mimics (the Son of God)' is the Antichrist of Christian eschatology. The

---

[1] Some of the books of Mani were illustrated by pictures. And see Origen c. Cels. 6. 24 on the διάγραμμα of the Ophiani.

[2] Zosimus drew diagrams of metallurgical apparatus further on in this same book περὶ ὀργάνων καὶ καμίνων.

ollowing words, θέλων ὡς τὸ πρῶτον (πρώην MSS.) πλανῆσαι ⟨τοὺς ἰνθρώπους?⟩, seem to be an allusion to the 'leading astray' of Eve ɔy the Serpent; and if so, Nicotheus must have considered Anti-christ to be an incarnation of the Devil.

23-24. ἐκ τῆς καταλήψεως τοῦ ὄντως υἱοῦ τοῦ θεοῦ. Does this mean that ὁ ἄνθρωπος καταλαμβάνει (takes hold of and clings to) τὸν υἱὸν τοῦ θεοῦ, or that ὁ υἱὸς τοῦ θεοῦ καταλαμβάνει (enters into and takes possession of) τὸν ἄνθρωπον?

ὁ ὄντως (ὢν) υἱὸς τοῦ θεοῦ is contrasted with ὁ (ψευδῶς) λέγων ἑαυτὸν υἱὸν θεοῦ.

24. δώσουσιν (δίδωσιν MSS.) αὐτῷ τὸν ἴδιον Ἀδὰμ εἰς φόνον. αὐτῷ probably means τῷ ἀντιμίμῳ, and not τῷ υἱῷ τοῦ θεοῦ. The followers of the Son of God will be persecuted by Antichrist; they will yield up to him their bodies (τὸν ἴδιον Ἀδάμ) to be slain, but save their φωτεινὰ πνεύματα, which will go back to 'Paradise' (i.e. to the incorporeal world), whence they originally came.

Eschatological predictions of the doings of Antichrist were partly based on historical persecutions of the Christians; he is an ideal figure of a persecuting Roman emperor.

109. 1. ⟨εἰς τὸν⟩ ἴδιον χῶρον. ἴδιον makes good sense; but it is sus-piciously near to τὸν ἴδιον Ἀδάμ, and for that reason I am inclined to think that it has been wrongly substituted for εὐδαίμονα or some equivalent word.

5-7. εἰσὶ δὲ τὰ στοιχεῖα τοῦ ὀνόματος αὐτοῦ ἐννέα, [τῆς διφθόγγου σωζομένης,] κατὰ τὸν τῆς εἰμαρμένης ὅρον. The forerunner of Anti-christ, who comes 'from Persia', is Manichaeus. The name Μανιχαῖος consists of nine letters, 'if you retain the diphthong'. The man who wrote τῆς διφθόγγου σωζομένης must have been accustomed to see the name spelt in two ways, Μανιχαῖος and Μανιχέος. But as τῆς διφθ. σωζ. breaks the connexion of κατὰ τὸν τῆς εἰμαρμένης ὅρον with what precedes, it is probably a note added by a reader.

κατὰ τὸν τῆς εἰμαρμένης ὅρον, 'according to the measure of εἰμαρμένη', means that the word εἰμαρμένη also consists of nine letters. This fact is taken to indicate that Manichaeus is connected with Heimarmene,—the connexion being that his teaching tends to bring or keep men under her dominion (περὶ τὴν εἰμαρμένην ἄγοντα τοὺς ἀνθρώπους).

§ 17 is connected with the contents of §§ 4-18 as a whole by the fact that it is concerned with subjection to εἰμαρμένη, which is the main topic of the whole digression. But was the mention of

Manichaeus taken over by Zosimus, together with the contents of the preceding sections 10–16, from the Apocalypse of Nicotheus, or was it added by Zosimus himself? Mani was put to death by king Bahram I, A. D. 274–277. Now we know from Porphyry that the Apocalypse of Nicotheus was in use at Rome in the lifetime of Plotinus, i. e. before A. D. 270. It must therefore have been written at least some years before that date; and it is hardly possible that Manichaeus can have been thus spoken of so early. Moreover, the paragraph on Manichaeus in the text of Zosimus is something of an interruption; and if it were omitted, the following words (εἶτα μετὰ περίοδον κ.τ.λ.) would fit on quite well to the end of § 16. This paragraph then was probably added by Zosimus himself to what he took from Nicotheus. By the time at which Zosimus wrote (soon after A. D. 300?), the Manichaean sect had doubtless grown strong in Egypt, and its founder might very well be regarded as a precursor of Antichrist by some of its opponents.

8–9. εἶτα μετὰ περίοδον πλέον ἢ ἔλαττον ἑπτὰ ⟨ἐτῶν?⟩ καὶ αὐτὸς ⌈ἑαυτῷ φύσει⌉ ἐλεύσεται. αὐτός means the Son of God, and not the ἀντίμιμος. The power of Antichrist will last for a certain time (seven years?); and at the end of that period, the Son of God will come.

Nicotheus must have gone on to say more about the παρουσία of the Son of God; but Zosimus ends at this point his report of the teaching of Nicotheus.

10–19. καὶ ταῦτα μὲν οἱ (ταῦτα μόνοι MSS.) Ἑβραῖοι [καὶ αἱ ἱεραὶ Ἑρμοῦ βίβλοι]. . . .· οἱ δὲ Ἕλληνες κ.τ.λ. ταῦτα is explained to mean 'the things concerning the φωτεινὸς ἄνθρωπος and his guide the Son of God, and the earthy Adam and his guide the ἀντίμιμος who blasphemously calls himself Son of God'. That is a summary of the contents of §§ 11, 12, 14, 15, ⟨⟨8⟩⟩, 16, and 17 fin.,—i. e. of the sections which contain the teaching of Nicotheus as reported by Zosimus. He calls this Christian-Gnostic system the teaching of 'the Hebrews', because he supposes that not only the Adam-doctrine, but the whole teaching of Nicotheus, including his doctrine of the Son of God, was derived from those sacred books of the Hebrews which had been translated into Greek and deposited in Egyptian libraries (§ 10),—that is, from what we call the books of the Old Testament.

If we suppose that the words καὶ αἱ ἱεραὶ Ἑρμοῦ βίβλοι were written here by Zosimus, it follows that he found this body of doctrine taught in a *Hermeticum* also, in the same or nearly the same form in which it was taught by 'the Hebrew' (that is, by his Christian-Gnostic authority). But that is incredible. A book in which the prehistoric Egyptian teacher Hermes was made to speak of Adam, —and of a Son of God who was incarnated as a man on earth, who suffered, and yet 'showed death to be trampled under foot', and who is to come again at the last,—and of a counterfeit and opponent of the Son of God, who leads men astray, and who is to appear on earth shortly before the coming of the true Son of God,—such a book would be a monstrosity. It may be added (though this is a less cogent argument) that αἱ ἱεραὶ Ἑρμοῦ βίβλοι is hardly a suitable phrase to be coupled to οἱ Ἑβραῖοι and contrasted with οἱ Ἕλληνες. Supposing that Zosimus had wished to refer to the teaching of Hermes here, we should have expected him rather to write οἱ Αἰγύπτιοι, as he writes οἱ Ἑβραῖοι when he means Nicotheus, and οἱ Ἕλληνες when he means Hesiod.

The words καὶ αἱ ἱεραὶ Ἑρμοῦ βίβλοι must therefore be bracketed. They may very likely have occurred further on in this section, in the lost passage which preceded πάντα ἑρμηνεύει. Zosimus may perhaps have written there something like ὅμοια [ ] ⟨δὲ παραινοῦσι ⟨⟨καὶ αἱ ἱεραὶ Ἑρμοῦ βίβλοι⟩⟩· ὁ γὰρ Ἑρμῆς τὰ περὶ τῆς εἱμαρμένης⟩ πάντα ἑρμηνεύει, κ.τ.λ. That is, the *Hermetica* agree with Hesiod in advising us not to accept the gifts of Heimarmene. (For the combination of Ἑρμῆς with πάντα ἑρμηνεύει, cf. Ἑρμῆς [ ] ⟨ὁ⟩ ἑρμηνεὺς πάντων τῶν ὄντων, in § 9.) Thus emended, § 18 would be a summary of all that has been said in §§ 4–17.

20–21. εὐτυχοῦντες, οὐδὲν ἕτερον ⌜λέγουσι⌝ (καταδέχονται ?) τῆς τέχνης. Cf. §§ 2 and 3. Zosimus here returns to the point from which he digressed in § 4. His opponents, when they happen to succeed by their method of καιρικαὶ καταβαφαί, refuse to admit the use of any other method.

21–23. τὸν ποιητὴν . . . λέγοντα " ἀλλ᾽ οὔπως ἅμα ⟨πάντα⟩ θεοὶ δόσαν ἀνθρώποισι" καὶ τὰ ἑξῆς. This appears to be an inaccurate quotation of Hom. *Od.* 8. 167, where Odysseus, answering the taunt of a Phaeacian, says οὕτως οὐ πάντεσσι θεοὶ χαρίεντα διδοῦσιν | ἄνδρασιν, and goes on to point out that different men are favoured by the gods in different ways ; one man, for instance, has eloquence or wisdom, and another, beauty.

24–25. εἰς μίαν τέχνην ἄνθρωποι διαφόρως εὐτυχοῦσι, καὶ διαφόρως τὴν μίαν τέχνην ἐργάζονται. Compare § 20 *init.* : ἔστιν ⟨εὑρεῖν⟩ . . . διαφόροις ἐργαλείοις καὶ ἀγωγαῖς τὴν αὐτὴν τέχνην ἐργαζομένους, καὶ διαφόρως (διαφόρους MSS.) ἔχοντας τὸ [νοερὸν καὶ] ἐπιτευκτικόν. The meaning is not very clearly expressed; but I think it may be inferred from the context that διαφόρως εὐτυχοῦσι (= διαφόρως ἔχουσι τὸ ἐπιτευκτικόν) means 'succeed by different methods'. In alchemy, one man makes use of καιρικαὶ καταβαφαί, another makes use of κάμινοι, and both succeed.

25-27. διὰ τὸ (διὰ τὰ ἤθη καὶ MSS.) διάφορα ⟨ὄντα τὰ⟩ σχήματα τῶν ἀστέρων ⟨διάφορον καὶ τὴν⟩ μίαν τέχνην ποιεῖν. Heimarmene works by means of the stars; and to say that a thing is determined by the positions of the stars is equivalent to saying that it is determined by Heimarmene. The meaning seems to be that the stars confer on one man the gift of using one method with success, and on another man the gift of using another method with success.

27-28. καὶ τὸν μὲν ἄκρον (ἄγων MSS.) ⟨εἶναι⟩ τεχνίτην, [τὸν δὲ μόνον τεχνίτην,] τὸν δὲ ὑποβεβηκότα, τὸν δὲ ⌊χείρονα⌋ ἀπρόκοπον. The success of a craftsman must of course depend, in part at least, on the degree of his proficiency in the craft; but the connexion of this with the context is obscure. Possibly καὶ τὸν μὲν ... ἀπρόκοπον ought to be bracketed. The words [τὸν δὲ μόνον τεχνίτην] and [χείρονα] have probably arisen out of τὸν μὲν ἀμείνονα τεχνίτην, τὸν δὲ χείρονα, written as an alternative for τὸν μὲν ἄκρον τεχνίτην ... τὸν δὲ ἀπρόκοπον.

110. 3-4. ἐν τῇ ἱερατικῇ. Alchemy is one branch of 'the hieratic art'; and the art of healing, as practised by Egyptian priests, is another branch of it.

4-12. φέρε εἰπεῖν κατεαγότος ὀστέου κ.τ.λ. This passage throws some light on medical practice in Roman Egypt. If you break your arm or leg, your friends first send for 'a bone-setting priest',—that is, probably, one of the priests employed in medical work in connexion with a temple of Imhotep or some other Egyptian god. This priest, we must suppose, pronounces a spell over the broken limb; and 'one hears the bones grate as they come together'. But if the priestly bone-setter cannot be found, then one sends for surgeons trained in a Greek school of medicine; and the surgeons bring with them their medical books and anatomical diagrams, and bandage the limb as the books direct.

The relation between the method of καιρικαὶ καταβαφαί and that of κάμινοι in alchemy is similar to the relation between the method of the Egyptian priest and that of the Greek surgeons in bone-setting; and the book περὶ ὀργάνων καὶ καμίνων corresponds to the books which the Greek surgeons use. If the one method cannot be employed, (or, in the case of alchemy, if the one fails to work rightly when employed,) you should have recourse to the other.

5–6. ⌜διὰ τῆς ἰδίας δεισιδαιμονίας ποιῶν⌝ κολλᾷ τὸ ὀστοῦν. It could not be said that the priest heals the fracture 'making (something) by means of his own fear of gods or daemons'. The meaning must have been that he effects a cure by means of some religious rite ; and this might be expressed by writing διὰ τῆς ἰδίας λειτ⟨ουργίας τοὺς⟩ δαίμονας ⟨εὐμενεῖς⟩ ποιῶν.

In §§ 3 and 4, those who make use of καιρικαὶ καταβαφαί are said to be dependent on the favour of 'their daemon' for success ; and as it is their method that is compared to the practice of the priestly bone-setter, perhaps it may be inferred that the use of the καιρικαὶ κατα-βαφαί was accompanied by some invocation of daemons, and that such an invocation was considered necessary to make these 'tinctures' do their work, whereas the method of κάμινοι was more purely scientific, and did not need to be supplemented by religious or magic rites. Compare Zosimus ii, where we are told that there were two kinds of καιρικαί, and it seems to be implied that the one kind was, and the other kind was not, connected with worship of daemons. Possibly the men against whom Zosimus is here contending used καιρικαί of the former kind alone.

7–8. [οὐ ⌜μὴ φοβηθῇ⌝ ἄνθρωπος ἀποθανεῖν, ἀλλά]. μὴ φοβηθῇ has probably arisen out of the preceding μὴ εὑρεθῇ ; and οὐ . . . ἄνθρωπος ἀποθανεῖν has come from οὐ δήπου ἀφίεται ὁ ἄνθρωπος ἀποθανεῖν below. [Zosimus means that all art is one, whatever the ἤθη of the practitioners. There seems to be some point in the repetition : the man doesn't resign himself to die because he can't get a priest ; far from it, he calls in the recognized practitioners and lives for ages (⟨συχνὸν ?⟩ χρόνον)—indeed he doesn't give up the struggle for want of . . .]

14. ἵνα μακάριοι γενόμενοι νικήσωσι πενίαν, τὴν ἀνίατον νόσον. This is a saying which occurs repeatedly in the alchemistic literature. The source from which Zosimus got it was probably a treatise on alchemy, attributed to Democritus, in which that philosopher was made to say (Berthelot, p. 59) ἐὰν ᾖς νοήμων, καὶ ποιήσῃς ὡς γέγραπται, ἔσῃ μακάριος· νικήσεις γὰρ μεθόδῳ πενίαν, τὴν ἀνίατον νόσον. Cf. Berthelot, p. 211 : if you do so-and-so, μακάριος ἔσῃ, ὦ Διόσκορε· τοῦτο γάρ ἐστι τὸ λυτρούμενον πενίας, τῆς ἀνιάτου νόσου. Berthelot, p. 212 : ἐμπεσὼν

εἰς τὰ μαθήματα ταῦτα, οὐκέτι ἔσῃ [1] ἀτυχής, ἀλλὰ γὰρ νικήσεις μεθόδῳ πενίαν, τὴν ἀνίατον [2] νόσον.

Zosimus here frankly admits that the alchemist's aim is to make money. How is this to be reconciled with the lofty sentiments of §§ 4–18, and especially with the exhortation to 'reject the gifts of Heimarmene'? For a possible answer to that question, see note on p. 141, ll. 15–16.

21–22. μὴ οἴου ἀξιοπιστότερον ἐμὲ τῶν ἀρχαίων ξυγγράψαι. Among the 'ancient' authorities known to Zosimus were books on alchemy that were supposed to have been written by the Egyptian Hermes,[3] 'the Jewess Maria' (i.e. probably Miriam the sister of Moses),[4] the Persian magician Ostanes, and the Greek philosopher Democritus.

25. βίκος ὑέλεος κ.τ.λ. Here follow technical details concerning apparatus.

26. τὸ πρῶτον βιβλίον τῆς τελευταίας ἀποχῆς. The reading ἀποχῆς is confirmed by Olympiodorus; it appears therefore that the work of Zosimus from which this extract was taken was entitled ἡ τελευταία ἀποχή. [ἀποχή appears to be a metaphorical use from the sense *receipt*; cf. L. and S.]

Ζωσίμου ⌐Θηβαίου⌐. Panopolis, the home or birthplace of Zosimus, was in that part of Egypt which was called Thebais. But Θηβαίου may have arisen, by corruption, out of the adjacent βεβαίωται, or out of Θεοσεβείᾳ.

III. 1. ὥστε ⟨τοῦτο⟩ καὶ σοὶ θέλουσι ποιῆσαι. Certain persons are trying to persuade Theosebeia to do something of which Zosimus disapproves. Who are these persons, and what is it that they want her to do? The preceding context is obscure; but the sense of it seems to be approximately as follows :—

(§6) There are two kinds of καιρικαὶ (βαφαί). The one kind is γνήσιον and φυσικόν; the other kind is false and ἀφύσικον. ⟨The latter kind (?)⟩ was made known by 'the local ἔφοροι' to their own priests.[5] They called them καιρικαί, because these processes were effective κατὰ καιρούς (i. e. at certain times), in accordance with the will of the (daemons?) but failed

---

[1] οὐκέτι ἔσῃ coni. Ruelle : οὐκ ἔστι ἔσοι cod.

[2] ἀνίατον Ruelle : ἀνίαρον cod.

[3] Agathodaemon (the teacher of Hermes) also is mentioned and quoted in the alchemistic texts as an authority on alchemy.
Zosimus, in Book VIII of this work (Syriac translation), says that the successors of Hermes have corrupted his (alchemistic) teaching by inaccurate commentaries.

[4] In the *Turba philosophorum*, an alchemistic compilation which was current in the middle ages (Berthelot, *La chimie au moyen âge*, Tome I), there is a reference to a dialogue of 'Aron' (Aaron?) 'cum Maria prophetissa sorore Moysis'.

[5] ἐξέδωκα[σι]ν οἱ (ἐκδεδώκασιν ἢ MS.) κατὰ τόπον ἔφοροι τοῖς ἑαυτῶν ἱερεῦσι.

when the (daemons?) were not willing to make them work.[1] But the γνήσιαι καὶ φυσικαὶ καιρικαί, i.e. those which operate φυσικῶς (and not by the intervention of daemons), were inscribed on the *stelae* by Hermes.[2] . . . These are kept secret; but when a man is initiated and learns them, he will get what he seeks.

(§ 7) The ἔφοροι then, being driven out by the men who were then in power,[3] took measures to suppress τὰ φυσικά, in order that they might not be driven out, but might be entreated and called upon for help by means of sacrifices. They concealed πάντα τὰ φυσικὰ καὶ αὐτόματα,[4] seeking thereby to ward off persecution, and to avoid the hunger which they would suffer if they did not receive sacrifices; and in place of the φυσικὴ (τέχνη), they introduced their own ἀφύσικος (τέχνη), and made it known to their own priests. . . . And their sacrifices were multiplied; but they did not fulfil their false promises.[5]

But when war arose . . .,[6] and their sanctuaries were laid waste, and their sacrifices were neglected, they fawned on the men who remained, . . . and urged them to cling to the sacrifices; and when they made the same false promises as before, all the pleasure-loving and foolish people were pleased.

This then is what they are seeking to do to you also, lady, by means of their false prophet, &c.

It appears from this that the thing which 'they' are urging Theosebeia to do is to abandon the 'natural' καιρικαί and make use of the 'unnatural' (or supernatural) καιρικαί, and, in connexion with the latter, to offer sacrifices to daemons. And accordingly, Zosimus goes on to say: 'invoke the supreme God alone, and employ sacrifices, not to propitiate the daemons, but only to drive them away, or to avert their maleficent influences.

---

[1] τούτου ἕνεκεν καὶ καιρικὰς (καιρικαὶ MS.) ἐκάλεσαν, ἐπειδὴ κατ(ὰ) καιροὺς ἐνήργουν (καὶ καιροῖς ἐνέργουν MS.), τῇ θελήσει τῶν ⌈δωκόντων⌉ (read δαιμονίων?) . . . . . ., μηκέτι δὲ θελήσασι (-σάντων?) τοὐναντίον ἐποίουν. (Is this sentence an explanatory note wrongly inserted in the text?).

[2] τὸ δὲ ἄλλο γένος τῶν καιρικῶν, ⟨τὸ⟩ γνήσιον καὶ φυσικόν (γνησίων καὶ φυσικῶν MS.), [τ] ὁ Ἑρμ(ῆς) ἀν[εν]έγραψεν (τὸ ἑρμὰν ἐνέγραψεν MS.) εἰς τὰς στήλας.

[3] οἱ οὖν ἔ[μ]φοροι, ἐκδιωκόμενοι [τότε] παρὰ τῶν τότε (ποτε MS.) μεγάλων ἀνθρώπων.

[4] I. e. the processes which worked 'of themselves', by the operation of natural forces, as opposed to those in which the aid of daemons was required.

[5] I. e. they promised to help those who offered sacrifices, but they did not do what they promised.

[6] ἀλλ' ὅτε ἐ[γ]ένετ(ο) (ἐγγένει MS.) ἄρα ⌈ἀποκατάστασις τῶν κλήματων⌉, καὶ διέφερετο τὸ ⌈κλῆμα⌉ πολέμῳ, καὶ ἐλείπετο ἐκ τοῦ ⌈κλήματος⌉ ἐκείνο[υ] τὸ γένος ἀνθρώπων, κ.τ.λ. What is the meaning of κλῆμα? Ought we to read κλίμα, in the sense of 'region of the earth'? [See Addenda.]

But who are the persons who sought in past times, and are still seeking in the present, to induce people to employ the ἀφύσικοι καιρικαί and to offer sacrifices? These persons are called οἱ κατὰ τόπον ἔφοροι (§ 6), and οἱ ἔ[μ]φοροι (§ 7). It is to their interest that sacrifices should be offered; and they suffer from hunger when the sacrifices are abandoned. This might be said either of the priests who live on the offerings, or of the gods or daemons to whom the sacrifices are offered; it could hardly be said of any one else. But the persons spoken of are not priests; for we are told that they revealed or entrusted certain things 'to their own priests' (τοῖς ἑαυτῶν ἱερεῦσι). It appears therefore that they must be gods or daemons; and perhaps οἱ κατὰ τόπον ἔφοροι means the local gods worshipped in Egyptian temples. If so, it would seem that these gods were called 'daemons' by Zosimus, as they were by the Christians of his time, and by some Pagans also. (Why daemons should be called ἔφοροι, I do not know. Possibly the word δαίμονες may have dropped out after ἔφοροι.)

We are told in § 7 that, at some past time, the ἔφοροι were expelled, or threatened with expulsion. In order to protect themselves, they introduced the ἀφύσικοι καιρικαί and the accompanying sacrifices; and their power, it seems, was thereby re-established. At some later time, there was a war, in the course of which their hold on the people was weakened; but they afterwards recovered some of their lost influence, and they are still maintaining their cause by means of 'their false prophet'. What are the historical events referred to in this passage? I have failed to find any satisfactory answer to that question. Perhaps the earlier 'expulsion' of the ἔφοροι may have been supposed to have occurred in the prehistoric past, and may have been connected with some mythical incident such as the war waged by Set against Osiris and Horus; or again, it may have been thought to have taken place in connexion with some historical event of remote date, such as the invasion and conquest of Egypt by the Persian king Cambyses. The later 'war' seems to be a comparatively recent incident; is it the rebellion of Egypt in the reign of Diocletian? It is probable that in the course of that rebellion some of the Egyptian sanctuaries were laid waste, and the worship of the gods was much interrupted; it is to be presumed that, after the suppression of the rebellion in A.D. 297, the Pagan cults were re-established on a firm footing; and we know that, a few years later, a resolute attempt was made by the Roman rulers to stamp out the Christian opposition to Pagan worship. Zosimus most likely wrote at a time when the rebellion in Egypt and its suppression by Diocletian were still fresh in men's memory; and it may be conjectured that these are the events of which he is thinking when he speaks of a temporary decline and subsequent revival of the practice of offering sacrifices to daemons.[1]

The meaning of this sketch of past occurrences is very doubtful; but it is clear that, in exhorting Theosebeia to invoke the supreme God alone, Zosimus sides with the Christians against the Pagan cults;[2] and the 'false prophet' must be some prominent advocate of Pagan polytheism. θυσίαι ἀποτρεπτικαί such as Zosimus speaks of with approval may perhaps have been in use among the Christian Gnostics with whom he was in contact.

2–3. κολακεύουσί σε (perhaps κολακεύει γάρ σε) τὰ κατὰ τόπον ⟨δαιμόνια?⟩, πεινῶντα οὐ μόνον θυσίας, ἀλλὰ καὶ τὴν σὴν ψυχήν. Zosimus has said earlier in § 7 that (οἱ ἔφοροι) ἔκρυψαν πάντα τὰ φυσικὰ καὶ αὐτόματα, ... ἵνα μὴ ... λιμῷ τιμωρῶνται, θυσίας μὴ λαμβάνοντες. And he now says to Theosebeia, 'the local (daemons?) are not only hungry for sacrifices, but are eager to devour your soul also'; that is, they seek to destroy your soul by inducing you to offer sacrifices to them instead of worshipping the supreme God alone.

4. ὡς καὶ ἐν τοῖς κατ' ἐν⟨εργ⟩ειαν ἐξεῖπόν σοι. A treatise of Zosimus entitled ἡ κατ' ἐνέργειαν βίβλος is mentioned elsewhere in the alchemistic texts (Berthelot, p. 89).

6. οὐκ ἐν τόπῳ ἐλαχίστῳ ὡς τὰ δαιμόνια. Each of the 'daemons' or local gods reside in some particular ἱερόν, and must be sought there by those who wish to worship him.

7–8. ταῖς ιβ' μοίραις (μύραις MS.) τοῦ θανάτου. Compare the list of twelve τιμωρίαι (i.e. evil passions) which is given in *Corp.* XIII. 7 b.

10. [μὴ τὰς προσφόρους]. προσφόρους has probably come from the preceding πρόσφερε.

12–13. ἃς προσεφώνησε Μεμβρῆς τῷ ... Σολομῶντι. Μεμβρῆς is doubtless a Greek transliteration of *Mēmrā* (Heb. *ma'amar*, 'word',) the name by which the hypostatized Word of God is denoted in the Targums. (As to the *Memra*, see Bousset, *Religion des Judentums,*

---

[1] Something resembling the revival of Pagan worship under Julian (A. D. 361–363) seems to be implied. Is it possible that the passage was written as late as that? Zosimus cannot be exactly dated; but it is commonly supposed that he wrote soon after A. D. 300, and before the time of Julian.

[2] Compare the passage (Syriac translation) quoted below, in which Zosimus says that the man who becomes perfect 'turns his face away from all that is called gods and daemons'.

1906, p. 399.) Zosimus must have known a document in which 'the Word of the Lord' was represented as speaking to Solomon (in the same sort of way that Νοῦς speaks to Hermes in *Corp.* XI), and giving him instruction concerning sacrifices by which daemons could be driven away or made powerless.[1]

13–14. αὐτὸς δὲ μάλιστα Σολομῶν ὅσας ἔγραψεν ἀπὸ τῆς ἑαυτοῦ σοφίας. This refers to another document known to Zosimus, which was supposed to have been written by Solomon, and in which sacrifices of the same kind were dealt with. It is implied that in this second document nothing was said about the *Memra* who took part, as Solomon's teacher, in the dialogue recorded in the first document.

In Book XII of his longest work (Syriac translation, Berthelot, *La chimie au moyen âge*, Tome II), Zosimus again speaks about writings ascribed to Solomon concerning daemons. He there says: 'Among the Egyptians there is a book called *The seven heavens*, attributed to Solomon, against the daemons; but it is not true that it is by Solomon. These bottles[2] were brought ⟨from Jerusalem⟩ long ago to our ⟨Egyptian⟩ priests. That is what the language used to denote them makes one suppose; for the term "bottles of Solomon" is a Hebraic expression. . . .[3] After these writings had spread everywhere, being still incomplete, they were corrupted. It is he (*sc.* Solomon) that invented them (*sc.* the talismanic bottles), as I said above. But Solomon only wrote a single work concerning the seven bottles; and people composed commentaries at different epochs to explain the things that this work contained. Now in these commentaries there was some fraud; ⟨but⟩ all ⟨of them⟩, or almost all, are in agreement on the work of the bottles directed against the daemons. These bottles acted ⟨in the same way⟩

---

[1] Reitzenstein (*Poim.* p. 214) reads Μαμβρῆς, and says that this Mambres is 'the Egyptian sorcerer'; that is, he identifies him with one of the two Egyptian magicians ('Jannes and Jambres', 2 *Tim.* 3. 8) who withstood Moses. [See the *Gospel of Nicodemus*. The Rabbinic forms of *Mambres* (Vulgate) vary between *Mmra*, *Yambres*, *Yombros*. In *Koran* ii. 96 Harut and Marut (who are probably identical with Yannes and Yambres) are two angels who teach men sorcery, and they are mentioned with Solomon, though the text does not exactly state that they taught him. This information I owe to the kindness of Professor Margoliouth. It is evident that no emendation is necessary in order to identify Membres with the magicians who contended with Moses.]

[2] The 'bottles', as is implied below, were vessels made for the purpose of shutting up daemons in them, and were inscribed with talismanic formulae. Some magic ritual, in which certain θυσίαι may have been included, would doubtless be employed to compel the daemons to enter the bottles.

[3] Here something is said about 'the great priests of Jerusalem'; but the sentence is corrupt and unintelligible.

as the prayer and the nine letters written by Solomon ; the daemons cannot resist them. . . . The seven bottles in which Solomon shut up the daemons were made of electrum. We must believe, in this respect, the Jewish writings concerning the daemons. The altered book which we possess, and which is entitled *The seven heavens*, contains, in summary, the following : ⟨. . .⟩.[1] The angel ordered Solomon to make these bottles. ⌈He⌉[2] adds ⟨that⟩ Solomon made the seven bottles, according to the number of the seven planets, in conformity to the divine prescriptions. . . . The wise Solomon knows also how to evoke the daemons ; he gives a formula of conjuration, and he indicates the electrum, that is, the bottles of electrum, on the surface of which he inscribed this formula.'

15–16. ταῦτα δὲ ποίει (ἐποίει MS.) ἕως ἂν τελειωθῆς (ἕως παντελειωθῆς MS.) τὴν ψυχήν· ὅταν δὲ ἐπιγνῷς ἑαυτὴν (ἐπιγνοῦσα αὐτὴν MS.) τελειωθεῖσαν, τότε [καὶ τῶν φυσικῶν] τῆς ὕλης κατάπτυσον (κατάπτησον MS.). The words [καὶ τῶν φυσικῶν] have probably come from τῶν γνησίων καὶ φυσικῶν above.

The τελείωσις here spoken of appears to be a transformation of the same sort as the παλιγγενεσία of *Corp.* XIII. When it has been accomplished, the soul of Theosebeia will have become pure νοῦς, and thenceforth she will necessarily reject with contempt the material world and all things in it.[3] But until this τελείωσις takes place in her, there is no reason why she should not take an interest in material things, and, *inter alia*, in the processes by which base metal can be transmuted into gold. For those who have not yet been ' made perfect ', gold has its uses.

One may compare Porphyry's *Vita Plotini*, c. 9, where we are told that Plotinus acted as guardian to a number of orphan children, and was careful in his administration of their properties ; ' for he said that, as long as they are not philosophers (ἕως ἂν μὴ φιλοσοφῶσιν,) their possessions and incomes must be kept unimpaired '. (When they became philosophers, property would cease to be of any use to them.)

In the quotation by Olympiodorus, as given in cod. M (eleventh century), this passage runs as follows : ὅταν δὲ ἐπιγνῷς σαυτήν, τότε

---

[1] The ' summary ' appears to have been omitted in transcription.
[2] Rather, ' The book '.
[3] In Book XI (Syriac translation), Zosimus says : ' Know that you will be ⌈tested for the spiritual and corporeal things⌉, until you arrive at perfection, acquiring patience⌉ with purity and love ; then you will find ⟨. . .⟩, abandoning the corporeal arts '.

ἐπιγνώσῃ καὶ τὸν μόνον ὄντως θεόν· καὶ οὕτως ἐνεργοῦσα ἐπιτεύξῃ τῶν γνησίων καὶ φυσικῶν, καταπτύουσα τῆς ὕλης. But that yields no satisfactory sense; and the order of the clauses in the text of Zosimus as given in cod. A (fifteenth century) seems preferable. The quotation might be emended thus : ⟨⟨καὶ οὕτως ἐνεργοῦσα ἐπιτεύξῃ τῶν γνησίων καὶ φυσικῶν⟩⟩ ⟨καιρικῶν⟩. ὅταν δὲ ἐπιγνῷς σαυτὴν ⟨τελειωθεῖσαν⟩, τότε [ἐπιγνώσῃ καὶ τὸν μόνον ὄντως θεόν] [[καὶ οὕτως . . . καὶ φυσικῶν]] κατάπτυσον τῆς ὕλης.

17. καταδραμοῦσα ἐπὶ τὸν Ποιμάνδρην (Ποιμένανδρα MS.), καὶ βαπτισθεῖσα τῷ κρατῆρι. There can be no doubt that in these words Zosimus refers to two of the *libelli* which have come down to us in the *Corpus Hermeticum*, viz. *Corp.* I (Ποιμάνδρης) and *Corp.* IV. ('Ο κρατήρ). Poimandres is ὁ τῆς αὐθεντίας νοῦς; and the κρατήρ is the tank or font filled with νοῦς into which men are invited to plunge. Thus both phrases alike mean 'betake yourself to νοῦς; attach yourself to τὰ νοητά, and abandon τὰ σωματικά'. And this agrees with the preceding injunction τῆς ὕλης κατάπτυσον.

If Zosimus read *Corp.* I, he must have found the name of the divine visitant there written in the form Ποιμάνδρης, and could have no reason for altering the spelling of it in his reference to that document ; it is therefore to be presumed that he wrote Ποιμάνδρην, and that this was changed into Ποιμένανδρα by a transcriber to whom the name Poimandres was probably unknown.

18. ἀνάδραμε ἐπὶ τὸ γένος τὸ σόν. The human soul, *qua* νοερά, is συγγενὴς τῷ θεῷ, or τοῖς ἄνω; consequently, Theosebeia, in ascending to the world of νοητά, will be rejoining her own γένος.

In this passage, Zosimus, in speaking of the τελείωσις of the soul, employs terms taken from philosophic *Hermetica*. In Book XII of his longest work (Syriac translation), he speaks on the same subject in the language of some sect of Christian Gnostics. Having mentioned a certain mirror, made of electrum, which seems to have been made use of in the ritual of some religious cult, he there goes on to say : 'This mirror represents the divine spirit.[1] When the soul looks at itself in the mirror, it sees the shameful things that are in it, and rejects them ; it makes its stains disappear, and remains without blame. When it (*sc.* the soul) is purified, it imitates, and takes for its model, the holy spirit ; it becomes spirit itself ; it possesses calm, and returns unceasingly[2] to that superior state in which one knows

---

[1] τὸ θεῖον πνεῦμα.

[2] I. e. 'returns to that superior state &c., and abides in it without cease' (?).

⟨God⟩ and is known ⟨by God⟩.   Then, having come to be stainless, it gets rid of its own bonds, and of those ⟨things⟩ which are common to it with its body, and it ⟨raises itself⟩ towards the Omnipotent. What says the philosophic word?   "Know thyself."   It indicates thereby the spiritual and intellectual[1] mirror.   What is this mirror then, if not the divine and primordial spirit?   Unless one says that it is ⌐the principle of principles⌐, the Son of God, the Word, he whose thoughts and sentiments proceed also from the holy spirit.[2]

'Such, lady, is the explanation of the mirror.   When a man looks in it and sees himself in it, he turns his face away from all that is called gods and daemons, and, attaching himself to the holy spirit, he becomes a perfect man;[3] he sees God who is in him, by the intermediation of this holy spirit.

'This mirror is placed above the Seven Gates,[4] on the eastern side, in such a way that he who looks in it sees the East, where burns the intellectual light[5] which is above the veil.   ⌐That is why it is placed also at the southern side, above all the gates which correspond to the seven heavens⌐,[6] above this visible world, above the Twelve Houses[7] and the Pleiades, which are the world of the Thirteen.[8]   Above them exists this eye of the ⌐invisible senses⌐, this eye of the spirit, which is present there and in all places.   One sees there this perfect spirit, in the power of which all is found, ⌐from the present time until death⌐.[9]

'. . . Transmit this, ⟨lady,⟩ to those of the philosophers[10] who are

---

[1] πνευματικὸν καὶ νοητόν.

[2] There seems to be some corruption in the sentence 'Unless . . . holy spirit'. As to 'the Son of God', see Zosimus i, §§ 14–18.

[3] τελειοῦται or τέλειος γίνεται.

[4] Zosimus has said shortly before that the material mirror of electrum, the mention of which gave occasion for this digression, was 'placed in charge of the priests, in the temple called the Seven Gates'.   The 'gates which correspond to the seven heavens' may be compared with the κλῖμαξ ἑπτάπυλος of the Mithraists.

[5] τὸ νοερὸν (or νοητὸν) φῶς.

[6] The meaning of the original was probably that the material mirror was placed at the eastern side of a certain temple or place of worship in Egypt, called 'the Seven Gates', but the metaphorical 'mirror' (also called 'the eye of the spirit'), of which Zosimus takes that material mirror to be a symbol, is situated above the visible heavens.

[7] I. e. the twelve Signs of the Zodiac.

[8] Compare the 'thirteenth Aeon', frequently spoken of in the Coptic-Gnostic documents edited by C. Schmidt.

[9] Zosimus may perhaps have said here that it is possible for us to see 'the perfect spirit' even during our present life on earth, but that we shall be more completely united with it after death.

[10] I. e. students of philosophy.   It seems that Theosebeia had gathered round her a group of pupils.

worthy of it, and teach them the things of the spirit. Turn yourself away from the ancient ⟨doctrines⟩, and recognize that all this exposition contains the type of the invisible things.[1]

'. . . Raise yourself by your thought out of the inferior sphere, which is a part of the ⟨material⟩ universe; behold your soul, by means of this spiritual mirror of ⁔electrum, ⌜made with⌝ the two intelligences, that is, ⌜with⌝ the Son of God, the Word, joined to the holy spirit, and filled with the spirituality of the Trinity. Communicate it (sc. the knowledge of "the things of the spirit") without jealousy[2] to those who are worthy of it and who shall ask it from you, in order that even here below you may possess a great good; I mean, the souls that you will save, and that you will direct towards the incorporeal and incorruptible nature.'[3]

Addenda. Among the numerous quotations from and references to Hermes which occur in the Greek alchemistic texts, there are a few which it seems worth while to append here, though they cannot be assigned to the class of 'philosophic or religious' *Hermetica.*

(a) The alchemist Olympiodorus, who probably wrote in the fifth century, quotes Zosimus as follows [4]:—

καὶ Ζώσιμος ἐν τῇ κατ' ἐνέργειαν[5] βίβλῳ ⌜τοῦ λόγου⌝[6] φησίν·[7] " ὅτι ἀληθῆ σοι προσφωνῶ, μάρτυρα καλῶ Ἑρμῆν λέγοντα·[8] Ἄπελθε πρὸς ⌜ἀχααβ⌝ τὸν γεωργόν, καὶ μαθήσῃ ὡς ὁ σπείρων σῖτον σῖτον γεννᾷ." οὕτω γάρ σοι κἀγὼ ἔλεγον[9] τὰς οὐσίας ἀπὸ τῶν οὐσιῶν βάπτεσθαι, κ.τ.λ.

According to Olympiodorus, then, the words Ἄπελθε κ.τ.λ. were ascribed by Zosimus to Hermes. But in another alchemistic document, in which the same saying occurs in a completer form, it is not ascribed to Hermes, but is put into the mouth of Isis. That document is extant in two different recensions, Berthelot p. 28 (cod. A) and p. 33 (cod. L). It begins thus :—

---

[1] This appears to mean that the metallurgical processes described by Zosimus in his work on alchemy may be taken as symbols of 'invisible things', and may be thus employed as means of teaching philosophic or religious truths. What he has just said about 'the mirror of electrum' is an instance of such teaching.

[2] φθόνος.

[3] τὴν ἀσώματον καὶ ἄφθαρτον φύσιν (= οὐσίαν).

[4] Berthelot p. 89 ; codd. ML.

[5] αὐτοῦ add. L.

[6] τοῦ λόγου M : τοῦ καταλόγου L.

[7] φησίν L : om. M.

[8] ὅτι ἀληθῆ . . . Ἑρμῆν λέγοντα M : οὕτως ἐγώ σοι προσφωνῶ, καὶ καλῶ τὸν Ἑρμῆν, ἀληθῆ μάρτυρα, λέγοντα L.

[9] ἔλεγον M : λέγω L.

Cod. A

Ἴσις προφῆτις τῷ υἱῷ Ὥρῳ.
Ἀπιέναι σου μέλλοντος, ὦ τέκνον,
ἐπὶ ἀπίστου Τύφωνος μάχης καταγωνίσασθαι περὶ τοῦ πατρός σου
βασιλείας, ⌜γενομένης μου Ὁρμα-
νουθὶ ἱερᾶς τέχνης Αἰγύπτου⌝ καὶ
ἐνταῦθα ἱκανὸν χρόνον διέτριβον.

κατὰ δὲ τὴν τῶν καιρῶν παραχώ-
ρησιν [2] καὶ τὴν τῆς ⟨σ⟩φαιρικῆς [3]
κινήσεως ἀναγκαίαν φοράν,

συνέβη τινὰ τῶν ἐν τῷ πρώτῳ
στερεώμ⟨α⟩τι [5] διατριβόντω⟨ν⟩ [τὸν
ἕνα τῶν] [7] ἀγγέλων, ἄνωθεν ἐπιθεω-
ρήσαντά με, βουληθῆναι [τῆς] [9] πρὸς
ἐμὲ μίξεως κοινωνίαν ποιῆσαι.[10]

φθάσαντος δὲ αὐτοῦ, καὶ εἰς τοῦτο
γίγνεσθαι μέλλοντος,[11] οὐκ ἐπέτρεπον
ἐγώ, πυνθάνεσθαι βουλομένη [12] τὴν
τοῦ χρυσοῦ καὶ ἀργύρου κατασκευήν.

ἐμοῦ δὲ τοῦτο αὐτὸν [13] ἐρωτη-
σάσης,

⟨οὐκ⟩ ἔφη [ὁ] αὐτῷ [14] ἐφιέσθαι
περὶ τούτο⟨υ⟩ [15] ἐξειπε⟨ῖ⟩ν,[16] διὰ τὴν
τῶν μυστηρίων ὑπερβολήν·

Cod. L

Ἴσις προφῆτις τῷ υἱῷ αὐτῆς Ὥρῳ.
Σὺ μὲν ἐβουλήθης, ὦ τέκνον, ἀπιέναι ἐπὶ τῆς τοῦ Τύφωνος μάχης,
ὥστε καταγωνίσασθαι περὶ τῆς τοῦ
πατρός σου βασιλείας· ἐγὼ δὲ μετὰ
τὴν σὴν ἀποδημίαν παρεγενόμην εἰς
Ὁρμανουθί, ὅπου ἡ ἱερὰ τέχνη τῆς
Αἰγύπτου μυστικῶς κατασκευάζεται.
ἐνταῦθα δὲ ἱκανὸν χρόνον διατρίψασα
ἐβουλόμην παραχωρῆσαι.[1]

ἐν δὲ τῷ ἀναχωρεῖν με,

ἐπ[ιτ]εθεώρησέ [4] μέ τις [τῶν
προφητῶν ἢ] [6] τῶν ἀγγέλων οἳ
διέτριβον [8] ἐν τῷ πρώτῳ στερεώματι·
ὃς προσελθὼν ἐμοὶ ἐβούλετο μίξεως
κοινωνίαν πρὸς ἐμὲ ποιῆσαι.

ἐγὼ δὲ οὐκ ἐπέτρεπον αὐτῷ εἰς
τοῦτο γίνεσθαι μέλλοντι, ἀλλ'
ἀπῄτουν ἀπ' αὐτοῦ τὴν τοῦ χρυσοῦ
καὶ ἀργύρου κατασκευήν.

αὐτὸς δέ μοι ἀπεκρίνατο οὐκ
ἐξεῖναι αὐτῷ περὶ τούτου ἐξειπεῖν,
διὰ τὴν τοῦ μυστηρίου ὑπερβολήν·

---

[1] Perhaps ἀναχωρῆσαι.
[2] Perhaps περιχώρησιν.
[3] σφαιρικῆς coni. Ruelle : φευρικῆς A.
[4] ἐπεθεώρησε scripsi : ἐπιτεθεώρηκε L.
[5] πρώτῳ στερεώματι Ruelle : πρωτοστερεόντι A.
[6] τῶν προφητῶν ἢ seclusi.
[7] διατριβόντων scripsi : διατρίβοντα τὸν ἕνα τῶν A.
[8] οἳ διέτριβον scripsi : ὃς διέτριβεν L. [9] τῆς seclusi.
[10] ποιῆσαι Ruelle : ποιήσας A.
[11] Perhaps φθάσαντος δὲ αὐτοῦ εἰς ⟨...⟩ (i. e. when he had arrived at the place where I was), καὶ συγγίνεσθαί ⟨μοι⟩ μέλλοντος.
[12] βουλομένη coni. Ruelle after L : βουλομένου A.
[13] αὐτὸν scripsi : αὐτῷ A.
[14] οὐκ ἔφη αὐτῷ scripsi (οὐκ Ruelle) : ἔφη ὁ αὐτὸς A.
[15] τούτου scripsi : τοῦτο A.
[16] ἐξειπεῖν coni. Ruelle : ἐξεῖπεν A.

τῇ δὲ ἑξῆς ἡμέρᾳ παραγενήϲεϲθαι[1]
[τὸν τούτου][2] μείζονα ἄγγελον,
⟨καλούμενον⟩[3] Ἀμναήλ, κἀκεῖνον
ἱκανὸν εἶναι [περὶ] τῆς [τούτων][5]
ζητήσεως ἐπίλυσιν ποιησάσθαι.

ἔλεγεν δὲ [περὶ][7] σημεῖον [αὐτοῦ]
ἔχειν[8] αὐτὸν ἐπὶ τῆς κεφαλῆς, [καὶ
ἐπιδείκνυσθαι][9] κεράμιον ἀπίσσωτον
ὕδατος διαυγοῦς πλῆρες.

⟨καὶ οὗτος μὲν οὐκ⟩[10] ἐβούλετο τὸ-
ἀληθὲς λέγειν·

τῆ⟨ς⟩ δὲ ἑξῆς ἡμέρα⟨ς⟩ ἐπεμφανεί-
σηϲ,[11] καὶ τοῦ ἡλίου μέσον δρόμον
ποιοῦντος,

κατῆλθεν ὁ τούτου μείζων Ἀμναήλ,
τῷ αὐτῷ περὶ ἐμὲ λ φθεὶς[13] πόθῳ.

⟨καὶ ὁ μὲν⟩[16] οὐκ ἀνέμενεν,[17] ἀλλ᾽
ἔσπευδεν ἐφ᾽ ὃ [υ][18] καὶ παρῆν·

ἐγὼ δὲ οὐχ ἧττον ἐφρόντιζον
⟨τοῦ⟩[19] περὶ τούτων ἐρευνᾶν.[20]

ἐγχρονίζοντος δὲ αὐτοῦ,

τῇ δὲ ἑξῆς ἡμέρᾳ ⌜ἦλθε πρός με
ὁ πρῶτος ἄγγελος καὶ προφήτης
αὐτῶν καλούμενος⌝ Ἀμναήλ.[4]

[ἐγὼ δὲ πάλιν αὐτὸν περὶ τῆς τοῦ
χρυσοῦ καὶ ἀργύρου κατασκευῆς
ἐπηρώτων.][6]
⌜ἐκεῖνος δέ μοι ἐπεδείκνυέ τι
σημεῖον ὅπερ εἶχεν ἐπὶ τῆς κεφαλῆς
αὐτοῦ, καὶ κεράμιόν τι ἀπίσσωτον
πλῆρες ὕδατος διαυγοῦς ὅπερ εἶχεν
ἐν ταῖς χερσί.⌝

καὶ ⟨οὗτος μὲν⟩ οὐκ ἐβούλετο τὸ
ἀληθὲς εἰπεῖν·

τῇ δὲ ἑξῆς ἡμέρᾳ

[πάλιν][12] ἐλθὼν πρὸς ἐμὲ ⟨ὁ
Ἀμναήλ⟩[14] κατελήφθη [τοῦ] ἔρωτι[15]
πρὸς ἐμέ.

καὶ ἔσπευδεν ἐφ᾽ ὃ παρῆν·

ἐγὼ δὲ οὐκ ἐφρόντιζον αὐτοῦ.

ἐκεῖνος δὲ ἀεί με ἐπείρα καὶ
παρεκάλει· ἐγὼ δὲ

---

[1] παραγενήσεσθαι scripsi : παραγίγνεσθαι A.
[2] τὸν τούτου seclusi.   [3] καλούμενον addidi.
[4] This sentence, as well as ⌜ἐκεῖνος δὲ ... ταῖς χερσί⌝ below, ought to be in *oratio obliqua*, as are the corresponding passages in A. The angel tells Isis that a greater angel, named Amnael, will come to her; and in order that she may be able to identify that greater angel when he comes, he mentions a certain mark by which Amnael may be known.
[5] περὶ τούτων was written as an alternative for τῆς ζητήσεως.
[6] ἐγὼ .. ἐπηρώτων seclusi.   [7] περὶ seclusi.
[8] ἔχειν scripsi : αὐτοῦ ἐλεῖν A.   [9] καὶ ἐπιδείκνυσθαι seclusi.
[10] καὶ ... οὐκ addidi.
[11] τῆς ... ἐπεμφανείσης scripsi : τῇ δὲ ἑξῆς ἡμέρᾳ ἐπεμφανήσας A.
[12] πάλιν seclusi.   [13] ληφθεὶς scripsi : λειφθεὶς A.
[14] ὁ Ἀμναήλ addidi.
[15] ἔρωτι scripsi : τοῦ ἔρωτος L.   [16] καὶ ὁ μὲν addidi.
[17] ἀνέμενεν coni. Ruelle : ἀνέμενον A.
[18] ὁ scripsi : οὗ A : ᾧ L.   [19] τοῦ addidi.
[20] Perhaps ἐρωτᾶν. This sentence was misunderstood by the writer of the L-recension.

οὐκ ἐπεδίδουν ἐμαυτήν, ἀλλ' ἐπεκράτουν τῆς τούτου[1] ἐπιθυμίας, ἄχρις ἂν
τὸ σημεῖον τὸ ἐπὶ τῆς κεφαλῆς αὐτοῦ[2] ἐπιδείξηται,[3] καὶ τὴν τῶν
ζητουμένων μυστηρίων παράδοσιν ἀφθόνως καὶ ἀληθῶς ποιήσηται.

λοιπὸν οὖν καὶ τὸ σημεῖον ἐπεδείκνυτο, καὶ τῶν μυστηρίων ⟨τ⟩η⟨ν⟩
παράδοσιν ἐποιεῖτο.[4]

⌈καὶ ἐπὶ παραγγελίας καὶ⌉ ὅρκους   ἀρξαμένου αὐτοῦ πρότερον λέγειν
⌈ἐκχωρίσας⌉ ἔλεγεν·[5]   ⌈παραγγελίας καὶ⌉ ὅρκους πρὸς ἐμὲ
                                         οὕτως·

Ὁρκίζω σε εἰς οὐρανὸν ⟨καὶ⟩ γῆν, ⟨καὶ εἰς⟩[6] φῶς καὶ σκότος.

ὁρκίζω σε εἰς πῦρ καὶ ὕδωρ καὶ ἀέρα καὶ γῆν.

ὁρκίζω σε εἰς ὕψος οὐρανοῦ [καὶ γῆς][7] καὶ Ταρτάρου βάθος.

ὁρκίζω σε εἰς Ἑρμῆν καὶ Ἄνουβιν.[8]

⟨ὁρκίζω σε εἰς⟩ [[ὕλαγμα]] τὸν   καὶ εἰς [[ὕλαγμα]] τὸν [κερκ]
[κερκ] ο⟨ὐ⟩ροβ⟨όρον⟩ δράκοντα.[9]   οὐροβόρον δράκοντα,

⟨ὁρκίζω σε εἰς⟩ ⟨⟨ὕλαγμα⟩⟩ ⟨Κερ-   καὶ ⟨⟨ὕλαγμα⟩⟩ κυνὸς τρικεφάλου
βέρου⟩, τοῦ φύλακο⟨ς τοῦ Ἅιδου.⟩[10] τοῦ Κερβέρου, τοῦ φύλακος τοῦ
                                       Ἅιδου.

ὁρκίζω σε εἰς τὸ πορθμ⟨ε⟩ῖον ἐκεῖνο[ν],[11] καὶ ⌈Ἀχέροντα⌉[12] ναυτίλον.

[1] τῆς τούτου A : αὐτὸν τῆς τούτων L.

[2] αὐτοῦ L : om. A.

[3] ἐπιδείκνυται A : ἐπιδείξηται L.

[4] τὴν παράδοσιν ἐποιεῖτο scripsi : ἤρχετο A : ἡ παράδοσις ἐποιεῖτο L. (Perhaps
καὶ τῆς τῶν μυστηρίων παραδόσεως ἤρχετο.)

[5] Perhaps something like πρότερον δὲ σιγᾶν παρήγγειλεν, ὅρκους λέγων. (Compare τούτοις με ἐφορκίσας παρήγγειλεν μηδενὶ μεταδιδόναι below.)

[6] καὶ γῆν, καὶ εἰς scripsi: γῆν AL.

[7] καὶ γῆς has come from καὶ γῆν in the preceding line; [or accus. omitted after
γῆς].

[8] Ἀννουβιν L.

[9] ὁρκίζω σε εἰς τὸν οὐροβόρον δράκοντα scripsi : ὕλαγμα τῶν κερκορου δράκοντα A :
καὶ εἰς ὕλαγμα τοῦ κερκουροβόρου δράκοντος L.

The οὐροβόρος δράκων, i. e. the snake swallowing its own tail (a symbol of the
cyclic and unendingly renewed activity of the cosmic powers), was well known in
Roman Egypt. There are pictures of it in the alchemistic documents. Olympiodorus (Berthelot p. 80) says that ἱερογραμματεῖς τινες τῶν Αἰγυπτίων, βουλόμενοι
⟨τὸν⟩ κόσμον ἐγχαράξαι ἐν τοῖς ὀβελίσκοις . . ., δράκοντα ἐγκολάπτουσιν οὐροβόρον;
and that this symbol signifies ⟨τὸν⟩ τὴν ἀρχὴν ἐν τῷ τέλει ⟨θέντα⟩, καὶ τὸ τέλος ἐν
τῇ ἀρχῇ.

Snakes do not bark; but dogs do. ὕλαγμα therefore, if that is the right reading,
must have been originally connected with Κερβέρου, and not with δράκοντα.—κερκ
may have come from κερβ⟨έρου⟩; and ὕλαγμα κερβ may have been shifted before
the two recensions diverged.

Lobeck Aglaophamus p. 740, quoting this ὁρκισμός (which he calls ' formulam
adjurationis e libro Isidos transscriptam a Borrichio in Hermet. Sap. p. 47 '), gives
καὶ τὸν νεκρῶν δράκοντα φύλακα in place of ὕλαγμα τῶν κερκορου δράκοντα τὸν
φύλακα (cod. A).

[10] τὸν φύλακα A.

[11] τὸ πορθμεῖον ἐκεῖνο Ruelle : τὸ πρόθμιον ἐκεῖνον A : τὸν πορθμέα ἐκεῖνον L:
πορθμίον ἐκεῖνο Lobeck.

[12] Ἀχαίροντα Lobeck. Read either καὶ τὸν Ἀχερόντιον (coni. Ruelle) or καὶ Χάρωνα.

ὁρκίζω σε εἰς τὰς τρεῖς ἀνάγκας καὶ μάστιγας καὶ ξίφος.[1]

τούτοις με ἐφορκίσας παρήγγειλεν μηδενὶ μεταδιδόναι εἰ μὴ μόνον τέκνῳ καὶ φίλῳ[2] γνησίῳ·	τούτοις πᾶσί με ἐφορκίσας παρ- αγγέλλειν ἐπεχείρησε μηδενὶ μετα- διδόναι εἰ μὴ μόνον τέκνῳ καὶ φίλῳ γνησίῳ.
⌐ἵνα εἰ αὐτὸς σύ, καὶ σὺ εἰ αὐτός⌐.[3]	σὺ δὲ αὐτός, ὦ τέκνον,
παρελθὼν οὖν [σκοπῆσον καὶ][4] ἐρώτησον ⌐ἀχαραν⌐ τὸν γεωργὸν [καὶ μάθε αὐτοῦ][5] τί μέν ἐστι τὸ σπειρόμενον, τί δὲ καὶ τὸ θεριζό- μενον·	ἄπελθε πρός τινα γεωργόν, καὶ ἐρώτησον αὐτὸν τί μέν ἐστι τὸ σπειρόμενον, τί δέ ἐστι τὸ θεριζό- μενον.
καὶ μαθήσ(ῃ)[6] ὅτι ⟨ὁ⟩ σπείρων ⟨σῖ⟩τον[7] σῖτον καὶ θερίσει, καὶ ὁ σπείρων [τὸν] κριθὴν[8] ὁμοίως καὶ κριθὴν θερίσει.	καὶ μαθήσῃ ἀπ' αὐτοῦ ὅτι ὁ σπείρων σῖτον σῖτον καὶ θερίζει, καὶ ὁ σπείρων κριθὴν κριθὴν καὶ θερίζει.

ταῦτα,[9] ὦ τέκνον, διὰ προοιμίου[10] ἀκηκοώς, ἐννόησον[11] τὴν [του] τῶν ὅλων[12] δημιουργίαν τε καὶ γέννησιν, καὶ γνῶθι ὅτι ἄνθρωπος ἄνθρωπον οἶδεν σπείρειν, καὶ [ὁ] λέων λέοντα, καὶ [ὁ][13] κύων κύνα· εἰ δέ τι τῶν παρὰ φύσιν συμβαίνει γενέσθαι, ὥσπερ τέρας γεννᾶται,[14] καὶ οὐκ ἔχει σύστασιν.[15] ἡ γὰρ φύσις τῇ φύσει τέρπεται, καὶ ἡ φύσις τὴν φύσιν νικᾷ.[16]

---

[1] τάς τρεῖς ἀνάγκας, ⟨πῦρ⟩ ('id est lumina vel taeda in quaestionibus adhibita') καὶ μάστιγας καὶ ξίφος coni. Lobeck.

[2] καὶ φίλῳ secludendum? ἢ φίλῳ Lobeck.

[3] Perhaps τοιοῦτος δὲ σὺ εἶ αὐτός.

[4] σκόπησον καὶ seclusi.

[5] καὶ μάθε has come from καὶ μαθήσῃ below.

[6] μαθήσῃ scripsi : μάθῃς A.

[7] ὁ σπείρων σῖτον scripsi : σπεῖρον τὸν A (σπείρων τὸν σῖτον Ruelle).

[8] κριθὴν scripsi (τὴν κριθὴν Ruelle) : τὸν κρίθον A.

[9] καὶ ταῦτα L.

[10] προοίμιον AL.

[11] ἐνόησον A.

[12] τὴν τῶν ὅλων scripsi : τὴν τούτων ὅλην AL.

[13] ὁ bis seclusi.

[14] τέρας γεννᾶται Ruelle : πέρασγεννᾷ τε A.

[15] οὐκ ἔχει σύστασιν scripsi (οὐχ ἕξει σύστασιν Ruelle) : οὐτεξεισίστασιν A.

[16] τῇ φύσει τέρπεται scripsi : τὴν φύσιν τέρπεται A : τὴν φύσιν τέρπει L. This aphorism, or a longer form of it (ἡ φύσις τῇ φύσει τέρπεται, καὶ ἡ φύσις τὴν φύσιν κρατεῖ, καὶ ἡ φύσις τὴν φύσιν νικᾷ), is frequently quoted by the alchemists. [For τέρπει cf. ἡ τῶν φύσεων συγγένεια τέρπει τὰς ὁμοουσίους φύσεις Berthelot, p. 210.] It was ascribed to Ostanes, and was supposed to be a compendium of the alchemistic truths which Democritus learnt from that teacher (Berthelot p. 57 and p. 41 ff.). Its obscurity was doubtless intentional. The alchemist Synesius, commenting on it (Berthelot p. 63), says μὴ ἄρα τοῦτο ἔλεγεν ὁ φιλόσοφος·—ὦ φύσεις οὐράνιοι, φύσεων δημιουργοί, ταῖς μεταβολαῖς νικῶσαι τὰς φύσεις;—ναί. The alchemist Stephanus, who wrote in the seventh century, begins his treatise περὶ χρυσοποιίας (published by Ideler, *Physici et medici graeci minores*, II, pp. 199–253) by expand- ing the saying ἡ φύσις τῇ φύσει τέρπεται κ.τ.λ. into a long rigmarole, the meaning of which (if there is any meaning in it) I have failed to discover.

⌜αὕτη οὖν δυνάμεως θείας μετε-
σχηκότες καὶ παρουσίας εὐτυχήσαντες κἀκείνοις προσλαμπομένοις
αὐτοῖς ἐξ αἰτήσεως¹ ἐξ ἄμμων καὶ
οὐκ ἐξ ἄλλων οὐσιῶν ⌜κατασκευά-
σαντες ἐπέτυχον¹ διὰ τὸ τῆς οὔσης
φύσεως ὑπάρχειν τὴν προβαλλομέ-
νην ὕλην τοῦ κατασκευαζομένου¹.

δεῖ οὖν ἐξ ἄμμων καὶ οὐκ ἐξ
ἄλλων οὐσιῶν κατασκευάζειν τὴν
ὕλην.

ὡς γὰρ προεῖπον ὅτι [ὁ]² σῖτος
σῖτον γεννᾷ, καὶ ἄνθρωπος ἄνθρωπον
[σπείρει],³ οὕτως καὶ [ὁ]⁴ χρυσὸς
χρυσὸν [θερίζει,] [τὸ ὅμοιον τὸ
ὅμοιον].⁵

ὡς γὰρ προεῖπον ὅτι ὁ σῖτος τὸν
σῖτον γεννᾷ, καὶ ὁ ἄνθρωπος τὸν
ἄνθρωπον, οὕτω καὶ ὁ χρυσὸς τὸν
χρυσόν.

ἐφανερώθη νῦν δὴ⁶ τὸ μυστήριον.⁷
λαβὼν οὖν ὑδράργυρον, πῆξον αὐτὴν κ.τ.λ.⁸

καὶ ἰδού σοι πᾶν τὸ μυστήριον.

In this document, as in much of the alchemistic literature, Graeco-Egyptian and Jewish traditions are intermingled. Isis and Horus are Egyptian, as are also Hermes (the god) and Anubis in the oath. Cerberus and Charon come from Greek mythology. But the story told by Isis to her son is based on a passage in the Jewish Book of

---

¹ If we retain the plurals μετεσχηκύτες, εὐτυχήσαντες, and κατασκευάσαντες, Isis is apparently made to speak of earlier alchemists. But that cannot be right; she has learnt the secret of alchemy directly from an angel, and can have had no human predecessors in the art. ἐπέτυχον must therefore be 1 pers. sing.; and the passage might perhaps be emended in some such way as this: αὐτὴ (αὐτῇ A) οὖν δυνάμεως θείας μετεσχηκυῖα, καὶ ⟨ἀγγέλου⟩ παρουσίας εὐτυχήσασα, κἀκείνου ⟨μοι⟩ προσεπιλαβομένου, τῆς ζητήσεως ⟪⟨ἐπέτυχον⟩⟫ (i. e. I succeeded in finding out how to make gold); ⟨καὶ ἔμαθον ὅτι δεῖ⟩ ἐξ ἄμμων καὶ οὐκ ἐξ ἄλλων οὐσιῶν κατασκευάζειν τὴν ὕλην [[ἐπέτυχιν]]. The writer of the L-recension probably had this paragraph before him in a form more or less similar to the text of A, and finding it corrupt and unintelligible, wrote briefly what he took to be the gist of it, and omitted the rest.
ἄμμοι are sands or earths containing gold. Zosimus, τελ. ἀποχή init., says that ὅλον τὸ τῆς Αἰγύπτου βασίλειον . . . ἀπὸ τῶν δύο τούτων τῶν τεχνῶν ἐστιν τῶν τε καιρικῶν καὶ τῶν ψάμμων (the two methods by which he thought the ancient kings of Egypt had supplied themselves with gold), and speaks of ψαμμουργική and ἀμμοπλυσία (' gold-washing '). Strabo (3. 2. 8, p. 146) says that the gold-diggers in Spain πλύσει τῆς ἄμμου τὸν χρυσὸν ἐκλαμβάνουσι.
² ὁ seclusi.   ³ σπείρει seclusi.
⁴ ὁ seclusi.   ⁵ θερίζει et τὸ . . . ὅμοιον seclusi.
⁶ δὴ scripsi : δὲ A.
⁷ The secret appears to be that ' gold generates gold ', and that consequently, in order to make gold, you must use, as your raw material, sand in which some gold is already present. The alchemists believed that it was possible to ' double ' or increase a given quantity of gold, and some of them give recipes for doing this. It might easily be thought that gold or other metal was ' generated ' or brought into existence, when in reality the metal was merely extracted from an ore or mineral deposit in which it was already present, but invisible.
⁸ καὶ λαβὼν A. Here follow technical details.

Enoch (cc. 6–8, Swete *Old Testament in Greek* III, pp. 791–793,[1] in which the old Hebrew legend about 'the sons of God' and 'the daughters of men' (*Gen.* 6. 1–4) is retold with large additions.

The writer regards Isis and Horus, not as deities, but as human beings. He assumes Isis to be one of the 'daughters of men' spoken of in *Gen.* 6. 1 and the Book of Enoch; she is a human queen and προφῆτις.

In its form, this alchemistic Isis-document resembles the *Kore Kosmu* and the group of *Isis to Horus* documents connected with it (*Exc.* XXIII–XXVII). The relation is similar to that between the alchemistic and philosophic writings in which the teaching was ascribed to Hermes. There was certainly imitation on the one side or the other; but it may be doubted whether the alchemists imitated the philosophic writers or *vice versa*. And the same question arises with regard to the numerous magic, astrologic, and 'iatromathematic' *Hermetica* also. Were they earlier or later than the philosophic or religious *Hermetica*? This question cannot be answered with certainty; but I am inclined to think that the practice of putting the

---

[1] Syncellus (Dindorf, 1829, p. 20) quotes that passage as follows: ἐκ τοῦ πρώτου βιβλίου Ἐνὼχ περὶ τῶν ἐγρηγόρων· " καὶ ἐγένετο ὅτε ἐπληθύνθησαν οἱ υἱοὶ τῶν ἀνθρώπων, ἐγεννήθησαν αὐτοῖς θυγατέρες ὡραῖαι, καὶ ἐπεθύμησαν αὐτὰς οἱ ἐγρήγοροι, κ.τ.λ. . . . πρῶτος Ἀζαὴλ, ὁ δέκατος τῶν ἀρχόντων, ἐδίδαξε . . τὰ μέταλλα τῆς γῆς καὶ τὸ χρυσίον πῶς ἐργάσωνται, . . . καὶ τὸν ἄργυρον. ἔδειξε δὲ αὐτοῖς καὶ . . . τοὺς ἐκλεκτοὺς λίθους, καὶ τὰ βαφικά. (The arts which are here said to have been taught by one of the angels who were enamoured of 'the daughters of men' are almost the same as those with which the alchemists dealt.) . . . πάντες οὗτοι ἤρξαντο ἀνακαλύπτειν τὰ μυστήρια ταῖς γυναιξὶν αὐτῶν καὶ τοῖς τέκνοις αὐτῶν," κ.τ.λ.

Syncellus *ib.* goes on to say: ἄξιον δὲ καὶ Ζωσίμου τοῦ Πανοπολίτου φιλοσόφου χρῆσίν τινα παραθέσθαι περὶ αὐτῶν ἐκ τῶν γεγραμμένων αὐτῷ πρὸς Θεοσέβειαν ἐν τῷ ἐνάτῳ τῆς Ἰμοὺθ βιβλίῳ, ἔχουσαν ὧδε· " φάσκουσιν αἱ ἱεραὶ γραφαὶ [ἤτοι βίβλοι], ὦ γύναι, ὅτι ἔστι τι δαιμόνων γένος ὃ χρῆται γυναιξίν. ἐμνημόνευσε δὲ καὶ Ἑρμῆς ἐν τοῖς φυσικοῖς ⌐καὶ σχεδὸν ἅπας λόγος φανερὸς καὶ ἀπόκρυφος τοῦτο ἐμνημόνευσε¬. τοῦτο οὖν ἔφασαν αἱ ἀρχαῖαι καὶ θεῖαι γραφαί, ὅτι ἄγγελοί τινες ἐπεθύμησαν τῶν γυναικῶν, καὶ κατελθόντες ἐδίδαξαν αὐτὰς πάντα τὰ τῆς φύσεως ἔργα· ὧν χάριν, φησί, προσκρούσαντες, ἔξω τοῦ οὐρανοῦ ἔμειναν, ὅτι πάντα τὰ πονηρὰ καὶ μηδὲν ὠφελοῦντα τὴν ψυχὴν ἐδίδαξαν τοὺς ἀνθρώπους. ἐξ αὐτῶν φάσκουσιν αἱ αὐταὶ γραφαὶ καὶ τοὺς γίγαντας γεγενῆσθαι. ἔστιν οὖν (ἀπ') αὐτῶν ἡ πρώτη παράδοσις [Χημεῦ] (περὶ) τούτων τῶν τεχνῶν. ⌐ἐκάλεσε¬ (ἐκάλεσαν ?) δὲ ταύτην τὴν βίβλον Χημεῦ (*al.* Χημᾶ), ἔνθεν καὶ ἡ τέχνη χημεία καλεῖται " καὶ τὰ ἑξῆς.

The passage here quoted from Zosimus by Syncellus occurs in Book VIII (Syriac translation) of the longest work of Zosimus; and it follows from the words of Syncellus that the title by which that work as a whole was known to him was *Imuth*. (Zosimus himself, in Book VII, Syriac transl., refers to 'the first and second books of Imuth'; and in Book I, Zosimus says 'All the work of the books of alchemy is in the book Imuth'.) But if the numbering of the books in the Syriac translation is right, the ἐνάτῳ of Syncellus must be a mistake for ὀγδόῳ.

The 'holy writings' of which Zosimus here speaks are evidently those ascribed to Enoch. The Book of Enoch then was known to Zosimus, as well as to the alchemist who wrote the Isis-document.

teaching into the mouth of Hermes or Isis was begun by teachers of philosophy, and was adopted from them by alchemists, magicians, and astrologers, who were apt to borrow and employ for their own purpose forms which originally had a higher meaning. But when the practice had once been established in all these different fields, it was carried on independently in each of them ; and this or that alchemistic, magic, or astrologic *Hermeticum* may be either earlier or later than this or that philosophic *Hermeticum*.

In this *libellus*, the words ' Go to the husbandman ' &c. are spoken by Isis. But Zosimus, as quoted by Olympiodorus, attributes that same saying to Hermes. It is possible that Zosimus found it in a document in which Hermes was the speaker ; but it seems more likely that he was referring to this Isis-document, and assumed that the discourse of Isis to her son had been written by Hermes. (Similarly, the *Kore Kosmu*, in which the teacher is Isis, is called ' a writing of Hermes ' in its superscription.) And if so, the words ἐμνημόνευσε δὲ καὶ Ἑρμῆς ἐν τοῖς φυσικοῖς (' Hermes also, in his φυσικά, spoke ⟨of daemons who have intercourse with women⟩ '), in the passage of Zosimus which Syncellus quotes, may be taken to refer to this Isis-*libellus*, and to imply that Zosimus regarded it as one of the φυσικοὶ λόγοι of which Hermes was the author.

The saying presents itself in three different forms, viz. παρελθὼν οὖν ἐρώτησον ⌜ἀχαραν⌝ τὸν γεωργὸν κ.τ.λ. (cod. A) : ἄπελθε πρός τινα γεωργὸν καὶ ἐρώτησον αὐτὸν κ.τ.λ. (cod. L) : ἄπελθε πρὸς ⌜ἀχααβ⌝ τὸν γεωργὸν κ.τ.λ. (Zosimus *ap.* Olymp.). Are ἀχαραν and ἀχααβ corruptions of the name of some mythical inventor or teacher of agriculture, or corruptions of some Egyptian place-name ? [Or proverbial, like Hodge the farmer ?] The writer of the L-recension apparently found the word unintelligible, and substituted τινα.

(*b*) Olympiodorus (Berthelot p. 100) : Ἑρμῆς τοίνυν μικρὸν κόσμον ὑποτίθεται τὸν ἄνθρωπον.

The statement that man is a microcosm may have occurred in a *Hermeticum* of any kind,—philosophic, alchemistic, or other.

(*c*) Olympiodorus (Berthelot p. 101) : ἄνθρωπον γὰρ εἶναί φησι τὸν ἀλεκτρυόνα ὁ Ἑρμῆς καταραθέντα ὑπὸ τοῦ ἡλίου.[1] ταῦτα λέγει ἐν τῇ ἀρχαϊκῇ[2] βίβλῳ. ἐν αὐτῷ[3] δὲ μέμνηται καὶ περὶ τοῦ ἀσπάλακος, ὅτι καὶ αὐτὸς ἄνθρωπος ἦν, καὶ ἐγένετο θεοκατάρατος, ὡς ἐξειπὼν τὰ τοῦ ἡλίου μυστήρια· καὶ ἐποίησεν αὐτὸν τυφλόν. ἀμέλει καὶ ἐὰν φθάσῃ θεωρηθῆναι

---

[1] Cf. ὅπερ ἐστὶ κατηραμένον ὑπὸ τοῦ ἡλίου in *Corp.* II. 17 a.
[2] Perhaps ἀρχαι(ολογ)ικῇ.   [3] αὐτῇ?

ὑπὸ τοῦ ἡλίου, οὐ δέχεται αὐτὸν ἡ γῆ ἕως ἑσπέρας. ⌜λέγει ὅτι ὡς καὶ⌝ γιγνώσκων τὴν μορφὴν τοῦ ἡλίου ὁποία ἦν. καὶ ἐξώρισεν αὐτὸν ἐν τῇ μελαίνῃ γῇ, ὡς παρανομήσαντα, καὶ ἐξειπόντα τὸ μυστήριον τοῖς ἀνθρώποις.[1]

We learn from this that a book ascribed to Hermes, and called ἡ ἀρχαϊκὴ (?) βίβλος, contained two edifying tales, the moral of which was that it is bad to reveal the mysteries of the sun. [For ἡλίου ὁποία A reads ποίας preceded by the common sign of the sun and of gold; i. e. the scribe meant to signify χρυσοποιίας. It seems likely, as Berthelot suggests (vol. iii, p. 111), that both tales have an alchemical bearing. If so, the *Hermeticum* from which they were drawn would be alchemical rather than philosophical.]

(*d*) Berthelot p. 115 (cod. M):[2] Ἑρμοῦ ἐὰν μὴ τὰ σώματα ἀσωματώσῃς καὶ τὰ ἀσώματα σωματώσῃς, οὐδὲν ⌜τὸ προσδοκώμενον⌝ (read τῶν προσδοκωμένων) ἔσται.

This is an alchemistic aphorism. It probably means that one must change solids into liquids or vapours, and liquids or vapours into solids.[3] But this use of the word ἀσώματα may have been suggested to the alchemists by philosophic *Hermetica* in which ἀσώματα were spoken of in another sense.

(*e*) Olympiodorus, Berthelot p. 84 (cod. M): ὁμοίως καὶ ὁ Χήμης,[4] τῷ Παρμενίδῃ ἀκολουθήσας, φησίν " ἓν τὸ πᾶν, δι' οὗ τὸ πᾶν· τοῦτο γὰρ εἰ μὴ ἔχοι τὸ πᾶν, οὐδὲν τὸ πᾶν "[5].

This aphorism is repeatedly quoted by the alchemists. It may

---

[1] There is some confusion in the text. The passage would be more coherent if rewritten thus: καὶ ἐγένετο θεοκατάρατος, ὡς ἐξειπὼν τὰ τοῦ ἡλίου μυστήρια. καὶ ἐπαίησεν αὐτὸν τυφλὸν (ὁ θεός), [ ] ὡς [καὶ] ΓΝΟΝΤΑ τὴν μορφὴν τοῦ ἡλίου ὁποία ἦν ⟨⟨καὶ ἐξειπόντα τὸ μυστήριον τοῖς ἀνθρώποις⟩⟩· καὶ ἐξώρισεν αὐτὸν ἐν τῇ μελαίνῃ γῇ ὡς παρανομήσαντα [[ ]]. The man's crime was that he discovered the true form of the Sun-god, and made known to other men that holy secret; and his punishment was that he was changed into a mole. The mole is blind, and lives in darkness underground (ἐν τῇ μελαίνῃ γῇ); thus it is unable to see the sun, and is deprived of the blessings which the sun confers.
The man who was changed into a cock must also have committed some offence against the Sun-god; but what his offence was we are not told.
[2] Also Cod. Bodleianus, Canon. Gr. 95, f. 35 a.
[3] Cf. Olympiodorus, Berthelot p. 89: (. . .) εἰς οὐδὲν ἄλλο διαιρεῖται εἰ μὴ εἰς σῶμα καὶ ἀσώματον. ἡ δὲ τέχνη αὕτη ἀμφότερα δέχεται. τὰ μὲν σώματα λέγει εἶναι τὰ χυτά, τὰ δὲ ἀσώματα λίθους· οἷον ἀνούσια λέγει τὰς ψάμμους· τὰ δὲ χωρὶς πυρός, διὰ τὴν πρώτην ἐργασίαν.
The alchemist Stephanus (seventh century) said ' Copper is like man; it has a soul and a body. . . . The soul is the most subtle part; . . . the body is the weighty thing, material, terrestrial, and having a shadow. After a series of suitable treatments, the copper becomes shadowless ' (Berthelot, *La chimie au moyen âge*, I, p. 261).
[4] This name was probably invented to denote the unknown author of the book called *Chema*, of which Zosimus speaks. Χύμης M : Χήμης L.
[5] τοῦτο γὰρ κ.τ.λ. M : καὶ εἰ μὴ τὸ πᾶν ἔχῃ τὸ πᾶν, οὐδέν ἐστι τὸ πᾶν L.

have been based on something that had been said by one of the philosophic Hermetists, or by some one who resembled them in his way of thinking. [In Berthelot, vol. i, p. 131, the first figure of the Κλεοπάτρης Χρυσοποιΐα, evidently representing the οὐροβόρος δράκων, has three concentric circles. In the outer ring is inscribed the saying: Ἒν τὸ πᾶν καὶ δι' αὐτοῦ τὸ πᾶν καὶ εἰς αὐτὸ τὸ πᾶν καὶ εἰ μὴ ἔχοι τὸ πᾶν οὐδέν ἐστιν τὸ πᾶν.]

MARCELLUS OF ANCYRA [1]

Eusebius *c. Marcellum* 1. 4. § 39 *sqq.*: ταῦτ' εἰπὼν (*sc.* ὁ Μάρκελλος) ἀπὸ τοῦ Ναρκίσσου ἐπὶ τὸν Εὐσέβιον μεταβαίνει, κατηγορῶν ὅτι τὸν λόγον τοῦ θεοῦ θεὸν [2] εἶναι ὁμολογεῖ. γράφει δὲ (*sc.* Marcellus) περὶ αὐτοῦ (*sc.* Euseb.) ταῦτα· "διελεῖν γὰρ τὸν λόγον τοῦ θεοῦ τολμήσας, καὶ ἕτερον θεὸν τὸν λόγον ὀνομάσαι, οὐσίᾳ τε καὶ 5 δυνάμει διεστῶτα τοῦ πατρός, εἰς ὅσην βλασφημίαν ἐκπέπτωκεν (*sc.* Euseb.) ἔνεστιν σαφῶς ἀπ' αὐτῶν τῶν ὑπ' αὐτοῦ γραφέντων ῥητῶν ῥαδίως μανθάνειν. γέγραφεν δ' (Euseb.) αὐταῖς λέξεσιν οὕτως· 'οὐ δήπου δὲ ἡ εἰκὼν καὶ τὸ οὗ ἐστιν ἡ εἰκὼν ἓν καὶ ταυτὸν ἐπινοεῖται, ἀλλὰ δύο μὲν οὐσίαι καὶ δύο πράγματα καὶ δύο δυνάμεις, ὡς καὶ τοσαῦται 10 προσηγορίαι.'" καὶ ταῦτα ὡς καλῶς διαβάλλων προστίθησι (*sc.* Marcellus) λέγων "πῶς οὖν οὐ τὴν αὐτὴν οὗτοι (*sc.* Narcissus and Eusebius) τοῖς ἔξωθεν [3] κακίστην ὁδὸν τραπέντες τὰ αὐτὰ διδάξαι τε καὶ γράψαι προύθεντο, τοῦ μὲν Εὐσεβίου Οὐαλεντίνῳ [4] τε καὶ Ἑρμῇ ὁμοίως εἰρηκότος, [5] τοῦ δὲ Ναρκίσσου Μαρκίωνί τε καὶ Πλάτωνι;"

15

[1] Edited by Klostermann, *Eusebius, Werke*, Bd. IV, 1906 (Griech. Christl. Schriftsteller der ersten drei Jahrhunderte).

The work in which occurred the passage quoted by Eusebius was written by Marcellus in A.D. 335 (Bardenhewer, *Patrologie* p. 240), and was a defence of the Nicene doctrine against the Arians. It was directed chiefly against Asterius; but others also were attacked by Marcellus as Arians, and among them Eusebius of Caesarea, who replied to these attacks in his *c. Marcellum*.

[2] Perhaps (ἕτερον) θεὸν?

[3] 'Those outside (the Church)' means heretics and Pagans.

[4] As to Valentinus, cf. Pseudo-Anthimus (*Testim.*) § 9, where it is said that Valentinus took from Hermes and Plato a doctrine which he set forth in a book entitled Περὶ τῶν τριῶν φύσεων, and that this same doctrine was afterwards taught by the Arians.

[5] According to Marcellus then, Hermes taught something like what he accuses Eusebius of teaching; namely, that the Logos is a second God, distinct from the supreme God, of whom he is an εἰκών. It may be inferred from this that Marcellus knew of passages in the *Hermetica* (such as *Ascl. Lat.* I. 8, quoted by Lactantius and Pseudo-Anthimus,) in which the Kosmos was spoken of as a second God distinct from the first God and subordinate to him, and that he assumed the 'second God' spoken of in those passages to be the Logos of Christian theology. It is possible, but not certain, that Marcellus also knew of some Hermetic passages (such as some of those quoted by Cyril) in which the Logos was spoken of *eo nomine*.

PSEUDO-ANTHIMUS[1]

Ἀνθίμου ἐπισκόπου Νικομηδίας καὶ μάρτυρος ἐκ τῶν πρὸς Θεόδωρον περὶ τῆς ἁγίας ἐκκλησίας.[2]

1. ὥσπερ εἷς θεὸς καὶ εἷς υἱὸς θεοῦ καὶ ἓν πνεῦμα ἅγιον, οὕτως εἷς ἄνθρωπος ὑπὸ θεοῦ καὶ εἷς κόσμος ἐγένετο, [καὶ μία καθολικὴ καὶ ἀποστολικὴ ἐκκλησία][3] καὶ ἓν βάπτισμα καθ' ὅλου ὑπάρχει τοῦ κόσμου, ὥς φησι Παῦλος· "εἷς θεός, μία πίστις, ἓν βάπτισμα."[4] 2. μία τοίνυν καθολικὴ καὶ ἀποστολικὴ ἐκκλησία ἐστι καθ' ὅλης τῆς οἰκουμένης, ἥ τις ἀπὸ τῶν ἀποστόλων παραλαβοῦσα τὴν πίστιν ἄχρι νῦν διαφυλάττει. καθολικὴ δὲ εἴρηται διότι καθ' ὅλου τοῦ κόσμου κεχυμένη ὑπάρχει, κατὰ τὸ εἰρημένον....[5] 3. αἱ δὲ αἱρέσεις οὔτε ἀπὸ τῶν ἀποστόλων ἔλαβον[6] οὔτε ἀπὸ τῶν μαθητῶν αὐτῶν ἢ τῶν τούτων διαδόχων ἐπισκόπων· — ἐπεὶ οὐκ ἂν

---

[1] This extract has been edited by G. Mercati, *Studi e Testi* 5, Rome 1901, pp. 87-98. Mercati, from whose edition I take the text, says that it has been preserved in two MSS., viz. A (Cod. Ambrosianus, saec. XIII), which is the better of the two, and S (Escurial, saec. XIV).

[2] This is the title as given in A. Anthimus, bishop of Nicomedia, was martyred under Diocletian in A.D. 302 (Euseb. *Hist. eccl.* 8. 6. 6; *Chron. Pasch.* Dindorf I. 516). But in §§ 8-18 of the extract the Arians are discussed, and are spoken of as a definite and well-known sect of heretics, which would hardly be possible before the date of the Council of Nicaea, A.D. 325; and the fact that Asterius is mentioned by name (§ 10), and no other Arian (except Eusebius) is named, makes it probable that this part of the extract (§§ 8-18) was written at a time not far from A.D. 350. There is, as Mercati points out, a sudden jump at § 8 *init.* from the Gnostics of the second century to the Arians of the fourth century, and nothing is said about the not unimportant heresies which arose in the third century. There seems then to be a breach of continuity at that point; and there is also a breach of continuity at § 18 *fin.*, where the passage about the Arians ends. In § 19, the topic dealt with in §§ 1-7 is resumed, as if nothing had intervened, and the heresies are again spoken of collectively. It is possible therefore that §§ 1-7 and § 19 occurred in a book *Ad Theodorum de sancta ecclesia* written by Anthimus before A.D. 302, and that about A.D. 350 some one inserted in this book a passage about the Arians (§§ 8-18).

Hermes is mentioned in § 7; but with that exception, it is in §§ 8-18 alone that Hermes is spoken of (if we disregard the obscure words οἱ Ἑρμοῦ καὶ Σελεύκου in § 6). The writer of §§ 8-18 must, for the reasons I have given, be called *Pseudo*-Anthimus. It is not impossible that § 7 was written by Anthimus; but if it was, the words Ἑρμοῦ καὶ in it may have been added by the same man who inserted §§ 8-18.

[3] I have bracketed καὶ μία ... ἐκκλησία, which inappropriately anticipates what is said in § 2. Perhaps the sentence may have been originally written thus: ὥσπερ εἷς θεὸς (ἔστι) ..., καὶ εἷς ἄνθρωπος ὑπὸ θεοῦ καὶ εἷς κόσμος ἐγένετο, οὕτω καὶ ἓν βάπτισμα κ.τ.λ.

[4] *Eph.* 4. 5: εἷς κύριος, μία πίστις, ἓν βάπτισμα, εἷς θεὸς καὶ πατὴρ πάντων.

[5] Here are quoted *Ps.* 18 (19). 5, *Malachi* 1. 11, and *Isaiah* 49. 6.

[6] The object of ἔλαβον (perhaps τὰ δόγματα, or τὰς ἀφορμάς,) has been omitted.

ἐκαλοῦντο αἱρέσεις· αἱρέσεις γὰρ κέκληνται ἀπὸ τοῦ αἱρεῖσθαί τι ἴδιον καὶ
τούτῳ ἐξακολουθεῖν.[1] — οὔτε πάλιν πανταχοῦ εἰσιν, ἀλλ' εἰς τύπους σφόδρα
βραχεῖς περιγεγραμμέναι, ἔνθα ἴσχυσεν ὁ διάβολος πλανῆσαί τινας διὰ
φιλαρχίας κενῆς, ⟨καὶ⟩ τούτους προστάτας καταστῆσαι τῆς ἑαυτοῦ κακοτεχ-
νίας· ὅθεν οὐδὲ καθολικαὶ κέκληνται αἱ παρ' αὐτῶν ἐκκλησίαι.   5

4. οὐκοῦν ἀναγκαῖον εἰπεῖν πόθεν καὶ παρὰ τίνων τὰς ἀφορμὰς λαβόντες
οἱ αἱρετικοὶ [παρὰ αἱρετικῶν][2] κατηνέχθησαν εἰς τὸ τῆς ἀπωλείας βάραθρον.
ἔθος γὰρ τοῖς αἱρετικοῖς τὰ ἀλλήλων ὑφαιρεῖσθαι καὶ προσεξευρίσκειν
καινότερα, αὐχοῦντες εἶναι διδάσκαλοι[3] ἀλλήλων. 5. καὶ πρῶτον μὲν
συγχωρήσει θεοῦ Σαδδουκαῖοι, ἐκ τῶν Ἰουδαίων ὄντες, ἐκήρυξαν μὴ εἶναι   10
ἀνάστασιν,[4] μήτε[5] πνεῦμα ἅγιον ὁμολογοῦντες μήτε ἀγγέλους μήτε
προφήτας· ἀφ' ὧν Κήρινθος μικρὰ παραμείψας[6] παραδίδωσι τοῖς Ἐβιωναίοις.
6. πάλιν οἱ ἀπὸ Σίμωνος γνωστικοὶ λεγόμενοι Μένανδρος καὶ Σατορνῖνος
καὶ Βασιλείδης, Μάρκος τε καὶ Κολόρβασος[7] καὶ οἱ λοιποὶ καινότερα
ἀλλήλων παρεπενόησάν τε καὶ παρέδωκαν τοῖς ὑπ' αὐτῶν ἠπατημένοις,   15
ὅθεν καὶ γνωστικοὺς ἑαυτοὺς προσηγόρευσαν· ἐξ ὧν ἔλαβον οἵ τε Ὀφῖται
καὶ Καϊανῖται, Σηθῖται τε καὶ οἱ Ἑρμοῦ καὶ Σελεύκου,[8] καὶ ὁ λοιπὸς ὄχλος
τῶν αἱρετικῶν τῶν τὰ τοιαῦτα ληρούντων, ὡς ἀπὸ Νικολάου Καρποκρᾶς καὶ

---

[1] There is a collection of *Quaestiones in Novum Testamentum*, printed in Migne
P. G. 28. 711 *sqq.* under the heading ' S. Athanasius—Spuria '; and among the
questions and answers there given are the following : (724 A) *Quaest.* 37, Κυρίλλου,
Διὰ τί ἡ ἐκκλησία καλεῖται ἐκκλησία, καὶ διὰ τί καθολική ; *Resp.* ἐκκλησία μέν, διὰ
τὸ πάντας ἐκκαλεῖσθαι· καθολικὴ δέ, διότι καθ' ὅλου τοῦ κόσμου κεχυμένη ὑπάρχει.
Quaest. 38, Πόθεν λέγεται αἵρεσις ; *Resp.* ἀπὸ τοῦ αἱρεῖσθαί τι ἴδιον καὶ τοῦτο
ἐξακολουθεῖν. I.e. the explanation of καθολική that is given in the Anthimus-
extract (and presumably that of αἵρεσις also) is attributed to Cyril by the collector
of these *Quaestiones*.

[2] περὶ αἱρετικῶν seclusi.

[3] " αὐχοῦντας εἶναι διδασκάλους ? " Mercati. The anacoluthon αὐχοῦντες κ.τ.λ.
is not impossible ; but the connexion of this sentence with the context is not clear,
and the passage would read better if ἔθος γὰρ . . . διδάσκαλοι ἀλλήλων, as well as
the preceding παρὰ αἱρετικῶν· ἔθος γὰρ τοῖς αἱρετικοῖς κ.τ.λ. are a note written by a reader as his answer to the
question παρὰ τίνων τὰς ἀφορμὰς λαβόντες κ.τ.λ.

[4] *Matth.* 22. 23.

[5] Why not οὔτε ? Perhaps ⟨οἱ⟩ μήτε ? Epiphanius says that the Sadducees
denied the Holy Ghost.

[6] μικρὰ παραμείψας A : τινα παραλείψας S.

[7] We might have expected Valentinus to be included in this list. He is omitted
here, but is incidentally mentioned in § 9, in connexion with the Arians.

[8] Perhaps οἱ ⟨ἀπὸ⟩ Ἑρμοῦ καὶ Σελεύκου. But who are these ? I have found no
record elsewhere of heresiarchs named Hermes and Seleucus. Is Ἑρμοῦ a copyist's
error for Ἑρμογένους ? (As to Hermogenes, see Hippol. *Ref. haer.* 8. 17.)—
Seleucus of Alexandria (*Abammonis resp.* 8. 1 b, pp. 31 and 53 above) was a
Pagan θεολόγος who interpreted in a Neoplatonic sense the old Egyptian ' books
of Hermes ', and was probably nearly contemporary with Anthimus. Is it possible
that the writer means by ' those of (or from) Hermes and Seleucus ' some Christian
heretics who had borrowed their doctrines from this Seleucus, or were thought by
him to have done so ?

Πρόδικος καὶ Ἐπιφανής,[1] οἳ καινότερα[2] καὶ αὐτοὶ ἐπενόησαν. 7. πάντες δὲ οὗτοι παρὰ Ἑρμοῦ καὶ Πλάτωνος καὶ Ἀριστοτέλους τῶν φιλοσόφων τὰς ἀφορμὰς τῆς ἀσεβείας εἰλήφασι.[3]

8. τῆς δὲ ⌈ἐπιφθαρείσης⌉[4] αἱρέσεως τῶν Ἀρειομανιτῶν τῇ ἐκκλησίᾳ τοῦ θεοῦ ⟨. . .⟩,[5] ἀναγκαῖον δηλῶσαι καὶ περὶ αὐτῆς, ἵν᾽ εἰδέναι ἔχοις ὅτι μετ᾽ ἐντέχνου σοφιστείας ὑφείλοιτο τὰ δόγματα τῶν ἀρχαίων. 9. καὶ οὗτοι τοίνυν[6] διδάσκουσι ⟨. . .⟩ τρεῖς ὑποστάσεις, ὡς Οὐαλεντῖνος ὁ αἱρεσιάρχης πρῶτος ἐπενόησεν ἐν τῷ βιβλίῳ τῷ ἐπιγεγραμμένῳ αὐτῷ Περὶ τῶν τριῶν φύσεων·[7] αὐτὸς γὰρ ⟨. . .⟩ τρεῖς ὑποστάσεις καὶ τρία πρόσωπα πατρὸς καὶ υἱοῦ καὶ ἁγίου πνεύματος πρῶτος ἐπενόησε·[8] καὶ οὗτος δὲ παρὰ Ἑρμοῦ καὶ Πλάτωνος ὑφελόμενος εὑρίσκεται.

---

[1] Carpocrates and his son Epiphanes are spoken of by Clem. Alex. *Strom.* 3. 2. 5-9 ; and Prodicus, *ib.* 1. 15. 69 ; 3. 4. 30 ; 7. 7. 41.

[2] Καρποκρᾶς . . . καινότερα A: Καρποκράτους καὶ Προδίκου καὶ Ἐπιφανίου καὶ Νοταρίου S. ᴇ copyist of S has thus made an imaginary heresiarch Notarius out of a misreading.

[3] The writer holds that the Christian Gnostics got their heretical doctrines from Pagan philosophers. In this he is partly right. Most of the Christian Gnostics were more or less influenced by Pagan Platonism.
The mention of Hermes together with Plato and Aristotle shows that the writer (whether Anthimus or the Pseudo-Anthimus of *c.* A. D. 350) knew enough about the Greek *Hermetica* to be aware that their doctrine is mainly Platonic. He probably supposed that this doctrine had been taught by Hermes in Egypt at an early time, that his teaching was recorded in the *Hermetica*, and that Plato learnt his philosophy from the *Hermetica*, or from Egyptian teachers to whom the Hermetic doctrine had been transmitted.

[4] Perhaps ἐπιφθόρου, or some equivalent epithet.

[5] Perhaps ⟨ἐπιφανείσης⟩.

[6] καὶ περὶ . . . οὗτοι τοίνυν om. S.

[7] What were the three φύσεις concerning which Valentinus wrote in this book ? Probably not the three Persons of the Trinity, though something which he said about the three φύσεις was assumed by disputants in the Arian controversy to have reference to the three Persons. Perhaps his three φύσεις were τὸ πνευματικόν, τὸ ψυχικόν, τὸ ὑλικόν. Hippolytus, *Ref. haer.* 6. 37, after quoting Plato *Ep.* 2 (περὶ τὸν πάντων βασιλέα πάντα ἐστί, . . . δεύτερον περὶ τὰ δεύτερα, καὶ τρίτον περὶ τὰ τρίτα), says τούτοις περιτυχὼν ὁ Οὐαλεντῖνος ὑπεστήσατο "τὸν πάντων βασιλέα", ὃν ἔφη Πλάτων, οὗτος πατέρα καὶ βυθὸν καὶ ⌈πᾶσι γῆν⌉ (προαρχὴν coni. D. and S.) τῶν ὅλων αἰώνων· "δεύτερον περὶ τὰ δεύτερα" τοῦ Πλάτωνος εἰρηκότος, τὰ δεύτερα Οὐαλεντῖνος ⌈τοῦ ἐντὸς ὅρου τὸν ὅρον ὑπέθετο πάντας αἰῶνας⌉· καὶ "τρίτον περὶ τὰ τρίτα" τὴν ἔξω τοῦ ὅρου καὶ τοῦ πληρώματος διαταγὴν συνέθηκε πᾶσαν. Hippol. *ib.* 6. 32 reports Valentinus as saying θνητή τις ἐστιν ἡ ψυχή, μεσότης τις οὖσα· ὑποκάτω γάρ ἐστι τῆς ὀγδοάδος . . . ὑπεράνω δὲ τῆς ὕλης. Compare the Naassenes as reported by Hippolytus, *ib.* 5. 6: ἔστι γὰρ τῶν ὅλων τρία γένη κατ᾽ αὐτούς (*sc.* the Naassenes), ἀγγελικόν (= πνευματικόν), ψυχικόν, χοϊκόν. Hippol. *ib.* 5. 8 (Naassene 'Attis-document'): λέγουσι δὲ "ὁ λέγων τὰ πάντα ἐξ ἑνὸς συνεστάναι πλανᾶται· ὁ λέγων ἐκ τριῶν ἀληθεύει, καὶ περὶ τῶν ὅλων ἀπόδειξιν δώσει."

[8] There is some strange mistake here. As the text stands, we are told that the Catholic doctrine of the Trinity was first invented by the heretic Valentinus, and that the Arians borrowed that Catholic doctrine from him. The author of the passage cannot have meant that ; I have therefore marked a lacuna before τρεῖς ὑποστάσεις in both places. What he probably did mean might be expressed by writing in both places ⟨τὸ ἑτερουσίους εἶναι τὰς⟩ τρεῖς ὑποστάσεις. With this alteration, the meaning would be ' The heretical doctrine of τὸ ἑτερούσιον which is taugh

10. [διὸ]¹ καὶ πάλιν πρὸ αἰώνων² ἀναπλάττουσι³ δεύτερον θεὸν ὑπὸ πατρὸς γεγενῆσθαι, ὡς ὁ πρόκριτος παρ' αὐτοῖς Ἀστέριος⁴ ἔφη, διδαχθεὶς ὑπὸ Ἑρμοῦ τοῦ ἐπικληθέντος Τρισμεγίστου, φάσκει γὰρ οὕτως⁵ πρὸς Ἀσκληπιὸν τὸν ἰατρόν·⁶ "Ἄκουε τοιγαροῦν, Ἀσκληπιέ.⁷ ὁ κύριος καὶ τῶν πάντων ποιητής, ὃν καλεῖν θεὸν νενομίκαμεν, ἔτι⁸ 5 τὸν δεύτερον ἐποίησε θεὸν ὁρατὸν καὶ αἰσθητόν." ὅθεν αὐτῷ καὶ "ὁ μονογενὴς θεὸς" παρὰ τὸν θεῖον Ἰωάννην λέγοντα "υἱὸν μονογενῆ"⁹ προσερρύη.¹⁰ 11. εἶτα πάλιν ὁ Τρισμέγιστός φησιν· "ἐπεὶ οὖν τοῦτον ἐποίησεν πρῶτον καὶ μόνον καὶ ἕνα, κάλλι⟨στ⟩ος δὲ¹¹ αὐτῷ ἐφάνη καὶ πληρέστατος πάντων τῶν ἀγαθῶν, ἠγάσθη τε καὶ 10 πάνυ ἐφίλησεν αὐτὸν¹² ὡς ἴδιον τόκον." 12. τοίνυν ἡ περὶ θεοῦ

by the Arians was borrowed by them from Valentinus, who was the first (of the Christians) to think of it; Valentinus however did not invent it himself, but filched it from Hermes and Plato'. [Mercati suggests that this passage is derived from some such account of Valentinus as that attacked by Tertullian in *adv. Valentin.* 4.] Cf. Marcellus of Ancyra (*Testim.* p. 154).

¹ διὸ seclusi. καὶ πάλιν introduces the discussion of another error of the Arians, namely, the doctrine that the Son is a 'second' God, subordinate to the Father. The quotations which follow are intended to prove that the Arians got this doctrine from Hermes and Plato.

² πρὸ αἰώνων seems to be out of place; it ought to stand nearer to γεγενῆσθαι, to which it belongs in sense.

³ *Sc.* the Arians.

⁴ This is 'the sophist' Asterius of Cappadocia, an Arian, against whom Marcellus of Ancyra wrote in A.D. 335. This passage was probably written not long after that date.

⁵ φάσκει γὰρ οὕτως A : λέγει γὰρ οὗτος S.

⁶ The writer assumes Asclepius the pupil of Hermes to have been a physician. Cf. *Ascl. Lat.* III. 37, 'avus enim tuus, Asclepi, medicinae primus inventor'; and Herm. *ap.* Stob. *Exc.* XXVI. 9, ἰατρικῆς δὲ ⟨βασιλεὺς⟩ Ἀσκληπιὸς ὁ Ἡφαίστου.

⁷ The passage ἄκουε τοιγαροῦν ... ἴδιον τόκον is quoted from the Λόγος τέλειος πρὸς Ἀσκληπιόν; it is the Greek original of *Ascl. Lat.* I. 8. The same passage is quoted in Greek by Lactantius *Div. inst.* 4. 6. 4 (vol. i, p. 298, and p. 15 above). Pseudo-Anthimus cannot have got the quotation from Lactantius; for he gives the introductory phrase, ἄκουε τοιγαροῦν, Ἀσκληπιέ, ('Audi ergo, Asclepi', *Ascl. Lat.*), which Lactantius omits.

In Lactant. *Div. inst.* and in *Ascl. Lat.*, the whole passage is one long sentence. Pseudo-Anthimus breaks it up into two separate sentences (as does Lactantius in his Latin translation of it in *Epit.* 37. 5, p. 20 above), writing ἔτι instead of ἐπεί before τὸν δεύτερον, and omitting the parenthesis (αἰσθητὸν δέ φημι ... εἰς ὅρασιν) after ὁρατὸν καὶ αἰσθητόν.

⁸ ἔτι Ps.-Anth.: ἐπεὶ Lactant.: quo (legendum quoniam) *Ascl. Lat.*

⁹ *Ev. Joh.* 1. 18 and 3. 16–18.

¹⁰ This sentence is obscure. It appears to mean 'Hence (i.e. because Hermes held this opinion about the second God?) it occurred to him (?) to use the phrase ὁ μονογενὴς θεός; and in that respect he is like St. John, who speaks of the μονογενὴς υἱός'. But that is not satisfactory; for it would almost amount to accusing St. John of Hermeticism, if not of Arianism.

In the last sentence of Pl. *Tim.*, the Kosmos is called μονογενής; and if a Hermetist used the phrase ὁ μονογενὴς θεός, he must have meant by it the Kosmos.

¹¹ κάλλιστος δὲ Mercati : κάλλιος δὲ A : καλός τε S : καλὸς δὲ Lactant.

¹² αὐτὸν om. Lactant.

πρώτου καὶ δευτέρου οἴησις ἐντεῦθεν[1] αὐτοῖς[2] τὴν ἀρχὴν εἴληφε. διὰ
τοῦτο καὶ " ἀγέννητον " Εὐσέβιος ὁ τῆς Καισαρείας γέγραφεν.[3] 13. ὁ δὲ
Πλάτων πρὸς Γοργίαν[4] οὕτω φάσκει· "ταῦτα δὴ πάντα[5] τότε ταύτῃ
πεφυκότα ἐξ ἀνάγκης ὁ τοῦ καλλίστου καὶ ἀρίστου δημιουργὸς ἐν τοῖς
5 γινομένοις παρελάμβανεν, ἡνίκα τε καὶ αὐτάρκη καὶ τελεώτατον υἱὸν γεννᾷ."[6]
καὶ πάλιν ἐν τῷ αὐτῷ λόγῳ φησί· "τούτων δὴ οὖν[7] οὕτως ἐχόντων ὁμολο-
γητέον ἓν μὲν εἶναι τὸ κατ' αὐτῶν[8] εἶδος ἔχον, ἀγέννητον καὶ ἀνώλεθρον,
οὔτε εἰς ἑαυτὸ εἰσδεχόμενον ἄλλο ἄλλοθεν οὔτε αὐτὸ εἰς ἄλλα ποιοῦν,[9]
ἀόρατον δὲ καὶ ἄλλως ἀναίσθητον τοῦτο, ὁ δὲ νοήσας εἴληφεν ἐπισκοπήν·[10]
10 τὸ δὲ ὁμώνυμον ὅμοιόν τε ἐκείνῳ δεύτερον, γεννητόν, αἰσθητόν, πεφορημένον."[11] 14. ταῦτα αἴτια τῆς πλάνης αὐτοῖς γέγονεν, οἳ μὴ προσέχοντες[12]
τῆς ὀρθῆς θεοσεβείας ἐξέπεσον.

πόθεν[13] δὲ καὶ τὸ "βουλήσει θεοῦ ὑποστῆναι τὸν τοῦ θεοῦ λόγον"
ἀπεφήναντο[14]; οὐχὶ καὶ τοῦτο παρὰ τοῦ Τρισμεγίστου μαθόιτες; 15. οὗτος

---

[1] *Sc.* from Hermes.

[2] *Sc.* the Arians.   That is, it was Hermes that originated this notion of a first
God and a second God, and it was taken over from him by Plato and by the
Arians.
It may possibly be true that Arius or some of his followers read the *Hermetica*,
and that they were to some extent influenced by them, as well as by other Platonic
writings in which a first God and a second God were spoken of.

[3] γέγραφεν A : ἔγραφεν S.   Does this refer to any passage in the extant writings
of Eusebius?   The meaning appears to be that Eusebius called the second Person
of the Trinity ἀγέννητος, and that he used this word 'because of' the Arian error
(διὰ τοῦτο).   Does that imply that the writer regarded Eusebius as an Arian?   In
reality, Eusebius wavered between the two sides in the controversy, but showed an
inclination towards Arianism, and was attacked as an Arian by Marcellus.   But if
he called the Son of God ἀγέννητος, that would be a declaration *against* Arianism.
It is possible that ἀγέννητος is a misreading for γεννητός, and that what Eusebius
wrote (or was accused of writing) was that the Son is γεννητός.   Cf. Marcellus *ap.*
Euseb. *c. Marcellum* 1. 4. 52 : 'Whence can they (*sc.* the Arians, including
Eusebius.) prove to us from Scripture ὅτι εἷς μὲν (*sc.* the Father) ἀγέννητος, εἷς δὲ
(*sc.* the Son) γεννητός, οὕτως ὡς αὐτοὶ γεγεννῆσθαι αὐτὸν πεπιστεύκασιν ; '

[4] The two passages here quoted are Pl. *Tim.* 68 E and 52 A.   Ps.-Anthimus
writes πρὸς Γοργίαν by mistake, instead of ἐν τῷ Τιμαίῳ.

[5] πάντα S (?) : πάντα ἃ A.

[6] ἡνίκα τὸν αὐτάρκη τε καὶ τὸν τελεώτατον θεὸν ἐγέννα (*al.* γεννᾷ) Pl.   The god
whom Plato says the Demiurgus begot is the Kosmos ; but Ps.-Anthimus took this
passage to be a statement concerning God the Son in the Christian sense, and
assumed that the Arians had so taken it.   [7] δὴ οὖν Ps.-Anth. : δὲ Pl.

[8] κατ' αὐτῶν A : καθ' αὐτὸ S : κατὰ ταὐτὰ Pl.

[9] εἰς ἄλλα ποιοῦν Ps.-Anth. : εἰς ἄλλο ποι ιόν Pl.

[10] τοῦτο ὃ δὴ νόησις εἴληχεν ἐπισκοπεῖν Pl.

[11] δεύτερον, αἰσθητόν, γεννητόν, πεφορημένον ἀεί Pl.   The two things contrasted
by Plato in this passage are the νοητὸν εἶδος (the 'idea'), which is changeless, and
the αἰσθητὸν εἶδος, which is subject to perpetual change.   Those who thought this
to have a bearing on the question in dispute between Arians and Catholics must
have taken the νοητὸν εἶδος to mean God the Father, and the αἰσθητὸν εἶδος to mean
God the Son.

[12] Is there a lacuna after προσέχοντες?   Or ought we to strike out μή, and write
τούτοις instead?   Cf. τούτοις προσέχοντες in § 16.

[13] πόθεν A : ὅθεν S.   [14] *Sc.* the Arians.

γὰρ μετὰ τὸν πρῶτον θεὸν περὶ τοῦ δευτέρου λέγων οὕτως¹ ἔφη· "εἰσόμεθα τὸν προεννοούμενον θεόν, ⟨...⟩² ὃς τὰ πάντα μὲν ἐκείνου
ὅμοια βουληθέντος ἔχει,³ δυσὶ δὲ λείπεται, τῷ εἶναι ἐν σώματι
καὶ ὅρατον ὑπάρχειν."⁴ 16. τούτοις προσέχοντες κακῶς ἀπεσφάλησαν
τῆς ἀληθοῦς γνώσεως οἱ Ἑρμοῦ τε καὶ Πλάτωνος καὶ Ἀριστοτέλους 5
αὐχοῦντες⁵ εἶναι μαθηταὶ ἢ⁶ Χριστοῦ καὶ τῶν ἀποστόλων αὐτοῦ.⁷

17. τὸ δὲ "δεύτερον αἴτιον υἱὸν λόγον", ἢν καὶ "δευτέραν ἀρχὴν"
νενομίκασιν,⁸ ἔλαβον παρὰ Ἀπελλῇ τοῦ μαθητοῦ Μαρκίωνος, ὃς στασιάσας
πρὸς τὸν ἑαυτοῦ διδάσκαλον οὕτως ἔφη· "ψεύδεται Μαρκίων λέγων εἶναι
ἀρχὰς δύο· ἐγὼ δέ φημι μίαν, ἥτις ἐποίησε δευτέραν ἀρχήν."⁹   10

18. πάλιν δὲ τὸ πνεῦμα τὸ ἅγιον βλασφημοῦσι,¹⁰ μὴ δεῖν τοῦτο προσ-
κυνεῖσθαι λέγοντες μηδὲ σέβεσθαι· δοῦλον γὰρ τοῦτο καὶ ὑπηρέτην [εἶναι]
ἀποκαλοῦσι. καὶ τοῦτο τὸ ἄθεον δόγμα παρὰ Δοσιθέου τοῦ αἱρεσιάρχου
τῶν Σαδδουκαίων¹¹ λαβόντες εἰς τὸν τῆς ἀθείας βυθὸν ἀπεπνίγησαν.¹²

19. ἰστέον δὲ καὶ τοῦτο ὅτι ἅμα τῷ ἀναχωρῆσαί τινας στασιάσαντας 15

¹ οὕτως om. S.

² See note on *Abammonis resp.* 10. 7 a, where τὸν προεννοούμενον θεόν appears to
mean the supreme God. In the Hermetic fragment quoted by Ps.-Anthimus, if τὸν
προεννοούμενον θεόν means the first God, there must be a lacuna after it; for in the
following words (ὃν ... ἔχει) it is the second God that is spoken of. Perhaps
εἰσόμεθα τόν ⟨τε⟩ προεννοούμενον θεὸν ⟨καὶ τὸν δεύτερον,⟩ ὃς τὰ πάντα κ.τ.λ. Fr. 36.

³ βουληθέντος ἔχει A: ἔχει βουληθέντος S. Perhaps ὃς τὰ μὲν ⟨ἄλλα⟩ πάντα
ἐκείνου (*sc.* τοῦ πρώτου θεοῦ) βουληθέντος ὅμοια ἔχει.

⁴ The 'second God' of whom the Hermetist speaks is the Kosmos; but those
who thought that the passage agreed with the Arian doctrine or gave support to it
must here again have taken the 'second God' to mean the second Person of the
Christian Trinity.

⁵ If there is any truth in this statement, some Arian must have said that he had
learnt his doctrine partly from Hermes (i.e. from passages in the *Hermetica* in
which the first God and the second God were spoken of).

⁶ ἢ means μᾶλλον ἢ.

⁷ οἱ Ἑρμοῦ ... ἀποστόλων αὐτοῦ om. S.

⁸ I.e. the Arians said that God the Son, the Logos, is the second αἴτιον, or
second ἀρχή (God the Father being the first αἴτιον or ἀρχή).

⁹ If Apelles said this, he contradicted himself; for he who speaks of a 'second
ἀρχή' says that there are two ἀρχαί. Perhaps some adjective, such as ἴσας or
ὁμοίας, has been lost after ἀρχὰς δύο. [Filastrius, *Haer.* 47 (19): 'Non mihi
opus est dicere a Marcione, ut duo principia adseram coaeterna: ego enim
unum principium esse praedico quem deum cognosco, qui deus fecit angelos,
fecit etiam *alteram uirtutem*, quem deum scio esse secundum, qui et uirtus dei
est, quae fecit mundum.]

¹⁰ A group of Arians, whose leader was Macedonius (deposed from his bishopric
in A.D. 360), were called by the Catholics πνευματομάχοι, 'fighters against the
Spirit'. See Didymus *De Trin.* 476 A (*Testim.* p. 168).

¹¹ The writer apparently took Dositheus to have been a Jew, and founder of the
sect of the Sadducees, who 'denied the Holy Ghost' (§ 5). Little is known about
Dositheus; but books ascribed to him were known to Origen (*Comm. in Joan.*
13. 27).

¹² S ends at ἀπεπνίγησαν, and omits § 19 (ἰστέον δὲ ... ἐκκλησίας), with which
A ends.

πρὸς τὴν ἐκκλησίαν καὶ τὸ ἀποστολικὸν κήρυγμα, εὐθέως οἱ πρὸς αὐτῶν πλανηθέντες καὶ τὸ ὄνομα τοῦ ἀποσχίσαντος¹ αἱρεσιάρχου ἐκαρπώσαντο, ἀπολέσαντες τὸ ὄνομα τῆς ἀναθρεψαμένης αὐτοὺς ἁγίας καθολικῆς καὶ ἀποστολικῆς ἐκκλησίας.

¹ Perhaps ἀποσχισθέντος.

EPHRAIM SYRUS

*Discourse against Mani.*¹ ' And if they should say for their shame that there were some of old time Teachers of the Truth,—for they¹ say about Hermes in Egypt, and about Plato among the Greeks, and about Jesus who appeared in Judaea, that ' they are 5 Heralds of that Good One to the world,'—(what does it prove)? For if so be that they³ did proclaim these (doctrines) of the Manichaeans as they say, if Hermes knew the Primal Man,⁴ the

¹ C. W. Mitchell, *S. Ephraim's Prose Refutations of Mani, Marcion, ana Bardaisan* (completed by *A. A. Bevan and F. C. Burkitt*), vol. ii, 1921, p. xcviii. —Date of writing, *c.* A. D. 365. (Ephraim died A. D. 373.) My thanks are due to Prof. Burkitt for his permission to make use of his translations of the Syriac text. For the footnotes I alone am responsible.

² ' They ' means the Manichaeans. Some Manichaean then must have spoken of Hermes as a teacher comparable to Plato and Jesus, and said that all three were ' heralds of that Good One to the world '. (' That Good One ' means God.) Mani first proclaimed his religion in A. D. 242, and was killed in A. D. 275; the Manichaean writing in which Ephraim found that statement may therefore have been of any date between *c.* A. D. 250 and 350.

³ Viz. Hermes, Plato, and Jesus. The Manichaean to whom Ephraim refers probably meant no more than that each of these three teachers made known some part of the truth which was afterwards more fully set forth by Mani. But Ephraim assumes the Manichaean's statement to have meant that the teaching of Hermes, Plato, and Jesus agreed in all details with that of Mani : and accordingly he seeks to refute it by mentioning some details of Mani's system which were not spoken of by Hermes, Plato, or Jesus.

Ephraim is sure that Hermes did not speak of these details; and this implies not only that he knew of the existence of a body of writings containing religious or philosophic teachings ascribed to Hermes, but also that he had either read those writings, or got information as to the whole of their contents from some one who had read them.

⁴ Ephraim takes it to be an ascertained fact that Hermes did not speak of ' the Primal Man '. But the author of *Corp. Herm.* I does speak of a ' Primal Man ' (Anthropos). Hence we may infer that *Corp. Herm.* I was either unknown to Ephraim, or known to him only as a document not ascribed to Hermes.

Father of the *Zīwânē*,[1] and if he knew the Pillar of Glory[2] and the . . . of Splendour,[3] and the Atlas and the rest of the others that Mani proclaimed and even worships and prays to ; and if Plato knew the Virgin of Light . . . and the Mother of the [Living],[4] or the war or . . ., — but he did know . . . and Hera and Athena and Aphrodite 5 the adulterous Goddess ! — and if Jesus proclaimed to them the Refining[5] in Judaea, and if He taught the worship of the Luminaries[6] that Mani worships, he who they say is the Paraclete, that comes after three hundred years[7]: and when we have found that the teachings of these or their followers agree the one to the other, or those of one 10 of them to those of Mani, there is justification ! But if they do not agree, refutation is at hand. But why is it that Astrology, even though it is a lie, agrees with itself in its teaching, and Magic with its tradition, and Geometry with its calculation, and Medicine with its book ?[8] And the disciples of Plato learned his teaching and teach 15 it to this day, and the disciples of Jesus both learned and taught

[1] Cf. Ephraim *op. cit.* vol. i, p. lxxix : 'Mani says that the Primal Man cast his five Bright Ones (Zīwânē) into the mouth of the Son of the Darkness, in order that, as a hunter, he might catch them in his [*net*].' *Ib.* p. xc : ' The Primal Man (is) the Father of the five Shining Ones, whom they call Zīwânē.' These ' five Bright Ones ' seem to be the five elements of which good soul-stuff is composed.

[2] In Mani's system, ' the Pillar of Glory ' seems to mean the Milky Way, regarded as the place to which redeemed souls are conveyed, and in which they wait until all is fulfilled (Burkitt, *op. cit.* vol. ii, p. cxxxvii).

[3] I. e. *Splenditenens* (Φεγγοκάτοχος), one of the five Powers by whom the material world is held in place. *Atlas* ('Ωμοφόρος) is another of these five Powers.

[4] ' The Virgin of Light ' and ' the Mother of the Living ' are two of the numerous divine persons to whom functions were assigned in Mani's mythical cosmology.

[5] ' The Refining ' is the process by which portions of ' Light ' (i. e. good soul-stuff) are continually being separated out from the mixture of Light and Darkness of which things in our present world consist, and are conveyed to the World of Light. It is the process of salvation, as pictured by Mani; and a Manichaean might have replied that Jesus did proclaim ' the Refining ', though not in the particular form in which it was imaged by Mani.

[6] I. e. Sun and Moon.

[7] Mani said he was the Paraclete whose coming had been foretold by Jesus (Augustine *c. Faustum* 13. 17. See Alfaric *Les écritures manichéennes* I. 47, 73 ; II. 37, 42, 120, 125). But why ' three hundred years ' ? Mani was born in A. D. 216, and began his public teaching in A. D. 242, i. e. not much more than 200 years after the death of Jesus. Perhaps Ephraim was thinking of his own time, and vaguely speaking as if Mani were almost contemporary.

Mani also called himself ' apostle of Jesus Christ '. Aug. *c. Faust.* 13. 4 : omnes eius epistolae ita exordiuntur, *Manichaeus apostolus Jesu Christi.*'

[8] What is the bearing of this sentence on the question under discussion ? Ephraim's argument is obscurely expressed, but his meaning seems to be this : ' In each school or sect of religion, as in each science or pseudo-science, there is a body of doctrine which has been handed down unaltered from the founder; therefore, if Hermes, Plato, and Jesus had taught " the Refining " (as the Manichaeans say they did), their disciples would be teaching it now. But we know that their disciples do not teach it now; therefore, Hermes, Plato, and Jesus did not teach it.'

what they heard from Him ; and so do the disciples of Marcion and
Bardaisan and Mani. If they also with Hermes and Plato and Jesus
and others from the Beginning were proclaiming a Refining in
succession, as Mani says,[1] how is it their disciples are not proclaiming
5 their teaching in Egypt [2] and in Greece and in Judaea like that which
Mani teaches to-day? For how is what Jesus teaches like what
Mani teaches? So that by this teaching of our Lord, which is open
and manifest, let that one be convicted who has much wronged God
and the Dead.[3]

[1] If Ephraim is here speaking accurately, it must have been Mani himself that
spoke of the teaching of Hermes together with that of Plato and that of Jesus ; and
it would follow from this that a collection of *Hermetica* was known in Babylonia
before A.D. 275. But perhaps ' as Mani says ' may mean no more than that some
Manichaean said this.

The beginning of one of Mani's writings, the book called *Shâpurakân*, is quoted
as follows by the Arab writer Biruni (Alfaric *Les écritures Manichéennes* II. 54) :
' Wisdom and good works have been brought (to men) in perfect sequence, from
one epoch to another, by the prophets of God. They were brought at one time by
the prophet named Buddha in the region of India, at another time by Zoroaster in
the land of Persia, at another time by Jesus in the West ; after which the present
revelation has arrived and the present prophesying has realized itself by me, Mani,
the messenger of the true God in Babylonia.' In that passage, Mani speaks of
Jesus as one of those who had taught truth before him, but joins with him Buddha
and Zoroaster, not Plato nor Hermes. But the *Shâpurakân* was addressed to King
Sapor, written in the Persian language, and intended primarily for Persian readers,
who would know much about Zoroaster, and something about Buddha, but little
or nothing about Plato and Hermes. In one of his other books, which were
written in Syriac, or in one of his epistles, Mani may possibly have spoken in like
manner of Plato, who would be better known in Syria than in Persia, and of Hermes
also, if the *Hermetica* were known to him ; but it is more likely that the man who
spoke thus of Plato and Hermes was one of Mani's followers in Syria or Egypt.

Hermes was mentioned by Faustus, one of the Manichaeans with whom Augustine
disputed. Aug. *c. Faustum* 13. 1 : Faustus said ' Nihil ecclesiae Christianae
Hebraeorum (*sc.* prophetarum) testimonia conferunt, quae magis constet ex Gentibus
quam ex Judaeis. Sane si sunt aliqua, ut fama est, Sibyllae de Christo praesagia,
aut Hermetis quem dicunt Trismegistum, aut Orphei, aliorumque in Gentilitate
vatum, haec nos aliquanto ad fidem iuvare poterunt, qui ex Gentibus efficimur
Christiani : Hebraeorum vero testimonia nobis, etiamsi sint vera, ante fidem
inutilia sunt, post fidem supervacanea, quia ante quidem eis credere non poteramus,
nunc vero ex superfluo credimus.' But this statement shows that Faustus knew of
Hermes Trismegistus only by report (' *ut fama est* '), and had not read the
Hermetica. His notion that Hermes was a prophet comparable to the Sibyl and
Orpheus, and that *praesagia de Christo* were to be found in his writings, may have
been derived from Lactantius.

[2] Ephraim here speaks of ' the disciples of Hermes ' as of a school or sect comparable to the Platonists and the Christians, and to the sects of Marcion and
Bardaisan : and his words seem to imply that men of this Hermetic school were
teaching in Egypt in his time. But we have no reason to think that there was at
any time a definite school or sect of Hermetists with a doctrine of its own, distinct
from that of the Platonists ; and perhaps Ephraim merely inferred the existence
of such a school from the Hermetic writings known to him.

[3] How did Mani ' wrong the dead ' ? Perhaps by denying the resurrection of
the body.

For Hermes taught[1] *that there was a Bowl,[2] filled with whatever it was filled with, and that there are souls excited by desire, and they come down beside it, and, when they have come close to it, in it and by reason of it they forget their own place.* Now Mani teaches that the Darkness made an assault on the Light and desired it,[3] while Hermes teaches that the Souls desired the Bowl; and this is a little (more) probable, even though both are lying, but it is (more) probable,

---

[1] Ephraim here gives a paraphrase or summary of a passage in a *Hermeticum*. Did he read it in Greek? Prof. Burkitt (Ephraim's *Refutations* II, p. cxxvi) is inclined to think that Ephraim did not know Greek, and had little or no first-hand knowledge of Greek writings. If so, he must have got the contents of this Hermetic passage from some one who had read it in Greek,—unless Greek *Hermetica* had already been translated into Syriac. *Fr. 22.*

[2] Prof. Burkitt tells me that the word *aggānā*, which he translated 'Bowl' (κρατήρ), might equally well stand for ὑδρία. But there can be little doubt that the word used by the Hermetist was κρατήρ.

The only mention of a κρατήρ in the extant *Hermetica* is in *Corp.* IV. 4, where Hermes says that God sent down a great *crater* filled with νοῦς, and invited 'the hearts of men' to dip themselves in it. But the bowl spoken of in the passage summarized by Ephraim is a *crater* of λήθη; its function is just the opposite of that of a *crater* of νοῦς, and there cannot have been any connexion between the one passage and the other.

Macrobius *Somn. Scip.* I. 12. 18 says that unembodied souls drink from 'the Crater of Dionysus' (which he identifies with the constellation called the Crater), and being thereby intoxicated, are drawn down to earth and embodied. The Hermetic passage must have been to the same effect, except that a Hermetist would doubtless omit the name Dionysus, and would speak rather of a *crater* filled with the wine of *lethe*.

It is not clearly stated by Ephraim whether the Hermetist said that the souls drink from the *crater* of *lethe*, or that they dip themselves in it; but it is to be inferred from the parallels elsewhere that drinking is meant. Cf. Virg. *Aen.* 6. 713–715: 'animae quibus altera fato | corpora debentur, Lethaei ad fluminis undam | securos latices et longa oblivia potant.' *Pistis Sophia* 336 (C. Schmidt, p. 217): when a disembodied soul is about to be sent down to earth and re-embodied, the Archontes give it a 'cup of oblivion out of the σπέρμα of κακία, filled with all kinds of ἐπιθυμίαι and all oblivion; and as soon as that soul drinks out of the cup, it forgets all the τόποι to which it has gone, and all the κολάσεις in which it has wandered.'

'The *Crater* of Dionysus' was spoken of (very likely in a similar connexion) in an Orphic poem; Proclus *In Tim.* 5. 316 A: καὶ Ὀρφεὺς οἶδε μὲν καὶ τὸν τοῦ Διονύσου κρατῆρα, πολλοὺς δὲ καὶ ἄλλους (sc. κρατῆρας) ἱδρύει περὶ τὴν ἡλιακὴν τράπεζαν. (The 'bowls placed round the table of the Sun' were presumably spoken of in another Orphic passage, unconnected with that in which 'the bowl of Dionysus' was mentioned.) The Hermetist may have got the notion of a bowl of *lethe* from some Platonist who had got it from an Orphic poem.

[3] Mani accounted for the embodiment of souls by saying that it resulted from the desire of 'the Darkness' to capture and appropriate 'the Light'; the Hermetist accounted for it by saying that it resulted from a desire felt by the souls themselves. Ephraim says that both are wrong, but that the Hermetic doctrine is less wrong than Mani's; for we know that embodied souls desire to continue in the body (or in other words, that men fear death), and that being so, it is not unreasonable to suppose that unembodied souls desire to be embodied, or that they desire the oblivion which is connected with embodiment. When Mani says that 'the Darkness desired the Light', it is as if he had said that 'the bowl of *lethe* desired the souls'.

because it, the Soul, desires to remain in the Body and delay in its
Habitation and dwell in its House and be fondled in its Bosom.
But Mani compels a man to hear him seriously though he is talking
nonsense, for ' the Darkness (he says) loved the Light its opposite '
5 — and how does Water love Fire that absorbs it, or Fire Water that
quenches it ?   And how did Fire love Light ?   How, pray, will it be
.benefited by it ?   For ' Fire loved Fire, and Wind Wind, and Water
Water '.[1]   Or, perhaps, are these Natures of Darkness male and
those from the Good One female ?   And if not, what is the sense of
10 this, that they loved one another ?

These things therefore Hermes did not teach,[2] nor did Jesus,
because Jesus taught the opposite of all of them.   For He quickened
bodies and raised the dead, whereas neither Hermes nor Plato believe
in the resurrection of the body.

[1] The Manichaean doctrine which is here criticized, and which Ephraim says
' Hermes did not teach ', seems to have been to this effect : ' the Darkness loved
(i. e. desired and sought to appropriate) the Light ; and each of the several
elements belonging to the Darkness (viz. bad fire, bad wind, bad water) loved the
corresponding element belonging to the Light (viz. good fire, good wind, good
water).'

[2] Here again, Ephraim's words imply that he knew what Hermes taught and
what he did not teach,—i. e. that he was acquainted with the contents of a collection
of *Hermetica*.

FILASTRIUS DIVERSARUM HERESEON LIBER[1]

HIC ITAQUE HERETICORUM EST NUMERUS A MUNDI INITIO ATQUE ORIGINE.

1. Primi sunt Ofitae, qui dicuntur ⟨et⟩ Serpentini. . . . 2. Alii sunt Caiani, qui Cain laudant fratricidam. . . . 3. Alia autem est heresis Sethianorum, quae Seth filium Adae . . . venerantur. [5] 4. Dositheus quidam postea, Iudaeus genere. . . . 5. Sadducei post ipsum, a Saddoc homine Iudaeo. . . . 6. Alia autem est Pharisaeorum. . . . 7. Alii autem Samaritani sunt. . . . 8. Alia est heresis Iudaeorum qui dicuntur Nazorei. . . . 9. Esseni autem alii sunt. . . . 10. Alii autem sunt Heliognosti, qui et De⟨in⟩uictiaci[2] dicuntur, [10] solem adorantes, atque dicentes solem scire omnia ⌜quae dei sunt⌝, homines etiam non alium nisi solem inluminare, solemque eis praebere omnia nutrimenta, non cognoscentes quod in seruitute positus cursum suum peragrat a deo patre per Christum dominum in sancto spiritu statutum co⟨t⟩tidie, de quo scriptum est: 'Qui dicit soli oriri, [15] et oritur, et non oriri, et non oritur.' ⌜Quem⌝ Hermes ille uanus paganus Trismegistus docuit post deum omnipotentem non alium nisi solem debere ⌜ipsum et⌝ homines adorare;[3] qui cum ad Celtarum prouinciam perrexisset, ipse eos dinoscitur docuisse, atque huic errori

---

[1] Ed. F. Marx (*Corp. script. eccl. Lat.* vol. xxxviii), 1898. This book was written by Filastrius of Brixia (Brescia) about A.D. 383. It was known to Augustine.

[2] *Deinvictiaci* means people who call the Sun *deus invictus*, and worship him under that title. *Deus invictus* (ἀνίκητος) was a term applied by Romans to Sun-gods of oriental origin, such as the god of Emesa (officially named *invictus Sol Elagabal*) whose cult was established at Rome by Elagabalus, A.D. 218, and the *deus Sol invictus* (probably the state-god of Palmyra) to whom Aurelian dedicated a temple at Rome in A.D. 274. Mithras also is called in inscriptions *Deus sol invictus Mithras*. The earliest dated instance of the term is *Soli invicto deo* in an inscription of A.D. 158. See Wissowa, *Religion und Kultus der Römer*, p. 305.

[3] There is some corruption in this sentence; but the meaning appears to be 'Hermes taught that, after almighty God, men ought to worship no other god except the Sun'. This implies (1) that the Sun is the 'second God', and (2) that men ought to worship no gods except the supreme God and the Sun. The first of these two statements is in agreement with *Corp.* XVI, and with numerous 'solar interpolations' in our *Hermetica*; compare especially Stob. *Exc.* II A. 14, ὃν (sc. τὸν ἥλιον) καὶ σέβομαι, . . . μετὰ τὸν ἕνα καὶ πρῶτον (θεὸν) τοῦτον δημιουργὸν γνωρίζω⟨ν⟩. But there is nothing in the extant *Hermetica* that resembles the second statement. It may be suspected that *non alium nisi* has been wrongly repeated from the preceding sentence, and that Filastrius wrote *docuit post deum omnipotentem* [ ] *solem debere* [ ] *homines adorare*; 'Hermes taught that, next after almighty God, men ought to worship the Sun'.

ut succumberent isdem suasisse.[1] Quem solem Iudaei captiuati
adorabant, ut Hiezechiel propheta[2] eosdem Iudaeos incusando con-
demnat, ac reos criminis maiestatis declarat et arguit contestando,
sicut scriptum est.

5 11. Alii sunt qui ranas colunt quas sub Faraone ira dei tunc
temporis Aegyptiorum terrae manauit. . . .

103 (75). Alia est heresis quae secu(n)dum paganorum uanitatem
siderum diuersa nomina profitetur, ut Hermes ille Trismegistus,[3] qui
uanus potius quam magnus iudicandus est, et poetae quidam ei
10 consimiles, qui cometas et pogonias et Hyadas, Haedos, et alia
huiusmodi adserunt nomine[4] delirantes, cum scriptura pauca nomina
siderum nobis edixerit dicente Iob beato propheta, ante quam pagani
e sanctis scripturis siderum nomina transtulissent. Dicit enim ipse
Iob[5]: 'Qui fecit Pliadas et Arcturum' inquit 'et Hesperum et
15 thesaurum austri et Oriona et Luciferum.' Haec itaque nomina e
sanctis scripturis accipimus nuntiata una: omnium siderum nomina
non dixit scriptura, sed potestati dei reseruauit per prophetam
declarans et dicens ita:[6] 'Qui numerat multitudinem stellarum, et
omnibus eis nomina uocans.' Haec itaque pauca nomina legentes e
20 sanctis scripturis poetae postea falsique filosophi ausi sunt usurpantes
suis mendaciis et alia plurima copulare atque impietatis semina
saeculo praedicare, ut ex his sperare putarent etiam omnium siderum
aut plurimorum nomina posse conprehendere,[7] cum omnium siderum

---

[1] Filastrius here speaks of a missionary journey of Hermes to 'the province of
the Celts' (i.e. Provence). There is no mention of anything of the sort elsewhere.
It would seem that Filastrius, or his authority, had heard of some group of Sun-
worshippers in southern Gaul, and, having also heard of *Hermetica* in which the
Sun was spoken of as 'second God', inferred that the Egyptian teacher Hermes
must have gone to Gaul and taught his doctrine there.

[2] *Ezech*. 8. 16.

[3] The 'heresy' (i.e. religious error) here attributed to Hermes is that of giving
names to stars or constellations which are not named in the Bible. Filastrius
assumes that Hermes and 'certain Pagan poets like him' (e.g. Aratus) borrowed
from the Bible those star-names which occur in it, and invented others which do
not occur in it. The names of the stars, he thinks, were assigned to them by the
Word of God at the Creation: it has pleased God to reveal to men the names of
a few of them only, and it is impious presumption to give names to any others.

It appears from this that Filastrius had heard that there were writings of Hermes
in which star-names were given. He tells us nothing else about these writings,
and probably knew little about them. There were many astrological *Hermetica*;
but it is not astrology, but merely the naming of stars, that he here condemns.

[4] nomine *Marx*: nomina *Fabricius*.

[5] *Job* 9. 9 and 38. 31.   [6] *Ps*. 146. 4.

[7] Cf. Stob. *Exc*. VI. 14, where Hermes, after speaking of the *Decani* and
Liturgi, says (emended text) μετὰ δὲ τούτους ἐστὶν ἄλλων ὄχλος (?) ἀστέρων, οὓς
ἡμεῖς μὲν προσηγοριῶν οὐ κατηξιώσαμεν· οἱ δὲ μεθ' ἡμᾶς ἐσόμενοι καὶ τούτοις προσηγορίας θήσονται.

nomina non alter nisi deus Christus, per quem fecit pater uniuersa, posuerit et scierit, atque eis singula nomina uocauerit, ut scriptum est.

DIDYMUS ALEXANDRINUS[1]

Migne
465 A

De Trinitate, lib. 2, cap. 3: μαρτυροῦσι τὰ λόγια[2] ὅτι διάφορα θεοπρεπῆ ὀνόματά ἐστι τῷ πνεύματι τοῦ θεοῦ, ... ἀναπλοῦντα ἔνια μὲν τὴν θεϊκὴν αὐτοῦ φύσιν, ἔνια δὲ τὴν αὐθεντικὴν δύναμιν, ... καὶ παρρησίαν παρέχοντα ἀκινδύνως ὁμοούσιον τοῦ θεοῦ καλεῖν αὐτό, καὶ πιστεύειν τῷ ἁγιασμῷ αὐτοῦ.

B καὶ οὐχ εὑρίσκομεν οὐδὲν τῶν ἄλλων πνευμάτων καταξιωθὲν κληθῆναι τοῖς 5 ὀνόμασι τούτοις. τὸ δὲ μόνως καὶ φύσει ὑπάρχον ταῦτα, οὐδέν ἐστι τῶν πάντων ἀλλὰ θεός. ...

476 A οἱ δὲ τὸ Μακεδονίου[3] πρεσβεύοντες δόγμα, τῆς αἱρέσεως αὐτῶν μᾶλλον ἢ τἀληθοῦς ⟨. . .⟩[4] γινόμενοι, οὐδέν τι συμβαῖνον τοῖς τῶν λογίων βλέπουσιν. συναρπακτικῶς[5] γὰρ μυθεύονται ῥήμασιν αὐτοῖς, ὡς οὐ χρὴ 10 ὁμωνυμίαις ἢ συνωνυμίαις ἢ ὁμοιολεξίαις προσέχειν. τοῦ γὰρ θεοῦ, φησίν, τὸ " ἀγαθός " ὄνομα τῷ " εἷς θεός " συμπέπλεκται· ἐπὶ δὲ τῷ ἁγίῳ πνεύματι, τῷ " ἀγαθός " ὀνόματι οὐ συνέζευκται τὸ " εἷς θεός ". καὶ πάλιν· " ἀγαθός ", φησίν, ἐγράφη εἶναι καὶ ἄνθρωπος. ... ὁμοίως δέ, φησίν,

---

[1] Edited by Mingarelli, 1769. Didymus of Alexandria died, at the age of 85, about A. D. 398. He lost his eyesight in childhood; but in spite of his blindness, he became eminent as a teacher and writer. He was head of the Catechetical School at Alexandria. He defended the orthodox doctrine of the Trinity against the Arians; but he was anathematized by the Church as a follower of Origen.

His work Περὶ τριάδος, in three books, 'was published very probably after 381, perhaps after 392' (Bardenhewer). It may be dated A. D. 380–398. It has been preserved in one MS. (eleventh-century) only, and was edited from that MS. by Mingarelli, 1769. Mingarelli's edition is reprinted in Migne *Patr. Gr.* 39.

[2] I.e. the Holy Scriptures. Didymus' argument is this: 'In the Bible, certain terms (such as ἀγαθός and ἅγιος) are applied to the Holy Spirit which are also applied to God the Father and to God the Son; therefore, the Holy Spirit must be God, and must be ὁμοούσιος with the Father and the Son.'

[3] Macedonius maintained that the Holy Spirit is not of one substance with the Father, but is a created thing (κτίσμα). He and his followers were called πνευματομάχοι ('fighters against the Spirit') by the orthodox. (See Socrates *Eccl. Hist.* 2. 45.) Didymus here goes on to quote verbally (ῥήμασιν αὐτοῖς) a passage (οὐ χρὴ ὁμωνυμίαις . . . καλεῖται καὶ ἄνθρωπος κ.τ.λ.) written by one of the followers of Macedonius.

[4] Lacunam signavi.

[5] συναρπακτικῶς probably means 'assuming the thing which is to be proved', i. e. 'employing a *petitio principii*'. Cf. Sext. Emp. *Hypot.* 2. 57: τὸ ζητούμενον συναρπάσουσι.

ἀγαθὰ ὁμωνύμως καὶ ἄψυχα.... ἀλλὰ καὶ ἐπὶ ἀνυποστάτων δῆθεν πραγμάτων εἴρηται· "ἀγαθὸν τὸ ἐξομολογεῖσθαι τῷ κυρίῳ". ὁμοίως ⟨δὲ⟩ B [ὁ]¹ "ἅγιος", φησί, καλεῖται καὶ ἄνθρωπος....

καὶ² τοῦτο μέν, φημὶ δὲ τὸ μὴ προσέχειν ὁμωνυμίαις καὶ ὁμοιολεξίαις,
5 λόγον ἔχει ἐπὶ τοῖς ἑτεροειδέσιν καὶ ἑτεροουσίοις, οὐ μέντοι ἐπὶ τοῦ ἁγίου πνεύματος καὶ ἐκείνου οὗ πνεῦμά ἐστιν, ἔτι μὴν καὶ τοῦ υἱοῦ. προστιθεῖσα γὰρ ἡ γραφὴ τὴν ἀπὸ ἑαυτῆς ἀσφάλειαν ταῖς ὁμωνυμίαις ἢ συνωνυμίαις συμφράζει τήν "μου" ἢ "σου" συλλαβήν, ἢ τὴν "ἅγιος" ἢ "ἀγαθός" λέξιν· τοῦτ' ἐστιν, ἢ ὡς ἀπὸ τοῦ θεοῦ λέγει "τὸ πνεῦμά μου", ἢ ὡς ἀπὸ
10 τοῦ Δαυὶδ καὶ ἡμῶν "τὸ πνεῦμά σου τὸ ἀγαθὸν ὁδηγήσει με". πείθεσθαι C οὖν δεῖ οἷς πολλῷ λυσιτελέστερον, ταῖς μνημονευθείσαις γραφικαῖς μαρτυ-ρίαις λέγω, καὶ εἰδέναι ὡς τὸ ἅγιον πνεῦμα τὴν ὁμωνυμίαν ἢ συνωνυμίαν καὶ τὰς ὁμοιολεξίας πρὸς τὸν θεὸν³ ἔχει καὶ τὸν μονογενῆ αὐτοῦ υἱόν, τοὺς τοῖς ὁμοίοις ὀνόμασιν ὑμνηθέντας, οὐ πρὸς τὰ κτίσματα διὰ τὴν εὑρισκομέ-
15 νην ἔσθ' ὅτε ἐν ἐκείνοις ὁμωνυμίαν.⁴ ταῦτα γάρ, εἰ καὶ δοίημεν ὀνόματί τινι ἢ λέξει θεῷ κοινωνεῖν, ἀλλ' οὐκ οὐσίᾳ, οὐδ' ἐνεργείᾳ δυνάμεως καὶ ἁγιασμοῦ. οὐδὲ γὰρ φύσει ταῦτα καθ' ἅπαξ⁵ ὑπάρχουσι, κατὰ 477 A σύγκρισιν δὲ τοῦ κακοῦ τὸ ἀγαθόν, καὶ τοῦ ἁμαρτήματος ἤγουν τοῦ πάθους τὸ ἅγιον τέτακται· τὸ γὰρ μὴ λίαν κακόν, καὶ ἁμαρτωλὸν
20 ἤγουν ἐμπαθές, ἀγαθὸν ἐνθάδε προσείρηται,⁶ ὡς γὰρ κακία, καὶ ἁμαρτία ἤγουν⁷ πάθος, καὶ ἀδυναμία ἐν τῷ ἑνὶ ἁγίῳ πνεύματι οὐχ εὑρίσκεται, ἅτε ἀγενήτῳ, οὕτως ἐν οὐδενὶ τῶν γενητῶν τὸ ἀγαθὸν καὶ ἅγιον καὶ δυνατὸν κατὰ τὸ τέλειον, ἀλλὰ κατὰ μετουσίαν· ὅπου δὲ οὐδαμοῦ ταῦτα κατὰ τὸ τέλειον, οὐδαμοῦ τὸ ἀγένητον. ἔνθα γὰρ σκότος, οὐδαμοῦ τὸ φῶς· καὶ ὅπου
25 νύξ, οὐχ ἡμέρα.⁸ ὅθεν εἴρηται καὶ τῷ Ἑρμῇ τῷ ἐπίκλην Τρισμεγίστῳ· "ἀδύνατον⁹ ἐν γενέσει εἶναι τἀγαθόν, ἐν μόνῳ δὲ τῷ ἀγενήτῳ.

¹ δὲ scripsi : ὁ cod.
² Here begins Didymus' answer to the argument of the πνευματομάχος. The connexion does not seem to be rightly expressed by καί.
³ Perhaps θεὸν ⟨πατέρα⟩.
⁴ The passage τὸ ἅγιον πνεῦμα . . . ἐν ἐκείνοις ὁμωνυμίαν is obscure. The statement τὸ ἅ. πν. οὐ πρὸς τὰ κτίσματα (sc. τὴν ὁμωνυμίαν ἔχει) is contrary to obvious facts, and inconsistent with the following words τὴν εὑρισκομένην ἔσθ' ὅτε ἐν ἐκείνοις (sc. τοῖς κτίσμασιν) ὁμωνυμίαν. Probably some phrase (connected with τὴν ὁμωνυμίαν . . . πρὸς τὸν θεὸν ἔχει) which would have made the sentence intelligible has dropped out.
⁵ Mingarelli says that καθ' ἅπαξ means 'absolutely'.
⁶ Cf. Corp. Herm. VI. 3 b, as emended : ἐν δὲ τῷ ἀνθρώπῳ κατὰ σύγκρισιν τοῦ κακοῦ τὸ ἀγαθὸν λέλεκται· τὸ γὰρ μὴ λίαν κακὸν ἐνθάδε ἀγαθὸν ⟨προσείρηται⟩. Didymus here borrows phrases from Corp. VI without saying whence he got them; but he mentions Hermes below, when he quotes a passage from that same libellus.
⁷ ἤγουν (ter) scripsi : ἤτ' οὖν (ter) Mingarelli.
⁸ Corp. VI. 2 a : ὅπου δὲ πάθος, οὐδαμοῦ τὸ ἀγαθόν· ὅπου δὲ τὸ ἀγαθόν, οὐδαμοῦ οὐδὲ ἐν πάθος. ὅπου γὰρ ἡμέρα, οὐδαμοῦ νύξ· ὅπου δὲ νύξ, οὐδαμοῦ ἡμέρα.
⁹ ἀδύνατον . . . τοῦ ἀγαθοῦ : Corp. VI. 2 a, b.

Β ὥσπερ δὲ μετουσία πάντων ἐστὶν τῇ[1] ὕλῃ δεδομένη, οὕτω καὶ
τοῦ ἀγαθοῦ".

ὅμοιον τοίνυν καὶ ἴσον τὸ ἅγιον πνεῦμα ⟨. . .⟩[2] τῆς τοῦ πατρὸς καὶ τοῦ
μονογενοῦς θεότητος· καὶ ἐκ τῆς τῶν τοιούτων δείκνυται κρίσεως αὐτὸ τῇ
φύσει ἀγιότης καὶ ἀγαθότης καὶ δύναμις ὑπάρχον, ἄτε ἓν ὂν ἐκ τοῦ ἑνός.   5

753 A   *De Trinitate*, lib. 2, cap. 27: ἀκουστέον δὲ — χαλεπὸν γὰρ οὐδὲν
ἐκ τούτου, ἀλλὰ καὶ ἐπωφελές — καὶ στίχων τῶν παρ' Ἕλλησι μετρίαν
περὶ τῆς πρὸς τὸν θεὸν πατέρα συντάξεως τοῦ υἱοῦ λόγου καὶ τοῦ πνεύματος
συναίσθησιν δεξαμένων, καὶ πρόσφορα καὶ ἀληθῆ θεωρησάντων εἶναι τὰ
ὀνόματα ταῦτα· καὶ ὡς οὐ διέζευκται τὸ παγκρατὲς ἅγιον πνεῦμα, οὐ φύσει,   10
οὐ δυνάμει, οὐ δόξῃ, τοῦ θεοῦ πατρός, ὡς οὐδὲ ὁ μονογενής, ἀλλὰ καὶ
πρόεισιν ἐξ αὐτοῦ ⌜οὐ συμμετρότερον⌝,[3] καὶ παρ' αὐτῷ μένει, πληροῦν τῇ
ἑαυτοῦ ὑπερτάτῃ καὶ ἀπλέτῳ χάριτι καὶ δυνάμει ἅπαντα, κατὰ τὸ κοινὸν
αὐτῷ τοῦ πατρὸς καὶ τοῦ υἱοῦ ἀγαθὸν βούλημα.

εἰσὶν δὲ οἱ στίχοι ⟨τοῦ⟩[4] χρησμοῦ οὗτοι·   15

Β
    " πνεῦμα μὲν ἀθανάτοιο θεοῦ πατρὸς ἐκπροπόρευμα,
     αὐτόθεν ἔνθεν ἔβη μένον ἔμπεδον,[5] οὔτι μεριστόν·
     ἀλλὰ θεοῖο λόγοιο μένον ζαθέοις ὑπὸ κόλποις
     πάντα τέλεια ποιεῖ[6] ὅσα μήδεται ἀρχέγονος φρήν,
     κτίσμασι δὲ ξύμπασι φέρει χάριν, ᾗ ὑπὸ πάντα   20

756 A
     ἔργα θεοῦ ζώει καὶ ἀ⟨ε⟩ίδιον ἔλλαχ' ἀρωγήν."[7]
καὶ πάλιν·

    " ὄφρα τὰ πάντα τριὰς συνέχῃ, κατὰ πάντα μετροῦσα."[8]

Ὀρφέως, τοῦ παρ' Ἕλλησι πρώτου θεολόγου·

    " πάντα γὰρ ἀθανάτοιο θεοῦ μεγάλῃ ὑπ' ἀρωγῇ   25
     ἄνθρωποι τελέουσι, σοφῇ ὑπὸ πνεύματος[9] ὁρμῇ."

Πλάτωνος τοῦ κωμικοῦ· ὃς ἀνθηρῶ[10] ἐν τοῖς ὑπογεγραμμένοις ἰάμβοις

---

[1] ἐστὶν τῇ cod. Didym.: ἐστὶν ἐν τῇ *Corp.* VI.

[2] Lacunam signavi.

[3] Perhaps οὐ συμμετρότερον is a corruption of something equivalent to οὔτι
μεριστόν in the verses. But if so, it is wrongly placed, and ought rather to stand
after παρ' αὐτῷ μένει.

[4] τοῦ addidi.

[5] Perhaps πνεῦμα μέν, ἀθανάτοιο θεοῦ πατρὸς ἐκπροπορευθέν, | αὐτόθεν ἔνθεν ἔβη
μένει ἔμπεδον.

[6] πάντα τέλεια ποιεῖ ὅσα μήδεται scripsi: πάντα τελεῖ ἅτε θεῖος ἀμήδεται cod.

[7] This χρησμός was evidently composed by a Christian. See note on *Artemii
Passio* § 46, where other oracles of the same kind are given.

[8] Perhaps κατὰ πάντ' ἀμέτρητος.

[9] πνεῦμα may here be taken to mean the breath of divine inspiration. The word
was used in that sense by Pagans, as well as by Jews and Christians.

[10] ἀνθηρῶς ('floridly' or 'brilliantly'?) can hardly be the right reading. [Perhaps
simply an expression of admiration.]

θεότητα ⟨. . .⟩¹ μοναδικῶς ἐκτεινομένην εἰς τριάδα, ἀφ᾽ ἧς τὰ ὅλα γέγονέ τε
καὶ σώζεται·

     " θεὸς γάρ ἐστιν εἷς πατὴρ ὑπέρτατος,

     λόγῳ τὰ πάντα πανσόφως καὶ πνεύματι

5   στήσας ὀλισθαίνοντα, κἀκ βυθοῦ πλάνης

     εἰς φῶς ἀνέλκων ἐκ μακρᾶς ἀταξίας." ²

Ἑρμοῦ Τρισμεγίστου,³ ἐκ ⟨⟨λόγου τρίτου⟩⟩ τῶν πρὸς τὸν Ἀσκληπιόν B
⟦λόγων τριῶν⟧.⁴ ἐρομένου τινὸς ⌜τὸν ἀγαθὸς δαίμονα⌝ περὶ τοῦ τρισαγίου
πνεύματος, ἔχρησεν οὕτως·⁵ " εἰ μὴ πρόνοιά τις ἦν τοῦ πάντων
10 κυρίου ὥστε με⁶ τὸν λόγον τοῦτον ἀποκαλύψαι, οὐδὲ ὑμᾶς

¹ The verb of which ὅς (perhaps ⟨οὗτ⟩ος?) is the subject has been lost.
² A Christian forgery.
³ The three following quotations from Hermes, and the quotation from Porphyry
(ἄχρι γὰρ τριῶν ὑποστάσεων κ.τ.λ.) which follows them, were taken over from
Didymus (but placed in a different order) by Cyril, c. *Julianum* 553 B–556 C.
The quotation from Porphyry is repeated by Cyril *ib.* 916 B.
    The genitive Ἑρμοῦ τρισμεγίστου, and the preceding genitives Ὀρφέως and
Πλάτωνος τοῦ κωμικοῦ, might be accounted for by assuming that Didymus took
these passages from a collection of extracts from various authors, and that in that
collection each passage was preceded by its author's name in the genitive, as
habitually in Stobaeus.
⁴ ἐκ τῶν πρὸς τ. Ἀσκλ. λόγων τριῶν cod. Didym. : ἐν τῷ αὐτῷ λόγῳ τρίτῳ τῶν πρὸς
Ἀσκλ. Cyril.   The proper title is undoubtedly λόγος τρίτος τῶν πρὸς Ἀσκλ.; and
it is more likely that the mistake of writing τῶν . . . λόγων τριῶν was made
by a copyist of Didymus' text, than that it was made by Didymus himself and
corrected by Cyril.
⁵ ἐρομένου τινὸς τὸν ἀγαθὸς δαίμονα περὶ τοῦ τρισαγίου πνεύματος, ἔχρησεν οὕτως
cod. Didym. : ὡς ἐρομένου τινὸς περὶ τοῦ θείου πνεύματος, φησὶν οὕτως Cyril.   How
is this mention of the Agathos Daimon to be explained? I am inclined to think
that Didymus wrote something like ⟨οὗτος (*sc.* Hermes) λέγει ὡς⟩ ⟨⟨ὁ Ἀγαθὸς
Δαίμων⟩⟩, ἐρομένου τινὸς ⟦ ⟧ περὶ τοῦ τρισαγίου πνεύματος, ἔχρησεν οὕτως.   In
support of this, it should be noticed that the verb ἔχρησεν implies as its subject
a god rather than a man ; and in the view of thé Hermetists, the Agathos Daimon
was a god (μακάριος θεός, *Corp.* XII. i. 13 b), but Hermes was a man. We may
suppose that the writer of the λόγος τρίτος πρὸς Ἀσκληπιόν made Hermes report to
his pupil Asclepius a dialogue in which the Agathos Daimon answered questions
put to him by some inquirer.   Cf. Cyril c. *Julianum* 553 A : (Ἑρμῆς), ὡς ἐρομένου
τινὸς τῶν ἐν Αἰγύπτῳ τεμενιτῶν, καὶ λέγοντος " διὰ τί δέ, ὦ μέγιστε Ἀγαθὸς
Δαίμων, τούτῳ τῷ ὀνόματι ἐκλήθη κ.τ.λ. ;" φησί· " καὶ ἐν τοῖς ἔμπροσθεν εἶπον
κ.τ.λ." Cyril. *ib.* 588 A : ἔφη γὰρ οὗτος (*sc.* Hermes) ἐν τῷ πρὸς Ἀσκληπιόν· " καὶ
εἶπε " φησὶν " Ὄσιρις· Εἶτα, ὦ μέγιστε Ἀγαθὸς Δαίμων, πῶς ὅλη ἡ γῆ ἐφάνη ; καὶ
εἶπεν ὁ μέγας Ἀγαθὸς Δαίμων κ.τ.λ."   In each of those two passages, a dialogue
in which the Agathos Daimon was the teacher is reported by Hermes. We are
told that the second of them (Cyril 588 A) occurred in a 'Discourse of Hermes
to Asclepius ' ; and it seems probable that this was that same ' Third Discourse to
Asclepius ' from which Didymus quotes the passage εἰ μὴ πρόνοιά τις κ.τ.λ. But
if so, it would appear that the inquirer of whom Didymus speaks (ἐρομένου τινός)
was named Osiris in the Hermetic documents. *Fr.* 24.
    The word τρισαγίου was probably added by Didymus.   The Hermetist wrote
τούτου τοῦ πνεύματος below, and may perhaps have used the term τὸ θεῖον πνεῦμα.
⁶ μοι cod. Didym. : με Cyril : μοι Malalas (who copied the passage from Cyril).
The Hermetist must have written με. We may suppose either that Cyril read με
in Didymus ; or that he read μοι in Didymus, but με in the Hermetic *libellus* (to
which he presumably had access, as he quotes other Hermetic passages which are

757 A τοιοῦτος¹ ἔρως κατεῖχεν ⟨ἂν⟩² ἵνα περὶ τούτου ζητήσητε. νῦν
δὲ τὰ λοιπὰ τοῦ λόγου ἀκούετε. τούτου τοῦ πνεύματος,³ οὗ
πολλάκις προεῖπον, πάντα χρῄζει· τὰ πάντα γὰρ ⌐βαστάζον
κατ᾽ ἀξίαν τὰ πάντα⌐⁴ ζωοποιεῖ καὶ τρέφει, καὶ ἀπὸ τῆς ἁγίας
πηγῆς ἐξήρτηται,⁵ ⌐ἐπίκουρον πνεύμασι⌐ ⟨. . .⟩⁶ καὶ ζωῆς 5
ἅπασιν ἀεὶ ὑπάρχον, γόνιμον ἓν ὄν."

not given by Didymus), and preferred με. If Cyril wrote με, the μοι of Malalas
cannot be derived from the μοι of cod. Didym., but must be a corruption of
Cyril's με.

The meaning appears to be 'You show a strong desire to learn the doctrine in
question; and that desire must have been implanted in you by the supreme God.
Hence I infer that it is God's will that I should reveal this doctrine to you'.
(πρόνοια seems to be used in the sense of βουλή, 'design' or 'purpose'.)

If the speaker is the Agathos Daimon, he speaks of himself as a subordinate
god, who is under obligation to obey the will of the supreme God. It must be
admitted, however, that these words would seem more appropriate if spoken by
the man Hermes than if spoken by a god. Moreover, they would seem more
suitable as a preface to an exposition of doctrine than as a remark interposed
in the midst of it; and we should accordingly have expected νῦν δὲ τὸν λόγον
ἀκούετε, 'but as it is' (i. e. since I am assured that God wills it), 'I will reveal
the doctrine to you', rather than νῦν δὲ τὰ λοιπὰ τοῦ λόγου ἀκούετε, which implies
that the speaker has revealed a part of the doctrine before he gives his reason
for revealing it. Perhaps the obscurities of the passage might be accounted for
by supposing that in the text of Didymus two pieces taken from different parts
of the Hermetic *libellus* have been wrongly joined together into one. On that
hypothesis, we might assume that the first piece (εἰ μὴ πρόνοια ἦν . . . νῦν δὲ
⟨. . .⟩) stood at or near the beginning of the *libellus*, and that Hermes is there
giving his reason for revealing a holy secret to his hearers; while the second piece
(τὰ λοιπὰ τοῦ λόγου ἀκούετε κ.τ.λ.) occurred in a later part of the *libellus*, where
Hermes 'revealed the λόγος' by reporting to his hearers a dialogue in which the
Agathos Daimon had given instruction to 'some one who asked questions'.

The plurals ὑμᾶς, ζητήσητε, and ἀκούετε show that, though the *libellus*
was entitled
πρὸς Ἀσκληπιόν, two or more pupils were present, as in *Ascl. Lat.*

τούτου τοῦ λόγου means either 'this doctrine', or (if we assume the speaker to
be, not the Agathos Daimon, but Hermes in his own person) possibly 'this discourse
of the Agathos Daimon'. But Didymus probably took τοῦ λόγου to mean 'the
Word of God', i. e. the second Person of the Christian Trinity; for if he had not
done so, he would have had no reason to quote the earlier part of the passage
(εἰ μὴ πρόνοιά τις . . . τοῦ λόγου ἀκούετε), and it would have served his purpose
better to quote only that part of it which begins with the words τούτου τοῦ
πνεύματος. Cyril and Malalas doubtless made the same mistake as to the meaning
of τοῦ λόγου.   ¹ Perhaps τοσοῦτος.

² ἂν addidi. The Hermetist must have written ἂν, which is needed to make
sense; whether Didymus wrote ἂν or omitted it, we have no means of knowing.

³ The πνεῦμα of which the Hermetist here speaks is the Stoic πνεῦμα which διὰ
πάντων διήκει (or possibly a blend of this with the divine πνεῦμα spoken of by
Jews). But the Hermetic writer, being a Platonist, regards this πνεῦμα as issuing
from a supreme and supracosmic God; and though he does not explicitly call it
a 'second God', it holds the same place in his system as the 'second God' in the
systems of other Platonists.

⁴ βαστάζον κατ᾽ ἀξίαν τὰ πάντα secludendum? βαστάζον κατ᾽ ἀξίαν is meaningless;
and τὰ πάντα looks like a doublet of the preceding τὰ πάντα. [βαστάζον, κατ᾽ ἀξίαν
Mingarelli.]

⁵ 'Hangs from a ount' is a strange metaphor; and it may be suspected that
the Hermetist wrote some verb meaning 'issues' or 'flows forth' (e.g. ἐξερρύηκεν).

⁶ Lacunam signavi. ἐπίκουρον πνεύμασι (πνεύματι Cyril) is impossible here; has

αὖθίς τε, τῇ εὐγενεστέρᾳ γνώμῃ καθυποτάττων τοὺς πολλοὺς καὶ οὐκ
ἀκριβεῖς περὶ τὴν γνῶσιν [τὴν ἕνεκα]¹ τῆς ἀχράντως, ἀμετρήτως, ἀφάτως,
καὶ ἀεὶ καὶ ὡσαύτως ἐχούσης αὐτοτέλους τριάδος, περὶ ἧς οὐδεὶς οὕτως
μεγαλοφρονέστατος οὐδὲ ⌜ὑψηλοπουστότατος⌝² ἀνθρώπων ἐστὶν ὃς ἄξιόν τι
5 τῆς τοσαύτης ὑπεροχῆς αὐτῆς θεωρῆσαι δύναται, ἀποφθέγγεται τοιάδε·³
"οὐ γὰρ ἐφικτόν ἐστιν εἰς ἀμυήτους τοιαῦτα μυστήρια παρέ- B
χεσθαι.⁴ ἀλλὰ τῷ νῷ⁵ ἀκούσατε. ἓν μόνον ἦν ⌜φῶς νοερὸν
πρὸ φωτὸς νοεροῦ⌝ καὶ ἔστιν ἀεὶ ⌜νοῦς νοὸς φωτεινός⌝.⁶ καὶ
οὐδὲν ἕτερον ἦν ἢ ἡ τούτου ἑνότης. ἀεὶ ἐν ⟨ἑ⟩αυτῷ⁷ ὤν, ἀεὶ
10 τῷ ἑαυτοῦ νοῒ καὶ φωτὶ καὶ πνεύματι πάντα περιέχει." καὶ 760 A
μεταξὺ ἄλλων ἐπάγει·⁸ "ἐκτὸς τούτου οὐ θεός, οὐ⟨κ⟩ ἄγγελος, οὐ
δαίμων, οὐκ οὐσία τις ἄλλη· πάντων γάρ ἐστι κύριος καὶ
πατὴρ ⌜καὶ θεὸς καὶ πηγὴ καὶ ζωὴ καὶ δύναμις καὶ φῶς καὶ

it come from a marginal note? The Hermetist may perhaps have written something like ⟨αἴτιον φωτὸς⟩ καὶ ζωῆς ἅπασιν ἀεὶ ὑπάρχον.

¹ τὴν ἕνεκα seclusi. It may be a corruption of some alternative for τὴν γνῶσιν
(e. g. τὴν ἐνέργειαν).

² ὑψηλονούστατος coni. Mingarelli. Perhaps οὕτω μεγαλόφρων οὐδὲ ὑψηλόνους.

³ Didymus does not give the title of the *libellus* from which he quotes this
passage (οὐ γὰρ ἐφικτόν κ.τ.λ.), but merely writes αὖθίς τε (Ἑρμῆς) . . . ἀποφθέγγεται
τοιάδε. But Cyril (c. *Julianum* 556 A) says that the passage occurred ἐν λόγῳ
τρίτῳ τῶν πρὸς Ἀσκληπιόν, i. e. in the same *libellus* from which the other extract
(εἰ μὴ πρόνοιά τις κ.τ.λ.) was taken. This shows that Cyril had that *libellus* before
him, and read in it the passage which he found quoted by Didymus,—unless
indeed he read Didymus carelessly, and mistakenly understood him to say that both
passages were taken from the same *libellus. Fr.* 23.

⁴ παρέχεσθαι, whether passive or middle, does not suit well with ἐφικτόν
('accessible' or 'attainable'). Perhaps the Hermetist may have written οὐ γὰρ
ἐφικτόν ἐστι τοῖς ἀμυήτοις τοιαῦτα μυστήρια παρ⟨αδ⟩έχεσθαι.

⁵ Perhaps ⟨ἐντεταμένῳ⟩ τῷ νῷ, or something of the sort. [Cf. p. 207, n. 11.]

⁶ The ἕν which 'alone existed (in the beginning)' must be the supreme God;
but the corruption of the text makes it doubtful by what name the Hermetist here
called the supreme God. Did he call him νοῦς, or φῶς νοερόν? Or did he apply
these terms, or either of them, to the second God only? The original text of the
Hermeticum, which had doubtless been corrupted before it came into the hands of
Didymus, might be conjecturally reconstructed in some such way as this : ἐν μόνον
ἦν [φῶς νοερὸν] [πρὸ φωτὸς νοεροῦ] καὶ ἔστιν ἀεί, νοῦς, νο⟨ερ⟩οῦ φωτ⟨εινὸ⟩ς ⟨αἴτιος⟩·
καὶ οὐδὲν ἕτερον ἦν ἢ ἡ τούτου ἑνότης. ⟨οὗτος⟩, ἀεὶ ἐν ⟨ἑ⟩αυτῷ ὤν (or possibly ἀεὶ
ἑαυτὸν νοῶν?), ἀεὶ τῷ ἑαυτοῦ [νοῒ καὶ] φωτὶ καὶ πνεύματι πάντα περιέχει. If this
attempt at restoration rightly expresses the Hermetist's meaning, he called the
supreme God νοῦς, and the terms φῶς (νοερόν) and πνεῦμα were used by him,
as synonyms, to denote a creative and life-giving force which is emitted by the
supreme God, and works upon the universe and all things in it.

⁷ ἑαυτῷ scripsi : αὐτῷ cod. Didym.

⁸ καὶ μεταξὺ ἄλλων ἐπάγει Didymus : καὶ μεθ' ἕτερά φησι Cyril. The passage
which follows (ἐκτὸς τούτου κ.τ.λ.) occurred in the same Hermetic *libellus* as the
preceding passage, i. e. in the 'third Discourse of Hermes to Asclepius'. τούτου
means the supreme God, who is spoken of in the preceding extract; and in the
Hermetic document the two passages may have been separated by one or two
intervening sentences only.

νοῦς καὶ πνεῦμα⌉,[1] καὶ πάντα ἐν αὐτῷ καὶ ὑπ' αὐτόν ἐστι."
νοῦν ἐκ νοῦ ⟨λέγων⟩,[2] καὶ φῶς νοερὸν ἐκ φωτὸς νοεροῦ,[3] ἔτι δὲ καὶ πνεῦμα
ὃ [4] πάντα περιέχει, τὸν θεὸν πατέρα καὶ τὸν μονογενῆ καὶ τὸ ἐν αὐτοῦ ἅγιον
πνεῦμα δηλοῖ· ὡς ἡ Σοφία λέγει "πνεῦμα κυρίου πεπλήρωκε τὴν οἰκουμένην". ἀγγέλους δὲ καὶ δαίμονας, καὶ τοὺς λεχθέντας μὲν ὑπὸ Ἑλλήνων 5
B οὐκ ὄντας δὲ ἀληθῶς θεούς, καὶ πᾶσαν φύσιν, ὑπὸ ταύτην ⟨φησὶν⟩ [5] εἶναι
τὴν ἀδιαίρετον ἐξουσίαν, τὴν μίαν πάντων δημιουργικὴν ἀρχήν.

καὶ Πορφύριος [6] δέ, καίτοι τὸ παράπαν οὐ σωφρονῶν περὶ τὸ ὄντως θεῖον,
ἀλλ' αὐτοχολωτῶν [7] ὡς εἰπεῖν, ὅμως Πλάτωνος ἐκτιθέμενος δόξαν,[8] καὶ
πώς ποτε συνελαθεὶς ὑπὸ τῆς ἀληθείας, ἢ τάχα καὶ τὸν Πλάτωνα αἰδεσθείς, 10
φάναι διενοήθη ταυτί· "ἄχρι γὰρ τριῶν ὑποστάσεων ἔφη Πλάτων τὴν
τοῦ θείου [9] προελθεῖν οὐσίαν· εἶναι δὲ τὸν μὲν ἀνωτάτω θεὸν τἀγαθόν, μετ'
αὐτὸν δὲ καὶ δεύτερον τὸν δημιουργόν, τρίτην δὲ καὶ τὴν [10] τοῦ κόσμου
C ψυχήν· ἄχρι γὰρ ψυχῆς τὴν θειότητα [11] προελθεῖν." [12] ⌈ὡς⌉ τὸ ἔνδον τεθολω-

---

[1] The words καὶ θεὸς καὶ πηγὴ καὶ ζωὴ καὶ δύναμις καὶ φῶς καὶ νοῦς καὶ πνεῦμα were probably thus written by Didymus, as they are repeated without variation by Cyril. But this long string of words, some at least of which are clearly inappropriate, cannot have been written by the Hermetist. It seems probable that in its original form the passage ran thus : πάντων γάρ ἐστι κύριος καὶ πατήρ, καὶ πάντα ἐν αὐτῷ καὶ ὑπ' αὐτόν ἐστι. We may suppose that καὶ πηγὴ ζωῆς καὶ φωτὸς καὶ πνεύματος was inserted by a later hand ; that this was corrupted into καὶ πηγὴ καὶ ζωὴ καὶ φῶς καὶ πνεῦμα ; and that, before the time of Didymus, καὶ θεός and καὶ δύναμις and καὶ νοῦς were added.

[2] λέγων addidi.

[3] Didymus apparently understood νοῦς νοός in his corrupt text of the *Hermeticum* to mean νοῦς ἐκ νοός, and took φῶς νοερὸν πρὸ φωτὸς νοεροῦ to imply that the latter of the two φάεα νοερά issued ' out of ' (ἐκ) the former. And thus interpreting the words, he identified the first νοῦς and φῶς νοερόν with God the Father, and the second νοῦς and φῶς νοερόν with God the Son. Compare Cyril *c. Julianum* 556 B : νοῦν μὲν γὰρ ἐκ νοῦ, καθάπερ ἐγῷμαι, φησὶ τὸν υἱόν, καὶ [ὡς] φῶς ἐκ φωτός. κ.τ.λ. The resemblance of Cyril's comment on this Hermetic passage to that of Didymus would, even if there were no other evidence, suffice to prove that Cyril had Didymus *De Trinitate* in his hands.

[4] ὃ scripsi : ᾧ cod. Didym. Cf. Cyril *ib*.: μέμνηται δὲ καὶ τοῦ πνεύματος ὡς πάντα περιέχοντος. [5] φησὶν addidi.

[6] Cyril (*c. Julianum* 916 B) tells us that the passage which follows (ἄχρι γὰρ τριῶν ὑποστάσεων κ.τ.λ.) occurred in the fourth book of Porphyry's Φιλοσόφου ἱστορία.

[7] αὐτοχωλωτων cod. [This seems to be a present participle balancing σωφρονῶν, and I have accented it accordingly. Translate ' being his own worst enemy ', and compare the new L. and S. *s.v.* αὐτοχόλωτος. For the form cf. ἀναισχυντεῖν.]

[8] The words Πλάτωνος ἐκτιθέμενος δόξαν are repeated by Cyril 553 B.

[9] θείου cod. Didym. and Cyril 553 B : θεοῦ Cyril 916 B.

[10] τρίτην δὲ καὶ τὴν cod. Didym. : τρίτον δὲ καὶ τὴν Cyril 553 B : τρίτην δὲ τὴν (which is probably what Porphyry wrote) Cyril 916 B.

[11] θειότητα cod. Didym. and Cyril (Aub.) 553 B : θεότητα Cyril 916 B. Porphyry most likely wrote θεότητα. Cyril apparently copied the passage from Didymus in 553 B, but took it directly from Porphyry in 916 B.

[12] τὸ ἀγαθόν was spoken of by Plato in *Rep.* VI 506 B–509 B, and the δημιουργός and ἡ τοῦ κόσμου ψυχή in the *Timaeus*. In the system of Plotinus there were three ὑποστάσεις, viz. τὸ ἀγαθόν (= τὸ ἕν), νοῦς, and ψυχή. Plotinus took τὸ ἀγαθόν

μένος καὶ βεβλαμμένος διορατικὸν¹ ὁ ἐπάρατος Πορφύριος, καὶ πρὸς τὴν **761 A**
τελεωτάτην ἀδυνατῶν θεολογίαν, ⌜ἅτε μήτε⌝² κατ' ἐπιθυμητικὴν² καὶ
φορτικὴν³ αὐτοῦ ὁρμὴν τὴν παροῦσαν ποιούμενος ἐξήγησιν, ἀμυδρῶς
τὸ ἓν καὶ σωστικὸν ἅγιον πνεῦμα τοῦ θεοῦ " ψυχήν " προσηγόρευσεν, οὐ
5 τὴν ἀνθρώπου δὲ ὅμως, ἀλλὰ τὴν ⟨ἐν⟩⁴ τῷ παντὶ διαπεφοιτηκυῖαν κόσμῳ.

ἔχεις οὖν καὶ τοὺς τῶν ἔξω σοφοὺς μαρτυροῦντας ὡς αἱ τρεῖς μακάριαι
ὑποστάσεις ἐν μιᾷ θεότητι ⟨. . .⟩.⁵ καὶ οὐκ ἄλλοτε καὶ ἄλλοτε ἐξεφάνησαν,
ἀλλ' ὅτε ἡ πρώτη, τότε σὺν αὐτῇ ἅμα καὶ ἐξ αὐτῆς καὶ ⌜ἡ ἄλλη καὶ ἡ
ἑτέρα⌝⁶ συναϊδίως, ὡς τὸ ἀπαύγασμα ⟨ἅμα⟩⁷ τῷ πυρί.

10 *De Trinitate*, lib. 3, cap. 1 : ψυχή, καθ' αὑτὴν ἐν τῷ νοητῷ ἀπαθὴς **773 B**
ὑπάρχουσα, τοῦ παθαίνεσθαί ποτε αἰτίαν ἔχει τὸ σώματι συνεῖναι, καὶ **C**
τὴν ἰδίαν αὐτῆς προαίρεσιν ἤγουν⁸ τῆς γνώσεως τὴν ἔφεσιν.⁹ τὸ μὲν
γὰρ σῶμα, ἐναποκεκλεισμένην ἔχον αὐτὴν ἐν ἑαυτῷ ὡς ἐν τυφλῷ φρουρίῳ,
διὰ τῶν ὑλικῶν παθῶν ἀπορρηγνύει τῆς τοῦ θεοῦ ὁμιλίας, καὶ καταφέρει
15 πρὸς γῆν καὶ τὰ γῆς, οἶμαι, φροντίσματα, καὶ οὕτω κατακρατεῖν ἐπιχειρεῖ **776 A**
τῆς φύσει κρείττονος, καὶ τοσούτῳ κρείττονος ὅσον τὸ ἀθάνατον
τοῦ θνητοῦ.¹⁰ ἡ δέ γε τῆς ἰδίας αὐτῆς προαιρέσεως ἢ γνώσεως πάλιν
ἐπιθυμία κ.τ.λ.

πολλάκις δὲ καὶ τὰ περὶ αὐτοῦ¹¹ ἢ παρ' αὐτοῦ μὴ λεχθέντα, ἢ δι'**780 C**
20 ἐπικρύψεως ᾐνιγμένα, ὡς κατ' αὐτοῦ ἢ παρ' αὐτοῦ ἀποπεφασμένα ἀβασανί-
στως διατιθέασιν,¹² καὶ πάντα σαθρὸν καὶ ἄναλκιν ἐκτετιμήκασι νοῦν,¹³ οὐδὲν

of Pl. *Rep.* to be the first of these three, the δημιουργός of Pl. *Tim.* to be νοῦς, the
second of them, and the cosmic ψυχή of Pl. *Tim.* to be the third; and Porphyry
followed Plotinus in thus explaining Plato's meaning.

Didymus identifies the ἀγαθόν of Plotinus and Porphyry with God the Father,
their νοῦς (= δημιουργός) with God the Son, and their cosmic ψυχή with God the
Holy Ghost. And Cyril follows Didymus in this.

¹ Perhaps ὁρατικόν.—τὸ ἔνδον ὁρατικόν or διορατικόν is ' the eye of the mind '.
² Perhaps ἅτε μὴ ⟨. . ., ἀλλὰ⟩ κατ' ἐπιθυμητικὴν κ.τ.λ.
³ φορτκὴν scripsi : φοιτικὴν cod.   ⁴ ἐν addidi.
⁵ Lacunam signavi.   ⁶ Perhaps [ἡ ἄλλη καὶ] ἡ ⟨δ⟩ε⟨υ⟩τέρα ⟨καὶ ἡ τρίτη⟩.
⁷ ἅμα addidi.   ⁸ ἤγουν scripsi : ἤτ' οὖν Mingarelli.
⁹ The phrase καὶ τὴν ἰδίαν αὐτῆς προαίρεσιν ἤγουν τῆς γνώσεως τὴν ἔφεσιν is of
Aristotelian origin ; it is based on Arist. *Metaph.* 1 *init.* (πάντες ἄνθρωποι τοῦ
εἰδέναι ὀρέγονται φύσει· σημεῖον δ' ἡ τῶν αἰσθήσεων ἀγάπησις, κ.τ.λ.), to which
Didymus expressly refers a few lines further on. But with that exception, the
passage ψυχὴ καθ' αὑτὴν . . . τὸ ἀθάνατον τοῦ θνητοῦ is wholly Platonic ; and as
its doctrine concerning the relation between soul and body is precisely that which
is again and again set forth in our *Hermetica*, and we know that Didymus had
read some of the Hermetic writings, it is not unlikely that he is here repeating
with little alteration the words of a *Hermeticum*.

¹⁰ The phrase τοσούτῳ κρείττονος ὅσον τὸ ἀθάνατον τοῦ θνητοῦ appears to be
a reminiscence of Herm. *ap.* Stob. *Exc.* I. 1 : ὅσον . . . τὸ ἔλαττον τοῦ κρείττονος
διέστηκε, τοσοῦτον τὸ θνητὸν τοῦ θείου (καὶ ἀθανάτου add. Cyril).

¹¹ *Sc.* περὶ τοῦ λυτρωτοῦ θεοῦ λόγου, i.e. Christ.
¹² The subject of διατιθέασιν is οἱ αἱρετικοί, i.e. the Arians.
¹³ Mingarelli translates ' et pravam quamlibet atque infirmam interpretationem
plurimi faciunt'. But the Greek is obscure, and perhaps corrupt.

καλλίους ἀλόγων ζῴων ἑαυτοὺς προσάγοντες τούτῳ τῷ περιποθήτῳ δεσπότῃ,
τῷ ἄγοντι δίχα βίας τοὺς πειθομένους εἰς τὴν τοῦ πατρὸς καὶ ἑαυτοῦ καὶ
τοῦ ἁγίου πνεύματος μίαν ἀδιαίρετον βασιλείαν, καὶ φειδοῖ τῇ πρὸς ἡμᾶς
παραινοῦντι " μὴ γίνεσθε ὡς ἵππος καὶ ἡμίονος, οἷς οὐκ ἔστιν σύνεσις ".[1]
τὰ γὰρ ἄλογα ζῷα, φησίν,[2] οἷς ἡ ψυχὴ τὸ ἐξ ὕλης αἷμα, κατὰ τὸν εἰπόντα   5
ἐν τῇ Γενέσει[3] " τὸ αἷμα αὐτοῦ ἡ ψυχὴ αὐτοῦ ", εἰς γῆν νένευκεν, ἀεὶ τῇ
D γαστρὶ μόνῃ δουλεύοντα, καὶ οὐκ ἀνέστηκεν τῷ σώματι καὶ τῷ νῷ, ὡς ὁ
ἄνθρωπος, ὁ καὶ τῶν ἐπιγείων αἰσθανόμενος καὶ τὰ μετέωρα βλέπων, καὶ
ἐπὶ τὴν ἄνω γαληνοτάτην καὶ ἀπαθεστάτην κατάστασιν σπεύδων, καὶ ὡς ἐν
πανδοκ⟨ε⟩ίῳ[4] τινὶ ἐν τῷ κόσμῳ ἡγούμενος καταλελυκέναι, καὶ παρασκευαζό-   10
μενος ⌈ἵν' εὖ φρονῇ⌉[5] ἐφ' ἑκάστης[6] πρὸς τὴν ἐκ τούτου ἔξοδον.   διά τε
τοῦτο ἁπλοῦς τὴν πίστιν καὶ τὴν γνώμην ὁ σοφὸς ὑπάρχει, κ.τ.λ.

---

[1] *Ps.* 31. 11 (9).

[2] Who is the subject of φησίν? The passage τὰ γὰρ ἄλογα ζῷα ... εἰς γῆν νένευκεν κ.τ.λ. down to ἐκ τούτου ἔξοδον (with the exception of the parenthesis οἷς ἡ ψυχὴ τὸ αἷμα ... ἡ ψυχὴ αὐτοῦ inserted by Didymus) is manifestly taken, in substance if not verbally, from some Pagan author; and it seems probable that this author's name was written after φησί by Didymus, but has accidentally dropped out. The passage is Platonic, and agrees in tone with many passages in our *Hermetica*; it is therefore not impossible that Didymus may have written φησὶν Ἑρμῆς.

[3] The passage meant is *Levit.* 17. 11 and 14: ἡ ψυχὴ πάσης σαρκὸς αἷμα αὐτοῦ ἐστι. But Didymus may have been thinking also of *Gen.* 9. 4: κρέας ἐν αἵματι ψυχῆς οὐ φάγεσθε.

[4] πανδοκίῳ cod.

[5] ἵν' εὖ φρονῇ (ἵν' εὐφρονῇ Mingarelli) is unintelligible. It is probably a corruption of ἐὰν εὖ φρονῇ or ὅ γ' εὖ φρονῶν.

[6] *Sc.* ἡμέρας, ' every day '.

AMMIANUS MARCELLINUS[1]

21. 14: In hoc rerum aduersarum tumultu,[2] haerens eius (*sc.* Constantii) fortuna iam et subsistens, aduentare casum uitae difficilem, modo non loquentibus signis aperte monstrabat. Namque et nocturnis imaginibus terrebatur, et nondum penitus mersus in
5 somnum, umbram uiderat patris . . . . Post haec confessus est iunctioribus proximis, quod tamquam desolatus, secretum aliquid uidere desierit, quod interdum adfuisse sibi squalidius aestimabat, et putabatur genius esse quidam, tutelae salutis adpositus, eum reliquisse mundo citius digressurum.[3] Ferunt enim theologi, in
10 lucem editis hominibus cunctis, salua firmitate fatali,[4] huius modi quaedam uelut actus rectura numina sociari, admodum tamen paucissimis uisa, quos multiplices auxere uirtutes.[5] Idque et oracula et auctores docuere praeclari. Inter quos est etiam Menander comicus, apud quem hi senarii duo leguntur :

15
ἅπαντι δαίμων ἀνδρὶ συμπαρίσταται
εὐθὺς γενομένῳ, μυσταγωγὸς τοῦ βίου.

Itidem ⟨. . . . .⟩ sempiternis Homeri carminibus intellegi datur, non deos caelestes cum uiris fortibus conlocutos, nec adfuisse pugnantibus uel iuuisse, sed familiaris genios cum isdem uersatos,[6] quorum ad-
20 miniculis freti praecipuis, Pythagoras enituisse dicitur et Socrates, Numaque Pompilius, et superior Scipio, et (ut quidam existimant)

[1] Edited by Clark (Weidmann, 1910). Date of writing, *c.* A. D. 390.
[2] At the time spoken of (A. D. 361) the emperor Constantius had just heard of Julian's rebellion against him.
[3] 'It was thought that (his visitant) was a genius appointed to watch over his safety, (and that this genius) had abandoned him because he was about to die.' Constantius himself, being an Arian Christian, would doubtless have said that the visitant was his guardian angel ; but Pagans would say that it was his ἴδιος δαίμων ; and Ammianus, being a Pagan, speaks of it as such, and goes on to give an account of Pagan beliefs concerning the ἴδιος ἑκάστου δαίμων.
[4] That is to say, this doctrine of the ἴδιος δαίμων must be so understood as not to conflict with the fixity of εἱμαρμένη. (Cf. *quoad licitum est* below.) It is εἱμαρμένη that determines the time at which the man must die ; and when that time comes, his ἴδιος δαίμων, who has till then watched over him, is compelled to abandon him.
[5] Every man has an ἴδιος δαίμων, but to few men only has he visibly appeared, and those few have been men of exceptional virtue. (Constantius, however, according to Ammianus' estimate of him, was hardly a man of that sort.)
[6] That is, when Homer says that Apollo or Poseidon or Athena appeared to a man and spoke to him, or helped him in a fight, we must understand that the being of whom this is said was not a celestial god, but the man's ἴδιος δαίμων.

Marius et Octauianus, cui Augusti uocabulum delatum est primo,
Hermesque Termaximus et Tyaneus Apollonius atque Plotinus,
ausus quaedam super hac re disserere mystica, alteque monstrare,
quibus primordiis[1] hi genii animis conexi mortalium, eas tamquam
gremiis suis susceptas,[2] tuentur, (quoad licitum est)[3] docentque maiora, 5
si senserint puras, et a conluuione peccandi, inmaculata corporis
societate discretas.

[1] Ammianus apparently says that Plotinus taught a 'mystic' doctrine (that
is, a religious doctrine unknown or unintelligible to the *profanum uulgus*) concerning the ἴδιος δαίμων, and explained from what sources (ἐκ τίνων ἀρχῶν) the
ἴδιος δαίμων issues or emanates. If any particular passage in the *Enneads* of
Plotinus is referred to, it may perhaps be *Enn.* 3. 4, περὶ τοῦ εἰληχότος ἡμᾶς
δαίμονος. (Ammianus, if he read that chapter, would probably not be able to
make out what Plotinus meant, but would see that it contained *mystica* and *alta*.)
In any case, the doctrine spoken of is presumably that of Pl. *Tim.* 90 A, τὸ δὲ δὴ
περὶ τοῦ κυριωτάτου παρ' ἡμῖν ψυχῆς εἴδους (that is, τοῦ ἐν ἡμῖν νοῦ) διανοεῖσθαι δεῖ
τῇδε, ὡς ἄρα αὐτὸ δαίμονα θεὸς ἑκάστῳ δέδωκεν. That notion frequently recurs in
later philosophic writings ; e. g. Plut. *De gen. Socr.* 22 : τὸ μὲν οὖν ὑποβρύχιον ἐν
τῷ σώματι ψυχὴ λέγεται· τὸ δὲ φθορᾶς λειφθὲν οἱ πολλοί, νοῦν καλοῦντες, ἐντὸς εἶναι
νομίζουσιν αὐτῶν, . . . οἱ δ' ὀρθῶς ὑπονοοῦντες, ὡς ἐκτὸς ὄντα, δαίμονα προσαγορεύουσιν.
Marc. Aurel. 5. 27 : ὁ δαίμων ὃν ἑκάστῳ προστάτην καὶ ἡγεμόνα ὁ Ζεὺς ἔδωκεν,
ἀπόσπασμα ἑαυτοῦ· οὗτος δέ ἐστιν ὁ ἑκάστου νοῦς καὶ λόγος. That is to say, a
man's ἴδιος δαίμων is the νοῦς in him, and the νοῦς in him is a portion of the
divine νοῦς, or of God. That doctrine, though perhaps not explicitly stated in
the same terms in any one sentence of Plotinus, is in accordance with his teaching,
and might very well be ascribed to him.

   Certain passages concerning νοῦς in the extant *Hermetica*, e. g. *Corp.* X. 23
(could.), could be so interpreted : οὗτός (*sc.* ὁ νοῦς) ἐστιν ὁ ἀγαθὸς δαίμων· μακαρία
ψυχὴ ἡ τούτου πληρεστάτη, κακοδαίμων δὲ ψυχὴ ἡ τούτου κενή.

[2] That is, the man's ἴδιος δαίμων takes charge of him *at his birth* (Plot. 3. 4. 3).
This sentence is a repetition in other words of what was said above, 'in lucem
editis hominibus cunctis . . . quos multiplices auxere virtutes'.

[3] [*Quoad licitum est*. Plot. 3. 4. 5 : οὔτε γὰρ πολὺ κατωτέρω ἐᾷ (ὁ δαίμων)
ἐλθεῖν εἰς τὸ χεῖρον ὑπερκαθήμενος, ἀλλ' ἐκεῖνο ἐνεργεῖ μόνον τὸ ὑπ' αὐτόν, οὔτε
ὑπεράνω αὐτοῦ οὔτε εἰς ἴσον· οὐ γὰρ δύναται ἄλλο γενέσθαι ἢ ᾗ ἔστιν.]

AUGUSTINUS

De civitate Dei[1]: . . . restat ut nullo modo credendum sit, quod **8. 2**
Apuleius persuadere nititur[2] et quicumque alii sunt eiusdem
sententiae philosophi, ita esse medios daemones inter deos et
homines tamquam internuntios et interpretes, qui hinc ferant peti-
5 tiones nostras, inde referant deorum subpetias; sed esse spiritus
nocendi cupidissimos, a iustitia penitus alienos, superbia tumidos,
inuidentia liuidos, fallacia callidos, qui in hoc quidem aere habitant,
quia de caeli superioris sublimitate deiecti merito inregressibilis
transgressionis in hoc sibi congruo uelut carcere praedamnati sunt;
10 nec tamen, quia supra terras et aquas aeri locus est, ideo et ipsi sunt
meritis superiores hominibus, qui eos non terreno corpore, sed electo
in auxilium Deo uero pia mente facillime superant. Sed multis
plane participatione᾿uerae religionis indignis tamquam captis sub-
ditisque dominantur, quorum maximae parti mirabilibus et fallacibus
15 signis siue factorum siue praedictorum deos se esse persuaserunt.
Quibusdam uero uitia eorum aliquanto adtentius et diligentius
intuentibus non potuerunt persuadere quod di sint, adque inter deos
et homines internuntios ac beneficiorum inpetratores se esse finxerunt;
⌈si tamen non⌉ istum saltem honorem homines eis deferendum
20 putarunt, qui illos nec deos esse credebant, quia malos uidebant,
deos autem omnes bonos uolebant, nec audebant tamen omnino
indignos dicere honore diuino, maxime ne offenderent populos, a
quibus eis cernebant inueterata superstitione per tot sacra et templa
seruiri.
25   Nam diuersa de illis Hermes Aegyptius, quem Trismegistum **23**
uocant, sensit et scripsit. Apuleius enim deos quidem illos negat;
. sed cum dicit ita inter deos et homines quadam medietate uersari, ut
hominibus aput ipsos deos necessarii uideantur, cultum eorum a
supernorum deorum religione non separat. Ille autem Aegyptius
30 alios deos esse dicit a summo Deo factos, alios ab hominibus.[3] Hoc
qui audit, sicut a me positum est, putat dici de simulacris, quia opera

---

[1] Edited by Hoffmann (*Corp. script. eccl. lat.* vol. xxxx, Pars i, sect. v), 1899.
Date, A. D. 413–426.
[2] Apuleius, *De deo Socratis*, 6 *sqq.*
[3] Herm. *Ascl. Lat.* 23 b–24 a and 37.

sunt manuum hominum; at ille uisibilia et contrectabilia simulacra
uelut corpora deorum esse adserit; inesse autem his quosdam spiritus
inuitatos, qui ualeant aliquid siue ad nocendum siue ad desideria
nonnulla conplenda eorum, a quibus eis diuini honores et cultus
obsequia deferuntur. Hos ergo spiritus inuisibiles per artem quan- 5
dam uisibilibus rebus corporalis materiae copulare, ut sint quasi
animata corpora illis spiritibus dicata et subdita simulacra, hoc esse
dicit deos facere, eamque magnam et mirabilem deos faciendi
accepisse homines potestatem. Huius Aegyptii uerba, sicut in
nostram linguam interpretata sunt,[1] ponam. 'Et quoniam de 10
cognatione, inquit,[2] et consortio hominum deorumque
nobis indicitur sermo, potestatem hominis, o Asclepi,
uimque cognosce. Dominus, inquit, et Pater uel quod est
summum, Deus ut effector est deorum caelestium, ita
homo fictor est deorum qui in templis sunt humana 15
proximitate contenti.' Et paulo post: 'Ita humanitas,
inquit, semper memor naturae et originis suae in illa
diuinitatis imitatione perseuerat, ut., sicuti Pater ac
Dominus, ut sui similes essent. deos fecit aeternos, ita
humanitas deos suos ex sui uultus similitudine figuraret.' 20
Hic cum Asclepius, ad quem maxime loquebatur, ei respondisset
adque dixisset: 'Statuas dicis, o Trismegiste?' tum ille,
'Statuas, inquit, o Asclepi; uides quatenus tu ipse diffi-
das; statuas animatas sensu et spiritu plenas tantaque
facientes et talia, statuas futurorum praescias eaque 25
sorte uate somniis·multisque aliis rebus praedicentes,
inbecillitates hominibus facientes easque curantes, tristitiam laetitiamque pro meritis. An ignoras, o Asclepi,
quod Aegyptus imago sit caeli, aut, quod est uerius,
translatio aut descensio omnium quae gubernantur adque 30
exercentur in caelo? Ac si dicendum est uerius, terra
nostra mundi totius est templum. Et tamen quoniam
praescire cuncta prudentem decet, istud uos ignorare
fas non est: Futurum tempus est, quo appareat Aegyptios

---

[1] Augustine does not name the translator. He cannot have supposed him to be
Apuleius; for if he had, he would necessarily have said so, seeing that he speaks
about Apuleius in this passage, and contrasts his teaching with that of 'Hermes'
(i. e. that of the *Ascl. Lat.*). See Introduction to *Ascl. Lat.* (vol i, pp. 78–79).

[2] *Ascl. Lat.* 23 b, 24 a b. There is reason to think that 24 b ('An ignoras
O Asclepi,' &c.), which is the beginning of the Prophecy, was originally unconnected
with 24 a, and was separated from it by something which is now lost; but Augustine
read the passage as it is given in our MSS. of *Ascl. Lat.*

incassum pia mente diuinitatem sedula religione ser-
uasse.'

Deinde multis uerbis Hermes hunc locum exequitur, in quo uidetur
hoc tempus praedicere, quo Christiana religio, quanto est ueracior
5 adque sanctior, tanto uehementius et liberius cuncta fallacia figmenta
subuertit, ut gratia uerissimi Saluatoris liberet hominem ab eis dis,
quos facit homo, et ei Deo subdat, a quo factus est homo.[1] Sed
Hermes cum ista praedicit, uelut amicus eisdem ludificationibus
daemonum loquitur, nec Christianum nomen euidenter exprimit, sed
10 tamquam ea tollerentur adque delerentur, quorum obseruatione
caelestis similitudo custodiretur in Aegypto, ita haec futura deplorans
luctuosa quodam modo praedicatione testatur. Erat enim de his, de
quibus dicit apostolus, quod ' cognoscentes Deum non sicut Deum
glorificauerunt aut gratias egerunt, sed euanuerunt in cogitationibus
15 suis, et obscuratum est insipiens cor eorum ; dicentes enim se esse
sapientes stulti facti sunt, et inmutauerunt gloriam incorrupti Dei in
similitudinem imaginis corruptibilis hominis '[2] et cetera, quae com-
memorare longum est. Multa quippe talia dicit[3] de uno uero Deo
fabricatore mundi, qualia ueritas habet ; et nescio quo modo illa
20 obscuratione cordis ad ista delabitur, ut dis, quos confitetur ab
hominibus fieri, semper uelit homines subdi et haec futuro tempore
plangat auferri quasi quicquam sit infelicius homine, cui sua figmenta
dominantur ; cum sit facilius, ut tamquam deos colendo, quos fecit,
nec ipse sit homo, quam ut per eius cultum di possint esse, quos
25 fecit homo. Citius enim fit, ut ' homo in honore positus pecoribus
non intelligens conparetur,'[4] quam ut operi Dei ad eius imaginem
facto, id est ipsi homini, opus hominis praeferatur. Quapropter
merito homo deficit ab illo qui eum fecit, cum sibi praeficit ipse
quod fecit.

30 Haec uana deceptoria perniciosa sacrilega Hermes Aegyptius,
quia tempus, quo auferrentur, uenturum sciebat, dolebat ; sed tam
inpudenter dolebat, quam inprudenter sciebat. Non enim haec ei
reuelauerat Sanctus Spiritus, sicut prophetis sanctis, qui haec praeui-
dentes cum exultatione dicebant : ' Si faciet homo deos, et ecce ipsi

---

[1] Augustine is right in taking the Prophecy (*Asct. Lat.* 24 b, 25) to be a predic-
tion of the victory of Christianity and the abolition of Paganism. But he assumes
that the man who predicted these things lived in the second millennium B.C., and
that the future events which he predicted were revealed to him by devils ('illi
spiritus indicauerunt,' &c., p. 182, l. 10).

[2] *Rom.* i. 21 *sqq.*   [3] *Sc.* Hermes, in *Ascl. Lat.*

[4] *Ps.* 48 (49). 13 and 20.

non sunt di;'[1] et alio loco: 'Erit in illo die, dicit Dominus, exterminabo nomina simulacrorum a terra, et non iam erit eorum memoria;'[2] proprie uero de Aegypto, quod ad hanc rem adtinet, ita sanctus Esaias prophetat: 'Et mouebuntur manufacta Aegypti a facie eius, et cor eorum uincetur in eis,'[3] et cetera huius modi. Ex 5 quo genere et illi erant, qui uenturum quod sciebant uenisse gaudebant; qualis Symeon,[4] qualis Anna,[5] qui mox natum Iesum, qualis Elisabeth,[6] quae etiam conceptum in Spiritu agnouit; qualis Petrus reuelante Patre dicens: 'Tu es Christus, filius Dei uiui.'[7] Huic autem Aegyptio illi spiritus indicauerant futura tempora perditionis 10 suae, qui etiam praesenti in carne Domino trementes dixerunt: 'Quid uenisti ante tempus perdere nos?'[8] Siue quia subitum illis fuit, quod futurum quidem, sed tardius opinabantur, siue quia perditionem suam hanc ipsam dicebant, qua fiebat ut cogniti spernerentur, et hoc erat 'ante tempus', id est ante tempus iudicii, quo aeterna damnatione 15 puniendi sunt cum omnibus etiam hominibus, qui eorum societate detinentur, sicut religio loquitur, quae neque fallit nec fallitur, non sicut iste quasi 'omni uento doctrinae hinc adque inde perflatus'[9] et falsis uera permiscens dolet quasi perituram religionem, quem postea[10] confitetur errorem. 20

24   Post multa enim ad hoc ipsum redit, ut iterum dicat de dis, quos homines fecerunt, ita loquens:[11] 'Sed iam de talibus sint satis dicta talia. Iterum, inquit, ad hominem rationemque redeamus, ex quo diuino dono [homo][12] animal dictum est rationale. Minus enim miranda etsi miranda sunt, quae 25 de homine dicta sunt. Omnium enim mirabilium uicit admirationem, quod homo diuinam potuit inuenire naturam eamque efficere. Quoniam ergo proaui nostri multum errabant circa deorum rationem increduli et non animaduertentes ad cultum religionemque diuinam, 30 inuenerunt artem, qua efficerent deos. Cui inuentae adiunxerunt uirtutem de mundi natura conuenientem, eamque miscentes, quoniam animas facere non poterant, euocantes animas daemonum uel angelorum eas indiderunt imaginibus sanctis diuinisque mysteriis, per quas 35

---

[1] *Jer.* 16. 20.   [2] *Zech.* 13. 2.
[3] *Isaiah* 19. 1.   [4] *Luke* 2. 25–35.
[5] *Luke* 2. 36–38.   [6] *Luke* 1. 41–45.
[7] *Matt.* 16. 16 *sq.*   [8] *Matt.* 8. 29.
[9] *Ephes.* 4. 14.   [10] I. e. in *Ascl. Lat.* 37, as misunderstood by Augustine.
[11] *Ascl. Lat.* 37.   [12] *om.* C d.

idola et bene faciendi et male uires habere potuissent.'
Nescio utrum sic confiterentur ipsi daemones adiurati,[1] quo modo
iste confessus est. 'Quoniam, inquit, proaui nostri multum
errabant[2] circa deorum rationem increduli et non anim-
5 aduertentes ad cultum religionemque diuinam, inuenerunt artem qua efficerent deos.' Numquidnam saltem
mediocriter eos dixit errasse, ut hanc artem inuenirent faciendi deos,
aut contentus fuit dicere ' Errabant ', nisi adderet et diceret ' Multum
errabant'? Iste ergo multus error et incredulitas non animaduerten-
10 tium ad cultum religionemque diuinam inuenit artem, qua efficeret
deos. Et tamen quod multus error et incredulitas et a cultu ac
religione diuina auersio animi inuenit, ut homo arte faceret deos, hoc
dolet uir sapiens tamquam religionem diuinam uenturo certo tempore
auferri. Vide si non et ui diuina maiorum suorum errorem praeteri-
15 tum prodere, et ui diabolica poenam daemonum futuram dolere
conpellitur. Si enim proaui eorum multum errando circa deorum
rationem incredulitate et auersione animi a cultu ac religione diuina
inuenerunt artem, qua efficerent deos : quid mirum, si, haec ars
detestanda quidquid fecit auersa a religione diuina, aufertur religione
20 diuina, cum ueritas emendat errorem, fides redarguit incredulitatem,
conuersio corrigit auersionem ?

Si enim tacitis causis dixisset proauos suos inuenisse artem, qua
facerent deos : nostrum fuit utique, si quid rectum piumque sapere-
mus, adtendere et uidere nequaquam illos ad hanc artem peruenturos

---

[1] It was believed that daemons sometimes confessed the truth about themselves
when expelled by exorcism from persons possessed by them. See ch. 26 *fin.*
below.

[2] The Greek must have been something like ἐπειδὴ πεπλανημένοι ἦσαν κ.τ.λ.,
'After our ancestors had been in error about the gods, and had not believed in
them nor worshipped them, they invented an art of god-making'; i. e. there was a
time when men were without religion (cf. *Kore Kosmu* 53 *sqq.*), but that state of
things came to an end when the art of making gods was discovered. But Augustine,
misled by the translator's rendering of ἐπειδή by *quoniam*, supposes the meaning of
the sentence which he quotes to be ' Our ancestors invented the art of making gods
because they were in error', &c. He is surprised to find Hermes making an
admission so damaging to his own cause; and he accounts for it by assuming that
Hermes was inspired by a devil ('malo spiritu instigatus') when he spoke of the
art of god-making with approval, but was at the same time compelled by God
('ui divina') to confess that this god-making was a result of error and irreligion.

Augustine agrees with the Hermetist in believing that 'souls' (i. e. incorporeal
living beings) are embodied in statues by means of certain rites; but he differs
from him as to the moral character of the souls thus embodied, and calls them
' unclean spirits' ('immundi spiritus eisdem simulacris arte illa nefaria conligati ').
He agrees with him in believing that they sometimes heal the sick, and predict
future events; but he thinks that, when they do so, these apparent benefits are
harmful ('quasi beneficia praestando magis nocentes, quia magis decipientes ').

fuisse, qua homo deos facit, si a ueritate non aberrarent, si ea, quae
Deo digna sunt, crederent, si animum aduerterent ad cultum
religionemque diuinam; et tamen si causas artis huius nos diceremus
multum errorem hominum et incredulitatem et animi errantis adque
infidelis a diuina religione auersionem, utcumque ferenda esset 5
inpudentia resistentium ueritati. Cum uero idem ipse, qui potestatem huius artis super omnia cetera miratur in homine, qua illi deos
facere concessum est, et dolet uenturum esse tempus, quo haec
omnia deorum figmenta ab hominibus instituta etiam legibus
iubeantur auferri,[1] confitetur tamen adque exprimit causas, quare ad 10
ista peruentum sit, dicens proauos suos multo errore et incredulitate
et animum non aduertendo ad cultum religionemque diuinam
inuenisse hanc artem, qua facerent deos: nos quid oportet dicere,
uel potius quid agere nisi quantas possumus gratias Domino Deo
nostro, qui haec contrariis causis, quam instituta sunt, abstulit? 15
Nam quod instituit multitudo erroris, abstulit uia ueritatis; quod
instituit incredulitas, abstulit fides; quod instituit a cultu diuinae
religionis auersio, abstulit ad unum uerum Deum sanctumque conuersio; nec in sola Aegypto, quam solam in isto plangit daemonum
spiritus, sed in omni terra, quae cantat Domino canticum nouum, 20
sicut uere sacrae et uere propheticae litterae praenuntiarunt, ubi
scriptum est: 'Cantate Domino canticum nouum, cantate Domino
omnis terra.'[2] Titulus quippe psalmi huius est: 'Quando domus
aedificabitur post captiuitatem.' Aedificatur enim domus Domino
ciuitas Dei, quae est sancta ecclesia, in omni terra post eam captiui- 25
tatem, qua illos homines, de quibus credentibus in Deum tamquam
lapidibus uiuis domus aedificatur,[3] captos daemonia possidebant.
Neque enim, quia deos homo faciebat, ideo non ab eis possidebatur
ipse qui fecerat, quando in eorum societatem colendo traducebatur;
societatem dico, non idolorum stolidorum, sed uersutorum daemo- 30
niorum. Nam quid sunt idola, nisi quod eadem scriptura dicit:
'Oculos habent, et non uidebunt,'[4] et quidquid tale de materiis licet
adfabre effigiatis, tamen uita sensuque carentibus dicendum fuit.
Sed inmundi spiritus eisdem simulacris arte illa nefaria conligati
cultorum suorum animas in suam societatem redigendo miserabiliter 35

[1] *Ascl. Lat.* 24 b: 'quasi de legibus a religione, pietate, cultuque divino statuetur
praescripta poena prohibitio.' Ib. 25: 'capitale periculum constituetur in eum qui
se mentis religioni dederit. Nova constituentur iura, lex nova.' Both those sentences
must be of later date than the rest of the Prophecy in which they are inserted;
but one of them, if not both, must have been present in the text as read by
Augustine.
[2] *Ps.* 95 (96). 1.   [3] *1 Pet.* 2. 5.   *Ps.* 114 (115). 5.

captiuauerant. Unde dicit apostolus: 'Scimus quia nihil est idolum ;
sed quae immolant gentes, daemoniis immolant, et non Deo ; nolo
uos socios fieri daemoniorum.'[1] Post hanc ergo captiuitatem, qua
homines a malignis daemonibus tenebantur, Dei domus aedificatur
5 in omni terra ; unde titulum ille psalmus accepit, ubi dicitur :
'Cantate Domino canticum nouum, cantate Domino omnis terra.
Cantate Domino, benedicite nomen eius, bene nuntiate diem ex die
salutare eius. Adnuntiate in gentibus gloriam eius, in omnibus
populis mirabilia eius ; quoniam magnus Dominus et laudabilis
10 nimis, terribilis est super omnes deos. Quia omnes di gentium
daemonia, dominus autem caelos fecit.'[2]

Qui ergo doluit uenturum fuisse tempus, quo auferretur cultus
idolorum et in eos, qui colerent, dominatio daemoniorum, malo
spiritu instigatus semper uolebat istam captiuitatem manere, qua
15 transacta psalmus canit aedificari domum in omni terra. Praenuntiabat illa Hermes dolendo ; praenuntiabat haec propheta
gaudendo. Et quia Spiritus uictor est, qui haec per sanctos
prophetas canebat, etiam Hermes ipse ea, quae nolebat et dolebat
auferri, non a prudentibus et fidelibus et religiosis, sed ab errantibus
20 et incredulis et a cultu diuinae religionis auersis esse instituta miris
modis coactus est confiteri. Qui quamuis eos appellet deos, tamen
cum dicit a talibus hominibus factos, quales esse utique non debemus,
uelit nolit, ostendit colendos non esse ab eis, qui tales non sunt,
quales fuerunt a quibus facti sunt, hoc est a prudentibus, fidelibus,
25 religiosis ; simul etiam demonstrans ipsos homines, qui eos fecerunt,
sibimet inportasse, ut eos haberent deos, qui non erant di. Verum
est quippe illud propheticum : 'Si faciet homo deos, et ecce ipsi non
sunt di.'[3] Deos ergo tales, talium deos, arte factos a talibus, cum
appellasset Hermes, id est idolis daemones per artem nescio quam
30 cupiditatum suarum uinculis inligatos cum appellaret factos ab
hominibus deos, non tamen eis dedit quod Platonicus Apuleius
(unde[4] iam satis diximus, et quam sit inconueniens absurdumque
monstra uimus), ut ipsi essent interpretes et intercessores inter deos,
quos fecit Deus, et homines, quos idem fecit Deus ; hinc adferentes
35 uota, inde munera referentes. Nimis enim stultum est credere deos,
quos fecerunt homines, plus ualere aput deos, quos fecit Deus, quam
ualent ipsi homines, quos idem ipse fecit Deus. Daemon quippe
simulacro arte inpia conligatus ab homine factus est deus, sed tali

[1] *I Cor.* 10. 20.
[2] *Ps.* 95 (96). 1 *sqq.*
[3] *Jer.* 16. 20.
[4] *De civ. dei*, 8. 18.

homini, non omni homini. Qualis est ergo iste deus, quem non faceret homo nisi errans et incredulus et auersus a uero Deo? Porro si daemones, qui coluntur in templis, per artem nescio quam imaginibus inditi, hoc est uisibilibus simulacris, ab eis hominibus, qui hac arte fecerunt deos, cum aberrarent auersique essent a cultu et 5 religione diuina, non sunt internuntii nec interpretes inter homines et deos et propter suos pessimos ac turpissimos mores, et quod homines, quamuis errantes et increduli et auersi a cultu ac religione diuina, tamen eis sine dubio meliores sunt, quos deos ipsi arte fecerunt; restat, ut, quod possunt, tamquam daemones possint, uel quasi 10 beneficia praestando magis nocentes, quia magis decipientes, uel aperte malefaciendo (nec tamen quodlibet horum, nisi quando permittuntur alta et secreta Dei prouidentia), non autem tamquam medii inter homines et deos per amicitiam deorum multum aput homines ualeant. Hi enim dis bonis, quos sanctos angelos nos 15 uocamus rationalesque creaturas sanctae caelestis habitationis 'siue sedes siue dominationes siue principatus siue potestates',[1] amici esse omnino non possunt, a quibus tam longe absunt animi affectione, quam longe absunt a uirtutibus uitia et a bonitate malitia.

25 Nullo modo igitur per daemonum quasi medietatem ambien- 20 dum est ad beneuolentiam seu beneficentiam deorum uel potius angelorum bonorum, sed per bonae uoluntatis similitudinem, qua cum illis sumus et cum illis uiuimus et cum illis Deum quem colunt colimus, etsi eos carnalibus oculis uidere non possumus; in quantum autem dissimilitudine uoluntatis et fragilitate infirmitatis miseri 25 sumus, in tantum ab eis longe sumus uitae merito, non corporis loco. Non enim quia in terra condicione carnis habitamus, sed si inmunditia cordis terrena sapimus, non eis iungimur. Cum uero sanamur, ut quales ipsi sunt simus; fide illis interim propinquamus, si ab illo nos fieri beatos, a quo et ipsi facti sunt, etiam ipsis fauentibus 30 credimus. —

26 Sane aduertendum est, quo modo iste Aegyptius, cum doleret tempus esse uenturum, quo illa auferrentur ex Aegypto quae fatetur a multum errantibus et incredulis et a cultu diuinae religionis auersis esse instituta, ait inter cetera: 'Tunc terra ista, sanctissima 35 sedes delubrorum adque templorum, sepulcrorum erit mortuorumque plenissima';[2] quasi uero, si illa non auferrentur, non essent homines morituri, aut alibi essent mortui ponendi quam in terra; et utique, quanto plus uolueretur temporis et dierum,

---

[1] *Col.* 11. 6.　　　　　　　　　　[2] *Ascl. Lat.* 24 b.

tanto maior esset numerus sepulcrorum propter maiorem numerum
mortuorum. Sed hoc uidetur dolere, quod memoriae martyrum
nostrorum templis eorum delubrisque succederent, ut uidelicet, qui
haec legunt animo a nobis auerso adque peruerso, putent a paganis
5 cultos fuisse deos in templis, a nobis autem coli mortuos in sepulcris.[1]
Tanta enim homines inpii caecitate in montes quodam modo
offendunt resque oculos suos ferientes nolunt uidere, ut non adtendant
in omnibus litteris paganorum aut non inueniri aut uix inueniri deos,
qui non homines fuerint mortuisque diuini honores delati sint.
10 Omitto, quod Varro dicit omnes ab eis mortuos existimari manes
deos et probat per ea sacra, quae omnibus fere mortuis exhibentur,
ubi et ludos commemorat funebres, tamquam hoc sit maximum
diuinitatis indicium, quod non soleant ludi nisi numinibus celebrari.

Hermes ipse, de quo nunc agitur, in eodem ipso libro, ubi quasi
15 futura praenuntiando deplorans ait: 'Tunc terra ista, sanctissima sedes delubrorum adque templorum, sepulcrorum
erit mortuorumque plenissima,' deos Aegypti homines mortuos
esse testatur. Cum enim dixisset proauos suos multum errantes
circa deorum rationem, incredulos et non animaduertentes ad cultum
20 religionemque diuinam, inuenisse artem, qua efficerent deos: 'Cui

---

[1] Augustine takes *mortuorum* to signify Christian martyrs, and *sepulcrorum* the
graves of the martyrs, and supposes Hermes to mean that the Egyptians, when
they cease to worship the Pagan gods, will worship Christian martyrs instead
According to him, Hermes in one place (*Ascl. Lat.* 24 b) says that worship of dead
men is a pollution of the land, and in another passage of the same book (*ib.* 37)
admits that the Pagan religion which he advocates is a worship of dead men.
Augustine accounts for this inconsistency by assuming that in ch. 24 the devil who
speaks through the mouth of Hermes is expressing his hatred of the Christian
martyr-worship, whereas in ch. 37 this same devil is reluctantly compelled by the
power of God to confess that the gods of the Egyptians are dead men.

Augustine's interpretation of the passage cannot be right; for it is impossible to
believe that the Hermetist can have been guilty of so gross a self-contradiction.
Seeing that he himself held that the gods worshipped in the Egyptian temples, or
some of them at least, were dead men, he cannot have spoken of the worship of
dead men as a horrible thing.

There is no reason to doubt that chs. 24 and 37 were written by the same
person; but even on the supposition that the two passages were written by different
hands, the difficulty would not be removed; for worship of dead men (e. g. former
kings and emperors), and of gods who were believed to have once lived on earth as
men, was so firmly established and so generally accepted by the Pagans in Egypt,
that no Hermetic writer could have spoken of it with detestation. Consequently,
the words *sepulcrorum erit mortuorumque plenissima* cannot mean what Augustine
supposed.

It is true that Julian (*Contra Christianos* I. 335 B Neumann) speaks in like terms
about Christian martyr-worship: ὅσα δὲ ὑμεῖς ἑξῆς προσευρήκατε, πολλοὺς ἐπεισά-
γοντες τῷ πάλαι νεκρῷ (sc. Jesus) τοὺς προσφάτους νεκρούς, τίς ἂν πρὸς ἀξίαν
βδελύξαιτο· πάντα ἐπληρώσατε τάφων καὶ μνημάτων· καίτοι οὐκ εἴρηται παρ' ὑμῖν
οὐδαμοῦ τοῖς τάφοις προσκαλινδεῖσθαι καὶ περιεπεῖν αὐτούς. But the sentiment
expressed by Julian is Hellenic, and not Egyptian; and there is no ground for

inuentae, inquit,[1] adiunxerunt uirtutem de mundi natura
conuenientem eamque miscentes, quoniam animas facere
non poterant, euocantes animas daemonum uel angelorum
eas indiderunt imaginibus sanctis diuinisque mysteriis,
per quas idola et bene faciendi et male uires habere 5
potuissent.' Deinde sequitur tamquam hoc exemplis probaturus,
et dicit: 'Auus enim tuus, o Asclepi, medicinae primus
inuentor, cui templum consecratum est in monte Libyae
circa litus crocodilorum, in quo eius iacet mundanus
homo, id est corpus; reliquus enim, uel potius totus, si 10
est homo totus in sensu uitae, melior remeauit in caelum,
omnia etiam nunc hominibus adiumenta praestans in-
firmis numine nunc suo, quae solent medicinae arte
praeberi.' Ecce dixit mortuum coli pro deo in eo loco, ubi habebat
sepulcrum, falsus ac fallens, quod remeauit in caelum. Adiungens 15
deinde aliud 'Hermes, inquit, cuius auitum mihi nomen est,
nonne in sibi cognomine patria consistens omnes mortales
undique uenientes adiuuat adque conseruat?' Hic enim
Hermes maior, id est Mercurius, quem dicit auum suum fuisse, in
Hermopoli, hoc est in sui nominis ciuitate, esse perhibetur. Ecce 20
duos deos dicit homines fuisse, Aesculapium et Mercurium. Sed de
Aesculapio et Graeci et Latini hoc idem sentiunt; Mercurium autem
multi non putant fuisse mortalem, quem tamen iste auum suum fuisse
testatur. At enim alius est ille, alius iste, quamuis eodem nomine
nuncupentur. Non multum pugno, alius ille sit, alius iste; uerum 25
et iste; sicut Aesculapius, ex homine deus secundum testimonium
tanti aput suos uiri, huius Trismegisti, nepotis sui.

Adhuc addit et dicit: 'Isin uero Osiris quam multa bona
praestare propitiam, quantis obesse scimus iratam!'
Deinde ut ostenderet ex hoc genere esse deos, quos illa arte homines 30
faciunt (unde dat intellegi daemones se opinari ex hominum mortuorum animis extitisse, quos per artem, quam inuenerunt homines
multum errantes, increduli et inreligiosi, ait inditos simulacris, quia
hi, qui tales deos faciebant, animas facere non utique poterant), cum

ascribing to the Hermetist a similar repugnance to the worship of dead men
as gods.

The writer of the Hermetic prophecy must have meant, not that there will be
much worship of martyrs, but that there will be much slaughter. The words
sepulcrorum erit mortuorumque plenissima may be an inaccurate translation of
ταφῶν (gen. pl. of ταφή) καὶ νεκρῶν πληρεστάτη ἔσται, 'the land will be full of
funerals and (unburied) corpses'.

[1] *Ascl. Lat.* 37.

de Iside dixisset, quod commemoraui, 'quantis obesse scimus iratam', secutus adiunxit: 'Terrenis etenim dis adque mundanis facile est irasci, utpote qui sint ab hominibus ex utraque natura facti adque conpositi.' 'Ex utraque natura'
5 dicit ex anima et corpore, ut pro anima sit daemon, pro corpore simulacrum. 'Unde contigit', inquit, 'ab Aegyptiis haec sancta animalia nuncupari, colique per singulas ciuitates eorum animas, quorum sunt consecratae uiuentes, ita ut eorum legibus incolantur et eorum nominibus nuncu-
10 pentur.' Ubi est illa uelut querela luctuosa, quod terra Aegypti, sanctissima sedes delubrorum adque templorum, sepulcrorum futura esset mortuorumque plenissima? Nempe spiritus fallax, cuius instinctu Hermes ista dicebat, per eum ipsum coactus est confiteri iam tunc illam terram sepulcrorum et mortuorum, quos pro dis
15 colebant, fuisse plenissimam. Sed dolor daemonum per eum loquebatur, qui suas futuras poenas aput sanctorum martyrum memorias inminere maerebant. In multis enim talibus locis torquentur et confitentur, et de possessis hominum corporibus eiciuntur.

Nec tamen nos eisdem martyribus templa, sacerdotia, sacra et **27**
20 sacrificia constituimus, quoniam non ipsi, sed Deus eorum nobis est Deus. Honoramus sane memorias eorum tamquam sanctorum hominum Dei.... Quaecumque igitur adhibentur religiosorum obsequia in martyrum locis, ornamenta sunt memoriarum, non sacra uel sacrificia mortuorum tamquam deorum. ...

25 Nos itaque martyres nostros nec diuinis honoribus nec humanis criminibus colimus, sicut colunt illi deos suos, nec sacrificia illis offerimus, nec eorum probra in eorum sacra conuertimus. Nam de Iside, uxore Osiris, Aegyptia dea, et de parentibus eorum, qui omnes reges fuisse scribuntur (quibus parentibus suis illa cum sacrificaret,
30 inuenit hordei segetem adque inde spicas marito regi et eius consiliario Mercurio demonstrauit, unde eandem et Cererem uolunt[1]), quae et quanta mala non a poetis, sed mysticis eorum litteris memoriae mandata sint, sicut Leone sacerdote prodente ad Olympiadem matrem scribit Alexander,[2] legant qui uolunt uel possunt, et
35 recolant qui legerunt, et uideant quibus hominibus mortuis uel de quibus eorum factis tamquam dis sacra fuerint instituta. Absit ut eos, quamuis deos habeant, sanctis martyribus nostris, quos tamen

---

[1] Cf. Herm. *ap.* Stob. *Exc.* XXIII. 65: οὗτοι (Osiris and Isis) ... τροφὰς θνητοῖς ... ἐχαρίσαντο.
[2] As to this 'epistle of Alexander', cf. Aug. *De ciu. dei* 12. 10.

deos non habemus, ulla ex parte audeant conparare. Sic enim non
constituimus sacerdotes nec offerimus sacrificia martyribus nostris,
quia incongruum indebitum inlicitum est adque uni Deo tantummodo
debitum, ut nec criminibus suis nec ludis eos turpissimis oblectemus,
ubi uel flagitia isti celebrant deorum suorum, si, cum homines essent, 5
talia commiserunt, uel conficta delectamenta daemonum noxiorum,
si homines non fuerunt. Ex isto genere daemonum Socrates non
haberet deum, si haberet deum;[1] sed fortasse homini ab illa arte
faciendi deos alieno et innocenti illi inportauerint talem deum, qui
eadem arte excellere uoluerunt. 10

18. 39 Nulla igitur gens de antiquitate suae sapientiae super patri-
archas et prophetas nostros, quibus diuina inerat sapientia, ulla
se uanitate iactauerit, quando nec Aegyptus inuenitur, quae solet
falso et inaniter de suarum doctrinarum antiquitate gloriari, quali-
cumque sapientia sua patriarcharum nostrorum tempore praeuenisse 15
sapientiam. Neque enim quisquam dicere audebit mirabilium
disciplinarum eos peritissimos fuisse, antequam litteras nossent, id
est, antequam Isis eo uenisset easque ibi docuisset. Ipsa porro
eorum memorabilis doctrina, quae appellata est sapientia, quid erat
nisi maxime astronomia et si quid aliud talium disciplinarum magis 20
ad exercenda ingenia quam ad inluminandas uera sapientia mentes
solet ualere? Nam quod adtinet ad philosophiam, quae se docere
profitetur aliquid, unde fiant homines beati, circa tempora Mercurii,
quem Trismegistum uocauerunt, in illis terris eius modi studia
claruerunt, longe quidem ante sapientes uel philosophos Graeciae, 25
sed tamen post Abraham et Isaac et Iacob et Ioseph, nimirum etiam
post ipsum Moysen. Eo quippe tempore, quo Moyses natus est,
fuisse reperitur Atlans ille magnus astrologus, Promethei frater,
maternus auus Mercurii maioris, cuius nepos fuit Trismegistus
iste Mercurius.[2] Frustra itaque uanissima praesumtione garriunt 30

[1] *De civ. dei* 8. 14.

[2] Augustine thinks that the Egyptian teacher Hermes Trismegistus was grandson
of the elder Hermes, who was grandson of Atlas, and that Atlas lived at the time
of the birth of Moses. He takes the elder Hermes spoken of in *Ascl. Lat.* 37 to be
the Hermes of the Greeks, who was son of Maia the daughter of Atlas. Cf. Aug.
Civ. dei 18. 8 : 'Cum ergo regnaret Assyriis quartus decimus Saphrus et Sicyoniis
duodecimus Orthopolis et Criasus quintus Argiuis, natus est in Aegypto Moyses....
Regnantibus memoratis regibus fuisse a quibusdam creditur Prometheus, quem
propterea ferunt de luto formasse homines, quia optimus sapientiae doctor fuisse
perhibetur. . . . Frater eius Atlans magnus fuisse astrologus dicitur. . . . His
temporibus etiam Mercurius (i. e. the elder Hermes) fuisse perhibetur, nepos
Atlantis ex Maia filia, quod uulgatiores etiam litterae personant. Multarum autem
artium peritus claruit, quas et hominibus tradidit; quo merito eum post mortem
deum esse uoluerunt siue etiam crediderunt.'

quidam dicentes, ex quo Aegyptus rationem siderum conprehendit, amplius quam centum annorum milia numerari. In quibus enim libris istum numerum collegerunt, qui non multum ante annorum duo milia [1] litteras magistra Iside didicerunt? Non enim paruus 5 auctor est in historia Varro, qui hoc prodidit.

Migne.
Patr. Gr.
tom. lxxvi,
col.

CYRILLUS ALEXANDRINUS

Contra Julianum [2] Lib. I: ἐκεῖνα [3] τέως παρείς, τετράψομαι μᾶλλον **541** *init.*
ἐπί γε τὸ δεῖν εἰπεῖν τὰ Ἑλλήνων, πολυπραγμονῆσαί τε τὰ παρ' αὐτοῖς,
καὶ τῆς ἑκάστου δόξης ἀκριβῆ ποιεῖσθαι τὴν βάσανον. [4]

[1] I. e. about 1600 B.C.

[2] My authority for what follows in this note is Neumann, *Juliani Imp. librorum contra Christianos quae supersunt*, 1880.

Julian wrote his work *Contra Christianos* in A. D. 362-363. It consisted of three books. Cyril's reply to it (*Contra Julianum*) was probably written in A. D. 435-441. Cyril apparently designed a work in thirty books, each decad of which was to be a reply to one of the three books of Julian. Cyril's first decad, in which he deals with Julian's Book I, is extant. Of his second decad, in which he probably dealt with Julian's Book II, only a few short fragments have been preserved. There is reason to think that he intended to write a third decad, dealing with Julian's Book III; but there is no evidence that he fulfilled that intention.

The chief MSS. of Cyril *c. Julianum* are M (Venetus Marcianus 123), saec. XIII; V (Venetus Marcianus 122), saec. XIV; Ψ (Scorialensis), saec. XIV-XV; and B (Monacensis), saec. XVI. Neumann says that all these MSS. are derived from the *Codex deperditus Capnionis* (saec. IX-XIII *init.*?), which was probably destroyed in 1648. The Greek text of the *Codex Capnionis* was translated into Latin by Oecolampadius, and his translation was published in Cratander's Latin edition of Cyril's works, Basileae 1528. This Latin translation by Oecolampadius. if we could be sure that its rendering of the lost *Codex Capnionis* is exact, would be the best authority for the text of Cyril. But as a good many inaccuracies and mistakes can be detected in it, it must be used with caution; and in some instances it is clear that the reading of Aubert's Greek MS. is preferable to that which the Latin of Oecolampadius appears to indicate. I have not been able to get access to the first edition of Oecolampadius' translation (Cratander 1528); but I have used in lieu of it the Latin text of *Opera D. Cyrilli Alex.*, Basileae 1546, which I take to be an unaltered reprint of that of Oecolampadius. ('Editiones Latinae usque ad Aubertianam [i. e. down to 1638] Oecolampadii interpretationem repetiverunt,' Neumann, *op. cit.* p. 152.)

The chief printed editions of the Greek text of Cyril *c. Julianum* are that of Book I alone by Borbonius, 1619, and that of Books I-X by Aubert, 1638. Aubert's edition is reprinted in Migne *Patr. Gr.* tom. 76. Aubert's text is taken from an *apographon* of cod. B.

In my revision of the extracts here printed, I have used the readings of Aubert's edition (which represents cod. B) and the Latin translation by Oecolampadius (which represents the lost *Codex Capnionis*). For a complete *apparatus criticus*, these ought to be supplemented by the readings of M, V, and Ψ; but I have no means of getting collations of those MSS.

[3] Viz. the theology of Moses, which, according to Cyril, is identical with that of the Christians.

[4] τετράψομαι . . . τὴν βάσανον Aubert: *vertam me potius ad Graecos, ut exacto iudicio quid illi senserint perscruter* (i. e. τετράψομαι μᾶλλον ἐπὶ τοὺς Ἕλληνας,

541 A　Ὀρφέα μὲν οὖν . . . φασι . . . ᾠδὰς δὲ καὶ ὕμνους τοῖς ψευδωνύμοις ἐξυφῆ-
ναι θεοῖς, . . . εἶτα τῶν ἑαυτοῦ δογμάτων κατεγνωκότα . . . μεταφοιτῆσαι
πρὸς τὰ βελτίω, καὶ τοῦ ψεύδους ἀνθελέσθαι τὴν ἀλήθειαν, φάναι τε οὕτω
περὶ θεοῦ· "φθέγξομαι οἷς θέμις ἐστί . . ."[1]

C　Ὅμηρον δὲ . . .[2]

5

544 C　ἴωμεν δὲ καὶ ἐπ' αὐτοὺς ἤδη τοὺς σοβαροὺς καὶ κατωφρυωμένους,
δοκησισοφίας τε δόξαν λαβόντας οὐκ ἀγεννῆ παρά γε τοῖς Ἑλλήνων
παισί. . . .

545 A　Θαλῆς[3] μὲν οὖν ὁ Μιλήσιος νοῦν τοῦ κόσμου φησὶν εἶναι τὸν θεόν.

Δημόκριτος δὲ ὁ Ἀβδηρίτης συμφέρεται μὲν κατά τι, προσεπάγει δέ τι　10
καὶ ἕτερον· νοῦν μὲν γὰρ εἶναι τὸν θεὸν ἰσχυρίζεται καὶ αὐτός, πλὴν ἐν
πυρὶ σφαιροειδεῖ, καὶ αὐτὸν εἶναι τὴν τοῦ κόσμου ψυχήν.[4]

ὥστε (?) τῆς ἐκείνων δόξης ἀκριβῆ ποιεῖσθαι τὴν βάσανον) Oecolampadius. Perhaps
τετράψομαι μᾶλλον ἐπὶ [γε] τὸ [δεῖν] εἰπεῖν τὰ Ἑλλήνων κ.τ.λ.

[1] Here follow two extracts from the Jewish ‘*Palinodia* of Orpheus’ (Abel,
Orphica, pp. 144 ff.). See Schürer, *Gesch. des jüd. Volkes*, 1909, III, pp. 595–608.
The *Palinodia* of Orpheus was one of a collection of extracts (some genuine and
some forged) from Greek poets, which was compiled for the purpose of giving
support to the Jewish religion, and included passages attributed to Aeschylus,
Sophocles, Euripides, Philemon, and other comedians, and some verses (on the
Sabbath) ascribed to Homer, Hesiod, and Linus. According to Schürer, this
collection of extracts can be traced back to Pseudo-Hecataeus ‘On the Jews’ or
‘On Abraham’—a book written by an Egyptian Jew before 200 B.C., and falsely
ascribed by its author to Hecataeus of Abdera, who lived in the time of the first
Ptolemy, and wrote a history of Egypt. Passages contained in the collection were
taken over from Pseudo-Hecataeus by the Alexandrian Jew Aristobulus (Euseb.
Pr. ev. 13. 12), *c.* 170–150 B.C., and by Christian writers (Clem. Alex. *Strom.*
5. 14 (quoted by Euseb. *Pr. ev.* 13. 13) and *Protrept.* 7. 74; Ps.-Justin *Cohort. ad
Graecos* 15 and 18; Ps.-Justin *De monarchia* 2–4). See note on 549 D below.

The *Palinodia* of Orpheus is given, with some variations, in Pseudo-Justin *De
monarchia* 2 and *Cohort. ad Gr.* 15; Aristobulus *ap.* Euseb. *Pr. ev.* 13. 12. 5;
Clem. Alex. *Protrept.* 7. 74, *Strom.* 5. 12. 18, and *Strom.* 5. 14. 123–127 = Euseb.
Pr. ev. 13. 13. 50–54; Theodoret. *Gr. aff. cur.* c. 2; and in *Excerpta e Theosophia
Χρησμοὶ τῶν Ἑλληνικῶν θεῶν*), edited by Buresch, *Klaros*, 1889, § 55 f. In the
Exc. e Theosoph. it is thus introduced: ὅτι Ὀρφεύς, ὁ Οἰάγρου τοῦ Θρᾳκός, πρότερον
μὲν ὕμνους τινὰς εἰς τοὺς ἐξαγίστους θεοὺς ἐξυφάνας καὶ τὰς μιαρὰς γενέσεις αὐτῶν
διηγησάμενος, εἶτα, συνεὶς ὥσπερ τὸ δυσσεβὲς τοῦ πράγματος, μετέθηκεν ἑαυτὸν ἐπὶ τὸ
μόνον καλόν, καὶ τὸν ὄντως ὑμνῶν θεόν, καὶ τὴν τῶν πάλαι Χαλδαίων σοφίαν, δηλαδὴ
τὴν τοῦ Ἀβραάμ, ἐπαινῶν, παραινεῖ τῷ ἰδίῳ παιδὶ Μουσαίῳ τοῖς μὲν φθάσασι μυθευθῆναι
μὴ πείθεσθαι, τοῖς δὲ ῥηθήσεσθαι μέλλουσι προσέχειν τὸν νοῦν. ἔστι δὲ τὰ ἔπη ταῦτα·
φθέγξομαι οἷς θέμις ἐστί, κ.τ.λ. (46 lines).

[2] Cyril here says that Homer’s gods are deifications of virtues and vices, and of
‘the parts of the Kosmos’ and the cosmic elements; but that Homer ‘was not
wholly ignorant of the truth’, inasmuch as he occasionally speaks of the one God
who is over all.

[3] These statements of the doctrines of Thales, Democritus, Anaximander,
Aristotle, and the Stoics are taken from Pseudo-Plutarch *Placita Philos.* (Diels
Doxogr. pp. 301–306), which is an abbreviated transcription of the *Placita* of
Aetius. Cyril may have got them from Eusebius, by whom the passage of
Ps.-Plutarch is quoted (*Pr. ev.* 14. 16. 6).

[4] Ps.-Plut. (Diels p. 302): Δημόκριτος νοῦν τὸν θεὸν ἐν πυρὶ σφαιροειδεῖ τὴν τοῦ
κόσμου ψυχήν. That is a corruption of the text of Aetius, which is given by

'Αναξίμανδρος δέ, οἷμον ὥσπερ ἑτέραν ὁλοτρόπως ἰών, θεὸν διορίζεται B
εἶναι τοὺς ἀπείρους κόσμους, οὐκ οἶδ' ὅ τι λέγων.[1]

ὁ δὲ πλείστην ἔχων καὶ οὐκ ἔξω θαύματος ⌜εἰς βασάνους ἐννοιῶν τὴν
· δείνωσιν⌝,[2] τὸν Ἀριστοτέλη λέγω τὸν Σταγειρίτην, τὸν Πλάτωνος φοιτητήν,
5 εἶδος μὲν χωριστὸν ὀνομάζει τὸν θεόν, ἐπιβῆναι δὲ διατείνεται τῇ τοῦ
παντὸς σφαίρᾳ.

καὶ μὴν οἱ καλούμενοι Στωϊκοὶ θεὸν εἶναί φασι πῦρ τεχνικὸν ὁδῷ βαδίζον
ἐπὶ γένεσιν[3] κόσμου.

γεγράφασι δὲ περὶ τούτων Πλούταρχός τε καὶ ἕτεροι τῶν παρ' αὐτοῖς
10 λογάδων, καὶ ὁ θρασὺς καθ' ἡμῶν Πορφύριος.[4]

ἆρ' οὖν οὐ διάφοροι μὲν ἀλλήλοις εἰσί, στοχασταὶ δὲ μᾶλλον ἢ[5] τῆς
ἀληθείας διαγνώμονες, οἱ πολυτρόποις οὕτω δόξαις καταμεθύοντες ;[6] καίτοι
τοὺς ἀληθῶς τε καὶ ἀπλανῶς ἐγνωκότας κατ' οὐδένα τρόπον ταῖς ἀλλήλων
ἐννοίαις ἐχρῆν ἀντιφέρεσθαι,[7] καθάπερ ἀμέλει καὶ ἐφ' ἡμῶν αὐτῶν[8] ἔνεστιν
15 ἰδεῖν. . . .

εἰ γὰρ δὴ βούλοιτό τις εὖ μάλα διαμαθεῖν[9] τὸν ὀρθῶς τε καὶ ἀκιβδήλως D
ἔχοντα λόγον περὶ τοῦ πάντων ἐπέκεινα θεοῦ, ⌜τὴν τίνος ἂν εἰσδέξηται
δόξαν καὶ⌝ οὐκ ἂν ἁμάρτοι σκοποῦ ;[10] Θαλῆς μὲν γὰρ καὶ Ἀναξίμανδρος, 548 A

Stobaeus (Diels *ib.*) as follows : Δημόκριτος νοῦν τὸν θεὸν ἐν πυρὶ σφαιροειδεῖ.
Διογένης καὶ Κλεάνθης καὶ Οἰνοπίδης τὴν τοῦ κόσμου ψυχήν. Cyril, misled by the
error of Ps.-Plut., thought that the words τὴν τοῦ κόσμου ψυχήν belonged to the
sentence about Democritus.

[1] οὐκ οἶδ' ὅ τι λέγων Aub. : *nesciens quid loquatur* (i. e. οὐκ εἰδὼς ὅ τι λέγει)
Oec.

[2] ὁ δὲ . . . τὴν δείνωσιν Aub. : *At ille qui apud eos* (i. e. παρ' αὐτοῖς) *maximam
et usque ad miraculum gravitatem sententiarum habet* Oec.

[3] ἐπὶ γένεσιν Ps.-Plut. : *ad nativitatem* Oec. : ἐπὶ γενέσει Aub., Aetius *ap.*
Stob.

[4] The doctrines of the Greek philosophers down to and including Plato were
reported by Porphyry in his Φιλόσοφος ἱστορία, to which Cyril repeatedly refers.

[5] ἆρ' οὖν οὐ . . . μᾶλλον ἢ Aub. : *Itaque inter se diversi sunt divinatores, magis
quam* (i. e. ἆρ' οὖν διάφοροι ἀλλήλοις εἰσὶ στοχασταὶ μᾶλλον ἢ) Oec.

[6] οἱ πολυτρόποις οὕτω δόξαις καταμεθύοντες Aub. : *qui tam multifariam*
(i. e. πολυτρόπως) *opinionibus inebriati sunt* Oec.

[7] ταῖς ἀλλήλων . . . ἀντιφέρεσθαι Aub. : *ita inter se diversis opinionibus ferri
oportebat* (i. e. οὕτως ἀλλήλων διαφόροις ἐννοίαις ἐχρῆν φέρεσθαι ?) Oec.

[8] ἐφ' ἡμῶν αὐτῶν Aub. : *apud hos* (i. e. ἐπὶ τούτων) Oec. With Aub.'s reading,
the meaning is that the Christians do not differ among themselves as the Pagan
philosophers do. Cyril maintains that all teachers whose authority was recognized
by the Christians, from Moses down to the Apostles and Evangelists, taught one
and the same theology (including the doctrine of the Trinity) ; and he adds, εἰ
δὲ δή τινες τῶν μετ' ἐκείνους (i. e. heretical Christians), οὐ συνιέντες τὰ αὐτῶν,
διημαρτήκασι τἀληθοῦς, οὐκ ἐκείνοις [[μᾶλλον]] ἕψεται, ⟨⟨μᾶλλον⟩⟩ δὲ τούτοις, κατά γε
τὸν ὀρθῶς ἔχοντα λογισμόν, ἢ τοῦ πεπλανῆσθαι γραφή (*crimen*).

[9] εὖ μάλα διαμαθεῖν Aub. : *ab his* (i. e. παρὰ τούτων) *discere* Oec.

[10] τὴν τίνος . . . ἁμάρτοι σκοποῦ ; Aub. : *cuius opinionem amplexaretur, ut non
aberret scopo ?* Oec. The sense required might be expressed by writing τὴν τίνος
εἰσδεξάμενος δόξαν [καὶ] οὐκ ἂν ἁμάρτοι σκοποῦ ;

ἕτεροί τε ὧν ἀρτίως διεμνημονεύσαμεν,[1] εἰκῆ πεφλυαρηκότες ἁλοῖεν ἄν
Πυθαγόρας δὲ καὶ Πλάτων, διατετριφότες ἐν Αἰγύπτῳ, καὶ πολλοῖς τῶν[2]
αὐτόθι περιτυγχάνοντες, ἅτε δὴ φιλομαθεστάτω τε ὄντε καὶ φιλοΐστορε,
οὐκ ἠγνοησάτην τὴν Μωσέως ἀρετήν· ἦν γὰρ Αἰγυπτίοις τὰ κατ' αὐτὸν
οὐκ ἐν μετρίῳ θαύματι.[3] ἐντεῦθεν οἶμαι τὸν περὶ θεοῦ λόγον οὐκ ἀκόμψως[4] 5
ἐκμεμαθηκότας ἐπιεικέστερόν πως παρὰ τοῖς ἄλλους τὰ[5] περὶ αὐτοῦ δοξάσαι
⌈καὶ μὴν καὶ ἑλέσθαι φρονεῖν⌉.[6] εὑρήσομεν δὲ καὶ τῶν Ἀθήνησί τινας
τοῖς παρ' αὐτῶν εὖ ἔχειν ὑπειλημμένοις συνενηνεγμένους.[7]

οἶμαι δὲ δεῖν ἀξιῶσαι λόγου καὶ μνήμης[8] τὸν Αἰγύπτιον Ἑρμῆν, ὃν δὴ
καὶ Τρισμέγιστον ὠνομάσθαι φασί, τετιμηκότων αὐτὸν τῶν κατ' ἐκεῖνο 10
B καιροῦ,[9] καί, καθά τισι δοκεῖ, τῷ ἐκ Διὸς καὶ Μαίας μυθολογουμένῳ γενέσθαι

---

[1] ἕτεροί τε ὧν ἀρτίως διεμνημονεύσαμεν Aub.: *aliter (sicut iam ostendimus) et
aliter* (i. e. ἑτέρως τε, ὡς ἀρτίως διεμνημονεύσαμεν, καὶ ἑτέρως?) Oec. The ἕτεροι are
Democritus, Aristotle, and the Stoics.

[2] τῶν scripsi: τοῖς Aub.: *familiares multis qui illic erant* (i. e. τοῖς αὐτόθι)
Oec.

[3] ἦν γὰρ Αἰγυπτίοις . . . θαύματι Aub.: *erant enim apud Aegyptios* (i. e. ἦν γὰρ
παρ' Αἰγυπτίοις?) *Mosaica non in parva admiratione* Oec. If the text is sound, τὰ
κατ' αὐτόν must mean 'the doctrines of Moses'. But perhaps the true reading may
be ἦν γὰρ Αἰγυπτίοις τοῖς κατ' αὐτοὺς κ.τ.λ.: 'Moses was much admired by the
Egyptians who lived in the times of Pythagoras and Plato.' Cf. Cyril *c. Jul.* 573 A:
φαίην ἂν ὅτι Πλάτων τε καὶ Πυθαγόρας δοξάζουσι μέν πως ἐπιεικέστερον περί τε θεοῦ
καὶ κόσμου. συνειλόχασι δὲ τὴν εἰς τοῦτο παίδευσιν εἴτουν ἐπιστήμην Αἰγυπτίοις
ἐμβεβληκότες, παρ' οἷς δὴ πολὺς ὁ περὶ τοῦ πανσόφου Μωσέως λόγος ἦν, καὶ τῶν παρ'
αὐτῷ δογμάτων τὸ θαῦμα ἐτετίμητο.

[4] οὐκ ἀκόμψως Aub.: *absque insolentia* (i. e. ἀκόμπως?) Oec.   [5] τὰ seclusi.

[6] ἐπιεικέστερόν πως . . . ἑλέσθαι φρονεῖν Aub.: *ut sentirent et loquerentur de eo*
(i. e. περὶ αὐτοῦ δοξάσαι καὶ λέξαι?) *aliquanto sanius quam alii* Oec.

[7] τῶν Ἀθήνησί . . . συνηνεγμένους Aub.: *Athenienses quosdam, cum illis, ad hoc
ut idem saperent quod ipsi, adductos* (i. e. τῶν Ἀθηναίων τινὰς ἐπὶ τὸ ταὐτὸ αὐτοῖς
φρονεῖν συνηνεγμένους?) Oec.
Who are these 'men at Athens'? Perhaps the Athenian school of Neoplatonists.
The earliest man of note in that school was Plutarchus, who died in A. D. 431-432
(Zeller III. ii, p. 808), i. e. a few years before the date of Cyril *c. Julianum.*

[8] οἶμαι δὲ . . . μνήμης Aub.: *Iam memoria et sermone dignum existimo* (i. e. οἶμαι
δὲ εἶναι ἄξιον μνήμης καὶ λόγου?) Oec.

[9] What time is meant by κατ' ἐκεῖνο καιροῦ? The time of Hermes? Or the
time of Pythagoras and Plato? Cyril does not explicitly say in what period he
believed Hermes to have lived; but he must have supposed him either to have
been a younger contemporary of Moses, or to have lived not long after him; for
on the one hand he says that Hermes learnt from Moses, and on the other hand he
quotes without dissent the statement that Hermes founded the institutions and
sciences of Egypt, which implies an early date. Do the words τῷ ἐκ Διὸς καὶ Μαίας
μυθολογουμένῳ γενέσθαι παρεικαζόντων αὐτόν mean that the name Hermes was given
to him *by his contemporaries* because they thought that he resembled the mythical
Hermes of the Greeks? If so, κατ' ἐκεῖνο καιροῦ would signify the time of Hermes
himself. But Cyril may have been aware that the name Hermes Trismegistus was
merely a Greek translation of an Egyptian name; and in that case, he may have
thought that the Egyptian teacher was first called Hermes in the age of Pythagoras
and Plato.
At any rate, Cyril holds that the Egyptian Hermes learnt something of the truth
from Moses, and that Pythagoras and Plato learnt something of the truth from the
Egyptian Hermes.

παρεικαζόντων αὐτόν. οὑτοσὶ τοιγαροῦν ὁ κατ' Αἴγυπτον Ἑρμῆς, καίτοι
τελέστης ὤν, καὶ τοῖς τῶν εἰδώλων τεμένεσι προσιζήσας ἀεί, πεφρονηκὼς
εὑρίσκεται τὰ Μωσέως, εἰ καὶ μὴ εἰς ἅπαν ὀρθῶς καὶ ἀνεπιλήπτως, ἀλλ'
οὖν ἐκ μέρους· ⌜ὠφέληται⌝ γὰρ καὶ αὐτός.¹ πεποίηται δὲ καὶ τούτου μνήμην
5 ἐν ἰδίαις συγγραφαῖς ὁ συντεθεικὼς Ἀθήνησι τὰ ἐπίκλην Ἑρμαϊκὰ πεντεκαί-
δεκα βιβλία.² γράφει δὲ οὕτως ἐν τῷ πρώτῳ περὶ αὐτοῦ· εἰσκεκόμικε δέ
τινα τῶν ἱερουργῶν λέγοντα· "ἵν' οὖν ἔλθωμεν εἰς τὰς ὁμοίας,³ ἆρ' οὐχὶ καὶ
τὸν ἡμέτερον Ἑρμῆν ἀκούεις τήν τε Αἴγυπτον εἰς λήξεις ⁴ καὶ κλήρους
ἅπασαν⁵ τεμεῖν, σχοίνῳ τὰς ἀρούρας καταμετροῦντα,⁶ καὶ διώρυχας τεμέσθαι
10 ταῖς ἐπαρδεύσεσι, καὶ νόμους θεῖναι, καὶ τὰς χώρας ἀπ' αὐτῶν προσειπεῖν,⁷ c
καὶ καταστήσασθαι τὰς συναλλάξεις τῶν συμβολαίων, καὶ ⌜νεωστὶ
φύσασθαι⌝ ⟨. . .⟩ κατάλογον τῆς τῶν ἄστρων ἐπιτολῆς,⁸ καὶ βοτάνας
τεμεῖν, καὶ πρός γε ἀριθμοὺς καὶ λογισμοὺς καὶ γεωμετρία , ἀστρονομίαν

¹ ὠφέληται γὰρ καὶ αὐτός Aub.: *etenim et ipsi fuit utilitas* Oec.

² Cyril here tells us that some one composed or compiled at Athens a work
entitled *Hermaica*, which consisted of fifteen books. It may perhaps have been
written by one of οἱ Ἀθήνησι spoken of above in 548 A. How long before Cyril
wrote his *c. Julianum* it was in existence, we do not know ; it may have been of
recent date, but there is no proof that it was not written some centuries earlier.
The first book at least was in the form of a dialogue ; one of the interlocutors in
the dialogue was an Egyptian priest (εἰσκεκόμικε δέ τινα τῶν ἱερουργῶν λέγοντα);
and this priest was made to speak of Hermes as a man who lived long before the
speaker's time, and was the founder of Egyptian culture. From the words καὶ τὸν
ἡμέτερον Ἑρμῆν it may perhaps be inferred that the man with whom the priest was
talking was not an Egyptian, but a Greek. Beyond this, we know nothing about
the contents of the work called *Hermaica*. In the extract from the first book
which is here given, nothing is said of Hermes as a teacher of philosophy or
religion. That does not prove that his philosophic and religious teaching was
ignored throughout the work ; but there is no reason to suppose that it contained
a collection of writings, whether philosophic and religious or of other kinds,
that were ascribed to Hermes. At any rate, Cyril apparently did not get his
Hermetic extracts from it, since he quotes some of them by other titles ἐν λόγῳ
πρώτῳ τῶν πρὸς τὸν Τὰτ διεξοδικῶν, 553 A : ἐν λόγῳ τρίτῳ τῶν πρὸς Ἀσκληπιόν,
556 A).

³ The words ἔλθωμεν εἰς τὰς ὁμοίας (*ut veniamus ad similes* Oec.) are obscure,
and perhaps corrupt.

⁴ λήξεις ('allotments') καὶ κλήρους scripsi: λῆξιν καὶ κλήρους Aub.: *sortes et
fines* Oec. What is the difference of meaning, if any, between λήξεις and κλήρους,
I do not know.

⁵ ἅπασαν om. Oec.

⁶ *funiculo mensum esse* (om. τὰς ἀρούρας) Oec.

⁷ Hermes made laws (νόμους) ; and he called the districts of Egypt 'nomes'
(νομούς). The writer seems to have thought that the latter word was derived
from the former. But the sense would be improved by cutting out καὶ τὰς χώρας
ἀπ' αὐτῶν προσειπεῖν, and thereby bringing 'contracts' (τὰς συναλλάξεις τῶν συμβολαίων) into juxtaposition with 'laws'.

⁸ νεωστὶ φύσασθαι κατάλογον τῆς τῶν ἄστρων ἐπιτολῆς Aub.: *nuper dixisse*
(φήσασθαι or φῆσαι?) *summam legis* (ἐντολῆς?) *astrorum* Oec. νεωστί is evidently
wrong. One might conjecture νεὼς ἱδρύσασθαι, (καὶ . . .). A verb in the infinitive
(ποιήσασθαι?) must have been lost before or after κατάλογον τῆς τῶν ἄστρων
ἐπιτολῆς.

τε¹ [ἀστρολογίαν]² καὶ τὴν μουσικὴν καὶ τὴν γραμματικὴν ἅπασαν εὑρόντα
παραδοῦναι ;"

    ποιήσωμεν τοίνυν τῶν ἑκάστου δοξῶν³ τὴν ἀφήγησιν· μεμνήσομαι δὲ
καὶ ἑτέρων⁴ οὐκ ἀθαύμαστον παρ' αὐτοῖς ἐπὶ παιδείᾳ λαχόντων ὄνομα. . . .

D   Πυθαγόρας γοῦν φησιν·⁵ "ὁ μὲν θεὸς εἷς· αὐτὸς⁶ δὲ οὐχ, ὡς τινες 5
ὑπονοοῦσιν, ἐκτὸς τᾶς διακοσμήσιος, ἀλλ' ἐν αὐτᾷ,⁷ ὅλος ἐν ὅλῳ τῷ κύκλῳ⁸
ἐπισκοπῶν πάσας γενεάς,⁹ ⌈ἐστὶ κρᾶσις ὢν⌉ τῶν ὅλων αἰώνων,¹⁰ καὶ [φῶς]
⟨ἐργάτας⟩¹¹ τῶν αὐτοῦ δυνάμεων καὶ ἔργων ἀρχὰ πάντων,¹² ἐν οὐρανῷ
φωστήρ, καὶ πάντων πατήρ,¹³ νοῦς καὶ ψύχωσις τῶν ὅλων, κύκλων πάντων
κίνασις."¹⁴ ἰδοὺ δὴ σαφῶς¹⁵ ἕνα τε εἶναι λέγει τὸν τῶν ὅλων θεόν, καὶ 10
πάντων ἀρχήν, ἐργάτην τε τῶν αὐτοῦ δυνάμεων, φωστῆρα¹⁶ καὶ ψύχωσιν
ἤτοι ζωοποίησιν τῶν ὅλων, καὶ κύκλων πάντων κίνησιν· αὐτοκίνητον γὰρ

---

¹ καὶ πρός γε ἀριθμοὺς . . . ἀστρονομίαν τε Aub.: et cum numeris et geometria
(i.e. καὶ πρός γε ἀριθμοῖς καὶ γεωμετρίᾳ?) etiam astronomiam Oec. Perhaps καὶ
προσέτι ἀριθμοὺς κ.τ.λ.

² ἀστρολογίαν seclusi: ⟨καὶ⟩ ἀστρολογίαν Aub.: et astrologiam Oec.

³ I. e. the doctrines of Pythagoras, Plato, and Hermes.

⁴ Viz. Sophocles (549 D) and Xenophon (552 A).

⁵ This extract is given by Clem. Alex., Protrept. 6. 72: οὐκ ἀποκρυπτέον οὐδὲ
τοὺς ἀμφὶ τὸν Πυθαγόραν, οἵ φασιν "ὁ μὲν θεὸς εἷς . . . πάντων κίνασις". Clement
ascribed the passage to 'those about Pythagoras'; Cyril ascribes it to Pythagoras
himself. It must have been written by a late Pythagorean. In the words οὐχ . . .
ἐκτὸς τᾶς διακοσμήσιος, ἀλλ' ἐν αὐτᾷ, the writer sides with the Stoics against the
Platonists. Cf. [Justin], Cohort., 19.

⁶ αὐτὸς Aub.: χοῦτος Clem. (Stählin).

⁷ αὐτῷ Aub.: αὐτᾷ Clem.

⁸ ὅλος ὁ κύκλος apparently means the Kosmos; cf. τῷ ὅλῳ κύκλῳ (Clem.) below.
But the words ἐν ὅλῳ τῷ κύκλῳ seem out of place here.

⁹ ἐπισκοπῶν πάσας γενεάς Aub.: omnes generationes considerat Oec.: ἐπίσκοπος
πάσας γενέσιος Clem.

¹⁰ 'ἐστὶ κρᾶσις forte ἐπίκρασις' Aubert) ὢν τῶν ὅλων αἰώνων Cyril (Aub):
contemperatio existens omnium seculorum (i. e. κρᾶσις ὢν τῶν ὅλων αἰώνων) Oec.:
κρᾶσις τῶν ὅλων, ἀεὶ ὢν (om. ἐστὶ) Clem. Neither κρᾶσις nor ἐπίκρασις can be
the word that the Pythagorean wrote. Possibly ἐπικρατῶν?

¹¹ φῶς Aub.: lux (i. e. φῶς) Oec.: ἐργάτας Clem. As Cyril repeats the phrase
below in the form ἐργάτην τε τῶν αὐτοῦ δυνάμεων, he must have written ἐργάτας
here, and φῶς must have come from φωστήρ by a copyist's error.

¹² ἔργων ἀρχὰ (principium Oec.) πάντων Aub.: ἔργων ἀπάντων (om. ἀρχὰ)
Clem. It is doubtful if C. referred to this phrase, if order is any guide; in any case
the balance of the clause demands ἔργων πάντων.

¹³ ἐν οὐρανῷ φωστήρ καὶ πάντων πατήρ Clement and Cyril. But the statement
that God is 'a luminary in heaven' does not suit well with the context; and it
may be doubted whether the words stood thus in the passage as originally
written.

¹⁴ ψύχωσις τῶν ὅλων, κύκλων πάντων κίνασις Cyril (confirmed by ψύχωσιν . . . τῶν
ὅλων καὶ κύκλων πάντων κίνησιν below): animatio omnium, circulorum omnium
motio Oec.: ψύχωσις τῶ ὅλω κύκλω, πάντων κίνασις Clem. The latter seems the
better reading. But possibly the author of the passage wrote κινατάς, or κίνασιν
followed by a nom. mas. participle.

¹⁵ ἰδοὺ δὴ σαφῶς Aub.: ecce quam (ὡς or πῶς?) manifeste Oec.

¹⁶ φωστῆρα Aub.: lucem (φῶς?) Oec. Perhaps some words connected with
φωστῆρα have been lost.

οὐδέν, παρῆκται δὲ τὰ πάντα παρ' αὐτοῦ, καὶ τὴν ἐκ τοῦ μὴ ὄντος εἰς τὸ
εἶναι κίνησιν λαχόντα φαίνεται.

ὁ δὲ Πλάτων ὧδέ[1] πη φθέγγεται·[2] "τὸν γὰρ πατέρα καὶ ποιητὴν[3] τοῦδε
τοῦ παντὸς εὑρεῖν τε ἔργον, καὶ εὑρόντα εἰς πάντας ἐξειπεῖν ἀδύνατον.[4]"
5 ὀρθῶς δὴ μάλα· . . . ἔστι γὰρ ἁπάσης ἐννοίας ἐπέκεινα. . . . Πορφύριος 549 A
δέ φησιν ἐν βιβλίῳ τετάρτῳ Φιλοσόφου ἱστορίας, δοξάσαι τε τὸν Πλάτωνα
καὶ μὴν καὶ φράσαι ⌜πάλιν⌝[5] περὶ ἑνὸς θεοῦ, ὄνομα δὲ αὐτῷ μηδὲν ἐφαρμόττειν,[6] μηδὲ γνῶσιν ἀνθρωπίνην αὐτὸν καταλαβεῖν,[7] τὰς δὲ λεγομένας
προσηγορίας ἀπὸ τῶν ὑστέρων καταχρηστικῶς αὐτοῦ κατηγορεῖς(θαι).[8] "εἰ
10 δὲ ὅλως[9] ἐκ τῶν παρ' ἡμῖν ὀνομάτων χρή τι τολμῆσαι λέγειν περὶ αὐτοῦ,[10]
μᾶλλον τὴν τοῦ ἑνὸς προσηγορίαν καὶ τὴν τἀγαθοῦ τακτέον ἐπ' αὐτοῦ. τὸ
μὲν[11] γὰρ ἐμφαίνει τὴν περὶ αὐτὸν ἁπλότητα καὶ διὰ τοῦτο αὐτάρκειαν· B
χρῄζει γὰρ οὐδενός, οὐ μερῶν,[12] οὐκ οὐσίας, οὐ δυνάμεων, οὐκ ἐνεργειῶν, ἀλλ'
ἔστι πάντων τούτων αἴτιος· τἀγαθὸν δὲ παρίστησιν ὅτι ἀπ' αὐτοῦ πᾶν ὅ τί
15 περ ἀγαθόν ἐστιν, ἀπομιμουμένων κατὰ τὸ δυνατὸν τῶν ἄλλων τὴν ἐκείνου,
⟨εἰ οὕτω⟩[13] χρὴ φάναι, ἰδιότητα, καὶ δι' αὐτῆς σωζομένων."

ὁ δέ γε τρισμέγιστος Ἑρμῆς οὕτω πώς[14] φησι·[15] "θεὸν νοῆσαι μὲν
χαλεπόν, φράσαι δὲ ἀδύνατον, εἰ ⟨τῳ⟩ καὶ νοῆσαι δυνατόν.[16]
τὸ γὰρ ἀσώματον σώματι σημῆναι ἀδύνατον, καὶ τὸ τέλειον
20 τῷ ἀτελεῖ καταλαμβάνεσθαι[17] οὐ δυνατόν, καὶ τὸ ἀΐδιον τῷ
ὀλιγοχρονίῳ συγγενέσθαι[18] δύσκολον. τὸ μὲν γὰρ ἀεί ἐστι, τὸ

[1] ὁ δὲ Πλάτων ὧδέ Aub. : *At Plato, et ipse* (καὶ αὐτὸς?) Oec.
[2] Pl. *Tim.* 28 c.
[3] τὸν γὰρ πατέρα καὶ ποιητὴν Cyril : τὸν μὲν οὖν ποιητὴν καὶ πιτέρα Plato.
[4] ἐξειπεῖν ἀδύνατον Cyril : ἀδύνατον λέγειν Plato.
[5] καὶ μὴν καὶ φράσαι πάλιν Aub. : *et dixisse quoque* (om. πάλιν) Oec. πάλιν is
meaningless; πολλὰ coni. Nauck.
[6] ὄνομα δὲ αὐτῷ μηδὲν ἐφαρμόττειν Aub. : *nomen quidem* (μὲν?) *illi nullum
congruere* Oec.
[7] μηδὲ . . . καταλαβεῖν Aub. : *neque humanam cognitionem posse* (δύνασθαι?)
comprehendere Oec.
[8] τὰς δὲ λεγομένας . . . κατηγορεῖν Aub. : *sed appellationes quae de eo dicuntur, a
posterioribus esse, abusiveque de ipso dici* (i. e. ἀπὸ τῶν ὑστέρων εἶναι, καταχρηστικῶς
τε αὐτοῦ κατηγορεῖσθαι?) Oec.
[9] εἰ δὲ ὅλως . . . δι' αὐτῆς σωζομένων is rightly taken by Nauck (*Porphyrii
opuscula selecta*, p. 13) to be a continuation, in *oratio recta*, of the quotation from
Porphyry. (Possibly φησί has dropped out.) τὸ ἕν and τὸ ἀγαθόν were the names
given by Plotinus to τὸ ἐπέκεινα νοῦ.
[10] εἰ δὲ ὅλως . . . λέγειν περὶ αὐτοῦ Aub. : *Quod si omnino aliquid, nominibus
quibus utimur, de eo dicere audendum* Oec. (Is *aliquid, nominibus* a misprint for
aliquid e nominibus?) [11] Sc. τὸ ἕν.
[12] μερῶν Aub. : *partibus* Oec. : τιμῶν coni. Nauck.
[13] εἰ οὕτω add. Nauck. ἐκείνου, χρὴ φάναι Aub. : *illius, si ita licet dicere* Oec.
[14] πώς Aub. : *alicubi* (i. e. πού) Oec. [15] See Herm. *ap.* Stob. *Exc.* I.
[16] εἰ καὶ νοῆσαι δυνατόν Aub. : *si cui etiam* (i. e. εἰ τῳ καὶ) *intelligere possibile*
Oec.
[17] καταλαμβάνεσθαι Aub. : *comprehendere* (καταλαμβάνειν?) Oec.
[18] συγγενέσθαι Aub. : *conferre* (συνενέγκασθαι?) Oec.

δὲ παρέρχεται· καὶ τὸ μὲν ἀληθές ἐστι, τὸ δὲ ὑπὸ φαντασίας
⌜σκιάζεται⌝.[1] ὅσον[2] οὖν τὸ ἀσθενέστερον τοῦ ἰσχυροτέρου καὶ
τὸ ἔλαττον τοῦ κρείττονος διέστηκε, τοσοῦτον τὸ θνητὸν τοῦ
c θείου καὶ ἀθανάτου."[3] ⟨καὶ ἑτέρωθι·⟩[4] "εἴ τῳ[5] οὖν ἀσώματος
ὀφθαλμός, ἐξερχέσθω τοῦ σώματος ἐπὶ τὴν θέαν τοῦ καλοῦ, 5
καὶ ἀναπτήτω καὶ αἰωρηθήτω,[6] [καὶ] ⟨μὴ⟩[7] σχῆμα, μὴ χρῶμα,[8]
[μὴ ἰδέας][9] ζητῶν θεάσασθαι, ἀλλ' ἐκεῖνο μᾶλλον τὸ τούτων
ποιητικόν,[10] τὸ ἥσυχον καὶ γαληνόν, τὸ ἑδραῖον, τὸ ἄτρεπτον,
⌜τὸ αὐτὸ πάντα καὶ μόνον⌝,[11] τὸ ἕν, τὸ αὐτὸ ἐξ ἑαυτοῦ,[12] τὸ αὐτὸ
ἐν ἑαυτῷ, τὸ ἑαυτῷ ὅμοιον[13] [ὃ μήτε ἄλλῳ ὅμοιόν ἐστι μήτε 10
ἑαυτῷ ἀνόμοιον]."[14] καὶ πάλιν ὁ αὐτός[15] "μηδὲν οὖν, περὶ ἐκείνου
[πώποτε][16] τοῦ ἑνὸς καὶ μόνου ἀγαθοῦ ἐννοούμενος, ἀδύνατον

[1] σκιάζεται Aub. : adumbratur Oec.

[2] ὅσῳ Aub. : quantum (i. e. ὅσον) Oec.

[3] τοσοῦτον ... ἀθανάτου Aub. : tantum etiam (i. e. τοσοῦτον καὶ?) a divino e immortali mortale Oec.

[4] καὶ ἑτέρωθι addidi. A passage which followed θεὸν νοῆσαι μὲν ... θείου καὶ ἀθανάτου in the Hermetic libellus is given by Stobaeus (see Exc. I). Cyril omits that passage, but appends a sentence (εἴ τις οὖν ἀσώματος ὀφθαλμὸς κ.τ.λ.) which he must have taken either from another libellus, or from another part of the same libellus. He probably wrote something like καὶ ἑτέρωθι (cf. 588 A) to indicate the beginning of this second quotation from Hermes. Fr. 25.

[5] εἴ τις ... ὀφθαλμός Aub. : Proinde si quis incorporeus oculus Oec. With that reading, the subject of ἐξερχέσθω would be the incorporeal eye itself. But that cannot be right; the subject of the verb ought to be the man who possesses an incorporeal eye. The sense required can be got by writing either εἴ τῳ οὖν ἀσώματος ὀφθαλμός, or εἴ τις οὖν ἀσώματον ὀφθαλμὸν ⟨ἔχει⟩. The ἀσώματος ὀφθαλμός is that which Hermetists frequently call ‘the eye of the mind’.

[6] αἰωρηθήτω Aub. : contempletur (i. e. θεωρείτω) Oec.

[7] μὴ σχῆμα scripsi : καὶ σχῆμα Aub. : non figuram Oec.

[8] χρῶμα scripsi : σῶμα Aub. : corpus Oec. σχῆμα and χρῶμα are the two visible properties of σώματα. Cf. Pl. Phaedr. 247 C : ἡ γὰρ ἀχρώματός τε καὶ ἀσχημάτιστος καὶ ἀναφὴς οὐσία ... ψυχῆς κυβερνήτῃ μόνῳ θεατὴ νῷ.

[9] μὴ ἰδέας (non species Oec.) seclusi.

[10] τὸ τούτων ποιητικόν Aub. : quod omnia facere potest (i. e. τὸ πάντων ποιητικόν) Oec. τούτων means σχήματος καὶ χρώματος, or τῶν σχῆμα καὶ χρῶμα ἐχόντων (i. e. τῶν σωμάτων).

[11] τὸ αὐτὸ πάντα καὶ μόνον (quod ipsum omnia et solum Oec.) is meaningless, and perhaps ought to be bracketed. τὸ αὐτό may have come from τὸ αὐτὸ ἐξ ἑαυτοῦ below; and in place of πάντα καὶ μόνον τὸ ἕν, one might conjecture τὸ ἕν καὶ μόνον πάντα ὄν.

[12] τὸ αὐτὸ ἐξ ἑαυτοῦ is equivalent to τὸ αὐτογέννητον.

[13] τὸ ἑαυτῷ ⟨μόνῳ⟩ ὅμοιον?

[14] ὃ μήτε ... ἀνόμοιον seclusi. The iteration (τὸ ἑαυτῷ ὅμοιον followed by μήτε ἑαυτῷ ἀνόμοιον) is intolerable.

[15] ὁ αὐτὸς Aub. : ille (i. e. οὗτος?) Oec. Fr. 26.
Aubert, by a strange mistake, includes the phrase καὶ πάλιν ὁ αὐτός in the preceding quotation from Hermes, of which he takes it to be the last clause, and ascribes what follows (μηδὲν οὖν ... φθαρτά ἐστιν) to Cyril, not seeing that this also is a quotation from Hermes.

[16] πώποτε seclusi. (Oec. has nothing to correspond to πώποτε. Perhaps we ought to read μηδὲν οὖν ⟨μηδέποτε⟩, περὶ ἐκείνου τοῦ ἑνὸς κ.τ.λ. Or is it possible that πώποτε has arisen out of ὦ Τάτ?

εἴπῃς· ἡ πᾶσα γὰρ δύναμις αὐτός ἐστι.[1] μηδὲ ἔν τινι αὐτὸν
διανοηθῇς εἶναι, μηδὲ πάλιν [κατ'] ἐκτός τινος·[2] αὐτὸς γὰρ
ἀπέραντος ὢν πάντων ἐστὶ πέρας, καὶ ὑπὸ μηδενὸς ἐμπεριεχό-
μενος πάντα ἐμπεριέχει.[3] ⟨. . .⟩[4] ἐπεὶ τίς διαφορά ἐστι τῶν D
5 σωμάτων πρὸς τὸ ἀσώματον,[5] καὶ τῶν γενητῶν πρὸς τὸ ἀγένητον [καὶ τῶν ἀνάγκῃ ὑποκειμένων πρὸς τὸ αὐτεξούσιον] [ἢ τῶν
ἐπιγείων πρὸς τὰ ἐπουράνια καὶ τῶν φθαρτῶν πρὸς τὰ ἀΐδια];[6]
οὐχ ὅτι τὸ μὲν αὐτεξούσιόν ἐστι, τὰ δὲ ἀνάγκῃ ὑποκείμενα;[7]
⟨. . .⟩[8] τὰ δὲ κάτω, ἀτελῆ ὄντα, φθαρτά ἐστιν."

10 ἀλλὰ μὴν καὶ Σοφοκλῆς οὕτω φησὶ περὶ θεοῦ·[9]

" ἐν ταῖς ἀληθείαισιν εἷς[10] ἐστιν θεός,
ὃς οὐρανόν τ' ἔτευξε, καὶ γαῖαν μακράν,
πόντου τε χαροπὸν οἶδμα, κἀνέμων βίας.[11]
θνητοὶ δέ, πολλὸν[12] καρδίᾳ πλανώμενοι,
15 ἱδρυσάμεσθα, πημάτων παραψυχήν,[13]
θεῶν ἀγάλματ' ἐκ λίθων, ἢ χαλκέων[14]

[1] αὐτός ἐστι Aub.: *ipse est* Oec.: perhaps αὐτῷ ἐστι.

[2] κατ' ἐκτός τινος Aub.: *quasi* (καθὰ?) *extra aliquem* Oec.: κατ' seclusi.

[3] *Ipse enim est qui sine termino. omnium est terminus: et qui a nullo compre-
henditur, omnia in se comprehendit* (i.e. αὐτὸς γάρ ἐστιν ὃς ἀπέραντος ὢν πάντων
ἐστὶ πέρας, καὶ ὃς ὑπὸ κ.τ.λ.?) Oec.

[4] Lacunam signavi. There is a breach in the sequence of thought. The
passage ἐπεὶ τίς διαφορά ἐστι κ.τ.λ. might perhaps be taken as written in support of
the preceding statement that there is nothing which God cannot do (the argument
being 'God is ἀσώματος and ἀγένητος. and consequently he is αὐτεξούσιος, and cannot be prevented by ἀνάγκη from doing anything which he thinks fit to do'); but
it has no apparent connexion with the clauses which more immediately precede it
(μηδὲ ἔν τινι αὐτὸν διανοηθῇς εἶναι κ.τ.λ.).

[5] τὸ ἀσώματον Aub.: *incorporea* (i.e. τὰ ἀσώματα) Oec.

[6] καὶ τῶν . . . αὐτεξούσιον et ἢ τῶν . . . τὰ ἀΐδια seclusi. The former at least
must certainly be struck out; for it is absurd to say 'the difference between τὰ
ἀνάγκῃ ὑποκείμενα and τὸ αὐτεξούσιον is this, that the one is αὐτεξούσιον and the
other is ἀνάγκῃ ὑποκείμενον', i.e. 'the difference between A and B is that the one
is B and the other is A'.

[7] τὰ . . . ὑποκείμενα scripsi: τὸ . . . ὑποκείμενον Aub.: *aliud autem necessitati
subditum* Oec.

[8] Lacunam signavi. τὰ δὲ κάτω κ.τ.λ. must have been preceded by something like τὰ μὲν γὰρ ἄνω, τέλεια ὄντα, ἀΐδιά ἐστι. But the connexion of this
sentence with what stands before it is not clear.

[9] The passage attributed to Sophocles is a Jewish forgery. It came from the
same source as the *Palinodia* of Orpheus (see note on 541 A). Clem. Alex.
Strom. 5. 14. 114: ὁ μὲν Σοφοκλῆς, ὥς φησιν Ἑκαταῖος ὁ τὰς ἱστορίας συνταξάμενος
ἐν τῷ κατ' Ἄβραμον καὶ τοὺς Αἰγυπτίους (i.e. the Jewish Pseudo-Hecataeus), ἄντικρυς
ἐπὶ τῆς σκηνῆς ἐκβοᾷ· " ἐν ταῖς ἀληθείαισιν . . . εὐσεβεῖν νομίζομεν" *Protr.* 7. 74.

[10] *Unus verissime unus* (i.e. εἷς ταῖς ἀληθείαισιν εἷς) Oec.: εἷς ταῖς Euseb. *Pr. ev.*
13. 13. 40.

[11] *vim* (i.e. βίαν?) Oec.: βίαν Clem. *Str.*: βίας Clem. *Protr.*

[12] *Plerique autem mortales* (i.e. θνητοὶ δὲ πολλοί) Oec.: πολλοὶ Clem.

[13] *extruimus in animarum iacturam* (i.e. εἰς πῆμα τῶν ψυχῶν?) Oec.

[14] *ex lapidibus et lignis* (i.e. ἐκ λίθων τε καὶ ξύλων?) Oec.

ἢ χρυσοτεύκτων ἢ ᾿λεφαντίνων τύπους,[1]
θυσίας τε τούτοις καὶ κενὰς πανηγύρεις
τεύχοντες, οὕτως εὐσεβεῖν νομίζομεν."[2]

552 A   καὶ μέντοι καὶ ὁ σοφώτατος Ξενοφῶν·[3] "ὁ γοῦν πάντα[4] σείων καὶ
ἀτρεμίζων[5] ὡς μὲν[6] μέγας τις καὶ δυνατός, φανερόν·[7] ὁποῖος δέ τις[8]
μορφήν, ἀφανές.[9] οὐδὲ[10] μὴν ὁ παμφαὴς[11] δοκῶν εἶναι ἥλιος,[12] οὐδὲ οὗτος[13]
ἔοικεν ὁρᾶν ἑαυτὸν ἐπιτρέπειν,[14] ἀλλ᾽ ἤν τις ἀναιδῶς αὐτὸν θεάσηται, τὴν
ὄψιν ἀφαιρεῖται."

εἷς μὲν οὖν ὅτι θεὸς κατὰ φύσιν τε καὶ ἀληθῶς ἐστι,[15] παντὸς ἀνώτερος[16]
νοῦ καὶ λόγου, ἀκατάληπτος, ἀνείδεος, ζωοποιὸς καὶ πάντων ἀρχή, ἀγένητος,
ἄφθαρτος, γενεσιουργὸς τῶν ὅλων, μεμαρτύρηται σαφῶς παρά τε τῆς
θεοπνεύστου γραφῆς καὶ διὰ φωνῆς τῶν παρ᾽ αὐτοῖς[17] ποιητῶν τε καὶ λογο-
γράφων. ὅτι δὲ τὸν ἐξ αὐτοῦ κατὰ φύσιν γεννηθέντα υἱόν, τὸν δημιουργὸν

---

[1] *vel elephantinis figuris* (i. e. ἢ ᾿λεφαντίνων τύπων) Oec.

[2] στέφοντες Clem. *eos* (i. e. τούτους ?) *colere arbitramur* Oec.

[3] This passage is twice quoted by Clem. Alex. (*Protrept.* 6. 71 and *Strom.* 5. 14.
109). It is given as an extract from Xenophon by Stobaeus also (2. 1. 33, vol. ii,
p. 15 Wachsm.), who presumably got it from some Pagan source. (In Stob., the
words ὁ γοῦν πάντα σείων κ.τ.λ. are preceded by an additional sentence, viz.
δαίμονες οἱ τὰ μέγιστα διαπρασσόμενοι ἥκιστα ἀνθρώποισιν ἐπιφαίνονται, which was
perhaps originally written as a heading.) It is not transcribed verbally from
Xenophon, but is a free paraphrase of Xen. *Mem.* 4. 3. 13 f.

[4] πάντα Aub., Clem. *Strom.*, Stob. : τὰ πάντα Clem. *Protr.*

[5] *omniaque* (a misprint for *omnia qui* ?) *concutiat et confirmat* Oec.

[6] ὡς μὲν Clem., Stob. : ὥσπερ Cyril (Aub.) : *quod* (i. e. ὡς) *magnus sit* Oec.

[7] φανερός Aub., Clem. : φανερόν Stob. : *manifestum* (φανερόν ?) Oec.

[8] δέ τις Aub., Clem. *Protr.* : δ᾽ ἐστὶν Clem. *Strom* : δὲ τὴν Stob.

[9] ἀφανής Aub., Clem., Stob. : *ignotum* (ἀφανές ?) Oec.

[10] οὔτε Aub. : οὐδὲ Clem., Stob.

[11] παμφαὴς Aub., Clem. : παμφανὴς Stob.

[12] *neque enim videtur* (a slip or misprint for *neque enim qui videtur* ?) *esse
lucidissimus sol* Oec.

[13] οὗτος Aub., Clem. *Strom.*, Stob. : *hic* (i. e. οὗτος) Oec. : αὐτὸς Clem. *Protr.*

[14] ἔοικεν ὁρᾶν ἑαυτὸν (αὐτὸν Clem.) ἐπιτρέπειν Aub., Clem. : *videtur permittere
ut ipse cernatur* Oec. : αὐτὸν ὡς ἔοικεν ὁρᾶν ἐπιτρέπει Stob.

[15] *quod unus naturalis verusque* (ἀληθὴς ?) *deus sit* Oec.
Cf. 556 C, πρόεισι γὰρ ἐξ αὐτοῦ κατὰ φύσιν. 597 D, τοῦ θεοῦ κατὰ φύσιν καὶ ἀληθῶς.
904 D, 905 A–B.

[16] ἀνώτερος scripsi : ἀνωτάτω Aub. : *longe super omnem mentem* Oec. God cannot be comprehended by human thought (νοῦ), nor described by human speech
(λόγου).

[17] *Sc.* τοῖς Ἕλλησι. By the preceding citations (541 A–544 C and 548 C–552 A),
Cyril has shown that some Pagans (including Hermes Trismegistus) have acknowledged the one God known to Moses and the Christians. He now goes on to show,
by the citations which follow, that some Pagans (including Hermes Trismegistus)
have acknowledged the three Persons of the Christian Trinity ; for they have
spoken of the Son (552 D–553 B), and of the Holy Spirit (553 B–556 A).
Oecolampadius gives *eorum qui apud illos clari sunt poetarum et scriptorum* ;
he must therefore have read after παρ᾽ αὐτοῖς in the Codex Capnionis some adjective
of similar meaning to *clari* (e.g. ὀνομαστῶν).

αὐτοῦ λόγον, ἐγνώκασι καὶ αὐτοί, δι' ὧν γεγράφασιν ἐπιδείξομεν. παραθέντες
τὰς παρὰ τούτων χρήσεις.[1]

φησὶ γὰρ ὁ Πορφύριος ἐν τετάρτῳ βιβλίῳ Φιλοσόφου ἱστορίας ὡς
εἰπόντος Πλάτωνος περὶ τοῦ ἀγαθοῦ οὕτως· "ἀπὸ δὲ τούτου,[2] τρόπον τινὰ
5 ἀνθρώποις ἀνεπινόητον, νοῦν γενέσθαι ⌜τε ὅλον καὶ⌝ καθ' ἑαυτὸν ὑφεστῶτα,[3]
ἐν ᾧ δὴ τὰ ὄντως ὄντα[4] καὶ ἡ πᾶσα οὐσία τῶν ὄντων. ὃ δὴ καὶ πρώτως
καλὸν καὶ αὐτόκαλον, παρ' ἑαυτοῦ τῆς καλλονῆς ἔχον τὸ εἶδος.[5] προῆλθε
δὲ προαιώνιος, ἀπ' αἰτίου τοῦ θεοῦ[6] ὡρμημένος, αὐτογέννητος ὢν καὶ αὐτο-
πάτωρ· οὐ γὰρ ἐκείνου κινουμένου[7] πρὸς γένεσιν τὴν τούτου ἡ πρόοδος
10 γέγονεν, ἀλλὰ τούτου παρελθόντος αὐτογόνως ἐκ θεοῦ,[8] παρελθόντος[9] δὲ
οὐκ ἀπ' ἀρχῆς τινὸς χρονικῆς· οὔπω γὰρ χρόνος ἦν.[10] ἀλλ' οὐδὲ χρόνου

---

[1] *apponemus et de his* (καὶ περὶ τούτων) *sententias* Oec.

[2] τούτου means τοῦ ἀγαθοῦ (neuter). The Neoplatonic doctrine that νοῦς issues
from τὸ ἀγαθόν was based on Pl. *Rep.* 508 A–509 B; but Porphyry's statement of
it in this passage was not derived immediately from anything in Plato's writings,
but was taken over by him from Plotinus. Cyril identifies the ἀγαθόν of the
Neoplatonists with God the Father, and their νοῦς with God the Son. See note on
Didymus *De Trin.* 760 B, p. 174, n. 3.
    At what point does the quotation from Porphyry end? In Migne's reprint of
Aubert's edition, it is made to end at οὐσία τῶν ὄντων, and what follows (ὃ δὴ καὶ
πρώτως ... αἰωνίας ὑποστάσεως) is printed in ordinary type, as if written by Cyril
in his own person. Nauck (*Porphyrii Opusc. sel.* p. 15) says 'προῆλθε δέ—
ὑποστάσεως verba videntur a Porphyrio esse aliena', which implies that he thinks
the quotation ends at τῆς καλλονῆς ἔχον τὸ εἶδος. But it seems to me evident that
the words προῆλθε δὲ ... ὑποστάσεως are such as would be spoken by a Pagan
Neoplatonist, and not such as would be spoken by Cyril himself; and it is to be
presumed that the Neoplatonist who speaks is Porphyry. I have therefore taken
the quotation as extending to ὑποστάσεως. The transition from *oratio obliqua* (νοῦν
γενέσθαι) to *oratio recta* (προῆλθε δέ) is no great difficulty.

[3] ἀπὸ δὲ τούτου ... ὑφεστῶτα Aub.: *ab hoc autem modo quandam hominibus
inexcogitabilem mentem factam esse totam, et secundum seipsam subsistentem* (i. e.
ἀπὸ δὲ τούτου τοῦ τρόπου τινὰ ἀνθρώποις ἀκατανόητον νοῦν γενέσθαι ὅλον καὶ καθ'
ἑαυτὸν ὑφεστῶτα) Oec. In the first part of this sentence, Aubert's reading (τρόπον)
is certainly right, and that of Oecolampadius (τοῦ τρόπου) is wrong. There are a
good many other instances also in which Aubert's reading seems better that Oec.'s
variant; and that being so, perhaps Neumann's statement that Aubert's MS. was
derived from the Codex Capnionis used by Oecolampadius ought to be recon-
sidered.
    τε ὅλον καί is unintelligible: perhaps an adjective or participle, to which καθ'
ἑαυτὸν ὑφεστῶτα was coupled, has been lost after γενέσθαι.

[4] As to ἐν ᾧ δή (sc. νῷ) τὰ ὄντως ὄντα, see note on *Abammonis Responsum* 8. 2 a,
p. 54 above.

[5] ὃ δὴ καὶ πρώτως καλὸν ... τὸ εἶδος secludendum? These words have no
apparent connexion either with what precedes or with what follows, and interrupt
the sequence of thought. Moreover, the use of the neuter (ὅ and ἔχον) is awkward,
since νοῦς is spoken of in the masculine both before and after.

[6] τοῦ θεοῦ means τοῦ πρώτου θεοῦ (i. e. τοῦ ἀγαθοῦ); and similarly, ἐκ θεοῦ below
means ἐκ τοῦ πρώτου θεοῦ.

[7] *non enim illo movente* (i. e. κινοῦντος?) Oec.

[8] For αὐτογέννητος ὢν ... ἐκ θεοῦ, cf. *Abammonis Resp.* 8. 2 a, p. 54 above.

[9] παρελθόντος ... παρελθόντος δὲ Aub.: *progrediente .... Processit autem*
(παρῆλθε δέ?) Oec.

[10] Cf. Pl. *Tim.* 37 D, where it is said that χρόνος was made by the Demiurgus as

C γενομένου πρὸς αὐτόν ἐστί τι ὁ χρόνος· ἄχρονος γὰρ ἀεὶ καὶ μόνος[1]
αἰώνιος ὁ νοῦς. ὥσπερ δὲ ὁ θεὸς ὁ πρῶτος καὶ[2] μόνος ἀεί, κἂν ἀπ' αὐτοῦ
γένηται τὰ πάντα, τῷ μὴ τούτοις συναριθμεῖσθαι,[3] μηδὲ τὴν ἀξίαν αὐτῶ⟨ν⟩[4]
συγκατατάττεσθαι δύνασθαι[5] τῇ ἐκείνου ὑπάρξει, οὕτω καὶ ὁ νοῦς αἰώνιος
μόνος καὶ ἀχρόνως ὑποστὰς καὶ τῶν ἐν χρόνῳ αὐτὸς ⌜χρόνος⌝ ἐστίν,[6] ἐν 5
ταυτότητι μένων τῆς ἑαυτοῦ αἰωνίας ὑποστάσεως."

καὶ μὴν καὶ Ὀρφεὺς αὖθις οὕτω πού φησιν·[7]

"οὐρανὸν ὁρκίζω σε. θεοῦ μεγάλου σοφὸν ἔργον·
αὐδὴν ὁρκίζω σε πατρός, ἣν φθέγξατο πρώτην,[8]
ἡνίκα κόσμον ἅπαντα ἑαῖς στηρίξατο βουλαῖς." 10

αὐδὴν δὲ πατρός, ἣν ἐφθέγξατο πρώτην,[9] τὸν μονογενῆ λόγον αὐτοῦ φησιν,
D ἀεὶ συνυπάρχοντα τῷ πατρί· οὐ γὰρ ἦν χρόνος ὅτε δίχα λόγου τοῦ ἰδίου
νοοῖτ' ἂν ὑπάρχων ὁ θεὸς καὶ πατήρ. ἐν ταὐτῷ[10] δὲ καὶ τῶν ὅλων δημιουργὸν ἀπέφηνεν ὄντα θεόν.[11]

ὁ δὲ τρισμέγιστος Ἑρμῆς οὕτω φθέγγεται περὶ θεοῦ·[12] "ὁ γὰρ λόγος 15
αὐτοῦ προελθών,[13] παντέλειος[14] ὢν καὶ γόνιμος καὶ δημιουργός,[15]
an εἰκὼν κινητὸς αἰῶνος. The statement οὔπω χρόνος ἦν is verbally self-contra-
dictory; πω and ἦν are words properly applicable only to things that take place in
a time-process, and the phrase implies that time came into existence at a certain
point in time. The writer expresses his meaning more correctly when he says that
νοῦς is ἄχρονος.

[1] *Absque tempore enim et sola, aeterna mens* Oec.
[2] *Sicut autem deus primus unus et* (i. e. εἷς καί) *solus semper* Oec.
[3] For ὁ θεὸς ὁ πρῶτος μόνος (ἐστίν) . . . τῷ μὴ τούτοις συναριθμεῖσθαι, cf. Cyril
c. Julianum VIII. 916 B : φάσκοντες μὴ δεῖν τἀγαθὸν συναριθμεῖν τοῖς ἀπ' αὐτοῦ·
ἐξῃρῆσθαι γὰρ ἀπὸ πάσης κοινωνίας, διὰ τὸ εἶναι ἁπλοῦν πάντῃ, καὶ ἄδεκτόν τινος
συμβάσεως.
[4] αὐτῶν scripsi : αὐτῷ Aub. : *cum illorum* (i. e. αὐτῶν or ἐκείνων) *substantia* Oec.
[5] *simul recensetur* (om. δύνασθαι) *eius dignitas* Oec.
[6] [Cf. *c. Jul.* 905 D : οὐδὲ γὰρ ἦν χρόνος, καθ' ὃν οὐκ ὄντα νοοῦμεν, μᾶλλον δὲ
αὐτός ἐστι τῶν αἰώνων ποιητής, καὶ χρόνον παντὸς ἀνῳκισμένην ἔχει τὴν ὕπαρξιν.]
[7] See Lobeck *Aglaophamus*, p. 737. These three verses are doubtless a Jewish
forgery, and probably of the same origin as the *palinodia* of Orpheus (541 A above);
but the Jew who forged them may have initiated the opening words of a Pagan
ὁρκισμός, in which Orpheus adjured his pupil not to reveal to others the holy secrets
which he was about to communicate to him. They are quoted, in connexion with
the *palinodia*, in Pseudo-Justin *Cohort. aa gent.* 15. Malalas (*Testim.*) took
them from Cyril, but by mistake ascribed them to Hermes Trismegistus instead of
Orpheus. [See O. Kern, *Orphicorum Fragmenta, fr.* 299.]
[8] *quam locutus est primum* (i. e. πρῶτον) Oec.
[9] *quam locutus est primum* (i. e. πρῶτον) Oec. [10] *in ipso* (i. e. ἐν αὐτῷ) Oec.
[11] 'He declared that God is maker of the universe'; a paraphrase of κόσμον
ἅπαντα ἑαῖς στηρίξατο βουλαῖς.
[12] *Fr.* 27. The Hermetic passage ὁ γὰρ λόγος . . . ὕδωρ ἐποίησε is quoted by
Malalas, by the writer of *Chron. Pasch.*, by Suidas, and by Cedrenus. (See *Testim.*)
Malalas got it from Cyril, and the three others got it from Malalas.
[13] προελθών om. Suidas.
[14] [Cf. Cyril *c. Jul.* 920 B : ἡμεῖς δὲ παντέλειον εἶναί φαμεν τὸν πατέρα· ὁμοίως δὲ
τὸν υἱόν, ὡς ἐκ τελείου τέλειον. 913 C : ἔστι ζῶν καὶ ζωοποιός. . . . εἶναι δέ φαμεν
αὐτὸν ἀόρατον, ἀναφῆ, ἄφθαρτον, ἀναλλοίωτον, αὐτοτελῆ, παντέλειον.]
[15] The best MSS. of Suidas give δημιουργικός.

⌜ἐν γονίμῃ¹ φύσει πεσὼν² ἐπὶ³ γονίμῳ ὕδατι⌝⁴ ἔγκυον τὸ⁵
ὕδωρ ἐποίησε."⁶ καὶ ὁ αὐτὸς αὖθις "ἡ οὖν ⌜πυραμὶς⌝" φησιν
"⌜ὑποκειμένη τῇ φύσει καὶ τῷ νοερῷ κόσμῳ⌝.⁷ ἔχει γὰρ⁸
ἄρχοντα ἐπικείμενον ⟨τὸν⟩⁹ δημιουργὸν λόγον τοῦ πάντων
5 δεσπότου, ὃς¹⁰ μετ' ἐκεῖνον πρώτη δύναμις, ἀγένητος, ἀπέραντος, ἐξ ἐκείνου προκύψασα, καὶ ἐπίκειται καὶ ἄρχει τῶν δι' αὐτοῦ¹¹
δημιουργηθέντων."¹² ἔστι δὲ τοῦ παντελείου πρόγονος¹³ καὶ τέλειος καὶ

¹ γονίμῃ Aub. : γονίμῳ Malalas, *Chron. Pasch.*, Suidas, Cedrenus.
² πεσὼν Cyril, Malalas, *Chron. Pasch.*, Cedrenus : παῖς ὢν MSS. Suidas.
³ ἐπὶ Aub. : *in foecundam naturam cadens et foecunda aqua* (i. e. καὶ γονίμῳ ὕδατι) Oec. : ἐν Malalas, *Chron. Pasch.*, Cedrenus : καὶ Suidas.
⁴ ἐν γονίμῃ φύσει and ἐπὶ γονίμῳ ὕδατι cannot have stood thus side by side. Perhaps the Hermetist may have written something like ὁ γὰρ λόγος αὐτοῦ προελθών, παντέλειος ὢν [καὶ γόνιμος ?] καὶ δημιουργ(ικ)ός, ⟨καὶ⟩ ἐν (or ἐπὶ) γονίμῳ φύσει (sc. τῇ τοῦ ὕδατος) πεσών [ ], ἔγκυον τὸ ὕδωρ ἐποίησε. The watery chaos was γόνιμος, in the sense that it was capable of bringing things forth when impregnated with God's λόγος.
⁵ ἔγκυόν τε Aub. : *foecundam aquam fecit* Oec. : ἔγκυον τὸ Malalas, *Chron. Pasch.*, Suidas, Cedrenus.
⁶ This passage must have occurred in a description of the *demiurgia* ; and the Hermetist who wrote it must have been directly or indirectly influenced by *Gen.* I. 2, καὶ πνεῦμα θεοῦ ἐπεφέρετο ἐπάνω τοῦ ὕδατος. The ὕδωρ of which he speaks is the watery chaos out of which the world was evolved ; and he took the πνεῦμα θεοῦ which 'moved (or brooded) upon the face of the waters' to be God's λόγος. In hypostatizing the λόγος, he followed Philo, or some Jew of the same school as Philo. Cf. *Corp. Herm.* I. 5 a : λόγος ἅγιος ἐπέβη τῇ (ὑγρᾷ) φύσει. *Ib.* 5 b, as emended : κινούμενα δὲ ἦν διὰ τὸν ἐπάνω τοῦ ὕδατος ἐπιφερόμενον πνευματικὸν λόγον.
⁷ *Fr.* 28. ἡ οὖν πυραμὶς ... κόσμῳ Aub. : *Itaque Pyramis inquit, subiacet* (ὑπόκειται ?) *naturae et mentali mundo* Oec. If πυραμίς is sound, the pyramid must have been mentioned as a symbol or type of the arrangement of the universe (God, or God's λόγος, being the apex), and we may suppose the sentence to have originally run somewhat as follows : ἡ οὖν πυραμὶς ὑποκειμένην (ἀποφαίνει) τὴν φύσιν (i. e. the material world) τῷ νοερῷ ⟨...⟩. But it seems more likely that πυραμίς is corrupt.
⁸ The subject of ἔχει must be ἡ φύσις or ὁ (αἰσθητὸς) κόσμος.
⁹ τὸν addidi.
¹⁰ ὅς refers to λόγον, and not to the nearer substantive δεσπότου. This awkward-ness might be avoided by writing ⟨τὸν⟩ [δημιουργὸν] τοῦ πάντων δεσπότου λόγον, ὃς κ.τ.λ.
¹¹ αὐτοῦ means τοῦ λόγου. In the beginning God made the world by the agency of his λόγος ; and his λόγος continues to govern the world which was thus made.
¹² ὃς μετ' ἐκεῖνον ... δημιουργηθέντων Aub. : *quod* (sc. *Verbum*) *post illum prima virtus, ingenitum absque termino* (i. e. ἀγένητος ἀπέραντος in agreement with λόγος, not with δύναμις), *ex illo prospectans* (προκύψας ?) *et incumbens* (καὶ ἐπικείμενος ?), *ac impetat* (misprint for *imperat*) *omnibus quae* (πάντων τῶν) *per ipsum formata sunt* Oec.
In his description of the hypostatized λόγος of God, the writer of this passage agrees closely with Philo. The use of the term 'God's λόγος' to denote the second God in the two following Hermetic extracts also is to be attributed to the same Jewish influence. Cyril, for his special purpose, picked out from the *Hermetica* known to him passages in which the word λόγος was thus used, and has here brought together four such passages ; to which must be added the passage quoted by him in 920 D. (See also 588 B.) But in the extant *Hermetica*, the use of λόγος in that sense is rare, and the second God is more usually called by other names.
¹³ πρόγονος Aub. (πρωτόγονος Reitzenstein) : *est autem et* (ἔστι δὲ καὶ) *e perfectis-simo progenitus* Oec.

γόνιμος γνήσιος υἱός.¹ καὶ πάλιν ὁ αὐτός, ὡς ἐρομένου τινὸς τῶν ἐν

553 A Αἰγύπτῳ τεμενιτῶν,² καὶ λέγοντος "διὰ τί δέ, ὦ μέγιστε Ἀγαθὸς Δαίμων, τούτῳ τῷ ὀνόματι ἐκλήθη³ ἀπὸ τοῦ πάντων κυρίου;" φησί·⁴ "καὶ ἐν τοῖς ἔμπροσθεν εἶπον· σὺ δὲ οὐ συνῆκας; ⟨ἡ⟩⁵ φύσις τοῦ νοεροῦ αὐτοῦ λόγου⁶ φύσις⁷ ἐστι γεννητική.⁸ ⌈τοῦτο 5 ὥσπερ αὐτοῦ ἡ γέννησις ἢ φύσις ἢ ἔθος ἤ⌉.⁹ ⟨σὺ δὲ⟩¹⁰ ὃ θέλεις αὐτὸ⟨ν⟩¹¹ καλεῖν κάλει, τοῦτο μόνον νοῶν, ὅτι τέλειός ἐστι[ν ἐν τελείῳ]¹² καὶ ἀπὸ τελείου, ⟨καὶ⟩¹³ τέλεια ἀγαθὰ ἐργάζεται, καὶ δημιουργεῖ καὶ ζωοποιεῖ. ἐπειδὴ οὖν τοιαύτης ἔχεται φύσεως, καλῶς τοῦτο προσηγόρευται."¹⁴ καὶ ὁ αὐτὸς ἐν λόγῳ πρώτῳ τῶν πρὸς 10 τὸν Τὰτ διεξοδικῶν¹⁵ οὕτω λέγει περὶ θεοῦ· "ὁ τοῦ δημιουργοῦ¹⁶ λόγος,

---

¹ The sentence ἔστι δέ . . . γνήσιος υἱός has usually been taken to be a continuation of the Hermetic passage ἡ οὖν πυραμὶς . . . δημιουργηθέντων. But as it contains the words παντέλειος and γόνιμος, which previously occur, not in that passage, but in the preceding quotation from Hermes (ὁ γὰρ λόγος . . . ὕδωρ ἐποίησε), it seems more likely that this sentence is a comment, written by Cyril, on both those Hermetic passages together. [For a similar comment, beginning with ἔστι δέ, compare p. 214, l. 7.]

² *Quum interrogasset quidem* (misprint for *quidam*?) *sacerdos Aegyptius* Oec. Cf. ὡς ἐρομένου τινός in 556 B.

³ *Fr.* 29. Compare Didymus 756 B and Cyril 588 A. Hermes is reporting an answer given by the Agathos Daimon to 'some one who asked a question'. If it is so, who is the subject of ἐκλήθη? From what follows, it appears that the person to whom the name in question was given (i.e. the subject of ἐκλήθη) is God's νοερὸς λόγος.

⁴ The grammatical subject of φησί is ὁ αὐτός, i.e. Hermes. But it is evident that the following words (καὶ ἐν τοῖς ἔμπροσθεν εἶπον κ.τ.λ.) are spoken by the Agathos Daimon, in answer to the question asked by the τεμενίτης. Cyril must therefore have meant 'Hermes reports the answer of the Agathos Daimon thus'.

⁵ ἡ addidi.

⁶ αὐτοῦ means τοῦ πάντων κυρίου, the supreme God.

⁷ φύσις secludendum?

⁸ *Natura Verbi eius natura est generativa, et condere potens* (i.e. γεννητικὴ καὶ δημιουργικὴ) Oec.

⁹ τοῦτο ὥσπερ αὐτοῦ looks like the beginning of a sentence the rest of which is lost; and ἤ (perhaps ἡ) γέννησις ἢ φύσις ἢ ἔθος ἤ may be a remnant of a marginal note.

¹⁰ σὺ δὲ addidi.

¹¹ αὐτὸν scripsi : αὐτὸ Aub.

¹² ἐστι scripsi : ἐστιν ἐν τελείῳ Aub.

¹³ καὶ addidi. ἀπὸ τελείου τέλεια ἀγαθὰ ἐργάζεται Aub.; but I can find no meaning in ἀπὸ τελείου ἐργάζεται. With my correction, ἀπὸ τελείου means ἀπὸ τελείου ὄντος τοῦ πάντων κυρίου προεληλυθώς.

¹⁴ τοῦτο (sc. τὸ ὄνομα) is the name spoken of in the pupil's question (διὰ τί . . . τούτῳ τῷ ὀνόματι ἐκλήθη;). The speaker means 'It does not matter what you call him, provided that you understand what sort of being he is; but it is well to call him by the name in question, because that name is one that describes him rightly'.

¹⁵ *Fr.* 30. Besides this extract, Cyril gives two others (588 A and 588 B) which are taken from the first of the διεξοδικοὶ λόγοι of Hermes to Tat.

¹⁶ In the preceding Hermetic extracts, the term δημιουργός is applied to God's λόγος. But in this fragment, and in 588 A (from the same *libellus*), it is the supreme God himself, and not his λόγος, that is called ὁ δημιουργός; and in 588 B (also from the same *libellus*), the λόγος is called δημιουργικός, but not δημιουργός.

ὦ τέκνον, ἀΐδιος, αὐτοκίνητος, ἀναυξής, ἀμείωτος, ἀμετάβλητος,
ἄφθαρτος ⌜μόνος⌝,[1] ἀεὶ ἑαυτῷ ὅμοιός ἐστιν, ἴσος δὲ καὶ ὁμαλός."[2] B
εὐσταθής, εὔτακτος, εἷς ὢν [ὁ][3] μετὰ τὸν προεγνωσμένον θεόν."[4]
σημαίνει δέ, οἶμαι,[5] διά γε τουτουὶ[6] τὸν πατέρα.

5   ἀπόχρη μὲν οὖν ταυτὶ πρὸς ἐντελεστάτην ἀπόδειξιν τοῦ ὅτι τὸν μονογενῆ
τοῦ θεοῦ λόγον ἐννενοήκασι καὶ αὐτοί. δεῖν δὲ οἶμαι οἷς ἔφην προσεπενεγκεῖν
καὶ τὰ περὶ τοῦ ἁγίου πνεύματος παρ' αὐτῶν εἰρημένα.

Πορφύριος γάρ φησι, Πλάτωνος ἐκτιθέμενος δόξαν,[7] "ἄχρι τριῶν ὑποστάσεων[8] τὴν τοῦ θείου προελθεῖν οὐσίαν· εἶναι δὲ τὸν μὲν ἀνωτάτω θεὸν
10 τἀγαθόν,[9] μετ' αὐτὸν δὲ καὶ δεύτερον τὸν δημιουργόν, τρίτον δὲ καὶ τὴν τοῦ
κόσμου ψυχήν· ἄχρι γὰρ ψυχῆς τὴν θειότητα[10] προελθεῖν". ἰδοὺ δὴ σαφῶς[11]
ἐν τούτοις ἄχρι τριῶν ὑποστάσεων τὴν τοῦ θείου[12] προελθεῖν οὐσίαν ἰσχυρί- C
ζεται· εἷς μὲν γάρ ἐστιν ὁ τῶν ὅλων θεός, κατευρύνεται δέ, ὥσπερ ἡ περὶ αὐτοῦ
γνῶσις, εἰς ἁγίαν [τε][13] καὶ ὁμοούσιον τριάδα, εἴς τε πατέρα φημὶ καὶ υἱὸν
15 καὶ ἅγιον πνεῦμα, ὃ καὶ ψυχὴν τοῦ κόσμου φησὶν ὁ Πλάτων.   ζωοποιεῖ δὲ

---

[1] μόνος Aub.: *Conditoris Verbum . . . solum* (i. e. μόνος) Oec.: perhaps μόνιμος.
(Or μόνῳ ἑαυτῷ ὅμοιος?)   [Cf. p. 198, l. 9 sq.]

[2] ἑαυτῷ . . . καὶ ὁμαλός Aub.: *sibi ipsi aequale est, simile et planum* (i. e. ἑαυτῷ
ἴσος ἐστὶν ὅμοιος καὶ ὁμαλός) Oec.   There is some slight corruption here.   Perhaps
ἐστιν ἴσος δὲ καὶ ὁμαλός ought to be bracketed.   For ἀεὶ ἑαυτῷ ὅμοιος, cf. τὸ ἑαυτῷ
ὅμοιον κ.τ.λ. in 549 C, where terms similar in meaning to those here applied to
God's λόγος are predicated of incorporeal deity in general.

[3] ὁ seclusi.   εἷς ὢν μετὰ τὸν . . . θεόν is equivalent to ὃς μετ' ἐκεῖνον πράτη
δύναμις in 552 D.

[4] τὸν προεγνωσμένον θεόν (*praecognitum deum* Oec.) denotes the supreme God; but
how προεγνωσμένον (if the reading is right) has come to mean this, I do not know.
See note on τὸν προεννοούμενον θεόν in *Abammonis Resp.* 10. 7 a, pp. 39, 99 above.

[5] οἶμαι om. Oec.

[6] τουτουί refers to τὸν προεγνωσμένον θεόν.   'By this term', says Cyril, 'Hermes
means God the Father'.

[7] This passage of Porphyry is quoted by Didymus, p. 171 above, whence
Cyril here transcribed it; and it is quoted again by Cyril, *c. Julianum* 916 B,
where he must have taken it directly from Porphyry.   In 916 B he writes as follows:
γράφει τοίνυν Πορφύριος ἐν βιβλίῳ τετάρτῳ Φιλοσόφου ἱστορίας· Ἄχρι γὰρ τριῶν
ὑποστάσεων ἔφη Πλάτων τὴν τοῦ θεοῦ προελθεῖν οὐσίαν· εἶναι δὲ τὸν μὲν . . . τὴν
θεότητα προελθεῖν. λοιπὸν δὲ (perhaps δὴ) τὸ ἄθεον ἀπὸ τῆς σωματικῆς ἐνῆρχθαι
(perhaps ἐνῆρκται) διαφορᾶς. (Is the last clause, λοιπὸν . . . διαφορᾶς, a continuation of the quotation from Porphyry, or a remark added by Cyril?   Migne prints
it as a part of the passage quoted; but Nauck, *Porph. opusc. sel.* p. 14, omits it,
and thereby implies that he does not ascribe it to Porphyry).

It appears from Didymus 760 B and Cyril 916 B, though we should not have
known it from Cyril 553 B, that ἄχρι τριῶν ὑποστάσεων . . . θεότητα προελθεῖν was
in *oratio obliqua* in the passage as written by Porphyry, being dependent on ἔφη
Πλάτων.

[8] *usque ad tres subsistentias* (i. e. ὑποστάσεων) Oec.: ἀποστάσεων Aub. here, but
ὑποστάσεων Aub. 916 B and Didymus.

[9] *esse autem summe quidem* (i. e. τὸ μὲν ἀνωτάτω?) *deum Bonum* Oec.

[10] θειότητα Aub. here, and Didymus: *deitatem* (i. e. θεότητα?) Oec.: θεότητα
Aub. 916 B.

[11] *Ecce quam manifeste* Oec.   [12] τοῦ θείου Aub.: *dei* (i. e. τοῦ θεοῦ) Oec.

[13] τε seclusi.   Cf. τὴν ἁγίαν καὶ ὁμοούσιον τριάδα in 553 D.

τὸ πνεῦμα, καὶ πρόεισιν ἐκ ζῶντος πατρὸς δι' υἱοῦ, καὶ " ἐν αὐτῷ ζῶμεν καὶ
κινούμεθα καὶ ἐσμέν ".[1] ἀληθεύει γὰρ λέγων ὁ κύριος ἡμῶν Ἰησοῦς Χριστός
" τὸ πνεῦμά ἐστι τὸ ζωοποιοῦν ".[2] καὶ πάλιν ὁ αὐτὸς Πορφύριος περὶ
Πλάτωνος· " διὸ ἐν ἀπορρήτοις περὶ τούτων αἰνιττόμενός φησι[3] ' περὶ τὸν
βασιλέα[4] πάντα ἐστι, καὶ ἐκείνου ἕνεκα πάντα, καὶ ἐκεῖνο αἴτιον[5] πάντων   5
καλῶν,[6] δεύτερον δὲ πέρι τὰ δεύτερα, καὶ τρίτον πέρι τὰ τρίτα ', ὡς [γὰρ][7]
πάντων μὲν περὶ τοὺς τρεῖς ὄντων θεούς,[8] ἀλλ' ἤδη πρώτως μὲν περὶ τὸν
D πάντων βασιλέα, δευτέρως δὲ περὶ τὸν ἀπ' ἐκείνου θεόν, καὶ τρίτως περὶ τὸν
ἀπὸ τούτου." δεδήλωκε δὲ[9] [[ἐμφαίνων]] καὶ τὴν ἐξ ἀλλήλων ὑπόστασιν,[10]
ἀρχόμενος ἀπὸ τοῦ βασιλέως,[11] καὶ τὴν ὑπόβασιν καὶ ὕφεσιν τῶν μετὰ τὸν   10
πρῶτον ⟨⟨ἐμφαίνων⟩⟩ διὰ τοῦ " πρώτως " καὶ " δευτέρως " καὶ " τρίτως "
εἰπεῖν, καὶ ὅτι ἐξ ἑνὸς τὰ πάντα,[12] καὶ δι' αὐτοῦ σώζεται.[13] τεθεώρηκε μὲν
οὖν οὐχ ὑγιῶς εἰσάπαν, ἀλλὰ τοῖς τὰ Ἀρείου πεφρονηκόσιν ἐν ἴσῳ διαιρεῖ

---

[1] *Act. App.* 17. 28.

[2] ζωοποιεῖ δὲ τὸ πνεῦμα ... " τὸ πνεῦμά ἐστι τὸ ζωοποιοῦν ". Cyril says this in
order to justify his identification of the Neoplatonic ψυχή (ἡ τοῦ κύσμου) with the
Holy Spirit. The argument is not very clearly stated, but seems to be to this
effect: ' the word ψυχή means τὸ ζωοποιοῦν; and Scripture tells us that τὸ
πνεῦμα is τὸ ζωοποιοῦν *Ev. Joh.* 6. 63 ; therefore, ἡ ψυχὴ = τὸ πνεῦμα.' Cf. 921 A.

[3] φησί, sc. Πλάτων. The passage quoted by Porphyry occurs in Pl. *Ep.* 2 (to
Dionysius), 312 E: φῂς γὰρ δὴ ... οὐχ ἱκανῶς ἀποδεδεῖχθαί σοι περὶ τῆς τοῦ πρώτου
φύσεως. φραστέον δή σοι δι' αἰνιγμῶν (hence Porphyry's words ἐν ἀπορρήτοις περὶ
τούτων αἰνιττόμενος), ἵν' ἄν τι ἡ δέλτος ἢ πόντου ἢ γῆς ἐν πτυχαῖς πάθῃ, ὁ ἀναγνοὺς
μὴ γνῷ. ὧδε γὰρ ἔχει· περὶ τὸν πάντων βασιλέα ... τρίτον πέρι τὰ τρίτα. ἡ
οὖν ἀνθρωπίνη ψυχὴ περὶ αὐτὰ ὀρέγεται μαθεῖν ποῖ' ἄττα ἐστί, κ.τ.λ.
These words of Plato had already been explained as referring to the Christian
Trinity by Justin, *Apol.* I. 60 (c. A.D. 145): καὶ (παρὰ Μωϋσέως ἔλαβε Πλάτων) τὸ
εἰπεῖν αὐτὸν (sc. τὸν Πλάτωνα) " τρίτον " ... δευτέραν μὲν γὰρ χώραν τῷ παρὰ θεοῦ
λόγῳ ... δίδωσι, τὴν δὲ τρίτην τῷ λεχθέντι ἐπιφέρεσθαι τῷ ὕδατι πνεύματι, εἰπὼν
" τὰ δὲ τρίτα πέρι (sic legendum) τὸν τρίτον ". Cf. Clem. *Strom.* 5. 14. 103 (quoted
in Euseb. *Pr. ev.* 13. 13. 29): ὥστε καὶ ἐπὰν εἴπῃ (Πλάτων) " περὶ τὸν πάντων
βασιλέα ... καὶ τρίτον πέρι τὰ τρίτα ", οὐκ ἄλλως ἔγωγε ἐξακούω ἢ τὴν ἁγίαν τριάδα
μηνύεσθαι· τρίτον μὲν γὰρ εἶναι τὸ ἅγιον πνεῦμα, τὸν υἱὸν δὲ δεύτερον, δι' οὗ " πάντα
ἐγένετο " κατὰ βούλησιν τοῦ πατρός.

[4] τὸν βασιλέα Cyril : τὸν πάντων βασιλέα Pl. *Ep.*

[5] ἐκεῖνο αἴτιον Cyril, Pl. *Ep.*

[6] πάντων καλῶν Cyril (Aub.): ἁπάντων τῶν καλῶν Pl. *Ep.*   [7] γὰρ seclusi.

[8] *Nam quum omnia quasi* (ὥσπερ in place of μὲν ?) *existant circa tres deos* Oec.

[9] Perhaps δή.

[10] *Manifestavit autem et subsistentiam quam ex seipsis inter se habent* (om.
ἐμφαίνων) Oec. I have bracketed ἐμφαίνων here, and inserted it below, where
some such word is needed to provide a construction for διὰ τοῦ ... εἰπεῖν.

The subject of δεδήλωκε must be the same as that of the verbs in the following
sentence (τεθεώρηκε κ.τ.λ.), and therefore must be Plato, not Porphyry. It is true
that it was not Plato, but Porphyry, that said πρώτως, δευτέρως, and τρίτως; Plato
said (or was represented by the writer of Pl. *Ep.* 2 as saying) δεύτερον and τὰ
δεύτερα, τρίτον and τὰ τρίτα. But Cyril, writing loosely, here ascribes to Plato
the form of words used in Porphyry's explanation of Plato's meaning.

[11] *inciperéque a rege* (ἄρχεσθαί τε in place of ἀρχόμενος ?) Oec.

[12] What does ὅτι ἐξ ἑνὸς κ.τ.λ. depend on? Perhaps something has been lost
before καὶ ὅτι.

[13] *et per ipsum omnia servantur* (τὰ πάντα σώζεται) Oec.

καὶ ὑφίστησιν, ὑποκαθημένας τε ἀλλήλαις τὰς ὑποστάσεις εἰσφέρει, καὶ
τρεῖς οἴεται θεοὺς εἶναι διῃρημένοις¹ τὴν ἁγίαν² καὶ ὁμοούσιον τριάδα·
πλὴν οὐκ ἠγνόηκεν ὁλοτρόπως τὸ ἀληθές. οἶμαι δ' ἂν³ ὅτι κἂν ὑγιῶς ἔφη 556 A
τε καὶ [π]εφρόνησεν.⁴ ἐξήνεγκε δὲ καὶ εἰς τοὺς ἄλλους ἅπαντας τῆς περὶ
5 θεοῦ δόξης τὸ ἀρτίως ἔχον, εἰ μὴ τάχα που⁵ τὴν Ἀνύτου καὶ Μελίτου
γραφὴν ἐδεδίει, καὶ τὸ Σωκράτους κώνειον.⁶

λέγει δὲ καὶ Ἑρμῆς ἐν λόγῳ τρίτῳ τῶν πρὸς Ασκληπιόν·⁷ " οὐ γὰρ
ἐφικτόν ἐστιν εἰς⁸ ἀμυ ν]ήτους⁹ τοιαῦτα μυστήρια παρέχεσθαι.¹⁰
ἀλλὰ τῷ νοΐ¹¹ ἀκούσατε. ἓν μόνον ἦν ⌜φῶς¹² νοερὸν πρὸ φωτὸς
10 νοεροῦ⌝ καὶ ἔστιν ἀεὶ¹³ ⌜νοῦς νοὸς φωτεινός⌝.¹⁴ καὶ οὐδὲν ἕτερον
ἦν ἢ ⟨ἡ⟩¹⁵ τούτου ἑνότης. ἀεὶ ἐν ἑαυτῷ¹⁶ ὤν, ἀεὶ τῷ ἑαυτοῦ¹⁷ νοΐ
καὶ φωτὶ¹⁸ καὶ πνεύματι πάντα περιέχει."¹⁹ καὶ μεθ' ἕτερά

¹ διῃρημένους scripsi : διῃρημένως Aub. : *distincte* Oec.
² *sanctamque* (ἁγίαν τε) Oec.
³ ἂν secludendum? One might write ἐξήνεγκε δ' ⟨ἂν⟩ below.
⁴ ἐφρόνησεν scripsi : πεφρόνηκεν Aub. : *intellexisset* Oec.
⁵ *fortassis autem et pronunciasset quod recte de deo sensit in aliis omnibus, nisi forte* Oec.
⁶ Cyril thinks that Plato really held the same opinion as Athanasius concerning the Trinity; but pretended that he held that of Arius, because he feared that the Athenians of his time (whom Cyril assumes to have been addicted to the Arian heresy) would put him to death if he openly taught a doctrine which differed from theirs.

In an edict issued by Constantine to give effect to the decisions of the Council of Nicaea, the Arians were called 'Porphyrians' (Gibbon ch. 21); which seems to imply that their doctrine was thought to agree with that of Plato as expounded by Porphyry. Cf. Pseudo-Anthimus, p. 158 above.
⁷ *Fr.* 23. The passage οὐ γὰρ ἐφικτόν ... πάντα περιέχει is given by Didymus, and by Malalas and *Chron. Pasch.* The latter part of it (ἦν φῶς νοερὸν ... πάντα περιέχει) is given by Suidas and Cedrenus also. See notes on Didymus p. 173 above.
⁸ εἰς Aub., Didymus, *Chron. Pasch.* : om. cod. Malal.
⁹ ἀμυνήτους Aub. : *non initiatis* Oec. : ἀμυήτους Didymus, Malalas, *Chron. Pasch.*
¹⁰ *Non enim comprehendi possent, si proponerentur non initiatis talia sacramenta* Oec. What was Oec.'s reading of the Greek? Did he read εἰ ἀμυήτοις ... παρέχοιτο?
¹¹ Possibly ⟨ἐντεταμένῳ⟩ τῷ νοΐ. [τῷ νοΐ)(τῇ αἰσθήσει. Cf. p. 227, l. 16.]
¹² ἦν φῶς (*erat lux* Oec.) Cyril, Didymus, *Chron. Pasch.*, Suidas, Cedrenus: ἐστὶ τὸ φῶς cod. Malal.
¹³ ἔστιν ἀεὶ (*est semper* Oec.) Cyril, Didymus: ἦν ἀεὶ cod. Malal., *Chron. Pasch.*, Suidas, Cedrenus.
¹⁴ νοῦς νοὸς φωτεινός (*mens mentis fulgida* Oec.) Cyril, Didymus, (*Chron. Pasch.*?), Suidas: νοῦς νόος φωτινὸς cod. Malal. : νοῦς νοῦ αἴτιον Cedrenus.
¹⁵ ἦν ἢ ἡ Didymus, Cedrenus: ἦν ἢ Cyril (Aub.): ἦν ἡ cod. Malal., *Chron. Pasch.*, Suidas.
¹⁶ ἐν ἑαυτῷ (*in seipsa* Oec.) Cyril, *Chron. Pasch.*: ἐν αὐτῷ codd. Didym., cod. Malal., Cedrenus.
¹⁷ τῷ ἑαυτοῦ (*sua mente* Oec.) Cyril, Didymus, *Chron. Pasch.*, Cedrenus : τῷ αὐτῷ cod. Malal.
¹⁸ ἀεὶ ἐν ἑαυτῷ ὤν, ἀεὶ τῷ ἑαυτοῦ νοΐ καὶ φωτὶ om. Suidas.
¹⁹ πνεύματι πάντα (ἅπαντα *Chron. Pasch.*) περιέχει Didymus, Cyril, Malalas, *Chron. Pasch.*, Cedrenus: πνεῦμα πάντα περιέχον Suidas.

φησιν[1] " ἐκτὸς τούτου οὐ θεός, οὐκ ἄγγελος, οὐ δαίμων, οὐκ οὐσία
τις ἄλλη· πάντων[2] γάρ ἐστι[3] κύριος καὶ πατὴρ καὶ θεὸς[4] καὶ πηγὴ
B καὶ ζωὴ καὶ δύναμις[5] καὶ φῶς καὶ νοῦς καὶ πνεῦμα,[6] καὶ πάντα
ἐν αὐτῷ καὶ ὑπ' αὐτόν[7] ἐστι". νοῦν μὲν γὰρ ἐκ νοῦ, καθάπερ ἐγῷμαι,
φησὶ τὸν υἱόν, καὶ [ὡς][8] φῶς ἐκ φωτός· μέμνηται δὲ καὶ τοῦ πνεύματος ὡς 5
πάντα περιέχοντος.[9] οὔτε δὲ ἄγγελον οὔτε δαίμονα, οὔτε μὴν ἑτέραν τινὰ
φύσιν ἢ οὐσίαν ἔξω κεῖσθαί φησι τῆς θείας ὑπεροχῆς [ἤγουν ἐξουσίας],[10]
ἀλλ' ὑπ' αὐτῇ τὰ πάντα καὶ δι' αὐτὴν εἶναι διορίζεται. καὶ πάλιν ὁ αὐτὸς
ἐν τῷ αὐτῷ λόγῳ, ⟨τῷ⟩[11] τρίτῳ τῶν πρὸς Ἀσκληπιόν, ὡς ἐρομένου τινὸς[12]
περὶ τοῦ θείου πνεύματος, φησὶν οὕτως· "εἰ μὴ πρόνοιά τις ἦν τοῦ[13] 10
πάντων κυρίου ὥστε με[14] τὸν λόγον τοῦτον ἀποκαλύψαι, οὐδὲ
ὑμᾶς νῦν ἔρως τοιοῦτος[15] κατεῖχεν ⟨ἂν⟩[16] ἵνα περὶ τούτου ζητήσητε.[17] νῦν δὲ τὰ λοιπὰ τοῦ λόγου ἀκούετε. τούτου τοῦ πνεύ-
C ματος, οὗ[18] πολλάκις προεῖπον, πάντα χρῄζει· τὰ πάντα γὰρ

[1] *Fr.* 23. The passage ἐκτὸς τούτου . . . αὐτόν ἐστι is given by Didymus, and by Malalas, *Chron. Pasch.*, Suidas, and Cedrenus. See notes on Didymus 760 A, pp. 173–4 above.

[2] *omnino* (i. e. πάντως) Oec.

[3] γάρ ἐστι (*enim est* Oec.) Cyril, Didymus : γὰρ (om. ἐστι) cod. Malal., *Chron. Pasch.*, Suidas, Cedrenus.

[4] κύριος καὶ πατὴρ καὶ θεὸς (*dominus et pater, et deus* Oec.) Cyril, Didymus, *Chron. Pasch.*, Suidas : κύριος καὶ θεὸς cod. Malal. : κύριος καὶ θεὸς καὶ πατὴρ Cedrenus.

[5] *veritas* (written by mistake for *virtus* !) Oec. : δύναμις cett.

[6] καὶ πηγὴ . . . καὶ πνεῦμα is given by Didymus and Cyril, but omitted by Malalas, *Chron. Pasch.*, Suidas, and Cedrenus.

[7] ἐν αὐτῷ καὶ ἐπ' αὐτόν Aub. : *in ipso et sub ipsum* (i. e. καὶ ὑπ' αὐτόν) Oec. : ἐν αὐτῷ καὶ ὑπ' αὐτόν Didymus, *Chron. Pasch.* : ὑπ' αὐτὸν καὶ ἐν αὐτῷ cod. Malal., Suidas : ὑπ' αὐτοῦ καὶ ἐν αὐτῷ Cedrenus. As Cyril writes ὑπ' αὐτῇ τὰ πάντα in his comment below, he probably wrote ὑπ' here.

[8] ὡς (*sicut* Oec.) seclusi. νοῦν ἐκ νοῦ φησὶ τὸν υἱόν is Cyril's comment on νοῦς νοός; and φῶς ἐκ φωτός (sc. φησι τὸν υἱόν) is his comment on φῶς νοερὸν πρὸ φωτὸς νοεροῦ. He takes φῶς νοερόν to mean God the Father, and φωτὸς νοεροῦ to mean God the Son (who was said by the Christians to be φῶς ἐκ φωτός, 'Light of Light'). In this explanation of the Hermetic passage, Cyril closely follows Didymus.

[9] ὡς πάντα περιέχοντος Aub. : *qui omnia contineat* (i. e. τοῦ πάντα περιέχοντος ?) Oec.

[10] ἤγουν ἐξουσίας Aub. : om. Oec.

[11] τῷ addidi.

[12] *Fr.* 24. See note on ἐρομένου τινὸς ⌜τὸν ἀγαθὸς δαίμονα⌝ in Didymus 756 B (pp. 171–3 above), where this Hermetic passage is quoted. Malalas took from Cyril the first part of this passage (viz. εἰ μὴ πρόνοια . . . τούτου ζητήσητε), but omitted the rest. The part given by Malalas is given in *Chron. Pasch.* also.

[13] ἦν τοῦ Cyril, Didymus, Malalas : ἦ τῶν *Chron. Pasch.*

[14] με Aub. : μοι cod. Didym., Malalas, *Chron. Pasch.* : *ita ut et verbum ipsum revelaret* (i. e. ὥστε καὶ αὐτὸν τὸν λόγον ἀποκαλύψαι ?) Oec.

[15] νῦν ἔρως τοιοῦτος Aub. : *nunc amor talis* Oec. : τοιοῦτος ἔρως Didymus, Malalas, *Chron. Pasch.*

[16] *tenuisset* Oec. : ἂν addidi.

[17] ζητήσητε Aub., Didymus, *Chron. Pasch.* : ζητήσετε cod. Malal.

[18] οὗ Aub. : *de quo* (περὶ οὗ ?) Oec.

βαστάζον, κατ' ἀξίαν¹ τὰ πάντα ζωοποιεῖ καὶ τρέφει, καὶ ἀπὸ
τῆς ἁγίας πηγῆς ἐξήρτηται ⌜ἐπίκουρον πνεύματι⌝² καὶ ζωῆς
ἅπασιν ἀεὶ ὑπάρχον, γόνιμον ἓν ὄν." οἶδεν οὖν αὐτὸν³ καὶ ὑπάρχον
ἰδιοσυστάτως, καὶ τὰ πάντα ζωοποιοῦν καὶ τρέφον, καὶ ὡς ἐξ ἁγίας πηγῆς
5 ἠρτημένον τοῦ θεοῦ καὶ πατρός· πρόεισι γὰρ ἐξ αὐτοῦ κατὰ φύσιν, καὶ δι'
υἱοῦ χορηγεῖται τῇ κτίσει.

πολυπραγμονήσαντες τοίνυν ὡς ἔνι τὰ παρ' ἐκείνοις βιβλία, διαφανεστά-
την πεποιήμεθα τὴν ἑκάστου δόξαν, ὡς ἂν εἰδεῖεν οἱ ἐντευξόμενοι ὅτι
πεπλάνηνται μὲν ἰδιογνωμονήσαντες τῶν παρ' Ἕλλησιν σοφῶν οὐκ ὀλίγοι,
10 καὶ ἀλλήλαις ἀντανισταμένας δόξας ἐσχήκασιν,⁴ εἰσὶ δὲ οἱ ⟨τῶν⟩ Μωσαϊκῶν
οὐκ ἠμοίρησαν[τες] λόγων,⁵ διὰ τὸ μέχρις Αἰγύπτου φιλομαθείας χάριν D
παρελθεῖν.⁶ οὗτοι ἄμεινόν πως ἢ οἱ λοιποὶ πεφρονήκασιν, ἐγγὺς μὲν γεγονότες τῆς ἀληθείας, οὐ μὴν ἀθόλωτον παντελῶς ἐσχηκότες τῆς διανοίας τὸν
ὀφθαλμόν·⁷ οὓς ἂν οἶμαί τις καὶ παραβλῶπας εἰπὼν οὐκ ἂν τοῦ εἰκότος
15 ἁμάρτοι λογισμοῦ.⁸

ὅτι τοίνυν καὶ πρεσβύτερα τὰ Χριστιανῶν, καὶ ἀληθείας ἔμπλεα, καὶ τοῖς
τῶν λογάδων⁹ ἐξειλεγμένοις εὖ ἔχειν ὑπειλημμένα, καὶ ἀσυγκρίτως ἐν
ἀμείνοσι τῆς Ἑλλήνων τερθρείας, ἀποχρών⟨τως⟩, οἶμαι, διέδειξε⟨ν ὁ⟩ λόγος.¹⁰

¹ omnia enim portat (βαστάζει?) secundum dignitatem Oec.
² πνεύματι Cyril: πνεύμασι cod. Didym. With either reading, the phrase is meaningless.
³ adiuvans spiritu, et vita omnibus semper existens foecundus. Unum igitur novit esse illum Oec.
⁴ quod errarint . . ., proprias sententias sequentes, et inter se diversas sententias habentes (ἐσχηκότες?) Oec.
As instances of Greeks who 'have gone astray, and held opinions mutually opposed', Cyril has mentioned Thales, Democritus, Anaximander, Aristotle, and the Stoics (545 A B), pp. 192–3 above.
⁵ εἰσὶ δὲ οἱ τῶν Μωσαϊκῶν οὐκ ἠμοίρησαν λόγων scripsi: εἰσὶ δὲ οἱ Μωσαϊκῶν οὐκ ἀμοιρήσαντες λόγων Aub.: non fuerint tamen expertes (om. οἱ?) eorum quae (τῶν?) in Mosaicis libris contenta sunt Oec.
The men of whom Cyril is here speaking are Pythagoras and Plato. He thought that Pythagoras and Plato had visited Egypt, and there learnt the doctrine of Hermes, who had learnt from Moses.
⁶ Nam ea propter (διὰ γὰρ τοῦτο?) etiam usque in Aegyptum disciplinarum studiosi peragrarunt (παρῆλθον?) Oec.
⁷ propioresque veritati sunt facti (ἐγγύς τε γεγόνασι τ. ἀ.?), non ita turbidum (οὐ θολωτὸν οὕτως?) mentis habentes oculum Oec.
⁸ non aberraverit (om. τοῦ εἰκότος λογισμοῦ) Oec.
⁹ Cyril apparently uses λογάδες in the sense of λόγιοι or λογοποιοί, 'men who produce λόγοι', i.e. authors of literary works of any kind. The term includes philosophers, but is not limited to them.
¹⁰ ὅτι τοίνυν . . . τερθρείας, ἀποχρῶν, οἶμαι, διέδειξε λόγος Aub.: Itaque satis (ἀποχρώντως) hic liber (οὗτος? ὁ λόγος) ostendit (om. οἶμαι) quod veriora sint et vetustiora (ἀληθέστερα καὶ πρεσβύτερα?) quae a Christianis traduntur, longeque melius habeant Graecorum nugis, etiam testantibus eloquentissimorum virorum sententiis Oec. ὁ λόγος (or οὗτος ὁ λόγος) means either 'my argument', or 'this book' (i.e. Lib. I. of Cyril's work).

580 *Contra Julianum* Lib. II. καὶ τοῦτο μὲν ἂν πρέποι τοῖς τὴν ἀγελαίαν
καὶ συρφετώδη καὶ ἀλόγιστον πάντως ψευδολατρείαν ἐξευρηκόσιν ...·[1]
ὅτι δὲ τῆς εἰς λῆξιν ἠκούσης ἐμβροντησίας ἀνάπλεῳ γεγονότες καταφωρα-
θεῖεν ἄν,[2] ἀμογητὶ κατοψόμεθα, τὴν τῶν μετ' αὐτοὺς πολυπραγμονήσαντες
δόξαν, ἔφη γάρ που περὶ αὐτῶν[3] ἰσχνὸς ὢν ἄγαν ὁ Πλούταρχος ἐν τῷ πρώτῳ 5
βιβλίῳ φυσικῶν δογμάτων συναγωγῆς·[4] " ἔλαβον[5] δὲ ἐκ τούτων ἔννοιαν
θεοῦ. ἀεί τε γὰρ ἥλιος καὶ σελήνη καὶ τὰ λοιπὰ τῶν ἄστρων, τὴν ὑπόγειον
⟨φορὰν⟩[6] ἐνεχθέντα, ὅμοια μὲν ἀνατέλλει τοῖς χρώμασιν. ἴσα δὲ τοῖς μεγέ-
B θεσι, καὶ κατὰ τόπους καὶ κατὰ χρόνους τοὺς αὐτούς."[7]   καὶ πάλιν ἐν τῷ
αὐτῷ βιβλίῳ·[8] " ὁρίζονται δὲ τὴν τοῦ θεοῦ οὐσίαν[9] οὕτως· πνεῦμα νοερὸν 10
καὶ πυρῶδες, οὐκ ἔχον μὲν μορφήν, μεταβάλλον δὲ εἰς ὃ βούλεται, καὶ
συνεξομοιούμενον πᾶσιν. ἔσχον δὲ ἔννοιαν τούτου πρῶτον μὲν ἀπὸ τοῦ
κάλλους τῶν ἐμφαινομένων,[10] προσλαμβάνοντες ὡς οὐδὲν[11] τῶν καλῶν[12] εἰκῆ
καὶ ὡς ἔτυχε γίνεται, ἀλλὰ μετά τινος τέχνης δημιουργούσης."[13]   προσεπ-

[1] Julian, in a passage quoted by Cyril (576 A-D), compared the *cosmogonia* of
Moses with that of Plato, to the disadvantage of the former. Moses, he said,
leaves questions of the greatest importance unanswered; e. g. he assumes the
existence of 'the abyss', 'the darkness', and 'the waters', but does not explain
how they came into being; and he says nothing about the origin of the angels.
According to Moses, God is merely ὕλης ὑποκειμένης κοσμήτορα, and not ἀσωμάτων
ποιητής.

Cyril's reply, of which the passage here printed is a part, may be summarized as
follows (if I rightly understand his ill-arranged and obscurely worded argument):
'Moses suited his teaching to the capacity of his hearers; and he was right in
doing so. If he had discussed profound philosophic problems, they would not
have understood him. In his time, all men on earth were sunk in utter ignorance;
they worshipped created things, and knew nothing of the Creator; and the aim of
Moses was to enlighten them on this one point. But in later times, some of the
Pagans have had glimpses of the truth which Moses taught, viz. that there is one
God, by whom all things have been created, and that men ought to worship him
alone.'

Thus Cyril divides the Pagans into two classes. The first class consists of those
(here called οἱ τὴν ἀγελαίαν . . . καὶ ἀλόγιστον πάντως ψευδολατρείαν ἐξευρηκότες)
who know nothing of God the Creator; to that class belonged all mankind in the
time of Moses (and presumably most of the Pagan Greeks down to Cyril's own
time, though he does not expressly say so). The second class (here called οἱ μετ'
αὐτούς) consists of those who have attained to a conception of God the Creator;
and in it are included Hermes Trismegistus, the Greek thinkers whose doctrine is
reported in the two extracts from Plutarch's *Placita*, and Julian himself.

[2] *Quod autem in summum stuporem pervenisse deprehensi sint* Oec.

[3] αὐτῶν apparently means τῶν μετ' αὐτούς, i. e. Pagans of the second and more
intelligent class.

[4] Ps.-Plutarch *Placita* (Aetius), Diels *Doxogr.*, p. 294.

[5] ἔλαβον Cyril : ἐλάβομεν Ps.-Plut.

[6] φορὰν Ps.-Plut. : om. Cyril (Aub.) : *sub terram euntes* Oec.

[7] *et in iisdem locis* (om. καὶ κατὰ χρόνους) Oec.

[8] Diels *ib.*, p. 292.

[9] οὐσίαν Aub. : *assertionem* Oec.   Post οὐσίαν add. οἱ Στωϊκοὶ Ps.-Plut.

[10] ἐμφαινομένων Aub. : *lucentium* Oec.

[11] ὡς οὐδὲν Aub. : οὐδὲν γὰρ Ps.-Plut.

[12] τῶν καλῶν om. Oec.

[13] *sed quod ista arte quadam formentur* ⟨δημιουργεῖται?⟩ Oec.

οἴσω δὲ τούτοις ἃ γέγραφέ ποτε¹ ὁ τρισμέγιστος Ἑρμῆς πρὸς τὸν ἑαυτοῦ
νοῦν, ὀνομάζεται γὰρ οὕτω τὸ βιβλίον·² "εἶτα φὴς[ιν]³ 'ἀόρατος ὁ
θεός'; εὐφήμησον. καὶ τίς αὐτοῦ φανερώτερος;⁴ διὰ τοῦτο
⟨πάντα⟩ πεποίηκεν,⁵ ἵνα διὰ πάντων τις αὐτὸν βλέπῃ.⁶ τοῦτό
5 ἐστι τὸ ἀγαθὸν τοῦ θεοῦ, τοῦτο ἡ ἀρετή,⁷ τὸ αὐτὸν φαίνεσθαι
διὰ πάντων." ὁμολογοῦντα δὲ τούτοις καὶ αὐτὸν ὀψόμεθα τὸν τῆς εὐαγοῦς C
ἡμῶν θρησκείας κατήγορον⁸ Ἰουλιανόν· διϊσχυρίζεται [μὲν]⁹ γὰρ ὡς ἀδίδα-
κτόν τι χρῆμα καὶ αὐτομαθὲς ἀνθρώποις τὸ εἰδέναι θεόν. φησὶ δὲ οὕτως·
"ὅτι δὲ οὐ διδακτόν, ἀλλὰ φύσει τοῦτο¹⁰ τοῖς ἀνθρώποις ὑπάρχει,¹¹ τεκμήριον
10 ἡμῖν ἔστω πρῶτον ἡ κοινὴ πάντων ἀνθρώπων ἰδίᾳ καὶ δημοσίᾳ καὶ κατὰ
ἄνδρα καὶ ἔθνη¹² περὶ τὸ θεῖον προθυμία. ἅπαντες [μὲν]¹³ γὰρ ἀδιδάκτως
θεῖόν τι πεπιστεύκαμεν,¹⁴ ὑπὲρ οὗ τὸ μὲν ἀκριβὲς οὔτε πᾶσι ῥᾴδιον ⟨γινώ-
σκειν⟩¹⁵ οὔτε τοῖς ἐγνωκόσιν εἰπεῖν εἰς πάντα⟨ς⟩¹⁶ δυνατόν."¹⁷ καὶ μεθ'
ἕτερα πάλιν· "ταύτῃ δὴ τῇ κοινῇ πάντων ἀνθρώπων ἐννοίᾳ πρόσεστι καὶ
15 ἄλλη. πάντες γὰρ [ἄνθρωποι]¹³ οὐρανῷ καὶ τοῖς ἐν αὐτῷ φαινομένοις θεοῖς D

¹ ποτε om. Oec.
² *Corp* XI. ii. 22 a. The title of *Corp.* XI is Νοῦς (or Νοῦ) πρὸς Ἑρμῆν. Cyril
either made a mistake about the title through carelessness, or found it altered into
something like Ἑρμοῦ πρὸς τὸν ἑαυτοῦ νοῦν in his copy.
³ "φής : in exemplo nostro φύσιν" Aub. I. e. Aubert's MS. gave εἶτα φύσιν,—
doubtless a corruption of εἶτά φησιν. *Deinde inquit* (i. e. εἶτά φησιν) Oec. But
the following εὐφήμησον shows that εἶτα φής is the right reading. ταφῆς codd. Corp.
⁴ *fulgidior* (φωτεινότερος ?) Oec.
⁵ διὰ τοῦτο πεποίηκεν Aub.: *propter hoc fecit omnia* (i. e. πάντα) Oec.: δι' αὐτὸ
τοῦτο πάντα ἐποίησεν codd. Corp.
⁶ τις αὐτὸν βλέπῃ Aub.: αὐτὸν βλέπῃς codd. Corp.
⁷ τοῦτο ἡ ἀρετή Aub. : τοῦτο δὲ αὐτοῦ ἀρετή codd. Corp.
⁸ *qui ita sanctam nostram religionem impugnat* (οὕτω κατηγοροῦντα ?) Oec.
⁹ μὲν seclusi.
¹⁰ Perhaps Julian wrote ὅτι δὲ οὐ διδακτὸν ⟨τὸ εἰδέναι θεόν⟩, ἀλλὰ φύσει
τοῦτο κ.τ.λ.
¹¹ ἀλλὰ φύσει τοῦτο τοῖς ἀνθρώποις ὑπάρχει om. Oec.
¹² καὶ ⟨κατ'?⟩ ἔθνη Neumann. But perhaps καὶ κατὰ ἄνδρα καὶ ἔθνη (*ubicunque
viri sunt et gentes* Oec.) ought to be bracketed; it is a needless repetition of ἰδίᾳ
καὶ δημοσίᾳ.
¹³ μὲν om. Neumann.
¹⁴ Cf. Julian *Or.* 6, 183 B (Hertlein): καὶ οὐδὲ τοῦτο μόνον ἀρκέσει αὐτῷ, ἀλλὰ
καί, εἴ τι τῆς ψυχῆς ἐν ἡμῖν ἐστι κρεῖττον καὶ θειότερον, ὅπερ δὴ ‖ πάντες ἀδιδάκτως
πειθόμενοι θεῖόν τι εἶναι νομίζομεν, καὶ τοῦτο ἐνιδρῦσθαι πάντες οὐρανῷ κοινῶς
ὑπολαμβάνομεν. (In that passage, the words πάντες ἀδιδάκτως ... ὑπολαμβάνομεν
have no connexion with the context. There is evidently a lacuna after ὅπερ δή;
and it appears that the gap has been filled by inserting πάντες ἀδιδάκτως κ.τλ.
taken from elsewhere.) Julian *Or.* 7, 209 C: ⟨νόμους⟩ τοὺς ἐκ τῶν θεῶν ἡμῖν ὥσπερ
ἐγγραφέντας ταῖς ψυχαῖς, ὑφ' ὧν πάντες ἀδιδάκτως εἶναι θεῖόν τι πεπείσμεθα.
¹⁵ γινώσκειν add. Neumann. *de quo diligenter loqui* (τὸ μὲν ἀκριβὲς εἰπεῖν ?)
neque omnibus facile est, neque iis qui noverunt (om. εἰπεῖν ?) *erga omnes* (πάντας)
possibile Oec.
¹⁶ πάντα Aub.
¹⁷ A reminiscence of Pl. *Tim.* 28 C, εὑρεῖν τε ἔργον καὶ εὑρόντα εἰς πάντας ἀδύνατον
λέγειν.
¹⁸ ἄνθρωποι delevit Neumann 'propter hiatum'.

οὕτω δή τι φυσικῶς προσηρτήμεθα,[1] ὡς καὶ εἴ τις ἄλλον ὑπέλαβε παρ᾽
αὐτοῖς τὸν[2] θεόν, οἰκητήριον αὐτῷ πάντως[3] τὸν οὐρανὸν ἀπένειμεν, οὐκ
ἀποστήσας αὐτὸν τῆς γῆς, ἀλλ᾽ οἷον ὡς[4] εἰς ⟨τὸ⟩ τιμιώτατον[5] τοῦ παντὸς
ἐκεῖνο, τὸν βασιλέα καθίσας τῶν ὅλων, ἐφορᾶν ἐκεῖθεν ὑπολαμβάνων τὰ
τῇδε."   5

ἄθρει δὴ οὖν ὅπως οἱ τὴν παχεῖαν[6] καὶ ἀγυρτώδη καί, ἵν᾽ οὕτως εἴπω,
βαναυσικὴν οὐκ ἀνασχόμενοι πλάνην, καὶ τῆς τῶν ἀγελαίων[7] ἀποφοιτήσαντες[8] δόξης, οὐκ ἠμοιρήκασι παντελῶς τῆς ἀληθοῦς ἐννοίας περὶ θεοῦ,[9]
81 A κατετεκμήραντο δὲ τίς τε καὶ ὅση τῆς ἐνούσης αὐτῷ δυνάμεως ἡ ὑπεροχή,
ὡς καὶ θεσμοῖς εὐταξίας τὴν οὕτω μεγάλην καὶ ἀξιάγαστον κτίσιν ὑπενεγ- 10
κεῖν. οἵ γε μὴν ἕτεροι, περὶ ὧν ὁ λόγος, οὔ⌈τε⌉ θεὸν ἐγνώκασι διὰ τῶν
κτισμάτων, ἀλλὰ γὰρ ἦσαν οὕτως ἐμβρόντητοι καὶ φρενὸς ἔξω γεγόνασιν
ἀνθρωποπρεποῦς, ὡς μὴ μόνον οὐρανῷ καὶ γῇ[10] καὶ σελήνῃ καὶ τοῖς ἑτέροις
τῶν ἄστρων ἑλέσθαι προσκυνεῖν, ἀλλὰ γὰρ καὶ ἐν σηκοῖς εἴδη[11] πολύμορφα
καθιδρῦσαι, ἐγχαράξαι τε μορφὰς αὐτοῖς οὐκ ἀνθρωπείας μόνον, ἀλλὰ καὶ 15
ζῴων ἀλόγων, καὶ πτηνῶν τε καὶ ἑρπετῶν, καὶ θεοὺς αὐτὰ καὶ σωτῆρας
ἀποκαλεῖν. . . .

85 D ὅτι δὲ τοῖς πανσθενεστάτοις τοῦ θεοῦ νεύμασι παρεκομίσθη πρὸς ὕπαρξιν
ἡ σύμπασα κτίσις, χαλεπὸν οὐδέν, ὥς γε οἶμαι,[12] διαμαθεῖν καὶ ἐξ ὧν γεγράφασιν οἱ τῆς αὐτοῦ δεισιδαιμονίας διδάσκαλοι.[13] ἐδόκει γὰρ ἅπασι καὶ 20
φρονεῖν καὶ λέγειν συλλήβδην ἅπαντα δεδημιουργῆσθαι παρ᾽ αὐτοῦ, νοητά
τε καὶ αἰσθητά, ἀόρατα καὶ ὁρώμενα. συνωμολογήκασι γὰρ ὅτι "περὶ
τὸν ἁπάντων βασιλέα καὶ κύριον πάντα [τε][14] ἐστί".[15] καὶ δὴ καὶ εἰπεῖν ὁ
Πλάτων διατείνεται "θεοὶ θεῶν, ὧν ἐγὼ δημιουργὸς πατήρ τε ἔργων".[16]

[1] natura quodammodo ita affecti sumus erga coelum et deos, qui in illo lucent
Oec.
[2] τὸν secludendum?
[3] πάντα Aub.: omnino (i. e. πάντως) Oec.
[4] οἷον ὡς (quodammodo quasi Oec.) can hardly be right. Perhaps οἷον ought to
be struck out.
[5] τιμιώτερον Aub.: id. quod in mundo dignissimum (i. e. τὸ τιμιώτατον) Oec.
[6] Perhaps οἱ ⟨μέν⟩ τὴν παχεῖαν κ.τ.λ., in contrast to οἵ γε μὴν ἕτεροι below.
The παχεῖα πλάνη is the error of the more stupid class of Pagans.
ἀγελαίων scripsi (cf. τὴν ἀγελαίαν . . . ψευδολατρείαν in 580 A): ἀγενναίων
Aub.: agrestium Oec.
[8] ἀποφοιτήσαντες Aub.: abducentes Oec.
[9] It is implied that Hermes was one of those who οὐκ ἠμοιρήκασι παντελῶς τῆς
ἀληθοῦς ἐννοίας περὶ θεοῦ, κ.τ.λ.
[10] γῇ Aub.: terram (i. e. γῆν) Oec.: perhaps ἡλίῳ.
[11] εἴδη Aub.: imagines Oec.: perhaps εἴδωλα.   [12] ὥς γε οἶμαι om. Oec.
[13] superstitionum doctores (i. e. οἱ ⟨τῶν?⟩ δεισιδαιμονιῶν διδάσκαλοι?) Oec.
[14] τε seclusi.
[15] Pl. Ep. 2. 312 E: περὶ τὸν πάντων βασιλέα πάντ᾽ ἐστι.   See Cyril above,
553 C.
[16] Pl. Tim. 41 A.

ἤδη μὲν οὖν τὰς Ἑλλήνων παρηγάγομεν χρήσεις,¹ τὰς ἐπί γε τούτοις φημί·²
καὶ παρήσω μὲν τὸ ταὐτὰ ⟨πολλάκις⟩³ εἰπεῖν, διαμεμνήσομαι δὲ τῶν Ἑρμοῦ
τοῦ τρισμεγίστου λόγων.⁴ ἔφη γὰρ οὗτος ἐν ⌈τῷ⌉⁵ πρὸς Ἀσκληπιόν· "καὶ **588 A**
εἶπε, φησίν,⁶ Ὄσιρις·⁷ 'εἶτα, ὦ μέγιστε Ἀγαθὸς Δαίμων,⁸ πῶς
5 ὅλη ἡ γῆ⁹ ἐφάνη;' καὶ εἶπεν ὁ μέγας Ἀγαθὸς Δαίμων· 'κατὰ
⌈τάξιν⌉¹⁰ καὶ ἀναξήρανσιν, ὡς εἶπον. καὶ ⟨γὰρ⟩¹¹ τῶν πολλῶν
ὑδάτων κελευσθέντων ἀπὸ τοῦ ⟨. . .⟩¹² εἰς ἑαυτὰ ἀναχωρῆσαι,
ἐφάνη [ὅλη]¹³ ἡ γῆ, ἔμπηλος καὶ τρέμουσα·¹⁴ ἡλίου δὲ λοιπὸν¹⁵
ἀναλάμψαντος, καὶ ἀδιαλείπτως διακαίοντος καὶ ξηραίνοντος,
10 ἡ γῆ ἐστηρίζετο ἐν τοῖς ὕδασιν,¹⁶ ἐμπεριεχομένη ὑπὸ τοῦ ὕδατος.'"¹⁷ καὶ μὴν καὶ ἑτέρωθι·¹⁸ "ὁ πάντων δημιουργὸς καὶ κύριος

---

¹ "ῥήσεις: in nostro exemplo χρήσεις" Aub. Either word might be used to
denote passages quoted. (Cf. χρήσεις in 552 A.) Among the passages meant are
those quoted from Ps.-Plut. *Plac.* in 580 A B.

² *sententias quas praeter illas dicunt* (ἃς . . . φασί?) Oec.

³ ταὐτὰ Aub. : *idem saepe* (i. e. ταὐτὸ πολλάκις) *dicere* Oec. ταῦτά alone would
not do ; but it would be possible to write either ταῦτα alone or ταὐτὰ πολλάκις (or
αὖθις).

⁴ *mentionem faciemus Hermetis termaximi* (om. τῶν λόγων) Oec.

⁵ *Fr.* 31. As Cyril elsewhere shows knowledge of at least three λόγοι addressed to
Asclepius, he cannot have written ἐν τῷ πρὸς Ἀσκληπιόν. He may have written
either ἐν τοῖς πρὸς Ἀσκλ., or ἐν τῷ ⟨τρίτῳ? τῶν⟩ πρὸς Ἀσκλ. See 701 A below.

⁶ φησίν om. Oec.

⁷ This is an extract from a *libellus* in which Hermes was made to report to
Asclepius a dialogue in which the Agathos Daimon had given instruction to Osiris.
See note on Didymus *De Trin.* 756 B, p. 171 above.
Osiris is spoken of, in connexion with Isis and Horus, in the *Kore Kosmu* ; but
the *libellus* from which this passage is quoted is the only *Hermeticum* known to us
in which he was brought into connexion with the Agathos Daimon, and he nowhere
else appears as a pupil receiving instruction from a teacher.

⁸ Both here and in B below Ἀγαθὸς Δαίμων is strangely used as a vocative
(*ὁ maxime bone daemon* Oec.). Perhaps we ought to read ὦ μέγιστε Ἀγαθοδαῖμον,
and εἶπεν ὁ μέγας Ἀγαθοδαίμων.

⁹ ὅλη ἡ γῆ apparently means 'the whole extent of land', or 'all the land there
is'; as opposed to this or that particular γῆ (e. g. the land of Egypt).

¹⁰ τάξιν (*ordinem* Oec.) is impossible. κατὰ διάκρισιν (separation of earth from
water) καὶ ἀναξήρανσιν would agree with what follows.

¹¹ γὰρ addidi : καὶ om. Oec.

¹² ἀπὸ τοῦ om. Oec. Sense might be made by writing either ἀπὸ τοῦ ⟨πάντων
κυρίου⟩ (to be taken with κελευσθέντων), or ἀπὸ τοῦ ⟨μίγματος⟩ (to be taken with εἰς
ἑαυτὰ ἀναχωρῆσαι). ¹³ ὅλη seclusi.

¹⁴ Perhaps ⟨τὸ μὲν πρῶτον⟩ ἔμπηλος καὶ τρέμουσα. For τρέμουσα, cf. *Kore Kosmu*
(Stob. *Exc.* XXIII) 51 : κραδαινομένη ἔτι γῆ ἡλίου λάμψαντος ἐπάγη.

¹⁵ λοιπὸν om. Oec. ¹⁶ ἐν τοῖς ὕδασιν Aub. : *propter aquas* Oec.

¹⁷ The *cosmogonia* which the Hermetist put into the mouth of the Agathos
Daimon must have been based, in part at least, on the first chapter of Genesis.
(Compare the cosmogonies of *Corp.* I and *Corp.* III.) In this passage, the writer
was evidently thinking of *Gen.* I. 9, καὶ εἶπεν ὁ θεός· Συναχθήτω τὸ ὕδωρ . . . εἰς
συναγωγὴν μίαν . . . . καὶ συνήχθη τὸ ὕδωρ . . ., καὶ ὤφθη ἡ ξηρά.

¹⁸ *Fr.* 32. In these two passages (καὶ εἶπεν Ὄσιρις κ.τ.λ. and ὁ πάντων δημιουργὸς
κ.τ.λ.) we have two different and independent descriptions of the origin of γῆ. The
word ἑτέρωθι must therefore mean, not 'in another part of the same *libellus*', but 'in
another *libellus*'. And as the wording of the second passage about γῆ (ὁ πάντων

ἐφώνησεν οὕτως, 'ἔστω γῆ, καὶ φανήτω στερέωμα[1]'· καὶ
εὐθέως ἀρχὴ τῆς δημιουργίας γῆ ἐγένετο." καὶ ταυτὶ μὲν περὶ
B τῆς γῆς. ἡλίου δὲ πέρι πάλιν ὧδέ φησι,[2] "καὶ εἶπεν Ὄσιρις· 'ὦ
[τρὶς][3] μέγιστε Ἀγαθὸς Δαίμων, ⟨πόθεν ἐφάνη ὁ μέγας οὗτος
ἥλιος;' καὶ εἶπεν ὁ μέγας Ἀγαθὸς Δαίμων· 'ὦ Ὄσιρι,⟩ ἡλίου   5
γένναν βούλει ἡμᾶς καταλέξαι [πόθεν ἐφάνη];[4] ἐφάνη προνοίᾳ
τοῦ πάντων δεσπότου.'"[5] [[ἔστι δὲ ἡ γένεσις τοῦ ἡλίου ἀπὸ τοῦ
πάντων δεσπότου,[6] διὰ τοῦ ἁγίου καὶ δημιουργικοῦ λόγου αὐτοῦ γενομένη.]][7]

δημιουργὸς κ.τ.λ.) closely resembles that of the second passage about the sun (ὁ δὲ
πάντων κύριος κ.τ.λ., §88 B), there can be little doubt that Cyril took it from the
same *libellus* from which he took that, i. e. from 'the first of the διεξοδικοὶ λόγοι οf
Hermes to Tat'.

[1] στερέωμα, 'firmament', has been borrowed from *Gen.* 1. 6-8. But the words
καὶ φανήτω στερέωμα seem out of place here. If στερέωμα means heaven (ἐκάλεσεν
ὁ θεὸς τὸ στερέωμα οὐρανόν, *Gen.* 1. 8), it would follow that γῆ means earth as
opposed to heaven, and consequently, that this passage has nothing to do with the
separation of land and water *Gen.* 1. 9), but is rather a paraphrase of *Gen.* 1. 1,
ἐν ἀρχῇ ἐποίησεν ὁ θεὸς τὸν οὐρανὸν καὶ τὴν γῆν. But if the writer is speaking of
the creation of earth and heaven together, why does he say that earth alone is
ἀρχὴ δημιουργίας? Perhaps then καὶ φανήτω στερέωμα ought to be bracketed?

It is possible, however, that the person who inserted καὶ φανήτω στερέωμα took
στερέωμα to mean, not 'heaven', but 'a solid mass of earth', i. e. 'dry land'
(being misled, perhaps, by the words γενηθήτω στερέωμα ἐν μέσῳ τοῦ ὕδατος,
Gen. 1. 6). On that assumption, γῆ would here again mean 'land', as in the
preceding passage, and φανήτω στερέωμα would be merely a repetition, in different
words, of ἔστω γῆ.

We may suppose the Hermetist to have gone on to say that fire and air rose as
exhalations from the separated land and water, and that the sphere of heaven was
formed out of the fire. If that was the order of events in his cosmogony, he would
be right in saying that γῆ was 'the beginning of the *demiurgia*', i. e. the first thing
made; for the only thing that existed before it was the undifferentiated watery
chaos, which was not made by God, but was already in existence when the
demiurgia began.

[2] *Fr.* 31. This passage about the sun is evidently taken from the same *libellus* as
the first passage about γῆ. Both of them are extracts from a reported dialogue in
which the Agathos Daimon told Osiris how the world was made. In this
cosmogony, the making of the sun (and presumably of the moon and stars also)
seems to have been placed after the separation of land and water, as it is in
Genesis. That is implied by the words ἡλίου δὲ λοιπὸν ἀναλάμψαντος in the first
passage; and that mention of the sun apparently led on to the question asked in
the other passage, 'What was the origin of the sun?' Of the answer given by the
Agathos Daimon to this question, only the opening words are quoted by Cyril; it
was enough for his purpose to show that the making of the sun was ascribed by
Hermes to the supreme God.

[3] τρὶς seclusi.   [4] πόθεν ἐφάνη seclusi.

[5] ὦ τρὶς μέγιστε ἀγαθὸς δαίμων, ἡλίου γένναν βούλει ἡμᾶς καταλέξαι, πόθεν ἐφάνη;
ἐφάνη προνοίᾳ τοῦ πάντων δεσπότου Aub.: *ô ter maxime bone daemon, unde
apparuit magnus iste sol? Et dixit magnus bonus daemon: Osiri, solis
nativitatem vis nos dicere unde apparuerit? Apparuit providentia omnium
domini* Oec. It is evident that ἐφάνη προνοίᾳ τοῦ πάντων δεσπότου is spoken
by the Agathos Daimon, and consequently must have been preceded by something
like καὶ εἶπεν ὁ μέγας Ἀγαθὸς Δαίμων. The words πόθεν ἐφάνη ... ὦ Ὄσιρι were
accidentally omitted in Aubert's MS., but can be restored from Oec.'s translation
of the Codex Capnionis.   [6] ἀπὸ τοῦ πάντων δεσπότου om. Oec.

[7] Where does the quotation from Hermes end? Aubert makes it extend to

ὁμοίως καὶ ⟨ὁ⟩ αὐτὸς[1] ἐν τῷ πρὸς τὸν Τὰτ διεξοδικῷ λόγῳ πρώτῳ φησίν·
"ὁ δὲ πάντων κύριος εὐθέως ἐφώνησε τῷ ἑαυτοῦ ἁγίῳ καὶ
νοητῷ[2] καὶ δημιουργικῷ λόγῳ[3] 'ἔστω ἥλιος'· καὶ ἅμα τῷ φάναι,
τὸ πῦρ,[4] [τῆς] φύσεως ἀνωφεροῦς ἐχόμενον,[5] λέγω δὴ τὸ ἄκρατον
5 καὶ φωτεινότατον καὶ δραστικώτατον καὶ γονιμώτατον,[6] ἐπεσπάσατο ⌈ἡ φύσις τῷ ἑαυτῆς πνεύματι⌉,[7] καὶ ἤγειρεν εἰς ὕψος

λόγου αὐτοῦ γενομένη.   But the words ἔστι δὲ ἡ γένεσις τοῦ ἡλίου ἀπὸ τοῦ πάντων
δεσπότου are merely a repetition of ἡλίου γένναν and ἐφάνη (ὁ ἥλιος) προνοίᾳ τοῦ
πάντων δεσπότου; and the Hermetist surely cannot have thus said the same thing
twice over.   It therefore seems better to make the quotation end at προνοίᾳ τοῦ
πάντων δεσπότου, and to take what follows, down to γενομένη, as a comment
added by Cyril.   If so, we must alter δέ into δή.   [But cf. p. 203, l. 7.]
   But if the quotation ends at προνοίᾳ τοῦ πάντων δεσπότου, it contains no mention
of God's λόγος; why then does Cyril speak of the λόγος in his comment on it?
This difficulty can be got over by assuming that the words ἔστι δὴ . . . λόγου αὐτοῦ
γενομένη have been transposed by a copyist's error.   If we place them after the
quotation which follows (ὁ δὲ πάντων κύριος . . . ἀπὸ (τοῦ) ὕδατος), all comes right.
Cyril comments on both extracts together, and summarizes the teaching of Hermes
concerning the origin of the sun by combining the contents of both: he takes the
phrase τοῦ πάντων δεσπότου from the first of them, and διὰ τοῦ ἁγίου καὶ δημιουργικοῦ
λόγου αὐτοῦ from the second.   And when the passage is placed there, the sentence
which follows (τὸ μὲν οὖν προστάξει θεοῦ διὰ τοῦ . . . λόγου κ.τ.λ.) fits on to it
excellently.
   [1] καὶ αὐτὸς Aub.: idem (i. e. ὁ αὐτὸς) Oec.   [2] καὶ νοητῷ secludendum?
   [3] Fr. 33. ἐφώνησε τῷ ἑαυτοῦ ἁγίῳ . . . λόγῳ probably means 'He spoke with his
holy speech', not 'He spoke to his holy Word'.   (Cf. Corp. I. 18: ὁ δὲ θεὸς εὐθὺς
εἶπεν ἁγίῳ λόγῳ· Αὐξάνεσθε κ.τ.λ.)   If so, God's λόγος is not hypostatized in this
passage, though it is fully hypostatized in 553 A B (from the same libellus), where
'the λόγος of the Maker' is spoken of as a divine Person who stands next after
the supreme God.
   [4] καὶ ἅμα τῷ φάναι, τὸ πῦρ Aub.: et simul apparuit ignis (i. e. καὶ ἅμα ἐφάνη τὸ
πῦρ) Oec.   It would be possible to account for both readings by assuming that the
original was καὶ ἅμα τῷ (εἰπεῖν) ἐφάνη (ὁ ἥλιος).   τὸ (γὰρ) πῦρ κ.τ.λ.
   [5] qui natura sursum fertur Oec.   τῆς seclusi.   Perhaps the Hermetist may
have written τὸ πῦρ, ἅτε φύσεως ἀνωφεροῦς ἐχόμενον, . . . ἐπεσπάσατο . . . καὶ
ἤγειρεν εἰς ὕψος.   'He (?) raised the fire aloft, inasmuch as it was of upward-
tending nature.'   For φύσεως ἀνωφεροῦς ἐχόμενον, cf. τοιαύτης ἔχεται φύσεως in
553 A, and δημιουργικῆς ἔχεται φύσεως in 921 A.
   [6] φωτεινότατον καὶ δραστικώτερον καὶ γονιμώτερον Aub.: fulgidissimum et effica-
cissimum (-τατον) et foecundissimum (-τατον) Oec.
   The writer distinguishes two different kinds of fire, one of which is, and the other
is not, ἄκρατον κ.τ.λ., and says that he is here speaking of the former kind only.
The ἄκρατον πῦρ must be the fire of which heaven and the heavenly bodies
(including the sun) consist, as opposed to terrestrial fire, which is a mixture of the
element fire with other elements.   [Cf. Corp. I. 5 a and b: ἐκ δὲ φωτὸς π(ροελθὼν)
λόγος ἅγιος ἐπέβη τῇ φύσει, καὶ πῦρ ἄκρατον ἐξεπήδησεν ἐκ τῆς ὑγρᾶς φύσεως
ἄνω εἰς ὕψος· κοῦφον δὲ ἦν καὶ ὀξύ, δραστικόν τε.   § 10. ἐπήδησεν εὐθὺς ἐκ τῶν
καταφερῶν στοιχείων . . . ὁ τοῦ θεοῦ λόγος εἰς τὸ καθαρὸν τῆς φύσεως δημιούργημα,
καὶ ἡνώθη τῷ δημιουργῷ νῷ· ὁμοούσιος γὰρ ἦν.   Corp. III. 2 a: πυρὶ τῶν ὅλων
διορισθέντων καὶ ἀνακρεμασθέντων πνεύματι ὀχεῖσθαι.]
   [7] ἐπεσπάσατο ἡ φύσις τῷ ἑαυτῆς πνεύματι Aub.: attracta est (ἐπεσπάσθη?) natura
suo spiritu Oec.   This is unintelligible.   What can be meant by a φύσις which
possessed a πνεῦμα of its own, and 'drew the fire to itself by means of its own
πνεῦμα'?   The subject of ἐπεσπάσατο and ἤγειρεν ought rather to be the Demiurgus.
The Hermetist may perhaps have said that 'God spoke, and therewith drew the
fire to himself by means of his own πνεῦμα, and raised it up aloft from the water'.

ἀπὸ ⟨τοῦ⟩¹ ὕδατος." ⟨⟨ἔστι δὴ ἡ γένεσις τοῦ ἡλίου ἀπὸ τοῦ πάντων δεσπότου, διὰ τοῦ ἁγίου καὶ δημιουργικοῦ λόγου αὐτοῦ γενομένη.⟩⟩ τὸ μὲν οὖν προστάξει θεοῦ διὰ τοῦ δημιουργοῦ² πεποιῆσθαι λόγου τὰ πάντα, πρέπον ἂν ⟨εἴη⟩³ ἀνθρώπῳ νοεῖν, καὶ ἀληθὲς εἰπεῖν·⁴ τὸ δὲ ὅπως, ἢ τίνα τρόπον, αὐτὸς ἂν εἰδείη καὶ μόνος.⁵ ὅτι δὲ τῶν γεγονότων ἑκάστῳ τὸ εἶναι 5 τοιῶσδε διανέμει κατ' ἐξουσίαν,⁶ καὶ ὁ τῆς ἁπάντων ὑπάρξεως τρόπος αὐτὸν ἔχει τὸν ὁριστήν, σαφὲς ἂν γένοιτο καὶ δι' ὧν ἔφη Μωσῆς, "γενηθήτω τὸ στερέωμα, καὶ ἐγένετο οὕτως,"⁷ καὶ "συναχθήτω τὸ ὕδωρ εἰς συναγωγὴν μίαν, καὶ ὀφθήτω ἡ ξηρά".⁸ ταῦτα γὰρ δὴ τὴν ἑκάστου τῶν εἰς γένεσιν παρενηνεγμένων ὁρίζει φύσιν. διαμνημονεύει δὲ καὶ τούτου πάλιν ὁ παρ' 10 αὐτοῖς τρισμέγιστος Ἑρμῆς· εἰσκεκόμικε γὰρ λέγοντα τὸν θεὸν τοῖς κτίσμασιν⁹ "ἀνάγκην δὲ ὑμῖν τοῖς ὑπ' ἐμὲ¹⁰ περιθήσω ταύτην τὴν διὰ τοῦ λόγου μου¹¹ ὑμῖν ἐντολὴν δεδομένην· τοῦτον γὰρ νόμον D ἔχετε".¹² ὡς γὰρ ἔφην ἀρτίως, τῶν γεγονότων ἑκάστῳ φυσικὸν ὥρισε[ν τὸν]¹³ νόμον ὁ δημιουργός, καὶ τοῖς αὐτοῦ νεύμασι τὸ εἶναι τοιῶσδε ⌜τυχὸν 15 ἢ μή⌝¹⁴ διαλαχόντα φαίνεται. . . .

597 D ὅτι δέ ἐστι τῶν ἄγαν ἐκτοπωτάτων ἑτέροις ἡμᾶς ἀναθεῖναι θεοῖς τῆς δημιουργίας τὴν ἐνέργειαν,¹⁵ ἀφιστῶντας αὐτὴν τοῦ θεοῦ κατὰ φύσιν καὶ

ἔστω ἥλιος ought to be followed by a description of the making of the sun; but this sentence seems to be rather a description of the making of the fiery sphere of heaven. Perhaps the Hermetist went on to say that a portion of the fire which was drawn up aloft was collected into a globe, and so the sun was brought into being.

¹ τοῦ addidi.   ² Perhaps δημιουργ⟨ικ⟩οῦ.   ³ εἴη addidi.

⁴ *decet hominem et intelligere ac dicere* (om. ἀληθὲς) Oec.

⁵ 'By what process God made things, He alone knows.' This is a criticism of the passage last quoted, in which Hermes tried to describe the process by which God made the sun.

⁶ κατ' ἐξουσίαν (*sua potestate* Oec.), if sound, must mean 'with unrestricted power'. ἔξεστι τῷ θεῷ διανέμειν ἑκάστῳ τὸ εἶναι τοιῶσδε· there is nothing to prevent God from determining that a thing shall be thus or thus.

⁷ *Gen.* I. 6.   ⁸ *Gen.* I. 9.

⁹ *Fr.* 34. This is an extract from a speech of God to his creatures, which must have more or less resembled God's speech to the new-made souls in Pl. *Tim.* 41 E–42 D (τὴν τοῦ παντὸς φύσιν ἔδειξεν, νόμους τε τοὺς εἱμαρμένους εἶπεν αὐταῖς, κ.τ.λ.), and God's speeches to the souls in *Kore Kosmu* (Stob. *Exc.* XXIII) 17 (λόγων ἐμῶν ὡς] νόμων τούτων ἐπακούσατε, κ.τ.λ.) and *ib.* 38–41. Compare also God's speech to πάντα τὰ κτίσματα καὶ δημιουργήματα in *Corp.* I. 18.

¹⁰ ἐπ' ἐμὲ Aub.: *sub me* (i. e. ὑπ' ἐμὲ) Oec.

¹¹ διὰ τοῦ λόγου μου means 'by my speech'.

¹² Perhaps ἕξετε.—τοῦτον means ταύτην τὴν ἐντολήν: 'you (shall) have for your law this commandment which I have given you.'

¹³ ὥρισε νόμον scripsi : ὥρισεν τὸν νόμον Aub. Perhaps ὥρισέ τινα νόμον.

¹⁴ *Esse vel non esse taliter* (om. τυχὸν) Oec. Aubert translates '*ut sint huiusmodi puta aut secus*'. But ἢ μή is meaningless; and perhaps it would be better to bracket τυχὸν ἢ μή.

¹⁵ Julian upheld, as better than the teaching of Moses, the doctrine of Plato *Tim.* 41 C and 69 C, that the supreme God did not himself make τὰ θνητά, but handed

ἀληθῶς,[1] κἀκ τῶν αὐτοῦ[2] διδασκάλων κατίδοι τις ἄν. γράφει γὰρ οὕτως
Ἀσκληπιῷ ὁ ἐπίκλην τρισμέγιστος Ἑρμῆς ⟨ἐν τῷ⟩[3] περὶ τῆς τοῦ παντὸς
φύσεως· "εἰ τοίνυν[4] δύο ὡμολόγηται τὰ ὄντα, τό τε[5] γινόμενον
καὶ τὸ ποιοῦν, ἕν ἐστι[6] τῇ ἐνώσει, τὸ μὲν προηγούμενον, τὸ
5 δὲ ἑπόμενον· προηγούμενον μὲν ὁ ποιῶν θεός, ἑπόμενον δὲ τὸ
γινόμενον, ὅ τι[7] ἂν ᾖ. καὶ μὴ διὰ τὴν ποικιλίαν τῶν γινομένων φυλάξῃ, φοβούμενος ταπεινότητα καὶ ἀδοξίαν θεῷ περι-
[γρ]άψαι.[8] μία γὰρ αὐτῷ ἐστι δόξα τὸ ποιεῖν πάντα·[9] καὶ τοῦτό **600** A
ἐστι [τὸ][10] τοῦ θεοῦ ὥσπερ τὸ σῶμα,[11] ἡ ποίησις. αὐτῷ δὲ τῷ
10 ποιοῦντι οὐδὲν κακὸν οὐδὲ αἰσχρὸν νομιζόμενον.[12] ταῦτα γάρ
ἐστι τὰ πάθη τὰ τῇ γενέσει παρεπόμενα, ὥσπερ ὁ[13] ἰὸς τῷ χαλκῷ, καὶ ὁ ῥύπος τῷ σώματι· ἀλλ᾽ οὔτε ὁ χαλκουργὸς τὸν ἰὸν[14]
ἐποίησεν,[15] οὔτε τὸν ῥύπον οἱ γεννήσαντες."[16] καὶ μεθ᾽ ἕτερα
πάλιν διὰ θερμοτέρων ἔρχεται λόγων, ἐναργὲς παράδειγμα τιθείς, καί φησιν·[17]
15 "εἶτα τῷ μὲν αὐτῷ ζωγράφῳ[18] ἔξεστι καὶ οὐρανὸν ποιῆσαι καὶ
γῆν καὶ θάλασσαν, [ταῦτα] καὶ θεοὺς καὶ ἀνθρώπους[19] καὶ

over the task of making them to the gods whom he had made (τῶν μὲν θείων αὐτὸς
γίγνεται δημιουργός, τῶν δὲ θνητῶν τὴν γένεσιν τοῖς ἑαυτοῦ γεννήμασι δημιουργεῖν
προσέταξεν, *Tim.* 69 C). Cyril is here contending against that doctrine.

[1] Perhaps τοῦ κατὰ φύσιν καὶ ἀληθῶς θεοῦ.

[2] Does αὐτοῦ mean Julian, or Plato? There is no evidence that Julian had
himself read the *Hermetica*; but Cyril believed that Plato's philosophy was
derived from the teaching of Hermes, and might in that sense call Hermes one of
the διδάσκαλοι of the Platonist Julian.

[3] ἐν τῷ addidi. *Corp.* XIV was probably headed by the superscription Περὶ τῆς
τοῦ παντὸς φύσεως in Cyril's copy of that *libellus*.

[4] εἰ τοίνυν . . . οἱ γεννήσαντες : *Corp.* XIV. 6, 7.   [5] τε om. *Corp.*

[6] 'In exemplo nostro scriptum erat ἔνεστι' Aubert : *unum esse* (ἓν εἶναι ?) Oec.:
ἕν ἐστι *Corp.*

[7] ὅ τι ἂν ᾖ Aub.: *Quod ita esse* (beginning a fresh sentence) Oec.: ὁποῖον ἂν
ᾖ *Corp.*

[8] 'In exemplo nostro περιγράψαι' Aubert : *ascribere* Oec. : φοβούμενος μὴ τ. κ.
ἀ. τῷ θ. περιάψῃς (*al.* φοβούμενος τ. κ. ἀ. τῷ θ. περιάψῃ) *Corp.*

[9] ποιεῖν τὰ πάντα *Corp.*   [10] τὸ Aub. : om. *Corp.*

[11] τὸ σῶμα Aub. : σῶμα (om. τὸ) *Corp.*: *et hoc est opus dei, sicut corporis effici*
(i. e. καὶ τοῦτό ἐστι τὸ ἔργον τοῦ θεοῦ, ὥσπερ τοῦ σώματος τὸ ποιεῖσθαι ?) Oec. The
Latin of Oec. yields the sense 'this (viz. τὸ ποιεῖν πάντα) is God's function, just as
τὸ ποιεῖσθαι is the function of body'. Was that the sense of the Greek text as
given in the Codex Capnionis ? Or is it merely Oec.'s guess at the writer's
meaning ?

[12] νομιζόμενον Aub., *Corp.* : *At facienti* (τῷ δὲ ποιοῦντι ?) *nihil vel mali vel foedi
imputamus* (νομίζομεν ?) Oec.

[13] ὁ om. *Corp.*   [14] οὔτε ἰὸν ὁ χαλκουργὸς *Corp.*

[15] ἐποίησεν Aub., *Corp.*: *neque aerarius rubiginem patitur* (ἔπαθεν or πασχει ?)
Oec.

[16] οἱ γεννήσαντες Aub. : *ii qui genuerunt* Oec. : ὁ ποιητὴς γεγέννηκεν *Corp.*

[17] εἶτα τῷ μὲν . . . καὶ κίνησιν : *Corp.* XIV. 8–10.

[18] *Ipsi pictori licet* (om. εἶτα τῷ μὲν) Oec.

[19] οὐρανὸν ποιῆσαι καὶ γῆν καὶ θάλασσαν ταῦτα καὶ θεοὺς καὶ ἀνθρώπους Aub. :
coelum ac terram pingere, et mare (om. ταῦτα), *ac deum* (θεὸν ?) *et homines* Oec.:
οὐρανὸν ποιῆσαι καὶ θεοὺς καὶ γῆν καὶ θάλασσαν καὶ ἀνθρώπους *Corp.*

πάντα τὰ ἄλογα καὶ ἄψυχα· τῷ δὲ θεῷ οὐ δυνατὸν πάντα[1]
ποιεῖν; ὦ πολλῆς[2] ἀνοίας καὶ ἀγνωσίας τῆς περὶ τὸν θεόν.
τὸ γὰρ πάντων δεινότατον[3] πάσχουσιν οἱ τοιοῦτοι. τὸν γὰρ
B θεὸν φάσκοντες εὐσεβεῖν τε καὶ[4] εὐλογεῖν τῷ μὴ τὴν πάντων[5]
ποίησιν ἀνατιθέναι αὐτῷ,[6] οὐδὲ[7] τὸν θεὸν ἴσασι·[8] πρὸς δὲ τῷ 5
μὴ εἰδέναι, καὶ τὰ μέγιστα εἰς αὐτὸν ἀσεβοῦσι, πάθος[9] αὐτῷ
περιτιθέντες ὑπεροψίαν ἢ ἀδυναμίαν. εἰ γὰρ μὴ πάντα ποιεῖ,
⟨ἢ⟩[10] ὑπερηφανῶν οὐ ποιεῖ,[11] ἢ μὴ δυνάμενος· ὅπερ ἐστὶν ἀσεβές,
ὁ γὰρ θεὸς ἐν μόνον ἔχει πάθος, τὸ ἀγαθόν· ὁ δὲ ἀγαθὸς οὔτε
ὑπερήφανος οὔτε ἀδύνατος. τοῦτο γάρ ἐστιν ὁ θεός, τὸ ἀγαθόν· 10
ᾧ πᾶσα δύναμις τοῦ ποιεῖν πάντα. πᾶν δὲ τὸ γεννητὸν[12] ὑπὸ
τοῦ θεοῦ[13] γέγονεν ὅπερ ἐστίν,[14] ὑπὸ τοῦ[15] ἀγαθοῦ καὶ τοῦ
πάντα δυναμένου ποιεῖν. εἰ δὲ[16] πῶς μὲν αὐτὸς ποιεῖ, πῶς δὲ
τὰ γινόμενα γίνεται βούλει[17] μαθεῖν, ἔξεστί σοι. ἴδε[18] εἰκόνα
καλλίστην καὶ ὁμοιοτάτην, γεωργὸν[19] σπέρμα καταβάλλοντα 15
εἰς τὴν γῆν, ὅπου μὲν πυρόν, ὅπου δὲ κριθήν, ὅπου δὲ ἄλλο τι
τῶν σπερμάτων. ἴδε τὸν αὐτὸν ἄμπελον φυτεύοντα καὶ μηλέαν
καὶ τἆλλα τῶν δένδρων. οὕτω καὶ ὁ[20] θεὸς ἐν μὲν οὐρανῷ
ἀθανασίαν σπείρει, ἐν δὲ γῇ μεταβολήν,[21] ἐν δὲ τῷ παντὶ[22] ζωὴν
καὶ κίνησιν." 20

---

[1] οὐ δυνατὸν πάντα ποιεῖν; Aub.: *impossibile ne fuerit acere?* (om. πάντα) Oec.:
ἀδύνατον ταῦτα ποιεῖν: *Corp.* The ταῦτα before καὶ θεούς in Aub. may have come
from ταῦτα written in the margin as a variant for πάντα before ποιεῖν.

[2] ὦ τῆς πολλῆς *Corp.*

[3] δεινότατον Aub.: καινότατον *Corp.*: *gravissime enim laborant* Oec.

[4] εὐσεβεῖν τε καὶ om. *Corp.*   [5] τὴν τῶν πάντων *Corp*

[6] ἀνατιθέναι αὐτῷ Aub.: αὐτῷ ἀνατιθέναι *Corp.*

[7] οὐδὲ Aub.: οὔτε *Corp.*

[8] ἴσασι Aub.: οἴδασιν *Corp.*—*Nam deum dicentes*] *se colere ac benedicere, non
tribuunt ei, quod fecerit omnia : neque deum sciunt* Oec. Possibly Oec. meant to
write *eo quod non tribuunt* &c., but omitted *eo quod* by a slip, and in consequence
of that omission, put a colon instead of a comma after *omnia*.

[9] πάθος Aub.: *affectiones* (πάθη) Oec.: πάθη *Corp.*

[10] ἢ *Corp* : *vel* (ἢ) Oec.: om. Aub.

[11] ὑπερηφανῶν οὐ ποιεῖ Aub.: *superbiens non facit* Oec.: ὑπερήφανός ἐστι *Corp.*

[12] πᾶν δὲ τὸ γεννητὸν Aub., *Corp.*: *quod autem genitum est* (om. πᾶν) Oec.

[13] ὑπὸ τοῦ θεοῦ om. Oec.   [14] ὅπερ ἐστίν om. Oec.

[15] ἐστὶν, ὑπὸ τοῦ Aub.: ἐστι τοῦ *Corp.*

[16] εἰ δὲ Aub.: *si autem* Oec.: ἴδε *Corp.*

[17] γίνεται, βούλει Aub.: *discere vis quomodo . . . fiant* (i. e. γίνεται, βούλει) Oec.:
γίνεται, καὶ εἰ βούλει *Corp.*

[18] ἔξεστί σοι. ἴδε Aub.: *vide* (om. ἔξεστί σοι) Oec.: ἔξεστί σοι ἰδεῖν *Corp.*

[19] γεωργὸν Aub.: ἴδε γεωργὸν *Corp.*—*Agricola semina in terram demittit*
(γεωργὸς . . . καταβάλλει?) Oec.

[20] οὕτω καὶ ὁ Aub.: *ita et* Oec.: οὕτως ὁ *Corp.*

[21] *in terra necessitudinem et mutabilitatem* (ἐν δὲ γῇ ἀνάγκην καὶ μεταβολήν?)
Oec.

[22] *in omnibus autem* (ἐν δὲ τοῖς πᾶσι?) Oec.

καὶ ταυτὶ μὲν οἱ πάλαι τῶν παρ' Ἕλλησι σοφῶν οὐκ ἄσημοι γεγονότες¹
πεφρονήκασί τε αὐτοί, καὶ μὴν καὶ ἑτέρους [ἑλέσθαι φρονεῖν ἠξίουν·² ὅ γε
μὴν ἐπιεικὴς καὶ ἀτιμαγέλης³ οὑτοσί. ταῖς τῶν ἄλλων δόξαις ἐρρῶσθαι
φράσας,⁴ μόνων⁵ ἡττᾶται τῶν τοῦ Πλάτωνος λόγων.

5   *Contra Julianum* Lib. IV. δαίμοσιν οὖν ἄρα πονηροῖς λελατρεύκασιν·⁶ 700 D
οὓς εἴπερ ἀναγκαῖον ἦν ἀποτροπιάζεσθαι, καθά φασιν αὐτοί,⁷ πῶς οὐκ ἔδει
τοῦτο πειρᾶσθαι κατορθοῦν διὰ τοῦ [φιλεῖν]⁸ προσερηρεῖσθαι τῷ τῶν ὅλων
πατρὶ καὶ δημιουργῷ ;⁹ τοῦτο δὲ ἂν γένοιτο καὶ μάλα ὀρθῶς, εἰ ἐν λόγῳ
ποιοῖτό τις τὸ διαβιῶναι θέλειν εὐσεβῶς¹⁰ καὶ ἀνεπιπλήκτως, καὶ διὰ τῆς εἰς
10 πᾶν ὁτιοῦν τῶν ἀγαθῶν ἐφέσεώς τε καὶ προθυμίας ἀφομοιοῦσθαι ζητεῖν¹¹ τῷ
παναγίῳ θεῷ. ἀμείνους γὰρ οὕτω τῆς ἐκείνων ἐσόμεθα¹² δυστροπίας, καὶ
ταῖς παρ' αὐτῶν ἐφόδοις ἀνάλωτοι.

   καὶ πλήρης μὲν ἡ γραφὴ τῶν εἰς τοῦτο μαρτυριῶν· γέγραπται γὰρ 701 A
ὅτι "παρεμβαλεῖ ἄγγελος Κυρίου κύκλῳ τῶν φοβουμένων αὐτόν, καὶ
15 ῥύσεται αὐτούς"·¹³ παροίσω δὲ καὶ τὰς αὐτῶν τῶν Ἑλλήνων φωνάς. ἤδη
μὲν οὖν διεμνημονεύσαμεν γεγραφότος ὡδὶ Πορφυρίου·¹⁴ "διὸ συνετὸς ἀνὴρ
καὶ σώφρων εὐλαβηθήσεται τοιαύταις χρῆσθαι θυσίαις δι' ὧν πρὸς ἑαυτὸν
ἐπισπάσεται τοὺς τοιούτους.¹⁵ σπουδάσει δὲ τὴν ψυχὴν καθαίρειν παντοίως·
καθαρᾷ γὰρ οὐκ ἐπιτίθενται ψυχῇ, διά τοι τὸ αὐτοῖς ἀνόμοιον." ἐδόκει δὲ¹⁶
20 οὕτω φρονεῖν καὶ τῷ κατ' αὐτοὺς τρισμεγίστῳ Ἑρμῇ· γράφει δὲ ὡδὶ καὶ

---

¹ *veteres Graecorum sapientûm non ignobiles* (om. γεγονότες) Oec. There is
some slight corruption here. Perhaps Cyril may have written καὶ ταυτὶ μὲν τῶν
πάλαι σοφῶν τινες, οὐκ ἄσημοι παρ' Ἕλλησι γεγονότες, πεφρονήκασι κ.τ.λ. The
'wise men of old' of whom he speaks are Hermes and his pupils. The meaning is
'Julian rejects the teaching of Hermes on this question, and accepts that of Plato;
but Hermes was right, and Plato was wrong'.

² *senserunt* (om. αὐτοί), *et alios sentire* (om. ἑλέσθαι) *voluerunt* Oec.

³ ἀτιμάγενος Aub. : *ab aliis secedens* (i. e. ἀτιμαγέλης) Oec. ἀτιμαγέλης meaus
'scorning the herd', i. e. going off on a line of his own, without regard to the
opinions of others.

⁴ *aliorumque* (ταῖς τε τῶν ἄλλων?) *opinionibus valedicens* Oec.

⁵ μόνων scripsi : μόνον Aub. : *solius* (μόνου) *Platonis* Oec.

⁶ Sc. οἱ Ἕλληνες, the Pagans.

⁷ φασιν αὐτοί Aub. : *ipse dicit* (i. e. φησιν αὐτός) Oec.

⁸ φιλεῖν seclusi. θέλειν would be better, but is not needed.

⁹ *quomodo non erat attentandum sic* (οὕτω in place of τοῦτο?) *recte agere ut per
hoc* (ὥστε διὰ τούτου?) *studerent* (φιλεῖν) *universorum deo et patri adhaerere?* Oec.

¹⁰ εὐσεβῶς Aub. : *recte* (ὀρθῶς?) Oec.

¹¹ καὶ διὰ τῆς ... ζητεῖν Aub. : *per desiderium* (*et?*) *alacritatem ad omne bonum
quaerendo assimilari* (διὰ τοῦ διὰ τῆς ... προθυμίας ἀφομοιοῦσθαι ζητεῖν?) Oec.

¹² ἐσόμεθα Aub. : *futuri essemus* Oec.

¹³ Ps. 33. 8.   ¹⁴ Porph. *De abst.* 2. 43.

¹⁵ Sc. τοὺς κακοεργοὺς δαίμονας. In the passage from which this extract is taken
(*De abst.* 2. 38 ff.) Porphyry divides the daemons into two classes, the beneficent and
the maleficent ; and it is of the latter that he is here speaking.

¹⁶ ἐδόκει δὲ Aub. : *Unde videbatur* Oec.

αὐτὸς¹ ἐν ⌜τῷ⌝² πρὸς Ἀσκληπιόν, περὶ τῶν ἀνοσίων δαιμόνων, οὓς δεῖ
B φυλάττεσθαί τε καὶ φεύγειν προτροπάδην·³ "μία δὲ φυλακή ἐστι, καὶ
αὕτη⁴ ἀναγκαία, ἡ⁵ εὐσέβεια. εὐσεβοῦς γὰρ ἀνθρώπου καὶ
ἁγνοῦ καὶ σεμνοῦ⁶ οὔτ' ἂν δαίμων τις κακὸς οὔτε εἱμαρμένη
κρατήσαι ποτὲ ἢ ἄρξειεν·⁷ ὁ⁸ θεὸς γὰρ ῥύεται τὸν τοιοῦτον, 5
ὄντα ὄντως εὐσεβῆ,⁹ ἐκ παντὸς κακοῦ."

τί τοίνυν, παρέντες ὅπερ ἐστὶν ὁμολογουμένως ἄξιον ἐπαίνου παντός,
ἀπονενεύκασι πρὸς τὰ χείρω, βδελυροῖς καὶ ἀποτροπαίοις δαίμοσι δεῖν
ἐπιτελεῖσθαι λέγοντες παρ' αὐτῶν τὰς θυσίας;¹⁰ ἐπειδὴ δέ, ὡς ἔφην, Κρόνῳ
καὶ Διῒ Διονύσῳ τε καὶ Ἀθηνᾷ καὶ μέντοι καὶ Ἄρει καὶ τοῖς ἑτέροις αὐτὰς 10
προσεκόμιζον, αὐτοὶ¹¹ δηλονότι, καὶ οὐχ ἕτεροι παρ' αὐτούς,¹² εἶεν ἂν οἱ πονηροί
τε καὶ ἀποτρόπαιοι καὶ φθονεροὶ¹³ δαίμονες, τὸ τῆς θεότητος ὄνομα παρα-
κλέπτοντες.

769 A *Contra Julianum* Lib. V. προσεπάγει δὲ τούτοις (*sc.* Ἰουλιανός)· "ὅτι
δὲ οὐχ Ἑβραίων μόνων¹⁴ ἐμέλησε τῷ θεῷ, πάντων δὲ ἐθνῶν κηδόμενος 15

¹ Perhaps οὗτος.
² See note on 588 A *init.* Cyril may here have written ἐν τοῖς πρὸς Ἀσκλ., or
ἐν τῷ (τελείῳ λόγῳ τῷ) πρὸς Ἀσκλ. *Videbatur . . . Hermeti, qui scribit ad
Asclepium* (om. ἐν τῷ) Oec.
   The passage is quoted by Cyril from the Greek original of *Ascl. Lat.* III. 29 b.
It is more correctly quoted by Lactantius, *Div. init.* 2. 15. 6 (p. 14 above). In the
text of Cyril, it is expanded by interpolations.
   Cyril writes γράφει (*sc.* Ἑρμῆς), not λέγει; i.e. he assumes that the *libellus* from
which he quotes, a dialogue in which Hermes is one of the interlocutors, was written
by Hermes himself.
³ οὓς δεῖ . . . προτροπάδην Aub. : *quos oporteat servare, et quos fugare et persequi*
Oec.   What was Oec.'s reading of the Greek?
   It is not clear whether the clause οὓς δεῖ . . . προτροπάδην is a part of what Cyril
says that Hermes wrote about the evil daemons, or a remark added by Cyril.
Possibly the Hermetist wrote τούτους δεῖ φυλάττεσθαι· μία δὲ φυλακή κ.τ.λ., and
Cyril added καὶ φεύγειν προτροπάδην after φυλάττεσθαι.
⁴ *ipsa* (αὐτὴ) Oec.   ⁵ καὶ αὕτη ἀναγκαία ἡ om. Lact.
⁶ καὶ ἁγνοῦ καὶ σεμνοῦ om. Lact.
⁷ οὔτ' ἂν . . . ἢ ἄρξειεν Aub. : *neque daemon malus neque fatum ipsum vincet vel
subditum faciet* (οὔτε δαίμων κακὸς οὔτε αὐτὴ ἡ εἱμαρμένη κρατήσει ἢ ἄρξει?) Oec. :
οὔτε δαίμων κακὸς οὔτε εἱμαρμένη κρατεῖ Lact.
⁸ ὁ om. Lact.
⁹ τὸν τοιοῦτον, ὄντα ὄντως εὐσεβῆ Aub. : *talem pium* (om. ὄντα ὄντως) Oec. : τὸν
εὐσεβῆ (om. τοιοῦτον ὄντα ὄντως) Lact.   It may be conjectured that the Hermetist
wrote τὸν τοιοῦτον (meaning thereby τὸν εὐσεβῆ); that εὐσεβῆ was inserted as an
alternative for τοιοῦτον; and that ὄντα ὄντως is a corrupted doublet of τὸν
τοιοῦτον.
¹⁰ δεῖν . . . θυσίας Aub. : *sua sacrificia* (τὰς παρ' αὐτῶν θυσίας?) *persolvi debere
aicunt* (a slip of the pen for *dicentes*?) Oec.   παρ' αὐτῶν seems pointless; and
perhaps παρ' αὐτῶν τάς ought to be bracketed.
¹¹ αὐτοὶ Aub. : *ipsi* (αὐτοὶ) Oec. : perhaps οὗτοι.
¹² παρ' αὐτούς om. Oec.
¹³ ἀποτρόπαιοι καὶ φθονεροὶ Aub. : *pestilentes et devastatores* (φθοροεργοὶ?) Oec.
¹⁴ μόνων scripsi : μόνον Aub. : *non solum Hebraeorum* Oec.

ἔδωκεν ἐκείνοις μὲν οὐδὲν σπουδαῖον ἢ μέγα, ἡμῖν δὲ μακρῷ[1] κρείττονα[2] καὶ διαφέροντα, σκοπεῖτε λοιπὸν τὸ ἐντεῦθεν. ἔχουσι μὲν εἰπεῖν καὶ Αἰγύπτιοι, παρ' ἑαυτοῖς ἀπαριθμούμενοι σοφῶν οὐκ ὀλίγων ὀνόματα, πολ- B λοὺς ἐσχηκέναι[3] τοὺς ἀπὸ τῆς Ἑρμοῦ διαδοχῆς,[4] Ἑρμοῦ δέ φημι τοῦ τρίτου,

[1] μικρῷ Aub. : _longe_ (i. e. μακρῷ) Oec.

[2] κρείττονα Aub. : _plura_ (πλείονα?) Oec.

[3] ἔχουσι μὲν ... ἐσχηκέναι Aub. : _Nam_ (μὲν γὰρ?) _et Aegyptii dicere possunt apud se numerari_ (ἀπαριθμούμενα?) _sapientium non paucorum nomina, multosque se habuisse_ (πολλούς τε ἐσχηκέναι?) Oec. Perhaps Julian wrote ἔχουσι μὲν (γὰρ) εἰπεῖν ... παρ' ἑαυτοῖς ἀπαριθμούμενα σοφῶν οὐκ ὀλίγων ὀνόματα, πολλοὺς ἐσχηκότες κ.τ.λ.

[4] Julian here speaks of Hermes as a philosopher or teacher of religion, and one whose teaching was transmitted through a series of successors. That much he might have learnt by report, without having read any writings attributed to Hermes. There is no evidence in this passage, nor, as far as I know, in any of Julian's writings, that he had himself read the Greek _Hermetica_, nor even that he knew of their existence. (The writer of _Artemii Passio_, § 34, makes Julian say that he was τῇ Ἑρμοῦ θεολογίᾳ ἐξησκημένος· but that can hardly be regarded as evidence.) He here speaks of Hermes as he speaks of Oannes and Belus, and of Cheiron ; and it cannot be supposed that he had read writings ascribed to these persons. But the _Hermetica_ must have been known to many people in his time ; and despite the absence of positive evidence that he had seen or heard of them, it is not likely that they had wholly escaped the notice of a student such as Julian, and one so keenly interested in the matters with which they dealt.

Julian says that the names of many Egyptian successors of Hermes are known. Who are the men of whom he is thinking ? Among the names known to him may have been Tat, Asclepius, and Ammon ; and he may have learnt from Greek sources the names of some Egyptian teachers (real or imaginary) of later times, such as those mentioned by Plutarch, _Is. et Os._ 10 : Εὔδοξον μὲν οὖν Χονούφεώς φασι Μεμφίτου διακοῦσαι, Σόλωνα δὲ Σύγχιτος (Σώγχεως?) Σαΐτου, Πυθαγόραν δὲ, Οἰνούφεως (Ὀννούφεως?) Ἡλιουπολίτου. Plut. _Vit. Solon._ 26 : Solon χρόνον τινὰ τοῖς περὶ Ψένωφιν τὸν Ἡλιουπολίτην καὶ Σῶγχιν τὸν Σαΐτην, λογιωτάτοις οὖσι τῶν ἱερέων, συνεφιλοσόφησε. In Plut. _De gen. Socr._ 5-7 it is said that Plato and Simmias studied under Χόνουφις the προφήτης at Memphis, and that this Chonuphis deciphered an ancient inscription which Agesilaus found in the tomb of Alcmene in Boeotia. Diog. Laert. 8. 8. 6. 90 : Eudoxus συνεγένετο ἐν Αἰγύπτῳ ⌈Ἰχονουφυ⌉ (read [ι] Χονούφει) τῷ Ἡλιουπολίτῃ. Clem. Alex. _Strom._ 1. 15. 69 : ἱστορεῖται δὲ Πυθαγόρης μὲν Σώγχηδι τῷ Αἰγυπτίῳ ἀρχιπροφήτῃ μαθητεῦσαι, Πλάτων δὲ Σεχνούφιδι τῷ Ἡλιουπολίτῃ, Εὔδοξος δὲ ὁ Κνίδιος Κονούφιδι (Χονούφιδι? or Ὀν(ν)ούφιδι?). Proclus (_in Tim._ I. 101 Diehl) says that Solon associated with _Pateneit_ of Sais, _Ochaapi_ of Heliopolis, and _Ethemon_ of Sebennytus. Most of these persons, if not all of them, are doubtless fictitious ; but it is possible that some of the names assigned to them may have been borne by real Egyptian priests. Ὀννουφις is _Wen-nofre_ (sometimes written by Greeks in the form Ὀννωφρις), a name of the god Osiris ; and Χόνουφις is one of the various forms in which the name of the god Chnum was written. A more likely form for a man's name is _Se-Chnuphis_ (Σέχνουφις in Clement) or _Pse-Chnuphis_ (Ψέ(χ)νωφις in Plutarch?), which would mean _son of Chnum_.

Among those who carried on the διαδοχή of Hermes in Egypt after Alexander's conquest of the country might be reckoned the Egyptian priests Manetho (third century B. C.), Chaeremon (first century A. D.), and Abammon, the writer (real or supposed) of the _Responsum ad Porphyrium_. And in a somewhat different sense, the Egyptian Platonists Ammonius Saccas and Plotinus might also be called _diadochi_ of Hermes.

⟨τοῦ ἐν⟩¹ τῇ Αἰγύπτῳ ἐπιδημήσαντος,² Χαλδαῖοι δὲ καὶ Ἀσσύριοι τοὺς ἀπ'
⟨Ὠ⟩άννου² καὶ Βήλου, μυρίους δὲ Ἕλληνες τοὺς ἀπὸ Χείρωνος·⁴ ἐκ τούτου
γὰρ πάντες ἐγένοιτο τελεστικοὶ ⌜φύσει⌝⁵ καὶ θεολογικοί, καθ' ὃ δὴ μόνον
Ἑβραῖοι δοκοῦσι⁶ τὰ ἑαυτῶν ἀποσεμνύνειν."

¹ τρίτου, τοῦ ἐν scripsi: τρίτου Neumann: τρίτον Aub.: De Hermete inquam,
qui tertio (τρίτον) venit in Aegyptum Oec.
² τῇ Αἰγύπτῳ ἐπιδημήσαντος V B¹ Aub. (ἐπιφοιτήσαντος B² marg.): ἐπιφοιτήσαντος τῇ Αἰγύπτῳ M.
Julian's 'third Hermes' corresponds to the fifth of the five Mercurii enumerated
in Cic. Nat. deor. 3. 56 (quoted by Lactantius, Div. inst. 1. 6 2): 'quintus
(Mercurius), . . . qui Argum dicitur interemisse, ob eamque causam Aegyptum
profugisse, atque Aegyptiis leges et litteras tradidisse. Hunc Aegyptii Theuth
appellant.' In a passage ascribed to Manetho (Syncell. I, p. 72 Dindorf, quoted
in note on Stob. Exc. XXIII. 7, vol. III, p. 491) Hermes Trismegistus is called
ὁ δεύτερος Ἑρμῆς, and is distinguished from Θώθ, ὁ πρῶτος Ἑρμῆς.
ἐπιφοιτᾶν means 'to visit repeatedly or habitually'. But Julian probably meant
to say that Hermes the teacher migrated from Greece to Egypt once for all, and
settled there, as is said in Cic. Nat. deor.; and if so, ἐπιδημήσαντος is better than
the variant reading ἐπιφοιτήσαντος. See note on Artemii Passio, p. 237, n. 1 below.
³ ἀπ' Ὠάννου Neumann: ἀπὸ ἀννου V: ἀπονίνου (i.e. ἀπὸ Νίνου) M: ἀπ' Ἀννου
Aub.: ab Ano Oec. For Ὠάννου, Neumann refers to 'ea quae de Oanne et Belo
Eusebius exposuit chron. I, pp. 14–16 Schoene, quae legisse Julianum haud
absonum'. Oannes is probably a name of the Babylonian god Ea, who was called
'the wise god' and 'the god of wisdom'. (Jensen takes Ὠάννης to be the Assyrian
word ummânu [pronounced uwwânu], which meant a wise or skilled man, an artist
or craftsman.) Berosus (quoted by Eusebius l. c.) says that Oannes rose out of the
sea in the form of a fish with human head and feet, and taught the people of
Babylonia γραμμάτων καὶ μαθημάτων καὶ τεχνῶν παντοδαπῶν ἐμπειρίαν, and all that
appertains to civilized life, and that 'since that time nothing has been discovered
that goes beyond his teaching'. Berosus also says that Oannes wrote a book περὶ
γενεᾶς καὶ πολιτείας, and gave this book to men. It may perhaps be inferred from
this that a sacred book, of which Oannes was the reputed author, was preserved in
some Babylonian temple. But if there was such a book, it can hardly have been
accessible to Julian.
Βῆλος, the Babylonian Bel, was the god to whom the function of Demiurgus was
assigned in the cosmogony of Berosus (Euseb. ib.). It does not appear that any
teaching was ascribed to him.
⁴ The Centaur Cheiron, the schoolmaster of Achilles and other heroes, is regarded by Julian as the earliest Greek theologian. Cf. Clem. Alex. Strom.
1. 15. 73: ὁ δὲ Βηρύτιος Ἕρμιππος (time of Trajan and Hadrian) Χείρωνα τὸν Κένταυρον σοφὸν
καλεῖ, ἐφ' οὗ καὶ ὁ τὴν Τιτανομαχίαν γράψας φησιν ὡς πρῶτος οὗτος "εἴς τε δικαιο-
σύνην θνητῶν γένος ἤγαγε, δείξας | ὅρκους καὶ θυσίας ἱλαρὰς καὶ σχήματ' Ὀλύμπου".
παρὰ τούτῳ Ἀχιλλεὺς παιδεύεται . . . · Ἱππὼ δὲ ἡ θυγάτηρ τοῦ Κενταύρου, συνοική-
σασα Αἰόλῳ, ἐδιδάξατο αὐτὸν τὴν φυσικὴν θεωρίαν, τὴν πάτριον ἐπιστήμην.
⁵ ἐγένοντο τελεστικοὶ φύσει (nati sunt natura sacerdotes Oec.) could only mean
'were born τελεστικοί'. But the sense required by the context is 'were made
τελεστικοί by teaching'. φύσις is commonly opposed to διδαχή, as ingenium to
ars or disciplina; and it is of διδαχή that Julian is speaking. φύσει is therefore
impossible. Perhaps Cyril wrote ἐγένοντο τελεστικοί, φησί (sc. Ἰουλιανός), καὶ
θεολογικοί.
⁶ μόνον Ἑβραῖοι δοκοῦσι V (teste Neumann), Aub.: δοκοῦσι μόνον Ἑβραῖοι
Neumann: id quod Hebraei sua magnifacientes sibi soli (μόνοι?) tribuunt Oec.:
(What was Oec.'s reading of the Greek?).
Theology, says Julian, is the one thing on which the Hebrews pride themselves;
yet in that very thing they are surpassed by other nations.

Contra Julianum Lib. VIII. πλὴν καὶ αὐτοῖς ἐνοῦσαν εὑρήσομεν[1] 920 c
τοῖς Ἑλλήνων σοφοῖς τῆς ἁγίας τριάδος τὴν γνῶσιν. προσεχέστατα γάρ,
καὶ μεσολαβοῦντος οὐδενός, ἀλλήλοις συνεῖναί φασιν αὐτά·[2] καὶ ἣν [ἂν]
ἔχει[3] τάξιν πρὸς [γε][4] τὸ πρῶτον ὁ νοῦς, ταύτην[5] ὁμοίως καὶ τὴν τρίτην
5 ψυχὴν ἐσχηκέναι φασὶν πρὸς τὸν ἀπὸ τοῦ πρώτου δεύτερον νοῦν.

ὅτι δὲ καὶ γεννήματος καὶ μὴν καὶ τεκόντος εἰσδέχονται φαντασίας,[6]
εἰσόμεθα, πάλιν ὡδὶ γεγραφότος αὐτοῦ·[7] "ποθεῖ δὲ πᾶν τὸ γεννῆσαν,[8] καὶ
τοῦτο ἀγαπᾷ, καὶ μάλιστα ὅταν ἐν ὦσι[9] τὸ γεννῆσαν καὶ τὸ γεννώμενον·
ὅταν δὲ καὶ [τὸ] ἀ⟨δι⟩όριστον[10] ᾖ τὸ γεννῆσαν, ἐξ ἀνάγκης σύνεστιν αὐτῷ,[11]
10 ὡς τῇ ἑτερότητι μόνον[12] κεχωρίσθαι." ἀκούεις ὅπως τὸ γεννηθὲν δεῖν ἔφη D
συνεῖναι πάντῃ τε καὶ πάντως τῷ γεγεννηκότι, διὰ [τοι τάχα που][13] τὸ
ἀδιόριστον ἤγουν προσεχὲς φυσικῶς, καὶ τὸ διὰ μέσου κεῖσθαι μηδέν, κεχωρίσθαι δὲ μόνῃ τῇ ἑτερότητι,[14] καὶ οὔτι που τάχα τῇ κατὰ τὴν φύσιν, ἀλλ'
ὅτι τὸ γεννῆσαν πρὸς τὸ γεννώμενον μίαν πως ἔχει διαφορὰν τὴν τοῦ ὅτι τὸ
15 μὲν γεγέννηκε, τὸ δὲ γεγέννηται.

ἔφη δέ που καὶ ὁ τρισμέγιστος παρ' αὐτοῖς Ἑρμῆς περὶ τοῦ πάντων
ἀριστοτέχνου θεοῦ· "καὶ[15] γὰρ ὡς τέλειος καὶ σοφὸς τάξιν [καὶ]
ἀταξίᾳ[16] ἐπέθηκε, ἵνα τὰ μὲν νοερά,[17] ὡς πρεσβύτερα καὶ κρείτ-

---

[1] εὑρήσομεν Aub. : *invenimus* (ηὑρήκαμεν?) Oec.

[2] The Ἑλλήνων σοφοί of whom Cyril is here speaking are Plotinus and
Porphyry. αὐτά means the three ἀρχικαὶ ὑποστάσεις of Plotinus, viz. τὸ ἀγαθόν,
νοῦς, and ψυχή.

[3] ἂν ἔχοι Aub. : *habet* (ἔχει) Oec.   [4] γε seclusi.

[5] ταύτῃ Aub. : *eundem* (sc. *ordinem*, i.e. ταύτην or τὴν αὐτὴν) Oec.

[6] i. e. that Plotinus and Porphyry held the second ὑπόστασις to be related to the
first as son to father.

[7] Plotinus 5. 1. 6. This passage of Plotinus is quoted by Eusebius, *Pr. ev.* 11.
17. 8.

[8] πᾶν is nominative ; τὸ γεννῆσαν is accusative.

[9] ὅταν ἐν ὦσι Aub. : *quando unum sunt* Oec. : ὅταν ὦσι μόνοι Plot. (Volkmann),
Euseb. (Dindorf).

[10] ἀδιόριστον scripsi : τὸ ἀόριστον Aub. : *indiscretum* Oec. : τὸ ἄριστον Plot.
(Volkmann), Euseb. (Dindorf). Cyril's comment (διὰ . . . τὸ ἀδιόριστον ἤγουν
προσεχὲς φυσικῶς) shows that he read ἀδιόριστον in Plotinus, and took the meaning
to be 'when there is no division between τὸ γεννῆσαν and τὸ γεννηθέν'.

[11] Sc. σύνεστι τῷ γεννήσαντι τὸ γεννηθέν.

[12] μόνον Aub. : *eo quod solum diversitate separetur* Oec.: μόνον Plot. (Volkmann),
Euseb. (Dindorf). But perhaps Cyril read and wrote μόνῃ ; cf. κεχωρίσθαι δὲ μόνῃ
τῇ ἑτερότητι in his comment.

[13] διά τοι τάχα που τὸ ἀδιόριστον Aub. : *et propterea fortassis* (καὶ διὰ τοῦτο τάχα
που?) *indiscretum* Oec. I have bracketed τοι τάχα που, which may perhaps be a
misplaced doublet of οὔτι που τάχα before τῇ κατὰ τὴν φύσιν below.

[14] *separatum autem esse dicit* (add. φησὶ?) *sola diversitate* Oec.   [15] Fr. 35.

[16] ἀταξίᾳ scripsi : καὶ ἀταξίαν Aub. : *et deordinationem* Oec. The statement that
God imposed order on ἄτακτος ὕλη was familiar to all Platonists. But what is the
connexion of thought between this and what follows (ἵνα τὰ μὲν νοερά κ.τ.λ.)?
Perhaps there is a lacuna before ἵνα ; the Hermetist may have written something
like (ἄρχοντα καταστήσας τὸν ἑαυτοῦ λόγον,) ἵνα κ.τ.λ.

[17] τὰ αἰσθητά are usually contrasted with τὰ νοητά ; but in this passage they are
contrasted with τὰ νοερά.

τονα, προεστήκῃ καὶ τὸν πρῶτον τόπον ἔχῃ,[1] τὰ δὲ αἰσθητά,
ὡς δεύτερα, ἵνα][2] τούτοις ὑποστήκῃ. τὸ οὖν κατωφερέστερον
τοῦ νοεροῦ καὶ βρῖθον[3] λόγον ἐν ἑαυτῷ σοφὸν ἔχει [δημιουρ-
γικόν]·[4] ὁ δὲ λόγος [αὐτοῦ][5] οὗτος δημιουργικῆς ἔχεται φύσεως,
γόνιμος ὑπάρχων καὶ ζωοποιός."[6] ὅτι γὰρ[7] ἐν πᾶσιν ἐστι τοῖς   5
⌜κεκινημένοις⌝[8] ὡς ζωοποιὸς ὁ τοῦ θεοῦ λόγος, ἰσχυριζόμεθα καὶ ἡμεῖς·
πιστώσεται δὲ γεγραφὼς ὁ πάνσοφος Παῦλος " εἷς θεὸς ὁ ἐπὶ πάντων καὶ
διὰ πάντων καὶ ἐν πᾶσιν".[9] οὐ γὰρ ἦν ἑτέρως δύνασθαι τὸ παρενεχθὲν εἰς
γένεσιν καὶ ἐξ οὐκ ὄντος ⟨εἰς τὸ [εὖ εἶναι]⟩[10] κεκινημένον τὴν [[εἰς τὸ εὖ
εἶναι]] διαμονὴν ἀκράδαντον ἔχειν. μὴ τοῦ ἀφθάρτου[11] καὶ ὄντος ἀληθῶς   ιc
μετεσχηκὸς θεοῦ. οἶδεν οὖν ἄρα[12] δημιουργικῆς ὄντα φύσεως τὸν υἱόν,
γόνιμόν τε καὶ ζωοποιόν, καὶ ἑτέρας ὄντα[13] φύσεως παρὰ πάντα τὰ τῆς παρ'
αὐτοῦ ζωῆς δεκτικά. ζωοποιεῖ δὲ[14] πᾶν τὸ ζωῆς ἐπιδεὲς ἐν ἁγίῳ πνεύματι.
ὡς γὰρ[15] αὐτός πού φησιν υἱός, "τὸ πνεῦμά ἐστι τὸ ζωοποιοῦν,"[16] καὶ πᾶσα[17]
τῶν γεγονότων ἡ πῆξις τελεῖται παρὰ πατρὸς δι' υἱοῦ ἐν πνεύματι,[18] ψάλλει   15
γοῦν[19] ὁ θεσπέσιος Δαβὶδ ὅτι " τῷ λόγῳ κυρίου οἱ οὐρανοὶ ἐστερεώθησαν,
καὶ τῷ πνεύματι τοῦ στόματος αὐτοῦ πᾶσα ἡ δύναμις αὐτῶν".[20]

---

[1] καὶ τὸν πρῶτον τόπον ἔχῃ secludendum ?   [2] ἵνα seclusi.

[3] *Itaque quod a mentali magis descendit, et est grave* Oec.

[4] δημιουργικόν (*quod formare possit* Oec.) seclusi.

[5] αὐτοῦ (*eius* Oec.) seclusi.

[6] Aubert makes the quotation from Hermes end at λόγον ἐν ἑαυτῷ σοφὸν ἔχει δημιουργικόν, and attributes the following words (ὁ δὲ λόγος . . . καὶ ζωοποιός) to Cyril. But Cyril says below οἶδεν οὖν ἄρα (*sc.* Hermes) δημιουργικῆς ὄντα φύσεως τὸν υἱόν, γόνιμόν τε καὶ ζωοποιόν; and that makes it evident that the words ὁ δὲ λόγος οὗτος δημιουργικῆς ἔχεται φύσεως, γόνιμος ὑπάρχων καὶ ζωοποιός were ascribed by him to Hermes, and belonged to the Hermetic passage which he quoted. That being so, it is necessary to bracket δημιουργικόν in the quotation, because it prematurely assumes what is stated in the following words δημιουργικῆς ἔχεται φύσεως.

In this *Hermeticum*, the λόγος is spoken of in terms similar to those used in the Hermetic passages quoted by Cyril in 552 D and 553 A. In the first of those passages, God's λόγος is called γόνιμος καὶ δημιουργ(ικ?)ός; in the second, it is said that (ὁ αἰσθητὸς κόσμος?) ἔχει ἄρχοντα ἐπικείμενον (τὸν) δημιουργὸν λόγον τοῦ πάντων δεσπότου, and that this λόγος ἐπίκειται καὶ ἄρχει τῶν δι' αὐτοῦ δημιουργη-θέντων; and in the third, we are told that God's νοερὸς λόγος δημιουργεῖ καὶ ζωοποιεῖ.

[7] γάρ is obscure; is there a lacuna before ὅτι γάρ?

[8] κεκινημένοις Aub.: *in omnibus quae producta sunt* Oec.: perhaps γεγεν(ν)η-μένοις. The word κεκινημένοις may have come from ἐξ οὐκ ὄντος κεκινημένον below.

[9] *Ephes.* 4. 6: εἷς θεὸς καὶ πατὴρ πάντων, ὁ ἐπὶ πάντων καὶ διὰ πάντων καὶ ἐν πᾶσιν. Nothing is there said about God's λόγος; but Cyril takes the statement 'God is ἐν πᾶσιν' to mean 'God's λόγος is ἐν πᾶσιν'.

[10] εἰς τὸ εἶναι huc transposui: εὖ seclusi.

[11] *dei corruptibilis* (a slip for *incorruptibilis*) Oec.

[12] Perhaps οἶδεν οὖν [ἄρα] ('Ερμῆς).   [13] *alterius existentis* (ὄντος ?) *naturae* Oec.

[14] δὲ Aub.: *enim* (γὰρ ?, Oec.   [15] γὰρ Aub.: *et* (δὲ ?) Oec.   [16] *Ev. Joh.* 6. 63.

[17] πᾶσα Aub.: *omnino* (πάντως ?) Oec.   [18] *in spiritu sancto* (add. ἁγίῳ) Oec.

[19] γοῦν Aub.: *unde* Oec.   [20] *Ps.* 32. 6.

ADDENDUM TO CYRIL.

Pitra, *Analecta Sacra et Classica*, Tom. V, gives two documents which contain some Hermetic fragments borrowed from Cyril *c. Jul.*

(*a*) Pitra *Anal. Class.*, p. 305 (from Cod. Vatican. 2200, p. 444):

Superscription : Συμφωνία [ἐκ] τῶν παλαιῶν φιλοσόφων τῶν Ἑλλήνων
πρὸς τὴν ἁγίαν καὶ θεόπνευστον νέαν γραφήν, ἤτουν (read ἤγουν) ἀπόδειξις
καὶ ἔλεγχος κατ᾽ αὐτῶν περὶ τῆς . . . τριάδος, κ.τ.λ.

περὶ τῆς ἁγίας καὶ πανσέπτου τριάδος.

Ἑρμοῦ πρὸς Ἀσκληπιὸν περὶ θεοῦ·[1] "οὐ γὰρ ἐφικτὸν[2] εἰς ἀμυήτους
τοιαῦτα μυστήρια παρέχεσθαι· ἀλλὰ τῷ νοῒ ἀκούσατε. ἐν μόνον ἦν φῶς
νοερὸν πρὸ τοῦ[3] φωτὸς νοεροῦ, καὶ ἔστιν ἀεὶ νοῦς νοὸς φωτεινός, καὶ οὐδὲν
ἕτερον ἦν ἡ τούτου ἑνότης· ἔστιν ἐν αὐτῷ ὄν, ἔστιν τῷ[4] ἑαυτοῦ νοΐ, καὶ φωτὶ
καὶ πνεύματι τὰ[5] πάντα περιέχει."

τοῦ αὐτοῦ ἐκ τοῦ αὐτοῦ λόγου·[6] "ἐκτὸς τούτου οὐ θεός, οὐ⟨κ⟩ ἄγγελος, οὐ
δαίμων, οὐκ οὐσία τις ἄλλη· πάντων γάρ ἐστι κύριος καὶ πατὴρ καὶ θεὸς
καὶ πηγὴ καὶ ζωὴ καὶ δύναμις καὶ φῶς καὶ νοῦς καὶ πνεῦμα, καὶ πάντα ἐν
αὐτῷ καὶ ὑπ᾽ αὐτόν ἐστι."

τοῦ αὐτοῦ πρὸς ⌜τὰ διεξοδικὰ⌝ πρώτου λόγου περὶ θεοῦ·[7] "ὁ τοῦ δημιουργοῦ λόγος, ὦ τέκνον, ἀΐδιος, αὐτοκίνητος, ἀναυξής, ἀμείωτος, ἀμετάβλητος,
ἄφθαρτος, μόνος αὐτῷ ὅμοιός ἐστιν,[8] εἷς ὢν μετὰ τὸν προεγνωσμένον θεόν."

τοῦ αὐτοῦ ἐκ τοῦ ὕμνου πρὸς τὸν παντοκράτορα πατέρα τῶν ὅλων καὶ θεὸν
ὄντα μόνον, ἀπ᾽ οὐδενὸς ἔχοντα ὅπερ ἔχει·[9] "ἀεὶ ἔγνωκα ἕνα μετὰ σοῦ,
⌜ὥστε⌝ τὸν ἐκ σοῦ γεραίρων υἱόν, ὃν ⌜ῥώμῃ⌝ ἀπορρήτῳ καὶ ὀξυτελανου (?)
φωνῆς ἴδιον, εὐθὺς ἀφθόνως καὶ ἀπειλῶς[10] (?) ἅτε νοῦς⌝ λόγον ἐγέννησας, θεὸν
ὄντα τὴν οὐσίαν ἐκ τῆς σῆς οὐσίας, ὃς σοῦ τοῦ πατρὸς εἰκόνα τὴν ἄφθαρτον
καὶ πανόμοιον[11] φέρει, ⌜ὥστε ἐστὶν ἐκεῖνον ἐνεργὲς ἐν ἐκείνῳ κάλλους
ἔσοπτρον, ἀλλ᾽ ἀνέκφραστον πρόσωπον⌝."[12]

[1] Cyril *c. Jul.* 556 A. *Fr.* 23.   [2] ἐφικτόν ἐστιν Cyril.   [3] τοῦ om. Cyril.
[4] ἀεὶ ἐν ἑαυτῷ ὤν, ἀεὶ τῷ Cyril.   [5] τὰ om. Cyril.   [6] Cyril *ib.* *Fr.* 23.
[7] Cyril *ib.* 553 A B. *Fr.* 30. πρὸς τά is doubtless a mistake for πρὸ. Τάτ (ἐν
λόγῳ πρώτῳ τῶν πρὸς τὸν Τὰτ διεξοδικῶν Cyril.)
[8] μόνος, ἀεὶ ἑαυτῷ ὅμοιός ἐστιν, ἴσος δὲ καὶ ὁμαλός, εὐσταθής, εὔτακτος Cyril.
[9] This extract from a hymn to the supreme God is not given in Cyril *c. Jul.*,
from which the preceding quotations are taken; and if τοῦ αὐτοῦ means Ἑρμοῦ, it
ought to be added to the collection of Hermetic fragments. But it is possible that
a passage which stood before it has been omitted, and that τοῦ αὐτοῦ referred to an
author named at the beginning of that passage.
[10] ἀπειλῶς : [fortasse ἀφειδῶς].   [11] πανόμοιαν Pitra.
[12] The meaning of this corrupt clause may perhaps have been something like ὥστε
φανῆναι ἐναργῶς ἐν ἐκείνῳ, ὡς ἐν ἐσόπτρῳ, τὸ ἀνέκφραστον κάλλος τοῦ σοῦ προσώπου.
There is a first God, (who is νοῦς?) ; and there is a second God, the λόγος, who
has been begotten by the first God, and 'bears his image', and in or through whom
the first God is manifested. The words λόγον ἐγέννησας, θεὸν ὄντα look rather
like a reminiscence of θεὸς ἦν ὁ λόγος in the prologue of the Fourth Gospel (which
was known to Numenius) ; but the doctrine is similar to that of some of the Hermetic
fragments quoted by Cyril, and the passage may have been written by a Pagan.

Πορφυρίου, ἐκτιθεμένου Πλάτωνος δόξα⟨ν⟩·¹ " ἄχρι γὰρ τριῶν ὑποστάσεων ἔφη Πλάτων ⌜τουτέστιν ἐκπροελθεῖν⌝² οὐσίαν· ⌜εἰδέναι⌝³ τὸν μὲν
ἀνωτάτω θεὸν ⌜ὄντα ἀγαθόν⌝,⁴ μετ᾽ αὐτὸν δὲ καὶ δεύτερον τὸν δημιουργόν,
⌜τρίτην δὲ κατὰ⌝⁵ τὴν τοῦ κόσμου ψυχήν· ἄχρι γὰρ ψυχῆς τὴν θεότητα⁶
προελθεῖν."

τοῦ αὐτοῦ·⁷ " γεννητὸς ὁ υἱός ἐστι, καὶ ἱκανὸς γνώμης ἀφανοῦς ἰδεῖν
⌜αἰσθητήριον· φύσει γὰρ⌝ μόνου θεοῦ, ὡς ⌜αἴτιον⌝⁸ τοῦ παντός, γυμνὴν
ὑχὴν ἰδεῖν δυναμένου. εἰς γὰρ ⟨ὁ ?⟩ αἴτιος τοῦ παντός, εἰς καὶ ἐξ αὐτοῦ
ἄλλος ⌜ὁ εἷς⌝, καί ⌜ποτε οὔ τις ὁ εἷς⌝, οὐκ ἐν χρόνῳ· ἀίδιος γὰρ ὁ εἷς, καὶ
⌜ἀναίδιος ὁ εἷς⌝, καὶ οὐδὲν τούτοις συναίδιον."⁹

Ἀριστοτέλους· " ἀκάματος φύσις θεοῦ, γεννήσεως οὐκ ἔχουσα ἀρχήν·
ἐξ αὐτῆς δὲ ὁ πανσθενὴς οὐσιῶται λόγος."

Πλουτάρχου· " ⌜τοῦ παρὰ τούτων ὅλων αἰτίου προεπινοεῖται· οὐδὲν⌝ ὅλος
δὲ ¹⁰ ἐξ ὅλου, ἄλλος δὲ ἐξ αὐτοῦ ὡσαύτως, ἀλλ᾽ οὐκ ἀλλοίως, καὶ μέσον
οὐδέν."

Ἀντιόχου, ἱερέως Ἡλιουπόλεως, ὃ ηὑρέθη ἐν ταῖς σύριγξι ταῖς Αἰγυπτίαις,
" ἦν νοῦς εἷς, πάντων νοητὸν τέλος,¹¹ τοῦ δὲ ἄπο ⌜παγγενεῖ τις⌝¹² νοερὸς
λόγος, ἄφθαρτος υἱός, ἀπαύγασμα νοεροῦ πατρὸς ἐών, αἰγλήεις, ὁμοιούσιος,
ἄφθιτος υἱός, ἐν μὲν ἐπωνυμίῃ διεστηκὼς¹³ ἀπὸ πατρός, εἷς δὲ πέλων ἐν πατρὶ
ἀεί, ἐξ ἑνὸς [ὁ] εἷς, μία ⌜τάξις ἐν πρώτῳ ἁγίῳ πνεύματι."¹⁴

¹ Cyril c. _Jul._ 553 B. (Πορφύριος γάρ φησι, Πλάτωνος ἐκτιθέμενος δόξαν Cyril.)
² τὴν τοῦ θείου προελθεῖν Cyril.　　　　³ εἶναι δὲ Cyril.
⁴ τἀγαθόν Cyril.　　　⁵ τρίτον δὲ καὶ Cyril.　　　⁶ θειότητα Cyril.
⁷ I. e. (as the text now stands) Πορφυρίου. But would Porphyry speak thus of
' the Son '?　　　　⁸ Probably αἴτιον.
⁹ Perhaps, ἀίδιος γὰρ ὁ εἷς, καὶ ϲγναίδιος ὁ γιός, καὶ οὐδὲν τούτοις συναίδιον. [Per-
haps καὶ αὖ ἀίδιος ὁ εἷς. Cf. ll. 9, 20, and p. 175, l. 9 above.]
¹⁰ Perhaps τοῦ γὰρ τῶν ὅλων αἰτίου προεπινοεῖται οὐδέν· ὅλος δὲ κ.τ.λ. ' Nothing
is conceived before the Cause of all '; i. e. there can be nothing prior to the
supreme God.
　Cf. c. _Jul._ 920 c.: προσεχέστατα γάρ, καὶ μεσολαβοῦντος οὐδένος, ἀλλήλοις συνεῖναί
φασιν αὐτά. _Adv. Anthropomorphitas_, 1117 a: ἔστι γὰρ ἐν τοῖς καθ᾽ ἑαυτὸν παντέ-
λεια, καὶ οὔτε τινὰ μείωσιν ἐπιδέχεται, διὰ τὸ ἐπιτρέπτως καὶ ἀναλλοιώτως ἔχειν ἀεί,
οὔτε μήν, ὡς ἔφην, προσθήκης ἂν δέοιτό τινος.]
¹¹ νοητὸν τέλος Pitra. [Read νοερώτερος. See n. 14.]
¹² παγγενεῖ τις Pitra. [Read παγγενέτης. See n. 14.]　　　¹³ διαστηκὼς Pitra.
¹⁴ [The pseudo-oracle (or a variant of it) which is mutilated here is given in Buresch
Klaros, χρησμοί, 49: ὅτι ἐν Αἰγύπτῳ κατὰ τοὺς λεγομένους Σηράγγας ἐγέγραπτο
χρησμὸς τοιοῦτος·

　　　⟨ἦ⟩ν νοῦς εἷς, πάντων νοερώτερος, ἄφθιτος ἀρχή.
　　　τοῦ δ᾽ ἄπο παγγενέτης νοερὸς λόγος, ἄφθιτος αἰεὶ
　　　υἱός, ἀπαυγὴ τοῦ νοεροῦ πατρός, εἷς ἅμα πατρί,
　　　ἐν μὲν ἐπωνυμίῃ γε διεστηκὼς ἀπὸ πατρός,
　　　εἷς δὲ πέλων σὺν πατρὶ καὶ ἐξ ἑνὸς εἷς· μία δόξα
　　　πατρός, υἱοῦ καὶ πνεύματος ἄφθιτος, αἰὲν ἐοῦσα.

　v. 1. ννους cod.　　v. 4. διεστώς ἀπὸ πατέρος cod.　　v. 6. υἱοῦ cod.
αἰγλήεις, ὁμο[ι]ούσιος, ἄφθιτος υἱός form five feet of another hexameter. ἀπαύγασμα
(cf. ἀπαυγή) is Christian commonplace for the Son in relation to the Father (φῶς);
cf. Cyril, c. _Jul._ 905 A and _passim_. The Σηράγγαι were a Lybian tribe.]

(Here follow in the MS. parallel texts from *Ev. Joh.* and *Ep. ad Hebr.*)

Ἑρμοῦ ἐκ τοῦ πρὸς Ἀσκληπιὸν λόγου γ΄.[1] "τούτου τοῦ πνεύματος, οὗ πολλάκις προεῖπον, πάντα χρῄζεται·[2] πάντα γὰρ βαστάζων[3] κατ' ἀξίαν, τὰ πάντα ζωοποιεῖ καὶ τρέφει, καὶ ἀπὸ τῆς ἁγίας πηγῆς ἐξήρτηται, ⌜ἐπίκουρον πνεῦμα ἦν⌝[4] καὶ ζωῆς ἅπασιν ἀεὶ ὑπάρχον γόνιμον, ἓν ὄν."

(Here 'sequuntur Cyrilli Alex. adversus Julianum fragmenta quatuor', says Pitra.)

(*b*) Pitra, *Anal. Class.* p. 291 (from Cod. Vatican. 1198) :

10 ἄλλος δέ τις τῶν Ἑλλήνων σοφός ⟨. . .⟩· ⌜μεθ' ἑτέρων τινῶν Ἀσκληπιοῦ λεγομένου αἰτησάντων ἑρμηνείαν τῶν πάντων φιλοσόφων φιλοσοφώτερον⌝ δοῦναι αὐτοῖς λόγον περὶ θεοῦ φύσεως· ὁ δὲ Ἑρμῆς[5] σιφέριον[6] ἔγραψεν οὕτως·[7] "εἰ μὴ πρόνοιά τις τοῦ τῶν πάντων[8] κυρίου ⌜οὐ μὴ⌝[9] τὸν λόγον τοῦτον ἀποκαλύψαι ἐβούλετο,[10] οὐδὲ ⌜ἡμᾶς τοιούτοις ἔργοις⌝[11] κατεῖχεν, ἵνα
15 περὶ τούτων ⌜ἐρωτήσεται⌝.[12] ‖[13] οὐ γὰρ ἐφικτόν ἐστιν εἰς ἀμυήτους τοιαῦτα παρασχέσθαι μυστήρια.[14] ἀλλὰ τῷ νοῒ [ἀκουσάντων] ἀκούσατε. ἓν μόνον ἦν φῶς νοερὸν πρὸ φωτὸς νοεροῦ ⌜καὶ ἦν αὐτὰ ἕνωσις ἐκ τοῦ νοῦ⌝ φωτὶ καὶ πνεύματι. ‖ τὰ πάντα ἐξ αὐτοῦ καὶ εἰς αὐτόν.[15] ‖ εἰς γόνιμον ἐκ γονίμου κατελθὼν ἐπὶ γονίμῳ ὕδατι[16] ἔγκυον τὸ ὕδωρ ἐποίησεν."

EXCERPTA E THEOSOPHIA

(Χρησμοὶ τῶν Ἑλληνικῶν θεῶν.)[17]

§ 44. ὅτι πρὸς τὸν ἐρωτήσαντα, εἰ δι' ἐπιμελείας βίου δύναται γενέσθαι

---

[1] Cyril *c. Jul.* 556 B. *Fr.* 24.

[2] χρῄζει Cyril.

[3] τὰ πάντα γὰρ βαστάζον Cyril.

[4] ἐπίκουρον πνεύματι Cyril.

[5] Perhaps, ἑτέρων τινῶν μετὰ τοῦ Ἀσκληπιοῦ λεγομένου αἰτησάντων Ἑρμῆν, τὸν πάντων φιλοσόφων φιλοσοφώτερον, δοῦναι αὐτοῖς λόγον περὶ θεοῦ φύσεως, ὃ δὴ Ἑρμῆς κ.τ.λ.

[6] A *libellus*, from Heb. *sepher*, 'a book'.

[7] Cyril *c. Jul.* 556 B. *Fr.* 24.

[8] τις ἦν τοῦ πάντων Cyril.

[9] ὥστε με Cyril.

[10] ἐβούλετο om. Cyril.

[11] ὑμᾶς νῦν ἔρως τοιοῦτος Cyril.

[12] περὶ τούτου ζητήσητε Cyril.

[13] Cyril *ib.* 556 A. *Fr.* 23. The two fragments are here joined together without any mark of division.

[14] μυστήρια παρέχεσθαι Cyril.

[15] The words φωτὶ καὶ πνεύματι occur (after two lines which are here omitted) in the fragment as given by Cyril; and πάντα ἐν αὐτῷ καὶ ὑπ' αὐτόν ἐστί occurs in another fragment which there follows.

[16] Cyril *ib.* 552 D (ἐν γονίμῃ φύσει πεσὼν ἐπὶ γονίμῳ ὕδατι) εἰς Pitra. *Fr.* 27.

[17] The document entitled Χρησμοὶ τῶν Ἑλληνικῶν θεῶν, preserved in a Tübingen MS., is edited by Buresch in his *Klaros*, 1889, p. 87 *sqq*. It consists of excerpts from a work entitled *Theosophia*, which the excerptor describes as follows: § 1. ὁ τὸ βιβλίον συγγεγραφώς, ὅπερ ἐπιγέγραπται ΘΕΟΣΟΦΙΑ, διαλαμβάνει κατ' αὐτὸ τὸ προοίμιον, ὅτι συνέγραψε μὲν πρότερον ἑπτὰ βιβλία περὶ τῆς ὀρθῆς πίστεως· ἄρτι δὲ τὸ ὄγδοον καὶ τὰ ἐφεξῆς συγγράφει, δεικνὺς τούς τε χρησμοὺς τῶν Ἑλληνικῶν θεῶν καὶ τὰς λεγομένας θεολογίας τῶν παρ' Ἕλλησι καὶ Αἰγυπτίοις σοφῶν, ἔτι δὲ καὶ

θεοῦ ἐγγύς, εἶπεν ὁ Ἀπόλλων· [1]

    ἰσόθεον δίζῃ γέρας εὑρέμεν, οὔ σοι ἐφικτόν.
    Αἰγύπτου τόδε μοῦνος ἕλεν γέρας αἰνετὸς Ἑρμῆς,

τῶν Σιβυλλῶν ἐκείνων ⟨τοὺς χρησμούς⟩, τῷ σκοπῷ τῆς θείας γραφῆς συνᾴδοντας, καὶ ποτὲ μὲν τὸ πάντων αἴτιον καὶ πρωτοστατοῦν, ποτὲ δὲ τὴν ἐν μιᾷ θεότητι παναγίαν τριάδα δηλοῦντας. § 2. ἐν μὲν οὖν τῷ πρώτῳ βιβλίῳ, ὅπερ ἐστὶ ⌜πρὸς προάγοντα⌝ (πρὸς ⟨ὀρθὴν πίστιν⟩ προάγον Buresch : rather, ⟨τῶν⟩ πρὸς⟨ὀρθὴν πίστιν⟩ προαγοντω⟨ν⟩.) τὸ ὄγδοον, καὶ τοῖς ἐφεξῆς δυσί, χρησμῶν τοιούτων μέμνηται καὶ θεολογιῶν. ἐν δὲ τῷ τετάρτῳ ἢ ἑνδεκάτῳ (i. e. in that book which is the fourth of those dealing with ' oracles and theologies ', and the eleventh of the whole work,) παράγει χρήσεις Ὑστάσπου τινὸς κ.τ.λ. In that part of his work in which he sought to show that the θεολογίαι τῶν παρ' Αἰγύπτοις σοφῶν agreed with Holy Scripture, the author of the *Theosophia* doubtless quoted Hermetic passages, such as are employed by Didymus and Cyril for the same purpose; but the excerptor did not transcribe these passages. That the author of the *Theosophia* was well acquainted with the name of Hermes Trismegistus, and probably knew of religious teachings or writings ascribed to him, is shown by § 31 of the *excerpta*: ὅτι ὁ Ἑρμῆς, οὐχ ὁ Τρισμέγιστος, ἀλλ' ὁ λόγιος καλούμενος θεός, χρησμὸν εἶπε τοιοῦτον· Εἷς θεὸς κ.τ.λ.

    A smaller group of excerpts from the *Theosophia* was published by G. Wolff in an appendix to his *Porphyrii de philosophia ex oraculis haurienda librorum reliquiae*, 1856. Another and fuller text of a part of the document edited by Buresch has been published by Mras, *Wiener Studien* 28, 1906, pp. 43 ff.

    Buresch gives sufficient reasons for thinking that the *Theosophia* was written in A.D. 474–491, and that the excerptor wrote after A.D. 692. Cf. *Hermes*, 1880, p. 605.

    Brinkmann, *Rheinisches Museum* LI (1896), pp. 273 ff., discusses an abjuration-formula (probable date A.D. 850–900) drawn up for the use of converts from Manichaeism. This formula was published by Cotelerius, *S. Patr. apostol. opera* (1672) i, pp. 368 ff. It contains a list of books condemned as being favourable to Manichaeism; and among those books is one which is described as follows : τὸν Ἀριστοκρίτου βίβλον, ἣν ἐπέγραψε Θεοσοφίαν, ἐν ᾗ πειρᾶται δεικνύναι τὸν Ἰουδαϊσμὸν καὶ τὸν Ἑλληνισμὸν καὶ τὸν Χριστιανισμὸν καὶ τὸν Μανιχαϊσμὸν ἓν εἶναι καὶ τὸ αὐτὸ δόγμα, καὶ ἵνα πιθανὰ δόξῃ λέγειν, καθάπτεται καὶ τοῦ Μανέντος ὡς πονηροῦ. This description of ' the *Theosophia* of Aristocritus ' agrees very well with what is known to us of the *Theosophia* from which were taken the excerpts edited by Buresch. (It is true that no mention of Manichaeism occurs in those excerpts; but we know that Buresch's *Theosophia* originally contained quotations from the Persian Hystaspes, and it is therefore not unlikely that it also contained some mention of the Persian Mani, who is said to have discussed the prophecies of Hystaspes in the second chapter of his ' Book of Secrets ', Flugel, *Mani*, pp. 102 and 357.) Hence Brinkmann concludes that the ' *Theosophia* of Aristocritus ' spoken of in the abjuration-formula is probably identical with Buresch's *Theosophia*. If we accept the identification, we get, besides the fact (apparently unknown to the Excerptor) that the author's name was (or was thought by some to be) Aristocritus, the additional information that this writer spoke of Mani, and called him πονηρός, but at the same time quoted or referred to passages in Mani's works which showed agreement with Christian doctrine.

  [1] If Buresch is right as to the date of the *Theosophia*, this oracle must have been in existence before A.D. 491. It was most likely composed some considerable time before that date. Its author puts Hermes Trismegistus on a par with Moses and Apollonius of Tyana, and mentions these three as the only men that have ' drawn near to God ', or ' seen God '. He must therefore have known the religious *Hermetica*, and valued their teaching highly. The man who spoke thus of Hermes and Apollonius must have been a Pagan; yet he regarded Moses with equal veneration. In that respect his attitude resembles that of Numenius

Ἑβραίων Μωσῆς, καὶ Μαζακίων[1] σοφὸς ἀνὴρ
ὅν ποτε δὴ χθὼν θρέψεν ἀριγνώτοιο Τυήνης.[2]
θνητοῖς γὰρ χαλεπὸν φύσιν ἄμβροτον ὀφθαλμοῖσιν
εἰσιδέειν, ἢν μή τις ἔχῃ σύνθημα[3] θέειον.

(A. D. 150–200), who said that Plato was 'Moses speaking in Attic Greek' (Clem. Alex. *Strom.* 1. 22. 150). No doubt he thought that Pythagoras and Plato learnt their philosophy partly from Hermes, and partly from Moses.

The prominence given to Apollonius, who is here placed above all other Greek philosophers, suggests a date in the third or fourth century—perhaps the fourth rather than the third. Apollonius lived in the first century p. C. For some time after his death, he seems to have been known chiefly as a miracle-worker or magician, and was hardly classed by general estimation as a philosopher or seer of the highest rank. It was the *Life of Apollonius* written by Philostratus (*c.* A.D. 220), —a work of fiction based on a small substratum of facts,—that established the high repute which attached to his name thenceforward. Philostratus (*Vita Apoll.* 1. 2) describes him as θειότερον ἢ ὁ Πυθαγόρας τῇ σοφίᾳ προσελθόντα; but he adds, οὔπω οἱ ἄνθρωποι γιγνώσκουσιν (αὐτὸν) ἀπὸ τῆς ἀληθινῆς σοφίας, ἣν φιλοσόφως τε καὶ ὑγιῶς ἐπήσκησεν· ... οἱ δὲ ... μάγον ἡγοῦνται αὐτόν, καὶ διαβάλλουσιν ὡς βιαίως σοφόν. In the time of Diocletian (*c.* A.D. 300) the fame of Apollonius was further enhanced by religious controversy. At that time Hierocles, one of the bitterest enemies of the Christians, wrote a book entitled *Philalethes*, in which he sought to disparage Jesus by drawing a comparison between him and Apollonius, to the advantage of the latter; and Eusebius wrote in reply a treatise πρὸς τὰ ὑπὸ Φιλοστράτου εἰς Ἀπολλώνιον τὸν Τυανέα, διὰ τὴν Ἱεροκλεῖ παραληφθεῖσαν αὐτοῦ τε καὶ τοῦ Χριστοῦ σύγκρισιν. (Buresch, *Klaros*, p. 91, says that Hierocles was not the first to draw this comparison, but merely worked it out more fully, and that Apollonius had previously been compared with Jesus by Porphyry; and in proof of this, he refers to Macarius Magnes, ed. Blondel, p. 51. But if it was so, Eusebius was not aware of it; for he says in his treatise, cap. 1 *fin.*, μόνῳ παρὰ τοὺς πώποτε καθ' ἡμῶν γεγραφότας ἐξαίρετος νῦν τούτῳ (sc. Ἱεροκλεῖ) γέγονεν ἡ τοῦδε (sc. Ἀπολλωνίου) πρὸς τὸν ἡμέτερον σωτῆρα παράθεσίς τε καὶ σύγκρισις.—It has been thought by some that Philostratus, in his *Vita Apoll.*, was tacitly comparing this Pagan worker of miracles with Jesus as described in the Gospels; but that opinion seems to me groundless, though it is defended by Zeller, *Philos. der Gr.* III. ii, p. 168.)

In what Eusebius says about the contents of the *Philalethes*, there is no evidence that Hierocles knew anything about Apollonius except what he had read in the *Vita Apoll.* of Philostratus.

Hierocles, inasmuch as his aim was to depreciate Jesus, would have diminished the force of his argument if he had exalted overmuch the man with whom he compared him; and accordingly, he said (Euseb. cap. 2) ἡμεῖς μὲν τὸν ταῦτα πεποιηκότα (sc. Ἀπολλώνιον) οὐ θεόν, ἀλλὰ θεοῖς κεχαρισμένον ἄνδρα ἡγούμεθα· οἱ δὲ δι' ὀλίγας τερατείας τινὰς τὸν Ἰησοῦν θεὸν ἀναγορεύουσι. (Eusebius, on his side, is ready to admit that Apollonius was σοφός τις τὰ ἀνθρώπινα, *ib.* cap. 5.) But others went beyond this; e.g. Eunapius, *Vitae sophist.* (*c.* A.D. 380), *prooem.* p. 3, says that Apollonius was οὐκέτι φιλόσοφος, ἀλλ' ἦν τι θεῶν τε καὶ ἀνθρώπου μέσον.

[1] Mazaca was the earlier name of Caesareia in Cappadocia. Μαζακίων therefore means Καππαδοκῶν; i.e. Apollonius is here called a Cappadocian.

[2] 'Wohl Τυήνης' Buresch: Τυήνας cod. The usual form of the place-name was Τύανα, neut. pl.

[3] σύνθημα apparently means a 'password' by which a man may get admittance to God's presence. If so, the term may have been suggested by the use of a password in certain mystery-rites; but it must here be understood metaphorically.

FULGENTIUS

Fulg. *Mytholog.*[1] 1. 15 (*Fabula de novem Musis*): Septima (*sc.* Musa appellata est) Terpsicore, id est, delectans instructione[m]; unde et Hermes in Opimandrae[2] libro ait 'eccurutrofes et cufusomatos',[3] id est, absque instructione escae et vacuo corpore.

JOANNES LYDUS[4]

De mensibus[5] 4. 7: ὅτι τὸ τῆς Τύχης καὶ Εἱμαρμένης ἐπὶ τῆς γενέσεως προβέβληται ὄνομα· καὶ μάρτυς Ἑρμῆς, ἐν τῷ καλουμένῳ τελείῳ λόγῳ οὕτως εἰπών· "αἱ καλούμεναι ἑπτὰ σφαῖραι ἔχουσιν ἀρχὴν τὴν καλουμένην τύχην ἢ εἱμαρμένην, ἥτις πάντα ἀλλοιοῖ[6] καὶ ἐπὶ τῶν αὐτῶν οὐκ ἐᾷ μένειν. ‖ ἡ δὲ εἱμαρμένη ἐστὶ καὶ ἡ εἱμαρτὴ 5 ἐνέργεια ἢ αὐτὸς ὁ θεὸς ἢ ἡ μετ' ἐκείνην τεταγμένη κατὰ πάντων οὐρανίων τε καὶ ἐπιγείων μετὰ τῆς ἀνάγκης τάξις. καὶ ἡ μὲν αὐτὰς κύει τὰς ἀρχὰς τῶν πραγμάτων, ἡ δὲ καταναγκάζει καὶ τὰ τέλη γίνεσθαι· ταύταις δὲ ἀκολουθεῖ τάξις καὶ νόμος, καὶ οὐδὲν ἄτακτον."[7]

10

ὅτι κατὰ τὰ Ἑρμοῦ δόγματα[8] μᾶλλον ὁ Πορφύριος δοκεῖ λέγειν περὶ τύχης, λέγων οὕτω· "τὴν τύχην οἱ παλαιοὶ τῷ ἑπτὰ ἀριθμῷ συνῆπτον, ὡς τὴν τῶν ἑπτὰ ἐπίκλωσιν ἔχουσαν, ὅσα εἰς τὸ ζῷον καὶ τὴν ἐκτὸς τούτου ἐνέργειαν ἀπ' αὐτῆς ἐπικλώθεται ταύτης κυρίας πάντων γινομένης."

4. 32. ὅτι ὁ Αἰγύπτιος Ἑρμῆς ἐν τῷ λόγῳ αὐτοῦ τῷ καλουμένῳ τελείῳ 15 φησὶ[9] τοὺς μὲν τιμωροὺς τῶν δαιμόνων, ἐν αὐτῇ τῇ ὕλῃ παρόντας, τιμωρεῖσθαι τὸ ἀνθρώπειον κατ' ἀξίαν· τοὺς δὲ καθαρτικούς, ἐν τῷ ἀέρι πεπηγότας, τὰς ψυχὰς μετὰ θάνατον ἀνατρέχειν πειρωμένας ἀποκαθαίρειν περὶ τὰς χαλαζώδεις καὶ πυρώδεις τοῦ ἀέρος ζώνας, ἃς οἱ ποιηταὶ καὶ αὐτὸς ὁ Πλάτων ἐν Φαίδωνι[10] Τάρταρον καὶ Πυριφλεγέθοντα ὀνομάζουσι· τοὺς δὲ σωτηρικούς, 20 πρὸς τῷ σεληνιακῷ χώρῳ τεταγμένους, ἀποσώζειν τὰς ψυχάς.

[1] Fabius Planciades Fulgentius, *Mitologiarum libri tres*, ed. Helm: Teubner, 1898. Date of writing, about A.D. 500.
[2] Opimandrae is genitive of Opimandres, which is ὁ Ποιμάνδρης read as one word.
[3] *Corp.* I. 1: ἐκ κόρου τροφῆς ἢ ἐκ κόπου σώματος. See cr. note on that passage.
[4] *c.* A.D. 550. Lydus held high offices under Anastasius and Justinian, fell into disfavour A.D. 552, and probably lived till a few years after 565.
[5] *Ed.* R. Wünsch: Teubner, 1898. No complete text of Lydus *De mensibus* has been preserved; we have only a series of extracts from it.
[6] αἱ καλούμεναι ... ἀλλοιοῖ: *Ascl. Lat.* 19 b, vol. i, p. 324.
[7] ἡ δὲ εἱμαρμένη ... οὐδὲν ἄτακτον: *Ascl. Lat.* 39, vol. i, p. 362.
Lydus has put together two passages concerning εἱμαρμένη, taken from different parts of the Τέλειος λόγος.
[8] Lydus appears to mean that Porphyry, in connecting τύχη with the influence of the seven planets on earthly life (τὴν τῶν ἑπτὰ ἐπίκλωσιν), accepted the teaching of Hermes on that subject.
[9] See *Ascl. Lat.* 28 and 33 b, vol. i, pp. 366, 370.   [10] Pl. *Phaedo* 112 A–114 B.

4. 53. ὅτι πολλὴ τοῖς θεολόγοις διαφωνὴ περὶ τοῦ παρ' Ἑβραίων τιμωμένου θεοῦ καὶ γέγονε καὶ ἔστιν· Αἰγύπτιοι γὰρ καὶ πρῶτος Ἑρμῆς Ὄσιριν ⟨. . .⟩[1] τὸν ὄντα θεολογοῦσιν αὐτόν, περὶ οὗ Πλάτων ἐν Τιμαίῳ λέγει·[2] "τί τὸ ὂν μὲν[3] ἀεί, γένεσιν δὲ οὐκ ἔχον, τί δὲ τὸ γινόμενον,[4] ὂν δὲ 5 οὐδέποτε ;" Ἕλληνες δὲ τὸν Ὀρφέως Διόνυσον,[5] κ.τ.λ.

4. 64. ἡ γὰρ τοῦ παντὸς αἰσθητοῦ φύσις . . . ἂν εἴη κατὰ τοὺς φυσιολόγους Ἀφροδίτη. . . . ὁ δὲ Χρύσιππος οὐ Διώνην ἀλλὰ Διδόνην αὐτὴν ὀνομάζεσθαι ἀξιοῖ παρὰ τὸ ἐπιδιδόναι τὰς τῆς γενέσεως ἡδονάς, Κύπριν δὲ ὀνομασθῆναι παρὰ τὸ κύειν παρέχειν, καὶ Κυθηρείην ὁμοίως, παρὰ τὸ μὴ 10 μόνον ἀνθρώποις ἀλλὰ καὶ θηρίοις τὸ κύειν ἐπιδιδόναι. ἔνθεν Ἑρμῆς ἐν τῇ κοσμοποιίᾳ τὰ μὲν ὑπὲρ ὀσφὺν ἄρρενα τῆς Ἀφροδίτης, τὰ δὲ μετ' αὐτὴν θήλεα παραδίδωσιν·[6] ὅθεν Πάμφυλοι καὶ πώγωνα ἔχουσαν ἐτίμησαν Ἀφροδίτην ποτέ.[7]

Ib. 4. 149.[8] . . . σα κατὰ τὸν Αἰγύπτιον Ἑρμῆν, ὃς ἐν τῷ[9] λεγομένῳ 15 τελείῳ λόγῳ φησὶν οὕτως· "αἱ δὲ παραβᾶσαι ψυχαὶ τὸν τῆς εὐσεβείας κανόνα, ἐπὰν ἀπαλλαγῶσι τοῦ σώματος, παραδίδονται τοῖς δαίμοσι, καὶ φέρονται κατὰ τοῦ ἀέρος σφενδονούμεναι καὶ κατὰ τὰς πυρώδεις καὶ χαλαζώδεις ζώνας, ἃς οἱ ποιηταὶ Πυριφλεγέθοντα καὶ Τάρταρον καλοῦσιν."[10] καὶ ὁ μὲν 20 Ἑρμῆς περὶ μόνου τοῦ καθαρμοῦ τῶν ψυχῶν,[11] ὁ δὲ Ἰάμβλιχος ἐν τῷ πρώτῳ

---

[1] Wünsch prints Ὄσιριν τὸν ὄντα κ.τ.λ. But that cannot be what Lydus wrote. Ὄσιριν τὸν ὄντα is meaningless ; and Plato does not speak of Osiris in the passage quoted from the *Timaeus.* The best remedy is to assume that there is a lacuna after Ὄσιριν, and that the meaning was 'The Egyptians, and first among them Hermes, say that the God worshipped by the Hebrews is Osiris ; (certain other persons say) that the God worshipped by the Hebrews is ὁ ὤν, that is, the Being whom Plato calls τὸ ὂν ἀεί'. Those who said that the God of the Hebrews was ὁ ὤν were doubtless thinking of *Exodus* 3. 14 : καὶ εἶπεν ὁ θεὸς πρὸς Μωυσῆν λέγων Ἐγώ εἰμι ὁ ὤν. καὶ εἶπεν Οὕτως ἐρεῖς τοῖς υἱοῖς Ἰσραήλ· Ὁ ὢν ἀπέσταλκέν με πρὸς ὑμᾶς.

The mention of Hermes implies that in some *Hermeticum* (perhaps one of the *Isis to Horus* documents) Osiris was said to be identical with the God of the Hebrews. It would not necessarily involve an anachronism to make Hermes speak of the Hebrews, as he was commonly believed to have been nearly contemporary with Moses.

[2] Pl. *Tim.* 27 D.   [3] μὲν om. Pl.   [4] καὶ τί τὸ γιγνόμενον μὲν ἀεί Pl.

[5] In Plut. *Quaest. conviv.* 4. 6, the God of the Jews is identified with Dionysus.

[6] Compare Stob. *Exc.* XXII, Ἑρμοῦ ἐκ τῆς Ἀφροδίτης. It is possible that the *Hermeticum* which is called ἡ κοσμοποιία by Lydus is the same that is called ἡ Ἀφροδίτη by Stobaeus.

[7] As to the notion of a bisexual Aphrodite, see Preller-Robert, p. 509.

[8] This passage, unlike the preceding extracts from the *De mensibus*, is preserved in a fragment of cod. O, which gives the unabbreviated text of Lydus. See Wünsch, *praefatio*, p. lxxxix.

[9] In cod. S (a series of excerpts) the passage begins thus : ὅτι ὁ Ἑρμῆς ἐν τῷ κ.τ.λ.

[10] See *Ascl. Lat.* 28 and 33 b.

[11] That is, the writer of the Τέλειος λόγος spoke only of the 'purgation' of souls in the atmosphere (the subject dealt with in *Ascl. Lat.* 28–33 b), and did not go on to describe the happier condition of the souls when their purgation has been completed, and they have risen out of the atmosphere into the region above the moon.

τῆς περὶ καθόδου ψυχῆς πραγματείας καὶ τῆς ἀποκαταστάσεως[1] αὐτῶν
μέμνηται, τὸν ὑπὲρ σελήνης ἄχρις ἡλίου χῶρον τῷ Ἅιδῃ διδούς, παρ' ᾧ φησι
καὶ τὰς ἐκκεκαθαρμένας ἑστάναι ψυχάς, καὶ αὐτὸν μὲν εἶναι τὸν Πλούτωνα,
Περσεφόνην δὲ τὴν σελήνην. ταῦτα μὲν οἱ φιλό⟨σοφοι⟩.

JOANNES MALALAS [2]

Dindorf, *Jo. Malalae Chron.* p. 45 f.; Migne *Patr. Gr.* tom. 97,

[1] The ἀποκατάστασις of the souls means their return to their original situation
and condition. This implies that, according to Iamblichus, the souls, before their
embodiment on earth, dwelt in heaven (above the moon) and not in the atmosphere
(below the moon).

[2] Joannes Malalas, of Antioch in Syria, wrote his Chronicle about A.D. 528–573.
His account of the reign of Sesostris, including the passage about Hermes, was
transcribed almost word for word by the writer of the *Chronicon Paschale*,
c. A.D. 629, and was repeated, with slight verbal alterations, by Cedrenus in his
Historiarum compendium, c. A.D. 1067. The passage about Hermes was transcribed from Malalas (or from some later chronicle based on that of Malalas) by
Suidas also in his Lexicon, c. A.D. 950.

Ducange, in a note on *Chron. Pasch.* (Migne *P. G.* 92. 169), says ' Haec eadem
verba [sc. the Hermetic passage ἦν φῶς νοερὸν κ.τ.λ.] descripsere Symeon Logotheta
in Chron. ms. et ex eo Cedrenus et Suidas in v. Ἑρμῆς'. According to Krumbacher,
Gesch. der byz. Litt. pp. 200 and 358, there are extant in manuscript two distinct
Chronica, one of which (cod. Messin. 85 &c.) is rightly, and the other (cod. Paris.
1712) wrongly, ascribed to ' Symeon, Magister and Logothetes' (who is probably
identical with Symeon Metaphrastes, A.D. 950–1000). Both these *Chronica* were
still unpublished in 1897. It is to be inferred from Ducange's note that either the
Chronicon rightly ascribed to Symeon or that of ' Pseudo-Symeon' contains a
transcript of the passage of Malalas here printed, and that Cedrenus may have got
it from that source.

The Chronicle of Malalas is extant in one manuscript only, viz. Cod. Oxon. Bodl.
Baroccianus 182, ' saec. forsan XII exeuntis'. I have seen the manuscript, and
verified from it Dindorf's printed text of this passage.

Malalas got the contents of his paragraph on Hermes from Cyril *c. Julianum*
552 C–556 C (*Testim.*). But he read Cyril carelessly, and blundered. Cyril gives
a quotation from Orpheus (οὐρανὸν ὁρκίζω σε κ.τ.λ.), followed by seven distinct
quotations from Hermes. Malalas, overlooking the words καὶ μὴν καὶ Ὀρφεύς in
Cyril's text, thought that the ὁρκισμός, as well as the extracts from *Hermetica*,
were ascribed by Cyril to Hermes; hence he says that Hermes (not Orpheus) ηὔξατο
λέγων " ὁρκίζω σε κ.τ.λ.". He picked out some of Cyril's quotations, and omitted the
rest; and he shifted those which he selected, giving the Hermetic extracts in the
order 7 (first part only), 5, 6, 1, and placing after them the Orphic ὁρκισμός, which
Cyril had placed before them. He says that the Hermetic passages which he quotes
occurred ' in different discourses addressed to Asclepius'; whereas Cyril said that
three of them occurred in one and the same discourse addressed to Asclepius (ἐν λόγῳ
τρίτῳ τῶν πρὸς Ἀσκληπιόν), and did not say to whom the fourth (ὁ γὰρ λόγος . . .
ὕδωρ ἐποίησε) was addressed. And though Malalas says that they occurred ' in
different discourses', he does not indicate the points at which one quotation ends
and another begins, but lumps them together as if they were continuous speech.

It is indeed possible that Malalas had not himself read Cyril, but got at second
or third hand his information as to what Cyril had said, and that he was misled by
the intermediaries. But as Malalas made strange mistakes in other matters (e. g.
he puts Sappho in the time of Cecrops, and Democritus in the time of Pelops, he

col. 92 : καὶ λοιπὸν ἐν τοῖς μετὰ ταῦτα χρόνοις ἐβασίλευσεν Αἰγυπτίων πρῶτος ἐκ τῆς φυλῆς τοῦ Χὰμ ⟨Σέ⟩σωστρις.¹ . . .

ἐν τοῖς χρόνοις τῆς βασιλείας τοῦ προειρημένου ⟨Σε⟩σώστρ⟨ι⟩ος² ἦν Ἑρμῆς ὁ Τρισμέγιστος ὁ Αἰγύπτιος, ἀνὴρ φοβερὸς ἐν σοφίᾳ· ὃς ἔφρασεν
5 τρεῖς μεγίστας ὑποστάσεις εἶναι ⌈τὸ τοῦ ἀρρήτου καὶ δημιουργοῦ ὄνομα⌉,³ μίαν δὲ θεότητα εἶπεν ⟨εἶναι⟩·⁴ διὸ καὶ ἐκλήθη ἀπὸ τῶν Αἰγυπτίων Τρισμέγιστος Ἑρμῆς. ἐμφέρεται γὰρ ἐν διαφόροις αὐτοῦ λόγοις πρὸς Ἀσκληπιὸν εἰρηκὼς περὶ θεοῦ φύσεως ταῦτα· " εἰ μὴ⁵ πρόνοιά τις ἦν τοῦ πάντων κυρίου ὥστε μοι τὸν λόγον τοῦτον ἀποκάλυψαι, οὐδὲ ὑμᾶς τοιοῦτος ἔρως
10 κατεῖχεν ἵνα περὶ τούτου ζητήσητε.⁶ ‖ οὐ γὰρ ἐφικτόν⁷ ἐστιν ⟨εἰς⟩⁸ ἀμυήτους τοιαῦτα μυστήρια παρέχεσθαι. ἀλλὰ τῷ νοῒ ἀκούσατε. ἐν μόνον ἦν [τὸ] φῶς⁹ νοερὸν πρὸ φωτὸς νοεροῦ, καὶ ἦν ἀεὶ νοῦς νοὸς φωτ⟨ε⟩ινός, καὶ οὐδὲν ἕτερον ἦν ἢ τούτου ἑνότης. ἀεὶ ἐν αὐτῷ ὤν, ἀεὶ τῷ αὐτοῦ¹⁰ νοῒ καὶ φωτὶ καὶ πνεύματι πάντα περιέχει. ‖ ἐκτὸς τούτου¹¹ οὐ θεός, οὐκ ἄγγελος,
15 οὐ δαίμων, οὐκ οὐσία τις ἄλλη· πάντων γὰρ κύριος ⟨καὶ πατὴρ⟩ καὶ θεός,¹²

makes Herodotus a successor of Polybius, and he describes Cicero and Sallust as great Roman poets), it is most likely that he was the man who blundered in this case also.

The mistakes of Malalas were repeated by the writer of *Chron. Pasch.*, by Suidas, and by Cedrenus, because they merely copied from him, and did not look up the passage in Cyril. The variant readings of *Chron. Pasch.*, Suidas, and Cedrenus in the Hermetic passages quoted are given in my notes on Cyril.

¹ Σῶστρις cod. Malal. : Σέσωστρις Cedrenus.
² Σώστρου cod. Malal. : Σεσώστριος *Chron. Pasch.*
³ ὃς ἔφρασεν . . . δημιουργοῦ ὄνομα cod. Malal. : ὅστις ἔφρασεν τρεῖς μεγίστας δυνάμεις εἶναι τὸ τοῦ ἀρρήτου καὶ δημιουργοῦ θεοῦ ὄνομα *Chron. Pasch.* : ὃς ἔφρασε τρεῖς μεγίστας εἶναι δυνάμεις τοῦ δημιουργοῦ τῶν ὅλων θεοῦ Cedrenus. The sense seems to be rightly given by Cedrenus; and the text of Malalas might be made to agree with that of Cedrenus by emending it thus: ὃς ἔφρασε τρεῖς μεγίστας εἶναι ὑποστάσεις (or δυνάμεις) [τὸ] τοῦ [ἀρρήτου καὶ] δημιουργοῦ ⟨τ⟩ῶν ὅλων ⟨θεοῦ⟩. If Malalas wrote τῶν ὅλων, it must have been corrupted into ὄνομα in the copy of Malalas which was used by the writer of *Chron. Pasch.*, but preserved unaltered in the copy used by Cedrenus.
⁴ μίαν δὲ θεότητα εἶπεν cod. Malal. : μίαν δὲ θεότητα εἶπεν εἶναι *Chron. Pasch.* : εἰπὼν ἐν τριάδι μίαν εἶναι θεότητα Suidas : μίαν θεότητα εἶναι εἶπε Cedrenus. But the clause μίαν δὲ θεότητα εἶπεν εἶναι looks like a later addition, the sense would be improved if it were cut out, and Τρισμέγιστος thereby brought nearer to τρεῖς μεγίστας. Perhaps Malalas wrote ἔφρασε τρεῖς μεγίστας εἶναι ὑποστάσεις τοῦ δημιουργοῦ τῶν ὅλων θεοῦ· διὸ καὶ ἐκλήθη Τρισμέγιστος.
⁵ εἰ μὴ . . . ζητήσητε, Cyril *c. Jul.* 556 B. εἰ μὴ . . . ἐν μόνον (i. e. the whole of the first quotation from Hermes and the beginning of the second) is omitted by Suidas and Cedrenus, who make the speech ascribed to Hermes begin with the words ἦν φῶς νοερόν.
⁶ ζητήσετε cod. Malal. : ζητήσητε Cyril, *Chron. Pasch.*
⁷ οὐ γὰρ ἐφικτόν . . . πάντα περιέχει, Cyril *c. Jul.* 556 A.
⁸ εἰς *Chron. Pasch.*, Cyril : om. cod. Malal.
⁹ ἦν φῶς *Chron. Pasch.*, Suidas, Cedrenus, Cyril : ἐστὶ τὸ φῶς cod. Malal.
¹⁰ τῷ αὐτῷ cod. Malal. : τῷ ἑαυτοῦ *Chron. Pasch.*, Cedrenus, Cyril.
¹¹ ἐκτὸς τούτου . . . ἐν αὐτῷ ἐστίν, Cyril *c. Jul.* 556 A B.
¹² κύριος καὶ θεός cod. Malal. : κύριος καὶ πατὴρ καὶ θεός *Chron. Pasch.*, Suidas : κύριος καὶ θεὸς καὶ πατήρ Cedrenus : κύριος καὶ πατὴρ καὶ θεὸς καὶ πηγὴ καὶ ζωὴ καὶ δύναμις καὶ φῶς καὶ νοῦς καὶ πνεῦμα Cyril.

καὶ πάντα ὑπ' αὐτὸν καὶ ἐν αὐτῷ ἐστιν. ‖ ὁ γὰρ λόγος¹ αὐτοῦ προελθών, παντέλειος ὢν καὶ γόνιμος καὶ δημιουργός, ἐν γονίμῳ φύσει πεσὼν ἐν γονίμῳ ὕδατι, ἔγκυον τὸ ὕδωρ ἐποίησε." καὶ ταῦτα εἰρηκὼς ηὔξατο λέγων· "⟨⟨οὐρανὸν⟩⟩ ὁρκίζω σε, [[οὐρανέ]],² θεοῦ μεγάλου σοφὸν ἔργον·³ [ἵλαος ἔσο]⁴ ὁρκίζω σε φωνή⟨ν⟩⁵ πατρός, ἣν ἐφθέγξατο⁶ πρώτην, ἡνίκα κόσμον 5 ἅπαντα ἐστηρίξατο βουλῇ."⁷ φωνὴν⁸ πατρός, ἣν ἐφθέγξατο πρώτην,⁹ τὸν μονογενῆ λόγον αὐτοῦ ⟨φησιν⟩.¹⁰ ταῦτα δὲ καὶ ἐν τοῖς κατὰ Ἰουλιανοῦ τοῦ βασιλέως ὑπὸ τοῦ ὁσιωτάτου Κυρίλλου συναχθεῖσιν¹¹ ἐμφέρεται, ⟨πρὸς ἀπόδειξιν σαφεστέραν⟩¹² ὅτι καὶ ὁ Τρισμέγιστος Ἑρμῆς, ἀγνοῶν τὸ μέλλον, τριάδα ὁμοούσιον ὡμολόγησεν. 10

ὁ δὲ ⟨Σέ⟩σωστρις¹³ βασιλεὺς μετὰ τὴν νίκην καταλαβὼν τὴν Αἴγυπτον τελευτᾷ· καὶ ἐβασίλευσε μετ' αὐτὸν τῆς τῶν Αἰγυπτίων χώρας Φαραὼ ὁ καὶ ⌜Ναραχὼ⌝¹⁴ καλούμενος. καὶ ἐκ τοῦ αὐτοῦ γένους ἐβασίλευσαν Αἰγυπτίων οἱ λοιποί.¹⁵

---

¹ ὁ γὰρ λόγος . . . ὕδωρ ἐποίησεν, Cyril c. Jul. 552 D.

² οὐρανὸν ὁρκίζω σε . . . λόγον αὐτοῦ φησιν, Cyril c. Jul. 552 C.

³ ὁρκίζω σε οὐρανὲ θεοῦ μεγάλου σοφὸν ἔργον cod. Malal., Suidas: οὐρανὸν ὁρκίζω σε θεοῦ μεγάλου σοφὸν ἔργον Chron. Pasch., Cyril: ὁρκίζω σε οὐρανοῦ μεγάλου ἐργάτα Cedrenus. It is to be inferred from the reading of Chron. Pasch. that Malalas copied the hexameter correctly from Cyril, and wrote οὐρανὸν ὁρκίζω σε; but this was altered into ὁρκίζω σε οὐρανέ before the time of Suidas.

⁴ ἵλαος ἔσο cod. Malal.: ἵλεως ἔσο Chron. Pasch. (ἵλεως, ἵλεως ἔσο post περιέχοντος πάντα Suidas: ἵλεως ἔσο post λόγον αὐτοῦ Cedrenus). The person who inserted the words ἵλεως ἔσο must have meant them to be addressed to God, or to the μονογενὴς λόγος, and not to οὐρανός. They are manifestly out of place in cod. Malal. and Chron. Pasch., but are better placed in the texts of Suidas and Cedrenus, in which they stand at the end of the ὁρκισμός.

⁵ ὁρκίζω σε φωνῇ cod. Malal.: ὁρκίζω σε φωνὴν Chron. Pasch., Suidas: ὁρκίζω σε φωνὴ Cedrenus: αὐδῇν ὁρκίζω σε Cyril.

⁶ ἐφθέγξατο cod. Malal., Chron. Pasch., Suidas, Cedrenus: φθέγξατο Cyril.

⁷ κόσμον ἅπαντα ἐστηρίξατο βουλῇ cod. Malal., Chron. Pasch.: τὸν πάντα κόσμον ἐστηρίξατο Suidas: κόσμον ἅπαντα ἑαῖς στηρίξατο βουλαῖς Cyril.

⁸ φωνὴν cod. Malal., Chron. Pasch.: αὐδῇν δὲ Cyril.

⁹ ἡνίκα κόσμον . . . ἐφθέγξατο πρώτην om. Cedrenus (homoioteleuton). φωνὴν πατρὸς ἣν ἐφθέγξατο πρώτην (post ἐστηρίξατο) om. Suidas.

¹⁰ φησιν Cyril: om. cod. Malal., Chron. Pasch., Suidas, Cedrenus. Suidas, taking the words τὸν μονογενῆ λόγον αὐτοῦ (which were written by Cyril as part of his comment on the ὁρκισμός) to be a part of the ὁρκισμός itself, has altered them into ὁρκίζω σε κατὰ τοῦ μονογενοῦς αὐτοῦ λόγου, and added καὶ τοῦ πατρὸς κ.τ.λ.

¹¹ συνταχθεῖσιν Chron. Pasch.

¹² πρὸς ἀπόδειξιν σαφεστέραν Chron. Pasch.: om. cod. Malal.

¹³ Σέσωστρις Chron. Pasch., Cedrenus: Σῶστρις cod. Malal.

¹⁴ Ναραχὼ cod. Malal.: Νάχωρ Chron. Pasch.: Ναρεχὼ Cedrenus. Perhaps Malalas wrote Νεχαώ (cf. Φαραὼ Νεχαώ, 'Pharaoh-Necoh', in 2 Kings 23. 29 ff.). He probably meant by 'Pharaoh' the earliest king called by that name in the Bible, i.e. the Pharaoh who was king of Egypt in the time of Abraham (Gen. 12. 15). Malalas would be quite capable of confusing him with the Pharaoh-Necoh of Josiah's time.

¹⁵ This sentence is obscure; and the meaning of what Malalas wrote is probably more correctly given by the corresponding sentence of Cedrenus, ἐκ τούτου οἱ ἀπὸ τοῦ γένους αὐτοῦ καταγόμενοι βασιλεῖς Φαραὼ προσαγορεύονται.

Chronicon Paschale (ed. Dindorf: Migne *Patr. Gr.* tom. 92, col. 169–171): ἐν τοῖς μετὰ ταῦτα χρόνοις ἐβασίλευσεν τῶν Αἰγυπτίων ... Σέσωστρις ... ἐκ τοῦ αὐτοῦ γένους ἐβασίλευσαν Αἰγυπτίων οἱ λοιποί.

Suidas [1] (ed. Bernhardy): Ἑρμῆς ὁ Τρισμέγιστος. οὗτος ἦν Αἰγύ-
5 πτιος σοφός· ἤκμαζε δὲ πρὸ τοῦ Φαραώ.[2] ἐκέκλητο δὲ Τρισμέγιστος, διότι
περὶ τριάδος ἐφθέγξατο, εἰπὼν ἐν τριάδι μίαν εἶναι θεότητα, οὕτως· " ἦν φῶς
νοερὸν πρὸ φωτὸς νοεροῦ ... ἔγκυον τὸ ὕδωρ ἐποίησε." καὶ ταῦτα εἰρηκὼς
ηὔξατο λέγων· " ὁρκίζω σε, οὐρανέ, θεοῦ μεγάλου σοφὸν ἔργον· ὁρκίζω σε
φωνὴν πατρός, ἣν ἐφθέγξατο πρώτην, ἡνίκα τὸν πάντα κόσμον ἐστηρίξατο·
10 ὁρκίζω σε κατὰ τοῦ μονογενοῦς αὐτοῦ λόγου, καὶ τοῦ ⌐πατρὸς⌐ [τοῦ μονογενοῦς λόγου, καὶ τοῦ πατρὸς][3] τοῦ περιέχοντος πάντα· ἵλεως, ἵλεως ἔσο.'

Cedrenus, *Hist. Compend.* (ed. Bekker: Migne, tom. 121, col. 64):
μετὰ δὲ τοῦτον Σέσωστρις τῶν Αἰγυπτίων ἐπὶ εἴκοσιν ἔτη ἐβασίλευσεν. ...

ἐπὶ τούτου Ἑρμῆν φασιν ἐν Αἰγύπτῳ θαυμαστὸν ἄνδρα γνωσθῆναι καὶ
15 φοβερὸν ἐπὶ σοφίᾳ· ὃς ἔφρασε τρεῖς μεγίστας εἶναι δυνάμεις τοῦ δημιουργοῦ
τῶν ὅλων θεοῦ, μίαν ⟨δὲ⟩ θεότητα εἶναι εἶπε· διὸ καὶ Τρισμέγιστος κατωνό-
μασται. ὃς οὕτω πρός τινα Ἀσκληπιὸν αὐτοῖς ῥήμασιν ἔφη· " ἦν φῶς
νοερὸν πρὸ φωτὸς νοεροῦ ... ἔγκυον τὸ ὕδωρ ἐποίησεν." οὕτως εἰπὼν ὁ
Ἑρμῆς ηὔξατο· " ὁρκίζω σε, οὐρανοῦ μεγάλου ἐργάτα, ὁρκίζω σε, φωνὴ
20 πατρός, ἣν ἐφθέγξατο πρώτην, τὸν μονογενῆ λόγον αὐτοῦ, ἵλεως ἔσο." τῶν
φωνῶν τούτων καὶ ὁ ἱερὸς Κύριλλος ἐμνήσθη, εἰπὼν ὅτι καὶ ὁ Τρισμέγιστος
Ἑρμῆς τριάδα ὡμολόγει.[4]

ὁ δὲ Σέσωστρις μετὰ τὴν νίκην τὴν Αἴγυπτον καταλαβὼν τελευτᾷ.
ἀνέστη δὲ μετ' αὐτὸν βασιλεὺς ἐπ' Αἴγυπτον Φαραὼ ὁ καὶ Ναρεχὼ καλού-
25 μενος, κρατήσας ἔτη, ὥς φασι, πεντήκοντα.· ἐκ τούτου οἱ ἀπὸ τοῦ γένους
αὐτοῦ καταγόμενοι βασιλεῖς Φαραὼ προσαγορεύονται.

---

[1] This article of Suidas was printed by Flussas as a part of ' Caput XV ' of his *Mercurii Trismegisti Pimandras.* Fr. 27. See pp. 202–203.

[2] ' Hermes flourished before the time of Pharaoh.' Suidas got this from Malalas, who said that Hermes lived in the time of Sesostris, and that Sesostris was succeeded by (the first) Pharaoh.

[3] κατὰ τοῦ μονογενοῦς αὐτοῦ λόγου, καὶ τοῦ πατρὸς τοῦ μονογενοῦς λόγου, καὶ τοῦ πατρὸς Bernhardy. But the words τοῦ μονογενοῦς λόγου καὶ τοῦ πατρός are omitted in the best MSS. of Suidas; and it is evident that the repetition of these words is a copyist's error. There can be little doubt that πατρός is a mistake for πνεύματος (abbreviated πν̄ατος), and that Suidas wrote ὁρκίζω σε κατὰ τοῦ μονογενοῦς αὐτοῦ λόγου, καὶ τοῦ πνεύματος τοῦ περιέχοντος πάντα. Cf. καὶ πνεῦμα πάντα περιέχον in the preceding speech of Hermes as given by Suidas. See p. 202.

[4] [This group of fragments is also given by Johannes Antiochenus. See Addenda.]

ARTEMII PASSIO [1]

§ 26. καὶ ὁ παραβάτης·[2] "ἀνόσιε[3] καὶ τῆς τῶν θεῶν εὐμενείας ἀλλότριε, χθιζὸς ὢν ὁ Χριστὸς καὶ ἐφήμερος, κἀκ τῶν τοῦ Καίσαρος Αὐγούστου χρόνων ἀρξάμενος, αἰώνιος βασιλεὺς ὑπὸ σοῦ κεχειροτόνηται σήμερον;"

[1] The *Artemii Passio* was published by Mai, *Spicilegium Romanum* 4. 340 sqq., and reprinted in the *Acta Sanctorum*, Oct. 8, 856 *sqq.*, and in Migne *P. G.* 96. 1251 *sqq.*; and parts of it, including the passages here printed, have been re-edited by Bidez, in his edition of the *Church-History* of Philostorgius (*Die griech. Christ-lichen Schriftsteller d. ersten drei Jahrhunderte*), 1913. It is preserved in ten or more Greek MSS. (saec. XI–XIII), and in Slavonic and Armenian translations; and it is transcribed, with some alterations, in the *Hagiographia* of Symeon Metaphrastes (Migne *P. G.* 115. 1159 *sqq.*). This text follows Bidez.

According to the title in the MSS., the author of *Art. Pass.* was Ἰωάννης μοναχὸς ὁ Ῥόδιος. Mai took this to mean Joannes Damascenus (A.D. 800–850); but Bidez rejects this identification, and says that 'John the monk of Rhodes' is a man of whom nothing else is known.

The writer of *Art. Pass.* based his narrative of the martyrdom of Artemius on a short *martyrium* of earlier date, written in simple and popular style, which is printed by Bidez (*Philostorgius*, Anhang II). This he supplemented by extracts from the *Church-History* of Philostorgius (*c.* A.D. 425), and by materials taken from other sources, and worked up the whole into a composition in ornate style. The story which he tells is this: Eugenius and Macarius, two Christian presbyters, were summoned before Julian at Antioch, and each of them in turn, after a disputa-tion with the wicked emperor, was tortured by his order. Artemius, *dux* of Egypt, who was present in the court, intervened on behalf of these two men, and protested against Julian's maltreatment of them; whereupon the emperor, after an argument with him, condemned him to torture and death.

The date of *Artemii Passio* is not precisely determined. Krumbacher (*Byz. Litt.* p. 199) puts it in the ninth century. Bidez says merely that *Art. Pass.* must have been written before the time of Symeon Metaphrastes (A.D. 950–1000), and fixes no *terminus a quo*; but as some time must be allowed for the development of the legend before the writing of the early *martyrium*, and that document is spoken of as 'ancient' (ἀρχαῖον) by the writer of *Art. Pass.*, the latter can hardly have been composed very long before A.D. 800.

Artemius is known to historians as a man who was made *dux* of Egypt by Constantius, and was put to death in Julian's reign. His trial and execution (A.D. 362) are spoken of by Ammianus Marcellinus, 22. 11: 'Artemius . . . Alexandrinis urgentibus atrocium criminum mole, supplicio capitali multatus est. . . . Perlato laetabili nuntio indicante extinctum Artemium, plebs omnis (of Alexandria), elata gaudio insperato', proceeded to lynch the much-hated bishop George, whom Artemius had helped and supported with the armed force under his command. It appears that one of the charges brought against Artemius was that he had been an accomplice in the murder of Julian's elder brother Gallus by Constantius (*Art. Pass.* §§ 36, 40, 44, presumably based on Philostorgius). The martyrologist's assumption that Julian put men to death merely because they professed the Christian religion is of course groundless; but it is very likely that the fact that Artemius had taken part in the sacking of a Pagan temple (Julian *Ep.* 10, 379 A B) made the emperor more disposed to treat him with severity. Gibbon (ch. 22) remarks that the Greek and Latin Churches have honoured Artemius as a martyr, though 'ecclesiastical history attests that he was not only a tyrant, but an Arian'.

Most of the statements about Hermes in *Art. Pass.* may have been derived indirectly from Cyril *c. Julianum*; but the immediate source of them was probably a writing of the same character as Buresch's *Theosophia*, and closely related to it, if not that very work itself.

[2] *Sc.* Julian.   [3] Addressed to Eugenius.

καὶ ὁ μάρτυς· "ναί, κατὰ τὸ ἀνθρώπινον καὶ τὸ τῆς ἀφράστου καὶ ἀρρήτου
οἰκονομίας αὐτοῦ μυστήριον, εἴτ᾽ οὖν σαρκώσεως, οὕτως ἔχει, βασιλεῦ· ἐπεὶ
κατὰ τὴν θείαν αὐτοῦ καὶ προαιώνιον γέννησιν οὐδεὶς εὑρεθήσεται χρόνος ὁ
ταύτης ὑπέρτερος."

5   καὶ ὁ παραβάτης, νομίσας ἀπαίδευτον εἶναί τινα τὸν τοῦ Χριστοῦ μάρτυρα
καὶ τῆς Ἑλληνικῆς σοφίας ἀμέτοχον, διαχλευάζων ἔφη πρὸς αὐτόν· "οὐκοῦν,
ὦ ταλαίπωρε, ὁ Χριστός σου δὶς ἄρα γεγέννηται; καὶ εἰ ἐπὶ τούτῳ κομπά-
ζεις, εἰσὶ καὶ παρ᾽ Ἕλλησιν ἄνδρες σοφώτατοι οὐ μόνον δὶς γεννηθέντες,
ἀλλὰ καὶ τρίς· ὅ τε γὰρ Ἑρμῆς, ὁ Τρισμέγιστος ἐπικαλούμενος, τρίτον
10 ἦλθεν ἐν κόσμῳ ἑαυτὸν ⌜ἐπιγνούς⌝,[1] καθὼς αἱ ἱεραὶ αὐτοῦ καὶ θαυμάσιοι
βίβλοι[2] διαγορεύουσι, καὶ διὰ τοῦτο Τρισμέγιστος ὀνομάζεται. ὁμοίως δὲ
καὶ Πυθαγόρας, ὁ τούτου μεταγενέστερος, καὶ αὐτὸς τρίτον ἦλθεν ἐν βίῳ,
πρότερον μὲν Αἰγύπτιος γεγονὼς ναύκληρος, ἔπειτα δ᾽ Εὔφορβος, ὁ ὑφ᾽
Ὁμήρου μνημονευόμενος, ἔσχατον δὲ Πυθαγόρας, Μνησάρχου υἱός, Σάμιος."

15   27. καὶ ὁ μάρτυς,[3] καταγελάσας τῶν ληρημάτων, μᾶλλον δὲ κομψευ-
μάτων, τοῦ σοφοῦ βασιλέως, καὶ τῆς τῶν ἀσεβῶν Ἑλλήνων μωρολογίας
ὑπονοήσας δὲ τὸν τύραννον τὴν τοῦ Χριστοῦ γέννησιν διὰ τουτωνὶ τῶν
ῥημάτων χλευάζειν πειρώμενον, ἔφη πρὸς αὐτὸν μετὰ πολλῆς αὐστηρίας καὶ
γενναιότητος·

20   "ἔδει τὴν ἀρχὴν μηδὲ ἀποκρίνασθαί σοι, παρανομώτατε, μηδὲ τῆς
οἱασοῦν ἀπολογίας καταξιῶσαί σε· ἀλλὰ διὰ τὸν παρεστῶτα ὄχλον, ὅτι τῆς
τοῦ Χριστοῦ ποίμνης οἱ πλείονες αὐτῶν τυγχάνουσιν, εἶπον ὅσαπερ εἶπον,
καὶ νῦν ἐπ᾽ ὀλίγον ἐρῶ, τῆς αὐτῶν κηδόμενος σωτηρίας, ὅτι τὸν Χριστὸν
ἄνωθεν καὶ πρὸ πολλῶν γενεῶν οἱ προφῆται προκατήγγειλαν, καὶ πολλὰ τῆς
25 παρουσίας αὐτοῦ τὰ μαρτύρια κᾀκ τῶν παρ᾽ ὑμῖν χρησμῶν καὶ τῶν Σιβυλ-
λείων γραμμάτων.[4] καὶ τῆς ἐπανθρωπήσεως αὐτοῦ ἡ αἰτία ἐπὶ σωτηρίᾳ

---

[1] ἐπιδεικνὺς M, Symeon Metaphr.: ἐπιγνοὺς codd. cett.
   Cf. Cyril *c. Julianum* 769 B: Ἑρμοῦ τοῦ τρίτον (legendum τοῦ τρίτου, τοῦ ἐν) τῇ
Αἰγύπτῳ ἐπιδημήσαντος (al. ἐπιφοιτήσαντος). The statement in *Art. Pass.* is
apparently derived from that passage. If so, the writer of *Art. Pass.*, or the author
of the book from which that writer got his information about Hermes, probably
read τοῦ τρίτον τῇ Αἰγύπτῳ ἐπιφοιτήσαντος in his text of Cyril, and supposed those
words to mean that Hermes was thrice incarnated on earth, and that his third birth
took place in Egypt. The notion that Hermes was thrice incarnated does not, as
far as I know, occur elsewhere.
   [2] The writer knows of the existence of 'holy books' ascribed to Hermes; and
he also knows (§ 28) that some of the discourses of Hermes were addressed to Tat,
and others to Asclepius. That much he might have learnt from Cyril *c. Julianum*.
There is no evidence that he had himself read any Hermetic writings; and his
statement that 'the books of Hermes say' that Hermes was thrice incarnated is
probably a groundless assumption.   [3] *Sc.* Engenius.
   [4] See § 46 below. The Sibylline writings, as well as numerous χρησμοὶ τῶν
Ἑλληνικῶν θεῶν, are cited in Buresch's *Theosophia*, but not in Cyril *c. Julianum*.
This makes it probable that the immediate source of this passage in *Art. Pass.*
was the *Theosophia* or some document closely related to it.

καὶ ἀνακλήσει τῆς τῶν ἀνθρώπων ἐκπτώσεως γέγονεν· ἐλθὼν γὰρ ἐπὶ τῆς
γῆς, πᾶσαν νόσον ἀπήλασε καὶ πᾶσαν μαλακίαν, . . . καὶ τὸ δὴ πάντων
θαυμασιώτερον, ὑπὲρ τῆς τοῦ κόσμου σωτηρίας παθὼν τὸ διὰ τοῦ σταυροῦ
πάθος, ἀνέστη τριήμερος ἐκ τῶν νεκρῶν . . . καὶ ἀναστὰς ἐκ τῶν νεκρῶν
ὤφθη τοῖς μαθηταῖς αὐτοῦ . . ., καὶ ὁρώντων αὐτῶν καὶ βλεπόντων ἀνελήφθη   5
εἰς τοὺς οὐρανούς, ἐξαποστείλας αὐτοῖς τὴν τοῦ ἁγίου πνεύματος δωρεάν τε
καὶ δύναμιν . . . . οἵτινες ἐξελθόντες ἐκήρυξαν αὐτὸν πανταχοῦ, μηδὲν
ἐπιφερόμενοι ἢ μόνην τὴν ἀόρατον αὐτοῦ δύναμιν, οὐκ ἀσπίδα καὶ δόρυ καὶ
ξίφος κατέχοντες, ἀλλὰ γυμνοὶ καὶ ἄοπλοι καὶ πένητες, πάντα τὸν κόσμον
ἐζώγρησαν, νεκροὺς ἐγείροντες, λεπροὺς καθαρίζοντες, δαιμόνια ἐκβάλλοντες.   10
καὶ ταῦτα τίνες ; ἁλιεῖς καὶ ἀγράμματοι καὶ τῆς τοῦ κόσμου σοφίας
ἀμέτοχοι.

§ 28. οὓς δὲ αὐτὸς παρεισήγαγες, ἐπικερτομῶν τὴν Χριστοῦ γέννησιν,
ἄνδρας σοφούς τε καὶ θεολόγους, ὡς νῦν εἴρηκας, εἰ καὶ δοίημεν ἀληθὲς[1]
γενέσθαι τοῦτο τὸ παραλήρημα, τί γεννηθέντες δίς τε καὶ τρὶς καὶ τετράκις   15
τὸν κόσμον ὠφέλησαν, ἢ μέρος τι τῶν τοῦ κόσμου μικρὸν ἢ ἐλάχιστον ; τίς
ἐκ τῶν βίβλων Ἑρμοῦ τε καὶ Πυθαγόρου νεκροὺς ἐξανέστησεν, ἢ λεπροὺς
ἐκαθάρισεν, ἢ δαίμονας ἀπήλασεν, οὓς ὑμεῖς θεραπεύετε ; ἀλλ᾽ Ἑρμῆς μέν,
ὁ Τρισμέγιστος ὑφ᾽ ὑμῶν προσαγορευόμενος, Αἰγύπτιος γέγονεν ἄνθρωπος,
καὶ τοῖς Αἰγυπτίων νόμοις τραφεὶς γυναῖκά τε γήμας παῖδας ἐτέκνωσεν, ὧν   20
τὸν πρεσβύτερον Τὰτ ὀνομάζουσι·[2] πρὸς ὃν αὐτὸς διαλέγεται καὶ τοὺς
ἑαυτοῦ λόγους ἀφοσιοῖ, πρός τε τὸν ἐξ Ἐπιδαύρου Ἀσκληπιὸν[3] τὸν προκα-
τάρξαντα καθ᾽ ὑμᾶς τῆς ἰατρικῆς ἐπιστήμης. ᾧ καὶ τὴν ἑαυτοῦ θεολογίαν
διασαφεῖ ἔχουσαν οὕτως· "θεὸν νοῆσαι μὲν χαλεπόν, φράσαι δὲ
ἀδύνατον."[4] ἔστι γὰρ τρισυπόστατος, ἀνερμήνευτος οὐσία καὶ φύσις,   25

---

[1] ἀληθὲς Bidez : ἀληθῶς Symeon Metaphr.

[2] Tat is the only son of Hermes that is mentioned in our *Hermetica*. What
reason the writer had for thinking that Hermes had other sons, I do not know.

[3] The writer identifies the Asclepius of the *Hermetica* with the Greek god of
healing.

[4] Herm. *ap.* Stob. *Exc.* I. The writer of *Art. Pass.* may have found this quotation in the *Theosophia* ; and the writer of the *Theosophia* may have got it from
Cyril *c. Julianum* 549 B. We know from Lactantius and Stobaeus that the words
θεὸν νοῆσαι μὲν χαλεπόν, φράσαι δὲ ἀδύνατον occurred in a discourse addressed to
Tat ; but Cyril does not say to whom they were addressed.
    The passage which follows these words in *Art. Pass.* (ἔστι γὰρ τρισυπόστατος . . .
ἐπεσπάσαντο) is printed by Bidez as a continuation of the quotation from Hermes.
But that passage certainly did not occur in the Hermetic *libellus* from which θεὸν
νοῆσαι μὲν χαλεπόν, φράσαι δὲ ἀδύνατον is quoted; and if Bidez is right, it would appear
that the writer of *Art. Pass.* must have found the words of Hermes (θεὸν . . . ἀδύνατον)
followed by the comment ἔστι γὰρ τρισυπόστατος . . . ἐπεσπάσαντο in his source, and
mistakenly thought that the whole passage was there ascribed to Hermes.
    For τρισυπόστατος in this connexion, cf. Ἑρμῆς ὁ Τρισμέγιστος . . . ὃς ἔφρασεν τρεῖς
μεγίστας ὑποστάσεις εἶναι κ.τ.λ. in Malalas, p. 233, l. 4 above (based on Cyril).

οὐκ ἔχουσα παρὰ βροτοῖς ἐξομοίωσιν·[1] οὓς δὲ θεοὺς ὀνομάζουσιν ἄνθρωποι, πολὺ τὸ μυθῶδες καὶ σφαλερὸν ἐφ' ἑαυτοὺς ἐπεσπάσαντο.

καὶ περὶ τῆς Χριστοῦ ἐλεύσεως καὶ αὐτὸς ἀμυδράν τινα προφητείαν διαγορεύει,[2] οὐκ ἐξ ἑαυτοῦ, ἀλλ' ἐκ τῆς Ἑβραίων θεολογίας ταύτην ἀπαρυσά-
5 μενος.[3]

ἀλλὰ τί μοι τῶν σαπρῶν τε καὶ ὀδωδότων Ἑρμοῦ ῥημάτων τῶν παρ' ὑμῖν τιμωμένων, ἤδη πρὸ πολλοῦ σεσηπότων καὶ ἀπερρυηκότων; οὐδὲ γὰρ ὅσιον περὶ τῶν ζώντων ἐρωτᾶν τοὺς νεκρούς, ἔχων[4] ἐκ τῶν θεοσόφων λογίων τοὺς ἀληθεῖς μάρτυρας, οἳ τὴν τοῦ Χριστοῦ παρουσίαν τε καὶ θεότητα προ-
10 κατήγγειλαν.

§ 29. Πυθαγόρας δέ, ὁ τῆς Ἰταλικῆς κατάρξας αἱρέσεως, τί μέγα καὶ θαυμαστὸν ἐν τῷ βίῳ τρὶς παραχθεὶς ἀπειργάσατο; ἢ ὅτι . . .; ταῦτα ὁ τρὶς γεννηθεὶς ἐθαυματούργει ἐν Ὀλυμπίᾳ γενόμενος, δοξομανῶν καὶ φαντασιούμενος ὁ τρισάθλιος, ...

15 § 30. ταῦτα τῶν σῶν φιλοσόφων τὰ προτερήματα, τῶν δὶς καὶ τρὶς γεννηθέντων ὡς αὐτὸς ἐρητορεύσας· κἀκεῖνα τοῦ ἐμοῦ Χριστοῦ ἐπὶ σωτηρίᾳ καὶ ἀνακλήσει τοῦ τῶν ἀνθρώπων γένους τὰ τερατουργήματα.

καὶ Πυθαγόρας μὲν καὶ Ἑρμῆς τὰς τῶν ἀνθρώπων ψυχὰς εἰς τὸν Ἅιδου πυθμένα κατάγουσι, μετεμψυχώσεις[5] δή τινας καὶ μεταγγισμοὺς παρεισά-
20 γοντες, ποτὲ μὲν εἰς ἄλογα ζῷα καὶ θηρία ταύτας μεταβιβάζοντες, ποτὲ δὲ εἰς ἰχθύας καὶ φυτὰ[6] καὶ ἄλλας τινὰς ἐπανακυκλήσεις καὶ περιόδους κατα- σπῶντες αὐτὴν καὶ ἀπορραπίζοντες· ὁ δὲ Χριστός, καθὸ θεὸς ὑπάρχων ἀληθὴς καὶ αἰώνιος, ἀθάνατον αὐτὴν καὶ ἀγήρω κατασκευάσας τῷ ἀπ' ἀρχῆς πνεύ- ματι θείῳ καὶ ἐμφυσήματι,[7] ὅτε τὸν πρῶτον ἐδημιούργησεν ἄνθρωπον, . . .
25 καὶ πεσοῦσαν[8] μετὰ τοῦ σώματος διὰ τῆς παρακοῆς καὶ τῆς ἀπάτης τοῦ

---

[1] Cf. Herm. *ap.* Cyril *c. Julianum* 549 C : τὸ ἑαυτῷ ⟨μόνῳ?⟩ ὅμοιον [ὃ μήτε ἄλλῳ ὅμοιόν ἐστι μήτε ἑαυτῷ ἀνόμοιον].

[2] This may perhaps be a vague reference to the Hermetic passages quoted by Cyril (552 B &c.) concerning God's λόγος. But the words περὶ τῆς Χριστοῦ ἐλεύσεως ἀμυδράν τινα προφητείαν διαγορεύει would apply better to the description of the *mundi regenitura* in the Prophecy of Hermes, *Ascl. Lat.* III. 26 a (which is explained by Lactantius as meaning 'missuiri a patre tunc filium dei, qui deletis omnibus malis pios liberet'). If that is the passage to which the writer of *Art. Pass.* is here referring, the source in which he found it must have contained a Hermetic extract not derived from Cyril.

[3] This agrees with Cyril's view that Hermes learnt from Moses.

[4] ἔχων Bidez : ἔχοντας Symeon.

[5] For μετεμψύχωσις, see note in vol. II, pp. 269 ff. The μετενσωμάτωσις of souls is asserted in some of our *Hermetica*, but not in any of Cyril's quotations from Hermes.

[6] The re-embodiment of human souls in plants is not, I think, mentioned in any of the extant *Hermetica*. It was not commonly taught by Platonists ; but it was spoken of by Empedocles, and by Plotinus. See *Corp.* X. 7.

[7] Perhaps πνεύματος θείου ἐμφυσήματι.

[8] πεσοῦσαν ⟨ἰδὼν⟩?

ψυχοφθόρου δράκοντος, ἐλθὼν ἐπὶ γῆς καὶ πολιτευσάμενος[1] καὶ ὑποδείξας
ἡμῖν ὁδὸν σωτηρίας διὰ τοῦ βαπτίσματος καὶ τῆς ἐκ νεκρῶν αὐτοῦ ἀναστά-
σεως, ἐκ τῶν τοῦ Ἅιδου πυθμένων εἰς οὐρανοὺς ταύτην ἐπανήγαγεν· καὶ
πάλιν ἐρχόμενος κρῖναι ζῶντας καὶ νεκροὺς ἐξαναστήσει τὰ σώματα καὶ
συνάψει ταῖς ἑαυτῶν ψυχαῖς, καὶ ἀποδώσει ἑκάστῳ κατὰ τὰ ἔργα αὐτοῦ. ... 5

§ 34. καὶ ὁ παραβάτης· " ἀλλὰ Κωνσταντῖνος, οἰκτρότατοι, νεωτερίσας[2]
διὰ τὰς προσπεσούσας αὐτῷ ἀνοσιουργίας ἀπέστη τῶν θεῶν, ὑφ' ὑμῶν τῶν
Γαλιλαίων ἐξαπατηθείς, ἅτε δὴ παιδείας ἀμέτοχος, καὶ μήτε τοῖς Ῥωμαϊκοῖς
νόμοις μήτε τοῖς Ἑλληνικοῖς ἔθεσιν ἐμπεδωθείς. ἐγὼ δέ, ὦ ἀνόσιε,[3] τῆς
Ἑλληνικῆς τε καὶ Ῥωμαϊκῆς παιδείας ἄκρως ἐπειλημμένος, καὶ ταῖς τῶν 10
παλαιῶν ἀνδρῶν θεολογίαις, Ἑρμοῦ[4] τέ φημι καὶ Ὀρφέως καὶ Πλάτωνος,
ἐξησκημένος, οὐχ ἥκιστα δὲ καὶ ταῖς Ἰουδαϊκαῖς γραφαῖς ἐξωμιληκὼς καὶ
τὴν τούτων τερθρείαν πεπατηκώς, πάλιν ἐπὶ τὸ πατροπαράδοτον καὶ ἀρχαιό-
τατον καὶ θεοφιλὲς τοὺς ἀνθρώπους ἔθος τε καὶ σέβας ⌐μένειν⌐ διακελεύομαι
ἢ ταῖς τῶν ἀπαιδεύτων καὶ νεωτεριζόντων ἀνοίαις ἀκολουθεῖν." [5]   15

§ 46 (*Artemius loquitur*): " τὸν Χριστὸν ἄνωθεν οἱ προφῆται προκατήγγειλαν, ὡς καὶ αὐτὸς κρεῖττον ἐπίστασαι. καὶ πολλαὶ τῆς αὐτοῦ
παρουσίας αἱ μαρτυρίαι κἀκ τῶν παρ' ὑμῖν σεβομένων θεῶν καὶ τῶν χρησμῶν αἱ προαγορεύσεις, τά τε Σιβύλλεια γράμματα καὶ ἡ τοῦ Βιργιλίου τοῦ
Ῥωμαίου ποίησις ἣν ὑμεῖς βουκολικὴν ὀνομάζετε·[6] καὶ αὐτὸς ὁ παρ' ὑμῖν 20
θαυμαζόμενος Ἀπόλλων ὁ μαντικὸς τοῖον δή τινα περὶ Χριστοῦ ἐξεφώνησε
λόγον. ἐρωτηθεὶς γὰρ παρὰ τῶν ἑαυτοῦ προπόλων, ἀποκρίνεται ὧδε·[7]

---

[1] πολιτευσάμενος. [See Addenda.]

[2] Κωνσταντῖνος οἰκτρότατα νεωτερίσας Symeon.

[3] Addressed to Macarius.

[4] On the question whether the *Hermetica* were known to Julian, see note on
Cyril *c. Julianum* 769 B.

[5] πάλιν . . . μένειν . . . ἤ is unintelligible. The sense required is given by
Symeon Metaphr., who writes πάλιν ἐπὶ τὸ . . . σέβας ἀνατρέχειν διακελεύομαι,
μακρὰ χαίρειν εἰπὼν ταῖς τῶν ἀπαιδεύτων κενολογίαις.

[6] Virg. *Ecl.* 4.

[7] The oracle μὴ ὄφελές πύματόν με . . . βιάζεται οὐράνιος φῶς is quoted, with some
variations, in the *Excerpta e Theosophia* (Buresch, *Klaros*), § 16 : ὅτι ἐρωτήσαντός
ποτε τοῦ ἱερέως τὸν Ἀπόλλωνα περὶ τῆς μελλούσης κρατεῖν θρησκείας, παράδοξον εἶπε
χρησμὸν τοιοῦτον· Μὴ ὄφελες . . . οὐράνιος φῶς. Another text of the same oracle
was found by Buresch (*Klaros* p. 130) in a MS. of the twelfth or thirteenth century
in the National Library at Athens : ὅτι ὁ ψευδώνυμος τῶν Ἑλλήνων θεὸς Ἀπόλλων,
⌐ὅτε⌐ ἐρωτήθη ὑπό τινος τῶν αὐτοῦ ἱερέων περὶ τοῦ Χριστοῦ, χρησμὸν ἔφησε τόνδε, ὃς
καὶ εὕρηται ἐν Δελφοῖς ⌐τῆς Ἰταλίας⌐ κατὰ τὸ α´ ἔτος τῆς βασιλείας Ἀναστασίου
[A.D. 491], γενομένης ἐπομβρίας μεγάλης κατακλυσμοῦ δύναμιν ἐχούσης, ἐγγεγραμμέ-
νος εἰς τὸ θεμέλιον τοῦ αὐτοῦ εἰδώλου· ἔχει δὲ ὁ χρησμὸς οὕτως· Μή μ' ὄφελες πύματόν
τε . . . βιάζεται οὐράνιος φῶς.
This oracle was evidently composed by a Christian. An oracle which resembles
it in containing distinctively Christian doctrine is quoted by Didymus *De trin.* 2. 27,
Migne 753 B (πνεῦμα μὲν ἀθανάτοιο κ.τ.λ.). In the *Excerpta e Theosophia* there is
a group of other oracles of similar character ascribed to Pagan gods, viz. :

§ 45. ὅτι ἐν Ὄμβροις (ὄμβραις MS.), τῷ φρουρίῳ τῆς ἐν Αἰγύπτῳ (Αἰγύπτου

μὴ ὄφελες πύματόν με[1] καὶ ὕστατον[2] ἐξερέεσθαι,
δύσμορ' ἐμῶν[3] προπόλων, περὶ θεσπεσίοιο θεοῖο[4]

Buresch᾽ Θηβαΐδος. ἦν χρησμὸς γεγραμμένος τοιοῦτος· "τὸν λόγον υἷα θεοῖο θεόν τε λόγον καλέουσι, | καὶ θεότης κοινή τις ἐν υἱῷ καὶ γενετῆρι." Ombros is another form for Ombos.

§ 46. ὅτι ἐν ⟨Κοπ⟩τῷ, τῇ πόλει Αἰγύπτου, ὁ χρησμὸς οὗτος ἦν γεγραμμένος, καὶ ἀποκρίσεως καὶ ἐρωτήσεως (perhaps καὶ ἐρωτήσεις καὶ ἀποκρίσεις ⟨ἔχων⟩?)· "ʿοὐρανὸς αὐτολόχευτος, ἐμέ ... νε τοῦτο δίδαξονˮ (perhaps σύ με, ⟨κοίρα⟩νε, τοῦτο δίδαξον)." | "ʿἀλλ' αὐτὸνˮ ἔτευξε λόγος (perhaps λόγῳ), λόγον υἷα φυτεύσας· | οἱ δύο δ' αὖ εἰς εἰσι, πατὴρ καὶ κύδιμος υἱός." | "ἀλλά μοι ἔννεπε τοῦτο· τίς ἐς χθόνα δῖαν ἱκάνων | ἄρρητος σοφίην βροτέην ἐδίδαξε γενέθλην;" (Read ἄρρητον σοφίην κ.τ.λ.: 'Who was it that came down to earth and taught mortal men wisdom that was (till then) unrevealed?')| "ἐκ προθύρων γενετῆρος, ἀπ' οὐρανίων κορυφάων | ⟨... κατελθὼν ⟩ υἱὸς ὕλην κόσμησε βροτῶν πολυτειρέα φύτλην, | καί μιν ἑοῦσ' ἄχραντος ἀπειρήτη θ' ὑμεναίων | παρθενικὴ ἐλόχευσε πόνων ἄτερ Εἰληθυίης." (It may be conjectured that the first question and answer were to this effect: 'Is heaven self-engendered?' 'No; God made it by his Logos, who is God's son.' Cf. *Orac. Sibyll.* I. 19 ff.: αὐτὸς (sc. θεός) ταῦτ' ἐποίησε λόγῳ, — καὶ πάντ' ἐγενήθη | ὦκα καὶ ἀτρέκεως, ʿὅδε γὰρ πέλετ' αὐτολόχευτοςˮ, — | οὐρανό(θε)ν καθορῶν· ʿὑπὸˮ (οὕτω?) τετέλεστο δὲ κόσμος. Sense might be made of that passage by writing [αὐτὸς] ταῦτ' ἐποίησε λόγῳ [καὶ πάντ' ἐγενήθη ὦκα καὶ ἀτρέκεως], — οὐ γὰρ πέλει αὐτολόχευτα, — | οὐρανόθεν καθορῶν.)

§ 47. ὅτι ἐν Ἐλεφαντίνῃ, τῇ πόλει Αἰγύπτου, χρησμὸς ἐγέγραπτο τοιοῦτος· "πνεῦμα θεόρρητον φυσίζοον εἰκόνα πατρὸς | ἀμφὶς ἔχει· γενετὴρ δ' ἔλαχ' υἷεα, παῖς δὲ τοκῆα· | οἱ τρεῖς, οἱ δ' αὖ εἰσι μία φύσις, αὐτοὶ ἐν αὐτοῖς."

§ 48. καὶ ἕτερος χρησμὸς τοιοῦτος· "τὸν θεὸν αὐτογένεθλον ἀείναον αὐδάξαντο | ἄνθρωποι, ʿλόγον ἁγνὸνˮ (perhaps λόγου ἁγνοῦ) ὅσοι σοφίην ἐδάησαν, | καὶ λόγον ἀγλαὸν υἷα πανομφαίοιο θεοῖο, | πνεῦμα δ' ἐν ἀμφοτέροισιν ἀκηράσιον ζάθειον· | εἰσὶ δέ τις τριὰς ἁγνὴ ἐν ἀλλήλοισιν ἐόντες."

§ 49. See n. 14 on p. 22. 6 above.

§ 51. ὅτι ἡ Ἄρτεμις ὀλοφυρομένη πρὸς τὸν ἑαυτῆς εἶπε τεμενίτην χρησμὸν τοιοῦτον· "παῖς Ἑβραῖος κέλεταί με, θεὸς μακάρεσσιν ἀνάσσων, | οὐρανόθεν καταβάς, βρότεον δέμας ἀμφιπολ[ιτ]εύων, | δύμεναι εἰς Ἀΐδαο καὶ ἐς Χάος ʿνῦνˮ (ἀψ?) ἀφικέσθαι. | κείνῳ δ' οὐκ ἔστιν τὸ δεδογμένον ἐξαλέασθαι. | χάζομαι, ὡς ἐθέλει· τί νυ μήσομαι, δαίμονες ἄλλοι;" (Another version of this is given by Malalas, p. 298 Dindorf, and repeated, with slight variations, by Cedrenus p. 205 B, I, p. 360 Bekker, and by Suidas: Αὔγουστος Καῖσαρ θυσιάσας ἤρετο τὴν Πυθίαν τίς μετ' αὐτὸν βασιλεύσει. She answered, "παῖς Ἑβραῖος κέλεταί με θεοῖς μακάρεσσιν ἀνάσσων | τόνδε δόμον προλιπεῖν καὶ (ἐς) Ἄιδην αὖθις ἵκεσθαι. | ʿλοιπὸν ἄπιθι σιγῶν ἐκ βωμῶν ἡμετέρωνˮ [perhaps σιγῶν λοιπὸν ἄπελθε θυρῶν ἐξ ἡμετεράων].")

To these may be added an oracle given by Malalas p. 27, *Chron. Pasch.* I. p. 84 (Dindorf), Cedrenus p. 20, Zonaras ann. p. 1048, and Suidas (Wolff *De noviss. orac. act.* p. 14): Θοῦλις ... πάσης Αἰγύπτου βασιλεὺς ... παραγέγονεν εἰς τὸ μαντεῖον τοῦ Σαράπιδος. καὶ θυσιάσας ἐρωτᾷ ταῦτα· "φράσον ἡμῖν ... τίς πρὸ τῆς ἐμῆς βασιλείας ἐδυνήθη τοσαῦτα· ἢ τίς ἔσται μετ' ἐμέ;" καὶ ἐδόθη αὐτῷ χρησμὸς ἔχων οὕτως· "πρῶτα θεός, μετέπειτα λόγος, καὶ πνεῦμα σὺν αὐτοῖς. | ταῦτα δὲ σύμφυτα πάντα, καὶ ἔντυπον εἰς ἕν' ἰόντα, | οὗ κράτος ἐστ' αἰώνιον. ὠκέσι ποσσὶ βάδιζε, | θνητέ, ʿἄδηλον δὴˮ (perhaps θνήτ', ἄδηλον ἄδην) ἀνύων βίον, ἆσσον ἐκείνων.

These oracles were presumably (like the Christian *Oracula Sibyllina*) forged by Christians in imitation of oracles of similar form which had been forged by Jews.

[1] μὴ ὤφελες πύματόν με Art. Pass. (Bidez): μὴ ὄφελες πύματόν με Exc. e Theosophia (Buresch *Klaros* p. 99): μὴ μ' ὄφελες πύματόν τε cod. Ath. (Buresch *Klaros* p. 130).

[2] The question which the priest has asked Apollo to answer is 'the last', because the god is about to be expelled from his temple, and the oracle will never be consulted again.

[3] δύσμορ' ἐμῶν Art. Pass. and cod. Ath.: δύστηνε Exc. e Th.

[4] θεσπεσίοιο θεοῖο Art. Pass. and cod. Ath.: θεσπεσίου γενετῆρος Exc. e Th. Post γενετῆρος add. ἀμφί τε τηλυγέτοιο πανομφαίου βασιλῆος Exc. e Th. The

καὶ πνοιῆς τῆς πάντα πέριξ βοτρυηδὸν ἐχούσης,[1]
τείρεα, φῶς, ποταμοὺς καὶ Τάρταρον,[2] ἠέρα καὶ πῦρ·
ἤ με καὶ οὐκ ἐθέλοντα δόμων ἀπὸ τῶνδε διώκει,[3]
ἡ δὲ ἐμὴ ⌜τριπόδων ἔτι λείπετο ἠριγένεια⌝.[4]
αἲ αἴ με,[5] τρίποδες, στοναχήσατε· οἴχετ' Ἀπόλλων,   5
οἴχετ', ἐπεὶ ⌜βροτός⌝[6] με βιάζεται οὐράνιος φώς.
καὶ ὁ παθὼν θεός ἐστι, καὶ οὐ θεότης πάθεν αὐτή.[7]

τηλύγετος βασιλεύς is God the Son ; and the epithet πανομφαῖος is meant to imply that he is the Logos. The author of the *Theosophia* explains the verse thus : καὶ τοῦ μονογένους καὶ ἀγαπητοῦ υἱοῦ αὐτοῦ, τοῦ πάσης θείας φήμης καὶ κληδόνος αἰτίου· ὀμφὴ γὰρ ἡ θεία κληδὼν καὶ προαγόρευσις ἡ τὸ ὂν φαίνουσα.

[1] τῆς πάντα πέριξ βοτρυηδὸν (or βοτρυδὸν) ἐχούσης *Art. Pass.* and cod. Ath.: ἡ πάντα πέριξ βοτρυδὸν εἴσχει *Exc. e Th.* The Holy Spirit encompasses all things, and 'holds them clustered together'.

[2] τείρεα, φῶς, ποταμοὺς καὶ Τάρταρον *Art. Pass.* and cod. Ath.: οὔρεα, γῆν, ποταμούς, ἅλα, Τάρταρον *Exc. e Th.*

[3] διώκει *Art. Pass.* and cod. Ath.: διώξει *Exc. e Th.*

[4] ἡ δὲ ἐμὴ τριπόδων ἔτι λείπετο ἠριγένεια *Art. Pass.*: ἡ δὲ ἐμὴ τριπόδων ἐπιλείπεται ἠριγένεια cod. Ath.: αὐτίκ', ἐρημαῖος δὲ λελείψεται οὐδὸς ἀφήτωρ *Exc. e Th.* [The oracle that follows in Buresch (18. v. 2) ends: οἲ οἴ, χρησμῶν ὑπολείπεται ἠριγένεια, where χρησμῶν has a variant τριπόδων.]

[5] αἲ αἴ με *Art. Pass.* and cod Ath.: οἴμοι ἐγώ *Exc. e Th.*

[6] ἐπεὶ βροτός με *Art. Pass.*: ἐπεί με βροτός cod. Ath.: ἐπεὶ φλογύεις (με add. Buresch) *Exc. e Th.* βροτός must have been inserted as a gloss on φώς The φλογύεις οὐράνιος φώς is Christ (ὁ ἐξ οὐρανοῦ κατελθὼν καὶ γενόμενος ἄνθρωπος, νοητὸν πῦρ ὑπάρχων, says the author of the *Theosophia*). Perhaps the Christian forger found in a Sibylline oracle the phrase φλογόεν με βιάζεται οὐράνιον φῶς (spoken. not by the god, but by the Sibyl—cf. Virg. *Aen.* 6. *init.*, and *Orac. Sibyll.* 3. 1-7 and 296 *sqq.*; 11. 322 *sqq.*; 12. 297 *sqq.*). and altered the words to suit his purpose.

[7] The verse καὶ ὁ παθὼν κ.τ.λ. has nothing to do with the oracle to which it is appended in *Art. Pass.* It is the first line of a *poematium* of different origin. in which the speaker is not the god Apollo, but a human worshipper of Christ (Χριστὸς ἐμὸς θεός ἐστιν). That *poematium* is given in full (as a continuation of the oracle μὴ ὄφελες . . . οὐράνιον φώς) in Buresch's Athens MS., and, in a less complete form, in one of the MSS. of *Art. Pass.* (viz. cod. T, Parisinus, saec. XII); but in the other MSS of *Art. Pass.* only the first verse of it has been retained, and it is altogether absent in *Exc. e Theosophia*. It must have stood next after the oracle of Apollo in the common source of the Athens MS. and of our text of *Art. Pass.*; and the transcribers mistakenly supposed it to be a continuation of that oracle. It may be reconstructed as follows :

καὶ ὁ παθὼν θεός ἐστι, καὶ οὐ θεότης πάθεν αὐτή·
ἄμφω γὰρ βροτὸς ἦεν ὅμως καὶ ἄμβροτος αὐτός,
ἀθάνατος θνητός τε, θεοῦ λόγος ἀνδρομέη σάρξ,
οὔτε ἀμειβομένων οὔτ' ἐς χύσιν ἄμφω ἰόντων
5   οὔθ' ἕκας ἀλλήλων· αὐτὸς θεὸς ἠδὲ καὶ ἀνήρ,
πάντα φέρων παρὰ πατρός, ἔχων δέ τε μητρὸς ἅπαντα,
ἀθανάτου παρὰ πατρὸς ἔχων φυσίζοον ἀλκήν,
μητρὸς δ' ἐκ θνητῆς σταυρόν, τάφον, ὕβριν, ἀνίην
[πανθ' ἅμα εἰσορόαν τε καὶ ⌜ἀμφιθέων⌝ καὶ ἀκούων.]
10   τοῦ καὶ ἀπὸ βλεφάρων ποτ' ἐχεύατο δάκρυα θερμά,
εὖτέ μιν ἀγγελίη λυγρὴ μόλεν οἷο φίλοιο·
αὐτὸς καὶ ⌜θρήνων πρόφασιν λύσεν ἐκ τοῦ Ἅιδου⌝
ἀνέρα τὸν θρήνησε, παλίσσυτον ἐς φάος ἕλκων·
ὡς βροτὸς ἐθρήνησε, καὶ ὡς θεὸς ἐξεσάωσε.
⟨ —— —— —— —— —— —— ·⟩

PSELLUS

Psellus,[1] Ἀλληγορία περὶ τοῦ Ταντάλου:[2] τοιαύτη μὲν καὶ ἡ δευτέρα δόξα περὶ τοῦ Διὸς τοῖς Ἕλλησιν. ἡ δὲ τρίτη[3] ἱστορικωτέρα καὶ ἴσως[4]

15   πέντε τε χιλιάδας πυρῶν ἐκ πέντ' ἐκόρεσσεν
    οὔρεσιν ἐν ταναοῖσι, τὸ γὰρ θέλεν ἄμβροτος ἀλκή.
    Χριστὸς ἐμὸς θεός ἐστιν, ὃς ἐν ξύλῳ ἐξετανύσθη,
    ὃς θάνεν, ὃς τάφον ἦλθεν, ὃς ἐκ τάφου ἐς πύλον ὦρτο.

Line 2. (ἄμφω . . . αὐτός) cod. T of *Art. Pass.*: om. cod. Ath. (Buresch)
3. θνητός τε cod. Ath.: θνητὸς (om. τε) T | ἀνδρομέη cod. Ath.: ἀνδρομαίη T
4. ἀμειβομέναν cod. Ath.: ἀμειβόμενος T | χύσιν T: σχίσιν cod. Ath.   5. οὔθ'
ἑκὰς cod. Ath.: ἀτεκὰς T   6, 7. ἔχων δέ . . . παρὰ πατρὸς cod. Ath.: om. T
7. ἀθανάτου scripsi: ἀθάνατος cod. Ath. | φυσίζοον cod. Ath.: φυσίζωον T   8. δὲ
ἐκ θνητῆς T: δὲ θνητῆς cod. Ath. | ὕβριν, ἀνίην cod. Ath.: ὑβριανίην T   9. πάνθ'
ἅμα cod. Ath.: πᾶν θαῦμα T | ἀμφιθέων, 'running round', is not a suitable word
to stand between 'seeing' and 'hearing'. Perhaps ἀμφαφάων. | This verse breaks
the connexion of thought between l. 8 and l. 10; I have therefore bracketed it.
10–14. Lazarus, *Ev. Joh.* 11.   12. Perhaps θρήνων πρόφασιν (?) ἐξ Ἅιδου ἔλυσεν.
The phrase θρήνων πρόφασιν ('the cause of his lamentations', in apposition to
ἀνέρα) might be allowed to stand: but in that case, we must suppose that τὸν
θρήνησε (which may easily have come from -τὸς ἐθρήνησε in the following line) has
been wrongly substituted for something else.   15. One or more lines must have
been lost before this verse. The sense may have been '(He felt hunger (*Matth.* 4.
2, *Luke* 4. 2; *Matth.* 21. 18), and therein is seen the frailty of his human nature;
he fed five thousand (*Mark* 6. 35 *sqq.*), and therein he showed the might of his
divine nature.' | Five πυροί (grains of wheat) have been substituted for the five ἄρτοι
of the Gospels.   17. ἐν ξύλῳ T: ἐς ξύλον cod. Ath.   18. ἐς πόλον ὦρτο cod.
Ath.: ἀπόλον ὄρτω T

[1] Born A. D. 1018; lived till after A. D. 1075. See C. Zervos, *Michel Psellos*,
Paris, 1920.
[2] This *opusculum* is an allegorical explanation of the myth of Tantalus. It has
been edited by Cramer, *Anecd. Gr.*, Oxon., iii, pp. 408–411, and by Boissonade,
Tzetzes-Psellos, Paris, 1851. Cramer used the Bodleian MS. Auct. T. II. 15;
Boissonade used Gesner's edition of A. D. 1544, and two Paris MSS., viz.
no. 1182 (A) and no. 3058 (B). Title, Ἀλληγορία περὶ τοῦ Ταντάλου τοῦ σοφω-
τάτου Ψέλλου Cramer: Μιχαὴλ τοῦ Ψέλλου ἀναγωγὴ εἰς τὸν Τάνταλον Boissonade.
[3] Psellus gives three opinions of the Greeks concerning Zeus, and is inclined to
accept the third, which is that Zeus and Kronos were men, and were deified after
death. With this third opinion, he says, Hermes agrees. But what is the 'myth'
that Hermes accepted? Apparently it is the story that Zeus and Kronos were
born and died on earth as men, and became gods after their death; but would that
be called a 'myth'?
The passage to which Psellus refers is probably *Corp.* X. 5. Hermes there
speaks of 'our ancestors Uranos and Kronos', not of Zeus and Kronos; but he
implies that they were formerly men living on earth, and says that after their
release from the body they have attained to the beatific vision; and when Tat says
'Would that we also might attain to it', Hermes replies 'Would that we might,
my son'. This might be described as 'inciting Tat to imitate them' (πρὸς τὴν
ἐκείνων μίμησιν τὸν ἑαυτοῦ παῖδα διερεθίζει).
Psellus speaks of the attitude of Hermes with respect to the myths in general.
This seems to imply that he had read a good many *Hermetica*; for unless he had
done so, he could hardly have made a general statement of this kind about the
teaching of Hermes. His meaning appears to be that Zeus and the other
individual gods of Pagan mythology are rarely spoken of in the *Hermetica*, and
that the stories told about them by the Greeks are hardly ever referred to; and
that is true.   [4] καὶ ἴσως Boissonade: ἴσως καὶ Cramer.

ἀληθεστέρα· αὐτόν τε γὰρ καὶ τὸν τούτου πατέρα τὸν Κρόνον οἱ μῦθοι[1]
ὁμόθεν ἀπὸ Κρήτης γεννῶσι, καὶ τὸν μὲν οὐκ ἴσασιν ὅπου[2] γῆς κατορώρυκται,
τοῦ δ' ἐπὶ τῷ τάφῳ δεικνύουσι κολωνόν· εἶτα τὴν θνητὴν ὑπεραναβάντες
φύσιν[3] ἀγχισπόρους ποιοῦσι τῆς οὐσίας τοῦ κρείττονος, καὶ πρὸς τὸ τῆς
θειότητος εἶδος μεταβιβάζουσι, τούτῳ δὴ τῷ λόγῳ καὶ Ἑρμῆς προστίθεται 5
ὁ Τρισμέγιστος· τἄλλα γὰρ παραθεωρῶν τοὺς μύθους,[4] τοῦτον δὴ μόνον
γυμνὸν ἐξεδέξατο, καὶ πρὸς τὴν ἐκείνων μίμησιν τὸν ἑαυτοῦ παῖδα διερεθίζει
τὸν Τάτ.[5]

Psellus, Ἀπολογία ὑπὲρ τοῦ Νομοφύλακος κατὰ τοῦ Ὀφρυδᾶ (Sathas,
Μεσαιωνικὴ βιβλ. V, p. 189): Ζωροάστρην δὲ ποῦ θήσεις τὸν Αἰγύπτιον,[6] 10
ἢ Ἑρμῆν τὸν Τρισμέγιστον, οὓς καί φασιν αὐτοδιδάκτους[7] γενέσθαι, τῆς
ψυχῆς μόνης ὥσπερ ἔκ τινος κεκρυμμένης φλεβὸς ἀναστομωσάσης αὐτοῖς
τὰ μαθήματα; ἀλλ' οὐδ' αἱ μακρόβιοι νύμφαι, εἰ δεῖ πιστεύειν τῷ Πλάτωνι,
δι' ἃς τὸ "νοῦ καὶ ἐπιστήμης δεκτικὸν" τῷ τοῦ ἀνθρώπου ὅρῳ προστεθεῖται,
διαδόσιμον ἔσχον τὴν γνῶσιν ἑτέροις σοφοῖς ὁμιλήσασαι, ἀλλ' ⌈Ὁμηρίδας 15
ὅ⌉ φασιν αὐτοφυεῖς αὐτὰς γεγενῆσθαι.[8]

Scholium on *Corp. Herm.* I. 18[9]: ἔοικεν ὁ γόης οὗτος τῇ θείᾳ γραφῇ
οὐ παρέργως ὡμιληκέναι· ὅθεν ἐκ ταύτης ὁρμώμενος τῇ κοσμοποιίᾳ ἐπιχειρεῖ,

---

[1] οἱ μῦθοι Boiss.: om. Cramer.

[2] ὅπου Boiss.: ὅποι Cramer.

[3] ὑπεραναβάντες φύσιν Boiss.: φύσιν ὑπεραναβάντας Cramer.

[4] παραθεωρῶν τοὺς μύθους Boiss. (θεωρῶν τοὺς μύθους A, παραθεωρῶν τοῖς μύθοις Gesner and B): θεωρῶν ὡς μύθους Cramer.

[5] Τάτ Cramer (i. e. Cod. Bodl.): Τάτ conj. Boiss.: τά A: μίμησιν διερεθίζει τὸν Τάνταλον Gesner and B. See also Lactant. *Div. inst.* I. 11. 6 (*Fr.* 5); see p. 10 above.

[6] Why does Psellus call Zoroaster an Egyptian? He was commonly thought by the Greeks to have been a Mede or a Persian; but Psellus seems to have usually regarded him as a Chaldaean, and the author of the doctrines taught in the *Oracula Chaldaica*.

[7] Psellus here says that Hermes was 'self-taught', i. e. that he did not learn his philosophy from any teacher, but was himself the originator of it; he, like the Nymphs, οὐ διαδόσιμον ἔσχε τὴν γνῶσιν ἑτέροις σοφοῖς ὁμιλήσας. Psellus is thinking of human teachers only, and says nothing about divine inspiration, or such instruction as, in some of our *Hermetica*, Hermes is said to have received from Νοῦς, from Poimandres, or from the Agathos Daimon. But his words are not necessarily incompatible with that; cf. Hom. *Od.* 22. 347, αὐτοδίδακτος δ' εἰμί, θεὸς δέ μοι ἐν φρεσὶν οἴμας | παντοίας ἐνέφυσεν. The κεκρυμμένη φλέψ out of which the thoughts of Hermes sprang up in him might be the working of the divine Νοῦς in his soul.

[8] See Addenda.

[9] This scholium is written by a later hand, with the superscription τοῦ Ψέλλου, in the margin of Cod. B of the *Corpus Hermeticum*, and is inserted (without superscription) in the text of *Corp.* I. 18, before the words ὁ δὲ θεὸς εὐθὺς εἶπεν, in Cod. M.

μηδὲ αὐτὰς ὀκνῶν τὰς μωσαϊκὰς λέξεις ψιλὰς ἐνίοτε ἀναγράφειν, ὡς καὶ τὸ
προκείμενον τοῦτο ῥητὸν ὅλον.[1] τὸ γὰρ " καὶ εἶπεν ὁ θεός Αὐξάνεσθε καὶ
πληθύνεσθε " σαφῶς ἐκ τῆς μωσαϊκῆς κοσμοποιίας ἐστίν. οὐ μὴν ἐνέμεινε
παντελῶς τῇ ἁπλότητι καὶ σαφηνείᾳ καὶ τῷ εὐθεῖ καὶ εἰλικρινεῖ καὶ ὅλως
5 θεοειδεῖ τῆς θείας γραφῆς, ἀλλ' εἰς τὸ εἰωθὸς ὑπερρύη πάθος τοῖς τῶν
Ἑλλήνων σοφοῖς, εἰς ἀλληγορίας καὶ πλάνας καὶ τερατείας ἐκ τῆς εὐθείας
ὁδοῦ καὶ ἀπλάνους ἐκτραπείς, ἢ ὑπὸ τοῦ Ποιμάνδρου συνελαθείς. οὐκ
ἄδηλον δὲ ὅστις ἦν ὁ τῶν Ἑλλήνων Ποιμάνδρης, ὁ καὶ παρ' ἡμῖν ἴσως
κοσμοκράτωρ ὀνομαζόμενος, ἢ τῶν ἐκείνου τις. κλέπτης γάρ, ⟨ὡς Βασί-
10 λειος⟩[2] φησίν, ὁ διάβολος, καὶ ἐκφερομυθεῖ τὰ ἡμέτερα, οὐκ ἵνα οἱ ἐκείνου
μεταμάθωσι τὴν εὐσέβειαν, ἀλλ' ἵνα τοῖς τῆς ἀληθείας ῥήμασι καὶ νοήμασι
τὴν ἑαυτῶν δυσσέβειαν ἐπιχρώσαντες καὶ μορφώσαντες πιθανωτέραν ἐργάσωνται καὶ τοῖς πολλοῖς εὐπαράδεκτον. οὐ γὰρ ἀληθεύει Πλάτων[3] τὰς
ἐκ τῶν βαρβάρων φήμας παραλαμβάνοντας κάλλιον ἀπεργάσασθαι τοὺς
15 Ἕλληνας λέγων παιδείᾳ χρωμένους καὶ μαντείαις ταῖς ἐκ Δελφῶν. ἀλη-
θεύουσι δὲ μᾶλλον οἱ λέγοντες[4] ἀταλαίπωρον εἶναι παρὰ τοῖς Ἕλλησι τῆς
ἀληθείας τὴν ζήτησιν, μάλιστα δὲ ἐν τῇ περὶ τοῦ θείου δόξῃ πλανᾶσθαι
αὐτούς. εἰσὶ δὲ οἱ ταῦτα λέγοντες οὐχ ἡμέτεροι, ἀλλὰ τῶν Ἑλλήνων οἱ
δοκιμώτεροι, εἴ τις ἐντετύχηκε καὶ οἷς ἔγραψεν ὁ Πορφύριος πρὸς Ἀνεβὼ[5]
20 τὸν Αἰγύπτιον· " παρ' ἐκείνου λοιπὸν ἐπιζητῶ μαθεῖν τὴν ἀλήθειαν, ἐπειδὴ
παρὰ τῶν Ἑλλήνων ἀπέγνων." εἰ μὲν οὖν τι καὶ ἄλλο βάρβαρον γένος
τὸν δημιουργὸν καὶ βασιλέα τοῦδε τοῦ παντὸς πατριώδει δόξῃ καὶ νόμοις
ἐθρήσκευεν, εἰπεῖν οὐκ ἔχω· ὅτι δὲ ἡ τῶν Ἑβραίων θεοσέβεια[6] περιβόητος
ἦν ἀνὰ πᾶσαν τὴν οἰκουμένην, καὶ ὅτι ἡ νομοθεσία αὐτῶν ἀρχαιοτέρα ἦν καὶ
25 Ἑρμοῦ τούτου καὶ εἴ τις ἄλλος παρ' Ἕλλησι σοφός, πολλοῖς ἀποδέδεικται.[7]

Psellus, Περὶ ἐνεργείας δαιμόνων διάλογος (Migne *Patr. Gr.* tom. 122,
col. 828 B): νῦν δέ, ὥσπερ ἐκκεκομμένοι τοὺς ὀφθαλμοὺς καὶ ἐκκεκωφη-

[1] Viz. the 'speech of God' in *Corp.* I. 18.   [2] ὡς Βασίλειος add. Reitz.
[3] *Epinomis* 987 E, 988 A.   [4] Thuc. I. 20.
[5] Ἀνεβὼ Boissonade: ἀναβαίνοντα MSS. See *Abammonis responsum*, p. 28
above.
[6] θεοσέβεια M : εὐσέβεια B².
[7] Psellus then (if the scholium is rightly ascribed to him) thought that the
author of *Corp.* I (whom he assumed to be Hermes) had read *Genesis*, but
corrupted the truth of Holy Scripture by intermixing with it the false notions of
Pagan Greeks; and that he was led into this error by his instructor Poimandres,
who is the Devil.
   We should hardly have expected Psellus the Platonist to speak so contemptuously
of the *Hermetica*, and show so little respect for the Greek philosophers. He may
have found it expedient at times to disguise his opinions, in order to guard himself
against accusations of heterodoxy; but it is going rather far to call Hermes a γόης,
and say that he was prompted by Satan. Psellus speaks in a different tone in his
letter to Xiphilinus (Sathas, Μεσαιωνικὴ Βιβλιοθηκή, Tom. V, Letter 175, p. 444 *sq.*;
Zervos, *Michel Psellos*, p. 217 *sq.*). In that letter, he does indeed admit that on

μένοι τὰ ὦτα καὶ νοῦ μηδαμῶς μετέχοντες ἔμφρονος,[1] οὔτε παρὰ τῆς τῶν
ὄντων συγγενείας ἕνα τὸν δημιουργὸν ὁρῶσιν, οὔτε τοῦτ' αὐτὸ λεγούσης
(τῆς γραφῆς) ἐπαΐουσιν, οὔτε λογισμῷ βασανίζουσιν, ὡς, εἰ δύο διεστῶτες
τῶν ὄντων ἦσαν δημιουργοί, οὐκ ἂν ἦν μία ἡ τὰ πάντα συνδέουσα τάξις καὶ
ἕνωσις.[2]   5

certain points Plato's opinions are in contradiction to the dogmas of the Church;
but he says that Plato (for instance, in his teachings concerning the Trinity, justice,
and the immortality of the soul) is in complete agreement with the fundamental
principles of Christianity, and that the reading of Plato is consequently profitable
for Christians.   In the same letter he says that he has not confined his attention to
Plato but has also studied Aristotle, whom he holds to be valuable for logic and
science, but useless for theology and metaphysic, because Aristotle was incapable
of quitting the earth and rising into the transcendental world, as did Plato and his
followers; and he adds that he has moreover deeply investigated the philosophy of
Chrysippus, that of the Chaldaeans, and that of the Egyptians.   By the philosophy
of the Chaldaeans he must have meant chiefly the teaching of the *Oracula
Chaldaica*, as interpreted by Proclus; and by the philosophy of the Egyptians he
probably meant chiefly the Greek *Hermetica*, but possibly also *Abammonis
responsum* (knowledge of which is implied in the mention of Porphyry's letter to
Anebo in the scholium).

[1] The people of whom this is said are a contemporary sect called Euchitae or
Enthusiastae.   The speaker in Psellus' dialogue says of them (824 A) πατὴρ αὐτοῖς
υἱοί τε δύο, πρεσβύτερος καὶ νεώτερος, αἱ ἀρχαί· ὧν τῷ μὲν πατρὶ τὰ ὑπερκόσμια μόνα,
τῷ δὲ νεωτέρῳ τῶν υἱῶν τὰ οὐράνια, θατέρῳ δὲ τῷ πρεσβυτέρῳ τῶν ἐγκοσμίων τὸ
κράτος ἀποτετάχασιν.   That is, they recognize two different Demiurgi, namely, the
supreme God's elder son, who is Demiurgus of τὰ ἐπίγεια, and his younger son,
who is Demiurgus of τὰ οὐράνια.   (The 'younger son' apparently corresponds to
the Christ of orthodox doctrine, and the 'elder son' to the Devil.)   Some of the
Euchitae defy and repel the 'younger son', and worship only the 'elder son'
(whom they call Satanael) and his subordinate demons.

[2] There is no mention of Hermes here; but in the words εἰ δύο διεστῶτες τῶν
ὄντων ἦσαν δημιουργοί κ.τ.λ., the argument is the same that is used in *Corp. Herm.*
XI. ii. 9 (μιᾶς δὲ κατὰ πάντων τάξεως τεταμένης (ταχύτητος τεταγμένης MSS.),
ἀδύνατον δύο ἢ πλείους ποιητὰς εἶναι· μία γὰρ ἐπὶ πολλῶν οὐ τηρεῖται τάξις· ... καὶ
εἰ ἕτερος ἦν ὁ ποιητὴς τῶν μεταβλητῶν κ.τ.λ.); and the resemblance is close enough
to make it probable that Psellus had read *Corp.* XI. ii, and was thinking of it when
he wrote this sentence.

NICEPHORUS GREGORAS

Niceph. Greg.,[1] *Explicatio in librum Synesii de insomniis* ;[2] Migne
Patr. Gr. tom. 149, col. 539 B–541 B.

539 B. καὶ φωνάς] ἀλλὰ γὰρ οὗτος μέν (*sc.* Synesius), ὡς πρὸς εἰδότα
λέγων, ἄκρως πως καὶ ἐπιπολαίως ἅπτεται τούτων· ἡμεῖς δ' οὐδ' ὀκνήσομεν
5 ἐξαπλῶσαι ταῦτα τῶν φίλων εἴνεκα, ἔκ τε χρησμῶν συλλεξάμενοι καὶ
Χαλδαϊκῶν παραγγελιῶν. . . . 541 A. περὶ δὲ τῶν ὀνομάτων ἃ φωνοῦσι,
παραγγέλλουσι (*sc.* οἱ Χαλδαῖοι) λέγοντες " ὀνόματα βάρβαρα[3] μήποτ'
ἀλλάξῃς. εἰσὶ γὰρ ὀνόματα παρ' ἑκάστοις θεόσδοτα, δύναμιν ἐν τελεταῖς
ἄρρητον ἔχοντες, ὥσπερ τὸ Σαβαώθ, τὸ Ἀδωναΐ, τὸ Χερουβὶμ καὶ τὸ
10 Σεραφίμ, τὸ Ἀβραὰμ καὶ Ἰσαὰκ καὶ Ἰακώβ,[4] καὶ ὅσα τοιαῦτα· ἅ, φησίν, ἐὰν
εἰς τὴν Ἑλληνικὴν μεταθῇς διάλεκτον, ἀφανίζεις τὴν αὐτῶν δύναμιν καὶ
ἐνέργειαν· " ὡς καὶ Ὠριγένει δοκεῖ τῷ σοφῷ.[5]

φησὶ δὲ Ἀσκληπιὸς ὁ τοῦ τρισμεγίστου Ἑρμοῦ μαθητὴς ἐν τῷ πρὸς τὸν
Αἰγύπτιον βασιλέα λόγῳ,[6] ὅτι " ὅσον δυνατόν[7] ἐστί σοι, βασιλεῦ,[8]
15 τὸν ὑφ' ἡμῶν παραδεδομένον σοι[9] λόγον διατήρησον,[10] ἵνα μήτε
εἰς Ἕλληνας ἔλθῃ τοιαῦτα μυστήρια, μήτε ἡ τῶν Ἑλλήνων
ὑπερήφανος φράσις κεκαλλωπισμένη[11] ἐξίτηλον ποιήσῃ τὸ
σεμνὸν καὶ στιβαρὸν καὶ τὴν ἐνεργητικὴν τῶν ὀνομάτων φράσιν. οἱ γὰρ τοιοῦτοι λόγοι, τῇ πατρῴᾳ διαλέκτῳ ἑρμηνευό-
20 μενοι, ἔχουσι[12] σαφῆ τὸν τῶν λόγων νοῦν· καὶ γὰρ αὐτὸ τὸ τῆς

[1] ' Nicephorus Gregoras, historian, astronomer, philosopher, theologian, and
poet, lived from 1295 to 1360' (Zervos, *Michel Psellos*, p. 231).
[2] ' Exstat ms. in codicibus Regiis; et in lucem editus est a Petavio cum Operibus
Synesii,' says J. Bouvinus, Migne 148. 53 A.
[3] See Addenda.
[4] The names Sabaoth, Adonai, Cherubim, Abraham, Isaac, and Jacob, repeatedly
occur in invocations in the Greek magic Papyri (written about A. D. 300). The
Hellenistic magicians, it seems, misunderstood the phrase ἐγώ εἰμι . . . θεὸς Ἀβραὰμ
καὶ θεὸς Ἰσαὰκ καὶ θεὸς Ἰακώβ (*Exod.* 3. 6), and supposed Ἀβραάμ, Ἰσαάκ, and
Ἰακώβ to be names of the God of the Jews.
[5] See Origen *c. Cels.* 1. 22–25.　　　　　　　[6] *Corp.* XVI. 2.
[7] ὅσον οὖν δυνατόν *Corp.*　　　　　[8] πάντα δὲ δύνασαι add. *Corp.*
[9] τὸν ὑφ' ἡμῶν παραδεδομένον σοι om. *Corp.*
[10] διατήρησον ἀνερμήνευτον *Corp.* The word ἀνερμήνευτον is needed to make
sense, and must have been accidentally omitted by Niceph. or by a transcriber of
his commentary.
[11] Perhaps φράσις (ἡ . . .) κεκαλλωπισμένη.—φράσις καὶ ἐκλελυμένη καὶ ὥσπερ
κεκαλλωπισμένη *Corp.*
[12] ὁ δὲ λόγος τῇ πατρῴᾳ διαλέκτῳ ἑρμηνευόμενος ἔχει *Corp.* But in *Corp.* this
passage (ὁ δὲ λόγος . . . τὴν ἐνέργειαν τῶν ὀνομάτων) is placed before the other (ὅσον
οὖν δυνατόν ἐστί σοι . . . τὴν ἐνεργητικὴν τῶν ὀνομάτων φράσιν).

φωνῆς ποιὸν καὶ ἡ τῶν Αἰγυπτίων ὀνομάτων δύναμις[1] ἐν αὐτῷ
τὴν τῶν λεγομένων ἐνέργειαν ἔχουσι·[2] διαστρεφόμενοι δὲ
ἀσαφεῖς τε γίνονται καὶ ἀνενέργητοι."[3]

AL·KINDÍ [4]　(c. A. D. 850)

An-Nadím, *Fihrist,*[5] Bk. 9, ch. 1 (Chwolsohn, *Die Ssabier,* vol. ii,
p. 3 *sqq.*):

§ 1. 'An extract from the autograph of Aḥmad b. ath-Thayyib,[6] in
which he gives the following account of the Sabians according to
al-Kindi :[7]

'The Sabians with one accord teach as follows : The world has
one First Author, who has never ceased to be,[8] who is unique[9] and
without plurality, and to whom none of the attributes of caused
things[10] are applicable.　He (God) imposed on those of his creatures
that are endowed with the faculty of judgement[11] the duty of acknowledging his supremacy ; he revealed to them the right way (of life and
thought), and sent emissaries (prophets)[12] to guide them aright, and
to establish the proofs (of God's existence ?).　He bade these prophets
summon men to (live according to) God's good pleasure, and warn
them of God's wrath.　They (i. e. these prophets) promised to the
obedient unending beatitude, and threatened the disobedient with
penal retribution, according to their deserts.　One of the earlier sages
of the Sabians[13] is reported to have said that God punishes men

---

[1] δύναμις om. *Corp.* (δύναμις Turnebus).

[2] ἐν ἑαυτῇ (ἐν αὐτῇ B) ἔχει τὴν ἐνέργειαν τῶν λεγομένων *Corp.*

[3] διαστρεφόμενοι . . . ἀνενέργητοι om. *Corp.*

[NOTE.—*For the transliteration of Arabic names, see vol. I. p. 97, n. 1.*]

[4] Al-Kindi is the earliest Arabic 'philosopher' of note.　The exact date of his
death is unknown ; but he is thought to have died between A. D. 850 and 873, and
must in any case have been dead before the establishment of the Sabian community
at Bagdad.　The 'Sabians' of whom he speaks must therefore be Pagans resident
at Harran.

[5] An-Nadím wrote the *Fihrist-el-'Ulûm* (Catalogue of learned men and their
writings) in A. D. 987.

[6] This man, a pupil of al-Kindi, lived in Bagdad, and died A. D. 898.　He
wrote a book entitled ' A treatise on the doctrines of the Sabians ' (Chwolsohn, ii,
p. xii), which is referred to by al-Maqdisi also (see following *Testim.*).

[7] i. e. Aḥmad b. ath-Thayyib cites al-Kindi as follows.

[8] Rather, ' has never *begun* to be ' ?　The supreme God is ἀγένητος.

[9] ' Einzig' (εἷς καὶ μόνος).

[10] τὰ γεγονότα or γιγνόμενα.　　　　　　　　[11] τὰ λογικὰ ζῷα, i. e. men.

[12] We learn from the texts which follow, that the chief ' prophets' recognized by
the Sabians of Harran, though not their only prophets, were Agathodaemon and
Hermes.

[13] This probably means some early Greek philosopher; it might be Pythagoras.

during 9,000 periods of time,[1] and thereafter the man attains to God's mercy: but this applies only to those people who have been summoned to God and the true religion, and have sworn to accept that religion.[2] The famous men and sages of the Sabians are ⌜Aráni⌝,[3] Agathodaimon, and Hermes ; to whom some of them add Solon, the maternal grandfather of Plato.'

(§§ 2–8, a description of religious rites and observances of the Sabians : e. g. § 8, 'A man must not take two wives at once' ; i. e. they do not permit polygamy, as the Mohammedans do. § 9. 'According to their opinion, the rewards and punishments will affect the spirit only, and will not be postponed to an appointed time' ; i. e. there is no resurrection of the body, and no one Day of Judgement for all mankind together. § 10 deals with 'the marks by which they say a prophet is to be recognized' ; this appears to be of Mohammedan rather than Pagan origin.)

§ 11. 'Their opinion about the primal matter, the elements, the form, the non-existent, time, space, and movement[4] agrees with that of Aristotle in his book Περὶ φυσικῆς ἀκροάσεως. As to heaven, they hold that it is a fifth element.

---

[1] [Cf. Barhebraeus below, p. 276. 18 : 'Autumant animas sceleratorum novies mille saeculis cruciari, deinde ad misericordiam Dei redire.' Perhaps a reference might be added to Proclus *In Timaeum*, I, 147 Diehl. See Addenda.]

[2] i. e. those only who have had the truth preached to them, and have accepted it and been converted to the true religion, will (after a purgatorial period of 9,000 years) 'attain to God's mercy'. What is the fate of those who have not heard the truth, or, having heard it, have rejected it, we are not told. But this clause looks like a Mohammedan addition.

[3] Who is Arani? This name, in various corrupt forms, occurs repeatedly in the Arabic texts. Chwolsohn thought that Aráni is a corruption of Orpheus ; but that seems hardly credible, even when due allowance is made for the blunders to which the Arabic script gives rise. De Goeje thought the name ought to be read Oráni, and took this to be an Arabic transcription of Οὐράνιος ; but who could Οὐράνιος be ? (Dudden, *Gregory the Great*, vol. i, p. 76, says 'Agathias, *Hist.* ii. 29. 32, gives an interesting account of a philosopher named Uranius' (in the time of Justinian ?) 'who served as a standing joke at Constantinople until he went to Persia' ; but it is unlikely that this man was regarded as a 'prophet' by the Sabians of Harran.)

Is there not more probability in the conjecture that Arani was a name invented by the Harranians, and meant the eponymous founder of their city? (Cf. Ṣabí, eponymous ancestor of the Sabians.) The absence of the guttural aspirate with which the name of the city begins (Χαρράν in LXX, Κάρραι elsewhere in Greek, the Χ being changed into Κ because of the aspirated ρ which follows,) is a difficulty; but this may perhaps have resulted from identification of the imaginary city-founder with Haran ('Αρράν in LXX) the brother of Abraham. We may suppose that Harranians who used the Greek language wrote 'Αρράνιος, and that this was transcribed as Aráni in Arabic. Dimeshqi (d. A. D. 1327: Chwols. ii, Text III, § 18) says 'Harran : the founding of this city is attributed to Arán, a son of Azar (Terah) the father of Abraham '. See *Introduction* IV.

[4] ἡ πρώτη ὕλη, τὰ στοιχεῖα, τὸ εἶδος, τὸ μὴ ὄν, χρόνος, τόπος, κίνησις.

§ 12. 'Al-Kindi says[1] that he has seen a book, the teaching of which is accepted by the Sabians, and which consists of treatises of Hermes concerning the acknowledgement of the unity of God, which treatises he (Hermes) wrote for his son,[2] with extremely thorough treatment of these doctrines,[3] from which, and from the recognition of which, no philosopher, whatever effort he may put forth, can withdraw himself.'

AL-MAQDISÍ (c. A.D. 950)

Muṭahhar b. Ṭáhir al-Maqdisí, '*The Book of Creation and History*'.[4]

Huart, vol. i, p. 130 (in a chapter entitled ' Of the beginning of the creation': heading of the section, ' Opinions of the philosophers reported by the Moslem authors '): ' It is reported of Galen that he believed in the existence of four natural forces[5] from which the world cannot separate itself, and that he added "The other philosophers admit the existence of these four natural forces joined to a fifth that is different from them, without which the natural forces could not be in agreement, since they are opposed to one another."[6] Hermes has an analogous opinion; he institutes the world as in repose, and then this (*sc.* the world?) moves itself.[7] Now this movement is purely

---

[1] We are explicitly told that § 1 and § 12 come from al-Kindi; but it is not clear whether §§ 2-11 were taken from al-Kindi or from other sources.

[2] That is, al-Kindi saw (at Harran?) a book which contained a collection of *Hermes to Tat* documents (it may have been the Γενικοὶ λόγοι, or the Διεξοδικοὶ λόγοι, or both together). He seems to have been struck by the fact that these Hermetic writings, accepted as authoritative by the Sabians, taught the unity of God, a doctrine which he would have expected the Pagan ' polytheists ' of Harran to reject.

[3] Rather, ' this doctrine ', viz. the unity of God ?

[4] This book (not mentioned by Chwolsohn) has been published and translated by Cl. Huart, 3 vols., 1899–1903. The book has been attributed to Abu-Zaid Ahmad b. Sahl al-Balkhí; but Huart found evidence which convinced him that its author was a man named Mutahhar b. Tahir al-Maqdisi, about whom nothing else is known.

[5] viz. the Hot, the Cold, the Moist, the Dry.

[6] This appears to mean that there is a force by which ' the four natural (or physical) forces ' have been harmoniously combined together, and that the Kosmos has been thereby brought into being.

[7] Here we have a statement ascribed to Hermes. The statement is obscure, but may perhaps be taken to mean that the world was at first motionless, i. e. was mere lifeless matter, but afterwards ' moved itself ', when ' soul ' or life had been infused into it by the Demiurgus. Something to that effect may have occurred in a Hermetic *libellus*; it may have been quoted by a Sabian of Harran, and al-Maqdisi may have got it from one of those who wrote about the doctrines of the Harranians (e. g. from ath-Thayyib).

The following sentence (' Now this movement ' &c.) appears to be al-Maqdisi's comment. What he meant by the word translated ' spiritual ', I do not know. (Possibly, ' effected by νοῦς ', or ' by ψυχή '!)

spiritual, and this is a fall (i. e. an abrupt change?) and a transference (to another order of things?); for repose is not an act.'

Huart, vol. ii, p. 83: 'It is told, according to 'Ali b. 'Abdallah al-Qasrí, in the *Book of celestial conjunctions*, ... that Hermes the elder, who is Enoch or Idris (may God bless and save him!) existed long before Adam, that he dwelt (in Egypt) from the higher part of Upper Egypt adjoining the Soudan down to Alexandria, and that he transported the human race thither, and thus saved it from drowning (in the Deluge). The same author maintains that Budásf' (i. e. Buddha) 'existed before Hermes; now the latter (ı. e. Hermes) is much more ancient than Adam; this is an opinion admitted by those who believe that there have been several Adams.'

Huart, vol. ii, p. 131 (heading of section, 'Of the ancients who believed that the world will come to an end'): 'The Harranians admit reward and punishment (*sc.* of men after death); but I do not know what they think about the destruction of the world; I only know that they trace back their origin to Agathodaimon, to Hermes, and to Solon the maternal grandfather of Plato. Some of them believed in the destruction of the world and the resurrection.'[1]

Ib., p. 137 : 'The same author (*sc.* Ibn Abdallah al-Qasrí, in his *Book of celestial conjunctions*) says "Hermes Trismegistus, who is Enoch or Idris the prophet, lived a very long time before Adam. He went down into Upper Egypt and the rest of the country as far as Alexandria, in order that the creatures (i. e. men) might take refuge there against the danger of being drowned; but the deluge and the volcanos more than once destroyed them (i. e. mankind), as well as the plants and the animals ". This is what I have found in the book of this author.'

Huart, vol. iii, p. 8 (heading of the section, 'Opinion of the Mazdeans and of the other religions concerning the prophets'): 'The Harranians say that the names of the prophets who have called mankind to God are innumerable; and that the most celebrated are Oraní (*al.* Aráni), Agathodaimon, Hermes, and Solon maternal grandfather of Plato. Among the ancients, some consider as prophets Plato, Socrates, and Aristotle, and say that prophetship is knowledge joined to works (i. e. combined with good deeds?).'

Huart, vol. iii, p. 12 (heading of the section, 'History of Idris the

---

[1] Does this mean that some of the Pagan Harranians held a doctrine of periodical destructions and restorations of the world, like that of the Stoics? Or are the men here spoken of the Christians of Harran, as opposed to the Pagans?

prophet') : 'Those who occupy themselves with this branch of knowledge say that Idris is no other than Enoch, son of Yared. son of
Mahaleel, son of Qenan, son of Enos, son of Seth, son of Adam. . . .
He was the first prophet who received a mission after Adam ; for he
had received from his predecessors the inheritance of the prophetship,
but not that of the mission. He is the first who traced characters by
means of the pen[1] after Adam, and the first who sewed garments
and put them on, for before him they used to clothe themselves in
the skins of beasts. The children of Adam were still living ; God
called him to the prophetship after the death of Adam, and revealed
to him the knowledge of astronomy and medicine. His name among
the Greeks is Hermes. His work each day was equivalent to that of
all men together ;[2] this won for him God's approval, and God exalted
him to a sublime rank ;[3] but as to the manner in which this exaltation took place, opinions differ.'

Huart, vol. i, p. 132 : 'As to the Harranians, it (*sc.* the question
how creation began, or how the Kosmos first came into being) is a
disputed question among them, according to what is told (about
them). Ahmad b. ath-Thayyib, in his treatise concerning this sect,
says that these people agree on this point, that the world has an
eternal cause ; they attribute to it[4] seven and twelve *demiurgi*.[5] And
with regard to matter, the non-existent,[6] form, time, space, movement,
and force, they accept the opinion of Aristotle in his book of the
Hearing of the nature of man.[7] According to Zorqán's report, their
doctrine is analogous to that of the Manichaeans ; some, however,
affirm that their doctrine is the glory of that of the philosophers :[8] no
one has yet ventured to show their contradictions.'

Huart, vol. i, p. 159 (heading of the section, 'Different opinions
of men concerning the nature of the angels') : 'The Harranians say
that the angels are the stars which govern the world ;[9] it is this that

---

[1] i.e. the first man who wrote. Writings ascribed to Enoch were known to
Jews and Christians ; and perhaps it was the belief that he was the earliest writer,
that led to his identification with the Egyptian Hermes, the inventor of writing.

[2] i.e. his deeds were equivalent in merit to the sum of all other men's deeds ?

[3] i.e. God took him up to heaven. Enoch 'was not, for God took him' (*Gen.* 5.
24) ; and it could be learnt from the *Hermetica* that Hermes became a god in heaven
when his life on earth ended.   [4] i.e. to the First Cause? or to the world ?

[5] This probably means that the world is governed by the seven planets and the
twelve *Zodia*, operating in subordination to the supreme God, who is the First
Cause of all.

[6] τὸ μὴ ὄν.   [7] Φυσικὴ ἀκρόασις. ('Of man' must be an error.)

[8] [For probable sense see p. 276. 17].

[9] i.e. the Sabians of Harran identified the angels spoken of by Jews, Christians,
and Mohammedans with the star-gods of their own doctrine.

led the Batenians[1] to maintain that they (*sc.* the angels) are seven and twelve in number.'

Huart, vol. i, p. 173 (heading of the section, 'Different opinions concerning Paradise and Hell'): 'I have read in the Laws of the Harranians[2] that the Creator has promised to those who are obedient delight without end, and has threatened the disobedient with a chastisement proportioned to their demerit; this is the law adopted by most of the ancients.'

Ib., p. 185: 'I have read in the Laws of the Harranians that the world has an eternal cause,[3] and that this cause is unique and does not multiply itself, and that it is incomparable with the things that are known. Men of discernment are compelled to acknowledge its divinity, and also the mission of the prophets destined to prove its existence and establish the arguments for it. They promise to the obedient an unlimited felicity, and threaten the disobedient with a chastisement proportioned to their demerit. This chastisement will, later on, be brought to an end. Some among the first[4] say that he with whom fault is found will be chastised during 7,000 revolutions (i. e. years?), and his chastisement will then be ended, and he will enter into the mercy of the Most High.'

MAS'ÚDÍ[5] (died A.D. 956)

Al-Maqrízí (who died A.D. 1442) quotes Masudi, *Kitábu 'l- Tambíh wa-'l-Ishráf*, as follows (Chwolsohn, ii, p. 604):

'One of these two pyramids (of Gizeh in Egypt) is the grave of Agathodaimon, and the other that of Hermes.[6] Between these two

---

[1] Bátiní ('Esoteric') was one of the names given to the Ismailís, an ultra-Shiite sect (Browne, *Lit. Hist. of Persia*, i. 311 and 407).

[2] 'The Laws of the Harranians' must have been a book about the religion or philosophy of the Pagans of Harran. It may have been one of the writings of Thabit b. Qurra, e. g. his *Liber de lege et canonibus ethnicorum*, or his *Liber de legibus Hermetis et de orationibus quibus utuntur ethnici*.

[3] viz. the supreme God.

[4] i. e. some of the chief or earliest teachers recognized by the Harranians? This might mean either Agathodaemon and Hermes, or early Greek philosophers such as Pythagoras. See notes on Al-Kindi, p. 248. 12, 13.

[5] Masudi, 'the Herodotus of the Arabs', wrote a Universal History. The book here cited contained a general survey of things more fully dealt with in his longer writings.

[6] The belief that the two great pyramids are the graves of Agathodaimon and Hermes occurs repeatedly in Arabic writings from the tenth century onwards. It must have originated among people who knew the *Hermetica* and revered the supposed authors of the Hermetic teaching, as there could hardly be any other ground for coupling these two names together; and as there is no reason to think

men there was an interval of about a thousand years,[1] and Agatho-daimon was the earlier of the two. The inhabitants of Egypt, i. e. the Copts, before Christianity arose among them, believed in the prophetship of both (Agathodaimon and Hermes), according to the view of the Sabians about prophecy, and not in the way of revelation.[2] According to their opinion (i. e. that of the Sabians), the prophets are pure souls, which, having been purified and cleansed from the defile-ment of the world, are united with higher substances,[3] so that they have knowledge of future things, of the secrets of the world, and the like. . . . But according to the opinions of those of the Sabians whom we have mentioned, the pyramids are graves of the pure bodies.'[4]

Masudi, *Murúju 'l Dhahab*,[5] (Chwolsohn, *Nachtr. zu Text II*); vol. ii,

that the *Hermetica* were generally known in Egypt after the fifth century, it is most likely that the notion first arose among the Sabians of Harran or Bagdad (who must have known of the pyramids by report, and in whose eyes Agatho-daimon and Hermes were the two greatest men of Egypt), and was conveyed thence to Egypt by Arabs. The fact that some Pagan rites of worship were practised at the pyramids down to the tenth century or later is well attested. It can hardly be supposed that Sabians of Harran or Bagdad habitually went on pilgrimage to the Egyptian pyramids; it is more likely that the worshippers were Copts, among whom some remnants of the ancient Pagan cults of Egypt still survived. But whether the worshippers themselves called the objects of their worship Agathodaimon and Hermes, is more doubtful. If they did, we must suppose that they had forgotten the names of the deified kings who had been worshipped at the pyramids in earlier times, and had picked up these new names from the Arabs, who had learnt them from the Sabians of Bagdad.

[1] This statement shows that Masudi had not himself read the *Hermetica*, and knew about them, and the supposed authors of the teaching contained in them, only by report, or by reading what others had written about them; for if he had seen the documents, he would have found among them dialogues in which Agathodaimon and Hermes talked together. He assumes that Agathodaimon, as well as Hermes, was a man; and in this he follows the Harranians, who held both of them to have been 'prophets' in the same sense. But in the view of the Hermetic writers themselves, the Agathos Daimon was not a man, but a god,—an impersonation of the divine νοῦς, – who gave instruction to the man Hermes.

[2] This appears to mean that the Sabians of Harran and Bagdad held Agatho-daimon and Hermes to have been inspired teachers, but did not suppose themselves to have received from them a written revelation of infallible authority, such as the Moslems believed themselves to have received, in the Koran, through their prophet Mohammed. Masudi is well informed (through the writings of Thabit b. Qurra or otherwise) about the views of these Sabians in his own time, and assumes, without evidence, that the pre-Christian Egyptians had held similar opinions.

[3] 'Higher substances' (αἱ ἄνω οὐσίαι) must mean either τὰ οὐράνια, or τὰ νοητὰ or ἀσώματα. This description of a 'prophet' is not unlike the descriptions of 'the man who has got *gnosis*' which occur in the *Hermetica*.

[4] 'The pure bodies' seems to mean the bodies of men whose souls were pure in the sense explained. Agathodaimon and Hermes were such men.

Maqrizi, after this quotation from Masudi, goes on to say that 'The Sabians (i. e. Pagans) did not cease to worship Abu 'l-Haul (i. e. the Sphinx), to sacrifice white fowls to it, and to make fumigations of sandarac-wood before it'.

[5] This book, an epitome of Masudi s great historical works, was written A. D. 943-944.

p. 621): 'Enoch is identical with the prophet Idris; the Sabians say he is the same person as Hermes. The meaning of Hermes is 'Uthárid' (i. e. the planet Mercury).

Ib., p. 642: Masudi gives various opinions concerning the causes of the fact that many people possess the faculty of divining, discovering hidden things, and predicting future events; and he then goes on to say: 'And the Sabians think that Orpheus (?)[1] the first and Orpheus (?)[1] the second, who are identical with Hermes and Agathodaimon, knew hidden things. As such (i. e. because they were believed to have possessed this faculty) they were held to be prophets by the Sabians, who denied that the *ginn* (i. e. daemons) are accustomed to impart many of the aforesaid hidden things;[2] for the souls of the prophets, they say, were so pure that they knew things which were hidden from other men.'

Ib., p. 622: Masudi speaks of the remains of a great temple of the Pagan Greeks at Antioch, and says 'The Sabians think that it was built by Asclepius.[3] . . . When the Caliph went to Antioch in the year 289 (A.D. 901), . . . the Sabian Thabit b. Qurra the Harranian saw this temple, showed veneration for it, and told about its nature what we have reported.'

Ib., p. 372: Masudi gives particulars about the temples and rites of the Sabians at Harran, and mentions an 'inscription from Plato' on the door-knocker of one of their places of worship. The words inscribed were 'He who knows his (God's) Being honours him also' (which may be taken to mean that true worship consists in learning to know God, or that γνῶσις brings with it εὐσέβεια).[4]

AN-NADÍM, *Fihrist*

(written A.D. 987)

Fihrist, Bk. 10 (Chwolsohn, i, p. 788): 'According to some, Hermes is said to have been one of the seven temple-priests who were appointed (by the Pagans of Harran?) to have charge of the seven temples (of the planet-gods); and it is said that the charge of the

---

[1] See p. 249, n. 3.

[2] This amounts to saying that the Sabians of Harran and Bagdad rejected magical methods of divination, in which the agency of daemons was employed.

[3] It may have been a temple of the Greek god Asclepius, or of a Syrian god identified with him; but to Harranian Sabians such as Thabit, the name Asclepius would rather mean the Egyptian Asclepius of the *Hermetica*.

[4] See vol. III, p. 36, n. 1.

temple of (the planet) Mercury was given to him, and that he was thence named Hermes. According to others, he is said to have gone to Egypt and become king of that land. His children were Tat, Ṣá, Ashmun,[2] Athríb,[3] and Qoft.[4] They say that he was a wise man, and that after his death he was buried in the building which is known in Cairo under the name Abu-Hermes, and which the people call "the two Hermae" (pyramids); one of the two being his grave, and the other that of his wife, or, according to others, that of his son, who succeeded him after his death.'[5]

IBN ZULÁQ (died A.D. 997)

(Chwolsohn, ii, p. 629.) Yáqút (who died A.D. 1229), in his *Geographical Dictionary*, quotes Ibn Zulaq as saying that 'among the wonders of Egypt are the two great pyramids, . . . of which the one is the grave of Hermes, i.e. Idris, and the other is that of Agathodaimon, the pupil[6] of Hermes; and the Sabians (i.e. Pagans) used to go on pilgrimage to these pyramids.'

IBN ḤAZM AL-QORTHOBÍ[7] (died A.D. 1064)

(Chwolsohn, ii, p. 526.) '*Concerning the Jews, and those Christians who deny the Trinity, and those of the Magians and Sabians who acknowledge the unity of God.* . . . The adherents of these religions agree with us (Moslems) in acknowledging the unity of God, and also in acknowledging the prophetic missions, the miracles of the prophets, and the sending down of the writing of revelation by God; but they dissent from us in this, that they recognize only *some* of the prophets. . . . The Magians believe in the prophetship of Zaradusht (Zoroaster), but refuse to recognize Moses, or Jesus, or any of the prophets of the Israelites, or Mohammed, and do not admit that any one of these

---

[1] Probably a mistake for Ṣabi.

[2] Is this Eshmunein, i.e. Hermopolis Magna in Egypt, which was called by Egyptians 'the city of the Light'?

[3] Athribis. a town in the Delta.   [4] The town Koptos in Egypt?

[5] It appears from this passage that an-Nadim knew little about Hermes and the *Hermetica*; but his mention of Tat son of Hermes shows that the vague and confused traditions which had reached him were derived in part from the Harranian Sabians, to whom the *Hermetica* were well known.

[6] A mistake; he ought to have said 'teacher'.

[7] Born at Cordova. This extract is taken from his ' Book of Religions and Sects'.

was a prophet. The Sabians are divided into several sects,[1] but they all deny the prophetship of those of whom I have said that the Magians do not believe in their prophetship, and they also deny that of Zaradusht. Some of them[2] recognize Abraham as a prophet, but others of them deny this. All the Sabians, however, recognize the prophetship of ⌈Nawadásp⌉,[3] ⌈Ilún (*al.* Eilún)⌉,[4] Hermes, his son Tat b. Hermes, Agathodaimon, ⌈Arani⌉ the elder and ⌈Arani⌉ the younger, and Asclepius; but about other prophetships they disagree.'

IBRÁHÍM BIN WASSÍF SHÁH

(not later than A.D. 1150)

Chwolsohn (ii, p. 534) gives the following extract from this man's book on the ancient history of Egypt: 'People named him (*sc.* Enoch = Idris) Hermes, after the name of 'Uthárid (the planet Mercury). He taught writing to his son Sábí;[5] and thence all who write after him (?)[6] are called Sábí. . . . Idris had handed over his testament, and the books (which he had written), to his son Methuselah, and had told Sabi to help him in his studies; for Sabi had attained to great wealth of knowledge.'

---

[1] It appears from this statement that Ibn Hazm understood by 'Sabians' Pagans in general. The Pagan Greeks (including the Harranian Pagans) would, in his view, be one sect of Sabians, and the Buddhists (about whom he cannot have known much) another sect of Sabians. But he must have got most of the names in his list of Sabian prophets from earlier writers who were speaking of the Sabians of Harran and Bagdad, that is, of that particular group of Pagans who knew the *Hermetica*, and recognized as prophets the supposed authors of the Hermetic teaching; and he mistakenly thought that these same prophets were recognized by all Pagans alike (e. g. that Buddha was recognized as a prophet by the Pagans of Harran and the Pagan Greeks in general, and Hermes by the Buddhists).

[2] Who are these? Possibly the Pagans of Harran, who would be specially interested in Abraham as one of their earliest and greatest citizens. It was commonly thought by Mohammedans that the true religion had been taught by Abraham, but had subsequently been corrupted, until it was taught anew in its purest form by Mohammed; and the Harranian Pagans may have adopted some such notion about Abraham from their Moslem rulers and neighbours.

[3] Probably a mistake for Budasp (Boddhisattwa, i. e. Buddha).

[4] Can this be Ἕλλην, eponymous ancestor of the Ἕλληνες (i. e. Pagans)?

[5] Sabi, eponymous ancestor of the Sabians, must have been invented after the Pagans of Harran took the name of Sabians, i. e. after A. D. 830. He was made a son of Hermes, and thus identified with Tat.

[6] This phrase would most naturally mean 'all who use the art of writing'; but the author must have meant rather 'all whose writings are in accordance with the doctrine which Hermes taught in his writings are called Sabians'.

AL·SHAHRASTÁNÍ[1] (died A.D. 1153)

Chw. § 6 (Haarbrücker, ii. 1). 'Not far removed from these[2] are others, who accept (legal and moral) ordinances and rational propositions, and often the fundamental principles on which these are based, from an inspired teacher, but limited themselves to the earliest of the inspired teachers, and did not go on to (accept the teaching of) the others. These are the first Sabians,[3] who accept ⌜Adsímún⌝[4] and Hermes—that is, Seth and Idris (= Enoch),—but do not recognize the other prophets.'

(In §§ 7–26 Chw., al-Shahrastani describes the philosophic doctrine of 'the Sabians', which he sets forth partly in the form of an imaginary debate between Sabians and adherents of Abraham (i. e. of the true religion). The philosophic system which he ascribes to 'the Sabians' (i. e. to Pagans in general) is, in the main, a Greek system based on Plato and Aristotle, i. e. a form of that Neoplatonism which the Arabic 'philosophers' had learnt from the Greeks.)

Chw. § 27 (Haarbr. II, p. 61). 'It is said that ⌜Adsímún⌝ (Agathodaimon) and Hermes were Seth and Idris. Concerning ⌜Adsímún⌝, the philosophers hand down the tradition that he said "that the first principles were five, namely, the Creator, Reason, Soul, Space,

---

[1] Shahrastani's *Book of religions and sects* has been translated by Haarbrücker, 1850. I take these passages from the extracts from Haarbrücker's translation which are given by Chwolsohn, ii, pp. 415–450.

[2] 'These' are the sects or schools of which Shahrastani has just been speaking, i. e. the adherents of philosophic systems. He says that these are people who rely on their own reason or judgement (as opposed to those who base their beliefs on a divine revelation).

[3] 'Sabians' here means Pagans in general. (Cf. § 31, where the Harranians are called 'a class of Sabians', i. e. one of the classes into which Pagans are divided.) But what is meant by 'the *first* Sabians'? Perhaps, 'the Sabians in the original or proper sense of the word'. Shahrastani has found it said in earlier writings that the prophets of 'the Sabians' (of Harran and Bagdad), are Agathodaimon and Hermes, otherwise called Seth and Idris (see § 34 below); and he mistakenly thinks that this applies to Pagans in general, i. e. that all Pagans alike recognize Agathodaimon and Hermes as their prophets, and that Paganism in all its forms is derived from the teaching of these two men. Agathodaimon and Hermes, being identical with Seth and Enoch, must be the earliest of all prophets (after Adam); and Pagans are people who have accepted the teaching of these earliest prophets, but rejected that of all prophets who came later (e. g. of Moses, Zoroaster, Jesus, and Mohammed).

[4] A miswriting of Agathodaimon. In the Arabic texts, the name Agathodaimon is frequently corrupted into some such form as Adsímún; but it now and then occurs correctly spelt, and there is no doubt that Agathodaimon is meant.

and Void,[1] and that the composite things came into being there-after ".[2] But this is not reported of Hermes.'

Chw. § 30 (Haarbr. ii, p. 73) ' *The Harranians*.[3] These are a class of the Sabians, who assert that the Creator to whom men pray is both one and many. He is one, they say, in virtue of his essence, primariness, originality, and eternity ; but he is many, inasmuch as he multiplies himself before men's eyes through the corporeal forms.[4] These corporeal forms are the seven governing planets, and the good, wise, and distinguished bodies on earth.[5] That is, he manifests him-self through them, and personifies himself by means of their bodies ; but his unity in his own being is not (thereby) annulled. They say he has made the sphere of heaven, and all the bodies and stars that are therein, and he has appointed these (i. e. the stars) to be governors of this world. They are the fathers, the element-stuffs[6] are the mothers, and (all) composite things are the offspring. The fathers (i. e. the stars) are living and rational beings, who make the influences[7] reach the elements, and the element-stuffs receive the influences into

---

[1] 'die Leerheit.' But we should rather have expected 'Space and *Time*'. E. G. Browne, *Lit. Hist. of Persia*, p. 408, describing the doctrines of the Ismaili sect, says that ' Intermediate between God and Man are the five Principles or Emanations (the Universal Reason, the Universal Soul, Primal Matter, Pleroma or Space, and *Kenoma or Time*)'. It would appear from this that in some Arabic writings Void was somehow identified with Time.

[2] The statement attributed to Agathodaimon (and, as we are explicitly told, not to Hermes) would, in Greek terms, be this : ' There are five ἀρχαί (or ἀγένητα), namely, ὁ δημιουργός, νοῦς, ψυχή, τόπος, and (χρόνος ?) ; and from these all σύνθετα came into being.' Something to that effect might very well occur in a *Hermeticum* (if the context made it clear that the supreme God, here called the Demiurgus, was the first ἀρχή of all, and the other four issued from him or were subordinate to him) ; and it probably did occur in one of those Hermetic *libelli* in which Agathos Daimon was the teacher ; for that is the only kind of document known to us from which a saying of Agathodaimon could have been got. Al-Shahrastani did not himself know the *Hermetica* ; but he found the saying ' handed down by the philosophers ', i. e. quoted by writers such as al-Kindi, al-Farabi, or Ibn Sina, who may have got it from one of the Sabians of Harran or Bagdad, if not directly from the *Hermeticum* in which it occurred.

[3] ' The Harranians ' means the Sabians of Harran and Bagdad. The account of their doctrine which is here given by Shahrastani is presumably a summary of the contents of some book or books written by Thabit b. Qurra, or by some other member of the Sabian community in Bagdad. As those men knew the *Hermetica*, and must have been more or less influenced by them, it is possible that some things in Shahrastani's account of their doctrine are ultimately derived from *Hermetica* not now extant ; but we have no means of knowing whether it is so.

[4] [*Corp.* XVI. 3 : τὸν θεὸν ἐπικαλεσάμενος τὸν τῶν ὅλων δεσπότην καὶ ποιητὴν καὶ πατέρα καὶ περίβολον, καὶ πάντα ὄντα τὸν ἕνα, καὶ ἕνα ὄντα τὰ πάντα κ τ.λ.]

[5] ' Bodies ' apparently here means ' men in the body '. God incorporates himself (1) in the seven planets, by which the sublunar world is governed, and (2) in good and wise men (such as Hermes) ; ' that is, he manifests himself through them ;' he is present in them, and works by means of them.

[6] τὰ ὑλικὰ στοιχεῖα !   [7] ' Die Einwirkungen ' Haarbr. : ἐνέργειαι !

their wombs, and thence results the birth of the offspring. When this takes place, it may come to pass that among the offspring produced is a being compounded of the pure parts of those element-stuffs without (any of) the impure parts of them, and that this being is so composed as to have a perfect temperament ;[1] so that through this being God personified himself in the world.

'Moreover, they[2] assert that, at the beginning of every period of 36,425 years,[3] Nature brings forth in each of the inhabited regions of the earth a pair, male and female, of each kind of animals, men, &c., so that the race continues through that space of time; but when the period comes to an end, the reproduction and procreation cease. Then begins another period, and there arises another race of men, beasts, and plants, and so on through the endless course of time.[4] This, they say, is (the true meaning of) the resurrection which was promised by the mouth of the prophets ;[5] for there is no dwelling-place (for men) other than this (earthly) dwelling-place, and ⌐only time destroys us⌐ ;[6] and a revival of the dead, an awakening of those who rest in their graves, is unthinkable. . . .[7]

'From these people is derived the doctrine of metensomatosis, and (also that of the) "indwelling" (of God in the planets in heaven, and

---

[1] Among the 'composite things' (i.e. living organisms) produced by the working of the stars on the elements, are men ; and a man is better and wiser than other men in proportion as he is made of purer elements, and these elements are more perfectly coadjusted in his composition. The man who has this superiority over other men in the highest degree is one 'through whom God personifies himself in the world'; i.e. he is one in whom God is present, and through whom God speaks to mankind ; he is an inspired teacher, a prophet. [For the influence of the stars on birth cf. Stob. Exc. xxii ; for temperament, Exc. xxvi. 13 *sqq.*]

[2] In this paragraph also, and in all that follows, 'they' apparently means the Harranians (i.e. Thabit and his associates and followers), and not Pagans in general.

[3] Doubtless a mistake for 36,525, which is one hundred times $365\frac{1}{4}$ (the number of days in the Egyptian year), or in other words, twenty-five times 1,461 (the number of the Egyptian 'Sothic period').

[4] There is no such doctrine as this in any of the extant *Hermetica*, nor in any other Pagan writings known to me. But it might possibly have been evolved out of a combination of the Stoic theory of periodical ἀποκατάστασις with the statement in *Corp. Herm.* I that sexual procreation of men and beasts first began 'at the beginning of the second period'.   [5] Jesus and Mohammed.

[6] Perhaps the meaning may have been 'our bodies necessarily perish by lapse of time'.

[7] It looks at first sight as if Shahrastani meant that the 'Harranians' of whom he is speaking denied life after death. But if their teaching was, as we have every reason to think, mainly Neoplatonic, they cannot have denied the immortality of the soul, or at any rate of the νοῦς ; and it is most likely that the Harranian writer whose doctrine Shahrastani here reports was speaking, not of the soul, but of the living organism, soul and body in one, and that what he denied was not the immortality of the soul, but the resurrection of the body, which Christians and Mohammedans asserted.

in individual men on earth).' Chw. § 32 (Haarbr. ii, p. 75):
'Metensomatosis consists in this, that the cycles and periods repeat
themselves without end, and that what came into being at the beginning comes into being again in each period;[1] that rewards and
punishments take place in this abode, not in another, in which the
action is not done;[2] and that the actions in the realm of which[3] we
find ourselves are only retributions for actions formerly done by us in
previous periods,'[4] &c.

Chw. § 33 (Haarbr. ii, p. 75): The 'indwelling' (of God in the
planets and in individual men) is the personification, as we have reported it.[5] Sometimes this takes place through indwelling of his[6]
(whole) being, and sometimes through indwelling of a part of it, according to the degree of perfection[7] of the temperament of the body
(in which God embodies himself). Sometimes they say that God
personifies himself only by means of the celestial 'habitations' (i. e.
the planets or planet-spheres) in general; but that he still remains
one, for it is only his action (and not his essential being) that manifests itself in each of the 'habitations', according to the measure of
his workings on it and his personification through it. It is as if the
seven 'habitations' were God's seven members, and as if our seven
members were God's seven 'habitations', in which he manifests himself,[8] so that he speaks by means of our tongue, sees by means of our
eyes, hears by means of our ears, grasps and reaches out by means of

[1] This is not μετενσωμάτωσις, but ἀποκατάστασις; so that if Haarbrücker is right
in translating the Arabic word (et-tanásuch) by metensomatosis, Shahrastani must
have misunderstood his source. [See on p. 260, n. 4.]

[2] This apparently means 'on earth, and not in a Paradise or Hell elsewhere'.
Men do good and ill on earth, and are rewarded and punished on earth.

[3] 'in deren Bereich' Haarbr.

[4] 'Periods' seems here to mean successive incarnations, and not the periods
spoken of above in connexion with ἀποκατάστασις. (The passage could be made
consecutively intelligible only by assuming that the Harranian writer held that
each human soul is reincarnated once in each apocatastasis-period; but such a
doctrine would be unexampled, and it would be difficult to work it out without
inconsistency.)
The statement 'that the actions' &c. looks rather like the Indian doctrine of
karma. But something to the same effect occurs in Plotinus 3. 2. 13 (cruel masters
become slaves when reincarnated, he who has been a murderer in a previous life is
murdered, and so on).

[5] I. e. 'the personification of which I have already spoken (in § 31)'. The word
'personification', as here used, seems to mean 'incorporation'.

[6] To whom does 'his' refer? Does this phrase mean 'the indwelling of God's
whole being in a man', or 'the indwelling of God in the man's whole being'? In
either case, it amounts to saying that there are different degrees of divine 'possession' or inspiration.

[7] 'Verrichtung' Haarbr.

[8] This is a special application of the analogy between the Kosmos and the

our hands, goes to and fro by means of our feet, and acts by means of our members.

They believe that God is too exalted to make things that are evil, mischievous, and loathsome, (e. g.) beetles, snakes, and scorpions; these are rather things that result from natural necessity, being conditioned by the conjunctions of favourable and unfavourable stars, and by the combination of pure and impure element-stuffs. All happiness, all that is good and pure, was purposed by creation, and is to be referred to the supreme Creator; but all unhappiness, all that is evil and impure, results from natural necessity,[1] so that it is not to be attributed to the Creator, but these things are partly incidental effects[2] brought about by necessity, and are partly grounded on ⌈the evil⌉,[3] and on the bad conjunctions (of the planets).'

Chw. § 34 (ii, p. 76 Haarbr.): 'The Harranians derive their doctrine from the four prophets ⌈Adsímún⌉ (Agathodaimon), Hermes, ⌈Ayáná⌉, and ⌈Awádsí (al. Erádí)⌉;[4] some derive it from Solon, the ancestor of Plato on the mother's side, and believe that he was a prophet. They also believe that ⌈Awádsí (al. Erádí)⌉ forbade them to eat onions, cabbage, and beans.'[5]

human microcosm. The system of the planet-spheres is God's body, in which he dwells (as the human soul dwells in the human body), and through which he acts in governing the sublunar world; and in like manner, God from time to time dwells in the body of this or that individual man, and speaks and acts through it. Such a man is ἔνθεος, i. e. 'has God inside him', in the same sense that the starry heavens are permanently ἔνθεοι.

[1] Cf. the ἀνάγκη of Pl. *Timaeus*, by which the νοῦς of the Demiurgus, aiming at the good, is to some extent thwarted. In the *Timaeus*, this ἀνάγκη is regarded as inherent in matter (to which the 'element-stuffs' here spoken of correspond); but here, as in some of the *Hermetica*, it is also connected with the operation of the stars (or of Heimarmene working through the stars.)

[2] 'Zufälligkeiten' Haarbr. They are things that occur κατ' ἐπακολούθησιν, as the Stoics said; i. e. they are not things purposed by God on their own account, but inevitable by-products of his working for good ends.

[3] Perhaps 'the evil nature of matter', or 'the impurity of the element-stuffs'?

[4] As Shahrastani said before (§ 6) that Pagans in general accept Agathodaimon and Hermes as their prophets, he probably thought that those doctrines which were peculiar to the Harranians, and in which they differed from other Pagans, were derived from the teaching of 'Ayáná' and 'Awádsí'. But these two names have been corrupted beyond the possibility of recognition. Probably one of the two is meant for the name elsewhere written Aráni.

[5] This was probably a regulation observed in one of the local cults of Harran, and may have been spoken of as such in one of Thabit's writings. Perhaps ⌈Awadsi⌉ may have been the name of the reputed founder of that particular cult.

'UMAR BIN CHIDHR IṢFAHÁNÍ [1]

(Chw. ii, p. 517). '*Concerning the principles of the religion of the Sabians.* There is no doubt that these people submit themselves to the spiritual beings, and follow the immaterial Lights, whom the philosophers call "Intelligences",[2] and the adherents of positive religion name "angels". The Sabians have ordinances, rules, and usages of worship, which consist in fasts, prayers, almsgiving,[3] and sacrifices. All (this, i. e. their whole cult) is not based on any positive religion and positive doctrine; moreover they have no proof (of the obligation to do these things), but they are things that they have established for themselves, and the practice of which they have found to be good, and which have thus come to be matter of law and usage among them.[4] The intermediaries between them and the spiritual beings are Hermes and Agathodaimon, i. e. Seth and Idris. The other prophets[5] are not recognized by them; they say "They[6] are like us in kind and form; ... (they eat, drink, sleep, &c., as we do;) ... what advantage have they over us, ... that we should follow their decisions, take their actions for our guidance, obey them, and subject ourselves to them? ..." Some Sabians believe in metempsychosis, and the repetitions of things in cycles and periods,[7] but others do not. These are the fundamentals of their religion.'

---

[1] 'When and where this author lived, we do not know,' says Chwolsohn; but he was probably later than al-Shahrastani, as he appears to have copied from him.

[2] I. e. the divine *νόες* by whom the celestial spheres are governed.

[3] The ordinance of almsgiving is Mohammedan rather than Pagan.

[4] I. e. they have no written text which they regard as an infallible authority, in the sense in which the Koran is so regarded by orthodox Moslems; they claim liberty to think for themselves, and their only criterion of good and bad, or right and wrong, is their own judgement. But this seems inconsistent with what is said about Hermes and Agathodaimon in the following sentence, which appears to mean that knowledge of the truth has been transmitted to them from the divine *νόες* by those two 'prophets'. [But see vol. I, pp. 97–101.]

[5] I. e. the other prophets recognized by the Moslems (including Moses and Jesus, as well as Mohammed).

[6] Does 'They' mean 'the prophets' (including Agathodaimon and Hermes), or 'the *other* prophets' (Agathodaimon and Hermes being excepted)?—This sentence looks like a quotation from Thabit b. Qurra or some other philosophic Sabian.

[7] ἀποκατάστασις.

SUHRAWARDÍ,[1] *The Philosophy of Illumination*

(written A.D. 1186)

Horten, p. 2: 'I will now set forth the truths which I learnt in hours of solitude, when I turned away from corporeal things, and turned to the purely spiritual things of Light, and entered into communication with the divine world, and with some of the spirits of the celestial realm. I first grasped a definite truth by mystic intuition, and then sought to demonstrate it by arguments; whereas the Peripatetics[2] follow the reverse method, letting themselves be led by (logical) demonstrations, without knowing beforehand the goal to which their arguments will lead them. *Our* master is Plato, especially in his works *Timaeus* and *Phaedo*; whereas Aristotle remains the loadstar of those who seek truth by the empirical method. But we find ourselves in agreement (also) with the father of the secular men of learning,[3] namely, Hermes of Egypt, who is known under the name of the prophet Idris, and was the founder of the *Harámisa* (i.e. Hermetists).[4] Intermediate in time between Hermes and Plato are the others, namely, Empedocles;[5] Pythagoras, pupil of Empedocles;

---

[1] Shaykh Shihábu 'd-Dín Yahyá Suhrawardí was a mystic who taught a doctrine called Ḥikmatu 'l Ishráq ('Philosophy of Illumination'). He was accused of 'atheism, heresy, and believing in the ancient philosophers', and was put to death at Aleppo by a scn of Saladin in A.D. 1191; whence he was called al-Maqtúl, 'the martyr' (Browne, *Lit. Hist. of Persia*, i, p. 423). See Carra de Vaux, *La Philosophie illuminative d'après Suhrawardi Maqtoul*, in *Journal Asiatique* 1902, Tome XIX, pp. 63–94.

M. Horten, *Die Philosophie der Erleuchtung nach Suhrawardi*, Halle a. S. 1912, has published a translation of selections from a book (lithographed at Teheran, 1895–1898) which contains the text of one of Suhrawardi's writings together with comments by Shirazi (†1311) and 'glosses' by another Shirazi (†1640). The passages here given are taken from Horten's translation.

[2] When Suhrawardi speaks of 'the Peripatetics', he means chiefly Avicenna, whose philosophic system was based mainly on Aristotle. Suhrawardi had, in his earlier life, accepted Avicenna's teaching, but he afterwards became dissatisfied with it. Horten, p vi, quotes a passage in which Suhrawardi says 'Before this work on the Philosophy of Illumination, . . . I have written other books . . . according to the method of the Peripatetics. . . . This mystic-Platonic method is a different kind of philosophy, and a shorter way than that of the Peripatetics, which loses itself in secondary questions'.

[3] 'Mit dem Vater der weltlichen Gelehrten' Horten. What is meant by the word translated 'weltlichen'? Perhaps the meaning is that Hermes was the founder of *Pagan philosophy*, as distinguished from *Moslem theology*.

[4] It is implied in what Suhrawardi says here and elsewhere that he was well acquainted with the teaching of the philosophic *Hermetica*. He must have either read Hermetic writings himself (in a Syriac or Arabic translation), or got information concerning their contents from Sabians or Moslems who had read them and written about them.

[5] I. e. Pseudo-Empedocles. Of the real Empedocles the Arabs knew little or nothing; but there was current among them a book ascribed to Empedocles,

Socrates, pupil of Pythagoras; and Plato, the seal and keystone of mysticism, who was pupil of Socrates. These men expressed their doctrine in oracular [1] utterances. [2]

'Related to this (Hermetic and Platonic) philosophy is that of Light and Darkness, which was set forth by the ancient Persians, e.g. Gámásp, Farshádshúr, and Buzurgmihr, [3] who lived before those Greeks (viz. Empedocles, Pythagoras, &c.). It was on the presuppositions of these Persians that the philosophers of Illumination built up their system. [4] The Persians taught the existence of two principles, Light

which was probably of similar origin and character to the numerous pseudonymous writings ascribed to early Pythagoreans, and must have contained Platonic or Neoplatonic doctrines. (It appears from what Suhrawardi says further on, p. 45 *sq*. Horten, that the Platonic 'ideas' were spoken of by 'Empedocles', i. e. in the book ascribed to him.) Suhrawardi makes Empedocles earlier than Pythagoras; this mistake seems to have been commonly made by Arabic writers. Some of them said Empedocles was a pupil of King David, and of the legendary sage Loqman (de Boer, *Gesch. der Philosophie im Islam*, p. 27).

[1] What does 'oracular' mean? Perhaps 'symbolic', or 'allegorical'; i. e. what these men said is not to be accepted in its literal sense, but yields truth when rightly interpreted. That might be said of Plato's 'myths', and of much of his *Timaeus*.

[2] This passage ('Our master is Plato ... oracular utterances') is translated as follows, from a MS. at Constantinople, by C. de Vaux, *Journal Asiatique* 1902, p. 68: 'This was the sentiment of the prince and chief of philosophy, Plato, possessor of force and of light. Likewise thought those who came before him, from the time of Hermes the father of sages down to his (Plato's) time, the great sages, pillars of wisdom, such as Empedocles, Pythagoras, and others. The words of the ancients are symbolic; the objections that are made against them, though valid against the exterior form of their words, are not valid against their meanings; a symbol cannot be refuted.'

I have no means of finding out how far the differences between Horten's rendering of this and other passages and that of C. de Vaux result from differences of reading in the texts used by them.

[3] Jámáspa and Frashaostra are spoken of in the Avesta as contemporaries and helpers of Zarathushtra. Jamaspa married one of Zarathushtra's daughters and succeeded him in the pontifical office. Tradition ascribed to Jamaspa the writing down of the 'Avesta'. Frashaostra was vizier of king Víshtáspa, and father-in-law of Zarathushtra.

There was a man named Buzurgmihr, who was vizier of the Persian king Anushirwan, in the sixth century A. D.; he is said to have sent for Indian books and had them translated into Pehlevi, and there may have been writings of which he was, or was thought to have been, the author. Can this be the man meant? If so, Suhrawardi made a mistake of something like twelve centuries as to his date; for he says Buzurgmihr, as well as Jamaspa and Frashaostra, lived before Pythagoras, and apparently puts all three together in the time of Zoroaster.

[4] The 'Philosophy of Illumination' was in existence before Suhrawardi's time; he was not its first founder or inventor, but he revived it, and expounded it afresh. C. de Vaux, *Avicenne*, pp. 151–153, speaks of a writing of Avicenna (apparently not now extant) called *The illuminative philosophy*, and quotes from Ibn Tofail, *Philosophus autodidacticus*, as follows: 'Avicenna composed the *Shifa* according to the doctrine of the Peripatetics; but he who wants the complete truth without obscurity ought to read his *Illuminative philosophy*.'

C. de Vaux *ib.* quotes from Hadji Khalfa, *Lexicon biographicum*, 'There are

and Darkness; but by this they meant nothing else than necessary being and contingent being; for the Light stands for necessary being, and the Darkness for contingent being.[1] They did *not* teach that the first principle of the universe is a duality, Light and Darkness. That is asserted by no man who has attained to normal use of his reason; and far less was it asserted by the famous philosophers of Persia, who penetrated into the depths of knowledge.[2] The wisdom of those ancient Persian teachers is not the infidel doctrine of the Magians, who assume two first principles, Light and Darkness; nor was it that of Hadi-Máni of Babylonia. He (i.e. Mani) was by religion a Christian, but by race a Magian; and from him are descended the dualists, who assume two Gods, namely, the God who is the good and works good, that is, the Light, and the other God, who is the evil and works evil, that is, the Darkness.'[3]

Ib., p. 3. 'Though Aristotle was a great philosopher, we must not exaggerate his importance in such a way as Avicenna does at the end of his Logic. Other great philosophers are Agathodaimon, i.e. Seth

---

two ways of attaining to knowledge of the Author of all things. The first is that of speculation and argument; those who follow it are called "theologians" (*motakallimun*) if they believe in the revelation (i.e. the Koran) and adhere to it, but "philosophers" if they do not believe in it, or if they disregard it. The other way is that of ascetic exercises; those who follow it are called "Sufis" if they are faithful Musulmans, but if they are not, they are called "the illuminated sages".' (This implies that the adherents of the 'Philosophy of Illumination' were not called Sufis. But the term Sufi is often used to mean mystics in general, whether orthodox Mohammedans or not; and in this wider sense, Suhrawardi also was a Sufi.)

[1] 'Necessary being' and 'contingent being' are technical terms of Arabic philosophy. 'Necessary being' denotes God; 'contingent being' denotes all else than God.

[2] The commentator Shirazi (d. A.D. 1311), in his note on this, says 'Suhrawardi awoke to new life the philosophy of those ancient Persians, and harmonized it with that of the Greeks.—Gamasp was the pupil of Zaradusht, Farshadshir, and Buzurgmihr. . . . Misfortunes, and above all the loss of the royal power, dug the grave for their wisdom; Alexander caused most of their writings to be burnt'.

It appears that Suhrawardi found the fundamental principles of his 'Philosophy of Illumination' in some Persian writings which were ascribed to contemporaries and associates of Zoroaster; but he found them also in Greek Platonism, and in the *Hermetica*, from which he supposed Greek Platonism to have been derived. C. de Vaux, *Journal Asiatique* 1902, p. 89, says 'The "Philosophy of Illumination" is merely a form of Neoplatonism; but the nomenclature employed in it' (e.g. the use of the term 'Light' in place of νοῦς) 'has rather Oriental origins, and specially Persian or Chaldaean'.

[3] According to Suhrawardi, 'Light' (i.e. God or good) is primal and supreme, 'Darkness' (i.e. evil) is derivative and subject. This, he thinks, was the doctrine taught by Zoroaster himself and his first followers; but the Magians (i.e. the later Zoroastrians) have corrupted their prophet's teaching, and fell into the error of putting the power of Darkness (Ahriman) on a par with that of Light (Ormuzd); and Mani, influenced by them, fell into the same error.

son of Adam; Hermes, i. e. the prophet Idris; and ⌜Aṣkalínús⌝ (Asclepius),[1] the servant of Hermes.'

Ib., p. 44. 'Those philosophers who released themselves from their bodies, and thereby freed themselves from matter, saw the incorporeal Lights (i. e. the divine νόες or νοητά). This is true of the prophets and sages, such as Plato, Socrates, and their predecessors Hermes, Agathodaimon, and Empedocles. Of most of these men it can be proved that they saw the spiritual world (i. e. the νοητὸς κόσμος). Plato tells about himself, that he stripped himself of the garment of Darkness, i. e. got rid of his connexions with corporeality, and saw the spiritual world;[2] and all the philosophers of India and Persia experienced such visions. If we believe the astronomical observations of a single person, e. g. of Ptolemy, or those of two persons, e. g. of ⌜Abrachos⌝ (Hipparchus?) and Archimedes, how can we do else than believe the assertions of the greatest philosophers?[3]

'The writer of these lines (i. e. Suhrawardi), when he first occupied himself with philosophy, zealously maintained the system of the Peripatetics, and accordingly denied these visions, and the existence of the spirits and ideas;[4] he maintained the Peripatetic doctrine, that there exist in the higher world only ten spirits.[5] But afterwards, he saw the proof of God, i. e. the vision of the incorporeal Lights, when he had, by means of continual solitude and many ascetic practices,

---

[1] It appears from this that Suhrawardi knew of some *Hermetica* in which Asclepius was the teacher; our *Corp.* XVI may have been one of them.

[2] There is nothing like this in Plato's writings; he does not speak about himself in his Dialogues. The name Plotinus, in Arabic script, is easily mistaken for Plato; and C. de Vaux is probably right in saying that Suhrawardi sometimes made this mistake, and was thus led to ascribe to Plato things that had been said by Plotinus. It is most likely that Suhrawardi is here thinking of passages in the *Enneads*, in which Plotinus describes the ecstatic state of union with the One, and says or implies that he has himself experienced it. (See Plot. 4. 8. 1 : Inge, *The Philosophy of Plotinus*, ii, pp. 134–142.)

[3] Hermes and Plato tell us that they have 'seen' God or τὰ νοητά; why not believe them, if you believe an astronomer when he says that he has seen a star in a certain position at a certain time?

[4] The 'spirits' are the divine νόες; the 'ideas' are the νοητὰ εἴδη of Platonism. But it seems that Suhrawardi (accepting Plotinus' identification of νοητόν with νοῦς, and working it out in his own way) takes the 'ideas' to be 'spirits'. He calls the νοητὰ εἴδη 'Lights' that issue from the 'Light of Lights'; and these 'Lights' he regards as living persons,—gods or angels that emanate from God.

[5] These 'ten spirits' are the divine νόες connected with the several spheres of heaven; and the doctrine of 'the Peripatetics' concerning them means that of Avicenna (as to which see de Boer, *Gesch. der Phil. im Islam*, p. 123, and C. de Vaux, *Avicenne*, p. 241 *sq.*). That doctrine was based on that of Aristotle *Metaph.* xii and *De caelo*, adjusted to the Ptolemaic system of astronomy. Suhrawardi would add to the ten νόες of Avicenna an indefinite number of νόες = νοητὰ εἴδη.

released himself from his connexion with corporeality, and made clear
to himself that all forms of being in this corporeal world are images
of pure Lights, which exist in the spiritual world.[1]   But if any one is
not satisfied with this proof,[2] he may devote himself to ascesis, and
to the service of the mystics ; and perhaps he will thereby acquire a
" natural disposition ", and will thereupon see the Light which radiates
in the world of divine Powers, and the substances of the celestial
realm, and also the Lights which Plato and Hermes saw, and moreover the Lights of Paradise, i. e. the spiritual Lights of which that
virtuous sage and perfect *Imam* Zarádusht (Zoroaster) of Azerbeijan
speaks in his book *Zend*.'

Ib., p. 45 *sq*. 'All the learned men of Persia agree that each
species of the heavens (?), stars, simple and composite elements, has
a " Lord " in the world of Light, who is an incorporeal spirit ($\nu o \hat{v} s$),
and governs the species that corresponds to him.   Those Persians
gave names to many of these " Lords " ; Hurdád corresponds to water,
Murdád to the trees, and Ardi Bihisht to fire.   These are the Lights
(i. e. $\nu o \eta \tau \grave{a} \ \epsilon i \delta \eta$) to which in former times Empedocles and the
theologians Hermes, Pythagoras, and Plato referred.'[3]

Ib., p. 47. 'The proof of these doctrines (i. e. of the truth of
certain statements concerning Platonic "ideas", and the distinction
between these " ideas " and logical universals) is not the conviction
of Plato and the philosophers of intuition, viz. Pythagoras, Empedocles,
and Hermes,[4] but the immediate certainty of the illumination itself.'[5]

Ib., p. 61. 'Hermes, Agathodaimon,[6] Empedocles, Pythagoras,

---

[1] The 'pure Lights' (i.e. the $\nu o \eta \tau \grave{a} \ \epsilon i \delta \eta$) are the $\pi a \rho a \delta \epsilon i \gamma \mu a \tau a$ of which corporeal things are $\epsilon i \kappa \acute{o} \nu \epsilon s$.

[2] 'This proof' appears to mean the assertions of Suhrawardi himself, and of earlier mystics such as Hermes and Plato, that they have 'seen' the $\nu o \eta \tau \acute{a}$.   If a man is not content to accept the doctrine on their authority, he may. by suitable training under the direction of one who has 'seen', acquire a faculty of mystic intuition (or, as the Hermetists said, an ' eye of the mind '), whereby he will ' see ' the $\nu o \eta \tau \acute{a}$ for himself.

[3] Shirazi 'the Glossator' (d. A.D. 1640) says, in a note on the sentence pre-ceding this passage, 'The philosophers Socrates, Pythagoras, Agathodaimon, and Empedocles taught that the pure Light is the spiritual world.' ($\acute{o} \ \nu o \eta \tau \grave{o} s \ \kappa \acute{o} \sigma \mu o s$).
Hurdad &c. are departmental gods or angels spoken of in Persian writings ; Suhrawardi identifies them with the $\nu o \eta \tau \grave{a} \ \epsilon i \delta \eta$ of the Platonists.

[4] This implies that ' these doctrines' concerning Platonic ideas were taught by Hermes,—i. e. that they were to be found in *Hermetica* known to Suhrawardi.

[5] The ' illumination ' (or ' irradiation ') means the infusion of divine $\nu o \hat{v} s$ into a man, whereby he is enabled to see $\tau \grave{o} \ \acute{o} \nu \tau \omega s \ \acute{o} \nu$ by immediate intuition.   He who is thus ' illuminated ' knows the truth with a certainty unattainable by those who merely accept it at second hand, as a doctrine taught by Plato and others.

[6] Horten, here and elsewhere, wrongly says that Agathodaimon is a miswriting for Anaximander.

Socrates, and Plato taught transmigration of souls (*metensomatosis*) as did also the philosophers of Egypt,[1] Persia, India, Babylon, and China.'

Ib., p. 62. 'The mystic philosophers, Plato and the earlier sages, viz. Socrates, Pythagoras, Empedocles, Agathodaimon, and Hermes, and even the Peripatetics, taught only a one-sided transmigration from man into beast, and not a reverse transmigration (from beast) into man.[2] Aristotle is said to have returned from his original doctrine, in which he denies the transmigration of souls, to that of his master Plato,[3] and to have accepted the transmigration of souls.'

Ib., p. 69. 'The spheres of heaven give forth sounds which are not produced by means of earthly things. This is the teaching of the ancient Greeks, Hermes, Pythagoras, Plato, and others.'

MAIMONIDES (died A.D. 1204)[4]

Chwolsohn, Text V, § 14, vol. ii, p. 461 : Maimonides, in his *Guide to the perplexed*, describes the religion of the 'Sabians' (by which he means Pagan polytheists in general). He gives a list of the books from which he got his knowledge of the 'Sabian' religion ; and among these are 'a book attributed to Hermes ;[5] a book of the Sabian Is'haq,[6] in which he undertakes the defence of the Sabian belief; and a large work by the same man concerning the usages of the Sabians and their several ordinances, their festivals, sacrifices, and prayers, &c.' 'All these books which I have mentioned,' says Maimonides,

---

[1] This looks as if Suhrawardi did not regard Hermes and Agathodaimon as Egyptians, but thought that they were Greeks. But if so, who were his 'philosophers of Egypt'? (On the other hand, in p. 2 above, he speaks of 'Hermes of Egypt'.)

[2] This is a mistake ; in *Corp. Herm.* X, for instance, transmigration in both directions is asserted. But it is true that in most Platonic writings comparatively little is said about transmigration from beast to man.

[3] This statement is doubtless based on pseudo-Aristotelian writings such as 'the *Theologia* of Aristotle'. Compare what Patrizzi said about Aristotle (see *Introduction*, p. 38).

[4] The Jewish philosopher Maimonides was born in Spain, A.D. 1092; he migrated thence to Egypt, where he died. He got his philosophy from Arabic sources.

[5] This may have been an Arabic translation of Greek *Hermetica*. But as Maimonides includes Pagans of all kinds under the term 'Sabians', we cannot be sure that the book he speaks of was of the same character as our philosophic *Hermetica*; it may have been a book on astrology or magic.

[6] Chwolsohn (i, p. 621) says 'this man is quite unknown to us'; but he assumes him to have been a Harranian Sabian, and suspects that the man meant is Sinan son of Thabit b. Qurra, who is known to have written on these subjects.

'treat of idolatry, and have been translated into Arabic. They are doubtless only a small part of those which have not yet been translated, or have perished in the lapse of time.'

AL-QIFTHÍ (died A. D. 1248) [1]

Chwolsohn i, p. 790 (see also Chw. ii, p. 529): Al-Qifthi, in his *Lives of wise men* gives a Life of Hermes. After saying that he will omit what the historians and the commentators on the Koran have said about Hermes, and will give only what the philosophers say about him, he proceeds thus: 'As to the birth, education, &c., of Hermes, there are different opinions. According to some, he was born in Memphis in Egypt, was called " Hermes Hermetum ", and was identical with Enoch and Idris; Agathodaimon is said to have been his teacher. . . . According to others, Hermes was born and brought up in Babylon; Seth, son of Adam, was his teacher. They say he then migrated from Babylon to Egypt, and exhorted the people of that land to do good and be obedient to God. And as men at that time spoke 270 different languages, God taught him all these languages, that he might be able to teach all peoples of the earth in their mother-tongues.[2] He also founded cities, gathered round him all men who desired knowledge, and taught them the principles according to which states are governed. Hermes also instructed men in philosophy and astronomy, and in the ordering of the year; for God had taught him the secrets of the spheres, the movements of the planets, &c. Moreover he gave laws to the nations in all countries; he divided the earth into four parts, appointed a king over each part, and charged these kings to take care that their subjects should live in accordance with the religion which he had founded.'[3]

Al-Qifthi also says that, after the death of Hermes, the most powerful of the four kings among whom he divided his realm was Asclepius. And in another passage (an extract from his 'Life of Asclepius') he

---

[1] Al-Qifthi was Saladin's vizier (Chw. i, p. 243).

[2] This may perhaps have been suggested partly by a reminiscence of the 'gift of tongues' conferred on the Apostles (*Acts* 2), and partly by the supposed connexion of the name Hermes with ἑρμηνεύειν. If the latter, it must have come from a Greek source.

[3] As the denotation of the name 'Sabians' widened, the range of operation assigned to Hermes ('prophet' of the Sabians) widened with it; so that by this time he could be described as the founder of all Pagan religion and all Pagan wisdom.

says that, when Hermes divided his realm into four parts, Asclepius received Greece as his share; that Asclepius, in his grief at the death of Hermes, set up an image of Hermes in a temple, and that in course of time this image came to be worshipped as a god; and 'it is said that thence arose the worship of idols' (Chw. vol. ii. p. 532).

AL-KÁTIBÍ (died A.D. 1276)[1]

Chwolsohn ii, p. 492 *sqq.*[1]: (*a*) 'The Hernanites[2] say that there are five primal beings,[3] of which two are living and active, one passive, and two neither living nor active nor passive. The two living and active beings are *God* and *Soul*.[4] The soul is the principle of life in material and celestial bodies, the cause of the appearance of the world. The third primal being is *matter*, which is passive, solely in virtue of the fact that it receives the forms from the distributor of forms. The two last of the primal beings are *time* and *space*.

'The primal existence of these beings is necessary for the following reasons:

'(1) A *God* that brings things into being is indispensable, because the things that are *possible* (or *contingent*) must be ultimately dependent on a being *necessary* of himself and by himself.[5]

'(2) *Soul* is primal; for if it were not, it would necessarily be material, since everything that comes into being in time[6] participates in matter and time; but a material soul is an absurdity.[7]

'(3) If *matter* were not primal, it would need another matter,[8] and this would need a third, and so on *ad infinitum*.

'(4) If *time* had had a beginning, it would have been preceded by a not-time. But that is a contradiction; for the non-existence of time would have been anterior (in time) to its existence, so that there

[1] Chwolsohn's French text, which I here translate, is reprinted from Schmölders, *Essai sur les écoles philosophiques chez les Arabes*, p. 227 *sqq.*

[2] *Hernanites* must be a miswriting for *Harranians*, i.e. Pagans of the school of Thabit b. Qurra.

[3] ἀγέν(ν)ητα; things without a beginning in time.

[4] θεός and ψυχή. This implies that the supreme God is νοῦς; there is here no recognition of τὸ ἐπέκεινα νοῦ (the ἕν or ἀγαθόν of Plotinus) as a distinct *hypostasis*.

[5] The terms 'necessary being' and 'contingent being' were in frequent use in the philosophic writings of the Arabs. They belong to a Neoplatonism that is later than the Greek *Hermetica*; but they may have been used by Thabit.

[6] τὰ γιγνόμενα. [7] ψυχή is ἀσώματος and ἄυλος.

[8] Things are brought into being by the imposition of form on ὕλη; therefore ὕλη, if not ἀγένητος, must have been brought into being by the imposition of form on a pre-existent ὕλη, and so on.

would have been, before (the beginning of) time, another time in which the non-existent time was contained. And just as time has no beginning, so also it has no end ; for if it no longer existed,' &c. (argument as before). 'Time then, is necessary of itself.

'(5) The same argument applies to *space*. If space had appeared when there was not yet an above and a below, a right side and a left side, where could it have manifested itself?

'God is perfect in knowledge and wisdom ; that is, his knowledge and wisdom are so exalted that there is nothing beyond them. He is perfect in knowledge, because he is eternal; for the attribute "eternal" implies that he must know all things, and that he cannot ever be without knowledge of them.[1] He is perfect in wisdom, because it is he that gives to the material elements the forms appropriate to them ; it is he that prepares the material elements, and disposes them to receive these forms.[2] He is not, however, compelled to act as he does ; it is wisdom only, and desire to diffuse the good,[3] that preside over all his actions.

(*b*) 'God is the cause of the existence of the immaterial substances,[4] which are formed by mind (or intellect),[5] which, in its turn, emanates from God.[6] The emanation is not operated by a free choice on God's part ; it is operated spontaneously, as the ray issues spontaneously from the sun-disk.[7] Mind is the only thing that has issued immediately from God, who, because he is one and simple, can only produce a single non-composite being.[8] All other created things are derived from God only by means of this mind.

---

[1] How does 'eternal' imply omniscience? Perhaps the writer was thinking chiefly of knowledge of the future. To men, the future is unknown ; but to God, who is 'eternal' (in the Platonic sense), i. e. not in time, what is future to men is present, and therefore is known.

[2] God, as Demiurgus, first brings the four στοιχεῖα into being (as in Pl. *Tim.*) by imposing the forms of fire, air, earth, and water on formless ὕλη, and then makes the various organisms out of these elements. Perhaps 'these forms' means the forms of the various things that are composed of the elements.

[3] God (*qua* νοῦς) aims at τὸ ἀγαθόν in his *demiurgia* (as in Pl. *Tim.*).

[4] τὰ ἄυλα or ἀσώματα ; among which ψυχαί are included.

[5] νοῦς.

[6] The text of the extract from Katibi (as given by Chwolsohn) runs on unbroken from beginning to end ; but the theology of the passage which I have marked (*b*) differs from that of the passage which I have marked (*a*), and the two passages must therefore have come from different sources. In (*a*), God is νοῦς, and there is nothing prior to νοῦς ; in (*b*), God is prior to νοῦς, and is the ἕν of Plotinus. The doctrine of (*a*) is pre-Plotinian ; that of (*b*) is Plotinian.

[7] So said Plotinus, using the same simile (*Enn.* 5. 1. 6 ; 5. 3. 12 and 15). *Ahamnionis resp.* 8. 2. The second God ἀπὸ τοῦ ἑνὸς ἑαυτὸν ἐξέλαμψε.

[8] νοῦς, the second God, is μονογενής and ἀσύνθετος.

'Soul is an immaterial substance, existent from all eternity,[1] cause of the life of ⌐the first types⌐,[2] but involuntary cause, in the same way that God is the cause of mind.

(c) 'The soul,[3] once turned towards matter, was enamoured of it, and burning with desire to enjoy corporeal pleasures, was thenceforward unwilling to detach itself from matter.[4] [It was thus that the world came into being.][5]

'From this moment, the soul forgot itself, forgot[6] its first abode, its true centre, its eternal existence ; and it became so completely ignorant that it no longer knew the truth, nor the essence (or real being) of things, nor even the demonstrative sciences, unless it studied them.[7] [God, always occupied in directing all towards the good, united soul to the matter of which he saw it so enamoured, diffusing in matter a multitude of forms.[8] Thence the composite bodies, the heaven, the elements,[9] &c.]

'But God, being unwilling to abandon the soul in the degradation (of its union) with matter, endowed it with intelligence (νοῦς) and the

[1] ψυχή is an ἀσώματον that emanates from νοῦς; but this emanation is not an event that has taken place at a certain time in the past; the term 'emanation' signifies a relation that has nothing to do with time-process.

[2] What are 'the first types'? ψυχή might be said to be the cause of the life of all living things; and the world-soul operating as φύσις, and, in that capacity, putting life into plants and animals, might perhaps be said to work 'involuntarily'.

[3] From this point onward (except in the clauses which I have bracketed) the 'soul' spoken of is not soul in general, or the world-soul, as in (a) and (b), but is the individual human soul,—the soul of this or that particular man. This passage (c) may possibly have come from the same Harranian source as (a) ; but if so, something which connected (c) with (a) must have been omitted.

The passage (c) closely resembles many *sententiae* of the Arabic *De castigatione animae* (Bardenhewer), and would serve as a summary of the contents of the *Castig. an.* as a whole.

[4] Cf. the descent of Anthropos and his marriage with φύσις in *Corp. Herm.* I.

[5] A 'desire to enjoy corporeal pleasures' could not be attributed to the world-soul, but only to individual human souls. The words 'It was thus that the world came into being' appear to have been inserted by some one who assumed that (c) was continuous with what preceded it, and that it was still the world-soul and the *demiurgia* that were being spoken of in (c). And the same is to be said of the other passage which I have bracketed ('God, always occupied ... the elements, &c.').

[6] The Platonic λήθη. From the moment of its descent and incarnation (i. e. at birth) the soul forgets the νοητὸς κόσμος from which it has come, and which is its true home.

[7] This may perhaps have been suggested by the illustration of ἀνάμνησις that is given in Pl. *Meno* by means of a geometrical problem.

[8] To 'impose forms on matter' is regarded as equivalent to putting soul (or life) into matter. God formed a multitude of living organisms, putting into each of them an individual ψυχή parted off from the world-soul.

[9] The elements, if spoken of at all here, ought to have been mentioned before 'composite bodies'.

faculty of (intellectual) perception, precious gifts, which were intended to remind it of its high origin, the spiritual (i. e. incorporeal) world, its former home; to restore to it consciousness (or knowledge) of itself; and to make it see that it is an alien here below, that it will never be free from pain in the world below, and that what it thinks to be pleasure is not true pleasure, but on the contrary, a blind attraction towards deadly things.   This gift (of νοῦς) was intended to make the soul understand that passing pleasures are no pure happiness, that each of them involves a series of evils and regrets, and that even the choicest pleasures—sexual intercourse, luxurious feasting, &c., —are precisely the causes of many diseases. As soon as the soul has received this instruction from perception and intelligence, as soon as it has recovered consciousness of itself, it desires the spiritual world, as a man transported to a foreign land sighs for his distant home. It becomes convinced that, in order to return to its primal state, it must detach itself from the bonds of this world, from sensual lusts, and from all material things, and that, when it is once freed from all this, it will abide for ever in the bliss of the spiritual world.'[1]

BARHEBRAEUS (died A. D. 1286)

Gregorius Abulfarag Barhebraeus, *Hist. dynastiarum*, transl. Pococke, Oxon. 1663; pp. 6 *sqq.*: 'Autumant Graeci antiquiores Ehnochum esse Hermetem qui Trismegistus cognominatus est, q. d. triplicis doctrinae autor, quod tribus attributis essentialibus Deum descripserit, viz. Existentia, Sapientia, et Vita. Arabes autem ipsum Edrisum appellant. Ac dicitur tres fuisse Hermetes; quorum primus fuit Hermes ille qui Saidam Aegypti superioris incoluit, ac primus omnium de substantiis superioribus loquutus est, et de diluvio praemonuit, veritusque ne perirent scientiae atque obliterarentur artes, Pyramides extruxit, quibus omnia artificia et instrumenta et in iisdem scientiarum ordines delineavit, eas conservatas posteris tradere cupiens. Secundus Hermes Babylonius, qui in Calwada Chaldaeorum urbe habitavit, ac post diluvium floruit, atque primus urbem Babelem condidit post

---

[1] This report of the teaching of 'the Harranians' was most likely got by al-Katibi, either immediately or through some intermediary, from writings of Thabit b. Qurra or one of his followers; and if so, it may be accepted as a specimen of the doctrines that were taught in the school of the Harranian Sabians, and were thought to be derived from the teaching of Agathodaimon and Hermes.   The doctrine reported is Platonic, and is closely akin to that of the Greek *Hermetica*.

Nimrodem Cushi filium. Tertius demum Hermes Aegyptius, qui
Trismegistus, i. e. sapientiae tertias occupans, vocatus est, quod Hermetum Sapientum tertius fuerit; et *translatum est e libris ipsius
pauxillum quid, viz. sermones ipsius ad discipulum suum Tatium, forma
interrogationum ac responsionum dispositi, nullo connexionis vel conse-
quentiae ordine, cum exemplar originarium vetustate exesum fuerit
Extat autem exemplar apud nos lingua Syriaca.*[1]

'Ac fertur Hermetem primum centum et octoginta urbes condidisse,
quarum minima Roha; ipsumque hominibus cultum Dei, ieiunium,
preces, eleemosynam, utque festa descendentibus in domibus suis
atque ascendentibus planetis agerent praescripsisse, necnon singulis
noviluniis, et quotiescunque Sol aliquid e duodecim signis ingredere-
tur; utque ex omnibus frugibus praemitias et e suffitibus et vinis
praestantissima offerrent, necnon ebrietate et cibis illicitis interdixisse.[2]

'Sabii autem autumant Sethum Adami filium Agathodaemonem
Aegyptium esse, Hermetis praeceptorem; fuitque Asclepiades[3] rex
unus (eorum) qui ab Hermete sapientiam hauserunt, quemque Hermes
quartae terrae tunc temporis habitatae parti praefecit, ei nempe quam
post diluvium incoluerunt Graeci. Cum autem Hermetem ad se
sustulisset Deus, magno eum ob casum moerore affectus est Asclepiades, eam quam passi sunt terricolae benedictionis et scientiae eius
iacturam dolens; et simulachrum sibi ad ipsius similitudinem con-
flavit, quod in templo ubi sacra peragere solebat statuit, ita comparato
simulachro, ut quantum fieri potuit, gravitatis apparatum et maiestatis
speciem prae se ferret. Deinde eundem in coelum sublatum effinxit,
atque alias coram eo stans, alias sedens, quaedam ex ipsius sapienter
dictis et praeceptis de cultu (divino) recitabat. Post diluvium vero
putarunt Graeci simulachrum illud Asclepiadis ipsius fuisse, illudque
maxime in honore habuerunt. Solebat enim Hippocrates, cum dis-
cipulos suos iureiurando adigeret, dicere: "Adiuro vos per Deum
Creatorem mortis et vitae, et patrem meum, patremque vestrum
Asclepiadem etc." . . .

'Dico autem, quicquid narrationum de rebus ante diluvium affertur,

---

[1] I.e. a Syriac translation of a collection of *Hermes to Tat* dialogues (presumably including the *Hermes to Tat* libelli that have come down to us in Greek,
or some of them, together with others that are now lost,) was extant in Syria in
A.D. 1250–1286.
[2] The statements in this paragraph were doubtless derived from writings of
Thabit or other Harranian Sabians concerning the local cults of Harran, which
were supposed to have been founded by Hermes. Compare Barhebraeus' account
of Thabit's writings in the following extract.
[3] In the Arabic, *asclibiadis*; a mistake for Asclepius.

T 2

quod Prophetico sermoni non innititur, meram esse coniecturam atque opinationem, cum nemo sit qui eas memoriae prodiderit.'

Ib., p. 184: 'Porro in aedibus Mohammedis Ebn Musa literis operam dedit Thabet Ebn Korra Ebn Merwan, Sabius Harranensis Bagdadi advena. Illi ergo benefacere studens Mohammed, ipsum ad Al Motadedum perduxit, et in Astrologorum numerum adscripsit. Thabet iste summum apud Al Motadedum dignitatis gradum maximosque honores consecutus est, adeo ut coram ipsum continue sederet, diuque cum ipso colloqueretur unaque rideret, magisque ad eum accederet quam Consiliarii ipsius aut amicorum praecipui. Multa scripsit in disciplinis Mathematicis, Medecina, et Logica. Sunt et illi libri lingua Syriaca scripti de iis quae ad Sabiorum religionem spectant, de eorum constitutionibus, praeceptis, et ritibus, de mortuis involvendis et sepeliendis, de munditia et immunditia, quaenam animalia sacrificiis idonea, quae inepta, de temporibus cultui divino destinatis, de ordinanda lectione inter orandum.

'Illud autem quod apud nos constat de Secta Sabiorum est, professionem eorum eandem prorsus esse cum Chaldaeorum antiquorum professione; Keblamque ipsorum polum Arcticum;[1] quatuor virtutibus intellectualibus ipsos diligenter studere;[2] illis ut ter orent iniunctum esse, primo ante ortum Solis, semihora aut minus, quo oriente 5 sole finiantur octo incurvationes, quarum singulae tres continent adorationes; secundo ita ut finiatur oratio meridie, declinare incipiente sole, constetque quinque ingeniculationibus, quarum unaquaeque tres contineat adorationes; tertio, oratione simili secundae, et finienda occidente sole. Ieiunia illis iniuncta esse, (ieiunium) triginta dierum, 10 quorum primus est octavus *Adari*; dein novem dierum, quorum primus est nonus *Al Canuni* prioris; necnon septem dierum, quorum primus *Shebati* octavus. Stellas invocare, multa offerre sacrificia, de quibus non comedunt, sed penitus igni absumenda tradunt. A fabarum et allii esu abstinere, nonnullos etiam a phaseolis, brassica, 15 crambe, et lentibus.[3]

'Dicta eorum affinia sunt dictis Philosophorum; argumenta eorum ad probandam Dei unitatem longe firmissima sunt. Autumant animas sceleratorum novies mille seculis cruciari, deinde ad misericordiam Dei redire.'

20

---

[1] I. e. they face towards the North when praying.

[2] What are 'the four intellectual virtues'? This looks like a fragment of Sabian *philosophy*, incongruously inserted into the description of Sabian *ritual*.

[3] These particulars may have been taken from one of Thabit's books concerning the rites of worship and religious usages of the Pagans of Harran (or of some one

HERMES DE CASTIGATIONE ANIMAE

This document is a discourse (or rather, a long string of short admonitions) addressed to the human soul, and is ascribed to Hermes. The Arabic text has been edited, with a Latin translation, by Bardenhewer (*Hermetis Trismegisti de castigatione animae libellus*, Bonn, 1873).[1] I here give an English rendering of Bardenhewer's Latin translation.[2]

Seven MSS. of the *Castig. an.* were known to Bardenhewer. Three of them give the whole text : viz. W, Leyden, A.D. 1654 ; H, Bodleian, in Syriac script ; P, Paris, *saec.* xv. The four others are mutilated.

There is in the *Castig. an.* no systematic order or arrangement, and no continuous sequence of thought. The Arabic text is divided into fourteen *capita*, which Bardenhewer has subdivided into sections ; but these divisions have no significance. The book consists of about ninety distinct and unconnected passages, each of which contains one leading thought, in many cases illustrated by a simile. These mutually independent passages are, as a rule, marked off from one another by phrases addressed to the soul, which stand at the beginning and end of each of them ('Convince yourself of this, O Soul, and reflect on it', or something of the sort). I call the several passages *sententiae* ; and I have separated them from one another by a slight space.

A book thus composed cannot properly be called a *treatise* ; it is rather an *anthologium*, put together by a compiler, who collected from various sources passages which he thought suitable for his purpose. The bulk of it may be described as a series of variations on one and the same theme. Any one who read it through continuously would soon get tired of the perpetual iteration ; and we may suppose that the

group or sect of them). What follows is a short description of the philosophy of the Harranian Platonists.

[1] There is an earlier edition, with a German translation, by Fleischer (*Hermes Trismegistos an die menschliche Seele*, Leipzig 1870). But in Fleischer's edition, only about half of the complete text is given, as the latter part of it (p. 316, sec. 9 to end) was omitted in the two MSS. used by him.

The *Castig. an.* is discussed by J. Kroll, *Die Lehren des Hermes Trismegistos*, 1914, pp. 390–405 ; and by Reitzenstein, *Die Göttin Psyché in der hellenistischen und frühchristlichen Literatur* (*Sitzungsber. d. Heidelberger Akad. d. Wissensch.* 1917, Abh. 10), pp. 51–66.

[2] For a thorough investigation of the *Castig. an.*, knowledge of the Arabic language, and of Arabic philosophic writings in general, would be required. These qualifications I do not possess ; but the character of the document, and the relation of the doctrine taught in it to Greek philosophy, can perhaps be seen clearly enough for the present purpose through the medium of a translation.

compiler rather intended each of the *sententiae* to be read separately (one a day, perhaps), and used as a subject for meditation.

The *sententiae* differ among themselves in form and style, and here and there in some point of doctrine; but most of them agree in inculcating a certain type of philosophic religion, a Platonism in which *contemptus mundi* is strongly emphasized; and this we must take to have been the creed of the compiler. But he was ready to include in his collection anything that seemed to him to tend to edification; and so we find a few *sententiae* that are distinctively Aristotelian,[1] and some pieces of gnomic or proverbial wisdom that have no connexion with any philosophic school.

At what date was the *Castig. an.* compiled? Bardenhewer says that the book must have been written before A.D. 1270, because a 'Book of admonition to the Soul', which he takes to be our *Castig. an.*, is referred to by Ibn Abí Useibi'a, who died in that year; and he thinks that it must have been written after the treatises of the *Fratres Sinceri*,[2] the date of which is said to be shortly before A.D. 1000.

---

[1] In some of the Platonic *sententiae* also, there are traces of Aristotelian influences, e. g. terms of Aristotelian logic, and the antithesis δυνάμει—ἐνεργείᾳ.

[2] The contents of the treatises of the *Fratres Sinceri* have been published by Dieterici, in his *Abhandlungen der Ichwân es-Safâ in Auswahl*, Leipz. 1883–1886, and in a series of other publications. Concerning the *Fratres Sinceri* ('Brothers of Purity') see de Boer, *Gesch. der Phil. in Islam*, pp. 76–89, and C. de Vaux. *Avicenne*, pp. 117–126. The association which bore this name had its headquarters at Basra, and flourished between A.D. 950 and 1000. R. A. Nicholson. *Lit. hist. of the Arabs*, p. 370 *sq.*, quoting from Ibnu 'l Qifti (d. A.D. 1248), gives the following account of the *Fratres Sinceri*: 'They formed a society for the pursuit of holiness, purity, and truth, and established amongst themselves a doctrine whereby they hoped to win the approval of God, maintaining that the Religious Law was defiled by ignorance and adulterated by errors, and that there was no means of cleansing and purifying it except philosophy, which united the wisdom of faith and the profit of research. They held that a perfect result would be reached if Greek philosophy were combined with Arabian religion. Accordingly, they composed fifty tracts in every branch of philosophy, theoretical as well as practical, added a separate index, and entitled them the "Tracts of the Brethren of Purity".' These treatises, which must have been written by some of the more learned members of the fraternity, form collectively a sort of encyclopaedia, extending over the whole range of philosophy and science as known to the Arabs of the time.

The liberal syncretism of the *Fratres Sinceri* is well illustrated by the following extract from one of their treatises, quoted by C. de Vaux from Dieterici, *The Macrocosm*, p. 91: 'Embark, like Noah, in the ship of salvation; we shall save you from the waves of the sea of matter, that you may not sink therein. Enter into the heavenly kingdom that was revealed to our father Abraham. Would you not wish to be present with Moses at the right-hand side of Mount Sinai? Would you not wish to be pure from the impurities of the flesh, like Jesus, who is so near to God? Would you not wish to come forth from the darkness of Ahriman, that you may see Jezdan?' (i. e. to attain to the 'Realm of Light', the Paradise of the Zoroastrians). 'Or again, would you not wish to be admitted to the temples of Ad and Tamud' (two mythical tribes of idolaters spoken of in the Koran), 'that

But it is not clear what reason he has for fixing on the latter date as the *terminus a quo*. He is doubtless right in saying that there is much similarity between the teaching of the *Castig. an.* and that of the *Fratres Sinceri* (that is, that the same kind of philosophic religion presents itself in both, and is frequently expressed in similar language); but that fact does not tell us which of the two is prior in time to the other. However, assuming that Bardenhewer's inferences are valid, we may take it that the *Castig. an.* in its present form was probably written at some date between A. D. 1000 and 1250.

Was the teaching contained in the *Castig. an.* ascribed to Hermes by the compiler? The name Hermes does not occur in the text, but in the title only; and there, in two MSS., another name stands in place of it. In four of the seven MSS. (R, L, P, U) the title is 'Commentatio Hermetis philosophi', &c., or something equivalent; but in W, it is 'Liber reprehensionis animae a *Platone* conscriptus'; and in H, it is 'Commentatio *Aristotelis* philosophi praestantissimi quae vocatur compellatio animae'. (In B, the title is lost.) Bardenhewer, however, concludes, for reasons which he holds to be sufficient, that in the title as written by the author (or, as I prefer to call him, the compiler) the teacher was named Hermes.

The compiler may be described as an Arab Platonist; that much can be inferred from the prevailing character of the *sententiae* collected by him (and from the contents of the prefatory passage 1. 1–4, if we take that passage to have been composed by him). The teaching of the collection as a whole differs considerably from that of Arab 'philosophers' such as Avicenna; on the other hand, it closely resembles that which Al-Katibi (d. A. D. 1276), in that part of the extract from him in *Testim.* which I have marked (*c*), ascribes to the 'Hernanites' (i. e. the Harranian Sabians). It therefore seems not unlikely that the compiler was a 'Sabian',—that is, that he was not, even in outward profession, a Mohammedan, but was a Pagan of the school of Thabit b. Qurra, and that the *sententiae* which he collected were taken chiefly from writings that were in use in that school. And this is confirmed by the ascription of the teaching to Hermes, the

you may there behold the celestial spheres of which Plato speaks, and which are not the (visible or material) spheres of the stars, but "intelligences" (νόες)'? But in this passage, the writer of which refers to the chief non-Moslem religions known to him,—Judaism, Christianity, Zoroastrianism, and philosophic Paganism,— the name which stands for Pagan philosophy is Plato, not Hermes; and this may perhaps be taken to indicate that he had learnt his philosophy not from the Sabians and their Hermetic scriptures, but rather from other Platonic sources.

'prophet' of the Harranian Sabians.   There seems to be no trace of
a survival of the Sabian school in Iraq after about A.D. 1050; it may
therefore be conjectured that the *Castig. an.* in something like its
present form was compiled by an adherent of that school about
A.D. 1000-1050. It must, however, be remembered that a collection
such as this would be open to additions at any time; and it may have
been begun much earlier, and grown to its present extent by degrees,
in the hands of successive transcribers.

Whence did the compiler get the *sententiae* which he collected?
That is a question to be considered separately in the case of each
sententia.   Some of them appear from internal evidence to have been
first written in an Arabic environment;[1] but there are some at least
which contain nothing that is necessarily of later date than A.D. 300,
and which may very well have been translated with little alteration
from documents of the same character as our Greek *Hermetica*.
Among these I would place, firstly, a few *sententiae* which contain a
blend of Platonism with Stoic physics, viz. 1. 8–11;[2] (3. 13?); 5.
2–5; 6. 7 b; and secondly, those which contain undiluted Platonism
of the same character as that of the Greek *Hermetica*.   In the latter
class may be placed 2. 5–8; 3. 12; 4. 4; 4. 14; 5. 9–11; 6. 2, 3;
6. 5; 6. 6, 7 a; 6. 8, 9; 7. 10, 11; 8. 1, 2; 8. 3; 11. 1–7; 12. 5–7;
13. 8, 9; 14. 7, 8; 14. 11, 12.

It cannot be affirmed with certainty that any one of these *sententiae*
has been translated from a Greek original; but it is at any rate evident
that the doctrines taught in them have been derived from the similar
doctrines taught in Greek writings; and it seems not unlikely that
some of them are more or less exact translations of Greek *Hermetica*[3]
which were written in Egypt before A.D. 300, and were included in

---

[1] Among these I would put the warnings against polytheism (2. 9 *sq.* and
12. 3 b *sq.*), and against women and strong drink (5. 7 *sq.*; 6. 10–12); those in
which the group *timor, tristitia, egestas* or some variation of it occurs (3. 3–7;
4. 9–11; 5. 6; 7. 1 *sq.*; 7. 10 *sq.*); gnomic maxims (2. 15 b; 4. 13; 7. 3; 9. 10;
12. 1 *sq.*; 12. 3 a); and a few specimens of simple Moslem piety (e. g. 9. 8). A
few slight traces of Zoroastrian or Manichaean influence may perhaps be found
(3. 8; 11. 6 b; 13. 6 *sq.*).

[2] 1. 8–11 stands first of the *sententiae*, if we set aside the three prefatory passages
which precede it; and it seems possible that it was the original nucleus of the
whole collection, other *sententiae* being successively appended. If this nucleus
was a translation of a Greek *Hermeticum*, that would account for the whole
collection being ascribed to Hermes.

[3] The hortatory tone of some of these *sententiae* resembles that of *Corp.
Herm.* VII. In some of them, statements about the soul in the third person
may have been altered by the compiler of the *Castig. an.* into sentences addressed
to the soul in the second person; and in some, perhaps, 'O Tat' or 'O Asclepius'
may have been altered by him into 'O Soul'.

the collection of *Hermetica* which the Harranian Sabians, in A.D. 830, put forward as their 'Scripture'.[1]

HERMES DE CASTIGATIONE ANIMAE

Preface (prefixed by a transcriber) : [2]

'In the name of God, preserver of the universe.[3]

'With God's help, . . . I begin to transcribe a treatise of that most eminent philosopher Hermes Trismegistus, in which the soul . . . is called away from the things below, and is urged to seek after the things above. . . . (By the teaching given in this treatise) the soul is restrained from sinking down into the turmoil of the perishable things of this world, and from being caught by their deceptive snares ; . . . and it is urged to . . . give its attention to those things by which it may draw nearer and nearer to Him who has created it, and be more and more closely conjoined with Him. . . .'[4]

I. I   Cap. I, §§ 1–4.   'I am about to set before you, O Soul,[5] the forms which mind (νοῦς) alone can apprehend, those forms which ever are ;[6] and I bid you represent them to yourself in thought.[7]   For when you

---

[1] It might be objected that, if it were so, we should most likely have found among the *sententiae* of the *Castig. an.* some extracts from Greek *Hermetica* that are still extant.   But that objection is not decisive, because the extant *Hermetica* are probably no more than a small fraction of the complete collection of *Hermetica* that existed in Egypt in A.D. 300, and was extant at Harran in A.D. 830, and presumably at Bagdad for some time after A.D. 900.

[2] Here and throughout the *Castig. an.*, the passages enclosed by quotation marks are translated by me from Bardenhewer's Latin translation of the Arabic. In the passages not thus marked I give, not a translation, but a shortened paraphrase ; and I omit, in most cases, the clauses addressed to 'the Soul' which stand at the beginning and end of the several *sententiae* (see e. g. 2. 9 *init.* and 10 *fin.*), and which I take to have been added by the compiler of the *Castig. an.*

[3] For this has been substituted, in one of the MSS., 'In the name of the Father, the Son, and the Holy Ghost'.   The man who wrote those words was a Christian ; and he must have accepted the book as sound and edifying.   Though there is nothing in it that is distinctively Christian, there is little with which a Christian monk might not have been ready to agree (except, perhaps, the pre-existence of the human soul ; and even that might have been accepted by a follower of Origen).

[4] That is a correct description of the contents of the *Castig. animae.*

[5] The 'Soul' to whom every paragraph of the *Castig. animae* is addressed by the compiler means any or every *man* who will listen to his teaching ; that is, it means the reader.   A man on earth consists of body and soul ; but the writer, consistently with his doctrine, ignores the body, and speaks to the soul alone.

[6] i. e. τὰ νοητὰ εἴδη, τὰ ἀεὶ ὄντα.   It is evident that the Arabic word which Bardenhewer, here and throughout the *Castig. an.*, translates by *ratio*, stands for νοῦς as used by Platonists and Hermetists.

[7] (*Species illas*) *cogitatione tibi informes et effingas* Bardenhewer.   The phrase *cogitatione aliquid sibi informare et effingere*, which occurs repeatedly in the *Castig. an.*, appears to mean 'to fashion by thought, and thereby reproduce in

represent things to yourself in thought, you understand them, and make them your own, and are convinced of the truth of them ; as you **2** are convinced, for instance, that ' &c.[1] . . . 'And if some of the things I am about to expound should be somewhat obscure to you, you must apply to them your faculty of representing things to yourself in thought, keeping that faculty vigorous and sound and free from confusion and inconsistency.

'You will be led to the knowledge of the internal things which are invisible to you,[2] by the external things which you see before you.[3] A man who looks at a painted picture infers thence the existence of the painter ; and seeing with his eyes the picture which has been made by the painter's hands, he is thereby led to know the invisible processes of the painter's thought in the designing and drawing of the picture, which corresponded to the forms that presented themselves **3** to his mind.[4] And in all cases alike (as in that of the painter), if the maker of a thing is not himself visible to us, we can form a notion of him from the thing he has made, when that thing is presented to our view. Even so then, we can represent to ourselves in thought the

one's own mind, something that already exists outside one's mind'. This phrase is used as equivalent to the one word νοεῖν (see 5. 1). The writer's meaning might perhaps be explained thus: the νοητὰ εἴδη (the παραδείγματα of which all αἰσθητά are imperfect copies) are God's thoughts or purposes ; and for a man, to attain to truth is to reproduce those εἴδη in his own mind, and 'make them his own',— i. e. to think those same thoughts which God thinks. It is to make his thought (and will) coincide with God's.

[1] Here are given some instances of things of which men 'are convinced', i. e. which they know beyond possibility of doubt : 'You are convinced that man (as an earthly organism) is ἔμψυχος, ἔμψυχα are ζῶντα, ζῶντα are σώματα, and σώματα are οὐσίαι (a specimen of logical classification by *species* and *genus* ; ζῶντα includes plants, σώματα includes lifeless bodies, and οὐσίαι includes incorporeal things) ; you are convinced that one (line) is straight and another curved ; that water quenches thirst, and is by nature cold and moist, and that fire burns things, emits light, and is by nature hot and dry ; in short, you are convinced of all things that you have understood in the world of thought, and of all that you have seen with your own eyes in the world of sense.' (The writer means that he would have his pupil attain to a like certainty concerning the truths set forth in the *Castig. an.*) Three of the instances of certain knowledge that are here given (properties of water, properties of fire, straight and curved lines) occur in a like connexion in 14. 6 ; the writer of 1. 1-4 may have got them thence, and added the classification-instance.

[2] τὰ ἀόρατα, τὰ νοητά, τὸ ἀφανές.   [3] τὰ αἰσθητά, τὰ φανερά.

[4] [Compare the teaching of *Corpus* V. For the figure of the painter cf. V. 7 : τίς πάντα ταῦτα ἐποίησε ; . . . καὶ ἀνδριάντα μὲν ἢ εἰκόνα χωρὶς ἀνδριαντοποιοῦ ἢ ζωγράφου οὐδείς φησι γεγονέναι· τοῦτο δὲ τὸ δημιούργημα χωρὶς δημιουργοῦ γέγονεν ; ὦ τῆς πολλῆς τυφλότητος κ.τ.λ.

§ 2: τὰ δὲ πάντα φαντασιῶν, διὰ πάντων φαίνεται, καὶ ἐν πᾶσι· καὶ μάλιστα οἷς ἂν αὐτὸς βουληθῇ φανῆναι. § 3: εἰ δὲ θέλεις αὐτὸν ἰδεῖν, νόησον τὸν ἥλιον κ.τ.λ. § 5: ὦ θέας ἐκείνης. τέκνον, εὐτυχεστάτης . . . θεάσασθαι . . . καὶ τὸν ἀφανῆ φαινόμενον δι᾽ ὧν ποιεῖ. Cf. *Corp.* XI. ii. 22 a.]

Author of all that is, by contemplating and admiring the (visible) things ⟨which He has made, and ever brings into being, and⟩ which are and have been produced by Destiny [1] .... [2]

'I bid you then, O Soul, to represent to yourself in thought all things that are either understood by thinking or perceived by sense.[3]

4 And know that it is the truly existent Being,[4] the First Cause,[5] perfect and full of light,[6] that bestows on men knowledge of the inner nature of things,[7] and of the finer distinctions between them,[8] [and of everlasting life,] and in short, knowledge of all things. And all things are, in relation to Him, *particulars*, but are not *parts* of Him; as He on the other hand is, in relation to them, the *universal*, but is not a mere *sum* of them.[9]

'Reflect on this, O Soul, and mark it well; and free yourself from the pollution of the physical world, and to that end, humble yourself;[10] and seek and strive earnestly to attain to Him who is the source and father of good, the root and originator[11] of intelligence,[12] the giver of life and wisdom,[13] Him who is perfect goodness and mercy,[14] that so you may come to partake of Life, and enjoy happiness and bliss.'[15]

---

[1] The physical world is governed by εἱμαρμένη (i. e. by natural law), which is God's working in the αἰσθητὸς κόσμος.
There seems to be something wrong in Bard.'s reading, *in contemplatione et admiratione rerum quae ex eis quae fati necessitate prodeunt iamiam prodierunt*. What I have written gives the sense required by the context.

[2] The words I have omitted are *non proponendis similitudinibus de rebus abditis et rebus promptis* (sc. *effingi potest rerum universitatis Auctor*) Bard.: 'Nicht aber durch Aufstellung blosser sinnbildlicher Allgemeinheiten über geheime und nicht geheime Dinge' Fleischer. What does that mean? Is it an allusion to attempts to represent the deity in visible form,—i. e. a protest against idols? *Res abditae* and *res promptae* must mean νοητά and αἰσθητά.

[3] I. e. not τὰ αἰσθητά alone, but τὰ νοητά also.

[4] *Ens vere substantiale*, i. e. τὸ ὄντως ὄν, which here denotes God.

[5] *Principale* Bard.

[6] *Lucidum* Bard. God is φῶς (the intellectual 'light' by which the mental eye sees), and as such, bestows 'light' or *gnosis* on men.

[7] 'Knowledge of the mysterious *Gründen* (causes or reasons?) and purposes of things' Fleischer.

[8] E. g. the distinction between good and bad?

[9] What is here meant by *particularia* and *universale*? Cp. *Corp. Herm.* XVI. 3 as emended: ⟨God is the One that is τῶν πάντων τὸ πλήρωμα·⟩ ἐὰν γάρ τις ἐπιχειρήσῃ τὰ πάντα τοῦ ἑνὸς χωρίσαι, ἐκδεξάμενος τὴν τῶν πάντων προσηγορίαν ἐπὶ πλήθους, οὐκ ἐπὶ πληρώματος, τὸ πᾶν τοῦ ἑνὸς λύσας ἀπολέσει τὸ πᾶν.

[10] *Animum demittas* Bard. Does this refer to ascetic practices?

[11] *Auctor* Bard.: perhaps ἀρχή.   [12] νοῦς.

[13] *Sapientia* Bard.: σοφία, or γνῶσις?

[14] God's 'mercy' was spoken of by Jews, Christians, and Moslems, but not often by Pagan Greeks. (God's ἔλεος occurs, however, in *Corp. Herm.* XIII.)

[15] This passage, I. 1–4, seems to have been written by the compiler of the *Castig. an.* as a preface to the whole collection of *sententiae*. It can hardly have been taken over from a Greek source in its present form; but the thoughts

5   Cap. 1, §§ 5, 6. 'The Author, Creator, and Founder of the universe,—to be revered beyond all is He, and holy are his names,[1] —created you, O Soul, out of nothing, and equipped you with the power of forming and fashioning things (in your mind) by thought. You *form* things by your thought in accordance with their reality as made by the Creator; but you *fashion* by your thought things which belong to the thought-world,[2] and the true form of which is hidden from you, fashioning them out of the things which you see before you in the sense-world,[3] like out of like, (thought-)form out of (sense-) form.[4] (You are thus led on to knowledge of that which truly is,) even as, by inference from the image stamped on the wax, you are brought to a knowledge of the real form of that image as it existed in the seal by means of which it was stamped on the wax, and from the image engraved on the seal you are led on to know its real form as it existed in the soul of the man who engraved the seal.[5] Or again, it is even as water leaves on sand and mud the shape of its undulating movements.[6]

6   'Believe me then, when I say that the things which I have set before you are true (*or* real); and know that all the shapes and images which you see with your bodily eyes in the world of things that come

expressed in it belong to a Platonism of the same kind that is found in the Greek *Hermetica*.

    The two following passages, 1. 5–6 and 1. 7, are also prefatory; but appear to be unconnected either with 1. 1–4, or with one another. The doctrine of 1. 5–6 is, like that of 1. 1–4, Platonic and Hermetic; that of 1. 7 is Aristotelian.

    [1] The notion that God's *names* are holy is Jewish, Christian, and Moslem, rather than Pagan-Platonic.

    [2] The νοητὸς κόσμος, i. e. the world of ὄντως ὄντα.

    [3] The αἰσθητὸς κόσμος.

    [4] The writer here makes a distinction between '*informare* res cogitatione' and '*effingere* res cogitatione'. He seems to mean by *informare*, to form concepts of τὰ ὄντως ὄντα by direct intuition; and by *effingere*, to form concepts of τὰ ὄντως ὄντα by inference from τὰ αἰσθητά, which are 'images' or copies of τὰ ὄντως ὄντα.

    [5] The wax is ὕλη. The image stamped on the wax is the αἰσθητὸν εἶδος of this or that thing in the material world (e. g. the sensible qualities of this or that particular horse). The form engraved on the seal is, I suppose, the general type, or universal, of a natural class of things (e. g. the *species* 'horse', i. e. the group of qualities which all horses have in common). The engraver of the seal is God; and the 'form (i. e. thought, design, or plan) that was in the engraver's mind' is the νοητὸν εἶδος, which is the παράδειγμα pre-existent in God's thought (e. g. the αὐτό-ιππος). We begin by perceiving the αἰσθητὸν εἶδος, and thence pass on to the apprehension of the νοητὸν εἶδος and of God.—The simile of seal and wax was a commonplace of Greek philosophy, from Pl. *Theaet.* onward. But the appended simile of the ripple-marks in sand does not occur in any Greek writing known to me.

    [6] The rippling water may perhaps be taken to stand for God's ἐνέργειαι imposing form on matter; the sand is ὕλη; and the ripple-marks are the αἰσθητὰ εἴδη, which we perceive, and from which we can infer God's ἐνέργειαι.

to be and cease to be[1] are mere semblances[2] and copies[3] of the forms which have real existence in the thought-world,[4] those forms which are eternal and will never cease to be.

'[For[5] the things that are in the spiritual[6] world can be seen by the eye of the mind[7] alone; and therefore every being that partakes of the nature of mind and also has a body, if such a being has arrived at particular existence,[8] must convince itself by thought that it is a reality that will never cease to be.[9]]

'(The human mind) then first ⌐forms for itself by thought a representation of itself in matter¬, and thereafter ⌐represents to itself its own forms¬.[10] And thereby it comes to pass that the man is captivated by love of his own being, and is filled with joy; for by thought he gets from himself intellectual enjoyment of his own being. This joy he gets not from anything outside him, nor from any accident attaching to him; from himself does he get enjoyment of himself. And this is pleasure that is real, ceaseless, and ever-lasting.'

7   Cap. 1, § 7. 'Seek, O Soul, to win sure knowledge of things by learning to know their *existence* and their *essence*;[11] but disregard their

---

[1] τὰ γιγνόμενα.

[2] *Simulacra*: εἴδωλα. [*Corp.* VI. 4 b: πάντα γὰρ τὰ ὀφθαλμῷ ὑποπίπτοντα εἴδωλά ἐστι, καὶ ὥσπερ σκιαγραφίαι.]

[3] *Effigies*: εἰκόνες.

[4] τὰ νοητὰ εἴδη, τὰ ὄντως ὄντα.

[5] This passage ('For the things … cease to be') is omitted in some of the MSS.

[6] πνευματικός. (The Arabic word is cognate with Heb. *ruach*.) The use of πνεῦμα and its derivatives in place of the Platonic and Hermetic νοῦς and its derivatives is usually a mark of Jewish or Christian influence.

[7] ὁ ὀφθαλμὸς τοῦ νοῦ. [*Corp.* X. 4 b: καὶ ὀλίγου δεῖν ἐσβέσθη (ἐσεβάσθη codd.: see Addenda) μου ὁ τοῦ νοῦ ὀφθαλμὸς ὑπὸ τῆς τοιαύτης θέας. § 5: οὐκ ἰσχύομεν ἀναπετάσαι ἡμῶν τοὺς τοῦ νοῦ ὀφθαλμούς, καὶ θεάσασθαι τὸ κάλλος τοῦ ἀγαθοῦ. IV. 11b: ἢν (τὴν εἰκόνα) ἀκριβῶς εἰ θεάσῃ καὶ νοήσεις τοῖς τῆς καρδίας ὀφθαλμοῖς. . . . εὑρήσεις τὴν πρὸς τὰ ἄνω ὁδόν. Cf. V. 2, VII. 1 a.]

[8] I. e. every νοερὰ ψυχή that has been parted off from the world-soul and incarnated; or in other words, every man, during his present life on earth.

[9] I. e. a man must, by use of the νοῦς of which his true self consists, convince himself that he is immortal. But perhaps rather 'Man must convince himself that, *in respect of* his νοῦς, he is a reality that will never cease to be'. It is in virtue of the νοῦς of which it partakes, that the human soul is immortal.

[10] *Ratione igitur se ipsum sibi ipsi in materia effingit, exinde per se ipsum suas ipsius species et formas* Bard. But in place of *Ratione*, Fleischer gives 'Die Vernunft', *nom.* (i. e. *Ratio*).—*Per se ipsum*, 'by itself', apparently stands in contrast to *in materia*, and so means 'apart from matter'.—The writer may perhaps have meant that a man begins by identifying himself with his material body, but passes on thence to regard himself as an incorporeal being, akin to the divine νοῦς. (He comes to 'know himself', in the sense in which self-knowledge is spoken of in *Corp. Herm.* I.)

[11] To know the *existentia* (ὕπαρξις?) of a thing is to know ὅτι ἐστι; to know its *essentia* (οὐσία) is to know τί ἐστι.

qualities and *quantities*.[1]   For the *existence* of a thing and its *essence* are simple (i. e. incomposite) and eternal, and there is nothing that intervenes between the soul and them;[2] but the *qualities* and the *quantities* are composite (or concrete),[3] and are circumscribed by limits of space and time.   And know, O Soul, that it will not be possible for you, when you depart from the sense-world,[4] to take with you any knowledge of the world of composite (or concrete)[3] things, as though such knowledge were (as in truth it is not) separated (from external things) and joined and mingled with the being of the soul itself.   Grasp then the knowledge of simple things, and abandon knowledge of composite things.'[5]

8   Cap. I, §§ 8–11. '(*a*) Of the cosmic elements, [O Soul,] *Earth* is the heaviest, inasmuch as it settles down below all other things. It is gross, thick, dense, and rigid, and is devoid of light and life.[6]

'(*b*) Next in order comes the element *Water*, which is subtler and

---

[1] τὸ ποιόν and τὸ ποσόν. The 'qualities' here spoken of are the *sensible* qualities of this or that particular thing, which vary with time and place (e. g. a thing is hotter at one time and colder at another). The *essential* qualities of a thing are included in the *essentia*, which is a universal, and is independent of time and place. [*Ascl.* I. 11 a : unde efficitur ut rerum diversitates, qualitates, effectus, quantitates suspiciosa indagatione sectetur, retardatus uero graui et nimio corporis vitio has naturae rerum causas quae uerae sunt proprie peruidere non possit. 34 b (p. 322) : scitote intelligibilem mundum, id est, qui mentis solo obtutu dinoscitur, esse incorporalem, nec eius naturae misceri aliquid posse corporale, id est, quod possit qualitate, quantitate, numerisque dinosci : in ipso enim nihil tale consistit.]

[2] I. e. the human soul can apprehend them immediately, without the intervention of the body and the bodily sense-organs.

[3] *Composita*, σύνθετα. Aristotle uses τὸ σύνθετον or ἡ σύνθετος οὐσία (and also τὸ σύνολον) to signify *id quod compositum est ex materia et forma* (Bonitz *Index Arist.*); e. g. Arist. *Metaph.* 4. 24. 1023 a 31 : τοῦ συνθέτου ἐκ τῆς ὕλης καὶ τῆς μορφῆς. *De an.* 2. 1. 412 a 16 : πᾶν σῶμα φυσικὸν οὐσία ἂν εἴη, οὐσία δ' οὕτως ὡς συνθέτη (a concrete thing). The Arabic writer uses the word 'composite' in this Aristotelian sense when he speaks of 'the world of composite things'. But he also says that 'the qualities and the quantities are composite'; and as qualities and quantities are not composed of form and matter, this must be taken to mean that the (sensible) qualities and quantities of which he is speaking are the qualities and quantities of 'composite' things (i. e. particular concrete things). Cf. 10. 7–9 and 11. 5 *sq.*

'Simple' means incomposite, i. e. consisting of form alone, and not of form and matter combined together.

[4] I. e. when the man dies.

[5] I. e. seek knowledge of universals, and disregard knowledge of particulars. This paragraph is a statement of Aristotle's doctrine that ἐπιστήμη is τῶν καθόλου and not τῶν καθ' ἕκαστα.

[6] 'Light and life'; cf. ζωὴ καὶ φῶς in *Corp. Herm.* I. As here used, 'light' perhaps means the principle of cognition (sense and thought), and 'life' the principle of self-movement or activity; these are the two chief aspects of what might be called *life* in the widest sense. Earth is utterly lifeless.

purer than earth, and is superior to earth. Water has more light in it than earth, and is nearer to life.[1]

'(c) Next comes the element *Air*, which is subtler than water, ⟨and has in it more light and life ;⟩

'(d) and next to air comes the element *Fire*, which is the subtlest of the four (sublunar) elements ; it is superior to the three others, and is the most largely endowed with light.

9 '(e) Next to fire comes *the Element of the Celestial Sphere*,[2] which ⌜contains the purest parts of the things placed below it⌝,[3] and is marked by peculiar excellence in comparison with the other elements,—firstly, in that it is subtle and light[4] in the highest degree, possesses light in abundance, is beautifully ordered and arranged,[5] and is near to[6] life, and is joined in vicinity to things excellent and participant of mind ;[7] secondly, in that it has that figure which is of all figures the most excellent, most perfect, and most symmetrical, namely, the figure of a sphere ; and thirdly, in that all the things enveloped by it are indued with that same figure, sphere following sphere in order downward even to the sphere of the earth.[8]

10 '(f) Next above the element of the celestial sphere, which is the outermost of all the (five) elements, follows (in ascending order) the substance of *Soul*,[9] which bestows on the celestial orbs ordered movement, and pure and brilliant light. Soul is subtler than all the things encompassed by it,[10] inasmuch as they are bodies and elements, but

---

[1] Water is not utterly lifeless ; there is in it some rudiment of sentient life and self-movement. (Cf. 5. 2–5.)

[2] This is Aristotle's 'fifth element'.

[3] We should have expected 'which is purer than the four elements situated below it'.

[4] *Levis* : ἐλαφρός, λεπτομερής.

[5] τάξις. Cf. e. g. *Corp.* V. 5, VIII. 4.

[6] *Vitae propinquus.* See vol. III, p. 40.

[7] τὰ μετέχοντα νοῦ. The celestial sphere 'adjoins' or 'is in proximity to' τὰ νοητά, which are pictured as situated in the boundless space outside the Kosmos. This way of speaking is, if taken literally, inconsistent with the incorporeality of τὰ νοητά.

[8] [*Corp.* VIII. 3 : τῇ δὲ ἀθανασίᾳ περιβαλὼν τό πᾶν σῶμα. This is the Aristotelian doctrine of the fifth body—κύκλῳ φερόμενον. See vol. III, p. 39].

[9] ἡ τῆς ψυχῆς οὐσία.—ψυχή, the lowest of τὰ νοητά, is placed next above the celestial sphere, which is the highest of τὰ αἰσθητά. The world-soul (that universal soul out of which individual souls are 'parted off') is here pictured as a stratum of quasi-gaseous and luminous soul-stuff situated immediately above or beyond the outermost sphere of heaven. It is self-moving and intelligent, and imparts movement and 'light' (i. e. both physical light and intelligence. the one being hardly distinguished from the other,) to the heavenly bodies situated below it.

[10] i. e. than the five elements spoken of above.

soul is wholly incorporeal.[1]	All things that are situated below soul[2] are unable to partake of life except by means of soul.[3]	Soul possesses in itself the powers of thought, will, and judgement;[4] and it extends its own properties to all things with which it is conjoined, so far as they are capable of receiving those properties;[5] and thereby they attain to life.	But those things with which soul is not conjoined[6] are utterly destitute of thought, will, movement, and judgement; and a thing that does not possess these properties in any degree is lifeless.

II	'(g) Next above the substance of soul comes *Mind* (νοῦς), which is exalted above soul, and encompasses it.[7]	Mind is the subtlest of all things discoverable;[8] it is superior to all the rest, and is situated in the highest place.

'(h) And Mind is inferior only to that *supreme Deity* who is eternal and most holy and most lofty.	From Him, without intermediary, does mind receive, and dispense to all things placed below it,[9] excellence[10] and light and life.[11]	Mind is the supreme mediator

---

[1] ψυχή is here said to be ἀσώματος.	Yet there is assigned to it a situation in space, which implies that it is *not* ἀσώματος in the strictest sense of that term; and it is called subtler (λεπτομερέστερον) than the five elements, which, if taken literally, implies that it is, like them, a σῶμα, and differs from them only in degree of rarity.	The statement that ψυχή is ἀσώματος is Platonic; the other view is Stoic; and the writer is trying, with imperfect success, to combine together these two ways of regarding things.

[2] I. e. the elements and the things composed of them.

[3] We were told above that all the elements, except earth, have in them some life, more or less; and it follows from what is here said that the life in them is conferred on them by the ψυχή (the world-soul) situated above the heavens, or comes to them from that ψυχή. [Stob. *Exc.* XX 1 (codd.): πᾶν γὰρ σῶμα δεῖται τοῦ εἶναι, δεῖται καί ζωῆς τῆς ἐν τάξει κειμένης. § 3: μετειληφὸς δὲ εἴδους ζωῆς, ζῇ, καὶ κοινωνεῖ τοῦ εἶναι τῇ ψυχῇ.]

[4] I. e. the world-soul is νοερά.

[5] The universal and supracosmic ψυχή possesses intelligence in its highest form; an animal on earth receives from this supracosmic ψυχή as much intelligence as the animal organism is capable of receiving (viz. sentience and instinct, which the writer regards as lower grades of intelligence).	Man is capable of receiving intelligence in its higher grades.

[6] τὰ ἄψυχα; e. g. stones, and perhaps plants.

[7] νοῦς is pictured as a still rarer and more 'subtle' gas, diffused through extra-cosmic space beyond the stratum of ψυχή.	The writer's notion of extracosmic νοῦς resembles that of the τύπος-νοῦς in *Corp. Herm.* II; but he differs from the author of *Corp.* II in interposing a ψυχή-stratum between the extracosmic νοῦς and the outermost sphere of the Kosmos.

[8] *Omnium quae reperiuntur.*	Is this phrase meant to except God (of whom it might be said that he *est*, but *non reperitur*, i. e. that there is no *place* in which he can be found)?

[9] Primarily and immediately to ψυχή, and through ψυχή, to all ἔμψυχα.

[10] *Praestantiam* Bard., *Adel* Fleischer: τὸ καλόν?

[11] φῶς καὶ ζωή.	'Light' must here mean *that which enables us to see* (both with the bodily eyes and with 'the eye of the mind'), i. e. the principle of *cognition* in

(between God and the Kosmos), the chamberlain who stands nearest (to the King).[1]

'[Contemplate this system then, O Soul, assure yourself of its truth, and be firmly convinced of it ; for thus it is that things are constituted, ordered, and arranged.]'[2]

2. 1–4 Cap. 2, §§ 1–8. It is not true that this world deceives men.[3] That would be true only if men enjoyed uninterrupted happiness in this life, and were not plunged into misery until after death ; but that is not the case. In this life men experience good fortune and ill fortune, happiness and misery, by turns. It is not the world then that deceives men ; but men deceive themselves, and so bring themselves to ruin. They think their happiness consists in the goods which this world gives, and think that these goods will last for ever, forgetting that life in this world is an alternation of good and bad.

5, 6 But though this world is a complex of contraries, good and evil

all grades ; and 'life', as distinguished from 'light', must mean chiefly *self-movement* or *activity*.

[1] νοῦς is prime minister or vizier of the supreme God, and dispenser (ταμίας) of the 'light and life' that issue from Him. *Corp.* XII. i, 1.

[2] This passage (1. 8–11) is a separate whole, complete in itself. It is unconnected with what precedes and follows ; and it is at variance with the hard-and-fast division and contrast between αἰσθητά and νοητά, things corporeal and things incorporeal, which is so strongly insisted on in nearly all the rest of the *Castig. an.* It sets forth a system in which things are placed in a continuous and unbroken series, ranging upward from lifeless matter to the supreme God ; and ψυχή and νοῦς are spoken of as if they were 'subtler' or rarer forms of material or corporeal substance. This is a compromise between the 'hylozoism' of the Stoics (who regarded πῦρ or πνεῦμα as a living and intelligent agent) and the Platonic conception of incorporeal entities. A compromise of the same kind presents itself in some of the Greek *Hermetica*; and *Castig. an.* 1. 8–11 may be described as an expansion of the sentence in *Corp. Herm.* XII. i. 14 a (repeated with slight variation in *Corp.* V *fin.*) : ἔστιν οὖν τῆς μὲν ὕλης τὸ λεπτομερέστατον ἀήρ, ἀέρος δὲ ψυχή, ψυχῆς δὲ νοῦς, νοῦ δὲ θεός.

God, νοῦς, and ψυχή, as here spoken of, correspond to the three divine *hypostases* (τὸ ἕν, νοῦς, ψυχή) of Plotinus; but the doctrine is here presented in a simple and popular form, as compared either with the more elaborate metaphysic of Plotinus, or the more complicated systems of Arab philosophers such as Avicenna (in which, in place of the one νοῦς, there is a hierarchy of some ten different νόες). Comparative simplicity is not in itself a decisive proof of earlier date, for simplification of a complex system is also possible; but it is at least highly probable that this passage (1. 8–11) was transcribed by the compiler of the *Castig. an.*, with little alteration, from a Syriac or Arabic translation of a Greek original of the third century A. D. ; and it is not unlikely that in that original the teaching was ascribed to Hermes,—that is to say, that we have here a more or less exact translation of one of the lost Greek *Hermetica.* If *Castig. an.* 1. 8–11 were translated back into Greek, with 'O soul' omitted or changed into 'O Tat', it might be placed among the *libelli* of the *Corp. Herm.* without seeming in any respect incongruous with them. (The 'fifth element', which does not often occur in the Greek *Hermetica*, may perhaps be a later addition.)

[3] Apparently a denial of what had been asserted by some particular teacher. Cf. 14. 4 *sq.*

being intermingled in it in mutual conflict, yet at the same time it contains semblances or shadows [1] (of things higher and more real), whereby the soul is awakened, and urged to turn its attention on itself; and thus the soul is enabled to gain clear intelligence, and to attain to knowledge of the truth. [2]

The soul descends into this world [3] in order that it may make trial of things and learn to know them; [4] but when it is here, it neglects its business of seeking and learning truth; it is drawn away to the pursuit of worldly goods and pleasures, and forgets the purpose for which it came down to earth.

7   Men use their senses amiss, and fail to attain to any true knowledge; but this world, rightly regarded, is a place for learning truth in. The visible forms of things which it presents to our senses are fleeting and perishable; but 'they are semblances or shadows of forms that are not apprehensible by sense, forms that are real and everlasting.' [5] There is in the thought-world nothing of which copies are not to be seen among the things which are brought into being by the process of nature in the sense-world; and on the other hand, all things that are found in the sense-world are merely varying semblances or copies of things in the thought-world. The deceptive and fleeting pleasures of the sense-world suggest to us that we should turn from them to the true and unceasing pleasures of the thought-world; the frail, transitory, and perishable forms of the sense-world bid us turn from them to the stable and constant forms of the thought-world; the mutual repugnance [and inconstancy] of all things in the sense-world urges us to turn to the concord [stability and constancy] of all things in the thought-world.

8   'Therefore, O Soul, as long as you are in the physical world, [6] seek not any pleasure (of sense), and suffer not yourself to be so occupied with any sensible thing as to be drawn away from learning to know,

---

[1] εἴδωλα or εἰκόνες. *Corp.* VI. 4 b.

[2] I. e. knowledge of the νοητά and of God,—the γνῶσις of the Hermetists.

[3] The Platonic doctrine of the pre-existence of the soul in a higher world is here assumed.

[4] But if the soul, before its incarnation, already knows τὰ νοητά, what more knowledge does it need? Perhaps the writer might have answered, that in the world above the soul has known τὰ νοητά *only*; but when incarnated on earth, it becomes acquainted with τὰ αἰσθητά also, and is enabled, by comparing the one with the other, to estimate τὰ νοητά at their true value. (The good cannot be fully known and understood unless contrasted with the bad.) Cf. 3. 7 and 6. 8.

[5] τὰ αἰσθητὰ εἴδη are εἴδωλα or εἰκόνες of τὰ νοητὰ εἴδη. [Stob. *Exc.* II. A. 3 (codd): πάντα οὖν . . . τὰ ἐπὶ γῆς ἀληθῆ μὲν οὐκ ἔστι· τῇ σοὲ ἀληθείας μιμήματα.]

[6] *In mundo naturae*: i. e. as long as your present life on earth lasts.

and representing to yourself in thought, and seeking out, those things [1] which (it is your true function to) aim at and desire and pursue ; that so you may be enabled to devote all your efforts to the one aim of getting knowledge. [2]

'If you desire true pleasures and unceasing joys, you must put off your unclean garment, [3] cast off the burden of your body, and guard against things repugnant to your (incorporeal) substance ; and having done so, turn to the world of true pleasures and unceasing joys, clothe yourself in garments [4] congruous with your true being, and surround yourself with forms appropriate to your own substance, forms everlasting and unchanging,—those forms, of which copies and semblances were seen by you while you were yet in the world of things that come to be and cease to be.' [5]

9 Cap. 2, §§ 9, 10. ['Convince yourself, O Soul, of the truth of all the things which I have hitherto expounded to you, and understand them ; and know this also : ']

There are three things that are pernicious in all their various forms ; viz. (1) *polytheism*, [6] (2) *injustice*, (3) *desire for (sensuous) pleasures*.

---

[1] viz. τὰ νοητά or τὰ θεῖα.

[2] The γνῶσις of the Hermetists,—that 'knowledge' of God which involves union with God.

[3] I.e. your body. Cf. *Corp. Herm.* VII. 2 b: δεῖ σε περιρρήξασθαι ὃν φορεῖς χιτῶνα, κ.τ.λ. You must 'put off' your body, not by dying, but by 'alienating yourself from' the body, i.e. ceasing to be concerned with or influenced by the body and bodily things. Cf. 3. 4.

[4] What are the 'garments' which the soul is to put on? I know of no exact parallel to this in Pagan Greek writings. In *Corp. Herm.* X. 16 it is said that the human νοῦς *when disembodied* 'puts on a garment of fire'; and some of the later Platonists said that souls. when not incarnated in a gross body on earth, are clothed in some sort of 'pneumatic' body of finer substance (an opinion which was held by Origen); but the writer of this passage appears to be speaking of the souls of men still living upon earth. The 'garments' which a soul in that condition puts on must be metaphorical; they are, I suppose, the νοητὰ εἴδη. Cf. 4. 6, where the beatified soul is described as 'stripped of the garments of evil and delusion, and clothed in garments of good, and of that which is everlasting'.

[5] 2. 1–8 is an exhortation to renounce the pleasures of sense, and seek the higher joys of the incorporeal world. The thoughts, in §§ 5–8, are Platonic, and must have been derived from Greek writings, some of which may have been *Hermetica*; and the exhortation somewhat resembles the Hermetic sermon-fragment *Corp.* VII. But whether the Arabic-speaking Platonist who wrote the passage translated it from a Greek original, or composed it afresh in his own language, we have no means of knowing.

[6] This could not have been said by a Greek Hermetist, or by any Pagan Platonist. It might have been said by a Jew or by a Christian; but it is more likely that the author of this passage was a Moslem. In the view of a Moslem, not only 'Sabians' and Zoroastrians. but Christians also were polytheists. In the Koran, Christians are included among those who 'add gods to God', and are reproached for making Jesus a God and son of God, and worshipping the Virgin

And all these three spring from one root, viz. *love of the things of this world*.[1] Shun then the things of this world, flee from them, and fear them, even as a bird shuns the fowler's snare.

10 'By shunning *polytheism*, you will be led upward to worship of the one true God; by guarding against *injustice*, you will be led upward to light,[2] sincerity, purity, and integrity; by guarding against *desire for pleasures*, you will be set free from the bitterness of *fear* and *anxious care* and *ignorance* and *sense of want*.[3]'[4]

['Assure yourself, O Soul, that these maxims are true, and seek to learn that they are right; that so you may attain to salvation, and be kept safe from destruction.']

11 Cap. 2, §§ 11–13. Man was created by God to this end, that man might get knowledge, and direct his action by it.

But man grows to the fulfilment of this purpose by degrees, even as a grape is formed and ripened by degrees.

12 Man may be regarded either as 'a thing perceptible by sense',[5] or as a being endowed with mind (νοῦς).

'Regarded as a thing perceptible by sense, man, when he first comes into the world (at birth), is unfit to discharge any of the functions for which he has been made; but by assimilating stuff supplied to him, he is brought on to a stage at which he is fit to be taught and instructed, though still unable to take thought for himself. And if at this stage he puts forth adequate exertion, there enters into

Mary. The Christian worship of saints, relics, and images might also be regarded as polytheism. Cf. 12. 3 b. *sq.*

The two evils with which polytheism is here put on a par are ἀδικία and ἀκολασία, the vices opposed to δικαιοσύνη and σωφροσύνη, which are two of the cardinal virtues of Greek ethics. (There is no mention here of ἀνδρεία, which is spoken of in 3. 10 a.)

[1] *Studium rerum humanarum* Bard.: 'die Liebe zur Welt' Fleischer. *Res humanae* may be taken to mean things connected with man's body and bodily senses. But what can be meant by saying that *polytheism* springs from love of bodily things? Possibly the writer took 'worship of many gods' to be equivalent to worship of idols, which are corporeal things.

[2] 'Light' presumably means mental clear-sightedness or intelligence; but it is not clear how this can result from shunning injustice.

[3] *Timor, tristitia, inscientia, egestas.* Perhaps *tristitia* in this connexion means 'anxious care', φροντίς (Horace's *atra cura*). As to *egestas*, see 3. 3. He who suppresses desire for sensuous pleasures is set free from all the cares, troubles, and griefs which result from fostering such desires and trying to satisfy them. That thought is a commonplace of Greek ethics (see e. g. Pl. *Gorg.*); but the terms in which it is here expressed differ from those usually employed by Greek writers.

[4] This *sententia* (2. 9, 10) cannot have been translated from a Pagan Greek original; it probably first took shape in a Moslem environment.

[5] I. e. as a corporeal being, an earthly organism. This term would seem properly applicable to the body alone; but the writer makes it include the mental faculties of the merely 'natural' man.

him stuff of the highest kind,[1] that stuff which is perfect and makes perfect, whereby he is enabled to take thought for himself, and by such thought to direct his action ; so that thenceforward he is a fully developed [2] man.

13 'And in like manner, regarded as a being endowed with mind, man is at first nothing more than a (vital) force which enters into the generative organ and is injected into the womb together with the *semen* ;[3] thereafter, there enters into the embryo, perhaps through the mediation of the heavenly bodies,[4] a force that shapes it, whereby it is made into a living being ($\zeta\hat{\omega}o\nu$) potentially ($\delta\upsilon\nu\acute{a}\mu\epsilon\iota$) capable of seeking and avoiding things ;[5] and lastly, there enters into the man a force that is perfect and makes him perfect, namely, mind ($\nu o\hat{\upsilon}s$), whereby his development is brought to its final stage, in which he employs all his faculties in actuality ($\acute{\epsilon}\nu\epsilon\rho\gamma\epsilon\acute{\iota}\alpha$).

'In the beginning then, the man had neither potential nor actual existence ; next, he advanced to the grade of potential existence ; and lastly, he rose from the grade of potentiality to that of actuality and completeness. And thenceforward, he acts by his own free will ; he is now a fully developed man ($\tau\acute{\epsilon}\lambda\epsilon\iota os$), and is able to represent things in thought both to others and to himself.[6]'[7]

14 Cap. 2, §§ 14, 15 a. 'The Maker of the universe—revered be his name !—is ever speaking and pouring forth his thoughts,[8] in the

---

[1] *Summa materia* Bard. I suppose the first kind of 'stuff' means food for the body, and the second and higher kind of 'stuff' means food for the mind.

[2] $\tau\acute{\epsilon}\lambda\epsilon\iota os$. The consummation to which the man here spoken of attains must be understood to be worldly wisdom,—i. e. a mature man's trained intelligence, applied to the affairs of earthly life.

[3] The fact that a man's life starts from a seminal germ is repeatedly insisted on in the Koran. In this passage, that reflection is expanded in accordance with Greek physiology as transmitted by Arabic writers, and is brought into connexion with the Aristotelian antithesis $\delta\upsilon\nu\acute{a}\mu\epsilon\iota$—$\acute{\epsilon}\nu\epsilon\rho\gamma\epsilon\acute{\iota}\alpha$.

[4] The notion that life is imparted to terrestrial organisms by the influence of the stars occurs habitually in the *Hermetica* and contemporary Greek writings. The Arabic writer here mentions it, but seems to hesitate about accepting it.

[5] $\check{o}\rho\epsilon\xi\iota s$ and $\phi\upsilon\gamma\acute{\eta}$, the two kinds of $\acute{o}\rho\mu\acute{\eta}$.

[6] *Res tum aliis tum sibi ipsi informare et effingere* Bard.: i. e. he knows the truth himself, and can teach it to others.

[7] This *sententia*, 2. 11–13, is not Platonic, but Aristotelian. It cannot have been derived from a Greek *Hermeticum*.

It is not clear what the writer meant by distinguishing 'man so far as he is perceptible by sense' from 'man so far as he is endowed with $\nu o\hat{\upsilon}s$', and giving parallel descriptions of the development of the one and the other. Did he get these two descriptions from two different sources?

[8] *Sententia* Bard. For a Platonist, God's creative thoughts would be the $\nu o\eta\tau\grave{a}$ $\epsilon\check{\iota}\delta\eta$. God's 'words' are the visible things he has created. All men can 'hear the words', i. e. see the visible things ; but not all can understand the thoughts which they express.

hearing of all beings that partake of intelligence ($\nu o\hat{\upsilon}s$ or $\lambda\acute{o}\gamma os$). But not all who hear the words understand the meaning of Him who speaks them; there are some who need an interpreter to convey the meaning to them, an intermediary between the Speaker and the hearer, because the hearer is unable to understand what is said by means of his own thought.' Such a man is like one who hears words spoken in a foreign language, and needs an interpreter to explain their meaning to him. 'But be not you one of those who need intermediaries. An interpreter is often untrustworthy; often he changes the sense of the words, and wrests their meaning. I bid you therefore make your way up from the grade of those who do not understand (God's) language to the higher grade of those who understand it.'[1]

5 a

Cap. 2, § 15 b. 'Seek, O Soul, to know before you act,—to know what fruit the tree will bear before you plant the tree[2] [in order that you may understand aright the things which are said]. Learn that you must be diligent in acquiring knowledge before you act; whereby you will win honour, much comfort, and goodly fruit.'[3]

3. 1

Cap. 3, §§ 1, 2. 'The accidents (or qualities) which inhere in gross (i. e. corporeal) substances are never consistent; they tend to be mutually discrepant and repugnant. Be on your guard against them then, O Soul, and turn away from them; they are the things that I would have you guard against, the things that I would have you fear. You, O Soul, are simple, they are multiple; you are consistent, they are in mutual conflict; you are devoid of guile,[4] they are deceptive; you are truly existent,[5] they have no true existence; you

2

---

[1] This *sententia* resembles Hesiod *Op.* 293 *sq.* (quoted in Ar. *Eth. Nic.* 1. 2): $o\hat{\upsilon}\tau os\ \mu\grave{e}\nu\ \pi a\nu\acute{a}\rho\iota\sigma\tau os,\ \delta s\ a\mathring{\upsilon}\tau\grave{o}s\ \langle al.\ a\mathring{\upsilon}\tau\hat{\omega}\rangle\ \pi\acute{a}\nu\tau a\ \nu o\acute{\eta}\sigma\eta\cdot\ |\ \grave{e}\sigma\theta\lambda os\ \delta'\ a\mathring{\upsilon}\ \kappa\mathring{a}\kappa\epsilon\hat{\iota}\nu os,\ \delta s\ \epsilon\mathring{\upsilon}$ $\epsilon\mathring{\iota}\pi\acute{o}\nu\tau\iota\ \pi\acute{\iota}\theta\eta\tau a\iota.$ It is probably a polemic against orthodox Mohammedanism. The orthodox Moslems maintained that it was impossible to get any knowledge of God, and of His thoughts and purposes, except through God's revelation to Mohammed (who was the chief 'interpreter' or 'intermediary' between God and men), and, to a smaller extent, through other prophets and apostles; the more liberal theologians, and the 'philosophers', disputed this, and, in varying degrees, asserted the validity of human reason. The writer of this passage says to his pupil 'be your own prophet and apostle', and hints that Mohammed may not always have interpreted God's meaning rightly.

[2] I. e. before you act, find out what the consequences of the proposed action will be. Cf. 4. 13.

[3] § 15 b is, I think, a separate and distinct *sententia.* The words which I have bracketed, 'ut ea quae (a Deo?) dicuntur recte intelligas', are irrelevant here, and may have been inserted by some one who was trying to connect this passage with the preceding *sententia.*

[4] *Sincera* Bard.: truth-telling? or truth-seeing?

[5] The $\psi\upsilon\chi\acute{\eta}$ is an $\mathring{o}\nu\tau\omega s\ \mathring{o}\nu.$

are [a good thing] lasting and stable,[1] they are [things falsely coloured, illusions,] mutable and perishable. Shun them then; be on your guard lest you be enslaved by them, and thus prevented from attaining to your appointed end. Abandon not, O Soul, your essential nature, which is simple, true (or real), and of high dignity; and trust not to these (corporeal) things, which are multiple, mutually repugnant, deceptive, base, and perfidious; lest you be led astray, and fall into destruction.'[2]

3   Cap. 3, §§ 3, 4, and 7. 'How long, O Soul, will you continue to be vexed by unsatisfied desires,[3] ceaselessly fleeing from each sensation to its contrary, now from heat to cold and now from cold to heat, now from hunger to satiety and now from satiety to hunger, and likewise . . . in respect of all things which you perceive by your senses in the sense-world? As long as you are in want of these (corporeal) goods, ⟨you are vexed by *unsatisfied desire* for them;⟩ if you get possession of them, then, all the time that you have them, you are tormented by *fear* of losing them; and if they quit you, and you no longer have them, then you are freed from that fear, but the loss of them affects you with *grief and sorrow*.

4   'Lay aside then, O Soul, that thing[4] whereby you feel these pains and griefs. Regret not that (in doing so) you are quitting *griefs and cares, fear*, and the pain of *unsatisfied desire*; and be not annoyed that you attain to *satisfaction, freedom from fear*, and *joy*.[5] For he who prefers unsatisfied desire to satisfaction, fear to absence of fear, and degradation to high dignity,[6] is a fool; he who is a fool goes astray; and he who goes astray comes to destruction.

7   '⟨⟨Here (below),[7] O Soul, is the physical world, the abode of *un-*

---

[1] *Tu bonum perpetuum et stabile* Bard.

[2] This *sententia* is a statement of the Platonic contrast between τὰ αἰσθητά and τὰ νοητά, and an exhortation to the human soul to abandon the αἰσθητά, and cleave to the νοητά, to which it is akin by its own nature. The thought is Platonic and Hermetic; but there is no reason to think that the passage is a verbal translation from a Greek original; it may have been written either by the compiler of the *Castig. an.*, or by an Arab Platonist from whom he borrowed it.

[3] 'Quousque, o anima, *egena* manebis' Bard. Cf. *egestas* in 2. 10. [For the diatribe form, cf. *Corp.* VII, *init.*]

[4] viz. the body. Cf. 2. 8.

[5] *Copia, securitas, laetitia*; the opposites of *egestas, timor, aegritudines (et curae)*.

[6] '*Vilitatem nobilitati* praefert' Bard. (τὸ αἰσχρόν and τὸ καλόν?). But it ought to be rather *aegritudinem* (or *tristitiam*) *laetitiae*.

[7] § 7 evidently belongs to the same *sententia* as §§ 3, 4; but it has been accidentally shifted, and placed after the distinct and unconnected *sententia* §§ 5, 6.

satisfied desire, fear, degradation, and *sadness* ;¹ there (above) is the thought-world, the abode of *satisfaction, freedom from fear, high dignity,* and *joy*.² You have seen both worlds, and had experience of both ;³ now make your choice between them,⁴ in accordance with your experience. You can dwell in which of them you will; you will not be repelled or rejected from either. But it is impossible for a man to be at the same time vexed with unsatisfied want and fully satisfied, tormented by fear and free from fear, exalted and degraded, joyful and sorrowful ;⁵ and therefore it is impossible for a man to combine love of this world⁶ with love of the other world.⁷ That cannot possibly be done.⟩⟩'⁸

5   Cap. 3, §§ 5, 6. 'You have grown forth, O Soul, from a certain tree-trunk; and of that tree you are a branch. However far the branch may go forth from its trunk, there is still connexion and contact between trunk and branch, whereby every branch seeks nutriment
6 from its trunk. . . .'⁹ If anything were interposed between the trunk and the branch, it would cut off from the branch its supply of nutriment, and so the branch would forthwith wither and die.'¹⁰

['Meditate on this, O Soul, and be assured that you are destined to return to your Creator, who is the trunk out of which you have grown; and for that reason, rid yourself of the defilements and burdens of the physical world, by which you are hindered from returning to

---

¹ *Egestas, timor, vilitas, tristitia.*

² *Copia, securitas, nobilitas, laetitia.* But perhaps *vilitas* and *nobilitas* (which are not mentioned in § 3, and seem inappropriate in § 4) are later additions.

³ The soul has known the νοητά before its incarnation, and seen the αἰσθητά since its incarnation. Cf. 2. 6 ; 6. 8 ; 7. 4.

⁴ Cf. 6. 6. The choice between the two worlds is similarly spoken of in *Corp Herm.* IV. 5-6 b.

⁵ *Egenus et copiosus, timore cruciatus et securus, nobilis et vilis, laetus et tristis.*

⁶ *Studium rerum humanarum* Bard. : 'die Liebe zu dieser Welt' Fleischer.

⁷ *Vitae futurae* Bard. : 'jener Welt' Fl. The latter seems better; for the choice spoken of is not between the present life and a future life, but between two different ways of living one's present life.

⁸ I know of no parallel in Greek writings to the use here made of the terms *egestas, timor, (vilitas), tristitia* and their opposites ; it therefore seems that this *sententia* must be ascribed to an Arab Platonist. See note on 5. 6.

⁹ Here follows a doublet, in which the preceding statements are repeated, with 'fruit (of a fruit-tree)' in place of 'branch'.

¹⁰ The thought is similar to that of *Ev. Joh.* 15. 1-6 : 'I am the vine, ye are the branches' &c. It has a slighter and more remote resemblance to Pl. *Tim.* 90 A, where it is said that τὸ κυριώτατον ψυχῆς εἶδος (i e the νοῦς in us) πρὸς τὴν ἐν οὐρανῷ συγγένειαν ἀπὸ γῆς ἡμᾶς αἴρει, ὡς ὄντας φυτὸν οὐκ ἔγγειον ἀλλ' οὐράνιον. [*Ascl.* I. 6 b (codd.): horum omnium generum, quae sunt animalia desuper deorsum radices pervenientes habent; inanimalia autem de imo in superna viva radice silvescunt.]

your own world (above), and to the trunk out of which you have grown.'] [1]

[[Cap. 3, § 7.]]

8   Cap. 3, § 8. 'If ⟨a soldier defeated in battle⟩ [2] lays down his arms, ceases to fight, and surrenders to the enemy, he must needs be taken prisoner ; if he fights on and defends himself, and refuses to surrender, he must needs be killed.   And even so, every soul which descends into the physical world must needs undergo either *death* or *captivity*. [3] He who chooses captivity, chooses long torments and degrading slavery. [4]   But he who chooses death, [5] dies gloriously ; by his death he wins back (true) life, and is released from captivity, with its humiliation and degradation.'

9   Cap. 3, § 9. 'If you wish to shun base and ignoble deeds fix your thought on the source whence they issue, and flee from it ; that source is *love of the things of this world*. [6]   If you aim at doing noble and divine deeds, fix your thought on the root whence they spring, and plant that root (in yourself) and foster it ; that root is *contempt for the things of this world*.   And in so doing, let there be no false pretence.' [7]

10 a   Cap. 3, § 10 a. 'Take care that you be not, through excess of

---

[1] This is a clumsy attempt to explain the application of the simile of trunk and branches.   Platonists held that the soul has issued from God and is destined to return to God ; but a branch does *not* return to the trunk out of which it has grown.

[2] It is assumed, but not explicitly said, that victory is impossible.   The descent of the soul into the sense-world is in itself a defeat ; and the only question is, how best to face the consequences of that defeat.

[3] This looks rather like a reminiscence of the Manichaean myth of the descent of the Primal Man (prototype of individual human souls) into the Realm of Darkness, and his capture by the Powers of Darkness.   But there is no close resemblance ; for there is nothing in the Manichaean myth to correspond to the alternative of *death*.

[4] The 'captivity' is that which is endured by the man who is (as Platonists and Hermetists said) 'a slave of Heimarmene' ; i. e. the man who lets his body and bodily things (which alone are under the dominion of Heimarmene) keep his higher self in subjection to them.

[5] A man here and there might have occasion to choose literal death, in the form of martyrdom.   But as the writer is speaking of '*every* soul' that is born on earth, the 'death' must be metaphorical.   It is that 'death' of the lower or corporeal self by which a man 'wins life' for his higher or incorporeal self. Cf. Luke 17. 33 (Matth. 16. 25 : Mark 8. 35 : Luke 9. 24) : ὃς ἐὰν ζητήσῃ τὴν ψυχὴν αὐτοῦ περιποιήσασθαι ἀπολέσει αὐτήν, ὃς δ' ἂν ἀπολέσῃ, ζωογονήσει αὐτήν.   The thought is common to Plato (*Phaedo, init.*) and Paul.

[6] *Studium rerum humanarum* Bard.

[7] I. e. despise them *sincerely*, and not merely in outward show.

caution, led on to *cowardice*, lest you lose *courage*[1] and the praise it wins, and undergo humiliation and the ignominy that goes with it.'

10 b Cap. 3, § 10 b. 'All that is immaterial (?)[2] is true being,[3] and all true being is immaterial. But ⌜the space of that which is immaterial⌝ always corresponds to the extent of the space of the matter that is assigned to it.'[4]

11 Cap. 3, § 11. 'As far as possible, *rationem particularem teneas*; but if you are led by the things themselves[5] *ad universalem quandam rationem*,[6] accept this willingly, and acquiesce in it; by so doing, you will be relieved from the trouble of care and toil.

'Even so, in the darkness of the night, a man seeks light from a lamp, which (it) gives him much trouble (to keep alight); but when the sun has risen, he no longer needs the lamp, and is released from that trouble.'

12 Cap. 3, § 12. 'Beware of applying yourself to[7] things that are low and unworthy,[8] lest the habit of doing so be established in your mind, and you acquire a character repugnant to your proper nature, and, by desire and appetite for these things, be cheated out of your return to your true home. The revered and exalted Maker of the universe is the highest[9] of all things; apply yourself then to high things,[10] and,

---

[1] δειλία and ἀνδρεία; cf. 2. 9 *sq*., where ἀδικία and ἀκολασία are spoken of.

[2] *Omne quod materia eget* Bard. : 'Alles was nicht aus der Materie Nahrung zieht' Fl.

[3] *Essentia.*

[4] What does this mean? ·If we take, as an instance of an 'immaterial' thing, a human soul, 'the matter that is assigned to it' might mean the man's body; and the thing asserted would in that case be that (something or other) corresponds to the size of the man's body. But 'the space of that which is immaterial' (*eius quod materia eget spatium*) seems quite inexplicable. (Is it possible that the writer was thinking of the parallel growth and development of the human body and the human mind, as described in 2. 11–13?)

[5] *Rebus ipsis.*

[6] What is meant by *ratio particularis* and *ratio universalis*? The *ratio particularis* must be the way of thinking or acting of the man who gets light from his own private lamp, and the *ratio universalis*, that of the man who avails himself of the light of the sun, which shines for all alike. But the simile might be applied in various ways. If the writer was thinking of the acquisition of knowledge (of God), his meaning might possibly be 'As far as you can, think things out for yourself; but if circumstances make it necessary, accept the creed of the community of which you are a member, and spare yourself the trouble of thinking for yourself'. (The *ratio universalis* would then be the way of the Catholic, and the *ratio particularis*, that of the Protestant.) But it is uncertain whether he meant this or something very different.

[7] I. e. concerning yourself about, or taking thought for.

[8] I. e. the 'corporeal' things of this world.

[9] *Praestantissimus.*   [10] *Sc.* τὰ νοητά.

by becoming like to the source of your being,[1] draw nearer and nearer to Him who created thee. [And know that high things always join themselves to high things, and low things to low things.]'[2]

13   Cap. 3, § 13. 'You are in the world of things that come to be, and yet you seek to be at rest. But how can anything be at rest in the world of things that come to be? A boat, as long as it floats on the water, cannot be still or at rest; or if at any moment it is still, it is so only by chance, and forthwith the water begins again to shake and toss the things which float upon its surface. Then only is the boat at rest, when it is taken out of the water, and drawn up on the land, which is the place of the boat's origin,[3] and is on a par with the boat in density and weight;[4] then, but not till then, is the boat truly at rest. And even so, the soul, as long as it is involved in the processes of the physical world,[5] cannot be still, nor be at rest, nor get any respite; but if it returns to its source and root,[6] then it is still and is at rest, and reposes from the misery and debasement of its wandering in a foreign land[7].'[8]

4. 1 a   Cap. 4, §§ 1, 2. The physical world is composed of pure things and foul things.[9] Drink then the foul things before the pure things;[10]

---

[1] *Generis assimilatione.* This is the Greek notion of ὁμοίωσις τῷ θεῷ.

[2] The thoughts are Platonic; and it is not impossible that this *sententia* may have been taken with little alteration from a Greek *Hermeticum*.

[3] *Quae fons et radix ipsius est.* The boat is made of wood that grew on land, and the boat was made on land.

[4] This seems to imply the notion that the soul is a thing of gaseous substance, and can be at rest only when it has risen to an atmospheric stratum that is of the same rarity (λεπτομέρεια) as itself,—a notion that can be traced back to Posidonius. Cf. 1. 8–11.

[5] *Quamdiu in cursu rerum naturae est.*

[6] I. e. to God.   [7] *Peregrinatio.*

[8] Cf. 14. 9 *sq.*, where it is implied that the soul cannot be 'at rest' as long as it is tied to the body.

In this *sententia*, the thought is Platonic (possibly with a slight touch of Stoicism); but I do not know that the simile of the boat occurs in any Greek writing.

[9] This statement is verbally contradicted by the first words of § 1 b, 'You must not think that there is in the physical world anything that is pure'. The only way to get rid of the contradiction is to take 'pure' in § 1 a as meaning 'apparently pure', or 'pure *in a lower sense*'. Possibly § 1 a originally stood alone, and §§ 1 b, 2 was afterwards added by another person.

By 'pure things' and 'foul things' the writer seems to mean *good* things and *bad* things; and if so, the 'pure things' and 'foul things' spoken of in § 1 a must be the (seeming) goods and evils of the corporeal world, i. e. the good fortune and ill fortune, or happiness and misery, which are mixed together in our earthly life, or come to men by turns (cf. 2. 4–8). These goods and evils are here spoken of metaphorically as pure and foul water which men drink.

[10] *Immundas (res) ante puras obducas* Bard. This means, I suppose, that (as a

that is the course a man must take if he wants to get happiness. Be assured that it is better to drink pure things after foul things than to drink foul things after pure things.

1 b   But you must not be led to think that anything (really) pure can be found in the physical world. If anything pure is found in this world, that thing is not *really* pure; for there can be no (true) purity in anything that is not everlasting. All things in the physical world are foul, and noisome in the highest degree.[1] (I am speaking figuratively (?).[2])

2   If you want something[3] that is really pure and wholesome, you must seek it elsewhere than in the world of things that come to be and cease to be. If you look for it in its own place,[4] you will find it; if you look for it elsewhere, you will not find it. And if you do not find that which you seek, and do not attain to that which you pursue, you will be afflicted by sorrow, and by the pain of unsatisfied desire;[5] and thence you will fall sick, and be brought to death,[6] and will lose happiness of mind[7] and everlasting life.

3   Cap. 4, § 3. 'The raft on which you are borne upon this great sea (of earthly life) is made of water frozen to ice; and it is only by chance that it serves to bear you. Soon the sun will rise and shine on it, and melt the ice, and it will turn into water again, and you will be left sitting on water. But you certainly will not be able to remain in that position; you must therefore look for something to bear you up. And there is nothing that will serve that purpose, except ability to swim and to direct your course aright until you shall have reached ⟨firm ground⟩.[8]'[9]

---

matter of worldly prudence) it is better to endure hardship first, and enjoy prosperity afterwards, than to enjoy oneself at first, and fall into adversity afterwards (the lesson that is taught by the fable of the ant and the grasshopper).

[1] *Quavis re gravi graviora* Bard. Cf. *Corp.* VI. 4 a: ἀδύνατόν ἐστι (τὸ ἀγαθὸν) ἐν τῷ κόσμῳ εἶναι· ὁ γὰρ κόσμος πλήρωμά ἐστι τῆς κακίας, κ.τ.λ.

[2] *Verum enimvero similitudinem tibi proposui* Bard.

[3] Perhaps 'If you want a draught to drink' &c., continuing the metaphor of § 1 a.

[4] I. e. in the νοητὸς κόσμος.   [5] *Egestas*; cf. 3. 3–7.

[6] Not literal death, but the destruction of the *higher* life.

[7] I. e. the bliss of νόησις, in contrast to *bodily* pleasure.

[8] *Quoad eas consecuta eris* Bard. (*Eas* apparently refers grammatically to 'facultates bene natandi et recti cursus tenendi'; but that would not make sense.)

[9] The ice-floe is the body. During the present life on earth, the soul is 'borne' by the body, or has the body for its 'vehicle'. But when death comes, the body will perish and be dissolved; the soul must therefore, while still embodied, learn to 'swim' (i. e. to live detached from the body), and to direct its course aright (i. e. towards the νοητά and God). Cf. 8. 1 sq. and 8. 3. Herm. *ap.* Stob. II B. 4:

4   Cap. 4, § 4. 'If water is pure and limpid, our eyesight can penetrate it and see all things that are in it; but if it is mixed with foul
mud, our eyesight is obstructed, and the things in the water are
hidden, so that we cannot see them. And again, when things are
illuminated by the sun, we can see them as they truly are; but if the
sun happens to be obscured by vapour, smoke, or dust, we cannot
see those things.

'Even so, if the brilliant and subtle light of Mind (νοῦς)[1] is mingled
with things gross, dense, and dark, it is made turbid by them, and
our minds are hindered[2] from seeing the forms and shapes that are
situated in Mind (νοῦς) itself.[3] We are thus deprived of the power of
representing things to ourselves in thought;[4] and so it comes to pass
that the soul can no longer[5] [. . .][6] get knowledge of the things it
ought to know, and hold the right course towards entering on the
way of its salvation.'

5   Cap. 4, §§ 5, 6. 'A man is not showing contempt for the house

(If you attain to *gnosis* in this life,) εὐδαιμόνως τεθνήξῃ, τῆς ψυχῆς σου μὴ ἀγνοούσης
ποῦ αὐτὴν δεῖ ἀναπτῆναι.

(It would be possible to interpret the parable in a different way, as applying
wholly to the present life, and having no reference to death. The ice-floe would
then mean worldly prosperity or good fortune. If you have it now, you have it by
mere chance, and it may at any time fail you; you must learn to do without it,
and seek the unfailing goods of the higher life.—But I think the first interpretation
is to be preferred.)

In what country was this written? Was there any region known to the Arabs of
Iraq in which ice-floes could be found? An incident such as is here described
might possibly occur in the northern part of the Caspian Sea.

[1] *Praestantia et subtilia rationis lumina* Bard.

[2] *Prohibentur* (subject, *rationis lumina*) Bard.

[3] The 'formae et figurae in ratione ipsa positae' are the νοητὰ εἴδη. They are
'situated in' the divine νοῦς; that is to say, they are God's thoughts. The νοητὸς
κόσμος is pictured as a world of which God is the sun, and which is illuminated by
the νοῦς poured forth from God as sunlight from the sun; and the things in that
world are the νοητὰ εἴδη. That is the *real* world; and if the νοῦς in us (which is
consubstantial with the divine νοῦς) were pure, we should see it as it really is.
But in the world as seen by our bodily eyes, both the light of the divine νοῦς by
which things are illuminated, and the νοῦς in us (that φῶς in us whereby we are
capable of seeing τὰ νοητά), are obscured by an intermixture of ὕλη, and therefore
we can see nothing clearly. Cf. 4. 14, and 5. 9–11.

Here, as often in Greek writings, 'light' (φῶς) seems to mean at the same
time that which sees (whether αἰσθητικῶς or νοερῶς), and the medium by means of
which things are seen. 'Like is apprehended by like'; and it is the 'light' in the
eye that sees the things on which the sunlight falls.

[4] *Facultas cogitatione sibi rerum informandarum*: i.e. the power of reproducing
the νοητὰ εἴδη (God's thoughts, or things as God thinks them, which are the realities)
in our own minds.

[5] *Sc.* when it has been intermixed with ὕλη, i.e. incarnated on earth. The soul
could and did apprehend the νοητά before its incarnation. It necessarily loses this
power at birth; but it may recover it, at least to some extent, by 'detaching itself
from corporeal things' during its life on earth.

[6] *Ea quae sibi parere* (produce? or acquire?) *oportet parere* Bard.

he lives in, if, while omitting to fit it out and adorn it, he nevertheless goes on living in it without reluctance ; he shows utter contempt for it only when he is eager to quit it, and is ready and willing to go out of it and live elsewhere. And even so, a man does not show contempt for the physical world, if, while putting away from him the pleasures and desires which belong to it, he nevertheless stays on in it without reluctance ; he shows true contempt for it only when he eagerly longs to depart from it, and to be at rest from it, and from its

6 hostility,[1] its contrariety, its discord,[2] and its darkness.[3] You ought therefore to fix firmly in your mind a longing and eagerness for physical death, and guard against being troubled at the prospect of it ; for by fear of death is wrought destruction, and by desire for it, salvation. Surely you know this, that by physical death you will migrate to another abode, where you will dwell, not (as now) in poverty, but at ease ; not in want, but fully satisfied ; not in fear, but without fear ;[4] not toiling, but at rest ; not it pain, but in pleasure ; not in sickness, but in health ; not in darkness, but in light. Do not therefore grieve overmuch at being stripped of the garments of evil and of delusive appearance,[5] and clothed in garments of that which is good and everlasting ;[6] grieve not at getting sure knowledge and experience of those things,[7] and, in virtue of your own simplicity and unity,[8] seeing them face to face.'[9]

---

[1] *Inimicitia.* Corporeal things are *at enmity with* the soul. Cf. *Corp. Herm.* VII.

[2] *Contrarietas, repugnantia.* Corporeal things are contrary or repugnant one to another ; the forces of the corporeal world, and the desires excited in us by them, pull different ways. and the man who is governed by them is 'distracted'.

[3] *Obscuritas.* The bodily senses perceive things dimly. It is in the world of νοητά alone that there is true φῶς ; or in other words, it is 'the eye of the mind' alone that can truly see.

[4] '(Migrabis) ex egestate ad copiam, e timore ad securitatem.' Cf. *egestas* and *copia, timor* and *securitas,* in 3. 5-7.

[5] *Vestimentis mali et fucati* : i.e. the body.

[6] *Vestimentis boni et perpetui.* Cf. 2. 8.   [7] i.e. of the νοητά and God.

[8] 'Qua es natura simplici atque unica.' At death the soul is parted from the body, and so gets rid of the accretions which have resulted from its embodiment (the θνητὸν εἶδος ψυχῆς of Pl. *Tim.*), and is restored to its original 'simplicity of nature' (or in other words, becomes pure νοῦς).

[9] In this passage, *contemptus mundi* reaches its highest degree. The man addressed is assumed to be already living an ascetic life (to have 'put away from him the pleasures and desires of this world') ; but that, he is told, is not enough. If he is merely *content* to die, that is too little ; he ought *eagerly to long for* death. A Christian monk might have spoken in this tone in a time of persecution, when martyrdom was to be expected ; (there are passages to nearly the same effect in Origen's *Exhortatio ad martyrium* ;) but no terms peculiar to Christianity are used here. It seems possible that this *sententia* was written by a Platonist under Arab rule (whether a 'Sabian', or a 'philosopher' who conformed to Islam in

7   Cap. 4, § 7. 'You seek friends and comrades in the world of things that come to be; but you know that it is impossible for you to find them there.   That which you seek is to be found only in the world of spirits;[1] for spirits are by nature simple, pure, and undefiled. If then that is what you are seeking, turn to that other world, that you may get what you want; and seek not, in the world of things that come to be, a thing that is not in it.   For its inhabitants are prisoners and slaves;[2] and how can one make a friend of a prisoner, or put trust in a slave?'[3] ['Be convinced of this, and hold to it firmly as a rule of conduct.']

8 a   Cap. 4. § 8 a. [. . .][4] 'It is very hard to be forced to abandon one's friends;[5] but it is harder still to be joined in friendship with one who is sure to abandon his friend.'[6]

8 b   Cap. 4, § 8 b. 'The dwellers in this world are wronged (by one another) and wrong (one another); they are led astray (by one another), and lead (one another) astray.   For instance, when a soul comes into this abode of cares and sorrows,[7] they welcome it with joy and gladness; and when it returns from this world (to its home above), they escort it forth with weeping and wailing.   In this is well seen how wrong men are,[8] and how much opposed to truth and right.'[9]

externals,' at a time when he and his associates had reason to think that they were likely to be put to death by orthodox Mohammedans.

[1] *In animorum mundo* Bard.: 'in der Welt der geistigen Wesen' Fl. Are these *animi* the νοητὰ εἴδη (or the νόες correlative with them), regarded as persons, and identified with the angels?   That is a notion that occurs in some Arabic writings. (See e.g. Suhrawardi, p. 267 above.)

[2] Men (as long as they remain merely 'natural' men) are shut up in the body as in a prison, and are 'slaves of Heimarmene'.

[3] Is the word 'friends' in this passage to be taken literally, as referring to *persons*?   Or is it used metaphorically, to denote *things* worthy to be loved and trusted, and is the writer's meaning that the goods and pleasures of this world are not to be loved?   The mention of 'prisoners and slaves' seems to show that *men* are meant. Yet it is difficult to understand how even the most unsociable Platonist could go so far as to deny that it is possible to find a human friend on earth.   Did the writer think that *all* men, except himself, were 'slaves'?   Might there not be at least one other man like-minded with himself?   Cf. 5. 12 *sq.*, 6. 1, 6. 2 *sq.*, and 6. 4; 7. 10–8. 2.

[4] Here Bard. gives two unintelligible sentences, which are omitted in Fleischer's MSS.

[5] *Ab amicis descri* Bard.: 'sich von wahren Freunden trennen zu müssen' Fl.

[6] Perhaps the meaning is that earthly friendships cause more sorrow than joy, because they are necessarily terminated *by death*.   A man is parted from his friends either by dying himself, or (what is yet harder for him) by their dying, and leaving him to live on without them.—I take this to be a distinct *sententia*, which was placed next to 4. 7 by the compiler merely because *friends* are spoken of in both.

[7] I.e. when a child is born.   Men are such fools that they rejoice at a birth, and mourn at a funeral.

[8] *In qua re satis cernitur iniuriae* Bard.

[9] The thought is old; μὴ φῦναι τὸν ἅπαντα νικᾷ λόγον, said Sophocles; and cf.

9, 10 Cap. 4, §§ 9–11. There are four things that are deadly, viz. (1) *inscientia* (ignorance); (2) *tristitia* ('anxious care', which is caused by striving to get 'external goods'); (3) *egestas* ('the pain of unsatisfied desire', which is caused by indulging the bodily appetites), (4) *timor* (fear of death).[1] The soul that is tormented by these four things is utterly miserable.

11 'If you were so far advanced that you could endure the bitterness of death with firmness, you would escape not only from *timor*, but also from *egestas*. Arm yourself with firmness then, and do not allow *egestas* and *timor* to be added to the *tristitia* of your wandering in a foreign land.'[2]

Cap. 4, § 12. 'To die with firmness is glorious; to die in fear and cowardice is shameful. *Dying* is but for a moment, and is quickly ended; but base endurance of *captivity* is a lasting condition. Be not unwilling then to undergo death, and thereby to quit the physical world; but suffer not yourself to be reduced to captivity; for that death is everlasting life, and this captivity is everlasting death.'[3]

Cap. 4, § 13. 'Men are of three grades. The lowest grade is that of the man who knows (what ought to be done), but does not do it. He is like a man that is armed but is not brave; and what can a coward accomplish by means of weapons?

'The second grade is that of the man who does (something), but does not know (what ought to be done). He is like a brave man that is unarmed; and how can he that is unarmed meet the foe in

---

Hdt. 5. 4: 'When a child is born (in a certain Thracian tribe), all its kindred sit round about it in a circle and weep for the woes it will have to undergo now that it is come into the world, making mention of every ill that falls to the lot of humankind; when, on the other hand, a man has died, they bury him with laughter and rejoicings, and say that now he is free from a host of sufferings, and enjoys the completest happiness.' It is a thought that might occur independently at any time and place; but it agrees well with the *contemptus mundi* of these Arab Platonists; cf. 4. 5 *sq.*

[1] Cf. *egestas*, *timor*, (*vilitas*,) *tristitia* in 3. 3–7. But *timor* was there explained as meaning fear of losing worldly goods or sensuous enjoyments; here, it is explained as meaning fear of death. See note on 5. 6.

[2] *Peregrinatio*, i.e. residence on earth, which is exile from your true home. (Cf. 3. 13.) It seems to be implied that during earthly life some degree of *tristitia* is inevitable, but *egestas* and *timor* can be avoided.

[3] This seems to be a distinct *sententia*, placed next to 4. 9–11 because 'facing death with firmness' is spoken of in both.

Death and *captivity* are spoken of in 3. 8; but there, they appear to be metaphorical. Here, death seems to be meant literally; it could hardly be said of the metaphorical 'death' of the lower self that 'it is over in a moment'. But if literal death is meant, what is the 'captivity' which is contrasted with it? Is it possible that this *sententia*, as well as 4. 5 *sq.*, is an *exhortatio ad martyrium*?

fight? But just as it is easier for a brave man to acquire arms than for a coward to acquire courage, even so he who acts without knowing (what he ought to do) is better than the man who knows (what he ought to do) but does not do it.

'The third and highest grade is that of the man who both knows (what he ought to do) and does it; he is like a brave man armed.'[1]

14   Cap. 4, § 14. 'The moon shines as long as it is illuminated by the sun; but if at any time the earth's shadow is interposed between moon and sun, then the moon is eclipsed and darkened. And even so, the soul is luminous and bright[2] as long as it is illumined by Mind (νοῦς); but if ⌜the causes of coming into being and ceasing to be⌝[3] are interposed between the soul and Mind (νοῦς), then the soul is deprived of its light, and is obscured.

'Moreover, the moon cannot escape from eclipse as long as the earth remains in its place in the universe; and even so, the soul, as long as it is held fast in the physical world,[4] cannot escape from darkness and loss (of power to see). Hence it is evident that the soul can come to be at rest[5] only when it quits the physical world and [hastily] departs from this life.'[6]

5. 1   Cap. 5, § 1. 'To use intelligence (νοεῖν) is nothing else than to represent things to oneself in thought.[7] Every soul then which refrains from doing this loses itself,[8] and he who loses himself is devoid of life.'

[1] This is a piece of proverbial wisdom that has no connexion with any particular school of philosophy. Cf 2. 15 b.

[2] I.e. is able to 'see' with the mental eye.

[3] *Causae exsistendi atque intereundi* Bard. Fleischer gives a different reading: 'treten aber *Blut, Schleim, und Galle* als Mittelursachen hemmend zwischen beide'. I suppose 'blood, gall, and phlegm' are regarded as the fluids which contain and supply the material of which the human body is composed, and the nutriment by which it is maintained. They may be called, in this sense, 'the proximate causes' of the existence of the human body, or of the πάθη by which the soul is affected through its conjunction with the body. In any case, the writer's meaning must have been that the πάθη which originate in the body are the obstruction (the 'earth-shadow') interposed between the embodied ψυχή and the divine νοῦς from which the ψυχή gets its 'light' (i.e. its power of 'seeing' the νοητά, which are the ὄντως ὄντα). It is the same Platonic theory of cognition that is stated in other words in 4. 4, and in 5. 9–11.   [4] *In rerum natura.*

[5] *Conquiescere.* It is assumed, but not explicitly said, that the soul can 'be at rest' only when it 'sees' τα ὄντως ὄντα, or God.

[6] This (if 'departs from this life' is to be taken literally) amounts to saying that *gnosis* is unattainable in this life. On that point, Platonists and Hermetists spoke variously; but most of them would have agreed that in this life men can, at most, see only δι᾽ ἐσόπτρου, ἐν αἰνίγματι, and not 'face to face' (1 *Cor.* 13. 12). See, for instance, *Corp. Herm.* X *init.*

[7] 'Cogitatione res sibi informare et effingere.'

[8] I.e. ceases to be a νοερά or λογικὴ ψυχή (that is to say, a human soul)?

'To represent things to oneself in thought is to use intelligence;[1] and to do that is to enjoy everlasting life, but desire for pleasures and for the (seeming) goods of this life is everlasting death.'

2   Cap. 5, §§ 2-5. All things that are of material substance and are devoid of intelligence (νοῦς)[2] move, by the law of their nature, towards their own homes; for there only is it well with them; there

3 only can they settle down and be at rest. 'Thus all things composed of *earth*, e. g. stones and the like, always, if not hindered, return to the earth, which is their root and source;[3] so that if one takes a piece of earth and lifts it up above the surface of the earth and then lets it go, it quickly returns, by its own natural movement, to (the earth, which is) its own element, and the root from which it sprang. And likewise all *waters*, moved by their own nature, are perpetually borne towards the main mass of their own element, unless there is something that holds them back; thus all watersprings ceaselessly flow into the rivers, and all rivers ceaselessly flow into and mingle with the sea. which is (the main mass of) the element water. And so it is with all other things also; *fire* and *air* at all times tend upward,[4] each of them returning to (the mass of) its own element.

4   Seeing 'then that each of the things that are devoid of intelligence (νοῦς)[5] and discernment, and are moved merely by a blind impulse and a natural desire,[6]—seeing that each of those things moves to the place where it thrives and is vigorous and strong, and refuses to remain apart and separated from its own fatherland and home,—why then do you, O Soul, who are endowed with intelligence and judgement, refuse to return to your fatherland and to your element,[7] in

[1] A doublet of the first sentence.

[2] I. e. the things that we should call *lifeless*. In this *sententia* the distinction between νοῦς and ψυχή is ignored. Things are divided into those that have νοῦς (*intelligent* life) and those that have not νοῦς. The former are, or include, what Platonists would call ἔμψυχα (living organisms); the latter are the cosmic elements (earth, water, air, and fire) or detached portions of these elements (pieces of inorganic matter). But the writer does not regard the latter (i. e. 'the things devoid of νοῦς') as wholly lifeless; he attributes to them some sort of blind sentience and instinctive self-movement. In this, his view partly agrees with that of 1. 8-11, in which the element earth alone is wholly devoid of 'light and life'. Compare also 8. 12-14.

[3] ῥίζα καὶ πηγή.

[4] Fire and air are τὰ ἀνωφερῆ στοιχεῖα.

[5] κρίσις, the power of distinguishing between good and bad, i. e. intelligent choice.

[6] ὁρμή or ὄρεξις φυσική, a desire implanted in them by φύσις, i. e. instinctive.

[7] As the one sea is 'the element' of this or that particular stream of water, so the world-soul, the universal (νοερὰ) ψυχή, is 'the element' of each particular human soul. Cf. 1. 8-11, where ψυχή has its place or region assigned to it next above the 'fifth element' in the ascending series, and next below νοῦς, which is in

which (alone) you (can) thrive and be vigorous? Why do you turn away from that, and desire to remain parted from your root and source?[1] Why do you prefer to tarry in a foreign land, and to en-
5 dure reproach and shame? Tell me, is it an instinctive desire that urges you to do so, or is it intelligent thought? If it is an instinctive desire, then you ought to imitate the behaviour of material things, which is implanted in them by nature; that is, their constant habit of returning to their own elements. But if you are impelled by intelligent thought and discernment, how can one who enjoys the power of intelligence and discernment induce himself to prefer a foreign country to his fatherland, to prefer the abode of degradation to that of high dignity,[2] to prefer endurance of reproach and shame to untroubled calm[3] and honour and authority?[4] One who is in that position[5] cannot be ranked either with material things[6] or with beings that partake of intelligence;[7] and that which belongs to neither of these two classes is nothing at all, and cannot be reckoned among things that have real existence.'[8]

6   Cap. 5, § 6. There are three things than which nothing more delightful can be found: viz. (1) *scientia* (knowledge—also called *cognitio* and *certitudo*); (2) *copia* (full satisfaction of desire); (3) *securitas* (freedom from fear).[9]

immediate connexion with God. Compare Herm. *ap.* Stob. XXV (*Isis to Horus*), in which we are told in detail how each soul, when it quits the body, goes back to ' its own place' (in the atmosphere).

[1] I. e. to remain in this world, where you are parted from the universal ψυχή, the divine νοῦς, and God. That is to say, why are you unwilling to die!

[2] *Vilitatis sedem sedi nobilitatis* (*praeferre*).

[3] *Quies.*

[4] *Auctoritas*: ἐξουσία, or perhaps τὸ αὐτεξούσιον.

[5] *Isto in gradu*: i. e. one who behaves as you do in this matter.

[6] *Res physicae*: τὰ φυσικά.

[7] τὰ μετέχοντα νοῦ.

[8] The cosmologic doctrine of this *sententia* is partly Stoic rather than Platonic (like that of 1. 8–11; cf. also 6. 7 b); it may perhaps have been derived from Posidonius. But that doctrine is not here given for its own sake, but is employed to lead up to an exhortation against fear of death,—an exhortation to the same effect as that in 4. 5 *sq.* (Cf. 4. 8 b and 4. 12.)

This piece may very likely have been translated from a Greek original of the third century A. D.; and it is possible that the Greek original was a *Hermeticum* (i. e. that its teaching was ascribed to Hermes).

[9] *Scientia, copia, securitas* (the opposites of *inscientia, egestas, timor*). Cf. the similar groups in other *sententiae*: in 2. 10, *timor, tristitia, inscientia, egestas* (the opposites of *securitas, laetitia, scientia, copia*): in 3. 3–7, *egestas, timor,* (*vilitas,*) *tristitia,* and their opposites *copia, securitas,* (*nobilitas*) *laetitia*: in 4. 9–11, *inscientia, tristitia, egestas, timor*: in 7. 2, *aegritudines* (*et*) *curae* (= *tristitia*), *timor, egestas*: in 7. 10, *egens, timore et tristitia cruciata*: in 12. 10, ' ignorance and oblivion' (= *inscientia*), ' desire for pleasures' (which corresponds to *egestas*), *tristitia, timor.*

Scientia [1] is to be got by 'the mind being called back to itself and gathered together into itself';

Copia is to be got by means of temperance; [2]

Securitas is to be got by 'fixing in one's mind a true opinion about physical death.' [3]

7   Cap. 5, §§ 7, 8. '[As long as you are in the world of things that come to be, O Soul,] beware of consorting with two things that are deadly to souls; be on your guard against them, dread them and flee from them. These two things are *women* and *strong drink*.

'He who falls into the snares of women is like a bird that falls into the hands of a little silly child; the child plays with it merrily and is glad, but meanwhile the bird endures the pains of death, and undergoes all manner of tortures.

8   'And you must likewise be on your guard against desire for strong drink, and against drunkenness; for drunkenness makes the soul like to a ship that is swept away over a stormy sea, without sailor or steersman to guide it.' [4]

['Even so the soul, if it falls away from intelligence (νοῦς), is swept away by the forces of nature, [5] and is tossed about at random, without order or law, so that it falls into destruction, and perishes.'] [6]

9   Cap. 5, §§ 9–11. 'If, when you have come to know a thing, you afterwards forget it, be assured that the knowledge of it comes to you

[1] Presumably knowledge of oneself and God, and of the relation between oneself and God,—the γνῶσις of the Hermetists.

[2] σωφροσύνη. I.e. by suppressing the sensuous or carnal desires. If a man tries to satisfy these desires, he thereby only enlarges them, and increases the torment of unsatisfied desire (*egestas*).

[3] I.e. by convincing oneself that death is not a thing to be feared. (This resembles the Platonic definition of ἀνδρεία.)—*Timor*, the opposite of *securitas*, is here explained as in 4. 9–11, and not as in 3. 3.

[4] This is a piece of gnomic wisdom which cannot have come from a Pagan Greek source. The warning against strong drink is presumably Mohammedan; and the warning against women also *may* have been written by a Mohammedan. Mohammed himself did not teach avoidance of women, either by precept or by example; but there were doubtless Moslems who differed from him on that point; and there were Moslem sects which took over and carried on the ascetic traditions of the Christian monks of Egypt and Syria, and of the Manichaeans. Cf. the description of a wife in 6. 11.

[5] *natura abripitur*: i.e. by the forces which operate in the material world, and act on the human body, and, through the body, on the souls. [Stob. *Exc.* XVIII. (codd.) 3: ἐχομένη γὰρ αἵρεσις τῶν κακῶν πλησιάζει τῇ σωματικῇ φύσει, διά (τε) τοῦτο τῷ ἑλομένῳ εἱμαρμένη δυναστεύει.]

[6] This sentence was probably added by an Arab Platonist, who made use of the warning against drunkenness as a simile, but had nothing to say about the parallel warning against women. (The first clause of the *sententia*, in which 'the world of τὰ γιγνόμενα' is spoken of, may have been added by the same man.) For 'drunkenness' employed as a simile or metaphor, cf. *Corp. Herm.* VII *init.*

from without, and that something material (or corporeal) is interposed between you and the knowledge of that thing.[1]   Therefore, if you forget the thing, that must be attributed to the nature of your body, which is dark, and at war with itself,[2] and heavy, and draws you to itself, and holds you in its grip[3] by means of the many mutually contrary things of which it is composed.   Thence it is that you forget what you had held in mind (before your incarnation), and become ignorant of what you knew.

10   'The relations (between the soul, the things it knows, and the causes of its knowing and forgetting them) are like the relations between the eye, the things it sees, and light and darkness.[4]   If the eye is surrounded by darkness, it does not see the objects, even if they are placed before it, and it cannot perceive them ; but if light falls on it, and it is illuminated, it is thereby enabled to perceive visible things which it could not see before.   It is the light then that has put the eye in communication with those things, and given it the power of perceiving them, and has brought it about that things which were only potentially present to it[5] before are now actually present to it. As long then as the eye feels the light, it feels and perceives the objects also ; but if it loses the light, and is again enveloped in dark-

[1] So Bardenhewer.   Fleischer translates thus : ' Between you, O Soul, and the knowledge (of a thing) which is conveyed to you through something material from the sphere outside of your being, there is only a mediate relation.'   The ' something material ' must be the body, or the bodily sense-organs.   Apparently Bard. takes the meaning to be that the body with its sense-organs is an *obstruction interposed* between the mind and its object, which *prevents* the mind from knowing the thing ; Fleischer takes it to be that the body with its sense-organs is a *medium of communication* between the mind and its object, by means of which the mind *is enabled to* know the thing.   Of these two interpretations, Bard.'s is to be preferred. Cf. 4. 14 (simile of eclipse of the moon), and 4. 4 (simile of things hidden from sight under muddy water).
   The thing to be known is τὸ νοητόν.   Knowledge of τὰ νοητά, τὰ ὄντως ὄντα, comes to the soul ' from without ', i.e. from the divine νοῦς, or from God.   Before its incarnation, the soul was in unbroken communication with the divine νοῦς, and consequently possessed that knowledge ; but when the soul is incarnated on earth, the body is interposed as an obstruction between the soul and the source of its knowledge, and the soul consequently loses or ' forgets ' the knowledge it possessed before.   This is the Platonic λήθη.
   [2] I.e. composed of mutually conflicting elements (and accordingly productive of mutually conflicting passions).
   [3] *Te retinet.*   Cf. *Corp. Herm.* X. 24 : τὴν [ἐν] τῷ σώματι προσηρτημένην καὶ ὑπ' αὐτοῦ ἀγχομένην κάτω (ψυχήν).
   [4] The simile of *light*, as employed by Platonists of all periods, can be traced back to Pl. *Rep.* VI. 507 *sqq.*   In this *sententia* it is set forth with exceptional fullness.
   [5] *In eo* (sc. *oculo*) *fuerunt* Bard.   The image of the object is *in* the eye ; and the object itself is thereby presented *to* the eye.   ' Potentially—actually ' is the Aristotelian δυνάμει—ἐνεργείᾳ.

ness, it forthwith loses (sight of) all things that are perceived by sight. If, however, the light were to abide with the eye unceasingly, the eye would continue to perceive things without cease, as long as the light remained and was unobscured.

11   'Now light comes to you, O Soul, from Mind ($\nu o\hat{u}s$),[1] and darkness from the body; and if you understand this, you ought not to grieve that you must quit the body.[2] For it is through the body[3] that you suffer the greatest loss, and are prevented from apprehending those things which it behoves you most to know.[4] Nay, you ought rather to grieve that you are separated from the thought-world;[5] for it is by the action of that world on you[6] that you enjoy the greatest gains and are enabled to attain to those things which it behoves you to seek after and to grasp. Turn away then from the physical world,[7] scorn and hate and fear it, and seek refuge in the thought-world, which is the root and source of your existence, and the abode appropriate to a being that stands so high in rank and authority as you;[8] that so you may partake of everlasting life, and attain to perfect bliss.'[9]

12   Cap. 5, §§ 12, 13. 'How long,[10] O Soul, will you go on straying and wandering hither and thither, to and fro, in the world of things that come to be? How long will you go on winning to yourself comrades and friends,—now putting a friend away, and now winning some one to you and making him your friend? Of all those with whom you join yourself in friendship, and who, at times, approve themselves to you, there is none that does not at other times show himself one that harbours in his mind disloyalty and treachery towards you, even while you are meaning to be loyal to him and to help him; none that does not deceive you by feigning, even while you are thinking him sincere; none that does not contaminate and defile you, even while you think him pure; and indeed, none that is not cease-

---

[1] I.e. from the divine $\nu o\hat{u}s$, which is here regarded as outside of and distinct from the soul. God is like the sun; and the divine $\nu o\hat{u}s$, by which the soul is 'enlightened', is like the sunlight which issues from the sun.

[2] I.e. you ought not to fear death. Cf. 4. 5 *sq*.

[3] I.e. through being incarnated on earth.   [4] Viz. the $\nu o\eta\tau\acute{a}$ and God.

[5] The $\nu o\eta\tau\grave{o}s$ $\kappa\acute{o}\sigma\mu os$.

[6] I.e. by the 'light' which is thence shed on you.

[7] *A natura avertaris.*

[8] *Propria sedes nobilitatis atque auctoritatis tuae* Bard. Perhaps *auctoritas* stands for $\dot{\epsilon}\xi o\upsilon\sigma\acute{\iota}a$.

[9] This Platonic *sententia* may be a translation of a Greek original; and the Greek original may possibly have been a *Hermeticum*.

[10] [Cf. *Corp.* VII. *init.*]

lessly opposed to you by his whole being and nature, even as you, by your whole being and nature, are ceaselessly opposed to him.   And in the end, after all this, he breaks and tears apart the bond of friendship by which he is joined to you, though you have done nothing to
13 deserve such treatment.   And (so) at all times you suffer grief and sorrow from partings.   [And you have no (true) friend or comrade, because those (whom you think to be your friends) are treacherous to you, while you are loyal to them ; they do you wrong, while you deal well and fairly with them.] [1]   For what you suffered at the first is not enough for you, but you wish to make yet further trial of them ; and you refuse to take warning from what you have learnt about them by long experience, and to be convinced thereby.

'How long will you go on seeking after those evil and unrighteous men, those traitors and deceivers ?   Are you *really* foolish and blind in this, or are you merely *feigning* folly and blindness ?' [2]

6. 1   Cap 6, § 1.   'If a man were to take but one drink of water, he would thereby get sure knowledge of the nature of all water ; for when one has had experience of a part, one thence gets light upon the whole.   And again, he who has looked at one handful of earth has therewith seen earth in general ; for though the kinds of earth are various, yet the essence [3] and concept [4] of earth is invariable.

'And even so, friends also are all of one nature and one essence ; [5] and he who attaches himself to them will find that (any) one of them throws light on all, and a few on many.' [6]

---

[1] This seems to be a doublet of what was said in § 12 ('Of all those with whom you join yourself . . . while you are thinking him sincere ').

[2] Compare 4. 7, which is to the same effect.   In both these *sententiae* alike, it may be doubted whether the writer is speaking literally or metaphorically ; that is, whether by 'friends' he means *men*, or the *things* of this world in which men mistakenly put their trust (the things spoken of in 6. 2 *sq.*).   The first sentence, with its mention of 'the world of τὰ γιγνόμενα', suggests the latter interpretation ; and so does the mention of 'contamination and defilement', and 'ceaseless opposition '.   But there are other phrases (e. g. 'those evil and unrighteous men ') which seem applicable only to human friends in the literal sense.   It is possible that the passage, as originally written, was meant to be taken literally, but that the first sentence, and one or two other phrases, were added by the compiler of the *Castig. an.* in order to make it applicable to all the seeming goods of the present life.

[3] *Substantia* : 'essence' in the logical sense (Aristotelian).

[4] *Notio*.

[5] What the writer presumably means, though he does not explicitly say it, is that all friends alike are untrustworthy.

[6] The four passages 5. 12 *sq.*, 6. 1, 6. 2 *sq.*, and 6. 4, appear to be four distinct *sententiae*, which the compiler of the *Castig. an.* has placed together because in all four 'friends' are spoken of.   But he has not placed here 4. 7 and 7. 10-8. 2, which also have to do with friendship.

2 Cap. 6, §§ 2, 3. I see that in all cases like seeks after like, and equal joins itself to equal; and you too ought to recognize the truth of this. Now you, O Soul, are luminous and bright;[1] you partake of life and speech;[2] you are intelligent[3] and righteous;[4] you are pure and stainless; you possess your own discernment[5] and rational will; do not then ally yourself (or make friends) with[6] (corporeal) things, which are foul and dark,[7] devoid of life and reason,[8] unintelligent and unrighteous, unclean and filthy, and are moved only by blind and random impulse and desire.

3 'If you distrust what I have now explained to you, show me, I pray, how these properties of yours that I have mentioned[9] can be in accord with the properties of things of the other kind (i. e. corporeal things); for you cannot possibly think that two things mutually opposed[10] can be included in one concept.[11] , [12]

4 Cap. 6. § 4. 'A man who is sinking in water does not try to catch fish; he has something more urgent to attend to. And even so, a dweller in this world, if he understands how grievous is his situation in it, is so fully occupied with saving his soul, that he disregards worldly goods and pleasures.

'As long as you are in the sense-world, O Soul, you will have enough to endure from your own body, with its conflicting forces[13] and its foulness. Do not then *add another person to your own body;*[14] lest

---

[1] I.e. you are able to see (mentally).

[2] '*Orationis* particeps' Bard.: 'redenbegabt' Fl. The human ψυχή is λογική or λόγον ἔχουσα.   [3] νοερά.

[4] The human soul was intellectually and morally perfect before its lapse and incarnation; and such it still is by its true nature.

[5] κρίσις, i e. the power of distinguishing between good and evil.

[6] *Societatem inire cum.*

[7] The body and bodily things are interposed as an opaque obstruction between the soul and the realities it seeks to see; cf. 4. 4.

[8] *Ratio* Bard., i.e. λόγος. If Bardenhewer has accurately translated the Arabic in writing *oratio* above, and *ratio* here, this is almost a decisive proof that the passage is a translation of a Greek original. The Arab translator must have read λόγος in both places, and rendered it by 'speech' in the first place, and 'reason' in the second.

[9] Viz. your luminosity and brightness, &c.

[10] Such as soul and body, or things incorporeal and things corporeal.

[11] *Notio.*

[12] This *sententia* has probably been translated, with little alteration, from a Greek original. It looks like an extract from a dialogue; and it does not seem unlikely that the original was a Greek *Hermeticum.*

[13] *Contrarietates.* The physical forces which act on and in the body (and, through the body, excite πάθη in the soul) are in conflict with one another, and with the soul; they might be called 'contraries' in either of these two senses.

[14] This may mean either 'do not marry a wife', or 'do not admit any one to friendship with you'

you be like one who has sunk under water, and at the same time is hampered and held down by a stone fastened to his neck. I think a man who has sunk under water cannot ⟨easily⟩ escape, even if he is alone ; and how can he hope to escape if he adds to his own weight by carrying some one else about his neck ?'[1]

5   Cap. 6, § 5. 'If, O Soul, you are about to enter on the road that leads to salvation,[2] you will have regard to the things you have come to know by experience, and you will seek after those things. If you have come to know only the things apprehensible by sense,[3] you will, when you have to quit the body, betake yourself to the things which are known to you, and turn towards them, and lay hold on them ;[4] but if you have come to know the things that are apprehensible by thought alone,[5] and prefer them to the others, you will (when you quit the body) turn towards these latter things, and betake yourself to *them*, and lay hold on *them*.[6][7]

6   Cap. 6, §§ 6, 7 a. 'You see before you, O Soul, the abode of things apprehensible by sense, and the abode of things apprehensible by thought alone. Both are placed before your eyes ; you have learnt by experience to know both the one and the other, and you have seen them both with your own eyes.[8] Choose now[9] which you will ;

---

[1] Here we have an extreme instance of the self-regarding and anti-social temper (as in 4. 7 and 5. 12 *sq.*, if those *sententia* are to be taken literally). The writer's attitude towards his fellow-men is like that of the early Christian hermits of Egypt and Syria.

[2] What is wanted here is something equivalent to *quum emigres necesse erit* below, 'When the time comes for you to quit the body', i.e. when you die. [The road of salvation—*Corp.* IV. 9 ; XI. ii. 21 ; Stob. *Exc.* II B, 5.]

[3] τὰ αἰσθητά.

[4] I. e. you will turn towards corporeal things, and will, *by your own desire*, be reincarnated on earth. In speaking of reincarnation, Platonists sometimes said that a soul seeks and enters into a fresh body voluntarily, and sometimes that it is reincarnated by compulsion, as a punishment ; the writer of this *sententia* takes the former view.   [5] τὰ νοητά.

[6] I. e. you will ascend to the νοητὸς κόσμος (and there dwell in union with God).

[7] This *sententia* is a concise statement of the Platonic doctrine of reincarnation (which is quite incompatible with Mohammedanism). It may perhaps be a translation of a Greek original.

[8] The soul has experienced τὰ νοητά before its incarnation (and, in some degree, in this life also, if and when it had attained to ἀνάμνησις of them) ; and it has experienced τὰ αἰσθητά since its incarnation. Cf. 1. 6 : 'the soul descends into this world in order that it may make trial of things and learn to know them'; and for the *choice* between the two worlds, cf. 3. 7.

[9] *Iam utrumvis eligas.* The choice is to be made *here and now*, i.e. *before* your present life on earth comes to an end. If you now choose τὰ νοητά, you will, when you come to die, return to your home in the νοητὸς κόσμος; if you now choose τὰ αἰσθητά, you will, when you come to die, be reincarnated upon earth. (That must, I think, be what is meant, though the meaning is not very clearly expressed.)

(whether you choose the one or the other,) you will not be repelled from it, nor will it be refused to you ; and (when you quit the body,) migrate into that abode which you think the pleasanter and the better of the two. If you prefer to go on dwelling in the world of things apprehensible by sense,[1] (you must) take up your abode there (again)[2] under the same conditions that you have learnt to know by experience (during your present life) ; but if you wish to depart to the world of things apprehensible by thought alone, you ought, before you quit this life, to picture to yourself in thought the road by which you will (have to) travel, and (inform yourself) how you are to proceed along that road from stage to stage in due succession, until you arrive at the stage of everlasting rest.[3]

7a　'If you keep in mind that road,[4] beware lest at the time of your departure from the body[5] you allow oblivion[6] and fear to interpose between you and the road,[7] that you may not wander from the road and go astray. But if you should (at any time) forget it, seek to recall it to your memory ; and to that end, make use of what is told you by those who have already travelled along that road, and know it by experience ;[8] for they are the masters of right guidance ;[9] they are lights in the darkness ; they will guide you and point out to you the path by which you may attain to that at which you aim.'[10]

7b　Cap. 6, § 7 b. 'Everything that looks and tends upward[11] must be light (*leve*) and clean and pure, so that it quickly arrives at the place

---

[1] I. e. to be reincarnated on earth when your present life has come to an end.

[2] *Sedem colloces* : i. e. you must enter into another body of the same kind as that in which you are now incarnated.

[3] A *gradual progress* towards the final rest in God is here spoken of. It is not clearly said whether it is a progress that takes place during the present life on earth, or a progress that is to take place after death ; but it suits best with what follows if we take it as meaning a progress in *gnosis* during the present life.

[4] *Si viam istam animo tenes.* But the meaning wanted is rather 'If you have chosen the νοητά, and wish to travel along the road that leads to the νοητὸς κόσμος and to God'.

[5] *Tempore emigrandi.*　　[6] λήθη.　　[7] *Inter te et ipsam* (sc. *viam*).

[8] This looks like a reminiscence of Pl. *Rep.* I. 328 E : χαίρω γε διαλεγόμενος τοῖς σφόδρα πρεσβύταις· δοκεῖ γάρ μοι χρῆναι παρ' αὐτῶν πυνθάνεσθαι, ὥσπερ τινὰ ὁδὸν προεληλυθότων, ἣν καὶ ἡμᾶς ἴσως δεήσει πορεύεσθαι, ποία τίς ἐστι, τραχεῖα καὶ χαλεπή, ἢ ῥαδία καὶ εὔπορος. The words are partly similar, but the application is different. [Stob. *Exc.* II. B, 4–5 (codd.): εὐδαιμόνως τεθνήξῃ, τῆς ψυχῆς σου μὴ ἀγνοούσης ποῦ αὐτὴν δεῖ ἀναπτῆναι· αὕτη γὰρ μόνη ἐστίν, ὦ τέκνον, ἡ πρὸς ἀλήθειαν ὁδός· ἣν καὶ οἱ ἡμέτεροι πρόγονοι ὥδευσαν, καὶ ὁδεύσαντες ἔτυχον τοῦ ἀγαθοῦ. *Corp.* IV. 11 b; VI. 6.]

[9] *Antistites recti ductus.*

[10] Among the 'guides' of whom the writer was thinking must almost certainly have been Plato and Hermes.

[11] ἀνωφερές.

towards which it tends.   But everything that looks ⟨and tends⟩ down-ward [1] must be heavy and foul; and the fouler and heavier it is, the more quickly does it arrive at the place towards which it tends.' [2]

8 a   Cap. 6, §§ 8, 9.   'Those illustrious strangers [3] come down from their own world into the physical world in order to make trial of it.' [4]

Bardenhewer.	*Fleischer's two MSS. (L and R).*
But if (when living in the physical world) they make use ⟨only⟩ of the (bodily) organs by means of which they perceive the objects of taste, smell, and sight, and all things that are perceived in the sense-world	But if you (O Soul) make use of the (bodily) organs by means of which the objects of taste, smell, and sight are immediately per-ceived, ‖ then, O Soul, therewith bethink you of your future, and
8 b and exist in it, [5] then they forget [6]	reflect that this world and its enjoy-

[1] κατωφερές.

[2] If the soul is to mount upward to the νοητά and to God, it must first be cleansed of the impurities which have adhered to it during its embodiment.   If, when it quits the body, it is still heavily weighted with these impurities, it will sink down to earth, and be reincarnated.

This *sententia* is based on Stoic physics, and implies something like the doctrine of Posidonius concerning disembodied souls.   In that respect, it is to be classed with 1. 8-11 and 5. 2-5 ; and like those *sententiae*, it may be a translation of a Greek original, which may perhaps have been Hermetic.

[3] *Illustres illi hospites*, i.e. human souls.   The life of the human soul in this world is a *peregrinatio*, a temporary sojourn in a foreign land.   The fatherland of the souls is the νοητὸς κόσμος ; and when they come down to live on earth, they come as ξένοι.   [Compare perhaps Stob. *Exc.* XXIV. 4.]

The abruptness of the opening words seems to show that this *sententia* is an extract from a longer document, in which the application of the word ξένοι was explained by what had been said before.

[4] I. e. in order to add experience and knowledge of τὰ αἰσθητά to the experience and knowledge of τὰ νοητά which they possess already.   Cf. 2. 6 ; 3. 7 ; 7. 6 b *sqq.*; 11. 1.

[5] From this point on, the two texts are entirely different ; and at the end of § 8 Fleischer's text of the *Castig. an.* ends.   As given by Bardenhewer, §§ 8, 9 present a continuous and coherent *sententia*.   As given by Fleischer, § 8 is incoherent ; the latter part of it (8 b) has no intelligible connexion with the beginning (8 a).   Hence it is evident that §§ 8, 9 originally stood as given by Bardenhewer.   In the arche-type of Fleischer's two MSS., the text of the *Castig. an.* was accidentally broken off at the end of 6. 8 a, and all that followed this was lost.   A transcriber, finding that the text before him ended abruptly at this point with an unfinished sentence, finished it off by adding a short passage of his own composition (§ 8 b as given by Fleischer), an exhortation to the soul, which he meant to serve as a fitting con-clusion to the whole of the *Castig. an.* as known to him (i.e. 1. 1–6. 8 a) ; and he made a clumsy attempt to connect his appended conclusion with what preceded it, by altering the third person plural in the unfinished sentence of § 8 a into the second person singular.   The archetype of Fleischer's MSS., before its mutilation, must have extended at least as far as the end of 6. 9, and may have included all that is given by Bardenhewer, down to the end of *cap.* 14.

The exhortation added by the transcriber in Fleischer's text (§ 8 b) is not in keeping with the tone of the *sententiae* in general ; there is nothing in the rest of the *Castig. an.* that resembles his list of moral virtues.

[6] The Platonic λήθη.   [Stob. *Exc.* XXIV. 6.]

their own world and all things in it, and think that there is nothing to be found except the things they see before them in the sense-world. They forget the thought-world, and lose all memory of it. Hence, if they cannot thereafter be brought back into the class of beings possessing intelligence (νοῦς),[1] they are said to be 'dead',[2] and to have perished, swept away by the course of nature.[3]

But if they return to their previous mode of existence,[4] and in some way recall to memory[5] their own world,[6] they are said to be no longer dead, but to have come to life again.'

ments and toyings and amusements are merely transitory things, and that nothing is permanent except the everlasting acquisitions, such as true knowledge, justice, forgiving kindness, mercifulness, uprightness, stedfastness, generosity, long-suffering, courage, liberality, and other praiseworthy qualities. But shun, O Soul, the blameworthy qualities; so will you keep yourself faultless, if you diligently meditate on that which I have so far set forth to you.

This is the end of my words and warnings to you. Let them ever stand before your eyes, and let their fulfilment become for you a habit and a second nature. Be this your task.

Praise to God! Amen.'

(*Here ends Fleischer's text of the Castig. an.*)

9   'And then, their thought is fixed on the archetypal form [7] which they have recalled to mind, and they strive to look into it deeply and

---

[1] *Ad speciem rerum rationis compotum referri* Bard. *Res rationis compotes* must mean νοεραὶ οὐσίαι, 'beings that possess νοῦς'; and if this term is rightly translated by Bard., it is necessary to take *speciem* as standing for εἶδος in the sense of 'class' or 'kind'. (Or, is *res rationis compotes*, i.e. νοερά, a mistake for νοητά? In that case, one might take *speciem* to mean 'sight', and translate 'they cannot be brought back to the sight of τὰ νοητά'.)

[2] Men who are completely unaware of τὰ νοητά are metaphorically 'dead'. This state is, in some of the *sententiae* of the Castig. an., called *mors perpetua*, 'everlasting death'. (Did those who used this term, or some of them, hold that such men cease to exist when their present life on earth ends? That is possible, but uncertain.)

[3] They are completely assimilated to the material world into which they have sunk, and are wholly subject to the physical forces which operate in it; and so the νοῦς in them, which is the true self, is extinct.

[4] *Ad priorem existendi rationem* : i.e. if they become νοεροί again.

[5] The Platonic ἀνάμνησις.

[6] Down to this point, 6. 8 (as given by Bardenhewer) is repeated in substance, and partly word for word, in 7. 4; but from this point onward, the two *sententiae* differ.

[7] *Speciei cuius recordati sunt inhaerent* Bard. The meaning appears to be that the man begins by 'recalling to mind' some one νοητὸν εἶδος, and then goes on from that to other νοητὰ εἴδη in succession, until at last he 'sees with the eye of mind' the νοητὸς κόσμος as a whole (and God, to whom the νοητὸς κόσμος is correlative).

search out its meaning;[1] and not that one form alone, but with it, all the forms which at first they had forgotten. And as often as they grasp in thought[2] some one of the things which they had forgotten, their (mental) eye is (more and more) freed from darkness; their health is strengthened, and they recover from their sickness. And therewith, they perceive with the eye of mind that[3] all things which they see before them in the sense-world are unreal,[4] and are merely images of things, not things that are real. An 'image' of a thing is a shadow or reflection of it, such as is seen on the ground, or in water. And since the soul had been caught[5] and held by love of semblances[6] of the various forms of things,[7] and not (by love) of the (real) things themselves, thence it came to pass that, when it descended into the sense-world,[8] at first it forgot the thought-world; but when it begins to contemplate those archetypal forms,[9] and recalls them to memory, it recovers from its sickness, and becomes of sound mind again after having known nothing;[10] and so it comes to pass that (when parted from the body by death?) it departs (from the sense-world), and returns to the contemplation of the real forms,[11] and to unceasing and everlasting life.'[12]

10   Cap. 6, §§ 10–12. 'Mind (νοῦς) is, as it were, the father of the soul,[13] and corporeal nature (φύσις)[14] the wife of the soul;[15] and the soul inclines both towards the one and towards the other. At one

---

[1] *Eamque penitus perspicere student atque exquirere.*

[2] *Intellegunt*: νοοῦσι.

[3] Perhaps: 'they see (things) with the eye of mind, (not, as before, with the bodily eyes alone,) (and become aware) that' &c. Cf. 7 a above.

[4] Cf. Herm. *ap.* Stob. II A.

[5] *Sc.* when it came down to be incarnated on earth. Cf. the description of the descent of Anthropos (prototype of particular souls) in *Corp. Herm.* I.

[6] *Simulacra*: εἴδωλα.   [7] *Variarum rerum specierum.*

[8] I.e. at birth. In babies, νοῦς is manifestly absent or dormant. (And some men remain children in this respect throughout their lives.)

[9] *Species istas*: the νοητὰ εἴδη.

[10] *Resipiscit postquam insciens fuit.* The soul which ἀναμιμνήσκει τὰ νοητά is compared to a sick man who gets well again, and recovers his senses, after having been unconscious or delirious.

[11] In this *sententia*, as in most of the others, the writer does not explicitly speak of 'seeing God' or 'being made one with God'; but when he speaks of seeing or knowing the νοητὰ εἴδη (which are God's thoughts, and are the only things that are real), that is merely another way of saying the same thing. In preferring to speak of the νοητὰ εἴδη rather than of God, the Platonists by whom these *sententiae* were written followed the example of Plato himself.

[12] This *sententia* contains nothing that need be of later date than A.D. 300; it may be a translation of a Greek original, which may possibly have been a *Hermeticum.*

[13] ψυχή issues or emanates from the divine νοῦς (as in the system of Plotinus).

[14] *Rerum natura.*

[15] Cf. the marriage of Anthropos with ἡ καταφερὴς φύσις in *Corp. Herm.* I. 14.

time it inclines towards Mind, by reason of the kinship between father and son ; and in this is seen its true and natural way of acting.[1] At another time it inclines towards corporeal nature, like a man burning with love of his wife ; and in this is seen an incidental and transitory way of acting.

11   'Now mark how a man's wife, when he is alone with her, welcomes him with play and laughter and fond words, and talks to him most sweetly and most gently ; but what she has in mind is other than her outward seeming ; for her design in thus behaving is only to enslave her husband, and make use of him to her own ends, and to drive him into dangers.[2]   She gives him honey to drink, but there is deadly poison mingled with it.

12   'On the other hand, mark how a father, when he is alone with his son, addresses him with stern warnings and grave reproofs, and speaks to him right harshly ; but what he has in mind is other than his outward seeming ; for in behaving thus, his only aim is that his son may thence get benefit and profit in all the concerns of life.   He gives his son a draught to drink that is bitter and nauseous, but there is mingled in it health and life and a happy issue.[3]'[4]

13   Cap. 6, §§ 13–15. 'Corporeal nature is your wife, O Soul, and intellect (νοῦς) is your father ; and a blow given by your father's hand is better than a kiss given by your wife.

14   'You cannot separate yourself from your father ; for the bond of kinship between you and him cannot be broken, whether you part from him or live with him, whether there is anger or goodwill between you ; under all conditions alike, kinship stands fast. A man can divorce his wife, and the bond that joins him to her is then broken ; but he cannot put away his father and take to himself another father.

---

[1] *Ratio naturalis et vera*: the way of acting which is in accordance with the soul's true nature.

[2] Wives are Delilahs. For the dislike of women that is here implied, cf 5. 7.

[3] Cf. *Corp. Herm.* XII. i. 3, where it is said that ὁ νοῦς ⟨τὴν⟩ ψυχὴν λυπεῖ, ἐξυφαιρῶν αὐτῆς τὴν ἡδονήν, and νοῦς is in that respect compared to a physician who inflicts pain on his patient, καίων ἢ τέμνων.

[4] This passage (6. 10–12) appears to be a distinct *sententia*, complete in itself; and it is marked off as such, in the usual way, by some words of exhortation appended at the end of it by the compiler of the *Castig. an.* ('Seek, O Soul, to understand these maxims; take to yourself those things which are true, and reject those things which are false').   But there is placed next to it another *sententia* (6. 13–15) which is little more than a doublet of it, the same subject being dealt with, and the same simile employed ; and in 7. 1–2 (which is similarly marked off from 6. 13–15 by interposed words of exhortation) the same simile of father and wife presents itself again in § 2.

15   'If you obey (your father) Mind, O Soul, you will partake of life and happiness; but if you disobey (your father) Mind, and obey (your wife) corporeal nature,[1] you will undergo death and misery.'[2]

7. 1   Cap. 7, §§ 1, 2. 'How long is this to last, O Soul,—that I go on urging you to enter on the road that leads to your salvation[3] and profit, but you refuse to yield to my urging; and that you go on urging me to enter on the way that leads to destruction and loss, but I refuse to yield to your urging to go your way together with you? If there needs must be this difference of opinion between me and you, nothing remains for us, O Soul, but separation; we shall have to part, O Soul, and each of us will have to go the way he wishes, and follow his own bent.'[4]

2   'You are not dealing fairly, O Soul; you are neither just nor wise.'[5]

'Your father (νοῦς) addresses you with teachings and warnings, the issues of which are salutary for you, and the fruits thereof full of delight; but you turn away from him, and turn to your wife (φύσις), and to her deceptions and her lures and her sweet flatteries, the fruits of which are cares and sorrows, and fear, and the pain of unsatisfied desire.'[6]

3   Cap. 7, § 3. 'If, when it is the time to act, O Soul, you miss the opportunity for acting rightly and fitly, you thereby lose the delight of reaping the fruit of good deeds, and winning the reward. If, in the season of planting, a man does not plant a tree, then, in the season of ripe fruit, he does not enjoy the fruit.'

4   Cap. 7, § 4. 'Convince yourself, O Soul, that those illustrious strangers[7] came down into the world of things that come to be, in order to make trial of it. But when they had arrived in it, and had acquired knowledge of the things in it, they forgot their own world, that is, the thought-world, and ceased to be aware of their own

---

[1] To obey φύσις would mean to be governed by the animal instincts, i.e. the blind desires which have their origin in the body.

[2] § 15 would serve as a suitable conclusion to §§ 10–12: and it is possible that there was originally one unbroken *sententia*, consisting of §§ 10, 11, 12, 15, and that a parallel passage (§§ 13, 14), taken from another source, was subsequently inserted.

[3] *Salus.* Cf. p. 313. 2 above.

[4] [From the context, especially 7. 2, this would appear to be an example of the exhortations addressed by νοῦς to the Soul.]

[5] It may be doubted whether it is best to take this sentence as a continuation of 7. 1, or as connected with what follows in 7. 2.

[6] *Aegritudines (et) curae* (equivalent to *tristitia*), *timor, egestas.* Cf. 5. 6.

[7] See 6. 8, of which the first part of this *sententia*, down to 'have forgotten', is a repetition.

immaterial being. But if they recall to memory the things they have forgotten, they see before them both the one state of life and the other, and note the difference between them, and see that the one is noble and the other base;[1] and seeing both, they are free to choose [2] whether they will abide in the one or in the other. If then they see with the mind's eye how much loftier and more exalted is the noble state of life than the base state, they prefer to return to those things to which they are akin by their own nature,[3] and they abandon with scorn and contempt the things (of the sense-world) with which they have been incidentally conjoined.'[4]

5 Cap. 7, §§ 5, 6 a. 'By warnings and reproofs souls are rubbed and polished, and are thereby cleansed from rust.[5] Now a (metal) mirror that has been stained with rust by some passing incident can be made bright again by rubbing and polishing; but when a mirror has been rusted by an incident[6] that persists and is slow to pass away, and that advances from the grade of potentiality to that of actuality, so that the mirror takes on the character of a different mirror, with a nature that is fixed and ingrained,—then the polisher's skill is of no avail, and the mirror cannot be cleansed from rust except by submitting it again to the refining fire. And even so, souls stained by some passing incident can be made bright again by warnings and reproofs —so that they recall to memory the state of life in which they were before;[7] but souls (that have become)[8] foul and unclean in their very nature can be made bright again only by being plunged in misery, and remaining long in that condition, and undergoing it again and again.[9]

---

[1] *Praestans, vilis.*

[2] As to this choice, cf. 3. 7.

[3] I. e. to the νοητά (and God).

[4] The writer of this *sententia* apparently had 6. 8 *sq.* before him, and starting from that, wrote in his own words a description of 'the choice'.

[5] [*Corp.* XIV. 7: ταῦτα γάρ ἐστι τὰ πάθη τὰ τῇ γενέσει παρεπόμενα, ὥσπερ ὁ ἰὸς τῷ χαλκῷ, καὶ ὁ ῥύπος τῷ σώματι. The figure has a different application, however.]

[6] [For the sense of *per accidens celeriter cessans* as distinguished from *accidens constans et tarde cessans* see p. 345, note 5.]

[7] [Cf. 7. 4 above.]

[8] All souls are, by their origin and true nature, bright and pure; the 'rust' is an accretion; and even in the worst cases, the foulness of the soul is only a '*second nature*'.

[9] What the writer of this *sententia* is asserting is the need of purgative suffering for souls that are badly defiled. But whether he means misery in this life, or purgatorial pains (in the form of penal reincarnations or otherwise) inflicted after death, or both, we are not told. Perhaps his insistence on the need of undergoing the suffering

6a   'How many times gold in which there is much alloy must be put into the fire again, before it comes forth pure and bright! How many times a bent rod must be heated in the fire, before it is made straight! How many times wheat must be passed through the sieve again, before the refuse that is mixed with it, and by which it is spoiled, is removed! And how many times defiled and rusted souls must undergo all manner of misery, before they recover right reason and are changed (back to their primal purity)[1]![2]

6b   Cap. 7, §§ 6 b–8. 'How much better is the sweetness of honey than the bitterness of aloes, no one can know unless he has tasted both . . .; and even so, the soul cannot know how much better is the sweetness of happiness than the bitterness of misery, unless it has

7   tasted both, and thereby learnt to know both. How great is the difference between the man who scorns and rejects a thing after he has tried and tasted it, and the man who draws near to it (for the first time), desiring to try and taste it![3] (For instance,) he who is fighting in a battle[4] longs to withdraw from it, because of the bitter stress of the fighting, and the heavy burden of his armour; but he who has never been in battle is eager to undergo it and to taste it.

'If then ⌐from those things which you have tried, O Soul, you think you have arrived at your last end (or aim), now return to your highest limit from those things in which you were before, and which you have

8   forgotten.⌐[5] But if you aspire to the highest quest of all, turn to the

'again and again' points rather to a series of reincarnations. See 10. 1–3, in which the simile of a rusted mirror is used again.

[1] *Rectam rationem capessunt et convertuntur.*

[2] This *sententia* may perhaps have been translated from a Greek original; but I know of nothing in the Greek *Hermetica* or other Platonic Greek writings that closely resembles it.

[3] The soul not yet incarnated knows τὰ νοητά, but knows nothing of τὰ αἰσθητά. It comes down to earth to be incarnated, 'desiring to try and taste' τὰ αἰσθητά (cf. 2. 6; 3. 7; 6. 8). When first incarnated, it forgets τὰ νοητά; but if, in the course of its life on earth, it recalls them to memory, thenceforward it knows both, and can choose between them; and comparing the one with the other, it 'scorns and rejects' τὰ αἰσθητά.

[4] The battle is life on earth. The 'heavy armour' is perhaps the body.

[5] 'Si igitur ab eis quae experta es, o anima, ad ultimum finem tuum pervenisse te existimas, iamiam ad summum terminum tuum ab eis in quibus antea fuisti quorumque oblita es redeas.' This obscure sentence stands in contrast to what follows it, viz. 'Sin autem maximam quaestionem appetis' &c., which appears to mean 'But if you aim at that which is highest of all, turn to the contemplation of God'. Hence the sentence 'Si igitur ab eis' &c. ought to mean 'If you aim at something short of the highest of all, do so and so'. But what is it that is spoken of as something short of the highest? Possibly the νοητὸς κόσμος. This writer in any case differs from the authors of most of the other Platonic *sententiae* of the *Castig. an.* in speaking explicitly of *God* as the object of men's aspiration; and perhaps he placed God above the νοητά, and spoke of the νοητὸς κόσμος as to which some men

contemplation of Him who is without end, and has had no beginning, who is seen present from an eternal past to an eternal future;[1] who calls things forth when they appear, and makes away with them when they disappear, who unfolds things and folds them together,[2] [calls things forth and makes away with them,] puts them there and takes them away,[3] whole after whole, and one particular thing after another.[4]'[5]

9   Cap. 7, § 9. 'Observe, O Soul, how particulars are incapable of stability and perpetuity; they disappear, and lose their own existence, and return to the universals to which they belong. And even so, the universals cannot equal in perpetuity that one First Principle which is one and alone and eternal;[6] and when their strength melts away and their time is ended, they all alike disappear.[7]

may be content to attain, and of God as a yet higher aim. Assuming this to be his meaning, one might conjecture that the sentence was originally to this effect; 'Si igitur, ab eis quae experta es (concludens), o anima, ad ultimum finem tuum *ita perventurum esse* te existimas, iamiam [ad summum terminum tuum] ab eis in quibus (nunc es ad ea) in quibus antea fuisti quorumque oblita es redeas.' 'If then, basing your opinion on the experience (of τὰ νοητά and τὰ αἰσθητά) which you have already acquired, you think *that you will in this way attain to* the utmost limit of your aspiration,—in that case, now at once return from (the world of αἰσθητά in which you now are, to) the world of νοητά in which you were before your incarnation, and which you have forgotten. But if' &c.

Or is the alternative spoken of in this sentence that of remaining content with the αἰσθητά? In that case, the text would have to be rewritten in some such way as this: 'Si igitur, ab eis quae experta es (concludens). o anima, (iamiam) ad ultimum finem tuum pervenisse te existimas [iamiam ad summum terminum tuum], (in rebus in quibus nunc es permaneas, neque) ab eis (ad ea) in quibus antea fuisti quorumque oblita es redeas.' 'If... you think that (in dwelling among τὰ αἰσθητά) you have already attained to your utmost aim, then stay where you are, and do not seek to return to the world of νοητά. But if' &c.

    [1] *Ab aeterno atque in aeternum (in rebus creatis) praesens conspicitur* Bard.

    [2] *Qui res explicat et complicat.* God is the author of the 'evolution' of the Kosmos as a whole, and that of each several organism from its germ (e.g. of a tree from a seed), and of the contrary process also (e.g. the production of a seed from a tree).   [3] *Ponit et tollit.*

    [4] *Totum* (τὸ ὅλον) *post totum, particulare* (τὸ καθ' ἕκαστον) *post particulare.* I suppose *totum* means the Kosmos as a whole, and *particularia*, individual organisms in it. [Possibly the opposition ὅλον)(τὸ καθ' ἕκαστον bears the same meaning as in *Ascl.* 290. 25, the kind as distinguished from the individual. The 'whole' would then be the 'res universalis' of c. 7, § 9.]

    [5] In this *sententia*, it may be conjectured that § 8 has been taken with little change from a Greek (and possibly Hermetic) source.

    [6] *Primum illud principium unum solum atque aeternum.* Perhaps 'that one First Principle or First Cause (ἀρχή) which alone is eternal'.

    [7] *Omnes simul evanescunt.*

    The *primum principium* must be God. But what is meant by the 'universals'? Bardenhewer says these *universales res* are the elements, and the *particulares res*, the individual things composed of the elements. But how could the elements be said to 'disappear'? If the verb were in the future tense ('omnes simul evanescent'), we might suppose these words to mean that the present world will one day be destroyed (as Jews, Christians, and Moslems agreed in believing).

'[And even so, the universals are found perpetually and everlastingly (?), now actually (ἐνεργείᾳ), and now potentially (δυνάμει).]'[1]

10   Cap. 7, §§ 10, 11. 'How great is the difference, O Soul, between friend (and friend)!

'(There is a friend of yours)[2] who increases his own wealth by robbing you; who bears malice against you and disparages you; who reduces you to poverty and want, and inflicts pain and grief and sorrow on you;[3] who seeks to make a fool of you and deceive you,[4] and to defile and pollute you;[5] who blinds you, while you desire to see, and leads you astray, while you wish to follow the right road; who imbues you with love of fleeting and perishable goods, in which is no truth, and makes you desire things false and low, in which is no reality. And from all this it results that you (O Soul) are ceaselessly distressed by poverty and want, and tormented by fear and sadness (or anxious care),[6] and that you are degraded and despised, surrounded by darkness,[7] stained with rust,[8] and reduced to slavery. As often as you enrich that friend, he becomes poorer than before;[9] as often as you cleanse him,[10] he becomes fouler and more unclean; as often as you heal his sickness, he becomes more sickly and infirm. You think that his friendship is lasting, and that he is constant; but he very soon makes up his mind to desert you and abandon you;[11] and when he does so, he inflicts on you the pains of parting[12] and mental derangement.[13] And it is through your own mistakes, through your own imprudence, blindness, and folly,[14] that all this befalls you.

---

[1] *Perinde universae res perpetue et sempiterne modo in actu inveniuntur, modo in potentia* Bard. This may perhaps have been written as an alternative for the preceding statement, which it appears to contradict; but I do not know what it means.

[2] This false 'friend' of the soul is the body. Cf. *Corp. Herm.* VII.

[3] The soul is compelled to concern itself about supplying the needs of the body, and in doing so, is vexed with anxiety, and tormented by the pain of unsatisfied desire. Cf. *Corp. Herm.* VI *fin.*: τὸ γὰρ πάντων χαλεπώτατον, ὅτι χρείαν αὐτῶν (sc. bodily goods) ἔχομεν, καὶ ζῆν τούτων χωρὶς οὐ δυνάμεθα.

[4] The bodily senses are fallacious.

[5] By giving rise to 'bodily passions'.

[6] Cf. *egestas, timor, tristitia* in 3. 3–7, and see note on 5. 6.

[7] Cf. 4. 4; 4. 14; 5. 9–11.   [8] Cf. 7. 5 *sq.*

[9] *Egenior fit.* I. e. every time that you give satisfaction to a bodily appetite, the strength of the bodily appetites is increased, and with it, the pain of still unsatisfied desire.

[10] Perhaps the writer (like early Christian ascetics) was averse to baths and washing.

[11] I. e. you will soon die.   [12] The pains of mortal sickness.

[13] *Mentis errorem*: derangement or delirium preceding death.

[14] I. e. all this results from your folly in cleaving to the body, or identifying yourself with it, and treating its interests as your own.

11 'How great is the difference between that friend and another[1] with whom you (may) join yourself in friendship; one who enriches you if you are in want, leads you back into the right road if you go astray, teaches and instructs you if you are ignorant, and restores your sight if you are blind. This friend will not (like that other) inflict on you manifold troubles and labours, cares and toils; moreover, he will abide with you for ever,[2] and you will never find that the bond of friendship between him and you is broken, or that he abandons and forsakes you. As often as you are in communion with him,[3] you win for yourself high dignity[4] from his high dignity, light from his light, and life from his life,[5] knowledge and intelligence from his knowledge and intelligence, satisfaction[6] and authority[7] from his satisfaction and authority. He bestows on you goods that cease not, and are everlasting; he pours forth upon you pleasures that are true, and have naught to do with the senses; and by uniting yourself with him, you get gain instead of loss. Deem[8] *him* then, O Soul, to be your friend; join yourself with *him*, and to *him* attach yourself.'[9]

8.1 Cap. 8, §§ 1, 2. 'If a man has a friend and loses him, but, at the time when he loses that friend, finds another that can take his place and act in his stead, the man will soon cast from him and put aside the memory of his first friend, especially if the new friend is more closely united with him, and is of higher standing[10] than the other. But if he loses a friend and can find no one to take that friend's place, he can hardly avoid suffering long sadness and heavy sorrow. If then, O Soul, you have a friend concerning whom you know with certainty that you will lose him and he will depart from you,[11] it is good advice to you[12] to bid you look out beforehand for some one that

[1] The true friend of the soul is the divine *voûs*.
[2] You will not be parted from *voûs* at death, as you will then be parted from the body. [3] *Una cum eo es.* [4] *Praestantia.*
[5] Cf. 'light and life' in I. 8–11 : ζωὴ καὶ φῶς in *Corp. Herm.* I.
[6] *Copia*, the opposite of *egestas*: τὸ ἀνενδεές. [7] *Auctoritas*: ἐξουσία?
[8] *Eum amicum cogitatione tuo effingas*: i. e. τοῦτον φίλον νόει.
[9] Compare the other *sententiae* concerning friends (4. 7; 4. 8 a; 5. 12 sq.; 6. 1–4). In some of them, it seems doubtful whether the word 'friends' is to be understood literally or metaphorically. But here, there is no doubt about the meaning. There is one false friend, and one true friend; the false friend is the body, and the true friend is *voûs*.
This *sententia* may perhaps be based on a translation of a Greek original, similar in character to *Corp. Herm* VII. But the group *egestas, timor, tristitia*, which occurs in it, is not likely to have occurred in a Greek *Hermeticum*.
[10] *Praestantior.* Or perhaps, 'a better friend'.
[11] This friend is the body, from which the soul will be parted at death. The friend that is to take his place is *voûs*.
[12] *Est hoc recte vivendi praeceptum.*

will act in his stead and take his place, and to tell you to seek one
2 that will be a comrade to you and an intimate friend. And this later
friend ought to be more closely joined with you, and of higher standing, than your earlier friend. For if a man loses something, and then
finds something better, his misfortune is changed into good fortune,
and his sorrow into joy and gladness.

'(And even so,) O Soul, before you quit the world of things that
come to be and cease to be, you must make yourself fit to be united
with the thought-world;[1] and before you depart from your [treacher-
ous and degraded and][2] short-lived companion, you must represent
to yourself in thought your departure from him,[3] and gradually dis-
connect yourself from him, and at the same time, hasten forward to
your union with your future friend, and grow accustomed to him,
and gradually attach yourself to him.'[4]

3   Cap. 8, § 3. 'If a man, O Soul, has come to hate the abode in
which he is living, and wishes to quit it, he ought, before he leaves
it, to seek out another place where he may dwell.[5] For he who quits
a place and knows no other place to which he can migrate,[6] can
hardly escape from wandering ceaselessly without (a home). For
being thus helpless, he is driven to settle at random and without
choice in any place at which he has arrived.[7] And it may be that he
is compelled to settle in a place which is worse than his former

[1] The νοητὸς κόσμος.

[2] Down to this point, nothing has, in this *sententia*, been said against the body,
except that the soul will be parted from it at death. It therefore seems probable that,
in the original text, nothing else was said against it throughout, and that the abusive
epithets *perfido, abiecto* were added by a transcriber who was influenced by the preceding *sententia*, 7. 10 *sq.*

[3] *Discessum ab eo cogitatione tibi informes atque effingas*: i.e. χρὴ νοεῖν τὴν
ἀποχώρησιν or τὸν χωρισμὸν (τῆς ψυχῆς ἀπὸ τοῦ σώματος). During your present
life, you must meditate on death, and so prepare yourself for the life to come.

[4] 8. 1 *sq.* is, I think, a distinct *sententia*, taken by the compiler from a source
closely resembling that from which he got 7. 10 *sq.*, and placed by him next to
7. 10 *sq.* because it deals with the same subject.

[5] The abode in which the man is now living is the body; and the abode
which he ought to seek out is the νοητὸς κόσμος. But men do not usually ' hate'
their bodies, and wish to die, until they have found the νοητά, or at least begun
to seek the νοητά; the first part of this sentence therefore does not agree well
with the second part. It ought to be rather 'If a man *knows that he will
have to quit* the abode in which he is living', i.e. that he will have to die
(as in the preceding *sententia*, 'if you know with certainty that you will lose your
friend ').

[6] Cf. Herm. *ap.* Stob. II B. 4 : εὐδαιμόνως τεθνήξῃ, τῆς ψυχῆς σου μὴ ἀγνοούσης
ποῦ αὐτὴν δεῖ ἀναπτῆναι.

[7] The soul which 'knows no other place to which it can migrate' will be
reincarnated on earth. Wandering at random, it will come upon some newly
generated human or animal body, and will enter into it.

abode; [1] whereby happiness is forbidden to him, and his life is thrown into confusion.' [2]

4 Cap. 8, §§ 4 and 9. 'No one, O Soul, dwells in an abode ⟨that is dark and confined and desolate⟩ without wishing to migrate to a place that is better and more roomy and more pleasant to look on.' [3]

9 '⟨⟨If ⟨then⟩, O Soul, you intend to quit the abode in which you are now dwelling, [4] migrate into one that is better. [5] . . . He who migrates from a house that is dark, confined, and desolate [6] into one that is bright and luminous, roomy, and pleasant to look on, [7] will always rejoice at his change of abode, and be glad of his happy departure. [8]⟩⟩' [9]

Cap. 8, § 5. If you have got sure knowledge of something else [10] besides the things which you perceive with your five senses, you have turned into the road which leads to your salvation ; but if you know nothing except what you perceive by means of the bodily senses, you are on the road which leads to destruction and misery.

6 Cap. 8, §§ 6-8. 'Caution, [11] O Soul, is a word the meaning of which you must learn.' If a man guards against things destructive of his own being, he is 'cautious'; if he seeks things destructive to him, he is 'incautious'. Be on your guard then, O Soul, against things destructive to you, and seek things salutary for you. Those things are salutary for you which are congruous with your own nature ; and those things are destructive to you which are repugnant to your own 7 nature. And there is nothing that is not either destructive or salutary.

If then you desire salvation (*salus*), seek things congruous with your own nature ; if you desire destruction, seek things repugnant to your own nature ; if you desire perturbation, distraction, and doubt, 8 seek things of both kinds at once. And therefore, if you, O Soul, are (by your own nature) luminous and bright, do not accustom your-

---

[1] E. g. the body of a beast.

[2] In this passage the same lesson is taught as in the preceding *sententia* (8. 1 *sq.*), but the simile employed is different. Cf. 4. 3 (a man on an ice-floe).

[3] *Praestantior* (but perhaps it ought rather to be *lucidior*), *amplior, amoenior*.

[4] I. e. to quit the body in which you are now incarnated.

[5] I. e. into the νοητὸς κόσμος.   [6] *Deserta, vasta.*

[7] *Amoena.*   [8] *Prospero exitu suo.* Cf. p. 325 n. 6 above.

[9] § 9 fits on well to § 4 (which does not fit on to § 3, though it deals with the same subject) ; and the verbal resemblance between § 4 and § 9 is so close, that there can be little doubt that these two sections originally formed a single *sententia*, which has been accidentally broken in two.   [10] I. e. knowledge of τὰ νοητά.

[11] [*Cautio* is a Mahommedan concept ; avoidance of things that may affect one's future life (Bardenhewer).]

self to dark things ; if you partake of life and speech,[1] do not become familiar with things devoid of life and speech ; if you are endowed with intelligence and discernment,[2] do not become familiar with things devoid of intelligence and 'mental light '.

10 [[Cap. 8, § 9 : see after § 4.]]

Cap. 8, § 10. The fruit of sins is unhappiness ; the fruit of right action and good training is happiness.

11 Cap. 8, § 11. If a man plants date-palms,[3] he gets dates, both fresh and dry, and is glad ; if he plants willows and briars, he gets no fruit, and loses his labour.

Therefore, O Soul, lay hold on things salutary for you, and abandon things destructive to you ; that so you may be received into the number of those souls who enjoy God's help, who follow the right way, and who will participate in everlasting happiness.[4]

12 Cap. 8, §§ 12–14. ['Convince yourself, O Soul, of those things which I am about to explain and expound to you.']

' I have had experience of this world and investigated it ; and I ascertained that the matter of which it consists was in being (or, came into being ?) from the beginning ;[5] and that thereafter there came to pass a separation of things subtle and fine[6] from things dense and coarse,[7] so that the former were borne upward, and the latter downward ;[8] and that next the matter of which this world consists was, by the movement of the heavens, divided into the four elements, fire, air, water, and earth.[9]

---

[1] *Oratio* (λόγος). I. e. if the ψυχή is λογική ; or in other words, if it is a *human* soul.　　　　　　　[2] νοῦς and κρίσις.

[3] Written in Mesopotamia ? This can hardly have come from the same region as the simile of the ice-floe in 4. 3.

[4] This *sententia* might have been written by a pious Moslem.

[5] *Materiam eius iam inde a rerum primordiis exstitisse.* But *exsistere* is ambiguous ; it may mean either εἶναι or γίγνεσθαι. Whether the Arabic is likewise ambiguous, I do not know ; but Bardenhewer's Latin leaves it uncertain whether the writer meant that ἐξ ἀρχῆς (or ἐν ἀρχῇ) ἐγένετο ἡ ὕλη, or that ὕλη is ἀγένητος. [B's *Dissertation* reads '(non ab aeterno esse, immo) initium cepisse '.]

[6] *Subtilia et praestantia.* But *praestantia* is hardly the right word.

[7] *Spissa et aspera.*

[8] I. e. the primal ὕλη, which was originally a homogeneous mass, was differentiated into τὰ ἀνωφερῆ and τὰ κατωφερῆ.

[9] There seems to be some confusion here. We should have expected to be told that τὸ ἀνωφερές was divided into fire and air, and τὸ κατωφερές into water and earth. But in this clause the writer ignores the preceding statement about τὰ ἀνωφερῆ and τὰ κατωφερῆ, and says that *the primal matter* was differentiated into the four elements. Possibly the statement about τὰ ἀνωφερῆ and τὰ κατωφερῆ, and that about the four elements, were alternatives, and were not originally meant to be combined together.

'I carefully considered how these four elements were moved, and what qualities they possessed; and I ascertained that they are moved by their own nature,[1] by a blind and lifeless[2] impulse, and not under 13 the guidance of reason and intelligence. But I found that there are also things,[3] composed of those elements, which are endowed with life and reason and intelligence.[4] I wondered how it could be that things lifeless and devoid of intelligence were the elements of beings that have life[5] and partake of intelligence;[6] and I came to think that perhaps these elements, when intermixed with one another in the bodies of beings possessed of life and reason,[7] generate life and intelligence in them.[8]

'But how can it reasonably be thought that a living being so produced out of two lifeless things intermixed with one another, or that a being that partakes of intelligence is produced out of two things 14 devoid of intelligence intermixed with one another? Hence I was forced to conclude that beings possessed of life and intelligence[9] are not composed of the matter of which this world consists,—I mean, the world of things that come to be and cease to be,—but that they have, for some reason or other,[10] come down into this world (from elsewhere), and that as they have come to it, so they will depart from it; and (I was forced to conclude) that it cannot be that a lifeless thing is the source of a living being, nor that a thing devoid of intelligence is the source of a being that partakes of intelligence.

'Be assured then [O Soul] that those beings possessed of life and

---

[1] I. e. by φύσις, in contrast to νοῦς. The force by which a stone is made to fall is called its φύσις, or the φύσις of the element earth of which the stone consists; and this force is not guided by any νοῦς residing in or belonging to the stone or the earth (though it may perhaps be guided by the divine νοῦς by which the whole Kosmos is governed).

[2] *Inanimus*: ἄψυχος?   [3] I. e. living organisms.

[4] *Vita, oratio, ratio*: i.e. ζωή, λόγος, νοῦς. Corporeal beings endowed with λόγος and νοῦς are, properly speaking, men alone. This writer does not speak of ζῶντα and ἔμψυχα, which are devoid of λόγος and νοῦς; i.e. he either ignores τὰ ἄλογα ζῷα and plants, or attributes to them also a lower grade of λόγος and νοῦς. Cf. 5. 2–5.

[5] *Rerum animatarum*: ἔμψυχα?   [6] μετέχοντα νοῦ.

[7] *Rerum vitae et orationis* (λόγου) *compotum*.

[8] I. e. that the life and intelligence of a man (or animal) is generated by the σύγκρασις τῶν στοιχείων in the body. Cf. Herm. *ap*. Stob. (*Isis to Horus*) XXVI. 13–29, where the various συγκράσεις and their effects are discussed in detail, and XX. 5–7.

[9] I. e. human ψυχαί. [Stob. *Exc.* XX. 4 (codd.) πῶς γὰρ οἷόν τέ ἐστι λέγειν ζῷον νοερόν, μὴ οὔσης οὐσίας τῆς καὶ παρεχούσης ζωήν; ἀλλ' οὐδὲ λογικὸν οἷόν τέ ἐστιν εἰπεῖν, μὴ οὔσης τῆς διανοητικῆς οὐσίας τῆς καὶ παρεχούσης νοερὰν ζωήν.]

[10] *Nescio quam ob causam*. The writers of some of the other *sententiae* (e. g. 6. 8 *sq*.) know the reason; they tell us that human souls come down into this world 'in order to get experience and knowledge' (of τὰ αἰσθητά).

intelligence are not composed of the elements of which this world consists, but are something quite different.[1]'[2]

['Investigate these things[3] then, O Soul, that you may come to know them; and seek to look into them deeply, that you may get experience of them; for thereby you will become happy and blessed, and will make your knowledge perfect and complete.']

9.1   Cap. 9, §§ 1–3. He who wishes to attain to knowledge and *exercitatio boni* (good conduct?) must cast aside *studium et cupiditas rerum humanarum* (love of the things of this world).

4   Cap. 9, §§ 4, 5. If you possess true knowledge,[4] O Soul, you will understand that you are akin to your Creator; and thence you will get true pleasure. But if you are devoid of knowledge, you will think that you belong to 'the worthless kinds of things',[5] and will seek after these things; and thence it will result that you will be afflicted with all manner of pains and torments.

5   Apply yourself then with all your energy to the attainment of true knowledge. Be ever occupied in meditation, that so you may come to see the truth, and be rightly guided by it in your ways of action; and rid yourself of ignorance and blindness, and the habit of sinning (which results from ignorance).

6   Cap. 9, § 6. Misery is brought about by this, that the soul sees and apprehends things that are in mutual conflict, and are subject to change;[6] happiness is brought about by this, that the soul sees and apprehends things that are mutually concordant, and are everlasting.[7] 'If then you wish to be at rest from misery, O Soul, migrate from the

---

[1] ψυχαί are ἀσώματοι or νοεραὶ οὐσίαι.

[2] This *sententia* differs in style and tone from all the others. It may perhaps be an extract from a dialogue. But who is it that is supposed to be speaking? It can hardly be Hermes; for the speaker talks about himself, and describes his earlier thoughts, and his gradual discovery of the truth, in a tone quite unlike that of the *ex cathedra* teaching of Hermes as reported in the Greek *Hermetica*. The piece is probably a translation of a Greek original, which might very well be of the third century A.D. or earlier. [See (with Bardenhewer) Plotinus' argument against the Gnostics, *Enn.* II. 9. 5.]

[3] *Res istas*: meaning *res vitae et rationis compotes*, i.e. human souls? Or τὰ νοητά in general? *Ut eas experiaris* seems applicable rather to the latter.

[4] The Hermetic γνῶσις.

[5] *Ad vilia rerum genera te pertinere*: i.e. that you belong to the world of αἰσθητά.

[6] I.e. fixes its attention on τὰ αἰσθητά (and sets its affection on them). The soul which does so is itself distracted by conflicting desires, and made miserable by the changes which deprive it of the things it loves.

[7] I.e. τὰ νοητά.

world of mutual conflict and mutability to the world of perpetuity [1] and stability.'

7   Cap. 9, § 7.   Merchants set forth their wares to be seen, not by the blind, but by men with sound eyes ; and story-tellers, and those who make speeches at cross-roads, speak to be heard, not by the deaf, but by men with sound ears.[2] 'And even so, philosophers [3] do not address, and seek to initiate in wisdom, souls that are walking on the road that leads to death ;[4] they address, and wish to imbue with wisdom, those souls (only) which are walking on the road that leads to life.'[5] And these latter are souls which come to them and seek to be taught ; but the souls which are walking on the road that leads to death are they that do not seek teachings, but recede from them and scorn them.[6]

8   Cap. 9, § 8.   If you wish to escape punishment, O Soul, beware of errors and avoid sins ; if you desire reward, let yourself be led to the right way of life.[7] 'For it needs must be that sin brings punishment and loss, and that the right way of life brings reward and gain.'

9   Cap. 9, § 9.   'If you join yourself to Mind ($\nu o\hat{u}s$), O Soul, your light [8] is increased, so that you see with your mental eye the right way of acting ;[9] but if you turn away from Mind ($\nu o\hat{u}s$) and join yourself to sense ($a\check{\iota}\sigma\theta\eta\sigma\iota s$), you lose the light of intelligence,[10] and are enveloped in darkness, and ⟨your mental eyesight is⟩ weakened,[11] so that in consequence of your blindness and darkness you give yourself up to sins.'

10   Cap. 9, § 10.   The physician tells his patient not to eat what is bad for him. If the patient obeys him, he does right, and as the fruit of his right doing, he recovers health ; if he disobeys him, he does wrong, and as the fruit of his wrong doing, he continues to suffer pain and torment.[12]

---

[1] It should rather be ' concord '.
[2] Cf. ' He that hath ears to hear, let him hear '.
[3] The man who wrote this must have called himself a ' philosopher '.
[4] *Animas mortis gradu incedentes.*   [5] *Vitae gradu incedentes.*
[6] Cf. *Corp. Herm.* I. 29: οἱ μὲν αὐτῶν καταφλυαρήσαντες (at my preaching) ἀπέστησαν, τῇ τοῦ θανάτου ὁδῷ ἑαυτοὺς ἐκδεδωκότες· οἱ δὲ παρεκάλουν διδαχθῆναι, κ.τ.λ.
[7] *Ad rectam rationem.*   [8] *Lumen*: φῶς, i. e. power of seeing.
[9] *Ita ut rectam rationem mentis acie perspicias.* Cf. c. 1, § 6 above.
[10] *Lucem rationalem*: τὸ νοερὸν φῶς.   [11] *Ad infirmitatem redigeris.*
[12] The 'philosopher' (or possibly νοῦς, as in *Corp. Herm.* XII. i) is the physician of the soul.

11   Cap. 9, § 11. If you wish to learn in what condition the soul will be when it has quitted the body, observe in what condition it is while it is joined with the body. If (while still in the body) it steadily pursues the right course of action,[1] then, when it has quitted the body, it will necessarily be led by its habit of right action to the right way of acting, and to a happy issue and reward ; but if it has been given up to sins, it will necessarily be led to sins by its habit, and from these sins it will reap the fruit of punishment [and blindness] and an unhappy condition in the future life.

10.1   Cap. 10, §§ 1–3. 'I will describe your state, O Soul, for I have long been wondering of it. You say and profess that you would fain escape from misery and sorrow ; but in reality you seek after them and pursue them, and envy those who possess them.[2] You say and profess that you desire happiness[3] and joys ; but in reality you shun them and turn away from them,[4] and refuse to set forth on the road that leads to them. Such behaviour[5] is in conflict with itself ; it is such as can come only from a being that is not one and simple, but partakes of a mixture and combination (of diverse elements).[6] For if a thing is simple, its way of action is necessarily simple and free from conflict ; but if a thing is mixed (i. e. composed of diverse elements), its way of action is necessarily mixed.[6]

2   'It is therefore clear that you are not yet cleansed from your vices, and are not yet freed from the evil (passions) with which you have been infected during earlier times and stages of life.[7] There is still

---

[1] *Rectam rationem sequitur.* Here and elsewhere, *recta ratio* stands in contrast to *peccata* ; and when thus used, it must mean 'the right way of acting', and can have nothing to do with *ratio* in the sense of νοῦς.

[2] I. e. you try to get the goods (as you think them) of this world, which cause misery and sorrow, and you envy those who have got them. Cf. *Corp. Herm.* VI. 6 : ἄνθρωπον . . . τὸ κακὸν πιστεύσαντα ἀγαθὸν εἶναι, . . . καὶ φοβούμενον αὐτοῦ στερηθῆναι, πάντα δὲ ἀγωνιζόμενον ἵνα μὴ μόνον ἔχῃ, ἀλλὰ καὶ ἐπαύξῃ.

[3] *Commoditas.*

[4] I. e. you shun τὰ νοητά, in which alone true joy is to be found.

[5] *Agendi ratio.*

[6] Cf. *Ascl. Lat.* I. 7 b : 'homo duplex est ; et eius una pars (viz. the ψυχή *qua* νοερά) simplex, quae, ut Graeci aiunt, οὐσιώδης, quam vocamus divinae similitudinis formam ; est autem (altera pars) (viz. the body, with which the θνητὸν εἶδος ψυχῆς is connected) quadruplex (i. e. composed of the four elements).' The soul is, by its proper nature, *simplex et una* (pure νοῦς) ; and such it was before its incarnation. But by its conjunction with the body, there has been added to it a θνητὸν εἶδος ψυχῆς (Pl. *Tim.*), in which the senses and the passions reside ; and so it is no longer *simplex*. It is this θνητὸν εἶδος ψυχῆς, the 'bodily' part of the soul, that desires τὰ αἰσθητά.

[7] *Per priora tempora atque aetates.* Does this mean 'during the earlier part of your present life', or 'in the course of previous incarnations'?

left on you therefore something of scurf[1] and rust,[2] and thence does it come to pass that your way of acting is in conflict with itself. If the rust that is on you has been caused by a passing incident, strive to get rid of it by rubbing, smoothing, and polishing, before it becomes inveterate; but if it has become inveterate, and is deeply ingrained, betake yourself to fire, and get yourself refined in it,[3] that you may

3 come forth from it clean and pure. For in the case of a mirror that is marred by [scurf and] rust of long standing, mere polishing is ineffectual, but its rust can be got rid of only by the refining fire.

'But when you are cleansed from your scurf and rust, your way of acting will be consistent with itself, and free from the mixture (of opposites), and from false pretence; so that then you will in very truth either seek after misery and sorrows, or else seek after joys and a happy life.'[4]

4   Cap. 10, §§ 4–6. First of all, assure yourself that 'physical death is nothing else than a departure of the soul from the body'.[5]

Next, reflect that a man who is wise and prudent in his own country is wise and prudent when he is abroad no less than when he is at home;[6] he will never quit his wisdom, wherever he may betake himself, and to whatever land he may travel.[7]

And after that, assure yourself that 'a good tree produces nothing

5 but good fruit, and a bad tree nothing but bad fruit'.[8] If trees pro-

---

[1] *Scabies.*

[2] From this point on, the simile of a rusted mirror is employed, as in 7. 5 *sq.* The writer of 10. 1–3 probably had 7. 5 *sq.* before him, and copied from that *sententia.*

[3] In 7. 5 *sq.*, the suffering needed to cleanse the 'rusted' or corrupted soul appears to be regarded as inflicted from without. But in this *sententia*, the soul is told to 'betake itself to the refining fire' (*ad ignem confugias*), i. e. to inflict the suffering on itself; and this presumably means that the man must employ ascetic practices, or painful kinds of penance. The 'polishing' may be taken in 10. 1–3 as meaning reflection and meditation; in 7. 5 *sq.*, it is explained as meaning 'warnings and reproofs'.

[4] *Vitae commoditas.*—It is left to the reader to add in thought 'and as it would be absurd to do the former, you will certainly do the latter'.

[5] A quotation from Plato, *Phaedo* 64 C: ἆρα μὴ ἄλλο τι (ἡγούμεθα τὸν θάνατον εἶναι) ἢ τὴν τῆς ψυχῆς ἀπὸ τοῦ σώματος ἀπαλλαγήν; *Gorg.* 524 B: ὁ θάνατος τυγχάνει ὤν ... οὐδὲν ἄλλο ἢ δυοῖν πραγμάτοιν διάλυσις, τῆς ψυχῆς καὶ τοῦ σώματος, ἀπ' ἀλλήλοιν.

[6] Probably a quotation, as the sentences which precede and follow are quotations.

[7] The fatherland of the soul is the νοητὸς κόσμος. The soul was wise when it dwelt there, before its incarnation; and it ought not to 'quit its wisdom', or lose its knowledge of τὰ νοητά, when it has come down into the αἰσθητὸς κόσμος.

[8] Matth. 7. 16–18: μήτι συλλέγουσιν ἀπὸ ἀκανθῶν σταφυλήν, ἢ ἀπὸ τριβόλων σῦκα; οὕτω πᾶν δένδρον ἀγαθὸν καρποὺς καλοὺς ποιεῖ, τὸ δὲ σαπρὸν δένδρον καρποὺς πονηροὺς ποιεῖ· οὐ δύναται δένδρον ἀγαθὸν καρποὺς πονηροὺς ἐνεγκεῖν, οὐδὲ δένδρον σαπρὸν

duced fruit other than that which it is their nature to produce, he who plants a vine ought to gather from it acorns, and he who plants an oak ought to gather from it grapes.   Things generate only what is like themselves.

6   Therefore, practise yourself in that which is good, and (in so doing) plant the good tree ; that your eyes may be freed from darkness, and from your knowledge you may gather knowledge, and from practising yourself in good [1] you may gather good, and from intelligence, intelligence and light and right training ; [2] that so you may make your way to those highest abodes, and attain to unceasing bliss and everlasting joys.[3]

7 a   Cap. 10, §§ 7–9. 'Suppose yourself, O Soul, to have put away from you your five senses ; and see whether you then apprehend anything other than the things which you were wont to apprehend by means of the five senses.   If you find that you apprehend something other than what you perceived by the senses, it is clear that you have returned to your fatherland,[4] and have turned your attention to that which is your (true) function.[5]

7 b   'For if mind (νοῦς) wishes to apprehend something, it separates that thing from the things conjoined with it,[6] and thereupon apprehends the thing by a simple (i. e. incomposite) act of apprehension, in virtue

8 of the mind's own simple nature.   For as sense (αἴσθησις) cannot apprehend a simple thing, so mind (νοῦς) cannot apprehend a composite (or concrete)[7] thing, and get knowledge of it by intellectual

---

καρποὺς καλοὺς ποιεῖν. The saying in its shortest form may have been proverbial long before the Christian era, and was doubtless often used in later times by people who knew nothing of the Gospels ; but as it is here illustrated, just as in Matth., by naming particular kinds of trees, it seems probable that it was transmitted to the Arabic writer from the Gospel text ; though it does not follow from this that he himself had read the Gospels.

Allusions to this saying occur repeatedly in the *Castig. an.*; e. g. 2. 15 b ; 7. 3 ; 8. 10 and 11 ; 12. 1 ; 14, 15 a.

[1] *Exercitatione boni* : i. e. by doing good deeds ?   Cf. 9. 1–3.

[2] *Rectam disciplinam.*

[3] This last paragraph (perhaps added by another writer) is an application of the saying 'a good tree produces nothing but good fruit'.   But what is the meaning of it ?   It seems to amount to this : 'Do good deeds and acquire knowledge (in this life ?), and you will be rewarded by doing good deeds and acquiring knowledge (in the life to come ?), even as he who plants a good tree is rewarded by gathering good fruit from it'.   But that is unintelligible.   Cf. 9. 11, which appears to be to the same effect, but is likewise obscure.

[4] The world of νοητά.

[5] *Munus* : viz. the contemplation of τὰ νοητά.

[6] I. e. forms a concept by abstraction from the particulars presented by sense.

[7] σύνθετον, i. e. a thing which consists of ὕλη and εἶδος combined together. (σύνθετον in this sense is an Aristotelian term.   See I. 7 and 11. 5 *sq.*) νοῦς

cognition, unless it separates the thing's properties from one another, and distinguishes them one from another, and separates everything else from them, so that it completely isolates that one thing ; and having done so, it apprehends all the thing's properties one by one. It is clear then that sense, being a composite thing, apprehends composite (or concrete) things; but intellect, being a simple and indivisible thing, apprehends simple and indivisible things (viz. universals).

9a   'Mark then how thought, when it deals with composite (or concrete) things, abandons simple things, and (abandons) simple apprehension, which is apprehension of the real, and (which alone is) [real pleasure and] true cognition ; but when it returns from them to simple things, and abandons things that are composite (or concrete) and mixed, then it apprehends things simple and everlasting, and dismisses things that are composite (or concrete) and are bounded by limits of time.

9b   'This explanation makes it clear that the soul's life is dependent on its departure from the physical world,[1] and the soul's death and lasting misery is effected by its abiding in the physical world.'[2]

11.1   Cap. 11, §§ 1-7. 'You have come down into this physical world, O Soul, and have learnt by experience what sort of place it is;[3] you have found in it nothing but things hideous to the sight, frightful to the hearing, nauseous to the taste, noisome to the smell, and filthy to the touch.[4] And yet, now that you have come to the place where these things are, you are overcome by love and eager desire for them ; you have placed your happiness in them, and have forgotten the high qualities that are proper to your nature.   And when you have recognized that you have sinned and gone astray, you have sought to associate others with you in your sin, and to lay the blame on others.[5]

apprehends the εἶδος (i. e. the universal) alone, and not the particular concrete things, which are 'composed of' ὕλη and εἶδος.

[1] *Mundus naturae*, 'the physical world', is *mundus rerum compositarum*, 'the world of particular concrete things'. The 'departure of the soul from the physical world' probably here means, not its separation from the body at death, but its turning away from τὰ αἰσθητά to τὰ νοητά during the present life; for in 7 a we were told that the soul which has learnt to apprehend τὰ νοητά has already 'returned to its fatherland'.

[2] §§ 7 a and 9 b are Platonic; but the statement of the theory of cognition which is given in 7 b, 8, and commented on in 9 a, is Aristotelian, and resembles I. 7.   The *sententia* in its present form seems to have been written by an Arab Platonist, who got the contents of 7 b, 8 from an Aristotelian source, and adapted them to his purpose by adding 7 a at the beginning, and 9 a, b at the end. (Or possibly 7 a and 9 a may have been added first, and 9 b later and by another person.)   [3] Cf. 6. 8 a.

[4] Hatred of τὰ αἰσθητά is here expressed in the strongest terms. Cf. *Corp. Herm.* VI and VII.

[5] What others ?   Other men (e.g. bad teaching and example)?   Or, God or

2 Not so !   The blame should fall on him alone who has deserved it ;
the sin is his alone who has committed it.   Seek then to amend your
sins and errors ; for as it is by your own free will that you have fallen
into the grievous state in which you now are, so by your own free
will alone can you escape from it.   As long as you have been in the
world of things that come to be, you have been afflicted by all manner
of troubles ; begin now to be convinced that it is in yourself, and in
your own sins and errors, that the cause and source of all those
troubles is to be found.   If you recall the past, you will remember
and acknowledge this ;[1] but if some trouble has befallen you the
cause and source of which you do not recognize, yet do not put the
blame for it on some one else, but deem that the cause of it is to be
found in that mistake[2] which you made at the beginning, and which

3 you have forgotten.   For if a man houses himself in an abode of
misfortunes,[3] the misfortunes that befall him and the afflictions that
he suffers have come to pass through his own mistake, in that he
came and took up his abode there ; for having so done, he could not
but undergo misfortunes.   And what makes it yet worse is this, that
he was bidden[4] to guard against these misfortunes, and he did not
guard against them ; he was told to fear them, and he did not fear
them ; he was warned, and would not take warning, but followed his
own will and desire.

4   'As long as you remained outside the prison,[5] O Soul, did you not
see all and hear all ?   But now that you have entered the prison, all
those things are hidden from you ; you are shut in and made a

Fate ?   For the latter, cf. Pl. *Rep.* X. 617 E : αἰτία ἑλομένου· θεὸς ἀναίτιος. [*Corp.*
IV. 6 b : δύο γὰρ ὄντων τῶν ὄντων, σώματος καὶ ἀσωμάτου, ἐν οἷς τὸ θνητὸν καὶ τὸ
θεῖον, ἡ αἵρεσις θατέρου καταλείπεται τῷ ἑλέσθαι βουλομένῳ, κ τ.λ. § 8 a : ἐπεὶ ὁ
μὲν θεὸς ἀναίτιος, ἡμεῖς δὲ αἴτιοι τῶν κακῶν, ταῦτα προκρίνοντες τῶν ἀγαθῶν.]

[1] I. e. if you reflect on your past life on earth, you will see that your unhappiness
has been caused by errors or sins committed by you during the course of it.

[2] *Peccatum* : ἁμαρτία, which might mean either *error* or *sin*.   The 'mistake
which the soul made at the beginning' is its coming down from the νοητὸς κόσμος
to be incarnated, which is here regarded as a wilful lapse.   Cf. the descent of
Anthropos in *Corp. Herm.* I.

[3] The body (or the αἰσθητὸς κόσμος) is a *domicilium casuum adversorum*.

[4] This seems to refer to errors and sins committed during the present life,—
those which the man ' will remember if he recalls the past ',—and not to the
' original mistake' of coming down to be incarnated ; for it is not recorded that
the soul was warned against the latter.   The man has been warned by his
teachers to avoid the sins by which misery is caused, and has disregarded their
warnings.

[5] I e. the body, which Platonists called a φρουρά (*Phaedo* 62 B) or a εἰρκτή
(*Axiochus* 370 D).   Cf. τὴν ἐν τῷ σώματι ἐγκεκλεισμένην ψυχὴν in *Corp. Herm.* VII,
where it is similarly said that the soul shut up in the body ' cannot hear the things
it ought to hear, nor see the things it ought to see '.

prisoner, vainly longing to hear and see something.   How were you induced to enter the prison?   Has not all this come to pass by your

5 own mistake (or sin)?   As long as you were in the world of simple (incomposite) things,[1] you had plenty of things to see and know; for you could see all the worlds[2] displayed before you, pure and bright and shining; and down below, at the bottom of all, was situated the world of things that come to be and cease to be,—a dark and murky world, having as little brightness in comparison with them[3] as has a black stone that is seen amidst transparent water.

'Well, you thought fit to enter this (dark) world, that you might find out by experience what sort of place it is; and having decided to do so, you forsook the high level of the simple things, and came down to the low level of the mixed things.[4]   And so, eagerly seeking[5] the things you longed for, you departed (from your home above),

6a and came into the world of things that come to be.   In thus forsaking the world of simple things, and seeking after and desiring the world of composite (or concrete) things, you were like a bird that makes for the snare, to take the berry that is placed there, and finds its own life taken by the snare; or like a fish that wants to eat the fisherman's bait, and is itself eaten by the fisherman.

6b   'Bright and luminous as you are, O Soul, by your own nature, you went to the world of darkness,[6] and engaged in combat with it; and the world of darkness obscured your light, and encompassed you with darkness, and blinded you, and made you lose sight of all that you

---

[1] I. e. the world of νοητά.   The terms *res compositae* (σύνθετα) and *res simplices* (ἀσύνθετα or ἁπλᾶ) are used here as in 1. 7 and 10. 7—9.   They are of Aristotelian origin, but have been adopted by the Platonist by whom this *sententia* was written, and are used by him as equivalent to αἰσθητά and νοητά.

[2] *Omnes mundos.*   What are the *mundi* (κόσμοι)?   The writer seems to have in his mind a picture of the visible universe as described by the Greek Hermetists, and by Stoics and Platonists in general; towards the circumference, the luminous heavens, consisting of a series of concentric spheres, and at the centre, the dark earth.   The phrases here employed are probably taken from a source in which the visible universe alone was spoken of; and in that connexion, the luminous κόσμοι would mean either the celestial spheres, or the sun, moon, and stars.   The words would then imply that the soul had its origin in the visible heavens, and has come down thence to earth.

[3] *Fulgens in eis ut . . . fulget* Bard.   The meaning of this phrase is doubtful.

[4] *Res mixtae* (things made of a mixture of different and mutually conflicting elements) denotes the same things as *res compositae*.   (It is possible that this writer took *res compositae* to mean 'things composed of diverse elements', rather than σύνθετα in the Aristotelian sense, viz. things consisting of ὕλη and εἶδος combined together.)

[5] *Cum motu quaerens.*

[6] *Tu igitur, O anima, luce et claritate tua mundum tenebrarum adiisti.*

had seen, and forget all that you had known ;[1] and in the end, you were captured and held prisoner.[2]

7   'All this has come to pass in consequence of the mistake you made (or, the sin you committed) in the beginning.[3]

'But if you wish to return (to your home above), fix your attention on the deadly things which ⌜were in your nature⌝,[4] and be on your guard against them.   For it is only by guarding against them that you can be saved ; only so is it possible for you to return (to your true home).   And in order that you may easily know what things you have to guard against, I will include them all under one term,[5] namely, *desire for bodily pleasures*.   Put away from you then and be on your guard against everything that you feel with your bodily senses to be pleasant ;[6] lay hold on and make use of everything that your mind (νοῦς) finds to be pleasant.[7]'[8]

8   Cap. 11, §§ 8, 9.   A fire can be extinguished ; but the flame of desire is never extinguished.   Pains affect the body for a while, then cease, and leave you at rest ; but from the pain of desire you never get rest, unless you cure it by the medicine of true intelligence (νοῦς), and put desire away from you, and learn to abstain (from the thing you have been desiring); for desire grows in strength if you follow it, but dies away if you turn from it and abstain.[9]

[1] The Platonic λήθη.

[2] This resembles Mani's myth of the descent of the Primal Man to combat with the Powers of Darkness, and his defeat and capture.   But it is not necessarily derived from Mani ; for Mani's myth may have been itself derived, in part at least, from Christian Gnostics, and through them, from Pagan Platonists.—The simile of a *combat* is hardly consistent with what is said in other parts of this *sententia*, viz. that the soul was induced to come down by *desire* for τὰ αἰσθητά (§§ 5 *fin.*, 6 a), or by *curiosity* (§ 5), and that, having come down, it still desires and loves τὰ αἰσθητά (§ 1).

[3] Viz. the mistake of coming down to be incarnated.

[4] *Res perniciosas quae in natura tibi erant* Bard.   Perhaps 'the deadly things which are contrary to your true nature': or 'the things of the physical world (*mundus naturae*), which are pernicious to you': or possibly, 'the deadly accretions that have grown upon you' (τὰ ὀλέθρια τὰ ἐμπεφυκότα σοι).   The last would suit well with *exuas*, 'strip them off you'.

[5] *In unam omnes tibi comprehendam notionem.*

[6] *Quod voluptarium esse corpore sentis*: i. e. everything that gives you a feeling of pleasure by acting on your bodily senses.

[7] *Quod voluptarium esse ratione intellegis.*   Bodily ἡδονή is bad ; but there is a ἡδονή (sometimes called χαρά) which accompanies νόησις, and is good.

[8] This *sententia* may have been translated from a Greek original with little alteration ; and it is not impossible that the original was a Hermetic *libellus*.   Perhaps § 6 b, which looks rather like a reminiscence of Mani's myth, may be a later edition.

[9] This would serve as an explanation of what is said about *egestas* and *copia* in some of the *sententiae* (3. 3 &c.).   This passage has been placed next after 11. 7, in which 'desire for bodily pleasures' was spoken of ; but it probably does not

9   [One of the desires of the sense-world is gluttony. It is not the
only one ; there are others also, but gluttony is the most deadly of
them all, because 'the body does not desire either (strong) drink or
res venereas[1] if it is not sated with food. And this applies[2] also to
(fine ?) clothes, and all the (seeming) goods by which the soul is
allured into those dangerous and terrible places[3] which bring it to
vicious habits, and lower and degrade it'.][4]

11. 10   Cap. 11, §§ 10, 11. I have now taught you, O Soul, how to act
aright ; do not pretend that you cannot avoid going wrong. I have
restored your eyesight ; do not feign to be blind. If a blind man
falls into a well, he is held blameless ; but if one whose eyes are
sound comes to a well and sees it, and throws himself into it of his
own free will, he is without excuse. And even so, if, despite my
warnings, you wilfully indulge your desires, you will be without excuse ;
and you will suffer worse than before, and pay double penalty.[5]

12   Cap. 11, § 12. If a man holds aloof from the desires of this world,
the misfortunes of this world hold aloof from him, and he departs
from this world safe and sound,[6] and destined to get profit (in the
world to come) ; and that profit consists in drawing near to God.[7]
If he pursues the desires of this world, the misfortunes of this world
pursue him, and he quits this world a sick man, and one doomed to
suffer loss (in the world to come) ; and that loss is that he is far
removed from God.

12. 1   Cap. 12, §§ 1, 2 a. If a man plants the tree of perseverance,[8] he
gathers from it the fruit of success, and wins victory ; he attains to
2 a that which he desires, and is happy. If he plants the tree of idleness

---

belong to the *sententia* 11. 1–7, which appears to be complete in itself. [*Corp.*
VI. 3 b (codd.) : ἡ γαστριμαργία, ἡ τῶν κακῶν πάντων χορηγός.]

[1] Cf. the warning against women and strong drink in 5. 7 *sq.*

[2] What applies? It could not be said that people do not desire clothes unless
they are sated with food. It therefore seems that 'this' must mean what was said
in § 8 ; i.e. the meaning must be that desire for (fine) clothes is, like other 'bodily'
desires, insatiable, and is only increased by indulgence.

[3] Is *loca* to be understood literally (e.g. courts and rich men's houses ? or taverns
and the like ?) or metaphorically ?

[4] This section may have been added to § 8 by the compiler of the *Castig. an.*, or
by some other transcriber.

[5] This appears to be the concluding paragraph of a didactic discourse. Perhaps
it was written to stand at the end of 11. 1–7, and was separated from that *sententia*
by the insertion of §§ 8, 9.

[6] *Salvus*, in contrast to *aegrotus*.

[7] *Propinquitas ad Deum*, in contrast to *longinquitas a Deo*.

[8] *Constantia*.

(or negligence),[1] he gathers from it the fruit of failure ; he does not attain to that which he desires, and is unhappy.

2 b   Cap. 12, § 2 b.   ['I am about to set before you, O Soul, several maxims ; learn them and make yourself sure of them.'][2]

'The soul is the desirer ;[3] *good*[4] is the thing desired ; perseverance[5] is that on which the desirer must lean for his support ; and that which aids the desirer to get the thing desired, is nothing else than (that same) *good* and *goodness*.[6]   For if the activity of the desirer is conjoined with the activity of the thing desired, then the desirer and the thing desired are necessarily brought together.'[7]

3 a   Cap. 12, § 3 a.   Perseverance is bitter to the taste, but it bears the fruit of sweetness and repose ; idleness is sweet to the taste, but it bears the fruit of bitterness and trouble.[8]

3 b   Cap. 12, §§ 3 b, 4.   Persevere and be steadfast[9] in worshipping the one true God ; and 'beware of being unsettled by distaste and weariness,[10] lest you abandon worship of the one God, and acknowledge many gods.   He who acknowledges many gods is obliged to worship many ; he undergoes grievous toils and troubles ;[11] he is distracted by cares and tormented by anxieties ; and in the end he incurs destruction.

4   'To be affected by weariness and distaste is (a mark) of beast-like souls ; to persevere and be steadfast is (a mark) of fully developed and (truly) human souls.   Beware then of letting yourself be turned away (from worship of the one God) by weariness and distaste ; and do not be induced to acknowledge more gods than one ; for if you do, you will be distracted and worn out and exhausted by your worship of them, so that your light[12] will be quenched, your strength will

---

[1] *Pigritia.*

[2] This sentence must have been written by the complier, and intended to apply to several of the following *sententiae* together.

[3] This 'desire' is the Platonic ἔρως (τοῦ καλοῦ or τοῦ ἀγαθοῦ).

[4] *Bonum* : τὸ ἀγαθόν, which seems here to mean God, or union with or nearness to God.

[5] *Constantia* : in this connexion, perseverance in prayer or contemplation.

[6] *Bonum et bonitas.*   This appears to mean that, for attainment to the *summum bonum*, there is need both of persevering effort on the man's part, and of God's grace.   [7] I. e. the soul is united with God.

[8] I. e. work hard and endure hardship now (in this world ?), and you will be happy later on (in the world to come ?).

[9] *Instruaris constantia et firmitate.*   [10] *Fastidio et taedio.*

[11] This looks rather like Clough's version of the First Commandment : 'Thou shalt have only one God ! Who | Would be at the expense of two ?'

[12] Your 'light' is that by means of which you see (with the mental eye), i. e. the νοῦς in you.

be weakened, your high rank [1] will go to nothing, and your dominion [2] will cease ; and that will be death to you.   Beware then of that death, and turn away from the things which cause it.' [3]

5   Cap. 12, §§ 5–7. 'You ought, O Soul, to get sure knowledge of your own being, [4] and of its forms and aspects. [5]   Do not think that any one of the things of which you must seek to get knowledge is outside of you ; no, all things that you ought to get knowledge of [6] are in your possession, and within you. [7]   Beware then of being led into error by seeking (elsewhere) the things which are in your possession.   Many men forget where these things are to be found, and look for them outside themselves, and are thereby led into error, but afterwards remember, and become aware that these things are within them, and not outside of them.

6   'The things of which you have to get knowledge exist for ever without cease ; [8] and none of those things is outside of you. [9]   But the things outside you are those which are from the first [10] distinct from you ; that is, they are things that take on varying qualities, [11] and are involved in the process of coming to be and ceasing to be ; [12] and nothing at all except such things is to be found ⟨outside you⟩.

7   'Call yourself back then to yourself, O Soul, and seek in yourself all that you ought to get knowledge of.   Do not go forth out of your-

---

[1] *Excelsitas.*

[2] *Imperium.*   Taken literally, this might mean 'You will cease to be a Moslem, and, as such, a member of the ruling class or caste'.   But perhaps the writer meant to suggest a metaphorical meaning.

[3] This *sententia* is, on the face of it, a Moslem warning against polytheism. (Cf. 2. 9 sq.)   But some of the phrases seem hardly to the point if applied to polytheism in the literal sense ; and perhaps the writer meant that term to be understood as including not only the religions of the Sabians, Zoroastrians, and Christians, but also devotion to the πολλὰ αἰσθητά, or the many and mutually conflicting objects of 'bodily' desire.

[4] γνῶθι σεαυτόν.   Cf. *Corp. Herm.* I. 19 : ὁ ἀναγνωρίσας ἑαυτὸν ἐλήλυθεν εἰς τὸ ⸢περιούσιον⸣ (ὑπερούσιον) ἀγαθόν.

[5] *Species et formas.*   This perhaps means the higher and lower, or better and worse, states of the soul under different conditions (e. g. the state in which it was before its incarnation, and, after its incarnation, the state of λήθη and that of ἀνάμνησις).   Cf. *Corp. Herm.* X. 7 : τῶν ψυχῶν πολλαὶ αἱ μεταβολαί.

[6] I. e. the νοητά and God.   [7] *Apud te et in te.*

[8] They are τὰ ἀεὶ ὄντα, in contrast to τὰ γιγνόμενα καὶ ἀπολλύμενα.

[9] The ψυχή, qua νοερά, is of one substance with the divine νοῦς, and has in it (potentially, if not actually) all that is in the divine νοῦς, i. e. all the νοητά.   In other words, the soul's thoughts (and will) are, if and so far as the soul realizes itself, identical with God's thoughts (and will).

[10] *In primo principio* : i.e. by their origin ?   These things are σωματικά, and the soul is ἀσώματος ; they are ὑλικά, and the soul is ἄυλος or οὐσιώδης.

[11] *Res accidentia suscipientes.*   These *accidentia* must be distinguished from the *formae et species* of the soul (if that phrase means varying states).

[12] *In cursu exsistendi atque intereundi.*

self, lest you fall into the surging tide of things that are in mutual conflict, and lest their varying qualities toss you about, even as a troubled and stormy sea tosses the ships that sail on it, and in the end you neither get any good nor attain to any knowledge.'[1]

['Be assured then of what I have told you, and reflect on it; and do not forget the things that are in your possession, and go to look for them in some other place; for all things that the soul needs to get knowledge of are in the soul, not elsewhere.

'And the cause of their not being seen does not come from the soul, but it is the body that is interposed.'[2]][3]

8 Cap. 12, §§ 8, 9. If a craftsman's tool is worn out or broken, it is of very little use; and it is best to throw it away, and take in its stead another that is more fit to work with.

If a craftsman has found a good tool, he must work with it, and seek to make profit by his work; but when he has acquired wealth, he leaves off working, and sells the tool for a very small price, and rests from his labours.

9 Take care, O Soul, to provide yourself with a good tool; and when you have found it, make good use of it, and work hard, and make profit; and when you have acquired wealth, then sell your tool for a very small price, and carry away your gains with you, and quit the house in which you have earned them.[4]

---

[1] This Platonic *sententia* may be a translation of a Greek original that may have been written before A. D. 300, and may possibly have been a *Hermeticum*.

[2] I. e. the body obstructs the soul's view of them. Cf. 4. 4 (simile of muddy water), 4. 14 (eclipse of the moon), and 5. 9–11.

[3] This passage ('Be assured . . . is interposed') was probably added by the compiler of the *Castig. an.* The only part of it which is not mere repetition is the last sentence; and that is inappropriate. The body is here said to be an obstruction interposed between the soul and the things the soul is trying to see, which implies that those things are *outside of* and *at a distance from* the soul; and that is inconsistent with the preceding sentence, and with what is asserted throughout the *sententia*, viz. that those things are *within* the soul.

[4] Does the 'tool' mean the body? (Cf. 13. 5: 'the body is the soul's tool'.) If so, the meaning of the parable is that the soul ought to make good use of the body in which it is incarnated (i. e. to do good deeds during its life on earth), and thereby acquire 'wealth' (virtue or merit); and that the soul that has done so will, when the body is worn out, throw it away, quit the 'house' in which it has been working (i. e. this world), and 'carry its gains (the merit it has earned) away with it' to the other world, and there 'rest from its labours', and enjoy its reward. But some of the things said are difficult to reconcile with that interpretation. What could be meant by exhorting the soul to 'find' and 'provide itself with' a good body, and telling it to take another and more serviceable body when its present body is worn out?

Perhaps it would be possible to take the tool as meaning a creed or doctrine (e. g. Mohammedanism or Platonism), or an authoritative book (e. g. the Koran or the *Hermetica*). Choose a good one to start with, and if one of them fails you,

Cap. 12, § 10.   When a man is sick of the jaundice, honey does not taste sweet to him, as it does to a healthy man.   And even so, true teachings are pleasant only to him who is in health of mind; only such a man can understand their meaning.

The diseases of the mind are *ignorance and oblivion, desire for pleasures, sadness,* and *fear*;[1] and he whose mind is sick of these diseases is prevented from tasting the savour of that which he is told and understanding its meaning.

13.1   Cap. 13, §§ 1–3.   True happiness is a thing that never gives rise to satiety.[2]   Everything that the soul meets with in the world of things that come to be gives rise to satiety; and a thing of that nature cannot be rightly called a pleasure.   If then the soul seeks pleasure in this world, it is seeking a thing that is not there, and cannot be found.   Many dwellers in this world are diligent in searching for
2 pleasures; but in vain do they seek them.   Men betake themselves to all stations of life, that they may taste them and make trial of them; and then they turn away from them, overcome by distaste and weariness.[3]   No one is content with his state of life.   Souls in this world search about, seeking a station that will match with their high rank and their proper qualities;[4] and failing to find it, they wander to and fro, seeking in vain a place where they may rest.   And seeing that this is so, the soul (if it is wise) will despair of getting satisfaction, and will abandon the quest for pleasure, as long as it is in the world of things that come to be.

3 Every position in which the soul is placed in this world demands steadfast endurance (of some evil);[5] and that is bitter to the taste; and everything that is mixed with something bitter becomes bitter itself.

throw it aside, and take in its place another that is better suited to your need; and make good use of it, and you will get much profit from it.   But a time will come when you will have learnt from it all that it can teach you; you will then have acquired the power of thinking things out for yourself (or attained to the certainty of mystic intuition), and will have no further need of any external authority; and you will quit the particular sect or school to which you have hitherto belonged, carrying your gains of wisdom with you, and 'rest from your labours' in knowledge of the truth.   Supposing that to be what the writer meant, this *sententia* would be partly to the same effect as 2. 14 *sq.*, the 'tool' of 12. 8 *sq.* corresponding to the 'interpreter' of 2. 14 *sq.*   But it is doubtful what he meant.

[1] *Tristitia, timor.*   Cf. *inscientia, tristitia, egestas, timor* in 4. 9–11; and see 5. 6.

[2] *Fastidium.*   [3] *Aspernatione et taedio.*

[4] *Excelsitati et proprietatibus.*   The soul properly belongs to the world above, and there is nothing in this world that is worthy of it.

[5] *Constantiam et tolerantiam.*

Hence it follows that a man must either spend his life wandering to and fro in misery, now tasting a thing and now rejecting it,—and that is a base and degraded way of living ;—or else remain in some one state of life, and steadfastly endure (the evils of) that state ; and if he does the latter, he must resign himself to the bitterness of such endurance. Now to pluck bitter fruit[1] and at the same time to win for oneself high rank and power,[2] is surely better than to pluck sweet fruit and at the same time to be degraded and put to shame.[3]

4   Cap. 13, §§ 4, 5.   It is fitting that the workman should use the tool, and not the tool the workman ; that the rider should guide and spur the horse, and not the horse the rider ; and that the sovereign should direct and govern the people, and not the people the sovereign. If in such things as these the natural order is maintained, the result is harmony and beauty ; but if the relations are reversed, the result is confusion, ugliness and distortion.

5   Now it is through the operation of the soul that the body lives, and possesses the powers of sight, hearing, smell, taste, and touch ; the body then is the soul's instrument or tool.   And it is shameful that the tool should rule over the workman and enslave him ; it is the workman, and not the tool, that ought to govern.

If a fool gets possession of an instrument, he is so much occupied with adorning and tending it, that he neglects to make use of it and work at his trade ; and so he becomes a slave to it.   (And even so, if the soul is occupied with adorning and tending the body, and so neglects to use it as an instrument, the soul becomes a slave of the body ; that is,) a thing that partakes of life, and is equipped with power of sight and hearing, and endowed with intelligence ($\nu o\hat{\upsilon}s$), and is of high rank,[4] becomes slave of a thing that is lifeless and blind and deaf and without intelligence, and is of little worth.[5]

When the people rule over the sovereign, the times are upside

---

[1] *Amaritudinem percipere.*   [2] *Excelsitatem et auctoritatem.*
[3] *Vilitatem et humilitatem percipere.*
This *sententia* may be summed up thus: ‘In this life, happiness is unattainable; and it is better, because more worthy of the soul's true nature, to recognize that fact, and resign oneself to the inevitable unhappiness of this life, than to go on vainly seeking pleasure.’ (The writer doubtless meant it to be understood that he who takes the better course in this life will be rewarded in the life to come, and will find true happiness in the other world ; but he does not say so, and only hints at it in the last sentence, where he speaks of ‘ winning for oneself high rank and power ’.)   There is nothing here that is distinctively Platonic, except the mention of ‘ the world of $\tau\grave{\alpha}$ $\gamma\iota\gamma\nu\acute{o}\mu\epsilon\nu\alpha$ ’ and the *excelsitas* of the soul ; and there is no reason to think that this *sententia* was derived from a Greek source.
[4] *Praestans.*   [5] *Vilis.*

down, and it cannot be but that both sovereign and people go to ruin ; and even so, if the body rules over the soul, both must needs go to ruin.

6   Cap. 13, §§ 6, 7. Sovereignty is a thing quite unsuited for created beings. It is a thing by which men are put to the test. If a man that is wise and follows the right way is tested by it (i. e. by having sovereign power entrusted to him), he understands that he is not able to administer the government himself ; he therefore humbles himself, and seeks the Ruler and First Cause of the universe, that (Power) which pours forth all goods on those who seek it ; and so, inasmuch as his soul attaches itself to the Good,[1] he gets good for himself, and acquires intelligence, and by God's help, is led to good ways of living, and is brought to strive to do right and keep himself free from sin.[2] Such a soul draws from the Source of good and righteousness, and thereafter pours forth the goods which it has in itself upon those who are subject to its rule ; and it is well with the ruler and the subjects also.

7   But if a fool is put to the test by (having) sovereign power (placed in his hands), he rejoices and exults in it, and thinks that his power resides in his own strength and his own nature ; and the result is that he neglects his work of governing, and devotes himself wholly to pleasures and enjoyments ; and the fruits they bear are ignorance and blindness, errors, and sins. Such a soul draws from the source of evil and unrighteousness,[3] and proceeds to pour forth what it has in it on those who are subject to its rule ; whence result evil and unrighteousness and ruin both for the ruler himself and for his subjects.[4]

8   Cap. 13, §§ 8, 9. If you enter the life of dreams,[5] O Soul, do not place your happiness in it, nor in the spectacle it exhibits to you, and

---

[1] God is τὸ ἀγαθόν.

[2] *Ducitur ad bonam vivendi disciplinam et studium rectae rationis.*

[3] This looks rather like Zoroastrian or Manichaean dualism. The only 'source of evil and unrighteousness' which Platonists recognized was ὕλη; and they seldom spoke of ὕλη as a 'source' co-ordinate with God.

[4] 13. 6 *sq.* has been placed next to 13. 4 *sq.* by the compiler of the *Castig. an.* because 'sovereignty' is spoken of in both ; but they are two distinct *sententiae.* In 13. 4 *sq.* the subject is the relation between soul and body, and political government is brought in merely as a simile or illustration. In 13. 6 *sq.*, the subject is political government; this latter *sententia* might be an admonition addressed to a young caliph or sultan. It is possible that the compiler of the *Castig. an.* meant it to be read as a parable, and applied to the relation between soul and body; but it is not well suited for that purpose; for the bad ruler described in it is not *enslaved* by his subjects, as the soul that neglects its function is in 13. 4 *sq.* said to be enslaved by the body.

[5] I. e. life in this world, or in the body.

do not suppose that it is real;[1] else, when you wake,[2] you will be a laughing-stock.

The world of things that come to be and cease to be is a world of dreams. He who is asleep and dreaming (in the literal sense) in this world is in reality dreaming doubly;[3] and when he wakes (in the literal sense), he is like a man who has been awakened from an 'incidental' sleep,[4] but has given himself up again to his 'natural' sleep. . . .[5]

9   In this world you are sleeping without cease, and all things that you see before you in this world are nothing else than dreams. Now when you wake up after sleeping and dreaming (in the literal sense), you disregard the things you saw in your dream, and again (as before you fell asleep) look upon the things of the physical world, which exist under stable conditions,[6] and you are more firmly convinced of the reality of these things than of the reality of those which you saw in your dream. And even so, if you wake from your 'natural' (or permanent) sleep, which is (life in) this world, and return to true waking life, which is (life in) the thought-world,[7] then you return to sights[8] and things of the reality of which you are more firmly convinced than of the reality of those things which you saw before you in the physical world.[9]

14. 1   Cap. 14, §§ 1-3.   Just as dreams are unreal in comparison with the things seen in waking life, even so the things seen in waking life in this world are unreal in comparison with the thought-world, which alone is truly real.[10]

---

[1] Cf. Herm. *ap.* Stob. II A.

[2] I. e. when you quit the body, and find yourself in the other world.

[3] I. e. a dream in the literal sense of the word is a dream within a dream.

[4] I. e. a sleep that comes and goes, in contrast to permanent or uninterrupted sleep.   What we call waking life in this world is sleep of the latter kind.

[5] Here follows an explanation of the distinction between an *accidens celeriter cessans* (of which literal sleep is an instance) and an *accidens constans* (of which the 'sleep' of waking life in this world is an instance).

[6] *Quae sunt per accidens constantia.*

[7] *Mundus rationis*: the νοητὸς κόσμος.   [8] *Species.*

[9] I take 13. 8 *sq.* and 14. 1-3 to be two distinct but very similar *sententiae*, dealing with the same subject, but taken from different sources by the compiler of the *Castig. an.*

The notion that this life is a dream is suggested in Pl. *Theaet.* 158: 'How can you determine whether at this moment we are sleeping, and all our thoughts are a dream; or whether we are awake, and talking to one another in the waking state? . . . A doubt about the reality of sense is easily raised, since there may even be a doubt whether we are awake or in a dream.'

[10] This must, I think, be what the writer meant. Bardenhewer translates thus: 'If the dreams of this world, O Soul, are referred to the causes of this world, they

2   Do not think then that your happiness consists in gazing at [1] the sights you see in the sense-world. If you place your happiness in that, you will be like one who has fallen asleep, and in his dreams has seen sweet and pleasant things, and has put his trust in them. Such a man, when he is awakened, is grieved and sorrow-stricken at being parted from the things which he saw in his dream ; and so, by reason of his weakness of intelligence and lack of knowledge, he gives himself up to sleep again,[2] in his longing for the things which he saw in his sleep. And even so, if the soul, while dwelling in the world of things that come to be, has been wont to gaze at (and fix its affection on) this world's enjoyments, pleasures, and delights, then, when it quits this world (at death), it suffers most intense pains and most grievous sorrows (by reason of the loss of those enjoyments) ; and moreover, it returns into this world,[3] seeking the things which it has been wont to gaze at, because it is overcome by longing for them, and puts its happiness in them.

3   But if the soul, while dwelling in this world, has been wont to gaze at the miseries and sorrows and distresses in it,[4] then, when it quits this world, it rejoices and is glad that it is departing from it ; just as, if a man sees in a dream things ugly, foul, and grievous, and then awakes out of his sleep, he rejoices and is glad that he has got away from the things he saw in his dream.[5] Moreover, he will refuse to give himself up to sleep again,[6] because of the distress and terror he suffered when he saw those hideous things in his dream.

4   Cap. 14, §§ 4, 5. If this world offers you anything, do not accept it ; for the world is mocking you, and its purpose is that you may laugh a little, and then weep much. That is nature's way ; not that she feigns,[7] for a physical thing cannot feign to be one thing when it is another. But the soul is endowed with life, intelligence ($\nu o \hat{\upsilon} s$), and discernment ($\kappa \rho \acute{\iota} \sigma \iota s$), and can be deceived or not deceived, according to her own free choice. If the soul marks the devices of him who is seeking to deceive her (viz. the world), and turns away from his wiles and guards against them, she escapes the evil that would otherwise

are not real ; and likewise, if the causes of this world are referred to the thought-world, which alone is real, they are not real.'

    [1] *Spectare.*
    [2] In this he corresponds to the disembodied soul which seeks to be reincarnated.
    [3] By voluntary reincarnation.
    [4] It is implied that this, and not the other, is the right way to look at things.
    [5] This life is a nightmare.   [6] I. e. the soul will refuse to be reincarnated.
    [7] Cf. 2. 1–4. ('It is not true that the world deceives men ; they deceive themselves.')

5 follow ; and if she yields to the world's wiles and frauds, she yields to them of her own free will.   As it is in her power to yield to them, so it is in her power not to yield; for she has free will, and according to her own will she either guards against perdition or goes to perdition.

6   Cap. 14, § 6. Lay hold on the things which you and all men know, and let go the things which you and all men know not.

For instance, you and all men know that fire is hot, and burns things, and emits light, and that water is cold and moist and fluid, and quenches thirst; you know that the whole is greater than a part of it, and that a straight line differs from a curved line.[1]

(With no less certainty) you know that . . . ; and that . . . .[2]   Now it is unhappiness to quit that which one loves, and happiness to quit that which one hates ; and it is certain that you must quit this world (i. e. that you will die); therefore it needs must be that unhappiness will befall you if you love this world, and happiness if you hate it.

7   Cap. 14, §§ 7, 8. 'Withdraw yourself in imagination, O Soul, from the physical world,[3] and then see whether you can find anything besides your own essence[4] and its existence.[5]   If you describe your essence, you would say that the soul is (1) a thing similar and cognate to thought,[6] and endowed with the faculty of representing things to itself in thought,[7] and (2) a thing that moves both other things and itself,[8] that has power of discernment (κρίσις),[9] and impels itself towards those things which it wills and desires [and that it is

---

[1] Cf. the similar list of instances of certain knowledge that is given in 1. 1.

[2] This sentence, as given by Bardenhewer, is unintelligible.

[3] Cf. 10. 7 a : 'Suppose yourself, O Soul, to have put away from you your five senses,' &c.

[4] *Essentia* (οὐσία, in the sense of ἡ κατὰ τὸ εἶδος οὐσία); the answer to the question τί ἐστι ;

[5] *Existentia* (ὕπαρξις ?). To 'describe the *essentia*' of a thing is to define it ; to affirm its *existentia* is to say that the thing defined is not a mere concept, but has objective existence. If one ignores the physical world, one finds that there is left in existence nothing except ψυχή, which is a thing to be defined as follows. (But what about νοῦς and νοητά ? They seem to be included in ψυχή, which here means νοερὰ ψυχή.)

[6] *Substantiam notioni similem et cognatam.*

[7] *Facultas rerum cogitatione sibi informandarum* ; i. e. the faculty of νόησις.

[8] ἡ ψυχή is αὐτοκίνητος, as all Platonists said. In Pl. *Phaedr.* 245 C, ψυχή is described as τὸ αὐτὸ κινοῦν, and τοῖς ἄλλοις ὅσα κινεῖται πηγὴ καὶ ἀρχὴ κινήσεως. Cf. Herm. *ap.* Stob. *Exc.* XVI. 1 : ἡ ψυχὴ οὐσία ἐστιν ἀσώματος, . . . αὐτοκίνητος. *Exc.* IV. A. 4.

[9] I. e. ability to distinguish between good and evil.

endowed with excellent and good qualities, namely, justice, equity, liberality, and mercy].[1]   And if you describe your essence thus, and (affirm that) these qualities belong to your essence and nature, then you must necessarily assert that you are a "subtle"[2] and governing[3] thing.

8   'Now if you go on to describe the other things,[4] can you find a description appropriate to their essence[5] in any other way than by assigning [a description and] attributes to them by transference,[6] and describing them by qualities that are alien to their nature?[7]   And if a thing does not admit of a description appropriate to its essence, and no attribute (can be assigned to it), are you not forced to assert that such a thing is devoid of life, and is destined by its own nature to be passive?[8]

'You must understand then that the soul makes in the physical world nothing else than copies of the things which Mind (νοῦς) makes in the soul itself;[9] and that Mind (νοῦς) makes in the soul nothing else than copies of the things which the First Cause of all makes in Mind (νοῦς).[10],[11]

---

[1] Evidently an interpolation; these social virtues cannot be included in the 'essence' of the soul.

[2] This probably means ἀσώματος, or immaterial; not composed of ὕλη, which is 'gross'. Cf. i. 8-11.

[3] *Res moderatrix*; i.e. the function of the soul is to govern things, not to be governed by them.

[4] I.e. the things of the physical world (*rerum natura*, § 1 *init.*); corporeal things, τὰ αἰσθητά.

[5] I.e. define them.

[6] *Per modum translationis*: i.e. by speaking metaphorically?

[7] What does this mean? . Possibly, that particular concrete things cannot be defined; definition is of universals only. If one tries to define a particular material thing, one can do so only by defining the εἶδος that is imposed on its ὕλη, and ignoring the ὕλη. But if that is what the writer means, he does not say it clearly.

[8] I.e. to be moved and governed by something other than itself; the opposite of *res moderatrix*. But how does this follow from the fact that the thing cannot be defined?

[9] *Animam in rerum natura nihil aliud efficere nisi species* (εἰκόνας or εἴδωλα?) *eorum quae ratio in ipsa efficit*. The ψυχή (which here appears to mean the world-soul) makes the αἰσθητὰ εἴδη of the things in the material world; and these αἰσθητὰ εἴδη are 'copies' of the νοητὰ εἴδη (the παραδείγματα) which the divine νοῦς 'makes in' (or puts into) the ψυχή.

[10] *Nec rationem in anima aliud quidquam efficere nisi species eorum quae causa prima in ipsa efficit*. The νοητὰ εἴδη which are in the ψυχή are made in it by νοῦς, and are 'copies' of the νοητὰ εἴδη which are in νοῦς; and those which are in νοῦς are made in it by (or issue from) τὸ ἕν, which is τὸ πρῶτον αἴτιον, the supreme God.

The doctrine here stated must have been derived from Plotinus. But it is not clear what (if any) is the connexion of thought between this last sentence and the rest of the *sententia*.

[11] This Neoplatonic *sententia* may perhaps have been translated from a Greek original.

9   Cap. 14, §§ 9, 10. If two birds of the same species were tied together with a cord, and were left thus tied, each of them would undergo great torment, and would be deprived of rest; and each could get ease and rest only by being separated from the other. And it would be yet more so, if creatures of different shape and nature were tied together, a camel and a wolf, for instance, or a bull and a lion; or if a living being were tied to a lifeless thing.[1] And can there be anything more miserable than a wise man who is tied to a fool?

10   The camel cannot rest unless it is released from the bond by which it is tied to the wolf; and so it is also in the case of the wolf and the lion, the living being and the lifeless thing, the wise man and the fool.[2]

11   Cap. 14, §§ 11, 12. 'The substance (οὐσία) of the (human) soul is of the highest eminence, for this reason, that it is connected with all the different worlds, and can lodge in any region.'[3]

'(a) For a time,[4] the soul belongs to the physical world. At this stage, the soul is ⌜(merely) human⌝;[5] it sees before it the things apprehensible by the senses, and it is concerned with food and drink, and with physical things alone.

---

[1] [The figure of the living tied to the dead was used by Aristotle in his *Protrepticus*, imitated by Cicero (*Hortensius*), and cited by Iamblichus (*Protr.*, p. 48, Pistelli) and Augustine *c. Iul. Pelagianum*, 4 (15), 78). Rose, *Fragmenta*, 60. Cf. *Corp.* VII. 2 b : τὸν ζῶντα θάνατον, τὸν αἰσθητ(ικ)ὸν νεκρόν, τὸν περιφόρητον τάφον, τὸν ἔνοικον λῃστήν. The Elizabethan dramatist George Chapman (or his source) combines the Hermetic passage just quoted with Aristotle's figure :

A quick corse, only sensible of grief,
A walking sepulchre, or household thief,
.   .   .   .
A slave bound face to face to Death till death.
          Byron's Tragedy, V. iv. 35–38.]

[2] The inference which the reader is intended to draw from this *sententia* is that the soul cannot be at rest until it is released from the body. Cf. 3. 13. (Possibly the 'two birds of the same species' may be meant to signify two human souls; if so, that sentence would be to the same effect as 6. 4 : ' do not hamper yourself with any human friendship.')

[3] Cf. *Ascl. Lat.* I. 5 : ' Multiformis variaque generis humani species ' &c.

[4] When first incarnated, and during childhood, all human souls are in this state ; and some, perhaps, remain in it throughout their life on earth.

[5] *Tum quidem humana est.* But the life here described is that which belongs to beasts and beast-like men in common; it is rather the grade of life (*b*) next above this that is distinctively ' human '. [Stob. *Exc.* III. 5 (codd.): παρέπονται δὲ τῇ ψυχῇ οὐκ ἀθρόως παραγιγνόμεναι (*sc.* αἱ ἐνέργειαι)· ἀλλὰ τινὲς μὲν αὐτῶν ἅμα τῷ γενέσθαι τὸν ἄνθρωπον ἐνεργοῦσι, ὁμοῦ τῇ ψυχῇ περὶ τὰ ἄλογα οὖσαι, αἱ δὲ καθαρώτεραι ἐνέργειαι κατὰ μεταβολὴν τῆς ἡλικίας, τῷ λογικῷ μέρει τῆς ψυχῆς συνεργοῦσαι. *Exc.* XIX. 5 (codd.): καὶ τὸ μὲν πνεῦμα τοῦ σώματος, ὁ δὲ λόγος τῆς οὐσίας . . . τὸ δὲ αἰσθητικὸν πνεῦμα τῶν φαινομένων κριτικόν ἐστι. διῄρηται δὲ εἰς τὰς ὀργανικὰς αἰσθήσεις, καὶ ἔστι τι μέρος αὐτοῦ πνευματικὴ ὅρασις, καὶ ἀκουστικὸν καὶ ὀσφρητικὸν καὶ γευστικὸν καὶ ἁπτικόν.]

'(b) At another time, the soul belongs to the world that is peculiar (or appropriate) to itself.[1] At this stage, the soul is a thing that perceives things and gets knowledge of them,[2] that originates movement,[3] that is capable of investigating things and reflecting on them,[4] and is endowed with free choice and will. These are the qualities that are proper to the soul. . . .[5]

12 '(c) At another time, the soul belongs to the thought-world.[6] At this stage, the soul separates forms from matter,[7] apprehends the first principles (ἀρχαί, causes or sources) of things, and distinguishes from one another and grasps in thought (νοεῖ) all the simple and indivisible forms.[8]

'[(d) And lastly, at another time again the soul belongs to the *divine* world. At this (highest) stage the soul has attained to the Good and goodness,[9] and wills [10] what is good; it is free from the bad and badness, and sets itself against [11] what is bad; it does wisely and acts prudently.][12]

[1] I.e. there is a κόσμος that might be called λογιστός (if that word were in use), intermediate between the αἰσθητὸς κόσμος and the νοητὸς κόσμος; and this 'rational world' is the abode appropriate to the λογικὴ ψυχή, the distinctively human soul. (The soul which rises above this grade becomes something more than human.)

[2] *Res sentiens et cognoscens.* In this connexion *sentiens* must mean something more than mere αἴσθησις, which the soul already possessed in grade (a).

[3] *Agitans et movens.* At this stage, the soul is an ἀρχὴ κινήσεως, or is αὐτο-κίνητος. In grade (a) it was moved only by blind instinct, i. e. impelled by forces acting on it, through the body, from without.

[4] *Inquisitionis et contemplationis compos.*

[5] *Eaedemque vitam efficiunt quae in omnibus rebus constituitur quascumque animae imperium complexum est* Bard. It may be conjectured that what the writer meant was this: 'And it is in virtue of these same qualities that soul puts life into all things that are included under its dominion' (i. e. into bodies). But this would be applicable to the world-soul rather than to particular human souls. It is not by my own rational and voluntary action that my body has been made a living body.

[6] The νοητὸς κόσμος.

[7] I. e. apprehends the νοητὰ εἴδη (the archetypal forms, the παραδείγματα, which are God's thoughts or purposes apart from material things, the αἰσθητὰ εἴδη of which are imperfect copies of the νοητὰ εἴδη. To do this is to see things as God sees them.

[8] *Species simplices atque individuas.* Each of the νοητὰ εἴδη is *one*, incomposite and indivisible; and the soul apprehends them one by one, and distinguishes each of them from the others.

[9] The Good (τὸ ἀγαθόν) is here either identified with God, or regarded as correlative with God. [*Corp.* VI. 1 a: τὸ ἀγαθὸν . . . ἐν οὐδενί ἐστιν εἰ μὴ ἐν μόνῳ τῷ θεῷ. μᾶλλον δὲ τὸ ἀγαθὸν αὐτός ἐστιν ὁ θεὸς ἀεί, κ.τ.λ. *Corp.* X. 1 b (codd.): ὁ μὲν οὖν θεὸς καὶ πατήρ, καὶ τὸ ἀγαθόν, ὦ Τάτ, τὴν αὐτὴν ἔχει φύσιν, μᾶλλον δὲ καὶ ἐνέργειαν. § 6: περιλάμψαν δὲ πάντα τὸν νοῦν καὶ τὴν ὅλην ψυχὴν ἀναλάμπει καὶ ἀνέλκει διὰ τοῦ σώματος, καὶ ὅλον αὐτὸν εἰς οὐσίαν μεταβάλλει.]

[10] *Iubet.*   [11] *Vetat.*

[12] This passage (d) is contradicted by what follows; for in the following paragraph we are told that when the soul has attained to the νοητὸς κόσμος

'That the soul is connected with and akin to the First Cause[1] is clearly shown by the (aspiration) implanted in its nature, inasmuch as the soul strives to grasp the sum of all things that are included under His supreme dominion.[2] For never will the soul be found to be at rest and perfectly content, unless it has attained to the thought-world, and (made its own) all things that are in that world. Then, and then only, will the soul be found to be in want of nothing,[3] calm and at rest, and perfectly content.'[4]

13 Cap. 14, §§ 13, 14. There is nothing, O Soul, more unhappy and unfortunate than you are. You have come, a solitary traveller, into a land of barbarians; you speak to them in your own tongue, pouring forth lamentations, but they do not understand your language; and they speak to you in their tongue, but you do not understand it.[5] [For if a thing is conjoined with something contrary to it,[6] it is left forlorn, and reduced to helplessness, being so much occupied with 14 something other than itself, that it cannot but neglect itself.][7] How distressing is your state, O Soul, when you find no one to hear you if you speak, and no one to pity you if you lament! What solace is there for him who is estranged from his fatherland,[8] remote from his home, separated from his root and source? And at the same time he is held captive by his own appetites, so that he takes no thought that he will have to reap the fruit of his own errors and sins; he is

---

(grade (*c*)) it will be at rest, and will want nothing more. The passage (*d*) must have been inserted by some one who (like Plotinus) recognized a supreme *hypostasis* (τὸ ἀγαθόν) above and distinct from νοῦς, but (unlike Plotinus) took attainment to τὸ ἀγαθόν to mean moral goodness rather than mystic union with the supreme God. If we cut out (*d*), we get a *sententia* that is consistent throughout, the writer of which regarded νοῦς as the supreme God, and took τὰ νοητά to mean God's thoughts.

[1] I. e. God, who (for this writer) is νοῦς.

[2] The soul has an innate desire to extend its knowledge (of τὰ ὄντως ὄντα) until its range of thought extends over the whole range of God's government (or in other words, until its thought coincides with God's thought, and it thinks all that God thinks). And this proves that the soul is akin to God; i. e. its aspiration to draw nearer and nearer to God in thought proves that it was originally one with God or close to God.

[3] *Nihil requirens*: ἀνενδεής.

[4] There is nothing in this *sententia* ((*d*) omitted) that might not have been written by a Pagan Platonist before A.D. 300; and the original may possibly have been a Greek *Hermeticum*.

[5] Does the writer mean by these 'barbarians' one's fellowmen, or τὰ αἰσθητά in general? Probably the latter.

[6] The soul is thus conjoined with the body. Cf. 14. 9 *sq.* (a camel tied to a wolf, &c.).

[7] I have bracketed this sentence, because it breaks the connexion of thought.

[8] The νοητὸς κόσμος.

borne along by deadly desires,[1] imbued with gross cravings for pleasures and delights, taking no account of his own ways, intent on his own destruction. He is floating on a vast sea, borne on a thing that falsely seems a commodious vessel;[2] but when it breaks up and melts away,[3] ⟨. . . .⟩[4] He has entered into partnership with one who will desert him,[5] and has trusted himself to one who has deceived and tricked him. How disastrous it is, when a man is deceived by a friend that defrauds him, and a partner that deserts him!

15 a   Cap. 14, § 15 a. 'He who plants sweet things eats sweet things; he who plants things good for naught (*vilia*) eats things good for naught. For the fruit of good deeds (*operae bonae*) corresponds to the root from which it grows, and the fruit of bad deeds corresponds to the root from which it grows.'[6]

15 b   Cap. 14, § 15 b. 'A little knowledge which you carry out in action is more profitable than much knowledge which you neglect to carry out in action. May God have mercy on him who knows and does, and teaches others; who reads (this book), and understands what he has read, and teaches others to understand; who attains to the appointed end,[7] and leads others to it; who rightly intercedes (or mediates),[8] speaks truly, and partakes of God's aid.'[9]

---

[1] *Perniciosarum cupiditatum vehiculo vehens.* The *vehiculum* which the writer pictures to himself is a boat or raft rather than a carriage; see below.

[2] *Per vastum mare vehitur in vehiculis simulatis et commodis.*

[3] The boat or raft is the body, which will 'break up and melt away' at death. Cf. 4. 3 (an ice-floe).

[4] Some words must have been lost here; the different simile that follows cannot have been included in the same sentence.

[5] *Destituit* (present or perfect?) Bard.: but the future seems to be required. The body is a false friend or partner of the soul; cf. 4. 7, 5. 12 *sq.*, 6. 2 *sq.*, 7. 10 *sq.*, and 8. 1 *sq.*

[6] Cf. 10. 4–6.

[7] I.e. the end for which man was intended by his Maker.

[8] *Recte intercedit*: i.e. acts as an intermediary between God and men, conveying to them knowledge which he has received from God?

[9] This concluding paragraph may have been added either by the compiler of the *Castig. an.*, or (more probably, I think, since it contains nothing Platonic,) by a subsequent transcriber.

ADDENDA

(References are given by page and line for volume i—thus, 114. 2; by volume and page for Mr. Scott's notes; and by volume, page, and line for texts in volume iv. Cross-references of the form, 'see (note) on 114. 2', are to other notes in the *Addenda*. Where the titles of the books are abbreviated, the full name will be found in the list at the end of the *Addenda*.)

CORPUS HERMETICUM

Libellus I. 114. 1. The text has been reissued by Reitzenstein, with some changes, in Reitz.-Schaeder, *Studien* I. 154–160. Also the prayer in *Pap. Berol.* 9794 col. 2, 42 is printed (p. 160) from a fresh collation by Prof. Schubart.

2. The condition of vision is that the senses should be completely lulled; then there is communication (συγκίνησις) with God. See 130. 3, 240. 26, 242. 18. The repetition of ἐννοίας, or διανοίας, etc., indicates that the mind of the narrator had achieved the necessary detachment. The point of the comparison with the sleep of weariness or satiation lies in its profundity, not in its cause.

20. μέρει: ἀέρι Kroll.

21. ἐσπειράμενον (Casaubon), ὡς εἰκάσαι γε ⟨δράκοντι⟩. εἶτα Reitz. Hippolytus *Refut.* 5. 9. 13: εἶναι δὲ τὸν ὄφιν λέγουσιν οὗτοι τὴν ὑγρὰν οὐσίαν.

23. See on 118. 12. The fire is a bad element: φίλον γὰρ πυρὶ τὸ σκότος (Ps.-Clem. *Homil.* 20. 9).

116. 1. φωνὴν φωτός. πυρός Reitzenstein, who contrasts the inarticulate βοή (φωνή) with the λόγος of the following sentence (*Poimandres*, p. 86. 3).

7. ὁ σὸς θεός. Cf. ὦ νοῦς ἐμός (126. 7), ἀπὸ τοῦ νοός μου (130. 6). God is in man, and man in God (116. 10, 128. 22). As son of the Father, the writer also naturally says υἱοὺς δὲ σοῦ (130. 27). For the formula ἐγώ εἰμι see Norden, *Agn. Theos*, 189 sqq.

9. φωτεινὸς Λόγος. See on *Fr.* 23. The writer is told to look into himself if he would know the Λόγος (reading βλέπον κ. ἀκοῦον). The clue is φωτισμός. See notes on 230. 7, 330. 21; cf. 216. 29. *Poimandres*, p. 38, *Zwei rel.-gesch. Fragen*, pp. 80 sqq. This hardly belongs to the same stratum of doctrine as the fiery Demiurge; see Bousset, *G. G. A.*, 1914, p. 713.

18. See on 118. 12, also 114. 23.

20. ἐμπλήξει. Apparently misprint for ἐκπλήξει.

24. στοιχεῖα.[1] If we follow the traditional order, and assume that the document contains inconsistent elements, the Will received the Word

[1] τὰ γοῦν Keil.

(seed) and was made into a world. It is supposed that the elements and the souls spring from Βουλή (a female deity) upon the entrance of the Λόγος.[1] See Reitzenstein's parallels from Plutarch (*Is. et Osir.* 53-4, Philo *de ebriet.* 30) and Bousset's critical remarks *G. G. A.*, 1905, p. 696. In l. 29 γεννημάτων. Perhaps bracket ψυχῶν (Reitz.)

118. 2. τε ἅμα καί Reitz.

7. θεωρεῖσθαι ⟨τὴν γῆν⟩ Reitz.

8. τὸν ἐμπεριφερόμενον πν. λόγον εἰς ἀκοὴν Reitz. This belongs to the Λόγος section, 116. 2 *sqq.*

12. θεὸς τοῦ πυρὸς κ. πνεύματος. This distinction between the God of Life and Light and the God of Fire and Pneuma is important. There is, on the theory of this tract, a region of Life and Light,[2] from which are derived Soul and Mind (122. 30). In 116. 18 the Fire is said to be held in by a mighty power; the demiurgic sphere is evidently below the sphere of Light and Life (120. 13), and the creation of the Demiurge is ἐν τῷ πυρί.[3] As Bousset points out, the purging character of fire should be taken in this connexion (126. 22).

24. ἄρχεται γὰρ οὗ λήγει. οὐ λ. δὲ ἡ τ. περιφορά Kroll. Change unnecessary. This may be a school phrase, suggested ultimately by Homer. In describing the number series, which perpetually starts from the monad[4] and returns to it, Philo writes ᾗ (τῇ μονάδι) πᾶς ἂν ἀριθμὸς εἴποι τὸ ποιητικὸν ἐκεῖνο

$$\text{ἐν σοὶ μὲν λήξω, σέο δ' ἄρξομαι} \ [Il. 9. 97].$$

λήγει τε γὰρ ἀναλυόμενος ὁ κατὰ σύνθεσιν ἀπειράκις ἄπειρος ἀριθμὸς εἰς μονάδα, ἄρχεται τε αὖ πάλιν ἀπὸ μονάδος εἰς ἀπερίγραφον συντιθέμενος πλῆθος (*quis rer. div. heres*, 189-90). There is no reason why the revolution of the heavens should not be said to produce living creatures; cf. 182. 6, 25. Colon after λήγει and retain text. See on 364. 14.

120. 5. The myth of Ἄνθρωπος is widespread. It is not possible here to do more than indicate its character and refer to the literature. If we retain the order of the text, the story here told is as follows. The God of Light generated Man in his image and loved his son. Man saw the Creation of his brother the God of Fire and wished to emulate him. So he entered the Demiurge's sphere, and watched his brother's creations (the planets), which loved him and gave him a share in their nature. Then he desired

---

[1] I. e., the Triad, Θεός, Βουλή, Λόγος. For Boule see e. g. 148. 20. See Bousset, *Hauptprobleme*, p. 334.

[2] See Index, and consult Bousset, *Kyrios*, pp. 208 *sqq.*, *G. G. A.*, 1914, 716-22; Wetter, ΦΩΣ *passim*. So Esaldaios, the Demiurge of this creation, is a fiery God in the Naassene sermon (Hippol. *Refut.* 5. 7. 5; cf. 7. 3⁸. 1, 8. 9. 7, 10. 20. 1). See also *Hauptprobleme*, p. 151. This fiery Demiurge appears in the Chaldaic Oracles (Kroll, p. 13) νοῦ γὰρ νοῦς ἐστιν ὁ κόσμου | τεχνίτης πυρίου.

[3] 120. 12. Zielinski's emendation; cf. l. 20. Compare also (with Bousset) 200. 28.   [4] The monad is a symbol of God.

to break the bounds of their circles and to subdue the power of the God of Fire.[1] Nature saw the fair form of God (cf. ll. 4-6) and smiled with love— she saw the Man's reflection [2] and shadow in water and earth, while he saw his own image reflected, and fell in love, and straightway entered the senseless shape. And Man and Nature mingled, and Nature bore seven Men, bisexual, with characters answering to the seven planets (122. 19). This myth explains why man is mortal and immortal, an ἐναρμόνιος δοῦλος.

For analysis of the elements here I must refer to the literature. The first step was taken by Reitzenstein, who connected the myth with the Attis hymn in Hippolytus *Refut.* 5. 9. 8, and the commentary prefixed to it (cc. 6 *sqq*).[3] In the last resort he claimed that the basis of the Naassene sermon was 'eine heidnische Ἄνθρωπος-Lehre'. Bousset [4] accepts this account in general, but brings in the story of Attis as allegorized by Julian and Sallustius.[5] By comparing the doctrine and the names of the Gnostics attacked by Plotinus he arrives at the hypothesis of a group of Gnostics, originating in Syria and Mesopotamia, pagan in belief, and by reason of their origin familiar with the tale of Attis and the Great Mother. Now the names given by Porphyry in his *Life of Plotinus* (c. 16) are, among others, Zoroaster, Zostrianus, and Nicotheus. But Zoroaster and Nicotheus are precisely the figures that meet us in Zosimus (vol. iv. 105-7) [6] in connexion with Ἄνθρωπος, and the account of Z. enables us to fill in the detail missing here. Thus the evidence points to a tale shaped under pagan Gnostic influence.

(1) In the tale as we have it there is an absolute Hellenistic dualism between Mind and Matter, Man the lover and Nature the beloved. (2) The Plotinian account (which speaks of Ψυχή, not Ἄνθρωπος) helps to explain the 'image' of Man in 120. 26-30: ψυχὴν γὰρ εἰπόντες νεῦσαι κάτω καὶ σοφίαν τινά, εἴτε τῆς ψυχῆς ἀρξάσης, εἴτε τῇ τοιαύτῃ αἰτίας γενομένης σοφίας, εἴτε ἄμφω ταὐτὸν θέλοντες εἶναι . . . ἐκείνην λέγουσι πάλιν αὖ μὴ κατελθεῖν, οἷον μὴ νεῦσαι, ἀλλ' ἐλλάμψαι μόνον τὸ σκότος, εἶτ' ἐκεῖθεν εἴδωλον ἐν τῇ ὕλῃ γεγονέναι, εἶτα τοῦ εἰδώλου εἴδωλον πλάσαντες ἐνταῦθά που δι' ὕλης

---

[1] ll. 21-2. κράτος . . . καταπονῆσαι Candolle; so κράτος in l. 23. (Enter εἰμαρμένη!) Cf. 118. 12 (note), 200. 1-2. For text: l. 7 end καὶ ⟨ᾧ⟩ Reitz.; l. 13 γενόμενος ⟨δὲ⟩ . . . ἔξων Reitz.; l. 25 κάλλος ⟨αὐτόν τε⟩ Reitz.; l. 27 retain ὡς ἄτε; l. 29 ἐν αὐτῇ Reitz.; cf. *Fr.* 27. R. assumes a lacuna after ἀναρρήξας ⟨αὐτὴν καταπονήσας τε τοῦ δαίμονος⟩.   [2] l. 30 ἐν αὐτῇ Reitz.

[3] *Poimandres*, pp. 81 *sqq.* (where the Naassene sermon is edited). Also see Reitzenstein-Schaeder, *Studien*, i, pp. 14 *sqq.*, 1926 (revised analysis). Critical text in Wendland, Hippolytus, vol. iii (*Die griech. christl. Schriftsteller*, 1916 ; also in *Studien*, i, p. 161). See further R., *H. M. R.*, pp. 12 *sqq.*

[4] For criticism of R.'s position see *G. G. A.*, 1905, and the full discussion of the 'Urmensch' in *Hauptprobleme*, c. iv, especially pp. 181-94, 323-4.

[5] Julian, *Or.* v. (esp. 165 C, 167 B, 168 A), Sallustius, *de diis et mundo*, c. 4. On the relation of these passages see Nock, *Sallustius*, l-lv.

[6] Cf. *Poimandres*, p. 103.

ἢ ὑλότητος ἢ ὅ τι ὀνομάζειν θέλουσι.[1] Though not identical, the two accounts are so far at one in the role assigned to the 'image'. (3) In the story of Thouth-Adam,[2] the first Man, also called Φῶς, Zosimus (106. 15 sqq. above) represents him as tempted (by the ἄρχοντες?) to put on their 'Adam', i.e. the Adam of the four elements. He does not fall; but it may be suspected that in the original form he yielded and entered his earthly image. (4) The fall precedes an act of generation; creation takes a new impulse. In the Persian myth of Gayomard it seems probable that Gayomard fell in love with his mirrored image;[3] anyhow, after his death, his seed fell upon the earth, and when the sunlight had purified it, the angel of Ahura-Mazda took two parts of it, and the Spirit of Earth one part, and guarded it; and there sprang from it the first human pair, from whom seven pairs were born, to inhabit the seven quarters of the world. (5) The evidence appears to show that (a) one line of tradition makes Ἄνθρωπος a figure who is overcome or slain by Ahriman,[4] and from his fall a new stage of the world begins; (b) another line, Gnostic in character, makes him will to mingle with matter; this descent is the beginning of becoming.[5] (6) This tale, the wraith of a myth, sets the problem of man's subjection to fate, of the way to freedom, of immortality. ' Der Mythus war für die Gemeinden, welche die Hermetica voraussetzen, ungefähr dasselbe, wie für die Christengemeinde die Verkündigung vom Kreuz' (Bousset, G. G. A., 1914, p. 739), a statement that does not err on the side of moderation.

Reitzenstein's analysis, upon which we cannot enter in detail, derives not merely the story of Anthropos, but the creation myth, from the canonical version of the Iranian story.

122. 7. [τὰ] Keil: τὰ θνητοῦ Reitz. Cf. 124. 17.

10. ⟨ὧν ὑφ' ὕπνου⟩ κρατεῖται Zielinski.

17. Cf. (with Kroll) Vettius Valens, l. 1 περὶ τῆς τῶν ἀστέρων φύσεως.

19. For the *seven* see note on 120. 5.

---

[1] *Enn.* 2. 9. 10 (199. 6 Volkmann). In the Gnostic account the Demiurge arose from a union of Psyche and Matter (*Enn.*, p. 200. 16, V.).

[2] ' Adam ' according to the Chaldaeans etc., as in the Naassene sermon.

[3] Cf. 122. 19–20. See further Bousset, *Hauptprobleme*, pp. 202 sqq., G. G. A., 1905, Reitzenstein, H. M. R., pp. 9 sqq., and references there. ' Gayo-maretan ' means ' mortal life'; but ' life ' is ' immortality ', which belongs to a god. Hence Anthropos consists of contradictory elements (cf. 122. 5). Divinity is ' Gaya ' or Life (ζωή). See *Studien*, i. 18–19. When Gayomard died, seven metals from his body flowed into the earth; these are the metals of the planets—evidence that Anthropos had taken on their nature. Reitzenstein (*ibid.*, i. 18, ii. 223, 225) takes this as proof of the Iranian origin of *Corp.* I.

[4] There are at least hints of a conflict in 120. 20–3. The Man is of Life and Light, like God; his brother, the Demiurge, is of Fire and Pneuma.

[5] *Hauptprobleme*, p. 208. For Philo's Ἄνθρωπος see Bréhier, *Philon*, pp. 121–6; *Hauptprobleme*, pp. 194–202; and for criticism Kroll, P.-W., 8. 819. 24, E. Meyer, *Urspr. u. Anf. d. Christentums*, ii. 351, 371 sqq.

21. καὶ ⟨τί⟩ Reitz.

25. First the four elements of which man's body is made are named.[1] Thus Nature produced the bodies after the shape of man (l. 28). But man himself is made of higher elements (life and light).[2] This double set of elements is characteristic of the Hermetist dualism; it is not a division between higher and lower in the physical universe, but between the realm subject to εἱμαρμένη and that which is above εἱμαρμένη. Bousset[3] connects with this distinction the position given to fire and the God of Fire and Pneuma,[4] the enemy; for fire and light are here opposites (212. 1), and the first is akin to darkness.

This is not Greek, and the parallels are to be found in the *Oracula Chaldaica*, *Abammonis Responsum* (*de myst.*), and in the Gnostics.[5]

124. 1. τὰ πάντα: πάντα τά Keil. τέλους ⟨καὶ⟩ (Β²) ἀρχῶν γενέσεων Reitz.

17. αἰσθητῶς: αἰσθητικῶς Α. D. N.

27–8. Retain text; αὐτόν means τὸν θεόν. The chief thing is to know oneself as a son of God. See on 116. 7.

126. 3. ἑαυτὸν . . . ὄντα: αὐτόν Reitz.

11. ⟨καὶ⟩ τοῖς Reitz.

14. τεταγμένοι, perhaps, ranked in worship (Bousset).

18. πυλωρός. Philo, *Quaest. in Genes.* 4. 1 (Abraham before his tent-door = νοῦς): decet autem virtute pollens consilium sedere prope ad sensus, ut ianitor, ne quidquam nocivi introrsum surripiens causa noxae sit animae, quum compos est eam insontem integramque servare et immunem ab omni malo. nam insipientium sensus sine custodia derelicti sunt etc. Reitzenstein, *G. G. A.*, 1918, p. 253. Nous is the πάρεδρος δαίμων of the senses. See also *Studien*, pp. 10-11.[6] In l. 15 R. suggests φυλάσσονται. Kroll (*ib.*) ⟨ἀ⟩ιδίῳ.

23. θρώσκει ⟨ἐπ'⟩ αὐτόν . . . καὶ αὐτὸν βασανίζει καὶ τὸ ἐπ' αὐτὸν πῦρ . . . αὐξάνει Reitz. Cf. 200. 28, and on 122. 25 for the nature of fire.

128. 1. Several strands appear to be interwoven here: (1) the soul leaves body, shape, ἦθος, and senses; (2) it leaves its irrational parts or powers (Platonic-Posidonian); (3) as it gained certain evil capacities from the planets (which are here powers of evil) in its descent, so it sheds them in its ascent, circle by circle. The descent is not mentioned here: see

---

[1] l. 27 ἐκ πυρὸς δὲ τὸ πέπειρον Reitzenstein. αἰθήρ here is ἀήρ.

[2] Cf. 124. 29, 126. 4, 6, 132. 1, 140. 24, 212. 1, 246. 1, 248. 1-2 (with πνεῦμα), 376. 5-7.

[3] *G. G. A.*, 1914, pp. 717 *sqq.*, *Kyrios*, pp. 208 *sqq.*

[4] 114. 24 *sqq.*, 116. 18, 118. 12, 120. 12, 20, 122 18.

[5] For references see on 114. 1, 118 12; add (with Bousset) *de myster.*, ii. 4, Clement, *exc. ex Theodoto*, 12, Hippol. *Refut.* 8. 12: ἦν ἄνθρωπος καὶ ἐγένετο υἱὸς αὐτοῦ, ὥς τις εἴποι· ἦν πῦρ καὶ ἐγένετο φῶς. Further traces of the double series of elements will be found in notes on 236. 12, 304. 16.

[6] Punctuate after εἰσόδους, and remove comma before τάς.

references in vol. ii. 61–2. Zielinski [1] noted that the seven evils depend upon the number of the planets; cf. the lists in 126. 20, 166. 5 (see note), 168. 10, 180. 12.[2] This is the characteristic Hermetic doctrine of the evil power of the planets, and of the two souls.[3]

15. Reitzenstein (*Studien*, i. 28) refers this passage to the Iranian Dāmdāδ-Nask: 'über das Garōōmān ist offenbart, zu ihm komme allezeit die Stimme, die melodische, süsse, die für die Seele Unsterblichkeit und Freude hervorrufe'.[4] Compare also the Manichaean fragments cited by R. *ad loc.*[5]

23. θεωθῆναι. The phrase ἐν θεῷ implies a mystic union; 152. 31, note on 190. 17, 192. 3, 224. 3, 246. 17–19, 248. 5, 338. 8, 376. 1; Reitzenstein, *Poimandres*, pp. 17. 11, 21. 11: see further Bousset, *Kyrios*, pp. 150-1, Norden, *Agn. Theos*, p. 23.

130. 5. ἐκφορά: ἐκφθορά Zielinski. This appears as the last of a catalogue of privations: λόγος gives place to σιγή, silent communion with God. Cf. *Corp.* I, *init.*, 130. 23, 150. 15, 238. 22. See also Bousset, *Kyrios*, p. 388, Bréhier, *Philon*, p. 102. γέννημα τῶν ἀγαθῶν Kroll.

8. Reitzenstein now accepts the text as it stands; cf. l. 26.[6]

25. ἐνδυνάμωσον. Cf. ἐπνευμάτωσον, δυνάμωσον, διαέγειρον τῇ δυνάμει τοῦ αἰωνίου θεοῦ τόδε τὸ σῶμα καὶ πυρὶ πατείτω ἐπὶ τόνδε τὸν τόπον (Dieterich, *Abraxas*, 190. 6). καίτοι οὐδὲ σαρκικοῖς ὀφθαλμοῖς τὸ φῶς ἑωράκεισαν …

---

[1] *Archiv*, 8, pp. 332 *sqq.* In this passage there are strictly six *vices*; but growth and decay belong to the sub-lunar world of change. Cf. 242. 2 (ὡς ψεῦδος). Reitzenstein connects this with the Iranian account, according to which the soul becomes a fifteen-year-old girl, and those who rise at the destruction of the world regain their youthful form. This seems remote from the technical expressions used by the Hermetist.

[2] In *Corp.* XIII (242–4) there are twelve torments of matter (zodiacal); but in 244. 19 the seven reappear, with seven corresponding virtues. Zosimus mentions the twelve; see 111. 8 above.

[3] Compare *Fr.* 16 (iv. 34. 28 above). For the ἄνοδος see 154. 10, 194. 27, 390. 23, 418. 16. An excellent short analysis in Bousset, *G. G. A.*, 1914, pp. 732 *sqq.*; and further *Archiv*, iv, *Hauptprobleme*, pp. 361 *sqq.* Reitzenstein's analysis (*Studien*, i 26–7) finds Iranian elements in the first part. For the citations from Arnobius (vol. ii, pp. 61–2) see on iv. 7. 8, below.

In detail: ἀνενέργητος is used, as Zielinski notes, of an inhibited priest; the repetition at the end of the clauses is rhetorical, and perhaps it should be supplied in ll. 10, 14; R. interchanges ἀπλεονέκτητον (l. 11) with ἀνενεργήτους (l. 13); l. 11 προθυμίαν (Reitz.), on the analogy of Servius' *regni desiderium* (vol. ii. 62).

[4] Hence he restores the reading of BCM ἡδείᾳ (l. 19); in l. 16 ⟨παρ⟩οῦσι.

[5] Reitzenstein, *Das mandäische Buch*, p. 46; *Das iran. Erlösungsmysterium*, p. 13, 'folge (mir) zur Stätte der gebetgepriesenen Erde', i.e. die ' von der Stimme gebenedeite', the Ogdoad.

[6] *Apparatus of Papyrus* (Schubart): 12 ἀπὸ τοῦ νούς. 17 ἐμόρφωσεν. 20 ὁ πάσης. Vielleicht α[πασης]. 22 λ(ιτανειας ἀγ)νάς. 23 ανατεταγ(γ or σ)μενας. 24 τῆς κατουφο . . . : κάτω φο(ρᾶς) κάτω φόρου (φύσεως)? 27 τὸ γὰρ πνεῦμά μου ⟨συλλιπαρεῖ or συμπνεῖ⟩.

ἀλλ' ὡς ἡ δύναμις καὶ ἡ βούλησις τοῦ σωτῆρος ἐνεδυνάμωσεν τὴν σάρκα εἰς τὸ θεάσασθαι (Clem. *exc. ex Theodoto* 5, 3 (107. 5 Stählin).

26. It is unnecessary to supply a participle for the genitive; cf. l. 8. Punctuate after γένους to give the antithesis in l. 27 (Reitz.).

132. 4. παρέδωκας ... ἐξουσίαν. In the language of the mysteries παραδιδόναι)(παραλαμβάνειν and *tradere*)(*accipere* are regular usage.[1] See, e.g., 120. 8, 128. 24, 238. 16, 19, 248. 24, 254. 15, 460. 2; vol. iv, 147. 3, 5. The words are particularly used of teaching a hidden doctrine,[2] and are commonly applied to the γνῶσις θεοῦ, or indeed to magical or alchemical lore. To betray the secret is to become a διάβολος.[3] Παράδοσις from parent to child was permitted,[4] and *Exc.* XXIII (474. 15) is an excellent example of such transmission, from father-god to son-god, from mother to son. The word ἐξουσία also has a special meaning. It involves the notion first of knowledge (γνῶσις) passed on, then of the authority conferred upon the initiate through the possession of this knowledge;[5] he becomes a κῆρυξ or ὁδηγός.[6] In such usage πάντα is commonly associated with the knowledge or the power,[7] as in this passage. I have reserved any reference to the rich material collected by Norden (*Agnostos Theos*, pp. 288 *sqq.*) till the end of this note. It is particularly important for the wealth of New Testament parallels. Here there is space only for his treatment of this passage. He notes the order:—reception of γνῶσις, exhortation, prayer of thanks (unless 132. 5 is counted as a prayer, which would place prayer before the sermon to men).

The basis of his argument is an analysis of the elements in *Ev. Matth.* xi. 25–30, and he brings evidence for a formal schema in such compositions. It must suffice here to quote his parallel between our libellus and *Ep. Rom.* xi. 25.[8]

---

[1] Lobeck, *Aglaophamus*, p. 39; Dieterich, *Mithrasliturgie*, p. 53, *Abraxas*, p. 162. Cf. the end of the Naassene hymn (Hippolytus, *Ref.* v. 10): αἰῶνας ὅλους διοδεύσω, | μυστήρια πάντα δ' ἀνοίξω, | μορφὰς δὲ θεῶν ἐπιδείξω, | καὶ τὰ κεκρυμμένα τῆς ἁγίας ὁδοῦ, | γνῶσιν καλέσας, παραδώσω. Also *Ref.* i. 2. (The Chaldaean Oracles were θεοπαράδοτα).

[2] See especially vol. iv. 145, *ad fin.*, and compare 122. 14, 254. 14. See also examples in *Abraxas*, 162–3.

[3] 254. 15. διαβάλλειν in sacral usage means 'to blab, to publish abroad' (Reitzenstein, *H. M. R.*, p. 140. 1). See on 254. 15, and cf. 288. 2 *publicare*.

[4] Vol. iv. 148. 3; the revelation is preceded by an oath. Cf. Diodorus, ii. 29 (of the Chaldaeans).

[5] Reitzenstein, *Poimandres*, p. 48. 3 (cf. *G. G. A.*, 1918, 257), *H. M. R.*, pp. 301, 363; cf. e. g. (with R.) Apuleius, *Apol.* 26: (magus) qui communione loquendi cum deis immortalibus ad omnia quae velit incredibili quadam vi cantaminum polleat. He who possessed the knowledge became a leader or guide— οὐχ ὡς πάντα παραλαβὼν καθοδηγὸς γίνῃ τοῖς ἀξίοις κ.τ.λ. (128. 24). Similarly (130. 24) the order is knowledge, power, preaching. Cf. 132. 6–9, 21–3.

[6] 132. 8, 150. 22, 172. 4.

[7] 120. 22, 122. 7.

[8] *op. cit.*, p. 296.

Logion und hermet. Traktat	*Paulus*
Offenbarung eines μυστήριον	Offenbarung eines μυστήριον
Dankgebet für die γνῶσις θεοῦ	Gebet mit Erwähnung der γνῶσις θεοῦ
Appel an die Menschen	Ermahnungen an die ἀδελφοί.

8. κηρύσσειν. The κῆρυξ appears in 150. 22, in connexion with the κρατήρ, as here with the ἀμβρόσιον ὕδωρ.[1] The evidence about the character and work of this figure has been analysed by Norden (*Agn. Theos*, pp. 3 *sqq.*). The κῆρυξ is καθοδηγός,[2] and the 'Way' releases the soul from the bond of Fate. It is hard to avoid the conclusion that the water protects the soul in its ἄνοδος through troops of foes that beset its passage (154. 10 and iv. 111).[3]

16. τοῦ σκοτεινοῦ ⟨σώματος· του⟩ φωτὸς κ.τ.λ. Bousset. Cf. 124. 24, 172. 10.

Libellus II. 134. 2 *sqq.* These notes deal mainly with some difficulties about Space. The peculiarity of the tract is its identification of the 'in which' with the 'by which'—the Container with the First Mover, in Aristotelian language. It appears to reflect a Stoic-Peripatetic debate on the question whether there is Void or Nonentity without the Cosmos—though that is not the whole story—and adopts a third alternative, that the surrounding space both encircles and moves the Cosmos.[4] The arguments used to sustain this thesis are drawn from the Stoic physical tradition, and the attributes assigned by them to Space the Container are embodied in the definition of Space the Mover arrived at in § 12. It will be convenient to depart from the order of the text and to follow out the physical arguments first. Throughout, the resemblance of Topos to Plato's World-soul (*Tim.* 34 B, and on 190. 23) and to Aion should be borne in mind.

§ 1. It is presupposed that the 'moved' is identical with body, and therefore needs an 'in which'[5] and a 'by which', as container greater, as mover stronger. The 'in which' has a nature opposite to that of the moved. §§ 2–4. It is further assumed that the Cosmos is the greatest body, and is packed with bodies (i. e. is continuous body).[6] This assumes the

---

[1] See iv. 111. 17.

[2] Cf. 172. 4 and *Index*, ὁδηγός, -έω, ὁδός; also on 132. 4.

[3] Bousset, *Hauptprobleme* pp. 294-5—Clem. *Hom.* 9. 19: ἀεννάῳ ποταμῷ ἢ πηγῇ ... ἀπολουσάμενοι ἐπὶ τῇ τρισμακαρίᾳ ἐπονομασίᾳ οὐ μόνον τὰ ἐνδομυχοῦντα ὑμῖν πνεύματα ἀπελάσαι δυνήσεσθε, ἀλλ' αὐτοὶ .. τὰ ἄλλων κακὰ πνεύματα καὶ δαιμόνια χαλεπὰ σὺν τοῖς δεινοῖς πάθεσιν ἀπελάσετε. Other references in Bousset. See also Reitzenstein, *Hist. Monachorum*, pp. 108 *sqq.*, Bräuninger, *H. T.*, pp. 18-19.

[4] Traces of this debate may be found in Philo, *de plantat.* 7-10 (ii. 134 Wendland), and Cleomedes, *de mot. circ.* i. 1. The dilemma is posed by Philo in the words ἀνάγκη τοίνυν ἐκτὸς ἢ κενὸν ἢ μηδὲν εἶναι. See in general Brébier, *Philon*, pp. 85-6. Cleomedes of course adopts the orthodox Stoic view that there is a void.

[5] Cleom., p. 4. 11 Ziegler: πᾶν σῶμα ἔν τινι εἶναι ἀναγκαῖον.

[6] Philo *op. cit.* 7.

Stoic definition of the Cosmos [1] and excludes void from the Cosmos. It follows that the container must be much greater than the contained and cannot be body. The argument about the size of Space depends (l. 15) upon the commonplace experiments about displacement of bodies in a vessel. [2] Space, then, is a receptacle. [3] For Cleomedes, as for the Hermetist, it is incorporeal. [4] So far, these statements apply equally to the Stoic Void; it is necessary to note that their substance reappears in the definition in § 12. The writer identifies the Container with the Mover.

§ 6b–8a. The thesis to be established is that the Mover-Container is stationary. This is plain from the statement in ll. 8–10 and the formal conclusion in 138. 4. The argument is physical and in the tradition; it is intended, however, to apply to the doctrine of Θεὸς Ἑστώς (140. 19). The writer assumes that the Cosmos, in virtue of its circular motion, does not change place. Topos is ἀκίνητος, and cannot be moved *with* what it moves.

Objection: the sphere of the fixed stars moves with the planets. [5] No, for the stars have (continuous) opposite (circular) motions, and these motions cancel out. That is, they have no local motion (so that the Cosmos remains in and is moved by a stationary Topos). [6] Such are the implications of the argument. If we take the argument and the illustration together, the historical background will be clear.

To illustrate from *Exc.* VI. 13 (412. 15 = 416. 6) : (τῆς ἄρκτου) ἡ ἐνέργειά ἐστιν καθάπερ ἄξονος, μηδαμοῦ μὲν δυνούσης μηδὲ ἀνατελλούσης, μενούσης δὲ ἐν τῷ αὐτῷ τόπῳ, τῆς περὶ ⟨τὸ⟩ αὐτὸ στρεφομένης, ἐνεργούσης δὲ

---

[1] Cleom., p. 2. 10 : οὗτος δὲ πάντα μὲν τὰ σώματα ἐμπεριέχει, οὐδενὸς ἁπλῶς ἐκτὸς αὐτοῦ ὑπάρχοντος.

[2] Cleom., p. 4. 17 *sqq.* Cleomedes uses the argument from the need of expansion and contraction (4. 15, 8. 1). See on 138. 19 below.

[3] L. 14. Cf. Cleom. 4. 13 : τὴν οὖν τοιαύτην ὑπόστασιν, οἵαν τε οὖσαν δέχεσθαι σῶμα καὶ κατέχεσθαι, κενὸν εἶναί φαμεν. Cf. 8. 7–10.

[4] ἀσώματον ὂν καὶ οἷον ἀναφές (4. 13). This depends upon the ambiguity of the term ἀσώματον, which is formed κατὰ ψιλὴν τὴν πρὸς τὰ σώματα στέρησιν (Porph. *Sententiae* xix.)

[5] In l. 15 it may be suspected that ἀντέρεισιν has a technical sense. Philo asks what is the base on which the Cosmos is supported (ἐρήρεισται, ἐπερείδοντος), and the answer is that the λόγος is its ἔρεισμα. Cleomedes uses ὑπερείδειν, and his answer is the ἕξις of the Cosmos itself. Here it is said that the contrariety (sc. of the two circular motions) keeps the basis of the motion stationary.

[6] Simplicius (*in phys.* 609) argues that anything contained by another is not moved in space or locally, unless it changes from place to place. So that, according to Aristotle, even the planets are not in space, although they are contained by one another and by the fixed sphere, because they do not change place. In other words, linear motion involves change of position, but circular motion not so. Thus the heavenly bodies and the μερικὰ ζῷα must have their motions distinguished. (But see also *ib.* 592. 1, 593. 6 *sqq.*) So the Hermetist's illustration is taken from the latter (l. 26). See in general Ar. *Phys.* 4. 4.

τὴν ⟨τοῦ⟩ ζωοφόρου κυκλοῦ ⟨περιφοράν⟩. The spaced phrase gives the answer to Hermes' question: circular motion is in the same Place, and the going round cancels the going beyond. You see the Bears circling; that is circular motion, and circular motion is kept in place by immobility. The singularity of this argument lies in the stress laid upon *opposite* circular motions. It may be suspected that there is a reference to the Great Year, and to the circles of the Same (undivided) and the Other in *Tim.* 36 C, 39 A–D. In the *Excerpt* it is the Bear that moves the heavens round, and a passage in Aetius associates this activity with the return of the Great Year: οἱ δ' ἐν τῇ λεγομένη κεφαλῇ τοῦ κόσμου[1] (τὸν μέγαν ἐνιαυτὸν τίθενται), αὐτὴ δ' ἐστὶ τῶν ἑπτὰ πλανητῶν ἐπὶ ταὐτὰ σημεῖα[2] τῆς ἐξ ἄρκτου φορᾶς ἐπάνοδος.[3] The perfect or great Year occurs ' when the planets come to the place from which they started': then the separate motions in the Cosmos have cancelled out in the κυκλοφορία. See on 364. 14.

This stress on oppositeness has a history from Heraclitus through the Stoics to Philo, who makes play with the notion in his doctrine of λόγος τομεύς.[4]

The illustration (l. 25) is sufficient evidence of the bearing of this argument. The swimmer[5] holds his ground against the stream—two equal and opposite linear movements[6] make a στάσις within a fixed receptacle or container: that is, in Aristotelian language, ὁ πᾶς ποταμός. But the illustration, *mutatis mutandis*, is applicable to the whole heavens: τὸ μὲν πᾶν ἤτοι τὸν ὅλον οὐρανὸν κύκλῳ μὲν κινεῖσθαι, μὴ κατὰ τόπον δέ, ὅτι μὴ μεταβάλλει τόπον ἐκ τόπου.[7] The Cosmos is moved in (and, for the Hermetist, by) a stationary Container.

§§ 8 b–9. This is an argument from analogy about the nature of the mover ' by which '. It presupposes the Platonic theory that the source of motion is what is self-moved, and that what is moved from without is inanimate.[8] In its present form the analogy proceeds from the individual to the Cosmos, as later believers in Pronoia constantly did.[9] Whatever

---

[1] Kroll: Κρόνου codd.

[2] Kroll: ταὐτῇ ἡμέρᾳ codd.

[3] See Boll, *Sphaera*, p. 163, n. 5, and (in the light of that note) Kroll in Proclus *In remp.*, ii. p. 387.

[4] *Quis rer. div. heres*, 208; *de plantat.*, 10, 12. For traces in *Hermetica* see notes on 304. 16, 158. 24, and 192. 28, and references there. The subject cannot be pursued here.

[5] οἷον τὸν ἄνθρωπον λέγω—the article signifies a familiar example (cf. 138. 21). Ar. *Phys.* iv. 4; Simplic. *op. cit.* 583. 31 *sqq.* and *passim*.

[6] ἀντιμετάστασις σωμάτων. Compare the opposite motions of planets and stars.

[7] Simplic. *op. cit.* 591. 6.

[8] *Phaedrus* 245 c–e. As the tradition, rather than the source, interests us, Cicero's translation may be quoted (*Tusc.* i. 54): inanimum est enim omne, quod pulsu agitatur externo; quod autem est animal, id motu cietur interiore et suo.

[9] Philo *de provid.* i. 40: etenim si nec providentia est nec universalis motor, nihil omnino in mundo moveri poterit. quis enim dicere potest, totius mundi

is moved is moved from within, not externally, whether the mover be soul or *pneuma*.[1] The next sentence should mean: it isn't *body* that moves a body that has a soul [2]—no, nor ever body at all, even though there is no soul within to move it. (Is this a paradox), since bodies are what move stones and logs? Not at all, the incorporeal within bears the double weight, its own body and the burden—you can see the soul oppressed by it. This childishly expressed argument becomes more intelligible if we recall Philo's analogical arguments for Providence—the arrow or spear that finds its mark.[3] The writer means that Topos is an ἀρχὴ κινήσεως for the Cosmos, and a soul (*Tim.* 34 C). Hence probably the phrase in § 12 τὸ ἀρχέτυπον τῆς ψυχῆς. The first part of the tract is formally concluded in ll. 17–18, where the text should be retained. It simply repeats the thesis of 134. 2, now regarded as proved.

§§ 10–11. The void denied here is within the Cosmos, and the question is suggested by the previous discussion of motion. As the phrase τῷ τῆς ὑπάρξεως λόγῳ indicates, the writer uses a traditional argument.[4] A vessel contains, not a void, but an ὕπαρξις: if not water, then air, and so on.[5] In short: τὸ ὑπάρχον is incompatible with τὸ κενόν (l. 24). § 11 depends on the Stoic view that each element, as we know it, is a σύγκριμα.[5] If there were not continuity within the Cosmos, συμπάθεια would be impossible. See on 316. 31. But equally there is, on the Hermetist's view, no Void without—there is no *body* without, but there is the incorporeal Topos.

---

compositio inanimata quum sit, animatos motus fieri posse in natura perfectae creaturae? quod si non constat, argumenti loco sit civis huius mundi homo ipse, qui tamquam parvus mundus in magno mundo factus est, quum sine anima nequeat corpus actiones suas perficere, nisi prius consilio eius optimo velut amici cuiusdam utatur. . . . . 41 . . quod si animalium brutorum et animalium rationalium actionis vim esse novimus factum, dicamus in omnibus mundi partibus animam quandam ac voluntatem (id est providentiam) operari, nec sine anima motum haberi.

[1] This *pneuma* is not considered to be corporeal.

[2] Corpus reading; otherwise perhaps read ἐμψύχου. The sentence in ll. 15–16 is an inference from what precedes, and is confirmed by the example that follows. Perhaps ἐπικινεῖ for ἐπεὶ κινεῖ, though the active voice does not occur elsewhere.

[3] Sticks and stones are examples of bodies held together by ψιλὴ ἕξις as opposed to those unified by ψυχή (ἡνωμένα); Sext. Emp. *adv. math.* ix. 81.

[4] Cleom. 4. 15; compare the phraseology of 136. 26–137. 1. Retain the order of the text.

[5] The text in 140. 1 has fallen into confusion. The evidence from *Corp.* and Stob. MSS. is that the original gave a triad of substantives, and it is a fair inference from *Corp.* that κενός was repeated with each, if we consider ποταμὸς ὅλος to be, not a corruption, but an intrusion that replaced, say, ληνὸς κενός; the intrusion was facilitated by homoeoteleuton with κέραμος. Is it possible that some one wrote the phrase because he was thinking of the other ἀγγεῖον argument about ὁ πᾶς ποταμός (138. 1)?

[6] L 14: retain the bracketed words and read ὑπάρξει.

§ 12.   If we collect the results of the physical arguments above, Topos is incorporeal, it contains the Cosmos, it is stationary while it is a source of movement.[1] These elements are embodied in the definition here, though we now learn that it is Νοῦς proceeding from Νοῦς.[2]

The transition from a physical conception of surrounding Space to the religious one of an encompassing Deity is not great. In Philo, *Quaest. in Exod.*, *Fragm.*, p. 73 (Harris) the λόγος encloses and fills all like Topos, which surrounds bodies and is their refuge. *Leg. Alleg.*, I. 44 θεοῦ γὰρ οὐδὲ ὁ σύμπας κόσμος ἄξιον ἂν εἴη χωρίον καὶ ἐνδιαίτημα, ἐπεὶ αὐτὸς ἑαυτοῦ τόπος καὶ αὐτὸς ἑαυτοῦ πλήρης καὶ ἱκανὸς αὐτὸς ἑαυτῷ ὁ θεός, τὰ μὲν ἄλλα ἐπιδεᾶ καὶ ἔρημα καὶ κενὰ ὄντα πληρῶν καὶ περιέχων, αὐτὸς δὲ ὑπ᾽ οὐδενὸς ἄλλου περιεχόμενος, ἅτε εἷς καὶ τὸ πᾶν αὐτὸς ὤν.[3]

The setting of the argument, it has been seen, is Greek tradition, and there are Greek elements in this definition.   But it must be recognized that the distinction between God and Topos, and the nature of the language about light (though affected by Platonic tradition), is not Greek. In the space available it is perhaps simplest to print a passage of Simplicius (*in phys.* 641. 31) that illustrates the fusion of ideas. I do not think it has been quoted in the endless discussion on Greek and Oriental influences: καὶ γὰρ αἱ νοηταὶ τάξεις ὡς τόπους διαφόρους ἐκληρώσαντο τὰς τοῦ νοητοῦ κόσμου διαφόρους ὑποδοχάς. λέγει γοῦν Ὀρφεὺς περὶ ἐκείνου τοῦ τὰς τῶν λήξεων διαφορὰς ἔχοντος

τοῖον ἑλὼν διένειμε θεοῖς θνητοῖσί τε κόσμον,

καὶ ἡ περιοχὴ δὲ τόπος ἐκεῖ λέγεται πολλάκις. διὸ καὶ τὴν Συρίαν Ἀταργάτην τόπον θεῶν καλοῦσιν καὶ τὴν Ἶσιν οἱ Αἰγύπτιοι,[4] ὡς πολλῶν θεῶν ἰδιότητας περιεχούσας. κατὰ δὲ τὴν ἑκάστου πρὸς τὰ ἄλλα τῆς θέσεως τάξιν ὁ Πλάτων ὑπερουράνιον καὶ νοητὸν τόπον ἐκεῖνόν φησιν κ.τ.λ. See also the discussion of Hesiod's Chaos as χώρα, τόπος as πρωτουργός τις καὶ ἀρχηγικὴ φύσις, *ibid.*, 527. 12 *sqq.*

In 140. 18 *sqq.* perhaps read νοῦς ὅλος ἐξ ὅλου, ἑαυτὸν ἐμπεριέχων, ἐλευθερὸς σώματος παντός, | ἀπλανής, ἀπαθής, ἀναφής, | αὐτὸς ἐν ἑαυτῷ ἑστώς, χωρητικὸς τῶν πάντων, καὶ σωτηρίος τῶν ὄντων, | οὗ ὥσπερ ἀκτίνες τὸ ἀγαθόν, ⟨καὶ⟩

---

[1] Cf. 136. 7, a passage not yet dealt with.

[2] Textual.   Retain σώματος παντός: this incorporeal, unlike those connected with body, is χωριστὸν τέλεον σώματος (Porph. *Sent.* xlii, cf. xix; cf. *Ascl. Lat.* 346. 26, quoted below). ἀπλάνης is needed to complete the rhetorical triad. In ll. 20–4 I take the tradition as a basis of discussion. In l. 18 the Corpus reading νοῦς, λόγος should be noted: cf. 116. 9.

[3] Cf. vol. ii, p. 90. For language 346. 24, where, however, the reference is to *deus exsuperantissimus.* ὁ περιέχων, 218. 33.   One may also compare Strabo's account of the Jewish God (Bk. 16, 35) and Reinhardt, *Poseidonios über Ursprung und Entartung*, pp. 6 *sqq.* Arnobius *adv. nat.* I. 31: prima enim tu causa es, locus rerum ac spatium.

[4] This passage is not included in Hopfner's *Fontes hist. relig. Aegypt.* We may perhaps compare the description of Isis as φύσις Αἰῶνος (Athenagoras). The position of Topos should be compared with that of Aion in *Corp.* XI and 348. 8 *sqq.* (see notes).

ἡ ἀλήθεια, | τὸ ἀρχέτυπον φῶς, τὸ ἀρχέτυπον πνεύματος, τὸ ἀρχέτυπον ψυχῆς. This light is not corporeal;[1] compare the language of 116. 7, and *Fr.* 23 φῶς νοερὸν ... τῷ ἑαυτοῦ νοὶ καὶ φωτὶ καὶ πνεύματι πάντα περιέχει.[2] For soul see on 190. 22, 208. 19. *Pneuma* is also here a higher element, as in the fragment. It is possible that the variation as between the Corpus and the Stobaeus codices indicates a triadic ending. Cf. 142. 8-10, 284. 2, and *fr.* 23 above. Perhaps we should read πνεῦμα[τος]; contrast 142. 9-10.

To return to the corrupt passage 4 b-6 a (134. 20): an ἀνουσίαστος θεός[3] is contrasted with the containing Topos. This God is *summus exsuperantissimus* (see on 374.1). But the account of God in 142. 8-10, which denies that he is mind, or light, or *pneuma*, is different in content from other Hermetic documents.

144. 5-9. Retain the text, with comma after θεοῦ. In l. 7 ὁ ἀγαθός is defined: then God is given the same attributes; and then the two are identified. See on 164.4.

Libellus III. **144.** 23 *sqq.* Reitzenstein (*G.G.A.*, 1911, p. 558) regards the 'title' and § 1ᵃ as an introduction in 'lapidary' style to the account of

---

[1] *Acta Thomae*, 34: εὖρον δὲ ἐκεῖνον οὗ τὰ ἔργα φῶς ἐστιν καὶ αἱ πράξεις ἀλήθεια. See Bousset, *Kyrios*, pp. 208 *sqq.*, *G. G. A.*, 1914, p. 718, also Wetter, ΦΩΣ, *passim.* For ἀκτῖνες see 202 .15, 158. 10, Numenius (in vol. ii, 78), Proclus *in Crat.* 101. 21 Pasquali, and *Oracula Chaldaica, passim.* The Platonic Good has at most a remote relation to our passage. This Topos is not the highest Good; it is the deity who vivifies and sustains the individual souls in the Cosmos. See on 348. 8, 438. 17, and compare the Chaldaic oracles *passim.* It might perhaps be noted that in Proclus' account, which bears traces of the influence of the Chaldaic oracles, Topos is the most refined of bodies, σῶμα ἀκίνητον, ἀδιαίρετον, ἄυλον, ἄπαθες, Light homocentric with the Cosmos and enveloping it; the Cosmos itself is moved in Topos, though as a whole it is unmoved. He makes play with the words τόπος-τύπος, and quotes the λόγια about the πηγαία ψυχή (Simplic. *in phys.* 611 *sqq.*, Diels).

[2] This I suspect to be an oracle in verse; see note *ad loc.*

[3] Hippolytus *Refut.* vi. 42, ὁ πατήρ ... ὁ ἀνεννόητος καὶ ἀνούσιος (of Marcus the Gnostic); and *Pistis Sophia*, pp. 358. 29, 362. 30, &c. We must retain νοητὸς πρῶτος (134. 23), since *Fr.* 16 and iv. 32. 18 guarantee it. And should we connect ὁ προεγνωσμένος θεός with the phrase (*Fr.* 30; cf. *Fr.* 12, 17, 36)? Then perhaps continue (136. 1) ἔστιν ἡμῖν, οὐχ ἑαυτῷ· τὸ γὰρ νοητὸν τῷ νοοῦντι αἰσθήσει (?) ὑποπίπτει. ὁ θεὸς [οὐκ]* οὖν οὐχ ἑαυτῷ νοητός—οὐ γὰρ ἄλλο τι ὢν τοῦ νοουμένου, ὑφ' ἑαυτοῦ (οὐ)* νοεῖται—ἡμῖν δέ. (εἰ δὲ) ἄλλο τί ἐστι, διὰ τοῦτο ἡμῖν νοεῖται. εἰ δὲ νοητὸς ὁ τόπος οὐχ (ὡς) ὁ θεός, ἄλλ(ο τι) ὁ τόπος· εἰ δὲ καὶ (νοητὸς) ὁ θεὸς οὐχ ὡς (ὁ) τύπος, ἀλλ(ο τι ὁ τύπος) ὡς ἐνέργεια χωρητική. That is, *Topos* is known to us as the container that moves—the ἐνέργεια it possesses from God. Cf. 140. 20. In l. 2 αἰσθήσει may possibly be right; γνῶσις is a θέα; cf. 180. 26 αἰσθόμενος τῆς γνώσεως (codd.).

---

* Zielinski.

Creation. The six ἀρχαί (ll. 25–6) [1] are, on this view, transmuted from some Oriental system of gods, after the manner of the Gnostics. But may not the 'lapidary style' of § 1 a simply indicate a muddled summary of contents? In l. 23 δόξα is 'glory' (Philo, N. T., Gnostics); l. 26 σοφίας εἰς δεῖξιν gains support from § 3 b; ἀρχή here should mean *principatus* (so Zielinski), as 148. 4 goes to show. The note is changed to τὸ θεῖον (l. 27) with the last paragraph, from which four other terms in ll. 27–8 have been extracted in a fit of pantheistic confusion. The 'title' I take to be a briefer summary.[2]

148. 2. μοίρας ὀχλουμένης. ἀχλυομένας A.D.N. ἀμοιβὰς κυκλουμένας γνῶναι ἀγαθῶν καὶ φαύλων? Diodor. 18. 59. 6 ὁ γὰρ κοινὸς βίος ὥσπερ ὑπὸ θεῶν τινος οἰακιζόμενος ἐναλλὰξ ἀγαθοῖς τε καὶ κακοῖς κυκλεῖται πάντα τὸν αἰῶνα.

4. ἄρχεται αὐτῶν. ἀρχὴ καὶ ⟨τέλος⟩ (144. 28) αὐτῶν βιῶσαί τε καὶ σοφισθῆναι, to begin life, to achieve wisdom and to die; and then ἀνανέωσις: "ἀνάγκη καὶ ἀνανεώσει φύσεως καὶ θεῶν ἐγκυκλίων . . . δρομήματι." See vol. iv, Introduction V.

Libellus IV. **148.** 17. οὐ χερσίν. Polemic against such passages as 466. 19, 474. 35 (Zielinski).

24 *sqq.* Perhaps: ἀλλὰ πάντα [τὰ] ὑπ' αὐτοῦ·[3] ἀγαθὸς γὰρ ὤν, ⟨οὐ⟩[4] μόνῳ ἑαυτῷ τοῦτο ἀναθεῖναι ἠθέλησε, ⟨ἀλλὰ⟩ καὶ τὴν γῆν κοσμῆσαι.[5] The meaning I take to be that God, being good, gives and does not keep to himself (144. 7–8, 164. 6). Cf. *Constitut. apostolicae*, 8. 12: καὶ οὐ μόνον τὸν κόσμον ἐδημιούργησας, ἀλλὰ καὶ τὸν κοσμοπολίτην ἄνθρωπον ἐν αὐτῷ ἐποίησας, κόσμου κόσμον ἀναδείξας. (Stoic source).[6] The remainder may be interpreted thus: he sent down man as the ornament of the divine body, a mortal creature to adorn an immortal. And the cosmos of the creatures (microcosms) had the better of the Creature[7] and the Cosmos because he had λόγος and νοῦς. Thus man became the spectator of God's works, and wondered, and came to know the Maker—'is qui solus est omnia omnibus se libenter ostendit' (370. 6). The order is seeing,

---

[1] He reads ἀρχαὶ τὸ θεῖον. I add R.'s other readings: l. 23 ⟨πᾶν⟩ θεῖον. φῶς: [ὕλη]. l. 24 stop after ὤν. 146. 4 ὕφαμμα. l. 5 καταδ⟨ύντες⟩ ἐρῶσι. l. 24 ἐσπερμοβόλουν. l. 29 τερατουργίας ⟨ἔκτισαν⟩. ll. 24–7 εἰς ἔργων . . . πλήθει an interpolation from *Corp.* I, as may happen in sacred texts. l. 25 ἐνεργείας: cf. 148. 1.

[2] For another fusion of a note with the text see 390. 1–5, which is apparently an anthologist's comment.

[3] The soul is ἀπ' αὐτοῦ, the Cosmos ὑπ' αὐτοῦ (Plut. *Plat. quaest.* 1001 c).

[4] Zielinski, who reads ἀναθεῖναι τοῦτο ἠθέλησε [ ] κόσμον δέ . . .

[5] ἀναθεῖναι is difficult. Is the play on κόσμος already there?—he did not wish to keep this Body as a delight to himself.

[6] This play on the word is commonplace; see on 304. 11, also 182. 30.

[7] It is tempting to take the divine Creature as ἡ ἱερὰ γῆ, as l. 6 suggests. But the contrast can hardly be other than the usual antithesis between microcosm and macrocosm, and the καί (l. 9) is a stylistic flourish. For adorning the earth, see 300. 20, 302. 1–6 (notes).

wondering, knowing God.[1]　The following passage restricts the gift of
νοῦς to the chosen.[2]　It is questionable if λόγος means *speech* either here
or in the parallel passage 230. 7, where they are ἰσότιμα τῇ ἀθανασίᾳ and
where God is their father (l. 24).[3]　For in 152. 2 the contrast is explicitly
between αὐτοὶ μὲν οἱ λογικοί (AQS), who do not know their nature or maker,
and those who receive mind, after due performance of a ritual.　An explanation may be sought in those Hermetic passages which make λόγος one
of a series of 'wrappings'.[4]　It distinguishes man from the Cosmos
(150. 9) and from the brutes (ἄλογοι; see 230. 7, and perhaps 200. 15 *sqq*).
Λόγος plays a disconcerting number of parts in the Hermetic documents.
Here the full series νοῦς, λόγος, ψυχή, πνεῦμα is not paraded, and there is
an explicit contrast of the two first.　It is natural to compare the opposition πνευματικοί) (ψυχικοί, as Bräuninger suggests, and to suppose that the
man who receives νοῦς is filled with πνεῦμα, whereas the λογικός (ψυχικός)
here plays his human part, but never becomes ὅλη νοῦς.　It may be, as
Professor Jaeger suggests, that the series νοῦς, λόγος, σῶμα answers to the
more usual distinction νοῦς, ψυχή, σῶμα.[5]

150. 26. γνωρίζουσα ἐπὶ τί γέγονας.　The condition is put last.　Cf. 152. 3.
Cf. (with Norden) Clem. *exc. ex. Theodoto*, 78: ἔστιν δὲ οὐ τὸ λουτρὸν μόνον
τὸ ἐλευθεροῦν, ἀλλὰ καὶ ἡ γνῶσις, τίνες ἦμεν, τί γεγόναμεν· ποῦ ἦμεν ἢ ποῦ
ἐνεβλήθημεν· ποῖ σπεύδομεν, πόθεν λυτρούμεθα· τί γέννησις, τί ἀναγέννησις
(Valentinian Gnostics).　*Acta Thomae*, c. 15.　Epict. 1. 6. 25: οὐκ
αἰσθήσεσθε τοίνυν, οὔτε τίνες ἐστέ οὔτε ἐπὶ τί γεγόνατε οὔτε τί τοῦτο ἔστιν, ἐφ'
οὗ τὴν θέαν (*sc.* τῆς φύσεως) παρελήφθη.　See *Agn. Theos*, pp. 99–109.　See
also on 178. 2, 390. 7.

28. τέλειοι Hippol. *Refut.* 5. 8. 29: οὐδεὶς οὕτων τῶν μυστηρίων
ἀκροατὴς γέγονεν εἰ μὴ μόνοι ⟨οἱ⟩ γνωστικοὶ τέλειοι.　*ib.* 5. 16. 10: τὸ ἐξεικο-
νισμένον τέλειον γένος ὁμοούσιον.　Common among the Orphics and
Gnostics for the initiated; see Bousset, *Kyrios*, p. 239; *H.M.R.*,
p. 338 *sq*.　See also on 132. 8 for κῆρυξ and κρατήρ, and on Arnobius,
note on iv. 7. 8.

152. 4 αἰσθήσεις.[6]　ὅταν γὰρ τὸ κρεῖττον ὁ νοῦς ἐνωθῇ τῷ χείρονι τῇ αἰσθήσει,
ἀναλύεται εἰς τὸ χεῖρον τὸ σαρκὸς γένος, τὴν παθῶν αἰτίαν αἴσθησιν . . . οὗτος μὲν
δὴ τοιοῦτος, τὸ φιλοπαθὲς προκρίνων τοῦ φιλοθέου (Philo, *Leg. Alleg.* ii. 50).
ἔχουσι γὰρ (οἱ σοφοὶ) κεκαθαρμένην ὅρασιν καὶ ἐξητασμένην ἀκοὴν καὶ πᾶσαν

----

[1] Cf. 256. 26, 310. 10, *Fr.* 15, also 390. 9; contrast 152. 6.

[2] Cf. 128. 7, 180. 32.　For φθόνος see note on 166. 4.

[3] See notes *ad loc.*, and Bräuninger, *H. T.*, p. 15.

[4] See 194. 27–9 (note).

[5] See Bräuninger, *H. T.*, pp. 16–17, Reitzenstein, *H. M. R.*, p. 51, and the
lexicographical analysis of ψυχή, λόγος, νοῦς, πνεῦμα in the latter work.

[6] In l. 6 delete the second οὐ; this is in explicit contrast to 150. 11, 152. 10.
Probably θαυμάζουσι should be the main verb.　For parallels with this θέα see
notes on 156. 15. 158. 19 *sqq.*, and Norden, *op. cit.*, p. 106. l. 5 is justified because
the πάθη depend on κρᾶσις.

αἴσθησιν (*id.*, *Quod det. potiori insid. soleat*, 171). See on 126. 18 and 172. 13. Such men do not see what they should see, and do not wonder at the sight of God's works; they make the end of man pleasure, not knowing for what end they were made (cf. 150. 26, 152. 3). But the good 'see' all,[1] hasten to the One, and despise the things of earth. In l. 14 the final words should be kept to express the rapture of flight—the ἐν καὶ μόνον cannot be classified. ἐν καὶ μόνον is liturgical; cf. Peterson, ΕΙΣ ΘΕΟΣ, p. 253.

In ll. 16-18 the text should be retained; perhaps ⟨ἡ⟩ . . . ἔννοια (114. 2, 380. 14) or θεωρία for ἐντορία. The vision of the One is the end of the flight (156. 15).

31. ἀποθεῶσαι. The climax is man's relation to God, not the happy consequences of the rite to the man. Retain the text, taking the clause as explanatory. See note on 128. 23, and 190. 19.

154. 2. ὅτι καθάπερ αἱ πομπαὶ μέσον παρέρχονται. A.D N. (*J. Egypt. Archaeology*, 1925, p. 130) suggests that πομπαί means the images borne in a procession. See his references and *Fr.* 19.

10. The account of this ascent is based on the 'two-soul' theory: the soul changes its 'body' at each stage, and pursues its way against opposing powers, whose influence is counteracted by the rite. Apuleius, *Met.*, xi. 24: mane factum est, et perfectis sollemnibus processi duodecim sacratus stolis; and (also from Reitzenstein) a late Manichaean text: 'le second jour c'est la semence pure de l'Homme nouveau. Les douze heures, ce sont les douze rois lumineux des transformations successives (*ou* de transformation secondaire), ce sont aussi les merveilleux vêtements de la forme victorieuse de Yichon (Jésus) qu'il donne à la nature lumineuse: au moyen de ces vêtements merveilleux il pare la nature intérieure et fait que rien ne lui manque; la tirant en haut, il la fait monter et avancer et se séparer pour toujours de la terre souillée.'[2] See note on iv. 7. 8. below, and on 132. 8.

21. δυσπιστεῖν. νόησις and πίστις go together, 150. 24-6, 184. 26, 370. 15 note.

24-7. Cf. *Frr.* 25, 30, and note on 210. 1.

30. ἀρχὴ δέ. Retain the text. It has been said that the Monad as a source, is in all as source—that is the kind of source it is. This is supported by the definition of ἀρχή. Compare the traditional definition:[3] 'principii autem nulla est origo; nam e principio oriuntur omnia, ipsum autem nulla ex re alia nasci potest, nec enim esset id principium quod gigneretur aliunde'. This covers l. 30-156. 1. Then perhaps ἀρχὴ γάρ

---

[1] l. 9 ἔργων cf. 150. 10, Ar. *de mundo*, 399 b 21 . . ἀθεώρητος ἀπ' αὐτῶν τῶν ἔργων θεωρεῖται. This is not merely Stoic piety; the initiate *becomes* the All (ll. 10-12; cf. 246. 17).

[2] *Journal Asiatique*, N.S., x. 18; *H. M. R.*, pp. 226 *sqq*; Bousset, *G. G. A.*, 733; Reitzenstein, *Archiv* iv (for Apuleius); Bräuninger, *H. T.*, pp. 19 *sqq*.

[3] Plato, *ap.* Cic. *Tusc.* i. 54; cf. Macrobius, *in Somn. Scip.* 1. 6. 7.

ἐστιν ... ἔτυχεν· μονὰς οὖν οὖσα ἀρχή,[1] πάντα κ.τ.λ.—since the Monad complies with the definition of ἀρχή... It is, in the strict sense, ἀρχὴ πόσου. Cf. ὡς δυνάμει πάντας περιέχουσαν τοὺς ἐν ἀριθμῷ λόγους (Iamblichus, *in Nicom. arithm.* 11. 16 Pistelli).

156. 14. εἰκών. The Cosmos (150. 9); the vision leads to God.

15. θέα of God is the end, and the characteristic word must be kept (132. 7, 190. 18, *Fr. 25*). For the magnet cf. Hippol. *Refut.* 5. 17. 9 and 21. 8-9.

Libellus V. **156.** 19 *sqq.* The general theme—God manifest in his works—is Posidonian. Cf. *de mundo*, 399 b 14; Cic. *Tusc.* i. 68, Firmicus Maternus, *Math.* v. *Praef.* 3; and in general Norden, *Agn. Theos*, pp. 24-9.

20. ὀνόματος. Cf. p. 415 below and *Fr.* 3. See Norden, *Agn. Theos*, p. 157, n. 1.

158. 9. This is a distinction between the supreme God (τὸ ἕν) and ὁ εἷς. See on 344. 14 and *Frr.* 28-30. Peterson, ΕΙΣ ΘΕΟΣ, p. 253.

19-21. A traditional argument: Cic. *Tusc.* 1. 70, Ar. *de mundo*, 399 b 14. It is said (l. 12) that *noesis* alone sees the hidden —i.e. light knows light, its kin. (Pray for the power), and if you gain the power (εἰ δύνασαι) God will become manifest to the eyes of your mind. For the Lord is ungrudging, he is manifest through all the Cosmos. The simplest remedy is to read νόησον, ἰδεῖν [2] κ.τ.λ.; then the writer merely says that man can see and touch God if he thinks. But an alternative may be mentioned. Read ⟨μὴ τί που τὴν σαυτοῦ⟩ νόησιν ἰδεῖν; κ.τ.λ. Can you see your own thought and touch it with your very hands and set eyes on God's image?[3] If even that which is within you is hidden from you, how will God in you be manifest to you through your fleshly eyes? But God *is* visible to the mind's eye[4] through the *order* of the heavens and the beauty of the body. (The Cosmos—one image of God—*is* visible to the bodily eye; what is visible only to the mind's eye is man's mind (*the* image of God) and order and beauty).

24. τάξις. This argument depends upon the conception of ἰσότης.[5] In

---

[1] οὖσα μονὰς οὖν Corp. μονὰς οὖσα οὖν Stob. Possibly οὖσα fell out by similarity with οὖν and was written above.   [2] Reitzenstein.

[3] Man is the image of God; cf. 160. 24 (retaining τοῦ ἀνθρώπου). Philo, *de opif. mundi*, 69: ὃν γὰρ ἔχει λόγον ὁ μέγας ἡγεμὼν ἐν ἅπαντι τῷ κόσμῳ, τοῦτον ὡς ἔοικε καὶ ὁ ἀνθρώπινος νοῦς ἐν ἀνθρώπῳ· ἀόρατός τε γάρ ἐστι, αὐτὸς τὰ πάντα ὁρῶν καὶ ἄδηλον ἔχει τὴν οὐσίαν ... (continuation resembles § 5). The theme is the text κατ εἰκόνα θεοῦ καὶ καθ' ὁμοίωσιν. The whole chapter (6) of *de mundo* should be compared with our tract. Note also the close resemblance that chapter bears to 504. 18, 509. 34 (see notes below). See further Norden, *Agn. Theos*, pp. 25 *sqq*

[4] See Gregory of Nyssa, *de anima et resurr.* 25 B-27 C Migne, esp. ὁ ταῦτα βλέπων τῷ διανοητικῷ τῆς ψυχῆς ὀφθαλμῷ.

[5] On ἰσότης see Bréhier, *Philon*, pp. 86 *sqq.*; Bousset, *Schulbetrieb*, pp. 23

Philo's account of 'equality' within the Cosmos (*quis rer. div. heres*, 141 *sqq.*) : λέγεται γὰρ ἴσον καθ' ἕνα μὲν τρόπον ἐν ἀριθμοῖς ... καθ' ἕτερον δὲ ἐν μεγέθεσιν, ὧν μήκη, πλάτη, βάθη διαστάσεις εἰσίν (§ 144 ; cf. ll. 24-5). On this view the sun, the greatest luminary, is in the midst of the planets (222-4). But there is also ἰσότης δι' ἀναλογίας (§ 145). Now in *de Cher.* 22 Philo says that three of the planets are equal in speed ; the others are ἀνισόδρομοι but have an ἀναλογία with the others and between themselves. One of the Cherubim is the sphere of the fixed stars, which do not leave their τάξις, the other is the inner sphere, ἣν ἐξαχῆ σχίσας ἑπτὰ κύκλους ἀναλογοῦντας ἑαυτοῖς εἰργάζετο τῶν πλανητῶν ἕκαστον εἰς αὐτοὺς ἁρμοσάμενος (ὁ γεννήσας πατήρ). We can therefore retain the reading of ll. 30-3. For the argument in general see Cic. *de nat. deor.* ii. 15, 16, 90, Philo, *de provid.* ii. 40 ; also Apuleius, *de deo Socr.* 2. It depends upon the constancy of order amid diversity of motion or kind. See on 328-30. For the diatribe style compare Ps.-Clement, *Recognitiones*, 8. 22, and Lactantius below. The sequence of the (Posidonian) argument is the same: first *inconfusa varietas*[1] in the heavens (c. 22), later (cc. 28-32) the art displayed in the bodily structure of man.

160. 2. ὄργανον. The Cosmos ; cf. 272. 6 : 342. 17. This is an integral part of the doctrine that the Cosmos is an ἁρμονία. Censorinus, *de die nat.* 13. 6 : praeterea multa quae musici tractant ad alias rettulit (Pythagoras) stelias et hunc omnem mundum enarmonion esse ostendit. quare Dorylaus scripsit esse mundum organon dei. Chalcidius, *in Tim.* 299 : eamque silvam et necessitatem cognominat (Numenius), ex qua et deo mundi machinam constitisse. Also Ps.-Clem. *Recogn.* 8. 21 : quod si vere hanc habeat similitudinem (*sc.* sphaerae) mundi machina, evidens est opus in ea divinum. This section bears throughout a close resemblance to our tract.

8. ἄτακτον. i. e. ὕλη ; cf. 176. 8.

15. τὴν ταχύτητα τὴν. τὴν ταχυτάτην περὶ ταῦτα περίβασιν Norden. N. compares Cicero, *Somn. Scip.* 5. 2 caeli ... conversio concitatior. Add *Tusc.* i. 68. The argument is similar, that man can know the unseen God through his visible works. Cf. 210. 23. For the Posidonian character of the proof see *Agn. Theos*, pp. 25 *sqq.*, 105 *sqq.*; Wendland, *Philo's Schrift*, p. 10. Greg. of Nyssa, *de anima et resurr.* 25 B : τὴν ὀξυτάτην τοῦ πόλου περιφοράν.

17. τὸν ἀκίνητον διακινούμενον. An intentional paradox, as the parallel τὸν ἀφανῆ φαινόμενον indicates. For the play upon the word κόσμος (l. 19) cf. 150. 6, 304. 11 (ornamento ?).

21. Brandt remarked the connexion between this passage and *Exc.* XXII on the one hand, and Lactantius and Varro on the other

---

sqq. See also notes on 304. 16. Possibly 160. 32 may conceal an allusion to the same notion. For the position of the sun see note on 266. 16.

[1] Cf. 162. 5-6.

(see vol. iii, p. 467). But Reitzenstein [1] and Norden [2] have since shown that the ultimate source is Posidonius. The marks of design that the general argument seeks are utility and beauty (Cic. *de nat. deor.* ii. 133-53).[3] Here the primary consideration is beauty and measure (162. 5). For the last word compare the (Posidonian) account of Nemesius (*de nat. hominis*, 697 B Migne): διαστέλλεται δὲ σφοδρῶς καὶ συστέλλεται ἡ ἀρτηρία καθ' ἁρμονίαν τινὰ καὶ λόγον. The argument proceeds from τάξις to the invisible Maker (cf. *Corp.* XI. ii). Although this argument explicitly mentions beauty alone, the other branch of it, from utility, is implied.[4] Thus, the question (l. 29)—τίς ὁ τοῖς ποσὶ βάσιν πλατύνας ;—has for background the contention that man's feet are shaped in order that he may stand erect.[5] Lactantius, *de opif. dei*, 13. 6 : 'in plantis uero eadem quidem, sed tamen longe dispar quam in manibus ratio est : quae quoniam totius operis quasi fundamenta sunt, eas mirificus artifex non rotunda specie, ne homo stare non posset aut aliis ad standum pedibus indigeret sicut quadrupedes, sed porrectiores longioresque formauit, ut stabile corpus efficerent planitie sua ; unde illis inditum nomen est.' The artist works with a purpose.

32. τίς ὁ τὰ νεῦρα συνθείς ; With some hesitation I suggest that νεῦρα (in either sense) cannot be repeated from l. 26, and that it is substituted for the name of an internal organ, as the context indicates. Perhaps τὼ νεφρώ ; the artistry is shown in making them a pair. Compare Lactantius, *ibid.*, 14. 3 : quid (*sc.* utilitatis) rienum gemina similitudo ? . . . quid splenis ? quid iecur ? . . . quid globus cordis ? The Ps.-Clementine account (cc. 28-30) should be compared. The whole argument forms a Stoic theodicy.

162. 8. ἀνδριάντα. Stoic cosmological argument. Sext. Emp. *adv. math.* ix. 92, 99 ; Cic. *de nat. deor.* ii. 87 (signum aut tabulam pictam cum aspexeris), 90 (see on 158. 24) ; Philo, *de provid.* i. 72 : ecce enim statuam videntes statuarium intelligimus et imaginem venuste pictam cernentes pictorem ipsum admiramur. See also vol. iv, 282. § 2. This is the argument from τέχνη.

18. κύειν πάντα. This is the 'bold saying'. As Bräuninger sees (*H. T.*, p. 26), it harmonizes with ll. 6-7, a conception Stoic and Oriental. Compare 332. 11-12 (*utraque sexus fecunditas, voluntas, parit, procreare,*

---

[1] *Zwei religionsgesch. Fragen*, p. 93.

[2] *Agn. Theos*, p. 277. 2 ; cf. p. 105.

[3] Lact. *de opific. dei*, 2. 7, &c. (see Brandt, *W. St.* 13, 270 *sqq.*) with the recurrent catchwords *pulchritudo, utilitas*. For parallels in the same tradition from Gregory of Nyssa's *de hominis opific.*, see Gronau, *Poseidonios*, pp. 161 *sqq.*

[4] For utility see e.g. *Exc.* XXVI, esp. 516. 24 *sqq.* with note, below. To the same context belong Momus' diatribe on man's intellectual powers (note on 482. 4) and the account of the origin of civilization from need (see on 492. 1).

[5] See on 294. 11.

see note) and **144. 11.** Otherwise πατήρ (l. 15) loses its point;[1] read τοσοῦτός ἐστιν. . . . ἢ γὰρ μόνος οὗτος—the Μόνος θεός formula.

27. Quid est deus? quod vides totum et quod non vides totum (Sen. *N. Q.* 1. 8). Perhaps we should read ὁ οὐχ ⟨⟨οὗτος⟩⟩ in l. 29, to keep the parallelism.

164. 1. τί τίς . . . εὐλογήσαι A.D.N., comparing for optative **184. 5, 25; 210. 4.**

3. οὐ τόπος ἐστὶ περί σε. God ἐμπεριέχει πάντα. God is ἀχώρητος: ὁ ἀόρατος ὃς τὰ πάντα ὁρᾷ | ἀχώρητος ὃς τὰ πάντα χωρεῖ.[2]

4. πάντα δὲ ἐν σοί, πάντα ἀπὸ σοῦ. The first of three symmetrical ascriptions. The connexion is clear from **218. 29, 33.** God gives all and takes naught because he is good; see on **144. 5–9.**

13. On the σὺ εἶ formula in magical and Gnostic writings see Norden, *Agn. Theos*, pp. 183 *sqq.*; Reitzenstein, *Poimandres*, pp. 15 *sqq.*; Bousset, *Kyrios*, pp. 61, 150; vol. iv, 148. 5. Analysis of style in Norden, p. 181.

15. Cf. (with Norden) Greg. Naz. εἰς θεόν:

> σοὶ ἔνι πάντα μένει, σὺ δ' ἀθρόα πάντα θεάζεις
> καὶ πάντων τέλος ἐσσί, καὶ εἷς καὶ πάντα καὶ οὐδείς,
> οὐχ ἓν ἐών, οὐ πάντα· πανώνυμε, πῶς σε καλέσσω;

Libellus VI. **164. 22.** The tract begins by identifying the φύσις of the Good and God; this enables the writer to define the Good at once. Retain ll. 22–3, and perhaps continue ὁ θεός, ἀεὶ ⟨ἐνεργῶν⟩[3] εἰ δὲ οὕτως, οὐσίαν εἶναι δεῖ π. κιν. κ. γενέσεως ⟨ἐνεργητικήν;⟩—ἔρημον δὲ οὐδέν ἐστιν αὐτῆς— περὶ δὲ αὐτήν . . . ἔχουσα⟨ν⟩, ἀνενδεῆ καὶ ἀπέριττον, πληρεστάτην χορηγόν. ἐν δὲ ἀρχὴ πάντων· πάντ' ἄρ⟨α⟩ τὸ χορηγοῦν ἀγαθόν—ὅταν λέγω "καὶ πάντα καὶ ἀεί", ἀγαθόν ἐστι. Cf. Philo, *de decal.* 81: οὐ γὰρ ἑτέρου χρεῖος ἦν ὁ αὐταρκέστατος ἑαυτῷ . . . ὅς (θεὸς) ἐστι τὸ πρῶτον ἀγαθὸν καὶ τελεώτατον, ἀφ' οὗ τρόπον πηγῆς ἄρδεται τῷ κόσμῳ καὶ τοῖς ἐν αὐτῷ τὰ ἐπὶ μέρους ἀγαθά. The point is that good being the essence of God, he gives all; see **144. 5, 186. 10,** l. 6 above. God in himself has no needs and no superfluities (cf. **166. 6**). One is the source of all—hence what provides all is good. Cf. **216. 15** *sqq.*

166. 4. Having neither defect nor excess (**164. 26**), God has no πάθη. On the subject see Pohlenz, *Vom Zorn Gottes* (*Forsch.* 12), and note on **150. 16.** In **260. 19** it is said that God's only πάθος is the Good.

13. ⟨τού⟩των *sc.* τῶν παθῶν; cf. ll. 11, 17 *sqq.* As the argument in § 1 b showed that God, having no passions, cannot but be good, so this paragraph contends that the presence of πάθος excludes the Good. The tone is widely different from that of 2 b and may indicate a revision (Zielinski).

27. κινητός. Contrast **164. 25–6.** In the Cosmos we principally

---

[1] *Ep. Jac.* i. 18 βουληθεὶς ἀπεκύησεν ἡμᾶς λόγῳ ἀληθείας (Reitzenstein).

[2] *Kerygma Petri*, 13 (Klostermann, *Apocrypha*, i); cf. Schmidt, *Kopt -gnost. Schr.* i. 333. 4. (The first reference is from Norden.)

[3] Or κινῶν. Cf. **256. 24.**

think of man in relation to good ; hence the lines about man. In man, by comparison with the Good, evil has its station ; for the good here (sc. ἀγαθὸν ἐν μέρει) is the moderately bad—the minimum of evil ; so our good cannot be entirely purged of evil. It becomes tainted ; when tainted ceases to be good ; and ceasing grows into evil.

168. 4 *sqq.* Argument from man's πάθη ; contrast 166. 4 *sqq.* l. 14 γαστριμαργία. It is *insatiable*, and therefore a constant theme of diatribe literature. αἱ ἑορτώδεις ἀνέσεις αὗται ... μυρίας ἤδη πολλάκις ἁμαρτημάτων ὁδοὺς ἀνέτεμον. ἄκρατος γὰρ καὶ μετ' οἰνοφλυγίας ὀψοφαγίαι τὰς γαστρὸς ἀκορέστους ἐπιθυμίας ἐξεγείρουσι καὶ τὰς ὑπὸ γαστέρα, καὶ ῥέουσαι καὶ χεόμεναι πάντη φορὰν ἀμυθήτων ἀπεργάζονται κακῶν (Philo, περὶ τῶν εἰς τὰς ἱερουργίας ζώων, p. 13. 11 Wendland, *Neuentdeckte Fr. Philos*). So often in Philo phrases like αἱ γαστρὸς ἀπολαύσεις καὶ αἱ μετὰ γαστέρα ; again, σχεδὸν ἀγγεῖον τῶν ἡδονῶν ἁπασῶν (ἡ γαστὴρ) ἐστι (*leg. alleg.* iii. 138). See vol. iv, 337-8, § 8-9.

    21. περὶ αὐτήν. αὐτοῦ Kroll.

    23. αἶται. αὐταὶ Kroll.

    24. ὅτι ⟨εἰ⟩ ἡ οὐσία τοῦ θεοῦ (εἴ γε οὐσίαν ἔχει) τὸ καλόν ἐστι, τὸ δὲ καλὸν καὶ ἀγαθόν, Kroll.

    32. ὧν ⟨μᾶλλον⟩ αὐτός A.D.N.

    34. τὸ ὑπέρλαμπρον (CM). Cf. Iamblichus, *de myster.* ii. 5 : τὸ ὑπέρλαμπρον ... μονίμως ἱδρυμένον. Retain the antithesis.

Libellus VII. **170.** 20. This is one of many imitations, found in the diatribe form, of the Platonic *Cleitophon*, 407 b : ποῖ φέρεσθε, ὦνθρωποι ; καὶ ἀγνοεῖτε κ.τ.λ. Compare the language of the Chaldaic oracle (Kroll, *De orac. Chald.* 15) :

οὐδ' ὅτι πᾶς ἀγαθὸς θεὸς εἰδότες, ἃ ταλαεργοί,

νήψατε.

Also 132. 13. See Reitzenstein, *G.G.A.*, 1911, pp. 554-7 (and *H.M.R.*, p. 292) for a discussion of the call to repentance in Hermetic literature, and compare (with R.) Epictetus, iii. 22. 26, Horace, *Epod.* 7, Persius, v. 142 ; Geffcken, *Kynika*, p. 17. For Philo see Lewy, *Sobria Ebrietas*, esp. pp. 73 *sqq.* For valuable remarks on the diatribe form in Hermetic literature see Nock, *J.E.A.*, 1925, pp. 128-33.

172. 13. τὸν δι' ὧν φιλεῖ μισοῦντα, καὶ δι' ὧν μισεῖ φθονοῦντα. An enemy through what it likes (earthly lusts), a jealous thwarter through what it hates (the beauty of Reality). Cf. 152. 20.

    17. τὸ ἐγκείμενον ἀγαθόν. Read ἓν καὶ μόνον.

Libellus VIII. **174.** 14. If no part of the immortal Cosmos can die, *a fortiori* man, as λογικόν, is immortal ; see 450. 18-20. Here λογικόν signifies not merely the Greek rational animal, but the sharer of ζωὴ νοερά.

    22. οὔποτε ⟨δὲ⟩ ἐγένετο, Kroll.

    23. τὸ γὰρ ἀίδιον οὐ ἀίδιόν ἐστι τὸ πᾶν ⟨αὐτόγονον⟩ Kroll.

176. 4. ἰδεῶν τὰ ποιά. qualitates specierum ; cf. 326. 13.

178. 1. ⟨καὶ⟩ τοῦ ἀγαθοῦ ?

178. 2. τί θεός. For this catechetical form see Norden, *Agn. Theos*, pp. 99 *sqq*; e. g. ὁ μὲν μὴ εἰδώς, ὅ τι ἐστὶ κόσμος, οὐκ οἶδεν ὅπου ἐστίν· ὁ δὲ μὴ εἰδώς, πρὸς ὅ τι πέφυκεν, οὐκ οἶδεν ὅστις ἐστίν κ.τ.λ. (Marc. Aurelius, 8. 52). See note on 150. 26.

Libellus IX. **178. 21.** ἐκφωνεῖται. Without the thought it expresses λόγος would be a mere ψόφος, and thought would be inaccessible apart from speech: ἐπεὶ οὖν νοερόν τι χρῆμα καὶ ἀσώματόν ἐστιν ὁ νοῦς, ἀκοινώνητον ἂν ἔσχε τὴν χάριν καὶ ἄμικτον, μὴ διά τινος ἐπινοίας φανερουμένης αὐτοῦ τῆς κινήσεως· τούτου χάριν τῆς ὀργανικῆς ταύτης προσεδεήθη κατασκευῆς, ἵνα πλήκτρου δίκην . . . ἑρμηνεύσῃ τὴν ἔνδοθεν κίνησιν (Gregory of Nyssa, *de hom. opif.* 149 B).[1]

180. 1. ⟨ἀ⟩πογεγονέναι? If we read in **178. 26** with A.D.N. ⟨οἱ μέν φασιν⟩ χωρὶς αἰσθ., the writer probably added that in his view both νόησις and αἴσθησις were absent during sleep. His argument is that they are conjoined; if one is absent, the other should be; it is for waking men that both are conjoined.[2] In the Stoic tradition to which this *libellus* is allied such is the theory: τοῦ νοῦ πρὸς τὸ αἰσθητικὸν εἶδος τῆς ψυχῆς οἰκειομένου, ἀκόλουθον ἂν εἴη καὶ κινουμένου τούτου, συγκινεῖσθαι λέγειν αὐτόν, καὶ ἠρεμοῦντος συγκαταπαύεσθαι.[3] The theory given by Sextus in the note makes the individual νοῦς dependent upon a κοινὸς λόγος, and conjoins νοῦς with αἴσθησις, which is the link between the individual mind and the κοινὸς λόγος. Therefore during sleep the connexion is interrupted. The decisive argument for this interpretation is the remainder of this tract. For the essence of Posidonius' theory is σύμφυσις of likes. The περιέχον is λογικόν; it is by μετοχή with the κοινὸς λόγος that we become λογικοί (Sext. Emp. i. 131, and see footnote). But the doctrine here explained is similar. The Cosmos itself has mind and sense,[4] and the mind and

---

[1] l. 20 ἀδελφή. Cf. λόγος (*sc.* προφορικός) ἀδελφὸς τῆς διανοίας Philo *quod deterius potiori*, 38: *de posteritate Caini*, 100. In Philo (Cohn, iii. 169. 17) the stream of *logos* flows from the spring of διάνοια.

[2] Perhaps in l. 2 ⟨ἀεὶ ἥνωται νόησις⟩ αἰσθήσει.

[3] Gregory of Nyssa, *de hom. opif.* 169 B Migne (Posidonian). He continues with the simile of the fire under the embers. Now compare Sextus Empiricus, *adv. math.* i. 129: τοῦτον δὴ τὸν θεῖον λόγον καθ' Ἡράκλειτον δι' ἀναπνοῆς σπάσαντες νοεροὶ γινόμεθα, καὶ ἐν μὲν ὕπνοις ληθαῖοι, κατὰ δὲ ἔγερσιν πάλιν ἔμφρονες. ἐν γὰρ τοῖς ὕπνοις μυσάντων τῶν αἰσθητικῶν πόρων χωρίζεται τῆς πρὸς τὸ περιέχον συμφυΐας ὁ ἐν ἡμῖν νοῦς, μόνης τῆς κατὰ ἀναπνοὴν προσφύσεως σῳζομένης οἱονεί τινος ῥίζης . . . ἐν δὲ ἐγρηγορόσι πάλιν διὰ τῶν αἰσθητικῶν πόρων ὥσπερ διά τινων θυρίδων προκύψας καὶ τῷ περιέχοντι συμβαλὼν λογικὴν ἐνδύεται δύναμιν. (Then follows the comparison of the embers) οὕτω καὶ ἡ ἐπιξενωθεῖσα τοῖς ἡμετέροις σώμασιν ἀπὸ τοῦ περιέχοντος μοῖρα κατὰ μὲν τὸν χωρισμὸν σχεδὸν ἄλογος γίνεται, κατὰ δὲ τὴν διὰ τῶν πλείστων πόρων σύμφυσιν ὁμοιοειδὴς (v.l. ὁμοειδὴς) τῷ ὅλῳ καθίσταται. This is Posidonian; see Reinhardt, *K. u. S.*, pp. 192 *sqq.* For the embers see also vol. ii, 209. 1. The function of sleep is to restore the τόνος of the body. See below, note on 410. 1, where another aspect of the same theory is put forward.

[4] **182. 9.** It is not 'like' man's mind and sense: καὶ τὰ μὲν κοινῇ φησι ('Ἡρά-

sense of all creatures enters from without, εἰσπνέουσα ὑπὸ τοῦ περιέχοντος (184. 6).[1] This is the technical language of Posidonius, and establishes the connexion. For further evidence see 296. 4 *sqq.*, and notes thereon.

4. Zielinski brackets τῆς αἰσθήσεως. This is unnecessary. The one word can be used to cover the πάθος both in the senses and in the soul. Ἔστι δὲ ἡ αἴσθησις οὐκ ἀλλοίωσις, ἀλλὰ διάγνωσις ἀλλοιώσεως.[2] ἀλλοιοῦται μὲν γὰρ τὰ αἰσθητήρια, διακρίνει δὲ τὴν ἀλλοίωσιν ἡ αἴσθησις (Nemesius, *de nat. hom.* 636 B Migne).

5. συμφωνήσῃ should be compared with ἡνῶσθαι, ἥνωται (178. 15, 16). They are *termini technici* of the theory, which implies a συμφυΐα of all parts of the Cosmos. The individual mind is in communion with the mind of the Cosmos; the parts of the individual are likewise bound together.

We should retain ἐκφωνεῖσθαι; for the point is probably the rapidity with which the body obeys the mind—*mentis interpres oratio.* In a similar context Nemesius, *op. cit.* 637 A: (of the parts of the soul some govern, others obey) ὑπουργικὰ δὲ τὰ αἰσθητικὰ καὶ ἡ καθ' ὁρμὴν κίνησις καὶ τὸ φωνητικόν. καὶ γὰρ ἡ κίνησις καὶ ἡ φωνὴ ὀξύτατα καὶ σχεδὸν ἀχρόνως ὑπακούει τῇ βουλήσει τοῦ λογισμοῦ.[3]

7. This paragraph and the next indicate that the school tradition is used as a convenient framework for characteristic Hermetic doctrine. Note the formal resumption of the thread in l. 30 (really in 182. 3), and compare 184. 25. The opening lines are not inconsistent with the doctrine of a θεῖος λόγος and its συμφυΐα with the individual mind; nor is τῷ ὑπὸ τοῦ θεοῦ πεφωτισμένῳ δαίμονι incompatible with Posidonius' account of the συγγενὴς δαίμων.[4] But the sharp contrast between the illuminated and the bad daemons, the identification of piety and γνῶσις, and the distinction between the elect and the many, are Hermetic. There is a Daemon (Νοῦς) that guides the pious, and daemons that lead astray,[5] or avenge. This is part of the doctrine which places man, save the illuminated, under the government of εἱμαρμένη; and we should probably

κλειτος) φαινόμενα πιστὰ ὡς ἂν τῷ κοινῷ κρινόμενα λόγῳ. τὰ δὲ κατ' ἰδίαν ἑκάστῳ ψευδῆ (Sextus, *ib* 134, cf. 131).

[1] Also 182. 26.

[2] So Galen, *de placitis,* 635 Mueller. See Jaeger, *Nemesios,* p. 14.

[3] See also on 178. 21.

[4] In περὶ παθῶν (Galen, *de placit.* 488 Mueller). It is unnecessary to decide here between the rival interpretations of the phrase: see Schmekel, *Phil. d. mittl. Stoa,* pp. 248, 256; Pohlenz, *Nachr. G. G.,* 1921; Reinhardt, *K. u. S.,* p. 281; Heinemann, *Poseidonios,* i, p. 60, ii, p. 19. In this context it is intelligible as the soul or the λόγος illuminated by the Ruler of the Universe, into which an evil spirit creeps. Cf. Epictetus, i. 16: αἱ ψυχαὶ μὲν οὕτως εἰσὶν ἐνδεδεμέναι καὶ συναφεῖς τῷ θεῷ ἅτε αὐτοῦ μόρια οὖσαι καὶ ἀποσπάσματα κ.τ.λ.

[5] Cf. 126. 24, note on 200. 29, 368 *T.*

connect with it the division of good and bad *numina* referred to by Arnobius.[1]

26. αἰσθόμενος τῆς γνώσεως—by vision with the eye of the soul.

180. 32–182. I. ὑλικός)(οὐσιώδης. He who has not νοῦς, and he who has. See on 148. 24 *ad fin.* For οὐσιώδης see 122. 6, 248. 15, 298. I. In 182. I ὑλικῶς ACM.

182. 6. ἀφορᾷ: perhaps ἐφορᾷ. We might retain δημιουργῶν πάντα, ποιεῖ μέν ⟨πάντα ?⟩. ὅμοια is consistent with ἀγαθά. Epictetus, I. 14: ὁ δὲ θεὸς οὐχ οἷός τ' ἐστὶ πάντα ἐφορᾶν καὶ πᾶσι συμπαρεῖναι καὶ ἀπὸ πάντων τινὰ ἴσχειν διάδοσιν; (because souls are συναφεῖς τῷ θεῷ). So ἐφορᾶν, ἔφορος constantly in Philo.

30. κοσμεῖ. See ll. 17–20; the usual play on Cosmos and adornment. See on 148. 24, 208. 12, where the Aion is distinguished from the Cosmos.

184. 12. ἐν τῷ θεῷ. Stoic; Norden, *Agn. Theos*, p. 19, and on 212. 19, 218. 24.

13. ἠρτημένα. The word suggests grades of *life* in the chain stretching down from God. The detail of interpretation is uncertain; but it may be suggested that the first class, with bodies, are star-gods, and the other three are orders of daemons, the last perhaps being those that receive souls after death to punish or to save. See Lydus, in vol. i. 368.

184. 25–186. The text should be retained.[2] The ἐννοῶν (ἔννους ὤν) is explicitly opposed to the ἀγνοῶν, and νοῆσαι is identical with πιστεῦσαι (186. 2, 370. 9 fiduciam, 15 credulitatis; see notes *ad loc.* and 154. 21), and τὸ ἀπιστῆσαι (*om.* τὸ ACM) is identical with τὸ μὴ νοῆσαι. For λόγος see on 230. 7. This passage is one of those that show a reaction against the λόγος;[3] 'λόγος (ist) zunächst mehr die *ratio*, dann aber auch das Wort.'[4] In 186. 2 R. reads ἐνανεπαύσατο, on the ground that the place where God sits enthroned is a κύκλος τῆς ἀληθείας καὶ πίστεως.[5]

Libellus X. 188. 22. ἐσεβ᾽σθη: ἐσβέσθη ... ὑπὸ τ. τ. θέας? Cf. 248. 13 ἀποσβεσθήσεται (Reitzenstein), and l. 24.

190. 9. καὶ θέα Plasberg.

17. Reitzenstein[6] reads ἀνθρώπου ⟨κειμένην⟩ ... ⟨τὸ⟩ κάλλος, ⟨ἀλλὰ

---

[1] See on iv. 7. 8. On daemons, Bousset, *G. G. A.*, 1914, pp. 722–4. 745–8, particularly the citations from the *Testament of the Twelve Patriarchs*, e. g. *Sebulon*, ix. 7: καὶ τὰ πνεύματα τῆς πλάνης πλανᾷ αὐτοὺς ἐπὶ πάσαις πράξεσιν. καὶ μετὰ ταῦτα ἀνατελεῖ ὑμῖν αὐτὸς Κύριος φῶς δικαιοσύνης, and *Asser*, vi. 5.

[2] For optative without ἄν see on 164. 1; but the word may have slipped out before ἀγνοοῦντι.

[3] l. 27 [μ]οὐ—a certain emendation, independently proposed by Zielinski and Scott. See on 130. 5.

[4] Reitzenstein, *H. M. R.*, pp. 235-6.

[5] *Ibid.*; Wessely, *Denkschr. d. Wien. Ak.*, 1888, p. 70, l. 1012; περινοεῖν is used with ἐποπτεύειν; and l. 3 τὰ ... θεοῦ is explained by reference to the τέλειος λόγος (178. 10). [6] *H. M. R.*, p. 289.

χωρίζεσθαι αὐτοῦ καὶ μεταβάλλεσθαι ἐν⟩ τῷ ἀποθεωθῆναι. For the last word see on 123. 23 ; *H. M. R.*, pp. 221-2 ; Bousset, *Kyrios*, pp. 200, 424 *sqq.* In the context the figure of φωτισμός is to be expected, as in ll. 14-15 (ἀναλάμπει).

23. αἱ ψυχαί εἰσιν, αἵ τε ⟨περὶ τὸν θεὸν συνηγερμέναι, αἵ τε⟩ ἐν τῷ π. κ. κ. ὥσπερ ἀπονενεμημέναι Reitzenstein (*Göttin Psyche*, p. 67). R. compares the doctrine of 'certain Platonists' given in Porphyry, *de abst.* 2. 37-43, where the Platonism is accommodated to Persian lore. There is the first God, then the Soul of the Cosmos. lapped round the physical world. Then there are souls engendered from the 'whole' soul inhabiting regions about the moon, good daemons that do good works and are messengers of God. Others send ills upon men and fill them with evil desires. So the harmful and the beneficent must be distinguished, and the Power over the bad must not be confused with the first God. As R. contends, the emphasis here lies upon ἀπὸ μιᾶς ψυχῆς—all individual souls spring from an original Soul.[1] The expression 'the Soul of the All' is Platonizing. See on 464. 30, 184. 13, Arnobius vol. iv, 480, c. 28.

192. 3. δόξα. Reitzenstein, *H. M. R.*, pp. 287 *sqq.*, 359 ; Bousset, *Kyrios*, pp. 188, 203, 425. Σὺ τὴν δόξαν τοῦ φωτὸς περιθέμενος ἔσῃ (Dieterich, *Abraxas*, l. 3. 67). l. 5, cf. 186 10, 192. 19, 168. 34, 170. 2.

28-9. See Philo, *quis rer. div. heres*, 207-14, and notes on 304. 16, 158. 24 ; also on 134. 2 *sqq.*

194. 3. [ὁ] καλὸς ⟨⟨ὁ⟩⟩ κόσμος, οὐκέτι δὲ ἀγαθός?

10. For this comparison of microcosm and macrocosm refer to Plato *Timaeus*, 33 B, 40 A, 44 D *sq.* For a detailed analogy see, e. g., Plut. *de facie*, 928 B. Here the sphericity of the human head is the starting-point of the analogy. Lactantius, *de opif. dei*, 8. 4: 'hanc eius (hominis) aulam deus non obductam porrectamque formauit ut in mutis animalibus, sed orbi et globo similem, quod orbis rotunditas perfectae rationis ac figurae. eo igitur mens et ignis ille diuinus tamquam caelo tegitur.' The argument is the Stoic commonplace from man's erect posture : this, it may be conjectured, is the sense of ll. 11-12: man's eyes are so placed that he sees the stars ('in summo capite tamquam in arce sublimi speculatur') ;[2] his feet rest on the ground. The motion of his head in its socket is rotatory, not like the other limbs. The Cosmos, by its shape and movement, is identified with a head, all below being material—and 'below' for the cosmic sphere means 'within'[3]—and nothing being material above. l. 12, perhaps ὑλικόν. ⟨ὑπὸ⟩ νοῦ δέ... The surrounding membrane (l. 14) is that which gives harmony and motion to the whole body.[4] Here the natural cosmic parallel is given by *Orac. Chald.* 22 (Kroll): ὡς γὰρ

[1] Cf. Orig. *c. Cels.* vi. 25 : the Ophitic diagram where Leviathan (ἡ τῶν ὅλων ψυχή, interpreted as the soul that pervades all things) encircles the nine spheres.

[2] See 296. 4; Cic. *de nat. deor.* ii. 140 ; Macrob. *in Somn. Scip.* I. 14. 9.

[3] See 216. 19.

[4] For school tradition see Gregory of Nyssa, *de hom. opif.* 244 C Migne.

ὑπεζωκώς τις ὑμὴν νοερὸς διακρίνει.[1] The (stars) fixed to the membrane are immortal, because their body is *in* soul. as it were, and they have more soul than body ... l. 18 perhaps ⟨τὸ⟩ πᾶν. This is the conclusion of the analogy.

194. 27. The doctrine of psychic wrappings; see on 148. 24, 230. 7, 296. 12.[2] *Pneuma* here takes the lowest place,[3] and in the next lines the writer follows school tradition, as the reference to blood shows.[4] But the whole passage is not Stoic in character; if the refutation is taken as it stands (196. 4-5), it means that the *pneuma*, which vivifies the blood when dispersed through the body, withdraws to the soul (l. 4), and that the departure of the soul leaves the body lifeless. The underlying theory is probably that the *pneuma* is left by the soul at some stage of the ascent, as it was received in the descent.[5] Porphyry, *Sententiae*, xxxii: ἐξελθούσῃ γὰρ αὐτῇ (τῇ ψυχῇ) τοῦ τερέου σώματος τὸ πνεῦμα συνομαρτεῖ, ὃ ἐκ τῶν σφαιρῶν συνελέξατο. Proclus notes that the followers of Porphyry agree with the Chaldaean oracles in this.[6] The writer holds to the two-soul theory (*Fr.* 16).

198. 4. This version omits λόγος (194. 28); but in a document that is a mosaic we cannot expect consistency. l. 7. For the heavenly garment of the stripped *nous*, a common Gnostic conception, see Bousset, *Hauptprobleme*, pp. 303-5. *Fire* is here not the power of darkness, as in *Corp.* I, but a higher element; and the soul (l. 9) is left probably to an avenging daemon,[7] perhaps as the ἦθος is in 128. 2. ll. 11-12: the ingenuous formal question, preparing for an exposition.

200. 15. It should be noted that this is the view of the *Oracula Chaldaica*; Proclus, *in remp.* ii. 336-7 Kroll.

28. 'Wohl ein Missverständnis von I. 23 (ὁ Νοῦς) τῷ τιμωρῷ ἐκχωρήσας δαίμονι' (Bousset). Contrast p. 202. 1 with ll. 29-30. The

[1] Further, Kroll, *P.-W.*, 8. 819. 38, and (with him) Bidez, *Rev. Philol.*, 1903, 80, Cumont, *Cosmogr. Manich.* 26.

[2] Cf. (with J. Kroll, *Schr. des. H. T.*, p. 262) Philo, *de migr. Abr.* 3: καθάπερ γὰρ ἀνδρὸς ἑστία, καὶ νοῦ λόγος ἐνδιαίτημα κ.τ.λ. πνεῦμα: see 198. 21 sqq., Porph. *de antro*, 25. Other references in *P.-W.* 8. 819. 48. The theory of wrappings is found in the Chaldaic oracles (p. 47 Kroll): νοῦν μὲν ἐνὶ ψυχῇ, ψυχὴν δ' ἐνὶ σώματι ἀργῷ κ.τ.λ.

[3] Cf. 448. 13.

[4] Nemesius, *de nat. hom.* 541 B Migne: ἐπειδὴ τοῦ αἵματος ἢ τοῦ πνεύματος χωριζομένου νεκροῦται τὸ ζῷον. See also on 296. 4, and 492. 24; Philo, *quaest. in Gen.* 59 (Harris, *Fragm.* p. 25).

[5] See on 126. 31 sqq.; also 154. 10.

[6] See vol. ii, 59; Kroll, *Orac. Chald.*, p. 47. Macrobius, *Somn. Scip.* I. 11. 12: in singulis enim sphaeris quae caelo subiectae sunt, aetheria obvolutione vestitur, ut per eas gradatim societati huius indumenti testei concilietur. Servius *ad Aen.* xi. 51, a caelo spiritum.

[7] But in 200. 10 the end of the soul is to become mind throughout; probably this belongs to a different stratum.

probable explanation of the contradictions is that the fire described in 198–200. 5 is a heavenly element, whereas here the fire is akin to darkness.   See on 118. 12.

202. 8 *sqq.* See on 288. 9, 292. 20.   The affinities of this passage are with the *Asclepius*—the chain of beings from God downwards—*continuatio.*

15. For a 'Chaldaean' theory of the action of the ῥεῖμα νοητόν cf. Porphyry (Ps.-Galen, πρὸς Γαῦρον), p. 57 Kalbfleisch, and note on 438. 17.

20. Supply ἐνεργοῦσι, and compare l. 14.   The thesis is *continuatio*; see references on l. 8.

Libellus XI. i. 208. 1. Professor Bidez has published in *Cat. des Manuscrits alchimiques grecs*, vi, p. 218 an extract from a MS. of Psellus[1] which refers to this tract.   It has some bearing, as he remarks, upon Reitzenstein's theory of the archetype, and gives evidence for the form of the title.   I transcribe the passage:

Ἐρῶ δὲ ὑμῖν καὶ λόγον τῶν κεκρυμμένων, ὃν Ἕλλην ἀνὴρ σοφὸς τὴν θεολογίαν ἐν ἀπορρήτοις ἐξέφηνεν· Ἑρμῆν φημι τὸν οὕτω παρ' Ἕλλησι Τρισμέγιστον κατονομαζόμενον· οὗτος γὰρ ἔν τινι τῶν αὐτοῦ λόγων ὃν ἐπέγραψεν Ἀκήρατον Νοῦν, μετὰ θεὸν τοὺς αἰῶνάς φησιν, εἶτα τὸν νοῦν, μεθ' ὃν[2] δὴ τὴν ψυχήν,[3] καὶ αὖθις οὐρανόν, μεθ' οὗ φύσιν καὶ χρόνον καὶ γένεσιν. τίθησι δὲ ὑπεξηρημένα τινὰ ἑκάστῳ τούτων· τῷ μὲν θεῷ τὸ ἀγαθόν, τῷ δ' αἰῶνι τὸ ταυτόν, τῷ δὲ νῷ τὴν νοερὰν κίνησιν, τῇ δὲ ψυχῇ τὴν ζωήν, τῷ δὲ οὐρανῷ τὴν ἀποκατάστασιν καὶ ἀνταποκατάστασιν, τῷ δὲ χρόνῳ τὴν κίνησιν καὶ μεταβολήν, τῇ δὲ φύσει τὸ εὐμετάβολόν τε καὶ ῥευστόν, τῇ δὲ γενέσει τὴν ζωὴν καὶ τὸν θάνατον, τὰ μὲν ταῦτα συμφιλοσοφῶν τοῖς Ὀρφικοῖς καὶ τοῖς Χαλδαϊκοῖς,[4] τὰ δὲ οἴκοθεν ἐπεμβάλλων.

10. (Ἀρχαὶ πάντων πέντε· ὁ) Reitzenstein ; cf. 352. 21, and 144. 25, as he interprets it.   See on 208. 19.

17. ταυτότης. Iamblichus, *de myst.* I. 19 : τὸ ὕψος καὶ τὴν ταυτότητα τῶν πρώτων.   Cf. *Fr.* 30 ἀεὶ ἑαυτῷ ὅμοιος.

22. διαμονή.   Retain the order, and compare 376 Pap. αἰώνιος διαμονή See also on 208. 12.   διαμονή is 'life'.

208. 12. κοσμεῖ οὖν.   Aion is οὐσία to the ὕλη of the Cosmos (l. 5).   For the play on κοσμεῖ see on 182. 30.   It is said that Aion gives immortality and permanence to the 'matter' that is the Cosmos, and that there are two kinds of γενέσεις. one of which (in heaven), like heavenly time, is immutable and imperishable.   These lines do not distinguish

---

[1] Codex Parisinus 1182, f. 265ʳ.   [2] μεθ' ὃν Nock.

[3] Νοῦς and Ψυχή : cf. (with Nock) 208. 18.   N. regards the extract 'as a somewhat vague reminiscence of the tractate which Psellus had read, but to which he had not again referred in writing and which is not before him at the moment of writing'.

[4] 'τοῖς Χαλδαϊκοῖς in codice evanida praeter paucissima litterarum quae quadrant vestigia una cum Nock conieci' (Bidez).

between the seats of immortality and duration, and διαμονή does not imply mere finite duration.[1] The heavens and the Cosmos are a product, with a beginning, but eternal. An object for κοσμεῖ is needed ; οὖν suggests οὐρανόν ($\overline{ουνον}$) : *Tim.* 37 D, διακοσμῶν ἅμα οὐρανὸν ποιεῖ μένοντος αἰῶνος ... αἰώνιον εἰκόνα ... χρόνον. In ll. 13-15 it is simply stated that the temporal process of the Cosmos depends upon Aion, as Aion depends on God. ἤρτηται is the characteristic Hermetic word for the *continuatio* throughout the universe.

19. [ἡ] ψυχή Reitzenstein (*Göttin Psyche*, p. 69). I give his interpretation of this obscure passage. It combines a doctrine of Aion with a doctrine of Soul as the uniting principle of Life. Every living body is made of Matter and Soul (214. 3). Hence Soul is an ἐνέργεια of God (206. 21) and answers in a sense to Aion, which is a power of God (208. 6) and is Sophia [2] (l. 10). Cf. *Ascl.* c. 30. Cf. 212. 13 and ll. 1-2. But there is no contrast here between the One Soul and the many as in 190. 22, but simply a question of the substance. In detail, αὐτό (l. 25) refers to τὸ ... σῶμα, and τοῦτον (l. 30, codd.) to the Cosmos. For νοῦς ἐν τῇ ψυχῇ (l. 21) cf. Pl. *Tim.* 30 B 4.

30. εἴτε δι' ἀνάγκην, κ.τ.λ. : instruments of Aion. καὶ εἴ τι ἄλλο, the ordinary compendious formula in ἀνάκλησις. Cf. *de mundo* 401 b 7, 362. 13 (n.) and *Fr.* 29.

210. 1. ἀνομοίῳ. Cf. *Fr.* 25 ; 148. 22 ; Philo (Ps.-Philolaus), *de opif. dei*, 100 : αὐτὸς αὑτῷ ὅμοιος, ἕτερος τῶν ἄλλων. The ἀνόμοιος is ἐν ταυτότητι.

12. δύναμις γὰρ ὢν ἐνεργής. This should sum up the argument for God's activity. The following words then become difficult. The sense should be that God is an active power in things, (which are not independent) but subject to him. Then follows (l. 23) an account of his works. Should we read οὐκ αὐταρκέσ⟨ιν ἐν⟩εστι?

Libellus XI. ii. 23 sqq. κάλλος (l. 24) Posidonian. Praise of the beauty of the Cosmos, beginning with the order of the stars, is a common Stoic *motif.*[3] The theme in what follows is τάξις, διαμονή, μεταβολή— nothing so old as the Cosmos, yet ever self-renewing. (Should ἔσται follow ἀκμαιότερον?) Punctuate by a dash before and after τὸ ... κατανόητον. The argument is that God is not idle, and that there is no second Creator (§§ 5-6 a) ; look at his works, one order in heaven and earth (§§ 6 b-8 b). And one order means one Maker (§ 9).

212. 1-24. The argument is from one τάξις [4] to one Maker—union of

---

[1] It is constantly used of the Cosmos itself, also of the heavens. Here cf. l. 28, διαμένουσα ἐν τῇ ταυτότητι, with 206. 17 and 22 (note).

[2] ὁ κύριος ἐπεμαρτύρησέ σου τῇ Σοφίᾳ, ὅ ἐστιν Αἰών (*Pap. Par.*, 1206, p 112 Preisendanz).

[3] Cic. *Tusc.* i. 68, *de nat. deor.* ii. 54, 98 ; *de mundo*, c. 6 ; see 158. 22, 162. 12 (notes). The tone is comparable to that of *de mundo*.

[4] See on 158. 24. Cleomedes, i. 1. 4, p. 8 Z. ; for opposites see on 192. 28, Ar. *de mundo*, 396 b. Retain the text.

opposites, the stars each in their station, and mortals too have their level.

1. Heavenly light)(fire, a lower element. Typical Hermetic doctrine in a Stoic framework. See on 122. 25. l. 15 is probably a short way of saying that the fixed stars hold to their course, and the planets to their contrary motion. In 502. 5 the east is the left, but usage varied. l. 16. The inhabitants of each zone keep their level—the stars in their degree and men in theirs. Cf. 466. 20, 470. 25.

19. κινεῖται—again a Stoic argument for a Maker; delete ⟨ἤ⟩. This sentence is equivalent to the Stoic commonplace, ἐν αὐτῷ γὰρ ζῶμεν καὶ κινούμεθα καὶ ἐσμέν (Act. apostol. v. 28). The movement gives to the thing its οὐσία, and all things, according to their kind, are moved by God. Cf. 450. 9 sqq. For the phrase see Norden, Agn. Theos, p. 19.

23. ταχύτητος sc. τῆς τοῦ παντὸς φορᾶς, which contains all these motions;[1] retain τεταγμένης. The point is σύνδεσμος.

214. 6. Soul (Aion ?) is a δύναμις of God (208. 6, 19 note), and can be spoken of as the cause of life. But life has one sole cause, the Maker of the immortals. Then follows what appears to be an a fortiori argument —perhaps πῶς οὖν—καὶ ⟨εἰ⟩ τὰ θνητὰ ζῷα ἄλλα τῶν ⟨μὴ⟩ θνητῶν—πῶς δε⟨ῖ τὸν⟩ τὸ ἀθάνατον καὶ ἀθανασίαν ποιοῦντα ζῷον ⟨θνητὸν⟩ μὴ ποιεῖν;

In ll. 12–16 the unity of Soul, Life, and Matter points to one Maker. As the argument proceeds from ζωή to ζῷα, retain the latter in l. 15. εἷς οὖν θεός is a conclusion recalling in form the Stoic arguments given in Sextus Empiricus. So πάντα ... ποιεῖ, l. 19; cf. l. 30, 216. 5, 13, 25.[2] These are the formal conclusions and must all be retained.

16. Another set of unities—probably an argument from τάξις. See 212. 23, a passage which suggests ταχύτητα for θειότητα. For the repeated μία formula see Peterson, ΕΙΣ ΘΕΟΣ.

24–218. 10. An argument against an idle God. The first stage answers the difficulty that one God cannot make diverse things—he has a multiplicity of activities, as even man has. This argument by analogy for (a) the unity of God, or (b) the simplicity of the soul, is commonplace.[3] E. g. the one Sun has many rays. 'Denn auch im Menschen ist Eine Seele und Eine Vernünftige Kraft, und sie ist zugleich die Fertigerin der vielen (Künste)[4] . . .'

Next (216. 1), deprivation of these activities means nonentity, and of

---

[1] Hanc igitur in stellis constantiam, hanc tantam tam variis cursibus in omni aeternitate convenientiam temporum non possum intellegere sine mente, consilio, ratione (Cic. de nat. deor. ii. 54).

[2] But γελοιότατον (l. 16), [ἐν] πολλῷ γελοιότατον (l. 19), and δεισιδαίμων ὡς ἀκούεις (218. 4) appear to be Christian glosses. I observe that Reitzenstein has noted the last to be such.

[3] See 260. 9, 26 (notes), 262. 2. We must keep Ζωὴν καὶ Ψυχήν (214. 24). See above.

[4] Eusebius, Theoph. i. 31, p. 51. 25 Gressmann.

any of them, for God, imperfection. If we retain the text, the argument is : but those (ἐκεῖνα) activities (214. 24–5) cannot be apart from God.[1] If you cease from *your* (τούτων) activities, you are not a living thing, and if God ceases from *his* (ἐκείνων), he ceases to be God. If it is proved that you are naught, if you can do naught,[2] how much more so with God? For if there is anything that he does not make,[3] he is less than perfect. But if he is nowise (μή τι) idle, then he is perfect. ⟨θεὸς⟩ ἄρα πάντα ποιεῖ.

ll. 9–28. Argument from fecundity ; the unity of God's work lies in his fecundity. It is the continuous and ceaseless production of life—past, present, and future ;[4] and this is Life, the Noble, the Good—in a word, God. The clue (14 a) to God's function is given by (the strength of) your own generative impulse, though God has no affects,[5] and needs no helper[6]— he is therefore sole creator, immersed in his work and one with it. Without God, no life. Therefore : if there is this ceaseless flow of lives, and Life is one, there is one God ; and conversely, if all are alive (in heaven and in earth), and the one Life above and below comes from God, and is God, then all things are made by God (and none by a Demiurge). These arguments, in short, contend that the diversity of God's work is a mark of his perfection, not of another Creator, and that the unity of that work excludes any but one Creator. The *motifs*—εἶναι, ζωή, κίνησις—show Stoic influence.

14 c. This definition is characteristically Hermetic, and the text in l. 29 should be kept ; note 116. 12. Read Ζωή, Νοῦ, Ψυχῆς.

In 15 b the argument that God cannot have made both change and immortality is probably taken up (214. 24) : It is said quite wrongly that change is death, through which[7] the body is dissolved and life disappears.[8] Well, I say that the Cosmos itself changes in just this way—every day a part ‘disappears’ but it is never dissolved ;[9] for the Cosmos has its πάθη, namely whirls and disappearances. Here again we are on Stoic ground —*et mundus speciem mutat.*[10] What are these μεταβολαί?—the great cosmic changes. It is perhaps simplest to take them of the revolutions (220. 9) and obscurations of the heavenly bodies, which bring about the

---

[1] They would be all apart from him if he were ἀργός—but then he is nothing ; and if *any* are apart from him, he is imperfect.

[2] l. 5, perhaps μηδὲν δυνάμενον ⟨μηδέν σε⟩ εἶναι.

[3] 210. 11.

[4] 316. 1, 326. 18, 332. 15 (see note).

[5] See, e.g., Pohlenz, *Vom Zorn Gottes*, p. 67. See also Philo, *de decalogo* 51, 107 for the analogy.

[6] l. 20 ἄλλον ACM.

[7] δι' οὗ Reitzenstein, who assumes also a lacuna after ζωήν.

[8] Cf. perhaps 508. 3.

[9] ⟨αὐτὸν δὲ⟩ Reitzenstein.

[10] 330. 4 (see note). The point is that immortals suffer change, so change among mortals is not death, but rebirth. See 210. 26, 148. 13.

changes of day and night, the seasons, and storms—στροφή meaning περιστροφή. The Cosmos has not its shapes put into it,[1] but changes within itself. Comma after ἔχων.

218. 16-17. εἰ . . . ἰδέα. See 222. 23-4.

20. A word and a picture 'mean' something that they are not—a word is not the physical object it betokens; a picture represents jutting ridges, though it is flat. Punctuate ἔστι γὰρ . . . καὶ ⟨αἱ⟩ . . . ἀκρώρειαι· . . .

24 sqq. This is the climax of the argument against an idle Deity. The οὐσία of a man is life (of a certain kind); the οὐσία of God is creating, and God is naught without it. The term κίνησις is used here because it is the specific mode of motion that determines the οὐσία of a thing, and the writer dares to ascribe an οὐσία to God. Then follows an explanation of technical terms. 'Being in God' is not like 'lying in space'; for space is a body without motion (unlike God), and things that 'lie' do not move (while 'being in' God means receiving from him the motion that is life). All things 'lie' differently 'in' an incorporeal mind.[2] Consider that which 'contains' all (scil., that in which)—it is in nothing, it is surpassingly swift and potent (repeated negatively and positively). This leads up to the analogy of the human mind, the swiftness and power of which is a school commonplace.[3]

220. 16. ἑαυτόν ⟨τε⟩ ὅλον Reitzenstein.

17. ἐξισάσῃς. Cf. the phrase ἰσόθεος φύσις. See H. M. R., pp. 44, 187.

18. ὅμοιον τῷ ὁμοίῳ. By συγγένεια; light (φωτοειδὴς ὄψις) seeks light. Sextus Empiricus, 7. 93: καὶ ὡς τὸ μὲν φῶς, φησὶν ὁ Ποσειδώνιος τὸν Πλάτωνος Τίμαιον ἐξηγούμενος, ὑπὸ τῆς φωτοειδοῦς ὄψεως καταλαμβάνεται, . . . οὕτω καὶ ἡ τῶν ὅλων φύσις ὑπὸ συγγενοῦς ὀφείλει καταλαμβάνεσθαι τοῦ λόγου. Manilius, 4. 886-907. For other references see Dieterich, Mithrasliturgie, pp. 56-7. See also on 158. 19, 370, below. The general theory is a double cognatio or συμπάθεια, of mind with mind, of bodies with bodies.

21. Αἰὼν γενοῦ. Reitzenstein refers to the Naassene doctrines, where Anthropos is Aion (H. M. R., p. 293. 1). R. quotes a magical text in Griffith, Stories of the High Priest of Memphis, i. 3. 13 (p. 92): 'reading the first formula, thou wilt charm the heaven, the earth, the underworld,

---

[1] D ἐγκειμένας, ACM ἐκκειμένας.

[2] φαντασίᾳ is required because it leads up to the analogy of God's mind and man's—ὥσπερ νοήματα (220. 15).

[3] Plato, Theaet., 173 E; de mundo, 391 a 8. See further on 482. 4. For the origin we must look to Posidonius. Gregory of Nyssa, de anima et resurr. 45 D: the elements, upward and downward-tending, differ; ἀλλ᾽ ὅμως οὐδεὶς πόνος τῇ νοερᾷ φύσει ἑκάστῳ παρεῖναι, οἷς ἅπαξ ἐνεφύη, διὰ κράσεως μὴ συνδιασχιζομένη τῇ τῶν στοιχείων ἐναντιότητι. οὐ γὰρ ἐπειδὴ κατὰ τὴν τοπικὴν διάστασιν καὶ τὴν ποίαν ἰδιότητα πόρρωθεν ἀλλήλων ταῦτα νομίζεται, διὰ τοῦτο κάμνει ἡ ἀδιάστατος φύσις τοῖς τοπικῶς διεστηκόσι συναπτομένη κ.τ.λ. See Gronau, Poseidonios, p. 241. Lactantius (see vol. ii, 326) is in the same tradition.

the mountains, the seas. Thou wilt discern what the birds of heaven, and the creeping things shall say, all (see l. 24). Thou shalt see the fish of the deep, there being power of god resting upon water over them. Reading the second formula, if it be that thou art in Amenti, thou art again on earth in thy (usual) form ; thou wilt see the Sun rising in heaven with his cycle of deities, and the Moon in his form of shining ' (*H. M. R.*, p. 167). This section goes far beyond the commonplace Stoic framework in which it is set.

24. ἐπιστήμην, παντὸς ζῴου ἦθος. Cf. 246. 18.

26. τὰς αἰσθήσεις τῶν ποιητῶν (*sc.* στοιχείων). The elements are ποιητοὶ θεοί (Reitz.) See 486. 23.

222. 1. τὴν θάλασσαν. The sea (θάλασσα τῆς φθορᾶς) that separates the world of becoming from the world of being ; it must be crossed as the Israelites crossed the Red Sea (Reitzenstein, *H. M. R.* 294, 244).

7. εὐθεῖα, διὰ . . . ῥᾳδία, ὁδεύοντί σοι Reitzenstein.

Libellus XII. i. **222.** 24–224. 1. (εἰ δέ τίς ἐστιν) καὶ ποία . . . οὗτος . . . αὐτὸς . . . ὡς περιηπλωμένος Reitzenstein. Perhaps ὡς ⟨ἱ⟩περηπλωμένος ; used by Proclus of the Aether ; and Schol. *in Procli remp.* ii. 372. 15 φανὸν δὲ τὸ ὅλον ὑπὸ τῷ Ἡλίῳ ἀτεχνῶς ὑπερηπλωμένον. Iamblichus, *de myst.* 7. 2. For the οὐσία of God, see 164. 22, 168. 24.

224. 3. Retain θεός . . . θεοί: Reitzenstein reads ὥσπερ ⟨⟨καὶ⟩⟩ ζωή, and brackets ἐν δέ . . . ἀγαθὸν (ll. 9–11) ; i.e. the νοῦς is a κοινὸς νοῦς (see on 180. 1), and the bracketed words protest against this idea. ζέουσιν (l. 15) is perhaps Stoic ; ζέσις enters into the definition of θυμός (Nemesius, *de nat. hom.* 692 A).

22. ἀθεότης, ἔπειτα δόξα, αἷς Kroll.

226. 10. ἔχον, ⟨χαιρέτω⟩ ὁ Kroll.

27. μεταβολῆς: death (cf. 234. 17) ; and perhaps κοινότητα for ποιότητα (A. D. N.). But cf. 210. 4, where the same dubious phrase is used.

228. 3. The Agathos Daimon says that all is one, καὶ μάλιστα ⟨τὰ⟩ νοητὰ ⟨ἀ⟩σώματα.[1] (?) As the text proceeds to state, what we live by are incorporeal : δύναμις, ἐνέργεια, and Αἰών, which is a δύναμις of God (208. 6) ; and the mind of Aion, which (ὅσπερ Reitz.) is also his soul, is good ; hence nothing that is νοητόν has extension—it is one (cf. 220. 15). l. 6. ὡς εἶναι Reitz. In l. 9 should we read ⟨καὶ⟩ τοῦ ν⟨όμ⟩ου, comparing 224. 33–225. 1, and l. 12 ? It is clear that νοῦς and ψυχή are identified here ; and the argument is that God can raise the good man *himself* above fate and penal law, or place the heedless under them. See further Reitzenstein, *H. M. R.*, p. 408.

17. Ἄριστα καὶ θείως. So Kroll ; place bracket after Δαίμονος.

230. 7. νοῦν καὶ . . . λόγον. These gifts confer immortality ; therefore λόγος is used here of a divine power, which is restricted—not common to all men, as in the parallel 150. 9. There the λογικοί (152. 2) had not

---

[1] Contrast τὰ ἐν σώματι ἀσώματα (l. 24).

accepted the preaching ; here the ἐλλόγιμοι[1] are the men who have νοῦς for their pilot, as opposed to the ἄλογοι. This interpretation is reinforced by l. 12, where *both* lead the good to the troop of the gods, and l. 24, where God is declared to be the father of νοῦς and λόγος, and λόγος is both image and νοῦς (= ψυχή) of God. The writer of the marginal note (l. 8)—τὸν δὲ προφορικὸν ἔχει[2]—evidently considered that the Stoic formulae, ἐνδιάθετος and πρ. λόγος, were in question. On this view, we should connect the function of λόγος with such phrases as συνυπάρχει δὲ τῷ λόγῳ ἡ τῶν τιμίων γνῶσις, where πνεῦμα is associated with opinion (448. 23), and ὁ δὲ λόγος τῆς οὐσίας (*ib.* 13).[3] Above all, the phrases in 116. 7 *sqq.* should be compared.[4] The material collected by Reitzenstein shows that λογικός could stand for πνευματικός (as ἐλλόγιμος does here).[5] The initiated became the Λόγος θεοῦ,[6] and λογικός is 'geistig, vergeistigt'. Compare the phrase ἐνδιάθετον ἄνθρωπον (244. 9 note) ; after the Rebirth he is purified by the powers of God εἰς συνάρθρωσιν τοῦ λόγου. Though the technical term is Stoic, it has been transported into an entirely different sphere, where the elect win rebirth by means of an influx from God.[7] This πνεῦμα is not of Stoic vintage.

22. Retain the text ; as we saw above, both νοῖς and λόγος give immortality, and both (τούτων) own God as Father.[8] The λόγος is an image[9] of God in man—it belongs to a philosophical train of ideas to say that body is the image of the idea, and the idea of the soul. For the 'wrappings' (ll. 22-3) see on 194. 27.

Libellus XII. ii. **234.** 22-236. 2. It may be suspected that this paragraph has its own unity, if we can suppose that it uses the theory of sympathy. Like knows like. Knowledge by divination is one way, and ordinary knowledge (through sight) another. The conversation of man with God (l. 24) presupposes the doctrine that dreams are *deorum adpulsu*, and appears to answer closely to the third alternative given by

---

[1] 226. 17, 21, 25)(ἄλογοι 226. 18.

[2] It has been supposed that the subject of the verb here is the writer of the treatise. But there seems no reason why a glossator should not mean ἔχει (ὁ ἄνθρωπος), if he recognized that the ἐνδιάθετος λόγος was in question. In what follows Tat misunderstands precisely this point.

[3] Also περινοητικὸς λόγος in *Exc.* XVII, and probably *intellegentia* (296. 12).

[4] ὁ δὲ ἐκ νοῦς φωτεινὸς λόγος υἱὸς θεοῦ.—τὸ ἐν σοὶ βλέπον καὶ ἀκοῦον· (ὁ) λόγος κυρίου (υἱός), ὁ δὲ νοῦς πατὴρ θεός. οὐ γὰρ διΐστανται ἀπ' ἀλλήλων κ.τ.λ. Also 252. 7 (associated with λογικὴ θυσία), 19 (λόγον γὰρ τὸν σὸν ποιμαίνει ὁ νοῦς, πνευματοφόρε ... ἀπὸ τοῦ (σοῦ) Αἰῶνος εὐλογίαν εὗρον). Frs. 23, 27, 29, 30.

[5] *H. M. K.*, pp. 328 *sqq.* The formation answers to ἔννους.

[6] ὁ σὸς Λόγος δι' ἐμοῦ ὑμνεῖ σε· δι' ἐμοῦ δέξαι, τὸ πᾶν, λόγῳ λογικὴν θυσίαν (252. 7-8); 244. 8 διὰ τοῦ Λόγου.

[7] See also Bousset, *Kyrios*, p. 386, n. 1 and 379 ; *G. G. A.*, 1914, pp. 728 *sqq.* ; Braüninger, *H. T.*, pp. 14 *sqq.* For the προφορικὸς λόγος see note on 330. 21.

[8] l. 24 (νόμιζε) πατέρα Reitzenstein.

[9] Compare l. 11 above.

Cicero, 'quod ipsi di cum dormientibus conloquantur'.[1]   The mention of past, present, and future [2] is consistent with the Posidonian theory that the power of divination is first from God, then from fate, and lastly from nature : for everything happens by fate—'causa aeterna rerum, cur et ea, quae praeterierunt, facta sint et, quae instant, fiant et, quae sequuntur, futura sint' (*de div.* i. 125-6 ; Posidonian).   § 20 a starts with the affinity of kinds to particular elements,[3] in contrast to the citizen of the Universe (the microcosm), who is at home with all.   The point is that sight, by symphysis, betrays his affinity with the heavens : ἐμοὶ δὲ δοκεῖ μάλιστα τοιαύτην πρὸς τὸ μαντικὸν πνεῦμα λαμβάνειν σύγκρασιν ψυχὴ καὶ σύμπηξιν, οἵαν πρὸς τὸ φῶς ἡ ὄψις ὁμοιοπαθὲς γινόμενον: . . . ἐξάπτει γὰρ καὶ προάγεται καὶ συνεξορμᾷ τῆς αἰσθήσεως τὴν ὁρατικὴν δύναμιν (ὁ ἥλιος), ὡς τῆς ψυχῆς τὴν μαντικήν ('Απόλλων).[4]   The *order* of the heavens is seen with the eye of the soul (236. 6, 212. 24 ; Plut. *ibid.*).

236. 10-11. The three orders are named because *continuatio* is the theme ; comma after καλῶν.

12. εἶθ' αἱ CMZ. εἰ . . . εἰσιν om. A.   15. μέρη M.   It may be suspected that this passage gave one of those lists of four upper and four lower elements which show the balance of opposites existing in the Cosmos— ἰσότης καὶ ἐναντιότης.   See on 122. 25, 304. 16 with references.   Here, as there, there is confusion because there is a double list of ' higher ' opposites, and they cannot simply be emended away.   We have—

1. οὐρανὸς καὶ γῆ | καὶ ὕδωρ [5] καὶ ἀήρ
2. ζωὴ καὶ ἀθανασία | καὶ ψυχὴ καὶ νοῦς
3. εἱμαρμένη καὶ ἀνάγκη | καὶ πρόνοια καὶ φύσις.

I have rearranged the order for comparison.   It is evident that (2) contains one set of ' parts ' relating to the soul, and (3) another set relating to the ἁρμονία.   Again, the three sets of four are themselves symmetrically divided into pairs—ἡ εἰς ἴσα τομή.   For ζωὴ κ. ἀθανασία cf. 214. 9 (note), 24.   It is tempting to connect the pair with ζ. κ. φῶς, and to recall 122. 30, 126. 3, which derive soul and mind from these elements.

17. διαμονή· Life.   Cf. 208. 28 διαμένουσα ⟨ἐν⟩ τῇ ταυτότητι, l. 13, **206.** 22, and 266. 24.

21. σωρόν.   The Cosmos is not an aggregate of atoms, but has a ἕξις.

---

[1] *de div.* i. 64.

[2] This indicates a source which used the example of Calchas (vol. ii, p. 364).

[3] This is Stoic commonplace : Cic. *de nat. deor.* ii. 42 ; Sext. Emp. *adv. math.* 9. 86 ; Apuleius, *de deo Socr.* 8 ; Philo, *de plantat.* 2 sqq. *de gigant.* 6 sqq., *de somn.* i. 133-45.   For analysis see Bousset, *Schulbetrieb*, pp. 14 *sqq.*, Jaeger, *Aristoteles*, p. 166.   It appears certain that Posidonius applied the theory of symphysis to divination, but much is still in controversy : see Reinhardt, *K. u. S.*, pp. 214 *sqq.* ; Heinemann, *Poseidonios*, ii, pp. 324 *sqq.*

[4] Plut. *de defectu*, c. 42, 433 D–E.   Cf. Posidonius *ap.* Sext. Emp., *adv. math.*, 7. 93.

[5] ὕδωρ κ. γῆ ACM.

Libellus XIII. **238.** 22. Σοφία νοερά is the Mother, the Will the Father, the seed the Good. After parents, the child—the transposition in ll. 24–6 is unneeded.[1] The initiate becomes the Λόγος—cf. 244. 15–16. See *Poimandres*, pp. 214 *sqq.*

240. 9. Zielinski connects the verse fragment with l. 30 τῶν ... φρενῶν, comparing Eur. *Bacch.* 944, 1269. It is reasonable to compare the sense of 248. 17 ἀγνοεῖς ὅτι θεὸς πέφυκας καὶ τοῦ ἑνὸς παῖς, l. 2 θεοῦ θεὸς παῖς, and perhaps l. 1 ἄμοιρος.[2] It is possible that l. 1 expresses Tat's reason for asking about the reborn—ἄμοιρος γὰρ τῆς ἐν νοῖ οὐσίας καὶ τῆς νοητῆς (= νοερᾶς) ⟨γενέσεως εἰμί⟩.[3] In l. 3 τὸ πᾶν, ἐν παντί, ἐκ πασῶν is a triadic formula that should be kept.

The natural parallel is given by those passages in Arnobius (Cornelius Labeo) which describe the soul as not subject to the laws of fate, and as returning to its father's seat. See on 244. 4.

14 *sqq.* Cf. ἆρ' οὐχ ὅτι μὲν σοὶ ἐγὼ οὐχ ὁ ἁπτὸς οὗτος καὶ τῇ αἰσθήσει ὑποπτωτός, ὁ δὲ ἐπὶ πλεῖστον ἀφεστηκὼς τοῦ σώματος, ὁ ἀχρώματος καὶ ἀσχημάτιστος, καὶ χερσὶ μὲν οὐδαμῶς ἐπαφητός, διανοίᾳ δὲ μόνῃ κρατητός; Porphyry, *Ad Marcellam*, 8 (see Reitzenstein, *Historia Monachorum*, p. 99).[4] R. explains this as concerned with the 'συνάρθρωσις τοῦ λόγου (cf. 244. 16)—des Gottwesens, zu dem der Myste wird (daher διαρθροῦν bei Porphyrius, c. 10)'.—c. 10. εἰ μελετῴης εἰς ἑαυτὴν ἀναβαίνειν ἀπὸ τοῦ σώματος πάντα τὰ διασκεδασθέντα σου μέλη καὶ εἰς πλῆθος κατακερματισθέντα ἀπὸ τῆς τέως ἐν μεγέθει δυνάμεως ἰσχυούσης ἑνώσεως. συνάγοις δ' ἂν καὶ ἑνίζοις τὰς ἐμφύτους ἐννοίας καὶ διαρθροῦν συγκεχυμένας καὶ εἰς φῶς ἕλκειν ἐσκοτισμένας πειρωμένη. Epiphanius, *Haer.* 26. 13: ὅτι ἐπέγνων ἐμαυτήν, φησί, καὶ συνέλεξα ἐμαυτὴν ἐκ πανταχόθεν ... καὶ συνέλεξα τὰ μέλη τὰ διεσκορπισμένα. In l. 19 διαμεμέλισταί (Keil) μοι τὸ πρῶτον σύνθετον εἶδος should be read. Cf. 246. 6 συνετέθη νοερὰ γένεσις καὶ ἐθεώθημεν τῇ γενέσει. This is after the reception of the ten powers. Cf. the four στοιχεῖα in Porph. c. 24: πίστις, ἀλήθεια, ἔρως, ἐλπίς. (My quotations are taken from R.). See further Procl. *in Tim.* i. 212. 17 (Diehl):

δηθύνοντι γὰρ βροτῷ κραιπνοὶ μάκαρες τελέθουσι

(*Orac. chald.* 56)

καὶ τὴν τάξιν τῶν θείων ἔργων ἀσάλευτον φυλάττειν ἀρετάς τε ἀπὸ τῆς γενέσεως καθαρτικὰς καὶ ἀναγωγοὺς προβεβλῆσθαι καὶ πίστιν καὶ ἀλήθειαν καὶ ἔρωτα, ταύτην ἐκείνην τὴν τριάδα, καὶ ἐλπίδα τῶν ἀγαθῶν ἄτρεπτόν τε ὑποδοχὴν τοῦ θείου φωτὸς καὶ ἔκστασιν ἀπὸ πάντων τῶν ἄλλων ἐπιτηδευμάτων, ἵνα μόνος τις τῷ θεῷ μόνῳ συνῇ καὶ μὴ μετὰ πλήθους τῷ ἑνὶ συνάπτειν ἑαυτὸν ἐγχειρῇ.

---

[1] The γενεσιουργός of 240. 27 is the teacher, the Will personified (Reitzenstein). Cf. 254. 1, and (with R.) 'complexus Mithram sacerdotem et meum iam parentem' (Apuleius, *Metamorph.* 11. 25). See also *H. M. R.*, p. 48.

[2] 130. 26 τοὺς ἐν ἀγνοίᾳ τοῦ γένους, ... υἱοὺς δὲ σοῦ.

[3] Cf. l. 17 ἐγεννήθην ἐν νῷ; 246. 6 νοερὰ γένεσις; 242. 16, 248. 5.

[4] Also in *Nachr. G. G.*, 1916, pp. 409 *sqq.*

27. See on 238. 22.

28. εἶς. The συνάρθρωσις τοῦ λόγου.

242. 23. See on 128. 1; the zodiacal twelve; but in **244.** 19 the planetary seven reappear.

244. 4. κακία. It is perhaps worth noting that the translator in *Asclepius* renders this word by *malignitas* (344. 17—and 308. 21?).

19–**246.** 1. Here the planetary seven recur: there are seven divine powers answering to them, and then three more are added in a group to make up the Decad, a misfit. See Bousset, *Hauptprobleme*, p. 364, *G. G. A.*, 1914, p. 732.

The references to father and son in connexion with the Rebirth may be referred to the theory that the soul has strayed, but may return to the Father's seat—πατρικὴ αὐλα. See especially Arnobius, *adv. nat.* 2. 62: deo esse se gnatos nec fati obnoxios legibus, si uitam restrictius egerint, aulam sibi eius patere, ac post hominis functionem prohibente se nullo tamquam in sedem referre patritam?[1]

9. ἐνδιάθετον ἄνθρωπον. Kroll emends to λόγον (ᾱνον) which gives the interpretation, but is not needed. He is the 'inner' man, the ἐλλόγιμος of *Corp.* XII. i (note on 230. 7), exposed to the torments of the body, but 'put together again' by the Λόγος (l. 15). Hence the odd phrase συνετίθη ἡ νοερὰ γένεσις (246. 6).[2] See also on 330. 21 *sqq*.

16. See on 240. 14.

24. The figure of the ascent of the soul, suggested by the mention of the seven stages; cf. 154. 10 (A. D. N.).

248. 1. ἡ γὰρ δεκάς . . . ἐστὶ ψυχογόνος. Proclus. *In Tim.* i. 87. 28 (Diehl): ἥ τε γὰρ δεκὰς τὴν ἐπιστροφὴν πάντων δηλοῖ τῶν ἐγκοσμίων τὴν ἐπὶ τὸ ἕν. 316. 16 *sqq.*: ὁ μὲν γὰρ ὁ πατὴρ ἦν μονάς, ὁ δὲ ὁ πατὴρ καὶ ποιητὴς τετράς, ὁ δέ, ὡς οἱ Πυθαγόρειοί φασι, δεκάς, καὶ αὕτη τῶν θείων ἡ τάξις

$$\text{ἔστ' ἂν ἵκηται}$$

(προϊὼν ὁ θεῖος ἀριθμός,

μουνάδος ἐκ κευθμῶνος ἀκηράτου)

τετράδα ἐπὶ ζαθέην· ἣ δὴ τέκε μητέρα πάντων,

πανδεχέα, πρέσβειραν, ὅρον περὶ πᾶσι τιθεῖσαν,

ἄτροπον, ἀκαμάτην· δεκάδα κλείουσί μιν ἁγνήν.

. . . ἡ δημιουργικὴ δεκάς . . . νοῦν μὲν ἐλλάμπουσα ταῖς ψυχαῖς, ἅτε νοῦς οὖσα ὁλικός, ψυχὴν δὲ σώμασιν, ὡς τὴν αἰτίαν αὐτῆς ἔχουσά τε καὶ περιέχουσα κτλ. (cf. ii. 53. 1). ii. 236. 12: δεκαδικῶς μέν, ἵνα κοσμικὴ ψυχὴ γένηται· κόσμου γὰρ ἡ δεκὰς ἀριθμός. Cf. Iamblichus, *De vita Pythag.* 228 Nauck, and in general Kern, *Orphic. frag., fr.* 309–16.

Hippolytus, *Refut.* 4. 43: Αἰγύπτιοι δὲ . . . ψηφίσαντες τάδε διαστήματα τῶν

---

[1] Further on Arnobius (Cornelius Labeo) below on iv. 7. 8. The 'father's hall' is also Chaldaic, and references to it are found in the Proclus-Tzetzes Scholia to Hesiod.

[2] *H. M. R.*, pp. 48–9.

μοιρῶν ἐξ ἐπιπνοίας θειοτάτης ἔφασαν τὸν θεὸν εἶναι μονάδα ἀδιαίρετον καὶ αὐτὴν
ἑαυτὴν γεννῶσαν καὶ ἐξ αὐτῆς τὰ πάντα κατεσκευάσθαι· αὕτη γάρ, φησίν,
ἀγέννητος οὖσα τοὺς ἑξῆς ἀριθμοὺς γεννᾷ, οἷον ἐφ' ἑαυτὴν ἡ μονὰς ἐπιπροσ-
τεθεῖσα γεννᾷ τὴν δυάδα καὶ ὁμοίως ... μέχρι τῆς δεκάδος, ἥτις ἀρχὴ καὶ τὸ τέλος
τῶν ἀριθμῶν, ἵνα γένηται πρώτη καὶ δεκάτη ἡ μονὰς διὰ τὸ καὶ τὴν δεκάδα ἰσοδυ-
ναμεῖν καὶ ἀριθμεῖσθαι εἰς μονάδα ... προσῳκείωται δὲ τῇ μονάδι τὸ φῶς, τῇ δὲ
δυάδι τὸ σκότος, καὶ τῷ μὲν φωτὶ κατὰ φύσιν ἡ ζωή, τῇ δὲ δυάδι ὁ θάνατος· καὶ τῇ
μὲν ζωῇ ἡ δικαιοσύνη, τῷ δὲ θανάτῳ ἡ ἀδικία.

It is evident from 246. 23 that the Twelve signifies the body, which is
produced by the Zodiac; and the Decad, which produces the soul, con-
quers it.   Reitzenstein [1] notes that in Chaldaic (and therefore late Persian)
lore the body is connected with the Zodiac. We must retain (l. 2) ἔνθα
... πνεύματος. The One contains the Decad and the Decad the One—it
is πνεῦμα, which here ranks with ζωὴ καὶ φῶς among the higher elements
received by the reborn.[2] R. notes that the sign of the Aion is the letter I,
which can mean the Decad, and also the One. (Cf. Monoimos in Hippol.
Refut. 8. 12-13). He takes this as support for the view that Tat's ecstasy
(246. 15-19) is 'das Empfindung, als Aion, als der Weltgott, der ja "der
Mensch" oder "die Seele" ist'.

9. See on 254. 15.

13. For Reitzenstein's reading see on 188. 22.

15. ἐνώσεως Kroll.

18. ὕμνον οὖν τῷ θεῷ τοῦτον ἀναθῶμεν, τὴν εἰς αὐτὸν ἐξομοίωσιν καταλιπῶ-
μεν τὴν ῥέουσαν οὐσίαν, ἐλθῶμεν ἐπὶ τὸν ἀληθῆ σκοπόν· γνωρίσωμεν τὸν δεσπότην, ἀγαπήσωμεν τὸν πατέρα· καλοῦντι πεισθῶμεν, τῷ θερμῷ προσδράμωμεν τὸ
ψυχρὸν ἐκφυγόντες· πῦρ γενώμεθα, διὰ πυρὸς ὁδεύσωμεν. ἔχομεν εὔλυτον ὁδὸν
εἰς ἀνέλευσιν· πατὴρ ὁδηγεῖ πυρὸς ὁδοὺς ἀναπτύξας μὴ ταπεινὸν ἐκ λήθης ῥεύσω-
μεν χεῦμα (Chaldaic Oracle *ap.* Procl. *exc. Vatic.* 193. 12: Kroll, *orac.
chald.*, p. 54). Olympiodorus *in Phaed.* 244. 21 Norvin: διὸ καὶ τὸ λόγιόν
φησι, τὰς ψυχὰς ἀναγομένας τὸν παιᾶνα ᾄ͜ειν. Cf. *Exc.* XXIII *ad fin.*

19. ἣν ἔφης ἐπὶ τὴν Ὀγδοάδα γενόμενον νοῦν ἀκοῦσαι τῶν δυνάμεων, καθὼς
Ὀγδοάδα ὁ Π. ἐθέσπισε Reitz. A. D. N. would bracket ὀγδοάδα in any case,
also the whole clause (καθὼς ... ἐθέσπισε), unless the words are possibly
spoken by the initiate.

250. 10 *sqq.* See *H. M. R.*, pp. 50 *sqq.*

21. ἐπι⟨σ⟩τάξαντα?

252. 11. σῇ βουλῇ ἀπὸ σοῦ, ἐπὶ δὲ τὸ πᾶν. The Will and the All are
identical.   τὸ θέλημα αὐτοῦ ἔργον ἐστὶν καὶ τοῦτο κόσμος ὀνομάζεται (Clem.
Paedag. 1. 6. 27. (114 P.). Cited by Bräuninger, *H. T.*, p. 26, n. 1 and
applied by Reitzenstein to this text). The βουλή is σοφία—see 238. 22?[3]

---

[1] *H. M. R.*, pp. 49-50. In the Valentinian system the Decad signified the ten
circles of heaven, the Duodecad the Zodiac (Irenaeus, i. 17. 1; Bousset, *Hauptprobleme*, p. 341).

[2] See 252. 4, 19-20, and Bousset, *G. G. A.*, 1914, p. 716.

[3] *H. M. R.*, p. 287.

19-20. πνεῦμα θεέ . . . πνευματοφόρε. πνευμά⟨τιζε⟩ Keil. One must distinguish between the corporeal πνεῦμα of the Stoics and the Νοῦς that is ζωή καὶ φῶς. Cf. note on 122. 25, 118. 12 (codd.) θεὸς τοῦ πυρὸς καὶ πνεύματος, 146. 2 πνεῦμα λεπτὸν νοερόν. So here φώτιζε . . . πνευμάτιζε are natural words for 'illuminate and inspire'.

σὺ εἶ ὁ θεός. Anacletic. Cf. 164. 14 sqq., and the rich material in Norden, *Agn. Theos*, pp. 176 sqq., *H. M. R.*, p. 177.

254. 3-4. σὺ ὁ Κύριος. See Bousset, *Kyrios*, p. 118; Index, s. vv. κύριος, dominus ; also Peterson, ΕΙΣ ΘΕΟΣ, *passim*.

15. διάβολοι. A mystery has been transmitted to the initiate, and he must not divulge it— be a 'blabber'. See on 132. 4; also 238. 9, 250. 2, *publicare*, 288. 2. It can stand, as a technical expression, without a genitive. For ἀρετῆς (l. 13) cf. (with Reitzenstein) 432. 28, and alchemical usage (μηδενὶ σαφῶς καταλέγων τὴν τοιαύτην ἀρετήν). τοῦ παντός (l. 21 = 248. 9) : *sc.* τοῦ ἑνὸς καὶ τοῦ παντός (250. 30).

16. ⟨ἑαυτοῦ⟩ ἐθεμελιώθη Reitzenstein. But perhaps the meaning is that silence is golden.

Libellus XIV. **256.** 1-10. Reitzenstein refers this introduction to the previous *libellus.* The point has some little importance because γνῶσις (l. 5) is a word peculiar to the 'Oriental' tracts, to which *Lib.* XIII belongs, unlike XIV (*Poimandres*, p. 191; Bräuninger, *H. T.*, p. 40).

20. ἄρχει is absolute ; retain the text, and compare 184. 1-4.

26-7. This is the *felix* formula; see on 390. 7, 418. 14.

260. 1. ὥσπερ σῶμα. In making, God becomes visible; 256. 23-4.

9. See on 214. 24.

Libellus XVI. **262.** 7 sqq. For this *libellus* see Reinhardt, *K. u. S.*, pp. 365 sqq. (Helios Demiourgos), to whose explanation these notes are indebted.

15. ἀντίδειξιν = refutation.

264. 9. ἀποδείξεων ἐνεργητικούς. It may be suggested that this means : the Greeks argue and produce mere conclusions, the Egyptian language has words of power (l. 2) that produce effects (l. 12).[1] The contrast lies between Greek style and Egyptian names, because the wonder-working force of ὀνόματα βάρβαρα is in question. Cf. the Chaldaic oracle : ὀ. β. μήποτ' ἀλλάξῃς.[2] Psellus, *Expos. orac. chald.* 1132 C (Migne) : εἰσὶν ὀνόματα παρ' ἑκάστοις ἔθνεσι θεοπαράδοτα δύναμιν ἐν ταῖς τελεταῖς ἄρρητον ἔχοντα·

---

[1] Tatian says (*c. Graec.*, c. 4) that the Greek philosophers are ψιλόψοφοι, not φιλόσοφοι, contradicting one another; cf. l. 10. It is not contended that the Greeks don't 'prove', but that their words don't perform. The addition of μόνον would make the sense less dubious.

[2] Kroll, *Orac. Chald.*, p. 58; *Pap. Lond.* 122. 20 : οἶδα σου καὶ τὰ ὀνόματα βάρβαρα ; Origen, *c. Celsum* i. 24-5, 28; Euseb. *Pr. ev.* 4. 1. 11 ; Proclus, *In Crat.*, p. 32 Pasquali (δραστήρια); Synesius, *calv. enc.* 1185 A (Migne). Reference may also be made to the lists given in 'Hermetica', *Cat. codd. astr. graec.* 8. 2, pp. 149 sqq.

μὴ οὖν μήτ᾽ ἀλλάξῃς αὐτὰ εἰς τὴν Ἑλληνικὴν διάλεκτον (e. g. Seraphim, Michael, etc.). οὕτω μὲν λεγόμενα κατὰ τὴν Ἑβραϊκὴν διάλεκτον, ἐνέργειαν ἐν ταῖς τελεταῖς ἔχει ἄρρητον· ἀμειφθέντα δὲ ἐν τοῖς Ἑλληνικοῖς ὀνόμασιν, ἀσθενῆ. In l. 9 should καινούς be retained? The point is not that the Greeks cannot argue, but that the language does not use the venerable forms. Cf. νεωτεροποιοί . . . κατὰ τὴν ἄστατον εὑρεσιλογίαν μεταπλάττουσι· βάρβαροι δὲ μόνιμοι . . . καὶ τοῖς λόγοις βεβαίως τοῖς αὐτοῖς ἐμμένουσι . . . διαμείβειν δὲ αὐτοὺς κατ᾽ οὐδένα τρόπον οὐδένι ἀνθρώπῳ θεμιτόν ἐστι (*Abamm. resp.* 7. 5).

15. This is ritual language: colon at end of l. 15, and comma after ἐν ἑνί. δευτεροῦντος (-όω) may just be possible in the sense that the One is not double, does not repeat itself (like Pharaoh's dream, *Gen.* 41. 32). In l. 20 keep τὸ πάντα καὶ ἓν δοκοῖν[τι] καὶ ταὐτὸν εἶναι; and l. 24 δεῖ, εἴ γε ἓν ἔστιν—ἔστι δέ—καὶ οὐδ. π. ἐν ὄντα. If there is a One at all—and there is—it must be the πλήρωμα of all things.

27. πολλὰς πηγὰς ὑδάτων καὶ πυρός. While 'air' is possible, in place of fire (ll. 27, 29), there is reason to believe that the phenomenon of hot mineral springs is used as evidence that the three elements may spring from one root.[1] The theory is that sea-water is filtered through the channels of the earth, driven by πνεῦμα, and may gather other qualities from the substances it passes through. Here in little is the cycle of the elements, a sign of the great cycle accomplished in the Cosmos by the power of the Sun (ἀναδρομή, καταδρομή, τροφή).[2] Seneca may point the moral (*N. Q.* 3. 10. 4) : omnia in omnibus sunt : non tantum aër in ignem transit sed nunquam sine aëre est . . . transit aër in umorem sed ⟨est⟩ nihilominus non sine umore . . . habet terra umorem ; hunc exprimit ; habet aëra etc.

266. 1. γῆν ⟨συν⟩δεῖ (Reinhardt) is textually preferable to συνάγει ; the meaning is the same—a reference to the σύνδεσμος. Cf. Hermippus in vol. ii. 433. 3.

2-7. There is a universal cycle—πάντα . . . πάντα . . . διδοὺς πᾶσι. The Sun's light penetrates to every part of the Cosmos. (This was one reason why Posidonius argued that the Sun was greater than the earth : Diog. Laert. 7. 144.) See Basil, *Hexaem.* 2. 7 ; Proclus, *in Crat.*, pp. 101-102 Pasquali. For l. 5 cf. Basil, *loc. cit.*: τῷ κόσμῳ τὴν τοῦ φωτὸς χάριν ἀθρόως ἐνέθηκε. The light reaches the heaven above, floods the air beneath,[3]

---

[1] See *de mundo*, 395 b 24 ; Sen. *N. Q.* 3. 4 ; J. Lydus, *de mens.* 4. 8 : ὅτι ὅσῃ ἂν πυρὸς νομὴ καίοιτο, σηραγγώδη ἀνάγκη τυγχάνειν τὴν ἐν βάθει γῆν, ἐξ ἧς αἰτίας τὰ θερμὰ ὕδατα, διὸ καὶ βλεννώδης ἡ φύσις τῶν τοιούτων ὑδάτων ; Basil, *Hexaemeros*, 5. 6. For Posidonius' theory of springs see Reinhardt, *Poseidonios*, pp. 116-19 ; Gronau, *Quelle f. B's Hex.*, p. 71, *Poseidonios*, p. 94.

[2] See Jaeger, *Nemesios*, pp. 68 *sqq.* In 264. 28 R. reads ⟨τὰς δὲ κεκρυμμένας⟩ ἐν τοῖς μεσαιτάτοις μέρεσι ; but the words may refer to distance from the source, the sea. l. 29 ὁρ⟨μ⟩ωμένας ? For l. 31 add (with R.) a reference to *N. Q.* 2. 5.

[3] Air is by nature dark, and needs sunlight : Sen., *N. Q.* 2. 10, frigidus per se et obscurus ; lumen illi calorque aliunde sunt.

and penetrates to the uttermost depth and abyss upon earth (the planet, not the element). Cleomedes (*de mot. circ.*, pp. 110–111, Ziegler) argued that there was no paradox in the theory that earth, a point, sent up nourishment to the heavens, because its density was so great in comparison. Thus the road up and down is continuous through the Cosmos.

7. This asserts that the Sun is *mens mundi* (so Reinhardt). The Sun himself is the νοητὴ (= νοερὰ) οὐσία, and the rays of light are the receptacle; but none save the Sun knows whence that substance comes, or whither it goes. Julian, *Or.* 4. 134 a: ἄχραντον εἶναι ἐνέργειαν αὐτοῦ τοῦ καθαροῦ νοῦ τὴν ἀπανταχῇ προϊοῦσαν αὐγὴν ἔφη (Reinhardt). The next lines are unintelligible as they stand. But it is distinctly stated that no conjecture is needed to see the Sun—it is the sight-ray itself (αὐτὴ ἡ ὄψις) that illuminates the whole Cosmos. This rests upon the theory that light sees with us; see on 268. 24.

16. It is probable that the Sun is said to hold the middle position for the reason given in ll. 24 *sqq.* His reins are life ... immortality and becoming, the links that bind the regions, above and below, to him; for the theme is still the σύνδεσμος (ἀναδήσας l. 19) that the Sun makes between heaven and earth. Julian, *Or.* 4. 138 c: ἐπεὶ καί, εἰ μέσον ἔφαμεν ἐν μέσοις ἱδρῦσθαι τὸν θεὸν τοῖς νοεροῖς θεοῖς, ποταπή τις ἡ μεσότης ἐστὶν ὧν αὖ χρὴ μέσον αὐτὸν ὑπολαβεῖν, αὐτὸς ἡμῖν ὁ Βασιλεὺς εἰπεῖν Ἥλιος δοίη. μεσότητα μὲν δὴ φαμεν οὐ τὴν ἐν τοῖς ἐναντίοις θεωρουμένην ἴσον ἀφεστῶσαν τῶν ἄκρων, ... ἀλλὰ τὴν ἑνωτικὴν καὶ συνάγουσαν τὰ διεστῶτα ... τίνα οὖν ἐστιν, ἃ συνάγει, καὶ τίνων ἐστὶ μέσος; φημὶ δὴ οὖν ὅτι τῶν τε ἐμφανῶν καὶ περικοσμίων θεῶν καὶ τῶν ἀύλων καὶ νοητῶν, οἳ περὶ τἀγαθόν εἰσιν, ὥσπερ πολυπλασιαζομένης ἀπαθῶς καὶ ἄνευ προσθήκης τῆς νοητῆς καὶ θείας οὐσίας. ... [140 B] πρόδηλον οὖν ὅτι καὶ τὸ γόνιμον τοῦ Βασιλέως Ἡλίου τῆς ζωῆς μέσον ἐστὶν ἀμφοῖν. For the chariot Pl. *Phdr.* 246 E; Philo *de somn.* 294, *de mundo* 400 l. 7; Arnobius, *adv. nat.* 3. 30; and Dion Chrysostom xxxvi. 55, quoted at p. 415, n. 3, below.

For 'reins' see Macrobius, *Sat.* I. 18. 15–16. physici Διώνυσον Διὸς νοῦν quia solem mundi mentem esse dixerunt, mundus autem vocatur caelum, quod appellant Iovem. ... Liber a Romanis appellatur, quod liber et vagus est, ut ait Naevius [1]

> hac qua sol vagus igneas habenas
> inmittit proprius iugatque terrae. [2]

The probable source is Cornelius Labeo; see on Arnobius below.

24–268. 10. The μεταβολαί are not simply death; they are the characteristic form of life here—continuous production of life true to type (292. 16), just as permanence is the characteristic of the upper universe. By changes the Sun refashions and transforms the living creatures in these parts of the Cosmos, like the turn of a screw, one generation into another, [3]

---

[1] *Laevius* L. Müller.   [2] So, Lydus, *de mens.*, pp. 73. 22, 72. 8.
[3] ἄλληλα is not reciprocal as ἀλληλοφαγία means eating others of your kind, and

change of one into another, exchanging kind for kind, individual for individual (292. 11); and likewise the Sun carries on his creative work with the stars (by a different kind of change). This ceaseless fecundity is Posidonian commonplace: Philo, *de op f. mundi*, 43-44; Cic., *de nat. deor.* 2. 121; vol. iv. 148; and 290. 24; 292. 15. Also (with Reinhardt) Diodorus II. cc. 49 *sqq.*, esp. c. 50: διὰ τῆς συγγενοῦς φιλοζωίας τὰς διαδοχὰς εἰς ἀίδιον ἄγουσα διαμονῆς κύκλον. τόπῳ (l. 9) probably refers to the *continuatio* of life throughout the Universe, as the next two paragraphs go to show. Cf. 290. 3; 292. 1.

24. πληροῖ αὐτὸν ὀγκῶν. The theory is that matter has no magnitude, mass, or other characteristics until the form gives it ὄγκος. Plot. *Enn.* 2. 4. 11: οὐ τοίνυν δεῖ ὄγκον εἶναι τὸ δεξόμενον τὸ εἶδος, ἀλλ' ὁμοῦ τῷ γενέσθαι ὄγκον καὶ τὴν ἄλλην ποιότητα δέχεσθαι καὶ φάντασμα μὲν ἔχειν ὄγκου εἰς ἐπιτηδειότητα τούτου ὥσπερ πρώτην, κενὸν δὲ ὄγκον. Similarly the sunlight makes this horse or Socrates (ἰδίως ποῖον) grow; the matter comes from food (itself ripened by the Sun), transformed into flesh and blood by the Sun. Beginnings of the doctrine: Pl. *Phdr.* 246 E, *Rep.* 508 B; the doctrine of the climates depends upon relation to the Sun (see on 328. 16). In l. 25 περιέχων refers to the 'reins' by which the Sun holds the Cosmos together (266. 21 and 272. 2). A thing can be 'in' its container otherwise than spatially; cf. 218. 33 and note *ad loc.*

270. 4. αἴτιοι . . . τῶν ἐπὶ γῆς θορύβων. Cf. πανικοὶ θόρυβοι . . . τοῦτο πολλάκις γενόμενον ἔκφρονάς τε αὐτοὺς ἀποδείκνυσι, καὶ γνώμης ἀκρατεῖς, Synesius, *de provid.* 1260 A (Migne).

6-11. A piece of Democritean lore, according to Diels, *Archiv f. Gesch. d. Philosophie*, vii. 154-7. D. compares ἐγκαταβυσσοῦσθαι τὰ εἴδωλα διὰ τῶν πόρων εἰς τὰ σώματα (Plut. *Quaest. conv.* 8. 10. 2): see vol. ii, 433 n. 8. But see on 344. 3.

24. ὁ λόγος, οὐκ ἔρως, ἐστὶν ὁ πλανώμενος καὶ πλανῶν. See on 130. 5; 184. 27. Zielinski interprets this as one of those passages which give λόγος a lower place as ecstatic Platonizing idealism gains ground. But the sentence expresses rather a characteristic idea of Oriental origin than Platonism. See Bousset, *Kyrios*, p. 388 n. 1. In this context it is unexpected to the point of irrelevance; but that is no reason for doubting a Hermetic text.

272. 15. This argument, such as it is, may be put thus. There are unbodied images of bodies; and bodies are images of unbodied forms. Thus it is possible for reflections to be given by unbodied images (in mirrors) answering to bodies, and by bodies answering to unbodied (forms)—i.e. by the sensible answering to the intelligible world, and by the intelligible answering to the sensible. (Chiastic arrangement.) The statues of the gods have forms that come from the intelligible world, and should be adored.

ἀλληλογονία begetting others of your kind. The screw comes round to the same as R. suggests—a spiral of life.

ASCLEPIUS

NOTE. It seems desirable to explain the method of annotating adopted here. The text designated as *Asclepius* III in this edition presupposes, and attempts to remedy by transposition, extensive dislocations in the manuscripts. In compiling the additional material presented below I found it impossible to use relevant evidence unless I followed the traditional order of the manuscripts. Thus, *mundana* in 316. 28 has little or no meaning if it is not interpreted in connexion with *mundus* and *donum caeleste* in 320. 14-15; and the *daemones* of 318. 22 have their place (if parallels are to be trusted) in the argument about the Void in pp. 316-20, whereas the *daemones* of pp. 366-70, to whose company they are transported, appear to belong to a different branch of the family. Again, I had either to renounce the attempt to explain the *sublimis ratio* in 323. 8, or to interpret the passage involved as a continuous whole. It seemed proper to offer the evidence and alternative explanations for the judgement of readers.

Where the text is printed in two places my notes are attached to the passage in its traditional place; e.g. the comments on c. 17 b will be found under 316. 12, not under 326. 24. Where a passage, continuous in the original, has been broken up in this edition, the note dealing with it as a whole has been written round its most striking or difficult part. Other methods could doubtless have been followed; I take leave to doubt whether they would have been less troublesome to the reader.

It may be convenient to give here a short list of these compendious notes on *Asclepius* III.

cc. 17 c-18 b *under* 316. 25.	cc. 27 e-29 b *under* 364. 25.
cc. 19-21 *under* 330. 21.	cc. 29 c-32 b *under* 348. 8, 350. 7.
cc. 24 b-26 a *under* 340. 4.	cc. 33 a-36 *under* 328. 16.

286. 7. Quem (*sc.* sermonem) **si intellegens videris** = κατανοῶν φαίνει A.D.N.

10. **consentaneum...conexum.** Here the theme of *coniunctio* is first stated. From the (redactor's?) note in 296. 19, the title of this first tract may be *de coniunctione deorum*. The thesis (l. 10) is: τὰ πάντα ἐξ ἑνὸς εἶναι, ἢ ἐν τὰ πάντα. See notes on 294. 11; 296. 4.

288. 9. more vel tempore. Souls may be immortal in different degrees,[1] and may have limited immortality, according to Hermetic and related doctrine.[2] At the opening of an argument that is not well-knit or clear, it may be convenient to indicate the general drift. Thesis: all human souls are immortal. Argument: the scale of existence, depending upon the One, displays a continuity of grades, all bound up together

---

[1] 466. 3 *sqq.*; *Exc.* XXIV; 508. 28.

[2] See Nock, *Sallustius*, lxv.

(*coniunctio, conexio, cognatio*).   As there are grades of demons, so there are grades of men,[1] and the higher kind of man, in virtue of νοῦς, ' prope deos accedit '.[2]   This explains why all souls are not of one quality.[3]   In this scale man has the middle position (ἐν μεθορίοις), akin to God and akin to the creatures below him ; for he is a microcosm.   It is *consortium* (συμφυΐα) that determines a man's lot.   Since man's νοῦς is of the same nature as God, he is immortal if he joins himself to what is eternal.   Hence the stress upon man's *medietas* (294. 20) and upon the fact that man alone rises to knowledge of the divine — we know that to which we are akin,[4] and that which is mortal cannot approach what is immortal.[5]

18. cuncta . . . in aera. Ignis solum (Thomas).   All life, in each of the three regions, each one with its own special forms of life.   τοῦ δὲ πυρὸς μόνον τὸ μὲν κατώθεν ἀνίον ζωτικόν, τὸ δὲ ἀνώθεν κατίον τοῦτο θεράπευον. πᾶν ἄρα τὸ ἀνώθεν ζωόγονόν ἐστι, τὸ δὲ κάτωθεν τρέφει.   The reference is perhaps to the theory that life depends on internal heat, while the Sun is the perpetual source of this vital heat.   Cic. *de nat. deor.* 2. 23 *sqq.*: sic enim res se habet, ub omnia, quae alantur et quae crescant, contineant in se vim caloris, sine qua neque ali possent nec crescere. Nam omne, quod est calidum et igneum, cietur et agitatur motu suo . . . omne igitur, quod vivit, sive animal sive terra editum, id vivit propter inclusum in eo calorem.   Ex quo intellegi debet eam caloris naturam vim habere in se vitalem per omnem mundum pertinentem.   Atque id facilius cernemus toto genere hoc igneo, quod tranat omnia, subtilius explicato.   Omnes igitur partes mundi . . . calore fultae sustinentur. Quod primum in terrena natura perspici potest . . . atque aquae etiam admixtum esse calorem primum ipse liquor aquae declarat et fusio . . . ipse vero aër, qui natura est maxime frigidus, minime est expers caloris. . . . iam vero reliqua quarta pars mundi, ea et ipsa tota natura fervida est et ceteris naturis omnibus salutarem inpertit et vitalem calorem. Ex quo concluditur, cum omnes mundi partes sustineantur calore, mundum etiam ipsum simili parique natura in tanta diuturnitate servari, eoque magis, quod intellegi debet calidum illud atque igneum ita in omni fusum esse natura, ut in eo insit procreandi vis et causa gignendi, a quo et animantia omnia et ea, quorum stirpes terra continentur, et nasci sit necesse et augescere.   It is

---

[1] Cf. 302. 20, 480. 5.   Not all men have νοῦς : 150. 15, 180. 31, 204. 8, 296. 22, 302. 19 ; but without it they are no better than animals.   See Bousset, *Kyrios*, 139.

[2] 294. 2-10, 298. 4, 302. 19, 304. 24, 308. 5, 13.

[3] 288. 10. Asclepius asks the question (οὐ γὰρ . . . ψυχή ;`, and the answer is conveyed not in a sentence but in the whole exposition that follows.   Beginning from the One, Hermes shows the scale of lives, and the characteristics of each in its grade.

[4] Posidonius *ap.* Sext. Emp. *adv. math.* vii. 92.

[5] *Fr.* 7 ; Cic. *Tusc.* i. 62 ; Nock, *Sallustius*, lxvi–lxvii ; Gronau, *Poseidonios*, pp. 223 *sqq.*

the fusion of fire with the three elements that is vivifying, and the fourth part is the perpetual fount of life. Earth, the mother, receives all seeds, and brings them forth generation after generation according to their kind —πάντων ὑποδοχή, πάσας ἰδέας ἃς ὑπεδέχετο ἀνταποδιδοῦσα (l. 22). See above and *ibid.* 2. 98 : terra. . . solida et globosa et undique ipsa in sese nutibus suis conglobata (cf. in se ipsa consistens) vestita floribus, herbis etc. ; 83 quippe quae gravidata seminibus omnia pariat et fundat ex sese, stirpes amplexa alat et augeat ipsaque alatur vicissim a superis externisque naturis.

23. **Hoc ergo** : τοῦτ' οὖν ἐστι τὸ πᾶν . . . τὸ πάντων ἢ πάντα ὄν. Cf. 342. 13 note.

290. 11. Caelum. This is the heaven of the fixed stars: *de mundo*, 398 b 6 : σεμνότερον δὲ καὶ πρεπωδέστερον αὐτὸν (τὸν θεόν) ἐπὶ τῆς ἀνωτάτω χώρας ἱδρῦσθαι, τὴν δὲ δύναμιν διὰ τοῦ σύμπαντος κόσμου διήκουσαν ἥλιόν τε κινεῖν καὶ σελήνην, καὶ τὸν πάντα οὐρανὸν περιάγειν, αἴτιόν τε γίνεσθαι τοῖς ἐπὶ γῆς σωτηρίας. Cf. Apuleius, *de mundo*, c. 27, summus exsuperantissimusque deorum, and *de Platone* i. 12. Cic. *Somn. Scip.* 4 : nouem tibi orbibus vel potius globis conexa sunt omnia, quorum unus est caelestis, extumus, qui reliquos complectitur, summus ipse deus, arcens et continens ceteros, in quo sunt infixi illi qui voluuntur stellarum cursus sempiterni. cui subiecti sunt septem etc. Cf. 302. 8, 324. 3. The view is Posidonian and 'Chaldaean'. The Hermetist differs by making *Caelum* the διοικητής,[1] while God is the Creator. See on the whole subject Cumont, *Jupiter summus exsuperantissimus* (*Archiv*, 9. 333). For the functions of the Sun see Diog. Laert. 7. 144 : Ποσειδώνιος (φησί) . . . πῦρ μὲν οὖν εἶναι (τὸν ἥλιον), ὅτι τὰ πυρὸς πάντα ποιεῖ. Gronau (*Poseidonios*, p. 17, 1) has collected references on the influence of the Moon.

20. ἰδεῶν. Cf. 316. 21.

22. Πάντα μὲν οὖν ἄνωθεν ἠρτημένα εἰς ἰδέας ἀπονενέμηται (190. 24). Here πάντα means all living creatures, and the participle refers to the continuous chain of life bound together by *cognatio* : 184. 12–16; 192. 1; 196. 9; 202. 8 (κοινωνία δέ ἐστι ψυχῶν), 21, Iamblichus, *de myst.* (*Abamm. resp.*) i. 17; v. 9 : πολλῶν δὲ οὐσῶν τούτων καὶ τῶν μὲν προσεχῶς συνηρτημένων ὥσπερ τῶν δαιμονίων, τῶν δὲ ἀνωτέρω τούτων πως τεταγμένων ὥσπερ τῶν θείων αἰτίων, ἔτι δὲ τούτων πρεσβυτάτης μιᾶς αἰτίας ἐξηγουμένης. The essence of this account is continuity—*de myst.* i. 5 : ἀρχῆς δὴ οὖν καὶ τελευτῆς τοιαύτης οὔσης ἐν τοῖς θείοις γένεσι, δύο τῶν ἄκρων ὅρων τούτων (gods and souls) μεταξὺ νόει μεσότητα, ὑψηλοτέραν μὲν τῆς τῶν ψυχῶν τάξεως, τὴν τῶν ἡρώων ἐπιτεταγμένην . . . τῆς δὲ τῶν θεῶν ἐξηρτημένην τὴν τῶν δαιμόνων . . . ταῦτα δὲ οὖν τὰ γένη μέσα συμπληροῦνται τὸν κοινὸν σύνδεσμον θεῶν τε καὶ ψυχῶν, καὶ ἀδιάλυτον αὐτῶν τὴν συμπλοκὴν ἀπεργάζεται, μίαν τε συνέχειαν ἄνωθεν μέχρι τοῦ

---

[1] As Topos is below the supreme God (who, however, has a different character) in *Corp.* II. Retain the text. See on 348. 8.

τέλους συνδεῖ, καὶ ποιεῖ τῶν ὅλων κοινωνίαν εἶνει ἀδιαίρετον κρᾶσίν τε ἀρίστην καὶ σύμμιξιν τοῖς ὅλοις ἔχειν σύμμετρον, πρόοδόν τε ἀπὸ τῶν βελτιόνων ἐπὶ τὰ ἐλάττονα καὶ ἀναγωγὴν ἀπὸ τῶν ὑποδεεστέρων ἐπὶ τὰ πρότερα ... ποιεῖ πάντα πᾶσι προσήγορα καὶ συναρμόζοντα κ.τ.λ. The reason of this continuity is ἡ τῆς ζωῆς ὁμοειδὴς συγγένεια. If we compare this with *Corp*. X (refs. above) there is evidently a specific doctrine of the hierarchy of life stretching down from the One,[1] and the daemons are an essential part of this chain. It is probable that this doctrine of *cognatio* is characteristically Hermetic. For the analysis of texts indicating that Philo and others knew such an early Hermetic doctrine see Bousset, *Schulbetrieb*, c. II.

292. 8. deo. Cf. 290. 11.

9–11. The continuity extends through the Cosmos right up to the places of those *kinds* (γενῶν), of all of which the individuals (ἰδέαι) are immortal. That is, beginning with vegetables, the chain of life ascends to the grades of gods. Probably *specierum* is a careless translation ; cf. l. 27, *speciem*.

15. τὰ δὲ τῶν ἄλλων γένη, οἷς δὴ ἡ διαμονὴ τοῦ γένους ἐστί, καὶ εἰ κατ' ἰδέας θνῄσκει, τῇ γεννητικῇ δυνάμει διασώζεται. καὶ διὰ τοῦτο αἱ μὲν ἰδέαι θνηταί, ⟨τὸ δὲ γένος ἀθάνατον⟩.[2]

27. fortuito coniuncti sunt alicui[us] speciei. There appears to be no authority for the order in the text. Emendation Kroll's. Cf. Plut. *de def. orac.* 415 B : οὕτως ἐκ μὲν ἀνθρώπων εἰς ἥρωας, ἐκ δ' ἡρώων εἰς δαίμονας αἱ βελτίονες ψυχαὶ τὴν μεταβολὴν λαμβάνουσιν, ἐκ δὲ δαιμόνων ὀλίγαι μὲν ἐν χρόνῳ πολλῷ δι' ἀρετῆς καθαρθεῖσαι παντάπασι θειότητος μετέσχον.[3] The daemons here mentioned belong to a different tradition from the *nocentes angeli* of 344. 3.[4] They are links in the chain, and only two kinds need be mentioned : θεοειδεῖς and φιλάνθρωποι. Cf. Diog. Laert. 7. 1. 151 : φασὶν (οἱ Στωικοί) εἶναι καί τινας δαίμονας ἀνθρώπων συμπάθειαν ἔχοντας, ἐπόπτας τῶν ἀνθρωπείων πραγμάτων. Maximus Tyrius, 8. 8 b (Hobein) ... θεῶν μὲν ὑπηρέται, ἀνθρώπων δὲ ἐπιστάται.[5] For origin see Pl. *Sympos.* 202 e. See p. 408, n. 4, and on 362. 1.

294. 11. *sqq.* This eulogy of man is a counterpart to Momus' attack in 482. 11, on which I have collected some of the diatribe parallels. The theme, there as here, is man's intellectual power. But the emphasis here

---

[1] Apuleius, *de Platone*, I. II. I add Plut. *de def. orac.* c. 10, 415 A : ἐμοὶ δὲ δοκοῦσι πλείονας λῦσαι καὶ μείζονα ἀπορίας οἱ τὸ τῶν δαιμόνων γένος ἐν μέσῳ θέντες θεῶν καὶ ἀνθρώπων καὶ τρόπον τινὰ τὴν κοινωνίαν ἡμῶν συνάγον εἰς ταυτὸ καὶ συνάπτον ἐξευρόντες. εἴτε μάγων τῶν περὶ Ζωροάστρην ὁ λόγος οὗτός ἐστιν, εἴτε ...; Macrobius, *Comm.* I, 14, 15.

[2] ⟨genera non sunt⟩ A. D. N.

[3] Cf. *De Is. et Os.* 361 e. ; Chalcidius, *in Tim.* c. 132 ; Nemesius, 776-7.

[4] See note on 340. 4 below.

[5] See vol. iii. 230, also Max. Tyr. 9. 3-4, Apuleius, *de Platone*, I. 12 : daemonas vero ... ministros deorum arbitra[n]tur custodesque hominum et interpretes, si quid a diis velint.

is upon man's position as a μέσον[1] within the continuous chain that binds the Cosmos from highest to lowest (σύνδεσμος, *cognatio*). In this chain man, the microcosm, occupies a peculiar position, as spirit related to God and the higher spirits, as composed of the four elements related to the lower creation, and in all a *parvus mundus*. It is evident from Firmicus Maternus (*Math.* III *Prooem.*) that 'Petosiris' and 'Nechepso' adopted this doctrine. For the chain cf. l. 4: consortio omnium aliarum specierum multas et prope omnium per necessitatem coniunctiones facit[2]; and for the 'mixture' l. 16: natura temperata.[3] *Suspicit caelum* (l. 20): this is the *spectaculum* theme.[4] But man is also, as intermediary, ruler of the earth (l. 22). For this see on 300. 20, 304. 9, 356. 4.

22 *sqq.* **Elementis velocitate miscetur** (l. 22). The reference is to the mind's swiftness in ranging the universe.[5] Philo, *quod det. potiori*, 89: μόνον γὰρ αὐτὸ τῶν παρ' ἡμῖν ὁ νοῦς ἅτε πάντων ὠκυδρομώτατος καὶ τὸν χρόνον, ἐν ᾧ γίνεσθαι δοκεῖ, φθάνει καὶ παραμείβεται, κατὰ τὰς ἀοράτους δυνάμεις ἀχρόνως τοῦ τε παντὸς καὶ μερῶν, καὶ τῶν τούτων αἰτίων ἐπιψαύων. ἤδη δὲ οὐ μόνον ἄχρι τῶν γῆς καὶ θαλάττης ἀλλὰ καὶ ἀέρος καὶ οὐρανοῦ περάτων ἐλθὼν οἰδ' ἐνταῦθα ἔστη, βραχὺν ὅρον τοῦ συνεχοῦς καὶ ἀπαύστου δρόμου νομίσας τὸν κόσμον εἶναι, προσωτέρω δὲ χωρῆσαι γλιχόμενος καὶ τὴν ἀκατάληπτον θεοῦ φύσιν ... καταλαβεῖν. κ.τ.λ.

296. 4. A classification of organisms underlies this chapter, according

---

[1] Medietate generis sui (l. 8); feliciore loco medietatis (l. 20). In the (Posidonian) tradition man is μεθόριος. See Philo, *de opif.* 135: διὸ καὶ κυρίως ἄν τις εἴποι τὸν ἄνθρωπον θνητῆς καὶ ἀθανάτου φύσεως εἶναι μεθόριον, ἑκατέρας ὅσον ἀναγκαῖόν ἐστι μετέχοντα. *De opif.* 145 (quoted vol. iii. 49 *ad fin.*). Nemesius, *de nat. hom.* 512 C (Migne): ἐν μεθορίοις οὖν τῆς ἀλόγου καὶ λογικῆς φύσεως ὁ ἄνθρωπος ταχθείς; 505 B: γνώριμον δὲ ὅτι καὶ τοῖς ἀψύχοις κοινωνεῖ, καὶ τῆς τῶν ἀλόγων ζῴων μετέχει ζωῆς, καὶ τῆς τῶν λογικῶν μετείληφε νοήσεως. κοινωνεῖ ... συνάπτεται δὲ ... δι' ὃ καὶ ὥσπερ ἐν μεθορίοις ἐστὶ νοητῆς καὶ αἰσθητῆς οὐσίας, συναπτόμενος ... ὁ γὰρ Δημιουργὸς ἐκ τοῦ κατ' ὀλίγον ἔοικεν ἐπισυνάπτειν ἀλλήλαις τὰς διαφόρους φύσεις, ὥστε μίαν εἶναι καὶ συγγενῆ τὴν πᾶσαν κτίσιν. Both Philo (*ib.* 141) and Nemesius (507 C) use the figure of a magnet to illustrate the chain of connexion through creation. One might (with reservations) compare ll. 6–10. On the whole subject see the admirable account in Jaeger, *Nemesios*, c. 2. For microcosmos, Bouché-Leclercq, *L'Astrologie grecque*, p. 77; Dieterich, *Mithrasliturgie*, pp. 55 *sqq.*

[2] So *nexu* (δεσμῷ), *necessarium* (ll. 18–19). So Philo *ibid.* 82: ὡς ἀναγκαῖα καὶ φίλτατα ἀρχὴν μὲν οὐρανὸν ἐποίει, τέλος δὲ ἄνθρωπον ... βραχὺν οὐρανόν.

[3] Omnium istorum coniunctio temperata (Firmicus).

[4] See on 482. 11 and 204. 16. Man is the spectator of the heavens because he stands erect, unlike all other animals. This is a fertile theme. See e.g. 406. 18; Cic. *de nat. deor.* 2. 140; Philo *quod det. potiori*, 85; Manilius, 4. 886. 7; Lactantius, *de opif. dei.* 10. 26. Hence the question (see on 160. 29): τίς ὁ τοῖς ποσὶ βάσιν πλατύνας; the theme began with Pl. *Tim.* 90 A, 91 E. For the interpretation of *colit terram* see 300. 20–302. 1 (*firmissimus nexus*) and *de nat. deor.* 2. 150–2.

[5] The elements are here probably heaven, earth, sea, air. See Cumont, *Relig. Orientales*, p. 298, n. 18.

to their 'nutriment'. (1) Roots from above and roots from below. The root from above is the πνεῦμα, which is breathed through the mouth.[1] For the metaphor see Sext. Emp. *adv. math.* i. 129, quoted on p. 374 above. *viva radice* (ζωτικῇ ῥίζα?) is explained by Cic. *de nat. deor.* 2 29. (cf. 33): in arborum autem et earum rerum quae gignuntur e terra, radicibus inesse principatus (*sc.* ἡγεμονικόν) putatur. (2) Food is of two kinds: according as it goes to the lungs and heart, or to the stomach, in an animal. 'sed cum homo constet ex corpore atque anima, illud quod supra dixi receptaculum soli corpori praestat alimentum, animae vero aliam sedem dedit. Fecit enim (pulmonem) ... quoniam ergo duo sunt in homine receptacula, unum aëris quod alit animam, alterum ciborum quod alit corpus, duas esse per collum fistulas necesse est' (Lactantius, *de opif. dei.* 11. 3. 5).[2] The *inquieta agitatio* (retaining text) is probably explained by—καὶ αὕτη ἐστὶ τῆς ἀπροαιρέτου ταύτης ἀναπνοῆς αἰτία, ἡ τοῦ ἀτρεμεῖν τὸ πυρῶδες ἀδυναμία. ἐπειδὴ γὰρ ἴδιόν ἐστι τοῦ θερμοῦ ἡ κατὰ τὴν κίνησιν ἐνέργεια, τούτου δὲ τὰς ἀρχὰς ἐν τῇ καρδίᾳ κατενοήσαμεν κ.τ.λ. (Gregory, *op. cit.* 248 A).[3] It is the perpetual movement of the sky (κόσμος) that keeps life in being. The text should be retained. Similarly, food from the earth[4] restores the body through its appropriate channels, as the teleologists explain in detail. In a full account it would be added that earth and water do not necessarily nourish the body directly, but διὰ μέσου τινῶν.[5] The sentence about *spiritus* covers all classes of living creatures; it is the source of *all* life, though in different degrees of refinement. So far distinction between animate and inanimate life, and the common element in animate life—which is the basis of sensation—have been discussed. It remains to show how man is differentiated from animals and what links him to God. The translation (l. 11) is confused, but the sense is perhaps as follows: πνεῦμα δὲ ... πάντα ζωοποιεῖ, προσημμένου τῷ τοῦ ἀνθρώπου λόγῳ[6] νοῦ, ὅστις ὢν πέμπτη μοῖρα μόνῳ τῷ ἀνθρώπῳ ἐξ αἰθ.ρος κεχορήγηται, ἐξ ἁπάντων δὲ τῶν ζῴων τὰς ἀνθρωπίνας μόνον αἰσθήσεις εἰς τὴν τοῦ θείου λόγου κατανόησιν κοσμεῖ καὶ ἕλκει καὶ ἀναίρει. Man has these two

---

[1] See 184. 7 note.

[2] Gregory of Nyssa, *de hom. opif.* 248 B (Migne). For the evidence that this is Posidonian teleology see Gronau, *Poseidonios*, pp. 206 *sqq.* Cf. note on 160. 19 *sqq.*

[3] καὶ ἀνθρώποις εἶναι πρὸς θεοὺς συγγένειαν κατὰ τὸ μετέχειν ἄνθρωπον θερμοῦ (Alexander Polyhistor, D. L. 8. 27).

[4] inferioris mundi alimentis; cf. 306. 16 and 320. 14 (note on 316. 28). In Cic. *Nat. deor.* 2. 134 the argument is that three things are voided—the dry, the moist, and *spiritus*, and that animals need and receive all three through the mouth. Philo uses the notion of food of body and (the *human*) soul upon the assumption that the soul has συγγενεῖς τροφάς, αἰθερίου φύσεως μοῖρα οὖσα, πάλιν αἰθερίους καὶ θείας; cf. vol. iii. 41, n. 1.

[5] Nemesius, *de nat. hom.* 517 B.

[6] So Bousset, *G. G. A.*, 1918, p. 728.

additional gifts from above (230. 7).[1] It is Stoic commonplace that the senses man has in common with the animals are raised to a higher pitch[2]; he becomes a spectator of the heavens, unlike the beasts that look down. It is likely that λόγος is conceived as the *differentia* of man,[3] and νοῦς as a *proprium*. Note that νοῦς (= αἰθήρ) and λόγος belong to the upper series of elements; compare ζωὴ καὶ φῶς in *Corp.* I and φῶς in vol. iii. 39 n. 1 (Plut. ii. 389 F). Bousset[4] has analysed the variations in Philo between two views of *aether* and soul. For our purpose such a sentence as *Quaest. in Exod.* 2. 46 is relevant: quia ille (Adam) de terra et una cum corpore in existentiam veniebat; is autem (the ideal man) ex aethere et sine corpore.[5] Philo rejects the naturalist view which would class this *aether* along with the other elements, and accepts a divine *aether*, which is spiritual—or (so far as he uses the first) is careful to deny its cruder implications. The 'naturalists' he takes to be stoicizing Jewish exegetes.[6] It should be noted that the doctrine of a fifth element appears in connexion with the five regular solids,[7] and was adopted in Egypt.[8] Here the context is Stoic, and the language such as we meet in the stoicizing passages of Philo; but the special Hermetic theory underlying is best explained by 304. 21.[9]

26-7. Redactor's addition. See on 310. 26; 314. 29; and 320. 14 (n. on 316. 28). In l. 25 *mentibus* = ψυχαῖς; cf. 314. 20 (n. on 310. 26).

298. 5. See on 126. 18.

300. 6. **ut tantus et bonus.** With Kroll's emendation this is sound— ὡς τηλικοῖτος καὶ ἀγαθὸς ὤν. For τηλικοῦτος see 158. 10; 236. 9. It is fundamental Hermetic doctrine that God created because he was good and had the power. See 332. 11, and *Timaeus* 29 e.

9. **Voluntas . . . perfectio.** Cf. Firmicus Maternus, *Math.* v. *praef.* 3: cuius voluntas perfecti operis substantia est. See on 252. 11.

22. The tone should be compared with the speech of Momus (diatribe

[1] Cf. 194. 28, 230. 22, 234. 19, and 304. 21 (see notes); also note on 316. 25.

[2] Interpretes ac nuntii rerum in capite tamquam in arce (*nat. deor.* 2. 153). For the spectator *motif* see 150. 10, 310. 13; transition from senses to speculation, *Nat. deor.* 2. 140 sqq., Philo *de opif. dei*, 147. See also on 194 e.

[3] ζῷον λογικόν. Cf. 358. 13, 450. 13, 19, 448. 13: τὸ μὲν πνεῦμα τοῦ σώματος, ὁ δὲ λόγος τῆς οὐσίας. The sense of λόγος and νοῦς here belongs to the characteristically Hermetic doctrine. Note that πνεῦμα is described as the food of the soul, and that νοῦς is a gift from above, as in 320. 14.

[4] *Schulbetrieb*, pp. 8 sqq., 40 sqq.; I use his references. See also Zepf in *Archiv*, 1928.

[5] See Philostratus in vol. iii. 41; Philo, *quod. det. pot.* 83, *de spec. leg.* 4. 123 (contrast of αἰσθητική and λογική).

[6] Quam *recentes* vocant quintam essentiam (*quaest. in Exod.* 2. 73); for other traces of their work see Bousset, *op. cit.*

[7] Aetius, *Dox. graeci*, p. 334, and Plut. *loc. cit.*

[8] Diodorus, I. 11, where πνεῦμα = Zeus-Ammon, and ἀήρ = Neith or Sais.

[9] Note the word οὐσιώδης in 298. 1, which implies γνῶσις.

material directed against man's use of his powers ; see note on 482) and
the account of the introduction of arts and crafts by Isis and Osiris (492.
30). The traditional (Posidonian) thesis is that the world was made
for man, for his use and for his enjoyment;[1] for man is a λογικὸν ζῷον,
unlike the animals, but with needs, unlike beings higher than himself.[2]
After an account of man's creation from the four elements and his needs
Nemesius continues (520 A) : διὰ ταῦτα μὲν οὖν τροφῆς καὶ ἐσθῆτος δεόμεθα·
οἰκήσεως δὲ ... ἐδεήθημεν ... χρεία τοίνυν ἀνθρώπῳ τροφῆς μὲν καὶ ποτοῦ, διὰ
τὰς κενώσεις καὶ διαφορήσεις· ἐσθῆτος δέ, διὰ τὸ μηδεμίαν ἔχειν ἐκ φύσεως
ἰσχυρὰν περιβολήν· οἴκου δέ...θεραπείας δέ... διὰ δὲ τὰς τέχνας καὶ ἐπιστήμας
καὶ τὰς ἀπὸ τούτων χρείας, ἀλλήλων δεόμεθα ... εἰς ταὐτὸ πολλοὶ συνελθόντες,
κοινωνοῦμεν ἀλλήλοις κατὰ τὰς τοῦ βίου χρείας ἐν τοῖς συναλλάγμασιν,[3] ἥντινα
σύνοδον καὶ συνοικίαν πόλιν ὠνομάσαμεν, ἵνα ἐγγύθεν καὶ μὴ πόρρωθεν τὰς παρ'
ἀλλήλων ὠφελείας καρπώμεθα. φύσει γὰρ συναγελαστικὸν καὶ πολιτικὸν ζῷον
γέγονεν ὁ ἄνθρωπος. εἰς γὰρ οὐδεὶς αὐτάρκης ἑαυτῷ πρὸς ἅπαντα.... 524 B.
ἰδίᾳ δὲ αὐτοῦ καὶ τὰ τῶν τεχνῶν τε καὶ ἐπιστημῶν μαθήματα, καὶ ἡ κατὰ τὰς τέχνας
ταύτας ἐνέργεια. The argument proceeds to show that the world was made
for man (cf. *gubernare terrena*, l. 20) and passes into that praise of his
activities quoted in note on 482. In l. 25 *qui* is the MSS. reading ; also
in 302. 1 keep *et . . . terrae*, contrasting 300. 21 *non aquam et terram*—
the simple elements.

302. 4-6. A conclusion justifying the exercise of the arts and sciences
against the doubt that they are impious. See on 482. 4, and 310. 5 *sqq.*

304. 3. It is possible that this begins a separate tract, extending to
310. 23. The subject may be shortly defined as man's duty to God, and
his task in the Cosmos. The *exordium*, perhaps, is *Aeternitatis dominus*,
which may be compared with the *exordium* of the tract with which it is
conjoined—*Dominus et omnium conformator* (298. 14).[4]

11. διαπράσσεται ὥστε καὶ αὐτὸς καὶ τὸν κόσμον ἑκατερὸν ἑαυτοῖς κόσμῳ
εἶναι—ὅθεν ἐκ ταύτης τῆς θείας συγκράσεως τοῦ ἀνθρώπου κόσμος κεκλῆσθαι
δοκεῖ. This is the common play upon macro- micro-cosmos, and cosmos,
beauty or adornment.[5] See on 148. 24 *sqq.* Man's function is to govern
and order the lower part of the Cosmos; in so doing, he makes himself
κόσμος κόσμου by fulfilling his function (302. 22), and makes the Cosmos
an ordered beauty for himself. An etymology is added, which appears to
justify his name as (βραχὺς) κόσμος. Cf. a similar attempt, for the Cosmos
itself, in 182. 30—184. 5. l. 13: see on 150. 26 ; 178. 2. Man is a microcosm

[1] *Nat. deor.* 2. 154 *sqq.* Cf. 302. 2 : cognitione atque usu.
[2] Nemesius. *de nat. hom.* 525 B. As Jaeger has shown, N. gives a fairly full
outline of the Posidonian argument.
[3] *commodationes alternae* (l. 25), not 'loans', as the dictionaries translate.
[4] Bousset suggests a tract extending from 298. 8 to 304. 2 : 'aber auch das
Folgende gehört zum Teil noch hierher' (*G. G. A.*, 1914, p. 750). But one cannot
be sure how far the joins are patches.
[5] 306. 31 : munde mundum servando.

and, knowing himself, knows the Cosmos and his functions—ἐπὶ τί γέγονε.
l. 14 *meminerit*: see next note, and 354. 16.

304. 16–306. 28 (cc. 10–11 a). οὐκ ἀγνοῶν ὅτι αὐτὸς καὶ δευτέρα ἐστίν εἰκὼν
τοῦ θεοῦ, οὗ δὴ δύο εἰσίν αἱ εἰκόνες, ὁ κόσμος καὶ ὁ ἄνθρωπος· ὅθεν συμβαίνει,
ἐπειδὴ μία αὐτοῦ ἐστὶν ἡ σύστασις, τῇ μὲν μοίρᾳ ᾗπερ ἐκ ψυχῆς καὶ νοῦ, πνεύματος καὶ λόγου θεῖος ὑπάρχει, ὡς ἐκ τῶν ἀνωτέρων στοιχείων ὄντα αὐτὸν εἰς οὐρανὸν
ἀναβαίνειν οἷόν τε φαίνεσθαι, τῇ δὲ ὑλικῇ μοίρᾳ, ἢ ἐκ ⟨γῆς καὶ⟩ πυρός, ὕδατος καὶ
ἀέρος συνέστηκε, θνητὸν ὄντα ἐπὶ γῆς διαμένειν, ἵνα μὴ πάντα τὰ τῇ αὐτοῦ ἐπιμε-
λείᾳ παραδεδομένα στεῖρά τε καὶ ἔρημα καταλείπῃ.[1] This is the theory of the
microcosm in a peculiar Hermetic setting. If we compare the lists of
elements here with the confused passage in 306. 17-24, it is possible to
infer the context from which this theory has been drawn.

{ 1. *Lower elements : ⟨terra et⟩ ignis, aqua et aer.* (304. 24.)
{ 2. *Higher elements: anima et sensus, spiritus et ratio.* (304. 21.)
{ 3. *Bodily pairs : manus et pedes utrique bini, aliaque corporis membra.*
        (306. 20.)
{ 4. *Parts of mind : animus sensus memoria providentia.* (306. 22.)

The members of the pairs of groups are plainly intended to be parallel.
In (1) and (2) higher and lower are opposed, but the number of elements
is equal. In the second passage, again, the groups of four are contrasted
(ll. 18-19), but the terminology for group (4) is so altered from (a) that no
violence can force it into identity with (2),[2] and (3), instead of repeating
(1), gives instances of symmetry in the body. This last is, however, evidence of the character of this argument.

In Philo the work of λόγος τομεύς is twice expounded from the text
'divisit ea per medium et posuit contra se invicem'. The principles are
ἡ εἰς ἴσα τομή and ἐναντιότης,[3] which Philo ascribes to Heraclitus, and
which may be taken as Stoic. The theme is : καθάπερ ἡμῶν τὴν ψυχὴν καὶ
τὰ μέλη μέσα διεῖλεν ὁ τεχνίτης, οὕτως καὶ τὴν τοῦ παντὸς οὐσίαν.[4] For our

---

[1] I supply γῆς καί. It might be held that *in terra* implies the fourth element ;
but that refers to position on the Earth as opposed to Heaven, and there is reason
to suppose a formal parallelism of elements. The reading *igne aqua* suggests
that in both clauses the elements were grouped in pairs. I assume that fire
answers to νοῦς ; cf. 122. 30.

[2] Compare 236. 12 with note.

[3] *Quis rer. div. heres*, 133-214; *Quaest. in Gen.* 3. 5 (cf. 3). For λόγος τομεύς
see Bréhier, *Philon*, pp. 86 *sqq.*, and for the elements Bousset, *Schulbetrieb*, pp. 23
sqq. See also on 158. 24, and 192. 29.

[4] *Quis rer. div. heres*, 133. For the symmetrical division of the body, *ib.* 151,
Quaest. in Gen. 3. 5 : vivifico conditore prae utilitate illud sic dividente, ut eppo-
natur altera (pars) cum altera atque iterum simul ad necessarium ministerium
mutuo serviant sibi invicem ... sic manus ... non aliter se habent et pedes ...
crura et scapulae et coxae et ubera partesque dextera et sinistra ... indicant har-
moniam. There follows a similar division of *animus—rationalis*)(*irrationalis* ;
rationalis into *mens*)(*verbum prolativum*, etc.

purpose it suffices to quote Philo's allegorization of the sacrifice of Abraham; it is immaterial that it does not correspond in detail to these divisions; [1] the insistence upon symmetry is enough. Now the Hermetic theory of ἐνδύματα gives the series νοῦς, λόγος, ψυχή, πνεῦμα; [2] sensus in (2) must be identified with νοῦς here, and anima can hardly be doubted in the context, if only because νοῦς and ψυχή are regularly conjoined as proceeding from ζωή καὶ φῶς.[3] There is also evidence that there is a higher and a lower fire,[4] and it is known that the Egyptian Stoic, Chaeremon, wrote of a double series of elements, male and female.[5] The problem here is why (2) and (4), which purport to be the same list, differ irreconcilably. If we use our clue of symmetry in (3)—a pair of hands and a pair of feet working together—it does not seem impossible that two pairs appear in (4)—memory of past and practical wisdom,[6] spirit and sensation. Sensus is αἴσθησις (including desire) and animus θυμός.[7] The sequence animus, sensus, memoria, providentia suggests this. Can we account for the difference between (2) and (4)? This appears to be a list of faculties, which may (as 302. 21, 306. 25-28 suggest) be turned to the affairs of earth. We see a hint of the same contrast in Philo's opposition of ἀνθρωπίνη and θεία σοφία. If this distinction is tenable, the first contrast (304. 21) refers to the οὐσία of man's two parts, which are opposed in nature and function; the second to the functions of man's mind with relation to the Cosmos: it may be turned aside by cupidity (306. 8)[8] or by curiosity (310. 1-23) instead of using knowledge of God's works to increase piety. This view is supported to some extent by 304. 14: 'is novit se, novit et mundum, scilicet ut meminerit ... quae sibi utenda ... non ignarus se etiam secundam esse imaginem dei'; and by 354. 15-16; 356. 2: 'intelligentia enim sensus humani ... tota in memoria est praeteritorum: per eam enim memoriae tenacitatem et gubernator effectus est terrae' (cf. 300. 20; 302. 2). Upon the interpretations suggested 306. 25-28 follow naturally—mere scientific curiosity does not lead to contemplation of the divine, when hampered by the lusts of the body.

[1]

Quaest. in Gen. 4. 3.		Q. r. d. h. 125–32.		
δάμαλις	terra	ψυχή		
αἴξ	aqua	αἴσθησις		
κριός	aer	λόγος		
τρυγὼν καὶ περιστερά	totum caelum { planetae et fixa astra	ἀνθρωπίνη θεία } σοφία		

[2] 194. 27; cf. 230. 22, 234. 19.   [3] 122. 30; cf. 126. 3, 246. 1, 248. 1.
[4] 114. 23, 116. 14, 18, 118. 13, 120. 11-12, 126. 22.
[5] Seneca, N. Q. 3. 12. 2. There appears to be a reference to Chaeremon's theory in Abamm. resp. (33. 1 above).
[6] Providentia = φρόνησις. Compare 302. 21, Philo above, Chalcidius, cc. 137, 187.
[7] See vol. iv, Introduction, p. xxiii, n. 3, p. xxviii, 3.
[8] For ll. 5-17 cf. Nemesius, de nat. hom. 512 B-513 B. Cf. 308. 1-4, 9-10 as contrasted with 308. 16-19.

310. 11. **qualitates, quantitates.** Cf. 306. 25. The qualities and quantities of 'earth' are essential for, e.g., alchemy. Here (l. 13) is the Hermetic sequence of seeing, wondering, knowing God. See on 256. 26.

17. **concentum**—the theme of συμφωνία. *De mundo*, 396 b 7; Philo *de migr. Abr.* 178 (2. 303. 5 Wendl.); Χαλδαῖοι τῶν ἄλλων ἀνθρώπων ἐκπεπονηκέναι καὶ διαφερόντως δοκοῦσιν ἀστρονομίαν καὶ γενεθλιαλογικήν, τὰ ἐπίγεια τοῖς μετεώροις καὶ τὰ οὐράνια τοῖς ἐπὶ γῆς ἁρμοζόμενοι καὶ ὥσπερ διὰ μουσικῆς λόγων τὴν ἐμμελεστάτην συμφωνίαν τοῦ παντὸς ἐπιδεικνύμενοι τῇ τῶν μερῶν πρὸς ἄλληλα κοινωνίᾳ καὶ συμπαθείᾳ, τόποις μὲν διεζευγμένων, συγγενείᾳ δὲ οὐ διῳκισμένων. (Astrological.) *Artifex ratio* is Stoic language—τεχνικὸς λόγος. See vol. iv, Introduction, pp. xxiv–xxv (note.)

23. **curiositate.** See Momus' diatribe against περιεργία (482. 4) and note, and also vol. iv, Introduction, pp. xxiv–xxv (note).

26–314. 27. (cc. 14 b–16 a). **Fuit deus et ὕλη.** The redactor describes this tract under the title *de spiritu et de his similibus*. In 296. 26 there was a promise by the redactor to write *de sensu (sc. νοῖς) et de omnibus similibus* when he wrote *de spiritu*. This undertaking is fulfilled in a way by cc. 16 a (314. 18–25) and 18 b (320. 14–24).[1] If we compare these passages with 296. 11–298. 7, there is a marked similarity between them. They almost appear to be orthodox Hermetic tags, added to an account of the functions of spirit and matter. The first (296. 12) is casually appended by an ablative absolute to an account of spirit, and has embedded in it an obvious redactor's summary; the second, explaining how man is protected from evil, is inserted between a summing up of the nature of matter (314. 7–10) and the function of *spiritus* (314. 25–7); the third follows a similar summing up: *mundus itaque nutrit corpora, animas spiritus* (320. 14). It is possible that these additions were pious supplements to material consisting largely of philosophical commonplace; but, as their manner suggests; they may have been added by a redactor,[2] and possibly mark the ends of separate tracts. The redactor's general title was perhaps 'de spiritu . . . et de his similibus'.[3] There may have been three tracts, beginning ἦν θεὸς καὶ ὕλη [4] (310. 26), Νῷ μόνῳ νοητός (314. 29), and the third with some such title as περὶ ἀρχῶν (320. 25, 322. 1) or even περὶ οὐσιαρχῶν (cf. 322. 21).[5] The subject of the first two is spirit and

---

[1] I assume the traditional text; see notes on 316. 25 below.

[2] I observe that Bousset (*G. G. A.*, 1914, p. 750. 4) suspects 296. 11–298. 7; 314. 7–25; 316. 25–320. 25 (cc. 17 c–18 b) to be the work of the final redaction. This covers the three passages named, though the joins do not quite coincide. I cannot entirely agree with him about some of the other suspected interpolations in this part of the *Asclepius*.

[3] περὶ τῶν τοιούτων (sc. ἀρχῶν)?

[4] Cf. 146. 1.

[5] The *sublimis ratio* (322. 8) of this tract deals with the *continuatio*. It ends on 332. 18, and c. 21 is perhaps an addition with a diatribe theme περὶ τεκνοποιίας.

matter; all three have in common the theme of fecundity. However that may be, both tracts (1) and (2) deal with spirit and matter.

If we accept the text, *Ascl.* II (our tract 1) opens before the διακόσμησις, and is an account of ἀρχαί with regard to fecundity. There was God, and spirit was even then 'smouldering'[1] (?) in matter, before God launched into creation. We must suppose the 'separation' that preluded the Cosmos, so that the things constituting the Cosmos were not yet in being,[2] though their ἀρχαί (matter and spirit) were: ἀλλ' ἐν αὐτῷ ἤδη ἐνῆν τὰ ἐξ ὧν ἔμελλε γεννήσεσθαι (310. 29). The three senses of ἀγέννητος (ungenerated, to be generated, and sterile) are noted (or implied) in order apparently to lead to the assertion that what is ἀγέννητος (or, like God, αὐτογέννητος) can be γεννητικός. Now matter and spirit (312. 12) are both ἀγέννητα and γεννητικά. (We must remember that they were together from the start.)[3] The translation darkens the sense of the following sentence (l. 14); but the important word is *qualitas*,[4] and it is meant that spirit, being *in* matter, gives a generative nature to matter so qualified. In 314. 3–9, 25–7 the tract is summed up. Matter, though ungenerated, contains (potentially) all things as a womb or ὑποδοχή; an expression which appears to imply that it is the passive partner: then (l. 6) τοῦτ' οὖν ἐστι τὸ πᾶν τῆς ποιότητος τῆς ὕλης, τὸ γεννητικὴν εἶναι, καίπερ ἀγέννητον οὖσαν· [ὥσπερ γὰρ ἐν τῇ Φύσει ἡ τῆς ὕλης ποιότης γεννητική τίς ἐστιν, οὕτω καὶ ⟨τοῦ καλοῦ⟩ καὶ τοῦ κακοῦ ἐστιν ὁμοίως γεννητική.][5] (l. 25) τῷ δὲ πνεύματι διοικεῖταί τε καὶ τρέφεται τὰ ἐν τῷ κόσμῳ πάντα, ὃς δὴ ὥσπερ ὄργανον[6] τῇ τοῦ ὑψίστου θεοῦ βουλήσει ὑπηρετεῖ. The 'quality' of matter is just its indifferent fecundity.[7] So far there is nothing that is not explained more intelligibly in 316. 3–27. The appendix[8] about evil gives the orthodox Hermetic answer to the problem. It turns on the distinction between what is *cosmic*, the source of

---

[1] ὥστε ἀμήχανον παλιγγενεσίαν τὸν κόσμον λαβεῖν, μηδενὸς ἐντυφομένου σπερματικοῦ λόγου (Philo, *de aet. mundi*, 93: vi. 101. 13 Cohn).

[2] τὸ πανταχοῦ κατεσπαρμένον πῦρ ἐπεσκοτεῖτο, τῷ πλεονάζοντι τῆς ὕλης ἐπιπροσθούμενον (Gregory of Nyssa, *Hexaemeros*, 73 A Migne). This passage, however, prefaces the 'separation'. That fire does lurk in matter is proved (for the Stoics) by the effects of friction.

[3] 310. 27.

[4] ἡ τοίνυν ἀρχὴ τῆς γεννήσεως ἐν τῇ τῆς ὕλης (or τῆς Φύσεως?) ποιότητι or ἐν τῷ ποιὰν γίγνεσθαι τὴν φύσιν (cf. 176. 2). The first seems preferable; cf. 314. 6; 316. 13, 16. 'Ego enim et in Natura[m] *esse* sensum et naturam, et mundum dico in se continere naturam et nata omnia conservare' (332. 23; see p. 416, n. 1, below).

[5] This sentence may well belong to the digression in c. 16 a. 'Aeque' suggests that 'malignitatis' should be balanced.

[6] *Organum* is regularly used of the Cosmos; see on 160. 2; 342. 17, Chalcidius, *in Timaeum* 299, 'ex qua (silua) et deo mundi machinam constitisse' (Numenius).

[7] Philo, *de opif. mundi*, 5. 21 (i. 6. 16 Cohn) τῆς ἀρίστης αὐτοῦ φύσεως οὐκ ἐφθόνησεν οὐσία, μηδὲν ἐξ αὐτῆς ἐχούσῃ καλόν, δυναμένη δὲ πάντα, γίνεσθαι.

[8] l. 10 Nec (*ed. Rom.*) ego (*edd. vett.*) dixi . . . dicitur: Non . . . malitiam? (Thomas).

life and growth, and the *heavenly* gift—above all, νοῦς [1]—that guards the good man against evil. What the gifts in ll. 19–20 are we cannot be certain, because the translation is loose ; certainly νοῦς, probably ἐπιστήμη, and (by analogy) λόγος ; but *mens* is certainly ψυχή.[2]

The first part of c. 15 has been left aside, because the text is corrupt. It may be asked whether the things referred to in ll. 19–20 are not simply male and female, as distinguished from the ἀρχαί. Again *locus* appears to be both ἀγέννητος, and *par excellence* γεννητικός (l. 22). This would be true of the *locus* identified with ὕλη in 316. 15, or of Topos in *Corp.* II. But the text is so damaged that speculation is hazardous.

314. 29. Νοῒ μὲν οὖν μόνῳ νοητὸς ὤν, ὁ Ὕψιστος [3] καλούμενος Θεὸς δεσπότης καὶ δημιουργός ἐστι τούτου τοῦ αἰσθητοῦ θεοῦ, ὃς ἐν ἑαυτῷ ἐμπεριέχει πάντα τόπον, ⟨καὶ⟩ πᾶσαν τὴν τῶν ὄντων οὐσίαν (*sc.* ὕλην), καὶ πᾶσαν τὴν τῶν τε φυομένων καὶ τῶν γεννώντων φύσιν,[4] καὶ πᾶν δὴ ὅποιον ⟨ἢ⟩ ὁπόσον τυγχάνει ὄν. There are two gods, and (it may be suggested) two *initia omnium* (316. 26)— *spiritus* and ὕλη [5] : πνεύματι μὲν γὰρ κινοῦνται ἢ διοικοῦνται πᾶσαι αἱ ἐν τῷ κόσμῳ ἰδέαι, ἑκάστη κατὰ τὴν αὑτῆς φύσιν τὴν ὑπὸ τοῦ θεοῦ αὐτῇ μεμερισμένην. ἡ μὲν οὖν ὕλη πάντων ἐστὶν ὑποδοχή, τὸ δὲ πάντα κινοῦν καὶ διῆκον (?) ⟨πνεῦμα⟩· ὧν ὁ θεὸς δημιουργὸς ὢν καὶ ταμιεύων πᾶσιν τοῖς ἐν τῷ κόσμῳ ὅσον ἑκάστῳ ἀναγκαῖον, πνεύματος δὴ πληροῖ πάντα, κατὰ τὴν ἑκάστου τῆς φύσεως ποιότητα εἰσπνεόμενα.[6] Cf. Hermippus, p. 36, 10–12 Kroll.

Without the εἰσπνοή matter is qualityless. See next note.

316. 12–24. The main substance of this paragraph is an identification of matter with Ἅιδης. Let us begin with the conception of ἄποιος ὕλη. It was commonplace to compare matter to the scentless oil used as a medium or to tasteless water,[7] or again to empty space.[8] As such, matter is invisible ; it becomes visible in a way only by the form impressed (ἐντετυπωμένη) upon it. Then it has shape and outline.[9] This theory is fortified by an etymological account of Ἅιδης–ὕλη that may be paralleled from Lydus, *de*

---

[1] Cf. *mundana*)(*dono caelesti*—316. 28 ; 320. 15 and note on 316. 25.

[2] *Mentes* ; cf. 296. 5 ; 320. 16–17. For λόγος see on 230. 7 ; 296. 12 (n. on l. 4). In 296. 24 *intelligentia* is probably λόγος. Compare also the list in 304. 21 —the upper elements.

[3] 'deus summus exsuperantissimus' (374. 1). See on 290. 11, 344. 14 for references.

[4] ἡ γεννητικὴ φύσις—i.e. what comes from τὸ ἀρχηγὸν καὶ πρωτόγονον πνεῦμα (Hermippus).

[5] Cf. 312. 12, retaining 'et spiritus'. The point is that the fecundity of the Cosmos depends on these two principles ; this is elaborated in the account of the *sublimis ratio* (see on 330. 21).

[6] *Inhalata* Goldbacher. Cf. 182. 26.

[7] Albinus, *Eisagoge*, c. 8.

[8] *Tim. Locr.* 94 b ; Simplicius, *In phys.* 643. 10 : τόπος οὖν ἢ ὕλη τῶν εἰδῶν καὶ ὡς ὑποδοχή (cf. 316. 7, *omnium receptaculum*, and l. 16), καὶ ὡς τῆς διαστατῆς θέσεως καὶ τῆς τοιαύτης τάξεως αἰτία.

[9] l. 18 : ὥσπερ ὁρατὴ νομίζεται, ἐπεὶ περιγεγραμμένη δηλοῦται.

mens. 175. 1 Wünsch: ὅτι οἱ φυσικοί φασι τόδε τὸ πᾶν ὕλην ἀνείδεον πρὸ τῆς διακοσμήσεως γενέσθαι ποτέ, ὅθεν καὶ τὴν ὕλην Ἅιδην οἱ φιλοσοφήσαντές φασι καὶ Τάρταρον, ὡς ταραττομένην καὶ οὐκ ἠρεμοῦσαν κατὰ φύσιν διὰ τὸ ἀνείδεον αὐτῆς.... ὅθεν ὁ Χαλδαῖος ἐν τοῖς λογίοις πατρογενῆ τὴν ὕλην ὀνομάζει. καὶ ὅπως ὁ Ἰάμβλιχος ἐν τῇ πρώτῃ τῶν Χαλδαϊκῶν φησι, ἀκοῦσαι ἄξιον· ἀΐδιον μέν ἐστιν ἡ ὕλη, ἐπείπερ συνυφίσταται μετὰ τῶν πρωτίστων αἰτίων[1] ἐξ ἀϊδίου, μετ' αὐτῶν τε καὶ συν αὐτοῖς ἔχει τὸ εἶναι κ.τ.λ.[2] Etymologically Ἅιδης is the unseen, the shapeless (ἀνείδεος)[3]; it is the σκοτεινὸς τύπος, the place we cannot see.   And contrariwise the αἰσθηταὶ ἰδέαι are connected with ἰδεῖν[4] —a Greek etymology that requires full explanation in the Latin version. Now the 'bottom' of a sphere is its centre,[5] and there is the 'unseen place', which still defies the gazer—proof positive. It may be noted that the Sun, disappearing under the earth, is called Pluto.[6] For the theory see on 314. 29 and 364. 24.

316. 25–30, 320. 14 (cc. 17 c–18 b). ταῦτ' οὖν ἐστι τὰ ἀρχικώτερα καὶ τὰ πρεσβύτερα καὶ ὥσπερ τὰ κεφάλαια πάντων, ἃ ἐν τούτοις ἢ διὰ ταῦτα ἢ ἐκ τούτων ἐστὶ πάντα.[7]

ΑΣΚΛ. αὐτὰ ταῦτ' οὖν ἃ λέγεις, ποῖα δὴ ἐστίν, ὦ Τρισμέγιστε;

ΤΡΙΣΜ. κοσμικήν γε δὴ λέγω πασῶν τε τῶν ἐνουσῶν[8] ἰδέων καὶ ἑνὸς ἑκάστου ὥσπερ ἔχει, τὴν συνόλην οὐσίαν, ὥστε (320. 14) καὶ τὴν μὲν ὕλην τὰ σώματα τρέφειν, τὸ δὲ πνεῦμα τὰς ψυχάς. ὁ δὲ νοῦς δὴ κ.τ.λ.

The two primordial principles *within* the Cosmos are πνεῦμα and ὕλη ; they are, as we have been told, ἀγέννητα and creative.[9] In the continuation (320. 14) their nutritive functions are discriminated (cf. 296. 7 note).   And then νοῦς is brought in from *without* the Cosmos.[10]   It is a *donum caeleste* (320. 15); this explains why *mundana* is used emphatically

---

[1] Cf. Pl. *Crat.* 404 b ; Cornutus, *Theol. graec.*, pp. 5. 2 Lang (Ἅιδης-ἀόρατος) ; 74. 5 (Ἅιδης-ἀειδής).   Chalcidius, c. 134.

[2] Cf. 316. 25.

[3] See Cornutus, *op. cit.* 74. 6 ; Porph. *Sent.* xxix : ἐν ᾅδου δὲ λέγεται ὅτι τῆς ἀειδοῦς φύσεως ἐτύγχανε τὸ πνεῦμα καὶ σκοτεινῆς.

[4] l. 21 : ὅθεν καὶ ἰδέαι κέκληνται, διὰ τὸ αὐτὰς αἰσθητὰς εἶναι ἰδέας.

[5] Cic., *de nat. deor.* ii. 116 ; Manilius, 1. 168, l. 19 : see Pl. *Tim.* 63A.

[6] Cornelius Labeo (see Lydus, *de mens.* 137, Porph. *ap* Euseb. *praep. ev.* 4. 11. p. 109 c).   The connexion in this case is fertility.   I have assumed throughout the paragraph that the bottom of the sphere is the centre ; but ll. 13–16 better suit the supposition that the lowest part is τὸ κάτω ἡμισφαίριον, where the sun goes in the passages cited above.   In ll. 22–4 perhaps διὰ μὲν τὸ ἀϊδῆ εἶναι, Ἅιδης· διὰ δὲ τὸ ἐν τῷ τῆς σφαίρας ἐνερτάτῳ εἶναι, ἔνεροι κέκληνται—if we can assume a substitution instead of an addition.

[7] It seems preferable to end this sentence with an emphatic πάντα.

[8] sc. τῷ κόσμῳ.

[9] 312. 12 *cold.* Everything can be said to be *in* pneuma and matter, or made *through* them, or made *out of* them.

[10] The same emphasis in 296. 12.   See also 364. 23 and note on 364. 14 *ad fin.*

in 316. 28—κοσμικὴ οὐσία)(οὐράνιον δῶρον. In 320. 15 after *autem*, and in l. 20, before *sensus*, a dash should be inserted.[1]

31 *sqq*. See on 328. 16.

320. 14-23. See on 316. 25-30.

328. 16-330. 20 (cc. 33 a-36). It will be convenient to trace the argument leading up to this passage upon the assumption that the traditional order is defensible. c. 33 a (316. 31). *There is no void.* The Cosmos is a plenum, and the bodies composing it have different determinations. (This is an argument from the conception of *continuatio*. It implies the Stoic distinction between οὐσία and ποιότης.) In broad outline the argument is in two stages: (*a*) for the intermediate, air, which gives rise to the mistaken notion of empty space;[2] (*b*) for the intermediate beings dwelling in the air, and usually unseen, like the air.[3] There is a continuity of life through the sensible world, as in the intelligible world. c. 33 b (318. 22). Here the argument is plain; it is a well-known point against a void—to each element its own life, and so by analogy there are daemons in the air (or aether, as the case may be). Without these intermediates there is a solution of continuity.[4] c. 33 c (318. 26). Interpretation of void. It means

---

[1] Thomas inserts the first dash after *humanitas*.

[2] See notes on *Corp*. II. The argument is allusive. not direct; but it may be suspected that the *adtrectatio* of *tenuiora* refers to experiments with narrow-necked bottles (θλῖψις), and to the wind.

[3] 318. 11. Possibly something like—ὥσπερ γὰρ τὸ ἔξω τοῦ κόσμου, εἴ γέ τι ἔστιν, —οὐδὲ γὰρ ⟨κενὸν εἶναι⟩ ἐκεῖνο πιστεύω—ὅτι μάλιστα πλῆρές ἐστι νοητῶν (= νοερῶν?) τῇ αὐτοῦ θειότητι ὁμοίων, οὕτω καὶ ὁ ἐνθάδε κόσμος ὁ αἰσθητὸς ἔστι πληρέστατος σωμάτων τε καὶ ζῴων τῇ αὐτοῦ φύσει καὶ ποιότητι οἰκείων. It may be suspected that the construction resembled that of 346. 18-23.

[4] The references are Philo, *de plantat*. 2-17, *de gigant*. 6-16, *de somn*. I. 133-45; Sext. Emp. *adv. math*. 9. 86 ; Apuleius. *de Platone*, 1. 11. For analysis of sources see Bousset, *Schulbetrieb*, pp. 14 *sqq*. Here two levels are inserted between the earth and (the moon?). A piece of Posidonian tradition is repeated from Varro by Augustine, *de civ. dei*, 7. 6 : 'ab summo autem circuitu caeli ad circulum lunae aetherias animas esse astra et stellas, eos caelestes deos non modo intellegi esse. sed etiam uideri ; inter lunae uero gyrum et nimborum ac uentorum cacumina aerias esse animas, sed eas animo non oculis uideri, et uocari heroas et lares et genios. Apuleius, *de deo Socr*. 8 : quippe nulla earum [avium] ultra Olympi verticem sublimatur ... cum sit aëris agmen immensum usque ad citimam lunae helicen, quae porro aetheris sursum versus exordium est. quid igitur tanta vis aëris, quae ab humillimis lunae anfractibus usque ad summum Olympi verticem interiacet? quid tandem? vacabitne animalibus suis atque erit ista naturae pars mortua ac debilis?' The end of *Exc*. XXIV. (512 2) should be compared. l. 23 *in terram*: Koziol *aethera* ; Rohde *aetheream*. l. 24 *nubilis* corrige : *nebulis*. But can we be sure that some such word as σελήνην was not corrupted? The great division lies between the moist atmosphere, which is affected by the stars, and the serene atmosphere above. Apuleius (*de deo Socr*. 9-11) argues for a class of creatures neither earthly nor aetherial, 'pro loci medietate media natura'; and daemons are posited. The clouds are cited as an instance of this 'librata medie-

empty *of* something—and there must always be something, at least the pervading *spiritus* or air. c. 34 a (320. 4). Similarly *locus* is place *for* a body; you must give spatial determinations to some body, if the word is to mean anything (ll. 11–13). *Locus* is here used in the strict Stoic sense—τόπος)(χώρα ; contrast *Corp.* II. c. 34 b (322. 14). On the other hand, the intelligible world, being incorporeal, is entirely free from such determinations—quality, size, or number. The categories do not apply to it (see on 348 8). See vol. iv, Introduction, pp. xvii, xxxi.

c. 34 c (326. 12). This sensible world receives the endless variety of determinations from the One who is All.[1] In l. 14 πάντα γὰρ ὁ θεός, καὶ ἀπ' αὐτοῦ πάντα, καὶ ⟨ὑπὸ⟩ τῆς αὐτοῦ Βουλήσεως[2] πάντα· τοῦτ' οὖν τὸ πᾶν ἐστι τὸ ἀγαθόν, τὸ καλόν, τὸ προνοῶν, τὸ ἀμίμητον, τὸ αὑτῷ μόνῳ αἰσθητόν τε καὶ νοητόν κ.τ.λ.—a Platonic-Stoic formula. It is for this dependence of everything upon the One that Asclepius is to thank God when he contemplates τὸ πᾶν (l. 21), and the metaphor that follows suggests how the intelligible world of c. 34 b enwraps and protects the sensible world with all its determinations. It is the picture of the heavenly garment enwrapping this world.[3] Hippolytus, *Ref.* v. 8: ἡ δὲ Φύσις (*sc.* Isis) ἑπτάστυλος, περὶ αὑτὴν ἔχουσα καὶ ἐστολισμένη ἑπτὰ στολὰς αἰθερίους κ.τ.λ.[4]

c. 35 (328. 16). There is individual variety within the genus. The generic form is compatible with distinctions between individuals. It may be suspected that this chapter reflects a discussion that arose out of Posidonius' theory of κλίματα.[5] The essential of this theory is the συμπάθεια between the seven zones on earth and the corresponding celestial zones, and the production of appropriate types of life on each.[6] The difference

---

tas'. The analogy illustrates the argument for daemons, who (unlike the clouds) are ordinarily invisible, since composed of the finest air; they have no solidity to stop the ray of sight. The ll. 16–21 are illustrated by this passage. It is not primarily an argument for daemons, but an argument against the view that there is a void. We do not in fact see *every*thing: some things we see bigger than they are (e.g. in a mist), some too small, because they are far off or because the sight ray is blunted. 'Bigger' and 'smaller' lead up to 'invisible': there are things we cannot see at all because they are too little (or too fine)—for example, daemons, in whom many disbelieve, but in whom the writer does believe. If daemons, then no breach of continuity.

[1] l. 13. Construe *qualitatum vel corporum* as referring to the distinction ποιότης)(οὐσία, and take *specierum* as dependent on both words. An αἰσθητή ἰδέα is an individual; cf. l. 20 παντομόρφους ἰδέας. In l. 20 retain *magnitudines*—e.g. huge as the sun.

[2] For Βούλησις, Pl. *Tim.* 30 A, Diogenian, 2. 1 (Chrysippus).

[3] Retain *vestimento contecta*, l. 24. The best general reference is Eisler, *Weltenmantel und Himmelszelt* (1910).

[4] Note on c. 17 b under 316. 12.

[5] Cf. l. 27 and see on 502. 32.

[6] l. 23. *Species*: the εἶδος impressed upon matter. ll. 25–6: *formae, corpora ⟨et⟩ incorporalia* Kroll.

of κλίμα depends upon the movements of the sun. But if each zon produces its own types, how do individuals vary? It is an easy stretch to bring in the influence of the stars. The relevant passage is Firmicus Maternus, *Math.* I. 5: (Why are all Ethiopians black and Germans fair, si figuras hominibus et colores stellarum cursus diversa radiationis commixtione largitur?) Et primum quidem vellem, ut quaerenti mihi respondeat, an in hoc ipso populo, in quo nunc constituti sumus, una sit omnium hominum similisque forma, licet sit omnium una natura . . . unde constat generis quidem nostri substantiam et ipsam nudi ac solius corporis formam ex quattuor elementorum commixtione providi numinis artificio esse formatam, colores vero ac formas, mores etiam et instituta de nulla re alia nisi stellarum perenni cursus agitatione distribui.

c. 36 (330. 4). This is an analogy from Stoic meteorology. It gives an account of the changes of weather, seasons, crops, and signs, which depends upon the doctrine of συμπάθεια. This may be inferred from the immediately preceding reference to the *conversio mundi* and from the parallels quoted below. The Hermetist's instances are in the widest sense meteorological, and tacitly assume that climatic change is motion. (1) *Caelum* (l. 8). This, I suggest, simply means even in one kind of climate the aspects of the sky vary from cloudy to serene,[1] etc. Cf. Sext. Emp. *adv. math.* 9. 83: ὁ δὲ κόσμος ἀξιολόγους ἀναδέχεται μεταβολάς, ὅτε μὲν κρυμαλέου τοῦ περιέχοντος γιγνομένου ὅτε δὲ ἀλεεινοῦ, καὶ ὅτε μὲν αὐχμώδους ὅτε δὲ νοτεροῦ, ὅτε δὲ ἄλλως πως κατὰ τὰς τῶν οὐρανίων κινήσεις ἑτεροιουμένου. οὐ τοίνυν ὑπὸ ψιλῆς ἕξεως ὁ κόσμος συνέχεται. (The (Stoic) argument is that the κόσμος is a ἡνωμένον σῶμα ὑπὸ φύσεως συνεχόμενον, leading by a further step to the conclusion that φύσις is νοερά—therefore there are gods.) (2) *Terra* (l. 11). Seasonal changes of plants (depending on the heavenly bodies). For the text: 'atque stationes aut cursus' (l. 14) must stand; it is a commonplace of Hermetic style to link four such substantives,[2] and here they must balance the four in l. 15. Restoration is doubtful; the translator was misled by the association of planetary motions, but we need words that express seasonal variations in the character of fruits. I suggest some such reading as βλαστήσεις ἢ φοράς > στάσεις ἢ φοράς. Philo *de opif. mundi*, 41: τίς γὰρ οὐκ οἶδεν ὅτι πρῶτον μέν ἐστι σπορὰ καὶ φυτεία . . .; ἔπειτα βλαστοὶ καὶ πετάλων ἐκφύσεις, εἶτ' ἐπὶ πᾶσι καρποῦ φορά. καὶ πάλιν καρπὸς οὐ

---

[1] l. 10: *una caeli species* (εἶδος) is one of the great divisions of climate, which determine generic type (cf. Strabo, 2. 5. 43); e.g. Egypt has a εὔκρατον κλίμα (cf. 504. 12). (Hence the medical term *mutatio caeli*, and Horace's answer to the strict determinists who derived character as well as physical type from climate—*caelum, non animum, mutant qui trans mare currunt.*) At the end of the line, *species* (ἰδέαι) are the particular variations such a climate may undergo from day to day. Cf. Cic. *de divin.* ii. 92–4 *esp.* 'quarum rerum (*sc.* tempestatum etc.) in proximis locis tantae dissimilitudines saepe sunt, ut alia Tusculi alia Romae eveniat saepe tempestas' (Panaetius).

[2] Cf. 306. 25, 312. 25–314. 1, 326. 19–21.

τέλειος, ἀλλ᾽ ἔχων παντοίας μεταβολὰς κατά τε τὴν ἐν μεγέθει ποσότητα καὶ τὰς ἐν πολυμόρφοις ἰδέαις ποιότητας ... σὺν δὲ τῷ μεγέθει καὶ τὰς ποιότητας ἀλλάττει. In l. 15 *species* = μορφάς. See also 346. 22. (3) *Elementa.* I begin with a retranslation : τὸ δὲ πῦρ παντοίας καὶ θείας ἔχει μεταβολάς· τοῦ μέντοι ἡλίου καὶ τῆς σελήνης παντόμορφά ἐστι τὰ εἴδωλα· εἰσὶ γὰρ τρόπον τινὰ ὅμοιοι τοῖς ἡμετέροις κατόπτροις, τάς γε τῶν εἰδώλων ἐμφάσεις ἀντιτύπῳ λαμπρότητι ἀνταποδιδοῦσι. Sun and moon (*elementa*, l. 7) change too. On the doctrine of συμπάθεια these bodies are not only light-givers, but prognosticate changes of season, weather,[1] etc. They do so by position, by their aspects, by the phenomena of rainbows, parhelia, haloes and 'streaks'. This doctrine of signs is a fertile topic in Stoic meteorology.[2] In this context the reference is primarily to changes in the ποιότης of these bodies through the phenomenon of ἀνάκλασις, as the figure suggests. These are the sun's variations of colour and size, the phases of the moon.[3] But if we do not press the figure, the changes of fire might also include the seasonal changes of position.

The unexpressed assumption of the whole argument is that cosmic τάξις underlies cosmic μεταβολή. See references on 330. 21.

330. 21. sqq. (cc. 19-21). The theme of this chapter is the creative Will of God. To begin by tracing the connexion with c. 19 (322. 1, 21 ; 326. 1). There is a *sublimis ratio*[4] almost beyond human comprehension. The object of 19 b is to explain that the diversity of individual forms (*species*) is not evidence of mere plurality, but depends upon a continuous chain of deities, visible and invisible, all of which in turn depend upon the One (19 c).

c. 19 b (322. 21). The purpose is to reveal the dependence of the chain of life upon the One, which acts through departmental deities, themselves using visible deities. But there is a *cognatio* stretching up to

---

[1] Philo *de opif. mundi*, 58. Compare also *de migr. Abr.* 178, *de mut. nom.* 67 (on the Chaldaeans).

[2] Cf. *de mundo*, 395 a 29-b 3 ; Serv. *N. Q.* 1. 5. 10, and in general cc. 2-13. Arius Didymus *ap.* Stob. *Ecl.* 1. 240 Wachsm. (Posidonian, though attributed to Aristotle). A convenient account of the prognostic functions of sun and moon is contained in Basil, *Hexaemeros*, vi. 4.

[3] E.g. Apuleius, *de deo Socr.* 1. § 117. For sun and moon Virgil, *Georg.* 1. 424 *sqq.* ... nam saepe videmus | ipsius in vultu varios errare colores : | caeruleus pluviam denuntiat, igneus Euros, etc. Cleomedes, *de mot. circ.* 2. 1. 67 ; μείζων δὲ ὁ ἥλιος ἡμῖν ἀνίσχων καὶ δυόμενος φαντάζεται κ.τ.λ. For *imago lunae = luna.* cf. Virgil, *Aen.* vii. 22.

[4] λόγος. 322.8 ; 330. 21 ('iterum ratio') ; 332. 17 ('haec ergo ratio'). In the first passage we presuppose some such original as σεμνὸς γὰρ ὁ λόγος, καὶ διὰ τοῦτο θειότερος ἢ κατ᾽ ἄνθρωπον νοεῖν τε καὶ κατανοεῖν ὑπάρχων. The figure of the fountain (l. 12) recalls Philo's account of the ἐνδιάθετος λ. (*de vit. Mos.* 2 (3). § 127): ἐν ἀνθρώπῳ δ᾽ ὁ μέν ἐστιν ἐνδιάθετος, ὁ δὲ προφορικός, (καὶ ὁ μὲν) οἷά τις πηγή, ὁ δὲ γεγωνὸς ἀπ᾽ ἐκείνου ῥέων. In the second passage (330. 21) *alia* belongs to 326. 11 (see below). In 322. 11 *acceperis* = παραλαμβάνειν. See on 132. 4, and cf. *pando*, l. 2.

the One (19 c). The ousiarchs control all 'kinds', and subordinate to them are sensible gods, each (or each group) under its ousiarch.[1] It may be suspected that this chapter represents a 'physical' attempt to express all in all degrees as a manifestation of the One.[2] Such an attempt is at bottom Stoic, however interfused with other elements. If we can assume —and the assumption is plausible—that 316. 12–24 and 346. 27–32 (= 324. 19–25) are derived from one tradition, if not from the same source,[3] then we appear to have an attempt (however worked over) to identify the departmental deities as manifestations of the One. There are signs that Stoic etymologies underlie some, at any rate, of these identifications.[4] The tradition is connected with the names of Posidonius, Varro, and Cornelius Labeo.[5] This note offers some material for comparison.

(1) Jupiter as sky : Δία δὲ οἱ μὲν τὸν οὐρανόν, οἱ δὲ τὸν αἰθέρα, οἱ δὲ τὸν ἥλιον . . ἐξεδέξαντο.[6] νῦν οὖν Ζῆνα τὸν αἰθέρα οἰητέον, τουτέστι τὸ πῦρ στοιχειωτικὸν τοῦ παντός· τοῦτο γὰρ ζωῆς αἴτιον,[7] καὶ δι' αὐτοῦ ζῶμεν, κινούμενοί τε καὶ ὑποθερμαινόμενοι. τὸ δὲ πῦρ, ὡς ζωογόνον μᾶλλον καὶ συστατικόν . . . πατέρα ὁ λόγος ἀνδρῶν τε καὶ θεῶν προσαγορεύει.[8] Vitam (l. 4) appears to presuppose the etymology—ἀπὸ τοῦ ζῆν . . . Ζῆνα.[9] (2) Sun. In the translation the ousiarch is lumen. It is difficult not to associate vita et lumen with the Hermetic god of Life and Light, from whom ψυχή and νοῦς are derived (118. 10). If we assume that the physical tradition identified all these δυνάμεις with the One, it is possible that the ousiarch of the Sun was also called Jupiter, and that he was identified with the gift of light. See Achilles above; Arnobius, adv. nat. iii. 30 : 'nam quid de ipso dicemus Ioue, quem

---

[1] l. 23 princeps οὐσία⟨s⟩ = οὐσιάρχης? Cf. 324. 13 sui principem = οὐσίας principem?

[2] Servius, ad Georg. i. 5 : Stoici dicunt non esse nisi unum deum, et unam eandemque esse potestatem quae pro ratione officiorum nostrorum variis nominibus appellatur. Macrobius, Sat. i. 17. 4. De mundo, 401 a 12–b 24.

[3] It does not follow that in a composite document like the Asclepius passages that bear an obvious family resemblance should be grouped together. We cannot be sure how the redactors united their material.

[4] See on 316. 12.

[5] See on iv. 7. 8 below.

[6] Achilles, Isagoge (Maas, Comment. in Aratum, 82. 8). These commentaries are derived ultimately from Posidonius.

[7] Cf. praebet vitam (l. 5).

[8] Joannes Diaconus, Alleg. in Theogoniam, p. 381 (Gaisford, Poet. min. graec. iii. ; cf. p. 293.

[9] Maas, op. cit., 82. 20; also 336. 2. In view of the qualification given to caelum (l. 3) note Macrobius, Sat., i. 18. 15–16 : physici Διόνυσον Διὸς νοῦν quia solem mundi mentem esse dixerunt, mundus autem vocatur caelum, quod appellant Iovem ; unde Aratus de caelo dicturus ait, ἐκ Διὸς ἀρχώμεθα. So Lydus, de mens. 108. 20 W., the same view, ending ὁ σύμπας κόσμος Ζεὺς ὀνομάζεται διὰ τὸ ἀείζωον καὶ ἀτελεύτητον. Probably from Labeo; see Kahl, Philologus, Suppl.-Band V (1889), p. 762. Cf. Cornutus, c. 2, quoted below.

solem esse dictitauere sapientes . . . aethera nonnulli flagrantem ui flam-
mea' &c.[1] (3) *Omniformis*. Compare 454. 19–20 with 328. 25–31 ; and see
on Aion, 348. 8. In ll. 11–12 ὃς ἄλλαις ἰδέαις ἄλλας μορφὰς ἐμποιεῖ. The
species are individuals,[2] and the purpose is to explain the diversity of
individuals belonging to the same kind. See Firmicus Maternus quoted
on 328. 16. (4) *Fortuna* is responsible for μεταβολή according to τάξις,
the regular succession of generations within the kinds—retain καὶ . . . μένειν.[3]
(5) *Aer*. Maas, *op. cit.* 335. 10 Schol. : Δία τὸν φυσικόν, ὅς ἐστιν ἀήρ . . . οὗτός
ἐστιν ⟨ὁ⟩ διὰ πάντων διήκων κατὰ τοὺς Στωικούς.[4] Should we read in l. 18
secundus ⟨deus⟩?[5] See 314. 30–316. 6. The distinction is between the
supreme God and that ἐνέργεια *within* the Cosmos through which life is
created and maintained.

19 c (326. 1). After explaining the diversity of individuals under
departmental powers of the One, the writer returns to the Unity manifested in the chain of *cognatio*.[6] This prepares for an explanation of the

---

[1] Common source with Macrobius, i. 23. 5—Labeo (Kahl, p. 771). When
heaven is conjoined with the sun as giving life and light, we approach a region
more amply exploited in (the late) *Corp*. XVI. See Macrobius, *in Somn. Scip.* i.
20. 6 : mens mundi ita appellatur ut physici eum cor caeli uocauerunt . . . iure
ergo cor caeli dicitur per quem fiunt omnia quae diuina ratione fieri uidemus. est et
haec causa propter quam iure cor caeli uocetur quod natura ignis semper in motu
perpetuoque agitatu est, solem autem ignis aetherii fontem dictum esse retulimus,
etc. So in Stoic etymology Ζεύς and ζέσις are connected (Maas, *op. cit.* 335. 10).
See in general Reinhardt, *K.u.S.*, pp. 359–85, 329 *sqq*.

[2] See on 292. 8, and on 326. 11 below.

[3] Compare the doctrine of cc. 35–6, and such a passage as Firmicus Maternus,
Math. i. 10. 5 : hae sunt duae zonae, quae omne animantium genus in terrae finibus ex illa tranquilla commixtionis moderatione progenerant, per quas ad omnium,
quae gignuntur, ortus et occasus per omne aevum oblicus signorum ordo convertitur, in quo Sol et Luna, quinque etiam stellae errantes, . . . certa ac definita semper
agitatione discurrunt ; et ⟨ad⟩ harum stellarum cursum omne animantium genus
perpetua sibi generis propagatione succedit. This is Posidonius' climatology (like
c. 36), and implies uniformity of type. Compare with this 376. 11 ; also 268. 1–10.

[4] *Ib*. 83. 3 ; 336. 8 αὐτὸν γὰρ ἐπισπώμενοι ἐξ αὐτοῦ ζῶμεν, καί ἐστι ζωτικός. See
on 296. 4 above. Also Reinhardt, *op. cit.* pp. 200 *sqq.*; Norden, *Agn. Theos*,
pp. 19 *sqq*. Maas, *op. cit.* 178 b : cum dicit Herodotus (i. 131) Iovem dictum
aera, et Crates eiusdem opinionis esse et testem Philemonem comicum dicit . . .
hoc autem constat et ipsum Aratum dicere τὸν οὐδέποτ', ἄνδρες, ἐῶμεν ἄρρητον
(v. 1). namque quoniam nihil aliud est vox quam percussus aer, auctoritatem
rei praestat 'plenas Iove vias' (v. 2) referens et 'omnis hominum conventus'
(v. 3). nihil eorum, quae in terra sunt, sine aere est . . . propter quod et Stoici
Iovem esse adfirmant, qui per materiam manat spiritus. See 330. 27.

[5] The world soul or φύσις τοῦ κόσμου? Aion is the source of life in 348. 20 ;
see on 348. 8.

[6] l. 6. The sense is that in this chain of life the totality of the creation obeys the
Creator—τὸ ὅλον τῆς δημιουργίας ἐκείνῳ τῷ ὑψίστῳ δεσπότῃ πείθεται, ἢ τοῦ εἶναι οὐ
πολλά, ἢ μᾶλλόν γε ἕν. This is the Hermetic doctrine of the ἐξηρτημένα.

l. 11 : *efficiuntur alia* (from 330. 21). Should we translate — καὶ ἐκ τῆς αὐτοῦ

'sublimis ratio' in 330. 21—'haec iterum ratio quae est?' The opening
(l. 22) bears a strong resemblance to the invocation in a prayer, and
there is some reason to suspect that this is not fortuitous. If we retain the
text,[1] place a colon after *sacratum*, and remove the colon after *contemplatione*, we have first a customary formula of invocation justified,[2] and then
a denial that any name is adequate for interior meditation upon God.
There is a reason for using names in mutual intercourse, but that is
human necessity. This raises the distinction between the ἐνδιάθετος and
the προφορικὸς λόγος as developed by Philo.[3] In brief the relevant doctrine
is this. The senses, and therefore speech, are unfit to deal with sacred
things.[4] The two λόγοι are related as monad to indeterminate dyad, father
to son, fountain to stream. Compare the frequent disparagement of
speech [5] in the Hermetists (and Gnostics), and the value set on silence.[6]
In 244. 9 after the rebirth the ἐνδιάθετος ἄνθρωπος is freed from the body,
and the neophyte is bidden to fall silent. It is striking to find a school
definition of speech in such a context. But the trait is markedly Philonic.[7]
The writer wishes to say that if a name is a physical sound, definitely

Βουλήσεως, ἧς τῷ θελήματι (or λόγῳ) ποιεῖται ἀλλοῖα? The theme is the variety of individuals in unity, and the Will exercises its creative activity through the Logos (cf.
116. 25; 118. 11, 17; 238. 24). Λόγος may be too definite in this context. But
c. 20 proceeds to deal with the λόγος, and emphasizes the bisexuality of God
(cf. 118. 20).

[1] Retain *vel* before *quocumque* (l. 23). Cf. 208. 31 and 352. 13. The text is
clearer with a dash before *quod*.

[2] On the form of invocations, see Norden, *Agn. Theos*, pp. 143 *sqq.*

[3] *De spec. leg.*, iv. 69: συγγενῆ δύναμιν ... ἣν ἐκάλεσε δήλωσιν, ἀμφοτέρων τῶν
ἐν ἡμῖν λόγων εἰκύνας, ἐνδιαθέτου τε καὶ προφορικοῦ· δεῖται γὰρ ὁ μὲν προφορικὸς
δηλώσεως, ᾗ τὰ ἀφανῆ τῶν καθ' ἕκαστον ἡμῶν ἐνθυμία γνωρίζεται τῷ πέλας, ὁ δ'
ἐνδιάθετος ἀληθείας, εἰς τελειότητα βίου καὶ πράξεων, δι' ὧν ἡ ἐπ' εὐδαιμονίαν ὅδος
ἀνευρίσκεται. For references and full exposition see Bréhier, *Philon*, pp. 101 *sqq.*

[4] *Quis rer. div. heres*, 71; *de ebriet.*, 70. See also *de migr. Abr.*, 70-81.

[5] 130. 4 (reading ἐκφθορά), 22; 238. 22; 270. 24 (note); 150. 15; 184. 27;
190. 8 (note). See Zielinski, *Archiv*, 8.

[6] Speech may be used well or ill: 230. 8; *quis rer. div. heres*, 109.

[7] *de Abr.* 83, and esp. *quod deus sit imm.* 18. 83: οὐ γάρ ἐστιν ὁ λόγος αὐτῷ (τῷ
θεῷ) γεγονὼς ἀέρος πλῆξις ... ἀλλ' ἀσώματός τε καὶ γυμνός ... τὸ γὰρ ἀφ' ἡγεμονικοῦ
πνεῦμα διὰ τραχείας ἀναπεμπόμενον ἀρτηρίας τυποῦται μὲν ἐν σώματι κ.τ.λ. Still
more striking is a prayer in the *Constitutiones Apostolicae*, viii. 12, which bears a
family resemblance to some prayers of Firmicus cited below: (ὁ ποιήσας ἀέρα)
ζωτικὸν πρὸς εἰσπνοὴν καὶ ἀναπνοὴν καὶ φωνῆς ἀπόδοσιν διὰ γλώττης πληττούσης τὸν
ἀέρα κ.τ.λ. See also Nemesius, *de nat. hom.* cap. 14 for school tradition. So,
of the Creator's fiat, Basil uses a Stoic definition: οὐ διὰ φωνητικῶν ὀργάνων ἐκπεμπόμενον ψόφον, οὐδὲ ἀέρα διὰ γλώττης ἐκπεμπόμενον, ἀλλὰ τὴν ἐν τῷ θελήματι ῥοπὴν
κ.τ.λ. (*Hex.*, ii. 45 B). Euseb. *Theophan. Fr.* 1, Gressmann: ὁ τοῦ παμβασιλέως
θεοῦ τέλεος λόγος ... οὐ προφορικῇ δυνάμει συνεστώς, οὐδ' ἐκ συλλαβῶν ὀνομάτων
τε καὶ ῥημάτων τὴν φύσιν κατεσκευασμένος, οὐδ' ἐν φωνῇ δι' ἀέρος, κ.τ.λ. Tertullian,
adv. Praxean, c. 7.

..mited for purposes of intercourse, the name of God would require the whole range of physical apparatus required to produce articulate sound. Perhaps (330. 27–332. 10) εἰ γὰρ φωνὴ τόδ᾽ ἐστίν — ἐξ ἀέρος πνεύματι πεπληγμένου ψόφος, δηλοῦσα πάντα τὰ ὑπ᾽ ἀνθρώπου βουληθέντα ἢ νοηθέντα, εἴ τι ἐξ αἰσθήσεων τῷ νοΐ φαντασάμενος τυγχάνει,[1] οὗ τοῦ ὀνόματος ἡ πᾶσα οὐσία ἐξ ὀλίγων συνθετὴ συλλαβῶν ὡρισμένη καὶ περιγεγραμμένη ἐστίν, ἵνα γίγνηται παρ᾽ ἀνθρώπῳ ἡ ἀναγκαία τῆς τε φωνῆς καὶ τῶν ὤτων συναλλαγή — τότε δὴ ἅμα τῆς τε αἰσθήσεως καὶ τοῦ πνεύματος καὶ τοῦ ἀέρος καὶ πάντων γε ὅσων ἐν τούτοις ἢ διὰ ταῦτα ἢ ἐκ τούτων τὸ σύνολον τὸ ὄνομά ἐστι τοῦ θεοῦ.   Not that any name can express God : αὐτὸν μέντοι ἀνώνυμον, ἢ μᾶλλον πανώνυμον ⟨καλεῖ⟩, εἰ ἄρα αὐτὸς εἷς καὶ πάντα ἐστίν, ὥστε δεῖν ἢ πάντα τῇ αὐτοῦ ἐπωνυμίᾳ εἶναι, ἤτοι αὐτὸν τοῖς πάντων ὀνόμασι καλεῖσθαι.

c. 20 b.   This describes God in his creative activity; that is, God as Father.[2] It is Hermetic commonplace that God, as good, creates, and his Will is identical with his Goodness.[3] This same Goodness is manifested in the genesis of lives (l. 14) :[4] αὐτὴ γὰρ ἡ τῶν πάντων ἀγαθότης ἐκ τῆς αὐτοῦ θειότητος φύσει γεγένηται, ὅπως ἔσται τὰ πάντα οἷα ἐστί τε καὶ ἦν, καὶ τοῖς εἰς ἀεὶ μέλλουσιν ἔσεσθαι[5] πᾶσιν ἡ γεννητικὴ δύναμις ἐπαρκέσει. This is the σπερματικὴ δύναμις, and the writer is describing the σπ. λόγος. Cf. Philo,

---

[1] The conditions of speech are (1) sense impression and τὸ φαντασθῆναι ; (2) νοῦς, selecting from τὸ ὑποκείμενον, gives each thing its appropriate sign; (3) νοῦς expresses τὰ νοηθέντα by the physical apparatus (Basil, *Hexaemeros*, iii. 53 D–55 A Migne). See further Gronau, *Poseidonios*, pp. 69–71. In Stoic doctrine ' interpres mentis oratio' (Cic., *de leg.*, i. 10).

[2] 332. 11 αὐτὸς οὖν μόνος, ὡς πάντα ὤν (Kroll).

[3] *Voluntatis* (l. 12) should be kept. Firmicus Maternus, *Math.* v, *praef.* 3 : quicumque es deus qui . . . solus omnium gubernator et princeps, solus imperator et dominus, cui tota potestas numinum servit (cf. 326. 6–8), cuius voluntas perfecti substantia operis est (332. 12), cuius incorruptis legibus conventa natura cuncta substantia perpetuitatis ornavit (332. 15, 353–354), tu omnium pariter pater et mater (332. 11), tu tibi pater et filius uno vinculo necessitudinis obligatus (326. 4-6). Note the parallel prayer in vii. i. 2 : qui omnia necessitate perpetuitatis excoluit . . . per immortalem aeternae perpetuitatis ordinem (ἀΐδιον αἰωνίου διαμονῆς τάξιν, cf. 376. 11). Valerius Soranus (Aug. *de civ. dei*, vii. 9) : Iuppiter omnipotens, regum rerumque repertor, | progenitor genetrixque deum, deus unus et idem. For Will, 116. 25 (Βουλή and Λόγος), 186. 19 *sqq.* God's essence is τὸ κύειν πάντα καὶ ποιεῖν (162. 18). Cf. 216. 15 ; 218. 24-7. For Philo the ἴδιον of God is creating (*leg. alleg.* i. 5), and God's Power as Maker has proceeding from it another Power—παραβλαστάνει γὰρ τῇ μὲν ποιητικῇ ἡ ἵλεως, ἧς ὄνομα εὐεργέτις (*Qu. in Exod.* ii. 68—Harris, *Fragm.* p. 67). Note also Dion Chrysostom, xxxvi. 55, ἔρωτα δὴ λαβὼν τῆς ἡνιοχήσεως ἐκείνης . . . ὥρμησεν ἐπὶ τὸ γεννᾶν καὶ διανέμειν ἕκαστα καὶ δημιουργεῖν τὸν ὄντα νῦν κόσμον. Ὁρμᾶν ἐπὶ τὴν κοσμοποιΐαν is the regular Stoic phrase (M. Aurelius, 7. 75 ; Cleomedes, p. 12. 2 Ziegler).

[4] Cf. the function of *aer* (*pneuma*) in 296. 11, 314. 25, 324. 17; add 148. 11, 176. 3; Bäumker, *Problem d. Materie*, pp. 354-9; Schmekel, *Gesch. d. Phil. d. mittleren Stoa*, pp. 241 *sqq.*

[5] Cf. 468. 18.

Qu. in Exod. ii. 68 (Harris, *Fragm.* pp. 66-7): ὑπὲρ δὲ τούτων κατὰ τὸ μέσον φωνὴ καὶ λόγος καὶ ὑπεράνω ὁ λέγων . . . τὸ πρῶτον ὁ καὶ ἑνὸς καὶ μονάδος καὶ ἀρχῆς πρεσβύτερος, ἔπειτα ὁ τοῦ ὄντος λόγος, ἡ σπερματικὴ τῶν ὄντων οὐσία κ.τ.λ. New life is perpetually poured forth, keeping to type. So this part of the theodicy ends (l. 17): οὗτος οὖν ὁ λόγος, ὦ Ἀσκληπιέ, σοι παραδεδόσθω, διὰ τί καὶ πῶς ποιεῖται τὰ πάντα.[1]

336. 10. *naturae*: i.e. τῆς ἄνω φύσεως. Cf. ll. 23-4 and 338. 15.

20. *bonum*: cf. *meliorem*, l. 23.

338. 7. *inluminatur* = ἀποθεοῦται (Bousset, *Kyrios*, p. 151).

340. 3. (cc. 24 b- 26 a). See following notes.

340. 4-**346.** 7 (cc. 24 b-26 a). *The Apocalypse.* These chapters are expressly apocalyptic, and show traces of a variety of influences. We need not trouble about inconsistencies or repetitions in such a document, which took its goods where it found them. The theme is not simply that Hermetists will be persecuted or Egypt laid waste by outer barbarians. It is cosmic. Τὸ θεῖον leaves the earth—that is the burden of this prophecy;[2] νοῦς (the divine in man) disappears,[3] (and man is left to his lower soul);[4] the Cosmos itself runs down; there is a *senectus* and *regenitura mundi*. The framework is Stoic doctrine, such as we find in similar documents.

To begin with the invasion of foreigners—' Scythes aut Indus . . . vicina barbaria '.[5] This is apocalyptic commonplace, and we may ask whether it refers to an historical invasion, or is simply traditional literary material, naming barbarians upon the Roman borders, who constituted an imminent threat to civilization (Horace, *Odes*, 4. 14. 42). Here there is a failure of nerve—the barbarian flood, the flight of the gods. Now contrast the ascending rhythm, when the golden age appears to dawn : ' iam Scythae responsa petunt superbi | nuper et Indi. | iam Fides et Pax et

---

[1] 332. 23-4. The sense should be that of 312. 12 *sqq.* Chalcid. *in Tim.* 293: essentia uero, quia princeps silua est omnium corporum, per quam ire dicunt rationem solidam atque uniuersam, perinde ut semen. . . . 294. seminum ratio incurrens aliquam concipientem comprehendentemque naturam totum mundum quaeque in eo sunt enixa sit. Professor Rose suggests to me that the second *et* is a scribal error for *esse* (ēē). We are in general agreement about the sense, and I add his version : ἐγὼ γὰρ καὶ ἐν τῇ φύσει εἶναι καὶ τὸ αἰσθάνεσθαι καὶ τὸ φύεσθαι, καὶ τὸν κόσμον λέγω χωρεῖν τὴν φύσιν καὶ τὰ φυόμενα πάντα σῴζειν. The rest of the chapter is in diatribe style; it should be compared with Stoic answers to the question εἰ δεῖ παιδοποιεῖσθαι. See e.g. Stobaeus, *Ecl.* ii. 94. 14, 109. 16 Wachsm.

[2] 340. 12 ad caelum recursura diuinitas; 340. 25 diuinitas repetet caelum. In *Kore Kosmu* also the theme (with a difference) is a world left to itself, and to ἀγνωσία (486. 10), see below.

[3] 344. 2 *mente* (τῷ νοΐ) is emphatic; cf. 342. 27.

[4] The doctrine of two souls is presupposed (*Fr.* 16). As will be seen, the daemons have power over the lower soul and no power over νοῦς (370. 4, which belongs to this context).

[5] 340. 25.

Honos Pudorque | priscus et neglecta redire Virtus | audet' (*Carmen Saeculare*, 55). The Indians indeed break in and the Conflagration over-whelms them, in the *Oracula Sibyllina*.[1]

νῦν δὲ πάλιν, Αἴγυπτε, τεὴν ὀλοφύρομαι ἄτην·
Μέμφι, πόνων ἀρχηγὸς ἔσῃ, πληχθεῖσα τένοντας·
ἐν σοὶ πυραμίδες φωνὴν φθέγξονται ἀναιδῆ.

· · · · ·

Συήνην δ' ὀλέσειε μέγας φῶς Αἰθιοπήων·
Τεύχιραν οἰκήσουσι βίῃ μελανόχροες Ἰνδοί.

· · · · ·

Ἰνδοί, μὴ θαρσεῖτε καὶ Αἰθίοπες μεγάθυμοι·
ἡνίκα γὰρ πυρόεις (?) τροχὸς Ἄξονος, Αἰγοκεράστης
Ταῦρός τ' ἐν Διδύμοις μέσον οὐρανὸν ἀμφιελίξῃ.[2]

· · · · ·

ἔσσεται ἐμπρησμὸς μέγης αἰθέριος κατὰ γαῖαν,
ἄστρων δ' ἐκ μαχίμων (?) καινὴ φύσις, ὥστ' ἀπολέσθαι
ἐν πυρὶ καὶ στοναχαῖσιν ὅλην[3] γῆν Αἰθιοπήων.[4]

This passage (with its Indian irruption, the Conflagration and Renovation) may carry us on to the cosmic theme. In 342. 11 the Cosmos itself becomes a burden, not simply because men weary, but because it is running down. τοῦτο ⟨γὰρ⟩ τὸ πᾶν, ἀγαθὸν ὄν, ... κινδυνευθήσεται, καὶ ἔσται βαρὺ τοῖς ἀνθρώποις, καὶ διὰ τοῦτο καταφρονηθήσεται (l. 13). With the *regenitura mundi* its face will be changed and it will once more be *adorandus atque mirandus*[5] (346. 2). See also vol. iv, Introduction II, pp. x–xvi.

The *senectus mundi* is described in 344. 3-12.[6] The *nocentes angeli* need special note. They succeed the departing gods. This appears to be a piece of Persian dualism inserted in a Stoic framework. The term *angelus*[7] is associated with a book under the name of Ostanes, who is repeatedly named along with Hermes and the *magi*. It was too widely distributed in Pagan usage to be merely the result of Jewish-Christian influence; the original Pagan sense probably referred in particular to

[1] v. 179–213; quoted in part by Clement, *Protr.* 4. 50.

[2] 344. 8 nec siderum cursus constabit in caelo. Cf. *Orac. Sibyll.* v *ad fin.* (quoted in part in vol. iii. 177).

[3] στοναχαῖς Ἰνδῶν Castalio.

[4] For Egypt the widow (340. 13, 26) see *Orac. Sibyll.* xi. 279. For the dumbness of the oracles (344. 9), ibid. v. 484: Ἶσι ... μενεῖς ἐπὶ χεύμασι Νείλου | μούνη, μαινὰς ἄναυδος.

[5] 342. 12 admirandus: the *felix* formula; see on 148. 24, 256. 26. l. 17 *machina*: see on 160. 2 and 314. 25. l. 20 *tenebrae*: possibly the Hermetic contrast φῶς)(σκότος. See on *nocentes angeli* below (344. 3).

[6] We need not suppose here a total conflagration or inundation. Cf. Dion Chrys. xxxvi. 50.

[7] For evidence on this word see note on iv. 5. 12.

chthonian deities.[1] Now these are bad angels, and the natural parallel is the doctrine of 'some Platonists' in Porphyry, *de abstin.* ii. 36–43, where the bad daemons are ranged under their head ($\pi\rho\omicron\epsilon\sigma\tau\tilde{\omega}\sigma\alpha$ $\delta\acute{\upsilon}\nu\alpha\mu\iota\varsigma$)[2] over against the good. Cumont argued that this is a piece of Persian demonology adopted by Porphyry's Platonists, and that the source was a book passing under the name of Ostanes.[3] Bousset[4] has reinforced Cumont's hypothesis by evidence collected to show the Zoroastrian elements in the pseudo-Clementine *Homilies*,[5] where the background (as he reconstructs it) is a tale of the fall of the daemons from heaven, their increase, and their subjection by Zoroaster.[6] Though this has been worked over by redactors under Jewish and Jewish-Christian influence, there is a strong resemblance to the dualistic demonology in Porphyry. It is characteristic of the bad daemons to delight "$\lambda\omicron\iota\beta\tilde{\eta}$ $\tau\epsilon$ $\kappa\nu\acute{\iota}\sigma\eta$ $\tau\epsilon$", from which they draw their strength.[7] Now in *Kore Kosmu*, a composite document, B. finds traces of an original half-obliterated tale of the fall of the daemons, who in their fallen state used men as instruments;[8] the complaints of the elements about pollution have their parallel in the *Homilies*.[9] Further, there is a strong presumption that Cornelius Labeo, who held that there were good and bad daemons, rested upon early Hermetic lore.[10] This roughly indicates the lines upon which Bousset argues for a characteristic dualistic demonology, found independently in Labeo and Porphyry, connected with the Gnostic movement, and at least as early as the first century of our era.

Our passage is apocalyptic. But does not the form it takes resemble the fragment describing the fall of the daemons (?) in *Kore Kosmu* (486. 11)? Both passages are indeed embedded in familiar Greek theory —the *senectus mundi*, the $\pi\rho\acute{\omega}\tau\eta$ $\kappa\alpha\tau\acute{\alpha}\sigma\tau\alpha\sigma\iota\varsigma$: the gods departed or the gods still unknown. The common element is $\dot{\alpha}\gamma\nu\omega\sigma\acute{\iota}\alpha$ (486. 10) and a

---

[1] M. Dibelius, *Geisterwelt im Glauben des Paulus*; e.g. the Ostia inscription, $\dot{\alpha}\nu\gamma\acute{\epsilon}\lambda\omicron\iota\varsigma$ $\kappa\alpha\tau\alpha\chi\theta\omicron\nu\acute{\iota}\omicron\iota\varsigma$ $^{\prime}E\rho\mu\tilde{\eta}$ $\kappa\alpha\tau\alpha\chi\theta\omicron\nu\acute{\iota}\omega$ $\kappa\alpha\grave{\iota}$ $^{\prime}E\kappa\acute{\alpha}\tau\eta$ $\kappa\alpha\tau\alpha\chi\theta\omicron\nu\acute{\iota}\alpha$, $\Pi\lambda\omicron\acute{\upsilon}\tau\omega\nu\iota$ $\kappa\alpha\grave{\iota}$ $K\acute{\omicron}\rho\eta$ (*Nachr. G. G.*, 1899, p. 105, cf. p. 128).

[2] See on 366. 11; also note on iv. 5. 12 (p. 474), Chalcidius, c. 136.

[3] *Religions Orientales*, p. 280, n. 53.

[4] *Zur Dämonologie d. späteren Antike, Archiv*, 1915, p. 134.

[5] *Hauptprobleme*, pp. 136–59.

[6] *Hom.* viii. 12–17, ix. 3.

[7] Aug. *de civ. dei*, 8. 13; the passages quoted in vol. iii. 245 should be consulted; they are relevant to this tradition, hardly to the god-making in c. 38. Cf. *Hom.* ix. 9, 14, 15. In ix. 10 these daemons are bodiless $\pi\nu\epsilon\acute{\upsilon}\mu\alpha\tau\alpha$, with a desire for bodily satisfactions; so they enter men's bodies, using them as $\dot{\upsilon}\pi\omicron\upsilon\rho\gamma\omicron\acute{\upsilon}\nu\tau\omega\nu$ $\dot{\omicron}\rho\gamma\acute{\alpha}\nu\omega\nu$. Cf. Minucius Felix, *Octav.*, c. 37, *irrepentes etiam corporibus*, and 270. 7.

[8] 486. 11 *sqq.*; l. 15 $\dot{\omicron}\rho\gamma\acute{\alpha}\nu\omicron\iota\varsigma$ $\chi\rho\acute{\omega}\mu\epsilon\nu\alpha\iota$; Ps.-Clem. *Hom.* viii. 16. See note *ad loc.*

[9] viii. 16, 17.

[10] See on Arnobius, below.

triumph of evil. These bad angels mingle with men (344. 4) ; that is, enter their bodies and use them as instruments ?[1] And they drive mankind to mutual slaughter, as in *K.K.*[2] Even the pollution theme, though not dramatically staged as in the complaint of the Elements, is not entirely wanting.[3] Here the restoration of civilized life and religion is not accomplished by divinely gifted men, as the gift of civilization is attributed to Isis and Osiris in *K.K.*,[4] or to Zoroaster in the Persian legend. This is a cyclical cosmic process, bringing in a failure of τάξις in the heavens and upon earth,[5] and God is the restorer. We cannot dismiss this passage with a mere reference to the fact that bad daemons are not unknown in Greek tradition. Here is a definite dualism, and Bousset's hypothesis is so far strengthened by comparing the two passages.

It should be added that ' Ostanes' ' angels are connected with the astral system. Iamblichus quotes Nicomachus of Gerasa as follows :[6] Βαβυλωνίων οἱ δοκιμώτατοι καὶ Ὀστάνης καὶ Ζωροάστρης ἀγέλας κυρίως καλοῦσι τὰς ἀστερικὰς σφαίρας, ἤτοι ... ἢ ἀπὸ τοῦ σύνδεσμοί πως καὶ συναγωγαὶ χρηματίζειν δογματίζεσθαι παρ' αὐτῶν τῶν φυσικῶν λογ⟨ι⟩ων, ἃς ἀγέλους κατὰ τὰ αὐτὰ καλοῦσιν ἐν τοῖς ἱεροῖς λόγοις, κατὰ παρέμπτωσιν δὲ τοῦ γάμμα ἐφθαρμένως ἀγγέλους. διὸ καὶ τοὺς καθ' ἑκάστην τούτων τῶν ἀγελῶν ἐξάρχοντας ἀστέρας καὶ δαίμονας ὁμοίως ἀγγέλους καὶ ἀρχαγγέλους προσαγορεύεσθαι.

In c. 26 a the purgation and rebirth is described. The God who is τοῦ πρώτου καὶ ἑνὸς θεοῦ δημιουργός is the *deus summus exsuperantissimus* of 374. 1 ;[7] cf. 314. 29, 346. 24. For the second God see on 158. 9, 346. 24, *Frr.* 23, 28-30 ; and for the phrase, *Abamm. respons.* (iv. 31. 25 above, with note, and iv. 32. 16). He is ' first ' from the supreme God.'[8] In 344. 15 *factaque †voluntaria†* is doubtless corrupted by *voluntate*. But some adjective is needed. Compare ll. 4-6 and perhaps read *violenta* (ἔργα βίαια).

346. 24. deus. See on 344. 14 ; Ar. *de mundo*, 397 b 26 : " ἀκροτάτῃ κορυφῇ " τοῦ σύμπαντος ἐγκαθιδρυμένος οὐρανοῦ. The order is *summus deus, Iuppiter, Iuppiter Plutonius*. This is of a piece with the passages

---

[1] 486. 15 ; and see above ; also 270. 2 *sqq.*, esp. l. 26.

[2] 486. 15.

[3] 340. 19-21, 27-30. An apocalyptic commonplace : ἀλλ' ὅταν Εὐφράτης μέγας αἵματι πλημμύρηται (*Or. Sib.* iv. 61).

[4] If my conjecture (δίκη νέμουσα) is right, God sends Δίκη to men in *K.K.* (490. 23).

[5] 344. 6 ; compare the astrological descriptions in *Orac. Sib.* v. 206 and 512. Also *Or. Sib.* iv. 152 : ἀλλ' ὅταν εὐσεβίης μὲν ἀπ' ἀνθρώπων ἀπόληται | πίστις καὶ τὸ δίκαιον ἀποκρύφθῃ ἐνὶ κόσμῳ—then the Conflagration. In l. 11 ἀσέβεια, ἀταξία, ἀλογία (confusion) πάντων ἀγαθῶν.

[6] *Theolog. Arithm.*, p. 56. 14 de Falco.

[7] See Cumont, *Archiv*, ix. 323 *qq.*, and (for Hermetism) Bousset, *G. G. A.*, 1914, pp. 708 *sqq*.

[8] See on *Fr.* 28, and note on iv. 31. 25 below ; also iv. 226. 8.

in 316. 12, 324. 3 (notes). There are different subalterns or satraps, but one God. Pluto is 'frugifer'.[1] It may be that both the 'dispensator' and the 'nutritor' are the Sun.

εἷς Ζεὺς εἷς ᾽Αίδης εἷς ῞Ηλιος εἷς Διόνυσος

χείματι μέν τ᾽ ᾽Αίδην, Δία δ᾽ εἴαρος ἀρχομένοιο
῾Ηέλιον δὲ θέρευς, μετοπώρου δ᾽ ἁβρὸν ᾽Ιαώ.[2]

Porphyry, περὶ ἀγαλμάτων, fr. 7 :[3] ἐπεὶ δὲ καὶ τῶν εἰς γῆν βαλλομένων σπερμάτων ἦν τις δύναμις, ἣν ἥλιος περὶ τὸ κάτω ἡμισφαίριον ἰὼν ἕλκει κατὰ τὰς χειμερίους τροπάς, Κόρη μὲν ἡ δύναμις ἡ σπερματοῦχος, Πλούτων δὲ ὁ ὑπὸ γῆν ἰὼν ἥλιος καὶ τὸν ἀφανῆ περινοστῶν κόσμον κατὰ τὰς χειμερίους τροπάς.

33. **Distribuentur.** Zielinski (*Archiv*, 8, p. 370) connects this with the city alluded to at 358. 27. From *litus, mons, Libya, templum* (and cult) he argues that the only answer is Cyrene. Admitting that no tradition survives of Asclepius' burial there, he invokes the tradition of a grave in Arcadia, and the relations of cultus between Arcadia and Cyrene. For the city mentioned in the text here he gives the same answer—coast city, in the West, on the border of Egypt.[4] He suggests that the translator or redactor has confused the old city and the new. So the Hermetic tradition, he infers, recognized an 'Urstadt' in which the race settled, viz. Cyrene. The fusion seems improbable and no explanation of *crocodillorum* is vouchsafed. Reitzenstein suggests that the Asclepeion at Thebes was the *templum* mentioned in 358. 27.[5] See vol. iv, Introduction, p. xiv.

348. 8–358. 2 (cc. 29 c–32 b). **Aion.** This may be a separate tract on Aion, or it may continue the tract *de immortali*, following the account of the supreme God with an argument about the second God, and closing with a description of the steps required to attain knowledge of God. See on 364. 25 and vol. iv, Introduction, p. xviii. The ultimate origin is *Timaeus* 39 D.

Aion is the second god (348. 8), the source of life as distinguished from νοῦς. This is the theme of c. 29 c—τὸν δεύτερον θεὸν τοιόνδε ἐννόει . . . τὸν πάντα δημιουργοῦντα[6] καὶ πάντα τὰ ζῷα φωτίζοντα,[7] εἴτε ἔμψυχα εἴτε καὶ

---

[1] *C. I. L.* viii. 840 : Plutoni Aug[usto] frugifero deo sacrum.

[2] Commented upon by Cornelius Labeo (Macrobius, *Sat.* i. 18. 18–22).

[3] Bidez, *Vie de Porphyre*, p. 9* (Eusebius, *Pr. ev.* 3. 11.9) ; cf. Lydus, *de mens.* p. 162. 14 Wünsch (vol. iv. 232).

[4] Hdt. iii. 31. Egyptian under the Persians, and again after Alexander (Callimachus, ii. 68).

[5] *H. M. R.*, p. 129, n. 4. See the account of the experience of Thessalus of Tralles (*loc. cit.*, and *Cat. cod. astrol. graec.* viii. 3. 134, 4. 253) ; also the list 'Escolapius, Podalirius et Machaon eius filii, Asclepius eius nepos Escolapi, Hermes Trismegistus ', etc. (*Cod. Laur.* 71, 3).

[6] *Gubernare* = δημιουργεῖν. But perhaps διοικοῦντα : cf. 344. 14.

[7] The second god is φῶς ἐκ φωτός ; cf. *Frr.* 23 sqq., 140. 24, and 266. 1.

ἄψυχα.[1] In this account Aion *is* life ; and the Cosmos, enclosed within it, is therefore itself full of life and Aion (ll. 14-15), and in turn the steward of life to all that is in it.

If this view is accepted—and the parallels in *Corp.* II and XI. i. support it—Aion is a deity *within* which the great animal, the Cosmos, is enclosed (ll. 18-25). In 350. 7-18 this order is repeated :[2] (l. 14) ὁ θεὸς οὖν ἔστηκεν, ἀεί[3] τε ὅμοιος[4] ὢν μετ' αὐτοῦ ὁ Αἰὼν συνέστηκε,[5] τὸν ἀγέννητον[6] κόσμον, ὃν εἰκότως αἰσθητὸν καλοῦμεν, ἐν ἑαυτῷ ἐμπεριέχων·[7] τούτου δὲ τοῦ θεοῦ (Αἰῶνος) εἰκὼν πεποίηται οὗτος ὁ κόσμος, τόν γε Αἰῶνα μιμούμενος. (*Tim.* 37 D, 39 A).

These pages become intelligible if it is seen that the writer is fumbling with the problem of Aion (the self-moving world soul) and its image, the Cosmos. The clue is τάξις, the cyclic recurrence of all things within the Cosmos according to law, so that Aion can be said to be in time.

1. Aion gives life to the Cosmos and to all within it.[8] This is a διπλοῦς ἐνέργεια :[9] from without to the great animal, and within by the agency of the Cosmos, differentiating[10] the creatures through the *energeia* of the Sun and the motions of the stars by determinate numbers and times.

2. This gives rise to the question of the relation between Aion and time. Time goes in ordered cycles, the succession of seasons (the year), the *apocatastases* of stars to their places[11] (348. 31-350. 2). The Cosmos (as ὕλη !) is the ὑποδοχή of time, through which things grow and have their

[1] This covers *everything* in the Cosmos, because a living creature, as the Cosmos is, can have no part that is not alive ; cf. 232. 17, Macrob. *in Somn. Scip.* 2. 12. 13. In l. 12 Kroll reads ' partis, quae est sicuti est in ipso[que] mundo'.

[2] For ll. 7-11 see next note.

[3] Word-play : ἀεὶ ὤν—Αἰών.

[4] *sc.* ἐν τῇ ταυτότητι ? Cf. 206. 17.

[5] See 208. 1.

[6] 208. 7. Compare εἰ δ' ἡ τοῦ κόσμου φύσις (cf. 436. 18) ἀγένητός τε καὶ ἄφθαρτος, δῆλον ὅτι καὶ ὁ κόσμος, αἰωνίῳ συνεχόμενος καὶ διακρατούμενος δεσμῷ (Critolaus, *ap.* Philo, *de aetern. mundi* 75, Cohn vi. 96. 14).

[7] 208. 2, 9-10 ; 438. 2 ; *Fr.* 23. I venture to suggest that the noetic character of Aion is not in question, but his relation to the Cosmos—as *intra se habens* (l. 16) suggests. He binds it together—συνέχει καὶ σώζει τὸ πᾶν ; cf. 136. 7, 140. 20, Macrob. *op. cit.* 1. 6. 8-9.

[8] 348. 9, 14, 19 *sqq.*

[9] 348. 27. In 208 25, where Aion is the subject, Ψυχή is said to fill the Cosmos within and to encompass it without, imparting life to the 'great animal' from without and to all creatures within. Ψυχή is Aion, the world-soul (208. 19). In relation to the first God, Aion is a δύναμις (208. 6) ; it is to the Kosmos as οὐσία to ὕλη (208. 5). ἐνέργεια is the sole word used here ; but in the parallel passage (436. 18) the one activity is called δύναμις, the other ἐνέργεια. They are exercised by ἡ φύσις τοῦ παντός—Aion again. Aion makes the Cosmos a unity by binding it together, and gives life throughout the Cosmos by pervading it (συνδεῖ, διήκει).

[10] *differens* = ποικίλλων. Cf. 182. 25, 184. 1.

[11] For the double time (348. 32), see 208. 15 (codd.).

renewal. Now if all is in flux (350. 5), and God and Aion are stable [1]
(350. 7–15), how are this torrent of life and this fixity related? The
answer is, by ἀποκατάστασις, return to *the same*, according to law. This
explains *remeare in aeternitatem* in l. 13.[2] Aion διαμένει ἐν τῇ ταυτότητι,[3]
and time returns things to ταυτότης. Hence (350. 18) ἔχει τοίνυν ὁ χρόνος
τὴν τῆς ἰδίας στάσεως δίναμίν τε καὶ φύσιν αὐτῇ ταύτῃ τῇ τοῦ ἀποκαθίστασθαι
ἀνάγκῃ, καίπερ αὐτός γε ἀεὶ κινούμενος. διὰ τοῦτο δὲ καὶ εἰ ὁ Αἰὼν ἐστιν ἐστὼς
καὶ ἀκίνητος καὶ ἀκλίνης, ὅμως— ἐπεὶ τοῦ χρόνου κινητοῦ ὄντος εἰς τὸν Αἰῶνα
ἀεὶ καθίσταται ἡ φορά, καὶ αὐτὴ κατὰ τὸν τοῦ χρόνου λόγον ἀνακυκλουμένη—
συμβαίνει δὴ ὅτι καὶ αὐτὸς ὁ Αἰών, ἀκίνητος μόνος ὤν, διὰ τὸν χρόνον (ἐν ᾧ
αὐτός ἐστιν ὥσπερ καὶ ἐν αὐτῷ πᾶσα φορά) φαίνεται φέρεσθαι.

3. It is now possible to suggest that Aion itself moves (352. 2–14). The
phrase *sic et deum* (l. 4) is a formal conclusion to this argument, and
should (I think) refer to Aion, not to the first God.[4] l. 7 : τοῦτ' οὖν (τὸ
μέγεθος), τοιοῦτον ὂν οἷον μὴ ταῖς αἰσθήσεσιν ὑποπίπτειν, . . . ἀμέτρητόν ἐστιν·
οὔτε γὰρ ὑπερείδεσθαι οὔτε φέρεσθαι οὔτε περιβάλλεσθαι δύναται . . . (the
categories [5] do not apply to it) . . . φέρεται γὰρ ἐν ἀκροτάτῃ στάσει, ὂν ἐν
ἑαυτῷ αὐτόστασις (?) αὐτή, εἴτε θεός, εἴτ' Αἰών, εἴτε καὶ ἑκάτερος—ἢ ἕτερος ἐν
ἑτέρῳ, ἢ ἕκαστος συναμφότερος.

What distinguishes Aion from time? It has not the delimitations of
time, which are three (ll. 15–17): by number,[6] or by succession,[7] or by a

---

[1] On ll. 7–11 see next note.

[2] Cf. 350. 1–2, and on 352. 15–17 in this note. ἀποκατάστασις is used in 176.
15 of the way in which the *order* of the heavenly bodies is preserved, and the sense
is extended there to cover organisms. Aristotle. *de caelo*, 279 a 23 : τὸ γὰρ τέλος τὸ
περιέχον τὸν τῆς ἑκάστου ζωῆς χρόνον, οὗ μηθὲν ἔξω κατὰ φύσιν, αἰὼν ἑκάστου
κέκληται. κατὰ τὸν αὐτὸν δὲ λόγον καὶ τὸ τοῦ παντὸς οὐρανοῦ τέλος καὶ τὸ τὸν
πάντα χρόνον καὶ τὴν ἀπειρίαν περιέχον τέλος αἰών ἐστι, ἀπὸ τοῦ ἀεὶ εἶναι εἰληφὼς
τὴν ἐπωνυμίαν, ἀθάνατος καὶ θεῖος. ὅθεν καὶ τοῖς ἄλλοις ἐξήρτηται, τοῖς μὲν ἀκριβέστερον, τοῖς δ' ἀμαυρῶς, τὸ εἶναί τε καὶ ζῆν. In 210. 27 the planets are said to be
κεκοσμημένοι τάξει αἰωνίῳ, καὶ δρόμῳ διαφόρῳ τὸν αἰῶνα ἀναπληροῦντες. Their
ἀνομοιότης comes back to the same. See vol. iv, Introduction II, pp. xxii–xxiii.

[3] 208. 28.

[4] In ll. 2–3 *et—et* places Aion and time on a basis of comparison ; then οὕτω καὶ
τὸν θεόν κ.τ.λ. Cf. 350. 17. The point is that Aion is παμμεγέθης (ll. 5–6, 134.
16), and in this magnitude lies his stability. See 134. 3, 350. 10.

[5] See 236. 30, 370. 7, *Fr. 26*, and contrast 322. 17–18. 'Infinitus ingenitus inmortalis perpetuus solus, quem nulla deliniat forma corporalis, nulla determinat
circumscriptio, qualitatis expers, expers quantitatis, sine situ motu et habitu . . .
qui ut intelligaris tacendum est atque ut per umbram te possit errans inuestigare
suspicio, nihil omnino muttiendum ' (Arnobius, *adv. nat.* I. 31).

[6] Cf. 348. 30. Cf. Arnobius' criticism of Labeo (?): 'incipiamus ergo solle-
mniter ab Iano et nos patre, quem quidam ex uobis mundum, annum alii, solem
esse prodidere nonnulli. . . . si Ianus est annus, deus esse nec sic potest. quis
enim annum ignorat temporis esse circumscriptionem statam, nec habere uim
numinis id quod spatiis mensum et dierum dinumeratione conclusum est ? . . . quis

mode described as *alterius per ambitudinem reditus*,[1] which is perhaps a clumsy rendering of δι' ἀποκατάστασιν. The answer is στάσις (l. 18)—ἡ γὰρ στάσις, ἅτε ἑστῶσα, ἵνα τοῖς κινουμένοις ἀντερείδειν[2] δύνηται, τῆς βεβαιότητος χάριν ἀξίως τὴν ἀρχὴν ἔχει. πάντων οὖν τῶν ὄντων ἀρχαὶ ὁ θεός ἐστιν—καὶ ὁ Αἰών· ὁ δὲ κόσμος, κινητὸς ὤν, οὐκ ἔχει τὴν ἀρχήν. Πλέον γὰρ ἔχει ἡ ἴδια κίνησις τῆς αὑτοῦ στάσεως κατὰ τὸν τῆς ἀϊδίου φορᾶς νόμον, ἔχουσα ἀκίνητόν γε τὴν βεβαιότητα.[3] c. 40 b, though appropriate to this context, can be interpreted in its traditional place ; see on 364. 14.

c. 32 b (354. 9). This section on νοῦς is appended to the discussion of Aion, who is the second Νοῦς. The first part enumerates four grades ; the second (it is suggested) tells how these can be apprehended by man. For ὅμοιος ὁμοίῳ νοητόν—the mind knows its kin. The following version assumes some errors in the Latin : 354. 9, πᾶς μὲν οὖν νοῦς τῷ θείῳ (sc. νῷ) ὅμοιός ἐστιν.[4] αὐτὸς μὲν ἀκίνητος ὢν ἐν τῇ ἰδίᾳ στάσει ἑαυτὸν κινεῖ, σεμνὸς καὶ ἄφθαρτος καὶ ἀίδιος ὤν, καὶ εἴ τινι ἄλλῳ κρείττονι ὀνόματι κεκλῆσθαι δύναται. τοῦ δὲ ὑψίστου Θεοῦ ἐν αὐτῇ τῇ Ἀληθείᾳ ὢν ὁ Αἰών, πληρέστατος πάντων τῶν αἰσθητῶν καὶ πάσης τάξεως,[5] καὶ ὥσπερ συνυφεστὼς μετὰ τοῦ θεοῦ.[6]

The text has been translated on the assumption that *si . . . nuncupari* ends an anacletic formula characterizing the *summus deus*, whereas *plenissimus*, etc., characterizes Aion. It has also been tentatively assumed that *sensibilium* refers to the αἰσθηταὶ ἰδέαι which Aion pours forth.[7] This agrees with the probable sense of 350. 16 (see above), and answers to the statement that the *sensus mundanus* is the *recipient* of these

est enim tam demens, qui tempus (*scil.* Κρόνος-χρόνος) esse dicat deum, quod mensura cuiusdam est spatii in continua serie perpetuitatis inclusi ?' (*adv. nat.* iii. 29). ὡς ἄρα ὁ τὴν τοῦ χρόνου φύσιν κατασκευάσας Θεός, μέτρα αὐτῷ καὶ σημεῖα τὰ τῶν ἡμερῶν ἐπέβαλε διαστήματα, καὶ ἑβδομάδι αὐτὸν ἐκμετρῶν, ἀεὶ τὴν ἑβδομάδα εἰς ἑαυτὴν ἀνακυκλοῦσθαι κελεύει, ἐξαριθμοῦσαν τοῦ χρόνου τὴν κίνησιν (Basil, *Hexaemeros*, ii. 49 C Migne).

[7] ἐναλλαγῇ ; 350. 5 (*alternatio* along with *innovatio* ; cf. 148. 10) ; 346. 21 ; 348. 33.

---

[1] *Ambitudinem* is Thomas's reading ; no authority for *ambitionem* in his apparatus. See 350. 1-2, 206. 23 ; also iv. 422, n. 2. The grand measure of time is astronomical. *Tim.* 39 D.

[2] Note on 136. 15. The question is : what is the ἀντέρεισις that holds the Cosmos together ? Philo said Λόγος, as the Stoics said ἕξις. Here the answer is Aion, σωτήρ (140. 20) and σύνδεσμος.

[3] The participial clause returns to the main point : the Cosmos, though full of motions, has a principle of stability and does not shift from its place.

[4] Cf. 222. 25-224. 6.   [5] Cf. 362. 15 ; also 350. 4, 206. 18.

[6] 116. 11 οὐ γὰρ διίστανται ἀπ' ἀλλήλων· ἕνωσις γὰρ τούτων ἐστὶν ἡ ζωή.

[7] Aion is Παντόμορφος ; see 324. 11, 328. 29. In 218. 8 the Cosmos itself is Παντόμορφος. Aion is ὁ μεταμορφούμενος εἰς πάντας ἐν ταῖς ὁράσεσιν, ἀόρατος Αἰὼν Αἰῶνος (Dieterich, *Abraxas*, 176. 12). Cf. Numenius : ὁ μὲν οὖν πρῶτος (θεός) περὶ τὰ νοητά, ὁ δὲ δεύτερος περὶ τὰ νοητὰ καὶ αἰσθητά (vol. ii. 80, § 20).

forms[1] and orders. If this rendering is right—and it is not beyond dispute—the last phrase recalls that Aion, in performing this creative function, is a δύναμις of God. That Aion is the source of τάξις[2] within the Cosmos is the main theme of the piece, and (as we shall see) it is from these forms that his nature is known. The *sensus mundanus* (l. 14) is just the recipient of these forms and of the various orders—recurrence of seasons, return of the stars to their former positions. In 182. 11 it is said that the αἴσθησις and νόησις of the Cosmos is one, τὸ πάντα ποιεῖν καὶ εἰς ἑαυτὸν ἀποποιεῖν—the cycle of birth, decay, renewal.

That the ἀνθρώπινος νοῦς (l. 15) is directed to the tendance of the earth[3] and depends on memory is the theme of c. 11 a, and there (if my interpretation is right)[4] it is named in connexion with a higher set of powers. Down to man, and no further, τὸ τοῦ νοῦ θεῖον pervades.

The second part (356. 2) is less straightforward, because the translation is loose. The grades are now taken in reverse order, because an ascent to apprehension of the highest Νοῦς is described. The question is, how can man know νοῦς?[5] (*a*) τὸ μὲν γὰρ τὸν ἀνθρώπινον νοῦν ἐννοεῖν, ποταπὸς ἢ πηλίκος ἐστίν, ὅλον ἐν τῇ τῶν παρεληλυθότων μνήμῃ ἐστί (l. 2). (*b*) τὸ δὲ κατανοεῖν τήν τε φύσιν καὶ τὴν ποιότητα τοῦ ὑλικοῦ νοῦ ἐκ πάντων ὅσων ἐν τῷ κόσμῳ αἰσθητά ἐστιν οἷόν τε ἔσται διιδεῖν (l. 4).[6] We know *what* the cosmic mind is like through its activity in producing sensible kinds. (*c*) τοῦ δὲ Αἰῶνος,[7] ὃς δεύτερός ἐστι (θεός), ὁ νοῦς ἐκ τοῦ αἰσθητοῦ κόσμου διαγιγνώσκεται, ποταπός ἐστι.[8] The στάσις which is characteristic of Aion is revealed in the order of the sensible Cosmos, as we have seen.[9] Further, the moved implies a mover (134. 2-3). Allowing for the different doctrines in the two documents, we may recall that the αἴσθησις and νόησις of God (pantheistic) is τὸ τὰ πάντα ἀεὶ κινεῖν (184. 19). It would appear to be beyond doubt that Aion is here, as above, represented as the second Nous. (*d*) ἀλλὰ τὸ νοεῖν τὸν τοῦ ὑψίστου Θεοῦ νοῦν, πηλίκος ἐστί, ἀλήθειά

---

[1] Cf. 326. 12.

[2] Compare Numenius (*mutatis mutandis*): τὴν προσοῦσαν τῷ πρώτῳ (θεῷ) στάσιν φημὶ εἶναι κίνησιν σύμφυτον, ἀφ' ἧς ἥ τε τάξις τοῦ κόσμου καὶ ἡ μονὴ ἡ ἀΐδιος καὶ ἡ σωτηρία ἀναχεῖται εἰς τὰ ὅλα (vol. ii. 81, § 21).

[3] 356. 4.

[4] See on 304. 16 *ad fin.*

[5] γνῶσις can only be used of knowing God. The clue is in l. 8, where *qualitas dinoscitur* might be more clumsily rendered *qualitatis intellegentia*. *Pervideri* (l. 6) confirms this interpretation. I have used νοεῖν-νόησις and compounds to express the apprehending by man of νοῦς; cf. 158. 12, 380. 2.

[6] Pleonasm; so l. 17 *sqq.*: intellectus . . . ad intelligendam pervenit.

[7] *aeternita(ti)s* Thomas.

[8] I have evaded the difficulty of the reading *datus*, l. 7 (*datur* Thomas), because it is not essential for establishing the general sense. The repetition of these clumsy phrases with slight variations exposed them to scribal corruption.

[9] 158. 22 *sqq.* (τάξις). Cf. Numenius, in vol. ii. 81, § 21. Also 208. 12, τὴν ἀθανασίαν καὶ διαμονὴν ἐνθεὶς τῇ ὕλῃ.

ἐστι μόνη, ἧς δὴ ἐν τῷ κόσμῳ οὐδεμία σκιά, οὐδ' ἀμυδρῶς περιληφθεῖσα, διαγιγνώσκεται.[1] ll. 12-16 draw the moral : there is no truth on earth, yet man
can know God's *Nous* ('qui me videndae divinitatis luminasti lumine').[2]
Without this the description of the ascent towards Nous would end with
negation ; with it, there is an affirmation of φωτισμός. But this mystery
must not be revealed—the disciples must not be διάβολοι (254. 15,
note).

The lines 17-20, though obscure, appear to confirm the view that
knowing the higher grades of νοῦς is the subject. Our apprehending can
penetrate (if we attend) to the 'apprehension' (*intellegendiam*) and
discernment of the nature of the ὑλικὸς νοῖς, and apprehending the
Cosmos leads to discernment of Aion and the other powers of God.
This ascent is possible even under the limitations of the ἀνθρώπινος νοῦς
(l. 22), for the reasons described above : we are reminded of the sequence
seeing, admiring, adoring.[3] See vol. iv, Introduction II, pp. xxvi-xxvii.

It is probable that this section, with Aion as its chief theme, is a
separate tract, embedded in the collection known as the τέλειος λόγος. Its
natural affinities are *Corp*. II (though the first God of that document is
above *Nous*), *Corp*. XI, and the set of fragments[4] quoted for their
own purpose by Didymus and Cyril. The general theory is closely allied
to that of the Chaldaic oracles : πάντα γὰρ ἐξετέλεσσε πατὴρ καὶ νῷ παρέδωκε |
δευτέρῳ.[5]

Whatever Eastern elements may have entered into the conception of
Aion,[6] the character of this theology is best illustrated by Hellenistic
philosophical-theological notions. It is not possible here to do more
than give references in particular to the identification of Janus with Aion.[7]
Marcus Messala *ap*. Macrob., *Sat*. I. 9. 14 : 'qui cuncta fingit eademque
regit, aquae terraeque uim ac naturam grauem atque pronam in profundum
dilabentem, ignis atque animae leuem in immensum sublime fugientem,
copulauit circumdato caelo : quae uis caeli maxima duas uis dispares
colligauit.' Lydus, *de mens*. 64. 6 W.: Λογγῖνος δὲ Αἰωνάριον (Ianuarius)
αὐτὸν ἑρμηνεῦσαι βιάζεται ὡσεὶ τοῦ Αἰῶνος πατέρα, ἢ ὅτι ἔνον τὸν ἐνιαυτὸν

---

[1] In 176. 20 man is said to have *nous*, and therefore to have ἔννοιαν τοῦ πρώτου
(θεοῦ . . . ὡς ἀσωμάτου). For the denial that any truth is on earth, see e.g. 384. 22
—Hermetic dualism.

[2] This is the theme of the opening : 370. 8-18.

[3] See 148. 24 (note), 310. 7-13.

[4] Not all Hermetic.

[5] Psellus, 1140 C Migne.

[6] For a full historical discussion see Reitzenstein, *Iranische Erlösungsmysterium*, Beigabe I. But consult also M. Zepf, *Der Gott* Αἰών *in der hellenistischen
Theologie* (*Archiv*, Jan. 1928), for Greek antecedents, especially the philosophical
element in this theology, and see vol. iv, Introduction II, pp. xviii *sqq*.

[7] Alii mundum id est caelum esse uoluerunt Ianumque ab eundo dictum, quod
mundus semper eat, dum in orbem uoluitur et ex se initium faciens in se refertur
(Macrobius, *Sat*. i. 9. 11).

Ἕλληνες εἶπον... ἢ ἀπὸ τῆς ἴας ἀντὶ τοῦ τῆς μιᾶς κατὰ τοὺς Πυθαγορείους. ὅθεν ὁ Μεσσαλᾶς τοῦτον εἶναι τὸν αἰῶνα νομίζει.... Φοντήϊος δὲ ... ἔφορον αὐτὸν οἴεται τοῦ παντὸς χρόνου τυγχάνειν.[1]

In 348. 16 (and in 370. 16) the Sun is identified with Aion, as Aion is identified with *Caelum* and with εἱμαρμένη.[2] They are different modes of interposing a second deity between the supreme deity and the Cosmos.

350. 7 *sqq.* Perhaps μόνος ὁ θεός, καὶ εἰκότως μόνος· αὐτὸς γὰρ ἐν ἑαυτῷ ἐστι, καὶ ἐξ ἑαυτοῦ ἐστι, καὶ περὶ ἑαυτόν ἐστιν ὅλος, πλήρης καὶ τέλειος ὤν. καὶ αὐτὸς βεβαία αὐτόστασίς (?) ἐστι, οὐδ' ἄλλου τινὸς πληγῇ ἐκ τόπου κινεῖσθαι δύναται, ἐπεὶ ἐν αὐτῷ πάντα καὶ ἐν πᾶσιν αὐτός ἐστι μόνος. These phrases ring the changes on μόνος, πάντα, ὅλος. They are common Stoic form, and tend to harden into religious formulae. For μόνος see 332. 11 (note), 370. 6, 288. 13, 16. Also 332. 8, *Frr.* 23, 25, vol. iv, 199. 11, 226. n. 14, 152-3, and compare (with Norden)[3] Tertullian, *adv. Praxeam* 5: ante omnia deus erat solus, ipsi sibi et mundus et locus et omnia.

358. 15 *sqq.* (c. 37). In this passage the writer begins from the school definition of man : man, ζῷον λογικὸν θνητόν, is marvellous ; but still more marvellous is his power of θεουργία. Our text is substantially that possessed by St. Augustine, and I shall try to interpret it as it stands. The discovery is said to fall into two parts (l. 19), τὴν θείαν φύσιν ἐξευρεῖν, and θεοποιεῖν.[4] In l. 20 suppose we read provisionally ᾗ ἐξευρεθείσῃ προσῆψαν δύναμίν τινα ἐξ ὑλικῆς φύσεως (or ἐξ ὕλης)[5] οἰκείαν. To leave the relative aside for the moment, the evidence to be quoted below (on 360. 17) shows that this refers to the ritual custom of compounding substances specially sympathetic to the god and attaching them to his statue as a lure. *Virtutem* I take to be abstract for concrete, a substance possessing a power or quality[6] that it imparts to the compound in which it is an ingredient ; there is a μῖξις of δυνάμεις, and the whole is then a *receptaculum* (ὑποδοχή) for the soul of the god,[7] which man cannot make (l. 23). The difficulty is to determine what *cui inventae* means.

[1] See further P.-W., *Suppl.*, iii. 1187 *sqq.*

[2] See on 364. 14 and Zepf, *op. cit.* For *Caelum* see 290. 11.

[3] *Agn. Theos*, pp. 240 *sqq.*, 347 *sqq.* Also Peterson, ΕΙΣ ΘΕΟΣ, p. 196 ; Reitzenstein, *H. M. R.*, pp. 27-8 ('Isis, una quae est omnia', *C. I. L.* x 3800).

[4] The account of the primitive ignorance bears some resemblance to the tale that Chaeremon tells of the origin of the Egyptian kingdom, when the first king, Oanes, used his astronomical knowledge to impose himself upon the people (Sathas, *Bull. de corresp. hellénique*, i. 201 ; also *Cat. des manuscr. alchim. grecs*, vi, p. 18, 164): ἀμαθεῖς τὰ πρῶτα τοῦ δαιμονίου καὶ ἐστασίαζον πρὸς ἀλλήλους. Cf. 486. 10 (l. ἀγνωσία) with note, below.

[5] ὕλη is translated by *mundi natura* in 312. 12.

[6] *Virtus*: cf. Euseb., *Pr. Ev.*, iv. 1. 6 : πολλὰ γὰρ εἶναι εἴδη ῥιζῶν καὶ βοτανῶν καὶ φυτῶν καὶ καρπῶν καὶ λίθων, ξηρῶν τε ἄλλων καὶ ὑγρῶν παντοίας ὕλης δυνάμεων ἐν τῇ τῶν ὅλων φύσει. (See on c. 38 below.) The phrase *divinitatis naturam in se habentibus* (p. 360. 19) is almost equivalent.

[7] Augustine, *de civ. dei*, 8. 23 and 24 (see iv. 180 5 and 184. 34). This

(1) If *cui inventae* refers to *arti*, the sense is impossible. For the *virtus* added or attached to the art is a thing possessing virtue, as context and parallel passages show, not a power exercised by the art. It is a 'power' to be manipulated *by* an art, and cannot be attached to it. (2) To refer *cui* to *divinam naturam* would give sense: the clause would then mean that the divine nature was 'mixed' with the ὑποδοχή prepared for it. But this is grammatically unnatural and (as Professor Rose reminds me) ignores St. Augustine's feeling for fourth-century style. In addition, such an interpretation anticipates. The clause describes the preparing of the receptacle for the god; the evocation follows. (3) It seems better to suppose a mistranslation, and to read as follows with Professor Rose: εὑρόντες δὲ συνῆψαν μίξαντες δύναμιν ὑλικῆς (or κοσμικῆς) φύσεως οἰκείαν, ψυχάς, ἐπειδὴ ποιεῖν οὐχ οἷοί τ' ἦσαν, δαιμόνων ἢ ἀγγέλων ἀνακαλέσαντες, ἃς εἰς τὰς εἰκόνας ἐνέθεσαν ἱεροῖς καὶ θείοις μυστηρίοις, ὥστε ἔχειν τὰ εἴδωλα ἀγαθοποιὸν καὶ κακοποιὸν ἰσχύν. Thus the order is: discovery, compounding, evocation, σύγκρασις, powers of idols, followed by examples of those powers.

The best parallel is given by Proclus' tract περὶ τῆς καθ' Ἕλληνας ἱερατικῆς τέχνης.[1] ἴδοις ἂν οὖν τὰς συνεσπειραμένας ἰδιότητας ἐν ἡλίῳ μεριζομένας ἐν τοῖς μετέχουσιν ἀγγέλοις, δαίμοσι, ψυχαῖς, ζῴοις, φυτοῖς, λίθοις. ὅθεν οἱ τῆς ἱερατικῆς ἡγεμόνες ἀπὸ τῶν ἐν ὀφθαλμοῖς κειμένων τὴν τῶν ἀνωτέρω δυνάμεων θεραπείαν εὑρήκασι, τὰ μὲν μίξαντες, τὰ δὲ οἰκείως ἀναιρούμενοι· ἡ δὲ μίξις διὰ τὸ βλέπειν τῶν ἀμίκτων ἕκαστόν τινα, ἔχον ἰδιότητα τοῦ θεοῦ, οὐ μὴν ἐξαρκοῦν πρὸς τὴν ἐκείνου πρόκλησιν· διὸ τῇ μίξει τῶν πολλῶν ἑνίζουσι τὰς προειρημένας ἀπορροίας καὶ ἐξομοιοῦσι τὸ ἐκ πάντων ἓν γενόμενον πρὸς ἐκεῖνο τὸ πρὸ τῶν πάντων ὅλον· καὶ ἀγάλματα πολλάκις κατασκευάζουσι σύμμικτα καὶ θυμιάματα, φυράσαντες εἰς ἓν τὰ μερισθέντα συνθήματα καὶ ποιήσαντες τέχνῃ ὁποῖον κατ' οὐσίαν τὸ θεῖον περιληπτικὸν καθ' ἕνωσιν τῶν πλειόνων δυνάμεων, ὧν ὁ μὲν μερισμὸς ἠμύδρωσεν ἑκάστην, ἡ δὲ μίξις ἐπανήγαγεν εἰς τὴν τοῦ παραδείγματος ἰδέαν. ἔστι δὲ ὅτε καὶ μία πόα καὶ λίθος εἰς ἀρκεῖ πρὸς τὸ ἔργον... διὰ μὲν οὖν τῆς συμπαθείας προσήγοντο, διὰ δὲ τῆς ἀντιπαθείας ἀπήλαυνον... They used ζῷα προσήκοντα κ.τ.λ. in sacrifices, and came to know τὰς δαιμονίας δυνάμεις, ὡς προσεχεῖς εἰσιν οὐσίαι τῆς ἐν τῇ φύσει καὶ τοῖς σώμασιν ἐνεργείας, καὶ ἐπηγάγοντο δι' αὐτῶν τούτων εἰς συνουσίαν· ἀπὸ δὲ τούτων ἐπ' αὐτὰς ἤδη τὰς τῶν θεῶν ἀνέδραμον ποιήσεις, τὰ μὲν ἀπ' αὐτῶν διδασκόμενοι, τὰ δὲ καὶ αὐτοὶ κινούμενοι παρ' ἑαυτῶν εὐστόχως εἰς τὴν τῶν οἰκείων συμβόλων ἐπίνοιαν. See also on 360. 17.

27. See on 346. 33.

360. 4. irasci. Since the discussion begins with the traditional definition of man (358. 13), Apuleius' corresponding definition of daemons may

___

binding of god to matter is a σύγκρασις or μῖξις. For ὑποδοχή see vol. iii, p. 244.

[1] This was known only in Ficino's translation *de sacrificio et magia*. Professor Bidez has now published the original text in *Catalogue des manuscr. alchimiques grecs*, vi. p. 148 (1928).

be noted: daemones sunt genere animalia, ingenio rationabilia, animo passiva, corpore aeria, tempore aeterna (*de deo Socratis*, 13). See *ibid.* 15 *ad fin.* Also note on Psellus, iv. 244. 10 below.

6. θεραπεύεσθαι δὲ ... τὰς ψυχὰς ὧν ζῶσαι καθιερώθησαν (Rose). It is perhaps worth noting a sentence of Cornelius Labeo, who was connected (as Bousset suggests) [1] with the early development of Hermetism: de quo dicit Labeo in libris qui appellantur de diis animalibus: in quibus ait esse quaedam sacra, quibus animae humanae vertantur in deos qui appellantur animales quod de animis fiant (Servius, *ad Aen.*, iii. 168).

17. Asclepius returns to the question: what is the nature of the receptacle: καὶ τούτων .. τῶν θεῶν, οἳ ἐπίγειοι κέκληνται, ποταπὴ ἡ ποιότης; [2] ΤΡΙΣΜ. συνέστηκεν ... ἐκ βοτανῶν καὶ λίθων καὶ ἀρωμάτων (spices) θείάν τινα φύσιν ἐχόντων. Cf. the passages from *Abamm. resp.* [3] and Origen quoted in vol. iii, p. 244, and Eusebius quoted above; also *Pr. ev.* v. 12: ὅτι δὲ καὶ τὰ ἀγάλματα αὐτοὶ ὑπέθεντο πῶς χρὴ ποιεῖν καὶ ἐκ ποίας ὕλης δηλώσει τὰ τῆς Ἑκάτης ἔχοντα τοῦτο τὸν τρόπον·

> ἀλλὰ τέλει ξόανον κεκαθαρμένον ὥς σε διδάξω·
> πηγάνου ἐξ ἄγροιο δετὰς ποίει, ἠδ' ἐπικόσμει
> ζώοισιν λεπτοῖσι κατοικιδίοις καλαβώταις·
> σμύρνης καὶ στύρακος λιβάνοιό τε μίγματα τρίψας
> σὺν κείνοις ζώοισι καὶ αἰθριάσας ὑπὸ μήνην
> αὔξουσαν τέλει, αὐτὸς ἐπευχόμενος τήνδ' εὐχήν.

Origen, *c. Celsum*, v. 38 (on a fragment of Numenius; the preparation of Sarapis is described): ὡς ἄρα πάντων τῶν ὑπὸ φύσεως διοικουμένων μετέχει οὐσίας ζώων καὶ φυτῶν, ἵνα δόξῃ μετὰ τῶν ἀτελέστων τελετῶν καὶ τῶν καλουσῶν δαίμονας μαγγανειῶν οὐχ ὑπὸ ἀγαλματοποιῶν μόνων κατασκευάζεσθαι θεὸς ἀλλὰ καὶ ὑπὸ μάγων καὶ φαρμικῶν καὶ τῶν ἐπῳδαῖς αὐτῶν κηλουμένων δαιμόνων. Cf. Psellus,[4] who evidently draws upon Chaeremon's *Aegyptiaca*: ἀπὸ δὲ τῆς τελεστικῆς ἐπιστήμης πόσα ἂν παραδοξότατα συμπορίσαιο; ἐκείνη γὰρ τὰ κοῖλα τῶν ἀγαλμάτων ὕλης ἐμπιμπλῶσα οἰκείας ταῖς ἐφεστηκυίαις δυνάμεσι, ζώων, φυτῶν, λίθων, βοτανῶν, ῥιζῶν, σφραγίδων ἐγγραμμάτων, ἐνίοτε δὲ καὶ ἀρωμάτων συμπα-

---

[1] See note on iv. 7. 8 below. The Greek probably explained ἱερὰ ζῷα by (ψυχαὶ) ζῶσαι; the Latin *animalia-animas* very nearly approaches the etymology suggested by Labeo.

[2] *Qualitas*, perhaps body possessing certain qualities or ingredients. The answer names the ingredients. Cf. Cic., *Acad.*, I. 7 6.

[3] Augustine's comments on this passage are in *de civ. dei*, x. 11.

[4] See also Psellus, *de operatione daemonum* (*Cat. d. man. alch. gr.* vi. 128. 26; Boissonade, p. 40); ἀνιχνεύουσα δὲ ἡ τοιαύτη δύναμις τῶν ὑπὸ τὴν σελήνην γενέσεων ἑκάστης οὐσίαν καὶ φύσιν καὶ δύναμιν καὶ ποιότητα, λέγω δὲ στοιχεῖα καὶ τούτων μερῶν, ζώων παντοδαπῶν, φυτῶν καὶ τῶν ἐντεῦθεν καρπῶν, λίθων, βοτανῶν, καὶ ἁπλῶς εἰπεῖν παντὸς πράγματος ὑπόστασίν τε καὶ δύναμιν, ἐντεῦθεν τὰ ἑαυτῆς ἐνεργάζεται. ἀγάλματά τε ὑφίστησιν ὑγείας περιποιητικὰ καὶ σχήματα ποιεῖται παντοδαπὰ κ.τ.λ. Diodorus, i. 21. 6; Plut., *Isis et Osiris*, 39, 366 C Professor Rose refers me to the Paris Papyrus (l. 3072, Preisendanz) and to *Pap. Mimaut* (l. 296, Preisendanz).

θῶν, συγκαθιδρύουσα δὲ τούτοις καὶ κρατῆρας καὶ σπονδεῖα καὶ θυμιατήρια, ἔμπνοα ποιεῖ τὰ εἴδωλα καὶ τῇ ἀπορρήτῳ δυνάμει κινεῖ, καί, τό γε θαυμασιώτερον, οἱ αὐτοὶ καιροὶ τοῖς μὲν οἰκείοι γίνονται πολλάκις, τοῖς δὲ ἀλλότριοι πρὸς τὰς ἀπορρήτους ἐνεργείας· εἶτα δὴ καὶ ὀνόματά τινα πρὸς τὴν παραδοξοποιΐαν δεδύνηνται, ὥσπερ τὸ τρικάρηνον καὶ τὸ δρακοντόζωνον καὶ τὸ ξιφηφόρον καὶ μαστιγοφόρον καὶ δᾳδοφόρον καὶ τρίμορφον· καὶ εἰ μή τις ταῦτα ἐρεῖ καὶ ὑποψελλῷ τῇ γλώσσῃ, ἢ ἑτέρως ὡς ἡ τέχνη διατάττεται, οὐκ ἂν τὸ καταβακχευόμενον ἐνεργήσειεν. (C. N. Sathas, *Bull. de corresp. hellénique*, i, p. 205.)

From l. 20 on the writer describes the rites necessary to retain the god once he has been lured within.

362. 1. Retain *fortuitos* (τύχῃ; cf. 364. 23): explained by *singillatim quaedam curantes*, etc. (l. 4); each one has his or her special province and does not work by chance. It is natural to take this with the reference to πάθη in 360. 3–5.[1] Compare Maximus Tyrius, 9. 7 a (Hobein) ἀλλ' οὐχὶ δαιμόνων πᾶς πάντα δρᾷ, ἀλλ' αὐτοῖς διακέκριται κἀκεῖ τὰ ἔργα, ἄλλο ἄλλῳ. καὶ τοῦτό ἐστιν ἀμέλει τὸ ἐμπαθές, ᾧ ἐλαττοῦται δαίμων θεοῦ, κ.τ.λ.[2]

From the gods through daemons to men there is σύνδεσμος. Cf. Apuleius, *de deo Socratis*, 4: habetis interim bina animalia: deos ab hominibus plurimum differentis loci sublimitate, ... nullo inter se propinquo communicatu. ... quid igitur? nullone conexu natura se vinxit, sed in divinam et humanam partem ⟨hiul⟩cam se et interruptam ac veluti debilem passa est? nam, ut idem Plato ait, nullus deus miscetur hominibus. ... 5 nullus, inquis, deus humanis rebus intervenit? ... quem miseris auxiliatorem, quem fautorem bonis, quem adversatorem malis in omni vita ciebo? ... 6 ... ceterum sunt quaedam divinae mediae potestates inter summum aethera et infimas terras in isto intersitae aeris spatio. ... eorum quippe de numero praediti curant singuli [eorum], proinde ut est cuique tributa provincia, vel somniis conformandis vel extis fissiculandis... vel vatibus inspirandis vel fulminibus iaculandis vel nubibus coruscandis ceterisque adeo, per quae futura dinoscimus. quae cuncta caelestium voluntate et numine et auctoritate sed daemonum obsequio et opera et ministerio fieri arbitrandum est. Iamblichus, *de myst.* i. 20: οἱ δὲ τὴν δαιμονίαν ἐπιστασίαν διαλαχόντες, μοίρας τινὰς μεριστὰς τοῦ κόσμου κατατεινάμενοι, ταύτας κατευθύνουσιν, ἔχουσί τε καὶ αὐτοὶ μεριστὸν τὸ τῆς οὐσίας εἶδος καὶ δυνάμεως.

9. catholicorum. See vol. iv, Introduction, p. xix, for the general theory of Fate.

364. 14. οὗτος (or αὐτὴ?) οὖν ἐστιν ὁ Αἰών, οὔτε ἀρχόμενος εἶναι οὔτε καταλήξων, ὅς, τεταγμένου τοῦ ἀμεταπτώτου νόμου τῆς φορᾶς, ἀΐδιά τε κινήσει στρέφεται, καὶ ἀνατέλλεταί τε καὶ καταδύνει ἐπαλλήλοις ἀεὶ μέρεσιν,[3] ὥστε κατὰ τὴν τῶν

---

[1] Contrast 364. 8.

[2] The daemons pursue their earthly interests still—ἀλλὰ καὶ Ἀσκληπιὸς ἰᾶται νῦν (cf. 358. 26–32) κ.τ.λ. Cf. Max. Tyr., 8. 8 a (quoted vol. iii, p. 230).

[3] *Scil.* alternis sēper membris *for* alternis saepe per membra (*codd.*).

καιρῶν διαφορὰν οἷς κατεδεδύκει μέρεσι τούτοις καὶ ἀνατέλλεσθαι. τοιαύτη γάρ
ἐστιν ἡ κύκλησις, λόγος τις οὖσα περιφορητικός, δι' οὗ εἰς ἑαυτὰ οὕτω συννεύει
πάντα, ὥστε τίς ἀρχή ἐστι τῆς περιφορᾶς ἀγνοεῖσθαι, ἐπεὶ πάντα ἑαυτῶν ἀεὶ καὶ
προϊέναι φαίνεται καὶ ἕπεσθαι.

This is the theme of returning to the same that has been illustrated in
the note on 348. 8, — the eternal return of the stars, which are both before
and after themselves, and are bound into a unity.[1]   The argument runs
from the nature of the circle, without beginning or end,[2] to the celestial
revolution, and so (though not in this passage) to the eternity of the
Cosmos.[3]   Basil, writing of the Creation, warns his readers against those
who reason from the circular motion of the heavens or the apparent end-
lessness of the circle to a visible Cosmos without a beginning.[4]   οἱ μὲν
συνυπάρχειν ἐξ ἀιδίου τῷ θεῷ τὸν οὐρανὸν ἀπεφήναντο.   οἱ δὲ αὐτὸν εἶναι θεὸν
ἄναρχόν τε καὶ ἀτελεύτητον, καὶ τῆς τῶν κατὰ μέρος οἰκονομίας αἴτιον (Hexaem.
12 A).   Compare the following:[5]

Lydus, de mens. 3. 4	Basil, Hexaemeros, ii
κύκλος παντὸς ἀριθμοῦ ἐστιν ἡ δεκὰς καὶ πέρας . . .	(9 A) οὐδὲ γὰρ ὁ κύκλος οὗτος,
ὁ ⟨δὲ⟩ κύκλος ἐπίπεδον σχῆμά ἐστιν	τὸ ἐπίπεδον λέγω σχῆμα
ὑπὸ μιᾶς γραμμῆς περιεχόμενον,	τὸ ὑπὸ μιᾶς γραμμῆς περιεχόμενον . . .
	(49 C)
καὶ ταύτῃ κυκλικὸν ὀνομάζεται σχῆμα	τοῦτο δὲ κυκλικόν ἐστι τὸ σχῆμα,
ἀφ' ἑαυτοῦ ἀρχόμενον καὶ εἰς	ἀφ' ἑαυτοῦ ἄρχεσθαι, καὶ εἰς
ἑαυτὰ κατάληγον, ὃ δὴ ἴδιον	ἑαυτὸ καταλήγειν, ὃ δὴ καὶ
τοῦ χρόνου εἰς ἑαυτὸν	τοῦ αἰῶνος ἴδιον, εἰς ἑαυτὸν
ἀναστρέφοντος καὶ μηδαμοῦ περατου- μένου . . .	ἀναστρέφειν καὶ μηδαμοῦ περατοῦ- σθαι.
διὰ τοῦτο τὴν κεφαλὴν τοῦ χρόνου οἱ Πυθαγόρειοι	διὰ τοῦτο τὴν κεφαλὴν τοῦ χρόνου
οὐχὶ πρώτην ἀλλὰ μίαν ὠνόμασαν.	οὐχὶ πρώτην ἡμέραν, ἀλλὰ μίαν ὠνόμασεν, ἵνα καὶ ἐκ τῆς προσηγορίας τὸ συγγενὲς ἔχῃ πρὸς τὸν αἰῶνα.

Probably εἱμαρμένη is finally identified with the second god Aion, as
Aion is identified with the wheeling Sky.[6]   We are not to suppose a rigid

---

[1] Cf. Basil, Hexaemeros, ii. 9 A Migne: εἰς ἑαυτὰ συννεύει τὰ κύκλῳ κινούμενα.
See also Cumont, Relig. orientales, pp. 120, 162.

[2] Cf. 118. 23, and 346. 6-9.

[3] Cf. 350. 16.

[4] op cit., 9 A.   ἐπειδὴ οὔτε ὅθεν ἤρξατο ἐξευρεῖν δυνάμεθα, οὔτε εἰς ὃ κατέληξεν,
ἤδη καὶ ἄναρχον αὐτὸν ὀφείλομεν ὑποτίθεσθαι.

[5] Parallel given by Gronau, Poseidonios, p. 40; for discussion of sources
see p. 37.   See also Macrobius, in Somn. Scip. 1. 6. 8.

[6] 'La notion d'éternité était correlative de celle de l'εἱμαρμένη' (Cumont, Rel.
orientales, p. 268).   See in general Zepf, Archiv, Jan. 1928.

consistency of language, and should accept 364. 9-10: ἀλλὰ πείθονται τῇ τοῦ
αἰωνίου λόγου ἀνάγκῃ, ὅς ἐστιν ὁ Αἰών, ἄτρεπτος καὶ ἀκίνητος καὶ ἀδιάλυτος ὤν.
The identification in 364. 14 follows from the alternatives offered in 362.
13-15. The texts are dubious ; but it is permissible to suppose that two
of the alternatives are *either* ὁ ὕψιστος θεός *or* ὁ μετ' ἐκεῖνον τεταγμένος
δεύτερος θεός.[1]

In conclusion note a parallel to the argument considered above.
Critolaus argued for the eternity of the Cosmos ; it proceeds from
εἱμαρμένη.[2] ἐπεὶ δὲ εἱμαρμένη . . . ἄναρχος καὶ ἀτελεύτητός ἐστι, εἴρουσα τὰς
ἑκάστων ἀνελλιπῶς καὶ ἀδιαστάτως αἰτίας, τί δήποτ' οὐχὶ καὶ τὴν τοῦ κόσμου
φύσιν λεκτέον εἶναι μακραίωνα, τὴν τάξιν τῶν ἀτάκτων, τὴν ἁρμονίαν τῶν ἀναρ-
μόστων . . . ; εἰ δ' ἡ τοῦ κόσμου φύσις, δῆλον ὅτι καὶ ὁ κόσμος.

364. 25-370. 18 (cc. 27 e-29 b). This tract half conceals a traditional
discussion on two kinds of death. Death is not defined as the separation
of body and soul, but as a natural process of the body, depending upon the
fulfilment of its ' number '. The sense is clear from Macrobius, *in Somn.
Scip*. 1. 13. 11-13 : ' Addit etiam (Plotinus) illam solam esse naturalem
mortem ubi corpus animam, non anima corpus relinquit. constat
enim numerorum certam constitutamque rationem animas sociare
corporibus. hi numeri dum supersunt, perseuerat corpus animari : cum
uero deficiunt, mox arcana illa uis soluitur, qua societas ipsa constabat, et
hoc est quod fatum et fatalia uitae tempora uocamus. anima ergo ipsa
non deficit quippe quae inmortalis atque perpetua est, sed impletis numeris
corpus fatiscit : nec anima lassatur animando, sed officium suum deserit
corpus cum iam non possit animari. hinc illud est doctissimi uatis

> explebo numerum reddarque tenebris. [*Aen*. vi. 545.]

haec est igitur naturalis uere mors, cum finem corporis solus numerorum
suorum defectus adportat, non cum extorquetur uita corpori adhuc idoneo
ad continuationem ferendi.' It is a question of ἁρμονία in the body, of the
fated length of years before the natural dissolution.[3] Natural life depends
upon a *corporalis ratio*. It can, however, be terminated prematurely by
force. ' Nec leuis est differentia uitam uel natura uel sponte soluendi.
anima enim cum a corpore deseritur, potest in se nihil retinere corporeum,
si se pure, cum in hac uita esset, instituit : cum uero ipsa de corpore uiolen-
ter extruditur, quia exit rupto uinculo, non soluto, fit ei ipsa necessitas occa-
sio passionis, et malis, uinculum dum rumpit, inficitur. . . . animas uero ex hac
uita cum delictorum sordibus recedentes aequandas his qui in abruptum

---

[1] In 362. 11 ἡ ἀναγκάζουσα πάντα τὰ γιγνόμενα ἀεὶ πρὸς ἄλληλα εἰρομέναις συμ-
πλοκαῖς δεδεμένα. A Stoic play on εἱμαρμένη—see, e.g., Immisch, *Agatharchidea*,
pp. 77-9. Lydus, 4. 7 (see 362 *T.*), may contain a reminiscence of this passage :
Εἱμαρμένη οἱον εἰρομένη . . . ἵνα ὁ εἱρμὸς τῶν ὑποκειμένων σώζηται.

[2] Philo, *de aet. mundi*, 75 (Cohn, vi. 96. 8).

[3] 366. 2. Retain *quo*. It is useless to labour in reconciling our text with that
of Stobaeus ; but perhaps ἁρμῶν answers to *membra—μερῶν*. Take ἁρμογή in the
sense of ἁρμονία.

ex alto praecipitique delapsi sint, unde numquam facultas fit resurgendi. ... pari autem constantia mors nec ueniens per naturam timenda est, nec contra ordinem cogenda naturae' (*ibid.* 14–19). The contrast is between those who live to the term of their life and the βιαιοθάνατοι.[1] We shall find this distinction at the end of c. 28, with some slight suggestion that the Hermetist's source might be 'magian'. To proceed with c. 28. The *summus daemon* sounds like a borrowing from Iranian sources.[2] In Porphyry (περὶ τῆς ἐκ λογίων φιλοσοφίας, ii, p. 147 Wolff)[3] Sarapis is said to be the head of the bad daemons, and is identified with Pluto.[4] With *pia iustaque anima* (l. 12) we strike a highway. It answers to the admonition

discite iustitiam moniti et non temnere divos (*Aen.* vi. 620).[5]

Further, the description of the soul stained in vices has a close parallel in Virgilian language:

non tamen omne malum miseris, nec funditus omnes
corporeae excedunt pestes, penitusque necesse est
multa diu concreta, modis inolescere miris.
ergo exercentur poenis, veterumque malorum
supplicia expendunt: aliae panduntur inanes
suspensae ad ventos, aliis sub gurgite vasto
infectum eluitur scelus, aut exuritur igni.[6]

In answer to Asclepius' naive question in the catechetical manner (l. 23), which sums up the previous teaching, it is said simply that all *die*: πρῶτον μὲν οὖν τὰ ἐπὶ γῆς πάντα ἐστὶ θνητά. It is true, on the theory involved, that souls carry their passions with them.[7] But *ea* (368. 1, 2) should refer to the beings that die, not to their passions. Does the sentence (ll. 1–2) specify the class who fulfil *numerorum certam constitutamque rationem* of Macrobius?—εἶτα καὶ τὰ κατά τε τὸν σωματικὸν λόγον ζῶντα καὶ τοῦ ζῆν ὡσαύτως ἀναπαύοντα. *All* are subject to penalty, the more if they escape *human* retribution[8]—the divine eye they cannot escape.

---

[1] θάνατος *naturalis et fatalis*)(*extrinsecus ui coactus*; Aulus Gellius, xiii. 1. See in general Norden, *Vergilius, Aeneis* vi, p. 11.

[2] See on 118. 12, 126. 22, 200 28, and especially on 340. 4.

[3] Euseb. *Pr. ev.*, 4. 22. 16.

[4] Cf. Plut. *de Is. et Os.* 361 F.

[5] See Norden's note *ad loc.*, also 200. 9.

[6] *Aen.*, vi. 736. This refers to purgation. The *Asclepius*, as we have it, distinguishes only the good and the bad here. The evidence of Lydus is dubious —καὶ ὁ μὲν Ἑρμῆς περὶ μόνου τοῦ καθαρμοῦ τῶν ψυχῶν (*de mens.*, 4. 148). As we shall see, there are other indications of shortening. In l. 18 *sententia* (codd.) = καταδίκη.

[7] 'hinc metuunt cupiuntque dolent gaudentque'—the four passions (*Aen.*, vi. 733).

[8] l. 4 ὅσῳ ἐν τῷ βίῳ ἔτυχε λαθόντα, ἕως ἔζη—pleonasm. I suppose a mistranslation.

castigatque auditque dolos, subigitque fateri
quae quis apud superos, furto laetatus inani,
distulit in seram commissa piacula mortem.[1]

Then an abrupt return from *mors naturalis* to *mors vi coacta*. If we accept the text, the heaviest penalties are reserved for men cut off for crime, who render up no *anima debita naturae*. There is evidence that Posidonius (?) enumerated sub-classes of the βιαιοθάνατοι, and traces of that classification can be found in Virgil.[2] These were placed in limbo till their allotted span was past.[3] We cannot be certain that the abruptness does not signify some cut or lacuna in the text, and there is a point in the contrast of criminals and the just man (l. 10). Perhaps the true parallel also comes from Virgil—

quique ob adulterium caesi ; quique arma secuti
impia, nec veriti dominorum fallere dextras,
inclusi poenam exspectant : ne quaere doceri
quam poenam, aut quae forma viros fortunave mersit.[4]

However that may be, the just man of 368. 10 is the *pia iustaque anima* of 366. 12, who has passed the judgement. The anthologists have cut off the connecting words. He is secure from fate and the daemons through piety (370. 4).[5] What is the reason ? *Deus pater* [6] (l. 5) illuminates the *minds* of the pious. He is not revealed through the categories, but by the direct apprehension of νοῦς ;[7] for like apprehends like. l. 13 ἕκαστος γὰρ (sc. ἀγαθὸς) τῇ εὐσεβείᾳ ... αὐγάζει, ὥσπερ αὐτοῖς τοῖς ὄμμασι [8] τὸν ἀληθῆ λόγον καθορῶν,[9] καὶ τῇ τῆς ἐλπίδος πίστει [10] κ.τ.λ. The last sentence draws the terms

---

[1] *Aen.* vi. 567.

[2] *Aen.*, vi. 430. See in general Norden's edition, p. 11.

[3] Tertullian, *de anima*, 56 : perinde extorres inferum habebuntur quas ui ereptas arbitrantur, praecipue per atrocitates suppliciorum, crucis dico et securis et gladii et ferae ; nec isti porro exitus uiolenti quos iustitia decernit, uiolentiae uindex, et ideo, inquies, scelestae quaeque animae inferis exulant. It is at least interesting to note that Tertullian immediately (c. 57) refers to the literature under the names of Ostanes, Typhon. and others (who are associated with Hermes) ; these *magi* call up the *aori* and *biaeothanatoi* from their limbo. See on 340. 4, iv. 5. 14.

[4] *Aen.*, vi. 612.

[5] *summa pietate*—ἀκροτάτῃ εὐσεβείᾳ ; cf. 390. 8. C. 33 b belongs to another context ; see on 328. 16 ; and vol. iv, Introduction, II, p. xvii.

[6] For the formula in l. 6 see on 350. 7.

[7] l 10 : perhaps ὅλῳ τῷ νοῒ ἑαυτὸν πρὸς τὸν θεῖον νοῦν συμμίγνυται.

[8] *oculis* ed. Rom. The eye of the soul : cf. 156. 13, 172. 6, 188. 21 and Ar., *de mundo* 391 a 15.

[9] Comma after *perspecta*, answering to *percepta* in l. 10.

[10] *Fiducia* = πίστις ; cf. Bousset, *Kyrios*, p. 177 ; and see on 184. 25-7. The phrase should be interpreted in the light of ll. 11-12. Compare Firmicus Maternus, *de errore*, 24, *f. bonae spei*, and Tertullian's *f. spei nostrae*.

of the analogy closer; the Sun,[1] like the pious, is holy—hence his power.

The tract περὶ τοῦ ἀθανάτου ἢ περὶ τοῦ θνητοῦ[2] (364. 25) ends here. But it is possible that the section on Aion is intended to continue the theme. For that ends with an account of the 'way' to knowledge of the supreme God, returning to the theme and language of c. 29 b. See note on 348. 8 and vol. iv, Introduction, p. xxvi.

375, 377. *Papyrus Apparatus* (readings from Preisendanz)[3] :—[3] κατὰ καρδίαν *Preis.* (ι in Pap. uncertain). [6] ὅσ⟨ι⟩ό⟨νητι, ῇ⟩ πρ[ὸ]ς *Preis.* [7] πρὸς πάντα *Preis.* [19] τῇ σεαυτοῦ γνώσει *Preis.*

STOBAEI HERMETICA

Excerpt. I. **380. 14.** ἐννοοῦμαι. Sudden vision of God; hence the repetition. Cf. 246. 12, 156. 11–16.

Excerpt. II A. **382. 8.** This may be a trace of the cult of the four elements. Cf. Philo, *de decal.* 53 (iv. 281. 1 Cohn), and Bréhier, *Philon*, p. 163. Compare note on 486. 22, 490. 16; also note on 304. 16–306. 28. Dieterich, *Abraxas*, p. 57, ὕδωρ ὕδατος τοῦ ἐν ἐμοὶ ὕδατος πρῶτον (*Pap. Par.* 713).

384. 11. καὶ οὐκ ἀσκόπως—gloss?

14. θεοπτία. Cyril, *c. Iul.* 533 A, 628 B, 852 D (Migne).

Excerpt. II B. **390. 1–5.** An anthologist's preface; see vol. iii. 321.

7. The thesis is that the deepest[4] piety implies 'philosophy', and this involves the ability to answer certain questions (ll. 9–11)[5]—the formulae are catechetical—and thus to give thanks to the provider of good things. In knowing God's works, man marvels and reverences the Maker, and that is piety. Norden has argued that this is connected with the language of the mysteries.[6] The Hermetist's formula is ἡ μετὰ γνώσεως εὐσέβεια.[7] The apparent Stoic parallel is Cic. *de nat. deor.* ii. 153: 'cognitio deorum, e qua oritur pietas, cui coniuncta iustitia est reliquaeque

---

[1] For the Sun see Pliny, *N. H.*, 2. 5. 12, Firmicus, *Math.* v, *praef.* 5, and note on 266. 7. Metaphor in Sen., *Ep.* 41. 5.

[2] The reading *aut* suggests that the redactor perhaps embodied the title of a tract in a connecting sentence.

[3] Vol. iii. 284 *Pap. Mimaut.* Read εὐάκοιαν for εὐωχίαν (with Fahz in Preisendanz). See also *Errata*.

[4] Cf. 370. 4.

[5] Cf. 124. 9–10; 150. 10, 26 (note); 152. 3; 178. 2 (note); 310. 7 *sqq.*; and in general *Corp.* V.

[6] *Agn. Th.* pp. 102 *sqq.* Cf. (with N.) Marc. Aurelius 8. 52, *Somn. Scip.* 17, and the *felix* formula in Virgil: 'felix qui potuit rerum cognoscere causas' (*Georg.* ii. 490). See 256. 26; 418. 14.

[7] 170. 6.

virtutes, e quibus vita beata exsistit par et similis deorum.' But the centre of gravity in Hermetic piety is widely different. From knowledge springs piety, according to the Stoics—*deum colit qui novit.* It is by piety towards God that the Hermetist hopes to attain to γνῶσις. For nothing here is real, and deep piety is the way to knowledge.[1] Such pious men are few, because only selected men have νοῦς.[2]

392. 5, 7. φυγόντος and φυγεῖν should be retained. The reference is to the flight of the soul from the body. Compare Porphyry, *de regressu animae* in Augustine, *de civ. dei,* x. 29: 'Porphyrium ... tam crebro praecipere, omne corpus esse fugiendum, ut anima possit beata permanere cum Deo.' (For other references of A. to Porphyry's doctrine see Bidez, *Vie de Porphyre,* p. 38*.) Proclus, *In Tim.* iii. 296. 10 Diehl: ἡ πρὸς τὸ νοερὸν εἶδος τῆς ψυχῆς ἀναδρομὴ καὶ ἡ φυγὴ πάντων τῶν ἐκ τῆς γενέσεως ἡμῖν προσπεφυκότων· ... ἔστι γὰρ καὶ ἐν αὐτῇ τῶν κύκλων ἑκάτερος καὶ αἱ διτταὶ δυνάμεις καὶ τῶν ἵππων ὅ τε ἀγαθὸς καὶ ἐναντίος, καὶ ὁ μὲν εἰς γένεσιν ἄγει τὴν ψυχήν, ὁ δὲ ἀπὸ γενέσεως ἐπὶ τὸ ὄν, καὶ ὁ μὲν γενεσιουργὸν περιάγει κύκλον, ὁ δὲ τὸν νοερόν. Proclus refers to the myth of the *Phaedrus,* which allegorizes the doctrine of the tripartite soul found in the Hermetic text. For Plato cf. *Theaet.* 176 A: διὸ καὶ πειρᾶσθαι χρὴ ἐνθένδε ἐκεῖσε φεύγειν ὅτι τάχιστα. φυγὴ δὲ ὁμοίωσις θεῷ κατὰ τὸ δυνατόν. Διάστασις)(σύστασις is defensible. l. 9 κατοικεῖ: καθέλκει Kroll.

Excerpt. III. **392.** 19-402. 16. The argument of this Excerpt is Stoic in character, and should be interpreted in connexion with the Posidonian theory of instinct (*Exc.* iv b), which precedes it in Stobaeus. We need not look for logical rigour or terminological consistency in the writer. But, leaving this aside, the argument is as follows, if we accept the traditional order.

The first stage is summed up in 396. 10-15. The Cosmos is always producing; and cosmic forces, using bodies as their instruments, are immortal.[3] This is the theme announced in 392. 19: forces, as incorporeal, are immortal, and they are correlated with the bodies they work upon. The powers that exercise these influences are Pronoia[4] and Ananke; and the processes (γινόμενα) dependent on them can never cease their appropriate activity—τὸ γὰρ ⟨γινόμεν⟩ον[5] ἀεὶ ἔσται (394. 2). This granted, bodies (as the instruments in which process recurs) must be immortal too—body-making implies this.[6] The mention of forces accompanying the soul shows that the doctrine is Stoic.[7] The presupposition is an unfolding of powers: αἰσθητικῶς δὲ (*sc.* κινεῖσθαι) ὅταν προκύψῃ καὶ

---

[1] Bousset, *Theol. Literaturzeitung,* 1913; Bräuninger, *H.T.* p. 13.

[2] 150. 16; 200. 5; 334. 17; 336. 27.

[3] 396. 14 ἀθάνατος; possibly ἀεί is an enthusiastic colloquialism.

[4] An astrological power, 'spread out in the heavens'; cf. 436. 9; 418. 28.

[5] Hence the future tense? Cf. 396. 9.

[6] 394. 5. εἱ[ς].

[7] For the astrological aspect see on 438. 17.

πάλιν λογικῶς ὅταν προέλθῃ κατὰ τὴν ἡλικίαν καὶ ὕστερον νοητικῶς, καὶ οὐδενὸς ἔξωθεν ψυχικοῦ ἐπεισκριθέντος, ἀλλὰ καθάπερ ἐν τῇ τῶν καρπῶν βλαστήσει πάντα ὁμοῦ συγκέχυται.[1] With the word συνεργοῦσαι (l. 13) we meet the doctrine of the helpmeet sensation: μετὰ γὰρ νοῦν εὐθὺς ἔδει δημιουργηθῆναι αἴσθησιν, βοηθὸν αὐτῷ καὶ σύμμαχον.[2] In § 6 the connexion of these forces with the soul embodied is stated[3]; it is bound up with the theory of *pneuma*.

There follows (§ 7) a classification based upon Stoic conceptions; and it must be remarked that this classification holds for the remainder of the excerpt, which is specially concerned with ἔμψυχα. Of the three types of ἡνωμένα, the highest is that unified by soul; but a body may *be*[4] without a soul and without a *principatus*.[5] In decay an organized body becomes formless[6] under a new set of forces. (This leads to the distinction between pure bodies and the σύγκριμα which breaks up[7].) In 396. 3 there appear the ἕξις κοινὴ καὶ τῶν ἀψύχων ... λίθων καὶ ξύλων, ἧς μετέχει καὶ τὰ ἐν ἡμῖν ἐοικότα λίθοις ὀστέα, ἡ δὲ φύσις διατείνει καὶ ἐπὶ τὰ φυτά ... ἔστι δὲ ἡ φύσις ἕξις ἤδη κινουμένη.[8] The conclusion is that force is (colloquially) just whatever happens in any and every body.

The remainder of this excerpt will be clearer if it is borne in mind that the writer's interest is in showing that sensation is corporeal. He is thinking of living bodies and souls. In a word: sensation has its οὐσία from the body (398. 35, 402. 9). Further, sensation and the πάθη are intimately connected.

§ 13. Granted that forces must work in bodies (as has been shown), and that bodies are numerous (*varied* would have more point), then there are numerous forces—nay, even in one body several unite, not counting the accompanying[9] universal forces. The σύστασις of a living body is in question—its φύσις or ψυχή,[10] and that φύσις is itself an example of a universal force.[11] Further, on the Stoic view in question, sensation and

---

[1] Porphyry (Ps.-Galen) Πρὸς Γαῦρον, 60. 5 Kalbfleisch (restored from Hermippus, *de astrologia*, p. 64. 4). See also (with A. D. N.) Iamblichus *ap.* Stob. I. 48. 8 (I. 317. 21 Wachsm). Read τὸ ἄλογον (Wachsm.) in 394. 11 and ἡλικίας in l. 12.

[2] Philo, *Leg. Alleg.* ii. 8. 24 (and 2.6, quoted below). Mind is 'naked' without sensation. We are here in the tracks of a school tradition. See especially Bousset, *Schulbetrieb*, i. 3.

[3] l. 16 [αἱ] Usener. l. 17 ⟨οὐ⟩ συγγίγνονται?

[4] Retain εἶναι δύναται l. 24. ἡνωμένα σώματα are unified either by ψιλὴ ἕξις (stones) or φύσις (plants) or ψυχή (Sext. Emp. *adv. math.* i. 78 sqq.). The ascending series is εἶναι, κινεῖσθαι, ζῆν. See on 450. 2 sqq.

[5] *De nat. deor.* ii. 29.   [6] ἀειδές.   [7] Cf. 382. 5, 9–13.

[8] Philo, *Leg. Alleg.* ii. 7. 22. The whole passage should be read.

[9] The reading is παρεπομένων. In l. 25 ὄντως σωματικάς may be right, with a controversial intention. Cf. 400. 3.

[10] Cf. 394. 23.   [11] 406. 1.

motion are given to animals, for self-preservation.[1] Hence the remark that a (living) body cannot maintain its σύστασις without sensation and motion (398. 26).[2] The individual activities have to be learned [3]—see on 406. 2. The relation of sensations to forces is then used (398. 31) to show the corporeality of the former. We may best explain ἀποτέλεσμα by recalling the distinction between αἴσθησις καθ' ἕξιν and κατ' ἐνέργειαν: ἀποτελεῖται δὲ ἡ κατ' ἐνέργειαν ὅταν ἡ καθ' ἕξιν κινηθεῖσα ταθῇ μέχρι τῆς σαρκὸς καὶ τῶν αἰσθητικῶν ἀγγείων.[4] ... ὁ δὲ (θεὸς) θεασάμενος ἣν πρότερον εἶχε δύναμιν, καὶ καθ' ἕξιν ἠρεμοῦσαν, νῦν ἀποτέλεσμα καὶ ἐνέργειαν γεγενημένην καὶ κινουμένην κτλ.[5] But if sensation is a somatic disturbance from without, the stars are of a nobler [6] substance than to require it. The point is that, being perfect, they have no needs [7]; and sensation, like the πάθη, answers a need.[8] Of the classification of grades of sensations [9] in ll. 17–24 it need only be said that the differentiae are rough and ready, and that the passive sensations of the ἄψυχα should be taken as referring to the αὐξητική or φυτικὴ δύναμις [10] of living bodies; it is primarily life that concerns the writer. The nature and source of the doctrine is clear from ll. 24–26. We have already met the theory of the 'helper', sensation: ἡ γὰρ αἴσθησις καὶ τὰ πάθη τῆς ψυχῆς εἰσι βοηθοὶ νεώτεροι τῆς ψυχῆς ... (8) μιᾶς γὰρ ἐστι ψυχῆς μέρη καὶ γεννήματα ἥ τε αἴσθησις καὶ τὰ πάθη.[11] Pleasure and pain alone cf the classical four are named. The point is perhaps that the πάθη have 'utility' value, and complete the work of sensation; thus pleasure

---

[1] 'Bestiis autem sensum et motum dedit et cum quodam adpetitu accessum ad res salutares a pestiferis recessum ' (Cic. *de nat. deor.* ii. 34; cf. ii. 122). *Adpetitus* or *conatus* is not mentioned here ; nor is it in Philo.

[2] οἱ τέλειοι τὰς μὲν ἀρχὰς ἔχουσιν ἀπὸ σώματος καὶ αἰσθήσεως καὶ τῶν ὑργανικῶν μερῶν, ὧν ἄνευ ζῆν οὐκ ἔνεστι (Philo, *quis rer. div. heres,* 315).

[3] οὔτε γὰρ ἡ ὅρασις ... οὔτε τις τῶν ἄλλων αἰσθήσεων διδακτή ... ὁ δὲ νοῦς ὁ διδασκόμενός ἐστιν (Philo, *Leg. Alleg.* iii. 50. 147). In l. 27 possibly δ' ἔ(π)εισιν.

[4] *Leg. Alleg.* ii. 10. 37.

[5] *Ibid.* 40. The cooperation of *nous* is in question here; see 394. 13. Needless to say, Philo does not use the word ἐνέργεια in the Hermetist's sense.

[6] 400. 8. Retain the text. Possibly σωματική in l. 9 might be saved by reading αἴσθησις, σωματικὴ οὖσα, οὐδ' in l. 8. The writer does use σῶμα in a loose way throughout.

[7] Cf. 408. 5 μηδεν(ὸς) ἐνδέοντα, ὡς ἀίδια.

[8] See Cicero quoted above. We must retain κακοῦ ... ἀγαθοῦ in l. 10.

[9] 423. 6 πᾶν τὸ πάσχον αἰσθεται. The origin is in *Timaeus* 77 B 3: μετέχει γε μὴν τοῦτο ὃ νῦν λέγομεν τοῦ τρίτου ψυχῆς εἴδους, ὃ μεταξὺ φρενῶν ὀμφαλοῦ τε ἱδρῦσθαι λόγος, ᾧ δόξης μὲν λογισμοῦ τε καὶ νοῦ μέτεστιν τὸ μηδέν, αἰσθήσεως δὲ ἡδείας καὶ ἀλγεινῆς μετὰ ἐπιθυμῶν. πάσχον γὰρ διατελεῖ πάντα κτλ. I append Porphyry's comment : μόνον φύσεως παθητικῆς μετέχει (Πρὸς Γαῦρον 39. 23 (Kalbfl.).

[10] 'Nasci, nutriri, crescere commune est hominibus cum ceteris' (Chalcidius, *in Tim.* 182).

[11] *Leg. Alleg.* ii. 2. 5–3. 8. Cf. *ibid.* 2. 6 τὸ δὲ ἄλογον αἴσθησίς ἐστι καὶ τὰ ταύτης ἔκγονα πάθη, καὶ μάλιστα εἰ μὴ κρίσεις εἰσιν ἡμέτεραι, καὶ νεώτερος οὖν οὗτος ὁ βοηθός κ.τ.λ.

contributes to preserving the kind and pain stings the soul into watchfulness.[1] The Hermetist possibly meant that man has the widest range of pleasures,[2] even as man[3] is the creature whom pleasure and pain mislead. It must be remembered that a πάθος is the proper helper to the mind, as brother and kin. This gives the transition from a physical argument to an ethical; for the passions lead men astray (402. 1).

The last paragraph has perhaps suffered textually from the repetition of σῶμα and its derivatives. The purpose is plain: to sum up the whole contention that sensation is corporeal. Read δ' ἄν (Heeren) in l. 6. Then (accepting Scott's attribution of πῶς . . . σῶμα to Trismegistus) should we read (l. 8) σῶμα;—⟨ˇΑρα σῶμα⟩ ἄν εἴη . . . ἡ αἴσθησις εἰ[4] ἐν σώματι οὖσα τυγχάνει;—Ἐὰν ⟨ἀσώματον⟩ ἐν σώματι αὐτὴν θῶμεν κτλ. That is: must sensation be a body if it is in body? Well, if we make it an incorporeal in a body, we shall make it similar to the soul or to the forces; these are the incorporeals we lay down as being in the body. But sensation is neither, and there is no third incorporeal. But it must be either corporeal or incorporeal—therefore corporeal. A triumphant *petitio*.

Excerpt. IV B. **406. 2.** This passage on instinct is Posidonian. It is best understood in connexion with the previous excerpts on ἐνέργειαι; compare especially 404. 7: ἰδέαι δὲ ψυχῶν θεία, ἀνθρωπίνη, ἄλογος. It was a main purpose of Posidonius to show the σύνδεσμος existing between all grades of beings in the universe. This comes out clearly in the following passage from Nemesius of Emesa (*de nat. hominis*, 585–8 Migne), where it is linked with the distinction between the general character of φύσις and the freedom of human action. φύσις is, he says, τέχνης εἰκών, σκιὰ λογική. This πανουργία has two reasons: safety, and the binding together (συνάψαι) of all creation. It is distinct from rational action ἐκ τοῦ κατ' εἶδος ἕκαστον ζῷον ὁμοίως τὰ αὐτὰ ποιεῖν. Men have freedom; τὰ δὲ φύσει ὁμοίως παρὰ πᾶσίν ἐστιν. Cf. τὰ φύσει γιγνόμενα ἐνεργείᾳ μὲν γίγνεται καθολικῇ (406. 16); εἰ δὲ πάντες ὁμοίως ἄγονται ὑπὸ τῆς φύσεως (l. 26). The immediate source of Nemesius was Iamblichus, who disputed the question with the vegetarian Porphyry whether animals had λόγος or not. For the series of related passages and the evidence that Posidonius was the ultimate source see Jaeger, *Nemesios von Emesa*, pp. 117 sqq. l. 19 ἄνω: unlike the animals κάτω κεκυφότα.

Excerpt. V. **408. 21.** ἐκ τῶν ὁμοίων στοιχείων. Retain ὁμοίων. This is the Empedoclean principle, *similia similibus nutriri*. Cf. Simplicius, *in physica* 460. 4 sqq.: πᾶν ὑπὸ ὁμοίου τρέφεσθαι. Plut. *Quaest. Conv.* 663 A: εἴτε γὰρ ἐξ ὁμοίων ἀναλαμβάνει τὸ οἰκεῖον ἡ φύσις, καὶ εἰς τὸν ὄγκον αὐτόθεν ἡ

---

[1] *Leg. Alleg.* ii. 8. Cf. *ibid.* 71 δυεῖν προγεγονότων, νοῦ καὶ αἰσθήσεως, καὶ τούτων γυμνῶν . . . ὑπαρχόντων, ἀνάγκη τρίτην ἡδονὴν συναγωγὸν ἀμφοῖν ὑπάρξαι πρὸς τὴν τῶν νοητῶν καὶ αἰσθητῶν ἀντίληψιν. . . . τίς αὐτὰ συνήγαγεν ὅτι μὴ δεσμὸς τρίτος ἔρωτος, καὶ ἐπιθυμίας; κτλ.

[2] *Ibid.* 74.

[3] Retain l. 29, ἰδέας (l. 30), and λογικῶν (l. 31).   [4] Canter.

ποικίλη τροφὴ πολλὰς μεθιεῖσα ποιότητας ἐξ ἑαυτῆς ἑκάστῳ μέρει τὸ πρόσφορον ἀναδίδωσιν, ὥστε γίνεσθαι τὸ τοῦ Ἐμπεδοκλέους

    Ὡς γλυκὺ μὲν ⟨ἐπὶ⟩ γλυκὺ μάρπτε . . .

. . . δὲ καὶ ἄλλου ἐπὶ πρόσφορον μένοντος τῇ θερμότητι ἐν τῷ πνεύματι τοῦ μίγματος σκεδασθέντος, τὰ οἰκεῖα τοῖς συγγενέσιν ἔπεται κτλ. Macrobius, *Sat.* vii. 5. 16 *sqq.*: '. . . cum corpora ipsa de contrariis qualitatibus fabricata sint. ex calido enim et frigido, de sicco et humido constamus. . . . scimus autem similibus similia nutriri. . . . 21. sic et elementa, quae sunt nostra principia, ex diuersitatibus et ipsa constant et nos nutriunt. est enim ignis calidus et siccus, aer . . . .'

    30. τὸν ὕπνον. Cf. Aristotle, π. ὕπνου, 454 b 8: ἀδύνατον γὰρ ἀεὶ ἐνεργεῖν; 455 b 18: τὴν ἀνάπαυσιν παντὶ τῷ πεφυκότι κινεῖσθαι, μὴ δυναμένῳ δ' ἀεὶ καὶ συνεχῶς κινεῖσθαι μεθ' ἡδονῆς. . . .

    410. 1. καὶ ἐπ' ἰσότητος. For the expression see Pl. *Theaet.* 158 d: καὶ δὴ ἴσου ὄντος τοῦ χρόνου ὃν καθεύδομεν ᾧ ἐγρηγόραμεν. With ἀνάπαυλα (rest) cf. 408. 27. The underlying theory is that tension and relaxation alternate: ὕπνος τὸ σύντονον τῆς ἐγρηγόρσεως ὑπεχάλωσεν, εἶτα ἐγρήγορσις τὸ ἀνειμένον ἐτόνωσε . . . οὕτω τοίνυν τετονωμένον διὰ τῆς ἐγρηγόρσεως τὸ σῶμα λαβοῦσα, λῦσιν ἐπινοεῖ διὰ τοῦ ὕπνου τῷ τόνῳ, τὰς αἰσθητικὰς δυνάμεις πρὸς καιρὸν ἐκ τῶν ἐνεργειῶν ἀναπαύσασα (Greg. of Nyssa, *de hom. opif.*, v. 44, 165 B Migne). The εὔκαιρος ἄνεσις (*ib.* § 3) is required for nourishment, no tension impeding its passage. The vapours from the food in digestion ascend to the head and penetrate the passages of the sense-organs, so that sensation is necessarily dulled.

    Excerpt. VI. **412.** 22. τὰς . . . ⟨σφαίρας⟩ καὶ πάντα τὸν κύκλον ⟨τὸν ζῳδιακὸν αὐτοῖς ὑποτετάχθαι⟩. Cf. ll. 5–7. First the writer names all *below* the Decans,[1] and then corrects himself. In ll. 25–7 there was perhaps a trio of participles: πάντα συνέχοντας καὶ τὰ πάντα ⟨ἐπισκοποῦντας⟩ κτλ. Cf. 414. 1.

    414. 6. καθολικῶς. Astrological term.

    9. ἄμπωτις. For this meaning see Basil, *Hexaemeros*, 144 B–C (Migne). The moon causes great and sudden storms, ὡς μαρτυροῦσιν . . . ἡ περὶ τὸν λεγόμενον ὠκεανὸν ἄμπωτις, ἣν ταῖς περιόδοις τῆς σελήνης τεταγμένως ἑπομένην ἐξεῦρον οἱ προσοικοῦντες. See on 416. 34.

    416. 34 *sqq.* Origen, *c. Celsum*, i. 59: ἐπὶ μεγάλοις τετήρηται πράγμασι καὶ μεγίσταις μεταβολαῖς τῶν ἐπὶ γῆς ἀνατέλλειν τοὺς τοιούτους ἀστέρας, σημαίνοντας ἢ μεταστάσεις βασιλειῶν ἢ πολέμους ἢ ὅσα δύναται ἐν ἀνθρώποις συμβῆναι, σεῖσαι τὰ ἐπὶ γῆς δυνάμενα. ἀνέγνωμεν δ' ἐν τῷ περὶ κομητῶν Χαιρήμονος τοῦ Στωικοῦ συγγράμματι, τίνα τρόπον ἔσθ' ὅτε καὶ ἐπὶ χρηστοῖς ἐσομένοις κομῆται ἀνέτειλαν, καὶ ἐκτίθεται τὴν περὶ τούτων ἱστορίαν. Compare with this **414.** 8 *sqq.*

    418. 14. Μακάριος. The *felix* formula; see on 390. 1.

---

[1] Cosmas Hierosolymitanus, *ad carm. Greg. Nanz.* 38. p. 462 (Migne): ἐκ δὲ τούτων (τῶν δεκανῶν) τὴν ἄπειρον κίνησιν τοῦ ζῳοφόρου κύκλου καὶ τῶν πλανήτων.

23. τοῦ θεοῦ τοῦ ὀνόματος A. D. N.   See 162. 26.

Excerpt. VII.   25. Δαίμων.   Proclus, *in Crat.*, c. 181 (p. 107 Pasquali) : οἶον ὅτι ἕπεται τῷ Διὶ Δίκη τοῦ θείου νόμου τιμωρός, καὶ τοῖς μὲν κεκοσμημένοις καὶ κατὰ νοῦν ζῶσιν εὐμαρής ἐστιν ἡ θεὸς αὕτη, τοῖς δ' ὑβρισταῖς καὶ ἀμαθίᾳ συμφέρουσι τὴν ζημίαν ἐπιβάλλει, ἕως ἂν αὐτοὺς καὶ οἴκους καὶ πόλεις ἄρδην ἀφανίσῃ.   See in general Kern, *Orphicorum Fragmenta*, *Fr.* 158–60, 181 (where Δίκη is set over the πλανώμενα).   As Δίκη follows Zeus, there seems to be no reason why εἰλουμένη should not be retained.

περιορῶσα.   Δίκης ὀφθαλμός, ὃς τὰ πάνθ' ὁρᾷ (Plut. *Adv. Col.* 2. 1124 F) ; τὴν ἔφορον τῶν ἀνθρωπείων (Philo, *in Flaccum*, 18. 146, etc.) ; τὸν οὐράνιον τῆς Δ. ὀφθαλμόν (*id. de vita Mosis*, 1. 10. 55).

28. Pronoia and Ananke should probably be regarded as one power (or two aspects of one), identical with Heimarmene (420. 9) and with Zeus (according to the Stoics) or with Phusis (cf. 434. 7).   The sense of Pronoia here appears from 436. 9.   For Pronoia-Zeus see on 482. 4.   Note the Cosmopoiia in Dieterich, *Abraxas*, 183. 54 : ἐφάνη Μοῖρα κατέχουσα ζυγόν, μηνύουσι ἐν ἑαυτῇ τὸ δίκαιον εἶναι. ὁ δὲ Ἑρμῆς συνηρίσθη αὐτῇ λέγων· " ἐν ἐμοί ἐστι τὸ δίκαιον." τῶν δὲ μαχομένων ὁ θεὸς ἔφη αὐτοῖς· " ἐξ ἀμφοτέρων τὸ δίκαιον φανήσεται· πάντα δὲ ὑπό σε ἔσται τὰ ἐν κόσμῳ."

Excerpt. VIII.   422. 1.   The text is bad ; but it may be suspected that the writer himself is thoroughly confused.   A tentative interpretation is offered on this assumption.   To begin with the list of accidents in l. 3, which are *seven* in number.   It may be useful to recall that there was a traditional (Pythagorean ?) list of seven visibles.[1]   Now on the theory of sensation given by Galen[2] the proper object of sight is colour ; of taste, χυμοί.   But *with* the colour we apprehend (συνδιαγιγνώσκειν) the size and shape of the object ; again we apprehend its position and distance.[3]   Again ἦν δὲ αὐτῶν (προσβολῶν) πρώτη μὲν ἡ κατὰ ὀξύτητα καὶ ἀμβλύτητα, δευτέρα δὲ ἡ κατὰ θερμότητα καὶ ψυχρότητα, κατὰ συμβεβηκὸς δὲ αἱ λοιπαί, μέγεθός τε καὶ σχῆμα καὶ κίνησις καὶ ἀριθμός, αἳ καὶ μετὰ συλλογισμοῦ καὶ μνήμης, οὐ μόνης αἰσθήσεως ἐδείχθησαν γινόμεναι κατά τε τὴν ἁφὴν κτλ.[4]   The thesis is that sensation is not ἀλλοίωσις, but διάγνωσις ἀλλοιώσεως.[5]   So far, then, on this theory we see colour first, and then 'see' e. g. size κατὰ συμβεβηκός.   Next, (ὄψις) συνδιαγιγνώσκει αὐτῷ (sc. τῷ πρώτῳ αἰσθητῷ) τὸ κεχρωσμένον σῶμα,[6] or extends through the air ἐπὶ τὸ κεχρωσμένον. . . τῇ δὲ οὖν ὄψει πρὸς τοῖς ἄλλοις ὑπάρχει

---

[1] Philo, *de opif. mundi*, 120–1 (1. 42. 5 Wendl.) ἑπτὰ γάρ ἐστι τὰ ὁρώμενα, σῶμα, διάστασις, σχῆμα, μέγεθος, χρῶμα, κίνησις, στάσις.   The same list and order in Nicomachus, *Theol. Arith.* 42 Ast (Anatolius).   Lydus, *de mens.* 35. 2 Wünsch: καὶ τὸ πᾶν δὲ τοῦτο ἐν ἑπτὰ θεωρεῖται· ἐν σώματι. . . καὶ παρὰ ταῦτα οὐδὲν ἕτερον συμβέβηκε τοῖς ὁρωμένοις.   A word may have dropped from the second list ; it is needless to alter our text, because the writer is not to be suspected of accuracy. ἐπιφάνεια occurs in Lydus' next list of seven (ἀ)σώματοι.   See in general, Jaeger, *Nemesios*, p. 48.

[2] *De placitis*, 623, Müller.   [3] *Ibid.* 643. 1.

[4] *Ibid.* p. 633.   [5] *Ibid.* 635. 5.   [6] 623. 11.

καὶ θέσιν καὶ διάστημα συνδιαγιγνώσκειν τοῦ κεχρωσμένου σώματος κτλ.¹ If we allow for muddle, this would appear to be the distinction the Hermetist failed to express.² The technical term ἰδίως ποιά is apparently misused; it seems to refer to the συμβεβηκότα by themselves, as distinguished from a body seen in possession of them.

Excerpt. XI. **430**. 10. The 'two times' are significant for man, because the soul enters at birth; cf. note on 438. 17. The continuity of organic life is secured by the cycle of individuals who begin independent life with birth, whereas the eternal bodies continue changeless, returning in due order each to its place (176. 13).

Excerpt. XIII. **434**. 17. οἱ δ' οὖν Χαλδαῖοι τὴν μὲν τοῦ κόσμου φύσιν ἀίδιόν φασιν εἶναι καὶ μήτε ἐξ ἀρχῆς γένεσιν ἐσχηκέναι μηθ' ὕστερον φθορὰν ἐπιδέξεσθαι, τὴν δὲ τῶν ὅλων τάξιν τε καὶ διακόσμησιν θείᾳ τινὶ προνοίᾳ γεγονέναι, καὶ νῦν ἕκαστα τῶν ἐν οὐρανῷ γινομένων οὐχ ὡς ἔτυχεν οὐδ' αὐτομάτως ἀλλ' ὡρισμένῃ τινὶ καὶ βεβαίως κεκυρωμένῃ θεῶν κρίσει συντελεῖσθαι. Diodorus, ii. 30. 1. Retain δύναμις; cf. l. 9.

Excerpt. XV. **436**. 18. The φύσις τοῦ παντός is the World-Soul,³ the motion⁴ that moves the whole. For the double motion, from without and within, see 348. 27 (n. on l. 8) and 208. 25. This φύσις, as περιέχουσα, may be identified with the περιέχον πνεῦμα of 438. 17. It holds the Cosmos together, but also penetrates it 'tamquam mel per favos'.

In 438. 3 read ἡ φύσις πάντων, φύουσα ... φυὴν παρέχει. This writer is playing on φύειν. The style throughout is a form of the λέξις εἰρομένη— use of δέ with linking participles⁵—a simple tale of creation. The substance may be thus explained. It depends upon the λόγος τῆς ἁρμονίας of l. 15. First the pneumatic Nature, which sows its seeds⁶ and produces (?)

---

¹ Cf. Nemesius, *de nat. hom.* 644 Migne: συνδιαγιγνώσκει δὲ αὐτοῖς (*sc.* χρώμασιν) καὶ τὸ κεχρωσμένον σῶμα καὶ τὸ μέγεθος αὐτοῦ, καὶ τὸ σχῆμα, καὶ τὴν χώραν ἔνθα ἐστὶ καὶ τὸ διάστημα καὶ τὸν ἀριθμὸν κίνησίν τε καὶ στάσιν. This passage follows, and may be part of, a citation from Porphyry arguing that the soul itself is the cause of vision. See also Plotinus, *Enn.* iv. 5 (ii. 103. 12 V.). The doctrine involved is fully discussed in Jaeger, *op. cit.* c. 2.

² It is superfluous to alter the text, except for Usener's [ἀ]μέτοχα, l. 9.

³ Cf. 208. 19, 25; also the Chaldaean theory in Porphyry (see next note): ῥεῦμα θεῖον ἐξ αἰῶνος νοητόν; this moves the Cosmos, καὶ πάντα ἐ(ν) αὐτῷ ψυχὰς πέ(μ)π(ον) οἰκείας ζῳογονεῖ. As it comes from the East, the East is ζωῆς τόπος (Πρὸς Γαῦρον 57. 4 Kalbfleisch).

⁴ Cf. 448. 8.

⁵ l. 6 κινητήν· κινουμένη δέ. l. 18 οὐκ ἠρεμεῖ ... οὐκ ἠρεμοῦν δέ, μεταβάλλει ... μεταβάλλον δέ. See on 486. 10.

⁶ The seeds here are probably not organic, but the seeds of the qualities: τοῦ τε κόσμου πάλιν τὸ πῦρ ὃ σπέρμα λέγουσιν εἶναι καὶ μετὰ τὴν ἐκπύρωσιν εἰς σπέρμα μετέβαλε τὸν κόσμον (Plut. *de comm. not.*, 2. 1077 B). Gregory of Nyssa, *Hexaemeros*, 109 C: ἡ ψυχρὰ δύναμις ... οἷόν τι σπέρμα τῆς τοῦ ὑγροῦ φύσεως γίνεται. Philo, *de aet. mundi* 94.

matter in motion.[1]   Once in motion it heats up, and the [2] matter becomes separated into fire and water (with the opposite qualities of warm and dry, cold and moist, l. 15).   These are, in Stoic language, agent and patient. Then the operation of the λόγος τῆς ἁρμονίας which binds the opposites by interposing intermediates, since each element has two qualities. ἐπειδὴ δὲ τὰ ἐναντία συνάπτεσθαι ἀλλήλοις οὐκ ἠδύνατο μὴ μέσου τινὸς δεσμοῦ τεταγμένου τοῦ συνδέοντος αὐτά, ἔταξεν ὁ δημιουργὸς ἐν μέσῳ μὲν τῆς γῆς καὶ τοῦ ἀέρος ἐναντίων ὄντων τὸ ὕδωρ.[3] With the drying of the water, we must think of earth appearing above the water (l. 11) and particles even being borne up in vapour.[4]   To state the matter in terms of σύνδεσμος, elements have a primary and a secondary quality ; and earth, being cold as well as dry, has a bond with water, which is cold as well as moist, and so forth. This is the cycle of the elements : καὶ οὕτω γίνεται κύκλος καὶ χορὸς ἐναρμόνιος συμφωνούντων πάντων καὶ συστοιχούντων ἀλλήλοις.[5]   It will be noted that the selection of fire and water as the primary elements recalls Corp. II.

438. 17 *sqq.* The question is, when and how the soul enters the body, and the answer is, at birth. Ps.-Galen Πρὸς Γαῦρον (i.e. Porphyry) sheds most light on this discussion.[6]   It is a polemic against the Stoics.   The general answer is the same : ὅλως δὲ εἰ σ(π)έρμα (δυνάμει ἄνθρωπος, λέγομεν δ' ὅτι) οὐκ ἔχει ψυχὴν δυνάμει (59. 7). In § 4 the stages of the development of the embryo are traced—it has the growth of a plant only.[7]   The (σύμφυτον) πνεῖμα by its activity changes and moulds the semen. This is a βλαστικὴ κίνησις.[8]   From l. 20 the διαμόρφωσις is described vaguely.

---

[1] It is the seed that changes matter ; the matter is qualityless.   See on 316. 12. Should we read γενεσιουργοῦσα for γένεσις ἔχουσα in 438. 6 ?   Cf. λόγος γενεσιουργός (Iamblichus *ap.* Stob. 1. 81. 12 Wachsm.).

[2] ⟨ἡ⟩ ὕλη.

[3] Nemesius, *de nat. hom.* 616A.   See the parallel with Basil (89 B) in Jaeger, *Nemesios*, pp. 88-9, and consult the whole chapter.   Also Gronau, *Poseidonios*, pp. 112 *sqq.*, from whom I take the references to Gregory.

[4] Retain περιξηραινομένου (*sc.* τοῦ ὕδατος) in l. 11.   Vapour appears through the action of heat upon moist earth and it contains particles of earth, as motes in the sunlight still testify (Greg. *ibid.* 104 C).   Therefore retain the text in ll. 12-13. Cf. ξηρός τις καὶ γεώδης ὁ ἀτμὸς γενόμενος τὴν ποιότητα τῇ ξηρότητι τῆς γῆς κατεμίχθη (104 D).   For ὀχουμένη (l. 11) cf. ὀχεῖσθαι μὲν γῆν ὕδατι ξηρὰν οὖσαν (Philo, *de plant.* 3 (ii. 134. 2 Wendl.).

[5] Basil, *Hexaemeros* 4. 5, p. 92 A Migne.

[6] I quote from Kalbfleisch (*Abh. der K. K. Ak.* Berlin, 1895) by page and line. Hermippus (*de Astrologia*) attempts to controvert Porphyry's views, 2. 17 (p. 61 Kroll and Viereck).

[7] l. 18 οὐκ ἠρεμεῖ ἐν τῷ σπέρματι.   Cf. Philo, *de opif. mundi*, 67 : ἀλλ' ὅταν εἰς τὴν μήτραν καταβληθὲν στηρίσῃ, κίνησιν εὐθὺς λαβὸν εἰς φύσιν τρέπεται· φύσις δὲ βέλτιον σπέρματος, ἐπεὶ καὶ κίνησις ἠρεμίας ἐν γενητοῖς.

[8] Cf. φυτικὴ δύναμις)(γνωριστικὴ κίνησις (Porph. 55. 3).   χρεία δὲ πλάττεσθαι (καὶ τρέφεσ)θαι καὶ αὔξ(εσθαι) καὶ ζῆν γε οὕτως ἀλλ' οὐ γνωριστικῶς (56. 19).

εἴδωλον σχήματος is an attempt to describe the first signs of figure in the embryo.[1]   Possibly σχηματίζεται marks the end of this process, when the embryo takes a definite form[2]—διακεκριμένον ὅλον τὸ σῶμα (Oribasius). This is the μορφή, which is distinguished from the τέλειον εἶδος: Galen, iv. 605 Kühn, λέγω δὲ τὸ μὴ μόνον ἐγγίνεσθαι τῇ ὕλῃ τὸ εἶδος, ἐξ οὗ γίνεται τὸ μὲν ἄνθρωπος, τὸ δὲ δρῦς . . . ἀλλὰ καὶ τὴν μορφὴν αὐτὴν ὑπὸ τοῦ σπέρματος τὴν ὕλην διαπλάττοντος ἀποτελεῖσθαι, στοχάζεσθαι δ' αὐτό φασι (sc. οἱ Πνευματικοί) κατὰ τὴν μόρφωσιν οὐ τοῦ σχήματος μόνον, ἀλλὰ καὶ τοῦ μεγέθους καὶ τῆς θέσεως ἑκάστου τῶν μορίων, ἔτι τε τῆς πρὸς ἄλληλα συμφύσεως.[3]   The εἶδος hovers (?) above the shape, and through it what is taking form is endued with form.[4]

What the σπερματικὸς λόγος does with the embryo is to give size and form[5]; it is denied that ζωτικὴ κίνησις and thought are given in the womb.   The efficient cause is the πνεῦμα in the σπέρμα.

In § 5 (if we trust the textual tradition) it is said that the *harmonia* tempered the organism (the vegetative motion) as the receptacle of the mental life.   It is not meant that the infant exercises its intellect, merely that the εἴσκρισις of the soul, which makes the human life,[6] takes place upon a prepared organism at birth, so that a new type of movement supervenes upon that which is already there.   In Porphyry's figure, the pilot comes on board when the ship is ready.   The dianoetic life of the soul has no parts and does not change, whereas the *pneuma* causes the growth and change by numbers.   There are two modes of motion. ἀριθμοῖς admits of Neo-Pythagorean parallels.[7]

[1] ἐν ὑμένι μυξώδει γίνεται φανερῶς ἀμυδρὸς ὁ τύπος τῆς ῥάχεως καὶ ὁ τῆς κεφαλῆς (Oribasius, iii. 78) ; 'quarta (hebdomade) humorem ipsum coagulari ut quiddam uelut inter carnem ac sanguinem liquida adhuc soliditate conveniat' (Macrobius, *Comm. in Somn. Scipionis*, i. 6. 65)—both from Diocles.

[2] 'quinta uero interdum fingi in ipsa substantia humoris humanam figuram magnitudine quidem apis' (Macrobius).

[3] Cf. Porph. 52. 24 : καὶ μὴν τῷ γε τἀληθὲς σκοπουμένῳ (ἀ)τελὲς ἔτι φανεῖται ἄχρι τοκετῶν τὸ ἔμβρυον· ἦν δὲ τὸ ζωϊκὸν σῶμα οὐχ ἡ (ἔ)ξωθεν πλάσις, οὐδέ γε τὸ εἶδος ἡ ἔξωθεν περικειμένη μορφή, ἀλλ' ἡ δι' ὅλου (τ)ελειότης τοῦ πλάσματος, ἡ τελεία τῆς ἔξωθεν μορφῆς καὶ τῶν σπλάγχνων καὶ τῶν (ἄ)λλων ἁπαντῶν . . . καὶ συμπάσης τῆς ὀργανοποιίας θεωρουμένη τελείωσις.   The argument is that imperfect organs cannot have αἰσθητικαὶ δυνάμεις, and that the child is imperfect till it drops naturally from its mother.

[4] I take Usener's reading.

[5] In the Pneumatic account the σπέρμα has a δύναμις διαπλάττουσά τε καὶ μορφοῦσα τὸ κύημα (Ps.-Galen, xix. *def.* 95, p. 371. 4).   Porph. 60. 1, ἴδιον δὲ τῶν σπερμάτων τὸ (ἀεὶ ὁδῷ τινι) καὶ τάξει προβαίνειν καὶ τὸ τόδε μετὰ τόδε προάγειν. Plotinus, *Enn.* iv. 3. 10 : οἷα καὶ οἱ ἐν σπέρμασι λόγοι πλάττουσι καὶ μορφοῦσι τὰ ζῷα οἷον μικρούς τινας κόσμους.   Porphyry uses the phrase σπερματικὴ ψυχή (54. 3) of the Stoic view, and σπ. λόγοι frequently occurs in his polemic : τὸ ἄλογον ὑπὸ λόγου ῥυθμίζεται (56. 27).

[6] See Iamblichus *ap.* Stob. i. 381 Wachsm. ; also 366. 2, with note.

[7] Proclus, *in remp.* ii, pp. 33 *sqq.* (Kroll) ; Censorinus, *de die natali*, 9 : 'Pythagoras autem . . . dixit partus esse genera duo, alterum septem mensium, alterum

In § 6 a Platonist doctrine of natural affinity is rejected; the nearest soul enters καθ' εἱμαρμένην.[1] Porphyry alludes to such a view (48. 9): ἐμβαίνει δὲ ὁ κυβερνήτης εἰς φῶς πρ(οε)λθούσης τῆς φύσεως μετὰ τοῦ ἔργου ⟨οὐκ⟩ ἀναγκαζόμενος. . . . οὔτ' οὖν ἀναγκαζομένη ἡ αὐτοκίνητος ψυχὴ εἴσεισιν εἰς τὰ σώματα οὔτ' ἔτι μᾶλλον ἐπιτηρο(ῦσ)α τὸ στόμα καὶ τὰς ῥῖνας, τὰ καταγέλαστα δὴ ταῦτα. . . . ἐφ' οἷς τινες τῶν Πλατωνικῶν σεμνύνονται· φυσικὴ γὰρ ἡ ἐμψύχωσις καὶ δι' ὅλου ἡ ἔξαψις κατὰ συμφωνίαν τῶν ἁρμοσθέντων πρὸς τὸ ἐναρμόσαι οἷόν τε. The illustrations are the theory of sight, which postulates an *harmonia* between sight and its object, naphtha flaring up from fire across a gap, and in general ὅταν μηδὲν ἐμποδίζῃ εἰς τὸ καὶ ἄνευ ἁφῆς τὰ ἡρμοσμένα συμπάσχειν ἀλλήλοις. For ll. 6–7 κατὰ τὴν συγγενικὴν ⌜οὐσιότητα⌝[2] compare Porphyry's next sentence: ἕλκει δὲ καὶ ἡ μαγνῆτις λίθος κατὰ συγγένειαν φύσει τὰ σιδήρια καὶ τὰ κάρφη, καὶ τὸ ἁρμοσθὲν πρὸς ψυχῆς κυβέρνησιν τὴν ἐπιτηδείαν ψυχὴν τῷ ἁρμοσθέντι, οὐδὲν οὔτε βουλίσεως οὔτ' ἐπιτημήσεως οὔτε προαιρέσεως πρὸς τὴν παρουσίαν συμβαλλομένης.[3] This view is rejected by the Hermetist in favour of a theory which makes the soul that is nearest enter the body of the new-born.[4] On his view it is by Destiny itself that the soul communicates dianoetic motion to the new-born (ll. 8–10), and the intelligent substance of life itself, i.e. the life proper to the soul.[5] The soul uses the *pneuma* as its envelope[6] (l. 14—theory of capsules). For the purpose of this Excerpt gradations like sensation and opinion are ignored, as they are by Porphyry.[7]

decem, sed priorem aliis dierum numeris conformari, aliis posteriorem. eos vero numeros qui in uno quoque partu aliquid adferunt mutationis, dum aut semen in sanguinem aut sanguis in carnem aut caro in hominis figuram convertitur, inter se conlatos rationem habere eam quam voces habent quae in musice σύμφωνοι vocantur.' Of the numbers (c. 11) it suffices to say that for the first the 35 days to the ' initium hominis formati' are divided into stages of 6, 8, 9, 12 days, i.e. 4 : 3, 3 : 2, 2 : 1—the fourth, the fifth, the diapason. The full numbers are 210 days (35 × 6) and 274 days (40 × 7–6). See Gronau, *op. cit.* p. 197 for further references.

[1] Cf. 508. 25 : ὅθεν δεῖ καὶ τὴν πρὸς τὸ σῶμα αὐτῆς (*sc. τῆς ψυχῆς*) σύνοδον, ἁρμονίαν θεοῦ, ὑπὸ ἀνάγκης γενομένην εἶναι.

[2] Meineke's οἰκειότητα (cod. Vatic.) gives the sense; but ἰδιότητα (P) suggests ἐπιτηδειότητα.

[3] Cf. *de abstin.* ii. 48 : ὁλκὸν τῆς ψυχῆς ἡ τοῦ συγγενοῦς σώματος φύσις.

[4] τὴν (in ll. 6 and 7) indicates that there are two well-known rival theories of affinity—natural and destined by mere proximity. Porph. ἀφορμαί, c. 35, p. 29. 18 Mommert: ἡ οὖν παρουσία οὐ τοπική, ἐξομοιωτικὴ δέ, καθ' ὅσον οἷόν τε σῶμα ὁμοιοῦσθαι ἀσωμάτῳ καὶ ἀσώματον θεωρεῖσθαι ἐν σώματι ὁμοιουμένῳ αὐτῷ. Porphyry denies the view that the soul enters ἀναγκαζομένη (48. 18).

[5] This is not mere ζωτικὴ κίνησις, but ζωὴ νοερά (450. 12; 448. 4) or τὸ ζῆν γνωριστικῶς, in Porphyry's phrase; or it answers to the ζωτικὸν ῥεῦμα of the Chaldaeans. See also 420. 16 *sqq.*, 122. 31 ; 126. 1–5.

[6] Cf. ὑποδοχήν in 438. 28; Porph. 49. 9.

[7] At the stage of nutrition and formation; the entry of the sensitive and opining faculty would obstruct the growth and be a superfluity (51. 23). For the doxographical tradition see Psellus, *de omnif. doctr.* 716 A Migne:

We may look to an astrological doctrine for the affinities of this account. Porphyry [1] quotes (though not with approval) a Chaldaic theory which makes the East the gate of souls and εἴσπνοια τοῦ παντός. The child at birth is charged, so to speak, from the ῥεῦμα θεῖον ἐξ αἰῶνος νοητὸν (τὸ καθ' ἐν ἀόρατον ῥεῦμα) ἕλκον τὸ οἰκεῖον εἰς ζωότητα ῥεῦμα ἐξ αὐτοῦ ψυχῆς, καθ' ὃν καιρὸν εἰς τὸν ἀέρα προὔκυψε τῇ γέννῃ τῆς φυτικῆς διοικήσεως ἀποβληθὲν τὸ ἔμβρυον. The reason for astrological inquiry about conception is not because the ζωτικὸν πνεῦμα enters then, but because the embryo is then prepared for the ῥεῦμα and would not be prepared to receive it unless its foundation were laid at that particular moment. Here is an affinity according to Destiny differing from the affinity favoured by Porphyry; the fated εἴσκρισις is dependent upon the κοινὴ φορὰ πάντων (l. 19); [2] and immediately after there is an elaborate comparison to the musical *harmonia*—when the προσλαμβανόμενος is contempered with the μέση, it σῴζει τὴν διὰ πασῶν συμφωνίαν. This is Porphyry's addition; but the common background is the doctrine of *concentus*. [3]

It would appear that an exposition based on current Pneumatic (Stoic) theories of embryology, with Neo-Pythagorean elements, and with affinities to the ' Platonists' derided by Porphyry, is elaborated for the purpose of advocating a strict astrological fatalism. The soul enters the body at birth, but enters as Destiny decrees. [4]

If we now turn to the beginning of this Excerpt (436. 16) the discrimination into two types of motion is intelligible. [5] The one (κατ' ἐνέργειαν) is the motion of *pneuma* which causes growth within the Cosmos; the other (κατὰ δύναμιν) is the motion that supervenes upon the first when the human body is prepared for the *harmonia* of body and soul. [6] To interpret by other Hermetic tracts, this is the work of Aion. [7]

It may be suggested that §§ 2–3 [8] are not an account of creation, but

(in contrast to the Christian Fathers, the Greeks put the soul into the body after completion and birth) πλὴν ὅτε μὲν ἔσωθεν ἢ κατερριζωμένον τὸ ἔμβρυον τὴν φυσικὴν ψυχὴν τούτῳ διδόασιν, ἐξελθόντι δὲ τὴν λογικήν, καὶ προϊόντι τὴν νοεράν.

[1] p. 57.

[2] τ. κ. φορὰν σχεδὸν πάντων, καθ' ἣν ... πεπίστευτο ἐμψυχία μετὰ τὴν ἐξ ὠδίνων πρό(κυψ)ιν τῶν κυομένων.

[3] See on ἀριθμοῖς above. Porphyry constantly uses ἁρμόττειν, ἁρμονία, ἀνάρμοστος (= ἀτέλης), συμφωνεῖν, etc. See e.g. 53. 19–26.

[4] 440. 14 presupposes the doctrine of psychic wrappings—the soul inside the *pneuma*. Cf. 194. 28.

[5] Κίνησις κινοῦσα τὸ πᾶν should be retained (cf. 448. 8).

[6] See especially 448. 4 *sqq.*

[7] 208. 12 *sqq.*; 348. 22; 206. 21–22; 140. 18–24 (see note); 218. 26 τοῦτο γὰρ ὥσπερ ζωὴ καὶ ὥσπερ κίνησίς ἐστιν τοῦ θεοῦ, κινεῖν τὰ πάντα καὶ ζωοποιεῖ (the colour here is more Stoic). Also the Chaldaean theory in Porphyry—ῥεῦμα θεῖον ἐξ αἰῶνος νοητόν; this moves the Cosmos, καὶ πάντα τὰ ἐ(ν) αὐτῷ ψυχὰς πέ(μ)π(ον οἰκείας ζῳογονεῖ. As it comes from the East, the East is ζωῆς τύπος.

[8] 438. 4 ἡ φύσις πάντων, φύουσα ... φυήν. For the phrase see 436. 18. L. 11

the relevant data to account for the formation of an organized body according to a λόγος. The σπερματικοὶ λόγοι are the clue, and the process of κρᾶσις is described in Stoic terms. This explains the phrase κατὰ τὸν τ. ἁρμονίας λόγον (438. 15),[1] and 438. 26-7, where the *harmonia* (of the developed embryo) prepared the motion proper to it as a fit receptacle for the supervening motion. Thus the *harmonia* of body and soul is achieved at birth.

Excerpt. XVI. **440.** 18. Albinus, *Eisagoge*, 10 (of God) τῷ νῷ ληπτός, ἐπεὶ οὔτε γένος οὔτε εἶδος οὔτε διαφορά, ἀλλ' οὐδὲ συμβέβηκέ τι αὐτὸ οὔτε κακόν ... οὔτε ἀγαθόν.

442. 1. The soul is not *in* space, time, or nature, like the body.[2] Nor does the category of relation apply : it is not a contemperament, or form or shape of something—i.e. it is ἀσχημάτιστος. Ar. *Cat.* 6 a 36, πρὸς τι τὰ τοιαῦτα λέγεται ὅσα αὐτὰ ἅπερ ἐστὶν ἑτέρων εἶναι λέγεται. l. 3, τὸ οὗ ἔνεκα explains 440. 19: the body is not the final cause of the soul, as it is of time, etc. In short, the writer goes through a number of needs, including ἁρμονία,[3] which differentiate the soul from body. The entities relative to body form a group with a tie ; the soul is independent. For the general sense cf. Porphyry, ἀφορμαί xl. p. 35 (Mommert): ὅταν λάβῃς ἀένναον οὐσίαν ἐν ἑαυτῇ κατὰ δύναμιν ἄπειρον καὶ νοεῖν ἄρξῃ ὑπόστασιν ἀκάματον, ἄτρυτον, οὐδαμῇ μὲν ἐλλείπουσαν, ὑπερεξαίρουσαν δὲ τῇ ζωῇ τῇ ἀκραιφνεστάτῃ καὶ πλήρει ἀφ' ἑαυτῆς, ἐν αὐτῇ τε ἱδρυμένη καὶ κεκορεσμένη ἐξ ἑαυτῆς καὶ οὐδ' ἑαυτὴν ζητούσῃ, ταύτῃ ἐάνπερ τὸ ποῦ ἐπιβάλῃς ἢ τὸ πρός τι, ἅμα τῷ ἠλαττῶσθαι ἐξ ἐνδείας τοῦ ποῦ ἢ πρός τι, εὐθὺς ἐκείνην μὲν οὐκ ἠλάττωσας, ἑαυτὸν δὲ ἀπέστρεψας κάλυμμα λαβὼν τὴν ὑποδραμοῦσαν τῆς ὑπονοίας φαντασίαν. Cf. Plot. *Enn.* vi. 5. 12.

Excerpt. XX. **450.** 2. Proclus, *in Tim.* ii. 64. 10 (Diehl): τὸ δὲ συστατὸν σῶμα τὸ σύνθετόν ἐστι καὶ ἑτεροκίνητον. τὸ μὲν οὖν αὐτοκίνητον ἑαυτοῦ σωστικόν.[4] The pair εἶναι, ζῆν belongs to Stoic terminology ; but the sense here is Hermetic, as ll. 11–12 show : for ἐν λόγῳ γενέσθαι should refer to the 'capsule' theory of the soul, and the 'life' of ll. 12–13 is the life of the fully developed man, possibly (though not certainly) the ἔννους. The argument is that body is by definition that which grows and disappears,

---

⟨γῆ⟩, ὀχουμένη. Cf. ὀχεῖσθαι μὲν γῆν ὕδατι ξηρὰν οὖσαν (Philo, *de plantat.* 3). l. 12 ἀτμός. Cf. 522. 19 ; 526. 22. The notion here, as in our passage, is *measure*.

[1] Cf. 452. 4, where ἁρμονία, as a well understood technical term, needs no specification.

[2] See note on 132. 2 *init.* and iv. 199. 1. Contrast 352. 11.

[3] καὶ γὰρ τὴν ἁρμονίαν κρᾶσιν καὶ σύνθεσιν ἐναντίων εἶναι (Ar., *de an.*, 407 b 30). ἔστι γὰρ ἁρμονία πολυμιγέων ἕνωσις καὶ δίχα φρονεόντων συμφρόνησις (Ps.-Philolaus, *fr.* 6).

[4] The contrast ἀσώματον)(σῶμα ἔχον appears to be justified by 448. 10. In ll. 14–15 ψυχὴ ἀσώματος ... δύναμιν the contrast is with the μεταβολή of body in l. 6. οὐ μὴν καὶ τῇ ψυχῇ καὶ τοῦτο συμβαίνει, ὅτι οὐκ ἦν ἐξ ἀζωίας καὶ ζωῆς συγκείμενον πρᾶγμα, ἀλλὰ ζωὴ μόνον, καὶ τοῦτο ἦν τῷ Πλάτωνι τὸ οὐσίαν εἶναι καὶ λόγον τῆς ψυχῆς τὸ αὐτοκίνητον (Porph. ἀφορμαί xxi).

whereas man (as defined) owes his νοερὰ ζωή to something that imparts life and mind. Hence there must be an οὐσία that imparts ζωὴ νοερά. Cf. 444. 10–15, 448. 8.

The reason for the differences between men is astrological: the structure of the body is related to the contemperament (of the stars).[1] The soul 'takes over' an (ἐπιτήδειον) σῶμα fashioned by the stars (452. 7). See on 438. 17. For astrological detail see iii. 459. It is Stoic commonplace that the heavens were made for man. We may supplement l. 13 as follows: 'iam vero circumitus solis et lunae reliquorumque siderum, quamquam etiam ad mundi cohaerentiam pertinent, tamen et spectaculum hominibus praebent; . . . eorum enim cursus dimetati maturitates temporum et varietates mutationesque cognovimus; quae si hominibus solis nota sunt, hominum facta esse causa iudicandum est' (Cicero, *de nat. deorum*, ii. 62. 155). οἵ γε μὴν πλάνητες , . . πλείστην ἐπιδεικνύμενοι συμπάθειαν πρὸς ἀέρα καὶ γῆν· τὸν μὲν γὰρ εἰς τὰς ἐτησίους ἐπικαλουμένας ὥρας τρέπουσι καὶ μεταβάλλουσι καθ᾽ ἑκάστην . . . καὶ μὲν δὴ τὰ ἐπίγεια πάντα, ζῷά τε αὖ καὶ φυτά, καρποὺς γεννῶντα, αὔξουσι καὶ τελεσφοροῦσι τὴν ἐν ἑκάστοις φύσιν δολιχεύειν παρασκευάζοντες, ὡς νέα παλαιοῖς ἐπανθεῖν καὶ ἐπακμάζειν πρὸς χορηγίας ἀφθόνους τῶν δεομένων. . . . ἐπεὶ δ᾽ ἐκ τῶν οὐρανίων τὰ ἐπίγεια ἤρτηται κατά τινα φυσικὴν συμπάθειαν, ὁ τῆς ἑβδομάδος λόγος ἄνωθεν ἀρξάμενος κατέβη καὶ πρὸς ἡμᾶς, τοῖς θνητοῖς γένεσιν ἐπιφοιτήσας (Philo, *de op. mundi*, § 113–17).[2] The doctrine is Posidonian. But the account in the Hermetic writings is different. The domination of the stars is an evil, from which man looks for salvation.

Excerpt. XXI. 452. 16. This is a classification of deities, intelligible, and visible; the best commentary is *Abamm. resp.*, vol. iv. 31-2. If this is so, the text will not bear the introduction of Platonic distinctions. In l. 16 read perhaps προόν. ⟨προ⟩ὸν γάρ ἐστι δι᾽ οὗ, and compare ἀπ᾽ αὐτοῦ ἡ οὐσιότης (iv. 32. 5). Then l. 19: τὰ δὲ ἐνάντια . . . ἐστι φύσις, οὐσία αἰσθητή (Wachsm.).[3] We should probably take τὰ δὲ δοξαστά as referring to the visible deities. There is a κοινωνία ψυχῶν from top to bottom of the scale. The relation appears to be indicated in what follows. The lowest deities are images of the νοημάτ⟨ικ⟩οί (?) as the sun is the image of the supreme creator. We must retain the triple final clause; the πνεύματα are spirits —another grade of beings.

Excerpt. XXII. 454. 9. ἡ γένεσις here perhaps means *genitalia virilia*, and τοῦ αὐτοῦ (l. 11) expresses the theory that the male (like the female) seed simply repeats the parent. Psellus, *de omnifar. doctr.* 737 D Migne: τὸ ἀποκρινόμενον σπέρμα . . . τὸ μὲν ἀπὸ τοῦ ἀνδρός, λόγους ἔχει τῶν ἐν αὐτῷ ἠθῶν καὶ τρόπων καὶ τῆς μορφῆς, καὶ ἀπὸ μητρὸς δὲ ὡσαύτως.

---

[1] Cf. 120. 22.

[2] See also Nemesius, *de nat. hom.* 528-9 Migne; Philo, *de opif. mundi*, 30. 13 C. In general Reinhardt, *K.U.S.*, p. 342.

[3] W. places a lacuna before μεταξύ (l. 22).

(Doxographical tradition.) See also Gregory of Nyssa, iii. 680 (Migne), Nemesius, *de nat. hom.*, 545 Migne, and (with A. D. N.) Hephaestion, p. 65. 17 Engelbr., F. Boll, *Memorie R. Accad. Bologna*, II. v–vii. (1923) 10. The hour of the horoscope over which the Decan presides is that of conception. See Bouché-Leclercq, *Astrol. grecque*, p. 391. 1.

Excerpt. XXIII. **456.** 1. *Kore Kosmu. General references.* See Zielinski, *Archiv*, 8. 356; Reitzenstein, *Poimandres*, 136, *Die Göttin Psyche, S.-B. Akad. Heidelb.* 1917, p. 70; Bousset, *Archiv*, 18. 165, *P.-W.* 11. 1386. See also Introduction III in this volume.

It may serve the convenience of readers if Bousset's analysis (*P.-W.*) of this piece is first summarized without comment. (1) **456.** 12–458. 8. Chaos; the upper and lower world unseparated; formless matter in fear of the heavens. (2) **458.** 8–15. Ἀγνωσία ruled the sum of things, till God implanted in the gods the desire to know. (3) **458.** 15–460. 18. Isis to her son: origin of this revelation. (4) **462.** 6–34. Order in upper world. (5) **464.** 13–466. 27. Doublet. Making of Ψύχωσις and the souls. (6) **466.** 28–470. 13. Making of the human figures in the Zodiac, then the animal ones. The souls use the stuff left over to make animals (though the underworld is still uncreated). (7) **470.** 20–7. Transgression of souls (cf. 5). (8) **470.** 28–474. 9. The souls are to be punished and Hermes is commanded to make men's bodies as a prison. (Same oversight as in 5.) Promises of planets. Making of bodies. (9) **474.** 11–476. 32. Theme of imprisonment of souls resumed. Isis tells her son of the revelation made by Kamephis, how the souls lamented their fate. (10) (*a*) **476.** 33–478. 21, and (*b*) 478. 22–480. 20. A double answer by God. In (*a*) it is forgotten that the souls are already fallen. The speech is addressed to the souls in general, who are divided into three groups, the first of which are sinless (478. 4), while the threat to the worst group (478. 17), that they will be made animals, is inconsistent with the second answer (480. 8). (11) **480.** 21–484. 17. *Momus episode*—an insertion. Warning against man's ὕβρις, and advice to burden him with πάθη. Hermes reveals his 'hidden instrument'. (12) **484.** 20–486. 9. The cosmogony at last taken up again. Again God's ἡγεμονία is ἀνεπίγνωστος, and sun and moon have not yet appeared. There follows the διάστασις: the sun solidifies the quivering earth, etc. God blesses his handiwork. (13) **486.** 10–end. Ἀγνωσία. Without warning, the last section describes a revolution of the imprisoned souls against the gods in heaven; they use as tools the men who are left (?), and they bring strife into the world. The polluted elements appeal to God. He determines to send an ἀπόρροια from his own nature on earth —Osiris and Isis. These bring the blessings of civilization, and end their mission with a hymn to the highest God.

The general conclusion from this analysis is that the *Grundschrift* has its starting-point in (12): Egyptian cosmogony. No. (1) (the gods before Chaos) harmonizes with this; so do the introduction of the gods in (2) and the soul-making (5). But the first document had nothing to say of *souls* imprisoned in human bodies; it dealt with δαίμονες or πνεύματα in the heavenly spheres (466. 13). The compiler fused this tale of πνεύματα imprisoned for disobedience with the Platonic myth of souls. B. links this interpretation with the Egyptian character of the ending, and especially with the reference to daemons in 492. 27.

On this hypothesis we have (1) Picture of chaos; (2) the highest God and the gods; (5) Creation of πνεύματα ruling over the middle region—syncretistic; (12) Creation of heaven, earth, and sun by separation of the μελαίνη ἔνωσις. [Perhaps then the fall of the πνεύματα and their imprisonment (7 and fragments from 9)]. Also an account of creation of man; cf. 8. Then (13) corruption of mankind and salvation. This tale is itself a compilation from Egyptian cosmogony, an oriental myth of the fall of the spirits, and a later Isis-Osiris myth. Then a redactor, influenced by the *Timaeus*, who is responsible for 4, 6, 8, 9–10, 11. The redactor is also responsible for such passages as 458. 15–460. 18, 474. 15–19. His hand is responsible for the character of the long speeches.[1]

If the general lines of this analysis are sound—as I believe them to be in principle—it is useless to attempt to harmonize discrepant passages in the document.

456. 8. Zielinski (*Archiv*, 8. 356) interprets τὸ τέλειον μέλαν as 'chemistry': Plut. *Is. et Osir.* 33; vol. iv. 145 (ἱερᾶς τέχνης Αἰγύπτου); Georg. Syncellus I. 23 (Dind.). However this may be, τέλειον probably has ritual significance; cf. τέλειος λόγος, and (from Bousset) τέλειον for baptisms (Clement, *Paed.* i. 6. 26).

13. τὰ ὑποκείμενα is the world below; so τὰ κάτω in 458. 1, and compare 472. 5. We must suppose the upper world still lying on the lower, and yet to be separated. See on 484. 22.

458. 1. The theme is the fear of the 'things below' for the things above, before the separation. The highest God (not yet distinguished from the Demiurge, as in Christian Gnosticism) is a θεὸς ἄγνωστος,[2] even to the gods. God implanted into the gods (l. 12) the desire to seek, to find, and the power to succeed (weak rhetoric). It was because of this divine knowledge that Hermes later was able to reveal to men (who did not yet exist and could never have known of themselves) what he knew.

462. 7–34. The theme is the barrenness of Nature. God is a King with his attendant gods, a conception we meet again in 484. 22 and 496. 7. This metaphor (often from the Great King) is commonplace in Hellenistic writings[3]: the best known example is Ar. *de mundo* 398a 10. If we accept

---

[1] Analysis of style in Norden, *Agn. Theos.*

[2] See Norden, *Agn. Theos.*, pp. 65 *sqq.*; Epiphanius, *adv. haer.* i. 31. 5: ὅτε γὰρ ἐξ ἀρχῆς, ὁ αὐτοπάτωρ αὐτὸς ἐν ἑαυτῷ περιεῖχε τὰ πάντα ὄντα ἐν ἑαυτῷ ἐν ἀγνωσίᾳ (from Norden). l. 2 ἐπικειμένων (ἰδόντα) Reitzenstein. l. 3 ἀγωνίας: cf. ll. 14–15; καταφανταζόμενον: being like.

[3] See Cumont, *Relig. orientales*, p. 299, n. 21.

the text, it is the upper world that is barren, and the upper world that is to be set in order. This prefaces an allegory, the outline of which is as follows, if we omit the interruptions in ll. 20-1, 23-5. A fair woman, Physis, proceeded from God's voice,[1] and God bade her be fruitful. Physis laughed,[2] and obeyed the command; she bore to Ponos (who is abruptly introduced) a daughter Heuresis; to her God gave the boon of knowledge,[3] giving this boon he divided the things that already were and filled them with stars (the things that were to be known); and he gave to Heuresis the mastery with regard to them.[4]

It is noticeable that, apart from the creation of Physis, there are two acts of creation in this account (ll. 23-5, 31-2), the second of which is integral to the story, whereas the first interrupts the sequence between God's command and its fulfilment: they are doublets. I suggest that the first is a stray insertion or relic of an older story, giving an account of the creation of πνεύματα, and that it is more primitive in character than the Platonically coloured version given in 464. 13 *sqq.* We have to account for the mention of air and aether as well as sky, and πνεύμασιν for ἅπασιν would cover all three realms. If any trust is to be given to the text, the spirits were in the upper region, and it is the upper region that is here in question. The souls, when threatened with the fall, address heaven and aether and air (474. 31), and speak of their kindred *spirits* in the air (476. 17), the element nearest to their new abode.[5]

The allegory, as it stands, is a frigid Hellenistic piece, meaning that Labour, with ' Nature ', produces (astrological?) Discovery. It is in line with those Hesiodic-Orphic personifications [6] of which the best-known instance is the tale of Aphrodite, Poros, and Penia in the *Symposium*—a

---

[1] *Sirach*, 24. 3 (Song of Sophia) ἐγὼ ἀπὸ στόματος ὑψίστου ἐξῆλθον.

[2] λαλήσασα (l. 26) is pointless; perhaps γελάσασα. For laughter is connected with procreation; see on 472. 20, 532. 8, and compare 120. 26 (Φύσις) ἐμειδίασεν ἔρωτι; also l. 17 above. ἑαυτῇ was written to conform with the verb; a preposition at least is needed, unless we suppose the gross corruption from ἔρωτι.

[3] ἐχαρίσατο ⟨τὸ⟩ εἰ⟨δέ⟩ναι. It will be argued below that the Σοφία literature may have some bearing on this allegory. *Wisdom of Solomon*, 9. 9 καὶ μετὰ σοῦ ἡ Σοφία, ἡ εἰδυῖα τὰ ἔργα σου καὶ παροῦσα ὅτε ἐποίεις τὸν κόσμονο. . . . οἶδε γὰρ ἐκείνη πάντα. Cf. 7. 17-22, where Solomon was given to know the constitution of the world and the working of the elements . . . the circuits of the years and the positions of the stars—for Wisdom was his teacher.

[4] l. 33. Bracket the first τούτων, with Heeren. Note that the phrase τὰ ἤδη γεγονότα (l. 31) recurs in 472. 6, where God proceeds to the ordering of the lower world. That, too, is an astrological piece, and Heuresis reappears with Hermes when he gives men wisdom and truth (l. 24).

[5] It may be convenient to collect here the evidence that the fall was from heaven; 464. 13 ὑπεράνω; 466. 12 τῆς ἄνω φύσεως (gloss οὐρανοῦ), 22 οὐρανός; 468. 8; 474. 37; 476. 2, 19; 478. 5, 17, 19.

[6] The story of Prometheus, which (as I shall argue) has influenced this Excerpt, belongs to the same tradition.

tale, be it noted, of the origin of Philosophy, as this is of Knowledge or Discovery. Its bearing appears from 472. 25 (τῇ Εὑρέσει συνών), where Hermes gives man his intellectual powers, and from Momus' stress on man's undaunted curiosity. The underlying thread of the Excerpt is indeed ζήτησις and εὕρεσις.[1] But the figure of Physis invites conjecture. She proceeds from God's voice ; she is before the world was made ; she is bidden to be fruitful ; the mythological figment that is her daughter has the mastery of the stars, and 'knowledge' is her domain. Note (with Scott) the figure of Γέννα in Dieterich's *Abraxas*,[2] who appears after Hermes-Νοῦς when God laughed the fourth time. Dieterich has compared Γέννα to the Orphic Aphrodite.[3] On the other hand, if we take the distinction between mother and daughter with no more seriousness than it deserves, there are obvious parallels between Sophia[4] and Physis-Heuresis. At this point reference must be made to the combinations of Reitzenstein, who brings out the characteristics of Isis[5] as Γέννα (γένεσις) and Σοφία.[6] In this Excerpt Isis is the teacher and civilizer ; there is no trace of the world goddess who appears in the Hymns of Andros and Cyme.[7] Zielinski interprets *Kore Kosmu* as 'Jungfrau der Welt', and Bousset assents.[8] The evidence is too fragmentary for safe conjecture ; but if we could know more fully the background of this allegory and the related parts of the Excerpt, it is not impossible that Φύσις, who proceeded from the mouth of God, was the Kore Kosmu.

464. 14 *sqq.* This describes the creation of πνεύματα for the upper region (ὑπεράνω) out of a deity (?) Psychosis. The conception is probably Oriental (see on 468. 5) ; but there is a Platonic colouring, and the terminology is alchemical, as Zielinski notes.[9] The materials used by the Deity are not the classical four elements, but higher elements of the kind met with in Hermetic and related writings.[10] Hence the stress laid upon

---

[1] See 458. 14–15, 19–20.   [2] p. 183. 50 (quoted in vol. iii. 501–2).

[3] *op. cit.* p. 72 ; γενέτειρα θεά (*Hymn.* 55. 2).

[4] *Proverbs,* 8. 22 : κύριος ἔκτισέ με ἀρχὴν ὁδῶν αὐτοῦ εἰς ἔργα αὐτοῦ πρὸ τοῦ αἰῶνος ἐθεμελίωσέ με κτλ.

[5] She is φύσις αἰῶνος (Athenagoras, 28. 2 Schwartz).

[6] *Zwei rel.-gesch. Fragen,* 107 *sqq.* See also Cumont, *Relig. orient.* 239, nn. 54–5. Reitzenstein's argument is based on the Wisdom literature in part.

[7] In the Cyrene inscription she says : Αὐτὴ γὰρ εὗρον πάντα καὶ εἱλόμην πόνον (*Notizario Archaeologico,* 1927, p. 210). Date 103 A.D.

[8] In Epiphanius iii, p. 483 Dind. there is an account of the Gnostic feast of the birth of Aion from Kore (Isis) at Alexandria (Zielinski). Bousset compares *Acta Thomae* c. 6 ; ἡ κόρη τοῦ φωτὸς θυγάτηρ.

[9] e.g. κρᾶμα, ἐπίπαγος, ἐξατμιζόμενον ἄνθος etc. l. 16 ⟨δε⟩ούσαις Reitzenstein. Remainder as codd.

[10] See on 122. 25 and the contrast in 212. 1 φῶς)(πῦρ. Also the oracle ψυχαῖον σπινθῆρα δυσὶ κράσας ὁμονοίαις | νῷ καὶ πνεύματι θείῳ, ἐφ' οἷς τρίτον ἁγνὸν Ἔρωτα | συνδετικὸν πάντων ἐπιβήτορα σεμνὸν, ἔθηκεν (Lydus, *de mens.* i. 11, p. 3, Wünsch). Cf. Kroll, *de orac. chald.,* p. 26.

their peculiar nature (ll. 18, 25-8).   The stuff did not 'run' through heat, being of (divine) fire, or grow cold,[1] being of (divine) *pneuma*, when it was finished (ll. 25-6).

30. Ψύχωσιν. Reitzenstein (*Göttin Psyche*, p. 71) refers this to a (probable) Oriental source, and compares the Chaldaean oracle quoted on l. 17.   It is used of 'the soul-substance as source of the individual souls,' as in 190. 23 (see note).   R. allows that the *Timaeus* influenced the account of the mixing and the conception of σύστασις (l. 30); but (according to him) mythological elements are inserted: for πνεῦμα θεῖον and νοῦς (πῦρ νοερόν) represent deities from which in the old Oriental account ψυχή emanates.   Thus Ψύχωσις is a deity.   For his attempt to find an Iranian cosmogony in this *Excerpt* see *op. cit.* and Bousset, *P.-W.* 11, 1391.

466. 13. If I am right in conjecturing (iii. 509) that the 'cylinder' refers to the axis of the universe, this is a Platonic touch.

19. χερσίν. Zielinski contrasts οὐ χερσίν, ἀλλὰ λόγῳ in 118. 17.

22. καταμένει Wachsm.

468. 5. The elements here and above (464. 18) are not material; they belong to the 'upper' world.   Here 'earth' and 'water' are used, the lower elements in that world.   The creatures like man are the human figures in the zodiac, just as God gives the souls as models for their work the animal figures (ll. 13, 16-17).   Then the souls make the animals from matter, and God promises to add to the 'visible works' the 'invisible spirit' (l. 20).[2]   Though the meaning of 'visible works' is clear, ll. 26-8 are inconsistent with it (Platonizing imitation).   So Reitzenstein, *Göttin Psyche*, p. 74.   For ll. 18-19 cf. 332. 15.

27. προσεκύνουν.   This is the wrong tone; the sentence has a touch of the burlesque that is apparent in 474. 20 *sqq.*   προσ may be a doublet of πατρός, and perhaps we should read ἐκύκων—first they looked, then they stirred the brew.

470. 1 *sqq.*   The order of the creatures in the codices is justified because the hot-blooded are taken first, and the cold-blooded last, from a mixture that is cooling.

l. 6: τὸ δὴ ἧττον κοῦφον καὶ ἐτέρας ὑγρασίας [υσιας or υγιας] δεόμενον. υσιας is perhaps dittography.   See 526. 25.

21. περίεργον . . . τόλμαν.   This should be linked with 482. 27, where the supreme audacity is a renewed assault on heaven; see note *ad loc.*

20-7. (Text as codd.).   Philo, *de somn.* ii. 114: μέμνημαι δὲ καὶ πρότερόν τινος ἀκούσας ἀνδρὸς οὐκ ἀμελῶς οὐδὲ ῥαθύμως τῷ μαθήματι προσενεχθέντος, ὅτι οὐκ ἄνθρωποι μόνοι δοξομανοῦσιν, ἀλλὰ καὶ οἱ ἀστέρες καὶ περὶ πρωτείων ἁμιλλώμενοι δικαιοῦσιν οἱ μείζους ἀεὶ πρὸς τῶν ἐλαττόνων δορυφορεῖσθαι.

---

[1] ἔψυχε, intransitive?

[2] (ἀ)όρατον πνεῦμα (l. 21) is an οὐσία of ὁμοιογονία.   l. 23 ποιεῖν (ἢ) P².

472. 5. The creation of the lower world begins here; the account is irreconcilable with the task given to the souls in 468. 12, and the theme of punishment is resumed in 474. 12. As will appear, this is an astrological document, and perhaps related to the allegory of Physis in 462. 17; cf. 472. 25 (τῇ Εὑρέσει συνών). The stars are idle (l. 6) because there are no men on whom to exercise their power. As Zielinski notes, the promises are double-edged; for Hermetism the planets are a menace. We might therefore keep epithets like ἀναφελῆ in l. 15[1]; memory may be unavailing as hope may be deceptive. The four gifts of the moon are deities, and with Phobos we should compare πρὸς δαίμονα⟨ς⟩ καὶ φόβους[2]—the Fears that walk by night.

12. Ἥλιος δὲ αὐγῆς (κύριος); i.e. αὐγή is the ἰδία οὐσία of the Sun (Vettius Valens, p. 5. 15 Kroll).

15. παρὰ δ' Αἰγύπτοις Νεμέσεως ἀστήρ (Κρόνος) Achilles Tatius, *Isag.* 17. Cf. Vettius Valens, p. 2. 22.

20-1. Retain the text. For the connexion of laughter with procreation see on 532. 8. καταδίκη is probably the doom following childlessness (A. D. N.). Cf. 144. 16.

22 *sqq.* ⟨ὁ⟩ δὲ τοῦ Ἑρμοῦ σημαίνει παιδείαν, γράμματα, ἔλεγχον, λόγον, ἀδελφότητα, ἑρμηνείαν, κηρυκείαν, ἀριθμόν, ψῆφον, γεωμετρίαν...ἔστι δὲ δοτὴρ καὶ διανοίας καὶ φρονήσεως... κυρίως δὲ ποιεῖ... ῥήτορας, φιλοσόφους (cf. πειθὼ καὶ ἀλήθειαν, l. 24).... οὓς δὲ τῶν οὐρανίων ἴδριας ἢ καὶ ἐρευνητὰς γινομένους, διὰ τέρψεως καὶ εὐθυμίας τὸ θαυμαστὸν ἔργον ἐνδοξοκοποῦντας τῆς ὠφελείας χάριν. οὗτος γὰρ ὁ ἀστὴρ πολλῆς μεθόδου δύναμιν ἔχων κατὰ τὰς τῶν ζωδίων[3] ἐναλλαγὰς ἢ καὶ τὰς τῶν ἀστέρων συμπλοκὰς ἑτεροσχήμονας παρέχει πράξεις, οἷς μὲν εἴδησιν.... (Vettius Valens, p. 4. 4-23). For σωφροσύνη (l. 24) cf. perhaps νόμου δὲ καὶ συνηθείας καὶ πίστεως ὁ τοῦ Ἑρμοῦ (*ib.* p. 5. 20).

474. 4 *sqq.* This is Greek in character, and partakes of burlesque. The stuff is watered down to make men's bodies weak; cf. 476. 7, 524. 8. From this point, it may be suggested, there are traces of the Prometheus legend embroidered upon the main theme. It is part of a discussion upon Pronoia. Cf. Ennius, *Epicharmus, fr.* 2: 'frigori miscet calorem atque humori aritudinem' (Varro, *Prometheus, fr.* 6). In the Promethean legend the material is clay, and one fanciful version makes him water it with tears (Themistius, *Or.* 32, p. 359 Pet.). Man's physical fragility (ll. 5-8) is a constant theme in Stoic and school discussions on Pronoia;[4] see e.g., Nemesius, *de nat. hom.* 517 C, Migne : he compensates for weakness

---

[1] Τύχην καὶ Ἐλπίδα (l. 17) are ambiguous; see 482. 32. It should have been said in the note on Fortune and Hope (vol. iii. 524) that the planet Zeus stood for Νίκη in the Hermetic Πανάρετος.

[2] Kaibel, *Inscr. graec. Siciliae et Italiae* 2413. 8; see further Dieterich. *Abraxas*, pp. 86 *sqq.*

[3] In l. 25 ζῷδια are the planets; see 122. 19.

[4] See on 516. 24; also on 482. 4 *ad fin.*

with intelligence (472. 23, and Momus' speech). 'Idem (*sc.* Epicurei) queruntur hominem morbis et immaturae morti esse subiectum, indignantur videlicet non deos esse se natos' (Lactantius, *de opif. dei*, 4. 1).

25. στασιάζειν καὶ οὐχ ὁμονοεῖν. The tone of the passage is semi-humorous, and this looks like an echo of a Platonic phrase; cf. *Rep.* 352 a.

31. The order is: Heaven their origin; the *higher* elements of which they are made, their fellow-powers in the heavens. Retain the text to πάσχομεν which ends an invocation. The souls lose their fellows and their rule, and are no longer to be 'eyes of the gods' (cf. 476. 8). We may compare the οὐρανοῦ κατόπται of Sanchuniathon (vol. ii. 114). After πάσχομεν there are perhaps three rhetorical questions: τί πλεονάζουσαι(?) ἀπὸ . . . λαμπρῶν . . . σκηνώματα; The περίχυμα is the aether.

476. 10. The Stoics attacked the Epicurean view that the sun was as great as it seemed, and this controversy had many echoes among the Neo-Platonists. There are three points here: (1) l. 8. That souls should be cramped behind fleshly eyes! Read ἄλογοι with Usener. (2) The smallness of distant objects. (3) The need for light if the eyes are to see at all. Cf. Chalcidius, *in Tim.* 237: 'sic etiam stellarum ignis exiguus adparet atque ipse sol multis partibus quam terra maior intra bipedalis diametri ambitum cernitur.' The souls' plaint is their imprisonment—the 'eyes of the gods' (474. 35) are now replaced with chinks, and the heart confines those who once swept through the upper world, so that they will hardly bear the sound of their kin, the spirits, without. In l. 16 Heeren's ὑπαί is probably right.[1] Orpheus was quoted in l. 12, and Orpheus gives the parallel here:

πᾶσι⟨ν⟩ γὰρ θνητοῖς θνηταὶ κόραι εἰσὶν ἐν ὄσσοις
μικραί, ἐπεὶ σάρκες τε καὶ ὀστέα ἐμπεφύασιν
ἀσθενέες τ᾿ ἰδέειν τὸν δὴ πάντων μεδέοντα.[2]

We have here another echo of the debate on Pronoia, concerning the feebleness of the human eye[3]; see on 474. 4 with references. The point of the quotation from Orpheus (l. 12) is that 'like sees like', and the fiery eyes are to be veiled. See further Dieterich, *Abraxas*, p. 58.

20. *sqq.* For analysis of rhythm see Norden, *Agnostos Theos*, p. 66, *Antike Kunstprosa*, p. 922.

21-2. ἰδὲ ἐπελεήσας with stop after κατέβημεν: Reitzenstein. ἐξ οἵης τιμῆς καὶ ὅσσου μήκεος ὄλβου. . . .

---

[1] Cf. Philo, *de migr. Abr.* 187-8; after his diatribe against the Chaldaeans, he bids them migrate to Charran, τὸ τῆς αἰσθήσεως χωρίον, ὃ δὴ σωματικίς ἐστιν οἶκος διανοίας: Χαρρὰν γὰρ ἑρμηνεύεται τράγλη, τρῶγλαι δὲ σύμβολα αἰσθήσεως ὀπῶν εἰσίν· ὑπὰς γὰρ καὶ φωλεοὺς τρόπον τινὰ ὀφθαλμοὺς μὲν ὁράσεως κτλ. (The codices read τόπων for ὀπῶν.) For the Chaldaeans cf. Kern, *Orphic. fragm.* 247, ll. 20 *sqq.*

[2] *Orphic. fragm.* 247, pp. 263-4. The text above is based on Aristocritus.

[3] Contrast Manilius iv. 923, and Lactantius, *de opif. dei*, 8. 2 with Lucretius iii. 359 *sqq.* on human eyes; see on 482. 4. The favourable view appears in 160. 25.

24. Reitzenstein compares Titus of Bostra I. 36, p. 23, 13: ἵνα μὴ τὸ ἑαυτοῦ ἀπεράντως ἀεὶ προσδεδεμένον τῇ ὕλῃ καὶ τιμωρούμενον διατελῇ.

33. As the text stands, with its future tenses, 476. 33–478. 21 is a formal address to souls who serve God in heaven. They are in heaven, and to heaven those who may fall can hope to return if they sin, but do not sin beyond forgiveness. This speech is parallel to the warning in 466. 15. (See summary *ad init.*) But the title λόγοι τοῦ θεοῦ (l. 32) suggests that more than one discourse is embodied in the text, and the second is a sentence (478. 23) decreeing a punishment for transgressions[1] already committed.

480. 5. Reitzenstein compares the Valentinian account of the children of Achamoth: they are more loved by the Creator—διὸ καὶ εἰς προφήτας, φασίν, ἔτασσεν αὐτοὺς καὶ ἱερεῖς καὶ βασιλεῖς (Irenaeus, i. 7. 3).

480. 6. ῥιζοτόμοι γνήσιοι. Cf. Preisendanz, *Papyri Graeci Magici* I. iv. 2969 (Paris Papyrus): παρ' Αἰγυπτίοις ἀεὶ βοτάναι λαμβάνονται οὕτως· ὁ ῥιζοτόμος καθαίρει πρότερον τὸ ἴδιον σῶμα ... ἀνασπᾷ τὸ φυτὸν ἐξ ὀνόματος ἐπικαλούμενος τὸν δαίμονα, ᾧ ἡ βοτάνη ἀνιέρωται κτλ. It may be suspected that the scribe's eye caught φιλόσοφοι γνήσιοι after he had written ῥιζοτόμοι, and that some such adjective as πιστοί was displaced; cf. σαφεῖς and ἀκριβεῖς below.

8. ἀετοί. Eagles were often confused with vultures. The περκνόπτερος was the bird of Isis. Horapollo, i. 11, describes it as ἐλεήμων. It is said to go without food while brooding ὅπως μὴ ἁρπάζῃ τοὺς τῶν θηρίων σκυμνούς, and he ascribes to it the traits of the pelican—τὸν ἑαυτῆς μηρὸν ἀνατεμοῦσα παρέχει τοῖς τέκνοις τοῦ αἵματος μεταλαμβάνειν. In l. 9 ἐκβο⟨ρ⟩ήσουσιν may be suggested. Cp. βοράω in *E.M.* and ἐκβόσκω.

482. 4 *sqq. Speech of Momus.* Momus rings the changes on ἀμεριμνία, ἀλυπία, περιεργία, ζήτησις, τόλμη. If man has the unimpeded use of his senses, there will be no limit to his audacity. He will search out the secrets of earth, sea and heavens, and may even dare to storm the heavens themselves. That man has a fragile body (474. 6) will not counterbalance his intelligence. For man that is ἄλυπος is as a god; so the passions must play him false. As will be seen, this oration is in the diatribe style. But we may perhaps go a step further, and venture a conjecture about its origin. There is some reason to believe that the material forms part of the debate upon Pronoia and man of which there are traces in Stoic literature—why is man's body so weak, his passions so powerful? what can he do with such eyes? why did Pronoia impose so great a burden upon him? There are grounds for supposing that the tale of Prometheus has been fused with this account of Hermes, the maker of man, that Prometheus-Pronoia was the hero of such a debate, and that Momus, who appears so unexpectedly here, may have appeared in the part of a critic of Prometheus. The evidence is fragmentary, but it must be considered.

---

[1] In 473. 23 πνεύματα are the 'garments' interposed between soul and body.

What Momus calls curiosity (περιεργία) [1] is Inquiry and Discovery. It is not hard to recognize in this speech an inverted panegyric upon man, recalling Manilius' climax *ratio omnia vincit*; [2] or indeed that chapter in the *Asclepius* which begins *magnum miraculum est homo* (294. 11). Those passages use material from the Stoic diatribe literature, and so does this. The same material may be used (as here) to chastise the audacity of man, or (as in *Asclepius*) to exalt his powers. The common elements are the use to which man will put his acute senses; [3] the especial power of man's eyes, the organs through which he becomes a spectator of the heavenly motions; [4] the suggestion that such speculation is, or may become, impious; [5] and the underlying doctrine that man is a microcosm, his spirit of divine origin, his body composed of the elements. [6]

It will be convenient first to cite diatribes in which the misuse of reason is chastised. In Philo, *quod omnis probus*, 65 (vi. 19. 15 Cohn) man is said to burrow into the depths of the earth and penetrate the

---

[1] Cf. 310. 23 and Philo on the Chaldaeans (*de migr. Abr.* 176 *sqq.*), esp. 187 : μεταναστάντες οὖν ἀπὸ τῆς κατ' οὐρανὸν περιεργίας ἑαυτοὺς κτλ.

[2] iv. 932. See note on 294. 11 *sqq.*

[3] 482. 4-7 ; 516. 25 (note). Cf. Cic. *de nat. deor.* ii. 140 : ' ad hanc providentiam naturae tam diligentem tamque sollertem adiungi multa possunt. . . . sunt enim ex terra homines non ut incolae atque habitatores, sed quasi spectatores superarum rerum atque caelestium. . . . sensus autem interpretes ac nuntii rerum in capite tamquam in arce mirifice ad usus necessarios et facti et conlocati sunt. nam oculi tamquam speculatores altissimum locum obtinent, . . . et aures, . . . itemque nares . . . iam gustatus, . . . tactus autem.' In l. 5 λάλον γλώσσῃ (if Heeren's reading is accepted) comes from the same Stoic teleology: *de nat. deor.* ii. 148, ' domina rerum . . . eloquendi vis, quam est praeclara quamque divina! quae primum efficit ut et ea quae ignoramus discere, et ea quae scimus alios docere possimus.' Manilius iv. 897 : ' proiecta iacent animalia cuncta | . . . et quia consilium non est, et lingua remissa. | unius inspectus rerum uiresque loquendi | ingeniumque capax.'

[4] See on 294. 11 *sqq.* ; 476. 10, and footnote above ; Manilius iv. 923 : ' nec contemne tuas quasi paruo in corpore uires ; | quod ualet, immensum est . . . | paruula sic totum peruisit pupula caelum, | quoque uident oculi, minimum est, cum maxima cernant', and ll. 905-7 quoted on 294. 11. Also Lactantius, *de opif. dei*, 8. 2. This is Stoic teleological controversy. For the other side see on 476. 10.

[5] l. 22 ; 306. 25 ; 310. 1-23 ; Manil. iv. 915 : ' atque adeo faciem caeli non inuidet orbi | ipse deus uultusque suos corpusque recludit | semper uoluendo seque ipsum inculcat et offert, | ut bene cognosci possit doceatque uidentis, | qualis eat, cogatque suas attendere leges. | ipse uocat nostros animos ad sidera mundus | nec patitur, quia non condit, sua iura latere. | quis putet esse nefas nosci, quod cernere fas est? . . . ratio omnia uincit.' Firmicus Maternus, *Math. V. praef.* 4: ' da ueniam quod siderum tuorum cursus eorumque efficacias explicare conemur ; tuum sit quod ad istam nos interpretationem nescioquod inpulit numen. pura mente . . . 6. non nos sacrilega cupiditas ad hoc studium aut profanae mentis ardor inpegit, sed animus divina inspiratione formatus totum conatus est quod didicerat explicare,' etc. (a Stoic prayer). See also note on 302. 5.

[6] See note on 294. 11.

abysses of the sea, exploring for money's sake.[1] We come nearer to
Momus' theme (περιεργία, ζήτησις) with *de migr. Abr.* 216 (ii. 311. 11
Wendl.): τί δέ ἐστι τὸ διοδεῦσαι, σκεψώμεθα· τὸ φιλομαθὲς ζητητικὸν καὶ
περίεργόν ἐστι φύσει, πανταχῆ βαδίζον ἀόκνως καὶ πανταχόσε διακῦπτον καὶ
μηδὲν ἀδιερεύνητον τῶν ὄντων μήτε σωμάτων μήτε πραγμάτων ἀπολιπεῖν δικαιοῦν.
λίχνον γὰρ ἐκτόπως θεαμάτων καὶ ἀκουσμάτων εἶναι πέφυκεν, ὡς μὴ μόνον τοῖς
ἐπιχωρίοις ἀρκεῖσθαι, ἀλλὰ καὶ τῶν ξενικῶν καὶ πορρωτάτω διῳκισμένων ἐφίεσθαι.
λέξουσι γοῦν, ὥς ἐστιν ἄτοπον ἐμπόρους μὲν καὶ καπήλους γλίσχρων ἕνεκα κερδῶν
διαβαίνειν τὰ πελάγη καὶ τὴν οἰκουμένην ἐν κύκλῳ περιιέναι ἅπασαν, μὴ θέρους,
μὴ χειμῶνα . . . μὴ νόσον σώματος, . . . μὴ χρημάτων καὶ κτημάτων καὶ τῆς ἄλλης
περιουσίας ἀσφαλῆ χρῆσιν . . . ἐμποδὼν τιθεμένους, τοῦ δὲ καλλίστου καὶ περι-
μαχήτου καὶ μόνῳ τῷ γένει τῶν ἀνθρώπων οἰκειοτάτου χάριν, σοφίας, μὴ οὐχὶ
θάλατταν μὲν ἅπασαν περαιοῦσθαι, πάντα δὲ γῆς μυχὸν ἐπέρχεσθαι, φιλοπευστοῦν-
τας εἴ πού τι καλόν ἐστιν ἰδεῖν ἢ ἀκοῦσαι, κτλ.

Momus' thesis is that Providence has not foreseen man's power. But
the same materials are an ordinary ingredient of the Stoic argument for
Providence. This background for the senses has already been indicated;
the clearest parallel for the triumphant use that the mind makes of those
senses is Cicero's continuation of the same passage (ii. 151–3): 'nos[2] e
terrae cavernis ferrum elicimus, rem ad colendos agros necessariam, nos
aeris, argenti, auri venas penitus abditas invenimus . . . arborum autem
consectione omnique materia et culta et silvestri . . . utimur. . . . Magnos
vero usus adfert ad navigia facienda, quorum cursibus subpeditantur omnes
undique ad vitam copiae; quasque res violentissimas natura genuit, earum-
que moderationem nos soli habemus, maris atque ventorum, propter
nauticarum rerum scientiam plurimisque maritimis rebus fruimur atque
utimur. . . . Nos campis, nos montibus fruimur, nostri sunt amnes, nostri
lacus, nos fruges serimus, nos arbores. . . . Quid vero? hominum ratio non
in caelum usque penetravit? Soli enim ex animantibus nos astrorum ortus,
obitus cursusque cognovimus. . . . Quae contuens animus accedit ad
cognitionem deorum, e qua oritur pietas, cui coniuncta iustitia est, reliquaeque virtutes, e quibus vita beata existit par et similis deorum, etc.
Cf. Nemesius of Emesa, 532 C Migne: τίς οὖν ἀξίως θαυμάσειε τὴν
εὐγένειαν[3] τούτου τοῦ ζῴου, τοῦ συνδέοντος ἐν ἑαυτῷ τὰ θνητὰ τοῖς ἀθανάτοις, καὶ
τὰ λογικὰ τοῖς ἀλόγοις συνάπτοντος, τοῦ φέροντος ἐν τῇ καθ' ἑαυτὸν φύσει τῆς
πάσης κτίσεως τὴν εἰκόνα, δι' ἃ καὶ μικρὸς κόσμος εἴρηται; . . . τίς δ' ἂν ἐξειπεῖν
δύναιτο τὰ τούτου τοῦ ζῴου πλεονεκτήματα; πελάγη διαβαίνει, οὐρανὸν
ἐμβατεύει τῇ θεωρίᾳ, ἀστέρων κίνησιν καὶ διαστήματα καὶ μέτρα κατανοεῖ, γῆν
καρποῦται καὶ θάλασσαν, θηρίων καὶ κητῶν καταφρονεῖ, πᾶσαν ἐπιστήμην καὶ
τέχνην καὶ μέθοδον κατορθοῖ.[4]

[1] This is the theme *auri sacra fames*. The same type of reproach is used in
diatribe against luxury: Philo, *de agric.* 23–5. Cf. ll. 6–7, 27.

[2] Cf. also 294. 22; 300. 20. Manilius, iv. 904–10.   [3] Cf. 486. 13.

[4] The comparison between Cicero and Nemesius has been made by Jaeger, who
derives this exaltation of man over the brute from Posidonius. I should add that

Here man is as a god, compared with the animals; that he should be so near a god is Momus' grievance. If we retain the order of the traditional text, the speech may be interpreted as a prophecy of man's ζήτησις. If man is ἄλυπος, no secret will be hidden from his thoughts.[1] He will pry into the properties of plants[2] and stones, and will dissect bodies, animal and even human,[3] to explore he will cut down virgin[4] forests and press to the very bounds of the sea.[5]

The heavens: men will *observe* the orbits.[6] But a final audacity: they

he has suggested the *Antigone* as the source of Posidonius' inspiration (*Nemesios*, pp. 134–5). One might also compare Boethus *apud* Euseb. *Pr. ev.* xi. 28. 13. and Philo, *de opif. mundi*, 69 (i. 23. 7 Cohn): τρόπον τινὰ θεὸς ὤν κτλ.

[1] Εἰ δὲ καὶ ποικιλομήτης γράφοιτο (ὁ Προμηθεύς), σημαίνει τὸν ποικίλας εἰληχότα νοήσεις, ἃς δωρεῖται καὶ ταῖς ἀνθρωπίναις ψυχαῖς εἰς τὸ σῶμα πεσούσαις, ὅτι τὸ προνοητικὸν τῶν ἀνθρώπων κρύπτει τὸν πλοῦτον, ἀνθ' ὅτου Πρ. αὐτὸν ἠπάτησεν (Proclus *ap.* Schol. in Hesiod. Gaisford, *Poet. min. Graec.* iii. 65).

[2] Retain ποιότητα⟨s⟩ . . . χυλῶν (l. 14). Extraction of juices is the point.

[3] Again diatribe material; see Tertullian in vol. iii. 540.

[4] αὐτοφυεῖς (l. 18). Cf. *silvestri* in Cicero above.

[5] ll. 17–19. Text confused: possibly some such phrase as μέχρι καὶ τῶν περ⟨άτ⟩ων τῆς θαλάσσης. Cf. πλεῖται δ' ἡ θάλασσα μέχρι περάτων (Musonius *ap.* Stob. iii 528. 2 Wachsm.). In the context it seems possible that l. 20 (τίς . . . ὑπάρχει) may refer to the second way of violating the sea—by penetrating forbidden depths. So Philo, *quod omnis probus*, 66: θεοπλαστοῦσα δὲ ἡ κενὴ δόξα τὸν τῦφον ἄχρι καὶ βυθοῦ κατέβη θαλάσσης διερευνωμένη, μή τι τῶν πρὸς αἴσθησιν ἀφανὲς ἐναπόκειταί που καλόν. For ἀδύτων cf. 486. 20.

[6] Cf. Cic. above and Manilius iv. 905: 'imposuitque uiam ponto, stetit unus in arcem | erectus capitis uictorque ad sidera mittit | sidereos oculos propiusque adspectat Olympum | inquiritque Iouem' etc. In l. 22 τὰ ⟨μετέωρα⟩ μέχρις ἄνω Reitzenstein. ll. 24–5 are puzzling. Reitzenstein compares Horace, *Odes*, i. 3. 36: 'perrupit Acheronta Herculeus labor.' The ode is in the same tradition; there are plain correspondences; and the common theme is *audacia*. But Horace's theme is *invasion* of the elements in turn; the *nefas* for Momus is intellectual *curiosity* culminating in an assault on the heavens. The motive is not quite the same, though the actions following from it coincide so far. It may be questioned whether the violation of the air by Daedalus (i. 3. 34) does answer to the discovery of the orbits by observation. R. presupposes a philosophical source where one wrests the secret of the heavens by flight, and another makes a descent to Hades. This may be so, but Momus insists upon the weapon man possesses in his unimpeded senses (cf. 294. 24): he may ultimately regain heaven because knowledge is power and the soul is not sufficiently handicapped. The attractive suggestion about a κατάβασις therefore remains uncertain. Though the mining arts (Scott) are commonly mentioned in such diatribes, the changes needed seem too great for an allusion to them to be likely here. The sequence may be: they will try to find out the order of the heavens. (Then perhaps a marginal note ἔτι . . . ἔσχατος). ἀλλὰ καὶ τούτων (sc. τῶν μετεώρων) . . . τῷ θέλειν ἐρευνήσουσι. θέλειν may be right; but it is θεωρεῖν that will bare the secrets of the heavens; cf. the pointed reference to truth in l. 26. The parallel in Nemesius is οὐρανὸν ἐμβατεύει τῇ θεωρίᾳ. In l. 27 τρυφήσωσιν refers to the ὕβρις that follows a life free from care,

will arm to recover their lost seats (ll. 27-9) unless they are crippled—Horace's climax too, *caelum ipsum petimus*. The souls (as spirits) have already rebelled (470. 20; cf. 486. 11).

The remedy is to burden the soul with the irrational passions and the body with disease—a nemesis on man's intelligence and audacity.

It may be suspected that the background of this section is a teleological debate on Πρόνοια, and that elements from the legend of Prometheus, which played a part in that debate, have been transferred to the Egyptian Hermes, who not only is ταμίας (as one would expect) but has the epithet προνοητής (484. 10) appropriate to Prometheus.[1] A problem so complex cannot be analysed at the end of this note. But it may be suggested that Momus' speech has for its background a criticism of Πρόνοια, directed to the familiar topic of man's helplessness and his intelligence.[2] The whole discussion justifies the imposition of εἱμαρμένη upon man, and later explains how the gifts of civilization were bestowed. (It is unnecessary to ask whether the narrative is self-consistent: there are the elements.) Hermes is the maker of man, Νοῦς,[3] and (to judge from 484. 10) Πρόνοια. Prometheus the maker became in Stoic allegory Προμηθεύς-Πρόνοια and Νοῦς, as the poets long before had written.[4] The Stoic debates justifying

and ἐπὶ καὶ τὰ στοιχεῖα (28) should be taken of the stars (294. 22). For l. 29 cf. 478. 25. l. 31 χρεοκοπεῖσθαι is used of an elephant docked of half his rations (Plut. *de soll. anim.* 968 D).

The style of ll. 29-484. 3 should be noted, a series of sentences beginning with imperatives in asyndeton; see on 486. 29. The text can be construed as it stands, but it is possible that πλάνης (πλαῦ) (l. 32) indicates πλανάτωσαν . . . ἔρωτες· νεμέσθωσαν ἐλπίδες . . . βαρείτω πυρετός.

[1] Hermes is associated with Prometheus in the Protagorean myth. He plays the part of civilizer ascribed to Hermes at the end of this Excerpt. For the connexion of Isis with both in this role, compare Plutarch, *de Is. et Os.* 352 A: ἔτι πολλοὶ μὲν Ἑρμοῦ, πολλοὶ δὲ Προμηθέως ἱστορήκασιν αὐτὴν θυγατέρα· ὧν τὸν μὲν ἕτερον σοφίας καὶ προνοίας, Ἑρμῆν δὲ γραμματικῆς καὶ μουσικῆς εὑρετὴν νομίζομεν διὸ καὶ τῶν ἐν Ἑρμοῦ πόλει Μουσῶν τὴν προτέραν Ἶσιν ἅμα καὶ Δικαιοσύνην καλοῦσι, σοφὴν οὖσαν . . . καὶ δεικνύουσαν τὰ θεῖα κτλ.

[2] Stoic teleology *passim*. The point is that man's mind is godlike, but the animals surpass him in strength. For our purpose the best reference is Dion, *Or.* vi. 21-31, Cynic-Stoic allegorization of the Prometheus legend. See on 516. 24, also on 474. 4, 476. 10.

[3] 472. 4; Zosimus, vol. iv. 107. 21 (Prometheus); *ib.* 109. 15. Pr. is the ἴδιος νοῦς of Epimetheus (the earthly Adam).

[4] Material in Roscher, *Lexicon*, s.v. Prometheus; also Norden, *Beiträge*, pp. 428-40, 453-7. The connexion may be illustrated by the first three lines of p. 484. For l. 2: Dion, *Or.* vi. 29 (result of Prometheus' gift): διώκοντας οὖν τὸ ἡδὺ ἐξ ἅπαντος ἀεὶ ζῆν ἀηδέστερον καὶ ἐπιπονώτερον, καὶ δοκοῦντας προμηθεῖσθαι σφῶν αὐτῶν κάκιστα ἀπόλλυσθαι διὰ τὴν πολλὴν ἐπιμέλειάν τε καὶ προμήθειαν. The ἐπίπονος βίος is the catchword of these mythologizing discussions of Providence that start from Hesiod's text. (Cf. Aesch. *P. V.* 250, where the sense of 'blind hopes' is, however, nearer to 488. 1.) But the reference to fever (l. 3) is perhaps more

Providence confront him with a critic. Norden[1] has strikingly analysed Varro's *Prometheus*, where the scanty fragments of such a debate survive. Now Momus, whose presence in this galley is a surprise, appears in Aesop as the critic of Prometheus' handiwork—the secrets of men's hearts, he says, should be legible.[2] The encounter is at the level of fable. But it is evident from the Proclus-Tzetzes Scholia to Hesiod[3] that the tale of Prometheus was represented as a struggle with Εἱμαρμένη, which is Zeus, and which hid the 'human life'.[4] The justification offered by Proclus is that Zeus imposed labour and suffering on men so that they might hate the place of their birth and turn to their Father's hall and to the divine life from which they fell.[5] This is a twist in the opposite sense from Momus' desire. It answers rather to the Father's promise in 478. 15. For evidence that the Prometheus legend found its way into Hermetic tradition and was fused with other elements we may refer to Zosimus.[6]

Postscript. The above note was drafted before I could procure Reitzenstein's *Göttin Psyche*, with its illuminating suggestions. In brief: he reconstructs the council of the gods (484. 22) from Lucian; the gods make animals from the mixture; then Hermes, who must water his mixture,

striking evidence. Reitzenstein happily compares Horace, *Od.* i. 3. 30: 'macies et nova febrium | terris incubuit cohors.' Fever was the counterpoise imposed after the theft of fire. (The Scholiast adds that Pr. stole the fire to animate his statues; see on 474. 4.) Can we say that Horace and the Hermetist draw not only from one tradition, but from one legend? Servius, *in Eclog.* 6. 42: 'Pr. . . . post factos a se homines . . . ignem . . . hominibus indicavit, ob quam causam irati dii duo mala immiserunt terris, febres et mulieres (*codd.* morbos), sicut et Sappho et Hesiodus memorant'. Translate: 'Let fever bear them down, that their hearts may fail and that they may curb desire'. Even desire shall fail.

[1] *Beiträge.* The eyes (cf. 482. 5) and the arts are named. For the former see also 476. 16, and Manilius (quoted above, p. 456, n. 4). See also Phaedrus, iv. 15 and 16. I may note an apparent fragment of a debate in Zosimus, 105. 16 above; see note in *Addenda*.

[2] Aesop, 155 H; this answers to Babrius quoted in vol. iii. 536. It should be added that Momus appears in Jewish literature (Zielinski, who refers to Hausrath, *Neutestamentl. Zeitg.* iii. 388).

[3] e.g. Gaisford, *Poet. min. graec.* iii, pp. 63 *sqq.*

[4] Zeus is explicitly identified with εἱμαρμένη in Zosimus (105. 14–21 above, see note). This brings the allegory into the circle of the Anthropos myth.

[5] *op. cit.,* p. 65. The phrase αἱ πεσοῦσαι ψυχαί recurs. In a version given by Joannes Diaconus, *Allcg. in Theogoniam,* Gaisf. *P.M.G.* iii. 459, Prometheus is the foreseer, Menoetius the irrational part of the soul, Epimetheus the παθητικὸς νοῦς, and so forth. In Zosimus Epimetheus is the earthly Adam (iv. 109. 13). Cf. Proclus, *In remp.* ii. 53. The ultimate origin of all this is Plato, *Protagoras,* 320 C *sqq.*

[6] *loc. cit.;* see note. This also bears on the relation of mind and body and Fate. For 'Chaldaic' evidence Proclus, *Theol. Plat.* 297. 34, τὸν Πρ. . . . προνοοῦντα τῆς λογικῆς ἡμῶν ζωῆς: reference to the 'baptism' of the flesh. See Kroll, *Or. Chald.,* p. 52, for Hermetic parallels.

makes men weaker than animals. In compensation he gives them the power of discussion. The criticism of Momus represents world-weary pessimism—are men better for their wisdom, or is it folly? (Cf. Horace, *Odes*, i. 3). If this assumption is right in principle, this making of the human race and animals should take place after the ordering of the material world, whereas the creation of Anthropos must be prior. But the redactor had before him a pure Greek source, since the many souls come from the one. So he cannot use the conception of Anthropos, and the two accounts cannot be reconciled.

Without entering here on the question of structure, it may be said that the account of the *ensomatosis* shows marked burlesque characteristics, and that R. must be right in positing a background of Stoic allegorical-mythical declamation; I have tried to give some of the evidence. But if we admit a common tradition, is the mood of Momus that of Horace? It is inverted praise of εὕρεσις, leading up to a justification of Εἱμαρμένη. Hermes knows better than to leave man unimpeded (cf. 480. 1–2). He appears in a double role, first as the forger of the controlling instrument, and then as the ' Prometheus ' who brings the gifts of civilization whereby man can overcome Fate.[1] See also Introduction to this volume, III.

484. 9. The divine Pneuma that surrounds the Cosmos,[2] not the atmosphere about the earth; Adrasteia is coupled with Hermes; appropriately here, because she chastises the overweening.[3] Cf. *Exc.* VII. For the secret engine Reitzenstein refers to the rule of Hermes and Moira in the Cosmogony published by Dieterich in *Abraxas* : Μοῖρα κατέχουσα ζυγόν. This is attractive, but the instrument should be Fate, to give meaning to l. 10. If my interpretation of Momus' speech is right, his demand for πάθη has as a background the debate about εἱμαρμένη.

22. On Bousset's analysis, this belongs to the *Grundschrift*. God's rule is still ἀνεπίγνωστος, and the sun and moon uncreated (458. 4). B. interprets this as an Egyptian cosmogony.[4] In the beginning Nut, the goddess of heaven, was not separated from the earth-god, Keb.[5] The Father Shu raised Nut aloft. This is the διάστασις τῆς μελαίνης ἐνώσεως

---

[1] The end of Momus' speech may be illustrated by Vettius Valens, 219. 26 (Kroll) : Νενομοθέτηκε γὰρ ἡ εἱμαρμένη ἑκάστῳ ἀμετάθετον ἀποτελεσμάτων ἐνέργειαν· περιτειχίσασα πολλαῖς αἰτίαις ἀγαθῶν τε καὶ κακῶν, δι' ὧν αὐτογέννητοι ὑπουργοὶ δύο θεαὶ φερόμεναι, Ἐλπίς τε καὶ Τύχη, διακρατοῦσι τὸν βίον καὶ μετὰ ἀνάγκης καὶ πλάνης φέρειν ἐῶσι τὰ νενομοθετημένα.... ἡ δὲ ... διὰ παντὸς ἀποκεκρυμμένη πανταχοῦ λεληθότως ἐπιβαίνει καὶ προσμειδιῶσα πᾶσιν οἷά τε κύλαξ πολλὰς αἱρέσεις ἀγαθῶν ἐπιδείκνυσιν ὧν οὐκ ἔστι λαβέσθαι· πλανῶσα δὲ τοὺς πλείστους διακρατεῖ· οἱ δὲ ... ἐλπίζοντες ἃ θέλουσι πιστεύουσιν. ἐπιτυγχάνουσι δὲ ἃ μὴ προσδοκῶσιν κτλ.

[2] Cf. *Fr.* 23. With φύσις τοῦ περιέχοντος compare φ. τοῦ παντός, 436. 18.

[3] L 11 ταγῆς Heeren. But perhaps ἐπόη[τε]τειρα τοίνυν ⟨καὶ⟩ ταγή[s] ἔσται τῶν ὅλων—two nouns as in l. 10 and 478. 27.

[4] P.-W. 11. 1389. 7.

[5] Isis is represented as the deity who separated earth from heaven in the Andros and Cyme Hymns. See on 492. 1.

(484. 33). Underneath lies Ḳeb (κραδαινομένη γῆ). B. compares the ἰσοστασίας χεῖρας of 486. 3 to the action of Shu in raising Nut with his mighty hands. He is thus so far in agreement with Scott that § 2 belongs to the same cycle of ideas. For the action of the sun on the quivering earth compare *Fr.* 31.

486. 10. καὶ ἀγνωσία. Wachsmuth; cf. 458. 11. This begins the last section of the fragment. On the face of it this is an account of the primitive κατάστασις, before men were civilized. It is an ἄγριος πολίτεια (l. 24), inhabited by an ἄθεος ἀπανθρώπων χορός (488. 31; see note), where the stronger rule and slaughter and enslave, and where sacrilege is rife. It is perhaps worth noticing that the style of § 53 is the λέξις εἰρομένη appropriate to such narratives.[1] Possible Greek elements are: (1) The reign of Βία.[2] (2) The origin of civilization from χρεία.[3] (3) The account of the benefits conferred by the civilizers—religion, law, food and shelter, the sciences—contains only what Isis and Osiris *taught*; there is no trace of Isis the supreme goddess, as in the *Hymn* quoted below.

The state of the text renders the interpretation of § 53 doubtful, and (if Bousset is right) it is in any case ambiguous. Let us see the elements that can be explained on the assumption that a πρώτη κατάστασις is described. First, εὐγενείας (l. 13) is at least consistent with the theory of imprisoned *souls*.[4] Then the rule of Force, as we shall see, belongs to a well-marked Hellenic tradition. But the use of ἀγνωσία, the enmity with star-gods, and the dubious sentence about using men as instruments at least raise the suspicion of another element. Bousset argues that the *Grundschrift* had a tale of fallen *spirits* or daemons, and that this was worked over by some one who used the Platonic myth of the *souls* imprisoned in the flesh.[5] With the first element he connects the lore taught

---

[1] καὶ ἀγνωσία . . . καὶ . . . καὶ . . . καί. See Norden, *Agn. Th.*, *Anh.* vii.

[2] For detailed references see below. Note especially the Orphic material in Kern, *Orphic. Fragm.* 292, and compare 476. 12–16 above.

[3] 300. 22; 486. 37; 492. 1 and notes *ad loca*. This strand of theory goes back ultimately to Democritus. For detail see e.g. Jaeger, *Nemesios*, pp. 123–5; K. Reinhardt, *Hermes*, 1912, pp. 492 *sqq*.

[4] See Nemesius quoted on 482. 4; also 533 B, εἰδότες οὖν ὅσης εὐγενείας μετειλήφαμεν καὶ ὅτι φυτόν ἐσμεν οὐράνιον. This is Platonic-Stoic.

[5] *Archiv*, 1915, p. 134; P.-W. ii. 1389–90. The general lines of his evidence are in brief as follows. He begins from a discussion of the dualist demonology in Porphyry, *de abst.* ii. 36–43 (see on 344. 3, iv. 7. 8). Then he brings in Ps.-Clement, *Homiliae* VIII–IX, *Recognitiones* IV, which contain a similar demonology, if the additions of Jewish and Christian redactors are removed. The centre of the story, it is argued, is Zoroaster, who was sent to fight the fallen daemons, limited their power on earth, and ushered in the Golden Age (*Hom.* VIII. 17, IX. 3; see *Hauptprobleme*, 135–54). The support for this view lies (1) in Persian tradition, (2) in our Excerpt (fall, emulaton with gods, pollution and complaint of Elements, and regeneration by Osiris and Isis = Zoroaster), (3) the Book of Enoch, where there is no Flood as in the Jewish additions to Ps.-Clement, but a Golden Age. How Isis

by Hermes in 492. 27, that the 'continent' was filled with daemons. With this compare the *Book of Enoch* (cc. 6-7, 18, 21), where the star-spirits are punished for disobedience. On this view the emulation with the gods can be accounted for—it is consistent with the conduct of the spirits before they fell (470. 20–2, 25–7)—and their using men as tools has its parallel in Ps.-Clement.[1] I venture to add the evidence of *Asclepius* (344. 3 note), which describes the reign of *nocentes angeli*: the tale is there combined with the Stoic theory of a *senectus mundi*, as here with a Greek account of the primitive barbarism. Further, it may not be with-out significance that if there is no direct connexion between the legend of Zoroaster and of Isis and Osiris here, Prometheus is connected with Zoroaster in the Hermetic material given by Zosimus,[2] and the Prometheus legend has influenced the last part of the *Kore Kosmu*, if my hypothesis is right. See further, Introduction III in this volume.

In similar accounts of primitive barbarism[3] cannibalism accompanied the reign of Force. Here the major sin is pollution.[4] Hence (l. 19) ἔκαιον refers to the pollution of Fire,[5] and the ἄδυτα must be the waters into which living and dead are flung.[6]

22. Bousset compares the complaint of the Elements[7] with that of the four archangels in the *Book of Enoch*, c. 9.[8] Reitzenstein refers to the complaint of Aion and the sending of Dionysus the comforter (Nonnus, vii. *init.*); also the account of Anthropos in Hippol. *Ref.* v. 8. 22 : παῦε, παῦε τὴν ἀσυμφωνίαν τοῦ κόσμου καὶ ποίησον εἰρήνην τοῖς μακράν. See *Göttin Psyche*, p. 81, and Introduction III in this volume.

29–32. Retain the text, apart from the transposition of σεβαστόν and κρυπτόν. Nock compares *Pap. Leid.* W, vii. 11 γενέσθαι ἐν ὀνόμασι πάντων κτισμάτων. Identification of the deity and his name. See *J.T.S.* XXVI 176 *sqq.*, and *J.E.A.* XI. p. 137. 1.

Upon κρυπτόν naturally follows ἀνάτειλον (l. 37),[9] metaphor proper to φῶς. Read μύησον εἰρήνῃ· χάρισαι κτλ. For the dative cf. 482. 26 and Suidas,

and Osiris and the Zoroaster legend came to be connected cannot be said. The whole article should be consulted.

[1] *Hom.* IX. 10. The daemons enter men's bodies and use them as ὑπουργοῦντα ὄργανα.

[2] pp. 105-7 above.   [3] See below on 490. 23, 492. 3, 10.

[4] *Hom.* VIII. 17 : ἐπὶ δὲ τῇ πολλῇ τῶν αἱμάτων ῥύσει ὁ καθαρὸς ἀὴρ ἀκαθάρτῳ ἀναθυμιάσει μανθείς κτλ.

[5] Cf. 488. 10 ; Pomponius Mela, i. 9. 57, 'nec cremare aut fodere fas est, verum arte medicatos inter penetralia conlocant.'

[6] See 340. 27–30 ; 488. 23 ; 482. 20.

[7] For the cult of the Elements see *Wisdom of Solomon*, xiii. 2 ; Dieterich, *Abraxas*, p. 61 ; Bréhier, *Philon*, p. 162 ; note on 382. 8.

[8] Also *Hom.* VIII. 16–17.

[9] τοῦτον μὲν γὰρ πρεσβύτερον υἱὸν ὁ τῶν ὅλων ἀνέτειλε πατήρ (Philo, *de cont. ling.* 63).

s.v. μητραγύρτης : ἐμύει τὰς γυναῖκας τῇ Μητρὶ τῶν θεῶν. l. 39. χρησμούς : oracles and dreams are connected. The sequence is: ἀνάκλησις 'identifying the deity and his name'; petition to the deity to reveal himself, with consequences—peace, the comfort of hopes [1] that are no longer illusions, justice, penalties, reverence for the oath,[2] sacrifices pleasing to the deity in return; complaint against pollution that perverts a holy element from its function.[3]

488. 19. Retain the ἀνάκλησις, comparing 486. 29, and 488. 26, and reading αὐτογενές (see *L. and S., s.v.*); ἀεὶ ῥεῖθρα ποτάμων (l. 21), elevated language; cf. τενόντων, 490. 3.

26. Earth's speech. (1) ll. 26-30 ἀνάκλησις appropriate to the Maker of the Elements. (2) ll. 31-490. 7. *Complaint*: men are brutal and godless because they defile the earth that gives all. Retain text, but read ἀπανθρώπων. Compare 490. 7 with l. 32: she gives all—and receives the slain (l. 34), a pretty recompense! In l. 35 ὁ ἐπὶ may be a false start for ὁ ἐπιχθόνιος.[4] Construe—the earth, abounding in everything, lacks yet one thing—God (cf. l. 32). Hence, with no divine vengeance to fear, men are killed [5] all over earth's broad plains and she reeks with their humours. (3) 490. 9-13 *Petition*. I contain what I should not ; give me God besides the abundance I produce (answering to 488. 32, 490. 1), or at least some effluence from him since God himself is too great.[6] (4) ll. 11-13 *Ground of plea*. It is the all-giving Mother who speaks, and to defile her is the last impiety. Cf. 486. 5-6.

In short, the Elements plead for a revelation and the civilized way of life in place of brutishness and pollution.

490. 19. ἀπόρροια. So *Wisdom of Solomon*, vii. 25 (of Sophia).

490. 23. διὰ γένους. There is deep corruption here. What is asked for is in the first place Justice (488. 2), and Law is to be established in place of Force. If we examine the usual language about Δίκη, e.g. in Exc. VII and Philo *passim*, and compare this passage, it seems not impossible that Δίκη is the 'watcher' and 'follower' here too. If so, γένους may conceal a particle and the structure may have been changed to give the verb a subject. Should we read : ἀκολουθήσει ⟨Δίκη⟩ διανέμουσα μίσθους ἐπαξίους—haplography, or simply Δίκη νέμουσα? Compare 488. 2-3, 498. 3. In Hellenistic writings Isis is identified with Δίκη. See Roscher,

---

[1] 488. 1 ; cf. 482. 32.

[2] 492. 18.

[3] For the series of imperatives ἀνάτειλον . . . φοβείσθωσαν cf. 482. 29 *sqq.*, and Norden, *Agn. Theos*, Anhang vi.

[4] Meineke connects ὑπὸ πάντων (as he emends) with the previous sentence. But (1) πάντων is needed with πεπληρωμένος—that is the keynote of earth's plea ; (2) the brevity of ἀτιμοῦμαι δὲ ἤδη answers to the style of the other complaints, 488. 10, 14 (reading μαίνομαι).

[5] καταπίπτουσι (490. 4) is understood as passive.

[6] l. 7 colon after χωρεῖν. ll. 9-10 dash before and after οὐ . . . ὑπομένω.

Lexicon, ii. 460. The theory of the primitive κατάστασις without Δίκη is found in the Orphics. Cf. Sext. Emp., *adv. math.* ii. 31 :

ἦν χρόνος, ἡνίκα φῶτες ἀπ' ἀλλήλων βίον εἶχον
σαρκοδακῆ, κρείσσων δὲ τὸν ἥττονα φῶτα δάϊξεν.

. . . ἐπιτέτραπται "ἔσθειν (ἐσθέμεν Clem.) ἀλλήλους,
ἐπεὶ οὐ δίκη ἐστὶ μετ' αὐτοῖς." See Kern, *Orph. fr.* 292.

492. I. Repetition of the thesis that *need* was the origin of civilization.[1] See on 486. 10. Osiris and Isis bestowed *all* the gifts of civilization, not simply religion, and were instructed by Hermes. This is supported by the parallel documents and by the general nature of the theory pre-supposed. Further, the style of this *aretalogia—parallelismus membrorum* —requires the presence of certain sections in the order given by the MSS.[2] In addition to the references given in vol. iii. 550, the *Hymn to Isis* recently discovered at Cyme in Aeolis, in the ruins of an Egyptian sanctuary, by Professor Salač of Prague must be mentioned.[3] The text has been republished by Professor Roussel, who devotes an article to it.[4] There is, as he affirms, a common basis for the inscriptions of Andros, Ios, and Cyme[5]. Our aretalogy, like the prose epitome in Diodorus i. 27, considers Isis only as a benefactor, not as the supreme goddess—a point of some weight. In the following notes *H. I.* refers to the Cyme version.

3. τὸ . . . ἄγριον.[6] *H. I.* (19) Ἐγὼ μετὰ τοῦ ἀδελφοῦ Ὀσίριδος τὰς ἀνθρωποφαγίας ἔπαυσα . . . (23) Ἐγὼ τυράννων ἀρχὰς κατέλυσα.—(24) Ἐγὼ φόνους ἔπαυσα. Cf. vol. iii, p. 550. The cannibalism has been softened into mutual slaughter in our text.[7] See note on l. 10 below.

9. τεμένη. *H. I.* 22 Ἐγὼ τεμένη θεῶν ἱδρυσάμην.

10. νόμους. Isis is above all θεσμοφόρα, θεσμοθέτις. See on 490. 23.

---

[1] Read τῷ[ν]?

[2] In l. 3 this explains the repeated οὗτοι, and necessitates the parallel aorists. In ll. 9–10 νόμους answers by position to τεμένη, and οὗτοι (Meineke) should replace αὐτοί. Keep the text of ll. 15–18 for the same reason. On parallelism see Norden, *Agnostos Theos*, Anhang v.

[3] *Bulletin d. corresp. hellén.* 1927, pp. 378 *sqq.*

[4] *Rev. d. études grecques*, 1929, pp. 137 *sqq.*

[5] The Ios inscription, in worse condition, answers fairly closely to lines 1–32 (less 5 and 6) of the hymn, which contains 54 lines. Roussel's judgement is that the original of all the texts is not later than the first century B.C., and may be earlier. For an attempt to carry back the Ios inscription to the time of Ptolemy Soter, see Dittenberger, *Sylloge*[3], 1267.

The various documents have now been brought together and annotated by W. Peek, *Der Isishymnus von Andros* (1930).

[6] Possibly ⟨τοῦ ὁ⟩σίου τὸν βίον ἐπλήρωσαν . . .

[7] The lines quoted enclose three sentences referring to the worship of the Gods (μυήσεις, τεμένη, ἀγάλματα), as if the institution of religion had ended anthro-pophagy, tyrants, and slaughter. This, *mutatis mutandis*, is the Hermetic theme.

H. I. 2 Ἐγὼ νόμους ἀνθρώποις ἐθέμην. Here 'a way of life' may be included, as the following words suggest. Moschion. *ap.* Stob. *Floril.* 1. 8. 38:

ἦν δ' ὁ μὲν Νόμος | ταπεινός, ἡ βία δὲ σύνθρονος Διί, | ὁ δ' ἀσθενὴς ἦν τῶν ἀμεινόνων βορά, | τόθ' εὑρέθη μὲν καρπὸς ἡμέρου τροφῆς | ... ἔτευξαν οἴκους· καὶ τὸν ἠγριωμένον βίον | εἰς ἥμερον δίαιταν ἤγαγον βίου.

τροφὰς καὶ σκέπην. *H. I.* 5 Ἐγώ εἰμι ἡ καρπὸν ἀνθρώποις εὑροῦσα. Diodorus, i. 14. 27; Servius, *in Georg.* i. 19; Tibullus, i. 3. 26–9. This is the decisive step in material civilization—see Moschion above.[1] The diatribe literature against luxury links τροφή and σκέπη; the latter includes clothing and houses—Philo, *de praem. et poen.* 98: πλοῦτος δὲ ὁ μὲν τῆς φύσεως εὐτελής ἐστι τροφὴ καὶ σκέπη· τροφὴ μέν. ... σκέπης δὲ διττὸν εἶδος, τὸ μὲν ἀμπεχόνη, τὸ δὲ οἰκία. The Clementine parallel (*Hom.* VIII. 17) gives first flesh-eating and then cannibalism as a mark of the reign of the daemons: τῶν δὲ ἀλόγων ζῴων τότε ἐπιλιπόντων, οἱ νόθοι ἄνθρωποι καὶ ἀνθρωπίνων σαρκῶν ἐγεύσαντο. See also p. 189. 27 above.

12. *H. I.* 1: Εἶσις ἐγώ εἰμι ἡ τύραννος πάσης χώρας καὶ ἐπαιδεύθην ὑπ[ὸ] Ἑρμοῦ καὶ γράμματα εὗρον μετὰ Ἑρμοῦ, τά τε ἱερὰ καὶ τὰ δημόσια γράμματα, ἵνα μὴ ἐν τοῖς αὐτοῖς πάντα γράφηται. Diod. i. 27: ἡ παιδευθεῖσα ὑπὸ Ἑρμοῦ. Andros Inscr. 10 (Kaibel, *Epigrammata*, 1028).

The form of this paragraph may indicate an earlier stage of the aretalogy, as a prophecy.

15. Institutions as well as laws. *H. I.* 14 Ἐγὼ τὸ δίκαιον ἰσχυρὸν ἐποίησα. Cf. 1, 26, 32, 33. Εὐνομία supplants the παρανομία (490. 3) of the state of barbarism (486. 24). Ll. 15–18 show that the prayer 488. 2–5 is answered. Cf. 490. 18–23. Isis was Δικαιοσύνη; see Plut. *de Is. et Osir.* 352A (quoted above, p. 459, n. 1).

17. The sequence ἀρχηγέται γενόμενοι ... εἰσηγάγοντο balances πρῶτοι δείξαντες ... ἐπλήρωσαν above. On the god see Hirzel, *Der Eid*, p. 145. *H. I.* 31 Ἐγὼ ὅρκου φοβερώτερον οὐθὲν ἐποίησα.

20. This section is ritually important, because the chief complaint of the Elements was that the dead polluted them. Cf. Moschion, *loc. cit.*:

κἀκ τοῦδε τοὺς θανόντας ὥρισεν νόμος
τύμβοις καλύπτειν, κἀπιμοιρᾶσθαι κόνιν
νεκροῖς ἀθάπτοις, μηδ' ἐν ὀφθαλμοῖς ἐᾶν
τῆς πρόσθε θοίνης μνημόνευμα δυσσεβοῦς.

An Egyptian could not mention burial. Retain the text. In l. 21 ἐδίδαξαν περιστέλλειν answers to ἐργάζεται λειποθυμίας (l. 26).

23. ὑποστρέφειν is used of a recurrent disease; if we attach the sense of recurrence to φιλυποστρόφου, the sentence should mean that while the life-breath normally returns to the body, its delay causes swoons that do not admit (ἔχουσας) of recovery. See L. and S., *s.v.* ἀνακτάομαι.

27. The existence of daemons was a revelation to the primitive

---

[1] In our text there is no mention of cannibalism, as in the other documents, unless the complaint of Fire contains a hint of it, which is doubtful.

barbarism. On Bousset's theory, the sentence is evidence that the *Grundschrift* dealt with a fall of disobedient πνεύματα ; see Introduction III to this volume.

29. νομοθεσίας— used of the laws of the Cosmos in Vettius Valens, p. 343. 33 Kroll. So νόμος in Philo. The last great gift to civilization was the arts and sciences, especially the lore of astrology, of which Isis and Osiris were the sole (l. 29) repositories.

494. 1. The presupposition of astrology is συμπάθεια between heavenly and earthly things (cf. 468. 15, 452. 12). προσκαθέτους: the phrase κατὰ κάθετον is used of a κλίμα directly beneath a given zone in the heavens— e.g. ἔτι μὴν καὶ τὴν γῆν εἰς δώδεκα κλίματα διῃρῆσθαι φάσκοντες, καὶ καθ' ἓν ἕκαστον κλίμα, ἀνὰ μίαν δύναμιν ἐκ τῶν οὐρανῶν κατὰ κάθετον ὑποδεχομένην καὶ ὡμοιωμένα τίκτουσαν τέκνα τῇ καταπεμπούσῃ [κατὰ] τὴν ἀπόρροιαν δυνάμει, τύπον ⟨εἶναι⟩ τῆς ἄνω δωδεκάδος (Hippolytus, *Refutatio*, vi. 53, of the Valentinians). An ἱεροποιία that is προσκάθετος to a given star or constellation is presumably in the most favourable position for receiving its influences. For κλίματα see on 500. 26 *sqq.*

4-5. Corruption makes the meaning uncertain. To preserve the parallelism it may be suggested that the text read οὗτοι ... ὡς ... ὄντων· ⟨οὗτοι ...⟩ ἵνα ... σῶμα. Isis, as Δικαιοσύνη, is (ἡ) δεικνύουσα τὰ θεῖα τοῖς ἀληθῶς καὶ δικαίως ἱεραφόροις καὶ ἱεροστόλοις προσαγορευομένοις. οὗτοι δ' εἰσὶν οἱ τὸν ἱερὸν λόγον περὶ θεῶν ... ἐν τῇ ψυχῇ φέροντες ὥσπερ ἐν κίστῃ καὶ περιστέλλοντες κτλ. (Plut. *de Is. et Osir.* 352 B), There may be some reference to the sacred books, which ensured the continuity of knowledge.[1]

8. φασὶ δ' Αἰγύπτιοι τὴν Ἶσιν φαρμάκων τε πολλῶν πρὸς ὑγίειαν εὑρέτιν γεγονέναι καὶ τῆς ἰατρικῆς ἐπιστήμης μεγάλην ἔχειν ἐμπειρίαν (Diodorus, i. 25).

Excerpt. XXIV. 27. ἱερωτάτη. Cf. 486. 5, 490. 11. It is Isis (the earth-goddess) who speaks.

496. 7. God as King with attendants; see on 462. 7. It is best to retain the text and take the king (l. 12) as a god : see vol. iii. 236.

500. 26 *sqq.* This is an essay in astrological ethnography, a pursuit the end of which is to make one's own race come out first. For the various devices used see Bouché-Leclercq, *L'astrologie grecque*, pp. 328–47. As astrologers specified the parts with amorous particularity, it is perhaps better to retain the full catalogue in § 11. I shall deal with the general character of this section below. But it may be remarked that §§ 12-13 deal with physical peculiarities and differences of function dependent thereon. The materials for illustration may be found in the *Sylloge*, vol. ii of Foerster's *Scriptores Physiognomonici*. εὐκορύφους (502, l. 10): cf. a less ingenuous statement in the same tradition : ' qui autem sunt proximi ad axem meridianum subiectique solis cursui, brevioribus corporibus, colore fusco, crispo capillo' (Vitruvius, vi. 1. 4). ⌜ἀσφαλεῖς⌝ (l. 13): the Libyan trait is cunning, as befits the left-handed ('Afri subdoli', 'subdolae

---

[1] Cf. Lucan, iii. 220-4.

mentes ', ' Afri versipelles '¹); but it may be suspected that a physical mark came first here. So perhaps with ⌜πρός τινα⌝ τοὺς πόδας (l. 16); men living under the Bear are described as παχυσκελεῖς.² The reproach in l. 21 is common form against neighbouring peoples; here too it is an inference from part to function, like the inference from the (Stoic) seat of the ἡγεμονικόν to Egyptian intelligence that completes the first stage of the argument.

502. 32 sqq. This account depends upon the theory of εὐκρασία, and the point is that Egypt has a εὔκρατον (or εἰλικρινές) κλίμα, as contrasted with the δύσκρατα κλίματα in other parts of the earth. εἰλικρινές (like ἀτάραχον) is a meteorological term, opposed e.g. to ἀχλυῶδες, ὀμβρῶδες, καυσῶδες, κρυσταλλῶδες, ψυχρόν. On the general theory the κλίματα of earth answer to the κλίματα of heaven, and the contemperation of the air affects life and character. Cicero, de nat. deor. ii. 6. 17: 'An ne hoc quidem intellegimus, omnia supera esse meliora, terram autem esse infimam, quam crassissimus circumfundat(ur) aër, ut ob eam ipsam causam, quod etiam quibusdam regionibus atque urbibus contingere videmus, hebetiora ut sint hominum ingenia propter caeli pleniorem ⟨umore⟩ naturam, hoc idem generi humano evenerit, quod in terra, hoc est in crassissima regione mundi, conlocati sunt.' Such is the common handicap; but there are distinctions. Servius, ad Aen. vi. 724: 'dicit non esse in animis dissimilitudinem sed in corporibus, quae prout fuerint vel vivacia vel torpentia, ita et animos faciunt ... adeo cum ad corpus venerit, non natura sua utitur, sed ex eius qualitate mutatur, inde Afros versipelles, Graecos leves, Gallos pigrioris videmus ingenii: quod natura climatum facit, sicut Ptolemaeus deprehendit, qui dicit translatum ad illud clima hominem naturam ex parte mutare.³ de toto enim non potest, quia in principio accepit sortem corporis sui. ergo anima pro qualitate est corporis.' Cf. de nat. deor. ii. 46. 96; Posidonius in Galen, de placitis (442 Mueller): καὶ γὰρ τῶν ζῴων καὶ τῶν ἀνθρώπων, ὅσα μὲν εὐρύστερνά τε καὶ θερμότερα, θυμικώτερα πάνθ' ὑπάρχειν φύσει ... καὶ κατὰ τὰς χώρας δὲ οὐ σμικρῷ τινι διενηνοχέναι τοῖς ἤθεσι τοὺς ἀνθρώπους εἰς δειλίαν καὶ τόλμαν ἤτοι φιλήδονόν τε καὶ φιλόπονον, ὡς τῶν παθητικῶν κινήσεων τῆς ψυχῆς ἑπομένων ἀεὶ τῇ διαθέσει τοῦ σώματος, ἣν ἐκ τῆς κατὰ τὸ περιέχον κράσεως οὐ κατ' ὀλίγον ἀλλοιοῦσθαι.⁴ Vitruvius, vi. I. 3: 'ex caelo roscidus aer in corpora fundens umorem efficit ampliores corporaturas vocisque sonitus graviores, ex eo quoque quae sub septentrionibus nutriuntur gentes immanibus corporibus ... ab umoris plenitate caelique refrigerationibus sunt conformati. 4. (see above on 500. 26). 9. item propter tenuitatem caeli meridianae nationes ex acuto fervore mente expeditius celeriusque moventur ad consiliorum

¹ Foerster, op. cit., Sylloge, §§ 170, 174.   ² id. i, p. 383. 5.

³ Not Horace's opinion: 'caelum, non animum, mutant qui trans mare currunt.' Caeli mutatio is medical for a change of air, or κλίμα.

⁴ The sober beginnings of what grew to be a cosmic theory may be seen in Plato, Tim. 86 E. Cf. Laws, v. 747 D.

cogitationes. septentrionales autem gentes infusae crassitudine caeli
propter obstantiam aëris umore refrigeratae stupentes habent mentes. ...
11. namque temperatissimae ad utramque partem, et corporum membris
animorumque vigoribus, pro fortitudine sunt in Italia gentes ... itaque con-
siliis refringit barbarorum virtutes, forti manu meridianorum cogitationes.'
With our author Egypt naturally carries off the prize; but the kind of theory
—astrology, climates, physical and mental types—is common property.[1]
The force at work is συμπάθεια. For the general doctrine see Reinhardt,
Poseidonios, pp. 67 *sqq.*, 382,[2] *K. U. S.* 56. To come to detail, κάπνος
(504. 4) was used of *terrenus vapor*, as distinguished from ἀτμίς, by
Aristotle (*Meteor.* 341 b 8). The account is perfectly naive—the East
is the place where the sun is *always* rising (συνεχεῖ ἀνατολῇ) and in the
West it is always setting—so both are hot and disturbed; there is not
the pure influence (ἐπίστασιν, l. 9) that the Egyptian atmosphere exercises.
In contrast to the perturbation of the elements elsewhere, the sky is
pure and tranquil. I suggest that the metaphor of a struggle of
elements[3] (δυσκρασία) is carried through. The climate in constant
tranquillity (ἀμεριμνία, l. 16) generates and perfects and educates (trio of
verbs stylistic). This is its only strife and only victory; recognizing
its victory it treats its subjects like a good satrap, and is bountiful to
them. With some doubt I suggest that this figure *may* have begun in
l. 13, and that ἑαυτῷ προλέγει may represent προ⟨πο⟩λεμεῖ, defends or protects. The point about the word σατράπης is that it is an established and
trite metaphor. It is on the way to become one in the Posidonian *de
mundo* (398 a 29), where a comparison between the Great King with his
officers and God is worked out at length. Egypt is a vice-gerent of God,
who works through the κλίμα by συμπάθεια. It is at least an interesting coincidence that the next passage in our text (504. 23) should closely
resemble that section of the *de mundo* which follows the simile of the
Great King.

504. 1. διὰ τὴν ... ἐκεῖ κατακομιδήν, the precipitation of the clouds in
rain? So in l. 4 κατεκόμισε. It may be suspected that ἐπικείμενον (l. 3)
expresses the relation of the moisture-laden air to the people beneath.

3. πάχνης. Cf. Didymus, *Expos. in Psalm.*, cxlvii: ὥσπερ γὰρ χιὼν εἴς
τινα καταρρυεῖσθαι (καταρρεῖ) τόπον, καὶ πάχνη μετὰ ταῦτα λύεται, καὶ ὕδατα
προχεῖ, οὕτως ὁ θεῖος Λόγος. See vol. iii. 577.

21. λόγος. Probably 'speech and even the power to reason; nay, the
soul itself is sometimes injured'. The theory is ἰσονομία of the elements.

[1] Philo, *de prov.*, *ap.* Euseb. *Pr. ev.* viii. 14. 66: μόνη γὰρ ἡ Ἑλλὰς ἀψευδῶς
ἀνθρωπογονεῖ, φυτὸν οὐράνιον. ... τὸ δ' αἴτιον· λεπτότητι ἀέρος ἡ διάνοια πέφυκεν
ἀκονᾶσθαι. Stoic, as the quotation from Heraclitus about the dry soul shows.

[2] These pages contain an analysis of the *Kore Kosmu*, so far as Posidonian
influence goes.

[3] In a different context: πόλεμον δὲ λέγει ἐν σώματι, ὅτι ἐξ μαχίμων στοιχείων
πέπλασται (Hippolytus, *Refut.* v. 8).

23. For this elaborate figure see *de mundo*, 398 b 30 *sqq*. Diodorus, i. 7. 5 (account of the origin of life): ἀναφυῆναι παντοδαποὺς τύπους ζώων. τούτων δὲ τὰ μὲν πλείστης θερμασίας κεκοινωνηκότα πρὸς τοὺς μετεώρους τόπους ἀπελθεῖν γενόμενα πτηνά, τὰ δὲ γεώδους ἀντεχόμενα συγκρίσεως ἐν τῇ τῶν ἑρπετῶν καὶ τῶν ἄλλων τῶν ἐπιγείων τάξει καταριθμηθῆναι, τὰ δὲ φύσεως ὑγρᾶς μάλιστα μετειληφότα πρὸς τὸν ὁμογενῆ τόπον συνδραμεῖν. (See Reinhardt, *Hermes*, 1912.) Cf. Hermippus, p. 35. 4 Kroll.

25. τὰ δὲ καὶ πρὸς τὰ ὅλα. This is consistent with the doctrine of the microcosm taken cheerfully. Man is at home with *all* elements in the universe, and so a convinced upholder of the doctrine, like Philo, argues: ἡ δὲ συγγένεια τίς ; πᾶς ἄνθρωπος κατὰ μὲν τὴν διάνοιαν ᾠκείωται λόγῳ θείῳ, . . . κατὰ δὲ τὴν τοῦ σώματος κατασκευήν, ἅπαντι τῷ κόσμῳ· συγκέκραται γὰρ ἐκ τῶν αὐτῶν, γῆς καὶ ὕδατος καὶ ἀέρος καὶ πυρός . . . καὶ προσέτι πᾶσι τοῖς λεχθεῖσιν ὡς οἰκειοτάτοις καὶ συγγενεστάτοις χωρίοις ἐνδιαιτᾶται, τόπους ἀμείβων καὶ ἄλλοτε ἄλλοις ἐπιφοιτῶν, ὡς κυριώτατα φάναι τὸν ἄνθρωπον πάντα εἶναι, χερσαῖον ἔνυδρον πτηνὸν οὐράνιον[1] κτλ. (*de opif. mundi*, 146, i. 51. 5 Wendl.). On the other hand, if the doctrine of εἱμαρμένη is taken tragically, it is consistent to contend that the soul, while bearing the normal pressure of the alien elements,[2] is overwhelmed when there is δυσκρασία. So τὰ δὲ τῶν ὅλων (l. 28) leads up to the explanation, and ζώντων in l. 23 should be retained.

506. 1. Philo, *quis rer. div. heres*, 237 (iii. 51 Wendl.) παρὰ φύσιν γάρ ἐστι τὸ καταβαίνειν ὄρνεα . . . καθάπερ γὰρ τοῖς χερσαίοις οἰκειότατον χωρίον γῆ καὶ μάλιστα τοῖς ἑρπετοῖς, . . . διὰ τὴν πρὸς τὰ κάτω συγγένειαν, τὸν αὐτὸν τρόπον καὶ τοῖς πτηνοῖς ὁ ἀὴρ ἐνδιαίτημα οἰκεῖον.

2. πολιτεύεται, take up their abode. Cf. 524. 27. The theory that the region of each element sustains a certain kind of life is implicit here; the argument proceeds from the known *cognatio* within the four elements to the *cognatio* of the soul with its region. Hence *flammida* appear (ll. 4–5) to clinch the argument ; Philo, *de gigant.* 7, ἀνάγκη γὰρ ὅλον δι' ὅλων τὸν κόσμον ἐψυχῶσθαι, τῶν πρώτων καὶ στοιχειωδῶν μερῶν ἑκάστου τὰ οἰκεῖα καὶ πρόσφορα ζῷα περιέχοντος, γῆς μὲν τὰ χερσαῖα . . . πυρὸς δὲ τὰ πυρίγονα. Cf. *de plantat.* 12.

11. μάχεται. It is customary to speak of the elements as at war with one another; and the soul, maintaining itself against them, may be said to fight. In l. 13 καὶ ταῦτα refers to the δυσκρασία of the στοιχεῖα. Gregory of Nyssa, v. 46, 512 D Migne, τότε ὁ νοῦς δυσφορῶν τε καὶ ἀνιώμενος παύεται, ὅταν ἔξω γένηται τῆς μάχης τῆς ἐν τῇ συμπλοκῇ τῶν ἀντιστοιχούντων συνισταμένης. ἐπειδὰν γὰρ ἢ τὸ ψυχρὸν ἡττηθῇ τοῦ θερμοῦ κατισχύσαντος ἢ . . ., τότε τοῦ ἐν ἡμῖν πολέμου διὰ τοῦ θανάτου λυθέντος εἰρήνην ὁ νοῦς ἄγει, καταλιπὼν τὸ τῆς μάχης μεταίχμιον. See Gronau, *Poseidonios*, p. 217.

14. φόβου. γίνεται δὲ ὁ φόβος κατὰ περίψυξιν, τοῦ θερμοῦ παντὸς

---

[1] An albatross would equally suit the second part of the argument. See also *op. cit.* 155, and note on 506. 1.

[2] Cf. 196. 2 ; 138. 16 ; 506. 7.

συντρέχοντος εἰς τὴν καρδίαν, ἐπὶ τὸ ἀρχικόν (Nemesius, *de nat. hom.* 689 A).
The Stoic doctrine of the πάθη. Cf. 224. 14 : σώματος γὰρ συνθέτου ὥσπερ
χυμοὶ ζέουσιν ἥ τε λύπη καὶ ἡ ἡδόνη, εἰς ἃς ἐμβᾶσα ἡ ψυχὴ βαπτίζεται. Compare also the frequent occurrence of *timor* in *de castig. animae.* The
doctrine of ἰσότης is derived from the *Timaeus*, and the mediating source
is Posidonius. See e.g. Philo, *quis rer. div. heres*, 152 sqq., *de spec. leg.*
iv. 237.

ἐν βυθῷ. Philo, *de gigant.* 13 : ὥσπερ εἰς ποταμὸν τὸ σῶμα καταβᾶσαι
ποτὲ μὲν ὑπὸ συρμοῦ δίνης βιαιότητης ἁρπασθεῖσαι κατεπόθησαν, ποτὲ δὲ πρὸς
τὴν φορὰν ἀντισχεῖν δυνηθεῖσαι τὸ μὲν πρῶτον ἀνενήξαντο, εἶτα . . . ἀνέπτησαν.
. . . αἱ δὲ καταποντωθεῖσαι κτλ. Cf. *de somn.* i. 147.

Excerpt. XXV. **508.** 4 *sqq.* For the metaphor of the soul dissipated
like water [1] cf. Nemesius on the Manichaeans (*de nat. hom.* 577 Migne) :
κυρίως αὐτὴν (τὴν ψυχὴν) ἐν τοῖς στοιχείοις εἶναι βούλονται, καὶ συμμερίζεσθαι
τούτοις ἐν τῇ τῶν σωμάτων γενέσει, καὶ πάλιν εἰς ταὐτὸ συνιέναι διαλυομένων
τῶν σωμάτων, ὡς ὕδωρ μεριζόμενον καὶ πάλιν συναγόμενον καὶ μιγνύμενον, καὶ
τὰς μὲν καθαρὰς ψυχὰς χωρεῖν εἰς τὸ φῶς, φῶς οὔσας, τὰς δὲ μεμολυσμένας ὑπὸ
τῆς ὕλης, χωρεῖν εἰς τὰ στοιχεῖα . . . καὶ οὕτω τὴν οὐσίαν αὐτῆς κατατέμνοντες . . .
ἀθάνατον εἶναί φασι. Cf. also a χρησμός in Stobaeus, i. 49. 46 (414. 16
Wachsm.) :

> σῶμα λυθὲν ψυχήν τε λιπὸν καὶ ⟨γαῖ⟩α γενηθὲν
> οὐκέτι πως βιότοιο παλίνδρομον οἶδε κέλευθον,
> ἀλλὰ τὸ μὲν λυθέν ἐστι κενὴ ⟨κόνι⟩ς, ἡ δὲ πρὸς αἴθρην
> σκίδναται, ὅππυθεν ἦλθε, μετήορος εἰς αἰθέρ' ἁπλοῦν,
> ἄλλος δ' ἐξ ἄλλου γεννώμενος ἠδ' ἀναβλαστῶν
> ψυχοῦται γονίμου φύσεως ἀροτρεύμασι καινοῖς.

We come closer to the argument in our text with Nemesius, *ibid.* 541 B.
After considering the general position that ψυχή is σῶμα, he continues :
ἰδίᾳ δὲ πρὸς τοὺς δοξάζοντας αἷμα [2] ἢ πνεῦμα εἶναι τὴν ψυχήν, ἐπειδὴ τοῦ αἵματος
ἢ τοῦ πνεύματος χωριζομένου νεκροῦται τὸ ζῷον, οὐκ ἐκεῖνο ῥητέον. . . . οὐκοῦν
ὅταν μέρος ἀπερρύη τοῦ αἵματος, μέρος ἀπερρύη τῆς ψυχῆς· κουφολογία γὰρ τὸ
τοιοῦτον· ἐπὶ γὰρ τῶν ὁμοιομερῶν καὶ τὸ ὑπολειπόμενον μέρος ταὐτόν ἐστι τῷ
παντί· ὕδωρ γοῦν, καὶ τὸ πολὺ καὶ τὸ βραχύ, ταὐτόν. . . . οὕτως οὖν καὶ τὸ
ὑπολειπόμενον αἷμα, ὅσον ἂν ᾖ, ψυχή ἐστιν, εἴπερ ψυχὴ τὸ αἷμα. There follows
a list of animals that have no blood, or can live without water (like some
eagles and the partridge), or do not breathe (like bees, wasps, ants, and
fishes) to show that ψυχή is not blood or water or air.

We may now interpret the argument. The view denied by Isis contends
that the soul is a substance (air or πνεῦμα), subject to the laws of fluids,
and that souls therefore are at once mingled indistinguishably with the
main volume when they leave the body, as water mingles with water

---

[1] See vol. iii. 587.
[2] Cf. 196. 3. Pneuma (Stoics), blood (Critias), water (Hippo).

irretrievably. She reveals[1] that it is to be classed with things having a definite organization, and that such things have and seek their own place. This is the point of the illustration in § 6, which cites living beings only.[2] The soul is a structure formed by the hands of God (ἰδιοφυὲς καὶ βασιλικόν[3], l. 22); cf. 464. 28. But water is ἄλογον; (it has no particular place) —ἐκ πολλῶν συγκριμάτων παρατεθλιμμένον εἰς χύσιν.[4] It can be squeezed from many συγκρίματα. Cf. πάλιν δ' ἀπὸ ταύτης (γῆς) διαλυομένης καὶ διαχεομένης πρώτη μὲν γίγνεται χύσις εἰς ὕδωρ (Stob. i. 10. 16, p. 129. 21. W.: of Chrysippus).[5] It seems best to keep ἐξ ἄλλου in l. 25. The argument is that the soul, being ἰδιοσύγκριτος, is ἀσύγχυτος and cannot share in a κρᾶσις, as water can.[6] We may perhaps interpret τὸ συνεστός (l. 3) in the light of ἰδιοφυές. Cf. 248. 11 : τὸ σῶμα τοῦτο τὸ ἐκ δυνάμεων συνεστὸς λύσιν ἕξει ποτε;

The general argument is that τὸ ὁμογενές seeks τὸ ὁμογενές. Cf. Plut. Epit. (Doxogr. 392. 14) ; ἐξιοῦσαν γὰρ εἰς τὴν τοῦ παντὸς ψυχὴν ἀναχωρεῖν πρὸς τὸ ὁμογενές—cognatio.

Hence (508. 33) the long similitude of animals that instinctively make for their own haunts. It may be suspected that the source insisted upon the power of φύσις.[7] The fertility of illustration is characteristic of Posidonius. Cf. de nat. deor. ii. 124 : 'sic dissimillimis bestiolis communiter cibus quaeritur. in quo admirandum est, congressune aliquo inter se an iam inde ab ortu natura ipsa congregatae sint. est etiam admiratio non nulla in bestiis aquatilibus iis, quae gignuntur in terra ; veluti crocodili fluviatilesque testudines quaedamque serpentes (l. 4)[8] ortae extra aquam, simul ac primum niti possunt, aquam persequuntur. . . . tantam ingenuit animantibus conservandi sui natura custodiam.' Cf. μετὰ τῶν ὁμοίων (510. 19). See also on p. 504 above.

32. πεπαχυμμένη. Cf. Porphyry, de antro, 64. 15 ; Synesius, de insomniis, 1292 B (Migne) : κακυνομένης δὲ παχύνεται καὶ γαιοῦται. A. D. N. compares 524. 14, Sallustius de diis, iv.

510. 4, 19. The essence of this analogy is that each animal seeks its own place[8]—and so does the soul. The argument is from συγγένεια (510.

[1] l. 17. ὥσπερ δὲ μύστις A. D. N.

[2] This simile should be compared with that on 504. 23. See note above.

[3] βασιλικόν. Cf. Philo, quod omnis probus, 126.

[4] This is Stoic language, but it is well not to interpret too technically. An element is μέρος ἐλάχιστον τοῦ συγκρίματος τῶν σωμάτων.

[5] Nemesius, De nat. hominis, 617 A : ὥστε τὰ στοιχεῖα καὶ εἰς ἄλληλα μεταβάλλεσθαι καὶ εἰς τὰ συγκρίματα, καὶ πάλιν τὰ συγκρίματα εἰς τὰ στοιχεῖα ἀναλύεσθαι—the cycle of elements.

[6] Soul a μῖγμα: see Schmekel, Gesch. d. mittl. Stoa, pp. 110, 121, Gronau, Poseidonios, p. 225. For the σύνοδος (l. 26) see on 438. 17.

[7] 510. 21-2 οἰκείαν χώραν.

[8] If we interpret ἐνύδρεις as ' water-snakes ', Cicero's list of three answers to the Hermetist's. The χελῶναι are river (or marsh) tortoises.

21). Cf. Philo, *de opif. dei*, 147; *quis rer. div. heres*, 237. I withdraw the suggestion that the συσχετήριον was suggested by the περιστερεών in *Theaet.* 197 C.

11. κύκνοι. In Aristotle, *H.A.* ix. 12 the swans are said to live about marshes and fens, but (as ᾠδικοί) fly out to sea; there are sailors' tales from Libya, how many swans were seen singing at sea, and some were seen to die. The text may possibly refer to *the* swan song. But it is a τόπος that birds have different haunts for song, and the tradition about the swan's power of song is sufficient to account for the phrase. Cf. *Anth. Pal.* 9. 363. 17: ἀλκυόνες περὶ κῦμα, χελιδόνες ἀμφὶ μέλαθρα, | κύκνος ἐπ᾽ ὄχθαισιν ποταμοῦ, καὶ ὑπ᾽ ἄλσος ἀηδὼν (ᾄδουσι). So Dion, *Or.* xii. 4. See D'Arcy Thompson, *Glossary of Greek Birds, s.v.* κύκνος.

19. μετὰ τῶν ὁμοίων. καὶ γὰρ ζῷα ὁμογενέσι ζῴοις συναγελάζεται ὡς περιστεραὶ περιστεραῖς καὶ γέρανοι γεράνοις, Democritus, B 164 (Diels). It is probable that this idea (applied also to man and to ἄψυχα) was developed by Posidonius. See Jaeger, *Nemesios*, pp. 135–6.

512. 23. ἑαυτοῦ. η᾽ αὐτοῦ A.D.N. Cf. l. 21 ὀκτώ.

Excerpt. XXVI. **516.** 16. φυράμματος. The ἄνω φύραμα is probably a mixture of the pneumatic ὄχημα and the irrational soul, given from the heavenly spheres and dissolved again into them. See Proclus *in Tim.* 3. 234. 18, quoted in vol. ii. 59. Perhaps γίγνηται ⟨φύλαξ⟩.

18. Empeiria fits each body to its appropriate soul—a theory of ἐπιτηδειότης; see on 438. 17.

24. The order here depends on the elements—air first, and so forth. The Posidonian argument states the means of self-preservation vouchsafed to man, who is born fragile and unprotected. Cf. Philo, *de somn.* i. 103; Cic. *de nat. deor.* ii. 121 *sqq.*; Porph. *de abst.* iii. 9; Nemesius, *de nat. hom.* 517 C–19 A.

27. εὐχαίτοις. The general argument from which this is drawn considered the covering of bodies as a means of defence, and it is not impossible that hairy animals like goats were contrasted with scaly reptiles, so that the word may have slipped in by confusion; see on 518. 3. The required word is εὐπεριχύτοις; cf. 524. 3.

518. 3. καὶ τοῖς ὀδοῦσιν. ἰστόκοις? I add Professor D'Arcy Thomson's suggestion: ἰστόκοις ὀδοῦσιν ἐχάραξεν, ὧν δὲ τοὺς ὀγκίνους ὀξυνύδοντας περιέθηκεν.

Excerpt. XXIX. **530.** 10. These verses are printed in Maass, *Commentariorum in Aratum Reliquiae*, pp. 170–2, together with a Latin version, and are attached to a much longer ἀπλανῶν σφαῖρα. The poems are called Ἐμπεδόκλεους σφαῖρα. It is not necessary to reproduce Maass's apparatus from the Paris and Ambrosian MSS.; but the following readings may be noted: l. 12 κανονίζεται αἰών volvitur *versio Lat.* 532. 2. γένος ἕλκουσ᾽ AP ἔλαχον γένος Pⁱⁱⁱ ἐλάουσι γένος Pⁱᵛ ἐλόωσι βίον coni. *Scaliger.*

532. 8. γελώς. As A.D.N. notes, procreation is connected with laughter.

See 120. 26, notes on 462. 17, 26. For the connexion of the sun with
γένεσις compare 144. 15–17, where childlessness is cursed by the Sun as
A. D. N. rightly interprets the passage.

FRAGMENTA, ET TESTIMONIA VOL. IV.

IV. 5. 12. Ostanes. He is named by Apuleius, *Apol.* c. 27 in company with Epimenides, Orpheus and Pythagoras ; *ibid.* c. 90 : ' Carmendas
uel Damigeron uel † his Moses uel I[oh]annes [2] . . . uel quicumque alius
post Zoroastren et Hostanen inter magos celebratus est ' ; Tertullian, *de
anima*, 57 ; ' Ostanes et Typhon et Dardanus et Damigeron et Nectabis et
Berenice ' ; in Hippolytus, *Refut.* v. 14 he is named in company with
Hermes Trismegistus, Petosiris, Zoroaster, and others. Now here the
doctrine of *angeli* is specially associated with him. Cf. Minucius Felix,
Octavius, 26 : ' magorum et eloquio et negotio primus Hostanes . . . angelos,
id est ministros et nuntios Dei sedem tueri eiusque uenerationi nouit
adsistere. Idem etiam daemonas prodidit terrenos uagos, humanitatis
inimicos.' ' Ostanes,' as Cumont argued, was the source of the dualistic
demonology expounded in Porphyry, *de abstin.* 2. 36–43,[3] and there are
traces of it in *Asclepius* and possibly in *Kore Kosmu* ; see notes on 340.
4–346. 7, 366. 11, and 486. 11, with references. Angels are noted as a
separate class from daemons in the *Oracula Chaldaica*,[4] and in the
Hermetica,[5] which are related to the *Oracula*. Porphyry[6] recognized
angels and archangels, and distinguished them from daemons, and there
is evidence that Cornelius Labeo knew the distinction.[7]

6. 4 (*Fr.* 2). Probably conflated from 290. 5 and 352. 9.

ARNOBIUS

7. 8. Further extracts from this author have been appended, because
they shed some light on the early history of certain characteristic Hermetic
doctrines. It was shown by Nigettiet[8] that the opponent attacked by
Arnobius in *adversus nationes* ii. 13–62 was Cornelius Labeo. The date
of Labeo was still, however, assumed to be late ; and one consideration

---

[1] References to pages in vol. iv are usually given with the number of the volume
prefixed ; but occasionally, where the context makes the sense clear, the page
number is given with ' p.' prefixed.

[2] See vol. iv, p. 140, n. 1 above. The materials on ' Ostanes ' are collected in
Bousset's article (*Archiv*, 1915).

[3] Quoted in part, vol. iii. 245 ; the reference to blood in this and other quotations on that page indicates that the *bad* daemons are meant.

[4] pp. 44, 53, 60 Kroll.

[5] 344. 4 ; 358. 24.

[6] Augustine, *de civ. dei*, 10. 9 ; Proclus, *in Tim.* 1. 152 Diehl.

[7] Arnobius, *adv. nationes*, 2. 35 (see below *ad loc.*) : Augustine, *op. cit.* 9. 19.

[8] *De Cornelio Labeone* (1908). The fragments of Labeo are collected and discussed by Kahl in *Philologus, Suppl.-Band. v.*

that appeared to support this hypothesis was the dualism between good and bad daemons known best from Porphyry's *de abstinentia* ii. 36–43, but found in Labeo. The agreement about this doctrine was assumed to prove Labeo's dependence upon Porphyry. It has, however, already been seen in these *Addenda* that this dualistic doctrine also appears in the Hermetic documents, and no inference can be drawn about Porphyry's priority. The fact to be interpreted is the presence of this peculiar demonology in Labeo, the Hermetists, and Porphyry.

Boehm proved[1] that A.D. 126 was the *terminus ad quem* of Labeo, since he was quoted by Suetonius and knew the Chaldaic Oracles. He also showed in detail that Labeo's general point of view was consistent with later Stoicism.

It remained for Bousset to take the third step by pointing out that Boehm's contribution threw light upon the earlier history of Hermetism. It could no longer be maintained that Labeo drew upon the views of certain 'Platonists' as reported by Porphyry. These and related doctrines were carried back towards the first century of our era, and Bousset suggested that Labeo in all probability rested upon Hermetic writings of some sort, and gave currency to their doctrines.[2]

The chain of argument, then, has three links: that Labeo was Arnobius' opponent; that his *floruit* was much earlier than the date traditionally assigned to him; that certain distinctive doctrines are common to him and to the extant Hermetic documents.

These doctrines concern the origin, nature, perils, and destiny of the soul. They have already been noted at one place or other in the *Addenda*. It will be convenient to summarize the main heads of the beliefs attacked by Arnobius.

1. The soul is of divine origin and immortal;[3] it shares the *principalis substantia*[4] and is superior to the sun and stars;[5] in respect of its reason it is superior to the animals[6]; its seat is in the heavens[7]; it is *sapiens, docta, bona, iusta, recta*[8]; it is not subject to the laws of fate.[9]

2. The soul, descending through the spheres, acquires certain qualities,[10] and is thereby brought under influences that make it subject to passions and render it evil. This is an astral pessimism closely connected with the dualism between good and bad powers.[11] It is necessary to placate

---

[1] *De Cornelii Labeonis Aetate* (1913).

[2] *G. G. A.* 1914; *Zur Dämonologie d. späteren Antike* (*Archiv*, 1915, p. 134).

[3] ii. 62 (Labeo), 15, 19, 22, 28, 29, 35, 36, 43, 45, 51 ('regias suboles, ab ipso animas rege descendere').

[4] ii. 22; compare 222. 25.

[5] ii. 19; compare 204. 11; 336. 23.   [6] ii. 16; compare 230. 7.

[7] ii. 15, 33, 36, 37, 43, 51 ('animas sede a supera et regione descendere').

[8] ii. 15, 19, 25.   [9] ii. 62 (Labeo), 29.

[10] ii. 16, 28. Compare Macrobius, *in Somn. Scip.* i. 12 (see vol. ii. 62).

[11] ii. 62 (Labeo), iv. 12.

these powers lest the soul should be prevented from returning to the paternal seat.[1]

3. The soul returns to heaven, to its Father's seat.[2]

Now the core of this doctrine is the descent and ascent of the soul, its fatal star-given burden, its distinctive demonology. It is known that the doctrine attacked in *adv. nationes* ii. 62 is that of Labeo; and this is the doctrine treated at length in the other chapters quoted below. What is distinctive in them can be illustrated by the extant *Hermetica*.

There are not merely the same high claim for the *anima docta*, but the same pessimistic view of the soul clogged by accretions from the stars in its descent, relieved in its return to the Father's hall. This doctrine appears in *Corp.* I (128. 1 *sqq.*) and in XIII (242. 21 *sqq.*).[3] In *Asclepius*[4] it was said that the just man's one safeguard—his safeguard from the daemons[5]—was piety. This is connected with the characteristic doctrine of the two souls,[6] the lower of which is the fatal gift of the stars.[7] Now the distinction between good and bad daemons attributed by Porphyry[8] to certain Platonists was traced by Cumont[9] to a Persian demonology contained in a book by 'Ostanes',[10] and his argument was strengthened by the evidence collected from the *Hermetica* and from Ps.-Clement in Bousset's article. In particular the use of such words as ἀντίθεος,[11] *daemoniarches*,[12] προεστῶσα δύναμις[13] in this tradition should be noted.

Such are in brief the considerations that led Bousset to seek in Arnobius the means of filling a blank in the early history of Hermetism. In *ad-*

---

[1] ii. 62 Labeo`, 13, 33.   [2] ii. 62 (Labeo), 13, 33.

[3] See notes on this *libellus* in *Addenda*. I add a reference to the following passages in Servius, *Aen.* vi. 127, 439, 713, xi. 51, and Macrobius, *in Somn. Scip.* i. 11, 12. Nigettiet has shown that Labeo is the source of these. The parallels between Servius and Arnobius are conveniently set out in Schmekel's *Gesch. d. mittl. Stoa*, p. 104 (see also vol. ii, pp. 61-2); but Schmekel proceeded upon the hypothesis that the common source was Varro (Posidonius). Bousset gathered the Hermetic parallels in the article mentioned above, where he also resumes the evidence for the theory of προσαρτήματα τῆς ψυχῆς in early Gnosticism; see also *Hauptprobleme*, p. 361. I add Bousset's principal references: Clement, *Str.* ii. 23, 112 προσαρτήματα, πνεύματα ... προσηρτημένα τῇ λογικῇ ψυχῇ; ii. 20. 14—bad spirits make man's soul a dwelling-place of daemons (Valentinian); ii. 20. 113—the son of Basilides περὶ προσφυοῦς ψυχῆς; Ephraem, *Hymn.* 53, p. 553 E— according to Bardesanes man has a soul from the Seven (cf. 128. 1-20); Porphyry, *de abstin.* ii. 31 and *apud* Stob. *Ecl.* ii. 388; τοῦ πρώτου βίου ἡ διέξοδος διὰ τῶν ἑπτὰ σφαιρῶν γιγνομένη.

[4] 368. 10-370. 4 (see on 364. 25-370. 18), and on 244. 19-246. 1.

[5] 366. 11.   [6] *Fr.* 16 (iv. 34. 28 note).

[7] See on 128. 1 with references; also 120. 5 (Anthropos).   [8] *op. cit.*

[9] *Rel. orientales*, p. 280, n. 53. See on 340. 4-346. 7.

[10] See on iv. 5. 14.   [11] See p. 482, n. 5 below.

[12] *Fr.* 9 (iv. 14. 2).

[13] *De abstinentia*, ii. 42. Note the ἀντίμιμος δαίμων in Zosimus, vol. iv. 108. 21.

versus nationes ii. 13 (p. 8. 1 above) the unnamed opponent is described as a follower of Mercury, Plato, and Pythagoras[1]; it would not be unfair to say that all these elements are found in Labeo,[2] and that the astral pessimism common to him and to the Hermetists is not Neo-Platonic, even though some 'Platonists' specially marked off by Porphyry were imbued with it.

The text given below is Reifferscheid's. It has not been thought necessary to reproduce his apparatus. The foot-notes have been kept brief, since this introductory note and previous references in the *Addenda* have brought out the main points. I wish to make here a general acknowledgement of my debt to the scholars named above. It is perhaps worth adding that the 9,000 'periods' mentioned by Al-Kindí (iv. 249. 1) and Barhebraeus (iv. 276. 19), during which God punishes men is probably to be connected with a double journey of the soul through the planetary spheres.

Adv. nationes, ii. 13 . . . quid Plato uester in Theaeteto,[3] ut eum potissimum nominem, nonne animo fugere suadet e terris et circa illum semper quantum fieri potis est cogitatione ac mente uersari? audetis ridere nos, quod mortuorum dicamus resurrectionem futuram, quam quidem nos dicere confitemur sed a uobis aliter quam sentiamus audiri? quid in Politico[4] idem Plato? . . . audetis ridere nos, quod animarum nostrarum prouideamus saluti id est ipsi nobis? quid enim sumus homines nisi animae corporibus clausae? uos enim non omnes pro illarum geritis incolumitatibus curas? non quod uitiis omnibus et cupiditatibus absti-netis, metus ille uos habet, ne uelut trabalibus clauis adfixi corporibus haereatis? quid illi sibi uolunt secretarum artium ritus, quibus adfa-mini nescio quas potestates, ut sint uobis placidae neque ad sedes remeantibus patrias obstacula impeditionis oppo-nant?[5]

15. quare nihil est quod nos fallat, nihil quod nobis polliceatur spes cassas id quod a nouis quibusdam dicitur uiris et inmoderata sui opinione

---

[1] Labeo quotes from Nigidius Figulus. In my note on 364. 25 I have not ven-tured to speculate on origins; but *Ascl.* cc. 27 e–29 b contains a suggestive blend of Neo-Pythagorean number theory and the doctrine of the soul and of daemons under discussion here. See also 246.–248. 4.

[2] 'Qui primum Pythagoram et qui postea Platonem secuti sunt' (Macrobius, *in somn. Scip.* i. 11); this is the beginning of the account of the soul referred to above, p. 476, n. 3.

[3] 173 E. This sentence continues the passage quoted in the *Testimonia* above, pp. 7–8. It does not necessarily follow that *vos* (p. 8. 1) and *vosque ceteros* (p. 8. 2) refer to two separate groups of persons. If Arnobius attacked a document, but a document embodying beliefs still held by contemporaries, the distinction is explained. For the rhetorical plural compare *sciolis nonnullis* in ii. 62.

[4] 270 E.

[5] The impediments to the ascent of the soul; see note on 154. 10–13, 180. 9, 222. 1–2, note on 364. 25–370. 18, iv. 14. 16 *sqq.*, and iv. 219. 20. Note also the τιμωρίαι of 126. 20; 242. 21; 246. 2, 21 *sqq.*

sublatis, animas immortales esse, domino rerum ac principi gradu proximas dignitatis,[1] genitore illo ac patre prolatas, diuinas sapientes doctas neque ulla corporis attrectatione contiguas. quod quia uerum et certum est, a perfecto sumus inemendabili perfectione prolati, inculpabiles et ideo inreprehensibiles uiuimus, boni iusti et recti, uitiositatis nullius rei. nulla cupiditas nos uincit, nulla libido dehonestat, uirtutum omnium seruamus atque integramus tenorem. et quia uno ex fonte[2] omnium nostrum defluunt animae, idcirco unum conueniensque sentimus, non moribus, non opinionibus discrepamus, idem omnes nouimus nec, quot in orbe sunt homines, nobis sunt sententiae totidem neque infinita uarietate discretae.

16. at dum ad corpora labimur et properamus humana, ex mundanis circulis[3] secuntur nos causae, quibus mali simus et pessimi, cupiditatibus atque iracundia ferueamus, exerceamus in flagitiis uitam et in libidinem publicam uenalium corporum prostitutione damnemur. et quemadmodum se possunt incorporalibus corpora coniungere aut a deo principe res factae ab infirmioribus causis ad uitiorum dehonestamenta traduci? uultis homines insitum typhum superciliumque deponere, qui deum uobis adsciscitis patrem et cum eo contenditis immortalitatem habere uos unam? uultis quaerere peruestigare rimari, quid sitis uos ipsi, cuius sitis, censeamini quo patre, quid in mundo faciatis, quanam ratione nascamini, quo pacto prosiliatis ad uitam? uultis favore deposito cogitationibus tacitis peruidere animantia nos esse aut consimilia ceteris aut non plurima differitate distantia? quid est enim, quod nos ab eorum indicet similitudine discrepare? uel quae in nobis eminentia tanta est, ut animantium numero dedignemur adscribi?[4] ... quod si et illud est uerum, quod in mysteriis secretioribus dicitur, in pecudes atque alias beluas ire animas improborum,[5] postquam sunt humanis corporibus exutae, manifestius comprobatur, uicinos nos esse neque interuallis longioribus disparatos. siquidem res eadem nobis et illis est una, per quam esse animantia dicuntur, et motum agitare uitalem.

17. sed rationales nos sumus et intellegentia uincimus genus omne mutorum.[6] crederem istud uerissime dici, si cum ratione et consilio cuncti homines uiuerent etc. ...

---

[1] 126. 2–5, and 128. 23 (note).

[2] πηγή. Chaldaic term, but also Hermetic; cf. Fr. 24, if that is Hermetic. Cf. c. 45 below, Macrobius, in Somn. Scip. i. 11. 1 'ipsam uero animam mori adserentes, cum a simplici et indiuiduo fonte naturae in membra corporea dissipatur' (Labeo?), vol. iv. 31. 29.

[3] This is the doctrine of the descent of the soul from the planetary spheres; cf. c. 28 below ('quas ex quibus circulis qualitates ... adtraxerint'). See introductory note above. Macrobius, op. cit. i. 12.

[4] 204. 10; 296. 12–15 (note on 296. 4); 320. 14 (note on 316. 25).

[5] Pythagorean; found in 192. 5 and 308. 12.

[6] Cf. 358. 12; 450. 13 (λογικὸν διὰ τὸ νοερόν). The counter-argument

19. ... numquam, inquam, crederent typho et adrogantia subleuati, prima esse se numina et aequalia principis summitati, quia grammaticam musicam oratoriam pepererunt et geometricas formulas : in quibus artificiis quidnam insit admirabile non uidemus, ut ex eorum inuentione credatur esse animas potiores et sole et sideribus cunctis,[1] hunc totum, cuius membra sunt haec, mundum et dignitate et substantia praeterire. ... ex quo apparet, ut saepius dictum est, inuenta haec esse locorum necessitate ac temporum neque diuinas et eruditas aduolauisse huc animas, quod neque omnes doctae sint neque discere omnes possint et sint in his plurimae acuminis obtunsioris et bardi et ad dicendi studium plagarum coercitione cogantur. ...

22. ... immo cum annos fuerit quadraginta permensus,[2] mortalium conciliis inferatur, et si uerum est, illum principalis esse substantiae portionem † iam laeta[3] ex fontibus[4] uitae deriuatum hic agere, antequam notitiam rei sumat alicuius aut sermone imbuatur humano, det responsum rogatus, quisnam sit ipse aut quo patre, quibus sit in regionibus editus, quo pacto aut quanam ratione nutritus, quid operis aut negotii celebrans ante acti temporis decurrerit aeuitatem etc.

25. quid dicitis, o uiri plus quam satis est uobis ex aliena generositate tribuentes? haecine est anima docta illa quam dicitis, immortalis perfecta diuina, post deum principem rerum et post mentes geminas[5] locum optinens quartum et affluens ex crateribus uiuis? hic est ille pretiosus et rationibus homo augustissimis praeditus, mundus minor[6] qui dicitur et totius in speciem similitudinis

advanced by Arnobius in cc. 17–19 is school commonplace : the power of instinct —*multa rationis et sapientiae simulacra*—on the general lines of Stob. *Exc.* iv B (see note on 406) ; the theme that *necessitas* is the mother of invention (Posidonian) —in short a later Stoic argument against the theory of a *docta anima*.

[1] Cf. 204. 11.

[2] A child brought to the age of twenty, thirty, or forty without any teaching whatever would know nothing ; but it should know if the theory of *anima docta* were true.

[3] *iam laetae* Vahlen.   [4] Chaldaic ; cf. c. 15 above.

[5] Reifferscheid reads *daemones et genios* after Klussmann. But emendation is unnecessary ; for the *geminae mentes* are Chaldaic. *Orac. chald. ap. Psellum,* 1140 C Migne πάντα γὰρ ἐξετέλεσσε πατὴρ καὶ νῷ παρέδωκε | δευτέρῳ ; 1144 A ὁ πατὴρ ἑαυτὸν ἥρπασεν | οὐδ' ἐν ἑῇ δυνάμει νοερᾷ κλείσας ἴδιον πῦρ. The triad is composed of Father, δύναμις νοερά (first νοῦς) and δεύτερος νοῦς. Kroll argued (*De orac. Chald.* p. 14) that the theory of the triad was a Neo-Platonic insertion, and this was a ground for Nigettiet's belief that Labeo was dependent on Porphyry. But the passages cited above suggest the contrary ; and the presumption is that Labeo is an early witness for the triad. See further in Bousset's article, *Archiv,* 1915. The *crateres uiui* are also Chaldaic. Compare also *Corp.* IV with references in vol. ii, 141–2, and *Fr.* 21.

[6] Platonic-Stoic commonplace ; cf. 304. 11 note.

mundi fabricatus atque formatus, nullo melior ut apparuit pecore, obtunsior ligno, saxo?

28. ... quod si animae quas uocatis membrorum impediuntur obstaculo, quominus artes suas atque antiquas reminiscantur, in corporibus ipsis quemadmodum constitutae meminerunt et sciunt animas se esse et corporalem substantiam non habere, inmortalitatis condicione mactatas, quem teneant in rebus gradum,[1] quo sint ordine a deo patre discretae,[2] ad infima haec mundi quanam ratione peruenerint, quas ex quibus circulis qualitates,[3] dum in haec loca labuntur, adtraxerint? quemadmodum, inquam, sciunt doctissimas se fuisse et obstructione corporum amisisse quae nouerant? ...

29. ... quis est enim hominum, quamuis ille sit indolis infamia semper atque ignominiosa fugientis, qui cum dici exaudiat uiris ab sapientibus maxime, immortalis animas esse nec fatorum esse obnoxias legibus,[4] non in omnia flagitia praeceps se ruat, non securus, intrepidus res obeat atque adgrediatur inlicitas, etc?

33. ... uos uestrarum animarum salutem in ipsis uobis reponitis fierique uos deos uestro fiditis intestinoque conatu; at uero nos nobis nihil de nostra infirmitate promittimus naturam intuentes nostram uirium esse nullarum et ab suis adfectibus in omni rerum contentione superari. uos cum primum soluti membrorum abieritis e nodis, alas uobis adfuturas putatis quibus ad caelum pergere atque ad sidera uolare possitis;[5] nos tantam reformidamus audaciam nec in nostra ducimus esse positum potestate res superas petere. cum et hoc ipsum habeamus incertum, an uitam accipere mereamur et ab lege mortalitatis abduci. uos in aulam dominicam[6] tamquam in propriam sedem remeaturos uos sponte nullo prohibente praesumitis; at uero nos istud rerum sine domino fieri neque speramus posse neque ulli hominum tantum potestatis attribui licentiaeque censemus. ...

35. ... et tamen, o isti, qui mediae qualitatis animas esse non creditis et in medio limite uitae atque interitus contineri, nonne omnes omnino, quos esse opinatio suspicatur, dii angeli daemones[7] aut nomine quocumque sunt alio, qualitatis et ipsi sunt mediae et in ambiguae sortis condicione nutabiles? ...

36. ... si enim forte nescitis et antea uobis incognitum propter rei nouitatem fuit, accipite sero ac discite ab eo qui nouit et protulit in

---

[1] Cf. c. 25.   [2] ἀπονενημέναι; see on 190. 23, and 290. 22.
[3] Cf. 128. 1–17 note, and c. 16 above.   [4] Cf. c. 62 below.
[5] Cf. 128. 15, 22–3; 190. 29–192·3; 154. 10 note; iv. 34. 28 note: cc. 13, 62.
[6] See introductory note, notes on 244. 19 and on *Kore Kosmu. ad fin.* Macrobius, *in somn. Scip.* i. 12. 2 'animae in propriae inmortalitatis sedem et in deorum numerum reuertuntur'; ib. 12. 16 'ad animae sedem et inmortalitatem'.
[7] This distinction is known to have been made by Labeo; cf. Augustine, *de civ. dei* 9. 19; also *Orac. chald.* pp. 44, 53, 60 (Kroll). See notes on 340. 4–346. 7; iv. 5. 12, and *P.-W.*, s.v. angelus.

medium Christo, non esse animas regis maximi filias nec ab
eo quemadmodum dicitur generatas coepisse se nosse atque in sui
nominis essentia[1] praedicari, sed alterum quempiam genitorem his
esse, dignitatis et potentiae gradibus satis plurimis ab imperatore diiun-
ctum. eius tamen ex aula et eminentium nobilem sublimitate
natalium.

37. quodsi essent ut fama est dominicae prolis et potestatis animae generatio principalis, nihil eis ad perfectionem defuisset
uirtute perfectissima procreatis, unum omnes intellectum habuissent
unumque consensum, aulam semper incolerent regiam nec prae-
termissis beatitudinis sedibus, in quibus augustissimas nouerant
retinebantque doctrinas, imprudenter adpeterent terrena haec
loca, tenebrosis ut corporibus inuolutae inter pituitas et sanguinem
degerent, inter stercoris hos utres et saccati obscenissimas serias umoris.
sed habitari oportuit et has partis, et idcirco huc animas tamquam in
colonias aliquas deus omnipotens misit. et quid homines prosunt mundo
aut ob rei cuius sunt necessarii causam, ut non frustra debuisse credantur
parte in hac agere et terreni esse corporis inquilini? ad consummandam
molis huius integritatem partem aliquam conferunt, et nisi fuerint additi,
imperfecta et clauda est uniuersitatis haec summa? quid ergo, si homines
non sint, ab officiis suis cessabit mundus, uicissitudines suas non peragent
sidera, etc.? . . . quemadmodum ergo iactatur, habitatorem debuisse regionibus his addi, cum ab homine liqueat nihil ad mundi perfectionem
redire omniaque eius studia commoditatem semper spectare priuatam
nec a finibus propriae utilitatis abscedere?

43. . . . ergone sapientes illae atque ex causis principalibus
proditae genera haec animae turpitudinum criminum malitiarumque
nouerunt atque ut exercerent, ut gererent, ut percelebrarent haec mala,
† habitare atque habitare iussae sunt has partes et humani corporis cir-
cumiectione uestiri? . . .

44. sed sua, inquitis, uoluntate, non regis missione uenerunt.[2]

45. . . . tunc deinde oblitae unius esse se fontis,[3] unius genitoris
et capitis, germanitatis conuellerent atque abrumperent iura, etc.

52. . . . unde, inquitis, homines et ipsorum hominum quid aut unde sunt
animae? unde sunt elephanti tauri cerui muli asini? unde leones equi
canes lupi pantherae eorumque quae uiuunt quid aut unde sunt animae?
neque enim fidem res habet, ut Platonico ex illo cratere[4] quem conficit
miscetque Timaeus aut horum animae uenerint aut lucusta mus sorex
blatta rana centipeda animata esse credantur et uiuere, quandoquidem ex
elementis ipsis causa est illis atque origo nascendi, si ad animalia gignenda,
quae in singulis his degunt, insunt abditae atque obscurissimae rationes.
nam et uidemus alios ex sapientibus dicere, tellurem esse horum matrem,

---

[1] *essentia* Urs *esse sententia* P.   [2] Platonizing; cf. 446. 8.
[3] Cf. c. 15 above.   [4] *Timaeus* 41 D.

aquam tum alios, aerium spiritum[1] his alios iungere, solem[2] uero nonnullos esse horum opificem et ex ignibus animatos eius uitali agitatione
motari.

62. neque illud obrepat aut spe uobis aeria blandiatur, quod ab sciolis
nonnullis et plurimum sibi adrogantibus dicitur,[3] deo esse se gnatos
nec fati obnoxios legibus, si uitam restrictius egerint, aulam sibi
eius patere, ac post hominis functionem prohibente se nullo
tamquam in sedem referri patritam ; neque quod magi spondent,
commendaticias habere se preces quibus emollitae nescio quae
potestates uias faciles praebeant ad caelum contendentibus
subuolare, neque quod Etruria libris in Acheronticis pollicetur, certo-
rum animalium sanguine numinibus certis dato diuinas animas fieri
et ab legibus mortalitatis educi.

iv. 12. si magi,[4] haruspicum fratres, suis in accitionibus memo-
rant antitheos[5] saepius obrepere pro accitis, esse autem hos

[1] An allusion to the πνεῦμα that enwraps the ψυχή during its descent through
the stars. Cf. Macrobius, *in somn. Scip.* I. 11. 12 : ' in singulis enim sphaeris,
quae caelo subiectae sunt aetheria obuolutione uestitur, ut per eas gradatim societati huius indumenti testei concilietur'. See note on 194. 27.

[2] Cf. 348. 16.

[3] This is the chapter upon which Nigettiet founds his proof that Labeo was
Arnobius' opponent. The reference to the *libri Acherontici* points straight to
Labeo (see on 360. 6). But the remainder of the chapter embraces precisely
those doctrines which we have marked as distinctive in the earlier chapters of *adv.
nat.* ii. References have already been given in the introductory note. Some
verbal parallels may be added here.

deo esse se gnatos	deum uobis adsciscitis patrem. c. 16.
nec fati obnoxios legibus	nec fatorum esse obnoxias legibus, c. 29.
aulam sibi eius patere . . . prohibente se nullo tamquam in sedem referri patritam	uos in aulam dominicam tamquam in propriam sedem remeaturos uos sponte nullo prohibente praesumitis. c. 33.
preces quibus emollitae nescio quae potestates vias faciles	secretarum artium ritus, quibus adfamini nescio quas potestates, ut sint uobis placidae neque ad sedes remeantibus patrias obstacula impeditionis opponant. c. 13.
praebeant ad caelum contendentibus subuolare	alas uobis adfuturas putatis quibus ad caelum pergere atque ad sidera uolare possitis . . . nos . . . an uitam accipere mereamur et ab lege mortalitatis
diuinas animas fieri et ab legibus mortalitatis educi.	abduci (habemus incertum). c. 33.

[4] Cf. ii. 62 above.

[5] The word occurs in Lactantius, *Div. inst.* ii. 9. 13, and in Heliodorus iv. 7,
p. 105. 27 Bekker : ἀντίθεός τις ἔοικεν ἐμποδίζειν τὴν πρᾶξιν. The reference is to
a magian doctrine (cf. iv. 5. 13) and suggests the dualism between good and bad
spirits described in the introductory note. For *obrepere* cf. 270. 7 and Minucius
Felix, *Octav.* c. 37 : *irrepentes etiam corporibus* ; and for *hostias caedi* the delight

quosdam materiis ex crassioribus spiritus, qui deos se fingant, nesciosque
mendaciis et simulationibus ludant, cur non ratione non dispari credamus
hic quoque subicere se alios pro eis qui non sunt, ut et uestras opinationes
firment et sibi hostias caedi alienis sub nominibus gaudeant?

LACTANTIUS. 9. 17 (*Fr.* 3). See on 156. 20, and note *Texte und Untersuchungen* iv. 3, ix. 60.

13. 25 *sqq.* This passage contaminates the story of the fallen angels in
Genesis with the dualistic demonology found in the Hermetic doctrines
and in Porphyry. It should therefore be compared with the Pseudo-
Clementine writings [1] in which a similar contamination appears.[2] The
references to the distinction between *caelestia* and *terrena*, to *daemoniarches*
(p. 14. 2), to δαίμων κακός (p. 14. 28) and to ἄγγελοι πονηροί (p. 15. 6),[3]
together with the use of the word ἄγγελος, show that Lactantius has
interpreted a Persian demonology in terms of Jewish and Christian legend.
Compare notes on 304. 4–346. 7, iv. 5. 14 and 7. 8. Cyprian (iv. 5. 9),
using the same pagan material, explicitly cites 'Ostanes' and the magi.[4]
In p. 14. 20, 24 *iustos . . . cultores dei* and *cognitio dei ac iustitia* may be
taken as a reference to 366. 12 *piam iustamque* (*animam*) and 368. 10–
370. 4 *iusto homini in dei religione et in summa pietate praesidium est,*
as pp. 14. 27–15. 3 indicate. See on 364. 25–370. 18. In p. 15. 3–6 the
reference is certainly to *Corp.* XVI (270. 4–28), and the phrase *in illo
sermone perfecto* may be an allusion to the claim advanced in 262. 12–13,
λόγον . . . πάντων τῶν ἄλλων ὥσπερ κορυφὴν καὶ ὑπόμνημα.

16. 2. See on 340. 4–346. 7 *ad fin.* and iv. 31. 25 for references.

13 (*Fr.* 11, 12). αἴτιου may quite properly refer to the second God, or
δημιουργός, as distinct from the supreme God; see iv. 203. 4 (*Fr.* 28). The
will of God is identified with τὸ ἀγαθόν in 332. 13, where the theme is
(as here in p. 17. 11 *sqq.*) the divine fecundity; see on 330. 21 (c. 20 b).
I do not attempt to emend p. 16. 14.

19. 11. This refers to p. 17. 1; a similar phrase, open to the same
misinterpretation, will be found in 322. 8–12.

23. 1–11. This is the Stoic contrast of the κάτω κεκυφότα and man who
looks to the stars. See on 294. 11 with references, and iv. 176. 9–14.

21. (*Fr.* 15). Cf. 150. 9–12 (with note on 148. 24). This is Hermetic
commonplace in the optimistic vein. It may be doubted whether 300.
of the bad daemons in blood is relevant. For references see on 340. 4.–346. 7,
and on 486. 10–21. It is known that Labeo held the distinction between the
two realms of daemons (*de civ. dei* viii. 13, *adv. nat.* 7. 23). In *Hermetica* see
366. 11 (*Fr.* 9 — iv. 14. 2), 344. 3 (iv. 15. 6), iv. 13. 25 and 14. 28 (= 370
testim.) with notes.

[1] *Hom.* viii–ix, *Recogn.* iv. 2; see vol. iv, Introduction III.

[2] Reconstruction by Bousset, *Archiv*, 1915.

[3] The use of *antitheus* in *div. inst.* ii. 9. 13 belongs to this tradition; see p.
482, n. 5 above.

[4] Cf. Arnobius iv. 12 above.

15-20 answers to this; the point of that passage is man's need of a body. We should expect an end of this character: ἵνα πάντα μὲν ὁρῶν πάντα θαυμάζῃ, ⟨πάντα δὲ θαυμάζων τὸν πατέρα γνωρίζῃ.⟩ Cf. 256. 26.

26. 11. See on 340. 4–346. 7 and iv. 31. 25.

31. 25. θεὸς εἷς. This is the first God of the Hermetic theology—*deus summus exsuperantissimus* (374. 1). Cf. *Frr.* 23, 28; 344. 14. 'deus primipotens et unius gubernator dei.' See note *ad loc.* and on 346. 24. For πρῶτος θεός compare the phrase ὃς μετ' ἐκεῖνον πρώτη δύναμις (*Fr.* 28).

33. 1. Chaeremon is named in l. 23, and it may be suspected that the doctrine of the male and female elements is his. See Bousset, *Schulbetrieb*, pp. 23 *sqq.*, and note on 304. 16. There is some evidence that we touch here upon an older layer of Hermetic doctrine.

34. 3. νοῦν τε καὶ λόγον. Cf. 116. 26; *Fr.* 23, 27, 28.

34. 28 (*Fr.* 16) δύο γὰρ ἔχει ψυχάς. Cf. iv. 38. 23. The characteristic mark of this theory is that one soul is subject to the stars and Εἱμαρμένη; and this may be regarded as determining the outlook of the Hermetic religion, which purported to free man from the bonds of Fate. As Zielinski pointed out, the soul, burdened with the evils the planets bestowed upon it, frees itself from them as it takes its way up to truth.[1] It will be sufficient here to cite Arnobius, ii. 16: 'at dum ad corpora labimur et properamus humana, ex mundanis circulis secuntur nos causae, quibus mali sumus et pessimi.'[2] The soul, seeking its Father's hall, in its flight sheds the effects of these cosmic influences. The emphasis on the relation between man and the Cosmos is far removed from Platonism.[3]

35. 26. μόνοι: ⟨μεταστρεφό⟩μενοι?

39. 24 (*Fr.* 17). Βίτυς. Cf. iv. 34. 14. The theory that Bitys was the man mentioned by Pliny, and is the Hermetic authority for this chapter and for 10. 7 (p. 39) is due to Dieterich (*Jahrb. f. Philol.*, *Suppl.-Band* xvi, p. 753). Its importance, if it is upheld, lies in the early date to which Hermetic teaching can be assigned. I now think that the suggestion given on iv, p. 129, n. 1 is improbable.

ZOSIMUS. **104. 5.** Νικόθεος. See on p. 120. 5.

105. 4 *sqq.* (*Fr.* 19). ἄνοας; only the pious have νοῦς. πομπάς: puppets borne in a procession (A. D. N.). See on 154. 2.

14 (*Fr.* 20). μήτε τὰ καλὰ δῶρα. This should be connected with τὰ δῶρα τοῦ Διός in iv. 109. 15, and the whole passage gives some support to the hypothesis set forth in notes on 482. 4 and 486. 10 that there are signs in the Hermetic writings of a tradition which used the tales of Hesiod for the purposes of a debate on Providence and Fate. That there was such a use of allegorical material is evident from the Proclus-Tzetzes Scholia to Hesiod, and there is reason to suspect traces of its influence in

[1] ἡ πρὸς ἀλήθειαν ὁδός (cf. 36. 19 below). See note on 128. 1 with refs.
[2] For Arnobius see additional citations above.
[3] Bousset, *G. G. A.* 1918, pp. 732 *sqq.* should be consulted on the doctrine of the two souls. See also Reitzenstein, *Historia monachorum*, pp. 201 *sqq.*

Kore Kosmu.[1] From this debate we can interpret Zeus as Εἱμαρμένη,[2] and in ll. 16-21 there appears to be an echo of a philosophical debate, after the model of those referred to in the note on 482. 4: the divine Man asks what is the greatest happiness, and the earthly Man replies, 'a pretty woman and lots of money'. But this is not merely a Stoic discussion based upon the Prometheus legend. It was inferred from the *Kore Kosmu* that Hermes had to some degree been fused with the Greek Prometheus, and the tale of Zoroaster's expulsion of the daemons was used to explain certain characteristics of the text. Here we find Zoroaster and Prometheus together in the same context of philosophical debate based upon fable. It was Zoroaster's service to expel the daemons and free men, as we saw; and here he gets rid of the ills of Fate, μερικὰ καὶ καθολικά; further we shall come upon traces of the Anthropos myth of *Corp.* I in p. 107. 6. When it is remembered that Nicotheus was also named in p. 104. 5 the presumption is that these pages carry us back to the Pagan Gnostics mentioned in Porphyry's Life of Plotinus.[3]

24 *sqq.* (*Fr.* 21). It seems preferable to read πορεύεσθαι δὲ κτλ. (iv. 106. 1). The whole passage concerning the struggle between the 'pneumatic' man and the power of Εἱμαρμένη is coloured by the Anthropos myth (see on 120. 5).[4] The Son sinks into matter, and assumes all shapes, confronting his adversaries, the daemons; Augustine, *de haeres.* 46: 'hunc primum hominem, quia mutabilis et mendacibus formis cum adversa gente pugnavit'; Clement, *Exc. ex Theodoto*, 59. 3: ἀλλὰ καὶ οὗτος ὁ ψυχικὸς Χριστός, ὃν ἐνέδυσατο, ἀόρατος ἦν, ἔδει δὲ τὸν εἰς κόσμον ἀφικνούμενον, ἐφ' ᾧ τε ὀφθῆναι, κρατηθῆναι, πολιτεύσασθαι, καὶ αἰσθητοῦ σώματος ἀνέχεσθαι. σῶμα τοίνυν αὐτῷ ὑφαίνεται ἐκ τῆς ἀφανοῦς ψυχικῆς οὐσίας, δυνάμει δὲ θείας ἐγκατασκευῆς εἰς αἰσθητὸν κόσμον ἀφιγμένον. Reitzenstein[5] quotes Euagrius, *Ep.* 29, p. 587 Fr.: μέμνησο τῆς ὀρθῆς πίστεως καὶ γνῶθι ὅτι ἡ ἁγία τριὰς οὐκ ἐν ὄψει τῶν σωματικῶν οὐδὲ ἐν θεωρίᾳ τῶν ἀσωμάτων σημειοῦται οὐδὲ τοῖς πράγμασιν συναριθμεῖται. . . . οὐ γὰρ συμφέρει ἀποβλέπειν εἰς τοὺς τῶν ἐθνῶν σοφοὺς τὸν θεὸν περιεκτικῶς καλοῦντας πνεῦμα γνωστικὸν καὶ πῦρ, ὡς δὴ οὐκ ἔχοντα εἶδος, ἀλλὰ μεταβαλλόμενόν τε καὶ ὁμοιούμενον οἷς ἂν θέλῃ. τοῦτο δὲ θεοῦ οὐκ οἰκεῖον. As R. points out, the question is whether the Trinity can be seen with bodily eyes, and whether God changes to what he wills. R. refers this passage to our text: 'in einer christlich-gnostischen Schrift war diese, selbst vielleicht schon etwas dem Christentum äusserlich angeglichene

---

[1] See evidence in notes cited above; add Synesius, *de insomn.* 1295 B (Migne): γοητευθεῖσα δὲ ὑπὸ τῶν δώρων τῆς ὕλης, πάθος πέπονθε.

[2] Guaranteed by l. 20 here.   [3] See on 120. 5.

[4] See Bousset, *Hauptprobleme*, p. 190; Reitzenstein, *Poimandres*, p. 105, *Historia monachorum*, pp. 189 *sqq.*

[5] He explains τριάδα by a reference to Porphyry, *de abstin.* ii. 37: the first God is incorporeal and needs nothing, οὐ μὴν οὐδ' ἡ τοῦ κόσμου ψυχὴ ἔχουσα μὲν τὸ τριχῇ διαστατὸν καὶ αὐτοκίνητον ἐκ φύσεως. . . . δέδεκται δὲ τὸ σῶμα εἰς ἑαυτὴν καὶ περιείληφεν, καίπερ ἀσώματος οὖσα.

Lehre benutzt.' We may also compare a mutilated passage in *Artemii Passio* (239. 18–240. 5 above). These explain the words (iv. 106. 6) θεάσῃ τὸν θεοῦ υἱὸν πάντα γινόμενον κτλ.

In iv. 106. 15 it is explicitly said that Anthropos had the name Thouth in Egyptian speech, while other peoples called him Adam—the latter was the name given to him in the Naassene document (Hippol. *Ref. haer.* 5. 7; see p. 127 above). Bousset connects the title ὀνοματόποιος (l. 16) given to the First Man with a passage in Clement, *Eclogae*, 32; Πυθαγόρας ἠξίου μὴ μόνον λογιώτατον ἀλλὰ καὶ πρεσβύτατον ἡγεῖσθαι τῶν σοφῶν τὸν θέμενον τὰ ὀνόματα τοῖς πράγμασιν.[1] It is worth noting that the martyr's speech in *Artemii Passio* (p. 239. 24 above) introduces the names of Pythagoras and Hermes in connexion with the First Man. In *Leg. Alleg.* ii. 15 Philo (in opposition to the Greeks) makes Moses his authority for the statement that there was only one giver of names, Adam.

According to the story on p. 107 the Adam made of the four elements was innocent and functionless, and the ἄρχοντες (?) persuaded Phos in Paradise to put on this body, innocent as it appeared to be, and thereby Phos was enmeshed in the bonds of εἱμαρμένη. The variant in *Corp.* I makes Anthropos fall through delight in his own image; here there is daemonic temptation.[2] l. 12. διαπνεόμενος: διακηλούμενος?

It has already been noted (on IV. 105. 14) that the Prometheus legend was drawn into the circle of this myth of freedom and necessity. For iv. 107. 22 cf. 472. 3 (God's address to Hermes-Prometheus (?)): Ὦ ψυχῆς ἐμῆ(ς) ψυχὴ καὶ νοῦς ἱεροῦ ἐμοῦ νοῖ(ς); Prometheus also took on the flesh, because Epimetheus disregarded his counsel.[3] This seems to give the transition to the Christian story in l. 25 (see also 106. 6 above): the Son of God became all things to rescue men—'Αδὰμ προσῆν Ἰ. Χριστός (p. 108. 1). In p. 108. 8 λάθρα καὶ φανερὰ συνών may refer, as Bousset suggests, to the Anthropos changing through generations.

107. 1. ἄλφα. See Bouché-Leclercq, *L'astrologie grecque*, p. 607.

108. 21. ἀντίμιμος δαίμων. For the dualistic demonology implied see on Arnobius, note on iv. 7. 8 above.

111. 4. μὴ περι(ρ)ρέμβου . . . οἴκαδε καθέζου. A familiar contrast in the language of askesis. καθέζου has the association of solitary withdrawal in a cell, and the attainment of ἀπάθεια, and thus of τελειότης (l. 15).[4] For the twelve (zodiacal) *moirai*, here added to the four classical *pathe*, see on 128. 1.

---

[1] See Bousset, *Schulbetrieb*, p. 184; Iamblichus, *vit. Pythag.* c. 82.

[2] See further *Hauptprobleme*, *loc. cit.* In p. 107. 7 Bousset brackets αὐτοῦ; ὁ ἔσω ἄνθρωπος is opposed to ὁ ἔξω ἄνθρ. of l. 16.

[3] l. 24 ὁ Νοῦς ἡμῶν, used of God; cf. *Corp.* I (126. 7, 10). A man who ἐν θεῷ γίνεται (128. 22) is ἔννους (126. 7).

[4] Reitzenstein, *Hist. monachorum*, pp. 108 *sqq.*, 97. R. infers from τῆς σῆς ἀτελειότητος (p. 112. 1) that ἡ σὴ τελειότης was the formal mode of addressing the 'perfected'.

137. n. 6. Psellus, writing of daemons, says: ἐνίους δὲ καὶ κλιματάρχας ποιεῖται, καὶ σωμάτων ἑτέρους προστάτας καὶ ὕλης φύλακας (π. δαιμόνων p. 37 Boissonade).   See also Lydus, *de mens.* p. 178.

151 (c). For καταραθέντα we should perhaps read καταφωραθέντα (Wellman).   The story is that Ares employed Alectryon to keep watch for the sun while he visited Aphrodite, and was cursed by Ares for failing (Lucian, *Gallus*, c. 3 ; cf. Aristophanes, *Birds*, 833 and scholiast).   The Ἀρχαϊκή βίβλος has now been shown by Wellman to be a collection dealing with the causes of the peculiarities of animals, and the hypothesis that it was alchemical must be set aside (*Philologus, Suppl.-Band,* xxvii. 2).   It is possible that the bestiary passage in *Kore Kosmu* (480. 5) belongs to the same tradition.

DIDYMUS. 171. 8 (*Fr.* 24). λόγων τριῶν. What is the 'third' λόγος to which Didymus refers ?   It is probable that he was dealing with a συμφωνία[1] of proof texts from the pagans, and it is certain that he attributed to Hermes sayings that were not Hermetic (see on 173. 9, *Fr.* 23, below).   Did a manuscript read by dittography λόγ΄ γ΄ (λόγων γων), and was the reading improved in the manuscript of Cyril ?   This is a χρησμός.   Is it certain that it is not a prose version of an oracle originally written in iambics ?   πηγή is commonplace in the Chaldaic oracles, and ἐξήρτηται is the regular term for the dependence of the chain of life upon its source.   The πνεύματα (spirits) were dependent in their turn upon the Πνεῦμα which was the immediate source of all life.   See on Aion (n. on 348. 8).   Also Reitzenstein, *H.M.R.* p. 28, *Iran. Erlös. Myst.,* p. 173 and vol iv, Introduction, IV.

173. 9 (*Fr.* 23). These fragments are not Hermetic prose, but oracular verse, beginning with the trite formula exemplified in—οὐ γὰρ ἐφικτὰ τὰ θεῖα βροτοῖς τοῖς σῶμα νοοῦσιν | ἀλλ᾽ ὅσσοι γυμνῆτες ἄνω σπεύδουσι πρὸς ὕψος.[2] The first lines are not easy to restore, though their type is evident ; but thereafter the original might have run somewhat as follows :

ἐν γὰρ φῶς μόνον ἦν νοερὸν νοεροῖο πρὸ φωτὸς
νοῦς τε νοὸς φωτεινός, ὅ τ᾽ ἔστι καὶ ἔσσεται ἀεὶ
κοὐδὲν ἔην ἕτερον πλὴν τούτου τῆς ἑνότητος
αἰὲν ἐν αὐτῷ ἐών, ἀεὶ νοΐ πάντ᾽ ἔχει ἀμφὶς . . .
      . . . τοῦ δὲ κατεκτὸς[3]
οὐ θεύς, οὐ δαίμων, οὐκ ἄγγελος, οὐδέ τις ἄλλος.
πάντων γὰρ κύριος καὶ πατὴρ ⟨μοῦνος⟩ θεύς ἐστιν,
πηγή τε, ζωή, δύναμις, φῶς, πνεῦμά τε νοῦς τε.
πάντα γὰρ εἰν αὐτῷ, αὐτῷ δέ τε πάνθ᾽ ὑπόκειται.[4]

176. 9. See on iv. 23. 1–11.

[1] See iv. 225 ; also note on iv. 207. 7.
[2] *Orac. chald.* (Proclus, *in Crat.* 88. 4) ; iv. 228. 2.
[3] Cf. *fr.* 26.
[4] There is a clear example of a turgid piece of oracular verse, turned into prose and attributed to Hermes, in iv. 225. 20.

AUGUSTINUS. **179.** For the convenience of readers a reference may be inserted here to the parallels between the *Confessiones* I and *Corpus* V, noted by W. Theiler, *Die Vorbereitung des Neuplatonismus*, pp. 128 *sqq.* The book was published too late to be used in these notes.

CYRILLUS. **198.** 4 (*Fr.* 25). εἴ τις. The incorporeal eye is the man himself. For the ὅμοιον—οὐχ ὅμοιον formula see 148. 22, 154. 24-6, 210. 1 (note), and iv. 205. 2 (*Fr.* 30); Ps.-Philolaus *ap.* Philo, *de opif. mundi* 100: Ἔστι γὰρ . . . ἡγεμὼν καὶ ἄρχων ἁπάντων θεὸς εἷς ἀεὶ ὤν, μόνιμος, ἀκίνητος, αὐτὸς αὑτῷ ὅμοιος, ἕτερος τῶν ἄλλων.

199. 1 (*Fr.* 26). ἐν τινι . . . κατέκτος τινος. The category of place does not apply to God; see on 442. 1. It appears better to retain the text throughout, since a Hermetist was as likely to beg the question as an interpolator in cold blood.

202. 15 (*Fr.* 27). The natural comparison is with *Corpus* I, myth of Anthropos (120. 24 *sqq.*; see on 120. 5). The λόγος is fecundating (Reitzenstein). Retain the text.

204. 5 (*Fr.* 29). τοῦτο . . . γέννησις ἢ φύσις ἢ ἔθος ἢ ὃ θέλεις αὐτὸ(ν) καλεῖν. The common formula of ἀνάκλησις—'seu Iane libentius audis'. (For the formula see 208. 30-2). The name was perhaps παντέλειος καὶ γόνιμος λόγος (iv. 202. 16, 203. 7-4. 1); at least the explanation fits this name. Retain τέλειός ἐστι ἐν τελείῳ κτλ. In general, for this δημιουργικὸς λόγος, turned to their own purposes by the Fathers, see on Aion, n. on 348. 8-358. 2.

205. 1-3 (*Fr.* 30). εἷς ὤν. See on 158. 9.

207. 7 (*Fr.* 23). τρίτῳ. See on iv. 171. 8. The presumption is that Cyril did not quote directly from the *Hermetica*; he misunderstood and elaborated a false reference. *Frr.* 23 and 24 are quoted by Didymus and by Cyril, but in reverse order. It is *Fr.* 24 (iv. 171. 8, 208. 10) that the text of Didymus derives ἐκ τῶν λόγων [τριῶν]; he is silent about the source of *Fr.* 23. Cyril assumes them to be from the same document and emends to ἐν λόγῳ τρίτῳ (cf. 208. 9). But his assumption is impossible: *Fr.* 23 is based upon an oracle in hexameters, while *Fr.* 24 is plain prose or possibly iambics turned into prose. Cyril's references should therefore be regarded with suspicion.

213. 6 (*Fr.* 31). τάξιν: πῆξιν? Cf. 146. 4, 484. 37 (ἐπάγη).

215. 4 (*Fr.* 33). This fire is the finer fire, like light, and belongs to the 'upper' elements; see on iv. 223. 17. This explains τ. φύσεως ἀνωφεροῦς ἐχόμενον. It is possible to make sense of l. 6 if ἡ φύσις is interpreted of the περίεχον πνεῦμα (438. 17)[1]; this is the Φύσις τοῦ παντός (436. 18) which animates the whole universe by its πνεῦμα. See references *ad loca.*

216. 12. If it is borne in mind that Cyril's references are dubious, it is not impossible that this is a hazy allusion to *Kore Kosmu*, 466. 19, 476. 33.

223. 17 (*Fr.* 35). τάξιν καὶ ἀταξίαν. The sensible may be described as

---

[1] Cf. i . 235. 11 (reading πνεύματος).

disordered in comparison with the 'upper' realm; cf. 160. 8 *sqq.*, 176. 12. If we retain τὸ κατωφερέστερον τοῦ νοεροῦ (224, l. 2), the sense would appear to be that the 'higher' elements (which are not material) also have their divisions, and that the life-producing πνεῦμα ranks among them.[1] This "φύσις" surrounds the Cosmos and penetrates it; see e.g. 436. 18. As it is the source of κίνησις (*ibid.*) and life, Cyril's κεκινημένοις (p. 224. 6) may be accepted. In l. 17 God is τέλειος because his perfection is the reason for his creative activity; cf. 300. 9.

225. 20. See on iv. 173. 9.

FULGENTIUS. **230.** *Mytholog.* III. 9 (*Fabula Apollinis et Marsyae*). A musicis haec reperta est fabula, ut Orfeus in teogonia scribit; musici enim duos artis suae posuerunt ordines, tertium uero quasi ex necessitate adicientes, ut Ermes Trismegistus ait, id est: adomenon, psallomenon, aulomenon, hoc est : aut cantantium aut citharidiantium aut tibiziantum.[2]

Virgiliana Continentia, p. 85. 19 Helm : nam non illa in tuis operibus quaerimus, in quibus aut Pitagoras modulos aut Eraclitus ignes aut Plato ideas aut Ermes astra aut Crisippus numeros aut endelechias Aristoteles inuersat.

ibid., p. 87. 23 : uide quid in sequentibus dictum sit, et quod 'fato profugus' et 'ui superum' quo intenderemus fortunae fuisse culpam, non uirtutis debilitatem ut fugiret et deos quam sapientiam esse culpabiles ut pericula sustentaret, illam nihilominus Platonis antiquam firmantes sententiam, ubi ait : νοῦς ἀνθρώπινος θεός· οὗτος ἐὰν ἀγαθός, θεὸς ⌜εὖ ἑρμένος,⌝ id est : sensus hominis deus est : is si bonus est, deus est propitius.

JOANNES LYDUS. **232.** 2. See on 346. 24.

235. The following Testimonia should be added to this group :—

I. JOHANNES ANTIOCHENUS.[4] τότε ὁ Τρισμέγιστος Ἑρμῆς ἀνεφάνη, ὃς καὶ ἐθεολόγησεν οὕτως "ἦν φῶς νοερὸν πρὸ φωτὸς νοητοῦ ... ἔγκυον τὸ ὕδωρ ἐποίησε." ὁ δὲ αὐτὸς Ἑρμῆς καὶ ἐπηύξατο λέγων· "ὁρκίζω σε οὐρανόν ... ἵλεως ἔσο."[5]

II. JOANNES DE NICIU.[6] 'Hermès, homme extraordinaire, crut au canon proclamé parmi les paiens, savoir : "trois puissances suprêmes constituent le créateur (δημιουργός) et une seule divinité." Or ce même Hermès proclama que la majesté de la Sainte Trinité consubstantielle était la source de la vie et la dominatrice de l'univers.'

---

[1] For the double series of elements see on 122. 25, 236. 12, 304. 16, iv. 33. 1.

[2] This is probably not Hermetic; conceivably it might be a missing portion of libellus XVIII, as Reitzenstein suggests : but there is no reason to place confidence in Fulgentius' accuracy.

[3] *Corp.* XII. i, p. 224. 3 : οὗτος δὲ ὁ νοῦς ἐν μὲν ἀνθρώποις θεός ἐστι· ... ὁ γὰρ νοῦς ψυχῶν ἐστιν εὐεργέτης ἀνθρώπων· ἐργάζεται γὰρ αὐτὰς εἰς τὸ ἀγαθόν.

[4] *Chronicon*, *fl.* 550 or later.

[5] For comparison with Suidas (ll. 10–11) it may be mentioned that J. A. reads ὀρκίζω σε κ. τ. μ. ἀ. λ. καὶ τοῦ πνεύματος τοῦ πάντα περιέχοντος.

[6] *Chronicon* ; *Versio Aethiopica*, c. 15 (ed. Zutenberg). His *floruit* was the seventh century. See 233. 5 above.

III. Cosmas Hierosolymitanus.[1] τρισάριστος δὲ κέκληται· τρισένα γὰρ θεὸν λέγειν πρῶτος ἐφεῦρε.

Artemii Passio. 239. 24 sqq. See on iv. 105. 24.

Psellus. 244. 10 sqq. This passage is based upon a school Division. ζῶον λογικὸν θνητόν is the normal definition of man (see e.g., Porphyry, *Isagoge*, 15. 2 Busse). Why then the προσθήκη often found[2] in the definition —νοῦ καὶ ἐπιστήμης δεκτικόν? The formula itself is modified from the Platonic *Definitiones*, 415 b: Ἄνθρωπος ... ὁ μόνον τῶν ὄντων ἐπιστήμης τῆς κατὰ λόγον δεκτικόν ἐστι. Hence Psellus' reference to Plato. But the form repeated here is that preferred by the commentators on Aristotle and others (e.g. Proclus, *in Tim*. ii. 315. 6 Diehl). This addition is not superfluous if beings intermediate between gods and men are supposed to exist. Such are δαίμονες, νύμφαι, and ἄγγελοι. The qualities ascribed to these beings vary,[3] but the ἴδιον of man is in any case required to distinguish him. In the division implied by Psellus the nymphs were long-lived, but not immortal,[4] had intuitive, not acquired, knowledge; that is, they were αὐτοδίδακτοι, not νοῦ καὶ ἐπιστήμης δεκτικαί, like all men save the chosen few.[5] Cf. Nemesius of Emesa (c. A.D. 400), *de nat. hominis*, 524 B (Migne): ἴδια δὲ αὐτοῦ (sc. τοῦ ἀνθρώπου) καὶ τὰ τῶν τεχνῶν τε καὶ ἐπιστημῶν μαθήματα, καὶ ἡ κατὰ τὰς τέχνας ταύτας ἐνέργεια. δι' ὃ καὶ τὸν ἄνθρωπον ὁρίζονται, ζῶον λογικὸν θνητὸν νοῦ καὶ ἐπιστήμης δεκτικόν ... τὸ δὲ "νοῦ καὶ ἐπιστήμης δεκτικόν", ὅτι διὰ μαθήσεως προσγίνονται ἡμῖν αἱ τέχναι καὶ αἱ ἐπιστῆμαι, ἔχουσι μὲν δύναμιν δεκτικὴν καὶ τοῦ νοῦ καὶ τῶν τεχνῶν, τὴν δὲ ἐνέργειαν κτωμένοις ἐκ τῶν μαθημάτων. Λέγουσι δὲ τοῦτο τῷ ὅρῳ προστεθῆναι ὕστερον. ἐρρῶσθαι μὲν γὰρ καὶ χωρὶς τούτου τὸν ὅρον· ἀλλ' ἐπειδὴ καὶ νύμφας καὶ ἄλλα τινὰ γένη δαιμόνων τινὲς εἰσάγουσι, πολυχρόνια μέν, οὐ μὴν ἀθάνατα, ἵνα καὶ ἀπὸ τούτων διαστείλωσι τὸν ἄνθρωπον, προσέθηκαν τὸ νοῦ καὶ ἐπιστήμης δεκτικόν. οὐδὲν γὰρ ἐκείνων μανθάνει, ἀλλὰ φύσει οἶδεν, ἃ οἶδεν. Philoponus (c. 530 A.D.) *in Anal. Post*. 97 a 35, p. 411. 2 Wallies: οὕτως ἀπήρτισται ὁ τοῦ ἀνθρώπου ὁρισμὸς ὡς αὐτῷ μόνῳ ὑπάρχων καὶ μὴ ἑτέρῳ τινί. καὶ εἰ μὲν λάβῃς ὅτι εἰσί τινα ζῶα λογικὰ θνητὰ φύσεις τινὲς αὐτομαθεῖς, ἤγουν μὴ ἀπὸ διδασκάλου ἔχουσαι τὰς ἐπιστήμας καὶ τὰς τέχνας ἀλλ' αὐτοδίδακτοι οὖσαι ὑπὸ τῆς φύσεως, οἷος λέγεται εἶναι ὁ Ἱπποκένταυρος ἢ ὁ Σάτυρος ἢ Πᾶνές τινες (λέγεται δὲ καὶ παρὰ τοῦ Πλάτωνος εὑρεθῆναι σῶμα Νηρηίδος νεκρὸν ἐριμμένον), εἰ μὲν οὖν τοιαῦται φύσεις εἰσίν, ἀναγκαίως πρόσκειται τῷ ὁρισμῷ τοῦ ἀνθρώπου τὸ νοῦ καὶ ἐπιστήμης δεκτικὸν ἀντιδιαστέλλον τὸν ἄνθρωπον ἐκείνων ... εἰ δὲ οὐκ εἰσὶ φύσεις τοιαῦται περισσὸν κεῖται ἐν τῷ ὁρισμῷ· ἀρκεῖ γὰρ εἰπεῖν τὸν ἄνθρωπον εἶναι ζῶον λογικὸν θνητόν. David, *Prolegomena Philosophiae*, 15. 16–27, Busse: διὰ δὲ τοῦ εἰπεῖν νοῦ καὶ

---

[1] *Comment. ad carmina Gregorii Nanzian*. ii. 7. 243, p. 496 Migne. *Fl.* VII. c.

[2] e.g. Ammonius, *in Porph. Isag.* 17. 12 Busse.

[3] See Hierocles, *in carmen aureum*, 418 a, 419 a, 423 sqq. (Mullach), and Ammonius, *in Porph. Isag.* 70. 17 Busse.

[4] Cf. Hesiod *apud* Plut. *de def. orac.* 415 C.

[5] In Philo Isaac is constantly called αὐτοδίδακτος or αὐτομαθής.

ἐπιστήμης δεκτικὸν ἐκ τῶν μακραιώνων νυμφῶν, τοῦτ' ἔστιν ἐκ τῶν θνητῶν δαιμόνων; cf. ib. 24. 5–19.

The last lines should read Ὁμηρίδαι (i.e. Ὁμηρίδε) σο(φὰς) φασιν αὐτοφυεῖς,[1] as Professor Rose suggests to me.

NICEPHORUS GREGORAS. **247.** n. 3. See on 264. 10.

AL-KINDI. **249.** 1. The number (9,000) may be connected with speculations about Plato's number in *Timaeus* 23 E. Material will be found in Proclus, *in Tim.* i. 147 Diehl. It is unnecessary to enter into the details of these interpretations. The significant fact is that the number is related to a progress of the soul through the five spheres. The 9,000 years meant nine lives, and there is a cycle of lives, a descent through the spheres and then an ascent. Such is Proclus' interpretation of Porphyry. See on 128. 1 and note on iv. 7. 8.

260. n. 4. At the end of the chapter examining Plato's (i.e. an early Neo-Platonist) view of Fate, Nemesius attacks those who reduce the Christian ἀνάστασις to the ἀποκατάστασις (*de nat. hominis*, 761 A); Tatian, *oratio*, 3. 13–4. For ἀποκατάστασις see on 348. 8.

AUTHOR-INDEX TO ADDENDA[2]

Archiv für Religionswissenschaft (*Archiv*).

Bäumker, Cl. *Das Problem der Materie in der griechischen Philosophie*, 1890.

Bidez, J. *Vie de Porphyre le philosophe néo-platonicien*, 1913.

Boehm, B. *De Cornelii Labeonis Aetate*, 1913.

Boll, F. *Sphaera*, 1903.

Bousset, W. *Hauptprobleme der Gnosis*, 1907.
  Jüdisch-christlicher Schulbetrieb in Alexandria und Rom, 1915.
  Kyrios Christos, 1913.
  'Zur Dämonologie der späteren Antike' (*Archiv*, 1915).

Brandt, S. 'Ueber die Quellen v. Lactanz' Schrift de Opificio Dei,' *Wiener Studien* 13.

Bräuninger, Fr. *Untersuchungen zu den Schriften des Hermes Trismegistos*, 1926.

Bréhier, E. *Les Idées philosophiques et religieuses de Philon d'Alexandrie*, 2me ed., Paris, 1925.

Catalogue des manuscripts alchimiques grecs.

Catalogus codicum astrologorum graecorum.

Cumont, F. *Les Religions Orientales dans le paganisme romain.* 4me ed. 1929.

Dieterich, A. *Abraxas*, 1891.
  Mithrasliturgie, 1903.

Dibelius, M. *Die Geisterwelt im Glauben des Paulus.* Göttingen, 1909.

Forschungen zur Religion und Literatur des Alten und Neuen Testaments (*Forschungen*), ed. W. Bousset and H. Gunkel. Göttingen.

Geffcken, J. *Kynika und Verwandtes*, 1909.

Göttingische Gelehrte Anzeigen (*G.G A.*).

Gronau, K. *Poseidonios, eine Quelle für Basilius' Hexaemeros*, 1912.
  Poseidonios und die jüdisch-christliche Genesisexegese, 1914.

---

[1] τὸ αὐτοφυές is commonly opposed to τὸ ἐκ τέχνης.

[2] This list is not a bibliography; it merely gives fuller references for books cited in abbreviated form in the Addenda.

Heinemann, I. *Poseidonios' metaphysische Schriften*, T. I, 1921. T. II, 1928.
Hopfner, Th. *Fontes historiae religionis Aegyptiacae*, 5 vols.

Jaeger, W. W. *Nemesios von Emesa*, 1914.
Journal of Egyptian Archaeolgoy (*J.E.A.*).
Journal of Theological Studies (*J.T.S.*).

Kalbfleisch, K. *Die neuplatonische ... Schift πρὸς Γαῦρον περὶ τοῦ πῶς ἐμψυχοῦται τὰ ἔμβρυα* (*Abh. d. K. K. Akademie*, Berlin, 1895).
Kern, O. *Orphicorum fragmenta*, 1922.
Kroll, J. *Die Lehren des Hermes Trismegistos*, 1914.
Kroll, W. *Oracula Chaldaica*.

Lewy, H. 'Sobria Ebrietas,' 1929. (*Zeitschr. f. d. neutestam. Wissenschaft*, Beiheft 8.)

Meyer, E. *Ursprung und Anfänge des Christentums*, 3 Bande 1921–23.

Nachrichten der Göttingischen Gesellschaft der Wissenschaften.
Nigettiet, F. *De Cornelio Labeone*, 1908.
Nock, A. D. *Sallustius*, 1926.
Norden, E. *Agnostos Theos*, 1923 (1912).
Beiträge zur Geschichte der griechischen Philosophie, 1892.
Die Antike Kunstprosa, 2.B. 1898.

Pauly-Wissowa. *Real-Enzyclopädie* (*P.-W.*).
Peterson, E. ΕΙΣ ΘΕΟΣ, 1926. (*Forschungen*, N. F., H. 24.)
Pohlenz, M. *Vom Zorne Gottes*, 1909. (*Forschungen*, H. 12.)

Preisendanz, K. *Papyri graecae magicae*, 1928.
Reinhardt, K. *Kosmos und Sympathie* (*K.U.S.*), 1926.
Poseidonios, 1920.
Poseidonios über Ursprung und Entartung, 1928.
Reitzenstein, R. 'Die Göttin Psyche,' 1917. (*Sitz.-Ber. der Ak. d. Wissensch. z. Heidelberg.*)
Das iranische Erlösungsmysterium, 1921.
'Das mandäische Buch des Herrn der Grösse und die Evangelienüberlieferung', 1919. (*S.-B. Heidelberg.*)
Die hellenistischen Mysterienreligionen (*H.M.R.*) ed. 3, 1927.
'Historia Monachorum' und 'Historia Lausiaca,' 1916. (*Forschungen*, N.F., H. 7).
Poimandres, 1904.
Zwei religionsgeschichtliche Fragen, ed. 1, 1901.
Reitzenstein–Schaeder. *Studien zum antiken Synkretismus—aus Iran und Griechenland*, 1926.

Schmekel, A. *Die Philosophie der mittleren Stoa*, 1892.
Schmidt, C. *Koptisch-gnostische Schriften*. 1. *Die 'Pistis Sophia'*, 1905.

Werter, J. P. ΦΩΣ (*Skr. K. Humanistiska Vetenskaps-Samfundet i Uppsala*, Bd. 17).
Wendland, P. *Neuentdeckte Fragmente Philos*, 1891.
Philos Schrift über die Vorsehung, 1892.
Wiener Studien (*W. St.*).

Zepf. M. 'Der Gott Αἰών in der hellenistischen Theologie' (*Archiv*, 1928).
Zielinski, Th. 'Hermes und die Hermetik' (*Archiv*, 8, pp. 320–372).

APPENDIX

VATICANUS GRAECUS 237 AND VATICANUS GRAECUS 951

As the editor stated in vol. i, pp. 21 and 23, readings from these manuscripts (C and M) have been used in this edition so far as Reitzenstein's published works made them accessible to him. The extreme generosity of Mr. A. D. Nock, as I noted in the Introduction, has enabled me to give a list of readings supplementing those which already appear in the apparatus. The readings are cited by page and line of this edition. From p. 134 to the end of *libellus* XI, A is the standard of comparison; on *libellus* XII variants from Q are recorded; and on *libellus* XIV variants from R.

Scott pagination	A	C	M
134. 23	γίνηται	γίνεται	γίνεται
	νοητῶς οὕτως	νοητὸν οὕτως	νοητὸν οὕτως
136 4/5	habet	om. ἡμῖν ... νοεῖται	habet
6	καὶ ὡς θεὸς οὐχ ὡς τόπος	καὶ ὁ θεὸς οὐχ ὡς τόπος	καὶ ὁ θεὸς οὐχ ὡς τόπος
9	ἀδύνατον	εὐδύνατον	ἀδύνατον
15	ἔχει ἐστῶσαν	ἐστῶσαν ἔχει	ἐστῶσαν ἔχει
22	ὑπὸ στάσεως	ὑποστάσεως	ὑπὸ στάσεως
24	οὕτω	οὕτως ? ex οὕτω	οὕτως
138. 1	θεωρία	θεωρεία	θεώρει (looks on the photograph as though -ει were superscribed on something)
4	ὑποστάσει	ὑποστάσει	ὑπὸ στάσει
5	ζῴου	κόσμου	κόσμου
12	ὦ ἀσκληπιέ	ὦ ἀσκληπιέ	οὐδαμῶς ὦ ἀσκληπιέ
20	οὐδὲν δὲ τῶν ὄντων	οὐδὲν δὲ τῶν ὄντων	οὐδὲν δὲ ὄντων, but :· over ὄντων perh. referring to margin, which is not visible on photograph.
140. 1	κέραμος	καὶ κέραμος	καὶ κέραμος
3	τὰ μᾶλλον	τὰ μᾶλλον	τὰ μᾶλλον
6	om. δὲ	habet	habet
7	κεκραμμένον	κεκραμμένον	κεκραμένον
8	ἐστι πάντα ἃ φῆς	ἐστι πάντα ἃ φῆς	ἐστι πάντα ἃ σὺ φῆς
	om. εἰ ... 12 ἀέρα	om.	habet
12	ἀναντίρρητος, Conybeare : I have no note	ἀναντίρρητος	ἀναντίρρητος
19	ἀναφὴ corrected to ἀφανὴς	ἀναφὴς	ἀναφὴς
142. 3	πλεῖον	πλέον	πλέον
8	ὁ νοῦς	οὐ νοῦς	οὐ νοῦς
12	προσωκειομέναις	προσωκειωμέναις	προσωκειωμέναις
16	γάρ εἰσι	γάρ εἰσι	γάρ εἰσι
25	οὐδὲ θεὸς	οὐδὲ ὁ θεὸς	οὐδὲ ὁ θεὸς
144. 6	γενόμενος	γένος	γένος
11	μέγιστον	μεγίστη	μεγίστη

Scott pagination	A	C	M
144. 16	Conybeare ἔχοντες: ego ἔχοντος	ἔχοντος	ἔχοντος
19	[μένει]	μενεῖ	μενεῖ
[24	θεία ἀρχὴ	θεία ἀρχὴ	θεία ἀρχὴ] ¹
146. 10	ἄμμω	ἄμμω	ἄμμω
16	περιελήγη	περιελίγη	περιελήγη, corrected from something else.
23	ἑαυτοῖς	αὐτοῖς	αὐτοῖς
24	γνῶσιν θείων	θείων γνῶσιν	θείων γνῶσιν
31	φύσεων	φύσεως	φύσεως
148. 3	πασῶν	πασῶν	πασῶν
9	ἔμψυχον καθ	ἐμψύχου	ἐμψύχου
14	συνέστηκεν	καθέστηκεν	καθέστηκεν
150. 6	ἠθέλησεν	ἠθέλησε	ἠθέλησε
	κοσμῆσα	κοσμήσας	κοσμήσας
7	καὶ κατέπεμψε	κατέπεμψε	κατέπεμψε
21	μέγαν	μὲν γὰρ	μὲν γὰρ
152. 8	om. τοῦ	habet	habet
[11	ἐπὶ γῆς	ἐπὶ γῆς	ἐπὶ γῆς]
22	καταλήψη	καταλήψη	μεταλήψη
154. 2	αὗται	αὗται	αὗται ?
[7	ὑμῶν	ὑμῶν	ὑμῶν]
12	δρόμον	δρόμους	δρόμους
13	om. θεὸν	om. θεὸν	om. θεὸν
21	φανερώτατα	φανερώτερα	φανερώτερα
26	τὸ ἀνομοίω	τὸ ἀνομοίω	τῷ ἀνομοίω
28	οὖσα πάντων	οὖσα πάντων	πάντων οὖσα
156. 5	γενομένη	γεννομένη	γεννωμένη
22	γενήσεται	γένηται	γένηται
158. 8	τέκνον τᾶτ	ὦ τέκνον τατ	τέκνον ὦ τατ, the supra-scribed β a being in a different hand, accord-ing to my note
14	ἑαυτὸν (not αὐτὸν)	ἑαυτὸν	ἑαυτὸν
29	πολεύοντας	πολιτεύοντας	πολιτεύοντας but as ιτ (? λιτ) seems dotted for deletion it must mean πολεύοντας)
160. 1	συμπεριφέρουσα	συμπεριφέρουσα	συμπεριφέρουσα, but with περι dotted for deletion.
2	τῆς θαλάσσης (so B)	τῇ θαλάσση	τῇ θαλάσση
10	ὑπὸ δεσπότην ἐστὶ τὸ (so B)	ὑπὸ δεσπότην ἐστὶ τὸν	ὑπὸ δεσπότην ἐστὶ τὸν
20	ἐπὶ γῆς	ἐπὶ τῆς γῆς	ἐπὶ τῆς γῆς
24	ταύτην τὴν καλὴν	ταύτην τὴν καλὴν	τὴν καλὴν ταύτην
162. 1	ὁ	ὁ	τίς ὁ
12	ἀποστερήσεις	ἀποστερήσῃς	ἀποστερήσῃς
14	om. καὶ	habet	habet
	κρεῖττον ἐστιν ὅσον	κρείττων ἐστιν ὅση	κρείττων ἐστιν ὅση
26	θεὸς	θεὸς	θεὸς or θεοῦ?
164. 15	ἄλλο οὐδὲν ὃ μὴ ἔστιν σὺ εἶ (so my notes: I feel unsure)	ἄλλο οὐδέν ἐστιν ὃ μὴ ἔστι· σὺ εἶ	ἄλλο οὐδέν ἐστιν ὃ μὴ ἔστι· σὺ εἶ

¹ Readings in square brackets are merely *ex silentio*.

Scott pagination	A	C	M
164. 24	γνώσεως	γνώσεως	γενέσεως
26	ἀπέριττον ego : ἀπείρι-τον Conybeare	ἀπέρητον	ἀπερίτον
166. 1	πληρεστάτην (notes not clear)	πληρέστατον	πληρεστάτην
	χορηγὸν	χωρηγὸν	χορηγὸν
6	γένηται ego : γενέσθαι Conybeare	γένηται	γένηται
10	αὐτοῦ	αὐτοῦ	αὐτοῦ
18	γενητὰ	γεννητὰ corr. to γεν.	γενητὰ
168. 9	ἐσφιγμένον	ἀφιγμένον	ἐσφιγμένον
		νο	νο
11	ἀνοήτοις	ἀρρητοις	ἀρρητοις
15	[ἐνθάδε]	ἐνθάδε δὲ	ἐνθάδε δὲ
22	εἰλικρινέσταται	εἰλικρινέσταται	εἰλικρινέσταται self-corr. out of -έστεραι
34	ὑπέρλαμπον	ὑπέρλαμπρον	ὑπέρλαμπρον
170. 1	ἀγαθὸν τὸ ἀμίμητον	ἀγαθὸν ἀμίμητον	ἀγαθὸν ἀμίμητον
11	[αὐτῷ]	αὐτὸ	αὐτῷ
170. 18	ἐν ἀνθρώποις	ἐν τοῖς ἀνθρώποις	ἐν τοῖς ἀνθρώποις
23	εἰ (hardly legible, perh. οἱ superscr. on it)	οἱ	εἰ
27	καὶ μὴ ἑῶσα	καὶ μὴ ἑῶσα	μὴ ἑῶσα
172. 3	ζητήσατε	ζήσατε	ζητήσατε
4	ὁδηγήσαντα	-αντα	-οντα ?
6	τὸ	τὸν (but ν perh. by later hand)	τὸν
13	λῃστὴν	λοιστὴν	λῃστὴν
18	μισήσῃς	μισήσῃς	μισήσεις
174. 3	θανάτους	θανάτους	θανάτους
11	om. τῷ	habet	habet
26	ὑποκείμενον	ἀποκείμενον	ἀποκείμενον
176. 4	ἐνάτρῳ	ἐν ἄντρῳ	ἐν ἄντρῳ
23	πρ̅σ̅αυτοῦ, as Cony-beare : probably.	πρώτου	πρώτου
178. 20	ἀν̅ο̅υ = ἀνθρώπου	νοῦ	νοῦ
	λ. ἢ ὄργανα	λ. ἢ ὄργανα	λ. ἢ ὄργανα
	ἀδελφὸς	ἀδελφὸς	ἀδελφὴ
180. 5	[συμφωνήσῃ]	συμφωνήσῃς	συμφωνήσῃ
8	τινων	τινος	τινος
	ε post		
9	καινοῦ	καινοῦ	καὶ νοῦ
17	om. ὁ	om. ὁ	habet
31	κοινῶσαι ἀν̅ω̅ (= ἀν-θρώπῳ)	κοινωνῆσαι αἴσθησιν	κοινωνῆσαι αἴσθησιν
182. 1	om. μὲν	habet	habet
	ὑλικῶς	ὑλικῶς	ὑλικῶς
9	ἰδία	ἰδίαν	ἰδίαν
19	παρέχῃ ego : -ει Cony-beare	παρέχῃ	παρέχῃ
21	ἐκ τῆς γῆς	ἐκ γῆς	ἐκ γῆς
30	[εἰκότως]	εἰκότος	εἰκότως
184. 27	om. τὸ	om. τὸ	om. τὸ
	μου	μοι	μοι
186. 5	om. κ. α.	om. κ. α.	habet καὶ αἰσθήσεως
	ἢ post		
21	εἰ τοῦ	εἰ τοῦ	εἰ τοῦ

Scott pagination	A	C	M
188. 25	ἐκλάμπειν	ἐκλάμπει	ἐκλάμπει
190. 2	ὥσπερ according to my note	ὕπερ	ὅπερ
9	καταρτία	καταρτία	καταρτία
12	om. τὸ	om. τὸ	τὸ
23	om. τῷ	τῷ	τῷ
29	ἀνθ. αἱ ἀθ.	ἀνθ. ἀθ.	ἀνθ. ἀθ.
192. 5	παλίσσυρτος	παλίσυρτος	παλίσυρτος
18	σκιομαχεῖ	σκιομαχεῖ	σκιομαχεῖ
28	om. τὰ	τὰ	τὰ
194. 6	μὲν ποτὲ	μὲν ποτὲ	ποτὲ μὲν
10	[? σφαίρα or σφαῖρα]	σφαίρα	σφαίρα
11	κεφαλὴ· κεφαλῇ δὲ (fere scr.)	κεφαλὴ· κεφαλῇ δὲ	κεφαλὴ· κεφαλῇ δὲ
16	πλὴν εἰ	πλεῖ	πλεῖ
196. 6	om. τὸ before αἷμα om. τὰς before ἀρτ.	habet habet	habet habet
16	ἔγγονος	ἔγκονος	ἔγκονος
19	’Ο. ἀ. οὕτω	’Ο. ἀ. οὕτως	’Ο. ἐστιν ἀ. οὕτως
24	ὑγκωμένον βλέπειν	ὑγκωμένου βλέπει	ὑγκωμένου βλέπει
25	τεθολωμένην	τεθολωμένη	τεθολωμένην
26	ἠρτημένη (not -ην as Scott implies)	ἠρτημένη	ἠρτημένην (?)
28	ὄγγους	ὕγκους	ὄγκους
198. 11	σοῦ	τοῦ	σοῦ ex τοῦ
14	ἔχει corr. A² to ἔχειν	ἔχειν	ἔχειν
25	[πύρινον ὂν οὐκ] probably wrong	πύρινον οὐκ	πύρινον οὐκ
29	ὃς	οὓς	οὓς
200. 1	σώματα πῦρ	σῶμα τὸ πῦρ	σῶμα τὸ πῦρ
2	πρὸς	om.	habet
15	ἀνθρώπινον (first time)	ἀνθρώπειον	ἀνθρώπειον
18	ψυχὴ ἀνθρωπίνη	ἀνθ. ψ.	ἀνθ. ψ.
19	τέκνον ἡ ἀσέβεια	τ ἡ ἀ.	τ. ἡ ἀ.
19, 20	ποῖον ... ἀσέβεια	om.	habet
21	λυμᾶναι	λυμάναι	λυμάναι
25	εἰσι	ἐστι	ἐστι
29	Conybeare εἰσδύνεται: ego εἰσδύνασα	εἰσδύνασα·	εἰσδύνασα
30	Conyb. μάστιξ. But a curl under μάστιξ may signify that μάστιξιν is intended.	μάστιξιν	μάστιξιν
202. 2	ἔχει	ἔχει	ἴσχει
3/4	ἔργοις καὶ λόγοις	ἐ. κ. λ.	λόγοις καὶ ἔργοις
27	λέγεις πάλιν	λ. π.	πάλιν λέγεις
28	τὸ ὑπ’	τ	τὸν
204. 7	πρὸς	ὑπ’	ὑπ’
10	ζῷόν ἐστι θεῖον	ζ. ἐ. θ.	ζ. θ. ἐ.
22	οὐράνιον	οὐρανὸν	οὐρανὸν
206. 7	ἂν καὶ μόνῳ	ἂν μόνῳ	ἂν μόνῳ
208. 7	ἀεὶ γενόμενος	ἀ. γιν-	ἀ. γιν-
10	τί	τίς	τίς

Scott pagination	A	C	M
208. 34	περιβάλλοι	παραβάλλοι	παραβάλλοι
210. 1	ἐκπεσῇ	ἐκπεσεῖ	ἐκπεσεῖ
10	ῥοπὴν	ῥοπὴν	ῥοὴν
212. 3	[ἀνομοίων]	ἀνομίων	ἀνομοίων
7	δ' ἐκείνων	δὲ ἐκείνων	δὲ ἐκείνων
11	τὰ ego τὸ Conybeare	τὰ	τὰ
17	ταῦτα πάντα	ταῦτα πάντα	ταῦτα παντά
	ὧ	om.	om.
21	ἐνδιαφόρω	ἐνδιαφόρων	ἐνδιαφόρων
22	κινήσεως	κινήσεων	κινήσεων
214. 1	οὐ	ὡς	ὡς
12	καὶ	δὲ καὶ	δὲ καὶ
14	δ' ἂν	δὲ ἂν	δὲ ἂν
	om. εἰς	om.	om.
29	δὲ ὀσφραινόμενος ἐκεῖνα	δὲ ὁ ὁ.	δὲ ὁ ὁ.
216. 1	οὐ δυνατὰ χωρὶς	οὐδὲ δυνατὰ ἐκεῖνα χ.	οὐδὲ δ. ἐ. χ.
20	ἀλλον	-ον	-ον
30	ἀπολεία	ἀπώλεια	ἀπώλεια
218. 3	τοῦτο	τούτω	τούτω
9	ἐκκειμένας	ἐκκειμένας	ἐκκειμένας
14	om. αὐτὸν	habet	habet
16	[ἄπορον]	ἄγορον	ἄπορον
	εἴ τις	εἴη τις	εἴη τις
17	τ' ὄψεσιν	τ' ὄψεσιν	τ'ὄψεσιν
	[ὑποσταίη]	ὑποστείη	ὑποστείη
20	ἀκρώρειαι	ἀκώρειαι	ἀκρώρειαι
34	οὐδέ ἐστι	οὐδ' ἐστι	οὐδ' ἐστι
35	ταχύτερον	παχύτερον	ταχύτερον ex παχ-
220. 5/6	om. μεταβᾶσα . . . ὡς	habet	habet
10	ἀνατεπτήσεται (πτ superscribed on something)	ἀναπτήσεται	ἀναπτήπεται
11	βουληθείη	-ης	-ης
19	σεαυτὸν ex -ῶ	-ὸν ex -ῶ	σεαυ τὸν [sic]
25	ὑψηλότατος γενοῦ	ὑψηλότατος γένους	ὑψηλότατος γένους
33	ἑαυτὴν	αὐτὴν	αὐτὴν
222. 1	οὐδὲ . . . οὐδὲ	οὐδὲ . . οὐδὲν	οὐδὲν . . . οὐδὲν
3/4	τὸν καλὸν καὶ ἀγαθὸν	τὸν καλὸν καὶ ἀγαθὸν	τὸν καλὸν καὶ ἀγαθὸν
4	φιλοσώματος ὢν καὶ κακὸς	φ. κ. κ. ὢν	φ. κ. κ. ὢν.
9	καὶ π.	καὶ π.	omits the καὶ before π.
10	space	γρηγορητὶ κοιμωμένω	γρηγορητὶ κοιμωμένω
18	om. ἐπὶ	habet	habet

In Tractate XII are given variants from Scott's record of Q.

Scott pagination	Q	A	C	M
222. 21	ἑρμοῦ τοῦ τρισμ.	om.	ἑρμοῦ τρισμ.	ἑρμοῦ τρισμ.
23	τῆς	τῆς	om.	om.
224. 8	καὶ ψυχή ἐστιν ·	καὶ ἡ ψυχὴ	καὶ ζωχὴ (ψ. supra-scr. in late hand) [suprascript: ψυχὴ]	καὶ ψυχή
11	om. γὰρ	[hab.]	hab.	hab.
15	συνθέτου	as Q	συνθέντου	as Q
	ἡ ἡδονή	ἡδ.	ἡδ.	ἡδ.
18	προσλήμμασιν	[προλ.]	προλ.	προλ.
20	αὐτῆς τὴν ἡδονὴν	αὐτὴν τῆς ἡδονῆς	-ν -s -s	-ν -s -s
25	ὁ	om.	ὁ	ὁ
	ὑγείαν	?	ὑγίειαν	ὑγίειαν
28	τὰς ἐπιθυμίας	[no note]	ταῖς -αις	ταῖς -αις
31	οὐδὲν	οὐδὲ	-ὲ	-ὲ
	γὰρ καὶ	καὶ γὰρ	καὶ γὰρ	κ. γ.
226. 8	τὸν κ. π. τὸ π.	τὸ κ. π. π.	τὸ κ. π. π.	τὸν κ. π. π.
11	μὲν	μὲν	δὲ	δὲ
13	ἠλλαγμένος	ἠλαγ-	ἠλλαγ-	ἠλλαγ-
15	ἀνόμοιος	[ἀνόμοιος]	ἀνόμοιος	ἀνόμοιος
18	om. οἱ	[οἱ]	om.	om.
22/3	om. πάσχουσιν ... ὄντες	hab.	hab.	hab.
30	ἐδεδώκει	ἐδεδ.	ἐκδεδ	ἐκδεδ.
228. 2	αὐτοῦ ποτε	ποτε αὐτοῦ	π. α.	π. α.
9	μου	μοι	μου	μου
15	εἶναι	εἶναι	οὖν	οὖν
28	νοῦ	νοῦν	νοῦ	νοῦ
34	μὲν γὰρ	μὲν	μὲν γὰρ	μὲν γὰρ
34/5	τὸ δὲ ... ἐνεργεῖ om.	hab.	hab. (35 ἑαυτὰ)	hab. (35 ἑαυτὰ)
230. 3	ταὐτόν	ταὐτόν	ταὐτό	ταὐτόν
7	παρὰ	[παρὰ]	περὶ	περὶ
	τὰ. θ. ζ.	τὰ ἔθνη ζωα, [suprascript: τῶν ων] the suprascribed readings being due to late hand	τὰ θ. ζ.	τ. θ. ζ.
13	χρᾶται	χρῆται	χρᾶται	χρᾶται
18	[οὕτως]	οὕτω	οὕτως	οὕτως
232. 6	om. τὰ	[τὰ]	om. τὰ	om. τὰ
13	συσσώζων	σώζων	συσσώζων	συσσώζων
15/6	τοῦ αἰῶνος ... παν-τὸς om.	hab.	hab.	hab.
19	εἶναι	εἶναι	οὖν	οὖν
21	εἶναι	εἶναι	οὖν	οὖν
234. 4	σοι	om.	σοι	σοι
5	μύνον	μόνη	μόνον	μόνον
	στασίμη	-οι	-η	-η
6	[εἶναι]	οὖν	οὖν	οὖν
7	ἀδ. γὰρ χ.	[ἀ. γ. χ.]	ἀδ. χ. γὰρ	ἀδ. χ. γ.
	φῦναι	φυῆναι	φάναί	φάναί
8	γελοιύτατον	-ύτερον	-ότατον	-ότατον
10	[πᾶν]	[πᾶν]	πᾶς	πᾶς
11	ἢ	[ἢ]	ἤτοι	ἤτοι
12	ζῆ	[ζῆ]	ζῆν	ζῆ

Scott pagination	Q	A	C	M
234. 13	εἶναι	[εἶναι]	οὖν	οὖν
	ὁ κόσμος ἀμ. ὦ τέκνον ἐστι.	ὁ κ. ἀμ. ὁ κόσμος ἐ. so my notes expressly, but I doubt the reading	ὁ. κ. ἀ. ὦ. τ. ἐ.	ὁ. κ. ἀ. ὦ. τ. ἐ.
17	ἡ	om.	ἡ	ἡ
19	τὸ πνεῦμα ὁ νοῦς ψυχή	τὸ πνεῦμα ψυχὴ ὁ νοῦς	τ. π. ψ. ὁ. ν.	τ. π. ψ. ὁ. ν.
27	προγεγεννημένα	γεγεννημένα	προγεγενν.	προγεγενν.
29	μὲν	μὲν γὰρ	μ. γ.	μ. γ.
236. 1	τούτοις πᾶσι	π. τ.	π. τ.	τ. π.
4	οὐδὲν δύσκ.	οὐδὲν δὲ δύσκ.	ο. δύσκ.	ο. δύσκ.
8	τῶν	om.	τῶν	τῶν
10	ἀγαθὸν	[-ῶν]	-ῶν	-ῶν
12	εἰ οὖν ἐνέργειαί εἰσιν	om.	αἱ οὖν ἐνέργειαι ὅλως εἰσιν	αἱ οὖν ἐνέργειαι ὅλως εἰσιν
14	ὥσπερ τοῦ κόσμου μέρη ἐστιν	ὑπερ ... ἐστὶν	ὅπερ ... ἐστιν	ὕπερ τοῦ κόσμου μέρη ἐστιν
	γῆ καὶ ὕδωρ	ὕ. κ. γ.	ὕ. κ. γ.	ὕ. κ. γ.
15	μέλη	μέλη	μέλη	μέρη
18	οὐκ ἔτι τι	οὐκέτι ἐστί τι	οὐκέτι ἐστί τι	οὐκέτι ἐστί τι οὖν
22	οἴει εἶναι μὴ [ὑπὸ]	ἢ εἶναι μὴ ἀπὸ	οἴει οὖν μὴ ἀπὸ	οἴει μὴ ἀπὸ
26	ὕλην	ὕλη	-η	-η
28	om. καὶ ... οὐσιότητα	hab.	hab.	hab.
238. 1	om. περὶ	hab.	hab.	hab.
4	εἶναι	[εἶναι]	οὖν	οὖν

In Tractate XIV are given variants from Scott's record of R.

Scott pagination	R	A	C	M
256. 1	Ἐ. πρὸς Ἀσκλ.	Ἐ. π. Ἀ.	Ἐ. τρισμεγίστου Ἀσκληπιῶ εὖ φρονεῖν	as C
4	ὁ υἱὸς	ὁ υἱ.	ὁ υἱ.	ὡς υἱ.
12	om. ὑφ' ἐαυτ[οῦ] ἀλλ'	ὑφ' ἐαυτῶν ἀλλ'	as A	as A
13	om. second τὰ	om.	om.	τὰ
19	μόνως	-ως	-ος	-ος
26	ἐστὶν ἄξιος	ἐστιν ἄξιον τι (sic)	ἐστιν ἄξιον	ἐ. ἀ.
258.1/2	om. καὶ πῶς αὐτὸν	[hab.]	hab.	hab.
8	[ἀπαλλαγέντας]	[-ας]	-ες	-ες
15	om. ἀπὸ	om.	om.	om.
16	οὐδὲ	οὐδὲ	οὔτε	οὔτε
21	ὡς γένεσις δὲ	as R	as R	ὡς γένεσίς ἐτσι
28	om. μὲν	[μὲν]	μὲν	μὲν
29	ἂν ex ἐὰν	ἐὰν	ῶσαν (ω being by later hand)	ζὰν (looks like σαν but may be for ἐὰν)

APPENDIX

Scott pagi-nation	R	A	C	M
31	[ταπεινότητα]	-ητα	-ητα	-ατα
	περιάψη	-ης	-ης	-ης
260. 1	δὴ	[δὲ]	δὲ	δὲ
2	παθητὰ	παθητὰ	πάθη τὰ	πάθη τὰ
5	γεγέννηκεν	ἐγέννησεν	ἐγέννησεν	ἐγέννησεν
12/13	om. man. pr. ὦ ... θεὸν	hab.	hab.	hab.
15	οἴδασιν	-ιν	-ι	-ι
	τὸ	τὺ	τῶ	τῶ
17	εἰ γὰρ μὴ	as R	as R	$\overset{\beta\ \ a}{\text{εἰ-μὴ γὰρ}}$ (doubtful if correction is from first hand)
28	$\overset{\lambda}{\text{καταβάλοντα}}$ sic	καταβάλοντα $_{\lambda}$ sic	καταβάλλοντα	καταβάλλοντα
	εἰς τὴν γῆν	εἰς τὴν γῆν	εἰς γῆν	εἰς γῆν [1]

[1] The responsibility for any errors in the printed apparatus is editorial.

INDICES[1]

I. INDEX GRAECITATIS

A iv. 107. 1.
ἀβλαβής 188. 28.
ἄβυσσος 146. 1, 266. 7.
ἀγαθοποιέω 180. 29.
ἀγαθός. τ. -όν 128. 23, 140. 23, 142.
16 s., 154. 13, 236. 18, 242. 6, 252. 3,
258. 5, 260. 19 s., 344 T., 390. 18, iv.
201. 4. ἄκρατον (= ἀλήθεια) 384. 23.
ci. ἀλήθεια 246. 1. ἀληθινόν 238. 23.
αὐτό iv. 39. 23. περιούσιον 124. 16.
(θεός, ἐν θεῷ) 142. 21 s., 164. 22, 168.
4, Fr. 17. οὐσία θεοῦ 168. 25, 206.
15. πάθος θεοῦ 260. 19. πλήρωμα τ.
θεοῦ 168. 19. *ἓν καὶ μόνον 172. 17,
Fr. 26 (cf. 372 T.). = δημιουργία 270,
31. ci. θεὸς κ. πατήρ 186. 10, 23, 192. 19.
opp. πάθος 166. 19. opp. φθόνος 244.
33. ὁρᾶν τ. -όν 152. 12. εὐσέβεια 370 T.
τ. ἐνθάδε 166. 29. ἀγαθά 254. 11. πάντα
298 T. ὅλα iv. 36. 28 s. ἀνθρώπεια
170. 13. v. δαίμων, θεός, κόσμος.
ἄγαλμα 272. 25.
ἄγαμαι 298 T.
ἀγαπ-άω 124. 16. -ητικῶς 126. 13.
ἀγγεῖον. γενέσεως 422. 24. ci. ψυχή
516. 12. τὰ κάτω 508. 13.
ἄγγελος. Fr. 23, iv. 106. 8. δορυφορή-
σαντες 498. 1. κομῆται 416. 36. ἐν τ.
πρώτῳ στερεώματι iv. 145 s.
ἀγεννησία 424. 4.
ἀγέννητος 174. 15, 256. 15, passim. ὁ
εἷς 158. 4. τὸ -όν 166. 22. τὸ θεῖον
134. 21.
ἅγιος 130. 12 s., 146. 4, 250. 32. λόγος
116. 2, Fr. 33.
ἀγνο-έω 152. 3, 196. 16, 248. 17, 390.
24. τ. θεῖον 222. 6. ἑαυτήν 192. 12.
οἱ -οῦντες 124. 19, 170. 7. -ία 132. 16,
142. 26, 242. 23, 244. 18, 268. 20, 364
T. opp. γνῶσις 244. 18. ἐν -ίᾳ 130. 26,
434. 5.
ἀγνός 130. 22.
ἀγνωμοσύνη 162. 11.
ἀγνωσ-ία 170. 20 s., 192. 9, 260. 12,
458. 11, *486. 10. τ. θεοῦ 132. 10.
περὶ τ. θεόν 260. 12. -τος 430. 1, 464.
19. θεός 458. 4.

ἄγριος 486. 24. τὸ -ον 486. 38, 492. 4.
ἀγχ-όνη 180. 13. -ω (metaph.) 172. 16
204. 7.
ἀγών 200. 8. *392. 15, *496. 22.
ἀγων-ία 458. 3, 472. 18. -ίζομαι 170.
12, 200. 8.
ἄδεκτος 384. 26.
ἀδελφ-ή. τ. λόγου 178. 20. -ός
(metaph.) 120. 14.
ἀδέσποτος 160. 7, 270. 16.
ἄδηλος. τὸ -ον 434. 5.
ἀδιά-βατος *154. 13. -λειπτος 184. 1,
268. 9. -λυτος 268. 6. σώματα 176.
17.
ἀδιόριστος 146. 6.
ἀδικ-έω 200. 10, 480. 10. -ία. τιμωρία
242. 27.
ἀδοξία 258. 31.
ἀδυνατ-έω 200. 5. -ος. εἰμι 242. 16.
ἄδυτον pl. 482. 20, 486. 21.
ᾄδω 248. 27.
ἀειδής 394. 28.
ἀεί-ζωος. dist. ἀίδιος 174. 19. -κίνητος.
ψυχή 404. 3, 440. 18.
ἀένναος 284. 2.
ἀέρ-ιος. ψυχαί 190. 28. -ώδης, 528. 7.
ἀετός 480. 8, 504. 29, 508. 35.
ἀήρ. elementum, v. πῦρ. αὐτοάηρ 382.
9. personif. 488. 14. origo 118. 2,
438. 13. σῶμα 140. 5 s. ci. αἰθήρ 462.
24, 474. 34. ci. πνεῦμα 140. 14. spiritus
164. 18, 230. 26 (cf. 234. 30), 300. 4
(ψυχῆς σῶμα). regio 160. 12, 266. 5,
368 T. 512. 20, v. οὐρανός. εἰς ἀέρα
ἀναχύνεσθαι 508. 7.
ἀθανασία. 1. caelestis 176. 6, 188. 28.
ἐν οὐρανῷ 262. 2. ci. αἰών 206. 22.
ci. ζωή 236. 16, 266. 21. siderum 176.
6. (concr.) 198. 18. 2. animae 124.
20, 132. 14 s., 192. 4. ἀρχὴ -ίας 190.
29.
ἀθανατ-ίζω. pass. κόσμος 174. 18,
236. 24. -ος. 1. κύκλος τ. θεοῦ 250.
17. μέρη τ. κόσμου 266. 27. ci. διαμονή 266. 24. ἀίδια σώματα (astra) 408.
7, 16. ci. ἀδιάλυτος 268. 5. θεοί 144,
3. ἀθάνατα 234. 18. ἐνέργειαι 392.

---

[1] References are by page and line for volume i, and by volume, page, and line
(if numbered) for the other volumes. The letter T. is used to indicate *Testimonia*
under the *Asclepius*. An asterisk is used to mark an emendation, whether included
in the printed text or not; words that are probably corrupt have been obelized.

21. 2. ψυχή 174. 5, 404. 5 (ci. ἀεικί-
νητος`. τ. λογικόν 426. 22. ci. οὐσιώδης
122. 5. ὁ ἔννους 124. 10. -οι ἀντὶ θνητῶν
152. 10. ἡ ἀ. φύσις 506. 24. σῶμα 240.
16. 248. 16. γεννήματα 254. 11.

ἄθε-ος 486. 33, 488. 11, 31. -ότης 224.
22.

ἀθεώρητος 460. 14, 484. 28.

ἄθλ-ησις 484. 2. -ον 150. 20.

αἰδέομαι 158. 29.

ἀίδιος. θεός 174. 15, 19. ψυχή 446. 20.
ἀ. σώματα 382. 6, 388. 6 (elementa),
408. 2 (astra). ἀ. διαμονή 266. 24.
τὸ -ον 380. 5. ἐνέργεια 394. 4 s., 426.
16.

αἰθ-ήρ 220. 9, 414. 31, 466. 15. ἐξ -έρος
τ. πνεῦμα 122. 28 (elementum superius). ci. ἀήρ 462. 24, 474. 34.

αἷμα. ψυχή 196. 3. ci. πνεῦμα 196. 1,
198. 6. ci. ὕδωρ 410. 9. νόστιμον
454. 8.

αἱματώδης. γῆ iv. 106. 18.

αἰνέω 254. 9.

αἴνιγμα 240. 5.

αἵρ-εσις 152. 26 s., 422. 15, 446. 7. -έω
m. 422. 14, 428. 20, 446. 5 s. ἐν ἀρχῇ
ἑλομένη βίον 442. 28. τῷ ἑλέσθαι βουλομένῳ, ἑλομένῳ 152. 26 s.

αἴρω pass. 160. 12.

αἰσθ-άνομαι 176. 24. οὐ χωρὶς νοήσεως
178. 25. τ. γνώσεως 180. 26. -ησις
178. 11 s. ἡ αἴσθ. ζωή, λήθη θάνατος
234. 17. (θάνατος) ἀφανισμὸς -εως
σωματικῆς 364 T., στέρησις τ. -εως
176. 18. -εις σωματικαὶ κ. θνηταὶ 400.
3 s. -εις ἀποτελέσματα τ. ἐνεργειῶν
398. 32. ci. πάθος 400. 24 s. ὀργα-
νικαί, ci. πνεῦμα 448. 16 s. ἀνθρωπεία
182. 10. λογικῶν, opp. ἀλόγων, ἐμψύ-
χων 400. 20. λογικὰ περισσαῖς -εσι
ἐκόσμησε 516. 25. (ἄνθρωπος) ἅπτεται
καὶ (οὐρανοῦ) αἰσθήσει 236. 2. τ.
ἀσώματον ὑπὸ τ. ἡμετέρων -εων κατα-
ληφθῆναι οὐ δύναται 380. 13. ἡ α. κ.
ἡ νόησις συμπεπλεγμέναι 178. 23. ci.
δόξα 444. 28. ci. φύσις (animalium)
178. 16. ὑλική, opp. οὐσιώδης νόησις
178. 13. opp. γνῶσις 192. 21. σωμα-
τικαί 114. 4, 190. 13, 246. 9. μυσάτ-
τονται 126. 16. ἐνεφράχθησαν 242. 9.
καταργία πασῶν τ. -εων 190. 9. καταρ-
γῆσον τ. -εις 242. 18. αἱ -εις τ. σώματος εἰς τ. ἑαυτῶν πηγὰς ἐπανέρχονται
128. 3. α. καὶ νόησις τ. θεοῦ 184. 19,
τ. κόσμου 182. 9. -εις τ. ποιητῶν 220.
26.

αἰσθητ-ήριον. pl. 172. 19. -ικός *426.
22, 524. 14. -ικῶς *124. 17, 126. 24,
244. 8. -ός. θεός 298 T. κόσμος 118.

14. *268. 23, 270. 29, 272. 23 s. -ά,
ci. νοητά 142. 20.

αἰσθομαι 428. 6. (metaph.) 180. 26.

αἰτί-α. ἑνιαία iv. 33. 13. -ος. θεός 142.
2, 188. 3 s. πρῶτον -ον iv. 31. 7. δεύτερον iv. 160. 7. αἴτιον τούτου τ. αἰτίου
Fr. 11. ὁ κόσμος 188. 1. δαίμονες
-οι 270. 3. ἡμεῖς -οι τ. κακῶν 154. 8.

αἰών 458. 22, 460. 14, iv. 40. 2, pl. iv.
196. 7. τ. πατρῴας ἀποκαταστάσεως
232. 13. ci. astra: ἀναπληροῦν 212.
1. τ. μέγαν αἰ. διέπειν 484. 25. 530.
12. Αἰών. ci. δύναμις, ἐνέργεια 228. 4.
ci. θεός, κόσμος 206. 10 s. Αἰ. γενοῦ
220. 21. σός 252. 23. v. aeternitas.

αἰώνιος. διαμονή 376 T. τάξις 210.
27.

αἰωρέω. m. 414. 31, 418. 9.

ἀκάματος. κίνησις 436. 11.

ἀκάνθη 518. 9.

ἀκατά-ληπτος 480. 22. -σκεύαστος 146.
6.

ἀκατονόμαστος Fr. 21.

ἀκήρατος 210. 25.

ἀκίνητος 160. 17, 228. 35, 426. 11. passim.

ἀκλινής 246. 12.

ἀκμαῖος 210. 26.

ἀκοή 116. 5, 250. 11, pl. 192. 18.

ἀκοπίαστος 184. 2.

ἀκόρεστ-ος 120. 24. -ως 126. 26, 170.
11.

ἀκούσι-ος. τ. κακόν 428. 19. -ως 446. 6.

ἀκου-στός 172. 7. -ω 114. 8, 132. 12,
172. 21. 248. 25 s.

ἀκρασία 242. 25.

ἄκρατος. ἀγαθόν 384. 23. λόγος (-ον
ποτόν?) 170. 21. πῦρ 116. 29, Fr. 33.

ἀκρίβ-εια 458. 27. -ῆς 460. 6, 480. 7.
compar. αἰσθήσεις 516. 25. -ῶς. εἰ
θεάσῃ 156. 12. κατανόησον 210. 24.
νοῆσαι τ. θεόν 418. 12.

ἄκριτ-ος 518. 16. -ως 508. 7.

ἀκρίς 504. 28.

ἀκροατής 432. 24.

ἀκρώρεια 218. 20.

ἀκτίς. τ. ἡλίου 188. 23. metaph. ci.
νοῦς 140. 23. τ. θεοῦ 158. 10, 202. 15,
270. 18 s. τ. κόσμου 202. 16 s.

ἀλγηδών 168. 10, 402. 3.

ἀλεκτρυών iv. 151 (c).

ἄληπτος 190. 7.

ἁλίσκομαι 156. 9.

ἀλήθ-εια 130. 8, 140. 23, 172. 17, 184.
28, 252. 2, 254. 11, 382. 2 s., 384. 4 s.,
390. 15. τελεωτάτη ἀρετή 384. 22 δύναμις 244. 31. τ. -ας μιμήματα 382. 18.
ἥλιος ἀ. 388. 16 s. ἡ πρώτη ἀ. 388. 20.
ci. τ. ἀγαθόν 246. 1. personif. 472. 24.

αὐτο-άηρ 382. 9. -γέννητος. *ci.* αὐτοπάτωρ iv. 201. 8. -γόνος *488. 20, iv.
39. 15. *ci.* αὐτοπάτωρ iv. 31. 27.
-δεής 194. 6. -δίδακτος iv. 244. 11.
-καλον iv. 201. 7. -κίνητος. ψυχή
440. 18. -μήτωρ *Fr.* 13. -πάτωρ *Fr.* 13,
iv. 31. 28, iv. 201. 8.
αὐτόπτης 418. 13.
αὐτό-πυρ 382. 8. -τελής. δύναμις iv.
39. 17. λόγος 434. 8. ψυχή 442. 27.
-φυής 434. 9, 482. 18, iv. 244. 16. -ύδωρ
382. 9.
αὐτός. τὸ -ὸ ἐξ ἑαυτοῦ *Fr.* 25.
αὐτουργός 216. 20.
ἀφαν-ής. τὸ -ές 156. 24, 158. 20, 218.
1, 380. 12. *v.* φαίνω. -ισμός 364 *T.*
ἀφαντασίαστος 158. 5.
ἀφασία 240. 29.
ἀφάτως 114. 22.
*ἀφερπετόομαι 526. 7.
ἄφεσις 410. 7.
ἀφθαρ-σία 460. 13. -τος αἰών 208. 8.
χεῖρες (θεοῦ) 460. 12, † 480. 20 (ἄφαν-
τος?). -τοι 208. 16.
ἄφθονος. ὁ κύριος 158. 16. φῶς 266. 4.
ἀφ-ίστημι 176. 8. -ομοιόω 454. 17.
-οράω. τ. καρδία 172. 6. † 182. 6
(διαφορά?).
ἄφραστος. ὄνομα 374 *T.*
ἄφυκτος. νόμος 436. 13.
ἀφύσικος. τέχνη iv. 137.
ἄχρονος iv. 202. 1.
ἀχρώματος 242. 4, 388. 22, 420. 17.
ἀχώριστος 168. 32, 170. 4.
ἀψίς 488. 27.
ἄψυχος. -α 138. 11, 272. 21, 404. 27.

βαθμός 244. 26, 466. 8.
βαπτ-ίζω. σεαυτόν 150. 23. m. τ. νοῦς
150. 27. (pass.) 152 19. τ. κρατῆρι iv.
111. 17. σαρκὶ κ. αἵματι 510. 27, 224.
16. -ισμός. *ci.* κόλασις 510. 29.
βαρ-έω 484. 2 *s.* -ύς 146. 9.
βασανίζω 126. 27, 424. 22.
βασιλ-εία. πολλαί 520. 4. 280. 14
(etym.). -εύω 496. 20 *s.*, 520. 3. -εύς
262. 7 *s.*, 272. 15 *s.*, 278. 7 *s.*, 480. 5,
496. 5, iv. 206. 5 (Pl. *Ep.* 2. 312 E).
ὁ ὕπατος β. τ. ὅλων 278. 17. τ. -έως
ἀπόρροιαι 496. 7. *v.* ἥλιος, θεός. -ικός.
ψυχαί 494. 24, 518. 31. comp. 496. 8.
-ίς. πρόνοια 460. 1.
βάσις 160. 29, 280. 12.
βαστάζω 138. 14, 198. 26. ψυχή 192.
13, 196. 2. τ. πάντα (πνεῦμα) βαστάζον *Fr.* 24.
βί-α. pl. 200. 32. -άζω. βεβιασμένα
240. 8.

βιβλ-ίον 262. 19, iv. 30. 7. -ος 286. 1,
460. 11.
βί-ος. τὸν θνητῶν βίον 472. 26, 486. 33.
(τ.) βίου (ὁσίου?) τὸν βίον ἐπλήρωσαν
492. 3. ἀμέριμνος 482. 27. νικῆσαι
τὸν ἐναγώνιον 392. 16. ὁ καθ' εἱμαρμένην 442. 28, 420. 11. -όω 148. 4.
βλάστ-η 282. 13. -ημα. pl. 282. 5.
-ικός. κίνησις 438. 27.
βλασφημ-έω 180. 25, 184. 10. -ία 200.
32.
βλέπω. ἄνω 406. 19. τὰ μετέωρα (opp.
νεύειν εἰς γῆν) iv. 176. 8.
βο-άω 200. 22, 252. 9, 21. -ή 114. 24.
βοήθ-εια 126. 12. -ός 492. 2.
βορρά 418. 5.
βουλ-ή. θεοῦ 116. 25, 124. 4, 130. 13.
ci. θέλημα 252. 25. *ci.* ἐνέργεια
122. 1. τ. Ἡφαίστου -αῖς 458. 26.
-ησις. τ. πατρός 176. 21, 232. 14.
τ. θεοῦ 182. 13, iv. 159. 13. = τ. ἀγαθόν 344 *T.*, *Fr.* 11. -ῆς βασιλεύς 520.
9. -ομαι. σοῦ (θεοῦ) -ομένου 254. 6.
-ηθέντος *Fr.* 36. ποιεῖν (sc. Αἰῶνα) ὕπερ
-εται 228. 7. μεταβάλλον εἰς ὃ -εται
iv. 210. 11 (*v.* θέλω).
βοῦς 510. 2.
βραβ-εῖον 280. 4. -εύω 280. 11.
βρέφος 454. 7.
βρέχω. pass. 490. 5.

γαστήρ 160. 22, 246. 19.
γαστριμαργία 168. 14.
γέλως 180. 21, 472. 20, 532. 5.
γεναρχ-έω. ὁ -ῶν ἄνθρωπος iv. 39. 1.
-ης τ. γενεσιουργίας 254. 1.
γενεσιουργ-έω 464. 31. -οῦσα? (γένεσιν
ἔχουσα) 438. 6. -ία 254. 1. -ός 482.
8. τ. παλιγγενεσίας 240. 27. τ. -οῦ
κυκλήσεως iv. 35. 5.
γένεσις. 1. opp. σπορά, θάνατος 430.
11. ἡ πρόνοια τ. -εις κατέστησε 124.
14. δαίμονες τ. -εως ὑπηρέται 270. 11,
122. 25, 532. 5. 2. genitalia virilia?
454 9. 3. ὕλη ἀγγεῖον -εως 422. 24.
διφυής 208. 15. = ὑλικὴ κίνησις 194.
9. *ci.* κίνησις 164. 24. *ci.* χρόνος 206.
10, 29, 208. 15. *ci.* φθορά 386. 3, 402.
26, 430. 18. *ci.* ἀθανασία 266. 21.
dist. μεταβολή 260. 6 *s.* *ci.* θεός 262.
6. *ci.* ποιεῖν 258. 21. παθητή 166. 18.
= τὸ ἐνεργεῖσθαι 424. 5. = φαντασία 158. 4. = αἴσθησις, dist. ζωή
234. 16. *ci.* εἱμαρμένη 226. 19, 420.
10. *ci.* κοσμικὴ φορά (ποιαὶ -εις) 182. 7,
25. *ci.* ποιότης 206. 25. γ. τ. ποιῶν
κ. τ. ποσῶν 194. 7. ἥλιος ὑγκοῖ πάντων
τ. -εις 268. 26. 4. νοερά 246. 6.

οὐσιώδης 248. 15. ἐν θεῷ, κατὰ θεόν 242. 16, 246. 9. τ. θεότητος 242. 19.

γενητός -ά 166. 18.

γεν-ικός 448. 5. λόγος, λόγοι 186. 8, 190. 22, 402. 19, 410. 14. -ος 268. 2, 22. τοὺς ἐν ἀγνοίᾳ τ. -ους 130. 26. καθοδηγὸς τ. -ους 132. 22. ἀνάδραμε ἐπὶ τὸ -ος τὸ σόν iv. 111. 18. υἱὸς τ. πατρικοῦ -ους 240. 10.

γενν-αῖος 524. 20. -άω. γῆν τ. -ῶσαν πάντα 234. 7. τ. ἀριθμόν 156. 5, 232. 10. pass. (ἐν νῷ) 240. 17. 238. 21. ὁ -ώμενος 240. 1. (θεός) οὐ -ώμενος ἐν φαντασίᾳ 158. 1. -ημα 116. 29, 130. 5, 254. 11, 468. 10. -ήτειρα 486. 6. -ητός 156. 24, 212. 17. τὸ -όν 134. 21, 388. 8. τὰ -ά 158. 3, 256. 11 s. -ήτωρ. παντὸς ἀγαθοῦ 212. 5.

γεωργός 182. 18, 260. 28, iv. 144 (a).

γῆ. 1. elementum. 198. 26. v. πῦρ. 2. ἔστω γῆ Frr. 31, 32. 120. 1. 3. ci. οὐρανός, αἰθήρ, ἀήρ 494. 27, 250. 12, 20, 266. 5. μέση 212. 8, 500. 28. πολυκίνητος 234. 4. τ. γῆν κοσμῆσαι 150. 6. ci. κακία 180. 24. ὕδωρ περικέχυται τῇ γῇ 198. 28, 160. 3. personif. 486. 5, 488. 25. Adam iv. 106. 18. -γενής. metaph. 132. 9 s. -ινον. σῶμα 198. 15 s.

γίνομαι 208. 4. τὸ -όμενον 232. 25, 426. 17. opp. ὁ ποιῶν 258. 9 s. τὸ γενόμενον 164. 15, 426. 17. τ. -ύμενα 142. 4, 256. 14, passim. τὰ γεγονότα 236. 8. ἐπὶ τί γέγονας 150. 26. ἀκλινὴς γενόμενος ὑπὸ τ. θεοῦ 246. 12. δυνά-μεις -όμενοι ἐν θεῷ -ονται 128. 22. πάντα ὅσα θέλει γίνεται iv. 106. 9 (6), iv. 107. 25.

γινώσκω. γνῶναι τ. θεόν, τ. θεῖον, τ. πατέρα, σεαυτόν 114. 12, 130. 14. 200. 9, 222. 7 (νοερῶς), 254. 17. ὁ γνοῦς, ἤδη θεῖος 192. 15. ἀρχὴ τ. γνωσθησο-μένου 154. 17. ci. μαθεῖν 114. 9, 116. 7 s.

γνήσιος. υἱός 240. 11. πατήρ 258. 1, 480. 5.

γνώμη (θεοῦ) 466. 21, 498. 7, 14.

γνώμων 496. 25.

γνωρίζω 376 T. ἴδιον τ. ἀγαθοῦ τ. -εσθαι 188. 19. θεὸς -ει κ. θέλει -εσθαι 196. 17. τ. πατέρα 256. 27. τ. πάντα 126. 12. τ. ποιήσαντα 150. 11. ἑαυτόν 246. 10. ἐπὶ τί γέγονας 150. 26.

γνῶσις. ἀρετὴ ψυχῆς 192. 15. ἐπιστή-μης τ. τέλος, opp. αἴσθησις 192. 21 s. τέλος τοῖς -ιν ἐσχηκύσι θεωθῆναι 128. 23. ἡ κατ' οὐσίαν 130. 24. ci. νοῦς, λόγος 374 T. εὐσέβεια 180. 17, Fr. 10. ci. εὐσέβεια 132. 9, 170. 6, iv. 255.

opp. ἄγνοια 244. 17. σωτήριον 196. 18. ἁγία 250. 32. ἐν τ. σῇ -ει 376 T. τὸ φῶς τ. -εως 374 T. τ. ἀγαθοῦ 168. 17, 190. 8. τ. θεοῦ (v. εὐσέβεια). τ. παν-τός 282. 32. ἔργων θείων 146. 24. θείας δυνάμεως 148. 2. τ. λογισμῶν 444. 17. τ. τιμίαν 448. 24. μετέχειν 150. 28. παρελθεῖν ἐπί 256. 5. ἐπὶ τ. τῆς -εως θύρας 172. 4. οἱ ἐν -ει ὄντες 180. 20. ἡμῖν δοκοῦν ἀρχὴν ἔχειν τὴν -ιν 154. 15. αἰσθύμενος τ. -εως 180. 26. iv. 37. 1, iv. 38. 27, iv. 175. 13.

γνωστικός. οἱ ἀπὸ Σίμωνος iv. 156. 13.

γόν-ιμος. λόγος Frr. 27, 35. ὕδωρ Fr. 27. πνεῦμα Fr. 25. πῦρ Fr. 33. -ος 454. 9.

γοώδης 114. 24.

γράμμα. τὰ κρυπτὰ τ. -άτων 492. 12.

γραφ-ή 218. 20, 382. 23. -ω. τ. γε-γραμμένα 262. 24.

γρηγορέω 222. 10.

γυμν-ός. ci. φανόν 242. 5, 384. 24. νοῦς 198. 16. -όω. metaph. pass. 128. 14.

Δ iv. 107. 2.

δαιδαλουργία 148. 3.

δαιμόνι-ον. ἴδιον iv. 104. 13 s. -α 180. 9, iv. 111. 6. -ος. ψυχή 200. 6.

δαίμων. 1. (Deus) αὐτόγονε δαῖμον 488. 20. ὦ δαῖμον 486. 32. 2. ci. θεοί, ἄνθρωποι. pl. 142. 13, 236. 11, 272. 4 s. ἀνθρώπειαι ψυχαὶ εἰς δαίμονας 190. 29. ἱεροί 468. 9. ci. θεός, ἄγγελος Fr. 23. δορυφορησάντων ἀγγέλων κ. δαι-μόνων 498. 1 s. (ἴδιος) iv. 104. 16, iv 177. 15. (-ονες) τὰ τ. ἀνθρώπων ἐφορῶσι 268. 11 s. -ονος οὐσία ἐνέργεια 270. 1. -ες ἐνέργειαι 414. 20 s. τὸ περιέχον -όνων ἐπληρώθη 492. 27. μηδενὸς μέρους τ. κόσμου κενοῦ ὄντος -ονος 180. 9. ὑπη-ρετοῦσιν ἑκάστῳ τ. ἀστέρων, ἀγαθοὶ κ. κακοὶ ὄντες 268. 32 s. -όνων τὸ ἐπαμύ-νειν 268. 18. τιμωρός 126. 22. δίκην δίδωσι μετὰ θάνατον τοῖς -οσιν 144. 15. νοῦς, ὅταν δ. γένηται 200. 28. τιμωροί, καθαρτικοί, σωτηρικοί 368 T. τὸ ἦθος τῷ -ονι παραδίδως 128. 2. κακὸς δ. ci. εἱμαρμένη 370 T. πόσους χοροὺς -όνων 154. 11. δ. ἔσπειρε τ. ἰδίας ἐνεργείας τὸ σπέρμα 180. 11. ἀπὸ τῶν -όνων τ. σπέρμα τῆς νοήσεως 182. 2. ἀντίμιμος iv. 108. 21. πλάνος iv. 39. 31. χορός, χοροί 268. 11, 28. 3. Ἀγαθὸς Δαίμων 224. 5, 226. 29, 228. 16. ὁ μακάριος θεός 230. 22. μέγας, μέγιστε, Frr. 29, 31. (νοῦς) ἐστιν ὁ ἀ. δ. 202. 25. 4. Δίκη 418. 25.

δακ-ετός 200. 20. -νηρός 482. 33.

δάκρυ 532. 5.

τ. -ον *Fr.* 25. -ασμα. δικαιοσύνης 244.
26.

ἔθνος 230. 17, 270. 5.

εἰδικός. ἐνέργειαι 398. 14s.

εἶδος. 1. τ. ἐ. ἀφανὲς γίνεται 128. 1.
ἐν τ. ὕδατι 120. 28. τ. θνητὸν ἐ. 242.
1. τ. πρῶτον σύνθετον ἐ. 240. 19. 2.
ci. σχῆμα 438. 22. ζωῆς 450. 9. πρός
τι 442. 2. συμβεβηκός, ἰδίως ποιόν 422.
3. 3. -η ἁρμονίας 452. 4. ἀσωμάτων
422. 1. κινήσεως 420. 24. 4. *ci.*
γένος 268. 2, 518. 30. 5. τὸ ἀρχέτυπον ἐ. 116. 21.

εἴδωλον. σχήματος 438. 21. τ. ὀφθαλμῷ
ὑποπίπτοντα 168. 27. ἐ. τ. νοήματος
420. 24. δόξα ψευδής 432. 14.

εἰδωλοποιέω. pass. 438. 23.

εἰκασμός. λογισμοῦ 444. 17.

εἴκω 158. 26.

εἰκών. 1. -ἀνδριάντα ἢ -όνα 162. 8. 280.
19, 382. 20 s. metaph. θείαν τ. ἀνθρώπου -όνα 160. 24. 2. dei. (Ἄνθρωπος)
τὴν τ. πατρὸς -όνα ἔχων 120. 6. κόσμος
232. 13s, (ὁ κατ' -όνα) 174. 17, 158. 19.
οὗ πᾶσα φύσις -ών 130. 18. οὐδὲν ἐστιν
ὃ οὐκ ἐστιν -όνι 222. 12. ὁ αἰών 216.
32. λόγος -ὼν καὶ νοῦς 230. 24, iv. 154.
9. ὁ κατ' -όνα ἄνθρωπος 262. 11. βασιλεῖς 278. 18. 3. ὁ ἄνθρωπος κατ' -όνα
τ. κόσμου 176. 20. τ. ἡλίου 216. 35.
(αἰσθητοὶ θεοὶ) -όνες εἰσὶ νοηματ(ικ)ῶν
(?) 454. 1. 4. ὑπογέγραπται τ. θεοῦ
εἰκών 156. 12s. 5. similitudo 260.
27.

εἰλέω. m. 176. 10. 530. 12. δαίμων
ἐν μέσῳ τ. παντὸς -ουμένη 418. 26.

εἰλικρινής 168. 22.

εἱμαρμένη. *v.* μείρομαι.

εἰμί. 1. θεός. ἀεὶ ἐστι, ὤν 156. 24, 148.
19, 388. 23. ἀεὶ ἐν ἑαυτῷ ὤν *Fr.* 23. ὁ
πανταχοῦ ὤν iv. 111. 5s. τ. προόντως
ὤν iv. 32. 7. σὺ εἶ 164. 13s, 252. 20.
2. ἐν οὐρανῷ εἰμι 246. 17. 3. εἶναι.
ci. ζωή 450. 4. *ci.* ἕξις 442. 15; *v.* ἕξις.
τ. εἶναι αἴτιος 142. 2. τ. ἐν λόγῳ γενέσθαι 450. 11. 4. τ. ὄν, opp. τ. μὴ ὄν 138.
22, 162. 22. κινούμενον 234. 10. παρὰ τ.
ὄν 384. 6. τ. μὴ ὄν 426. 10. 5. τ. ὄντα.
(*a*) τ. ὄντως ὄ. 452. 16, iv. 31. 25, iv.
201. 6. θεός 184. 21. θεὸς κ. γένεσις 262. 6. *ci.* θεός, τ. ἀγαθόν 166. 6,
142. 19. γνῶναι, μαθεῖν, νοεῖν 114. 12,
192. 10, 256. 3, 384. 18. (*b*) δημιουρ-
γήσαντος τ. ὄ. 148. 20. λόγῳ συστησάμενος τ. ὄ. 130. 16. νοῦς σωτήριος τ.
-ων 140. 20. τ. ὄ. ἐφανέρωσε 162. 24.
κόσμος κυΐσκει τ. ὄ. 396. 12. κινεῖται
426. 10. opp. τ. μὴ ὄντα 142. 4. τ.
-ων τάξις 420. 2. ἡσυχία 462. 11.

εἰρήν-η 280. 1 s, 486. 39. personif. 472.
17. -ικός 498. 9. εἰρηνοποιέω. m.
498. 10.

εἰς. 1. θεός. *ci.* μόνος, μόνον. κρείττων κ. εἰς κ. μόνος 256. 19. τοῦ πάντα
ποιήσαντος κ. ἑνὸς μόνου 148. 19. τ.
ἀνομοίῳ κ. μόνῳ κ. ἑνί 210. 2. (τ. πρώτην
ἀλήθειαν) ἕνα κ. μόνον 388. 21. σπεύ-
δειν πρὸς τὸν ἕνα κ. μόνον θεόν 154. 12.
ἐπὶ τὸ ἓν κ. μόνον 152. 15. τ. ἐν κ. μ.
ἀγαθόν *Fr.* 26 (fortasse 172. 17). τ.
κυρίῳ κ. πατρὶ κ. μόνῳ κ. οὐχ ἑνὶ ἀλλ'
ἀφ' οὗ ὁ εἷς 158. 9. ἡ δὲ ἀρχὴ ἐκ τ.
ἑνὸς κ. μόνου ... τὸ δὲ ἓν μόνον ἔστηκεν
196. 9. ἐξ ἑνὸς εἷς iv. 226. n. 14. ἓν
μόνον φῶς νοερόν *Fr.* 23. ἀπὸ τ. ἑνὸς ὁ
θεὸς ἑαυτὸν ἐξέλαμψε iv. 32. 3. (ἥλιος)
μετὰ τ. ἕνα κ. πρῶτον 388. 18. ὁ εἷς
ἀγέννητος 158. 4. τ. ἑνὸς παῖς 248. 17.
τ. ἓν *Fr.* 25. ἀμερές iv. 32. 16. τ. ἐν τ.
ἀγαθῷ iv. 197. 11. εἷς θεός iv. 31. 25,
vi. 155. 3, 168. 12, iv. 199. 11. νοῦς εἷς
iv. 226. 17. 2. = τ. πᾶν, τ. πάντα 228.
3, 250. 15, 30, 264. 15s., iv. 152 (*e*). 3.
(κόσμον) πρῶτον κ. μόνον κ. ἕνα 298 *T.*
4. εἷς θελήματι θεοῦ 240. 28. 5. ὁ λόγος
εἷς 230. 18. χρόνος 424. 17. ἡ ὕλη
μία 232. 11. μιᾶς τ. ὕλης κ. μιᾶς τ. ψυχῆς
212. 29. μία τάξις 212. 25. *v.* unus.

εἰσ-δύνω. εἰς τ. ψυχήν 200. 29. -έρχο-
μαι. εἰς σῶμα 192. 4. -ηγητής 492.
31. -οδος. metaph. 126. 19. -πνέω.
184. 7.

ἐκ. τινος 402. 24.

ἐκ-γονος 196. 16. -δέχομαι 264. 21.
-δικία 488. 2.

ἐκεῖ 418. 17.

ἐκκαθαίρω 344 *T.* -κακέω 484. 3. κόπτω
126. 20. -λέγω. m. 256. 8. -λάμπω
158. 11, 188. 25, iv. 32 3. -λυτος 474.
5. -λύω. -λελυμένη φράσις 264. 6.

ἑκούσιος 428. 19.

ἐκ-πέτομαι. metaph. 246. 3. -πηδάω
118. 1. -πίνω. metaph. 170. 21.
-πληξις. (lege) 116. 20. -πνέω 454.
10. -πυρώδης. compar. 522. 25.
-τασις 204. 20. -τείνω 160. 26. -τελέω
126. 18.

ἐκτός. τὰ ἐ. 220. 12.

ἐκ-τρέχω 122. 23. -φαίνω 254. 14. -φημι
250. 2. †-φορά (-φθορά?) 130. 5. -φωνέω
178. 21, 180. 5.

ἐλαττόω 152. 28.

ἐλαφρός 118. 2, 146. 7.

ἐλεγχ-ος. *ci.* τιμωρός 224. 33. 530. 2.
-ω 530. 3.

ἐλε-ήμων 126. 11. -ος. θεοῦ (masc.)
240. 15, (neut.) 244. 14. -έω 144. 18.
τ. ἐλεηθέντος ὑπὸ τ. θεοῦ 244. 10.

9. θ. εἰς. opp. πρῶτος κ. βασιλεύς iv. 31. 25. πρῶτος κ. μόνος. opp. νοῦς iv. 202. 2. πρῶτος. ci. λόγος 446. 14. ci. προεγνωσμένος Fr. 30. προεννοούμενος Frr. 12, 17, 36. ἐπουράνιος δημιουργός. opp. ἥλιος 454. 2. ἐπ. θ. ci. πρόνοια 434. 9. ci. νοητὴ οὐσία 422. 10. ci. αἰών 206. 10 s. ci. κόσμος. τ. πρώτου κ. ἑνὸς -οῦ δημιουργός 344 T. πρῶτος κ. δεύτερος iv. 158. 11. πρῶτος Fr. 36. ci. κόσμος, ἄνθρωπος 176. 23, 426. 19. ci. νοητὸς κ. αἰσθητὸς κόσμος 270. 29. opp. τ. θεῖον 134. 20. 2. deus unus est. 154. 13, 214. 16, Fr. 3, iv. 31. 25, iv. 196. 5, iv. 200. 9, iv. 205. 13. v. εἷς, μόνος. deus omnia, in omnibus. v. πᾶς. 3. natura dei. οὐσία 162. 18, 164. 24, 206. 15. 222. 23. = τ. ἀγαθόν 142. 22, 144. 2, 162. 18, 164. 23, 168. 4. 186. 10, 206. 15. πλήρωμα τ. ἀγαθοῦ 168. 19. καλόν 418. 22. νοῦς 118. 10, 254. 4, 530. 9, iv. 32. 14. νοῦ τ. λεπτομερέσ-τερον, -τατον 164. 19, 230. 27. ὁ νοῦς ἐν τ. -ῷ 252. 20. ὁ θ. ἐν τ. νῷ 208. 21. opp. νοῦς etc. 142. 1. ci. ζωή, φῶς, πνεῦμα 252. 20. μέλη, μέρη τ. -οῦ 168. 31, 236. 15, 23. θ. οὐκ ἀναίσθητος 184. 9. ἀνουσίαστος 134. 22. ἀρρενόθηλυς 118. 10. πάγκρυφος iv. 7. 2. προών 422. 25. ci. μορφή 120. 7 s. σοφός 256. 19. τ. -οῦ σοφία 208. 10. 4. creator, pater, rex, etc. τοῦ εἶναι αἴτιος 142. 2. αὐτο-πάτωρ, -μήτωρ Fr. 13. δημιουργός 174. 16, 454. 3, 530. 8, iv. 39. 6 (v. 1 supra). ἀρχή. πηγή 144. 25, 208. 5. ἐνεργῶν 164. 16, 208. 32. ὁ ποιῶν 258. 28. ὁρᾶται ἐν τ. ποιεῖν 222. 17. ci. γένεσις 262. 5. v. βασιλεύς, δεσπότης, δημιουργός, κύριος, πατήρ, περίβολος, ποιητής, πρύτανις, υἱός, ὕπατος. 5. δυνάμεις τ. θεοῦ. v. βουλή, βούλησις, δύναμις, ἐνέργεια, θέλημα, θέλησις, λόγος, μείρομαι, πρόνοια. 6. nomen dei. 144. 10, 156. 20, 258. 2, 374 T., 418. 23. 7. deus alter. πρῶτος θ. κ. βασιλεύς iv. 31. 25. θ. τ. πυρὸς κ. πνεύματος 118. 12. v. αὐτάρκ(χ)ης, αὐτοπάτωρ, ἀρχή, μονάς, νοῦς, πηγή. 8. sol 158. 25, 212. 4. 9. cosmos. ὁ ὑλικὸς θ. 194. 3. δεύτερος 174. 11, 298 T., iv. 158. 1 s. ὁ μονογενής iv. 158. 7 (v. 1 supra). (caelum) ὁ κύκλος ... τ. -οῦ 250. 17. 10. μουσικὸς θ. 274. 14. 11. homo deus. -οἱ πρόγονοι 492. 9. -οί 458. 12. ὁ βασιλεὺς τ. ἄλλων -ῶν ἔσχατος 496. 12. 12. pl. νοηματικοί. opp. αἰσθητοί 452. 23. νοητοί iv. 35. 6.

ὑπερουράνιοι iv. 35. 11. περι-, ὑπερκόσμιοι iv. 36. 4. αἰθέριοι κ. ἐμπύριοι iv. 32. 10. ἐγκύκλιοι 146. 28. οὐράνιοι, ἐν οὐρανῷ, κατ' οὐρανόν, etc. 146. 30, 158. 25 s., 204. 11, 470. 22, 472. 7, 486. 12, 494. 28. πολεύοντες iv. 35. 29. στρέφονται 436. 10. 146. 5, 14 s., 272. 8, 462. 19, 476. 2. οἱ τριάκοντα ἕξ 414. 24. ἡ θέα τ. -ῶν iv. 38. 24. χοροὶ δύο -ῶν 192. 2. ci. ἄνθρωποι, δαίμονες 142. 13, 236. 10. ci. δαίμονες 272. 9. ci. ἄνθρωποι 142. 26, 250. 25. τ. ἀγαθῶν δοτῆρες iv. 39. 10. συγγενεῖς 458. 23. 13. deus et homo. ὁ νοῦς ἐν ἀνθρώποις θ. 224. 3. ὅμοιον τ. -ῷ 496. 16. τ. λογικὸν μέρος τ. ψυχῆς ἐπιτηδεῖον εἰς ὑποδοχὴν τ. -οῦ 270. 17. τ. ἄνθρωπον θνητὸν -όν 204. 22, (pl.) 224. 3. θ. πέφυκας 248. 17. νοῆσαι τ. -όν 168. 33, 380. 2. ἐν ᾧ γίνομαι 128. 22. θ. ἀναίτιος 154. 8. σὺ εἶ ὁ θ. 252. 20. v. ἐν.

θε(ι)ότης. opp. θεός 178. 18. ci. ἀνθρωπότης 224. 4. π. θειότητος 238. 9, 242. 19. ἀληθής 496. 14. μία iv. 233. 6. ἄχρι ψυχῆς iv. 175. 1.

θεοσεβής, 180. 26.

θεουργ-ία. ἱερατική iv. 34. 10. -ικός. δύσις iv. 39. 5. ψυχή iv. 39. 20. -ός iv. 39. 27.

θεόω. pass. 128. 23, *246. 8.

θερμός 522. 24. τὸ -όν 438. 15, 450. 24, 500. 8, 526. 23, 528. 7.

θεσπίζω 248. 21.

θεωρ-έω 474. 10, †118. 7, 460. 5. metaph. τ. θεόν 236. 5. ἐν τ. νοΐ 116. 16, 252. 33. -ητικός. τ. καλοῦ 448. 16. -ητός. τ. νοΐ 162. 27. -ία. οὐρανία 458. 27 (cf. l. 2). (doctrina) 256. 7. ἀπλανής 484. 13. κρυπτή 474. 15. παρέδωκεν ὁλοτελῆ -ίαν 460. 3. τ. -ίας μύστης 506. 21. ἵνα τ. -ίας ταύτης πλῆρες τ. περιέχον γένηται 494. 13 (cf. 460. 3 s.).

θῆλ-υ 462. 18. -υκός 122. 26, 124. 6, 498. 28. στοιχεῖα iv. 33. 3. -υς 498. 32 s.

θηρ-ιάζομαι 200. 27. -ίον 120. 3, 146. 20.

θλίβω 134. 15.

θνητός 120. 21. opp. ἀθάνατος 122. 5, 152. 10, 268. 6 s. opp. θεῖος 152. 24, 380. 9. τ. ἄνθρωπον εἶναι -ὸν θεόν 204. 21. v. ἀθάνατος.

θολόω. pass. 488. 14. ψυχὴ τεθολωμένη 196. 25. τ. μὴ -ούμενον 242: 3, 384. 23.

θόρυβος. pl. 270. 4.

θρησκ-εία 238. 4. -εύω 238. 3.

θρόνος. τ. ἀληθείας 476. 32. pl. ἀρετῆς πεπληρωμένοι 466. 23.

θρύπτω 396. 7.

θρώσκω 126. 24.

θύελλα 268. 14.

θυμ-ικός 522. 26. τὸ -όν 226. 16. -ός 404. 14, 444. 1. pl. 128. 5, 224. 31. -όω. m. 224. 30.

θύρα. τῆς γνώσεως -αι 172. 4. πρὸς θεόν iv. 39. 5.

θυσία. ἀποτρεπτικαί iv. 111. 10. δεκτή 254. 7. λογική 252. 8, 15; pl. 130. 22, 254. 2. pl. 488. 8, 492. 9.

θύτης 480. 7.

ἰατρ-ικός. -ή 494. 8, 520. 10. -ός 224. 18.

ἰδέα. 1. ἠλλάγη τῇ -ᾳ 114. 16. αὐτοῦ τ. -αν 116. 16. i. ἐξ -ας 386. 21. ci. χρῶμα Fr. 25. παντόμορφοι 246. 25, 268. 24. τ. -ῶν τὰ ποιά 176. 4. (ὕλη) -ας εἶχε μορφοποιουμένη 424. 2. ἐν ἄστρων -αις 146. 15. ἀσώματοι 272. 19 s. ci. σώματα, ἐνέργειαι 430. 22. (θεός) μίαν ἔχει -αν 218. 16 s. 2. -αι τ. παθῶν 400. 31. ψυχῶν 404. 7. 3. μία ἰ. ἐγένοντο (ψυχή) 444. 30. ci. σῶμα, ψυχή 230. 25. 4. (θεὸς) πρὸ τ. -ῶν iv. 32. 1.

ἰδιογενής 464. 27.

ἴδιος. (θεοῦ) δυνάμεις 130. 13. μέρη 168. 31. μορφή 120. 7. τύκος 120. 5, 298. T. οἱ -οι (θεοῦ) 130. 15. αἴσθησις (κόσμου) 182. 9. δαίμων iv. 104. 16. ἐξουσία 490. 26. φύσις 498. 14, 508. 32, 518. 22. -ον ψυχῆς 448. 2. τὰ τ. σώματος 422. 6.

ἰδιοσύγκριτος 464. 28.

ἰδιότης 442. 22 s.. 448. 2.

ἰδιό-τυπος 464. 28. -φυής 508. 22.

ἰδρύω 150. 20, 266. 16, Fr. 15. -υμένος 210. 10, 212. 9.

ἱέραξ 508. 35.

ἱερο-γραμματεύς iv. 28. 16. -ποιία 494. 3.

ἱερός 460. 7, 468. 9, 472. 4, 474. 35 s., 482. 20 (cf. 486. 19), 490. 10, 494. 27, 500. 27, 502. 25.

ἱεροσυλ-έω 226. 3. -ία 180. 13.

ἱκέτης 238. 11.

ἱλαρός 114. 18.

ἱλάσκομαι 126. 13.

ἵλεως 158. 9.

ἰός 260. 3 (rust); 480. 15 (venom).

ἰσάριθμος 268. 30.

ἰσοδυναμέω 204. 14, 412. 8.

ἴσος. ἄνθρωπον (θεῷ) -ον 120. 5. τὸν ὅμοιον ἢ -ον δρόμον 158. 31.

ἰσο-στάσιος 480. 3. -τιμος 230. 8.

ἵστημι. στῆτε 250. 16. ἕστηκε: τ. ἓν μόνον 196. 10; ὁ αἰών 208. 1; τ. κινοῦν 136. 9 s; χρόνος οὐχ ἑ. 426. 4. αὐτὸς ἐν ἑαυτῷ ἑστώς 140. 19. ἐν ἑστῶτι 136. 9.

ἰσχυροποιέω 268. 26.

ἰσχ-υρός 480. 21. οἱ -οί 486. 18. compar. 130. 19, 402. 4, 518. 5. -ύς 486. 17, 518. 16, 520. 11. ἐκ ψυχῆς κ. -ύος ὅλης 130. 10. -ύω 190. 5, 458. 19.

ἴσχω 182. 2.

κάδος 138. 25.

καθαίρω 182. 8, 242. 20. κεκαθαρμένος 248. 22.

καθαρ-εύω 166. 31. -μός. τ. ψυχῶν iv. 231. 20. -ός 118. 17, 168. 22, 198. 7. σκότους 172. 5. -τικός. δαίμων 368 T.

καθ-έζομαι. οἴκαδε iv. 111. 5 s. -είργνυμι. pass. 486. 11. -έλκω 392. 6. -ηγητής 520. 9. -ήκω. λόγου τ. καθήκοντος 466. 1. -ιερόω 492. 10 -ίζω 476. 32. -ικνέομαι 188. 27.

καθ-οδηγός 128. 24, 132. 22. -οδος. ψυχῆς iv. 36. 16 s., iv. 232. 1. -ολικός. ἀποτελέσματα 416. 36. ἐνέργειαι 398. 14, 24 (l. παρεπομένων καθολικῶν), 406. 16. -ολικῶς 234. 10, 468. 19. ci. ἐνέργεια 414. 6. -όλου 452. 17. -υπερτερέω 454. 13. -υπερτέρησις *454. 16.

καιν-ός. λόγοι 264. 9. superl. 260. 13. -ουργέω 470. 13.

καιρ-ικός. καταβαφαί iv. 104. 11, iv. 109. 20. φυσικά iv. 111. 14. -ός. -οῦ παρατήρησις iv. 34. 13.

καίω 224. 19, 486. 19. m. 200. 23, 464. 25.

κακ-ία. λύπη -ίας μέρος 166. 7. οὔτε τ. -ίαν ὁ θεὸς (ἐποίησε) 260. 6. τιμωρία 244. 4. ἀγνωσία, τ. ἀγνοεῖν 192. 9, 222. 6. ἀσέβεια 268. 16. κόσμου 168. 19, 428. 24. καθαρεύειν τ. -ίας 166. 31. τ. -ίαν ἐκκαθάρας 344 T. ci. εἱμαρμένη 226. 10, 262. 8. pl. 224. 32. -ίζω. pass. 224. 14.

κακο-δαίμων. ψυχή 192. 11, 202. 26. -ποιός. δαίμων iv. 104. 17.

κακ-ός. θρησκεία τ. θεοῦ μία, μὴ εἶναι -όν 238. 4. τ. ἐνθάδε ἀγαθόν 166. 30 s. οὐδὲν -ὸν ἐν τ. οὐρανῷ 428. 17. κόσμος οὐ κ. 194. 25. ὁ ἄνθρωπος κ. 194. 24, 428. 18. ὕλη 420. 7 passim, v. δαίμων. -όω. pass. 168. 2. -ωτικός 402. 1 s.

καλιά 406. 11.

καλλί-θριξ 502. 11. -μηρος 502. 19.

κάλλος. τ. κόσμου 210. 24. τ. εὐσεβείας 132. 9. τ. ἀληθείας, τ. ἀγαθοῦ

νοῦς ἀπεκύησε -ῳ ἕτερον νοῦν δημιουργόν 118. 11. -ῳ συστησάμενος τ. ὄντα
130. 16. τ. κόσμον ἐποίησε οὐ χερσὶν
ἀλλὰ -ῳ 148. 18. -ῳ τ. πάντα κ. πνεύματι στήσας iv. 171. 4. ci. βουλὴ θεοῦ
116. 26. γεννητικὴ φύσις, γόνιμος,
ζωοποιὸς Frr. 27, 29, 35. δημιουργ-ός,
-ικός, τ. δημιουργοῦ Frr. 27, 28, 30, 33,
35. iv. 201. 1. ci. δημιουργὸς νοῦς 118.
11. ci. νοῦς, ζαή 116. 11. νοερὸς Fr. 29,
iv. 226. n. 14. πανσθενής iv. 226. 12.
παντέλειος Fr. 27. πνευματικός 118. 9.
προ-ελθών, -κύψασα (δύναμις) Fr. 27,
Fr. 28. τέλειος Fr. 29. υἱὸς θεοῦ
116. 9. μονογενής iv. 202. 11. φωτεινός, ci. φῶς 116. 2, 9. ὁ λ. ἐστὶν εἰκὼν
κ. νοῦς τ. θεοῦ 230. 24. ἐπήδησεν ἐκ τ.
καταφερῶν στοιχείων ὁ τ. θεοῦ λ. 118.
17. οὐ γὰρ ἔτι εἶχε τ. -ον (ἡ φύσις)
118. 26. τ. θεοῦ iv. 154. 3 s., iv. 159.
13. iv. 170. 18. 4. rationis divinae
cum hominibus commercium. ἀνα-
καθαιρύμενος εἰς συνάρθρωσιν τ. -ου 244.
16. ὁ σὸς λύγος 252. 7. -ον τ. σὸν ποιμαίνει ὁ νοῦς 252. 19. τὸ ἐν -ῳ γενέσθαι
450. 11. δέξαι τ. πᾶν -ῳ 252. 8. προσ-
δεξάσθω μου τ. -ον 250. 18. θυσία διὰ
τ. -ου 254. 8. τ. ἀιδίῳ -ῳ συνηνωμένη
(ψυχή) iv. 39. 14. ci. νοῦς, γνῶσις
374 T. θεὸς παντὸς ἀνωτάτω νοῦ κ.
-ου iv. 200. 9. ὁ θεὸς ἐχαρίσατο τ. τε
νοῦν κ. τ. -ον, ἰσότιμα τ. ἀθανασίᾳ 230.
8; 150. 9.
λοιβή 488. 8.
λοιμός 414. 9.
λοχάω 518. 18.
λοχεύω 440. 4.
λύκος 510. 2.
λυμαίνω 200. 21.
λυπ-έω 224. 20. m. 428. 8. -η. ἐνέργεια
400. 28. τιμωρία 242. 24. κακίας
μέρος 166. 7. ci. ἡδονή 224. 14 s. opp.
χαρά 400. 28 s., 482. 30 s.
λύρα 276. 24 s.
λύ-σις 248. 12, iv. 35. 5, iv. 38. 26. -τήρ
iv. 35. 21. -ω 248. 22, 514. 21. τ. πᾶν
τ. ἑνός 264. 23.

M iv. 107. 4.
μαγεία 494. 7, Fr. 21.
Μαγνῆτις. λίθος 156. 16.
μάθημα. pl. 446. 4, 458. 25.
μαίνομαι 180. 21, 242. 7.
μαιόομαι. pass. 440. 4. metaph. 466.
18.
μάκαρ. ci. θεοί 230. 12. -ίζω 256. 27.
-ιος. ψυχή 202. 25. θεός 230. 22.
θεασάμενον -ιον γενέσθαι 418. 14.
μανθάνω. ci. γνῶναι 114. 8 s. τ. ἀληθές

206. 6, 210. 19. ci. εὐσέβεια 390. 9 s.
παρ' ἐμοῦ 254. 13. τ. προπάτορα 390.
20. ci. ἐπιστήμη 406. 22. ἀκριβῶς
204. 18.
μανία 240. 23.
μαντ-εία iv. 37. 27. -ις 418. 6.
μαρτυρ-έω 132. 1. -ία 146. 25.
μαστ-ίζω. -ιζομένη ψυχή 200. 31. -ιξ
200. 30.
ματαιολογία 258. 8.
μάχ-η. metaph. 392. 6. -ομαι 474.
25. metaph. 506. 11 (v. 392. 6).
μεγαλό-δοξος 474. 20, 488. 26. -φυής.
superl. 510. 32. -ψυχος 488. 18, 494.
21.
μέγεθος 158. 33. ci. αὔξη 438. 20.
συμβεβηκός 422. 3. ἀμέτρητον 220.
20. ἄρχει τ. πλήθει κ. τ. -ει (ὁ Ποιῶν)
256. 21.
μεθερμηνεύω 230. 19, 262. 23.
μέθ-η. metaph. 132. 9. -ύω 170. 20.
μειδιάω 120. 26, 462. 17.
μείρομαι. 1. εἵμαρται 226. 3, 8. ἡ εἱμαρτὴ ἐνέργεια 362. 1. τὰ εἱμαρμένα
226. 20. 2. εἱμαρμένη. ἐπικρατεῖ ὁ νοῦς
-ης κ. νόμου 228. 12. ἡ διοίκησις (τῶν
ἑπτά) εἱμ. καλεῖται 118. 15 (270. 27).
συμπάθειαν καθ' -ην (τ. ἀστέρων) 452.
13. ὑποκεῖσθαι τ. -η 122. 7, 420. 9
(dist. δίκη). τ. -ης πομπὰς Fr. 19.
τ. ἑλομένῳ -η δυναστεύει 446. 9, 17.
ἐν ἀρχῇ ἑλομένη βίον τ. καθ' -ην 442.
28. ἐγγυτάτω ψυχὴ οὖσα οἰκειοῦται
καθ' -ην 440. 7. εὐσεβοῦς οὐ κρατεῖ
370 T. (ci. δαίμων). τὸ φιλοσόφων
γένος ἀνώτερον τ. -ης Fr. 20. ἐὰν τ. -ην
ὁ θέλει[ν] ποιεῖν τῷ ἑαυτῆς πηλῷ Fr. 21.
λύσις τῆς -ης iv. 35. 6. τῆς -ης δῶρα
iv. 105. 20, iv. 104. 16, iv. 107. 12.
= ἀνάγκη 268. 20. ci. ἀνάγκη 362. 8.
οὐσιάρχης = τύχη 324 T., ci. ἁρμονία
124. 13. περὶ -ης 226. 1, 262. 8, 530.
10. v. πρόνοια.
μεί-ωσις. v. αὔξησις. -ωτικός 128. 8.
-ωτός 156. 7.
μέλλω. τὸ -ον 424. 15.
μέλος 382. 4. -η θεοῦ 236. 15. v. μέρος.
μένω. part. 168. 3. 384. 29, 386. 18.
μερ-ίζω 150. 16, *502. 1. -ικός 398. 17.
μέριμνα 466. 17.
μέρος. 1. (elementum) 234. 8, *382.
4, (?) 128. 4. 2. -η τ. θεοῦ 168. 31,
236. 23. 3. -η τ. κόσμου 128. 4, 174.
3, 236. 14. μεταβλητά 234. 14. ἀθάνατα 266. 27. opp. μέλη (?) θεοῦ 236.
14. 4. τὰ δύο -η τ. ψυχῆς. opp. ἐν
λιγικὸν 270. 14 s., 392. 4, 11. ἄλογα
400. 35 (opp. θεῖον), 404. 11. λογικὸν
394. 13. -η [τ. αἰσθήσεως] (αἴσθησις,

-ά. opp. αἰσθητά *Fr.* 35. compar.
502. 30. -ῶς. ἔγνως σεαυτόν 254. 17.
νοέω 124. 21, 156. 20, 218. 33, 506. 12.
ci. αἰσθέσθαι 178. 25. *ci.* θαυμάσαι
256. 26. *ci.* πιστεῦσαι 184. 26. τί
ἀγαθόν 142. 24. τί θεός 178. 2. τ.
νοοῦν, opp. τ. νοητόν, νοούμενον 136.
25. τ. πρῶτον νοοῦν, opp. τ. πρῶτον
νοητόν iv. 32. 17. ἀληθ-ές, -ῆ 384. 75.
τ. θέαν 116. 5. τ. θεόν 168. 33. 170.
2, 220. 17, 236. 5, 374 *T.*, 380. 2,
418. 12. τ. ὄντα 114. 85., 390. 4.
πάντα 248. 24. (τ. σύμπαντα) 458. 20.
τ. φῶς 116. 14. *ci.* θεᾶσθαι 156. 12,
190. 10.

νόημ-α 242. 10. τ. ψυχῆς 444. 3. *ci.*
δ ἄνοια 444. 26. *ci.* λόγος 446. 20,
448. 1. τ. δημιουργοῦ 420. 25. νοῦς,
ὀξύτατος ὢν πάντων τ. θείων νοημάτων
(ὀχημάτων ?) 198. 30. pl. 180. 7, 220
15, †174. 7. -ατικός. λόγος 446. 3.
οὐσία *446. 10. θεοί. opp. αἰσθητοί 452.
22, 24.

νόησις. *ci.* αἴσθησις: τ. θεοῦ 184. 19. τ.
κόσμου* 182. 9. ν. κ. αἴσθησις τ. ἀνθρώπου, ἡνῶσθαι 178. 15: συμπεπλεγμέναι
178. 24. ἀδελφή τ. λόγου 178. 19. *ci.*
λόγος 448. 10. οὐσιώδης. opp. αἴσθησις
178. 13. ὁρᾷ τ. ἀφανές 158. 12, *17.
θεῖαι 180. 18.

νοητ-άρχης iv. 32. 7. -ικός. ψυχὴ -ἡ
οὐσ⟨ί⟩α (?) 446. 20. -ἡ οὐσία, *ci.*
κινοῦσα κίνησις 448. 8. -ἡ διὰ δυνάμεων
ἐνέργεια, opp. ὅρασις 246. 13. -ός.
ν. πρῶτος ὁ θεός 134. 23. τ. πρῶτον ν.
Fr. 16 (*ci.* θεοπτικὴ ψυχή), iv. 32. 18.
οὐρανὸν ἡ ν. οὐσία διοικεῖ 272. 7 ; 262.
9. εἴ τις ἔστι κ. ν. οὐσία, *ci.* φῶς
ἡλίου 266. 8. ἡ ν. στάσις 194. 9. ν.
φῶς 250. 33. ἡ ν. οὐσία (sc. ψυχή)
πρὸς τ. θεῷ γενομένη 422. 10. ν.
κόσμος, opp. αἰσθητός 252. 28, 268.
23, 270. 29, 272. 23. τ. νοοῦν 136. 2. -α, opp. αἰσθητά
142. 20. opp. ὑλικόν, -ά 192. 27, 194.
12, 18. τ. -ῶν οὐσία ταυτότης 232. 4.
νομο-θεσία. pl. τ. θεοῦ 492. 29. -θετέω
466. 10. -θέτης 492. 31.
νόμος. 1. χάρισ -ους τ. βίῳ 486. 39 ;
492. 10. νόμος ἡ ἰσχύς 518. 16, 428.
225. 2. dei. λόγων ὡς -ων ἐπακούσατε
466. 20. -ον διὰ τ. λόγου *Fr.* 34. θεοῦ ν.
200. 17. θεῖος ν. 514. 24. ἀπαράβατος
ν. 494. 26. *ci.* εἱμαρμένη : ἄφυκτος 436.
13. εἱμαρμένης κ. τ. *νόμου 228. 9. 12.
τοῖς τ. θεοῦ νόμοις δουλεύειν 486. 1.
ci. τάξις 362 *T.* τιμωρός 224. 33.
νοσ-έω 428. 10. -ος 224. 19, 504. 21,
506. 14, 524. 10. ψυχῆς 224. 21.

νόστιμος 454. 8.
νότος 250. 5, 418. 6.
νοῦς. 1. substantia. φῶς 116. 7. ζωὴ
κ. φῶς 120. 4. ψυχὴ κ. νοῦς = ζωὴ κ.
φῶς 122. 30. *ci.* ψῶς, πνεῦμα *Fr.* 23.
ψυχῆς (τ. λεπτομερέσ-τερον, -τατον) ν.,
νοῦ δὲ θεός 164. 18, 230. 27. ὁ ἐν ἡμῖν
ν. θερμόν τι 526. 2. καπνὸς ἐμπόδιον
νοῦ 504. 5. 2. deus mens est : deus
primus mens non est. ὁ ν. πατὴρ θεός
116. 11 (opp. λόγος). ὁ πάντων πατήρ,
ὁ ν. 120. 4. ὁ ν. ὁ θεός, ἀρρενόθηλυς
ὢν 118. 10. ὁ ἐκ νοὸς φωτεινὸς λόγος
116. 9. ν. νοὸς φωτεινός *Fr.* 23. τοῦ
(πρώτου θεοῦ) ἔννοιαν λαμβάνει ὡς ἀσωμάτου κ. νοῦ ⟨καὶ⟩ τ. ἀγαθοῦ 178. 1. ὁ
θεὸς ⌈ἄφθαρτος⌉ ν. γίγνεται 480. 20. θεός·
σοφώτατος ν. κ. ἀίδιος 530. 9. ν. αὐτὸς
ἑαυτὸν νοῶν iv. 32. 14. καθαρὸς ν. iv.
34. 6. ν. εἷς iv. 226. 17. ὁ θεὸς οὐ ν.
ἐστιν, αἴτιος δὲ τ. (ν.) εἶναι 142. 8. θεὸς
παντὸς ἀνωτάτω νοῦ κ. λόγου iv. 200. 9.
3. deus alter, mens dei, creator, locus.
ἕτερος ν. δημιουργός 118. 11, 18, 20, 25.
δημιουργικὸς ν. iv. 32. 20. ὁ ν. ὀργάνῳ
τ. πυρὶ πρὸς τ. δημιουργίαν χρῆται 200.
2. (Τύπος) ν. ὅλος ἐξ ὅλου 140. 18. *ci.*
ἀλήθεια, τ. ἀρχέτυπον τ. ψυχῆς 140. 23.
ἀπὸ (τ. ἀγαθοῦ) νοῦν γενέσθαι τε ὅλον
καὶ καθ᾽ ἑαυτὸν ὑφεστῶτα iv. 201. 5 s.
ν. ἱερὸς (sc. λόγος-Ἑρμῆς) ἐμοῦ (sc. τ.
θεοῦ) νοῦ 472. 4. v. *infra.* 4. νοῦς
κοινός 222. 21. ὁ ν. ἐξ αὐτῆς τῆς τ.
θεοῦ οὐσίας ἐστὶν . . . *ὡς περιπλω-
μένος 222. 23. (a) ὁ μὲν θεὸς ἐν τ. νῷ, ὁ
δὲ ν. ἐν τ. ψυχῇ, ἡ δὲ ψυχὴ ἐν τ. ὕλῃ
208. 21. ὁ μὲν θεὸς περὶ πάντα κ. διὰ
πάντων, ὁ δὲ ν. περὶ τ. ψυχήν, ἡ δὲ ψυχὴ
περὶ τ. ἀέρα, ὁ δὲ ἀὴρ περὶ τ. ψυχήν
(sc. κόσμου) 230. 27. ν. = ἡ τ. θεοῦ
ψυχή 228. 7, 11. πάντων ἄρχων, ἐπικρατεῖ 228. 6, 11. ὁ ν. (τ. αἰῶνος)
ἀγαθός ἐστιν, ὕ(σ)περ ἐστὶν αὐτοῦ κ.
ψυχή 228. 4. ὁ (ν.) τ. παντὸς τ. πάντων (δημιουργός) 200. 2. ν. δέ, κεφαλὴ
αὐτὴ σφαιρικῶς κινουμένη 194. 12.
membrum dei : ἀθάνατον (*ci.* ὕλη, ζωή,
πνεῦμα, ψυχή) 234. 19 ; *ci.* πρόνοια,
φύσις, ψυχή 236. 17. ἐνέργεια τ. θεοῦ
(*ci.* ψυχή) 206. 21. ἀρχή (*ci.* θεός,
φύσις, ὕλη) 144. 25. ὅπου γὰρ ψυχή,
ἐκεῖ κ. ν. ἐστιν 224. 7. ζωή ἐστιν ἕνωσις νοῦ κ. ψυχῆς 216. 29. ν. κ. ψύχωσις
τ. ὅλων iv. 196. 9. ἡ τ. παντὸς διοίκησις, ἠρτημένη ἐκ τῆς ἑνὸς φύσεως, κ.
διήκουσα δι᾽ ἑνὸς τ. νοῦ 202. 21. τ.
ἀσώματα κινεῖται ὑπὸ τ. νοῦ 228. 27.
δύνατον νοῦν . . . ποιεῖν ὅπερ βούλεται
228. 6. (b) οὗτος ὁ ν. ἐν ἀνθρώποις θεός

ἐστι 224. 2. οὗτός ἐστιν ὁ ἀγαθὸς δαίμων 202. 25. καλοῦ τ. νοῦ τυχεῖν 202. 5. ci. ψυχή: εὐεργέτης. κυβερνήτης 224. 10. 26. ἐπιστατεῖ 224. 14; εὐεργέτης 224. 10; κυβερνήτης 224. 26; λυπεῖ 224. 20; ἐμβὰς ὁδηγεῖ 202. 1; τ. ἀγαθὸν περιποιεῖται 224. 23. τ. νοῦν (τ. ἐλλογίμων) ἡγεμονεύειν 226. 21. (c) τ. νοῦν ἐν τ. ἀλόγοις ζῴοις φύσεως δίκην ἐνεργεῖν, συνεργοῦντα αὐτῶν τ. ὁρμαῖς 228. 18 (224. 6, 27). 5. mens res divina est, vehiculis divinis circumdata. ὁ ν. ἐν τ. λόγῳ, ὁ λόγος ἐν τ. ψυχῇ, ἡ δὲ ψυχὴ ἐν τ. πνεύματι (ὀχεῖται) 194. 28. νοῦν ἐν ψυχῇ, λόγον δὲ ἐν τ. νῷ· τ. οὖν θεὸν τούτων πατέρα 230. 23. ἔνδυμα εἶναι τ. μὲν νοῦ τ. ψυχήν, τ. δὲ ψυχῆς τ. πνεῦμα 198. 11. ν., ὀξύτατος ὢν πάντων τ. θείων *ὐχημάτων (codd. νοημάτων), ... ἔχει σῶμα, τ. πῦρ 198. 29. ἐξίσταται τ. ψυχῆς 204. 2. καθαρὸς τ. ἐνδυμάτων 198. 4. ψυχὴ ὅλη ν. γίνεται 200. 10. ci. σῶμα, χιτὼν πύριν-ον, -ος 198. 7, 25, 200. 28. 6. ci. λόγος 150. 9 s., 178. 18, 184. 28. ὁ λόγος ἐστὶν εἰκὼν κ. νοῦς τ. θεοῦ 230. 25. ci. λόγος, γνῶσις 874 T. 7. mens divina visitat homines εἰμὶ ὁ Ποιμάνδρης, ὁ τ. αὐθεντίας ν. 114. 10: 130. 7, 248. 23. παραγίνομαι ἐγὼ ὁ ν. 126. 10. αὐτὸς ὁ ν. 126. 7. σὺ ὁ ν. 254. 4. ὦ ν. (ἐμός) 126. 7, 29. Νοῦ πρὸς Ἑρμῆν 206. 1. τ. θεῖον νοῦν ἐνοχλεῖν iv. 39. 27. λαβόντι ἀπὸ τ. νοός μου 130. 6. φησὶ ὁ ν. ἡμῶν iv. 107. 24. allegor. ποτὲ μὲν ψυχῆς ἔχει εἰκόνα ὁ Προμηθεύς, ποτὲ δὲ νόος iv. 107. 21; συμβουλεύων διὰ τ. νοὺς αὐτῶν iv. 108. 9; Ἐπιμηθέα συμβουλευόμενον ὑπὸ τ. ἰδίου νοῦ iv. 109. 14. 8. commercium hominis cum deo. γεννᾶσθαι ἐν νῷ 240. 17. τ. νοῦν δέχεσθαι 150. 28. βαπτίζεσθαι τ. νούς 150. 27. περιλάμψαν πάντα τ. νοῦν 190. 14. ci. φωτίζειν, ἐπιφωτίζειν 252. 30, iv. 106. 10. νοῦν ἔχειν 152. 21. 202. 28, 226. 28. ἐν τ. νῷ (νοΐ) θεωρῶ, ὁρῶ 116. 16, 21, 248. 5, 252. 33. πάντα ἐμπεριλαμβάνειν τ. νοΐ 152. 11. τ. νοΐ ἀκούσατε Fr. 23. ὁ τ. νοΐ θεωρητός 162. 27. ἔχε νῷ σῷ 114. 14. ἡ τ. νοῦ ἐπιστήμη 152. 16. ὁ τ. νοῦ ὀφθαλμός 188. 22, 248. 14, 250. 28; pl. 158. 15, 190. 6. σὺ ὁ ν. 254. 4. 9. ὑπηρετικὸς ν. (ὁ καταπεμπόμενος ὑπὸ τ. δίκης) 202. 29. ὁ ν., ὅταν δαίμων γένηται ... εἰσδὺς εἰς τ. ἀσεβεστάτην ψυχήν, αἰκίζεται 200. 28. 10. non omnibus mentem impertit deus 150. 19. ἡ τοιαύτη ψυχὴ νοῦν οὐκ ἔχει 204. 8. οἱ νοῦν μὴ ἔχοντες,

προσειληφότες 150. 17, 152. 2. 11. facultates. vires mentis humanae. (ἐπιστήμη) ὀργάνῳ χρωμένη αὐτῷ τ. νοΐ, ὁ δὲ ν. τ. σώματι (χρῆται) 192. 26. ἡ νόησις ὑπὸ τ. νοῦ (γίνεται) 178. 19. ὁ ν. ὅραται ἐν τ. νοεῖν 222. 17. ὁ ν. κύει πάντα τ. νοήματα 180. 6. 12. sensus verborum 262. 21, 264. 1. 13. consensus εἰς ν. 280. 23.

νυκτιφανής 530. 13.

νύμφη. μακρόβιοι iv. 244. 13.

νύξ 234. 24, 408. 27, 486. 39.

νυχθήμερος 414. 2.

νωθρός. ψυχή 204. 6.

νωχελής 450. 25.

ξηρ-αίνω 438. 10. -ός 438. 15, 500. 7.

ὀβελίσκος 492. 14.

ὀγδο-αδικός 128. 15 s. -άς 248. 19.

ὄγκ-ος 196. 28, 266. 8, 476. 20, 518. 3. -όω 176. 1, 196. 24 s.. 268. 24 s.

ὁδεύω 222. 11. metaph. 154. 18, 170. 7, 222. 8, 390. 27, 508. 18.

ὁδηγ-έω. metaph. 156. 14. 172. 4, 184. 29, 202. 1, 230. 11, 508. 24, iv. 106. 12. -ός iv. 109. 11.

ὁδός. metaph. 156. 14, 170. 6 s., 222. 7, 418. 18, iv. 34. 14. πρὸς ἀλήθειαν 390. 27. εἰς εὐδαιμονίαν iv. 38. 20. ἱερατικαί iv. 38. 31. τ. θανάτου 132. 20. ἐπὶ τ. ἑρπετά 192. 5.

ὁδούς 516. 26.

ὀδύνη 402. 3.

ὀδύρομαι 474. 22.

οἶδα. τ. θεόν, οἷ. ποῖα, τίς 204. 17, 222. 2, 25. τ. εἰ(δέ)ναι (?) 462. 30.

οἰκεῖ-ος 124. 24, 168. 31, 464. 27. τ. -ον 410. 8. -ότης. συγγενική 440. 7, 442. 5. ci. συντροφία 528. 20. -όω 440. 6, 448. 8.

οἰκ-έω. ἡ -ουμένη 250. 22. -ησις. metaph. 200. 5.

οἰκονομία 262. 10, 436. 1, 466. 14.

οἴστρησις 240. 24.

οἰωνοσκόπος 480. 7.

ὀκνέω 206. 4.

ὀλέθριος 414. 27.

ὀλιγο-μετρία 526. 18. -χρόνιος 380. 5.

ὁλόκληρος 168. 31.

ὅλος. ἀρχαί iv. 31. 25. λόγος 446. 15. νοῦς -ος ἐξ -ου 140. 18. ψυχὴ -η νοῦς γίνεται 200. 10. τό 220. 11. τά 126. 1, 130. 12, 132. 6, 174. 16.

ὁλοτελής. θεωρία 460. 2.

Ὀλύμπ-ιος 530. 11. -ος 196. 19.

ὄμβρος 250. 12.

Ὁμηρίδης. pl. iv. 244. 15.

σκοτεινός. metaph. 132. 16, 172. 11.
σκοτομαχέω 126. 27.
σκότος. 114. 19 s., 116. 8, 124. 17, 24,
146. 1. metaph. 172. 5 ; τ. -ους τιμω-
ρία(ι) 246. 2, 21.
σκώληξ 416. 23.
σοφ-ία 132. 24, 144. 26, Fr. 12. τ.
θεοῦ 206. 16, 208. 10. νοερά 238. 22.
personif. 472. 23. -ίζομαι. pass. 148.
4. -ος 242. 8. θεὸς μόνος ὄντως σ.
256. 19 ; τέλειος κ. σ. Fr. 35. λόγος
ibid.
σπείρω. metaph. 132. 23, 180. 11 s.,
238. 23. ἀθανασίαν 262. 2. φύσις
-ουσα 438. 5. τ. σπαρέν 430. 8.
σπέρμ-α 260. 28. ci. πνεῦμα 438. 17.
ci. γένεσις, φύσις 422. 25, 438. 6.
metaph. τ. θεοῦ -ατα 180. 8, 15, 182.
15. τ. νοήσεως 182. 2. τ. παλιγγενεσίας 146. 22. -ατίζω. metaph. 414.
26.
†σπερμογονέω 146. 23.
σπεύδω. metaph. 248. 21, 392. 8 s.,
iv. 176. 12. ἐπὶ (πρὸς) τ. ἐν κ. μόνον
(θεόν) 152. 15, 154. 13.
σπινθήρ 198. 27.
σπλάγχνον. pl. 234. 26, 270. 9.
σπλήν 160. 30.
σπορά 146. 21, 148. 9, 188. 6, 430. 10,
458. 16, 490. 31. metaph. 238. 21 s.
σταθμός 522. 2.
στασ-ιάζω 474. 25, 486. 14. -ις. -ιν
ἐσχηκέναι 116. 19. φορᾶς 136. 16.
κίνησις ἐν -ει κ. ὑπὸ -εως κινεῖται 138.
4. ἡ νοητὴ σ. 194. 9.
στατικός. -ὴ ἐνέργεια (τ. ἀγαθοῦ) 164.
25.
στεῖρος 462. 8.
στενάζω 458. 1, 474. 22.
στενότης 134. 15.
στενοχωρέω. pass. 140. 11.
στερε-ός 160. 13. -ωμα Fr. 32. pl.
514. 12.
στερ-έω. pass. 170. 12. 406. 7. -ησις
174. 9, 404. 25. τ. αἰσθήσεως 176. 18.
στερροποιέω 160. 28.
στεφανηφορέω 266. 16.
στήλη 492. 14.
στήρ-ιγμα 172. 11. -ίζω 412. 30. pass.
136. 25.
στιβαρός 264. 8.
στιγμή 270. 11 s.
στοιχεῖον. 1. elementum (a) 116.
24 s., 118. 16 s., 146. 5, 184. 4, 202. 20,
518. 6, 522. 18, 526. 16, 528. 17.
ὄμμα 408. 21. personif. 486. 23,
488. 28 (cf. 220. 26 αἰσθήσεις τ. ποιητῶν). (b) superius. ἡγεμονία τ. ὅλων
-ων, ὁ μὲν ἀρρενικῶν, ὁ δὲ θηλυκῶν

iv. 33. 2, 466. 29. πῦρ, ci. νοῦς 200.
1 s. 2. corpus, vehiculum animae. ὁ
οὐρανὸς πρῶτον σ., ἡ γῆ ὕστατον σ. 432.
10 (cf. ἔσχατον σῶμα 220. 11). πλαστὸν 240. 18. (astra) 482. 28. τ. ἱερὰ τ.
κοσμικῶν -ων σύμβολα 460. 7. 3. littera.
τ. Ω σ. iv. 104. 2 s. διὰ -ων (Α Δ Α Μ)
iv. 106. 25 s.
στόμα 160. 26, 522. 11.
στοργή 126. 14, 374 T.
στοχ-άζω. m. 266. 13. -ασμός 266.
12.
στρατ-ιά. δαιμόνων, θεῶν 268. 11,
272. 9. -ιώτης. astrol. 414. 30.
στρέφω 118. 21. m. 118. 22, 136. 20,
158. 34, 436. 10.
στροβέω. 270. 15.
στρουθός 510. 1.
στροφή 218. 8.
στυγν-άζω 474. 12. -ός 114. 20, 124.
24.
σύ. σὺ (εἶ) 164. 3, 13 s., 252. 20, 254.
3 s., iv. 148.
συγ-γενής. θεοί 458. 23. πνεύματα
476. 17. τ. -ές 526. 15. 466. 29.
-γενικός. οἰκειότης 440. 6, 442. 5.
-γεννάω. pass. 400. 5. -γίγνομαι
394. 17. -γραμμα. Ἑρμοῦ -ατα iv.
28. 7. -καταφέρω 138. 3. metaph.
172. 1. -κινέω 136. 10. -κίνησις
136. 13. ci. συμπάθεια iv. 37. 26.
-κλείω. ψυχὴ -ομένη 500. 8. -κλητος.
τ. θεῶν 484. 22. -κοινωνέω. τ. ἀγνοίᾳ
132. 15. -κοσμέω 416. 2. pass. 456.
16, 462. 11, 484. 35. -κραμα 528. 22.
-κρασις. τ. ἀστέρων, ἄστρων 452. *7,
10. τ. ἐναντίων 212. 3. -κριμα 500.
6, 508. 21. -κρίνω. pass. 204. 11.
-κρισις. κατὰ σ. 152. 9, 166. 28, iv.
169. 18. -χρωτίζω *228. 22. pass.
198. 19. -χωρέω. pass. 120. 12.
-χωρητικός. τ. ὄντων 140. 20.
σύζυγος 166. 9.
συμ-βαίνω. -βεβηκός, -ότα 422. 2, 19.
-βολον. ἱερά 460. 7. διὰ -ων 234.
25. -βουλος. ὁ λόγος σ. τ. οὐσίας
444. 15. -μετρος. *σύστασις 524. 18.
-μίγνυμι. pass. 118. 7. -παγία 528.
13. -πάθεια. πρὸς τ. δεύτερον θεόν
176. 22. ψυχῆς τ. -αν ἐχούσης τοῖς
οὐρανοῦ μυστηρίοις 458. 17. γεννᾶν
-αν καθ' εἱμαρμένην 452. 12. ci. συγκίνησις iv. 37. 25. -πάσχω. τὰ κάτω
-παθεῖν τοῖς ἄνω 494. 1. -περιφέρω
160. 1. pass. 404. 12. -πλέκω. pass.
αἴσθησις κ. νόησις ὥσπερ -πεπλεγμέναι
178. 24. 468. 28. -πνέω. metaph.
198. 13. -πνοια 438. 16. -φέρω. pass.
412. 8, 418. 10. -φορά 152. 13. -φωνέω,

metaph. 180.5. -φωνία (titulus) iv.
225.4. -φωνος 186.1. ἐνέργεια 472.
28.

σύν. ἑαυτῷ 266.23.

συν-ᾴδω 250, 31. -αγιάζω 132.3. -άγω
*266.1, 400.25. ὁ -ων 212.20.
-αϊδίως iv.175.10. -αποθνήσκω 400.
5. -άπτω 424.16, iv.39.11. -ῆπται
τ. ἀνθρωπίνη ψυχῇ τ. ἄλογα 404.13.
-ομένη, τ. θεοῖς iv.38.1. -άρθρωσις.
τ. λόγου 244.16. -αριθμέω. pass.
iv.202.3. -αυξάνω. σεαυτὸν τ.
ἀμετρήτῳ μεγέθει 220.19. -αύξω
458.7. -αφή. ἐπὶ τ. ὄν iv.35.20.
-δεσμος. ἴδιος 524.10. πάντων 124.
4. τ. σαρκῶν 478.16. τ. σωμάτων
408.20. †-δετος 410.7.

σύν-ειμι. σοι πανταχοῦ 114.11. -έδριον
484.22. -ενόω. pass. 424.8, iv.39.
14. -εξομοιόω. -ούμενον πᾶσιν iv.
210.13. -επεισρέω 178.24. -εργέω
224.12, 228.19, 394.13. -εργός 216.
20. νοῦς 224.27. -έρχομαι. εἰς ἕν
212.19. -εσις 526.1. -ετός 474.7,
500.14. -έχεια. τ. φορᾶς 134.14.
δαιμόνων 154.12. τ. ποιήσεως 256.22.
χρόνου 424.19. -έχω. ὑπὸ τ. θεοῦ
-όμενος 174.17. τοὺς ἑπτὰ πάντα
-οντας 412.25. ἡ -ουσα ἀνάγκη ἐστίν
436.4. ἐντὸς -ει 438.1. -ει (τ. κόσμον) ὁ αἰών 208.30. -θεσις. τ. ἐνδυμάτων 198.14. -θετος. πάντα 182.
23. σῶμα 224.15, 232.8. τ. πρῶτον
σ. εἶδος 240.19. -θημα. θέειον iv.
229.4. -ίστημι. λόγῳ συστησάμενος
τ. ὄντα 130.16. -εστάναι. opp. εἶναι
394.23. χωρὶς τ. καθολικῶν ἐνεργειῶν
τὸ σῶμα συστῆναι οὐ δυνατόν 398.26,
442.6 s. ἐξ ἀντιθέσεως τ. πάντα
-εστάναι 192.29. -έστηκε 124.25,
29. ἐκ πολλῶν 386.19. ἐκ δυνάμεων
-εστός, -ιστάμενος 248.11, 246.10.
τ. συνεστός 508.3. -νοέω 198.12.
ψυχὴ -οῦσα 446.21. -οδεύω. τ.
πλάνη 132.15. -οδία. ἱερά 498.9.
-οδος. ἡ πρὸς τ. σῶμα (ψυχῆς) σ.
508.26. ci. κρᾶσις (τ. στοιχείων)
522.17, 526.21, 528.16. -οικος.
δαίμονες 268.12. -ουσιαστικός. τ.
θεῷ 234.23. -ταξις. rhet. 262.19.
-τίθημι. -ετέθη ἡ νοερὰ γένεσις 246.
6. -τροφία. ci. οἰκειότης 528.21.
-τροφος 432.30. τ. ἡμετέρας ἀρχῆς -α
474.37.

σύ-σκηνος. -α τ. ψυχῆς 528.8. -σταθμία.
τ. φυράματος 522.16.

σύστ-ασις. τ. στοιχείων *184.3.
σώματος: ci. ἁρμονία 442.9. 450.23.
opp. διάλυσις 174.6, 176.16. ci.

ἀριθμός 232.9. ci. ἀλήθ-εια, -ές 382.
14, 386.18. ψυχῆς 514.2. τ. ὕλης
(τ. ψυχῶν) 474.5. ἐξ ὕλης κ. ψυχῆς
τ. -ιν ἔχοντος 214.2. σ. πάντων ὁ θεός
178.5. ἀρχή 460.18. -ατικός. τ.
στοιχείων κρᾶσις 528.3. -ατός 442.
15.

συστέλλω. pass. 198.5.

σύστημα. τ. τῶν ἀνθρώπων 470.32.
-ατα (ψυχαί) 460.16.

συσχετήριον 508.34.

σφαῖρ-α. κόσμος 176.4, 194.10. ἡ
δημιουργικὴ 120.13. ὀκτὼ 272.1.
ἑπτά 324 Τ. πλανώμεναι. opp.
ἀπλανής 136.12. -ικῶς 194.13.

σφαιροειδής. τ. πᾶν 176.2.

σφάλλω. σφαλῆναι τ. γνώσεως 130.
24. τ. τοιούτου (βίου) 376 Τ.

σφενδονέω 368 Τ.

σφίγγω 486.5. ἐσφιγμένον κακίᾳ
168.9.

σχῆμ-α. συμβεβηκύς 422.2. ἴδιον τ.
σώματος, ἐσχηματισμένον σ. 422.7.
πρός τι 442.2. ci. μέγεθος, εἶδος 438.
21. ci. χρῶμα 418.21. -ατα τ.
ἀστέρων iv.109.26. -ατίζω. pass.
422.7, 438.21. -ατότης. pl. 420.
21.

σχολάζω 192.17.

σώζω. (ὁ κόσμος) -ων τ. τάξιν 232.13.
τ. φωτί σου σωθέντες 374 Τ. σῷζε
ζωή, φώτιζε φῶς 252.17. ὑπὸ (τ.)
θεοῦ -εσθαι, σωθῆναι 128.26, 182.3.
μηδένα δύνασθαι σωθῆναι πρὸ τ. παλιγγενεσίας 238.10. πῶς σωθήσονται
132.23. νοητὴ οὐσία ἐξουσίαν ἔχει τ.
σώζειν ἕτερον, αὐτὴν -ουσα 422.11.

σῶμα. passim 1. -ατα ἀπὸ ὕλης 182.
21. -ατος ἴδια 422.6. -ατα ἀεὶ εἶναι
394.3. τριχῇ διαστατόν 248.7. ci.
ἁρμονία etc. 442.9. 2. ἔμψυχα. opp.
ἄψυχα 396.4. κίνησις (τ. φθαρτῶν
-άτων) 402.29 s. 3. hominum. γήϊνον
198.15. διαλυτά 408.10. θνητά.
ib. ἄνθρωπος θνητὸς διὰ τ. σ. 122.5.
παθητόν 198.19. σύνθετον 224.14.
ὑλικόν 126.32, 168.9. φυσικόν 446.
22. τ. αἰσθητὸν τ. φύσεως 248.
14. v. ψυχή. 4. mundus. οὗ μεῖζον
οὐκ ἔστι σ. 134.8. τ. πᾶν σ. 176.
7. δημιουργὸς ἐν -ατι ὤν 408.9.
5. caelum. σῶμα ἔσχατον 220.11. τ.
οὐρανοῦ 418.10. 6. astra. θεῖα. opp.
θνητά 394.15. ἀθάνατον ἐκ μιᾶς ὕλης
394.31. θεῖα, τέλεια, ἀΐδια 398.12 s.
ἀΐδια 430.12. 7. elementa. ἀΐδια 382.
7 s., 388.6. 8. terra. θεῖον 150.6.
9. mentis, animae. πύρινον σ. 198.7,
200.29. θεῖον σ. ci. ψυχή 404.11,

18. ἐμαυτὸν ἐξελήλυθα εἰς ἀθάνατον σ. 240. 16. πόσα ἡμᾶς δεῖ -ατα διεξελθεῖν 154. 11. 10. αἴσθησις σῶμα 402. 8 s. 11. metaph. τ. θεοῦ ὥσπερ σ. ἡ ποίησις 260. 1.

σωματ-ίζω. pass. 496. 26. -ικός. αἰσθήσεις 114. 4.

σωματο-ποιέω. τ. πᾶν 176. 1. -οῦσαι ἐνέργειαι 394. 16. τ. ἐνέργειαν -ήσασα 400. 1. -ποίησις 394. 7.

σωματ-ότης 236. 28. -ουργία 518. 29. -ωσις 394. 4, 408. 14. -⟨ωτ⟩ικός 398. 25.

σωρός 236. 21.

σωστικός 450. 3.

σωτ-ήρ. ἥλιος 268. 22. -ηρία. metaph. 170. 27. -ηρικός. δαίμονες 368 T. -ήριον. ἡ γνῶσις 196. 18. -ήριος. τ. ὄντων 140. 20, 414. 27.

σωφροσύνη 180. 16, 444. 5. personif. 472. 24.

ταμί-ας. ci. προνοητής 484. 10. -εῖον. ὕλης 264. 31. -α *466. 12, 470. 25.

†τανας 414. 26.

ταξίαρχος 476. 34.

τάξις. περιώρισται ἀριθμῷ κ. τύπῳ 158. 24 (cf. 160. 6?). ci. πρόνοια, ἀνάγκη 418. 27, 420. 2. ci. πρόνοια 432. 12. ci. εἱμαρμένη, ἀνάγκη, νόμος 362 T. τ. κόσμου 206. 18, 160. 19, 236. 6. κοσμική iv. 35. 10. κόσμος σώζων τ. τάξιν 232. 13. πᾶσα 212. 6. τ. ἀστέρων 158. 23 s. μία τ. 176. 13, 212. 24. αἰώνιος 210. 27. ci. οἰκονομία 466. 14. τ. γινομένων 184. 4. τ. ὕλης 232. 3. τ. ἐπιτιθέναι Fr. 35. τ. τάξιν ποιουμένη 514. 8. τάξει 128. 20. ἰδία τ. 120. 17. κατὰ -ιν. (πῆξιν?) Fr. 31.

ταπειν-ός 204. 18. -ότης 258. 31. -όω 220. 33.

ταράσσω. pass. 114. 23.

ταραχή 270. 4.

τάσσω. τεταγμένος 126. 14 (v. 128. 19), 268. 28, 368 T., 160. 10, 212. 23, 362 T.

ταυτότης. τ. αἰῶνος 206. 17. (δια)-μένουσα (ἐν) τ. -ότητι 208. 28, iv. 202. 6. οὐσία τ. νοητῶν 232. 5 s. χρόνου 424. 18.

τάφος. metaph. περιφόρητος 172. 13.

τάχ-ος. τ. φορᾶς 182. 25. (νοήσεως) 220. 13. -ύς. τ. ἀσώματον 218. 35. οὐρανοῦ τ. -υτάτην (?) περίβασιν 160. 15. -ύτης 212. 23.

τεῖχος. metaph. 198. 28.

τέκν-ον 158. 8, 252. 28 s., iv. 148. -όω. m. 460. 16.

τέλ-ειος. deus 216. 7, Fr. 35. τ. -ον 156. 7, 380. 4. λόγος Fr. 29. -οι ἄνθρωποι 150. 28. τ. -ον μέλαν 474. 18. †τ. ἐν ἅπασι -ον 494. 5. v. λόγος. -ειόω. pass. iv. 111. 16. -εσιουργέω. pass. 464. 26. -έω. ci. βουλή, θέλημα τ. θεοῦ 130. 13, 252. 10, 254. 6. -ος. opp. ἀρχή 118. 23, 272. 14. ci. ἀνανέωσις 144. 28. τῆς τ. ἀστέρων ἁρμονίας 452. 12. τ. εὐσεβείας 390. 22. θεωθῆναι 128. 23. ἐπὶ τ. τοῦ παντὸς τέλει 250. 2 (v. 252. 10). καθῆκον 478. 18. pl. ci. ἀρχαί (fines) 362 T. (mors) 392. 16.

τεμενί-ζω. pass. 460. 18. -ίτης Fr. 29. -ος 492. 9.

τένων 490. 3.

†τερασπορίας 146. 29. v. vol. iv, p. xlvi.

τέρπω 466. 14, 472. 21.

τετράπους. ζῷα, θηρία, τὰ -ποδα 120. 2, 146. 20, 406. 11, 470. 5, 516. 26.

τέττιξ 276. 36.

τέχν-η. ci. ἄνθρωπος 202. 17. ci. τ. λογικόν 406. 3. ci. ἐνέργειαι 398. 28. βασιλεῖαι -ης 520. 5, 220. 23, 492. 30. τ. δημιουργήματος 160. 23. -ιτεία. ἱεραί 464. 16. -ιτεύω 424. 3, 466. 27. -ίτης. τ. συμπάντων 458. 10, 490. 34. τ. κόσμου 486. 30. 464. 24. -ῖτις. φῦσαι 522. 10. -ούργημα 148. 7. -ουργία 148. 10

τήκω 396. 6.

τηρέω. ci. τάξις 158. 24, 176. 14, 212. 24, 412. 26. τ. ψυχὰς 516. 8.

τίθημι 252. 27.

τιθήνη. γῆ 212. 10.

τιμ-άω. τετιμημέν-ος (-οι) τῇ τ. θεοῦ προσηγορίᾳ 144. 3, 374 T., 474. 19. -ή. κατὰ -ήν, opp. κατὰ φύσιν 144. 4.

τιμωρ-έω. m. δαίμονες 368 T. pass. 392. 13. -ία. ci. δαίμων 126. 22. -ία, -αι. τ. σκότους 246. 2, 21. pl. ὕλης 242. 21. 126. 25, 144. 15 s. -ός. δαίμων 126. 22, 368 T. δίκη 420. 5. νόμος 224. 32. τ. τῶν ὑπὸ γῆν τύραννος 490. 22. pl. 242. 21.

τλημόνως 470. 31.

τμῆμα. pl. 466. 12, 470. 25.

τόκος. ἴδιος 120. 6, 298 T., 299 T.

τόλμ-α 268. 19. περίεργος 470. 21, 482. 28. -άω 268. 19. -ήσαντα εἰπεῖν 418. 13. -ηρός. τ. ἔργον ποιῆσαι τὸν ἄνθρωπον 482. 4. -ὰς χεῖρας 482. 17. -ηρῶς. compar. 162. 17.

τοξότης 406. 21.

τόπος. 1. ὁ τ. ἐν ᾧ (τὸ πᾶν) κινεῖται 134. 12, 140. 16. ἀσώματος 134. 19. νοῦς ὕλος 140. 18. ἐνέργεια χωρητικὴ 136. 7. 2. συμβεβηκός 422. 2. ἰδίως

benignitas 344. 15. omnipotens iv.
166. 17. primipotens 344. 14. utriusque sexus 332. 19. *v.* conformator,
dispensator, dominus, effector, gubernator, pater, voluntas. 3. nomen -i
330. 23, 332. 5 s., 374. 3. vox -i iv. 9.
16, iv. 18. 16. 4. unius -i (τ. πρώτου
κ. ἑνός) 344. 14. qui secundus effectus
est deus 362.14. secundum-um (solem)
348. (mundus) secundum sensibilem
300. 1 s. caelum, sensibilis deus 290.
11. aeternus (Aion) 348. 19. 5. *pl.*
-orum genera 322. 3. principes dii
dist. sensibiles 322. 21. aeterni 338.
22. caelestes 362. 2 s. ex (de) mun-
dissima parte naturae 336. 9, 338. 14.
ex inmortali natura 336. 23. *dist.*
homines. daemones 292. 22. di boni,
ci. angeli iv. 186. 15. terreni, terrestres
360. 3, 17, 362. 1, 10, iv. 14. 8. humana
omnia respiciunt 336. 26. -orum secessio 344. 3. -os figurare, efficere
338. 20 s., 358. 20. *v.* fictor. -orum
species (ἀγάλματα) 338. 16. qualitas
360. 18. *v.* homo. 6. (homo) in
naturam -i transit 294. 12. religio,
veneratio -i 370. 4, 14. colere 306. 31.
orare 372. 3 s. rogare 372. 1. consortium hominum deorumque 338. 3.
*diexodicus. -a 286. 19.
di-lectio. (στοργή) 374. 6. -lectus,
ci. cultus 302. 8 s. *ci.* philosophia
308. 22. -ligenter 308. 10. -ligen-
tia 300. 8, 304. 11, 308. 1 s. -ligo
300. 12, 342. 15. -mensio. temporum
356. 10. *pl.* 310. 10.
discessio animae 366. 10.
disciplina. (ἐπιστήμη) 314. 24, 334.
26, 336. 2 s. pl. 302. 2, 310. 5.
(τάξις) 354. 13 s., 362. 15.
dis-cursus. stellarum 348. 31. -pen-
sator 346. 19 s., 348. 18 s. -penso
316. 9. -pono 364. 13. -positio.
caelestis 294. 18. -putatio (λόγος)
298. 14, 322. 7. -solutio 366. 2.
-tribuo. *pass.* (μεμερισμέναι) 346. 32.
-tributor 346. 19.
diversitas. *pl.* 306. 25.
divin-atio 362. 4. -itas. (τ. θεῖον)
298. 5, 302. 14, 318. 14, 336. 2, 340.
12, 25, 372. 2. utriusque naturae 334.
14. -us. humanitas 306. 2. *compar.*
ratio 322. 9 *passim.*
doctrina. perfecta *Fr.* 5.
domin-or. terrae (sc. οἱ τ. γῆν διοι-
κοῦντες δαίμονες) 346. 33. -us. deus
(δεσπότης, κύριος). summus 326. 7.
ci. pater 330. 22. 332. 6, 336. 3, 338. 5,
22, 344. 13, 370. 6, *Fr.* 3, iv. 21. 9.

ci. conformator (ποιητής) 298. 14.
aeternitatis 304. 6.
domus. (σκῆνος) corporea 300. 13.
donum. caeleste 320. 15.
duplex. (διπλοῦς), animal 296. 8. effectus 348. 28. natura 302. 21.

†eccurutrofes. (ἐκ κύρου τροφῆς) iv.
230. 3.
effect-or. deus (ποιητής, ἐνεργῶν) 290.
15, 304. 8, 332. 6, 338. 6, 346 2. -rix
(ἐνέργεια) 362. 13. -us (ἐνέργεια) 306.
25, 310. 12, 314. 1, 334. 12, 346. 31,
348. 31. duplex 348. 28. (τέλος) 362.
18, 364. 12, 302. 5 (?).
effic-acia. (ἐνέργεια) 374. 7. -io 326.
11, 358. 17 s.
elementum. (στοιχεῖον). 1. quattuor
290. 4, 21, 300. 22, iv. 12. 16. -a in-
feriora 302. 22. (superiora), *opp.* in-
feriora 304. 22. quaternis utriusque
partis -is 306. 19. 2. (astra). elementis velocitate miscetur 294. 22. *ci.* caelum, terra 330. 7 (*v. l.* 17).
error 344. 16. *pl.* 320. 23, 356. 11,
370. 9.
eventus. (τύχη) 364. 23.
ex. se *Fr.* 4.
examen 366. 10.
existentia. *ci.* sapientia, vita iv. 274.
exsuperantissimus 374. 1.

facies 318. 16.
facio. deos iv. 180. 8, iv. 181. 25.
fatum. -a (εἱμαρμένη) 362. 8.
fecunditas 312. 3 s., 332. 11 s.
fel-ix 320. 15. -icitas 296. 20, 338.
12, 356. 24.
fictor. deorum 338. 6, 360. 25.
fiducia 370. 12 s.
firmitas. (βεβαιότης) 352. 20.
flumen. (Nilus) 340. 27.
fons. *metaph.* 322. 12.
forma (αἰσθητὴ ἰδέα). visibiles -ae 316.
22. *ci.* qualitas 316. 13, 318. 4. di-
versae 324. 12. duo ex quibus constant forma(e), [et] corpora (et) incorporalia 328. 25.
fors. (τύχη) 364. 23.
Fortuna. (εἱμαρμένη) 324. 14.
frequ-ens. obtutus 308. 23. -entatio.
1. obsequiorum 302. 10. usu et -ione
360. 23. 2. f. fertur influens per mundum et per animam omnium generum
290. 17. omnium agitatio atque f.
(πνεῦμα πάντα κινοῦν κ. πληροῦν ?) 316.
8. -entator. f. vel dispensator 348.
17 (πληρῶν ἢ χορηγῶν).

III. INDEX LOCORUM [1]

[1] References to editions have been regularized as far as possible. The notes contain many catenae of quotations illustrating the sense of words or ordinary doxographical tradition. It has not been thought necessary to give a full list of such places.

---

[1] See also vol. i, pp. 378–9.

114.	20	ἐν μέρει :	ἐν ἀέρι Kroll
	21	πεπειραμένον ὡς εἰκάσαι με εἰδότα :	ἐσπειραμένον (Casaubon), ὡς εἰκάσαι γε δράκοντι. εἶτα Reitzenstein
116.	1	φωνὴν φωτός :	φωνὴν πυρός Reitz.
118.	7	θεωρεῖσθαι :	θεωρεῖσθαι ⟨τὴν γῆν⟩ Reitz.
120.	7	καὶ παρέδωκε :	καὶ ᾧ παρέδωκε Reitz.
	13	γενόμενος . . . ἐξ ὧν :	γενόμενος δὲ . . . ἔξων Reitz.
	21	κατανοῆσαι :	καταπονῆσαι Candolle
	25	κάλλος :	κάλλος αὐτῶν τε Reitz.
	29	ἐν ἑαυτῷ :	ἐν αὐτῇ Reitz.
122.	10	ἄυπνος ἀπὸ ἀύπνου :	ἄυπνος ὢν ὑφ' ὕπνου ἀπὸ ἀ. Zielinski
	21	καὶ :	καὶ τί Reitz.
	27	τὸ δὲ ἐκ πυρὸς πέπειρον :	ἐκ πυρὸς δὲ τὸ πέπειρον Reitz.
124.	1	τὰ πάντα . . . γενῶν :	πάντα τὰ (Keil) . . . τέλους καὶ ἀρχῶν γενέσεων Reitz.
	17	αἰσθητῶς :	αἰσθητικῶς Nock
126.	3	ἑαυτὸν . . . ὄντα καὶ :	αὐτὸν κ.τ.λ. Reitz.
	11	τοῖς :	καὶ τοῖς Reitz.
	15	ἰδίῳ θανάτῳ μυσάττονται :	ἀιδίῳ (Keil) . . . φυλάσσονται Reitz.
	23	θρώσκει αὐτὸν :	θρώσκει ἐπ' αὐτὸν Reitz.
128.	11	προφανίαν OQ Turn. :	προθυμίαν Reitz.
	16	τοῖς οὖσι :	τοῖς παροῦσιν Reitz.
130.	5	ἐκφορά codd :	ἐκφθορά Zielinski
		γεννήματα ἀγαθῶν :	γέννημα τῶν ἀγαθῶν Kroll
132.	16	σκοτεινοῦ φωτός codd :	σκοτεινοῦ σώματος· τοῦ φωτὸς Bousset
136.	3	ὁ θεὸς οὐκοῦν κτλ. :	vid. iv. 365
146.	29	⌜τερασπορίας⌝ εἰς κατοπτίαν οὐρανοῦ καὶ δρομήματος οὐρανίων θεῶν :	εἰς κατοπτίαν οὐρανοῦ καὶ ἱερᾶς πορείας οὐρανίων θεῶν (v. vol. iv, xlvii)
148.	2	μοίρας ὀχλουμένης :	ἀμοιβὰς κυκλουμένας
	4	ἄρχεται αὐτῶν . . . σοφισθῆναι :	ἀρχὴ καὶ τέλος αὐτῶν κ.τ.λ.
150.	3	μόνῳ :	οὐ μόνῳ
	6	καὶ :	ἀλλὰ καὶ
152.	16	ἐπιστήμη, τῶν θείων ἐντορία, καὶ ἡ . . . :	ἐπιστήμη, ἡ τῶν θείων θεωρία, καὶ ἡ . . . vel aliquid simile
154.	30	ἀρχὴ δὲ ἐξ οὐδενὸς ἀλλ' ἢ ἐξ αὐτῆς . . . αὐτὴ γάρ ἐστιν ἐπεὶ . . . ἔτυχεν οὖσα· μονὰς οὖν ἀρχή (μονὰς οὖσα οὖν Stob.) :	ἀρχὴ δὲ ἐξ οὐδενὸς ἄλλου ἢ ἐξ αὐτῆς . . . ἀρχὴ γάρ ἐστιν ἐπεὶ . . . ἔτυχεν. μονὰς οὖν, οὖσα ἀρχή, κ.τ.λ.
158.	17	νόησιν ἰδεῖν :	μή τί που τὴν σαυτοῦ νόησιν ἰδεῖν
160.	15	τὴν ταχύτητα τὴν . . . περίβασιν :	τὴν ταχυτάτην . . . περίβασιν Norden
	32	τὰ νεῦρα :	an τῷ νεφρῷ ?
162.	29	οὗτος ὃ οὐκ ἔστι :	ὃ οὐχ οὗτος ἔστι
164.	1	τίς οὖν :	τί τίς οὖν Nock

164. 23 fortasse τὸ ἀγαθὸν αὐτός ἐστιν ὁ θεὸς ἀεὶ ⟨ἐνεργῶν⟩. εἰ δὲ οὕτως, οὐσίαν
εἶναι δεῖ πάσης κινήσεως καὶ γενέσεως ⟨ἐνεργετικήν⟩—ἔρημον δὲ οὐδέν ἐστιν
αὐτῆς—περὶ δὲ αὐτὴν στατικὴν ἐνέργειαν ἔχουσα⟨ν⟩, ἀνενδεῆ καὶ ἀπέριττον,
πληρεστάτην χορηγόν. ἐν δὲ ἀρχῇ πάντων· [π_ἓν γὰρ τὸ χορηγοῦν, ἀγαθὸν
ὄν· ἀγαθὸν δ' ὅταν λέγω, καὶ πάντα καὶ ἀεὶ ἀγαθόν ἐστι.

166.	13	ὥσπερ γὰρ οὐδὲν τῶν :		ὥσπερ γὰρ οὐδὲν τούτων
168.	21	περὶ αὐτήν :		περὶ αὐτοῦ Kroll
	23	αὗται :		αὐταὶ Kroll
	24	ὅτι :		ὅτι εἰ Kroll
	32	ὧν ἢ αὐτὸς :		ὧν μᾶλλον αὐτὸς Nock
170.	21	λόγον :		ποτόν nesciocuius
172.	17	τὸ ἐγκείμενον ἀγαθόν :		τὸ ἓν καὶ μόνον ἀγαθόν
174.	22	οὔποτε ἐγένετο :		οὔποτε δὲ ἐγένετο Kroll
	23	τὸ γὰρ ἀίδιον οὗ ἀίδιόν ἐστι τὸ πᾶν :		supplet αὐτόγονον Kroll
178.	1	καὶ νοῦ τοῦ ἀγαθοῦ :		καὶ νοῦ καὶ τ. ἀ.
180.	1	τὸ γεγονέναι :		ἀπογεγονέναι
182.	6	⌈αφορα⌉ :		γίνεται διάφορα.
186.	2	ἐπανεπαύσατο :		ἐνανεπαύσατο Reitz.
188.	22	ἐσεβάσθη :		ἐσβέσθη
190.	9	καὶ θεῖα :		καὶ θέα Plasberg
	23	εἰσιν αὗται :		ἤρτηνται (incaute Reitz. Platonicorum doctrinae Orientalia hic inmiscere videtur ; v. vol. iv. xxvi)
194.	3	ὁ καλὸς κόσμος :		καλὸς ὁ κόσμος
198.	30	τῶν θείων νοημάτων		τῶν θείων ὀχημάτων
206.	8	ὁ χρόνος :		suspicor nomen personae dialogi latere, ὁ νοῦς, nisi audeas ⟨ὁ Κρόνος et Κρό⟩-νου (l. 1), cum Kronos ipse (sive Akmon) perfectae doctrinae vir esset
208.	12	κοσμεῖ οὖν τὴν ἀθανασίαν :		κοσμεῖ οὐρανόν, τὴν κ.τ.λ.
210.	12	οὐκ αὐτάρκης ἐστὶ :		οὐκ αὐτάρκεσιν ἔνεστι
214.	7	πῶς οὖν καὶ τὰ θνητὰ ζῷα κ.τ.λ. :		πῶς οὖν—καὶ εἰ τ. θν. ζ. ἀλλὰ τῶν μὴ θνητῶν—πῶς δεῖ τὸν τὸ ἀθάνατον ... ποιοῦντα ζῷον θνητὸν μὴ ποιεῖν ;
	16	γελοιότατον glossatoris.		
	19	ἐν πολλῷ γελοιότατον glossatoris.		
216.	5	μηδὲν δυνάμενον εἶναι :		μηδὲν δυνάμενον μηδέν σε εἶναι
	7	τέλειος δὲ ἄρα :		τέλειος. θεὸς ἄρα
	36	διὰ τὸ τὸ :		δι' οὗ τὸ Reitz.
218.	4	δεισιδαίμων ὡς ἀκούεις glossatoris.		
222.	7	εὐθεῖα, ἰδία τοῦ :		εὐθεῖα διὰ τοῦ Reitz.
	8	ῥᾳδία ὁδεύοντί σοι :		ῥᾳδία, ὁδεύοντί σοι Reitz.
	24	καὶ ποία . . . :		εἰ δέ τις ἔστιν καὶ ποία . . . οὗτος μόνος ἀκριβῶς οἶδεν Reitz.
224.	1	ὥσπερ ἡπλωμένος :		ὡς περιηπλωμένος Reitz.
	22	ἀθεότης, ἔπειτα δόξα εἰς :		ἀθεότης, ἔπειτα δόξα, αἷς Kroll
226.	10	ἔχον ὁ :		ἔχον, χαιρέτω ὁ Kroll

228. 3 μάλιστα νοητὰ σώματα :   μάλιστα τὰ νοητὰ ἀσώματα
      4 ὅπερ :   ὥσπερ Reitz.
      6 ὡς οὖν :   ὡς εἶναι Reitz.
      9 τοῦ νοῦ :   καὶ τοῦ νόμου
     16 Δαίμονος ἄριστα. Καὶ θείως :   Δαίμονος. Ἄριστα καὶ θείως Kroll
230. 24 πατέρα :   νόμιζε πατέρα Reitz.
240. 1 ἐν ἐμοὶ :   ἐν νοΐ
      2 τῆς νοητῆς :   adde γενέσεως εἰμί
     21 ὁρᾷς με ... ὀφθαλμοῖς, ὅτι δὲ   ὁρᾷς με ... ὀφθαλμοῖς, ὅτι δὲ εἰμὶ οὐ
         (Q) κατανοεῖς :   κατανοεῖς Reitz.
248. 19 γενομένου μου: γενόμενον νοῦν Reitz.
     20 ὀγδοάδα secl. Nock
250. 21 ἐπιτάξαντα :   ἐπιστάξαντα
252. 19 πνεῦμα :   πνευματίζε Keil
     23-26 εὐλογίαν εὗρον.   εὐλογίαν εἶπον,
         καὶ ὃ ζητῶ   καὶ ὃ ζητῶ εὗρον·
         βουλῇ τῇ σῇ ἀναπέπαυμαι   βουλῇ τῇ σῇ εἶδον·
         εἶδον· θελήματι τῷ σῷ.   θελήματι τῷ σῷ ἀναπέπαυμαι
254. 16 ἐπεμελήθη :   ἐθεμελιώθη Reitz.
264. 29 ὑρωμένας :   ὁρμωμένας
266. 1 ἀεὶ :   συνδεῖ Reitz.
      5 ἀγαθαὶ :   ἅπασαι αἱ Kroll
288 18 aera ignis :   aera. Ignis *Thomas*
288. 25-290. 3 Anima et mundus a na-   Anima et mundus a natura conprehensa
         tura conprehensa agitantur,   agitantur, licet (*Bradwardine*) om-
         ita omnium multiformi ima-   nium multiformi imaginum inaequa-
         ginum aequalitate variata, ut   litate (*Ferguson*) variata et infinitate
         infinitae qualitatum ex inter-   (*Bradwardine*) qualitatum ex inter-
         vallo species esse noscantur,   vallo (ἐκ διαιρέσεως) species esse no-
         adunatae tamen ad hoc, ut   scantur, adunatae tamen, etc.
         totum unum et ex uno omnia
         esse videantur (*codd.*) :
290. 22 visibus :   iussibus *Kroll*
292. 15 sunt :   sunt, genera non sunt *Nock*
     27 alicuius :   alicui *Kroll*
310. 14 cunctarum omnium :   coniunctarum (iunctarum *Bradwardine*)
                                             omnium
320. 25 quorumque :   antiquiorumque
326. 6 gubernationis :   gubernatorum superiorum et inferiorum
                                             Bradwardine
328. 25 forma et corpora incorporalia : formae, corpora et incorporalia *Kroll*
332. 23 et sensum :   esse sensum *Rose*
334. 1 percepto :   percipito *Bradwardine*
342. 17 suo operi *G* :   summo suo operi *Bradwardine*
344. 15 voluntaria :   violenta
346. 6 per coacta temporis cursu :   peracto temporis cursu *reddit* πεπληρω-
                                             μένης τῆς τοῦ χρόνου περιόδου (*sc.* τῆς
                                             ἀποκαταστάσεως)
     27 dispensator :   Vitae dispensator *Scott*
     32 distribuentur. Distribuentur : distribuuntur.   Restituentur

348.	12	partis quae est ... in ipsoque mundo :	partis. quae est ... in ipso mundo *Kroll*
350.	15	fuit semperque :	fuit semper, semperque *Thomas*
356.	6	aeternitas :	Aeternitatis *Thomas*
358.	30	vitae, melior :	vitae melioris *Bradwardine*
364.	17	alternis saepe per **membra** : *Test.* ἀρμῶν :	alternis semper membris μερῶν
366.	6	est alia 2 *B* : et alia *cett.* :	est et alia *Bradwardine*
374.		*Test.* εὔνοιαν	εὐακοίαν Fahz
384.	11	καὶ οὐκ ἀσκόπως glossatoris.	
392.	9	κατοικεῖ :	καθέλκει Kroll
394.	1	τὸ γὰρ ὄν :	τὸ γὰρ γινόμενον
	11	τὰ ἄλογα :	τὸ ἄλογον Wachsmuth
	16	αἱ secl. Usener	
	17	συγγίγνονται :	οὐ συγγίγνονται
402.	13	παρὰ τὰ προειρημένα glossatoris.	
406.	17	εἰδόσι :	ἰδίοις
410.	7	τῶν συνδέτων μελῶν P : habet τῶν ante μελῶν F :	τῶν συντεταμένων μελῶν vel aliquid simile
412.	23	τὰς τῶν ἑπτὰ :	supplendum σφαίρας
	24	κύκλον :	supplendum τὸν ζῳδιακὸν αὐτοῖς ὑποτετάχθαι
	25	καὶ τὰ πάντα :	supplendum ἐπισκοποῦντας
418.	23	τὸ ὄνομα :	τοῦ ὀνόματος Nock
422.	9	ἀμέτοχα :	μέτοχα Usener
432.	8	τὰ ἐν οὐρανῷ ὑπόκειται :	τὰ ἐν οὐρανῷ νῷ ὑπόκειται
	29	πᾶν τὸ ζῷον τῶν ἀνθρώπων :	παντὸς ζῴου τὸ τῶν ἀνθρώπων γένος
434.	16	Ἑρμοῦ ἐκ τῶν Πλάτωνος ἄκμονα Πυθαγόρου :	Ἑρμοῦ ἐκ τῶν Ἄκμονος (v. vol. iv, xliv)
438.	6	γένεσις ἔχουσα :	γενεσιουργοῦσα
440.	4	τὸ δ' ἐν τῇ νηδύι :	τὸ δὲ πνεῦμα τὸ ἐν τ. ν.
	7	οὐσιότητα F : ἰδιότητα P : οὐ γὰρ ⌈ερωταν⌉ ἐστὶν αὐτῇ μετὰ σώματος εἶναι :	ἐπιτηδειότητα οὐ γὰρ πρῶτον ἔστιν αὐτῇ ... εἶναι (sc. non ante partum licet animae corpus habitare)
442.	15	τοῦ δὲ εἶναι σῶμα οὐχὶ συστατόν :	τ. δ. εἰ. σ. οὐχί—συστατὸν γάρ.
	27	οὐσία αὐτοτελὴς ἐν ἀρχῇ· ἑλομένη βίον :	οὐσία αὐτοτελής, ἐν ἀρχῇ κ.τ.λ. (Pl. *Rep.* 617 D)
446.	11	ἐστιν. ὁ περινοηματικὸς λόγος :	ἐστιν, ὥσπερ ὁ π. λ., Wachsmuth
	23	αὐτὴ ἑαυτῆς οὖσα :	αὐτὴ ἑαυτῆς ἄρχουσα
	24	ἐν secludendum.	
448.	1	ὀνόματι ζωὴν :	τῷ σώματι
450.	4	τῆς ἐν τάξει :	τῆς ἐν ἕξει
	9	εἴδους ζωῆς	supplendum ἑτέρου
452.	16	προόν· ὂν γάρ :	προόν· προὺν γάρ
458.	2	τῶν ἐπικειμένων :	supplet ἰδόντα Reitz.
462.	7	ἱκανὸς δὲ ὁ μέσος ἦργει χρόνος ἐκέκρυπτο :	ἱκανὸν δὲ ὁ κόσμος (vel μέσος κόσμος) ἦργει χρόνον καὶ ἐκέκρυπτο
	24	ἅπασιν :	πνεύμασιν

462. 26	ἑαυτῇ λαλήσασα :	[ἑαυτῇ] ἔρωτι (?) γελάσασα
30	ἐχαρίσατο εἶναι :	ἐχαρίσατο τὸ εἰδέναι
464. 16	οὔσαις :	δεούσαις Reitz.
466. 22	καὶ μένει :	καταμένει Wachsmuth
468. 27	πατρὸς προσεκύνουν :	πατρὸς ἐκύκων
474. 38	πλέον οὐδ᾽ ὅτι :	τί πλεονεκτοῦσαι
476. 21	ἀεὶ δὲ ἀπολύσας :	ἰδὲ ἐπελεήσας Reitz.
480. 9	ἐκβοήσουσιν :	ἐκβορήσουσιν
484. 11	τὰ γῆς :	καὶ ταγὴ
486. 10	ἄγνωστα :	ἀγνωσία Wachsmuth
488. 31	ἀπ᾽ ἀνθρώπων :	ἀπανθρώπων
35	ὁ ἐπὶ secludendum	
490. 12	μετεποίησαν. μόνῃ γὰρ αὐχεῖν τῶν ἀπὸ σοῦ πρέπει :	μεταποίησον· (Patricius) μόνῃ γὰρ ἀτυχεῖν τῶν ἀπὸ σοῦ οὐ πρέπει
23	διὰ γένους μισθὸς ἐπάξιος :	Δίκη νέμουσα (vel διανέμουσα) μισθοὺς ἐπαξίους
492. 1	τῶν πάντων :	τῷ πάντων
3	βίου τὸν βίον :	τοῦ ὁσίου τ. βίον
26	ἔχουσαν :	ἔχουσας
494. 11	λοιπὸν ὑπὸ :	οἶκον
504. 13	προλέγει :	προπολεμεῖ
508. 13	ἐπέχειν :	ἐπιχεῖν
17	μύστης δὲ ὥσπερ :	ὥσπερ δὲ μυστίς Nock
512. 23	ἑαυτοῦ :	ἡ᾽ αὐτοῦ Nock
516. 16	φυράματος τοῦ ἄνω γίγνεται :.	φ. τ. ἄ. μέμνηται (sc. τὸ φ. τῆς ψυχῆς)
520. 1	καὶ θάλλονται :	καθάλλονται Heeren
9	βουλῆς δὲ ὁ πατὴρ πάντων· καὶ καθηγητὴς ὁ τρισμέγιστος Ἑρμῆς :	βουλῆς δὲ ὁ πατὴρ (sc. σου), καὶ πάντων καθηγητὴς ὁ τρ. Ἑρμῆς. Vix convenit Deo Summo inter homines numerari ; itaque credo auctorem iterum Osiridis persona usum esse, regia illa consilii virtute omnibus antecellentis, quippe cui Hermes ipse Dei leges absconditas tradidisset (492. 29). Talis enim erat ratio inter regem et vatem. Nec iniuria Hermes πάντων καθηγητής nominatur, qui πάντα γνοὺς . . . ἴσχυσε δηλῶσαί τε καὶ δεῖξαι (458. 18). Cf. vol. iv, xl
17	τὴν :	supplet τάξιν Wachsmuth
526. 3	ἐπίσταται :	ἐπισπᾶται
538. Fr. 15	θαυμάζῃ :	supplendum πάντα δὲ θαυμάζων τὸν πατέρα γνωρίζῃ vel aliquid simile
546. Fr. 31	τάξιν :	πῆξιν
Vol. II. 253. 6	ἀγγελιώδους :	ἀγγειώδους
Vol. III. 491. l. 4 from foot	Ἀγαθοδαίμονος υἱοῦ :	Ἀγαθοδαίμονος, υἱοῦ
Vol. IV. 2. 8	τὸ ἀΐδιον :	τὸ ἀνθρώπειον (ANION)
7. 1	Ἄκμωνος retinendum.	
35. 26	μόνοι :	μεταστρεφόμενοι

38. 23	ὁ θεατὸς **νοούμενος** ἄν-θρωπος :	ὁ ἐνδιαθέτως ν. ἀ.	
151. (c)	**καταραθέντα** :	καταφωραθέντα Wellman	
176. 11	ἵν' εὖ φρο**νῇ** ἐφ' ἑκάστης:	[ἴν'] εὐφρύνης ἐφ' ἑκάστης	
195. 4	ὠφέλη**ται** :	τετύφλωται	
11	νεωστὶ **φύσασθαι κατά-λογον** :	ἀναγράψασθαι κατάλογον vel aliquid simile	
244. 15	'Ομηρίδας ὅ φασιν :	'Ομηρίδαι σοφάς φασιν Rose	
423. 13 (on 354. 9) : potius πᾶς μὲν οὖν νοῦς, θεῖος ὤν, ὅμοιός ἐστιν			

ERRATA
VOLUME I

116. 20	ἐμπλήξει	ἐκπλήξει	
126. *appar.* 14	Reitz.	Kroll	
144. 27	κατ'	κατ'	
160. 32	ἧπαρ	ἦπαρ	
230. 12	τὴν	τὸν	
258. 7	γινέσθαι	γίνεσθαι	
288. 4	completo	conpleto	
300. 25	quae	qui	
318. 24	nubilis	nebulis	
326. 25	spherae	sphaerae	
352. 16	ambitionem	ambitudinem	
370. 2	nubilis	nebulis	
11	quae	qua	
371. n. 1	*daemouas*	*daemonas*	
377. n. 3	πσατός	παντύς	
390. 20	ἐρῶτα	ἔρωτα	
398. 24	ἐπομένων	παρεπομένων	
430. 16	διαλυτὴ	διαλύτη	
452. 19	ἐνάντια	ἐναντία	
456. 14	πολυστέφους	πολυστεφοῦς	
19 *appar.* μυστηρίους		μυστηρίοις	
464. 23	ἐγίνετο	ἐγένετο	
27	κρᾶματος	κράματος	
32	ἐπάνθουν	ἐπανθοῦν	
470. 6	ἑτερᾶς	ἑτέρας	
480. 18	ἐμπνοῦς	ἔμπνους	
496. 5	βασιλεύς	γενόμενος βασιλεύς	
520. 3, 25	ὁμοιοπάθους	ὁμοιοπαθοῦς	
542. *Fr.* 25	Cyril *ib.* 9	Cyril *ib.* 549 c	

VOLUME II

59. (*last line*)	συνέχονται	συννήχονται	
137. (*titulus*)	III	IV	
141. *par.* 2, *l.* 4	617	Gaisford, *Poet. min. graec.* 3. 462	
par. 2, *l.* 6	950	,, ,, ,, ,, 3. 494	

270. 2	407 b	407 b 20
307. § 7, *l.* 10	p. 43	p. 343
l. 18	*In Tim.* 3	*In Tim.* 2
460. *par.* 5, *l.* 2	77	76

VOLUME III

50. *l.* 9 *from foot*	3. 7	3. 4
52. 1	quae	qui
72. *l.* 2 *from foot*	294	296
73. *l.* 1	295	297
l. 7	modice	incondite
111. 8	9. 2	9. 1. 2
10	5. 117	5. 116
23	Aesch. fr. 295	Aesch. fr. 70 Sidgwic
120. *l.* 6 *from foot*	πανrουργοὺs	πανουργοὺs
136. *par.* 1, *l.* 5	6. 4	6. 5
l. 3 *from foot*	10. 7. 316	10. 17
137. 2	*In Tim.* 2	*In Tim.* 1
4	*ib.* 2	*ib.* 1
268. *par.* 2, *l.* 8	nubilis	nebulis
284. *l.* 4 *from foot*	ἔλθε	ἐλθέ
l. 3 *from foot*	δεῖνα	δεῖνα ζωήν
509. *par.* 5	'But . . . intransitive.'	*dele*; *v.* vol. iv, p. xxxv, n. 2
577. *par.* 2, *l.* 8	*Erdbeschreiburg*	*Erdbeschreibung*
587. 1	An	[An
4	anology	analogy
589. *par.* 2	[Was . . . 197 c?]	*dele*
601. *par.* 3, *l.* 5.	φυχῶν	ψυχῶν
609. 19, 25	ὁμοιοπάθους	ὁμοιοπαθοὺς

VOLUME IV

39. 14	αἰδίῳ	ἀιδίῳ
16	τῇ πρὸs	⟨τῇ⟩ πρὸs
178. *n.* 1, *l.* 12	σώματι	σώματι φερόμενον
182. 26	uicit	uincit
187. *n.* 1, § 4	I. 535 D	p. 225
414. *n.* 7, *l.* 1	*imm.* 8	*imm.* 18. 83
447. *par.* 3, *l.* 5	ἐνάντια	ἐναντία

Retractata retractandave Addenda praebet 'Supplementum Lectionum'.